"*Philosophia* literally means 'love of wisdom,' but from the ancient Greek schools to the present-day halls of academia, philosophers' writings have more often reflected the wisdom of the world than the wisdom of the Word, and many have cast more shadow than light. Not so for John Frame's latest masterpiece. No other survey of the history of Western thought offers the same invigorating blend of expositional clarity, critical insight, and biblical wisdom. Supplemented with study questions, bibliographies, links to famous quotes from influential thinkers, twenty appendices, and a chapter-indexed glossary, this book would be an excellent choice as the main textbook for a seminary-level course. Overtly and unrepentantly Christian in its perspective, it will be my first recommendation for believers seeking a trustworthy guide to the labyrinthine history of philosophy and theology."

—**James N. Anderson**, Associate Professor of Theology and Philosophy, Reformed Theological Seminary, Charlotte

"The history of secular Western philosophy traces man's many attempts at great thoughts about God's creation but without God. This has resulted in varied thought-systems that possess fragments of truth capable of appealing to our natural curiosity about the world. Yet without the truth of Scripture acting as the authority over beliefs and values, not only are those fragments unable to provide us with the full picture, but even the little bit they do say is not fully true. In the end, all we are left with is a lie. This was Satan's subterfuge with the first woman. He tempted her to accept the hollowness of his lie as the truth. Since that day in the garden, Satan's strategy has remained essentially the same. Either he presents for our consideration fraudulent evaluations of the creation in the name of philosophy or he finds ways to mix the tares of false philosophies with the truth of God's Word in our own hearts and minds, thus confusing us about what is right. In either case, his goal is to tempt us to question what God has said. Responding to this attack, John Frame has provided an invaluable ministry to the church. He puts the history of Western philosophy in its proper context: spiritual warfare. Here we learn that philosophy is more than a set of courses in a college curriculum. It is a field of battle for the hearts and minds of billions. In these pages are exactly the resources you need to bring every thought captive to the obedience of Christ and to be a champion for truth. May this book help prepare you for such a time as this."

—**John Barber**, Pastor, Cornerstone Presbyterian Church, Palm Beach Gardens, Florida

"With this volume Frame offers his many devoted readers a 'triperspectival' take on the history of Western philosophy and modern theology. Based on a course that he has been teaching at Reformed Theological Seminary for many years (the text is keyed to lectures available at itunes.rts.edu), and a lifetime of reading and thinking, this volume is the next fat Frame book by P&R Publishing. Although his interpretations of the many thinkers covered in this survey admittedly follow popular conventions, his assessment is distinctly his own. Frame's devotion to Van Til, the dedicatee, is evident throughout as he reads this history as the story of the antithesis between Christian thought and all other belief systems. Here, Western thought becomes a narrative of errors, deviations, and idolatry and its study an exercise in preparing oneself for spiritual warfare in the life of the mind. *A History of Western Philosophy and Theology* rounds out Frame's corpus and is required reading for anyone interested in the contours of his thought."

—**Bruce P. Baugus**, Associate Professor of Philosophy and Theology, Reformed Theological Seminary, Jackson

"We now have an answer to the question of what would happen if John Frame became something of a Frederick Copleston and did a whole 'history of philosophy.' It is now possible to know, because it has been done. It would combine all the qualities that actually exist in Dr. Frame. It would be a fascinating combination of an irenic but prudent interaction with the whole gallery of thinkers through the ages, and would at the same time be an exercise in the casting out of the demons of humanistic autonomy, self-reference, and self-determination. I have felt since my student days when Dr. Frame was one of my professors that if I could choose anybody to evaluate anything in the intellectual realm (beginning with my own efforts as a student), it would be Dr. Frame. He was the best evaluator I ever sat under. That same quality has now been applied to the whole history of philosophy. Dr. Frame is gentler than Van Til, but (interestingly) just as incisive, with more of an eye for the finer contours and details than the old master himself."

—**Richard Bledsoe**, Metropolitan Missionary, Boulder, Colorado; former PCA pastor

"'If only!' If only I had had this volume from John Frame when I studied philosophy at Vanderbilt as an undergraduate in the late 1960s! That was a time when it seemed that every college student was 'into' philosophy, but most philosophy either was dark and cynical (existentialism) or seemed to ignore the serious evils of those days by seeking to explain everything through clearer language (logical positivism). Frame knows and explains well all the various strands of philosophy, and he puts the world and the history of philosophy in its proper perspective as seen through the lens of the Scriptures, God's truth about the world and about us. I was not privileged to have Dr. Frame's help when I first studied philosophy, but you do have that counsel available to you. Use it."

—**Robert C. Cannada Jr.**, Chancellor Emeritus, Reformed Theological Seminary

"When I was a young man, I plowed through Bertrand Russell's 1945 classic, *A History of Western Philosophy*. A couple of years ago I read the much shorter (and more interesting) work of Luc Ferry, *A Brief History of Thought*. Between these two I have become familiar with many histories of Western thought, each written out of deep commitments, some acknowledged, some not. But I have never read a history of Western thought quite like John Frame's. Professor Frame unabashedly tries to think through sources and movements out of the framework (bad pun intended) of deep-seated Christian commitments and invites his readers to do the same. These commitments, combined with the format of a seminary or college textbook, will make this work invaluable to students and pastors who tire of ostensible neutrality that is no more neutral than the next volume. Agree or disagree with some of his arguments, but John Frame will teach you how to *think* in theological and philosophical categories."

—**D. A. Carson**, Research Professor of New Testament, Trinity Evangelical Divinity School

"For this work of great scope, John Frame begins with the simple foundation of a disciple. Eschewing vain promises of value-free consideration of Western thought regarding philosophy, theories of knowledge, and ethics, he freely confesses the Christian necessity of weighing the divine *ought* behind all human thought and endeavor. As waters run in a furrow, so the mind of the Christian necessarily considers theory, assertion, and imperative in accord with the lines plowed by the Word of God. Frame knows that such presuppositions will marginalize his analysis for secularists blind to their own biases, but he submits thought and praxis to his Master in order to give masterful consideration to the thought and ethics of those who have contributed (both for good and for ill) to our culture's perspectives and priorities."

—**Bryan Chapell**, Pastor, Grace Presbyterian Church, Peoria, Illinois

"As a younger theologian I benefited enormously from John Frame's outline, an extensive syllabus on the history of philosophy. He managed in a succinct, yet most competent manner to summarize the most significant moments in this history and to evaluate them theologically, that is, biblically. Here, in *A History of Western Philosophy and Theology*, Frame puts flesh on the bones of his earlier outline. And what a treasure it is! Among other virtues, he puts into question the supposed opposition between philosophy and theology, believing as he does that applying biblical theology to the issues raised by philosophers is an authentic and authoritative answer to those questions. For those who view philosophy as an alien world, this volume will challenge their concerns. For those who are already committed to the proper interface between theology and philosophy, these pages will confirm and deepen their construal."

—**William Edgar**, Professor of Apologetics and John Boyer Chair of Evangelism and Culture, Westminster Theological Seminary

"The Bible as God's self-attesting Word provides the foundations indispensable both for doing sound philosophy and for determining the proper relationship between philosophy and theology. Works written with this crucial conviction are few and far between. This volume is a major and welcome exception. Bringing together the author's extensive thinking, past and present, in these areas, it is a valuable resource, especially for those concerned to follow the apostolic commitment to destroy arguments and everything lofty raised against the knowledge of God, and to bring every thought captive in obedience to Christ (2 Cor. 10:5)."

—**Richard B. Gaffin Jr.**, Professor of Biblical and Systematic Theology, Emeritus, Westminster Theological Seminary

"I come from a tradition that says about philosophy, 'Handle with care!' That is exactly what John Frame does in this important book, which connects in an exemplary manner the history of philosophy with biblical studies and Christian theology. To read this book with care is an education in itself."

—**Timothy George**, Founding Dean, Beeson Divinity School, Samford University; General Editor, Reformation Commentary on Scripture

"Professor Frame has done the church a great service in producing this history of philosophy and theology—two disciplines that continually interact and react with each other. He has done so with his usual clarity of thought and commitment to absolute truth. His summaries are concise but coherent, and he is unafraid to demonstrate the inherent contradictions that lie behind many modern constructs. This will be an indispensable guide for students and an invaluable tool for apologists."

—**Liam Goligher**, Senior Minister, Tenth Presbyterian Church, Philadelphia, Pennsylvania

"John Frame's *A History of Western Philosophy and Theology* is a delightful gift to the church and the academy. I have shelves full of books on philosophy and many more shelves of theology books. None, however, moves between these two disciplines with the facility, insight, and grace exhibited by Dr. Frame in this new work. His analysis of philosophers and their systems is always clear, conversational, and, most importantly, biblical. In spring 2015, I taught History of Philosophy and Apologetics to a very bright class of high school seniors at a nearby Christian school. I am so thankful to have had access to the digital review copy of this work because it has informed and enhanced my teaching at every point. Having experienced firsthand the utility of this work, I recommend it enthusiastically to seminarians, pastors, and teachers—or simply to anyone interested in the history of ideas in the West. The many teaching aids alone are worth the purchase price. This has become my favorite John Frame publication, and I look forward to highlighting and dog-earing my bound copy of this most interesting read!"

—**R. J. Gore Jr.**, Professor of Systematic Theology and Dean of the Seminary, Erskine Theological Seminary, Due West, South Carolina

"Everything that Frame writes about philosophy is worth careful consideration."

—**Howard Griffith**, Associate Professor of Systematic Theology and Academic Dean, Reformed Theological Seminary, Washington, D.C.

"Since the mid-twentieth century, Christians interested in pursuing the history of philosophy have often turned to Catholic scholarship, such as Frederick Copleston's multivolume *A History of Philosophy* and James Collins's *History of Modern European Philosophy*. Therefore, it is a sincere pleasure to commend John Frame's *A History of Western Philosophy and Theology* as a much-needed Reformed treatment of this important academic discipline. Frame traces the history of Western philosophy, a daunting task in itself. In the process, however, he also relates to Christian theology the great philosophical systems from the Greeks to the present. Frame connects this study to his larger corpus by adapting his perspectivalism to yet another discipline. The result, as we have come to expect from his previous scholarship, is another weighty volume.

"More than heft, however, Frame delivers clear, cogent, and coherent discussion. A prominent feature is how thoroughly Frame treats modern philosophy, which since the advent of Kant has exercised enormous influence on theology. Throughout the volume, Frame looks backward and forward. He makes connections, poses questions, and provides poignant illustrations, while acknowledging significant contributions of key figures. But he also faithfully demonstrates weaknesses in argument and contends that under the principle of human autonomy in its many forms, the Western philosophic mind has one great need—the gospel."

—**W. Andrew Hoffecker**, Emeritus Professor of Church History, Reformed Theological Seminary, Jackson

"John Frame has been one of the most insightful and rigorously honest philosopher-theologians of the last three decades. Not only is he prolific, but he has an uncanny ability to analyze the themes and the subtle nuances of Western philosophy and theology. Yet there is more. John has a pastoral sensibility. As one of his students over twenty-five years ago, I recall coming to class to find a single profound sentence on the blackboard: 'Theology is life.' John could never separate theology or philosophy from the realities of everyday life. His new textbook, *A History of Western Philosophy and Theology*, is one of those rare books that will both stimulate your mind and warm your heart."

—**Frank A. James III**, President and Professor of Historical Theology, Biblical Theological Seminary

"What a privilege John Frame gives his reader: to sit through a detailed and rich course on Western history and theology that only full-time graduate students usually get. Frame has done a wonderful job of giving a thoroughly Christian, Reformed, and masterful interpretation of all the major thinkers in Western history, from the Greeks to the present, within the covers of one book. For this *tour de force*, we are all in his debt."

—**Peter Jones**, Executive Director, truthXchange; Scholar-in-Residence, Westminster Seminary in California

"*A History of Western Philosophy and Theology* is a sweeping survey of the great thinkers who have shaped philosophical inquiry from its beginnings to contemporary thought. John Frame's mastery of this intellectual domain and his penetrating philosophical and theological critique yield a comprehensive and accessible guide to philosophy for Christian-worldview investigation. This work should be in pastors' libraries and readily available for seminary students, theologians, and philosophers who interact with the relationship between philosophy and Christian thought."

—**Peter A. Lillback**, President, Westminster Theological Seminary

"John Frame has done it again! He has written another superb and comprehensive book that will be of great and lasting value to the church. Seminaries and theological colleges in the West will want to require entering students to read this book before they matriculate. And graduates of those institutions will keep it close at hand for future reference. Thank you, Professor Frame!"

—**Samuel Logan**, International Director, World Reformed Fellowship

"John Frame has done it again. This book is a gift to the church. Students of all ages now have a dependable and trustworthy resource for use in evaluating Western philosophy from a Christian point of view. The prevailing perspective of the secular classroom will be challenged as Frame's work becomes more widely circulated in this generation."

—**Rod Mays**, Executive Pastor, Mitchell Road Presbyterian Church, Greenville, South Carolina; former National Coordinator, Reformed University Fellowship

"This book brings back memories of my own entrée into philosophy via the tradition that John Frame epitomizes. I was blessed to hear much of this as his student. No wonder I have always presumed that doing philosophy was a necessary implication of Christian discipleship. In fact, to be human is to be philosophical. Understanding things philosophically makes our engagement of everything better—humanness, creation, and culture, Christian theologizing included. It is to take seriously, and respond responsibly in, the world of ever-consequential ideas. This well-conceived book helps us to understand John Frame philosophically, as well as tantalizing many, I hope, to launch out into the philosophers themselves. Wonder calls us; wonder, in wisdom, awaits. And the love of wisdom proves to be the love of God. In this world of which he is Lord, we should expect to find truth everywhere. And wherever we find it, we may count that truth God's (something that I also learned from John Frame)."

—**Esther Lightcap Meek**, Professor of Philosophy, Geneva College, Beaver Falls, Pennsylvania

"The sheer magnitude, scope, and erudition of this volume are breathtaking. Virtually all aspects of Christian and secular philosophy and theology from the classical Greek period to the present are outlined in painstaking detail with lavish documentation. There can be no doubt that Professor Frame's insightful analysis of the human condition and his survey of historical attempts to resolve it will command attention both as a thesaurus of information and as a practical guide on how to live life in light of the revelation of God through his written Word."

—**Eugene H. Merrill**, Distinguished Professor Emeritus of Old Testament Studies, Dallas Theological Seminary

"Western civilization is passing through a remarkable time that may be remembered by future historians as a milepost in the ragged journey to a place that we have never been before. Christians, as well as reflective observers of all traditions and faiths, will need a faithful guide to help make sense of the philosophical movements that carried them along. Dr. John Frame is eminently qualified to be that guide. The noted theologian is also a first-class philosopher and student of philosophy. I am therefore most thankful to learn of the new book by Dr. Frame and P&R Publishing: *A History of Western Philosophy and Theology*. I commend this new work to the church—and beyond—as not merely a good book to read, but a trusted text to study and a stalwart sword to wield in the present crucial contest for the minds of men."

—**Michael A. Milton**, President, Faith for Living, Inc.; Chancellor Emeritus, Reformed Theological Seminary

"With over forty-five years of study in theology, apologetics, and philosophy, Frame gives the reader a well-rounded work on philosophy from a Christian and decisively Reformed perspective. This textbook on philosophy defends the Christian faith. The teacher of philosophy/theology will find the work—including its study questions, extensive bibliographies, lists of free audio lectures, and links to great quotes—invaluable. The student of Scripture and philosophy will find the work detailed and encouraging, and will be better able to defend and live out the Christian faith after partaking of and digesting Frame's extensive work. Frame gives an excellent overview of philosophers and their thought from the beginning to the present. In addition, he takes large philosophical ideas and simplifies them even for the average reader of philosophy. He does so in a clear, unambiguous writing style that is a pleasure to read. Overall, the book provides a wealth of knowledge, without ever becoming bogged down by lifeless descriptions or irrelevant information."

—**Joseph R. Nally**, Theological Editor, Third Millennium Ministries

"John Frame has done it again! This book is the very best of two worlds in two ways: great history of philosophy as that is informed by great theology; great history of theology as that is informed by great philosophy. This book is pedagogically creative, too. What more could a believer ask for? If you read it, you will learn a lot and become a lot. How many fantastic works are in this man?"

—**David Naugle**, Distinguished University Professor and Chair and Professor of Philosophy, Dallas Baptist University

"If attacks on Christians in America increase, so will what John Frame calls 'the attempt to make Christianity intellectually respectable.' He's right that this ignores our sinful repression of the truth and our need to receive from God new hearts and minds—and he shows in this book how philosophies that exalt either autonomous rationality or existential irrationality have taken a wrong turn. Philosophy majors and graduate students, most seminary students as well, and millions overly impressed by Platonists and Barthians need this book."

—**Marvin Olasky**, Editor in Chief, *WORLD* magazine

"John Frame has done it again! In the lucid and comprehensive style of his Theology of Lordship volumes, he here presents a full overview of Western thought about knowledge of God as it must appear to all who receive Holy Scripture, as he does, as the record, product, and present reality of God speaking. And the solid brilliance of the narrative makes it a most effective advocacy for the Kuyper–Van Til perspective that in a well-digested form it represents. It is a further outstanding achievement by John Frame. The book deserves wide use as a textbook, and I hope it will achieve that. My admiration for John's work grows and grows."

—**J. I. Packer**, Board of Governors' Professor of Theology, Regent College, Vancouver, British Columbia

"The apostle Paul told Timothy to stir up the gift that was in him. Professor John Frame has devoted a lifetime to stirring up his complementary gifts of penetrating Western philosophy, uncovering its religious dimensions, and bridging the gap between expert and layman, to produce in *A History of Western Philosophy and Theology* a volume practical for engaging in spiritual warfare."

—**Andrée Seu Peterson**, Senior Writer, *WORLD* magazine

"Few in our day champion a vision of God that is as massive, magnificent, and biblical as John Frame's. For decades, he has given himself to the church, to his students, and to meticulous thinking and the rigorous study of the Bible. He has winsomely, patiently, and persuasively contended for the gospel in the secular philosophical arena, as well as in the thick of the church worship wars and wrestlings with feminism and open theism. He brings together a rare blend of big-picture thinking, levelheaded reflection, biblical fidelity, a love for the gospel and the church, and the ability to write with care and clarity."

—**John Piper**, Founder and Teacher, desiringGod.org; Chancellor, Bethlehem College and Seminary

"This is the most important book ever written on the major figures and movements in philosophy. We have needed a sound guide, and this is it. Philosophy has many ideas and systems that are attractive but poisonous. Over the centuries people have fallen victim again and again. Frame sorts out the good and the bad with clarity and skill, using the plumb line of Scripture. Along the way he also provides a devastating critique of liberal theologies, showing that at bottom they are philosophies of human autonomy masquerading as forms of Christianity."

—**Vern S. Poythress**, Professor of New Testament Interpretation, Westminster Theological Seminary; Editor, *Westminster Theological Journal*

"Everyone familiar with the work of John Frame expects his books to challenge long-standing assumptions and to move discussions forward in creative ways. This book will not disappoint. John displays his expertise as a philosopher and his devotion to Scripture as the standard by which all philosophies should be evaluated. He points toward old paths that are sure and opens new ways to pursue the relevance of philosophical discussions for scholars, students, and motivated laypeople alike."

—**Richard L. Pratt Jr.**, President, Third Millennium Ministries

"John Frame begins his study of Western philosophy and theology with a quotation about the 'fear of the Lord' from the biblical book of Proverbs. Few intellectual historians operating today better embody such a biblically sagacious stance toward the philosophical and theological output of the Western world. In this work, Frame has bestowed a rich resource on his audience in the form of a sustained, thoughtful, and faithful witness to the development of the great ideas that populate so much discourse in the West and, for that matter, around the world. What is more compelling, however, is that Frame does not feign objectivity, like so many others, but engages his subjects from a Christian perspective, weighing each according to the teaching of Scripture."

—**John Scott Redd Jr.**, President and Associate Professor of Old Testament, Reformed Theological Seminary, Washington, D.C.

"For many Christians, philosophy connotes little more than the exercise of autonomous speculation. Viewed in only negative terms, the whole philosophic enterprise stands to be summarily dismissed. Although far more able than most to identify and engage the non-Christian assumptions governing so much of Western philosophy, Professor Frame is neither dismissive nor unappreciative. On the contrary, Frame winsomely engages the major philosophers of the Western tradition and the fundamental questions they raise. He exhibits deep familiarity with the history of philosophy, critical awareness of trends impacting theological development, and humble submission to the Word of God, thereby modeling the way in which a deep commitment to 'thinking God's thoughts after him' is beneficial for maintaining and advocating for the gospel today. For many students (and not a few teachers), Frame's *A History of Western Philosophy and Theology* will serve as a reliable map of the unexplored terrain of metaphysics, epistemology, axiology, and liberal theology. For others, it will serve as a walking staff, enabling the Christian man or woman to reenter philosophical discussion, maintain balance, and even prevail against hazardous forms of unbelief. I am glad for this volume and look forward to pointing theological students and others who lack philosophical grounding toward it."

—**Mark P. Ryan**, Adjunct Professor of Religion and Culture, Covenant Theological Seminary; Director, Francis A. Schaeffer Institute

"If Frame's Lordship Series is his magnum opus, the present work may be his crowning achievement. It's a remarkably extensive survey for a single volume, and Frame's knowledge of philosophers and philosophical schools is wide, deep, nimble, and analytical. More importantly, his impregnable grounding in the Christian (biblical!) worldview ensures that he offers from that distinctively Christian perspective a full, penetrating analysis and criticism of every major philosopher in the Western tradition. This, in fact, has never been done before, though many fine Christian books assessing philosophy have been written. What Frame has done here is to evaluate the entire basic canon of Western philosophy from a rigorously biblical viewpoint. That is simply unprecedented."

—**P. Andrew Sandlin**, President, Center for Cultural Leadership, Coulterville, California

"Not only does the nominal Christian of our modern era seek to avoid philosophical and theological writings, but to a great extent this world seeks to rebuff all analytic thought from a Christian perspective. The world is filled with so-called scholars who have no knowledge of the importance of philosophy and theology in the development of Christianity and in the context of our modern society. This simply should not be the case for biblical Christians who desire to bring all things under the crown rights of King Jesus. In order for Christians to rightfully understand the origin and development of civilization, a study of both philosophy and theology in their historical context ought to be fundamental, especially for those who want to become productive advocates for Christ's kingdom. In this present volume, Dr. Frame completes a solid analysis of the development of Western thought from a distinctly Christian perspective and ascertains its impact on man. His purpose is to expose the fact that what man is facing is nothing less than spiritual warfare in the life of Western society. If Christianity is to bring all things captive to the cause of Christ, then a very good place for every pastor, scholar, and Christian to begin is with the study of this book!"

—**Kenneth Talbot**, President, Whitefield College and Theological Seminary

"Many Christians today mistakenly think of philosophy as an esoteric endeavor irrelevant to Christian theology and discipleship. But Colossians 2:8, among other verses, indicates that we must learn to discern the ways in which human philosophies can be deceitfully empty and captivating. Furthermore, it implies that there is such a thing as 'philosophy . . . according to Christ.' In this fascinating survey, John Frame walks us through the history of philosophy to show the varied ways in which both secular philosophies and deficient Christian attempts at philosophy exhibit signs of both irrationalism and rationalism. The result is not only a historical overview of the key players and their philosophies, but also a model for how to integrate philosophy and theology in a way that honors the Lord by taking every thought captive so that we can obey Christ and submit to his lordship (2 Cor. 10:5). Highly recommended!"

—**Justin Taylor**, Senior Vice President and Publisher for Books, Crossway

"Getting the relationship between theology and philosophy right is vital if we are going to do either well. John Frame's *A History of Western Philosophy and Theology* offers tremendous help in getting it right. We never think in a historical vacuum but are profoundly shaped by our context and predecessors. This book helps us to locate ourselves historically so that we can be more aware of our blind spots and tendencies to err. The interpretation of history is explicitly evangelical, which I find refreshingly honest and helpful. Frame wonderfully shows that thinking Christianly makes profound sense. Once again, this intellectual sage has done a great service to the church and academy in bringing greater clarity to our understanding of the most important questions of life."

—**Erik Thoennes**, Professor of Theology and Chair, Undergraduate Theology, Biola University/Talbot School of Theology; Pastor, Grace Evangelical Free Church, La Mirada, California

"Drawing both on his background in philosophy and theology and on his forty-five years of reading, thinking, and teaching, Professor Frame has provided a history of Western philosophy and theology as stimulating as it is informative. His summary of the thought of substantial thinkers in both disciplines over the course of the past millennia (with the exception of Roman Catholic and Eastern Orthodox thinkers) is a wonderful gift to the church. His tome will be a particular blessing to would-be historians, philosophers, theologians, and apologists of the Christian faith. They are the ones searching for a point of entrance into the connected fields of philosophy and theology, and needing a biblically reliable and insightful analysis of the related disciplines. Their wait is over. Here they have the indispensable mapping to aid them as they start or make sense of the journey.

"Defining *philosophy* as 'the disciplined attempt to articulate and defend a worldview [aka *metanarrative*],' and arguing on the basis of the one found in Scripture, the philosophical credentials of theology ('the application of the Word of God, by persons, to every aspect of human life'), Professor Frame posits the view that the two disciplines are distinctive, yet 'profoundly interdependent.' But instead of following the notion, originating with Philo the Jew, that philosophy is the handmaid of theology, he offers a biblical view of philosophy—one in which inscripturated revelation is foundational as both the substance and the assessment of true philosophy. On this understanding, Scripture needs no helping hand from philosophy, for the former governs the latter when rightly pursued.

"Supporting this view are the known distinctives of Professor Frame's theological method: the supremacy of God's lordship, the consistent application of his 'something close to biblicism,' presuppositionalism, and triperspectivalism (as seen in three subdivisions of philosophy: metaphysics, epistemology, and value theory). The application of these distinctives to the history of Western philosophy and theology renders Professor Frame both an attractive narrator and a clearheaded challenger of man's claim to his 'autonomous' conceptualization of the world.

"Add to all this the user-friendly study questions, glossaries, and bibliographies, and the more novel list of online sources and links to famous quotes, and we have at hand a tome that many of us will undoubtedly wish had been available when we set out in earnest on our own studies. May God bless it not only to the individual inquirer after truth, but to fulfill Professor Frame's expressed aspiration—a new level of respect for evangelical Christianity, for the Bible, and for Christ!"

—**Tim J. R. Trumper**, Senior Minister, Seventh Reformed Church, Grand Rapids, Michigan

"This is an excellent primer that surveys the history of Christian thought from a thoroughgoing Christian and Van Tillian perspective—the fruit of many years of pedagogical experience. Of particular value are the spiritual conflicts that Frame identifies in every era and domain of Western worldview thinking, from the ancient Greeks to the present postmoderns. Those who read and digest Frame's work will grow in wisdom and, by God's grace, will avoid the doom of repeating earlier mistakes."

—**Kevin J. Vanhoozer**, Research Professor of Systematic Theology, Trinity Evangelical Divinity School

"How's your thought-life? Yes, Scripture is concerned about impure thoughts, but what about the manner of our thinking? What about the gulch of deceitful thinking? Scripture warns against deception, especially self-deception. This is particularly Paul's burden for the Colossians and the Laodiceans, believers who had been 'taken captive' through philosophy rooted not in the divine-preeminent Creator Christ, but in some aspect of creation, whether that be man's mind, his tradition, humanly plausible but deluding arguments, or some materialist or Gnostic pagan construct. And this captivity spawns real-world consequences: robbing Christians of encouragement, love, assurance, understanding, and knowing 'real reality.' How can we combat this sort of deceitful intellectual enemy who cunningly does not use guns and bazookas? By putting intellectual boots on the ground. But as any seasoned military officer knows, one cannot put boots on the ground in a hot zone without first knowing and understanding the ground. John Frame has again brilliantly served the body of Christ by providing a fresh, cogent, robust, informed, lucid, accessible, panoramic, practical, sound, faithful, doxological, honest, and historical treatment of philosophy and theology—good, bad, and sometimes ugly—all aimed at joining and supporting Paul's struggle for those whom he has perhaps not seen face to face, but whom he longs to see more firmly rooted in Christ. This volume is already indispensable, and will be increasingly so as postmodern fads infect and delude the church. Note carefully, however: this is not a work for professional theologians, though they would certainly benefit from it; nor is it a work for just ecclesiastical 'spiritual work,' though it will benefit all facets of 'church life.' This is a work for all Christians living in God's world, who are saved from something for something. This volume shows them how to think faithfully in God's redeemed world, so that they will in fact take every thought captive to the obedience of Christ—and that's not a suggestion; it's a command. This work wonderfully facilitates following Christ, who is to be preeminent in all things, including our thought-life."

—**Jeffery J. Ventrella**, Senior Counsel and Senior Vice President, Alliance Defending Freedom

"Christian apologist Cornelius Van Til pioneered the strategy of discerning a 'rationalist/irrationalist dialectic' in the various secular alternatives to the Christian faith, but he never wrote a comprehensive history of philosophy that sought to prove the point. John Frame now has. In this volume the evangelical world finally has a contemporary history of philosophy that is explicitly written from a Christian perspective, that is exceptional in its clarity and organization, and that *gets the details right*. I first encountered Frame's massive philosophy outlines as his graduate student back in the early 1990s, and I always wondered when such obvious labors of love would find the wider audience that they richly deserve. While it is impossible to provide in one volume (even one of this size!) a thorough exposition and assessment of every major thinker in intellectual history, Frame's detailed summaries and trenchant analyses constantly inspire the imagination to consider further what would be a genuinely Christian *alternative* to the thinker under discussion. Readers will surely need to continue for themselves the hard work that Frame has begun—the hard work of actually arguing out that Christian alternative. But often the very planting of seeds—seeds of doubt about idolatry, seeds of faith in the triune Creator, providential Sustainer, and Redeemer—is what is needed to get that process going for disciplined, attentive, and thoughtful Christian readers, and Frame plants such seeds again and again. I pray that his philosophic magnum opus finds a wide audience among college and seminary students, who are desperately in need of these accurate summaries that neither distort primary sources nor shrink back from articulating essential contrasts between influential philosophers and central biblical ideas."

—**Greg Welty**, Associate Professor of Philosophy and Program Coordinator, M.A. Philosophy of Religion, Southeastern Baptist Theological Seminary

"John Frame's *A History of Western Philosophy and Theology* should become an indispensable resource for Christian scholars, pastors, campus ministers, and lay leaders. There are volumes on theology and philosophy, but a volume that deals clearly and forthrightly with both is rare. Not only that, Dr. Frame, who is superbly equipped in each discipline, shows how they are interdependent. A strength of this volume is that he devotes major attention to the modern period that has been so challenging to many Christians who have had great difficulty understanding and responding to secular thought, especially as it developed in the twentieth century. The combination of his profound understanding and pastoral bent sets his books apart from the usual theological writings. This may well be his finest volume."

—**Luder G. Whitlock Jr.**, President Emeritus, Reformed Theological Seminary, Orlando

A HISTORY OF WESTERN PHILOSOPHY AND THEOLOGY

A HISTORY OF WESTERN PHILOSOPHY AND THEOLOGY

John M. Frame

P&R
PUBLISHING
P.O. BOX 817 • PHILLIPSBURG • NEW JERSEY 08865-0817

Page design by P&R Publishing
Typesetting by TAShumaker Graphic Services

Printed in the United States of America

ISBN: 978-1-62995-084-6 (cloth)
ISBN: 978-1-62995-085-3 (ePub)
ISBN: 978-1-62995-086-0 (Mobi)

Library of Congress Cataloging-in-Publication Data

Frame, John M., 1939-
A history of western philosophy and theology / John M. Frame. -- 1st ed.
pages cm
Includes bibliographical references and index.
ISBN 978-1-62995-084-6 (cloth.)
1. Christian philosophy--History. 2. Theology--History. I. Title.

BR100.F676 2015
261.5'1--dc23

2014036234

In Memory of

Cornelius Van Til

(1895–1987)

The fear of the Lord is the beginning of wisdom; all those who practice it have a good understanding. His praise endures forever! (Ps. 111:10)

My son, if you receive my words and treasure up my commandments with you, making your ear attentive to wisdom and inclining your heart to understanding; yes, if you call out for insight and raise your voice for understanding, if you seek it like silver and search for it as for hidden treasures, then you will understand the fear of the Lord and find the knowledge of God. For the Lord gives wisdom; from his mouth come knowledge and understanding; he stores up sound wisdom for the upright; he is a shield to those who walk in integrity, guarding the paths of justice and watching over the way of his saints. Then you will understand righteousness and justice and equity, every good path; for wisdom will come into your heart, and knowledge will be pleasant to your soul; discretion will watch over you, understanding will guard you, delivering you from the way of evil, from men of perverted speech, who forsake the paths of uprightness to walk in the ways of darkness, who rejoice in doing evil and delight in the perverseness of evil, men whose paths are crooked, and who are devious in their ways. (Prov. 2:1–15)

Trust in the Lord with all your heart, and do not lean on your own understanding. In all your ways acknowledge him, and he will make straight your paths. (Prov. 3:5–6)

And coming to his hometown [Jesus] taught them in their synagogue, so that they were astonished, and said, "Where did this man get this wisdom and these mighty works?" (Matt. 13:54)

Oh, the depth of the riches and wisdom and knowledge of God! How unsearchable are his judgments and how inscrutable his ways! "For who has known the mind of the Lord, or who has been his counselor?" "Or who has given a gift to him that he might be repaid?" For from him and through him and to him are all things. To him be glory forever. Amen. (Rom. 11:33–36)

For the word of the cross is folly to those who are perishing, but to us who are being saved it is the power of God. For it is written, "I will destroy the wisdom of the wise, and the discernment of the discerning I will thwart." Where is the one who is wise? Where is the scribe? Where is the debater of this age? Has not God made foolish the wisdom of the world? For since, in the wisdom of God, the world did not know God through wisdom, it pleased God through the folly of what we preach to save those who believe. For Jews demand signs and Greeks seek wisdom, but we preach Christ crucified, a stumbling block to Jews and folly to Gentiles, but to those who are called, both Jews and Greeks, Christ the power of God and the wisdom of God. For the foolishness of God is wiser than men, and the weakness of God is stronger than men. For consider your calling, brothers: not many of you were wise according to worldly standards, not many were powerful, not many were of noble birth. But God chose what is foolish in the world to shame the wise; God chose what is weak in the world to shame the strong; God chose what is low and despised in the world, even things that are not, to bring to nothing things that are, so that no human being might boast in the presence of God. And because of him you are in Christ Jesus, who became to us wisdom from God, righteousness and sanctification and redemption, so that, as it is written, "Let the one who boasts, boast in the Lord." (1 Cor. 1:18–31)

Yet among the mature we do impart wisdom, although it is not a wisdom of this age or of the rulers of this age, who are doomed to pass away. But we impart a secret and hidden wisdom of God, which God decreed before the ages for our glory. None of the rulers of this age understood this, for if they had, they would not have crucified the Lord of glory. But, as it is written, "What no eye has seen, nor ear heard, nor the heart of man imagined, what God has prepared for those who love him"—these things God has revealed to us through the Spirit. For the Spirit searches everything, even the depths of God. For who knows a person's thoughts except the spirit of that person, which is in him? So also no one comprehends the thoughts of God except the Spirit of God. Now we have received not the spirit of the world, but the Spirit who is from God, that we might understand the things freely given us by God. And we impart this in words not taught by human wisdom but taught by the Spirit, interpreting spiritual truths to those who are spiritual. The natural person does not accept the things of the Spirit of God, for they are folly to him, and he is not able to understand them because they are spiritually discerned. The spiritual person judges all things, but is himself to be judged by no one. "For who has understood the mind of the Lord so as to instruct him?" But we have the mind of Christ. (1 Cor. 2:6–16)

Let no one deceive himself. If anyone among you thinks that he is wise in this age, let him become a fool that he may become wise. For the wisdom of this world is folly with God. For it is written, "He catches the wise in their craftiness," and again, "The Lord knows the thoughts of the wise, that they are futile." So let no one boast in men. For all things are yours, whether Paul or Apollos or Cephas or the world or life or death or the present or the future—all are yours, and you are Christ's, and Christ is God's. (1 Cor. 3:18–23)

In [Christ] are hidden all the treasures of wisdom and knowledge. (Col. 2:3)

See to it that no one takes you captive by philosophy and empty deceit, according to human tradition, according to the elemental spirits of the world, and not according to Christ. (Col. 2:8)

Who is wise and understanding among you? By his good conduct let him show his works in the meekness of wisdom. But if you have bitter jealousy and selfish ambition in your hearts, do not boast and be false to the truth. This is not the wisdom that comes down from above, but is earthly, unspiritual, demonic. For where jealousy and selfish ambition exist, there will be disorder and every vile practice. But the wisdom from above is first pure, then peaceable, gentle, open to reason, full of mercy and good fruits, impartial and sincere. And a harvest of righteousness is sown in peace by those who make peace. (James 3:13–18)

CONTENTS

ANALYTICAL OUTLINE

RTS
on
iTunes U

CORRELATION OF BOOK CHAPTERS WITH FREE ONLINE LECTURES

The chapters in this book are complemented by my free audio lectures on the History of Philosophy that are located at Reformed Theological on iTunes U. The table below correlates chapters in this book (column 1) with corresponding iTunes U lectures (columns 2 and 3). The second row of the table is the link to the free lectures. The "Listen Online" section at the end of each chapter in this book lists the appropriate lectures for that chapter. Information about Reformed Theological on iTunes U may be found here: http://itunes.rts.edu/.

Link to Lectures: http://itunes.apple.com/us/course/legacy-history-philosophy/id694658914

Ch. #	Lec. #	Lecture Title on iTunes	Length
1	01	Why Study Philosophy—Metaphysics, Epistemology, and a Biblical Worldview	53:51
1	02	Comparison of Biblical and Nonbiblical Worldviews	31:42
2	03	The Milesians and the Eleatics	24:55
2	04	Eleatics Continued and Early Alternatives to Parmenides	54:47
2	05	Plato and Aristotle	56:59
2	06	Plotinus and Gnosticism	31:34
3	07	Original Opponents of Christianity, Second-Century Apologetics, and Irenaeus	52:15
3	08	Tertullian, Clement of Alexandria, Origen, and Athanasius	1:05:08
3	09	Saint Augustine	31:55
4	10	Christian Neoplatonism and Anselm of Canterbury	44:59
4	11	Thomas Aquinas—Faith, Reason, and Epistemology	36:14
4	12	Thomas Aquinas Continued and Late Medieval Developments	57:10
5	13	John Calvin and Seventeenth-Century Orthodoxy	20:39
5	14	Continental Rationalism and British Empiricism	1:06:08
6	15	Blaise Pascal and Joseph Butler	1:09:56
6	16	Joseph Butler Continued, William Paley, and Thomas Reid	44:21
6	17	Introduction to Liberal Theology, Enlightenment Rationalism, and Gotthold Lessing	36:40
7	18	Immanuel Kant: Transcendental Method, Phenomena, Noumena, and Critique	1:07:39
7	19	Immanuel Kant Continued and Idealism	57:39
7	20	Karl Marx	17:57
8	21	Friedrich Schleiermacher and Albrecht Ritschl	56:28
8	22	Albrecht Ritschl Continued, Wilhelm Herrmann, Adolf Harnack, and Søren Kierkegaard	58:29
8	23	Søren Kierkegaard Continued	20:40
9	24	Friedrich Nietzsche, Charles Sanders Peirce, and William James	53:23
9	25	Edmund Husserl, Martin Heidegger, and Jean-Paul Sartre	41:06
10	26	Karl Barth: Direction and Fundamental Structure of Thought	55:29
10	27	Karl Barth Continued, Emil Brunner, and Rudolf Bultmann	1:09:49
10	28	Rudolf Bultmann Continued, Paul Tillich, the New Hermeneutic, and Christian Atheism	57:07
10	29	Christian Atheism Continued and Dietrich Bonhoeffer	27:48
12	30	Hans-Georg Gadamer, Ferdinand de Saussure, Claude Lévi-Strauss, and Deconstruction	36:30
11	31	Jürgen Moltmann and the Theology of Liberation	1:01:11
11	32	The Theology of Liberation Continued and Wolfhart Pannenberg	1:08:28
11	33	Process Philosophy, Process Theology, and Open Theism	52:38
12	34	Introduction to Language Analysis, Logical Atomism, and Logical Positivism	1:01:26
12	35	Logical Positivism Continued and Ordinary-Language Philosophy	57:50
12	36	Ordinary-Language Philosophy Continued and Contemporary Epistemology	55:07
13	37	Abraham Kuyper, Herman Dooyeweerd, and Alvin Plantinga	1:08:02
13	38	Gordon Clark and Cornelius Van Til	56:59
13	39	Cornelius Van Til Continued	34:45

FOREWORD

INTELLECTUAL CHANGE TAKES PLACE at different paces. Rarely has any model for intellectual change taken place with the velocity that is currently being experienced in Western societies and in the rest of the world as it is influenced by the West. This change is taking place before watching eyes to an extent that is largely misunderstood and vastly underestimated.

Some prophetic voices have recognized the scale and scope of the intellectual changes taking place in the West. Francis Schaeffer, for example, spent most of his ministry educating Christians about the worldview shift that was occurring around them as most people moved from a vaguely Christian worldview to one that was thoroughly secular. This new worldview was based on the idea that final reality is impersonal matter or energy shaped into its present form by impersonal chance.

Significantly, Schaeffer observed that Christians in his time did not see this new worldview as taking the place of the Christian worldview that had previously dominated European and American cultures either by personal conviction or by cultural impression. These two worldviews, one generally Christian and the other barely deistic, stood in complete antithesis to each other in content and also in natural results. These contrary ways of seeing the world would lead to disparate convictions on matters ranging from abortion to sexuality, economics to politics, as well as legislation and public policy.

In 1983, writing just a few years after Francis Schaeffer wrote of a worldview shift, Carl F. H. Henry described the situation and future possibilities in terms of a strict dichotomy:

> If modern culture is to escape the oblivion that has engulfed the earlier civilizations of man, the recovery of the will of the self-revealed God in the realm of justice and law is crucially imperative. Return to pagan misconceptions of divinized rulers, or a divinized cosmos, or a quasi-Christian conception of natural law or natural justice will bring inevitable disillusionment.

> Not all pleas for transcendent authority will truly serve God or man. By aggrandizing law and human rights and welfare to their sovereignty, all manner of earthly leaders eagerly preempt the role of the divine and obscure the living God of Scriptural revelation. The alternatives are clear: we return to the God of the Bible or we perish in the pit of lawlessness.[1]

When Henry released the first volume of his magnum opus *God, Revelation, and Authority* in 1976, he began with this first line: "No fact of contemporary Western life is more evident than the growing distrust of final truth and its implacable questioning of any sure word."[2] This obstacle to the return to the authority of a Christian worldview is really part of a vicious circle that begins with the departure from at least a cultural impression of God's revealed authority: leaving a Christian worldview leads to a distrust of final truth and a rejection of universal authority, which then blockades the way back to the God of the Bible.

The rejection of biblical authority invariably leads to the secularization of society. *Secular*, in terms of contemporary sociological and intellectual conversation, refers to the absence of any binding theistic authority or belief. It is both an ideology and a result. *Secularization* is not an ideology; it is a theory and a sociological process whereby societies become less theistic as they become more modern. As societies move into conditions of deeper and more progressive modernity, they move out of situations in which there is a binding force of religious belief, and theistic belief in particular. These societies move into conditions in which there is less and less theistic belief and authority until there is hardly even a memory that such a binding authority had ever existed. Western culture has secularized beyond the authority of the God of the Bible and almost beyond the memory of any such authority.

The problem of authority is a problem of belief. In his book *The Secular Age*, Canadian philosopher Charles Taylor confirms this problem of belief in Western civilization in terms of three sets of intellectual conditions. Every society and every individual operates under certain intellectual conditions, self-consciously or not. On the question of God, Taylor traces three Western intellectual epochs: pre-Enlightenment impossibility of unbelief; post-Enlightenment possibility of unbelief; late modern *impossibility* of belief.[3]

After the Enlightenment, Western intellectual conditions changed to make it possible for one not to believe in God. For most of human

1. Carl F. H. Henry, *God, Revelation, and Authority*, vol. 6, *God Who Stands and Stays, Part 2* (Wheaton, IL: Crossway, 1999), 454.

2. Carl F. H. Henry, *God, Revelation, and Authority*, vol. 1, *God Who Speaks and Shows, Preliminary Considerations* (Wheaton, IL: Crossway, 1999), 1.

3. See Charles Taylor, *A Secular Age* (Cambridge, MA: Harvard University Press, 2007).

experience in Western civilization, it has been impossible not to believe in God. That does not mean that everyone was individually Christian or that everyone had experienced conversion and was a regenerate believer. And it does not mean that there were no skeptics or heretics. Before the Enlightenment, however, one could not explain the world without the Bible and its story. There was no alternative account of how the world had come to be. There was no naturalistic worldview available to people who lived in Western civilization throughout most of its centuries. Until Charles Darwin presented an alternative to Genesis, the Christian worldview prevailed without a serious rival. It was impossible not to believe: it was impossible to explain life, from order in the universe to justice between two individuals, without explicit reference to revealed truth.

But this situation changed with the Enlightenment and the availability of alternative worldviews by which one could frame a comprehensive account of the world set over against the Christian worldview. Any worldview must answer at least four central questions: Why is there something rather than nothing? What has happened and is broken in the world? Is there any hope, and if so, what is it? Where is history headed? With the Enlightenment came answers to these questions from a non-Christian framework (scientific naturalism, materialism, Marxism, etc.).

The intellectual conditions of Western culture have now secularized such that it is seemingly impossible for those operating under such conditions to believe in God. As Charles Taylor observes, to be a candidate for tenure at a major American university is to inhabit a world in which it is virtually impossible to believe in God or to acknowledge that belief. Under the first set of Western intellectual conditions, not everyone was a Christian, but all were accountable to a Christian worldview because there was no alternative. Secularization in American culture has reversed the conditions: not everyone is a non-Christian, but all must apparently operate under a secular worldview that denies the legitimacy of a Christian worldview. In a mere three hundred years, Western intellectual conditions have moved from an impossibility of unbelief to an impossibility of belief.

Significantly, Charles Taylor pinpoints this unbelief as a lack of cognitive commitment to a self-existent, self-revealing God. Secularization is not about *religion*. Taylor urges that people in the current hypersecularized culture in America often consider themselves to be religious or spiritual. Secularization, according to Taylor, is about belief in a personal God, One who holds and exerts authority. He describes the secular age as deeply "cross-pressured" in its personal experience of religion and rejection of the personal authority of God.[4] The issue is binding authority.

4. See ibid.

Change does not emerge from a vacuum. This is certainly true of Western culture's rejection of binding authority. In order to understand the ideological confusion of the Western mind in this postmodern age, we must look at its intellectual history and come to terms with the significant ideas that shaped its thought and produced its worldview. Without this, ideas appear without context and meaning.

The role of history in the life of a Christian is indispensable. To cut ourselves off from the past is to rob ourselves from understanding the present. We know that this is true, yet few of us ponder the consequences of this deliberate ignorance. But beyond this deliberate ignorance is the sometimes nondeliberate or accidental misunderstanding of history that can come to us in ways that are almost equally injurious. Getting the past wrong is almost as problematic as not getting the past into our minds at all. Christians have a particular stewardship of the mind and of the intellect that should lead us to understand that our discipleship to Christ is at stake in terms of our understanding of the past. Furthermore, the history of philosophy traced so well in this volume is a monumental cultural and intellectual achievement—and one that Christians have both shaped and been shaped by.

As we consider the issues and developments in Western philosophy, there is real debate to be had—and a real risk of misunderstanding. But part of this is a theological debate, part of it is a historical debate, and much of it is a cultural and political debate. It takes a good, intellectually rigorous historian of philosophy such as John Frame to present these issues in a manner that allows the past to speak to us as authentically as possible.

On the other hand, history is not the end of the story—it is not the final authority. For our final authority, Christians must consider the facts of history and then turn to theology and to our understanding drawn from the Scriptures to understand how we should live today in light of the past. John Frame points to this reality in powerful ways.

Reading a book such as this is to enter a world of intellectual conversation that involves a cast of hundreds by the time you finish this book. But you also enter into a narrative that gets clearer and more important as it becomes more accurate and more fully understood. We cannot go back to the past, and given the vast array of controversies and struggles that have occurred, we probably would not want to. Indeed, our task is not to go back, but rather in the present to consider what an understanding of the past now gives us the opportunity to do: to think more clearly and live more faithfully in light of God's authority over our lives.

R. Albert Mohler Jr.
President
The Southern Baptist Theological Seminary

PREFACE

IN THE CURRICULUM of Reformed Theological Seminary, where I have taught since 2000, there is a required course called History of Philosophy and Christian Thought. The course has been taught by a number of my colleagues as well as by me over the years. This book represents my version of it.

I am better known as a theologian than a philosopher, though as the book indicates I don't see a very big difference between these two disciplines. But I did major in philosophy at Princeton University, studied philosophical apologetics with Cornelius Van Til at Westminster Theological Seminary, and did graduate work in the philosophical theology program at Yale University. Over forty-five years I have taught philosophical subjects in both theological and apologetics courses, and my publications have often dealt with philosophical topics.[1] So although I tend to write in ways more typical of theologians than philosophers, philosophy is never far from my mind.

What should be included in a course called History of Philosophy and Christian Thought? The first part, "History of Philosophy," is a fairly standard course designation. There is a widespread consensus as to what thinkers should be discussed under that topic. "Christian Thought," however, is not easy to circumscribe for pedagogical purposes. Christians have written on all sorts of subjects and in all kinds

1. My first book, *The Doctrine of the Knowledge of God* (Phillipsburg, NJ: Presbyterian and Reformed, 1987), attempted to develop an epistemology based on Scripture. Similarly the other books in my Theology of Lordship series: *The Doctrine of God* (Phillipsburg, NJ: P&R Publishing, 2002) deals with such issues as divine sovereignty, human freedom, and the problem of evil. *The Doctrine of the Christian Life* (Phillipsburg, NJ: P&R Publishing, 2008) deals with three traditions of non-Christian philosophical ethics. *The Doctrine of the Word of God* (Phillipsburg, NJ: P&R Publishing, 2010) returns again to epistemology, as does my *Systematic Theology: An Introduction to Christian Belief* (Phillipsburg, NJ: P&R Publishing, 2013). And of course, there is a lot of philosophical reflection in my apologetics books, *Apologetics to the Glory of God* (Phillipsburg, NJ: P&R Publishing, 1994) and *Cornelius Van Til: An Analysis of His Thought* (Phillipsburg, NJ: P&R Publishing, 1995). The appendices at the end of this volume include some of my philosophical reviews and papers.

of genres. One could argue that in a course such as this, the students should hear about Ignatius of Antioch, Dante Alighieri, Isaac Newton, John Donne, John Milton, John Wesley, Charles Hodge, Herman Bavinck, Dorothy Sayers, J. R. R. Tolkien, George MacDonald, G. K. Chesterton, Malcolm Muggeridge, Billy Graham—the list could go on and on. Christians have participated in all walks of life and have influenced all of them. But we must have a plan that will narrow the list.

My plan leads to the exclusion of all the names in the preceding paragraph. Not that I disrespect any of these people; indeed, they are all impressive thinkers and wonderful servants of God. But this book needs to "tell a story," as we like to say today, and it needs to be a philosophical story. So I have chosen to deal with those Christian thinkers who have either made substantial contributions to the general history of philosophy or developed distinctive philosophical ideas that have influenced the theology of the church.

But what mainly provides the continuity of the story is my attempt to analyze and evaluate this whole history from a Christian point of view. I believe that the Bible should govern our philosophical thinking, as indeed it must govern every other area of human life (1 Cor. 10:31). Some, to be sure, doubt that the Bible has anything to say about philosophy. The best way of replying to these doubts is to show what in fact the Bible does say on this subject. That will be the main theme and emphasis of this book.

In any case, this will not be an "unbiased" account of the history before us. Some will say that it is propaganda, rather than an objective study. Certainly I have tried to get the facts right, though my work is not, on the whole, individual research into original source documents. You won't find in this book many (if any) new interpretations of the philosophers and theologians. I have followed, for the most part, the consensus interpretations, because I want to mainly assess the impact that each thinker has had on the consensus. But in this book there will be many *evaluations* of thinkers that I suspect will be found unconventional. My whole idea is to expose the fact that the history of philosophy and theology is nothing less than spiritual warfare in the life of the mind.

So this book will differ from most other histories of thought, even Christian ones, especially in these ways: (1) Its Christian perspective is quite overt; I've made no effort to be subtle about it. (2) Indeed, it can be understood as an extended apologetic, making the case that non-Christian systems of thought, even inconsistent Christian ones, inevitably lapse into the intellectual bankruptcies of rationalism and irrationalism. (3) It deals with philosophy and theology in the same volume, to make the point that these two disciplines are profoundly interdependent even if they are distinguishable. (4) It focuses on the modern period more than most other books of this kind, because I want to prepare students for the spiritual warfare as it exists in their own time, without neglecting the background of this battle in earlier times. Chapters 5–8 deal with "modern" thought, and 9–13 with the twentieth and twenty-first centuries.

To make this book as useful as possible as a textbook for class, group, and individual study, I have included the following chapter-specific teaching and study helps at the end of each chapter: Key Terms, Study Questions, a Bibliography (print and online resources), Read for Yourself (a list of primary sources), Listen Online, and Famous Quotes. The Listen Online sections correlate the appropriate free audio lectures in my History of Philosophy series with the current chapter (see "Correlation of Book Chapters with Free Online Lectures" immediately before this book's Foreword). The Famous Quotes sections provide links to well-known quotations on Wikiquotes (and occasionally on Goodreads and Wikipedia) from the philosophers and theologians discussed in the current chapter.[2] Additionally, at the end of this volume, a Glossary, an Annotated Bibliography of Philosophy Texts, a General Bibliography, and three indices provide additional help.

My dedication is to the memory of Cornelius Van Til, who has had more influence on my philosophical thought than any other noncanonical writer. The theological and philosophical public has not begun to make use of the brilliant and profound insights of Van Til. He is not a mere apologist, but a substantial thinker with, I think, a great many cogent answers to our current questions. His often-obscure language should not be used as an excuse for dismissing him. Van Til is one thinker who repays diligent efforts to understand.

All my books are deeply influenced by Van Til, and I reflected on the nature of that influence especially in *Cornelius Van Til: An Analysis of His Thought*. The present volume is the first book, however, that I have explicitly dedicated to him. The reason is that in this book I am seeking to reflect some particular emphases of Van Til's teaching. Van Til was a professor of apologetics, but his apologetics was unique, not only in "method," as he liked to say, but also in emphasis. Most apologists write for the man on the street. That is fine, and there is still great need for that. Van Til did that occasionally.[3] But most of Van Til's work aimed at the great thinkers who have had the most impact on Western civilization. And so his apologetic writing and teaching emphasized

2. In chapters 1 and 13, I quote directly from several P&R Publishing publications.

3. As in the fascinating booklet "Why I Believe in God," available at http://www.thehighway.com/why_I_believe_cvt.html.

the history of philosophy and theology.[4] He believed that if you can deal seriously with such thinkers as Plato, Aristotle, Kant, and Hegel, you will be in much better shape to deal with the village atheists who capture the popular mind for a week or two. Interaction with the greatest thinkers does much to explain the intellectual developments of our own time, and only such debate can display the full strength of the Christian position. In that conviction I agree with Van Til, and I hope in this book to follow his lead.

My thanks again to P&R Publishing, with which I have worked for many years, and especially to John J. Hughes, my longtime friend, who shepherded this volume through the publishing process and who has helped me much on my past writing projects. In this book, he has worked together with Karen Magnuson, an outstanding copyeditor who has also done excellent work on my past projects. Thanks also to my RTS colleague John Muether, who has produced the Index of Names, Index of Subjects, and Index of Scripture. And I also acknowledge the work of Joseph E. Torres, who checked through all the URLs of my online sources.[5] Thanks also to my students at the two Westminster Seminaries and at Reformed Theological Seminary who have provided valuable encouragements and challenges over the years, and to my wonderful family: dearest Mary, Debbie, Doreen and Dennis, Skip and Sharon, Justin and Carol, Johnny, and all the grandkids.

4. See especially his treatment of Greek philosophy in his *Survey of Christian Epistemology* (Philadelphia: Den Dulk Foundation, 1969). This emphasis of Van Til underscores the silliness and ignorance of William Lane Craig's comment in Steven B. Cowan, ed., *Five Views on Apologetics* (Grand Rapids: Zondervan, 2000): "Van Til, for all his insights, was not a philosopher" (235). Van Til earned a Ph.D. in philosophy from Princeton University, and his writings are full of references to philosophers and close analyses of philosophical ideas. Although I criticized Craig's comment, he has not retracted it or apologized, to my knowledge.

5. All URLs were rechecked May 29, 2015.

ABBREVIATIONS

AJCB	John M. Frame, *Apologetics: A Justification of Christian Belief* (Phillipsburg, NJ: P&R Publishing, 2015)
CD	Karl Barth, *Church Dogmatics* (New York: Charles Scribner's Sons, 1936)
CSR	Common Sense Realism
CVT	John M. Frame, *Cornelius Van Til: An Analysis of His Thought* (Phillipsburg, NJ: P&R Publishing, 1995)
DCL	John M. Frame, *The Doctrine of the Christian Life* (Phillipsburg, NJ: P&R Publishing, 2008)
DG	John M. Frame, *The Doctrine of God* (Phillipsburg, NJ: P&R Publishing, 2002)
DKG	John M. Frame, *The Doctrine of the Knowledge of God* (Phillipsburg, NJ: Presbyterian and Reformed, 1987)
DWG	John M. Frame, *The Doctrine of the Word of God* (Phillipsburg, NJ: P&R Publishing, 2010)
ESV	English Standard Version
Institutes	John Calvin, *Institutes of the Christian Religion*, ed. John T. McNeill, trans. Ford Lewis Battles, 2 vols. (Philadelphia: Westminster Press, 1960)
JETS	*Journal of the Evangelical Theological Society*

KJV	King James Version
NASB	New American Standard Bible
NOG	John M. Frame, *No Other God: A Response to Open Theism* (Phillipsburg, NJ: P&R Publishing, 2001)
NT	New Testament
OT	Old Testament
RO	Radical orthodoxy
ST	John M. Frame, *Systematic Theology: An Introduction to Christian Belief* (Phillipsburg, NJ: P&R Publishing, 2013)
WCF	Westminster Confession of Faith
WTJ	*Westminster Theological Journal*

A History of Western Philosophy and Theology

Spiritual Warfare in the Life of the Mind

1

PHILOSOPHY AND THE BIBLE

THE WORD *PHILOSOPHY* means, etymologically, "love of wisdom." *Wisdom*, in turn, is "a kind of heightened knowledge, a knowledge that penetrates to deep significance and practical relevance."[1] In the ancient world, there was a genre called *wisdom literature* found in the biblical books of Job, Proverbs, Ecclesiastes, and the Song of Solomon,[2] but also in many cultures outside Israel. The method of the wisdom teachers was to gather the sayings of the wise, from many generations and locations, for the guidance of their own communities. What distinguishes wisdom in Israel from that of other cultures is the conviction that "the fear of the LORD is the beginning of wisdom" (Ps. 111:10).

Philosophy, however, should not be understood as an extension of the tradition of wisdom literature. In many ways, as we will see, philosophy is historically a revolt against traditional wisdom.

Philosophy, however, should not be understood as an extension of the tradition of wisdom literature. In many ways, as we will see, philosophy is historically a revolt against traditional wisdom.

I define *philosophy* as "the disciplined attempt to articulate and defend a worldview." A *worldview* is a general conception of the universe. The sciences generally seek understanding of particular aspects of the universe: chemistry the chemical, biology the biological, and so on. But philosophy deals with the most general truths of reality: what is, how we know it, how we should act. The term *worldview*, therefore, is an appropriate designation for the subject matter of philosophy.

Today, many prefer the term *metanarrative* when they wish to refer to such a comprehensive vision. *Metanarrative* sees the universe as an ongoing *story*, *worldview* as a collection of things, facts, or processes.

1. *DG*, 505. See my discussion there on 505–9.

2. Other parts of Scripture also have characteristics of wisdom literature—for example, Psalms 1; 104; Matthew 11:25–30; 1 Corinthians 1–3; and the Letter of James.

But the two ideas presuppose each other. If there is a narrative, it must be about something—namely, things (including persons), facts, or processes. If there are things, facts, or processes, then they have a history and can be described in a narrative, however dull that narrative might be at times.

Some have denied that worldviews and metanarratives are possible, or that if they do exist (perhaps in God's mind), we have no access to them. Jean-François Lyotard defined "postmodern" thought, which he embraces, as "incredulity toward metanarratives."[3] Certainly we can understand why some would think arrogant the claim to know the general structure of the universe. On the other hand, we should also be able to understand that worldviews are quite indispensable, at least as working assumptions. For example, why should we engage in discourse at all if we are not assuming that the universe is accessible to rational thought? Why should even postmodernists believe that there is some value in writing books, making rational arguments to defend their postmodernism? Inevitably, we make at least the assumption that the world is accessible to the human mind. And that assumption is a belief about the world as a whole, a worldview.

Lyotard may argue against it, but in doing so, he necessarily assumes a different world—a world in which most of the universe is irrational, not accessible to the mind, but in which, unaccountably, there are little pockets of rationality ("little narratives") that enable us to live and talk together. The irrational vastness, plus the pockets of rationality, constitutes Lyotard's worldview. He has not done away with metanarratives, but has only substituted one for another.

There might seem to be a kind of circularity in presupposing what I argue for. But that is inevitable when we are dealing with worldviews. Lyotard assumes his worldview when he argues for it. Rationalists defend their rationalism by appealing to reason.

As a Christian, I am committed to a worldview that comes from the Bible: God the Creator, the world as his creation, man made in his image, sin and its consequences as our predicament, Christ's atonement as our salvation, his return as the consummation of all things. I will be presupposing that worldview in this volume, but also arguing for it in dialogue with the philosophers whom we will consider. There might seem to be a kind of circularity in presupposing what I argue for. But that is inevitable when we are dealing with worldviews. Lyotard assumes his worldview when he argues for it. Rationalists defend their rationalism by appealing to reason. Idealists defend their idealism by constructing arguments informed by idealism. Empiricists, in the end, must defend empiricism by appealing to sense experience, though they rarely try to do that, and it is hard to imagine how that defense could be successful. That's the way it is in philosophy and in all of life: we can't step out of our skins. The best we can do is to show one another

3. Jean-François Lyotard, *The Postmodern Condition: A Report on Knowledge* (Minneapolis: University of Minnesota Press, 1984), 7.

why our worldview makes sense to us and makes sense (to us) of all of life. And of course, we have the right to suggest that another person's worldview might not make sense and might even deconstruct upon examination.[4] That is an example of a philosophical discussion.

WHY STUDY PHILOSOPHY?

One doesn't study philosophy these days with the goal of landing a high-paying job. What use is it? Aristotle's answer, at the beginning of his *Metaphysics*, is perhaps best: "all men by nature desire to know." As Edmund Hillary and Tenzing Norgay climbed Everest "because it is there," so all normal human beings have a desire to understand their environment. Some confine their search to Lyotard's "little narratives," but as we've seen, it is not easy to observe that restriction. Socrates, the great saint of philosophy, said that "the unexamined life is not worth living."[5]

Philosophers are in the business of thinking clearly, cogently, and profoundly. To understand and evaluate their work is excellent mental exercise.

But let's make the question more specific: why should anyone study the *history* of philosophy? And since this book seeks to look at questions from a Christian perspective, let me ask why a Christian, specifically, should study the history of philosophy.

Of course, not all Christians are obligated to study this topic. Not all are suited to it by ability, education, interest, and calling. But for those who are, the subject promises a number of benefits:

Philosophy over the centuries has had a major influence on Christian theology. The concepts nature, substance, *and* person *found in the doctrines of the Trinity and the person of Christ, for example, are philosophical terms, not found in the Bible.*

1. Philosophers are in the business of thinking clearly, cogently, and profoundly. To understand and evaluate their work is excellent mental exercise. People involved in nonphilosophical fields can benefit from exposure to the rigor of philosophical formulations and arguments. That includes Christians. And in my view, Christian theologians, preachers, and teachers generally need to improve the quality of their thinking, particularly their argumentation.[6]
2. Philosophy over the centuries has had a major influence on Christian theology. The concepts *nature*, *substance*, and *person* found in the doctrines of the Trinity and the person of Christ, for example, are philosophical terms, not found in the Bible. This is not necessarily a bad thing. When we apply Scripture to situations and controversies, we must often translate Scripture

4. I have discussed this type of circularity in more detail in many places. See *DKG*, 130–33; *AJCB*, 10–15; *DWG*, 24–25.

5. Plato, *Apology*, 38a.

6. Many theologians seem to think that in a dispute it is sufficient to take issue with an opponent's *conclusions*, without refuting the *arguments* that led to those conclusions. That is one reason why theological literature today is often unpersuasive, and divisions persist unnecessarily.

into language relevant to those situations.[7] Of course, fields of study other than philosophy have also influenced Christian discourse: science, history, literature, and so on. But remember that the work of philosophers is to formulate and examine worldviews. Insofar as Christian theology is also the articulation of a worldview, its interaction with philosophy is especially important.

3. Sadly, through most of the history of Western civilization, philosophy has been governed by non-Christian assumptions. The dominance of these presuppositions was interrupted during the medieval period, and there have been Christian philosophers since the beginning of the church. But from around 600 B.C. to A.D. 400, and from around 1650 to the present, the dominant influences in philosophy have been non-Christian.

   Now, since the business of philosophy is to think clearly, cogently, and profoundly about the world, the hardest challenges to Christian thought have come from the discipline of philosophy. So when Christians study philosophy, they become acquainted with the most formidable adversaries of the gospel: non-Christian thought in its most cogent form. Acquaintance with these is very beneficial for gospel witness.

In this book, I will be especially concerned to describe the interaction, the dialogue, between Christian theology and non-Christian philosophy.

PHILOSOPHY, THEOLOGY, AND RELIGION

Sadly, through most of the history of Western civilization, philosophy has been governed by non-Christian assumptions.

I define *theology* as "the application of the Word of God, by persons, to every aspect of human life."[8] On this definition, and on my previous definition of *philosophy*, there is a strong affinity between the two disciplines. The Word of God is, among other things, the authoritative statement of the Christian's worldview. And because it describes a historical sequence, it may be called a *metanarrative* as well. *Application* in my definition of *theology* includes the "formulation" and "defense" in my definition of *philosophy*. So we may say that Christian theology is Christian philosophy, or philosophy with a Christian worldview.

It might be argued that philosophers, unlike theologians, do not work from authoritative texts. But if that is true, it is true only for secular philosophers, not for Jewish, Muslim, or Christian ones. And even secular philosophers, as we have seen, presuppose worldviews, so that the worldview becomes for them the authoritative text.

7. Even the translation of Scripture from, say, Greek to English is an application of Scripture to a group of situations, the situations encountered by English speakers.

8. For exposition and defense of this definition, see *DKG*, 76–85; *DWG*, 272–79; *ST*, chap. 1.

I define *religion* as "the practice of faith," as in James 1:26–27:

> If anyone thinks he is religious and does not bridle his tongue but deceives his heart, this person's religion is worthless. Religion that is pure and undefiled before God, the Father, is this: to visit orphans and widows in their affliction, and to keep oneself unstained from the world.

I do not follow theologians such as Barth and Bonhoeffer, and many preachers, who use *religion* to refer to self-righteousness, man's attempt to justify himself before God by his works. Dictionaries never define it that way. More commonly, dictionaries equate the term with *faith*, *belief*, or *creed*, as does the definition of Clouser, to be discussed later in this chapter. But my definition catches, I think, the nuance of James 1:26–27—not faith as such, but its outworking in godly speech and compassionate behavior. *Religion* is a perfectly good word, and there is no justification for redefining it in order to make a theological or rhetorical[9] point.

On my definition, then, Christian philosophy is part of the Christian religion, an outworking of Christian faith. Christians are servants of Jesus Christ. He is their Lord. Scripture calls them to "do all to the glory of God" (1 Cor. 10:31). Their thinking, their philosophizing, is part of that.

On my definition, then, Christian philosophy is part of the Christian religion, an outworking of Christian faith. Christians are servants of Jesus Christ. He is their Lord. Scripture calls them to "do all to the glory of God" (1 Cor. 10:31). Their thinking, their philosophizing, is part of that. It is remarkable that Christians so readily identify the lordship of Christ in matters of worship, salvation, and ethics, but not in thinking. But as I indicated by the great number of Bible verses prefacing this book, God in Scripture over and over demands obedience of his people in matters of wisdom, thinking, knowledge, understanding, and so forth. Whenever the Christian engages in study, of philosophy or anything else, his first question must be: "How is this related to Christ?" And of course, everything is related to him, for he is the Creator of all (John 1:3), and

Whenever the Christian engages in study, of philosophy or anything else, his first question must be: "How is this related to Christ?" And of course, everything is related to him, for he is the Creator of all (John 1:3).

> he is the image of the invisible God, the firstborn of all creation. For by him all things were created, in heaven and on earth, visible and invisible, whether thrones or dominions or rulers or authorities—all things were created through him and for him. And he is before all things, and in him all things hold together. And he is the head of the body, the church. He is the beginning, the firstborn from the dead, that in everything he might be preeminent. For in him all the fullness of God was pleased to dwell, and through him to reconcile to himself all

9. I have in mind here the rhetoric of some young evangelists: "You hate religion? Well, I do, too. I hate religion, but I love Jesus." I agree with the point and, to some extent, the attitude. But there are better ways of stating it. Don't criticize "religion," but criticize formalism, traditionalism, church bureaucracy, and the like.

> things, whether on earth or in heaven, making peace by the blood of his cross. (Col. 1:15–20)

So Paul is able to say that in Christ "are hidden all the treasures of wisdom and knowledge" (Col. 2:3).

So we normally distinguish Christian from "secular" philosophy. *Secular* usually means "nonreligious." But is there such a thing as nonreligious philosophy?[10] "Secular" philosophies, of course, do not demand church attendance or participation in religious ceremonies. But in other respects, they are religious. Roy A. Clouser, in *The Myth of Religious Neutrality: An Essay on the Hidden Role of Religious Belief in Theories*,[11] discusses the difficulty of defining *religion*. What, he asks, do the great religions of the world have in common? That question is more difficult than it might seem, Clouser argues.[12] We might think that all religions include ethical codes, but Shinto does not. We might think that all religions acknowledge a personal supreme being, but Buddhism and Hinduism do not. Or we might propose that all religions demand worship. But Epicureanism and some forms of Buddhism and Hinduism do not. Clouser concludes, however, that it is nevertheless possible to define *religious belief*,[13] and he suggests the following:

> A religious belief is any belief in something or other as divine.
>
> "Divine" means having the status of not depending on anything else.[14]

A religious belief is any belief in something or other as divine. . . . "Divine" means having the status of not depending on anything else.

Clouser's definition of *divine* does not suffice to fully define the biblical God—or, for that matter, the gods of other religions. But it does define an attribute of the biblical God,[15] an attribute also ascribed to absolutes of other religious traditions. All systems of thought include belief in something that is self-sufficient, not dependent on anything else. In Christianity, the self-sufficient being is the biblical God. In Islam, it is Allah; in Hinduism, Brahma. Clouser points out that in Greek polytheism the gods are not divine according to his definition, because they depend on realities other than themselves. The flux from which all things come, called Chaos or Okeanos, is the true deity of the

10. The next three paragraphs are taken from my *DCL*, 55–57.

11. Notre Dame, IN: University of Notre Dame Press, 1991.

12. See his discussion in ibid., 10–12.

13. Note that Clouser's question is not the meaning of *religion*, as I discussed it earlier, but the nature of a *religious belief*, that is, a belief that is religious in character.

14. Ibid., 21–22.

15. Called *aseity* in *DG*, chap. 26.

ancient Greek religion.[16] Even purportedly atheistic religions such as Theravada Buddhism have deities in Clouser's sense. Theravada holds that the Void, the ultimate Nothingness, sometimes called Nirvana, is not dependent on anything else.[17]

But such a definition of *religion* makes it impossible for us to distinguish sharply between religion and philosophy, or indeed between religion and any other area of human thought and life.[18] Philosophies also, however secular they may claim to be, always acknowledge something that is divine in the sense of "not depending on anything else." Examples would be Thales's water, Plato's Form of the Good, Aristotle's Prime Mover, Spinoza's "God or Nature," Kant's noumenal, Hegel's Absolute, the Mystical of Wittgenstein's *Tractatus*. In the epistemological sphere, also, philosophers typically acknowledge human reason as self-sufficient in the sense that it requires no justification from anything more ultimate than itself. When they appear to deny autonomous reason (as with the Sophists, Duns Scotus, Hume, existentialism, and postmodernism), they typically exalt autonomous will or feeling, as we will see later, so that will or feeling becomes divine.

Such a definition of religion *makes it impossible for us to distinguish sharply between religion and philosophy, or indeed between religion and any other area of human thought and life.*

The biblical point to be made here is that nobody is really an atheist, in the most serious sense of that term. When people turn away from worship of the true God, they don't reject absolutes in general. Rather, instead of the true God, they worship idols, as Paul teaches in Romans 1:18–32. The great division in mankind is not that some worship a god and others do not. Rather, it is between those who worship the true God and those who worship false gods, idols. False worship might not involve rites or ceremonies, but it always involves acknowledgment of aseity, honoring some being as not dependent on anything else.

So I will argue through this book that the basic questions of philosophers are religious in character. Both philosophers and religious teachers explore the great questions of metaphysics (being), epistemology (knowledge), and value theory (value). Under metaphysics, both philosophers and religious teachers discuss the question of God and the world. Under epistemology, they both concern themselves with the justification of truth claims. Under value theory, both are interested in how we should live and what we should regard most highly.

I will argue through this book that the basic questions of philosophers are religious in character. Both philosophers and religious teachers explore the great questions of metaphysics (being), epistemology (knowledge), and value theory (value).

16. Clouser, *Myth*, 25.

17. Ibid., 26–27.

18. The same result follows from some other recent attempts to define *religion*, such as Paul Tillich's definition of *religion* as "ultimate concern," and William Tremmel's "affirmation of unrestricted value." Clouser opposes these definitions in ibid., 12–16, but they also imply that all human thought is religious. I defined *religion* earlier as "the practice of faith," and that definition coincides with Clouser's, when we understand that to accept anything as "not depending on anything else" is an act of faith, though not necessarily Christian faith.

In current culture, there is a strong bias against "religious" views, in science, politics, and literature. If my argument above carries weight, we should reprove such bias. Insofar as *religion* is a meaningful category, it cannot be sharply distinguished from philosophy or science. When people oppose the teaching of "religious" concepts, they are not presenting a criterion that can logically distinguish between true and false ideas. Rather, they are using the term *religion* as a club to arbitrarily exclude consideration of viewpoints that they don't happen to like.

That is, of course, blatantly unfair, indeed "un-American," as we say in the States. Some, of course, appeal to the "separation of church and state" as formulated in the First Amendment to the U.S. Constitution. But that amendment (courts to the contrary notwithstanding) does not require a total separation of religion from the political sphere. It does not even forbid government-established churches, except on the federal level. When the Constitution was written, a number of the colonies had established churches, and the purpose of the amendment was not to forbid these, but to forbid the federal government from establishing a church in competition with the state churches.

In a truly free society, people in every field would be free to express their views whether called religious or not, and the marketplace of ideas would be free to sort them out.

In a truly free society, people in every field would be free to express their views whether called religious or not, and the marketplace of ideas would be free to sort them out.

SUBDIVISIONS OF PHILOSOPHY

Metaphysics

Let me say some more about the three subjects mentioned in the previous section. *Metaphysics* is the study of the most general features of the universe. Philosophers have sometimes called it "the study of being itself" or "the study of being qua being." That is to say, other disciplines including the sciences explore different sorts of *beings*, various types of being or various kinds of beings, but philosophy asks what is meant by *being* in general, in distinction, of course, from *nonbeing*.

This is a difficult set of questions. Hegel proposed this thought-experiment: close your eyes and think of *being*; then close your eyes and think of *nonbeing*. Notice any difference? It seems that whenever we try to think of nonbeing, we are thinking of *something*, and therefore of being. Same when we try to define *nonbeing*, or list things that are not beings. When we do that, they all turn out to be beings of some kind. Unicorns, for example, don't exist in jungles, but they do exist in literature. If being cannot be distinguished from nonbeing, however, how can it be anything at all?

Yet philosophers should be admired for their courage in fielding such apparently impossible questions.

Metaphysics includes the question "why is there something rather than nothing?"—which Heidegger thought was the most central question of all philosophy. It also asks about the present configuration of being: "why are things the way they are?" And "what are the most basic features of reality?"

Philosophers have varied in their appreciation of and interest in metaphysics. Since Kant, many secular philosophers have rejected metaphysics as baseless speculation. The language analysts of the twentieth century often said that the only function of philosophy was to clarify language, that philosophers had no means to know the structure of the universe beyond the methods of science. But some of the analysts differed with this assessment, saying that a careful analysis of our language in fact reveals metaphysical truths.[19] And process philosophy carries on a vigorous discussion of metaphysics to this day.

Philosophers have varied in their appreciation of and interest in metaphysics. Since Kant, many secular philosophers have rejected metaphysics as baseless speculation. The language analysts of the twentieth century often said that the only function of philosophy was to clarify language, that philosophers had no means to know the structure of the universe beyond the methods of science.

Specific questions discussed by metaphysicians, and their varying answers, include these:

1. Is the universe one or many? Parmenides, Plotinus, Spinoza, and Hegel said that beneath all the apparent plurality in the world there is a oneness, and the world is that oneness. These are called *monists*. Others, such as Democritus, Leibniz, and the early Wittgenstein, thought that the world was made of tiny components, distinct from one another and each irreducible to anything else. These are called *pluralists*. Still others, known as *dualists*, hold that the world is made up of two more or less equally ultimate realities; typically one is good and the other is evil, and they fight for supremacy. Examples of this are found in the Zoroastrian religion and the Manichaean sects that sought influence among early Christians. There are also other mediating positions. Some philosophers, such as Aristotle and Locke, have held the commonsense view that there are many things in the world, but that these things can be understood in general categories, so that the universe has both unity and plurality.
2. What is the basic composition of the universe? Thales said water, Anaximenes air, Anaxagoras something "indefinite," Heraclitus fire, Pythagoras number. Democritus thought the world was composed of tiny, indestructible material bits called *atoms*. These, and later thinkers such as Karl Marx, are called *materialists*, because they believed that everything in the world is material in nature. Plato and Aristotle said that the world is a combination of matter and form. Berkeley, Leibniz, and Hegel said that the world is mind and that matter is an illusion. This

19. One example is Peter F. Strawson, *Individuals: An Essay in Descriptive Metaphysics* (London: Methuen, 1959).

David Hume denied that there was any necessary connection between cause and effect. Immanuel Kant said that there was such a connection, but that the connection is imposed by the human mind, not to be found in nature.

view is called *idealism*. Plotinus, Spinoza, and Hegel said that the world is divine, a view called *pantheism*.

3. Are universals real, or only particulars? In our language, some terms refer to general or abstract realities: *redness, triangularity, manhood, virtue*. These are called *universals*. They are contrasted with *particulars*, which refer to individual things: *this man, this tree, this cookie, this bear.* Some philosophers (as William of Occam) have said that only particulars exist. These are called *nominalists*, for they say that universals are only names, words by which we refer to a lot of particulars at once. Others (Plato, Aristotle) say that universals have a distinct existence (if they don't, what do universal terms mean?). These are called *realists*. Some of these, such as Plato, questioned whether material things have any reality at all, so they believed that only universals are real. Among those who think universals exist, there is some disagreement as to *where* they exist: In another world (Plato)? As a component of things in this world (Aristotle)? In God's mind (Augustine)?
4. Do things in the universe change, or are they static? Parmenides said that the universe was entirely unchanging. Heraclitus said the opposite, that everything was constantly changing, in flux. Plato and Aristotle taught that some things were unchanging (forms), others constantly changing (matter).
5. Do the events of nature and history work toward goals (teleology), or do they simply occur, without any rationale or direction? Plato and especially Aristotle taught that the course of nature was teleological, that every motion or process had a purpose. Bertrand Russell and Jean-Paul Sartre denied that any purposes exist, except those that human beings themselves create.
6. What is the connection between cause and effect? Some, like Democritus, Hobbes, and Spinoza, have been *determinists*: that is, they taught that every event is necessitated by another event, forming an inexorable causal chain. Epicurus, the Church Fathers, Descartes, Arminius, Whitehead, and others have held to a view of *libertarian freedom* in which human beings are capable of performing acts that are not caused by other events. David Hume denied that there was any *necessary connection* between cause and effect. Immanuel Kant said that there was such a connection, but that the connection is imposed by the human mind, not to be found in nature.
7. Do human beings have souls? Minds distinct from their bodies? Plato said yes, followed by most traditional Christians, such as Augustine and Aquinas. Descartes agreed. Aristotle, however, said that the soul is "the form of the body." Thales, Epicurus, Thomas Hobbes, Karl Marx, and Bertrand Russell

were *materialists*, believing that all events can be explained in terms of matter and motion. On this view, there is no immaterial soul. If there is something that we can call *soul*, it is either material (the Stoic view) or an aspect of the body.

8. How does the human mind operate? How should it? Philosophers have made various distinctions within the sphere of human thought and experience: intellect, will, emotions, imagination, memory, intuition, perception, ideas, impressions, and so on. *Intellectualists* (such as Plato, Aquinas, Descartes, Hegel, Gordon H. Clark) believe that when the mind is working properly, all aspects of the mind are subject to the intellect. *Voluntarists* (Duns Scotus, William of Occam, Arthur Schopenhauer, Friedrich Nietzsche) note that believing something often if not always requires a choice, a decision of will. For them, will, not intellect, is fundamental. *Subjectivists* (such as the Sophists, Hume, Schelling, and Schleiermacher) believe that the mind does and should follow its feelings. Others develop more sophisticated theories of the interaction of these "faculties."
9. Is there a god? As I said earlier, in the most important sense there are no atheists. But there are great differences among philosophers as to *what kind* of god there is. Some, such as Xenophanes, Spinoza, and Hegel, believed that the world was god. (That view is called *pantheism*.) Whitehead and Hartshorne believed that the world was divine, an aspect of god, but that god was somewhat more than the world. (That view is called *panentheism*, "everything is *in* god.") Some seventeenth- and eighteenth-century thinkers held that God created the world to run according to "natural laws" and never again intervened. They are called *deists*. Plato used theological terms to describe his Idea of the Good, and in reference to the "Demiurge" who formed the world in the image of the Forms. Aristotle applied the term *god* to his Prime Mover. Anselm defined *God* as "that than which nothing greater can be conceived" and defined that, in turn, in biblical terms. People who hold a biblical view of God are called *theists*.

Is there a god? As I said earlier, in the most important sense there are no atheists. But there are great differences among philosophers as to what kind of god there is.

Epistemology

Epistemology is theory of knowledge. It asks: "What is knowledge?" "How is knowledge possible?" "How should we go about knowing?" "How do we distinguish truth from falsity, reality from appearance?"

Typically, philosophical epistemology deals with the *subject* of knowledge (a person), an *object* of knowledge (what he knows), and some sort of rule that determines whether the subject *knows* the object. Plato

Typically, philosophical epistemology deals with the subject of knowledge (a person), an object of knowledge (what he knows), and some sort of rule that determines whether the subject knows the object.

described that rule as an *account*, so he defined *knowledge* as "true belief with an account." More recently, the account has been called *justification*, and, still more recently, *warrant* (Alvin Plantinga).

Epistemologists have differed over the question to what extent knowledge is possible. Parmenides was sure that knowledge was possible, so that if anything appeared unknowable, it could not exist. But the Sophists denied that we had any knowledge, at least any knowledge that is objective and universal. One of them, Protagoras, said that "man is the measure of all things," referring to the individual man. For him, there is no universal truth, nothing that is true for everybody, only truth for the individual—truth for me and truth for you.

Those who are optimistic about the prospect of knowing truth, such as Parmenides and Plato, are often called *rationalists*. That is, they believe that human reason is the final judge of what is true and false, and that therefore it is always trustworthy. Others, such as the Sophists, have less confidence in reason. They may be called *irrationalists* or *skeptics*.

Epistemologists also differ as to the *ground* of knowledge. In the previous section, I distinguished a number of "faculties" of the human mind. Theories of knowledge discuss the interaction of these faculties, one of the overlaps between metaphysics and epistemology. In the quest for the most fundamental ground of knowledge, the main contenders are reason, sense experience, and our general subjectivity (including feelings, will, intuition, mystical insight). *Rationalists* (see above) believe that human reason is the final judge of what is true or false. *Empiricists*, such as John Locke and David Hume, believe that sense experience has the ultimate word and that all reasoning must be based on that. *Subjectivists*, such as the Sophists and perhaps modern existentialists, believe that we find meaning and knowledge within ourselves.

In my analysis, there are three general types of secular ethics: deontologism, teleologism, and existentialism.

Value Theory

Value theory, or *axiology*, includes ethics, aesthetics, and other kinds of value insofar as they are of interest to philosophers (e.g., some aspects of economic value). It asks, "What should we value most highly?"—the question of the *summum bonum* or highest good. Also, of course: "How should we make value judgments?" "Are values objective or subjective?" "What things, events, actions are good and bad? Right and wrong?" and so on.

In my analysis, there are three general types of secular ethics: deontologism, teleologism, and existentialism. *Deontological* ethicists such as Kant (and to some extent Plato) believe that we should make our decisions based on *duty*. *Teleological* ethics (such as that of Bentham, Mill, and to some extent Aristotle) argues that we should make our decisions first by identifying an ethical goal (usually individual or corporate happiness) and then seeking the best means of reaching that goal. *Existential* ethics (Sophism, Sartre) tells us to do what we most want to do in our heart of hearts, to express what we really are.

I will not be discussing value theory to a great extent in this book, because I need to conserve space, and I have discussed ethical philosophy in some detail in *DCL*: non-Christian ethics in chapters 5–8, Christian ethical philosophy in chapters 9–21. But the reader should take note (in the following section) of the importance of integrating metaphysics and epistemology with ethics. I will be emphasizing that point throughout this book.

RELATIONS OF THE THREE SUBDIVISIONS

A novice philosopher might look at these three disciplines—metaphysics, epistemology, and value theory—and wonder where to start.

A novice philosopher might look at these three disciplines—metaphysics, epistemology, and value theory—and wonder where to start. Perhaps he thinks that he might study metaphysics exclusively for a year, learning all he can about the structure of the world, and only after that turn to epistemology and ethics. After all, it seems, the subjects and objects of knowledge are part of the world. So you need to know the world before you consider those specific parts.

On the other hand, how can you gain a knowledge of metaphysics if you have no knowledge about knowledge? So evidently metaphysics presupposes epistemology, as epistemology presupposes metaphysics.

My general conclusion is that metaphysics, epistemology, and value theory are not independent of one another. Rather, they presuppose one another and influence one another. So, for example, one type of epistemology will lead to one kind of metaphysics, another to another kind.

What about value theory (focusing specifically on ethics)? Well, if you have no sense of right and wrong, no sense of obligations or rights, you really won't get far in a study of knowledge or being. For metaphysics and epistemology are human activities, human studies, and every human activity can be ethically evaluated. There are right and wrong ways to study philosophy, and these are expressed in ethical values. The ethics of study include discipline, diligence, respect for truth, avoidance of falsehood, honesty in reporting conclusions, humility in admitting error and inadequacy, acceptance of responsibility to give evidence for one's claims, where evidence is rightly demanded. When someone rejects or fails to exemplify such virtues, his philosophy (as a metaphysician or epistemologist) will suffer correspondingly. So the proper conclusions of philosophical study are the conclusions that we *ought* to have; and that *ought* is an ethical *ought*.

My general conclusion is that metaphysics, epistemology, and value theory are not independent of one another. Rather, they presuppose one another and influence one another. So, for example, one type of epistemology will lead to one kind of metaphysics, another to another kind. To Aristotle, for example, knowledge is a knowledge of individual things (epistemology), so in his metaphysics the world is a collection of things. To the early Wittgenstein, knowledge is a knowledge of facts expressed in propositions, and as he said, "The world is the totality of facts, not of things."[20] So for him as well, epistemology and metaphysics determine one another.

Indeed, all epistemologies presuppose that the human subject is somehow connected to the world so that knowledge is possible; that is a metaphysical presupposition. Similarly, value theory makes little sense unless there is a source of value. But to affirm that there is such a source and to identify it is a metaphysical task.

Another way of putting it is that metaphysics, epistemology, and value theory are *perspectives* on the whole discipline of philosophy.[21] We may picture that whole discipline as a triangle, and the three subdivisions as corners of the triangle; see fig. 1.1.

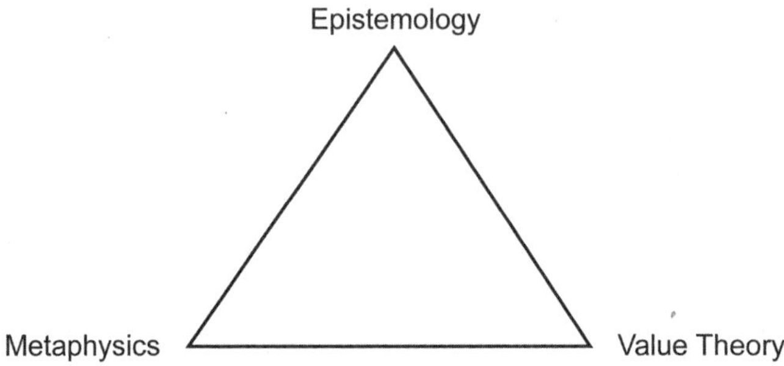

Fig. 1.1. Perspectives on the Discipline of Philosophy

You can begin the philosophical task at any corner of the triangle. But shortly you will run into content emanating from one of the other corners. In practice, you will go round and round the triangle: enriching your metaphysics with epistemological insights, enriching your epistemology with value theory, and so on. So metaphysics, epistemology, and ethics are not best understood as *parts* of philosophy, but as *aspects*. Each is a *perspective* on the whole discipline of philosophy.

Another way of putting it is that metaphysics, epistemology, and value theory are perspectives on the whole discipline of philosophy.

BIBLICAL PHILOSOPHY

In our historical approach to philosophy, we should begin at the beginning. And on a Christian view of things, the beginning is the

20. Ludwig Wittgenstein, *Tractatus Logico-Philosophicus* (London: Empire Books, 2011), 1.1.

21. Readers familiar with my previous books know that I use quite a number of triangular perspectival diagrams. Usually they form a pattern derived from God's lordship attributes, which we will consider later in the chapter. The present diagram does not align easily with the lordship pattern, but in general I see metaphysics as the "situation," epistemology as furnishing the "laws" or "norms" of thought, and value theory as bringing the person into the equation. But I'm aware that value theory also contains laws, that persons are a component of metaphysics, and so forth.

creation of the world by God. The biblical doctrine of creation establishes a worldview that antedates the views of all other religions and philosophies and is also unique among them.

Creator and Creature

The first element of this worldview is the Creator-creature distinction itself. In the biblical metaphysic, there are two levels of reality: that of the Creator and that of the creature. Van Til illustrated this relationship by two circles, the larger one representing God, the lower (and smaller) circle creation; see fig. 1.2.

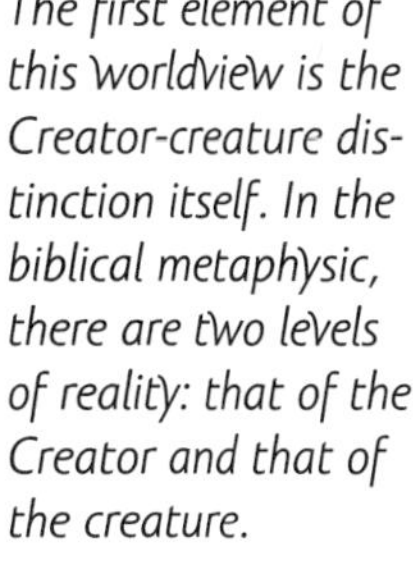
The first element of this worldview is the Creator-creature distinction itself. In the biblical metaphysic, there are two levels of reality: that of the Creator and that of the creature.

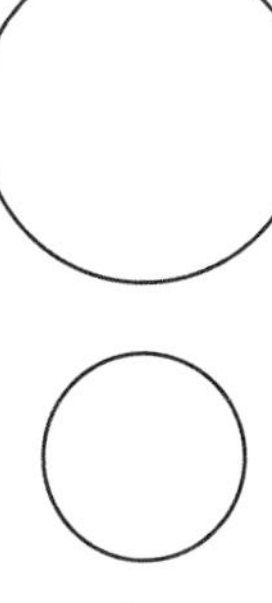

Fig. 1.2. The Distinction between Creator and Creature

These may never be confused (as in Spinoza, who believed that nature could be called God: *Deus sive natura*): the Lord is always Lord, and the creatures are always his servants. In Christianity, creation is *ex nihilo*, "out of nothing." The world is not an emanation from God's essence, a piece of God, as it were (as in Gnostic philosophy, for example). It is entirely and irrevocably distinct from God. But as a creature of God, it is capable of fellowship with God.

Someone might object that this distinction between God and the world is not compatible with the union of God and man in Jesus Christ.

Nor is there anything in between the two levels (also as in Gnosticism, which posited a continuum of mediators between the highest being and the material world). Van Til did sometimes put two vertical lines between the two circles, meaning that God was able to "connect with" his creation, that he was free to act in the world and communicate with it. But there is no third level of being, only two.[22]

Someone might object that this distinction between God and the world is not compatible with the union of God and man in Jesus Christ. But it is in Christology that the church has made the most zealous efforts

22. My good friend Peter Jones has noted that violation of the Creator-creature distinction is rife in modern neopaganism ("New Age thought"), which (parallel to ancient Gnosticism) tries to argue that all things are one. In that context, he describes the Christian worldview as *Twoism* and neopagan pantheism as *Oneism*. That distinction enables him to clearly communicate some of the major problems in modern culture. See Peter R. Jones, *Capturing the Pagan Mind* (Nashville, TN: Broadman and Holman, 2003); Peter R. Jones, *One or Two: Seeing a World of Difference* (Escondido, CA: Main Entry Editions, 2010).

to keep God and man distinct. The Council of Chalcedon (A.D. 451) declared that in Jesus there are two distinct natures, divine and human:

> So, following the saintly fathers, we all with one voice teach the confession of one and the same Son, our Lord Jesus Christ: the same perfect in divinity and perfect in humanity, the same truly God and truly man, of a rational soul and a body; consubstantial with the Father as regards his divinity, and the same consubstantial with us as regards his humanity; like us in all respects except for sin; begotten before the ages from the Father as regards his divinity, and in the last days the same for us and for our salvation from Mary, the virgin God-bearer as regards his humanity; one and the same Christ, Son, Lord, only-begotten, acknowledged in two natures which undergo no confusion, no change, no division, no separation; at no point was the difference between the natures taken away through the union, but rather the property of both natures is preserved and comes together into a single person and a single subsistent being; he is not parted or divided into two persons, but is one and the same only-begotten Son, God, Word, Lord Jesus Christ, just as the prophets taught from the beginning about him, and as the Lord Jesus Christ himself instructed us, and as the creed of the fathers handed it down to us.[23]

Notice the four Greek adverbs that are translated "no confusion, no change, no division, no separation." In Christ there is the most intimate possible union between God and man, which the *Chalcedonian Declaration* expresses by saying that in him there is "no division, no separation." But even in Christ, God and man are distinct. They are not "confused"; neither is "changed" into the other.

I believe that the doctrine of creation ex nihilo *is unique to biblical religion. Judaism and Islam give some respect to it, but that is because of the influence of the Bible on those faiths. Among "secular" thinkers, creation* ex nihilo *is nowhere to be found.*

I believe that the doctrine of creation *ex nihilo* is unique to biblical religion. Judaism and Islam give some respect to it, but that is because of the influence of the Bible on those faiths. Among "secular" thinkers, creation *ex nihilo* is nowhere to be found.[24]

Absolute Tripersonality[25]

Let us look now at the upper level of reality according to Scripture. What sort of being has created the world out of nothing? Of course,

23. *Dogmatic Definition of the Council of Chalcedon*, available at http://www.ewtn.com/faith/teachings/incac2.htm.

24. My exegetical argument of creation *ex nihilo* is in *DG*, 298–302.

25. At this point I begin to expound the *triperspectival* understanding of the world that I have previously argued in *DKG* and elsewhere. It can also be accessed in the writings of my friend Vern S. Poythress, for example in his *Redeeming Philosophy: A God-Centered Approach to the Big Questions* (Wheaton, IL: Crossway, 2014). I will discuss Poythress at the very end of this book.

many things can be said about the nature of God. But of particular philosophical importance is that God is *absolute personality*. To say that he is absolute is to say that he is self-sufficient, self-existent, or, as theologians say, *a se*. He therefore does not depend on anything else,[26] but everything else depends on him. He is, as the doctrine of creation implies, the origin of all things, the First Cause.

Absolute beings are fairly common in religious and philosophical literature. The Greek Fate, the Hindu Brahma, Parmenides' Being, Plato's Idea of the Good, Aristotle's Prime Mover, Plotinus's One, and Hegel's Absolute may fairly be described as absolute beings, possessing the attribute of *aseity*.[27]

The biblical God also has the attributes of personality. He is not only absolute, but personal: he knows, loves, speaks. So not only is he the fundamental cause of everything, but our relationship with him is the most important of all our personal relationships.

But the biblical God also has the attributes of *personality*. He is not only absolute, but personal: he knows, loves, speaks. So not only is he the fundamental cause of everything, but our relationship with him is the most important of all our personal relationships. He not only makes us, but tells us his will, expresses his love, provides salvation from sin, and tells us what he has done to redeem.

Belief in personal gods can be found in many religions.[28] The old polytheisms of Greece, Rome, Egypt, Babylon, Canaan, India, Scandinavia, Germany, and elsewhere are religions of personal gods. But those personal gods are never absolute beings. Zeus and Hera, for example, had parents, and were subject to fits of anger and jealousy. The gods of polytheism are not *a se*, not all-powerful, and certainly not paragons of morality and truth.

Only biblical religion acknowledges an absolute being who is also personal.[29] So for the Christian, the Creator of the universe is also our Lord, our ultimate Judge, and our dearest friend. So the God of the Bible is not only the First Cause, but also the ultimate standard of truth and of right.

Only biblical religion acknowledges an absolute being who is also personal. . . . More than this: the biblical God is not only personal, but tripersonal.

More than this: the biblical God is not only personal, but tripersonal.[30] He is one God in three persons, Father, Son, and Holy Spirit. His oneness is important philosophically: the world has only one First Cause, one ultimate standard of truth and right. But God's threeness is

26. Recall that this is Clouser's definition of *divine*.

27. Recall Clouser's definition of God as a being who is "not depend[ent] on anything else." The term *aseity* comes from the Latin *a se*, "from himself."

28. Not, however, in many philosophies. Of course, philosophies associated with religions that honor personal gods sometimes acknowledge them. (Epicurus admitted their existence, but did not allow them to play any role in his philosophy.) But even that is rare in the history of philosophy.

29. Of course, that includes Christianity, which in my view is the only true interpretation of the Bible. But as I noted earlier, there are also religions, such as Judaism, Islam, and the Christian heresies such as the Mormons and Jehovah's Witnesses, that carry some vestige of absolute-personality theism.

30. For my exegetical account of the doctrine of the Trinity, see *DG*, 619–735.

also important. As we saw earlier, philosophical metaphysicians have argued among themselves about monism and pluralism: whether the universe is one or many. Van Til's view was that because God is both one and many, he has made a world that is both one and many: that is, no unity without particulars, nor vice versa. Philosophical attempts to reduce the universe to one something, or to chop the world into "ultimate constituents," either procedure as an attempt to gain exhaustive knowledge of the world, are bound to fail.[31]

Lordship

What, then, is the relationship between Creator and creature, between the absolute tripersonality and those who depend on him? I believe that the most fundamental biblical description of this relationship is *lordship*: God is Lord, and creation is his servant.[32] In my analysis, the nature of God's lordship can be summarized by the terms *control*, *authority*, and *presence*. God's control is his power to bring all things to pass according to the counsel of his will (Eph. 1:11). His authority is his right to be obeyed, so that his control has a moral basis. His presence is his nearness to his creation and his intimate relationships with it. The most profound relationship is the covenant, in which God says, "I will be your God, and you will be my people" (Ex. 6:7; Lev. 26:12; Rev. 21:3).

I describe these three terms as the *lordship attributes*, and they are perspectivally related; see fig. 1.3.

What, then, is the relationship between Creator and creature, between the absolute tripersonality and those who depend on him? I believe that the most fundamental biblical description of this relationship is lordship*: God is Lord, and creation is his servant.*

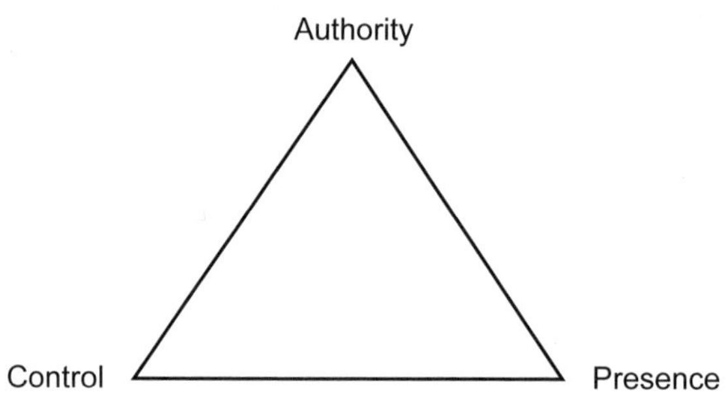

Fig. 1.3. The Lordship Attributes

Each of these attributes implies the others. If God is in control of all things, then he controls the standards for truth and right, so his control

31. I will discuss this in more detail in my discussion of Van Til in chapter 13.

32. For my argument for the centrality of lordship in Scripture and the nature of lordship in terms of control, authority, and presence, see *DG*, 21–115, and *ST*, chaps. 2–6. Other biblical designations of God are also important, especially *King* and *Father*. In my view, these are perspectivally identical with *Lord*.

implies his authority. And if he controls all things, he exercises his power everywhere, and (for an immaterial being) that constitutes his presence.

If God has authority over all things, then he has control, for he has the right to command anything (personal or impersonal), and it must obey. For example, even in the original creation he made the world by issuing commands. He commanded even nonexistent things to spring into existence ("let there be light," Gen. 1:3; cf. Rom. 4:17). And his authority implies his presence, for his authority extends to all things.

If God has authority over all things, then he has control, for he has the right to command anything (personal or impersonal), and it must obey. . . . And his authority implies his presence, for his authority extends to all things.

His presence means that nothing in the universe can escape from his control or authority (Ps. 139).

The threefold pattern suggests that this account of God's lordship may be importantly related to God's Trinitarian nature, and I believe it is. The three persons of the Trinity are, of course, "distinct but not separate." They work together in all of world history. But they do play distinct roles, particularly in their relation to the world, in the metanarrative of creation, fall, and redemption. In general, God the Father is prominent in biblical accounts of God's eternal plan. The Son, not the Father, becomes incarnate to implement that plan in obedience to the Father. Then the Spirit comes to be "with" and "in" God's people as he bears witness to the work of Christ. These distinctions suggest that the Father is the "authority," the Son the "controller," and the Spirit the "presence" of God.

Of course, in all aspects of God's work, the three persons are involved together. The Son is "in" the Father and the Father in him. The Spirit is in the Father and the Son, and they are in him. This mutual indwelling is what theologians call *circumcessio* or *perichoresis*.

PERSPECTIVES OF HUMAN KNOWLEDGE

If God is Lord, then human beings are persons subject to his lordship: servants, children, friends, citizens. In all our decisions and activities, the first consideration is our relation to God.

In the study of epistemology, for example, our knowledge is related to God's lordship in three ways: it must take account of God's control, authority, and presence. To take account of God's lordship attributes, in my view, is to think according to certain perspectives.

So in the study of epistemology, for example, our knowledge is related to God's lordship in three ways: it must take account of God's control, authority, and presence. To take account of God's lordship attributes, in my view, is to think according to certain *perspectives*. Earlier we considered the discipline of philosophy made up of the perspectives of metaphysics, epistemology, and value theory. Now I focus on epistemology and note important perspectives within that field.[33]

When we take account of God's *control* of nature and history, we can see that our entire situation is governed by his foreordination and

33. In a perspectival understanding of knowledge, there are perspectives within perspectives within perspectives.

providence.[34] As we explore that situation (both our individual situations and the whole course of nature and history), we are seeking to know the world by the *situational perspective*.

When we consider the world as standing under the *authority* of God, we can learn that everything in creation reveals him and his will (see my study of Romans 1 in the following section). To study the world this way is to focus on the *normative perspective*.

When we consider the world as the locus of God's *presence*, both outside us and within us, we are focusing on the *existential perspective*; see fig. 1.4.

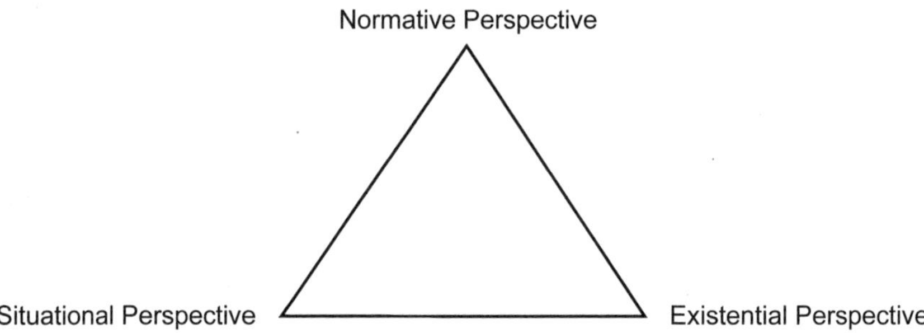

Fig. 1.4. Perspectives on Human Knowledge

I describe these as *perspectives* because they cannot be separated from one another. If we are to understand the situation rightly, we must understand it as the location of God's revelation, his norms; so the situational includes the normative. To understand God's norms rightly, we must understand how they apply to situations and to ourselves; so the normative includes the situational and existential. To understand God's relationship to ourselves rightly, we must understand ourselves as part of a God-created environment (situational) and as covenant subjects made to live under God's law (normative); so the existential includes the normative and the situational.

A Christian philosopher should understand that we cannot have a philosophy based on fact (situational) unless those facts are interpreted by God's norms (normative) and through the faculties of our minds (existential).

Though none of these perspectives can be separated from the others, it is helpful to distinguish them, if only to maintain a balanced view of things. A Christian philosopher should understand that we cannot have a philosophy based on *fact* (situational) unless those facts are interpreted by God's norms (normative) and through the faculties of our minds (existential). Nor can we maintain a philosophy that reduces all reality to *forms* or *logic* (normative) without relating these to the

34. *Foreordination* includes God's eternal plan and decrees for the course of history. *Providence* is God's action within history to bring his plan to fulfillment. See *DG*, chaps. 14, 16. In foreordination, God rules "from above"; in providence, he rules "from below." So his sovereignty envelops his creation.

facts of the world and the inwardness of the human subject. Same for philosophies of *feeling* (existential), which often fail to do justice to norms and to objective facts.

So no one of these three concepts is competent to be the foundation of a philosophy, separated from the others. Each is a perspective on the whole of reality and therefore a perspective on all philosophy. Each includes the other two, and none is intelligible apart from the other two.

No one of these three concepts is competent to be the foundation of a philosophy, separated from the others. Each is a perspective on the whole of reality and therefore a perspective on all philosophy. Each includes the other two, and none is intelligible apart from the other two.

SIN AND PHILOSOPHY

We have seen that the Bible teaches a distinct and unique worldview: the Creator-creature distinction, God as absolute tripersonality, and divine lordship as his relation to the world. But many fail to acknowledge the biblical worldview. The Bible itself gives a reason for this, namely, sin. In Romans 1:18–32, the apostle Paul says this:

> For the wrath of God is revealed from heaven against all ungodliness and unrighteousness of men, who by their unrighteousness suppress the truth. For what can be known about God is plain to them, because God has shown it to them. For his invisible attributes, namely, his eternal power and divine nature, have been clearly perceived, ever since the creation of the world, in the things that have been made. So they are without excuse. For although they knew God, they did not honor him as God or give thanks to him, but they became futile in their thinking, and their foolish hearts were darkened. Claiming to be wise, they became fools, and exchanged the glory of the immortal God for images resembling mortal man and birds and animals and creeping things.
>
> Therefore God gave them up in the lusts of their hearts to impurity, to the dishonoring of their bodies among themselves, because they exchanged the truth about God for a lie and worshiped and served the creature rather than the Creator, who is blessed forever! Amen.
>
> For this reason God gave them up to dishonorable passions. For their women exchanged natural relations for those that are contrary to nature; and the men likewise gave up natural relations with women and were consumed with passion for one another, men committing shameless acts with men and receiving in themselves the due penalty for their error.
>
> And since they did not see fit to acknowledge God, God gave them up to a debased mind to do what ought not to be done. They were filled with all manner of unrighteousness, evil, covetousness, malice. They are full of envy, murder, strife, deceit, maliciousness. They are gossips, slanderers, haters of

We have seen that the Bible teaches a distinct and unique worldview: the Creator-creature distinction, God as absolute tripersonality, and divine lordship as his relation to the world.

> God, insolent, haughty, boastful, inventors of evil, disobedient to parents, foolish, faithless, heartless, ruthless. Though they know God's righteous decree that those who practice such things deserve to die, they not only do them but give approval to those who practice them.

As I indicated earlier, God's lordship applies to all human activities, and knowing is one of those. So abandoning God's lordship leads to the corruption of human life in ethics and worship, but also in knowledge. In this passage, we learn that God has revealed himself clearly to human beings (Rom. 1:19–20). If people claim to be ignorant of him, they cannot claim innocence: their ignorance is their own fault. The revelation is clear, but they have willfully repressed it (vv. 18, 21, 23, 25, 28). For that repression they have no excuse (v. 20).

The sin of these people begins, then, in the area of knowledge. When they repress the knowledge of God, that leads to the sin of idolatry (Rom. 1:22–23), then to sexual sins (vv. 24–27), and then to "all manner of unrighteousness" (vv. 28–31). They not only do wrong themselves, but also approve of others who do the same.

Here, metaphysics (recognition of God's lordship), epistemology (knowing God from his revelation), and ethics (sins of all sorts) are intertwined. So it is not surprising that sinners reject the tenets of biblical philosophy that we have discussed earlier and substitute other ideas for it.

Sinners at heart do not want to live in God's world, though they have no choice about it. They recognize the truth to some extent, because they need to get along and to make a living. But they would very much like the world to be different, and often they either try to make it different or pretend that it is. In the unbelieving fantasy world, the Lord of the Bible does not exist, and man is free to live by his own standards of truth and right. In a word, the unbeliever lives as if he were *autonomous*, subject only to his own law. Nobody can be really autonomous, because we are all subject to God's control, authority, and presence. But we pretend that we are autonomous; we act as though we were autonomous, in the unbelieving fantasy world.

In the unbelieving fantasy world, the Lord of the Bible does not exist, and man is free to live by his own standards of truth and right. In a word, the unbeliever lives as if he were autonomous, *subject only to his own law.*

In Van Til's illustration, the first person who sought to live this way was the first woman, Eve, the mother of us all. God had told her not to eat of a certain fruit. But she thought about it:

> So when the woman saw that the tree was good for food, and that it was a delight to the eyes, and that the tree was to be desired to make one wise, she took of its fruit and ate, and she also gave some to her husband who was with her, and he ate. (Gen. 3:6)

At some level, she knew that she should obey God and reject the contrary words of Satan. But she preferred to trust her own senses and judgments, to make her decision as though she were autonomous. It was as though God had his opinion, Satan had his, and Eve was to cast the deciding vote. So the fall was first an event in Eve's mind, only second an event in her mouth and throat. It was philosophical before it was practical. We are cautioned again that God must be Lord of our thought, not just of our behavior.

Eve judged by her own metaphysic (the tree was "good for food"), aesthetic (a "delight to the eyes"), and epistemology ("desired to make one wise"), and she embarked on carrying out her own ethic: disobedience.

Eve judged by her own metaphysic (the tree was "good for food"), aesthetic (a "delight to the eyes"), and epistemology ("desired to make one wise"), and she embarked on carrying out her own ethic: disobedience.

So the history of non-Christian philosophy is a history of would-be autonomous thought. And of course, if people presuppose their own autonomy, they cannot acknowledge God as the absolute-personal Creator, the Lord.

I should note that although the fall involved Eve's thinking about metaphysics, epistemology, and ethics, the fall itself was in one sense ethical and *not* metaphysical. Most non-Christian philosophers and religions recognize that there is something wrong with the human condition. But they tend to think that the problem is with our metaphysical finitude, or even our failure to attain deity. But in Scripture, the human plight is personal, relational. It is based on our own disobedience to God.

The history of non-Christian philosophy is a history of would-be autonomous thought. And of course, if people presuppose their own autonomy, they cannot acknowledge God as the absolute-personal Creator, the Lord.

CHRISTIAN AND NON-CHRISTIAN PHILOSOPHY

Because of the fall, there is an antithesis between believers and unbelievers in every area of life: believers seek to glorify God in all areas of life (1 Cor. 10:31), while nonbelievers seek to live autonomously (Gen. 8:21; Isa. 64:6; Rom. 3:10, 23). That includes the area of thought, reasoning, seeking wisdom. If "the fear of the LORD is the beginning of wisdom" (Ps. 111:10), then those who do not fear God do not even have the beginning of wisdom. So Paul argues that "the wisdom of this world is folly with God" (1 Cor. 3:19; cf. 1:20) and that the wisdom of God is foolishness to the world (1 Cor. 1:18, 21–22). The larger context of these verses is instructive, and the summation is in 2:14–16:

> The natural person does not accept the things of the Spirit of God, for they are folly to him, and he is not able to understand them because they are spiritually discerned. The spiritual person judges all things, but is himself to be judged by no one. "For who has understood the mind of the Lord so as to instruct him?" But we have the mind of Christ.

Antithesis does not mean that Christians and non-Christians disagree on every proposition. Believers and unbelievers can readily agree that the sky is blue, that the earth revolves around the sun, and so on. But the intellectual activities of each must be seen in the context of their life purpose. The believer seeks to know the world in order to glorify God. The unbeliever seeks to know God in order to oppose God's kingdom, by exalting his own autonomy.

Neither, of course, is fully consistent with his life project. Believers are sometimes unfaithful to their Lord and must seek forgiveness (1 John 1:9). Unbelievers must seek to survive and prosper in a world that, contrary to their desire, is God's world, so they must often recognize God's reality despite themselves. God will not allow them to be perfectly consistent with their sinful impulse, for if they were, they would destroy themselves and create chaos around them. And if they did not continue to recognize the truth at some level, then they would no longer be without excuse (Rom. 1:20). Their continuing knowledge serves as a basis for their moral responsibility. So God regularly restrains sin and its effects, as in the Tower of Babel episode (Gen. 11:1–8).

When the believer, the unbeliever, or both are inconsistent with their general life-direction, they can agree. But such agreements may be short-lived. In any case, both agreements and disagreements are part of the larger context of spiritual warfare, the battle between the kingdom of God and the kingdom of Satan. Sometimes even Satan serves his purposes by speaking truth, as when he quotes Scripture in Matthew 4:6.[35]

The history of philosophy, therefore, describes one phase of spiritual warfare, as it has developed over the centuries.

Antithesis *does not mean that Christians and non-Christians disagree on every proposition. . . . But the intellectual activities of each must be seen in the context of their life purpose.*

THE ANTITHESIS IN METAPHYSICS

Let us then consider the antithesis in philosophy as it appears in the three subdivisions of philosophy that I distinguished earlier in the chapter: metaphysics, epistemology, and value theory. First, metaphysics.

As I mentioned, the biblical worldview emphasizes the Creator-creature distinction, the absolute tripersonality of God, and his lordship over the world, understood as control, authority, and presence. Non-Christian philosophy, though it takes many forms, uniformly seeks to oppose the biblical worldview, though it might paradoxically express agreement with it at various points and for various purposes.

I have found it useful to describe the antithesis in metaphysics by use of the terms *transcendence* and *immanence.* These terms are commonly used in Christian theology as representations of two biblical emphases.

35. For more discussion of the nature of antithesis, please see my discussions of Kuyper and Van Til in chapter 13, also *DKG*, 49–61, and *CVT*, 187–238. It is not easy to describe the ways in which nonbelievers do and do not "suppress the truth."

Transcendence evokes the biblical picture of God as "high," "lifted up," "exalted," and so on (Pss. 7:7; 9:2; Isa. 6:1). *Immanence* draws on biblical language about God's being "near" and "with us" (Gen. 21:22; 26:3, 24, 28; 28:15; Deut. 4:7; Isa. 7:14; Matt. 1:23).

In theological writing, *transcendence* sometimes takes on the meaning that God is so far removed from the creation that we cannot know him or speak truly of him. But the God of Scripture is not transcendent in that sense. In the Bible, God is eminently knowable; indeed, eternal life is knowing him in a certain way (John 17:3). And in the Bible, God speaks to his people, so that they can speak truly of him (17:17). When Scripture speaks of God's being high or lifted up, it refers to his position on the throne of the universe as Lord and King. If we use the term *transcendence* for his exaltation in this sense, then it refers to his lordship, particularly his control and authority.

Immanence in theology is usually used to refer to God's omnipresence, which is uncontroversial among Christians, but I think it is better to use the term with more covenant nuance. God is omnipresent, yes, but with personal intentions toward people, either blessing or judgment. God's immanence is his covenant presence.

I think it is better to use the term [immanence] with more covenant nuance. God is omnipresent, yes, but with personal intentions toward people, either blessing or judgment. God's immanence is his covenant presence.

What we must strenuously avoid is what some theologians do: to say that God becomes so "near" that he cannot be distinguished from the world, and that he therefore abandons his divine nature. That either reduces God to the level of man or raises man to the level of God, in either case violating the Creator-creature distinction.[36]

These biblical and nonbiblical concepts of transcendence and immanence may be illustrated by the following diagram; see fig. 1.5.

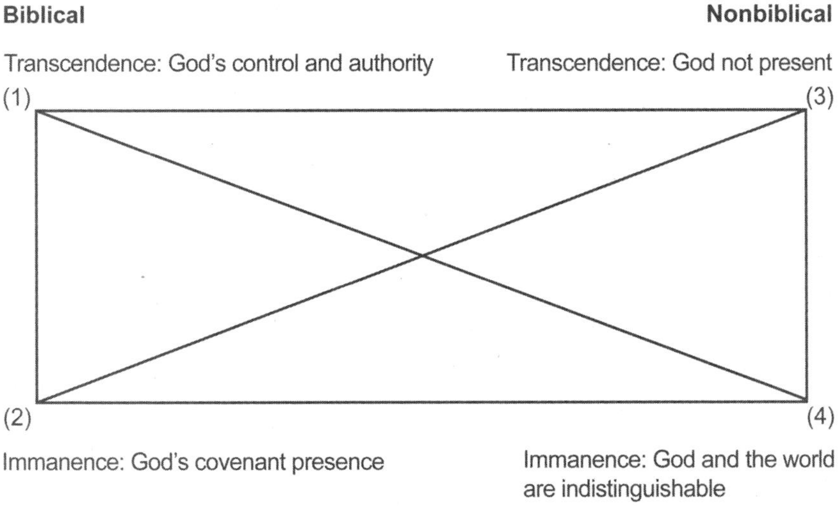

What we must strenuously avoid is what some theologians do: to say that God becomes so "near" that he cannot be distinguished from the world, and that he therefore abandons his divine nature.

Biblical **Nonbiblical**

Transcendence: God's control and authority

Transcendence: God not present

(1) (3)

(2) (4)

Immanence: God's covenant presence

Immanence: God and the world are indistinguishable

Fig. 1.5. Concepts of Transcendence and Immanence

36. This kind of argument led Thomas Altizer to his *Christian atheism* in the 1960s. See chapter 10.

The left side of the rectangle[37] represents the biblical views of transcendence and immanence that we have discussed. (1) is biblical transcendence: God's rule. Included in God's rule are his lordship attributes of control and authority. (2) is biblical immanence: God's covenant presence. The right side of the rectangle represents the nonbiblical views that we have noted. (3) is nonbiblical transcendence: that God is so far "above" us that we cannot know him or identify him in history. As Barth would say, he is wholly hidden or wholly other. (4) is nonbiblical immanence: that the immanence of God is in effect the autonomy of creatures, God as wholly revealed. On this view, man in effect becomes God, or God is reduced to the level of man.

The diagonal lines are lines of opposition. (1) and (4) are contradictory, for to say that creatures are autonomous (4) is to contradict the assertion that God is the supreme ruler of the world (1). (2) and (3) are also opposed, because to insist that God cannot be identified in history (3), that he is unknowable and unspeakable, contradicts the biblical teaching concerning God's presence (2).

The vertical lines draw our attention to the relative consistency of the two approaches. The biblical view is consistent and without tension.[38] The nonbiblical view is full of tension: How can God be both ineffable and identical with the world, as in Gnosticism? How can he be wholly hidden and wholly revealed, as in Barth? But although this system is contradictory, we can understand how this view of transcendence *generates* this particular view of immanence, and vice versa. If God is the nameless beyond, then necessarily we are left as masters of our own destiny. For, practically speaking, he cannot rule us. We cannot take account of him in our values, our decisions, or our worldviews. Still, we cannot live without ultimate values, so we become god ourselves. The universe cannot exist without ultimate powers of causation, so it becomes its own cause. Removing God from the world enables human autonomy. And conversely, if our goal is to be autonomous,[39] then we either must deny God's existence altogether[40] or must convince ourselves that God is too far beyond us to have any practical influence in our lives. So (3) and (4) require each other in a sense, even though bringing them together creates tension and paradox.

If God is the nameless beyond, then necessarily we are left as masters of our own destiny. For, practically speaking, he cannot rule us. We cannot take account of him in our values, our decisions, or our worldviews. Still, we cannot live without ultimate values, so we become god ourselves.

The horizontal lines lead us to consider the similarity of the two ways of thinking at the verbal level. Both views of transcendence may appeal

37. The next four paragraphs are taken from *ST*, chap. 3.

38. This is not to deny that there is mystery. Our knowledge of God is not exhaustive. But what God reveals of himself is not contradictory.

39. Remember that Scripture teaches that autonomy is always the goal of fallen man. So it is not arbitrary to ascribe this sort of thinking ultimately to human rebellion against God.

40. Atheism is an extreme version of transcendence (3). For it asserts that God is *so* far from the real world in which we live that he should not even be counted among real beings.

to the biblical language of God's exaltation and height. Both views of immanence describe his involvement in all things. But beneath the verbal similarity, there are enormous conceptual differences, indeed contradictions, as we have seen, between the two systems. The verbal similarities indicate why the nonbiblical positions have attracted many Christians. But these issues are so important that we must penetrate beneath the surface similarities to recognize the antithesis between these two ways of thinking.

How, then, is the antithesis relevant to the philosophical questions I outlined earlier in the chapter?

To have a comprehensive explanation of everything is to have a kind of knowledge available only to God himself. That is impossible for human beings.

1. Is the universe one or many? The reason why this question has been important is that philosophers have wanted to find an absolute *in* the world, belonging to the world, that is, rather than the God of Scripture. Non-Christian philosophers have wanted such an absolute to serve as a comprehensive explanation for everything (which indicates the connection between metaphysics and epistemology). They have tried to do that in two ways: (a) by identifying a *oneness* to which everything can be reduced (as Thales's "all is water") and (b) by seeking an ultimate *plurality*: chopping things down into their smallest parts to detect the ultimate constituents of the universe (Democritus's "atoms"). But Christians believe this cannot be done (Rom. 11:33–36). To have a comprehensive explanation of everything is to have a kind of knowledge available only to God himself. That is impossible for human beings. The impossibility of it is displayed by the fact that, as with the Trinity, there is in the world no oneness without plurality and no plurality without oneness. The world is both one and many, because God, who is one and many, has made the world in such a way that it reflects him.

   The world is both one and many, because God, who is one and many, has made the world in such a way that it reflects him.

   In non-Christian thought, it is difficult to relate the ultimate oneness to the pluralities of the world. Thales evidently understands "all is water" to state the discovery of a transcendent principle, a principle that explains everything. But this transcendent water cannot be real water, the stuff that makes other things wet. It is an abstract concept that combines all the qualities of everything else in the universe, but somehow stands apart from them. The big question for Thales is: How does water as a superprinciple give rise to the rest of the world? Does it somehow get transformed into other things? Or are the other things, in the end, illusory, as Parmenides claimed for his own superprinciple, Being? Plato struggled with the question of how the world of perfect, changeless Forms could give rise to the changing, imperfect world. In other words, on these views, how can the principle of oneness, defined by its transcendence over the world, become immanent enough to account for the many, without itself becoming many?

The same is true for philosophers who seek an ultimate plurality as the final explanation for everything. The "atoms" of Democritus, though plural, are transcendent in an important way. Nobody has ever seen an atom. These, as much as Parmenides' Being or Plato's Forms, are abstractions from the flow of our ordinary experience. So atomists need to explain how the atoms give rise to the world of that ordinary experience. The atoms are too transcendent to explain the world, and at the same time too immanent, too worldly, to provide the world with governance.

2. What is the basic composition of the universe? This question is the same as the previous one, but more specific. Philosophers who believe that the world is essentially one need to explain what that oneness is like, what kind of oneness it is. Is it divine, mental, material, or what? Same for philosophers who believe that the universe is essentially many. And as with the previous question, there is an overlap between metaphysical and epistemological concerns. For the philosophers who ask these questions are seeking exhaustive knowledge of the world.

   But again, the qualities singled out as the comprehensive nature of the world (water, air, fire, number, form, matter . . .) take on an abstract quality when used as philosophical ultimates. When Thales uses water as a transcendent principle, he is thinking of it as something different from the ordinary stuff that we drink and wash with. Essentially, he is using water to play the role of God, to serve as the ultimate explanation of everything. But Scripture calls this *idolatry.* And idols cannot do the job of God. The notion that trees, planets, people, minds, lungs, music, fish are "really" water is ludicrous on its face. So either water becomes a transcendent reality that cannot be described or it is an immanent reality that cannot perform any transcendent function.

Philosophers who believe that the world is essentially one need to explain what that oneness is like, what kind of oneness it is. Is it divine, mental, material, or what?

3. Are universals real, or only particulars? Let us consider apples as an example. Every apple is different from every other. But all apples are alike in some respects. Same for lemons and pears, men and women, political theories, scientific laws, literary movements, moral virtues, subatomic particles, galaxies . . . same for all objects. All classes of objects exhibit samenesses and

> differences, and that, as we have noted throughout this book, generates the "problem of universals and particulars." Plato thought that the samenesses among things had to be located in a special place, the world of Forms. Aristotle thought that these samenesses were aspects of things here on the earth.

But the relation between sameness and difference, form and matter, has always been problematic. Both Plato and Aristotle, known as "realists," thought that the real nature of an apple, its essence, is its sameness to other apples. The differences were "accidental." Indeed, in one sense, the differences don't really exist.[41] Hegel, too, thought that sameness was the essential thing, and that the dialectic, in the end, would wipe out all differences, exposing them as merely apparent. And what is merely apparent is incapable of rational analysis.

The biblical philosophy I outlined evades both realism and nominalism. In that worldview, God is equally one and many. He is always the same, one God, but among his three persons there are real differences. In him there is no sameness without difference and no difference without sameness.

Others, philosophers in the nominalist tradition, say that the samenesses of things are merely a verbal shorthand. It is easier to talk about a bushel of apples by referring only to their samenesses (they are "apples") than by describing all the differences among them: this one has a bump two inches from the stem, for instance. But in reality, the differences make everything what it is. To understand a particular apple is to understand the location of every bump and the composition of every bruise. To the nominalist, reality is particular and concrete, not general and abstract. So it is the differences that really exist. The samenesses are only conceptual and verbal.

The biblical philosophy I outlined evades both realism and nominalism. In that worldview, God is equally one and many. He is always the same, one God, but among his three persons there are real differences. In him there is no sameness without difference and no difference without sameness.

Particulars are collections of generalities, and generalities are collections of things. Universals and particulars define one another.

Similarly, he has made the world to be one and many. Reality in the world exhibits sameness and difference. It is one world, with many genuinely different aspects and objects. We cannot advance our understanding of the world by seeking, as Hegel did, how it is all the same, discarding the differences. For the general realities—apple, tree, man, woman, solar system, law of gravitation, virtue—are what they are because of the particulars that constitute them. And we can identify the particulars only with the use of general concepts. To identify the bump two inches from the stem of the apple requires us to think of the general concepts *apple*, *stem*, and *bump*. Particulars are collections of generalities, and generalities are collections of things. Universals and particulars define one another.

41. Both Plato and Aristotle located differences in "matter." But they defined *matter* as that which lacks form, and without form there is no being, no reality.

So we cannot accurately understand the universe by reducing it to generalities (as Plato, Aristotle, Hegel), or by dividing it into ultimate particulars (Democritus, Epicurus, Roscellinus, Occam, the early Wittgenstein). Universals and particulars are perspectivally related. I believe this fact destroys any human dreams of achieving exhaustive knowledge. There is no ultimate universal or ultimate particular that explains everything. Exhaustive knowledge is the prerogative of God alone.

Similar things can be said in response to the other questions I referred to earlier, about change, teleology, cause, mind, mental faculties, and God. I will take them up in the course of our historical discussions. In general, the questions themselves reflect the antithesis: non-Christian philosophers are seeking alternatives to God, making the discipline of philosophy an exercise in idolatry.

Christians, when they are consistent with their faith, seek answers to these questions within the biblical worldview: (1) The world is both one and many, reflecting the Trinity. There is no unity without plurality, and no plurality without unity. (2) The universe cannot be reduced to any single type of object.[42] The human body, for example, contains chemical fluids, bones, brain matter, nerves, nails, hair, and so forth, but it cannot be reduced to any of these. Nor can human thought be reduced to some faculty of the mind, such as reason or will. Thinking is an act of the whole person. Man is essentially the image of God. It cannot be said that he is "only" something else. Similarly for the creation as a whole. It is essentially God's creature.

THE ANTITHESIS IN EPISTEMOLOGY

Since God is the authority of all things, he is the ultimate criterion of truth and falsity, right and wrong (normative). If it is possible for human beings to know anything, their knowledge must meet these criteria.

As I indicated earlier, the Bible has much to say about wisdom, knowing, understanding, foolishness. The biblical doctrine of human knowledge comes out of the general biblical worldview. God's lordship has clear epistemological implications.

Since God is the *controller* of all things, it is for him to determine whether or not we gain knowledge, and under what conditions. The objects of knowledge are God himself and the world he has made. The human subject of knowledge is God's creature and God's image. Can the subject (existential) enter into a fruitful relation to the object (situational) so that knowledge takes place? That is for God to determine.

Since God is the *authority* of all things, he is the ultimate criterion of truth and falsity, right and wrong (normative). If it is possible for human beings to know anything, their knowledge must meet these criteria.

It is the *presence* of God, however (existential), that makes human knowledge actual. For part of the biblical meaning of God's presence is

42. That includes those objects of scientific discussion, such as quarks, bosons, and superstrings.

that he reveals himself to his creatures, specifically to human beings. We know God and the world because he has taken the initiative to reveal himself. Otherwise, we could have no knowledge at all.

So epistemology as well as metaphysics depends on God's transcendence (control and authority) and immanence (presence). And the non-Christian distortions of transcendence and immanence also create distortions in epistemology. If the absolute being is transcendent in the nonbiblical sense of being inaccessible to the world, then of course we cannot know him. And we cannot know the world either because God furnishes the only criteria by which we can discover truth. Similarly, if the absolute is immanent in the nonbiblical sense of being identical with the world, then our knowledge is autonomous and human reason becomes an absolute.

If the absolute being is transcendent in the nonbiblical sense of being inaccessible to the world, then of course we cannot know him. And we cannot know the world either because God furnishes the only criteria by which we can discover truth.

So we can interpret our rectangular diagram in epistemological terms; see fig. 1.6.

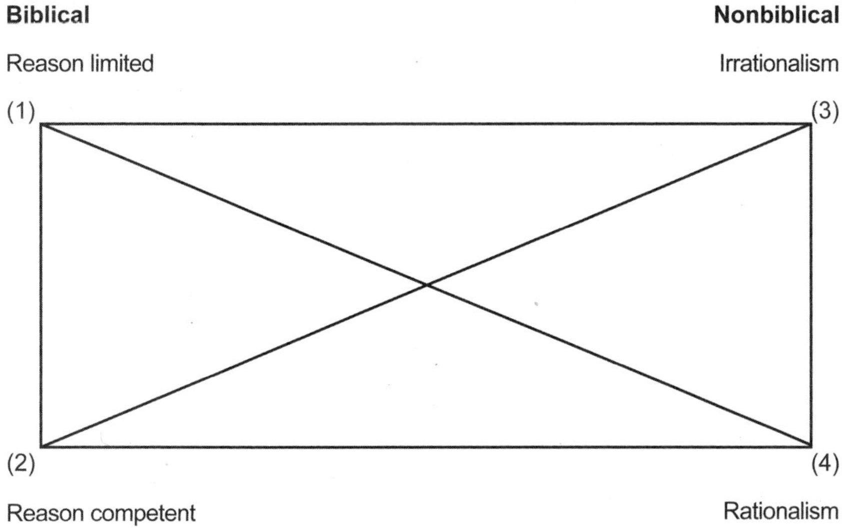

Biblical | **Nonbiblical**

Reason limited | Irrationalism

(1) | (3)

(2) | (4)

Reason competent | Rationalism

Fig. 1.6. Concepts of Rationalism and Irrationalism

If the absolute is immanent in the nonbiblical sense of being identical with the world, then our knowledge is autonomous and human reason becomes an absolute.

(1) tells us that our reason is limited because of God's transcendence. He, not we, is the ultimate controller of and authority for knowledge. Our knowledge is an aspect of our discipleship, that is, a *servant knowledge*. It is subject to God's control, and his authoritative revelation constitutes the highest laws of thought for us.[43]

43. In philosophy, the *laws of thought* are generally identified as the basic laws of logic: the law of noncontradiction (nothing can be both A and not-A at the same time and in the same respect), the law of identity (everything is what it is), and the law of the excluded middle (everything is *either* A *or* not-A; nothing can be both at the same time and in the same respect). What I am claiming is that God's revelation has higher authority even than any human system of logic.

(2) tells us that although our reason is limited, it is competent to know truth. It is competent because God has become immanent and has revealed himself and has revealed truths about the world, history, and ourselves.

(3) is an epistemological corollary to the non-Christian understanding of transcendence. If the absolute is so far from the world that we cannot know it, then human beings have no reason to think that they have access to truth, that their reason is competent to know the world.

(4) is an epistemological corollary to the non-Christian understanding of immanence. If the immanence of the absolute establishes human wisdom as absolute, then the human mind is the final determinant of truth and falsity. That is, we are autonomous.

Now, non-Christians routinely speak of Christian thought as rationalistic and irrationalistic. When a Christian speaks of the limits of human thought, the need to bow to God's revelation (1), non-Christian respondents are appalled at their surrender of autonomy. To non-Christians, to surrender autonomy is to abandon reason itself. Kant made much of this argument in his *Religion within the Limits of Reason Alone*.

But when a Christian speaks of the competence of human reason to know truth, non-Christians regard him as a rationalist. To postmodernists, for example, the very claim to know absolute truth is necessarily wrong. It is an arrogant claim.[44]

So both Christians and non-Christians charge each other with being rationalist and irrationalist. As a Christian, I believe that the non-Christians are guilty of this criticism, the Christians nonguilty, for reasons that should be evident from my description of these two positions.

When a Christian speaks of the limits of human thought, the need to bow to God's revelation, non-Christian respondents are appalled at their surrender of autonomy.

To consider the non-Christian position more fully: As we look at the history of philosophy, we will see that the non-Christian intellectual traditions vacillate between rationalism and irrationalism. As with the metaphysical tension of transcendence and immanence, non-Christian rationalism and irrationalism are inconsistent with each other, but they also, paradoxically, reinforce each other.

Parmenides' rationalism failed to impress later generations of thinkers, leading to the skepticism and relativism of Sophism and the Middle Academy. But few could rest content with skepticism and relativism, leading to a new form of rationalism in Neoplatonism. So the philosophical community over the centuries has vacillated from rationalism to irrationalism and back again.

The greatest philosophers have tried to combine rationalistic and irrationalistic principles in a single system. So Plato is rationalistic

44. In the postmodernist narrative, the modernists claimed that Christians were irrational because they did not have sufficient evidence for their claims. The postmodernists claim that Christians are rationalist because they claim to know absolute truth.

about the Forms, irrationalistic about the material world. Same for Aristotle and Plotinus. Kant is rationalistic about phenomena, irrationalistic about the noumenal world. Wittgenstein is rationalistic about his perfect language, irrationalistic about his "mystical" world. We will see other examples throughout this book.

The dynamic between the two positions is as follows: If rationalism is true, the mind should not make errors in its quest for knowledge. But it does. When it does, philosophers do not want to blame their autonomous reason (the subject of knowledge). Rather, they blame the world, the object of knowledge. The mind cannot attain perfect knowledge because the world is not perfectly knowable. So rationalism leads to irrationalism. But how do we know that the world is irrational? By our would-be-autonomous knowledge, of course. So irrationalism leads back to rationalism. Or, to shorten the discussion: Philosophers assert rationalism irrationally, for there is no adequate ground for asserting it. And philosophers assert irrationalism rationalistically, on the basis of their autonomous intellect. So in the end, the two positions, inconsistent as they are, are based on each other and are in one sense identical.

Irrationalism leads back to rationalism. Or, to shorten the discussion: Philosophers assert rationalism irrationally, for there is no adequate ground for asserting it. And philosophers assert irrationalism rationalistically, on the basis of their autonomous intellect.

It was Van Til's great accomplishment to narrate the history of philosophy as a movement from rationalism to irrationalism and back again, a description of non-Christian thought and a critique of it at the same time. I will frequently mention this pattern in the historical chapters of this volume.

THE ANTITHESIS IN VALUES

As I said earlier, I will not be focusing on value theory in this book, having dealt with it in much detail in *DCL*. But values are an important aspect of metaphysics and epistemology, since perspectives are inseparable from one another. So I want to sketch a bit in this section how value theory functions in my critique of philosophy.

Nothing impersonal has the authority to impose ethical norms. Only a person can do that (e.g., a mother, father, teacher, policeman), and only an absolute person can impose ultimate, universal norms.

I mentioned earlier that epistemology presupposes ethics, since the quest for knowledge requires ethical values: "discipline, diligence, respect for truth, avoidance of falsehood, honesty in reporting conclusions, humility in admitting error and inadequacy, acceptance of responsibility to give evidence for one's claims." And I have also argued that ethical values presuppose God.[45] In brief: nothing impersonal has the authority to impose ethical norms. Only a person can do that (e.g., a mother, father, teacher, policeman), and only an absolute person can impose ultimate, universal norms.

45. *AJCB*, 95–123; John M. Frame and Paul Kurtz, "Do We Need God to Be Moral?," *Free Inquiry* 16, 2 (1996). Courtesy of the Council for Secular Humanism, http://www.secularhumanism.org. Also available at http://www.frame-poythress.org/frame_articles/1996Debate.htm.

Many non-Christian thinkers (such as Paul Kurtz, in the dialogue referenced below) think they can affirm absolute ethical norms without God. But their attempt inevitably fails. That failure can be remedied either by embracing the ethic of biblical theism or by denying that absolute norms are possible. So non-Christian ethical absolutism (a form of rationalism) leads to non-Christian ethical relativism (a form of irrationalism). But again, irrationalism is based on rationalism and vice versa.

The Christian finds ethical certainty in God's revelation. But he often runs into difficulty trying to apply that revelation to the issues of life. He accepts that he doesn't have all the answers, and bows the knee to God's mystery. So in the area of values, the rectangle looks like this; see fig. 1.7.[46]

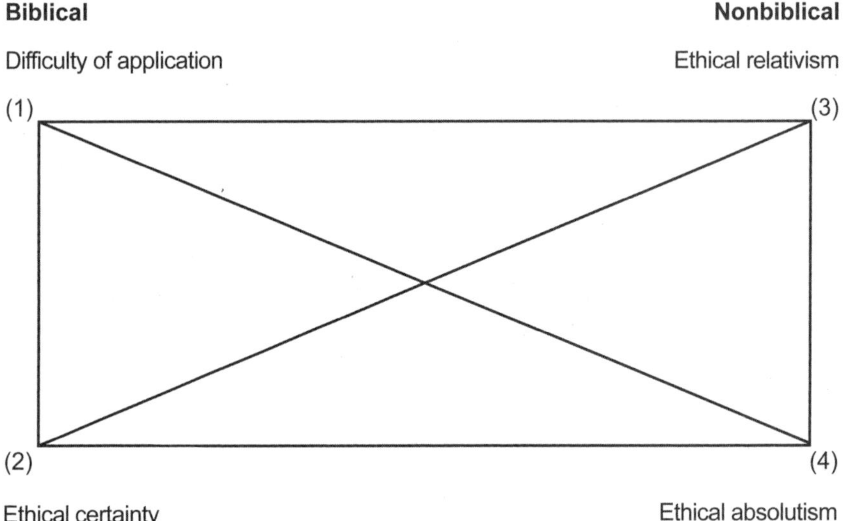

Fig. 1.7. Ethical Relativism and Absolutism

The Christian finds ethical certainty in God's revelation. But he often runs into difficulty trying to apply that revelation to the issues of life. He accepts that he doesn't have all the answers, and bows the knee to God's mystery.

Earlier I mentioned the three perspectives of Christian thought: situational, normative, and existential. These three perspectives play important roles in Christian ethics. (1) Christian ethics is normative, applying the moral laws of God given in Scripture and nature. (2) It is also situational, in that it analyzes the world that God has made to know how best to apply God's norms to a given situation. And (3) it is existential, in that it deals with the ethical agent to understand his role in making ethical decisions, how he takes the norms of God

46. For other applications to ethics of the rectangular diagram, see *DCL*, 45–49. These include the absoluteness and relevance of the moral law, divine sovereignty and human responsibility, objectivity and inwardness, humility and hope, and freedom and authority in society.

and applies them to his situation. In making decisions, the Christian goes round and round the triangle, interpreting the situation by the moral law, applying the moral law by investigating the situation, and understanding both of these through his subjective faculties; see fig. 1.8.

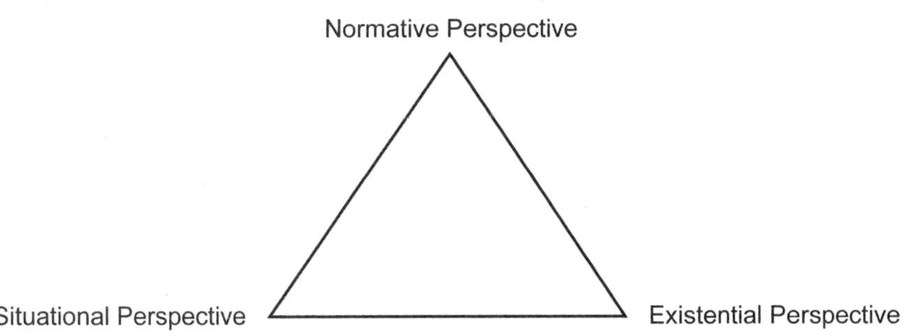

Fig. 1.8. Perspectives on Ethics

There are three general types of secular ethics: deontologism, teleologism, and existentialism. These correspond, more or less, to the three perspectives of Christian thought: deontological to the normative, teleological to the situational, and existentialist to the existential.

Non-Christians live in the same ethical world as Christians (situational), surrounded by God's laws (normative), made in God's image (existential). But they choose not to follow God, "exchang[ing] the truth about God for a lie" (Rom. 1:25). As philosophers, they develop systems of ethics that do not acknowledge God's laws, his world, and themselves as his image. They do not want to be confronted with God, but prefer an ethic that honors their own autonomy.

I mentioned earlier that there are three general types of secular ethics: deontologism, teleologism, and existentialism. These correspond, more or less, to the three perspectives of Christian thought: deontological to the normative, teleological to the situational, and existentialist to the existential. But in Christian ethics, there is no tension between the law, the situation, and the person, because the same God has made all three. God has made the person to live in his world, under his norms. We might have difficulties in applying his ethical norms to ourselves and our situations, but we may not blame that problem on the nature of God's creation.

Non-Christians, however, do not generally recognize the need to reconcile the three perspectives. They assume that because the biblical God does not exist, there may be inconsistency between the moral law, the world situation, and the moral agent.

Non-Christians, however, do not generally recognize the need to reconcile the three perspectives. They assume that because the biblical God does not exist, there may be inconsistency between the moral law, the world situation, and the moral agent. So many non-Christian philosophers adopt one or two of these perspectives and deny the other(s). So Kant the deontologist embraces the moral law and claims that morality has nothing to do with our environment or our personal inclinations. Mill the teleologist embraces what he considers to be the goal of ethics (human happiness) and denies that we are bound by rules or personal inclinations that fail to make people happy. And Sartre the existentialist says that ethics is the expression of personal integrity, but not the affirmation of moral law or the objective world.

I argued in *DCL* that these systems are incoherent. My point here is that ethical philosophy is subject to the same difficulties as epistemology and metaphysics. In my earlier discussion of the metaphysics of the human mind, I mentioned the division among philosophers between intellectualists, voluntarists, and subjectivists. In discussing schools of thought in epistemology, I mentioned rationalism, empiricism, and skepticism. In Christian philosophy, the members of each triad are best seen as perspectivally related. In the epistemological triad, human beings understand the world as whole persons. *Intellect* refers not to some faculty of the mind separate from others that wars with others for supremacy. Rather, it refers to the capacity of the person to reason and gain knowledge, which is, of course, influenced by will and subjectivity. *Will* refers not to an adversary of the intellect, but to the whole person from another perspective: the person as making choices and decisions. Those choices are influenced by his knowledge, and they in turn influence his thought processes. But non-Christian philosophy, which does not recognize divine coordination of these faculties, often feels that it must choose which one is "primary."

Same for the triad rationalism, empiricism, skepticism. In Scripture, this triad also describes the whole person in his quest for knowledge. Reason takes sense experience and feelings into account; sense experience can be defined only by reason; and so on. The Christian can trust that God has designed these faculties to work as one. But non-Christian thinkers cannot assume that, so for them one must choose which member of the triad to follow if and when there is conflict. This leads to philosophical partisanship and division.

In philosophy itself, thinkers today discuss essentially the same questions that Plato and Aristotle did. That interesting fact suggests that the history of philosophy might be to an extent a history of wrong turns.

That partisanship is what drives the history of philosophy. As in politics, one party prevails at first. But then another party scores argumentative points against the first and becomes dominant.

Yet in secular philosophy, none of these questions is ever answered. In other disciplines, such as astronomy, history, geology, and linguistics, one can trace progress to some extent (except when their questions are linked to philosophical questions). But in philosophy itself, thinkers today discuss essentially the same questions that Plato and Aristotle did. That interesting fact suggests that the history of philosophy might be to an extent a history of wrong turns.

KEY TERMS

Philosophy (etymology)
Philosophy (Frame's definition)
Wisdom
Wisdom literature
Worldview
Metanarrative
Theology
Religion (Frame)
Religion (Clouser)
Divine (Clouser)
Secular
Aseity
Metaphysics
Epistemology
Value theory
Being
Monism
Dualism
Pluralism
Atomism
Materialism
Idealism
Universals
Particulars
Nominalism
Realism
Teleology
Determinism
Libertarian freedom
Necessary connection
Intellectualism
Voluntarism
Subjectivism
Theism
Pantheism
Panentheism
Deism
Demiurge
Subject of knowledge
Object of knowledge
Account
Justification
Warrant
Rationalism
Irrationalism
Skepticism
Autonomous reason
Ground of knowledge
Empiricism
Summum bonum
Creator-creature distinction
Creation *ex nihilo*
Emanation
Oneism
Twoism
Council of Chalcedon
Absolute
Tripersonality
Lordship
Control
Authority
Presence
Lordship attributes
Circumcessio
Perichoresis
Situational perspective
Normative perspective
Existential perspective
Antithesis
Transcendence (biblical)
Immanence (biblical)
Transcendence (nonbiblical)
Immanence (nonbiblical)
Laws of thought
Ethical relativism
Ethical absolutism
Deontologism
Teleologism
Existentialism
Law
Situation
Person (ethics)

OUTLINE

Why Study Philosophy?
Philosophy, Theology, and Religion
Subdivisions of Philosophy
Metaphysics
Epistemology
Value Theory
Relations of the Three Subdivisions
Biblical Philosophy
Perspectives of Human Knowledge
Sin and Philosophy
Christian and Non-Christian Philosophy
The Antithesis in Metaphysics
The Antithesis in Epistemology
The Antithesis in Values

STUDY QUESTIONS

1. What distinguishes the wisdom literature in the Bible from that outside of it?
2. What is the difference between *worldview* and *metanarrative*? Why does Frame think that these are indispensable? How does he reply to Lyotard?
3. Summarize the Christian worldview.
4. Why study philosophy?
5. "Theology is Christian philosophy." Explain; evaluate.
6. How does Frame differ from Barth on "religion"? Evaluate these positions.
7. Many argue that religion must be separated from philosophy, education, or politics. What do you think? Discuss the arguments pro and con.
8. "Nobody is really an atheist." Explain; evaluate.
9. "The basic questions of philosophers are religious in character." Explain, using examples.
10. Why is it difficult to study "being qua being"?
11. Why is there something rather than nothing?
12. Of the metaphysical questions listed in this chapter, which do you find the most intriguing? Present your own analysis.
13. Same for the epistemological questions.
14. How are metaphysics, epistemology, and value theory related in the study of philosophy? Is there one of these that you should study before the others?
15. "Someone might object that this distinction between God and the world is not compatible with the union of God and man in Jesus Christ." Reply.
16. Define and discuss the four adverbs used in the *Chalcedonian Declaration* to describe the relation of Christ's divine and human natures. Why is this important for Christian philosophy?
17. Frame says that the doctrine of God's absolute tripersonality is unique to biblical religion. Is that true? Consider some non-Christian religions in this regard.
18. How do Van Til and Frame relate the doctrine of the Trinity to philosophical discussions of oneness and manyness?
19. How are the persons of the Trinity related to the lordship attributes?
20. Explain and evaluate Frame's distinction between three epistemological perspectives.

21. What does Romans 1:18–32 say about the effects of sin on human knowledge? On human philosophy? Show how the fall of Eve in Genesis 3 affected her philosophy.
22. "The fall itself was on one sense ethical and *not* metaphysical." Explain; evaluate.
23. "The history of philosophy, therefore, describes one phase of spiritual warfare." Explain; evaluate.
24. Show on Frame's rectangular diagram the opposing views of transcendence and immanence. How do the lines in the diagram display the relationships between these?
25. Describe and evaluate Frame's responses to the metaphysical questions of "the one and many" and the "basic composition of the universe."
26. Show how the lordship attributes of God are related to human epistemology. Expound the Frame rectangle in terms of rationalism and irrationalism.
27. Frame says that non-Christian thought vacillates between rationalism and irrationalism. Explain; evaluate.
28. Interpret the rectangle in terms of ethical relativism and absolutism.
29. Show how non-Christian ethics violates the triperspectival character of ethical choice.

BIBLIOGRAPHY OF PHILOSOPHY TEXTS

I have listed here texts in philosophy that I consider to be useful for the student, beyond those in the footnotes. I am including some comments about their distinctive content and approaches. Some of these volumes are historical, some topical, some readings translated from primary sources. The list begins with general philosophic texts that bear on all the chapters of this book. I will also, after every chapter, list some texts particularly relevant to the content of the chapter.

Histories of Philosophy: General

Allen, Diogenes. *Philosophy for Understanding Theology.* Atlanta: John Knox Press, 1985. Allen analyzes the thought of various philosophers to show how their work bears on the concerns of Christian theology.

Audi, Robert, ed. *The Cambridge Dictionary of Philosophy.* Cambridge: Cambridge University Press, 1995. Reference work on philosophers, ideas, and movements. Secular.

Edwards, Paul, ed. *The Encyclopedia of Philosophy.* New York: Macmillan/ Free Press, 1967. Eight volumes of essays (later published as four) by experts on philosophical issues, movements, and thinkers. Highly authoritative, as of its publishing date. Most of the writers approach their subjects from secular points of view.

Gottlieb, Anthony. *The Dream of Reason: A History of Philosophy from the Greeks to the Renaissance.* New York: W. W. Norton, 2002.

Kenny, Anthony. *A New History of Western Philosophy.* New York: Oxford University Press, 2010. A secular thinker, Kenny is well known as a philosopher in his own right.

Palmer, Donald. *Looking at Philosophy: The Unbearable Heaviness of Philosophy Made Lighter.* Mountain View, CA: Mayfield Publishing, 1994. Accurate secular history of philosophy written in an engaging, witty style, illustrated with cartoons. I have often used it as a text in my seminary course on the history of philosophy.

Placher, William. *Readings in the History of Christian Theology.* 2 vols. Philadelphia: Westminster Press, 1988. Primary source readings for many of the thinkers discussed in this book.

Strimple, Robert. "Roman Catholic Theology Today." In *Roman Catholicism*, edited by John Armstrong, 85–117. Chicago: Moody Press, 1994. An accurate and concise summary of post–Vatican II Roman Catholicism.

Stumpf, Samuel Enoch, and James Fieser. *Socrates to Sartre and Beyond: A History of Philosophy.* Boston: McGraw-Hill, 2003. Definitive, detailed, and often difficult secular treatment. Later, this book was combined with a group of primary-source readings in *Philosophy: History and Readings.* 8th ed. New York: McGraw-Hill, 2011.

Tarnas, Richard. *The Passion of the Western Mind: Understanding the Ideas That Have Shaped Our World* (NY: Ballantine Books, 1993). Tarnas is a non-Christian writer who is highly respected among academic philosophers. His explicitly pagan work provides an interesting contrast with the historic Christian viewpoint.

Thilly, Frank, and Ledger Wood. *A History of Philosophy.* New York: Henry Holt, 1957. This was the textbook used at Princeton where I first studied the history of philosophy. It is a comprehensive secular text, very clearly written, judicious in its selections, generally well organized.

Online

Internet Encyclopedia of Philosophy. http://www.iep.utm.edu.
Stanford Encyclopedia of Philosophy. http://plato.stanford.edu.

Readings in Philosophy: General

Abel, Donald C., ed. *Fifty Readings in Philosophy.* New York: McGraw-Hill, 2011. Readings in primary sources with brief introductions. A companion volume to the text in the next entry.

Abel, Donald C., and Eric O. Springsted. *Primary Readings in Philosophy for Understanding Theology*. Louisville, KY: Westminster John Knox Press, 1992.

Christian Analyses of the History of Philosophy

Bartholomew, Craig G., and Michael W. Goheen. *Christian Philosophy: A Systematic and Narrative Introduction*. Grand Rapids: Baker, 2013. An analysis of the whole history of philosophy, with an emphasis on Christian philosophy in the modern period. Bartholomew and Goheen are most indebted to the Christian philosophy of Herman Dooyeweerd, discussed briefly in chapter 13 of the present volume.

Brown, Colin. *Christianity and Western Thought: A History of Philosophers, Ideas, and Movements from the Ancient World to the Age of Enlightenment*. Downers Grove, IL: InterVarsity Press, 2010.

———. *Philosophy and the Christian Faith*. Downers Grove, IL: InterVarsity Press, 1968. Excellent textbook written from a Christian point of view. Brown says, "The aim of this book is to make a survey of the main thinkers and intellectual movements of western thought of the past thousand years, with a view to showing how they affect Christian belief." His limitation to the past thousand years keeps him, in my view, from giving sufficient attention to the thinkers from Thales to Plotinus, who certainly had a major effect on Christian belief. Deals with some modern theologians as well as philosophers.

Clark, Gordon H. *Thales to Dewey: A History of Philosophy*. Boston: Houghton Mifflin, 1957. Clark was a Reformed Christian philosopher who defended biblical inerrancy. He sought to encourage more respect for logic and reason. See chapter 13 of the present volume. Clark's book is clearly written and focuses somewhat more on epistemology than on other areas of philosophy. It contains a fairly subtle Christian apologetic.

Copleston, Frederick C. *A History of Philosophy*. 9 vols. Garden City, NY: Image Books, 1962–65. Nine-volume work by a scholarly Roman Catholic priest.

Hicks, Peter. *The Journey So Far: Philosophy through the Ages*. Grand Rapids: Zondervan, 2003. Discussion of the history of philosophy as a dialogue between Christian thought and philosophical schools.

Hoffecker, W. Andrew, ed. *Revolutions in Worldview: Understanding the Flow of Western Thought*. Phillipsburg, NJ: P&R Publishing, 2007. Generally excellent essays on the history of Christian thought as it responds to the developments of intellectual history.

Holmes, Arthur. *Philosophy: A Christian Perspective*. Downers Grove, IL: InterVarsity Press, 1975.

Moreland, J. P., and William Lane Craig. *Philosophical Foundations for a Christian Worldview*. Downers Grove, IL: InterVarsity Press, 2003. Large, thorough discussion of philosophical problems from a Christian point of view. Topical rather than historical.

Nash, Ronald H. *Life's Ultimate Questions: An Introduction to Philosophy*. Grand Rapids: Zondervan, 1999. Christian interpretation of several major philosophical issues and several major philosophical thinkers.

Naugle, David K. *Philosophy: A Student's Guide*. Wheaton, IL: Crossway, 2012. A brief topical discussion of philosophical issues (prolegomena, metaphysics, philosophical anthropology, etc.) from a Christian point of view. Quite valuable.

Schaeffer, Francis A. *How Shall We Then Live?* Wheaton, IL: Crossway, 2005. Schaeffer was an evangelist rather than an academic scholar, but he popularized a broadly presuppositional apologetic that frequently appealed to the history of philosophy and culture. Many came to believe in Christianity through his work. He wrote many books, but this one summarizes his use of the history of philosophy.

Sire, James W. *Habits of the Mind*. Downers Grove, IL: InterVarsity Press, 2000.

———. *The Universe Next Door: A Basic World View Catalogue*. Downers Grove, IL: InterVarsity Press, 1975. Sire influenced many to think of the Christian faith as a worldview, in competition with other worldviews.

Van Til, Cornelius. *A Survey of Christian Epistemology*. Philadelphia: Den Dulk Foundation, 1969. Van Til's work has had much influence on the present volume. Van Til often refers in his many books to philosophers and philosophical issues. But this one, a revision of his early *Metaphysics of Apologetics*, is one of the few that deals with the history of philosophy in a systematic way. This book deals extensively with Plato, and then with Plato's repercussions through history.

———. *Who Do You Say That I Am?* Nutley, NJ: Presbyterian and Reformed, 1975. This is much shorter than the previous title, and gives the gist of Van Til's critique of non-Christian philosophical thought. The three sections deal with ancient, medieval, and modern replies to the titular question.

Wolterstorff, Nicholas. *Reason within the Bounds of Religion*. 2nd ed. Grand Rapids: Eerdmans, 1984. Note the reversal of Kant's title. This is a very important work on the nature of Christian thought. I discuss Wolterstorff in chapter 13 of the present volume.

READ FOR YOURSELF

After each chapter of this book, I will list some primary source materials from the writers discussed in the chapter. Usually these will be the writings of historical figures. But since chapter 1 is primarily a systematic rather than a historical discussion, the "read for yourself" titles for this chapter will suggest books and articles that you can read to become more familiar with the approach to philosophy described here.

Frame, John M. *Apologetics to the Glory of God.* Phillipsburg, NJ: P&R Publishing, 1994.

———. *Cornelius Van Til: An Analysis of His Thought.* Phillipsburg, NJ: P&R Publishing, 1995.

———. *The Doctrine of the Knowledge of God.* Phillipsburg, NJ: Presbyterian and Reformed, 1987.

Frame on the Web: http://www.frame-poythress.org.

Poythress, Vern S. *Inerrancy and Worldview: Answering Modern Challenges to the Bible.* Wheaton, IL: Crossway, 2012.

———. *In the Beginning Was the Word: Language: A God-Centered Approach.* Wheaton, IL: Crossway, 2009.

———. *Logic: A God-Centered Approach to the Foundation of Western Thought.* Wheaton, IL: Crossway, 2013.

———. *Philosophy, Science, and the Sovereignty of God.* Phillipsburg, NJ: P&R Publishing, 2004.

———. *Redeeming Philosophy: A God-Centered Approach to the Big Questions.* Wheaton, IL: Crossway, 2014.

———. *Redeeming Science: A God-Centered Approach.* Wheaton, IL: Crossway, 2006.

Poythress on the Web: http://www.frame-poythress.org.

Van Til, Cornelius. *A Christian Theory of Knowledge.* Nutley, NJ: Presbyterian and Reformed, 1969.

———. *The Defense of the Faith.* Edited by K. Scott Oliphint. 4th ed. Phillipsburg, NJ: P&R Publishing, 2008.

———. *A Survey of Christian Epistemology.* Philadelphia: Den Dulk Foundation, 1969.

———. *Who Do You Say That I Am?* Nutley, NJ: Presbyterian and Reformed, 1975.

Van Til on the Web: http://www.vantil.info.

LISTEN ONLINE

After each chapter of this book, I will list the related free audio lectures on the History of Philosophy that are located at the Reformed Theological Seminary iTunes University website. (See the table "Correlation of Book Chapters with Free Online Lectures," found earlier in this book, for the complete list.) These are lectures that I have

OUTLINE

given as part of RTS's online learning program, and they are described at the link below this way:

> Spanning the timeframe from centuries before Christ to the present day, . . . [this course] explores the intersection between philosophical and Christian theological reflections in the ancient Greeks, early Christian Fathers, Medieval Christianity, the Reformation, the Enlightenment, and post-Enlightenment periods. This course will guide the listener through the thoughts and writings of major philosophical and theological thinkers, enabling the student to become more conversant with what has developed in these areas over the centuries.

Link: http://itunes.apple.com/us/course/legacy-history-philosophy/id694658914

- Why Study Philosophy—Metaphysics, Epistemology, and a Biblical Worldview: 53:51 minutes.
- Comparison of Biblical and Nonbiblical Worldviews: 31:42 minutes.

FAMOUS QUOTES

- **Aristotle:** http://en.wikiquote.org/wiki/Aristotle
- **Clouser:** http://www.metanexus.net/essay/excerpt-myth-religious-neutrality
- **Frame:** Theology is "the application of the Word of God by persons to all areas of life." (*Doctrine of the Knowledge of God* [Phillipsburg, NJ: Presbyterian and Reformed, 1987], 81)
- **Frame:** Nobody is really an atheist, in the most serious sense of that term. (This chapter)
- **Frame:** So I will argue through this book that the basic questions of philosophers are religious in character. (This chapter)
- **Lyotard:** http://www.goodreads.com/author/quotes/126575.Jean_Fran_ois_Lyotard
- **Van Til:** Arguing about God's existence, I hold, is like arguing about air. You may affirm that air exists, and I that it does not. But as we debate the point, we are both breathing air all the time. (*Why I Believe in God* [Chestnut Hill, PA: Westminster Theological Seminary, 1976], 3)
- **Van Til:** We always deal with concrete individual men. These men are sinners. They have "an axe to grind." They want to

suppress the truth in unrighteousness [Roms 1:18]. They will employ their reason for that purpose. (*The Defense of the Faith*, ed. K. Scott Oliphint, 4th ed. [Phillipsburg, NJ: P&R Publishing, 2008], 107)

- **Van Til:** Seeking to string beads that cannot be strung because they have no holes in them, with string of infinite length neither end of which you can find; such is the task of the educator who seeks to educate without presupposing the truth of what the self-attesting Christ has spoken in the Scriptures. (*Essays on Christian Education* [Nutley, NJ: Presbyterian and Reformed, 1971], 16)
- **Van Til:** But the best and only possible proof for the existence of such a God is that his existence is required for the uniformity of nature and for the coherence of all things in the world. We cannot *prove* the existence of beams underneath a floor if by proof we mean that they must be ascertainable in the way that we can see the chairs and tables of the room. But the very idea of a floor as the support of tables and chairs requires the idea of beams that are underneath. But there would be no floor if no beams were underneath. Thus there is absolutely certain proof for the existence of God and the truth of Christian theism. Even non-Christians presuppose its truth while they verbally reject it. They need to presuppose the truth of Christian theism in order to account for their own accomplishments. (*The Defense of the Faith*, 126)
- **Van Til:** In other words, the non-Christian needs the truth of the Christian religion in order to attack it. As a child needs to sit on the lap of its father in order to slap the father's face, so the unbeliever, as a creature, needs God the Creator and providential controller of the universe in order to oppose this God. Without this God, the place on which he stands does not exist. He cannot stand in a vacuum. (*Essays on Christian Education*, 89)

2

GREEK PHILOSOPHY[1]

THE ANCIENT GREEKS were not the first civilization in the West, but they made such immense contributions to art, architecture, science, politics, warfare, education, poetry, history, and philosophy that many discussions of these subjects, even today, begin with them. Until the twentieth century, when Eastern religion and philosophy began to make a major impact, Western thought had two roots: the Greek and the biblical. Some thinkers tried to synthesize these traditions in various ways. Others saw an antithesis between them and sought to be consistent with one or the other.

The ancient wariness about "Greeks bearing gifts" should be applied to the study of Greek worldviews. The chief benefit in studying Greek thought is to better understand the philosophical and cultural consequences of rejecting biblical theism.

Although I greatly admire the creative brilliance of the Greek thinkers, I believe it is a serious mistake to adopt their worldviews or to try to synthesize their thinking with the worldview of the Bible. The Greeks and the biblical writers did explore many common themes: God and gods, the nature of reality, the origin of the world, human nature, wisdom, knowledge, ethics, politics, even salvation. We can still learn much from the Greek discussions of these topics. But the ancient wariness about "Greeks bearing gifts" should be applied to the study of Greek worldviews.[2] The chief benefit in studying Greek thought is to better understand the philosophical and cultural consequences of rejecting biblical theism.

The word *rejecting* might seem harsh. Did the Greeks have access to Scripture? And if not, how could they have rejected it? The early

1. This chapter is a revision of my article "Greeks Bearing Gifts," previously published in *Revolutions in Worldview: Understanding the Flow of Western Thought*, ed. W. Andrew Hoffecker (Phillipsburg, NJ: P&R Publishing, 2007), 1–36.

2. The phrase "beware of Greeks bearing gifts" paraphrases text from Virgil's *Aeneid* and other sources. The allusion is to the Trojan horse. The Greeks sent a huge wooden horse as a supposed gift to the Trojans. After it was brought into the city, Greek soldiers emerged from the wooden structure, wreaking havoc.

Christian writer Justin Martyr thought that Plato got the idea for his Demiurge (a godlike figure in the dialogue *Timaeus*) from the writings of Moses. Justin's hypothesis is historically unlikely, and it is a symptom of Justin's overestimation of the coherence between Platonism and the Bible. But whatever we may say about the commerce in ideas between Greece and the Near East, the Bible does tell us that the Greeks, like all other people, had the resources for formulating a theistic worldview. We saw in chapter 1 that according to Paul in Romans 1:18–32, God has revealed himself clearly so that all people, Greeks included, know the biblical God, based on his revelation in creation. Yet they have rejected this knowledge and come to worship images of created things.

The world is not governed by impersonal fate . . . or by impersonal . . . movements of atoms . . . , but by a personal God who "has fixed a day on which he will judge the world in righteousness by a man whom he has appointed; and of this he has given assurance to all by raising him from the dead."

The same Paul once visited Athens and found it "full of idols" (Acts 17:16). He preached there to an audience that included Epicurean and Stoic philosophers and concluded by demanding their repentance for the sin of idolatry. Actually, neither the Epicureans nor the Stoics had much use for the traditional Greek gods. But Paul evidently believed that Stoic materialistic pantheism and Epicurean atomism were no better than the worship of Zeus and Apollo. To Paul, the world is not governed by impersonal fate (Stoicism) or by impersonal (occasionally random) movements of atoms (Epicurus), but by a personal God who "has fixed a day on which he will judge the world in righteousness by a man whom he has appointed; and of this he has given assurance to all by raising him from the dead" (v. 31). When Paul said this, some mocked, some withheld judgment, and a few believed.

The biblical God tolerates no rivals. It is wrong to worship Baal, Moloch, Dagon, Marduc, Zeus, Apollo, or Aphrodite. It is also wrong to regard the natural order as absolute, as an uncreated, self-sufficient reality. For both the "religious"[3] and the "secular" alternatives deny God the worship due to him alone. In this sense, both the materialistic Stoics and Epicureans and the spiritualistic Plato are idolaters.

The biblical God tolerates no rivals. . . . It is . . . wrong to regard the natural order as absolute, as an uncreated, self-sufficient reality. For both the "religious" and the "secular" alternatives deny God the worship due to him alone.

GREEK WORLDVIEWS: ONE AND MANY

We sometimes speak of "Greek philosophy" or even "Greek thought" as if it represented a single worldview. But at first glance, at least, there seem to be vast disagreements among the Greek thinkers. Besides the disagreement between materialists and spiritualists, we note that Homer and Hesiod believed in the traditional gods; Heraclitus, Xenophanes, and Epicurus had little use for them. Parmenides believed that nothing changes, Heraclitus that everything changes—well, almost everything. Plato despised sense experience; Heraclitus, the Stoics, and Epicurus affirmed it. Protagoras denied, and Plato affirmed, the

3. I put "religious" in quotes, for as I argued in chapter 1, all worldviews are religious, even those called "secular."

OUTLINE

possibility of objective knowledge. Parmenides and Plotinus believed that reality is a perfect oneness; Democritus and Epicurus believed that the world is irreducibly plural. Epicurus advised people to avoid politics; the Stoics encouraged such involvement. The tragedians and Stoics were fatalists; the Epicureans were not.

But the Greeks had much in common. First of all, none believed in the God of the Bible, despite the revelation of God to them mentioned earlier. None of the Greek philosophers even considered the theistic worldview, so far as we can tell from their writings. Since the theistic hypothesis was excluded from the outset, the Greek thinkers had the common task of explaining the world without reference to the biblical God, that is, of explaining the world by means of the world.

Unbelief in the biblical God meant also that the human mind had to do its work without help from any higher mind. Anaxagoras did teach that the world was directed by *nous* ("mind"). But according to Plato's *Apology*, Socrates expressed his disappointment that Anaxagoras didn't make much use of this idea. Nor did Heraclitus, who taught that the world was ordered by *logos* ("word" or "reason").

Aristotle also believed in a higher mind, the Unmoved Mover: a being whose entire activity consists in thinking about his own thoughts. But this god did not reveal his thoughts to Aristotle. Rather, it is a hypothesis of Aristotle's own reason and thus an idol.

To consider the issue more broadly: none of the Greeks believed that the world was created and directed by a personal supreme (absolute) being. The idea of an absolute being who is also personal is virtually unique to the Bible.[4] Hinduism, like Aristotle and Plato, teaches the existence of an absolute being, but that being (like those of the philosophers) is impersonal. The Homeric gods (as those of the Canaanites and other polytheists) are personal, but they are not absolute. Only the biblical God is both absolute and personal.[5]

None of the Greeks believed that the world was created and directed by a personal supreme (absolute) being. The idea of an absolute being who is also personal is virtually unique to the Bible.

THE GREEK WAY OF WORSHIP

In Greek religion, the absolute was fate, sometimes symbolized by the three women (*Fates*) who together weave and terminate the fabric

4. I say "virtually" to interject a note of caution. I have not studied all the religions and the philosophies of the world so as to prove the negative proposition that no other worldview includes a personal absolute. But I do believe this generalization is true. Scripture itself teaches that idolatry is universal among fallen people. God's revelation and grace, revealed only through the gospel of Christ, are the necessary antidote.

5. The god of Islam is absolute, and is often presented as personal. But (1) this emphasis comes ultimately from the Bible, from Muhammad's respect for the "peoples of the book." (2) Muslim theology compromises absolute-personality theism when it takes divine predestination in a fatalistic sense and when it presents its god as a supertranscendent being about whom nothing may truthfully be said in human language.

of human life,[6] but literally impersonal. The tragic heroes of Aeschylus and Sophocles are propelled by fate to transgress the proper boundaries of human life, whereupon they are destroyed, again, by fate. The dictates of fate might agree with those of morality in some measure, but not necessarily. Fate is an impersonal force like gravity or electricity, and even the gods are subject to it.

Dooyeweerd says that the older, pre-Homeric Greek religion

> deified the ever-flowing stream of organic life, which issues from mother earth and cannot be bound to any individual form. In consequence, the deities of this religion are amorphous. It is from this shapeless stream of ever-flowing organic life that the generations of perishable beings originate periodically, whose existence, limited by a corporeal form, is subjected to the horrible fate of death, designated by the Greek terms *anangke* [and] *heimarmene tuche*. This existence in a limiting form was considered an injustice since it is obliged to sustain itself at the cost of other beings so that the life of one is the death of another. Therefore all fixation of life in an individual figure is avenged by the merciless fate of death in the order of time.[7]

Homer

He later describes the "central motive" of this religion as "that of the shapeless stream of life eternally flowing throughout the process of birth and decline of all that exists in a corporeal form."[8]

For the tragedians, however, fate governs not only life and death, but everything in between as well. A fate that governs birth and death must govern all the events leading to birth and death. But then how can we reconcile such a comprehensive fatalism with the amorphousness of the stream of life? One of these, it seems, will have to yield to the other. Maintaining both leads to an unstable worldview. And neither fate nor the "shapeless stream" gives any meaning to the historical process. Things happen just because they happen (the shapeless stream) or because they were made to happen (fate), for no rational or moral purpose. We often draw a contrast between fatalistic worldviews and worldviews based on chance, but in the end these coincide: Both leave history meaningless and human beings helpless. Both types of worldview present a world that is not governed by purpose, goodness, or love.

We often draw a contrast between fatalistic worldviews and worldviews based on chance, but in the end these coincide: Both leave history meaningless and human beings helpless. Both types of worldview present a world that is not governed by purpose, goodness, or love.

But gradually the old nature-religion gave way to the religion of the Olympian gods. The transformation was not too great, for the

6. Clotho spun the thread, Lachesis measured it, and Atropos cut it.

7. Herman Dooyeweerd, *In the Twilight of Western Thought* (Nutley, NJ: Presbyterian and Reformed, 1960), 39.

8. Ibid.

gods were basically personifications of the various forces of nature: Poseidon of the sea, Hades of the underworld, Apollo of the sun, Hephaestus of fire, Demeter of the earth, and so on. Then the gods became patrons of human activities: Hera of marriage, Ares of war, Athena of education, Artemis of the hunt, Aphrodite of love, Hermes of commerce, and so on.[9] Zeus was the most powerful, but not all-powerful. He had a father and mother, the Titans Cronos and Rhea. He gained knowledge by consulting the Fates and suffered irrational fits of jealousy and rage.

Dooyeweerd describes this "younger Olympian religion" as "the religion of form, measure and harmony."[10] The Olympians lived far above the "shapeless stream of life." So worship of these gods became the official religion of the Greek city-states, which, of course, preferred order to chaos. Apollo especially became the embodiment of orderliness. But "in their private life the Greeks continued to hold to the old earthly gods of life and death."[11]

Dionysus, god of wine and revelry, was one of the Olympian gods, but not one honored much by Homer or by the politicians. For his worship was an intentional violation of the form, order, and structure: a religion of drunken revelry, of sexual orgy. So Dionysus, for all his Olympian transcendence, came to be seen as the patron of the old religion, the religion of shapelessness, of chaos.

The Olympian religion improved somewhat on the older one by providing some meaning to history, some reason why things happen as they do. Now, not only impersonal fate, or the chaotic life stream, but rational thought, the thinking of the gods, became part of the process. Yet ultimately history was still in the hands of irrational fate, which was superior to the gods, and of the stream of life, over which the gods had little control.

Both the old religion and the Olympian religion, therefore, have pessimistic implications for human life. Human beings are essentially pawns, of fate, of chaos, and/or of the Olympians. Unlike the God of the Bible, none of these elements of Greek religion has a moral character, nor is any of these beings "a very present help in trouble" (Ps. 46:1).

A new movement began around 600 B.C., when some thinkers began to try to understand the world without the help of religion. These were called philosophers, *lovers of wisdom.*

PHILOSOPHY, THE NEW RELIGION

A new movement began around 600 B.C., when some thinkers began to try to understand the world without the help of religion. These were called *philosophers*, lovers of wisdom. There had been wisdom teachers

9. One is reminded of how the later church appointed dead saints as patrons of human endeavors.

10. Dooyeweerd, *Twilight*, 40.

11. Ibid.

earlier in the ancient world, in Egypt, Babylon, and elsewhere. The wisdom literature in Scripture (Proverbs, Song of Solomon, Ecclesiastes) is similar to extrabiblical wisdom literature in many ways, but unlike it, the biblical wisdom teachers declare that "the fear of the LORD is the beginning of wisdom" (Ps. 111:10; Prov. 9:10; cf. Prov. 15:33; Eccl. 12:13).

What distinguishes the Greek philosophers from the Greek religions and from other ancient wisdom teachers is their insistence on the supremacy of human reason, what I will call *rational autonomy*. Wisdom teachers in other cultures treasured the traditions of fathers and mothers, the teachers of past generations (as in Prov. 1:8–9; 2:1–22; 3:1–2). They saw themselves as collectors and guardians of such traditions, occasionally adding something, and passing on the collection to their sons and daughters. The philosophers, however, wanted to accept nothing on the basis of tradition. Though Parmenides and Plato occasionally resorted to myth, they considered mythological explanations second best and in the end rationally inadequate. Reason must be autonomous, self-authenticating, subject to no standards other than its own.

What distinguishes the Greek philosophers from the Greek religions and from other ancient wisdom teachers is their insistence on the supremacy of human reason, what I will call rational autonomy. *Wisdom teachers in other cultures treasured the traditions of fathers.*

Though the philosophers disagreed on much, they all agreed that the good life was the life of reason.[12] To them, reason, not the fear of the Lord, was the beginning of wisdom. As such, for them, reason itself became something of a god, though they did not describe it as such: an object of ultimate allegiance, the ultimate standard of truth and falsity, of right and wrong.

The philosophers' attitudes toward the traditional Greek religion, therefore, ranged from ridicule (Xenophanes) to genial acceptance (Epicurus, who affirmed belief in the gods but denied that they caused anything to happen on earth). Socrates, considered the most admirable model of the philosophic temperament, was executed for his failure to believe in the gods of Athens, as well as for corrupting the youth. So Greek philosophy was a revolution in worldview. It represented a radical break from what had gone before.

Reason itself became something of a god, though they did not describe it as such: an object of ultimate allegiance, the ultimate standard of truth and falsity, of right and wrong.

A SURVEY OF GREEK PHILOSOPHY

But we must now look at the philosophers more specifically and in roughly chronological order. Note in the following discussion some themes that will apply to most of the individual figures, some of which

12. The Sophists of the fifth century (Protagoras, Gorgias, Thrasymachus) and the skeptics of the later Academy (Pyrrho, Timon, Arcesilaus) denied the possibility of knowing objective truth. But (paradoxically) they offered rational arguments for this conclusion. They never considered abandoning reason. For Plotinus, ultimate knowledge is mystical, not rational. But the path to mystical experience is rational. For him (also paradoxically), it is reason that teaches us how to transcend reason.

OUTLINE

I have mentioned already: (1) the supreme authority of human reason, (2) the consequent attempt to make rational claims about the nature of *all* reality, (3) the consequent claim that all reality is basically one, but (4) the continuing problem of dualism: the antagonism between impersonal fate and the shapeless stream of life. And (5) the shapeless stream challenges the power of reason to grasp reality. The philosophers try to deal with this problem in various ways, without compromising their fundamental allegiance to autonomous reason. But (6) the philosophers' inability to maintain the rationality of their enterprise indicates failure of their attempt to understand the world autonomously. For in the end we must conclude that they have set themselves an impossible task: imposing autonomous reason on an essentially irrational world. (7) These difficulties invalidate much of what they say about the soul, ethics, and society.

The Milesians

We have only fragments of the teachings and writings of the first group of Greek philosophers, named for their city, Miletus, in Asia Minor. Most of what we know about them comes from other writers, particularly Aristotle, who were not entirely sympathetic. Still, it is less important for us to know what these philosophers actually said or meant than to know how they were understood by later thinkers, for it was by these later interpretations that the Milesians influenced the history of philosophy.[13]

The philosophers' inability to maintain the rationality of their enterprise indicates failure of their attempt to understand the world autonomously.

Thales (approximately 620–546 B.C.) taught that "all is water" and that "all things are full of gods." **Anaximenes** (d. 528 B.C.) believed that "all is air." **Anaximander** (610–546) taught that "all is indefinite" (*apeiron*, "boundless"). To understand this, it helps to remember that the Greeks in general thought the universe consisted of four elements: earth, air, fire, and water. So the Milesians were seeking to discover which of these, if any, was the fundamental one, the element of the elements, the basic constitution of the universe.

Thus, they sought answers to three questions that continue to be of interest to scientists and philosophers: (1) What is the fundamental nature of reality? (2) Where did everything come from? (3) How did the universe get to be as it is?

For Thales, (1) the fundamental nature of the universe is water. That is the essence of everything, what everything really is, despite

13. Similarly in regard to other thinkers discussed in this book. For the most part, I will be assuming traditional interpretations of these thinkers, even though I know that many of these are controversial among specialists. I cannot here enter into detailed interpretive controversies, and I think the traditional interpretations tell us the nature of the impact that these philosophers have had on later history.

appearances to the contrary. (2) Everything came from water and will return to water. (3) The world developed out of water by various natural processes. Perhaps by saying that "all things are full of gods" he meant to indicate that these natural processes were governed by thought or mind in some way.

Anaximenes thought similarly about air, doubtless provoking arguments about whether water or air was the most plentiful element, the element most able to account for other phenomena, and the like. For him, the diversity in reality results from the condensation and rarefaction of air. Heraclitus would later make the case for fire. To my knowledge, nobody hypothesized the primacy of earth, perhaps because earth seemed to be less changeable than the others. Anaximander believed that none of the four elements could explain the variety of the world, so he said that the essence of things was a substance without a definite nature (in that sense "unbounded") that takes on limitations to create the visible world.

The all-statements of these thinkers represent human reason as vastly exceeding its limits. This is rationalism, an awe over the power of reason that turns it into a god.

Commentators sometimes describe the Greek philosophers as children looking at the world in wonder. This picture, however, is far from that of the apostle Paul, who, in the passage I mentioned earlier, says that those without the biblical God are suppressing the truth in unrighteousness. It is hard not to sympathize with Thales and his colleagues as they forge ahead to look at the world in a new way. We cannot hold against them the fact that modern science has transcended their perspectives. But if we consider seriously what they are doing, we may evaluate their work differently.

Thales's statement that all is water does not arise from what we would call scientific research. Doubtless Thales's observations influenced his view: the vast amount of water in the world, the need of water to sustain life, and so forth. But the *all* goes far beyond any possible observations. It is the language of a man sitting in an armchair, dogmatically asserting what the whole universe must be like. The *all*-statements of these thinkers represent human reason as vastly exceeding its limits. This is rationalism, an awe over the power of reason that turns it into a god.

Thales

On the other hand, water (and air, and even more obviously the "boundless") represents the "shapeless stream" of the old religion. Water moves in waves and currents. It cannot be leashed or controlled. There is a randomness about it that calls into question the power of reason to give an account of it. Thales's statement about everything being "full of gods" could be an attempt to give a rational direction to the random flow. But that raises further questions: are the gods, too, made of water? If not, then his hypothesis fails to explain *all*. If they are water, then they, like Zeus and Apollo, are victims of the flowing stream, not controllers of it. And we cannot ignore the fact that on Thales's basis the human mind, too, is water. My thoughts are essentially waves and wavelets, occurrences that just happen to take place in the movements of my inner sea. So why should we think that one wave is more true than another, more valid, more illuminating, more profound? Mechanistic natural processes can account for waves, but they cannot account for the truth or falsity of human thoughts.

So Thales is an extreme rationalist, whose worldview calls his reason into question. He is both a rationalist and an irrationalist. He calls to mind Cornelius Van Til's philosophical reading of Genesis 3: Our mother Eve was faced with two claims. God told her that she would die from eating the fruit. Satan told her that she would not die, but would become as God. Eve should have disregarded Satan's claim at the outset. Instead, she asserted her own right to make the final judgment (rationalism). But this claim presupposed that God did not exist as the ultimate determiner of truth and meaning, and that therefore there was no absolute truth (irrationalism). Van Til says that every unbeliever is caught in this tension between rationalism and irrationalism. Some emphasize the former, others the latter. But when they get uneasy with one, they leap to the other.[14] I will mention this pattern with other philosophers, both among the Greeks and in other traditions. I mention it not just as a fact of possible interest, but to show that the main inadequacies of Greek philosophy, in the end, are not to be blamed on primitive science, incomplete observations, or remediable logical mistakes, but on religious rebellion. These thinkers all absolutize the human intellect, but their nontheistic worldviews call the intellect itself into question.

These thinkers all absolutize the human intellect, but their nontheistic worldviews call the intellect itself into question.

The Milesians' epistemological failure is linked to a metaphysical failure. For the *all* of the Milesians excludes the biblical relation between Creator and creature. If all is water, then God, if he exists, is also water, and we are water. There is no fundamental difference between him and us. God and the world are one stuff. There is no creation. God has no intrinsic sovereignty over the world. The Milesians' scheme, therefore, rules out the biblical God. And if the biblical God is the only possible ground of meaning or truth in the world, the Milesians also rule out meaning and truth.

Heraclitus (525–475)

Heraclitus, who lived in Ephesus, not far from Miletus, thought that the most fundamental element was fire, the most dynamic and

14. Van Til's discussion can be found in his *A Christian Theory of Knowledge* (Nutley, NJ: Presbyterian and Reformed, 1969), 41–71. For his application to Plato, see Cornelius Van Til, *A Survey of Christian Epistemology* (Philadelphia: Den Dulk Foundation, 1969), 14–55. Cf. my *CVT*, 231–38 and passim.

changeable of the four. But he was less concerned with identifying the fundamental substance than with describing the pervasiveness of change, with the ways in which fire changes into other things and others into still others. He is often quoted as saying, "You cannot step into the same river twice," meaning that when you step in the second time, you are stepping into different waters. Since the waters are different, it is a different river. Actually, what he said was this: "On those stepping into rivers staying the same, other and other waters flow."[15] The river stays the same, but the waters constantly change. Evidently his view was that the elements of things are indeed constantly changing, but that such change makes it possible for sameness to occur at other levels of reality.[16]

The source of stability Heraclitus called the logos, probably the first philosophically significant use of this term.

So the world is constantly changing, but somehow these changes occur in regular patterns. If absolutely everything were in constant change, rational thought would be impossible. For rational thought requires stability: objects that remain themselves long enough to be examined. Horses must remain horses; houses, houses; people, people; rivers, rivers.

The source of stability Heraclitus called the *logos*, probably the first philosophically significant use of this term. *Logos* has a variety of meanings: "word," "reason," "rational account." Heraclitus believed in a principle governing change, to keep that change within rational bounds.

Reason must be our guide, Heraclitus tells us, even if we don't see how it can be reliable. Rationality must exist not only in our minds, but as an aspect of the universe. But he thus invokes reason, in effect, by an act of faith.

We can take Heraclitus's philosophy as common sense. When we look at the world, nothing seems to be perfectly at rest. Everything moves and changes, even if ever so slightly. Yet there is enough stability that we can talk about rivers, horses, houses, people, and many other things. The question is whether Heraclitus sheds any light on this change and stability. To say that there is a *logos* is to say that the stability in the world must have a source. But what is that source? Is *logos* really an explanation of anything, or is it just a label for an unknown? Heraclitus's writings are paradoxical, multilayered, full of symbols. They are fascinating, but in the end it just isn't clear (to me, at least) what he is trying to tell us.

We do see here another assertion of the Greek rationalism in the *logos*. Reason must be our guide, Heraclitus tells us, even if we don't see how it can be reliable. Rationality must exist not only in our minds, but as an aspect of the universe. But he thus invokes reason, in effect, by an act of faith. On the other hand, the changing flux amounts to

15. Hermann Diels and Walther Kranz, *Die Fragmente der Vorsokratiker* (Zurich: Weidmann, 1985), DK22B12. Translated by Daniel W. Graham in "Heraclitus," in *Internet Encyclopedia of Philosophy*, http://www.utm.edu/research/iep/h/heraclit.htm. I have inserted a comma for clarification.

16. See ibid.

irrationalism. For Heraclitus virtually concedes that reason cannot deal with reality unless it is somehow constant. But at the elemental levels, reality is anything but constant. Yet, rationalistically, he tries to develop a rational analysis of the elemental change.

Like the Milesians, Heraclitus rejects biblical theism and therefore the One who originates and sustains change. He is left with a world that is *somehow* changing and a rational constancy that is *somehow* there. The God who alone can give meaning to constancy and change is not a part of Heraclitus's philosophy.

Parmenides (c. 510–430)

Parmenides, who lived in Elea in southern Italy, agreed with Heraclitus that reasoning requires something changeless. So, swinging 180 degrees from Heraclitus, he denied the existence of change altogether. He wrote a poem describing an encounter with a goddess, who reveals to him that "Being is." The goddess, however, does not deliver this revelation on her own authority, but rather appeals to reason as a properly philosophical goddess should do.[17]

"Being is" means that nothing can change from what it "is" to what it "is not." Red cannot change to green, for then red would be changing into non-red, or non-green would be changing into green. And how can that be? Where does the green come from, if the previous state is non-green? So change cannot be real. It must be an illusion.

Indeed, the very idea of "nonbeing" must be rejected. There is no change from nonbeing to being, for there is no such thing as nonbeing. Nonbeing simply is not. Similarly non-red, non-green, and all other negative expressions.[18]

Parmenides tries to describe what a world would be like without nonbeing, and therefore without change. It is ungenerated, homogeneous, solid, symmetrical, spherical.

What is the real world, then? Parmenides tries to describe what a world would be like without nonbeing, and therefore without change. It is ungenerated, homogeneous, solid, symmetrical, spherical. If it is not homogeneous, for example, it must be a combination of one element and what it is not: for example, water and non-water. But that cannot be. Similarly with the other characteristics that Parmenides ascribes to reality.

This worldview, however, which Parmenides calls the *way of truth*, is so far from common sense that it gives us no help in living in the world

17. Parmenides is usually considered a follower of the religious teacher Xenophanes (570–475), who rejected the Olympian gods in favor of a kind of pantheistic monism. Parmenides' "Being" is roughly equivalent to Xenophanes' god.

18. Critics of Parmenides have pointed out that there is a difference between the existential (e.g., "horses are" = "horses exist") and the predicative ("horses are mammals") senses of the verb *to be*. Parmenides evidently confuses these. It is obviously contradictory to say, "Being is not," for in that phrase *Being* refers to existence. It is not obviously contradictory to say, "The horse is not green," for *is* in that sentence is used predicatively rather than existentially.

of our experience. It requires us to reject our experience to a drastic extent, to dismiss it as illusion. Parmenides' poem does, however, also include an elaborate cosmology, which another goddess calls the *way of belief* or *way of opinion*. This cosmology includes change and is very different from the way of truth. Most likely, Parmenides regards the way of belief as an error to be rejected. But he might also have intended for us to use the way of belief as a practical guide, as a way to think about the world that our senses present to us.

Parmenides

Parmenides is perhaps the most consistent rationalist in the history of philosophy. He said that there is no difference between "what is" and "what can be thought." So that, having determined what can be thought by human reason, he thought he had discovered the true nature of the world. In the service of reason he was willing to deny almost entirely the testimony of our senses, asserting the existence of a world vastly different from anything we have seen or heard. But what happens to reason in this unchanging world? Human reason is temporal, or seems to be. We think one thought after another. Our minds experience change, even in our most intellectual activities. How can we think at all, if we cannot advance from less adequate to more adequate ideas? So Parmenides' rationalism actually invalidates reason, leading to irrationalism.

Perhaps Parmenides knew this and provided the way of belief as an alternative philosophy, to account for the structure of our sense experience.[19] Then we can see rationalism in Parmenides' way of truth, irrationalism in his way of belief. On this understanding, Parmenides would have anticipated Plato's distinction between the world of Forms, which really "is," and the world of our sense experience, which is less knowable and less real.

Parmenides is perhaps the most consistent rationalist in the history of philosophy. He said that there is no difference between "what is" and "what can be thought." So that, having determined what can be thought by human reason, he thought he had discovered the true nature of the world.

Again we must ask how Parmenides' thought might have been different had he started with the existence of the biblical God and listened to his revelation.

The Atomists

Parmenides is classified as a *monist*, someone who believes that the universe is basically one. Indeed, Parmenides systematically excluded all diversity from the world in his attempt to exclude "nonbeing." In the way of truth, there cannot be different things, one that is red (for instance) and one that is not.

Other philosophers have been pluralists, maintaining that the universe is fundamentally many, rather than one. In ancient Greece,

19. Plato also introduced myths (as in *Republic* and *Timaeus*) to deal with subjects that his philosophy was unable to treat adequately. We might compare here the *custom* of David Hume, the *practical reason* of Immanuel Kant, *the Mystical* of Wittgenstein.

those who argued this position most thoroughly were the atomists, **Empedocles** (major work around 450), **Anaxagoras** (500–428), **Leucippus** (fifth century), **Democritus** (460–360), and **Epicurus** (341–270).[20]

Empedocles thought that the world was originally something like Parmenidean Being: one, homogeneous, and so on. But the opposing forces of love and strife start things in motion, separating out the four elements, and combining them in different ways. The four elements are "roots" of all reality, in effect the atoms, the basic stuff of which everything is made.

For Anaxagoras, there was an indefinite number of elements. Fire could not produce earth, he thought, unless there was some earth already in fire. Nor can a person's bread become muscle and hair unless there are little bits of muscle and hair in the bread already. Anaxagoras also taught the existence of *nous* or mind, a principle that maintains the rationality of change, similar to Heraclitus's *logos* and Empedocles' love and strife. Socrates complained in Plato's *Apology* that he had hoped to find in Anaxagoras some account of how mind directed the world, but he was disappointed to find in his writings only mechanistic explanations of nature.

Empedocles and Anaxagoras are called *qualitative atomists*. That is, they believed that the world is made up of elements with different qualities, either four (Empedocles) or indefinitely many (Anaxagoras). The elements are unchanging, somewhat like Parmenidean Being. But reality as a whole changes by the varying combinations of these elements.

Leucippus, Democritus, and Epicurus were *quantitative atomists*. Their atoms, or elements, all had the same qualities, except for size and shape (Democritus) or weight (Epicurus). These atoms moved through space and collided with one another to form objects. On this view, reality consists entirely of atoms and empty space.

Epicurus is probably the first philosopher to identify human freedom with causal indeterminacy, and to make this indeterminacy the basis of moral responsibility.

Since the atoms of Epicurus had the quality of weight, they tended to fall in one direction, a sort of cosmic "down." Normally they fell in lines parallel to one another. How, then, did they ever collide to form objects? Epicurus posited that occasionally an atom would "swerve" from the vertical path. The swerve is entirely uncaused, and accounts for the formation of objects. It also accounts for human free choice. Human beings are able to act apart from causal determination, for the atoms of their bodies sometimes swerve inexplicably.

Epicurus is probably the first philosopher to identify human freedom with causal indeterminacy, and to make this indeterminacy the basis of moral responsibility. This view of freedom is sometimes

20. The atomists were pluralists only in a sense. They were monists in that like Thales they believed there was only one *kind* of thing in the world, namely, atoms.

called *libertarianism* or *incompatibilism*.[21] A number of theologians have advocated free will in this sense, including Pelagius, Molina, Arminius, and the recent open theists.[22] But the question must be posed: how does the random swerve of atoms in my body make my acts morally responsible? If I walk down the street and some atoms in my head swerve and collide, making me rob a bank, why am I to blame? I didn't make them swerve; indeed, the swerve had no cause at all. It seems more plausible to say that the swerve *happened* to me, and therefore that I am *not* responsible for its consequences. It is like a chemical imbalance in my brain, making me do strange things. It is an odd kind of determinism, rather than freedom. Should we not say, then, that such a swerve precisely *removes* our responsibility?

How does the random swerve of atoms in my body make my acts morally responsible? If I walk down the street and some atoms in my head swerve and collide, making me rob a bank, why am I to blame? I didn't make them swerve; indeed, the swerve had no cause at all.

The question of responsibility leads us to think of ethics. Writing after the time of Plato and Aristotle, Epicurus is eager to apply his atomism to moral questions. One wonders indeed what sort of ethics can emerge from such a thoroughgoing materialism.

Essentially, Epicurus's ethic is that we should avoid pain and seek pleasure (which he defines as the absence of pain). Unlike the Cyrenaics and some later Epicureans, Epicurus distinguishes short-term from long-term pleasures and teaches that on the whole a quiet, peaceful, contemplative life is the most pleasurable. This view of ethics is called *hedonism*, from the Greek word meaning "pleasure." But there are several problems with it: (1) In the normal sense of *pleasure*, there are many things that human beings value more highly. One example is sacrificing one's life to save the life of another. Epicurus gives us no good reason to pursue pleasure rather than some other value. (2) If we define *pleasure* so broadly as to include all other values, including self-sacrifice, then it loses its meaning. It doesn't distinguish pleasurable from nonpleasurable activities. (3) Even if it is true that people value pleasure in some sense above all else, it is a logical jump to say that we *ought* to value pleasure above all else. But the *ought* is what ethics is all about. I doubt that anyone can derive an ethical *ought* from a materialistic philosophy. Matter in motion simply cannot tell us what we ought to do.

The ought *is what ethics is all about. I doubt that anyone can derive an ethical* ought *from a materialistic philosophy. Matter in motion simply cannot tell us what we ought to do.*

Atomism, then, tries to account for everything by matter, motion, and chance. If Thales was unable to account for human thought by means of water, how can the atomists expect to account for it by means of nondescript bits of matter in motion? The atomists are rationalistic in trying through their reason to reduce all reality to its smallest

21. It is called *incompatibilism* because it is incompatible with determinism. Other views of freedom are compatible with determinism. For example, the view called *compatibilism* is the view that freedom is simply doing what you want to do.

22. I have extensively criticized libertarianism in my *NOG* and in *DG*.

components. But having done that, they have left us little if any reason to trust our minds. So rationalism and irrationalism again combine. The problem becomes even more difficult when we try to account for human responsibility and moral obligation on a materialistic basis.

The religious roots of all this become especially clear in Epicurus's writings, for he is most explicit in wanting to exclude the supernatural from any role in the world. But without a personal God, how can one account for the validity of thinking and the authority of moral principles?

Pythagoras (572–500)

We know little of the specific views held by Pythagoras, but he influenced a school of thought that in turn influenced other philosophers. Plato visited the Pythagorean religious community in southern Italy and reworked many of their ideas in his own writings. The Pythagoreans followed a religion known as *Orphism*, which taught that the human soul was a divine being imprisoned in the body. On their view, the soul undergoes reincarnation until it is sufficiently purified to return to the divine realm. Our souls are divine because they are rational, so salvation comes through knowledge. Thus, the Pythagoreans followed the common Greek emphasis on the autonomy of the intellect. They also divided human beings into three classes: lovers of wisdom, lovers of honor, and lovers of gain—which could be the source for Plato's similar threefold distinction in the *Republic*. And they developed an elaborate cosmology, similar to that of Anaximander and of Parmenides' *way of belief*.

But we remember Pythagoras chiefly for his work in mathematics, including the Pythagorean theorem found in every high school geometry book. That theorem tells us that in a right triangle, the square of the hypotenuse is the sum of the squares of the other two sides. In a right triangle whose sides measure 3, 4, and 5 inches, the squares of the shorter sides would be 9 and 16, equaling 25, the square of the longer side. Pythagoras and/or his disciples also most likely discovered that harmonious combinations of musical notes arise from different vibrations related by simple fractions. If A on the scale is 440 vibrations, the next higher octave is 880, and so on.

These data might have suggested to the Pythagoreans that everything in the universe can be described as the application of a mathematical formula. . . . Since everything is the outworking of a mathematical formula, mathematics is the most ultimate reality.

These data might have suggested to the Pythagoreans that everything in the universe can be described as the application of a mathematical formula. Hence the slogan "all is number," reflecting the *all* formulae of the Milesians. Since everything is the outworking of a mathematical formula, mathematics is the most ultimate reality. This was the Pythagorean version of the common Greek theme that reason is the nature of reality as well as the nature of thought.

The Pythagoreans, however, did not ask, so far as we can tell, where the formulae came from. The existence of such formulae would seem to be a remarkable fact. Indeed, it should have suggested a personal creator, for the natural home of numbers and formulae is in the mind of a person. For the Pythagoreans, numbers "just are." They exist as brute facts. For the Pythagoreans, like other Greeks, were unwilling to acknowledge a rational person higher than themselves. The greatest mind is the mind of the human mathematician.

But the cost of this rationalism is the loss of cogency. If mathematical formulae just are, why should we trust them? Is it perhaps an accident that mathematical formulae neatly apply to right triangles and some musical intervals? And by what process do abstract numbers get converted into concrete things? Like that of other Greek philosophers, the Pythagoreans' rationality terminates in irrationality.

The cost of this rationalism is the loss of cogency. If mathematical formulae just are, why should we trust them? Is it perhaps an accident that mathematical formulae neatly apply to right triangles and some musical intervals? . . . Like that of other Greek philosophers, the Pythagoreans' rationality terminates in irrationality.

The Sophists

The Sophists were traveling educators in fifth- and fourth-century Greece who went from one city to another teaching young men the skills needed for success in public life: rhetoric, grammar, history, science, art, and the virtues of character that lead to public admiration. These teachers had many clients, for the traditional aristocracy was losing ground to the mercantile class, creating opportunities for upwardly mobile sons of wealthy families. Also, there was much political upheaval, raising philosophical questions about the ground and legitimacy of political rule.[23]

Thus philosophy took a new turn. No longer were philosophers mainly concerned with the structure of the natural world. Now human nature and the problems of human society became prominent.

If one's main concern is getting along with various political factions, then relativism will have a strong appeal, as we know from contemporary politics. If there is no absolute or objective truth, no truth that everyone must acknowledge, then one's convictions are free to move here and there, with every wave of political opinion. So it is not surprising that the Sophists were relativists.

Pythagoras

We learn about them mainly through the dialogues of Plato—an unsympathetic witness, to be sure, but most likely a fair one. The Sophist **Protagoras**, for example, advocated acceptance of traditional ways of thinking, not because they were true, but because we need to use them to gain power and acceptance. **Gorgias** denied the existence of objective truth and so wanted to substitute rhetoric for philosophy.

23. For more extensive discussion of the political and social background of Sophism, see Gordon H. Clark, *Thales to Dewey: A History of Philosophy* (Boston: Houghton Mifflin, 1957), 46–48.

Thrasymachus taught that "justice is the interest of the stronger," so that laws are (and should be) means by which the strong keep the masses subordinate. **Callicles** held, on the contrary, that laws are the means used by the masses to check the power of the strong.[24] **Critias**, later described as the cruelest of the thirty tyrants, said that a ruler must control his subjects by encouraging fear of nonexistent gods.

Socrates, as Plato presents him in the same dialogues, replies that indifference or hostility to objective truth is unacceptable. For one thing, the Sophists themselves are making assertions of fact. If there is no objective truth, then the Sophists' positions are not objectively true, and there is no reason for anyone to listen to them. This argument has been a standard answer to relativism ever since, and we still hear it used over against, for example, contemporary postmodernism.

Further, Socrates argues, justice cannot merely be the interest of the stronger. For the interest of the stronger is not what makes it *just*, as opposed to unjust. There must be some other quality that *defines* justice, that serves as a criterion to evaluate the conduct of rulers.

Thus Socrates refutes the irrationalism of the Sophists, or rather shows that such irrationalism is self-refuting. But the Sophists were also rationalists in the typical Greek way. Protagoras said that "man is the measure of all things." This statement expresses the Sophists' irrationalism: reality is what any man thinks it is. But it is also rationalistic, for it makes human reason the ultimate criterion of truth and falsity, right and wrong. One wonders how Protagoras could *know* this, especially given his overall relativism. He asserts rational autonomy arbitrarily. That is, he asserts rationalism irrationalistically, as he asserts irrationalism rationalistically—by the measure of his own mind.

If there is no objective truth, then the Sophists' positions are not objectively true, and there is no reason for anyone to listen to them. This argument has been a standard answer to relativism ever since, and we still hear it used over against, for example, contemporary postmodernism.

No other course was open to the Sophists, for they were skeptical about the traditional gods and would not consider the God of biblical theism.

Socrates (470–399)

But Socrates did more than refute the Sophists. He is a figure of such towering importance that all the other thinkers discussed to this point traditionally bear the label *pre-Socratic*. He is a major saint in the religion of philosophy, a martyr. He was executed in 399 by the Athenian state for disbelief in the official gods[25] and for corrupting the youth.

24. The distinction between Thrasymachus and Callicles reminds us of the differing attitudes of Marx and Nietzsche to Christianity. Marx considered Christianity an "opiate" by which the strong kept the poor in their place. Nietzsche considered it a "slave religion" by which lesser people inhibited those with ability and power. That such opposite conclusions can be derived from the same (relativistic) premises indicates some problem with the premises themselves.

25. Though Plato says that one of his last acts was to ask someone to deliver a cock to Asclepius, the god of healing.

Socrates is revered not so much for his ideas (which are hard to disentangle from those of his student Plato, our major source of information about him) as for his way of life, his style of argument, his passion for truth. Having rejected the relativism of the Sophists, he insisted on getting to the roots of philosophical questions, exploring first here, then there. And he insisted on living in accord with his philosophy. He refused opportunities to escape death, wanting to show himself loyal to the government of Athens.

Socrates is revered not so much for his ideas (which are hard to disentangle from those of his student Plato, our major source of information about him) as for his way of life, his style of argument, his passion for truth.

The Oracle at Delphi, he says, told him that he was the wisest of men because he alone was aware of his own ignorance. So he sought out people who he thought might be able to answer important questions, and he interrogated them rigorously. He regularly exposed flaws in the reasoning of the experts. Then he sought to define terms: what is *justice*, really? What is *virtue*? Characters in the dialogue would bring up examples of these qualities, but Socrates wanted to know more than examples. What is common to the examples of justice that makes them just? Usually, his interrogation yielded nothing definitive. But his use of dialogue (the technical term is *dialectic*) as a way of finding truth has inspired philosophers and other educators for centuries. Hence all disciplines have adopted his slogan, "The unexamined life is not worth living."

For Socrates, however, the use of dialogue was subordinate, as a source of truth, to something inward, to the human soul itself. He claimed that within him was a *daimon*, a divinity, and he believed that everyone could find the truth by looking within. So another Socratic slogan is "Know yourself."

Dialectic and introspection together, then, constitute the Socratic epistemology. The emphasis on dialectic renews the Greek rationalistic tradition. The emphasis on introspection, however, locates truth in individual subjectivity.

Dialectic and introspection together, then, constitute the Socratic epistemology. The emphasis on dialectic renews the Greek rationalistic tradition. The emphasis on introspection, however, locates truth in individual subjectivity.[26] This subjectivism is uncomfortably like that of the Sophists. If we are not to dismiss it as irrationalistic, we need to know how human subjectivity is related to the objective world, and to the Author of truth.

Plato (427–347)

Plato was the greatest student of Socrates and one of the greatest philosophers of all time. The greatest philosophers (among whom I include also Aristotle, Aquinas, Kant, and Hegel) tend to be those who bring together many ideas that at first seem disparate. As an example: Parmenides said that Being is fundamentally changeless, Heraclitus that the elements of reality are in constant change. Plato's genius is to

26. So Socrates has been compared to Søren Kierkegaard.

see truth in both of these accounts and to bring them together into a broader systematic understanding. Similarly, Plato provides distinct roles for reason and sense experience, soul and body, concepts and matter, objects and subjects, and, of course, rationalism and irrationalism.

Plato's epistemology begins with the observation that we can learn very little from our sense organs. So far, he agrees with the Sophists. Our eyes and ears easily deceive us. But the remarkable thing is that we have the rational ability to correct these deceptions and thus to find truth. It is by our reason also that we form concepts of things. We have never, for example, seen a perfect square. But somehow we know what a perfect square would be like, for we know the mathematical formula that generates one. Since we don't learn the concept of squareness by sense experience, we must learn it from reason. Similarly concepts of treeness, horseness, humanity, justice, virtue, goodness, and on and on. We don't see these, but somehow we know them.

These concepts Plato calls *Forms* or *Ideas*. Since we cannot find these Forms on earth, he says, they must exist in another realm, a world of Forms, as opposed to the world of sense. But what are Forms, exactly? In reading Plato we sometimes find ourselves thinking of the Form of treeness as a perfect, gigantic tree somewhere, which serves as a model for all trees on earth. But that can't be right. Given the many different kinds of trees, how could one tree serve as a perfect model for all of them? And even if there were a gigantic tree somewhere, how could there be a gigantic justice, or virtue, or goodness? Further, Plato says that the Forms are not objects of sensation (as a gigantic tree would be). Rather, they are known through intelligence alone, through reason. Perhaps Plato is following the Pythagoreans here, conceiving the Forms as quasi-mathematical formulae, recipes that can be used to construct trees, horses, virtue, and justice as the Pythagorean theorem can be used to construct a triangle. I say "quasi" because Plato in the *Republic* said that "mathematicals are a class of entities *between* the sensibles and the Forms."[27] Nevertheless, he does believe that Forms are real things and are the models of which things on earth are copies.

Plato's epistemology begins with the observation that we can learn very little from our sense organs. . . . But the remarkable thing is that we have the rational ability to correct these deceptions and thus to find truth. It is by our reason also that we form concepts of things.

The Forms, then, are perfect, immaterial, changeless, invisible, intangible objects. Though abstract, they are more real than the objects of our sense experience, for only a perfect triangle, for example, is a real triangle. And the Forms are also more knowable than things on earth. We might be uncertain whether a particular judge is just, but we cannot be uncertain as to the justice of the Form Justice. Thus, the Forms serve as models, exemplars, indeed criteria for earthly things. It is the Forms that enable us to know the earthly things that imitate

27. Diogenes Allen, *Philosophy for Understanding Theology* (Atlanta: John Knox Press, 1985), 20. Allen's further comments on this issue are helpful.

them. We can know that someone is virtuous only by comparing him with the norm of Ideal Virtue.

The Forms exist in a hierarchy, the highest being the Form of the Good. For we learn what triangles, trees, human beings, and justice are when we learn what each is "good for." Everything is good for something, so everything that exists participates in the Form of the Good to some extent. The world of Forms, therefore, contains not only formulae for making objects, but also norms defining the *purposes* of objects.

Plato

In *Euthyphro*, Socrates argues that *piety* cannot be defined as "what the gods desire." For why should they desire it? They must desire it because it is good. So piety is a form of goodness, and goodness must exist independently of what gods or men may think or say about it. So it must be a Form. We should note, however, that if courage, virtue, goodness, and so forth are abstract Forms, then they have no specific content. To know what is good, for Plato, is to know the Form of the Good. But Good is what all individual examples of goodness have in common. How, then, does it help us to know specifically what is good and what is bad?

Anytime we try to define *goodness* in terms of specific qualities (justice, prudence, temperance, etc.), we have descended to something less than the Form of the Good. The Form of the Good serves as a norm for human goodness, because it is utterly general and abstract. Any principle that is more specific is less normative, less authoritative. Such is the consequence of trying to understand goodness as an abstract Form rather than, as in biblical theism, the will of a personal absolute.[28]

The Form of the Good serves as a norm for human goodness, because it is utterly general and abstract. Any principle that is more specific is less normative, less authoritative. Such is the consequence of trying to understand goodness as an abstract Form rather than, as in biblical theism, the will of a personal absolute.

The world of sense experience is modeled on the world of Forms. Plato's *Timaeus* is a sort of creation account in which the Demiurge, a godlike figure, forms matter into patterns reflecting the Forms, placing his sculpture into a *receptacle* (perhaps empty space, or an indeterminate "stuff" anticipating Aristotle's *matter*). The Demiurge is very different from the God of the Bible, for he is subordinate to the Forms and limited by the nature of the matter. The matter resists formation, so the material objects cannot be perfect, as the Forms are. So the Demiurge must be satisfied with a defective product. It is not clear whether Plato intended this story to be taken literally. He sometimes resorted to myth when he could not come up with a properly philosophical account of something. But it is significant that he saw the need for some means to connect the Forms with the sensible world. And it is significant that he made that connection personal rather than impersonal.

28. And if anyone asks the relation of goodness to the God of the Bible, the answer is as follows: (1) Goodness is not something above him, that he must submit to; (2) nor is it something below him, that he could alter at will, but (3) it is his own nature: his actions and attributes, given to human beings for imitation. "You therefore must be perfect, as your heavenly Father is perfect" (Matt. 5:48).

OUTLINE

But how do we know the Forms, located as we are in this defective, changing world? Here Plato reflects the subjectivism of the Sophists and Socrates: we look within. We find within ourselves recollections of the Forms. Recollections? Then at one time we must have had experience of the Forms. When? Not in this life, where our experiences are limited to imperfect and changing things, but in another life before this one. So Plato embraces the Pythagorean-Orphic doctrine of reincarnation. We lived once in a world in which the Forms were directly accessible to us. Then we "fell" from that existence into the sense-world, into bodies. Our knowledge of the Forms remains in memory, but sometimes it has to be coaxed out of us by Socratic questioning. One famous example is in Plato's *Meno*, where Socrates asks questions of an uneducated slave boy, leading him to display a knowledge of geometry that nobody expected him to have.

The world of sense is not strictly knowable. Plato compares it to the shadows cast by a fire in a cave. Prisoners chained in the cave all their lives can see the shadows, but they mistake them for the truth, so in fact they know virtually nothing. Their notions are *conjecture*, not *knowledge*. We can move beyond conjecture to *belief* by distinguishing between images (such as shadows and pictures) and actual objects. Thus we come to know the visible world. But we do not "understand" the visible world until we see the things of the world as instances of general concepts. Thus we move from conjecture, to belief, to understanding. Pure knowledge is still a fourth stage: intuitive vision of the Forms. The first two stages Plato calls *opinion*, the last two *knowledge*. The first two come through sense experience, the last two through reason. Our sense experience is illumined by the sun; our knowledge of the intelligible world is illumined by the Form of the Good.

[According to Plato,] we lived once in a world in which the Forms were directly accessible to us. Then we "fell" from that existence into the sense-world, into bodies. Our knowledge of the Forms remains in memory, but sometimes it has to be coaxed out of us by Socratic questioning.

In *Phaedrus*, Plato considers knowledge from another perspective: knowledge is motivated by love. In beautiful objects,[29] we see an echo of true beauty, and we are moved by passion to seek the Form of Beauty itself. Here is another example of the Greek focus on inwardness. People have sometimes said that the search for knowledge must be disinterested, without passion. Although Plato advocated the dominance of intellect over the appetites, he saw a positive use of the passions, even in philosophy.

29. His example is the beauty of a boy, as a pederastic love interest. As did many other Greek thinkers, Plato favored homosexual relationships between men and boys, another indication of how far the Greeks were from the biblical revelation. Paul's argument in Romans 1 presents homosexuality as a particularly vivid example of the depths to which people fall when they reject God's revelation.

Since we once lived apart from the body in the world of the Forms, it must be the case that the human soul can exist separately from the body. In *Phaedo*, as Socrates prepares for death, he bases his hope for immortality on this epistemological argument. Plato divides the soul into three parts. The lowest is the appetitive, which seeks physical necessities and pleasures. Next higher is the spirited, which includes anger, ambition, desire for social honor, and so on. The highest is the rational, which seeks knowledge for its own sake.[30] We can see how, with a bit of emendation, these divisions correspond to the later common distinction between emotions, will, and intellect, respectively. They correspond even more closely to Freud's distinction between id (appetitive), ego (spirited), and superego (rational). In *Phaedrus*, Plato sees the spirited part as a driver with two horses, white (the rational) and black (the appetitive). The spirited is swayed sometimes by the appetitive, sometimes by the rational. The more it subordinates its appetites to its intellect, the better off it will be; see fig. 2.1.

Since we once lived apart from the body in the world of the Forms, it must be the case that the human soul can exist separately from the body. In Phaedo, *as Socrates prepares for death, he bases his hope for immortality on this epistemological argument.*

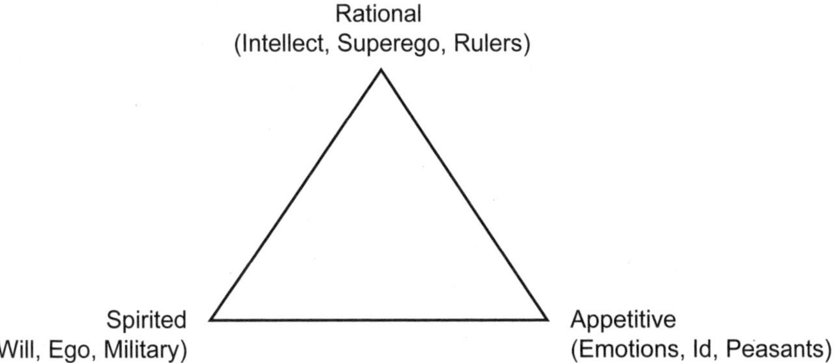

Fig. 2.1. Plato's Analysis of the Individual Soul, with Comparisons

Plato's major interest, like that of Socrates, was to tell us how to live. His metaphysics and epistemology are all a prelude to his ethics and political theory. Yet it is in these areas that he is most disappointing.

But Plato's major interest, like that of Socrates, was to tell us how to live. His metaphysics and epistemology are all a prelude to his ethics and political theory. Yet it is in these areas that he is most disappointing. His Socrates discusses at length the nature of justice and courage, but comes to no firm conclusion. He does conclude that the definition of *virtue* is "knowledge." One never does wrong except out of ignorance. If one knows what is right, he will necessarily do it. But most of Plato's readers through the centuries (including his pupil Aristotle) have dismissed this statement as naive, and

30. In *Phaedo*, the soul is only the higher part, but in *Phaedrus*, the soul includes all three parts, even prior to its bodily existence.

Christians have found it superficial in comparison with the Bible's view of human depravity.

And if virtue is knowledge, knowledge of what? Knowledge of the Good? But *good* is more difficult to define than *virtue* is. Like all other Forms, it is abstract. So how can it settle concrete ethical disputes, such as whether abortion is right or wrong? For Plato, to live right is to know the Good. But to say that is to leave all specific ethical questions unanswered.

Plato did come to some specific recommendations in the area of politics. But these recommendations have been almost universally rejected. In the *Republic*, he divides the body politic into groups corresponding to the divisions of the soul. In his ideal state, the peasants are governed by the appetitive soul, the military by the spirited, and the rulers by the rational. So the rulers of the state must be philosophers, those who understand the Forms. Such a state will be totalitarian, claiming authority over all areas of life. The upper classes will share their women communally, and children will be raised by the rulers. Art will be severely restricted, because it is a kind of shadow of which one can have only conjecture, the lowest form of opinion. Images detract from knowledge of Beauty itself (the Form), and they can incite to anarchy. Donald Palmer says that Plato's *Republic* "can be viewed as a plea that philosophy take over the role which art had hitherto played in Greek culture."[31]

If virtue is knowledge, knowledge of what? Knowledge of the Good? But good *is more difficult to define than* virtue *is. Like all other Forms, it is abstract. So how can it settle concrete ethical disputes, such as whether abortion is right or wrong?*

Most modern readers look at these ideas with distaste. Where did Plato get them? It would not be credible for him to claim that he got them by contemplating the Good. Rather, the whole business sounds like special pleading. Plato the philosopher thinks that philosophers should rule. He is rather like a Sophist here, claiming to be the expert in the means of governance. But he certainly has not shown that philosophers in general have any of the special qualities needed to govern. And the Sophists denied what Plato claims: access to absolute truth. We may applaud Plato's rejection of relativism. But his absolutism is what makes him a totalitarian. He thinks the philosophers have Knowledge, so they must rule everything.

Plato engages in special pleading because he has no nonarbitrary way of determining what is right and wrong. But as we've seen, once one identifies Goodness as an abstract Form, one cannot derive from it any specific content. So Plato's ideas about ethics and politics lack any firm basis or credibility.

The best thing that can be said of Plato is that he knew and considered seriously the criticisms that could be made against his system. He

31. Donald Palmer, *Looking at Philosophy: The Unbearable Heaviness of Philosophy Made Lighter* (Mountain View, CA: Mayfield Publishing, 1994), 73.

treats a number of these in the *Parmenides*, without actually answering them. In this dialogue, Parmenides asks the young Socrates whether there are Ideas (Forms) of such things as mud, hair, and filth. He might also have asked whether there are Ideas of evil, of imperfection, of negation. But how can there be a Form of imperfection, if the Forms by definition are of perfection? But if there is no Form of imperfection, then the Forms fail to account for all the qualities of the material world.

Another objection (called the *third man*): if the similarity between men requires us to invoke the Form Man to account for it, then what of the similarity between men and the Form Man? Does that require another Form (a Third Man)? And does the similarity between the second Form and the third Form require a fourth, ad infinitum?

The first objection shows that the Forms are inadequate to account for experience. The second objection shows that on Plato's basis the Forms themselves require explanation, and that they are inadequate to provide that explanation themselves.

The first objection shows that the Forms are inadequate to account for experience. The second objection shows that on Plato's basis the Forms themselves require explanation, and that they are inadequate to provide that explanation themselves.

Plato also explores other objections to his theory that I can't take the time to describe here. The main problem is that the Forms cannot do their job. The Forms are supposed to be models for everything in the sensible world. In fact they are not, for perfect Forms cannot model imperfection; changeless Forms cannot model change. So the imperfection and change of the experienced world have no rational explanation. Plato tries to explain them by the story of the Demiurge in *Timaeus*. But that, after all, is myth. Plato gives us no reason to believe in a Demiurge, and in any case the Demiurge does not account for the existence of matter or the receptacle. So the changing world of matter and space is for Plato, as for Parmenides, ultimately irrational. Parmenides had the courage to say that the changing world is therefore unreal. Plato does not go quite this far; rather, he ascribed a greater *degree* of reality to the Forms than to the sense-world. But we must question Plato's assumption that there are degrees of reality. What does it mean to say that one thing is "more real" than another?

Plato is rationalistic about the Forms, irrationalistic about the sense-world. For him, reason is totally competent to understand the Forms, incompetent to make sense of the changing world of experience.

The picture should be clear by now. Though Plato is far more sophisticated than the pre-Socratics, his position, like theirs, incorporates rationalism and irrationalism. He is rationalistic about the Forms, irrationalistic about the sense-world. For him, reason is totally competent to understand the Forms, incompetent to make sense of the changing world of experience. Yet he tries to analyze the changing world by means of changeless Forms, an irrational world by a rationalistic principle. Eventually, in the *Parmenides*, he has the integrity to admit that his fundamental questions remain unanswered; see fig. 2.2.

OUTLINE

Greek Worldviews: One and Many

The Greek Way of Worship

Philosophy, the New Religion

A Survey of Greek Philosophy

The Milesians
Heraclitus (525–475)
Parmenides (c. 510–430)
The Atomists
Pythagoras (572–500)
The Sophists
Socrates (470–399)
Plato (427–347)
Aristotle (384–322)
Stoicism
Plotinus (A.D. 205–70)

Conclusion

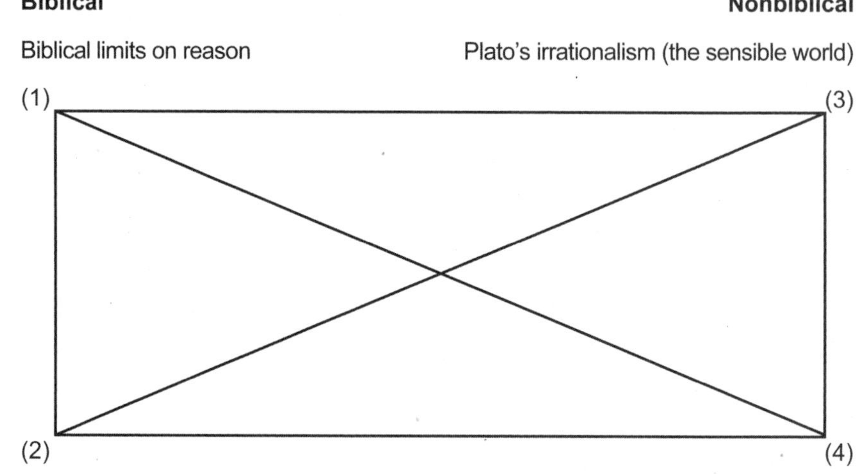

Fig. 2.2. Plato's Rationalism and Irrationalism

With Plato as with the pre-Socratics, the tension between rationalism and irrationalism has a religious root. If Plato had known the God of Scripture, he would have known in what fundamental ways our reason is competent, yet limited. And he would have understood that the world of change is knowable, but not exhaustively, because God made it that way. He would also have been able to consult God's revelation for ethical guidance, rather than teaching his students to rely on the abstract Form of the Good, which has nothing specific to say to them.

Aristotle (384–322)

Aristotle

Aristotle, Plato's student, was certainly Plato's equal in terms of brilliance, comprehensiveness, and influence on later thought. Someone has said that no pupil has had a greater teacher and no teacher a greater student.

Aristotle demythologizes Plato. He continues to distinguish between form and matter, but for him form is not found in a separate world (hence, I am no longer capitalizing the term). Rather, form is an element of things in the world we perceive.

The main category[32] of Aristotle's philosophy is the *substance*. A *substance* is an individual thing: a rock, a tree, a table, an animal, a person. With one exception that we will examine later, all substances contain both form and matter. In general, the matter is what something

32. For Aristotle, *categories* are the general types of subjects and predicates, the things we talk about and the things we can say about those subjects. He gives different lists of categories in different places in his writings, but the lists include such things as substance, quality, place, relation, time, posture, state, action, and passion.

is made of: the ingredients of bread, the clay of the statue. The form is the *whatness* of a thing, the qualities that make the thing what it is: bread, tree, statue, person. The matter is the *thisness*. The matter is what distinguishes one piece of bread from another, one brick from another, one person from another. Socrates and Plato share the same form, the form *man*, but not the same matter. So *man* or *manness* includes both Socrates and Plato, but *this man* points to one or the other.

Form and matter are usually relative. In a brick, clay is matter and the form is its brickness, the qualities that make it a brick rather than something else. But when the brick is used to build a house, the brick itself can be considered matter and the house itself (or rather its houseness) is the form. So the brick is form in one relationship, matter in another.

Thus the matter that underlies all reality, the stuff of which all reality is made, is indistinguishable from nonbeing. Aristotle avoids saying that, but the consequence is hard to avoid.

Yet it seems that there must be some kind of absolute matter or *prime matter*. The house is made of bricks; the bricks are made of clay; the clay is made of various other things. Each of these can be described as a form, because each is a substance, bearing various qualities. But this sequence cannot go to infinity. Let's say that we reach the smallest possible particle, perhaps one of Democritus's atoms. What is *that* made of? Presumably a kind of matter that has no qualities, but that is only a bearer of qualities. But something without qualities is not a substance. It is nothing. Thus the matter that underlies all reality, the stuff of which all reality is made, is indistinguishable from nonbeing. Aristotle avoids saying that, but the consequence is hard to avoid.

Aristotle insisted that such prime matter is not actually found in nature. In the natural world, there are only substances, and matter exists only in conjunction with form. But the problem reoccurs in every substance. For in every case we must ask: what is the form the form of? What is the stuff that the forms are attached to? And the answer must be, ultimately, nothing.

For Aristotle, the combination of form and matter in individual things injects an element of purposiveness or teleology into everything. Form is what each thing is, but it is also the purpose of the thing: for Aristotle, the nature and purpose of a thing are the same.

That is the main problem in Aristotle's philosophy. But we must continue to follow his thinking. For Aristotle, the combination of form and matter in individual things injects an element of purposiveness or teleology into everything. Form is what each thing is, but it is also the purpose of the thing: for Aristotle, the nature and purpose of a thing are the same. So the form of bread defines it as food, a statue as art. Recall that for Plato, too, purpose and essence were closely related: everything partook of Goodness and therefore was good for something. So form is not just what things are; it is also what they should be, what they strive to be. Form is a normative category as well as a descriptive one.

So an acorn bears the form of an oak. The acorn is not currently an oak, but it has the *potentiality* to be one, and in the normal course of events it will become an *actual* oak. So potentiality and actuality are important aspects of reality for Aristotle. The form directs the matter to realize its potential. As potentiality becomes actuality, the object becomes fully formed: it becomes what it inherently is. So Aristotle says that in potentiality matter is prominent, but in actuality form is prominent.

For Aristotle, the distinction between potentiality and actuality is a general explanation (or perhaps description) of change. Change, which bewildered previous philosophers, is for Aristotle simply the movement from potentiality to actuality. When my car moves from Atlanta to Orlando, it changes from being potentially in Orlando to being actually there.

Aristotle also uses the form-matter distinction to describe human nature. For him, the soul is the form of the body. This is a radical departure from Plato, for whom the soul was quite independent of the body, though presently confined to the body. This idea would suggest that for Aristotle, soul and body are inseparable and that the soul vanishes when the body dies. Certainly Aristotle doesn't affirm personal immortality as Plato does. But some interpreters think that his epistemology, like that of Plato's *Phaedo*, contains an argument that leads from epistemology to personal immortality.

So we should look at Aristotle's epistemology. For Aristotle, there are two givens that we must start with in order to know anything. The first is the *first principles*, principles of logic, as well as general propositions such as "the whole is greater than any part." These first principles cannot be proved; they are known intuitively. The second given is the *substance*, presented by sense experience. For Aristotle, both these starting points are important. He criticizes the "definition mongers," who try to derive everything from first principles without paying attention to the facts of experience. And he criticizes those who look only at facts as "no better than plants."

The passive intellect receives data from the senses. The active intellect examines, analyzes, tries to understand that data by abstracting the forms from the material things given in the data.

Now, for Aristotle, the intellect has two aspects, *passive* and *active*. The passive intellect receives data from the senses. The active intellect examines, analyzes, tries to understand that data by abstracting the forms from the material things given in the data. In Plato's terms, the active intellect tries to bring conjecture to the levels of belief and understanding. For Aristotle as for Plato, true knowledge is a knowledge of form, not matter. True knowledge is an understanding of what things are.

There has been much interpretive controversy over the nature of the active intellect in Aristotle's thought. The most common understanding is that each human being has his own active intellect. But in *De Anima*, Aristotle speaks of the active intellect (as he would not speak of the individual soul) as something separable from the body. So some have thought that for Aristotle there was only one active intellect, common to mankind: either a cosmic principle of intelligence, as in Heraclitus, Anaxagoras, and Plotinus, or a kind of god.[33] Perhaps Aristotle did not try to reconcile the apparent contradiction between *De Anima* and his general view of the soul.[34] But an Aristotelian who wanted to make a case for personal immortality would have to begin here.

Aristotle believed that the process of movement from potentiality to actuality must begin somewhere. Each motion is caused by another. But the chain of causes cannot go back to infinity. So at some point there must be an unmoved mover who starts the process going. Like the other Greek philosophers, Aristotle did not believe the world had a beginning. So his unmoved mover is not like the biblical God, who creates the world at the first moment of time. Rather, for Aristotle, every state of affairs at each moment is ultimately explained by a Prime Mover.[35]

Like the other Greek philosophers, Aristotle did not believe the world had a beginning. So his unmoved mover is not like the biblical God, who creates the world at the first moment of time. Rather, for Aristotle, every state of affairs at each moment is ultimately explained by a Prime Mover.

The Prime Mover[36] is pure form, the one exception to the rule that every substance contains both form and matter. If there were a material component in his nature, then he would have some unrealized potentiality, and that would move him toward actuality. Then he would not be unmoved. Similarly, he must not, in Aristotle's view, be influenced in any way by the world, or else he will be the moved, not the mover. So this being must not know the world (since to know is to be influenced in some way by the object of knowledge), or love the world, or act in the world.

How, then, does he cause motion? Aristotle's answer is that he is supremely attractive and thus influences things in the world to turn toward him. Interpreters of Aristotle have compared the Prime Mover to a goal to which runners run, or to a magnet attracting iron to itself. This writer thinks of a rock concert, in which frenzied fans throw

Interpreters of Aristotle have compared the Prime Mover to a goal to which runners run, or to a magnet attracting iron to itself.

33. For a helpful discussion of these interpretations, see Ronald H. Nash, *Life's Ultimate Questions: An Introduction to Philosophy* (Grand Rapids: Zondervan, 1999), 111–12.

34. For epistemological reasons also, it is regrettable that Aristotle did not clarify the relation between the active intellect and the soul. If the active intellect is a cosmic principle of intelligence, how does it enter into relation with the individual person? How does the cosmic intellect illumine my mind? And if each individual has his own active intellect, how can that intellect be separable from the body while the soul is not separable?

35. It helps to consider that causal sequences are either sequential (as one domino toppling the next) or simultaneous (as the gears of a watch moving one another alone). Aristotle's view of a chain of causes is more like the watch than like the dominoes. So it is not necessarily a *temporal* sequence and does not require a first mover at the beginning of time. Rather, each event requires a Prime Mover at the very time it is taking place.

36. Although Aristotle speaks of one Prime Mover as explaining all motion in the universe, he also maintains that every circular motion in the heavens requires an unmoved mover to get it started. Since he believes that the universe consists of a number of concentric spheres revolving around the earth, he postulates that there is an unmoved mover for each (either forty-seven or fifty-three). So Aristotle is a philosophical polytheist.

themselves at the performer's feet, while the performer himself remains (apparently) in a daze.

Aristotle distinguished four kinds of causation: formal, final, efficient, and material. These are "causes" in a broad sense, four ways of answering the question "why is something as it is?" They involve four meanings of the word *because*. Let us see how the four causes answer the question "Why is Bill thinking?" The formal cause tells what something is: Bill thinks because he is a man. The final cause tells the purpose, the reason something happened: Bill thinks because he wants to complete his philosophy paper. The efficient cause tells what made something happen: Bill thinks because his brain generates thoughts. The material cause tells what something is made of: Bill thinks because his brain is composed of materials that generate thinking. Now, on Aristotle's account, the Prime Mover causes motion as the final cause, rather than the efficient. But that leaves open the question of what is the efficient cause of motion in the world.

What does the Prime Mover do, if he does not efficiently cause things to happen, and if he does not know or love the world? Aristotle's answer is that he thinks. One wonders why Aristotle suddenly starts using personal language here, when his argument so far proves at most an impersonal principle. But what does this god think about, if not the world? Aristotle replies: he thinks of himself. But what facts about himself does he contemplate? Aristotle replies: his thoughts. The Prime Mover is "thought thinking thought." If the Prime Mover were to think of something about himself other than his thoughts, then his thoughts would be moved by that something else. For his thoughts to be entirely unmoved, they can be caused only by themselves.

The Prime Mover is a quasi-philosopher. As Plato believed that philosophers should be kings, Aristotle believes that his god is a philosopher.

What shall we make of this? First, the Prime Mover is a quasi-philosopher. As Plato believed that philosophers should be kings, Aristotle believes that his god is a philosopher. Further, though, Aristotle's deity reduces to tautology. He cannot know the world, lest he be relative to it. His thought cannot be of anything other than itself, lest it be relative to something else. It cannot be about any quality he has except his thinking, lest his thinking be moved by something else. So in the end his thought is a thought of a thought of a thought, or, to put it differently, a thought of nothing in particular.

Plato thought he had found the ultimate philosophical principle in the Form of the Good, but the Form of the Good turned out to be abstract and empty. Though bearing rational authority, it tells us nothing specific. So Aristotle's Prime Mover: it is so abstract that its mind is virtually nothing.

We can see that Aristotle's Prime Mover is vastly different from the biblical God. The biblical God is not only the final cause of the world, but the efficient cause as well. He is not only the logical beginning of the universe, but its temporal beginning as well. And he knows and loves the world, without endangering his own absolute nature. This is possible because the world itself is the expression of his eternal thought. His mind contains real content, which he freely reveals to human beings.

We should also consider Aristotle's ethics. For Aristotle, each being should act in accordance with its form, that is, its nature and purpose. He defines human beings as rational animals, so for him, as with all the other Greek philosophers, the good life is the life of reason.

For Aristotle, each being should act in accordance with its form, that is, its nature and purpose. He defines human beings as rational animals, so for him, as with all the other Greek philosophers, the good life is the life of reason.

Reason tells us that the goal of human life is happiness. Happiness is not pleasure, at least not in the narrow sense of Epicureanism. Happiness is general well-being. Pleasure is at most a means to the end of happiness. In general, Aristotle sees the good life as contemplative, philosophical (again, Aristotle exalts his particular vocation to a universal principle).

Aristotle, like Plato, distinguishes three aspects of the soul: the *vegetative*, the *sensitive* (perhaps roughly equivalent to Plato's *spirited*), and the *rational*. We share the first with plants, the second with animals; the third is unique to human beings. He also distinguishes moral from intellectual virtues. Moral virtues pertain to the will, intellectual to reason; see fig. 2.3.

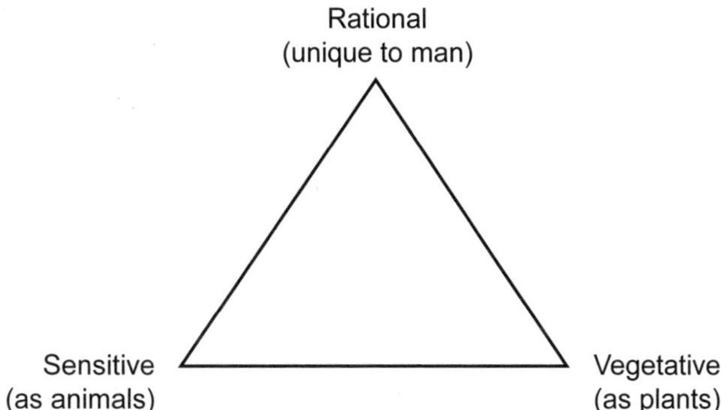

Fig. 2.3. Aspects of the Soul, according to Aristotle

We learn the moral virtues—courage, temperance, and justice—from imitating others who exemplify these qualities. Such imitation leads us in time to form good habits, and those habits form a good character. The intellectual virtue is prudence, and that comes from teaching. Aristotle distinguishes philosophic wisdom (disinterested, contemplative) from practical wisdom (wisdom to make decisions leading to happiness). One who has wisdom, he thinks, will seek moderation in all things. It is often possible to determine our specific duties by calculating the mean between two extremes. For example, a buffoon

We learn the moral virtues—courage, temperance, and justice—from imitating others who exemplify these qualities. Such imitation leads us in time to form good habits, and those habits form a good character. The intellectual virtue is prudence, and that comes from teaching.

makes a joke out of everything; a boor takes everything too seriously. But wit is the *golden mean* between these extremes. Aristotle didn't offer any precise formula for defining the extremes or locating the mean. Doubtless he knew that with a bit of cleverness, any act could be justified as being between two extremes (e.g., robbing one bank as the mean between robbing many and robbing none). And he did see that sometimes a right decision might be on one extreme, such as the very decision to do right rather than wrong. But he assumed that the wise man would be able to furnish a proper context for these judgments.

The State is the whole of which individuals and families are parts. Thus its interests take precedence over theirs. Yet the ruler ought to seek the happiness of his subjects. Aristotle was nothing if not balanced! Yet his impulse, like Plato's, is toward statism and totalitarianism, an impulse that might have influenced his most famous pupil, Alexander the Great.

There is a question as to how we can begin to acquire moral virtues. Aristotle teaches that we need to have virtuous dispositions to perform virtuous acts, but that we need to perform moral acts in order to form the habits that produce virtuous dispositions. Aristotle is aware of this circularity and counsels readers to begin the process by doing things that "resemble" virtuous acts. But how one gets from resemblance to actuality is a mystery.

The Christian revelation has an answer: God's grace creates moral dispositions in sinners and enables them to follow those dispositions. And it also answers another major problem in Aristotle's ethics. For Aristotle assumes that we can learn our moral obligations simply by observing our own natures and what makes us happy. This is the root of the "natural law" tradition in ethics. But as David Hume pointed out, one cannot derive moral obligations from natural facts. One can't infer what we *ought* to do from statements of what is the case; we cannot derive *ought* from *is*. The fact that we are rational does not prove that we ought to live according to reason; the fact that we seek happiness does not imply that we ought to seek it. Scripture points to God's revelation as the source of our knowledge of ethical obligation. For God is both fact and value. To know him is to know at the same time the ultimate source of reality and the ultimate source of ethical obligation.

One cannot derive moral obligations from natural facts. One can't infer what we ought to do from statements of what is the case; we cannot derive ought *from* is. *The fact that we are rational does not prove that we ought to live according to reason; the fact that we seek happiness does not imply that we ought to seek it.*

To summarize, the fundamental contrast in Aristotle's philosophy, as in Plato's, is that between form and matter. But form at the highest level (as illustrated in the Prime Mover) is entirely contentless and abstract: a kind of "being in general." And matter in its purest form is nonbeing. We see again the contrast between the Olympian order and the "shapeless stream" of the old religion. But in Aristotle the order is empty. He cannot really account for motion on its basis, or for ethical obligation. And the shapeless stream, in Aristotle, is more shapeless than ever. The lack of an absolute-personal God leaves Aristotle's system in incoherence.

Stoicism

The Epicurean and Stoic schools arose during the Hellenistic period, the time when Greek culture spread throughout Western and Near Eastern civilization. Alexander the Great (356–323), whose tutor was Aristotle, conquered most of the known world, doubtless his means of seeking happiness.[37] His empire broke up quickly after his early death, being divided among his lieutenants, eventually passing to the Romans. Although Greek culture attained a kind of supremacy during this time, its most creative period was past. Yet philosophical schools continued the discussions begun by their predecessors.

Zeno

I discussed Epicurus with the atomists at an earlier point, so I will here focus on the Stoics, a school founded by **Zeno of Cyprus** (334–262). The Stoics, like the Epicureans, were materialists, teaching that only physical objects were real. But they acknowledged many differences within the broad category *matter.* The soul was made of very fine matter, rocks and dirt out of coarser matter. Even virtues are material, but they can exist in the same place as other matter, so virtues can be in the soul. Gordon Clark suggests that the Stoics' *matter* is more like a field of force than like a hard stuff.[38] Or perhaps: for the Stoics, to say that something is material is simply to say that it really is, that it has being. Perhaps for them (whether or not they were aware of it), the proposition "reality is material" was tautological.

For the Stoics, knowledge begins in self-authenticating sensations. General skepticism about sense experience defeats itself, for it can be based only on the experiences that it presumes to doubt.

For the Stoics, knowledge begins in self-authenticating sensations. General skepticism about sense experience defeats itself, for it can be based only on the experiences that it presumes to doubt.

The world is a single reality, governed by its own world soul. This pantheistic God rules all by natural law. As Plato's Republic was ruled by a philosopher-king, so the world of the Stoics is ruled by a divine philosopher-king.

Everything happens by law, so the Stoics took a fatalistic attitude toward life. Aristotle, like present-day open theists, had said that propositions about the future were neither true nor false, because the future was not an object of knowledge. The Stoics held, on the contrary, that if I say, "The sun will rise tomorrow," and it does, that proposition was already true when I uttered it. Therefore, the rising of the sun *had* to happen.

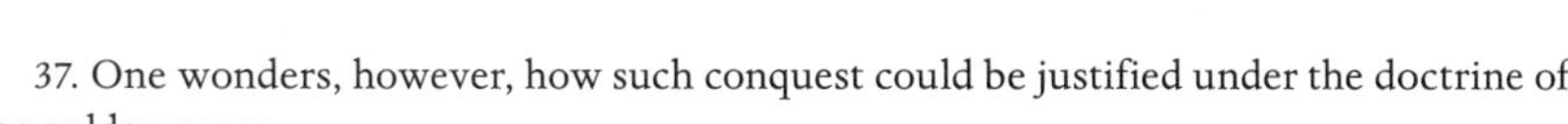

37. One wonders, however, how such conquest could be justified under the doctrine of the golden mean.

38. Clark, *Thales*, 158–60.

So the Stoics sought to act in accord with nature. They sought to be resigned to their fate. Their ethic was one of learning to want what one gets, rather than of getting what one wants. But they did not advocate passivity. Contrary to Epicurus, they sought involvement in public life (the emperor Marcus Aurelius was a Stoic). They taught, as did all other Greek thinkers, that one should live according to reason, which is also according to nature and according to the universal structure of society. They considered human society to be a universal brotherhood.

Stoicism is one major source, after Aristotle, of natural-law thinking in ethics. Again, I ask David Hume's question: how does one reason from the facts of nature to conclusions about ethical obligation? The lack of a true theistic position made the answer to this question, for the Stoics as for Aristotle, impossible.

Stoicism is one major source, after Aristotle, of natural-law thinking in ethics. Again, I ask David Hume's question: how does one reason from the facts of nature to conclusions about ethical obligation? The lack of a true theistic position made the answer to this question, for the Stoics as for Aristotle, impossible.

Even though the Stoics tried to overcome the form-matter dichotomy by making the whole world material, there remains a secondary dichotomy between the world soul and the beings within it. The Stoics failed to answer how the world soul accounts for individual facts, or how it gives moral direction to finite creatures.

Plotinus (A.D. 205–70)

The school of thought begun at Plato's Academy continued for many centuries, but it endured some radical philosophical shifts. In the third century B.C., a number of its members were skeptics: Pyrrho (d. 275), Timon (d. 230), and Arcesilaus (315–241). This was odd, because Plato himself had expended considerable energy refuting skepticism. But his dialogues rarely ended with cogent definitions of philosophical terms, and the *Parmenides*, as we have seen, leaves the theory of Forms itself hanging in uncertainty. So perhaps the skeptical turn of the Academy was not entirely a surprise.[39]

The period of "Middle Platonism" (100 B.C.–A.D. 270) was a time of world-weariness. Politics and economics gave people little reason to treasure the affairs of this life, much desire to escape from it. The mystery religions and Gnosticism[40] offered people various means of transcending the space-time world and being absorbed into divinity. The Platonic school also turned in a religious direction, emphasizing Plato's teaching that the soul belonged to a world other than this one and needed to return to that world through the exercise of mind. Into this tradition came **Plotinus**, the founder of the movement known as *Neoplatonism*.

39. It is interesting to note that there was a parallel history of rationalism and skepticism in Hindu and Buddhist philosophy. See David E. Cooper, ed., *Epistemology: The Classic Readings* (Oxford: Blackwell, 1999), 43–96.

40. For an account of Gnosticism, and the response to it by early Christian thinkers, see chapter 3.

Plotinus opposes the materialism of the Epicureans and Stoics, using various arguments: Materialism cannot explain thought. Materialism cannot identify the subject of knowledge, the one who knows, the one who uses the senses to gain knowledge. As Plato said, the most real beings are immaterial, including the human soul.

Plotinus describes a chain of being with a supreme being ("the One") at the top of the scale, and descending levels in order: Mind (*nous*), Soul (*psyche*), and the material world. He conceives of this ladder as a downward path and an upward path.

Materialism cannot explain thought. Materialism cannot identify the subject of knowledge, the one who knows, the one who uses the senses to gain knowledge. As Plato said, the most real beings are immaterial, including the human soul.

To examine the downward path, we will start at the top of the scale, with the highest being, the One. The One cannot be described in human words. Even the term *one* is not literally applicable. But Plotinus thinks that the idea of oneness, unity, captures much of what he wants to say about this being. The One has no qualities, no properties (or else there would be a division between subject and predicate). The only way to know the One is through being mystically united to him, in a trance that itself cannot be described.

Yet Plotinus does say a great deal about the One: that it exists, that it does not have the qualities of beings in the material world, that it is immaterial, that souls may enter a mystical relation with it. He particularly emphasizes that the One communicates its excellence to lower beings. This communication is an emanation, like light coming from a fire. The One does not freely choose to emanate; rather, it cannot help but do so.[41] To emanate is its nature. The emanations produce the lower beings. In the end, all reality is an emanation of the One. So in one sense, all reality is divine in character. Plotinus is fundamentally a monist.

Plotinus

The first product of the emanation, and the second level of reality, is *nous*, or Mind. Plotinus represents it as the result of the One's thought. It corresponds to Plato's world of Forms and, perhaps, to Aristotle's active intellect. Here, some multiplicity enters in: the distinction between subject and object, the many things of which there are Ideas.

The third level is that of Soul (*psyche*). Mind generates objects of its thought and thus produces Soul or life. Plotinus's Soul is like Plato's Demiurge, Heraclitus's *logos*. It governs the world from within the world. Plotinus describes three aspects of Soul: (1) the world Soul (compare the Stoic world soul), which explains motion and change; (2) the middle Soul, which gives life to particular souls; and (3) the lower Soul, which gives rise to bodies. Human souls are immortal.

41. This is in contrast with the God of the Bible. In Scripture, (1) God is not constrained to create. He creates the world freely and voluntarily. (2) The product of creation, the world, is not divine in character, not in any sense a part of God.

The fourth level is the material world. We are souls, contained in material bodies. This condition is the result of a "fall," which results because our souls have accepted the guidance of sensation and become entangled with the material.[42] Union with the body in itself is not evil, unless we linger too long in this condition. But we should seek to rise from it as soon as possible by knowledge and virtue. At the bottom level of the material world is prime matter (compare Aristotle's teaching on this). Prime matter is really nothing, or empty space (compare Plato's *receptacle*). As rays of light disappear into the darkness, prime matter represents the furthest extent of the emanation of the One.

We can ascend on the ladder of being as we first descended, being absorbed into Soul, then Mind, then the One. The method of ascent is gaining knowledge, which is also growth in virtue.

Plotinus probably noticed that Plato's Forms did not account for all reality. So he advocated a broader principle, higher than the Forms, that would account for all reality, including mud, hair, filth, evil, negativity, and imperfection. So the One can be understood as the result of a rationalistic impulse. Plotinus commends Parmenides' statement that "to be and to be thought are the same."

Significantly, however, it turns out that the One cannot be described at all. It has no qualities. It is not tall or short, because it is the principle of tallness and shortness. It is not good or evil, because it is the principle of good and evil, and therefore beyond good and evil. It is not even literally one, for it is the principle underlying both unity and plurality. So the One explains everything, and nothing. The explanation of everything turns out to be the greatest unexplained mystery of all.

The One explains everything, and nothing. The explanation of everything turns out to be the greatest unexplained mystery of all.

Ultimate knowledge, therefore, comes not from reasoning, but from mysticism, from ineffable union with the One. Thus Plotinus's extreme rationalism devolves into irrationalism. As Plato's Good was empty, and Aristotle's Prime Mover a self-referential tautology (thought of thought of thought), so Plotinus's One communicates to us no knowledge at all.

CONCLUSION

Recall the general themes I listed under the introduction. We have now seen many specific examples of the "form-matter scheme" (Dooyeweerd's phrase) that unites the various strains of Greek thought. Though very different in many ways, these philosophies all seek to understand reality without the guidance of an absolute person. Therefore, they affirm the autonomy of their own reason. Yet they note, as

42. It is not clear in Plotinus whether or not this fall is the result of a free choice. Given that the whole movement from the One to the material world is a necessary emanation, it would seem that the fall, too, was necessary. But when speaking of the fall and redemption of the human soul, Plotinus refers to choices we make.

they must, that their reason is fallible, not omnicompetent. There are areas of reality that defy rational analysis (change for Parmenides, the world of sense for Plato, prime matter for Aristotle, etc.). The Greek response to these mysteries is to say that part of the world is essentially unknowable, essentially irrational. We can't know it because it can't be known.[43] It is the chaos of the "shapeless stream." It is illusion (Parmenides), nonbeing, or nothingness. But the shapeless stream is found everywhere, as Aristotle's matter underlies all substances. So if matter is irrational, the whole universe is irrational. Thus the irrationalism of the Greeks undermines their rationalism, and when they (as Parmenides) force their way to a consistent rationalism, they end up denying the entire world of experience.

The Greeks' project was to impose autonomous reason on an irrational world. That project was bold, even revolutionary, as we have seen, but it could not hope to succeed.

Their project was to impose autonomous reason on an irrational world.[44] That project was bold, even revolutionary, as we have seen, but it could not hope to succeed.

The only ultimate alternative is the absolute-personality theism of Scripture. God has created a knowable world and has given human beings the power to know it. But they can never hope to know it exhaustively as he does. So there are mysteries—not because there is an irrational element in the world, not because there is an element of nonbeing that somehow is and exists in order to frustrate philosophers—but because God has hidden from us some of his rational understanding of his creation.

We can learn today from the questions the Greeks asked, from their failures, for the insights they express in matters of detail. But we should rigorously avoid the notion of rational autonomy and the form-matter scheme as a comprehensive worldview.

Combining the Christian perspective with the Greek is not advisable. We can learn today from the questions the Greeks asked, from their failures, from the insights they express in matters of detail. But we should rigorously avoid the notion of rational autonomy and the form-matter scheme as a comprehensive worldview.[45] Unfortunately, during the medieval period and beyond, Christian theologians relied extensively on Neoplatonism and (beginning with Aquinas) Aristotelianism. Aquinas, for example, distinguished between natural reason (which operates apart from revelation) and faith (which supplements our reason with revelation). Then he referred over and over again to Aristotle as "the Philosopher" who guides us in matters of natural reason. The problems generated by this combination of Christian and pagan thought will occupy our studies of the medieval period.

43. We recall the slogan "What my net can't catch isn't fish." See Cornelius Van Til's pamphlet *Why I Believe in God* (Philadelphia: Orthodox Presbyterian Church, n.d.).

44. As Van Til often says, imposing abstract forms on abstract particulars, stringing beads without holes.

45. It is sometimes useful to distinguish form and matter on a microlevel. It is not wrong to distinguish what things are made of (matter) from what they are (form). It is wrong to try to bring all reality under this schema. For to do that either would leave God out of our worldview or would make him a form (as Aristotle), matter, or both.

OUTLINE

KEY TERMS

Fate	Shapeless stream
Old nature-religion	Religion of the Olympian gods
Wisdom	Wisdom literature
Rational autonomy	Milesians
Apeiron	*Logos*
Way of truth	Way of belief
Atomism	Qualitative atomism
Quantitative atomism	Swerve
Hedonism	Determinism
Incompatibilism	Compatibilism
Libertarianism	Sophists
Dialectic	*Daimon*
Forms	Ideas
Form of the Good	Demiurge
Receptacle	Matter (Plato, Aristotle)
Recollection (Plato)	Conjecture
Belief	Understanding
Intuitive vision	Plato's three parts of the soul
Third man	Substance
Whatness	Thisness
Prime matter	Potentiality
Actuality	First principles
Passive intellect	Active intellect
Four causes	Prime Mover
Golden mean	Matter (Stoics)
World soul	Natural law
Skeptical Academy	Middle Platonism
Gnosticism	Neoplatonism
The One	*Nous*
Psyche	Emanate
Form-matter scheme	

STUDY QUESTIONS

1. Is it fair to say that the Greeks rejected the biblical worldview? Discuss.
2. Is it fair to speak of "Greek thought"? Is there anything on which all Greek philosophers were agreed?
3. Compare (a) the old Greek nature-religion, (b) the religion of the Olympian gods, (c) Plato's philosophy of Form and matter.
4. Describe and evaluate the philosophies of the Milesians.

5. Did Thales do scientific research? Why is that an important question?
6. Van Til says that Thales is both rationalist and irrationalist. On what ground? How does that affect the success of his philosophy?
7. Describe and evaluate the philosophy of Heraclitus.
8. Same for Parmenides. Why does he find the idea of nonbeing problematic?
9. Parmenides: "to be and to be thought are the same." Explain; evaluate. Why did Plotinus use this slogan to express his own philosophy?
10. Same for Epicurus. Explain his doctrine of the *swerve.*
11. Why did the Pythagoreans think that "all is number"?
12. What argument can be made against epistemological relativism?
13. Protagoras said that "man is the measure of all things." Explain; evaluate.
14. What was so important about Socrates? Evaluate.
15. "Dialectic and introspection together, then, constitute the Socratic epistemology." Explain; evaluate.
16. "Plato's genius is to see truth in both of these accounts [change, no change] and to bring them together into a broader systematic understanding." Explain; evaluate.
17. Describe and evaluate the argument of Socrates in Plato's *Euthyphro* about the nature of goodness.
18. Briefly summarize Plato's political views. Evaluate.
19. Describe Plato's difficulty with "mud, hair, and filth." Also the *third man.*
20. "The main problem [for Plato] is that the Forms cannot do their job." Explain; evaluate.
21. "Aristotle demythologizes Plato." Explain.
22. What does Frame describe as "the main problem in Aristotle's philosophy"? Can you solve it?
23. Compare Aristotle's view of the soul with that of Plato.
24. Compare Aristotle's Prime Mover with the God of Scripture.
25. Frame says that Aristotle cannot account for motion or ethical obligation. Explain; evaluate.
26. Describe and evaluate several doctrines of the Stoics.
27. Describe the upward and downward paths taught by Plotinus.
28. "Thus Plotinus's extreme rationalism devolves into irrationalism." How? Explain; evaluate.

BIBLIOGRAPHY: GREEK PHILOSOPHY

Print

Barnes, Jonathan, ed. *The Complete Works of Aristotle*. Princeton, NJ: Princeton University Press, 1984.

Cohen, S. Marc, Patricia Curd, and C. D. C. Reeve, eds. *Readings in Ancient Greek Philosophy: From Thales to Aristotle*. 4th ed. Indianapolis: Hackett Publishing, 2011.

Cooper, John M., and D. S. Hutchinson, eds. *Plato: Complete Works*. Indianapolis: Hackett Publishing, 1997.

Curd, Patricia, and Daniel W. Graham, eds. *The Oxford Handbook of Presocratic Philosophy*. Oxford: Oxford University Press, 2009.

Graham, Daniel W. *The Texts of Early Greek Philosophy: The Complete Fragments and Selected Testimonies of the Major Presocratics*. Cambridge: Cambridge University Press, 2010.

Kirk, G. S., J. E. Raven, and M. Schofield, eds. *The Presocratic Philosophers: A Critical History with a Selection of Texts*. Cambridge: Cambridge University Press, 1983.

McKeon, Richard, ed. *Basic Works of Aristotle*. Modern Library Classics. New York: Modern Library, 2001.

Plotinus. *The Enneads: Abridged Edition*. Edited by John Dillon. Translated by Stephen McKenna. New York: Penguin Classics, 1991.

Online

Burnet, John, trans. Fragments of Heraclitus. Available at http://en.wikisource.org/wiki/Fragments_of_Heraclitus.

Internet Classics Archive. "Select from a list of 441 works of classical literature by 59 different authors, including user-driven commentary and 'reader's choice' Web sites. Mainly Greco-Roman works (some Chinese and Persian), all in English translation." Generally older translations than in the collections cited in the Bibliography above. Includes the works of Plato, Aristotle, and Plotinus. http://classics.mit.edu/index.html.

Parmenides. "On Nature." Edited by Allan F. Randall from translations by David Gallop, Richard D. McKirahan Jr., Jonathan Barnes, John Mansley Robinson, et al. Available at http://rhetcomp.gsu.edu/~gpullman/2150/parmenides.htm. Also see John Burnet's older translation at http://philoctetes.free.fr/parmenidesunicode.htm.

Sophists. Selections from the Sophists are available at http://bingweb.binghamton.edu/~clas381a/sophists-readings.htm.

READ FOR YOURSELF

For books of primary source readings in this era and others, see the Annotated Bibliography of Philosophy Texts toward the end of this volume.

Presocratics: The work of these thinkers is found mainly in short fragments quoted by others. Collections of these may be found in the readings lists of various titles in the Bibliography above.

For your further study, I recommend that you read the fragments of the Milesian philosophers, Heraclitus, and the poem of Parmenides.

To understand the **atomist** school (Democritus, Epicurus), you might find it helpful to look at the poem *On the Nature of Things* by the Roman poet Lucretius, who sympathized with the earlier atomists. See http://classics.mit.edu/Carus/nature_things.1.i.html.

In **Plato**, read the *Apology* (Socrates' testimony at his death), *Phaedo* (Socrates' argument for life after death), *Meno* (the argument that learning is recollection), *Euthyphro* (the argument that piety-goodness must be something greater than what any god says or thinks), *Timaeus* (Plato's creation account), *Republic* (Plato's mature epistemology, including the cave analogy), and the *Parmenides* (Plato's recognition of unresolved problems in his philosophy).

In **Aristotle**, read the *Categories* (Aristotle's description of substance and its attributes), *Physics* book 2 (the four causes), book 3 (motion, potentiality, and actuality), *Metaphysics* 12 (the Prime Mover).

LISTEN ONLINE

Link: http://itunes.apple.com/us/course/legacy-history-philosophy/id694658914

- The Milesians and the Eleatics: 24:55
- Eleatics Continued and Early Alternatives to Parmenides: 54:47
- Plato and Aristotle: 56:59
- Plotinus and Gnosticism: 31:34

FAMOUS QUOTES

- **Heraclitus:** http://en.wikiquote.org/wiki/Heraclitus
- **Protagoras:** http://en.wikiquote.org/wiki/Protagoras
- **Socrates:** http://en.wikiquote.org/wiki/Socrates
- **Plato:** http://en.wikiquote.org/wiki/Plato
- **Whitehead:** http://en.wikiquote.org/wiki/Alfred_North_Whitehead (his quote about Plato)
- **Aristotle:** http://en.wikiquote.org/wiki/Aristotle
- **Plotinus:** http://en.wikiquote.org/wiki/Plotinus

3

EARLY CHRISTIAN PHILOSOPHY

AS I INDICATED in chapter 1, Christian philosophy begins in Scripture itself, with the two-level worldview of Genesis 1. God is the Creator, the world the creature. God is absolute tripersonality, and he is Lord of all that he has made. His lordship entails his control, authority, and presence. Sin leads people to think they can replace God's lordship with their own autonomy, and their rebellion extends to their philosophical thinking. The natural consequence is that their thinking becomes what Scripture calls *foolish*. We can see the foolishness of unbelief in many areas of metaphysics, epistemology, and value theory. Unbelieving thought is caught up in a dialectic of rationalism and irrationalism—principles that conflict with each other but nevertheless require each other.

God is absolute tripersonality, and he is Lord of all that he has made. His lordship entails his control, authority, and presence. Sin leads people to think they can replace God's lordship with their own autonomy, and their rebellion extends to their philosophical thinking.

The biblical writers themselves recognized that philosophy was one area of spiritual warfare (as Col. 2:8). The apostle Paul himself debated Epicurean and Stoic philosophers on Mars Hill in Athens (Acts 17:16–34), and he warned against the world's wisdom in the First Letter to the Corinthians (1 Cor. 1–3). After the biblical canon was complete, that spiritual battle continued, but the intellectual leaders of the church did not always fight it in the most effective way.

THE APOSTOLIC FATHERS

The first generation of postcanonical writers was called the *Apostolic Fathers* because they had direct knowledge of the apostles. These included Clement of Rome (d. A.D. 98), Ignatius of Antioch (d. 107), Polycarp of Smyrna (d. c. 153), the author of *The Shepherd of Hermas* (c. 140–55), and the writer of the *Didache* (probably mid–first century). These writings are preoccupied with the reality of persecution and martyrdom, and the demands in that situation of Jesus' ethic of love. They give us glimpses of the developing life of the churches as the gospel spread from one nation to another, particularly their worship and government. Theologically, they testify strongly to the deity of Christ and his incarnation, but surprisingly the Pauline doctrine of justification by grace alone through faith alone is largely absent.[1] And there is not much in this corpus of writings that we would be inclined to call *philosophy*, except that, as we have seen, theology as such is philosophical.

Theologically, the Apostolic Fathers testify strongly to the deity of Christ and his incarnation, but surprisingly the Pauline doctrine of justification by grace alone through faith alone is largely absent.

THE APOLOGISTS

But later in the second century came a group of Christian thinkers commonly known as the *apologists*. One early member of this group introduces himself in a letter to the Emperor Hadrian as "Aristides the philosopher." Another, Justin Martyr, is said to have worn a "philosopher's mantle." And indeed, Greek philosophy is a major influence on these thinkers. Among them were:

Quadratus of Athens (c. 124)
Aristides of Athens (d. c. 134)
Justin Martyr (d. 165)
Tatian the Syrian (d. c. 172)
Athenagoras of Athens (c. 177)
Theophilus of Antioch (c. 180)
Melito of Sardis (c. 170)

To these may be added the anonymous documents *The Preaching of Peter* and *The Letter to Diognetus*, both likely from the early second century. These thinkers dealt with similar themes and arguments, so I will focus our attention on Justin.

To understand any philosophical or theological movement, it is important to be aware of its environment, particularly the issues under discussion at the time, and the parties to the discussion.

To understand any philosophical or theological movement, it is important to be aware of its environment, particularly the issues under discussion at the time, and the parties to the discussion. The apologists, particularly, dealt with the following opponents:

1. The **Jews** opposed Jesus because they believed that his claim to be God was blasphemous. In response, the apologists sought to prove from Scripture that Jesus was the Messiah and, indeed, God in the flesh.

1. I have felt that the striking decline in theological depth between the biblical canon and the Apostolic Fathers is persuasive evidence that the former documents are divinely inspired and the latter are not.

2. The **Romans** opposed Jesus because they thought his claim to be King was an insurrection against the emperor's authority. So they persecuted Christians as potential revolutionaries. In response, the apologists tried to show that Christians were good citizens and that Jesus' kingdom was not of this world. Further, the Christians had to refute popular charges that they engaged in cannibalism (a misunderstanding of the Lord's Supper) and incest (a misunderstanding of Christian references to "the holy kiss" among "brothers" and "sisters").
3. **Greek philosophy**, as we saw in the previous chapter, was an intellectual revolt against religious ways of explaining the world. In the view of the Greek philosophers, reason was sacred, and intellectual autonomy the new ultimate. Thus, it foundered on the shoals of rationalism and irrationalism. The apologists often discussed Greek philosophy, especially Platonism, but they rarely invoked *antithesis*. In the apologists' writings there is little warning about the "wisdom of the world" or the spiritual warfare of Colossians 2:8. Rather, the apologists' approach is to seek common ground with philosophy, to wear the philosophers' mantle, to seek intellectual respectability as defined by the philosophical community.
4. **Heresy**, particularly **Gnosticism**, was gaining influence in the church. Gnosticism was a religious movement, somewhat predating Plotinus's Neoplatonism, but resembling it in many ways.[2] In Gnosticism, as in Neoplatonism, there is a scale of being. At the top there is a supreme being (actually nameless, but sometimes given a name, such as *Bythos*), connected to the material world by semidivine intermediaries. These are called *aeons*, with names such as *Logos*, *Zoe*, *Pneuma*, and *Psyche*. The "fall" occurs when the least of these beings mistakenly creates a material world. We are trapped in that world and must be reabsorbed into the nameless supreme being by various intellectual and moral disciplines taught by the Gnostic teachers.[3] These constitute the secret knowledge connoted by the term *Gnostic*. Despite the parallels between Neoplatonism and Gnosticism, Plotinus opposed the Gnostics. I'm inclined to regard that as a

In Gnosticism, as in Neoplatonism, there is a scale of being. At the top there is a supreme being (actually nameless, but sometimes given a name, such as Bythos*), connected to the material world by semidivine intermediaries.*

2. I am describing the form of Gnosticism most often referred to in the literature of the early church. There were other forms of it that were rather different, particularly a variant rather like *Manichaeism*, the view that there is not one supreme being in the world, but two great forces contending for opposite goals—good and evil.

3. Recall my distinction in chapter 1 between *metaphysical* and *ethical* concepts of the human plight and salvation from it. Gnosticism is a good example of a metaphysical concept. Our problem is that we are trapped in a world of material finitude, and our salvation is to be lifted out of it and to become indistinguishable from God.

family quarrel. We can see that Gnosticism and Neoplatonism represent a common way of thinking, a common worldview (with variations, of course) that was in the air during the early centuries of the Christian era.[4]

Neoplatonism and Gnosticism are particularly good examples of the transcendence-immanence and irrationalism-rationalism dialectics that I described in chapter 1; see fig. 3.1.

Neoplatonism and Gnosticism are particularly good examples of the transcendence-immanence and irrationalism-rationalism dialectics.

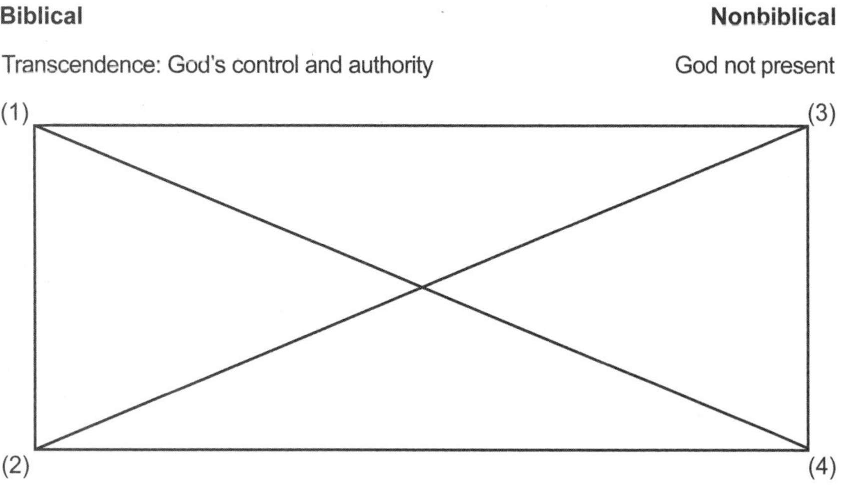

Fig. 3.1. Transcendence and Immanence in Gnosticism

Gnosticism uses the rhetoric both of extreme transcendence and of extreme immanence. Bythos is so far removed from us that we cannot even imagine him (transcendence), but all other reality emanates from him as light from a candle, so that somehow we are all divine (immanence).

Gnosticism uses the rhetoric both of extreme transcendence (3) and of extreme immanence (4). Bythos is so far removed from us that we cannot even imagine him (transcendence), but all other reality emanates from him as light from a candle, so that somehow we are all divine (immanence). This means that we cannot know Bythos at all (irrationalism), and/or that we can know him perfectly through our union with his nature (rationalism), and we can learn how to realize that union through the secret teaching of the Gnostics (rationalism). But ultimately our knowledge of Bythos is by union with him, rather than by propositional knowledge about him. That is the ultimate level of knowledge. It may be described as *rational*, for it is ultimate knowledge, or as *irrational*, because it is not propositional.

Gnosticism might be the source of still other forms of heresy in the early church, such as **Docetism**, the view that Jesus had no material

4. The idea that God and man are on a continuum and we can become God by various means is still in the air today. See Peter R. Jones's comparison between Gnosticism and the "new spiritualities" in *The Gnostic Empire Strikes Back* (Phillipsburg, NJ: P&R Publishing, 1992) and *Spirit Wars* (Escondido, CA: Main Entry Editions, 1997).

body, but only "seemed" (*dokeo* in Greek) to have one. Docetism comes from the Gnostic aversion to the material world. But the apostles themselves opposed this view, as in 1 John 4:2–3: "By this you know the Spirit of God: every spirit that confesses that Jesus Christ has come in the flesh is from God, and every spirit that does not confess Jesus is not from God. This is the spirit of the antichrist, which you heard was coming and now is in the world already."

The heretic **Marcion** (c. A.D. 85–c. 160) might also have been influenced by Gnosticism. In Gnosticism, typically the lowest of the aeons made the cosmic mistake of creating a material world. Marcion identified this inferior aeon with the Creator God of Genesis. He taught that this god had been replaced in the NT by the Father of Jesus Christ. So he taught a radical disjunction between the Testaments. He rejected the canonical authority of the OT, and of most of the NT, accepting only the Gospel of Luke (in a version revised by him) and a collection of ten letters of Paul as authoritative.

JUSTIN MARTYR (100–165)

In his *Dialogue with Trypho*, **Justin** tells a story about himself similar to other stories told by philosophers and would-be philosophers of his time. He searched here and there for the truth, he says, from city to city, from philosophy to philosophy, until in Ephesus he was finally convinced that Christianity was the greatest philosophy of all. He then defended Christianity until his martyrdom at the hands of the Romans.

In his *First Apology*, he seeks to persuade the Romans that Christians are good citizens of the empire. He argues the injustice of persecuting Christians just because they are Christians. He denies the charge that Christians are "atheists": Although they do not worship the gods of Rome, they do worship one God, the Author of all being and life. Christ is a King, but not an earthly ruler, so Christians cannot be regarded as insurrectionists. Justin describes the moral standards of Christianity to indicate their benefit to Roman society.

Justin Martyr

Much of his argument for the truth of Christianity in *First Apology* and *Dialogue with Trypho* (Trypho is a Jew) comes from the Scriptures: that the OT predicts the coming of Jesus and such details as his birthplace. But he also says that Christ is anticipated among the pagan philosophers:

> We have been taught that Christ is the first-born of God, and we have declared above that He is the Word of whom every race of men are partakers; and those who lived reasonably are Christians, even though they have been thought atheists; as among the Greeks, Socrates and Heraclitus, and men like them.[5]

5. Justin Martyr, *First Apology*, 52.

The Greek philosophers are in effect Christians, says Justin, because they lived according to the *logos*. In Greek philosophy, the *logos* is the principle of rationality that directs the course of the universe and makes it accessible to human reason. In John 1:1–14, the *logos* is Christ. Thus, when someone lives rationally, *meta logou*, he is living according to Christ. So philosophy prepares the Greeks and Romans for Christianity, just as the OT prepares the Jews. The *logos* is *logos spermatikos*, reason as the seed of truth that can be found among all peoples.

So as we might anticipate, there is in Justin little sense of antithesis between Christianity and Greek philosophy. As an apologist, Justin seeks to minimize the differences between these worldviews so as to make it as easy as possible for a learned pagan to make a transition to faith in Christ. And he wants to show that Christians are not ignorant barbarians, but are intellectually respectable, able to discuss issues with the greatest minds of the culture.

There is in Justin little sense of antithesis between Christianity and Greek philosophy. As an apologist, Justin seeks to minimize the differences between these worldviews so as to make it as easy as possible for a learned pagan to make a transition to faith in Christ.

In my judgment, the attempt to make Christianity intellectually respectable, and therefore easy to believe, is one of the most common and deadly mistakes of Christian apologists and philosophers throughout history. It ignores the fundamental biblical principle that people sinfully repress the truth and need to be given new hearts and minds by God's Spirit. Further, this common-ground approach leads to distortions in Christian theology itself.

Justin says that God is "without name."[6] When speaking of God, he prefers negative predicates to positive ones. God is not this, not that. This emphasis became known later as *negative theology* or the *via negativa*. But these principles are not biblical. Scripture itself does not hesitate to ascribe names and positive descriptions to God. The denial of meaningful speech about God is more characteristic of Gnosticism and Neoplatonism than of the Bible. Justin's emphases suggest the nonbiblical concept of transcendence that I mentioned in chapter 1: God is so far from us that we cannot rightly speak of him.

The attempt to make Christianity intellectually respectable, and therefore easy to believe, is one of the most common and deadly mistakes of Christian apologists and philosophers throughout history.

Of course, Justin cannot maintain the doctrine of the nameless God consistently, for his mind is saturated with Scripture. He regularly speaks of God as the Father, the Lord, the Holy One, the Creator, as Scripture does. But when he gets into a philosophical mood, he prefers to speak of God as *being* (using a Greek term, sometimes in the masculine, *ho on*, sometimes in the neuter, *to on*).[7] Further, in his hurry to credit Plato with a knowledge of Moses, he claims that the doctrine of the world's formation in Plato's *Timaeus* is the same as that in Genesis: the deity makes the world out of preexisting substance.[8] The church

6. Justin Martyr, *Second Apology*, 6.

7. Theologians have often justified the identification of God with being by citing Exodus 3:14. I and others have argued that this is a misreading of that text. See *DG*, 37–40.

8. Justin, *First Apology*, 59. Cf. Justin, *Second Apology*, 9.

would eventually reject this view in favor of the doctrine of creation out of nothing.

In fact, Justin's doctrine of creation is like the Gnostic in another way: for him, God does not create the world directly, but brings forth first subordinate beings to accomplish the task. In Justin's argument, these are the Son and the Holy Spirit. The Father cannot get his hands dirty, in effect, by coming into direct contact with matter. (Here the influence of Greek philosophy and/or Gnosticism is evident.) Of course, this idea also distorts the doctrine of the Trinity, for it makes the Son and the Spirit different in nature from the Father and ontologically subordinate to him.[9]

In his view of human nature as well, Justin moves away from Scripture toward a philosophical concept. He rightly seeks to reject Stoic fatalism and to defend human responsibility. But to do that, he appeals to the view that the human will is entirely indeterminate, entirely independent of God or of any other cause. In this sense, he adopts a view of human free will (*autexousion*) that was to damage many later theological systems, such as Pelagianism and Arminianism. This view is sometimes called *libertarian freedom*.[10] This notion is inconsistent with the Bible's teaching about God's sovereignty (Rom. 11:36; Eph. 1:11).

Recall from chapter 2 that Greek religion held to a "shapeless stream" of being, which the philosophers refined into the idea of formless matter. Because matter has no form, it is inherently unruly and unpredictable. In Epicurus, this indeterminacy appears in the random *swerve* of atoms from their normal course. These Greek notions, rather than anything in the Bible, stand behind the patristic notion of free will.[11]

Justin is so eager to show that Christianity fulfills the philosophical tradition that he distorts the biblical message at points. This weakness starts an unfortunate trend that continues throughout the history of the encounter between Christianity and philosophy.

So Justin's apologetic and philosophy are of mixed value. He clearly and emphatically corrects the misunderstandings of the Romans as to the doctrine and practices of Christian believers. His arguments from prophecy and miracle appeal to the data of Scripture itself.[12] His use of philosophy shows an impressive knowledge of the literature. This is all to the good. But he is so eager to show that Christianity fulfills the philosophical tradition that he distorts the biblical message at points. This weakness starts an unfortunate trend that continues throughout the history of the encounter between Christianity and philosophy.

9. Justin, *Second Apology*, 6.

10. I have offered many criticisms of this concept in my past writings and will offer some later in this one. For a summary, see *DG*, 138–45.

11. Calvinists who put great weight on the antiquity of doctrines should pause here. Among Christian writers who commented on divine sovereignty and human freedom, the most ancient held views contrary to those later held by Calvin and the Reformed confessions.

12. His interpretations of Bible texts, however, are not always accepted by modern scholars and readers.

Justin was, however, impressive in his personal faith and in his allegiance to Jesus. The title *Martyr* sealed the testimony of his life. Christians today sometimes ask how someone could have been a genuine believer and get so many things wrong (in Justin's case, including the Trinity, creation, and free will). We should remind ourselves that in one sense the "church fathers" were, in the words of a friend of mine, the "church babies." They were only beginning the long, hard task of understanding and applying God's revelation in Scripture. After A.D. 325 (and even more so after 381), the church would not have tolerated in its teachers[13] a view of the Trinity like Justin's. That is because the church had advanced further in its corporate level of knowledge. But salvation itself is not the ability to give an accurate formulation of biblical mysteries. (If it were, only the educated could be saved.) It is a commitment to Jesus Christ as Lord. Justin was one of the earliest in a long line of Christian thinkers who sought to defend the lordship of Christ in the world of human philosophy. God raised him up to do that. It was not easy for Justin to take on this task during a time of intense persecution. However he might have succeeded or failed, Christians should be thankful for what he achieved.

Irenaeus

IRENAEUS (130–200)

Irenaeus was Bishop of Lyons in modern France, but born in Smyrna, Asia Minor. He heard Polycarp, the disciple of the apostle John. He opposed the Gnostics and particularly Marcion.

His approach to Gnosticism and to non-Christian thought generally is more antithetical than Justin's. Irenaeus has little interest in proving his philosophical credentials. His whole interest is to warn his flock against dangerous teaching. Still, he knows the Gnostics well, and his treatment of them is biblically and philosophically astute.

Irenaeus has little interest in proving his philosophical credentials. His whole interest is to warn his flock against dangerous teaching. Still, he knows the Gnostics well, and his treatment of them is biblically and philosophically astute.

He addresses these issues in a book known today as *Against Heresies*. In the book, Irenaeus distinguishes a great number of different Gnostic systems and the names and functions of many aeons in each one, as well as their relations to the most high god (known as *Bythos*, *Proarche*, or *Propator*). In the Valentinian system, Bythos, though supposedly supertranscendent, deposits seed in his consort *Sige*, and she has children known as *Nous* (= *Monogenes*), *Aletheia*, *Logos*, *Zoe*, and others.[14] Eventually there are thirty aeons in the whole divine continuum (*pleroma*), and there must be thirty, because the

13. It is, of course, one thing to be a Christian believer, another thing to be qualified as a Christian teacher.

14. Notice that these sort out in pairs, each with one masculine partner (as Bythos) and another feminine partner (as Sige). Following Bythos and Sige, there are Nous and Aletheia, Logos and Zoe.

Scriptures say so. The scriptural argument illustrates the Gnostic use of allegorical exegesis: there must have been thirty aeons, because Jesus did no work during the first thirty years of his life. Further, in the parable of the laborers in the vineyard, workers were sent in the first hour, the third, the sixth, the ninth, and the eleventh, numbers that add up to thirty.

These thirty (and the other beings outside the pleroma) engage in a bizarre drama, similar to the dramas of the Olympic gods, similar indeed to the modern soap opera. There is love, sex, betrayal, ignorance, disobedience, number magic, symbolism upon symbolism. Eventually there is the story of the making of the material world by a wayward aeon. Irenaeus's evaluation:

> They have good reason, as seems to me, why they should not feel inclined to teach these things to all in public, but only to such as are able to pay a high price for an acquaintance with such profound mysteries. For these doctrines are not at all similar to those of which our Lord said, "Freely ye have received, freely give." They are, on the contrary, abstruse, and portentous, and profound mysteries, to be got at only with great labour by such as are in love with falsehood.[15]

Irenaeus's first argument against Gnosticism is found in his mere description of it. The Gnostic doctrine is weird, unbelievable. He does not need to advance sophisticated philosophical arguments against it. But part of the absurdity of it all is significantly philosophical: Bythos is supposedly far beyond anyone's understanding, and yet the Gnostics are somehow able to narrate his behavior in intricate and gross detail.

Irenaeus's first argument against Gnosticism is found in his mere description of it. The Gnostic doctrine is weird, unbelievable. He does not need to advance sophisticated philosophical arguments against it.

Bythos is both supertranscendent and superimmanent. For although he exceeds anyone's knowledge, he emanates beings that are as divine as he is.[16] But if he is supertranscendent, how can the other aeons, let alone the Gnostic teachers, gain that special knowledge that they sell at such great prices? And if he is superimmanent, why do we need teachers to enlighten us? Are we not as divine as they are? Irenaeus traces the Gnostic drama, from its "profound mysteries" to its all-too-humanness. In recognizing that transcendence-immanence dialectic, Irenaeus, almost unintentionally, proves himself to be a true philosopher; see fig. 3.2.

15. Irenaeus, *Against Heresies*, 4.3.

16. The beings emanated by Bythos are *homoousios* with him, of the same nature. The word *homoousios* is the same word later used in the Nicene Creed to indicate the relationship between the Son and the Father in the Trinity.

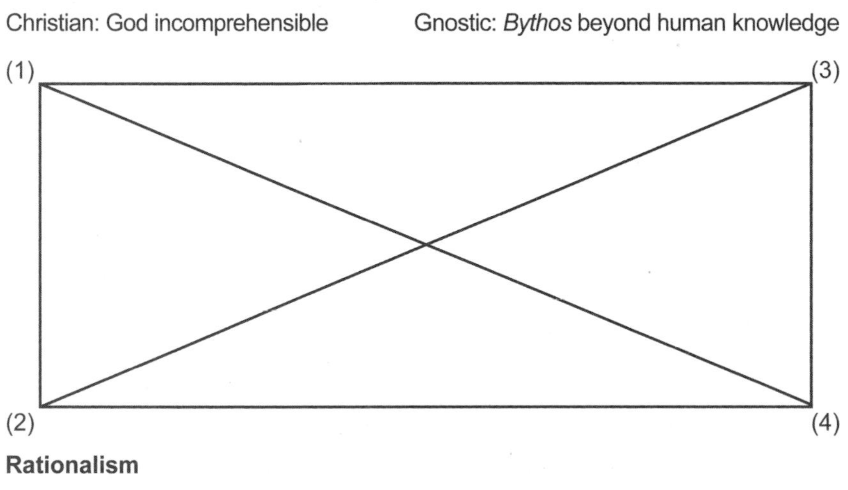

Fig. 3.2. Irrationalism and Rationalism in Gnosticism

Against these diverse Gnostic systems, Irenaeus cites the unity of the orthodox faith throughout the world. The churches of Germany, he says, believe the same thing as the churches of Spain. That common doctrine comes from the apostles and their *rule of faith*. This phrase evidently refers to doctrinal formulae given to candidates for baptism, which eventually take the form of statements such as the Apostles' Creed. Irenaeus also refers to writings of the apostles and others. Marcion, under the influence of Gnosticism, had denied the OT and many of the NT writings. Irenaeus, however, quotes almost all the books of our present NT canon as authoritative texts. The only books he does not quote are Philemon, 2 Peter, 3 John, and Jude. He does also mention 1 Clement and Shepherd of Hermas (which the church did not finally recognize as canonical) as worth reading. He dismisses the Gnostic Gospel of Truth as heretical. So the NT canon of Irenaeus is very close to that recognized today.

Against these diverse Gnostic systems, Irenaeus cites the unity of the orthodox faith throughout the world. . . . That common doctrine comes from the apostles and their rule of faith.

This emphasis on divine revelation plays, for Irenaeus, the role of a philosophical epistemology. The Gnostics derived their system by speculation and allegorical exegesis. Irenaeus, on the contrary, believes that we know God only through his revelation of himself. At one point he criticizes the Platonic doctrine of reminiscence: if all of us have forgotten the world of Forms, why should we trust Plato's recollection of it? So knowledge of God is not through memory, but through revelation. And the conflict with Marcion has sharpened Irenaeus's doctrine of revelation to a greater focus on the biblical canon.

This emphasis on divine revelation plays, for Irenaeus, the role of a philosophical epistemology. The Gnostics derived their system by speculation and allegorical exegesis. Irenaeus, on the contrary, believes that we know God only through his revelation of himself.

So when Irenaeus presents his positive theology, it is much more directly and literally biblical than that of the Gnostics. Nor is it encumbered by philosophical abstractions, as was the theology of Justin Martyr. Irenaeus rarely if ever describes God as *being*, but rather presents him as concrete and personal. Contrary to the philosophical doctrine of God's abstract transcendence, the God of Irenaeus interacts with human beings in history. Irenaeus describes the biblical drama as a history of redemption, and on that account is sometimes reckoned the father of biblical theology.

For Irenaeus, God needs no semidivine mediators to create the world. He does it himself, by his Word and Wisdom, *ex nihilo*. Word and wisdom are attributes of God himself, not subordinate beings as in Gnosticism and in Justin. We can see here how a number of theological conceptions reinforce one another: the sufficiency of Scripture, the concept of God as absolute tripersonality, the immanence of God in the world, creation *ex nihilo*. Certainly, Irenaeus's conflict with Gnosticism enables him to see the shape of the biblical worldview more clearly.

So in my view Irenaeus, more than Justin, understands the distinctive nature of the biblical worldview. Yet he is not perfect in this respect. Some problems:

1. At points he seems to confuse sin with finitude.
2. He understands salvation in terms more of the incarnation than of the atonement: in his incarnation, Christ "recapitulated" all stages of human life and thereby united all human flesh to God. This view, similar to the position that later developed in Eastern orthodoxy, is universalist in its implications.
3. He uses the language of deification when speaking of salvation, also similar to the development in Eastern Orthodoxy. Certainly neither Irenaeus nor the later theologians who followed him intended to compromise the Creator-creature distinction. But the use of such language is confusing in that regard. Second Peter 1:4 does speak of believers' becoming "partakers of the divine nature," but in my view this language is ethical, not metaphysical: a way of describing the image of God in which we are created and renewed.
4. Like Justin, Irenaeus affirms *autexousion*, the libertarian form of free will.

For Irenaeus, God needs no semidivine mediators to create the world. He does it himself, by his Word and Wisdom, ex nihilo. *Word and Wisdom are attributes of God himself, not subordinate beings as in Gnosticism and in Justin.*

TERTULLIAN (C. 160–220)

Tertullian represents the beginning of the Latin theological literature. (Irenaeus and earlier Fathers wrote in Greek.) Living in Carthage, he also initiates the North African tradition in Christian thought that culminated in Augustine's work. He was of Berber descent, possibly trained as a lawyer, converted around 197.

Around 213, Tertullian broke with the established church and joined the Montanist sect, which was eventually ruled a heresy. Montanus believed that the Holy Spirit had given direct revelations to him and to other believers who lived after the time of the apostles. He traveled with two women, Prisca and Maximilia, who also claimed visions and prophecy. In that respect, Montanism anticipates some movements in Reformation-era Anabaptism and modern charismatic theology. But Montanus claimed more than postapostolic special revelation. He presented himself as the *paraclete*, the Helper mentioned by Jesus in John 14:16, usually understood by Christians to be the Holy Spirit. Tertullian's particular group of Montanists returned to the orthodox church by the time of Augustine, and Augustine said that Tertullian himself returned to orthodoxy before his death, but that statement is unconfirmed.

Tertullian says that the heretics and the Greek philosophers have no right even to enter debate with the church, for they reject the apostolic rule of faith, the only criterion of Christian truth.

Whatever might be said about Tertullian's Montanist connection, many of his writings have had great influence on the theology of the church. The most important feature of these, in my judgment, is a greater sense of the antithesis between Christian and non-Christian thought. As we have seen, there was almost no sense of antithesis in the writings of Justin Martyr. In Irenaeus, there is some, for he adopts a very polemical stance toward Gnosticism and Marcion and he self-consciously presents the distinctives of the Christian worldview as opposite to the views of the heretics. But in Tertullian, the concept of antithesis becomes explicit, even an epistemological principle.

One of his earlier works is called *The Prescription of Heretics*. *Prescription* referred to a legal document claiming that a person had no right to address the court in its deliberations. So Tertullian says that the heretics and the Greek philosophers have no right even to enter debate with the church, for they reject the apostolic rule of faith, the only criterion of Christian truth. His words on this subject have become famous:

Tertullian

> What has Jerusalem to do with Athens, the Church with the Academy, the Christian with the heretic? Our principles come from the Porch of Solomon, who had himself taught that the Lord is to be sought in simplicity of heart. I have no use for a Stoic, or a Platonic, or a dialectical Christianity. After Jesus Christ we have no need of speculation, after the Gospel no need of research.[17]

With this passage we may compare a passage in his later writing *On the Flesh of Christ*. This book is a defense of the incarnation of Christ

17. Tertullian, *Prescription of Heretics*, 36.

against the spiritualism of Platonism and Gnosticism. These teachers condemned as impossible the idea that the divine should come into time and take human flesh. Tertullian defends this doctrine by saying (1) that nothing is impossible for God,[18] (2) that incarnation does not destroy God's divine nature, for he can become flesh while remaining himself,[19] and (3) that although the incarnation is contrary to worldly wisdom, it exemplifies the superior wisdom of God to redeem us through the physical means of death and resurrection.[20] In chapter 5, he is sometimes thought to renounce reason itself, by saying that he believes in the incarnation because it is absurd (*credo quia absurdum*). Actually, however, he does not say this, nor does he use the Latin word *absurdum*, though he uses the terms *ineptum* and *impossibile*. It reads as follows:

> *Crucifixus est dei filius; non pudet, quia pudendum est.*
> *Et mortuus est dei filius; credibile prorsus est, quia ineptum est.*
> *Et sepultus resurrexit; certum est, quia impossibile.*

In the translation of Ernest Evans:

> The Son of God was crucified: I am not ashamed—because it is shameful.
> The Son of God died: it is *immediately* credible—because it is silly.
> He was buried, and rose again: it is certain—because it is impossible.[21]

Tertullian did not entertain the irrationalist notion that we should believe absurd things because of their very absurdity. Rather, he sees a remarkable kind of rationality in the gospel: God is able to save by means that are foolish to the world, and that very foolishness is, to Christians, a mark of their credibility.

Clearly, Tertullian did not entertain the irrationalist notion that we should believe absurd things because of their very absurdity. Rather, he sees a remarkable kind of rationality in the gospel: God is able to save by means that are foolish to the world, and that very foolishness is, to Christians, a mark of their credibility.

This is an advance in Christian epistemology. Like Irenaeus, Tertullian starts with Scripture and stands firm on its foundation. More than Irenaeus, he sees the rule of faith and the foolishness of the gospel as the *presupposition* of all theological debate.

Although God is incomparably great, he can be clearly known by the works of his hands, according to Tertullian.[22] Tertullian does not despise the knowledge of sense experience as did Plato. He points out, rather, that sense and intellect are mutually dependent. But "ampler

18. Tertullian, *On the Flesh of Christ*, 3.1.
19. Ibid., 3.5–6.
20. Ibid., 4, 5.
21. Ernest Evans, trans., *Tertullian's Treatise on the Incarnation* (London: SPCK, 1956), 5.4.
22. Tertullian, *Apology*, 17.

and more authoritative" knowledge of God comes through his "written revelation."[23] As did earlier apologists, Tertullian points out the evils and ugliness of idolatry, he assures the Romans that Christians are loyal and beneficial to the state, and he argues that OT prophecy testifies to Christ.[24]

Beyond his interaction with unbelief, Tertullian developed doctrinal formulations for the church. He was the first to formulate in Latin what became the standard terminology for the Trinitarian and Christological distinctions (*substance, person, nature*). Some of his formulations, however, are subordinationist, because like Justin he sees the *logos* as a semidivine mediator between God and the world.

Tertullian . . . was the first to formulate in Latin what became the standard terminology for the Trinitarian and Christological distinctions (substance, person, nature)*.*

He rejects the Platonic-Gnostic idea that the soul of man is essentially divine but is trapped in a material body.[25] If the soul is essentially divine, he asks, how can we be ignorant of anything? And if union with the body eliminates knowledge, how can anything be known? The first question attacks the non-Christian principle of immanence (rationalism), the second transcendence (irrationalism). Showing some Stoic influence, Tertullian believes that the soul is material, but somehow simple.[26] In any case, for Tertullian the soul is not eternal, as in Plato, but created by God. Nor is there inherent irrationality in it. Here, Tertullian again asserts the distinctiveness of the Christian worldview.

He is one of the first to develop the doctrine of original sin. A *traducianist*, he believes that a person's soul is inherited from his parents, as is his body.[27] So our union with Adam through our parents transmits to us an uncontrollable subjection to temptation. But how was it possible for Adam to sin in the first place? Here Tertullian turns to speculation: the soul is a mixture of being and nonbeing, and the nonbeing introduces the possibility of sin. God does not prevent sin from taking place, because (as Justin and Irenaeus said) man has free will in the sense of *autexousion*. Here, in my judgment, Tertullian is not consistent with his intention to reason in accord with the rule of faith. He confuses the metaphysical and the ethical, explaining sin as a metaphysical derangement, a lack of being.

He is one of the first to develop the doctrine of original sin. A traducianist, *he believes that a person's soul is inherited from his parents, as is his body. So our union with Adam through our parents transmits to us an uncontrollable subjection to temptation.*

Tertullian is always interesting to read, vigorous, provocative, and (usually) cogent in his writing and reasoning. He makes significant progress toward a consistently biblical philosophy. It is amazing how much he accomplished in a time of persecution. But as with Justin and Irenaeus, it is plain that he left some philosophical work undone.

23. Ibid., 18.

24. Tertullian, *An Answer to the Jews*.

25. Tertullian, *On the Soul*.

26. See the account of Stoicism in chapter 2. When the Stoics said that the soul or God was "material," they might have meant only that it had a distinct reality.

27. This is opposed to *creationism*, the view that God creates a new soul out of nothing when the body is conceived.

OUTLINE

CLEMENT OF ALEXANDRIA (155–220)

We now shift our attention to still another geographical region. Justin traveled in Palestine, Asia Minor, and Rome. Irenaeus was born in Asia Minor, but was Bishop of Lyon in present-day France. Tertullian lived in Carthage, North Africa. Now we complete our trip around the Mediterranean.

Clement is one of the first of many Christian teachers to be located in Alexandria, in Egypt. Alexandria was one of the chief centers of Greek and Hellenistic Jewish culture in the ancient world, and would become, with Jerusalem, Antioch, Constantinople, and Rome, one of the chief centers of the Christian faith. The city had earlier been home to **Philo Judaeus** (20 B.C.–A.D. 50), a Jewish writer deeply influenced by Plato and the Stoics, who sought to reconcile the Jewish Scriptures to Greek philosophy by means of allegorical interpretation. Philo wrote of the *logos* as a semidivine mediator between God and the world and accommodated the creation story of Genesis 1 to Plato's *Timaeus*. As we have seen, Justin Martyr, among other church fathers, held similar positions.

Clement, after a period of travel, in which he may have been taught by some of the Christian apologists, settled in at the catechetical school in Alexandria, where he studied with Pantaenus and eventually succeeded him as the leading figure at the school.

Clement read widely in Greek philosophy and other non-Christian writings. His main surviving works are the *Protrepticus*, an apologetic addressed to pagan thinkers; *Paidagogos*, instruction to Christians, chiefly on ethical matters; and *Stromata*, a miscellaneous collection of teachings, somewhat more philosophical and theological in nature.

Like Justin, Clement prefers a rather impersonal vocabulary in speaking about God. God is nameless: you cannot properly speak of him. The closest we can come to describing him is to say that he is being.

His view of the relationship of faith and philosophy is much like that of Justin Martyr. Philosophy doesn't produce faith, he says, but it does support faith, clarify it, and make it attractive. As Aristotle said, the first principles of philosophy cannot be proved. Clement infers that these principles are intuitions of faith, so he says that faith is the indispensable basis of philosophy. Of course, he speaks here not of specifically Christian faith, but of a commitment to rational thought. Still, he believes that philosophy is God's covenant with the Greeks as the law was God's covenant with the Jews. (The river of truth, he says, has many streams.) So philosophy at its best leads to Christ. Of course, not all philosophy is worthy of the name. The Sophists, for example, are not true philosophers. But Clement also despises those Christians who reject all philosophy in the interest of orthodox doctrine. He calls them *orthodoxastai* (perhaps, *orthodoxists*), and you can almost hear Clement's contempt as you say that word.

Like Justin, Clement prefers a rather impersonal vocabulary in speaking about God. God is nameless: you cannot properly speak of him. The closest we can come to describing him is to say that he is being. Still, to avoid error, it is useful to use certain predicates to speak of God—a kind of conceptual scaffolding. For this purpose, negative names are better than positive ones: the *via negativa*.

Properly, however, human beings can know God only by way of mystical experience. Clement is perhaps the first Christian thinker to bring mysticism into his theological epistemology. It is not always easy to understand the meaning of *mystical experience* in such contexts. One sometimes suspects that it is an experience that (as in Gnosticism or Neoplatonism) erases the Creator-creature distinction and makes the human being identical with God. But mystics, especially Christian ones, often deny such an interpretation. At least, mysticism is a state of mind beyond rational thought, beyond language and logic, a place where knowledge is immediate and intuitive.

Clement of Alexandria

For Clement, as for Philo and for Justin, the *logos* is an intermediary between God and the world, subordinate to God. Clement regarded the *logos* as identical with Christ, so his view of the Trinity is one that would not be considered orthodox following the Nicene and Constantinopolitan Councils. As with Justin, the *logos* is also *spermatikos*, the means of divine revelation to the whole human race.

Clement also agrees with Justin's view of free will (*autexousion*). According to Clement, Adam was not created perfect, but was adapted to the reception of virtue. Human beings do not know God by nature, but they are equipped to learn of God by their own efforts. As did Adam, we have the capacity to obey God or to disobey, and God favors those who attain virtue. So Clement's view of sin and salvation has been described as *moralistic*.

Human beings can know God only by way of mystical experience. Clement is perhaps the first Christian thinker to bring mysticism into his theological epistemology.

Clement and Tertullian were near-contemporaries, but they lived in two different intellectual worlds as well as in two different geographical areas. Tertullian saw mostly discontinuity between pagan philosophy and Christianity, Clement mostly continuity. Likely, Clement never read Tertullian. If he had, perhaps he would have called him an *orthodoxist*. Clement had virtually no concept of intellectual antithesis between belief and unbelief. Rather, he reverted to a kind of theology very similar to that of Justin, as though all theological work since Justin had to be done again.

ORIGEN (185–254)

Origen was born in Alexandria, though he traveled widely and spent part of his life in exile in Caesarea. He was schooled by his Christian father and later studied philosophy with the Platonist Ammonius Saccas, who was also the teacher of Plotinus. It is tempting to imagine Origen and Plotinus arguing with each other during Ammonius's seminars, but the chronology doesn't support that scenario.

In 202, Origen's father was martyred during the persecution by the emperor Septimus Severus. The story is told that Origen wanted to join the martyrs, but was forbidden by his mother, who hid his clothes. In 203 he revived the catechetical school where Clement had taught, which had been discontinued for a time during the persecution.

Eusebius, the early-church historian, says that Origen castrated himself, in literal obedience to Matthew 19:12. However we evaluate this action, it indicates the depth of Origen's commitment to Christ, as does his continuous support of Christians suffering persecution. He was also an extremely hard worker. According to Epiphanius, Origen wrote six thousand works. Others have estimated a figure closer to two thousand. But on any account, his output was extremely impressive, though of course many of those writings have not survived.

Origen was a biblical scholar, apologist, and theologian. As a biblical scholar, he wrote commentaries and sermons on most of Scripture. In this field he is best known for supervising production of the *Hexapla*, which placed six versions of Scripture in parallel columns.[28] He held to a strong view of verbal inspiration, but for him this conviction warranted allegorical interpretation, for he believed that every text had to teach something worthy of God. He distinguished three senses of every text: (1) the somatic or literal, (2) the psychical or moral, and (3) the pneumatic or speculative. So although Origen had a high respect for Scripture as the Word of God, his allegorical interpretation could make it teach a wide variety of speculative, indeed philosophical, ideas.

Although Origen had a high respect for Scripture as the Word of God, his allegorical interpretation could make it teach a wide variety of speculative, indeed philosophical, ideas.

Origen's chief work as an apologist is *Contra Celsum*. Celsus was a second-century Platonist who wrote *The True Word*, an attack on Christianity. Origen's rebuttal is a painstaking reply to every point and subpoint in Celsus's book.

But Origen's most influential work is *On First Principles*. I noted that Irenaeus's work is sometimes described as Christianity's first biblical theology; Origen's *On First Principles* is sometimes described as Christianity's first systematic theology.

Origen distinguished three methods of knowing God, more commonly associated in later times with the work of Thomas Aquinas:[29] (1) *synthesis* (what Aquinas called *the way of causation*), coming to know God as the causal origin of earthly realities, (2) *analysis* (in Aquinas, *the way of negation*), denying to God anything inappropriate, anything

28. The six columns were (1) Hebrew, (2) Hebrew in Greek characters, (3) the Septuagint, and the Greek versions of (4) Theodotion, (5) Aquila of Sinope, and (6) Symmachus. Most of this is no longer extant.

29. For Aquinas, *analogy* was a more general principle, applicable to all knowledge of God. Aquinas's third method was called *the way of eminence*, the reverse of the way of negation. In the way of eminence, we attribute to God the highest degree of what we consider to be excellent or perfect in this world.

that suggests weakness, materiality, evil, and (3) *analogy*, determining the proportion or extent to which any attribute pertains to God (in Aquinas, *the way of eminence*). Though God is beyond all predication, some predicates are more true of him than others. It is more true, for example, to say that God is just than to say that he is unjust. Given the influence of Platonism on Origen and his allegorical use of Scripture, it is not clear how much these methods are governed by Scripture and how much by autonomous speculation.

His doctrine of God follows the model developed by Philo, Justin, and Clement under the influence of Gnosticism and Neoplatonism. God is being, and beyond being. None of our predications suit him, but it is right for us to conceive him as personality.

Origen formulates the terminology used for Trinitarian distinctions in the Greek-speaking world, as Tertullian had previously developed that vocabulary for the Latin-speaking churches. God is one ousia, *three* hypostaseis.

Origen formulates the terminology used for Trinitarian distinctions in the Greek-speaking world, as Tertullian had previously developed that vocabulary for the Latin-speaking churches. God is one *ousia*, three *hypostaseis. Ousia* means "being," and was generally accepted as synonymous with the Latin *substantia*, "substance." *Hypostaseis* distinguished what in the West were called the three "persons" (*personae*) of the Godhead. But the meanings of *hypostasis* and *persona* were more problematic. As far as the Greek language was concerned, there was not a great difference between *ousia* and *hypostasis*; the use of them for the unity and diversity of the Trinity, respectively, was a convention rather than a linguistic necessity. But *persona* in Latin had the theatrical connotation "mask" or "role," suggesting to the Easterners that the Western formulae veered toward Sabellianism, the view that God was one person who played several roles.[30] And to the Westerners, Origen's "three *hypostases*" sounded like "three gods." As long as all the Christians were willing to accept both the Greek and the Latin terms as conventional designations of the Trinity, there would be no problem. But later, when confronted by heresy, mutual suspicions abounded.[31]

Origen

One inconsistency in Origen's doctrine of the Trinity was fateful for later controversy. When Origen expounds Jesus' words in John 10:30, "I and the Father are one," he points out that *one* in Greek is the neuter *hen*, "one thing." That most naturally means that they are of the same being, though distinguished in the text as persons. Here, Origen comes close to saying that the Son and the Father are *homoousios*, of the same substance, the term that later distinguished Nicene orthodoxy. On the other hand, in other discussions readers have accused Origen of subordinationist views of the Son's relation to the Father, similar to the *logos* theology of Philo, Justin, and Clement. On this view, the Son derives his being from the Father. So Origen's view of John 10:30

30. Sabellianism was, after all, a heresy that developed primarily in the West.

31. I have discussed this misunderstanding at greater length in *DG*, 696–705.

sets a precedent for Nicene orthodoxy; his subordinationism sets a precedent for Arian heresy.

In Origen's view, creation of the world has been going on eternally; it should not be considered a particular act as in the literal understanding of Genesis 1. Since God could not create evil, he created all things ethically equal. Some of them fell into sin by their own free will (*autexousion*—as we have seen, the usual patristic libertarian view of freedom). But why are people born sick, or deformed, or poor? Origen speculates that they must have committed sins in a previous life, so he embraces a doctrine of the preexistence of souls.[32]

In redemption, Jesus overcomes the demonic powers (sometimes called the *Christus Victor* view of atonement), teaches righteousness to human beings, and gives us in his life and death a moral example. Origen does not emphasize the atoning death of Jesus and does not teach any clear doctrine of penal substitution. He hopes for universal salvation, even of the devils (a doctrine sometimes called *apokatastasis*). Nevertheless, even universal salvation will not bring the redemptive drama to an end. Even in heaven, men and angels will still have free will. So God will not be able to prevent them from falling again, and history might then have to continue on to another cycle of redemption.

We can see here the far-reaching effects of Origen's speculative method. In effect, Origen's theology is a synthesis between biblical thought and Platonism. That synthesis became extremely widespread in the Eastern Christian world. There, everyone was an Origenist, but some preferred his orthodox emphases, others his speculative ideas. These are sometimes called *right-wing* and *left-wing Origenists*, respectively. It was this division that led to the fourth-century wars over the Trinity.

ATHANASIUS (290–373)

Athanasius

Athanasius came to prominence through his role in the Arian controversy. **Arius** (c. 256–336) and his disciples were left-wing Origenists who believed that the Son of God (often called the *Word* after John 1) was not God in the highest sense, not fully God. They believed, therefore, that the Word was a creature, not the ultimate Creator, though they acknowledged that the Word was involved in the creation of all the other things in the universe (John 1:3). They used the slogan (which sounds catchy in Greek) *en pote hote ouk en*, literally "there was once when he [the Son] was not." This was not quite the same as saying that "there was a *time* when he was not": the slogan uses *pote* (literally "a when") rather than *chronos* ("a time"). The Arians intended a subtle distinction. They did not believe that if you went far enough back in time, you would find yourself in a universe (an extended period of time) in which the

32. Recall the precedent for this in Pythagoras and Plato.

Father existed without the Son. They conceded that the Son had existed through all the ages. Perhaps they thought the Son's beginning was also the beginning of time itself. But in the end they regarded the Word as a lesser being than the Father, worthy of a lesser degree of worship. He may be called "a god" (*theos*) but not "the God" (*ho theos*). In this regard, the Arian terminology, and the arguments for using it, is very similar to those of the Jehovah's Witnesses sect in the modern period.

In their view, the Father is by definition simple, without personal distinctions. He created the Word as a means of creating the material world. He could not create matter by himself, for that would defile him. The Holy Spirit was a still lesser being. So the three persons of the Trinity were hierarchically related. We should recall that the Gnostics used a very similar argument for their hierarchy of aeons: the supreme being could not come into direct contact with matter. Creating the material universe could be done only by an aeon of lesser dignity. We should also recall that such hierarchical views of the Trinity were taught earlier in the church, by Justin, Tertullian, Clement, and possibly Origen. But Arius was the first to clearly state that the Word and Spirit were creatures of God, rather than being fully God.

The term homoousios *turned out to be a watchword. The Arians denied that the Word and the Father were* homoousios, *that is, of the same substance, the same nature. The orthodox affirmed that they were.*

The term *homoousios* turned out to be a watchword. The Arians denied that the Word and the Father were *homoousios*, that is, of the same substance, the same nature. The orthodox affirmed that they were.[33]

In 325 was held the great Council of Nicaea, called chiefly to deal with the Arian controversy. Remarkably, the church was in relative peace because the emperor Constantine, who had himself become a Christian sometime before 315, had ended the persecution of Christians by the Roman Empire. The emperor presided over the council. In part the council was a celebration of God's preservation of his church despite terrible odds. Many of the delegates were wounded and disfigured, tortured for Christ—wounded warriors, as we would say today.

The council rejected Arianism and affirmed that God and the Word, his Son, were homoousios.

The council rejected Arianism and affirmed that God and the Word, his Son, were *homoousios*. The creedal statement as revised by the Council of Constantinople in 381 was as follows:

> We believe in one God the Father Almighty, Maker of heaven and earth, and of all things visible and invisible.
>
> And in one Lord Jesus Christ, the only-begotten Son of God, begotten of the Father before all worlds, God of God, Light of Light, Very God of Very God, begotten, not made, being of one substance [*homoousios*] with the Father, by whom all things

33. A middle-way party said that the Father and the Word were *homoiousios*, which differs from *homoousios* only by a letter *i*. *Homoiousios* means "of *like* substance," as opposed to *homoousios*, "of the *same* substance."

> were made; who for us men, and for our salvation, came down from heaven, and was incarnate by the Holy Spirit of the Virgin Mary, and was made man, and was crucified also for us under Pontius Pilate. He suffered and was buried, and the third day he rose again according to the Scriptures, and ascended into heaven, and sitteth on the right hand of the Father. And he shall come again with glory to judge both the quick and the dead, whose kingdom shall have no end.
>
> And we believe in the Holy Spirit, the Lord and Giver of Life, who proceedeth from the Father,[34] who with the Father and the Son together is worshipped and glorified, who spoke by the prophets. And we believe one holy catholic and apostolic Church. We acknowledge one baptism for the remission of sins. And we look for the resurrection of the dead, and the life of the world to come. Amen.

The creed does affirm the "eternal generation" of the Son from the Father, and the "eternal procession" of the Spirit, but it denies that the One generated is anything less than the One who generates, or that the One who proceeds is anything less than the One from whom he proceeds.[35]

The creed does affirm the "eternal generation" of the Son from the Father, and the "eternal procession" of the Spirit, but it denies that the One generated is anything less than the One who generates, or that the One who proceeds is anything less than the One from whom he proceeds.

Athanasius was present at the 325 council as an assistant to Alexander, Bishop of Alexandria. He spoke on that occasion to oppose the Arian position. In 328, he himself became Bishop. A few years later, Arianism reemerged, supported by the power of Constantine's successors, and the church's years of peace came to an end. Arians and Nicene orthodox were at each other's throats. Athanasius held firm to the Nicene position and was persecuted as the great enemy of the Arians. He was often deposed and exiled (on one estimate, seven times), but through God's providence he always returned to his position and died peacefully in 373. In 381 the Council of Constantinople reaffirmed the Nicene doctrine.

Athanasius was not a sophisticated intellectual as was Origen, but he was remarkably tenacious and had a good understanding of the issues at stake. He held firmly to the *homoousios* doctrine, but he was able to make common cause with those who preferred not to use that term[36] but who expressed the same doctrine in different words.

34. The Western churches (under the influence of Augustinian theology) added "and the Son" at this point, the famous *filioque*. Together with other issues, this addition led to the division of the Eastern and Western churches in A.D. 1054.

35. For more on eternal generation and procession and the *filioque*, see *DG*, 707–19.

36. We should recall that *homoousios* had some bad associations from the past. Some Gnostics used it to refer to the relationship between the aeons and Bythos. It was also part of the vocabulary of Paul of Samosata, who was accused of heresy. Athanasius understood that some Christians, who were not themselves heretics, could have good reasons for objecting to *homoousios*. Would that contemporary Christians had such flexibility with regard to technical, extrabiblical theological language.

For Athanasius, rather, the basic issues had to do with fundamental convictions of Christian faith:

1. Arianism encourages worship of a creature. Christians have long worshiped Christ as God. If Arianism were true, Christians either would have to abandon their worship of Jesus or would have to confess the sin of idolatry—giving divine worship to a mere creature.
2. Arianism teaches that our salvation depends on a creature, rather than wholly on God.

For Athanasius, . . . the basic issues had to do with fundamental convictions of Christian faith.

Worship and salvation: the fundamental issues of our faith.[37] In this regard, Athanasius is rather like Luther in the sixteenth century. Luther criticized the Roman church for its worship (the "idolatry" of the Mass) and for its doctrine of salvation (in effect, justification by works).

I have noticed the following parallel between the fourth century and the sixteenth century, periods that I consider to be times of fundamental reform for the church. In both periods the dominant theology was a kind of synthesis between biblical thought and Greek philosophy: in the fourth century, Origenism; in the sixteenth, the theology of Thomas Aquinas. In both periods there came a heresy that upset the balance: in the fourth century, Arianism; in the sixteenth, the sale of indulgences by people such as John Tetzel. Then came a reformer: in the fourth century, Athanasius; in the sixteenth, Luther. Then came a consolidator, someone who would rethink the whole of the church's theology in the light of the gains of the reformation: in the fourth and fifth centuries, Augustine; in the sixteenth, Calvin.[38]

Athanasius and Luther are similar in that they emphasized and reemphasized the fundamentals of worship and salvation. On those points they were uncompromising, eloquent, and emphatic.

Parallel Histories of Reformation			
Synthesis	*Heresy*	*Reformer*	*Consolidator*
Origen	Arius	Athanasius	Augustine
Thomas Aquinas	Tetzel	Luther	Calvin

Athanasius and Luther are similar in that they emphasized and reemphasized the fundamentals of worship and salvation. On those points they were uncompromising, eloquent, and emphatic.

I have also thought that there are important parallels between Athanasius and Irenaeus. Both focused on biblical, rather than philosophical,

37. Worship is our fundamental stance toward God as creatures. Salvation is our fundamental relation to God as sinners.

38. This scheme raises the question what a reformation might look like in our own time. I would think the issue would be the authority of Scripture. As Athanasius struggled for the deity of Christ, and Luther struggled for the divine character of salvation, so God might call a modern reformer to struggle for the divine character of revelation. In all these cases, the issue is the supremacy of God.

terms and arguments. Both avoided subordinationism in their representations of the Trinity. Both put a strong emphasis on the directness of God's relationship to the world. For Irenaeus and Athanasius, God does not get his hands dirty when he touches creation directly. He does not need a mediator to create, but does it himself, *ex nihilo*. The Son and Spirit are also involved, but because they are fully God, creation is a direct encounter between God and the world. God is not, therefore, supertranscendent, as in Gnosticism. He is present with us because the world is his creation and his dwelling place.

Together with the strengths of Irenaeus's theology, Athanasius repeats some of its weaknesses. As with Irenaeus, Athanasius believes in free will of the *autexousion* type. And as with Irenaeus, salvation has more to do with Jesus' incarnation than with his blood atonement: he saves us by taking our flesh to himself, so that we may be deified, however that is understood: "The Son of God became man so that we might become God."[39] But all in all, Athanasius was a genuine reformer and a valiant defender of the truth of Christ.

AUGUSTINE (354–430)

In the diagram I presented in the last section, Augustine is the "consolidator." He takes the gains of the Trinitarian controversy and rethinks the whole range of Christian theology in the light of that reform. That work required a thinker of great knowledge and intellectual genius, and Augustine certainly possessed those qualifications. He consummates the work of all the church fathers, bringing their best insights into a comprehensive system, much as Plato critically synthesized all the Greek philosophers previous to him. Moreover, Augustine lays a foundation for future philosophy such that for centuries his successors pay homage to him, as was also true of Plato. Indeed, Augustine is largely responsible for the fact that from his death in 430 until around 1650, Christianity dominates philosophic thought in the West.

Augustine is largely responsible for the fact that from his death in 430 until around 1650, Christianity dominates philosophic thought in the West.

Augustine was born and lived many years in North Africa, not far from where Tertullian worked in an earlier time. Born in Thagaste (now Souk Ahras, Algeria) to a pagan father (Patricius) and a devout Christian mother (Monica), he was raised as a Christian, but when he went to Carthage at seventeen to study rhetoric, he left the church to embrace the Manichaean religion. Manichaeism taught that the universe consisted of two worlds, warring against each other: light and darkness, good and evil. At that time Augustine followed a hedonistic lifestyle. In his *Confessions* he quotes a prayer he spoke at that time: "Grant me chastity and continence, but not yet."[40]

39. Athanasius, *On the Incarnation of the Word of God*, 8.54.
40. Augustine, *Confessions*, 8.7.17.

He taught rhetoric at Thagaste and Carthage, then at Rome, and then at Milan. He came to reject Manichaeism and embrace first the skepticism of the New Academy, then Neoplatonism. But eventually the influence of Ambrose, Christian Bishop of Milan, prevailed on him. In a period when some other prominent pagans were becoming Christians, Augustine came to a point of decision. He says that he was in the garden of his house when he heard children singing, "*Tolle lege, tolle lege*," "Take and read, take and read." He picked up a Bible, and his eyes fell on Romans 13:13–14:

> Let us walk properly as in the daytime, not in orgies and drunkenness, not in sexual immorality and sensuality, not in quarreling and jealousy. But put on the Lord Jesus Christ, and make no provision for the flesh, to gratify its desires.[41]

Augustine

Augustine recounts this as the occasion of his final conversion.[42] His mother Monica was overjoyed that her prayers for him of many years had been answered. In 387 he was baptized by Ambrose. He became a priest in 391 and Bishop of Hippo in 396.

Manichaeism

Augustine, who had once embraced Manichaeism, quickly became one of its strongest critics. Already before his conversion, he had moved away from this sect, convinced by the Neoplatonists that there can be only one supreme being. As a Christian, he came to see further that the world was not an emanation from the essence of the supreme being, as the Neoplatonists thought, but a creation out of nothing. Augustine's God was not the impersonal *One* of Plotinus or, alas, of some of the church fathers. Rather, Augustine always spoke of him in personal terms, a personalism enhanced by his understanding of the interpersonal relations of the persons of the Trinity.

Where does evil come from? If God is all-good, he must have the desire to prevent evil; and if he is omnipotent, he must have the power. Yet there is evil. What account can we give of that fact, if we are not to agree with the Manichaeans that it is a power equal and opposite to that of God?

But then where does evil come from? If God is all-good, he must have the desire to prevent evil; and if he is omnipotent, he must have the power. Yet there is evil. What account can we give of that fact, if we are not to agree with the Manichaeans that it is a power equal and opposite to that of God?

41. It is interesting that Romans 13:13–14 is not a "gospel" text like John 3:16, Romans 6:23, or Ephesians 2:8–9. It does not specifically speak of grace or atonement; rather, it makes a moral demand. So it doesn't fit the traditional evangelical pattern for Christian conversion. Doubtless by this time, however, Augustine knew the biblical teaching about saving grace. His stumbling block was his hedonistic lifestyle, which prevented him from embracing Christ as Lord. Augustine's conversion helps us to better understand the variety of ways in which God changes people's hearts.

42. Augustine, *Confessions*, 8.28–29.

Augustine says that evil is a form of nonbeing. It is not one of the things that God made, because God said that everything he made was good (Gen. 1:31). But of course, there are "lacks" in God's creation. Cows don't have wings. Oak trees don't bear fruit. Water does not burn. Normally, these lacks are not a problem. Beings incorporate nonbeing as doughnuts have holes. But sometimes nonbeing exists where being *ought* to be: a grapevine that bears no fruit, a robin that cannot fly, a boy born with no legs. In such cases, nonbeing becomes what Augustine called *privation*. The worst kind of evil, and the origin of the others, is moral privation, the sin of angels and man. God made Adam good, but out of excessive self-love, and by his own free will, he disobeyed God.

Augustine was never satisfied with standard answers to philosophic problems. For him, it was not enough to identify evil with nonbeing,[43] as a Neoplatonist would have done. Rather, he searched the Scriptures to find a distinctively Christian response to the problem. The biblical account of the fall makes it clear that evil is essentially moral, not metaphysical. Evil is not an aspect of God's good creation. It is personal rebellion against God's commands. And the natural evils of this world are God's curse on mankind for that rebellion.

But if evil is ethical, not metaphysical, why do we need the metaphysical argument about evil as nonbeing and privation? This argument is essentially a theodicy, an attempt to show that God is not to blame for evil. The theodicy is that in creation, God makes being, not nonbeing. So he cannot be held responsible for privations of being. But this is a little bit like a baker of doughnuts who, when people complain that the holes are too big, replies that he makes only doughnuts, not the holes in them. Applied to God's creative work, of course, this notion is laughable. Surely God's sovereignty in creation is such that he makes all the beings in the universe, and if there are also items in the universe identified as *nonbeing*, he makes those as well.

If evil is ethical, not metaphysical, why do we need the metaphysical argument about evil as nonbeing and privation? This argument is essentially a theodicy, an attempt to show that God is not to blame for evil.

The privation argument inevitably creates confusion, suggesting that evil is at least partly explainable as part of the metaphysics of the universe. Best to say unambiguously that God created a good world, but angels and men rebelled against him and brought evil into it. That does raise the further question of what there was about angels and men that made such rebellion possible. But I know of no biblical answer to that question. And the speculative answers tend to some extent to take the blame off the creature and place it on the Creator. Better to leave the issue shrouded in mystery.

43. And Scripture certainly forbade him to take the further step of Neoplatonists and Gnostics, to identify nonbeing with matter.

So the privation theory neither explains the fall (the root evil) nor exonerates God from being blamed for evil. It creates some confusion between ethics and metaphysics, and therefore in my view should be abandoned.

Augustine will eventually learn that God is sovereign over all aspects of his creation. If there is nonbeing and privation within the universe, it is there because God wills it to be there. Scripture does in fact teach that evils, even sins, come from God's will (as Acts 2:23; 4:26–28; Eph. 1:11), without detracting from the responsibility of sinful human beings.[44] Realization of that will require Augustine to modify his view of free will, from the patristic *autexousion* to one more in keeping with divine sovereignty.

Augustine will eventually learn that God is sovereign over all aspects of his creation. If there is nonbeing and privation within the universe, it is there because God wills it to be there.

Epistemology

Very soon after his conversion, Augustine wrote *Contra Academicos*, criticizing skepticism, another philosophic alternative that he had once embraced. If, as the academics claimed, certainty is impossible, then one cannot even know the most basic truths, such as the truth of one's own existence. Augustine countered that we can never doubt that we are doubting; we can never think that we are not thinking.[45]

In *Soliloquies*, a group of "dialogues with Reason," Reason asks:

> R. What then wouldst thou know? . . .
> A. God and the soul, that is what I desire to know.
>
> R. Nothing more?
> A. Nothing whatever.[46]

If, as the academics claimed, certainty is impossible, then one cannot even know the most basic truths, such as the truth of one's own existence. Augustine countered that we can never doubt that we are doubting; we can never think that we are not thinking.

But to know God and the soul, one must first learn truth.[47] And truth is by nature imperishable, for even if it perishes, it is still true that truth has perished; therefore, truth has not perished.[48] So truth is immutable and eternal—that is, divine. And as we saw earlier, the soul cannot be deceived as to its own existence. So God and the soul exist, and the truth exists in both.

In *De Magistro* ("On the Teacher"), Augustine says that teaching (particularly by signs) is impossible unless the learner already knows something of what he is being taught. If the learner does not know

44. I have argued this point at length in *DG*, especially chapters 4 and 9.

45. This is the root of Descartes' famous argument, *cogito, ergo sum*, "I think, therefore I am."

46. Augustine, *Soliloquies*, 1.2.7.

47. Ibid., 1.15.27.

48. Ibid., 2.2.2.

anything of the subject matter, how does he know where to look in order to gain more knowledge? So learning is possible only because each human being already possesses some truth. We are never in a position of having to start from nothing, from total ignorance.[49]

Augustine, like Plato, is therefore somewhat skeptical as to what can be learned by sense experience. Sense experience prods the mind, but the most important truths, the universals, the general concepts, are in the mind already. Otherwise, we could make nothing of the shapes and sounds that we see and hear. But where do these truths come from? Augustine does not follow Aristotle, who said that the mind abstracts these from sense experience. Nor does he follow Plato, who says that we recollect them from a previous existence in the world of Forms. Rather, these truths are located first of all in the mind of God. We know them because he has illuminated our minds to recognize them.

So Augustine is much influenced by Plato and Plotinus, as were the earlier church fathers. But we see that Augustine, much more than previous Christian teachers, seeks distinctly Christian answers to the subjects he considers. For him, truth is not a set of abstract concepts as in Plato. Rather, as in the Bible, the truth is personal, the person of God in Christ (John 14:6), the *logos* of John 1. Knowledge occurs when the personal God illuminates the minds of human persons to understand him and to understand the world he has made. So Augustine maintains the Creator-creature distinction and makes our thought a servant knowledge, part of our discipleship.[50]

Hence his employment of the formula *crede ut intelligas*, "believe that you may understand."[51] As we will see, this became the slogan of Anselm of Canterbury, in the form *credo ut intelligam*, "I believe that I might understand." For Augustine and for Anselm, faith is not the conclusion of a neutral rational process, but the foundation of understanding.

The human mind is daunted by the complexity of the doctrine of the Trinity and darkened by its own sin. God's inner nature far transcends the scope of human reason and sense experience. What understanding is available to us is thoroughly dependent on God's revelation to us.

The Trinity

Augustine believes that the doctrine of the Trinity is not directly accessible to human reason. The human mind is daunted by the complexity of the doctrine of the Trinity and darkened by its own sin. God's inner nature far transcends the scope of human reason and sense experience. What understanding is available to us is thoroughly dependent on God's revelation to us.

49. As in John Locke's later view of the mind as *tabula rasa*, an empty slate to be written upon by experience.

50. Cf. Cornelius Van Til, *A Christian Theory of Knowledge* (Nutley, NJ: Presbyterian and Reformed, 1969), 118–42. But I commend some things in Augustine that Van Til criticizes.

51. Augustine, *Treatise on the Gospel of John*, 29.6.

Augustine accepts wholeheartedly the church's formulations at Nicaea and Constantinople: There is one God in three persons, Father, Son, and Holy Spirit.

But how are these persons related to one another, and to the one divine being? The Cappadocian fathers, Basil of Caesarea, Gregory of Nazianzen, and Gregory of Nyssa,[52] who followed Athanasius in working out the doctrine of the Trinity in the Eastern church, began with the observation that the divine substance is a generality, a universal of which the three persons are particulars, just as three people are all human beings, but differ from one another by their particular properties. So the Cappadocians gave attention to the distinctive properties of each person of the Trinity: The Father is unbegotten but begets the Son. He is the *fountain of deity.* The Son is begotten. The Holy Spirit proceeds from the Father. The Cappadocians emphasized, then, the distinctions between the persons. The Arians had claimed that the orthodox were Sabellian, that they had failed to recognize the distinctness of the persons. The Cappadocians put that criticism to rest.

Augustine accepts wholeheartedly the church's formulations at Nicaea and Constantinople: There is one God in three persons, Father, Son, and Holy Spirit. . . . Augustine, however, felt a need to reemphasize the unity and equality of the persons in the one Godhead.

Augustine, however, felt a need to reemphasize the unity and equality of the persons in the one Godhead. He thought that to use the Latin term *substantia* for the unity of God was misleading, since it could suggest (as in Aristotle's distinction between substance and accidents) that God has properties accidental to him, properties that he could possess or not possess. Rather, Augustine suggested, it was better to speak of God as one *essentia,* "essence." An essence has no *accidents,* only necessary properties. So that if God is wise, he does not merely "have" wisdom, as if he could possibly be without it. Wisdom belongs to his essence. In the essence of something, there is nothing accidental; rather, everything in the essence is itself essential. So God *is* his wisdom, power, goodness, and so forth. In that sense, God is *simple.*

In the doctrine of the Trinity, then, the Father's begetting of the Son is a necessary act. Without it, God is not God, just as he would not be God without his wisdom. The same is the case for the procession of the Holy Spirit.

In the doctrine of the Trinity, then, the Father's begetting of the Son is a necessary act. Without it, God is not God, just as he would not be God without his wisdom. The same is the case for the procession of the Holy Spirit.

So Augustine stressed the unity of God more than the Cappadocians. He stressed, therefore, the doctrine of *circumcessio,* that each person was "in" the others, and that they were together in all the events of nature and history. For Augustine, the best analogy of the Trinity is the human mind, made in the image of God. Each of us has a single mind, but within that mind are memory, understanding, and will (which Augustine relates closely to love). These faculties are mutually dependent; none can exist or function without the others.

52. Basil (330–79) was Bishop of Caesarea. Gregory of Nyssa (332–95), his brother, was Bishop of Nyssa, and Gregory Nazianzen (329–89), their close friend, became Patriarch of Constantinople.

Today there is theological controversy between "social" Trinitarians such as Jürgen Moltmann and Cornelius Plantinga (who claim to follow the Cappadocians) and "psychological" Trinitarians such as Herman Bavinck and other more traditional theologians (who claim to follow Augustine). The social Trinitarians think that the Trinity can be best understood by analogy to human social relationships. The psychological Trinitarians think that the best analogy is to individual human thought and love. The social Trinitarians think that Augustine veered too close to Sabellianism. The psychological Trinitarians think that the Cappadocians veered too close to Arianism. (Is the Cappadocian view of the Father's *begetting* the Son too close to the Arian view of the Father's *creating* the Son?)[53]

The doctrine of the Trinity is a very deep mystery. Its incomprehensibility is evident to anyone who ventures into Augustine's *De Trinitate*. In my judgment, Augustine's understanding is more profound than that of the Cappadocians, and far more profound than that of the contemporary social Trinitarians. But it is baffling how the three persons of Augustine's conception can come into history and enter interpersonal transactions with one another. In the end, it might not be possible for present-day believers to formulate a view of God's unity and plurality that is perfectly balanced and that reproduces every nuance of the biblical teaching.

The doctrine of the Trinity is a very deep mystery. Its incomprehensibility is evident to anyone who ventures into Augustine's De Trinitate.

Pelagianism

Pelagius was a British monk who, like Augustine himself, was appalled by the moral state of the people of Rome. He preached and counseled them, teaching that through their free moral effort they could improve their lives. One of his texts was Augustine's own early book, *On the Freedom of the Will*. He encouraged his hearers to believe that there was nothing hindering them from moral success. Particularly, the fall of Adam had no effect on his descendants. Although indeed the habit of sin can be hard to break, nevertheless success comes through diligent effort. And if we are good enough, Pelagius said, we can merit heaven.

Augustine's own conversion, as we have seen, occurred in a crisis over his moral state. Romans 13:13–14 showed him the way, but as he reflected later he came to believe that his transformation was not the result of his own decisions but was completely the work of God's grace in him.

53. These contrary charges are more understandable when we consider that Sabellianism developed mainly in the West and Arianism in the East. But of course, to say that either emphasis is geographically or culturally determined is unwarranted, and to base criticism on that geographical distinction is a genetic fallacy.

Augustine argued that original sin was a reality. The sin of Adam had corrupted his descendants so that they had no hope of redemption apart from the work of Christ on their behalf. This conviction led to a rethinking of Augustine's concept of free will. He did not abandon the concept of free will, but he made two important revisions. First, he turned his attention away from metaphysical freedom (*autexousion*, the ability to act without causation) to the realm of moral freedom (the ability to do good). (Certainly the latter is the more important concept within the Bible itself.) Second, Augustine provided a biblical history of moral freedom, in four stages: (1) As originally created, Adam had the freedom to sin or not to sin (*posse peccare et posse non peccare*). (2) After the fall, Adam and his descendants became spiritually dead and therefore lacked the freedom not to sin. They could not stop sinning (*non posse non peccare*). (3) Those who are in Christ regain the freedom to do what is right (*posse non peccare*), though they still commit sin. (4) In heaven, believers are confirmed in righteousness, free to do good without ever again committing sin (*non posse peccare*).

Augustine argued that original sin was a reality. The sin of Adam had corrupted his descendants so that they had no hope of redemption apart from the work of Christ on their behalf. This conviction led to a rethinking of Augustine's concept of free will.

This discussion has proved valuable in teaching Christians the implications of salvation. In the Pelagian controversy, Augustine develops a strong doctrine of grace. From this point on, Western theology, both Catholic and Protestant, is preoccupied with grace, though there is much disagreement as to how God's grace comes to human beings.[54]

Augustine's description of moral freedom is also enormously influential, but we should remember that it does not solve the metaphysical problem of free choice. Whether human beings are able to make causeless choices (*autexousion*) is a problem left unresolved by Augustine's treatment,[55] though he plainly teaches that *some* causes do indeed constrain the will, particularly our regenerate or unregenerate moral nature (as in Matt. 12:35; Luke 6:45). If Augustine is right, we *cannot* make righteous choices apart from God's grace.

Augustine's description of moral freedom is also enormously influential, but we should remember that it does not solve the metaphysical problem of free choice.

The City of God

The City of God is often considered Augustine's greatest work. He labored at it from 413 to 426. It addresses the complaint that Christianity had weakened the Roman Empire so that there was inadequate

54. Though Augustine in his later writings is a great theologian of divine grace, he does not clearly teach justification by faith alone, as Luther and Calvin were later to do. He understands the term *justificare* (Latin translation of the Greek *dikaioo*) to mean "make righteous" rather than, as the Reformers later understood it, "declare righteous." So he never made the sharp distinction between justification and sanctification characteristic of Protestant theology.

55. For some reason, in my experience, students often confuse the metaphysical problem of freedom from causation (compatibilism vs. libertarianism) with the ethical problem of moral freedom. The two are related, as I have indicated, but they are not the same.

defense against the barbarian invasions. His reply has sometimes been called the first philosophy of history.

Augustine argues that society comprises two "cities," distinguished by the allegiance of their people: the heavenly city and the earthly city. He says:

> Accordingly, two cities have been formed by two loves: the earthly by the love of self, even to the contempt of God; the heavenly by the love of God, even to the contempt of self. The former, in a word, glorifies in itself, the latter in the Lord. For the one seeks glory from men; but the greatest glory of the other is God, the witness of conscience.[56]

The distinction between the two cities is not between church and state, though we might naturally expect to find a greater percentage of God-lovers in the church than in civil government. So Augustine's view is certainly not an anticipation of Luther's "two kingdoms" doctrine, as some have recently understood it.[57] Augustine is concerned with an antithesis between those who honor God and those who hate him, which cuts through all institutions of society and all phases of culture. Among modern thinkers, Augustine anticipates most closely Abraham Kuyper, who found a principle of *palingenesis* ("regeneration") affecting all aspects of human life.[58] So the weakening of Rome was due to its paganism and unbelief, rather than to the Christians within it.

As with Kuyper, Augustine believed that on some matters Christians and unbelievers could join in a common cause. But ultimately the two cities were headed in different directions—one to the culmination of God's blessing, and the other to eternal condemnation.

Perhaps Augustine's most famous and widely read book is the Confessions, *written from 397 to 400. There is no other book quite like it in literature.*

The Confessions

Perhaps Augustine's most famous and widely read book is the *Confessions*, written from 397 to 400. There is no other book quite like it in literature. It begins as theological autobiography, perhaps the first instance of that genre, in which Augustine seeks to understand God's role in his preconversion life and eventual turning to Christ. From autobiography, he passes into an examination of morality (we recall how important morality was in his conversion) and then to an account

56. Augustine, *The City of God*, 14.28.

57. In the two-kingdoms view, God himself authorizes both a sacred and a secular kingdom and provides that only the former be governed by Scripture. In that form I have argued against the two-kingdoms theory, both in *DCL* and in *The Escondido Theology* (Lakeland, FL: Whitefield Media Publications, 2011).

58. See my discussion of Kuyper in chapter 13.

of God's sovereignty in creation. It is fascinating to read Augustine's account in which God's grace extends from his personal experience, to the moral sphere, to the whole cosmos. As a devotional text, the *Confessions* is unsurpassed, much of it a conversation between Augustine and God. Here is its famous beginning:

> *Great art thou, O Lord, and greatly to be praised; great is thy power, and thy wisdom is infinite.* And man wants to praise you, man who is only a small portion of what you have created and who goes about carrying with him his own mortality, the evidence of his own sin and evidence that *Thou resisteth the proud.* Yet still man, this small portion of creation, wants to praise you. You stimulate him to take pleasure in praising you, because you have made him for yourself, and our hearts are restless until they find peace in you.[59]

As a devotional text, the Confessions *is unsurpassed, much of it a conversation between Augustine and God.*

KEY TERMS

Apostolic Fathers	The apologists
Gnosticism	Bythos
Aeons	Docetism
Marcion	*Meta logou*
Logos spermatikos	*Via negativa*
Nameless God	*Autexousion*
Libertarian freedom	Church babies
Rule of faith	Canon
History of redemption	Biblical theology
Creation *ex nihilo*	Deification
Montanism	Prescription
Presupposition	Traducianism
Philo Judaeus	*Orthodoxastai*
Mysticism	*Hexapla*
Somatic sense	Psychical sense
Pneumatic sense	Synthesis (Origen)
Analysis (Origen)	Analogy (Origen)
Ousia	*Hypostasis*
Subordinationist	*Apokatastasis*
Left-wing Origenists	Right-wing Origenists
Arianism	*Homoousios*
Council of Nicaea	Council of Constantinople
Eternal generation	Eternal procession
Synthesis	Heresy

59. Augustine, *Confessions*, 1.1.

Reformer
Tolle lege
Privation
Crede ut intelligas
Fountain of deity
Circumcessio
Social Trinitarianism
Pelagius
Metaphysical freedom
The city of God
Palingenesis
Consolidator
Manichaeism
Theodicy
Cappadocians
Essentia
Simplicity of God
Psychological Trinitarianism
Posse peccare
Moral freedom
The earthly city

STUDY QUESTIONS

1. Summarize the opponents of the second-century apologists, and the apologists' responses to those opponents.
2. "Gnosticism and Neoplatonism represent a common way of thinking." Summarize that common way of thinking and evaluate. (Use Frame's diagram if that helps.) In what way do these views offer a "metaphysical" rather than an "ethical" view of salvation?
3. How did the apostles themselves respond to Docetism?
4. How did Justin Martyr argue that the Greek philosophers are in effect Christians? Evaluate.
5. "In my judgment, the attempt to make Christianity intellectually respectable, and therefore easy to believe, is one of the most common and deadly mistakes of Christian apologists and philosophers." Is Justin guilty of trying to make Christianity intellectually respectable? If so, how? What were the consequences?
6. Explain and evaluate Justin's views that (a) God is being, (b) God created the world by preexisting substance, (c) God brought forth subordinate beings to create the world.
7. Describe Justin's concept of free will and its background in Greek philosophy.
8. With Justin and other church fathers, people often ask, "How could he have been a genuine believer and still get so many things wrong?" Respond.
9. Why did Irenaeus describe the Gnostic mysteries as "abstruse, and portentous"? Give some examples.
10. Show how Irenaeus in effect accuses the Gnostics of transcendence-immanence dialectic.
11. How did the particular opponents of Irenaeus motivate him to comment on the nature of the biblical canon? How do they motivate him toward a redemptive-historical framework?

12. "We can see here how a number of theological conceptions reinforce one another [in Irenaeus]: the sufficiency of Scripture, the concept of God as absolute tripersonality, the immanence of God in the world, creation *ex nihilo*." Explain; evaluate.
13. "[Irenaeus] understands salvation in terms more of the incarnation than of the atonement." Explain; evaluate. Is it appropriate to speak of salvation as deification?
14. "But in Tertullian, the concept of antithesis becomes explicit, even an epistemological principle." Explain, noting the contrast between Tertullian and earlier church fathers.
15. Explain Tertullian's famous rhetorical question, "What has Jerusalem to do with Athens?" Evaluate. Did he think we should believe the Christian faith even though it is logically absurd?
16. What does Tertullian contribute to the doctrine of the Trinity? How are his formulations inadequate?
17. How does Tertullian show an understanding (in different words) of the rationalist-irrationalist dialectic in non-Christian thought?
18. How did Clement of Alexandria understand the relationship of faith to philosophy? Evaluate.
19. "Rather, [Clement] reverted to a kind of theology very similar to that of Justin." Compare Clement and Justin in some theological areas.
20. "So although Origen had a high respect for Scripture as the Word of God, [he] could make it teach a wide variety of speculative, indeed philosophical, ideas." Explain; evaluate.
21. "[Origen's] doctrine of God follows the model developed by Philo, Justin, and Clement under the influence of Gnosticism and Neoplatonism." Explain; evaluate.
22. Frame says that suspicions developed between Western and Eastern Christians about the terminology chosen in Greek and Latin for the Trinity. Explain.
23. Frame suggests a possible inconsistency in Origen's view of the Trinity. Explain.
24. Describe and evaluate Origen's distinctive teachings about creation, preexistence of souls, the work of Christ, *apokatastasis*, second fall.
25. Compare Arianism to the teaching of the Jehovah's Witnesses sect, also to Gnosticism.
26. Review the chief events of the Arian controversy.
27. "[Athanasius] held firmly to the *homoousios* doctrine, but he was able to make common cause with those who preferred not to use that term but who expressed the same doctrine in different words." Explain; evaluate.

28. According to Athanasius, what were the most important issues at stake in the Arian controversy?
29. Describe and comment on Frame's comparison between the controversy of the fourth century and that of the sixteenth. Discuss a possible extension of that parallel to our own time.
30. "I have also thought that there are important parallels between Athanasius and Irenaeus." List these and comment. Does Athanasius repeat any of Irenaeus's weaknesses as well as his strengths?
31. Is Augustine's conversion story moralistic? Discuss.
32. Describe and evaluate Augustine's response to Manichaeism and to the problem of evil. Does he try to separate the ethical from the metaphysical? If so, how? Does he succeed?
33. Compare and contrast the views of Augustine and Plato on epistemology.
34. "But we see that Augustine, much more than previous Christian teachers, seeks distinctly Christian answers to the subjects he considers." Give some examples. Evaluate.
35. How does Augustine's view of the Trinity differ from the Cappadocian? Discuss.
36. Contrast social Trinitarianism with psychological Trinitarianism. Evaluate these.
37. Describe the views of Pelagius and Augustine's response.
38. Describe the four stages of human moral freedom, according to Augustine. Why does Frame say that this "does not solve the metaphysical problem of free choice"?
39. How does Frame compare Augustine with Kuyper? Evaluate that comparison.
40. What is the main content of Augustine's *Confessions*?

BIBLIOGRAPHY: EARLY CHRISTIAN PHILOSOPHY

Print

Holmes, Michael W., ed. *The Apostolic Fathers: Greek Texts and English Translations.* Grand Rapids: Baker, 2007.

Schaff, Philip, et al., eds. *Ante-Nicene Fathers.* 10 vols. Peabody, MA: Hendrickson Publishers, 1996.

———, eds. *Nicene and Post-Nicene Fathers.* 14 vols. Peabody, MA: Hendrickson Publishers, 1996.

Online

Bible Study Tools has most of the writings of the Ante-Nicene, Nicene, and Post-Nicene Fathers. Available at http://www.biblestudytools.com/history/early-church-fathers/.

Christian Classics Ethereal Library. Site hosts almost all the significant Christian writings of this period (and later periods, too), including the writings of Boethius, Abelard, Anselm, Aquinas, and others. http://www.ccel.org.

Schaff, Philip, et al., eds. *Ante-Nicene, Nicene, and Post-Nicene Fathers.* Christian Classics Ethereal Library. Optimized for Kindle. http://www.ccel.org/node/70.

Wikisource also has many writings of thinkers discussed in this period. http://www.wikisource.org/.

READ FOR YOURSELF

Read here and there in the titles cited in the chapter and in the editions listed in the Bibliography above. I say "here and there" because some of these authors write at greater length than is edifying for modern readers. I recommend especially the following:

Martyr, Justin. *First Apology.*
———. *Dialogue with Trypho.*
———. *Hortatory Address to the Greeks* (including comments on Plato).
Irenaeus. *Against Heresies.*
Tertullian. *Prescription against Heretics.*
———. *On the Flesh of Christ.*
———. *Apologetic.*
Origen. *On First Principles.*
———. *Against Celsus.*
Athanasius. *On the Incarnation of the Word.*
Augustine. *Confessions.*
———. *The City of God.*
———. *On Christian Doctrine.*
———. *Handbook on Faith, Hope, and Love (Enchiridion).*
———. *Soliloquies.*
———. *Anti-Pelagian Writings.*

LISTEN ONLINE

Link: http://itunes.apple.com/us/course/legacy-history-philosophy/id694658914

- Original Opponents of Christianity, Second-Century Apologetics, and Irenaeus: 52:15
- Tertullian, Clement of Alexandria, Origen, and Athanasius: 1:05:08
- Saint Augustine: 31:55

OUTLINE

FAMOUS QUOTES

- **Justin Martyr:** http://en.wikiquote.org/wiki/Justin_Martyr
- **Tertullian:** http://en.wikiquote.org/wiki/Tertullian
- **Origen:** http://en.wikiquote.org/wiki/Origen
- **Athanasius:** http://en.wikiquote.org/wiki/Athanasius_of_Alexandria
- **Augustine:** http://en.wikiquote.org/wiki/Augustine_of_Hippo

4

MEDIEVAL PHILOSOPHY

FROM AUGUSTINE UNTIL the mid-seventeenth century, Christianity was the strongest influence on philosophy in the West. Representatives of Islam and Judaism also made their case. But certainly there has not been a period in Western thought when religion had as much influence on philosophy.

When Augustine was dying in A.D. 430, the Vandals attacked Hippo, where he served as Bishop. Symbolically, the Western world entered a new era, in which the Roman Empire was no longer the glue that held civilization together. The maintenance of Western culture and civilization fell to the church.

The medieval period, then, represented a parenthesis—an interlude in history—between two eras, the ancient and the modern, in which secularism dominated Western thought. It was a time of relative peace, between two wars.

But the church transformed Western learning while preserving it. What emerged from this process were various syntheses between Christian theology and ancient philosophy. Such synthesizing was not new, as we have seen from the church fathers, especially Origen. But the medieval syntheses were more elaborate and, in the later medieval thinkers such as Aquinas, Duns Scotus, and Occam, vast in their scope and complexity. Christian philosophers at this time, unlike the church fathers, were not constricted by persecution or by a living tradition of pagan philosophy. But they never separated themselves sharply from Greek philosophy.

The propriety of such synthesis was not challenged among Christians until the Protestant Reformation, which insisted on a more radically biblical theology. But as we will see, Protestantism and Catholicism alike faced, soon after that, the formidable challenge of radical secularism, the beginning of modern thought. In the modern period, as in the ancient world, Christian thought had to compete with philosophy that claimed to be nonreligious. The medieval period, then, represented a parenthesis—an interlude in history—between two eras, the ancient and the modern, in which secularism dominated Western thought. It was a time of relative peace, between two wars. But of course, without a secularist enemy, many Christians found opportunity to fight among themselves.

Boethius teaching his students

BOETHIUS (480–524)

Boethius was born in Rome. His stepfather and eventual father-in-law was Symmachus, a consul under the ruler Theodoric, who was an Ostrogoth and an Arian. In time, Boethius was also appointed consul, but he was later arrested for sedition, imprisoned, and executed.

Besides his civic duties, Boethius was a noted philosopher and theologian. He translated the *Isagoge* of the Neoplatonist Porphyry and the *Organon*[1] of Aristotle. He wrote commentaries on Aristotle's *Categories* and *On Interpretation*. Until the work of Aquinas, most medieval thinkers, like the church fathers and Augustine, were more greatly influenced by Plato than by Aristotle. But Boethius, anticipating Aquinas, is more Aristotelian in some ways, as can be seen both from his translation interests and from his concern for sharp definitions of terms. He believed that the divergent views of Plato and Aristotle could be reconciled, but he evidently did not live long enough to publish that reconciliation.

We remember Boethius today chiefly for two definitions. First, he defined God's *eternity* as "the complete, simultaneous and perfect possession of everlasting life."[2] Augustine had also reasoned that God was not only without beginning or end, but also, in some sense, beyond time itself, though Augustine admitted difficulty in expressing that concept. But Boethius in a typically succinct way taught that doctrine with its implication: finite creatures lose part of their lives as their experiences fade into the past. But God never loses any part of his life. The fact that he is above time enables him to possess it all at once. So God's eternity is related to his sovereignty and self-existence.

Second, Boethius discussed the controversy over the divine and human natures of Christ. The Council of Chalcedon (451) had said that Christ had two *natures* in one *person*. These terms had also been used in the doctrine of the Trinity, defined by the Councils of Nicaea (325) and Constantinople (381): God has one being (nature, substance) and three *persons*. But the term *person* was especially problematic. It had been used by Sabellians to describe divine "masks" or "roles," and that was certainly not what the orthodox believers wanted to say in referring to the person of Christ. Boethius seeks to clarify this, and to bring the Latin *persona* closer to the Greek *hypostasis*, by defining *person* as "the individual substance of a rational nature."[3] For the Christological controversy, this definition is

1. *Organon* is a summary name for Aristotle's six works on logic and interpretation: *Categories*, *On Interpretation*, *Prior Analytics*, *Posterior Analytics*, *Topics*, and *Sophistical Refutations*. Significantly, it was not until the later medieval period that Aristotle's more substantive works, such as *Physics*, *Metaphysics*, and *On the Heavens*, were translated and became known in the Latin-speaking world. Until Aquinas, Christian thought in the West was far more greatly influenced by Plato than by Aristotle.

2. Boethius, *The Consolation of Philosophy*, 5.

3. Boethius, *A Treatise against Eutyches and Nestorius*, 4.

helpful. But applied to the Trinity, it confuses the use of *substance* for the one being of God. If each person is a *substance*, then the whole Trinity is one substance and three substances.

Boethius's most famous work is *The Consolation of Philosophy*, written during his final imprisonment. It is a curious volume, discussing matters of philosophical and religious interest, but with no reference to Jesus, Scripture, or Christian doctrine. Some have thought that Boethius abandoned his faith at this difficult time of his life, but that is a small minority view among scholars. He does often refer to God, but in a general philosophical way rather than a specifically religious spirit.

Boethius teaches that people are essentially good, but sometimes by their free will they choose wickedness. It does not seem that Boethius was much moved by Augustine's later reflections about grace.

In form, the book is a dialogue between Boethius himself and "Lady Philosophy." One subject is the relation of evil to providence. God foreknows but does not cause evil, he says, which reveals his somewhat libertarian view of human freedom.

Further, the greatest good is within us, the life of the mind, which fortune cannot take from us. Boethius teaches that people are essentially good, but sometimes by their free will they choose wickedness. It does not seem that Boethius was much moved by Augustine's later reflections about grace.

The classical scholarship of Boethius establishes a model for later medieval thinkers. Even more significantly, and unfortunately, later thinkers learned from him that it is possible to discuss philosophical and theological subjects without any reference at all to the Christian revelation. In this way, Boethius anticipates Aquinas's doctrine of *natural reason*.

PSEUDO-DIONYSIUS (5TH–6TH C.)

Pseudo-Dionysius was heavily influenced by Neoplatonism. As with Plotinus, the supreme being, the One, is the source of all things.

Writing sometime during the late fifth and early sixth centuries[4] was a mysterious figure, probably a Syrian, who took the name of "Dionysius the Areopagite," the convert of the apostle Paul mentioned in Acts 17:34. Some have described his use of this name as a "forgery"; others have defended it as a literary device. Most scholars today are convinced that this ascription was not literally true. Nevertheless, it caused all sorts of confusion through the Middle Ages. Most thought that this writer was in fact the convert of Paul, and so they accorded him a high level of respect. He became one of the most revered thinkers in the Eastern church, and also had considerable influence in the West. Thomas Aquinas considered him a major theological authority, citing him around seventeen hundred times.

But Pseudo-Dionysius was heavily influenced by Neoplatonism. As with Plotinus, the supreme being, the One, is the source of all things. But Plotinus held that everything *emanates* from God, as light from a candle, so that all things are in effect divine. Dionysius recognized that

4. But some sources list his dates as A.D. 650–725. I have no wisdom on his chronology.

this view was not compatible with the Christian doctrine of creation, but he struggled to find language to differentiate the two ideas. He also resisted the monism of Neoplatonism, affirming that things in creation are really different from one another. It is not that the many things in the universe are merely appearances of the One (as in Plato), but that the many are attracted to God as their goal and purpose (as in Aristotle).

This is all very mysterious, of course. Dionysius is willing to say that God has the attributes of goodness, light, wisdom, and so forth. In fact, it is God who has them literally; creatures possess them in a lesser degree and therefore analogically. In the final analysis, only God's perfect wisdom is true wisdom; the perfections of men are less real, more mixed with nonbeing. Like Plato, Dionysius affirms that there are degrees of being, and that God alone "is" in the fullest sense.[5] Yet he tries to overcome the pantheistic implications of this view.

In the end, Dionysius reverts to ignorance. God is fundamentally unknown to us, a darkness. The being behind all things is not himself a thing; the being behind all concepts cannot himself be conceptualized. Of God himself, then, we have only negative knowledge: what he is not. This is the *via negativa* that we noted in the thought of Justin Martyr and Clement of Alexandria in chapter 3. But below the divine realm there is increasing plurality and therefore greater possibility of conceptualization. So Dionysius presents elaborate categories of angelic hierarchies and finite beings.

So the rational mind cannot conceptualize God, though it ascends in his direction. Our only hope of knowing him is mystical—a kind of union with God himself, in which we abandon all words and concepts about him, even negative ones. After the Gnostics and Clement of Alexandria, Pseudo-Dionysius is the writer most responsible for bringing mysticism into Christian theology. We may well question whether this is a healthy development, considering that Scripture has no hesitation in speaking positively about God's nature and attributes, and since knowledge of God in the Bible is by revelation rather than by some kind of metaphysical union.

The rational mind cannot conceptualize God, though it ascends in his direction. Our only hope of knowing him is mystical—a kind of union with God himself, in which we abandon all words and concepts about him, even negative ones.

JOHN SCOTUS ERIGENA (800–877)[6]

Erigena translated Dionysius into Latin and was himself a diligent exponent of Christian Neoplatonism. He came from Ireland, one of the few parts of Europe where ancient culture had been preserved from barbarian destruction. Erigena was one of the few scholars of the time

5. One apparent advantage of this view is that, as in Augustine, evil in some sense is unreal. It is in the category of nonbeing rather than being.

6. *Eriugena* in some sources. Both *Scotus* and *Eriugena* are geographic designations, locating him in Ireland.

in western Europe who knew Greek, and he was also a gifted philosopher and theologian. Stumpf and Fieser say that "his systematic writing set him apart as the most impressive thinker of his century."[7] In 851 he entered the court of Charles the Bald to take part in the flowering of culture known as the Carolingian Renaissance.

His chief philosophical work is *The Division of Nature. Nature,* in Erigena's title, includes both God and the creation. God is the only true reality; all else flows from him and back to him. Like Dionysius, Erigena tries but finds it difficult to distinguish his position from Neoplatonic pantheism.

Erigena was also a gifted philosopher and theologian. Stumpf and Fieser say that "his systematic writing set him apart as the most impressive thinker of his century."

The flowing of things from God and back to him occurs in four "divisions":

(1) *Nature that creates and is not created*: God himself. For Erigena as for Dionysius, our knowledge of God is primarily negative. God's attributes are, he says, *super* attributes—super-goodness, super-truth, super-wisdom—so they cannot be confused with the attributes of creatures. But like Dionysius, Erigena finds it difficult to distinguish between the biblical concept of creation and the Neoplatonic doctrine of emanation. He equates God's creation of all things with his omnipresence, the fact that "God is in all things." For him, creation is not an event at the beginning of time, as in Genesis 1, but the continuing dependence of all things on God.

Recall our discussion in chapter 1 of the biblical vs. nonbiblical concepts of *transcendence* and *immanence.* There I used the diagram in fig. 4.1.

For Erigena as for Dionysius, our knowledge of God is primarily negative. God's attributes are, he says, super *attributes—super-goodness, super-truth, super-wisdom—so they cannot be confused with the attributes of creatures.*

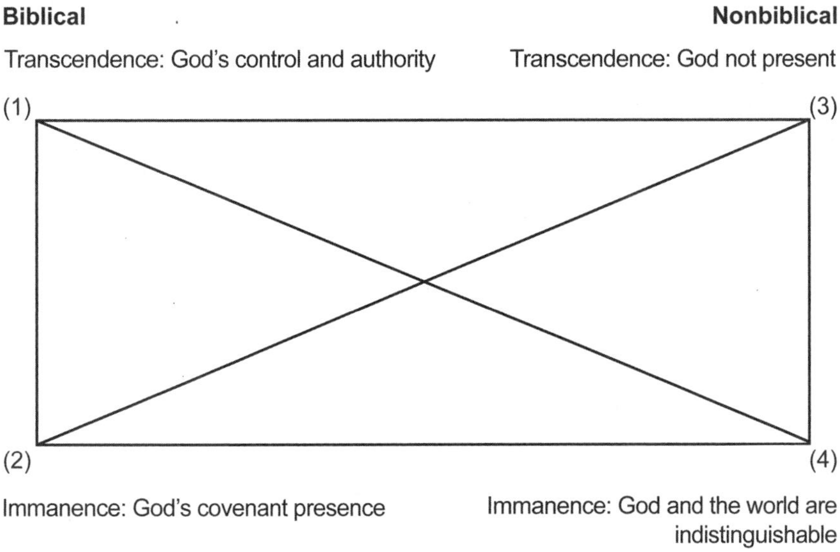

Fig. 4.1. Transcendence and Immanence in Erigena

7. Samuel Enoch Stumpf and James Fieser, *Socrates to Sartre and Beyond: A History of Philosophy* (Boston: McGraw-Hill, 2003), 148.

OUTLINE

Boethius (480–524)
Pseudo-Dionysius (5th–6th c.)
John Scotus Erigena (800–877)
Anselm of Canterbury (1033–1109)
- Faith and Reason
- *Monologium*
- *Proslogium*
- *Cur Deus Homo*

Toward Scholasticism
Thomas Aquinas (1224–74)
- Faith and Reason
- The Existence of God
- The Nature of God
- Epistemology
- Language

John Duns Scotus (1274–1308)
William of Occam (1280–1349)

Erigena, like the Gnostics and Neoplatonists, uses both the rhetoric of extreme transcendence (God is utterly beyond us and therefore unknowable) and the rhetoric of extreme immanence (God and the world are aspects of each other).

(2) *Nature that is created and creates*: the Forms of all things (as in Plato), which Erigena equates with *logos*. These are God's attributes and God's thoughts.[8] They "create" things on the earth, but again not in the sense of Genesis 1:1. They create, rather, in the sense that they are the patterns after which everything else exists, and in the sense that all other things "participate" in them.

(3) *Nature that is created and does not create*: the finite world of our experience, including angels, persons, animals, and things, existing according to the patterns of the Forms, and therefore participating in them.

(4) *Nature that neither creates nor is created*: God again, but this time as the final goal of all things.[9] Unlike Erigena's thinking about creation, this concept of consummation seems to be temporal and historical—as if the world were working its way toward a consummation in which evil will be judged, and all will be united to God.

Dionysius and Erigena are examples from the medieval period of how far thinkers can depart from the biblical worldview and still be accepted by many as great theologians. Pope Honorius III did condemn Erigena's *The Division of Nature* in 1225, but Pseudo-Dionysius, the main source of Erigena's philosophy, was accepted for centuries more as a theological authority. But neither of these men understood the biblical doctrine of creation or, therefore, the biblical Creator-creature distinction. Their negative theology substituted a divine darkness for God's clear revelation in creation and Scripture. Negative theology left them with a nonbiblical concept of divine transcendence, and their general Neoplatonic worldview left them defenseless against pantheism, the nonbiblical concept of divine immanence.

Dionysius and Erigena are examples from the medieval period of how far thinkers can depart from the biblical worldview and still be accepted by many as great theologians.

ANSELM OF CANTERBURY (1033–1109)

Although Anselm was influenced by Plato, as were all other Christian thinkers of the medieval period, he was much more orthodox

8. I disagree with the notion implicit here that God creates his own thoughts and attributes. Rather, God's attributes are what he *is*, and his thoughts are his eternal reflections. If God's attributes are created, then he must be in himself a being without attributes, a nothingness. That would be consistent with the supertranscendence of Plotinus, but it is not a biblical concept.

9. For Aristotle, there were four kinds of cause: formal, final, efficient, and material. Erigena has earlier described God as the efficient cause (2, 3) and the formal cause (2). Now he presents God as the final cause, the purpose of all things. At this stage, God no longer creates, for the work of creation is finished. There is no material cause, because for Erigena as for the Neoplatonists (and, at one level, Aristotle), matter is essentially nonbeing.

theologically than either Pseudo-Dionysius or Erigena. His thought is much closer to Augustine's than theirs, and much further removed from Neoplatonism. Indeed, Anselm is sometimes called "the second Augustine."

Faith and Reason

Anselm of Canterbury

In my view, Anselm's most interesting contribution is his description of the relation of faith and reason. As we have seen, this has been a major problem for Christian thought since the church fathers. Christian philosophers have often looked to Greek philosophy as supplying standards for rationality, while committed also to the Christian rule of faith. For many, such as Justin and Clement, faith and Greek philosophical reason work together nicely, reinforcing each other's claims. But occasionally, as with Tertullian, there is a protest against this relationship. And at least once, in the Trinitarian controversy, the church fought a major battle to liberate its doctrine from distortions that were due to Greek philosophy.

Augustine did not wrestle with the problem in a formal way, though his loyalty to the biblical teaching usually overwhelmed his genuine respect for Greek philosophy. At one point he invoked the slogan *crede ut intelligas*, "believe that you might understand."[10] Anselm, in his *Proslogium*, employs this formula in the first person: "I believe that I might understand."[11] Indeed, he considered *Fides Quaerens Intellectum* ("Faith Seeking Understanding") as a title for the book *Proslogium*, before (on advice from others) settling on the simpler one-word title.

Anselm's most interesting contribution is his description of the relation of faith and reason.

I take these formulae to be expressions of *presuppositionalism*.[12] In chapter 1, I indicated that on a biblical view of things human thought is not neutral, autonomous, or independent, but it presupposes criteria from whatever source it takes to be most authoritative. For some, the ultimate criteria of truth may come from human reason, or sense experience, or a religion or ideology. For a Christian, the ultimate standard of truth is God himself, as he is revealed in his creation and in Scripture. The patristic and medieval philosophers show in their thought loyalty to Scripture in some measure, but they sometimes contradict this loyalty by their appeals to Greek thought. To say "I believe that I might understand" makes our faith to be the basis, the presupposition, of rational inquiry. Anselm is quite explicit that his slogan is opposed to the idea of "understanding that I might believe." Faith is the foundation of knowledge, not a conclusion of it.

10. Augustine, *Treatise on the Gospel of John*, 29.6.

11. Anselm, *Proslogium*, 1.

12. I will expound this concept more fully in connection with Gordon H. Clark and Cornelius Van Til. See chapter 13.

But this reading of Anselm is difficult to defend in the light of some other things Anselm says. In the *Monologium*, for example, he announces his purpose as follows:

> that nothing in Scripture should be urged on the authority of Scripture itself, but that whatever the conclusion of independent investigation should declare to be true, should, in an unadorned style, with common proofs and with a simple argument, be briefly enforced by the cogency of reason, and plainly expounded in the light of truth.[13]

And in *Cur Deus Homo*, he expresses the purpose of the first part of his book, directed to unbelievers, as follows:

> in fine, leaving Christ out of view (as if nothing had ever been known of him), it proves, by absolute reasons, the impossibility that any man should be saved without him.[14]

In these prefaces, he seems to set aside the authority of Scripture and the revelation of Christ to argue his position by reason independent of revelation, that is, autonomously. Even in the *Proslogium*, which contains most of the evidence for my presuppositional interpretation of his epistemology, he describes the genesis of his writing thus:

> I began to ask myself whether there might be found a single argument which would require no other for its proof than itself alone; and alone would suffice to demonstrate that God truly exists, and that there is a supreme good requiring nothing else, which all other things require for their existence and well-being; and whatever we believe regarding the divine Being.[15]

Anselm looks for an argument that is self-attesting, that proves itself. What can that mean other than an argument that does not rest on Scripture or tradition—an argument based on itself, on human autonomy?

Anselm looks for an argument that is self-attesting, that proves itself. What can that mean other than an argument that does not rest on Scripture or tradition—an argument based on itself, on human autonomy?

So what is the basis of Anselm's thought? Faith in Christ revealed in the Bible, or trust in autonomous human reason? Some combination of the two? And whichever answer we give, how do we explain the data of Anselm's writing that suggest a different answer? I would not claim that Anselm is perfectly consistent in these matters, but I think

13. Anselm, *Monologium*, preface.

14. Anselm, *Cur Deus Homo*, preface.

15. Anselm, *Proslogium*, preface.

all his statements can be reconciled with a Christian presuppositional epistemology. Note first that the *Proslogium* not only contains the slogans *credo ut intelligam* and *fides quaerens intellectum*, but also contains many other indications of revelation-based thinking:

1. The whole document is written as a prayer, as reasoning in the presence of God. It is clear, then, that although the book is intended as a proof of the existence of God, Anselm has no real doubts as to God's existence. And in that prayer he *declares* that he has no doubts. So Anselm's "argument" is designed first to function in a prayer, one in which Anselm is already overwhelmed by God's reality and presence.

Anselm's "argument" is designed first to function in a prayer, one in which Anselm is already overwhelmed by God's reality and presence.

2. In the context of the prayer, Anselm repeats the *credo ut intelligam* formula, confessing his faith and love for God's truth:

   > I do not endeavor, O Lord, to penetrate your sublimity, for in no wise do I compare my understanding with that; but I long to understand in some degree your truth, which my heart believes and loves. For I do not seek to understand that I may believe, but I believe in order to understand. For this also I believe,—that unless I believed, I should not understand.[16]

3. Anselm's definition of *God*, "that than which nothing greater can be conceived" (which for Anselm is sufficient to prove God's existence), is a datum of revelation:

   > And so, Lord, do you, who do give understanding to faith, give me, so far as you knowest it to be profitable, to understand that you are as we believe; and that you are that which we believe. And indeed, *we believe that* you are a being than which nothing greater can be conceived.[17]

   The source of this definition is "that which we believe,"[18] that is, the faith of the church.

Anselm's definition of God, "that than which nothing greater can be conceived" (which for Anselm is sufficient to prove God's existence), is a datum of revelation.

4. When the monk Gaunilo replies to Anselm, he speaks "on behalf of the fool" (who says, "There is no God," Ps. 14:1). But Anselm's response begins:

16. Ibid., 1.

17. Ibid., 2 (emphasis mine).

18. Karl Barth stresses this point in his book *Anselm: Fides Quaerens Intellectum* (Richmond, VA: John Knox Press, 1960). I disagree with Barth on many matters, but on Anselm he is very illuminating.

> It was a fool against whom the argument of my Proslogium was directed. Seeing, however, that the author of these objections is by no means a fool, and is a Catholic, speaking in behalf of the fool, I think it sufficient that I answer the Catholic.[19]

Anselm tells Gaunilo that if he claims not to have the idea of God as defined in the *Proslogium*, he violates his "faith and conscience."[20] Faith and conscience, therefore, are the real ground of the argument. So it appears that the whole argument of the *Proslogium*, including Anselm's response to an objector, presupposes the truth of the Christian revelation.

5. In *Cur Deus Homo*, following the preface in which he claims to be "leaving Christ out of view," he says this:

> I HAVE been often and most earnestly requested by many, both personally and by letter, that I would hand down in writing the proofs of a certain doctrine of our faith, which I am accustomed to give to inquirers; for they say that these proofs gratify them, and are considered sufficient. This they ask, not for the sake of attaining to faith by means of reason, but that they may be gladdened by understanding and meditating on those things which they believe; and that, as far as possible, they may be always ready to convince anyone who demands of them a reason of that hope which is in us.[21]

Anselm intends all his writings to consist of rational discourse and arguments. The question is not whether Anselm appeals to reason, but rather what kind of reason Anselm appeals to.

So in the book, Anselm claims to offer proofs for his conclusions, but he disavows the idea that his readers can attain to faith by means of reason. The purpose of the book is not that, but "that they may be gladdened by understanding and meditating on those things which they believe" as well as being able to convince those who demand reasons (1 Peter 3:15). Anselm assumes, then, that his readers already believe his conclusions.

Now, to say all these things is not to cast any aspersion upon human reason. Certainly Anselm intends all his writings to consist of rational discourse and arguments. The question is not whether Anselm appeals to reason, but rather what kind of reason Anselm appeals to. Anselm was, of course, a medieval writer. Although in the *Proslogium* he addresses the atheist of Psalm 14:1, he was not writing there for an

19. Anselm, *Apologetic*, preface.
20. Ibid., 1.
21. Anselm, *Cur Deus Homo*, 1.

audience dominated by the radical unbelief of the later "Enlightenment." He was writing for an audience of Catholic Christians. He was able to assume their ability to appeal to "faith and conscience." In writing the *Proslogium*, he believed that anyone who took seriously his faith and conscience would accept Anselm's definition of God, and therefore, at least implicitly, believed in God. Or, in the language of *Cur Deus Homo*, he presented his arguments to people he assumed would already believe his conclusions, as a gladdening exercise in meditation on these truths.

For Anselm it is important for faith to seek understanding. Indeed, for him this is the very nature of theology. It is one thing to believe in God. It is another thing to understand how belief in God fits into a general Christian worldview.

Then why the appeal to "independent" reasoning (i.e., independent of Scripture) in his books? Because for Anselm it is important for faith to seek understanding. Indeed, for him this is the very nature of theology. It is one thing to believe in God. It is another thing to understand how belief in God fits into a general Christian worldview.

In *Cur Deus Homo*, note the question Boso asks to begin the dialogue in chapter 2:

> for what necessity and cause God, who is omnipotent, should have assumed the littleness and weakness of human nature for the sake of its renewal?

Boso does not ask this question out of a general unbelief. He believes in God, believes that God is omnipotent, and believes in the incarnation. But he does not understand *why* God became incarnate in Christ. This is a theological question, and Anselm answers it theologically. He answers it using concepts in Scripture that he and Boso both believe. In subsequent chapters, Anselm appeals to the nature of sin, of Satan, of angels, of eternal life and death. These are all biblical concepts.[22] So when Anselm "leav[es] Christ out of view," he does not leave the whole biblical revelation out of view.

Think of biblical doctrine as a series of puzzle-pieces: creation, divine love, Christ's two natures, sanctification, the church, and so on. Christians presume that they all fit together neatly, at least in the mind of God.

We can imagine this as a theological exercise: Think of biblical doctrine as a series of puzzle-pieces: creation, divine love, Christ's two natures, sanctification, the church, and so on. Christians presume that they all fit together neatly, at least in the mind of God. But now let us remove one of these pieces, the incarnation, and see whether we can reconstruct its shape from consideration of the other pieces. Can we show from a biblical understanding of sin, divine justice, divine mercy, Jesus' two natures, and so forth why it was necessary for him

22. Anselm also refers to specific Bible verses. For example, chapter 9 begins, "*How it was of his own accord that he died, and what this means: 'he was made obedient even unto death;' and: 'for which cause God has highly exalted him;' and: 'I came not to do my own will;' and: 'he spared not his own Son;' and: 'not as I will, but as you will.'*" Here Anselm assumes that these Bible passages are authoritative and that one's view of the incarnation must be consistent with them.

to be incarnated? *Cur Deus Homo* intends to give the answer. That is the nature of Anselm's "reasoning." In a sense, this involves "leaving Christ [or at least his incarnation] out of view." But that means only that he is temporarily removing one piece from the puzzle, in order to better describe its coherence with the other pieces. It does not involve any departure from commitment to the Christian faith, its revelation, or its worldview. So we can see that there is no contradiction between Anselm's commitment to "faith seeking understanding" and his method of offering rational arguments for individual parts of the Christian system of truth.

Similarly, in the preface to the *Monologium*, when Anselm proposes that "nothing in Scripture should be urged on the authority of Scripture itself," he is not denying the self-attestation of Scripture as a doctrine. Rather, he is indicating his method in this particular book: that he will argue his conclusions not by citing Scripture texts, but by expounding in extrabiblical language the rationale of the biblical doctrines, a rationale consistent with and implicit in the biblical worldview that Anselm believes.

So in the phrase "faith seeking understanding," Anselm sees "faith" as something objectively given to Christians by revelation. That faith is assumed in any exercise of Christian reasoning. The arguments he uses, though they might depart from biblical language, and though they might "set aside" some element of biblical teaching for the sake of argument, are themselves often taken from Scripture and in any case must be made consistent with it.

In the phrase "faith seeking understanding," Anselm sees "faith" as something objectively given to Christians by revelation. That faith is assumed in any exercise of Christian reasoning.

Monologium

Having explored Anselm's view of faith and reason, we should also look at the content of his major books. The *Monologium* presents arguments for the existence and nature of God. These are similar to arguments later and more famously propounded by Thomas Aquinas, and when I discuss Aquinas I will treat them in more detail.

Anselm's arguments deal with causality (God as the First Cause, the cause of all causes) and levels of reality. In the second area, Anselm deals with both levels or degrees of qualities (goodness, greatness) and levels of being (plants, animals, people). In both areas there is a hierarchy, and Anselm argues that the hierarchy implies a highest member. The roots of his argument from causality can be found in Aristotle and Augustine. The roots of his argument from degrees of reality can be found in Plato. Plato argued that goods in various degrees imply a highest good that serves as their cause and criterion. Plato also thought that being itself is a matter of degree, so that lesser beings imply a highest being, a Form of being in which the lower beings participate.

Anselm, of course, does not believe that the First Cause is an abstract form (as Aristotle) or that the highest being is an abstract Form (as Plato). He believes, rather, that the God of the Bible is both the First Cause and the highest being. So he adds arguments to show that the true God has attributes and qualities beyond those of Aristotle's Prime Mover and Plato's Form of the Good. He even develops arguments for the Trinitarian character of God, drawing on Augustine.

Proslogium

Anselm's best-known contribution to philosophy is the argument for the existence of God presented in the *Proslogium*. This argument was called the *ontological argument* by Immanuel Kant, but Anselm did not use any particular name for it. In the preface, he recalls his dissatisfaction with the complexity of arguments in the *Monologium*, and reports:

Anselm's best-known contribution to philosophy is the argument for the existence of God presented in the Proslogium. *This argument was called the* ontological argument *by Immanuel Kant, but Anselm did not use any particular name for it.*

> I began to ask myself whether there might be found a single argument which would require no other for its proof than itself alone; and alone would suffice to demonstrate that God truly exists, and that there is a supreme good requiring nothing else, which all other things require for their existence and well-being; and whatever we believe regarding the divine Being.[23]

The answer to this inquiry came to Anselm almost as a revelation: "it began to force itself upon me, with a kind of importunity."[24]

In chapter 1, he confesses his sins and asks for a small measure of illumination, for he believes that he might understand, not the reverse. In chapter 2, he notes that God is "that than which nothing greater can be conceived," a title, as we noted earlier, given by the Christian revelation. Now, the fool who says that "there is no God" in Psalm 14:1 does not believe that such a being exists. But at least he has a *concept* of this being "in his understanding." The problem is that the fool does not think this being exists in reality. But that position, says Anselm, is impossible:

Now, the fool who says that "there is no God" in Psalm 14:1 does not believe that such a being exists. But at least he has a concept of this being "in his understanding." The problem is that the fool does not think this being exists in reality. But that position, says Anselm, is impossible.

> Therefore, if that, than which nothing greater can be conceived, exists in the understanding alone, the very being, than which nothing greater can be conceived, is one, than which a greater can be conceived. But obviously this is impossible. Hence, there is no doubt that there exists a being, than which nothing greater can be conceived, and it exists both in the understanding and in reality.[25]

23. Anselm, *Proslogium*, preface.
24. Ibid.
25. Ibid., 2.

In chapter 3, he presents a further conclusion: Not only does God exist, but he cannot be conceived not to exist. And a being who cannot be conceived not to exist is greater than one who can be conceived not to exist. So God must be like that: a being who not only exists, but cannot be conceived not to exist. In philosophy, such a being is called a *necessary being*, as distinguished from a *contingent being*. A necessary being is one that *must* exist, rather than merely happening to exist. So a necessary being is one who depends only on himself or itself; a contingent being depends on something other than himself or itself.

In chapter 4, Anselm deals with an objection, and then in subsequent chapters he expounds the nature of God. His basic argument is that God is "whatever it is better to be than not to be."[26] So God must be self-existent, he creates all things from nothing,[27] he is sensible, compassionate, passionless,[28] omnipotent,[29] and so on.

Attached to the *Proslogium*, as we saw earlier, is an essay by the first critic of the argument, the monk Gaunilo, together with Anselm's *Apologetic* in answer to his critic. Gaunilo first expresses doubts about whether we can have in our minds the idea of one than which no greater can be conceived. To that argument, Anselm replies that Gaunilo (being a Catholic, not a fool) himself has such a concept, since that concept is part of the Christian faith.

Gaunilo also argues that if Anselm's argument is true, one could as easily prove a perfect anything—say a perfect island. We could define a perfect island as one than which no greater can be conceived, and that island must exist. Anselm's reply is that an island, no matter how perfect, is not a being than which no greater can be conceived. Only one being fits that definition, namely, God.

A being who cannot be conceived not to exist is greater than one who can be conceived not to exist. So God must be like that: a being who not only exists, but cannot be conceived not to exist.

But perhaps Gaunilo's argument is stronger than Anselm is willing to grant. For when he suggests that you could prove the existence of anything with Anselm's argument, he is really suggesting that there is something wrong with the whole procedure of reasoning from a concept to reality. To say that Anselm's argument could prove the existence of a perfect island, a perfect hamburger, or a perfect political system is to say that this procedure is never right, whatever the subject matter. One cannot reason from a mental concept of a perfect something to its real existence.

Plato, of course, would have disagreed. For him, it is rationally legitimate to reason from perfections in our concepts to the real existence

26. Ibid., 5.
27. Ibid.
28. Ibid., 6. He adds, however, that though God is passionless, he is "not improperly said in some sort to feel."
29. Ibid., 7.

of perfect Forms. For that reason, scholars have often commented that Anselm's proof shows Platonic influence. But for Plato, the argument from concept to reality works for many things, such as goodness, humanity, courage, and wisdom, and not for a personal absolute such as the Christian God.

Certainly we cannot rule out in a general way arguments that reason from our concepts to reality. In one sense, we know reality only through our concepts. To say that we can *never* reason from concept to reality is to say that we cannot trust our concepts to be reliable guides to truth. That is to say that we cannot trust our own minds to ascertain the truth.

Certainly we cannot rule out in a general way arguments that reason from our concepts to reality. In one sense, we know reality only through our concepts.

One particularly important argument from concept to reality is the argument that concepts such as *good*, *bad*, *perfect*, and *imperfect* presuppose standards of valuation. If those standards are to be valid, they must be objective, not limited to an individual human subjectivity. The highest standard of perfection, in other words, must really exist. In that sense, existence is a perfection and perfection is an existing reality. That is what we can learn from Anselm's argument.[30]

Anselm's argument has been subjected to many other criticisms throughout history, but to the surprise of many it has also had defenders in every age, including the present. After Gaunilo, Aquinas, Hume, Kant, Bertrand Russell, Michael Martin, and many others rejected the proof. But Descartes, Spinoza, Leibniz, Hegel, Whitehead, Hartshorne, Norman Malcolm, and Alvin Plantinga accepted various forms of it. Those who look at the argument with skepticism often find it difficult to take seriously. But even if it is seriously wrong, showing what is wrong with it is terribly difficult. As is typical of philosophical arguments, each attempt to refute the argument has attracted its own refuters. Let us consider some of these debates.

Expressed in a tidy syllogism, Anselm's argument looks like this: God has all perfections. Existence is a perfection. Therefore, God exists.

Expressed in a tidy syllogism, Anselm's argument looks like this:

God has all perfections.
Existence is a perfection.
Therefore, God exists.

Kant thought it was illegitimate to treat existence as a perfection. In his view, it was not even a proper predicate. That seems to mean that for Kant, existence doesn't "add" anything to a concept: my concept of an existent apple is no different from my concept of a nonexistent apple.

30. And also from the arguments from gradation found in the *Monologium*. Another parallel to the *Proslogium* argument is the "moral argument" developed by later philosophers and theologians, also based on gradations of value, but in this case moral value. For my attempt, see *AJCB*, 95–123.

But I think that in one sense there is certainly a difference. Seabiscuit was an existent horse; Silver, the Lone Ranger's steed, was not, most likely. Among the differences between Seabiscuit and Silver, one of them is existence. And that difference is evident both in concept and in the world.

In my view, a stronger critique will grant that existence is a proper predicate but will question whether it is a perfection. A Buddhist, for example, might well believe that existence is an evil. Since in Buddhism life is suffering, it is actually better not to exist than to exist. On that basis, Anselm's argument would prove the *nonexistence* of God: God has all perfections; nonexistence is a perfection; therefore, God does not exist.[31]

As we can see, the concept *perfection* (*greatness* in Anselm) is problematic. Anselm's belief that existence is a perfection is understandable in a Christian context, for in Genesis 1:31 God declared all creation, all existing things, to be good. Anselm, as we have seen, presupposes the Christian revelation and therefore presupposes a Christian scale of perfection. Others, such as Buddhists, do not share Anselm's presupposition.

Anselm's belief that existence is a perfection is understandable in a Christian context, for in Genesis 1:31 God declared all creation, all existing things, to be good. Anselm, as we have seen, presupposes the Christian revelation and therefore presupposes a Christian scale of perfection.

And there have been other disagreements about what constitutes a perfect being. Charles Hartshorne believes that a perfect being would not be changeless, as Anselm's, but would rather change to adjust to circumstances outside himself.[32] That view of God, of course, presupposes a theology very different from Anselm's. So evidently Anselm's argument presupposes a particular view of what is and is not perfect. Someone with a different presupposition will not find the argument persuasive. Or, like Hartshorne, he might reconstruct the argument to prove the existence of a god very different from that of Anselm.

So the history of criticism validates my earlier assessment, that Anselm's argument presupposes the worldview of the Christian revelation.

Cur Deus Homo

The third book of Anselm that we will consider asks why God became man in Christ. His answer is, essentially, that Christ came to save human beings from sin. He develops this answer in terms of medieval feudalism: Sin is an offense to God's "honor." God will not be reconciled unless man makes "satisfaction," paying the debt he owes.

31. Cf. J. N. Findlay et al., "Can God's Existence Be Disproved?" in *New Essays in Philosophical Theology*, ed. Antony Flew and Alasdair C. MacIntyre (London: SCM Press, 1955), 47–75.

32. Charles Hartshorne, "The Formal Validity and Real Significance of the Ontological Argument," *Philosophical Review* 53 (May 1944): 225–45. Cf. my discussion of process theology in chapter 11.

But to offend God's honor is a crime of infinite weight, one that man cannot possibly remedy.

The only remedy is for God the Son to come into the world as a man and to give his life. Now, the sinless Jesus did not himself owe this debt to God. So when he gave his life, he *exceeded* what he owed, doing something far beyond what was required. He merits a reward, therefore, and he passes that reward on to mankind.

Anselm's theory of the atonement set aside the theory held by Origen and Gregory of Nyssa, that Christ's atonement paid a ransom to the devil and thus freed mankind from his grip. Anselm argued that the devil had no claim on mankind; the controversy was between man and God himself. By connecting the atonement directly to man's rebellion against God, Anselm laid the foundation of almost all future thinking on the subject in the Western church.

Anselm argued that the devil had no claim on mankind; the controversy was between man and God himself. By connecting the atonement directly to man's rebellion against God, Anselm laid the foundation of almost all future thinking on the subject in the Western church.

Still, some Reformed and evangelical thinkers have found Anselm's formulation inadequate. Among Louis Berkhof's criticisms, the following has been the most influential:

> 2. The theory really has no place for the idea that Christ by suffering endured the *penalty* of sin, and that his suffering was strictly vicarious. The death of Christ is merely a tribute offered voluntarily to the honor of the Father. It constitutes a supererogatory merit, compensating for the demerits of others; and this is really the Roman Catholic doctrine of penance applied to the work of Christ.[33]

It is true that Anselm does not emphasize the law-court model that governs Reformation thinking about the atonement. But he clearly equates dishonor to God with sin:

It is true that Anselm does not emphasize the law-court model that governs Reformation thinking about the atonement. But he clearly equates dishonor to God with sin.

> This is the debt which man and angel owe to God, and no one who pays this debt commits sin; but every one who does not pay it sins. This is justice, or uprightness of will, which makes a being just or upright in heart, that is, in will; and this is the sole and complete debt of honor which we owe to God, and which God requires of us. For it is such a will only, when it can be exercised, that does works pleasing to God; and when this will cannot be exercised, it is pleasing of itself alone, since without it no work is acceptable. He who does not render this honor which is due to God, robs God of his own and dishonors him; and this is sin.[34]

33. Louis Berkhof, *Systematic Theology* (London: Banner of Truth, 1949), 386.
34. Anselm, *Cur Deus Homo*, 1.11.

In chapter 12, then, Anselm considers "whether it were proper for God to put away sins by compassion alone, without any payment of debt." The answer is no, because

> to remit sin in this manner is nothing else than not to punish; and since it is not right to cancel sin without compensation or punishment; if it be not punished, then is it passed by undischarged.

So Anselm is certainly thinking in terms of sin and punishment. In chapter 14, he says that "the honor of God exists in the punishment of the wicked." In chapter 15, he argues that God does not allow "his honor to be violated even in the least degree." In subsequent chapters, he indicates that man is not capable of repairing this breach by anything he does.

So although he does not say explicitly that "Jesus paid the penalty that we deserved," the idea of penal substitution is certainly implicit in his formulations. I wish he had put that more pointedly. On the other hand, modern evangelicals also need to stress more explicitly something that Anselm emphasized: The reason why transgression of God's law is so enormously wrong is that it dishonors God himself. Ultimately, we deal not with a law in the abstract, but with the absolute-personal God. Our problem is the breakdown of a relationship. It is for that reason that transgression of his law is such an evil and that the penalty for sin can be only death. And it is for that reason that the Son of God had to die in our place.

The reason why transgression of God's law is so enormously wrong is that it dishonors God himself. Ultimately, we deal not with a law in the abstract, but with the absolute-personal God. Our problem is the breakdown of a relationship.

TOWARD SCHOLASTICISM

We saw in the previous chapter and in this one a tendency among Christian writers to seek academic respectability, primarily by their expertise in Greek philosophy. Anselm is one of the least guilty in this respect, particularly as indicated by his resolve to base all his reasoning on the foundation of Christian faith. But Boethius, and much more Dionysius and Erigena, illustrates the danger of ignoring or compromising biblical teaching in the pursuit of philosophical enlightenment.

Peter Leithart explains that in the later Middle Ages, a division appeared in the church between two groups of theologians: those of monastic schools and those of cathedral schools. He says:

> The social differences between the monkish theologian and the school theologian could hardly be starker: Monks were rooted to a single place, while the masters of the schools were mobile, the original of the rootless Western intellectuals who later populated Russian novels. Monks were bound to

> obedience; masters made a living in a competitive environment, which encouraged innovation in order to win students. Monks were scholars of Scripture and used rhetoric and grammar as means for making Scripture plain; masters employed dialectic (logic) to resolve "questions." Monks sought union with God through meditation and a kind of unbounded free association on the text; masters pursued propositional truth through the application of logic and the concoction of disputations, and attempted to summarize Christian truth and organize it in systematic ways.[35]

Scholasticism is "school theology." It gathers together all the authorities of past ages, compares them to determine their consistency with one another, and where there is inconsistency seeks to determine who is right. The authorities included the church fathers, especially Augustine, but also the Greek philosophers: Plato, followers of Neoplatonism, and eventually Aristotle. Recall that Boethius had translated the logical works of Aristotle, the *Organon*. But in the late Middle Ages, the church also gained access to Aristotle's metaphysical and scientific writings.

Scholasticism is "school theology." It gathers together all the authorities of past ages, compares them to determine their consistency with one another, and where there is inconsistency seeks to determine who is right.

These were first available through Arabic translations and interpretations, for this period was also the high point of Muslim academic scholarship. **Avicenna** (980–1037), a Persian scholar, developed a composite of Aristotelian philosophy with Qur'anic theology. For him, as for Aristotle and Origen, creation is an eternal act of God, not an event at the beginning of time (as both Genesis and the Qur'an present it). As in Neoplatonism, Avicenna describes the world as a series of emanations into a hierarchy of beings.

Al Ghazali (1058–1111), also Persian, opposed this attempt to synthesize Islam with philosophy. He argues against the questionable opinions of Avicenna noted in the previous paragraph and rejects even the Aristotelian concepts of causality. For him, God is the only causal agent. He teaches that reason has a role in combating heretical positions, but that it should not be used to develop metaphysical ideas independent of revelation. Indeed, the highest knowledge of God is by mystical union, not reason. In this belief, Al Ghazali invokes the Sufi mystical tradition of Islam, but also the Neoplatonism that entered Christian theology through writers such as Dionysius and Erigena.

Al Ghazali invokes the Sufi mystical tradition of Islam, but also the Neoplatonism that entered Christian theology through writers such as Dionysius and Erigena.

35. Peter J. Leithart, "Medieval Theology and the Roots of Modernity," in *Revolutions in Worldview: Understanding the Flow of Western Thought*, ed. W. Andrew Hoffecker (Phillipsburg, NJ: P&R Publishing, 2007), 147. In a footnote, he adds that Anselm of Canterbury was *sui generis*: he reasons in meditation and prayer, but rarely cites Scripture at all. I agree, but I would add that although Anselm does not *quote* Scripture extensively, his main purpose is to expound and defend the doctrines of Scripture that constitute the faith Christians believe. His concern is pastoral and devotional rather than academic.

Peter Abelard

Averroes (1126–98), a Spaniard, distinguished between three kinds of thinkers: (1) the common people, who are capable of understanding the literal sense of the Qur'an and its moral exhortation, (2) theologians, who use reason to systematize their theology, but are not able to formulate true demonstrations, and (3) philosophers, who are able to use reason alone to demonstrate metaphysical truth. Each group is to be respected, but those in lower-numbered groups have no right to criticize those in a higher class of thinkers. Averroes, therefore, encourages the most sophisticated level of philosophical inquiry. But he was accused of holding a "theory of twofold truth," namely, that an idea can be true in one discipline, false in another. For example, it is true in theology, but false in philosophy, to say that there is a hell.

Averroes was closer to Avicenna than to Al Ghazali. It is not always easy to determine his views, but he combines Aristotle's view of God as the First Cause of the world with a quasi-Neoplatonic view of the world as a series of emanations from God. Although human beings are united in a single "active intellect" identified with God, there seems to be no such thing as individual immortality.

Moses Maimonides (1135–1204) adapted the newly available Aristotelian writings to the Jewish community, as the thinkers above had done for the Muslims. He, too, wrestles with the relation between philosophy and faith. He believes that there is no basic conflict between these, but that they deal with somewhat different topics and forms of experience. He believes that philosophy can demonstrate the existence of God, but cannot tell us what God is like. God's creation of the world, for example, is a doctrine of faith. Maimonides tries to show that Aristotle's arguments for the eternity of the world are respectable, but not strong enough to overturn the scriptural doctrine. He agrees with Averroes that after death our minds return to the universal "active intellect." Stumpf and Fieser comment, "If this is a doctrine of immortality, then it is one in which the unique characteristics of each individual have been greatly diminished."[36]

In the Christian community, one of the most influential writers in the movement toward scholasticism was Peter Abelard (1079–1142). Leithart says:

> For my purposes, Abelard is of interest for his contribution to the separation of theology and philosophy and the development of new ways of pursuing theology. Abelard was one of the early thinkers to treat "theology" as a "scientific" pursuit. He established the "summary" (*summa*) as the unit of theology,

36. Stumpf and Fieser, *Socrates to Sartre and Beyond*, 162.

and he organized theology around topics, rather than following the contours of the biblical text.

Anselm, following Augustine, had said that his theology was a matter of "faith seeking understanding." In his autobiography, Abelard says that his students demanded from him theology in precisely the opposite direction, for one cannot believe what he does not first understand. Though Abelard coyly puts the demand for rational theology in the mouths of his students, it is clearly his own theological agenda.[37]

In his autobiography, Abelard says that his students demanded from him theology in precisely the opposite direction, for one cannot believe what he does not first understand.

Abelard developed theology as a way of resolving questions, both about the text of Scripture and emerging from philosophical reflection. One of his writings is called *Sic et Non*, "Yes and No," in which he poses 185 questions and presents positive and negative answers to these questions from the church fathers. The first five questions are:

1. Must human faith be completed by reason, or not?
2. Does faith deal only with unseen things, or not?
3. Is there any knowledge of things unseen, or not?
4. May one believe only in God alone, or not?
5. Is God a single unitary being, or not?

The prologue commends Aristotle as "the most clear-sighted of all the philosophers," and notes that Aristotle "was desirous above all things else to arouse this questioning spirit."

Abelard's *Introduction to Theology* was condemned at the Council of Sens in 1140, mainly because of its speculative discussion of the doctrine of the Trinity. Among other descriptions, Abelard identifies the Father as Goodness, the Son as his Ideas (*logos*), and the Spirit as the world soul.

Abelard [taught that] the death of Jesus is God's way of winning our affections by an example of reconciling love. This has been called the moral-influence theory *of the atonement and in modern times has been the common view of many theological liberals.*

He is also known for a doctrine of the atonement very different from that of Anselm of Canterbury: The death of Jesus is God's way of winning our affections by an example of reconciling love. This has been called the *moral-influence theory* of the atonement and in modern times has been the common view of many theological liberals. But Abelard never adequately answered the question of how Jesus' death can be a moral influence if it is not a sacrifice for sin. Without atoning significance, Jesus' death can be understood only as a tragedy, or even a suicide. To say that such an act is a moral example is to call believers to take their own lives, a principle far removed from biblical morality.

After Abelard, many others followed his method of contrasting opinions (called *sentences*) of various authorities on theological questions. The four books of *Sentences* by **Peter Lombard** (1095–1161) became a

37. Leithart, "Medieval Theology," 153.

core curriculum for theology, and many (including Thomas Aquinas) wrote commentaries on them.

THOMAS AQUINAS (1224–74)

By consensus, however, it is the work of Aquinas himself that is the culmination of medieval theology. During his remarkably short life, he put together a huge collection of closely reasoned writings, constituting a brilliant synthesis of Christian theology with Aristotelian and Neoplatonic philosophy. Named *doctor of the church*, he has been recognized as the leading philosopher of Roman Catholicism and one of the three or four most influential philosophers of all time.

Faith and Reason

We have seen that Christian thinkers have often been concerned about the relation of faith to reason. Anselm used Augustine's formula, "I believe that I might understand." But Abelard quoted favorably the desire of his students to understand that they might believe. The question becomes even more difficult when *reason* is correlated with non-Christian philosophy in some way.

Aquinas, here as in other areas, seeks to reconcile various impulses of past thinkers. For him, both faith and reason are important for human knowledge. But it is important that we distinguish them clearly and identify the proper sphere in which each one functions.

Aquinas's greatest work, the unfinished *Summa Theologica*, begins with a discussion of "The Nature and Domain of Sacred Doctrine." The First Article deals with the question "whether, besides the philosophical disciplines, any further doctrine is required." Aquinas identifies the "philosophical disciplines" as those "investigated by human reason." He answers yes, we also need a doctrine given by divine revelation.

Aquinas defines philosophy as a discipline in which human reason is sufficient. Sacred doctrine is the discipline in which we receive the truth by revelation and faith.

First, man is directed to God "as an end that surpasses the grasp of his reason." Even though God surpasses reason, we need to know him. Therefore, the knowledge comes by revelation. Further, there are some truths about God that reason can investigate (and thus are the subject matter of philosophy). But knowing them by reason requires work, maturity, and intelligence. Not everyone is able to gain such knowledge, so God provides some of this knowledge, the most fundamental parts of it, by revelation.

In summary, then, Aquinas defines *philosophy* as a discipline in which human reason is sufficient. Sacred doctrine is the discipline in which we receive the truth by revelation and faith.[38] We would be inclined, then, to equate sacred doctrine with theology. But in 1.1.R Obj. 2, he distinguishes a kind of "theology" that is "part of philosophy" and

38. Aquinas, *Summa Theologica*, 1.1.1 R Obj. 1.

another kind that is "included in sacred doctrine." Here, he evidently uses the etymological definition of *theology*, "the study of God."

For Aquinas, then, there is some overlap between philosophy and theology, because these both deal with God. But is there overlap between philosophy and sacred doctrine? Aquinas does not suggest in this context that reason has a role to play in sacred doctrine, or that faith has a role to play in philosophy.

Thomas Aquinas

So many have concluded, I think rightly, that Aquinas here differentiates two very distinct realms of study: not philosophy and theology, but philosophy and sacred doctrine. Philosophy is governed by human reason, sacred doctrine by faith. Sacred doctrine, but not philosophy, is based on revelation. For Aquinas, however, revelation does have a veto power over philosophy. For example, Aquinas rejects Aristotle's proof that the world is eternal, because he believes it inconsistent with the biblical doctrine of creation. So when philosophy contradicts revelation, revelation must prevail, even in philosophical matters. Thus, there is some small measure of overlap between sacred doctrine and philosophy. But for the most part, they operate according to different authorities.

The two disciplines have different subject matters. Sacred doctrine deals with "man's salvation."[39] Presumably, then, philosophy deals with other subjects. Aquinas describes the scope of philosophy, or *natural reason*, to include the affairs of this life. For someone satisfied to learn about this world, make a living, marry, raise children, and die, natural reason is sufficient. But one who seeks to know God and thereby to find forgiveness of sins and eternal life must also attend to sacred doctrine.

Philosophy is governed by human reason, sacred doctrine by faith. Sacred doctrine, but not philosophy, is based on revelation. For Aquinas, however, revelation does have a veto power over philosophy.

Here we find an outline of the distinction between *nature* and *grace* found through the writings of Aquinas and other medieval thinkers.

Grace: revelation—faith—Scripture—eternal life—salvation—the church

---

Nature: natural reason (philosophy)—Aristotle—form and matter—this world—the state[40]

In chapter 2, I mentioned Herman Dooyeweerd's view that Greek religion and philosophy are dominated by a "form-matter scheme."

39. Ibid., 1.1.1.

40. I will not say much about the distinction between church and state here, except to mention that in my view the nature-grace distinction underlies the sharp distinction found in Lutheran and other Protestant theology between the "two kingdoms," the secular and the sacred, the realm of the common and the realm of the holy. For my critique of this distinction, see my *DCL* and *The Escondido Theology* (Lakeland, FL: Whitefield Media Publications, 2011).

Dooyeweerd regards medieval thought, particularly that of Aquinas, as dominated by a "nature-grace scheme." What that second scheme does is to take the Greek form-matter distinction and place that into the lower level, supplementing it with an upper level described by the term *grace*. So at the lower level, the medieval Christian was able to take Greek thought pretty much as it was, regarding revelation as a supplement to natural reason, dealing with a subject matter beyond the reach of natural reason. On this view, Aristotle is generally sufficient to teach us about earthly matters. But to learn of heaven, we need a word from God.

Aquinas himself, however, understands that these two realms do not fit seamlessly together. At times the upper level must veto ideas generated at the lower level. And I, like Dooyeweerd, believe that the conflict between the two levels, defined by medieval theology, is much more extensive than Aquinas imagines. The very supposition that these realms are independent is subversive of both.

According to Scripture, God's revelation is not needed for only one area of human life and knowledge. It is, rather, needed for all areas of life. God's revelation in Scripture itself does not tell us only how to obtain eternal life. It also instructs us about marriage, finances, society, music, art, scholarship—about everything human. Indeed, matters of this life cannot be strictly separated from matters of the next. For the Bible calls on us to live in this world with an eye to eternity. Everything we do should be done to the glory of God (1 Cor. 10:31).

According to Scripture, God's revelation is not needed for only one area of human life and knowledge. It is, rather, needed for all areas of life.

Aquinas begins his early work, *On Being and Essence*, by quoting Aristotle's *On the Heavens*: "a small error in the beginning grows enormous at the end." The nature-grace distinction appears to be a small matter. We do often see Scripture as a supplement to our other forms of knowledge. It is hard to see anything wrong with that.

But as Aquinas and his successors develop this notion, it becomes an enormous problem. For the realm of "nature" is, for Aquinas, essentially a realm in which autonomous reason (the reason that Aristotle advocated) is relatively unhindered. (Relatively, because it is subject to the occasional veto power of revelation.) And since Aquinas even develops his doctrine of God out of natural reason (following Aristotle's discussion of the Prime Mover), he is not able to insulate his theology, even his discipline of "sacred doctrine," from the effects of would-be autonomous thought.

The Existence of God

Chapter 2 of Aquinas's *Summa Theologica* deals with the existence of God. He first asks whether the existence of God is "self-evident," that is, known without evidence or argument. He concludes that God's existence is self-evident to one who knows the essence and existence of God, but not to us, since "we do not know the essence of God."[41] On this ground, Aquinas in effect rejects Anselm's proof, which is a proof from God's essence (definition) to his existence.

But we can know God through other means. His existence "needs to be demonstrated by things that are more known to us, though less known in their nature—namely, by His effects."[42] Moving, then, to proofs from God's effects, he says, "The existence of God can be proved in five ways."[43] Let us look at these briefly.

We can know God through other means. His existence "needs to be demonstrated by things that are more known to us, though less known in their nature—namely, by His effects."

1. *The Argument from Motion*: Aquinas argues that everything in motion must be moved by something else.[44] But the sequence of motion and movers cannot go back to infinity, "because then there would be no first mover, and, consequently, no other mover, seeing that subsequent movers move only inasmuch as they are moved by the first mover."[45] Perhaps Aquinas is thinking this way: Let's say that C moves B, which in turn moves A. In this sequence, B is not in the fullest sense the *mover* of A, because B is not the complete explanation for the movement of A. Nor is C the mover of A, unless it is truly the *first* in the sequence. But if the sequence goes back to infinity (to D, E, F, without end), then there is no first motion and therefore there is no complete explanation for A's movement. A does not really have a mover. But there must be a mover, and that means that there must be a *first* mover, "moved by no other; and this everyone understands to be God."[46]

Aquinas argues that everything in motion must be moved by something else. But the sequence of motion and movers cannot go back to infinity, "because then there would be no first mover, and, consequently, no other mover, seeing that subsequent movers move only inasmuch as they are moved by the first mover."

2. *The Argument from Efficient Cause*: This argument merely substitutes *efficient cause*[47] for *motion* in argument 1. "Therefore," says Aquinas, "it is necessary to admit a first efficient cause, to which everyone gives the name of God."[48]

41. Aquinas, *Summa Theologica*, 1.2.1, Answer.

42. Ibid.

43. Ibid., 1.2.3, Answer. There are many proofs of God's existence in Aquinas's other writings, such as the *Summa contra Gentiles*. But these five proofs—the *five ways*—have become famous for their conciseness and clarity.

44. He explains that this statement is based on Aristotle's analysis of motion in terms of potentiality and actuality. I won't go into this argument except to say that it is not generally accepted among modern thinkers. Aquinas assumes that rest is normal and that motion requires explanation. In modern physics, motion is normal, and rest (if there is any such thing) is what requires explanation.

45. Aquinas, *Summa Theologica*, 1.2.3, Answer.

46. Ibid. Of course, the God of the Bible is more than just a "first mover." Aquinas knew that. He was not using this argument to prove everything there is to know about God. But certainly God is, among other things, the ultimate cause of the motions found in the creation.

47. Aristotle distinguished four meanings of *cause*: The *formal* cause is the nature or form that makes something what it is. The *final* cause is the purpose for which something is made. The *material* cause is the "stuff" out of which something is made. The *efficient* cause is what makes something to exist or to behave in some way.

48. Aquinas, *Summa Theologica*, 1.2.3, Answer.

OUTLINE

Boethius (480–524)

Pseudo-Dionysius (5th–6th c.)

John Scotus Erigena (800–877)

Anselm of Canterbury (1033–1109)

Faith and Reason
Monologium
Proslogium
Cur Deus Homo

Toward Scholasticism

Thomas Aquinas (1224–74)

Faith and Reason
The Existence of God
The Nature of God
Epistemology
Language

John Duns Scotus (1274–1308)

William of Occam (1280–1349)

3. *The Argument from Possibility and Necessity* (sometimes called the argument "from the contingency of the world, *e contingentia mundi*"): A *necessary being* is a being that cannot fail to exist. A *contingent* (or, as Aquinas says here, "possible") *being* is one that can either exist or not exist. For a contingent being, existence is possible and nonexistence is possible. Now, let us assume that all beings are contingent. Over a course of infinite time,[49] all possibilities are realized at one time or other. One of those possibilities is the simultaneous nonexistence of all things. So at some time or other, nothing would exist. Say that happened on December 4, 1925. But then nothing would exist today, for out of nothing nothing comes. But things do exist today. So there must be some necessary being, not only contingent being. (And, Aquinas adds, by the reasoning of argument 2, there must be a necessary being that has its necessity caused by itself.) That necessary being is what "all men speak of as God."[50]

4. *Argument from Gradation*: Aquinas says, "Among beings there are some more and some less good, true, noble, and the like. But *more* and *less* are predicated of different things according as they resemble in their different ways something that is the maximum."[51] So things are hot, he says, insofar as they resemble fire, "the maximum of heat."[52] The maximum, he thinks, is the cause of all lesser manifestations of the quality, so fire is the cause of all hotness.[53] The maximum in being, goodness, and other perfections, he says, can be no other than God. Although he cites Aristotle in this argument, he evidently assumes a Platonic view of "degrees of being." Then he makes the Platonic maximum into an Aristotelian efficient cause. I would find the argument more plausible if he had kept it in a Platonic mode: the *nature* of imperfect goodness can be found only in perfect goodness, so perfect goodness must exist as a real universal. That sort of argument would be similar to the proof from degrees in Anselm's *Monologium*, and even to Anselm's argument in the *Proslogium*. But that does not appear to be Aquinas's argument. Rather, he wants to say that maximum goodness is the (Aristotelian) efficient cause of relative goodness, a proposition that I find implausible without a Christian theological context.

Aquinas wants to say that maximum goodness is the (Aristotelian) efficient cause of relative goodness, a proposition that I find implausible without a Christian theological context.

49. Aquinas doesn't mention the premise of infinite time, but I think he presupposes it. The argument isn't plausible without it. Of course, the notion that the world is eternal is an Aristotelian thesis that Aquinas elsewhere rejects as unbiblical.

50. Aquinas, *Summa Theologica*, 1.2.3, Answer.

51. Ibid.

52. Ibid.

53. Again, modern science would accept a more complicated view of universal warming. But perhaps Aquinas's argument can be recast to make that complicated process the true maximum and therefore the true cause.

5. *Teleological Argument*: Aquinas points out that "things which lack knowledge, such as natural bodies, act for an end."[54] I presume that he is thinking about objects such as the heavenly bodies, which move in regular motions. Then he reasons:

> Now whatever lacks knowledge cannot move towards an end, unless it be directed by some being endowed with knowledge and intelligence; as the arrow is directed by the archer. Therefore some intelligent being exists by whom all natural things are directed to their end; and this being we call God.[55]

The fifth way, the teleological, is an argument that has remained popular since Aquinas's time, associated with apologists such as William Paley and F. R. Tennant. The contemporary "intelligent design" movement . . . seeks to show that this argument survives the challenge of evolutionary theory.

The first three "ways" are sometimes called *cosmological arguments*, since they reason from the general nature of the world to God. These arguments have been used in Christian apologetics down to the present. The fourth way has no standard technical designation. I have sometimes called it *criteriological*, since I think the most plausible way to take it is to regard Aquinas's "maximums" as *definitions*, *criteria*, or *norms* for relative qualities. Then the proof of God would arise from the necessity of a criterion for goodness, and so on. I like that argument, but at present I don't think it was what Aquinas had in mind. The fifth way, the *teleological*, is an argument that has remained popular since Aquinas's time, associated with apologists such as William Paley and F. R. Tennant. The contemporary "intelligent design" movement of Phillip Johnson, William Dembski, Michael Behe, and others seeks to show that this argument survives the challenge of evolutionary theory.

The Nature of God

After proving that God exists, Aquinas discusses the nature of the God he has proved. Of course, we already know some things about him: he is the unmoved mover, the First Cause, a necessary being (who has his necessity of himself), the maximum of all good qualities, and the One who designs the processes of the world.

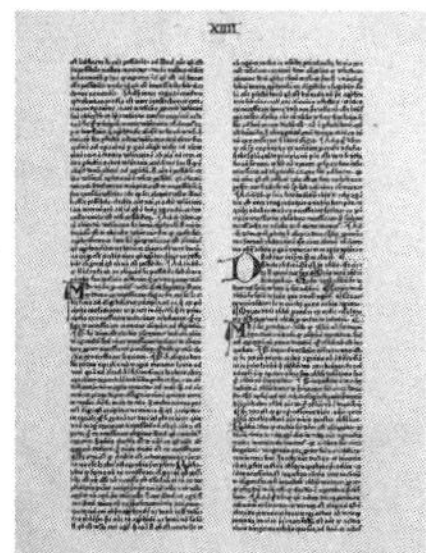

Summa Theologiae

Proofs 1–3 and 5 teach us God's nature by what the medievals called the *way of causality*. Proof 4, like Anselm's *Proslogium*, incorporates the *way of eminence*, in which we ascribe to God the maximum of what seem to us to be perfections. But there is also a third way in which the medievals attempted to gain knowledge of God. This is the *way of negation* or *way of remotion*. The way of negation is the opposite of the way of eminence in that it deals with imperfection rather than perfection. The way of eminence ascribes perfections to God; the way of remotion denies imperfections.

54. Aquinas, *Summa Theologica*, 1.2.3, Answer.

55. Ibid.

The way of remotion recalls the Gnostic-Neoplatonic principle that "we don't know what God is, only what he is not." Aquinas, we recall, denies at least that we can know God's *essence*.[56] But if the Neoplatonists' principle means that we cannot make positive predications concerning God, the Neoplatonists were not consistent with it, nor is Aquinas.

At any rate, after Aquinas has proved, to his satisfaction, the existence of God, in 1.2 of his *Summa Theologica*, he moves on in 1.3 to determine what we can know of God through those proofs, and through the principles of remotion and eminence. Question 3 of Part 1 of the *Summa* deals with the *simplicity* of God. Under *simplicity*, Aquinas denies that God is a body (for physical things are not simple; they can be cut into parts).

Then he discusses specific ways in which God is not "composed" of parts. He is not composed of matter and form, for since he is incorporeal, there is no matter in him. Further, he is not to be distinguished from his essence or nature; rather, he *is* his essence.[57] In Article 4, Aquinas argues that God's essence and being (*esse*, sometimes translated "existence"[58]) are not divided either, for any such division will make God dependent on something other than himself. In Article 5, Aquinas denies that God is contained in any genus. In Article 6, he argues that God is a substance without accidents.[59] So (Article 7) God is "altogether simple" and (Article 8) he never "enters into the composition of other things."

The way of remotion recalls the Gnostic-Neoplatonic principle that "we don't know what God is, only what he is not." Aquinas, we recall, denies at least that we can know God's essence.

56. It is not clear to me what it means to deny knowledge of God's essence. *Essence* might mean "definition," in which case the denial is plausible; who of us would be bold enough to define God? But if *essence* is what something really and truly is, and what distinguishes it from other beings, then I think any of the defining attributes of God revealed in Scripture can be called his *essence*, and those are knowable, not unknowable. What I seek to avoid is the Gnostic-Neoplatonic picture in which "what God really is" is a kind of impenetrable darkness of which we can have no knowledge. That represents the nonbiblical concept of transcendence that I criticized in chapter 1, and it leads to an irrationalism that invalidates all statements about God and leads to mysticism. For more discussion of this matter, see *DKG*, 30–33. I do think that Aquinas errs in this direction, though he doesn't carry out this error consistently. See Aquinas, *Summa Theologica*, 1.3.4, especially objection 2 and Aquinas's answer.

57. The argument, essentially, is that in human beings their essence (humanity) is distinguished from the characteristics of individual humans (legs, brains, etc.). These characteristics differ from one another by variations in their matter. But God has no matter, so the term *God* does not designate a general species in which the individuals differ from one another by their matter. It is, rather, God's essence itself that distinguishes him from other beings. So he is his own essence, his own deity.

58. The *esse* is the way in which the being realizes his or its essence in his or its concrete existence. Human beings realize their essence (rational animals, according to Aristotle; image of God, according to Scripture) in their decisions and actions, in their concrete life. In such contexts, we may not live up to our essence, and we may be pushed off course by factors outside ourselves. That cannot be the case with God. So there is no discrepancy between God's essence and his existence. They are, indeed, the same.

59. *Accidents* are anything not part of the essence. If man is "image of God," by essence, the fact that he has two legs is an *accident*.

This doctrine of the simplicity of God presents a picture of him rather like the Neoplatonic *One*, and raises questions about biblical affirmations of his numerous attributes and especially of his Trinitarian plurality.[60] But in the following discussions of the divine attributes, Aquinas clearly seems to be dependent on the Scriptures and the formulations of Christian orthodoxy. Essentially he shifts there from the way of remotion to the way of eminence. So God is perfect,[61] good,[62] infinite,[63] omnipresent,[64] and so on. Keep in mind that even in describing God's positive attributes, Aquinas still intends to work in the realm of natural reason, though one suspects that his knowledge of Scripture and Christian tradition often influences his formulations.

Aquinas, in the dimension of natural reason, *seeks to reason apart from divine revelation, that is, autonomously.*

Epistemology

Aquinas often speaks of knowledge in an Aristotelian way: Sense experience impacts the *passive intellect*, and the *active intellect* abstracts from that data the *forms* that constitute genuine knowledge. But in his writing there are also suggestions that knowledge comes through divine illumination, in an Augustinian or even Neoplatonic way (recall that Aquinas thought Pseudo-Dionysius was the real Dionysius, and quoted him often).

However that might be, Aquinas, in the dimension of *natural reason*, seeks to reason apart from divine revelation, that is, autonomously. Even the theistic proofs and proof of divine attributes discussed above are attempts to show from natural reason that God exists. As we have seen, they are examples of the three ways of medieval theology: causality, remotion, and eminence.

When Aquinas turns from discussions of God's existence and simplicity to discussions of the traditional divine attributes, the influence of Scripture on his discussion is apparent. But he never suggests a role for Scripture in his philosophical epistemology.

Certainly, at least when Aquinas turns from discussions of God's existence and simplicity to discussions of the traditional divine attributes, the influence of Scripture on his discussion is apparent. But he never suggests a role for Scripture in his philosophical epistemology. Within the sphere of natural reason, there is no place for it. So the way of causality tells us to reason autonomously concerning the powers needed to cause this or that event to happen. The ways of remotion and eminence call on us to deny or affirm of God what *we* take to be imperfections or perfections.

But these methods do not alleviate the general problem that one encounters when he tries to gain knowledge of God through natural

60. Aquinas understands the persons of the Trinity as "relations" within God in *Summa Theologica*, 1.27–43. I think that the relation between the plurality of the persons and the divine simplicity is difficult for him to formulate consistently.

61. Ibid., 1.4.

62. Ibid., 1.5–6.

63. Ibid., 1.7.

64. Ibid., 1.8.

reason alone. For autonomy itself is the problem. What competence do human thinkers have to identify what is perfect or imperfect, apart from divine revelation? I indicated that this was the weakness of Anselm's ontological argument, that the concept of perfection is problematic, that different people have different views of it. Nothing in Anselm's argument resolves the differences between Christians and Buddhists, or between, say, Anselm and Hartshorne, as to what would constitute a perfect being. The same problem attaches to any philosophical attempt to determine the nature of God from the concept of perfection or imperfection, or from the nature of causality.

To say a bit more about causality: philosophers today are more reluctant than Aquinas to dismiss the possibility of an infinite series of causes generating an event.[65] I am convinced, though it would be hard to prove this from the text of Aquinas, that his main motive for denying infinite series is epistemological.[66] He is convinced of what Leibniz called the *principle of sufficient reason*, that there is a reason for everything. *Cause* is the metaphysical correlate of *reason*. To say that event A was caused is to say that A has an explanation. If behind A there is an infinite series of causes, then there is no explanation for A, because no cause ends the series. That is a species of irrationalism (see chapter 1). A Christian cannot countenance this view, because according to Scripture there is a complete explanation for everything that happens—in the divine mind. In that sense, Aquinas's affirmation is biblical. But he does not appeal to Scripture; rather, since he is reasoning in the sphere of *natural reason*, he uses an argument of secular rationalism. But for the secular rationalist, the doctrine that everything has a full explanation is a presupposition, a postulate of faith. And that faith itself does not have the grounding of Christian faith. And secular rationalism, as we have seen, devolves into secular irrationalism, for it does not itself have a meaningful rational ground. And the rationalism and irrationalism together devolve into nihilism.

For the secular rationalist, the doctrine that everything has a full explanation is a presupposition, a postulate of faith. And that faith itself does not have the grounding of Christian faith.

Language

The philosophy and theology of Aquinas are so vast that I will be able to touch on only some basic features of them that have been especially important in the history of thought. But we should look at what Aquinas says about the language we use about God, for it is an essential ingredient of his thinking on the topics we have considered so far.

65. I have written about this in my article "Infinite Series," Appendix B in this volume, available at http://www.frame-poythress.org/infinite-series/.

66. I warn the student that my reduction of Aquinas's causal metaphysics to epistemology is anathema to the Thomists who follow Étienne Gilson and Jacques Maritain. But they have not persuaded me.

Aquinas says that since we do not know "the very nature of God as it is in itself,"[67] we know God's nature only "according to some idea of causality, or excellence, or remotion."[68] Therefore, terms such as *wise*, *powerful*, *good*, and even *God* itself do not designate God *univocally*, which would mean "with absolutely the same meaning"[69] as in their application to other beings. *Wise* applied to a man, evidently, does not have absolutely the same meaning that it has applied to God. Nor is the meaning *equivocal*, "absolutely diverse," in the two cases.[70] Rather, the meaning is somewhere between the two: an *analogical* meaning.

[According to Aquinas], terms such as wise, powerful, good, *and even* God *itself do not designate God* univocally, *which would mean "with absolutely the same meaning" as in their application to other beings.*

Aquinas is not very precise in the *Summa Theologica* as to what analogous predication is. Medieval philosophers in general distinguished various kinds of analogy, such as (1) the analogy of proper proportionality, for example, God's wisdom is related to God's nature as human wisdom is related to man's; (2) the analogy of attribution, for example, God's wisdom is analogous to man's because God's wisdom is the cause of man's; (3) the analogy of resemblance, for example, God's wisdom is analogous to man's because God's is like man's in some ways. Aquinas discussed each of these in earlier books, but in the *Summa Theologica* he seems to operate with (3), the simplest of these concepts: we can say that God is wise because there is a resemblance between our wisdom and his.

I would agree that because of the Creator-creature distinction, nothing in man is precisely the same as anything in God. Yet man is in God's image, and perhaps *resemblance*, vague as it is, is the best general term to describe the relation between the wisdom of the original and the wisdom of the image.[71]

Operating out of his conception of natural reason, *Aquinas says nothing about the biblical teachings concerning God's word and man's. Rather, he assumes that human language is fit in itself only to deal with the natural world.*

But I believe that Aquinas here presupposes an unbiblical view of language. Operating out of his conception of *natural reason*, he says nothing about the biblical teachings concerning God's word and man's. Rather, he assumes that human language is fit in itself only to deal with the natural world. *Univocally*, literally, it refers only to this world.[72] To make it apply to God, we must adjust it, twist it, use it in extraordinary

67. Aquinas, *Summa Theologica*, 1.13.10, R Obj. 3.

68. Ibid.

69. Ibid., general answer. I take it that we speak "univocally" when we affirm wisdom of Socrates, and then of Plato. But given the differences between the wisdom of the two thinkers, it is not clear how different they must be before univocal predication becomes inappropriate.

70. It is not clear in context what sorts of predication are "absolutely diverse." He denies that to use *animal* of a real animal, and then of a pictured animal, is equivocal, for he points out that there is a resemblance between the two. Perhaps an example of equivocal language would be a pun: *pen* being used to denote both a writing implement and an enclosure for pigs.

71. But compare my treatment of "Man in the Image of God" in my *ST*.

72. This is also the presupposition of much *language philosophy* in the twentieth and twenty-first centuries. See chapter 12.

ways (*analogously*). On a biblical basis, however, we need to affirm that although God is very different from us, we can speak of him in very ordinary language. God made language so that we could speak not only of the world and to each other, but also of God and to him. And he has given us his Word in Scripture, which guides us in the use of our language in all these areas. When Scripture says that "God is love" (1 John 4:8), it describes a love that is greater than we can imagine. But I don't believe it uses the *term* "love" in a nonliteral sense. In other cases, too, biblical language about God is clearly univocal. When Scripture says that God "never lies" (as Titus 1:2), it distinguishes God from literal liars, not analogous or figurative ones.

Another problem with the view that all language about God is nonliteral is that it affects everything we say about God. For example, Aquinas's cosmological argument asserts that God "caused" the world in the same sense that any event causes another. If we say that *cause* is analogous rather than univocal, the argument fails. Same for all his arguments for the divine nature, since they are based on remotion, eminence, and causality. To argue that division is unworthy of God but that goodness is worthy of him is to assume that *division* and *goodness* have the same meanings when applied to God as when applied to earthly beings.[73]

In summary, it will not do to confine ourselves to the supposed sphere of natural reason and reason about the divine causality and perfections as if God had never revealed himself to us. Without presupposing the worldview of Scripture, the rational argumentation proposed by Aquinas falls apart.

Aquinas, of course, was a Christian first and foremost, as was Justin Martyr and as were many other philosophers whom we have considered. And there are places in his work where he is primarily a biblical exegete. Even those, however, are problematic because they are built on a foundation established primarily in the realm of natural reason, reason without revelation. "A small error in the beginning grows enormous at the end."

John Duns Scotus

JOHN DUNS SCOTUS (1274–1308)

One of the party divisions in medieval philosophy was between philosophers of the Dominican and Franciscan orders. Aquinas was Dominican. Duns Scotus (not to be confused with John Scotus Erigena) was Franciscan. Earlier Franciscan teachers were Alexander of Hales

73. Aquinas's early book, *On Being and Essence*, to which I referred earlier, contains no reference to any doctrine of analogy. He follows the pattern: God has essence, angels have essence, man has essence. It is hard to imagine what that book would have been like if Aquinas had admitted that *essence*, *being*, and other important terms are analogous rather than literal.

(1185–1245) and Bonaventura (1221–74). Their school of thought was less Aristotelian and more Platonic than Aquinas, more Augustinian, more practical and mystical, less theoretical. Note, of course, that all these differences are differences in degree and emphasis. Both parties affirmed Plato, Aristotle, and Augustine.

Duns Scotus differs from Aquinas most notably in his view of the relations between faith, reason, and the will. Aquinas thought that reason (even natural reason) could demonstrate many propositions about God's nature and purposes. Duns Scotus believed that real demonstration should meet the standards of mathematical reasoning.[74] And on that ground he taught that only faith can give us certainty about God. Frank Thilly and Ledger Wood comment:

Duns Scotus differs from Aquinas most notably in his view of the relations between faith, reason, and the will.

> In this teaching a clean separation is made between revealed theology and philosophy, which if consistently adhered to leads to the emancipation of philosophy from its servitude to theology. Duns Scotus made the separation in the interest of faith, but, in so doing, he opened the way for the liberation of philosophy.[75]

This *liberation* is what I have called the *autonomy of thought*. Aquinas had allowed room for autonomy under the category of natural reason, but had allowed theology to have a veto power over philosophy. Duns Scotus also gives theology precedence over the sciences, but he presses the distinction between philosophy and theology more sharply than Aquinas did. Duns Scotus gives both faith and reason increased authority within their assigned spheres.

Duns Scotus holds strongly to a libertarian view of freedom, and he cannot accept that the will is determined by anything.

Duns Scotus is best known for his view of the will, both in man and in God. Aquinas had made the will subordinate to the intellect in both cases: the intellect directs the will as to which choices it should make. But this implies that the will is determined by knowledge.[76] Duns Scotus holds strongly to a libertarian view of freedom, and he cannot accept that the will is determined by anything. So he believes that the human will, even after the fall, can choose to act according to moral law, but he still believes that God's grace strengthens the will in these endeavors.

74. The theme that philosophy should emulate mathematics goes back to Plato's association with the Pythagoreans and can be frequently found among modern philosophers, beginning with the Continental rationalists (chapter 5).

75. Frank Thilly and Ledger Wood, *A History of Philosophy* (New York: Henry Holt, 1957).

76. I believe that Aquinas holds to a *compatibilist* view of free will—that free choice is doing what we want to do—rather than incompatibilist or libertarian (such as the *autexousion* of the church fathers that I discussed in chapter 3). See *Summa Theologica*, 1.83. Note also his strong view of divine predestination in 1.23. This view deviates from what was common among Aquinas's predecessors and anticipates the view of John Calvin. Duns Scotus reverts to a libertarian view of free will.

Now, Duns Scotus extends this view to the divine nature: God's will, too, is superior to his intellect. God's actions are not constrained by a divine reasoning process. God could have chosen not to create, or to create a different world from this one. He could also have given us different moral commandments. His laws are not rationally necessary. They are right because he commands them, not vice versa.[77] But Duns Scotus treats the first four commandments of the Decalogue differently: they are necessary, and God could therefore not have prescribed their opposites. Same for some general propositions: God must reward the just and condemn the wicked. Some interpreters find these exceptions to contradict Duns Scotus's general voluntarism.

And more seriously, Duns Scotus's voluntarism violates Scripture. In the Bible, God's moral law for human beings is essentially a command to image God, to be like him (Lev. 19:2, 24; Matt. 5:48; 1 Peter 1:15–16).[78] Duns Scotus's voluntarism comes not from the Bible's teaching on divine sovereignty, but from a view of human freedom that contradicts divine sovereignty.

And it is helpful to note that the Bible does not present the divine or human mind as battlegrounds where intellect and will (throw in emotions for good measure) fight for supremacy. Decisions are made by persons. *Intellect* is the person thinking, *will* the person deciding. Every thought is a thought we have decided to have, and every decision is a decision we consider to be knowledgeable.[79]

WILLIAM OF OCCAM (1280–1349)

As Duns Scotus is primarily known for his voluntarism, so Occam is primarily remembered for his view of universals, often called nominalism *or* conceptualism.

As Duns Scotus is primarily known for his voluntarism, so Occam is primarily remembered for his view of universals, often called *nominalism* or *conceptualism*.

We know that some expressions in language typically refer to individual or particular things, animals, or people—for example, *this book*, *Rover*, *Betty Jones*. But other expressions apply to many individuals at once, such as *book*, *dog*, and *girl*. Expressions of the latter kind are called *universals*, because they apply to anything in the universe that fits the relevant category. Now, in general, we know how to find individuals: for example, look for Rover in the backyard. But it is not so clear where one should go to find *dog*, or *book*, or *girl*, let alone such higher-order universals as *virtue*, *courage*, and *humanity*. But where would we be without them?

Plato and Aristotle were preoccupied with this question, and their reflection gave rise to what Dooyeweerd called the *form-matter scheme*,

77. Here Duns Scotus takes a view opposite to Plato in *Euthyphro*.

78. For more argument on this matter, see *DCL*, 133–35.

79. On this understanding of the mind, see *DKG*, 319–46; *DCL*, 361–82.

which provided the general structure of their philosophies. For both Plato and Aristotle, the knowledge of universals is a higher form of knowledge than the knowledge of particulars.[80] But clearly, universals cannot be seen and heard in the way that particulars can be seen and heard. Plato reasoned that since the referents of universal terms cannot be found in this world, they must be found in a higher world, the world of Forms or Ideas. Aristotle disagreed and taught that universals-forms are found in this world. For him, they are discovered as the active intellect abstracts them from sense experience. Both Plato and Aristotle are said to hold *realistic* views of universals. They believe that universal terms designate real entities; they disagree only on the question where those entities can be found.

William of Occam

Now, the debate over universals preoccupied medieval philosophers. Since they were Christian, they discussed not only general epistemology, but also theological issues such as original sin (can we explain that by the corruption of the universal "humanity" found in our first parents?) and the Lord's Supper (is the universal "body of Christ" found in consecrated bread and wine?).

The medievals argued various positions. Odo of Taurnai (1060–1113) and William of Champeaux (1070–1121) argued for what was called *extreme realism*, the view that the universal is a reality found in all particulars of the class it designates. Roscellinus (1050–1125) was a *nominalist*, holding that universals are not real things, but only names that we attach to things. He even said that the universal was nothing but a "breath of sound," *flatus vocis*, earning him the title of *extreme nominalist*. Peter Abelard (1079–1142), who studied with both William of Champeaux and Roscellinus, is sometimes called a nominalist, but it is more helpful to describe him as holding a midway position called *conceptualism*: universals are concepts in the mind, symbolized by words. Anselm of Canterbury is usually considered a realist because of the nature of his ontological argument and of the gradation arguments of the *Monologium*. He also wrote against Roscellinus.

The debate over universals preoccupied medieval philosophers. Since they were Christian, they discussed not only general epistemology, but also theological issues.

Aquinas, as was typical in his thought, brought together many of these viewpoints. For him, universals exist (1) *ante rem*, outside of things, but as concepts in the mind of God, not as elements of a world separate from ours, (2) *in re*, as the concrete essences of things belonging to the designated species, (3) *post rem*, in the human mind as it abstracts the universal concept from its experiences of particular things.

Nominalism comes naturally to us now in the modern period, given the influence of empirical philosophy and science. We look around us, and we see individual horses, but we don't see *horse*. So

80. That is, someone who knows about horses in general is considered more expert than somebody who knows about only one horse.

it is plausible to deny its existence. But certainly *horse* is, as Abelard said, at least a concept in the mind, so it is not hard to reason from nominalism to conceptualism. After all, words are not just breaths of sound; they convey meaning. But let us think further: when we say that "a horse has four legs," are we merely spelling out the meaning of a concept, or are we saying something *true*? Does the concept *horse* really describe a class of beings that exist in the world? Is *horse* merely a name, or do the beings in the class named by it really resemble one another? This is the kind of reasoning that leads us toward a realistic position: the affirmation that there are *real* resemblances and not only fictional ones.

Occam, the "invincible doctor,"[81] believed that human reason was limited to the realm of individual things. Universal terms are names for classes of individual things,[82] but they don't designate any realities beyond the individual things. To assert such realities is to violate the principle that became known as *Occam's razor*: choose the simplest solution to a problem, positing no more entities than necessary. But don't universals exist *ante rem* in God's mind, as Aquinas said? No, says Occam. Things exist as they are simply because God chose to make them as they are. By Occam's razor, we should not postulate that God made them according to a pattern in his mind. So Occam subscribes to a voluntarism like that of Duns Scotus: things in this world exist because of God's will, his choice, not his rational thought.

Such a view leads to empiricism, the view that sense perception is the foundation of human knowledge.[83] In Occam's view, knowledge is first a knowledge of particular things, and so empirical. That empirical knowledge does not imply propositions about a realm beyond experience, as Plato, or even Aquinas, thought. Occam does not believe that we can prove the existence of God by natural reason. Occam did think that the existence of God could be rendered probable by natural reason, but he did not think that the truths of revelation such as the Trinity were even intelligible to natural reason. They could be known only by revelation and through faith.

Occam subscribes to a voluntarism like that of Duns Scotus: things in this world exist because of God's will, his choice, not his rational thought. Such a view leads to empiricism, the view that sense perception is the foundation of human knowledge.

81. It is amusing to recall the titles or solemn nicknames given to various medieval philosophers. Augustine was the *doctor of grace*, Bernard of Clairvaux the *mellifluous doctor*, Anselm the *magnificent doctor*, Albert the Great the *universal doctor*, Aquinas the *angelic doctor*, Duns Scotus the *subtle doctor*, Bonaventure the *seraphic doctor*. Students might enjoy associating these titles with doctors of their own faculties, and making up new ones.

82. The "classes" exist, certainly, for Occam, as concepts in the mind. So many call Occam a conceptualist (like Abelard) rather than a nominalist. Certainly Occam was not Roscellinus.

83. It is interesting that as empiricism developed later as a distinct philosophical movement, its main representatives, Locke, Berkeley, and Hume, lived in the British Isles, as did Occam.

So Occam takes a step beyond Duns Scotus in setting science free from metaphysics and speculation. Within the sphere of natural reason, human thought is more autonomous than ever before.

But ironically, as Occam and Duns Scotus relegate philosophy and science to the realm of autonomy, they reconstitute theology on a Biblicist foundation. Our knowledge of Christian doctrine is by faith and Scripture alone. Occam also becomes a critic of the tradition and claims of the organized church. In these respects, Occam (and his followers, such as Gabriel Biel and, later, Johann von Staupitz) influenced Martin Luther, who once claimed, "I am from Occam's school."

Ironically, as Occam and Duns Scotus relegate philosophy and science to the realm of autonomy, they reconstitute theology on a Biblicist foundation. Our knowledge of Christian doctrine is by faith and Scripture alone.

What remains to be done is to reconstitute philosophy and science as well on a Biblicist foundation.

ECKHART VON HOCHHEIM (1260–1329)[84]

"Meister" Eckhart was a Dominican, and in his formal theological work very close to Thomas Aquinas. But especially in his popular writing and preaching, he was preoccupied with concepts that were more dependent on Neoplatonic mysticism.

The Godhead, for Eckhart, is eternally dark, inexpressible, unknown even to himself. But in him there is a *fecundity*, a love that overflows in the procession of the Son and Holy Spirit, and then flows back into the Godhead. God needs the Trinity and the world in order to think. The idea of the world is an eternal creation, but the temporal world is created out of nothing, in God, but is not identical with God.

Man's task is to ascend beyond a knowledge of particulars to unity. He must negate his individuality to return to God. Like the Buddha, Eckhart urges detachment from earthly things, so that in some sense we may become God, but that cannot be done apart from the grace of God. Like many other theologians influenced by Neoplatonism, Eckhart seeks to avoid any pantheistic reduction of the Creator-creature distinction. He compares our final unity with God with the transformation of the bread and wine into the body and blood of Christ. But in my mind, that analogy contributes no additional clarity.

Though Eckhart was a serious philosophical theologian, he was less interested in precise formulations than in religious experience.

Though Eckhart was a serious philosophical theologian, he was less interested in precise formulations than in religious experience. Our union with God, he thought, cannot be realized through reason, but only through feeling, for God is beyond all concepts and reasons.

Eckhart was a major influence in the thought of Johannes Tauler and Rulman Merswin, and, perhaps most significantly, on the anonymous author of *A German Theology*, which made a great impression on Martin Luther. But Eckhart himself was taken before the Inquisi-

84. In some sources he is given the first name Johannes, but that seems to be inauthentic. He is commonly known as "Meister" Eckhart, *Meister* ("Master") being an academic title.

tion and excommunicated in 1329.[85] There is no record of his having received this verdict, or of his death or burial site.

EPILOGUE

The medieval period was a great opportunity for Christian philosophers. Christian thinkers were free from persecution, and they lived in a culture and under governments that were professedly Christian. But they never quite freed themselves from the church fathers' ambition to achieve intellectual respectability. Although the medievals critically analyzed Greek philosophy in its details, they never fully broke away from its commitment to human autonomy and its attempt to contain divine transcendence within a form-matter scheme. Medieval philosophers did seek to do justice to God's grace, but (especially with Thomas Aquinas) they regarded the realm of grace not as God's lordship directing all of life, but as a supplement to a realm of nature, which in turn was subject to an autonomous natural reason.

So as the medieval period gave way to the Renaissance and Reformation, Christian philosophy was still limited by its own tendency to compromise. In the next periods of history, the autonomous realm of nature will be liberated from grace and will give rise to a new secularism: like Greek philosophy and without the constraints of Christianity. The realm of grace, however, also becomes free in Reformation theology to seek a more radically biblical way of thinking. The antithesis between Christian and non-Christian thought becomes more evident. But the new conditions will bring even more occasions of compromise. So the spiritual warfare in philosophy continues down to our time.

The medieval period was a great opportunity for Christian philosophers. Christian thinkers were free from persecution, and they lived in a culture and under governments that were professedly Christian.

KEY TERMS

Eternity (Boethius)	Person (Boethius)
Degrees of being (Dionysius)	*Via negativa*
Mysticism	*Credo ut intelligam*
Fides Quaerens Intellectum	Presuppositionalism
Argument from gradation	Ontological argument
Concept	Necessary being
Contingent being	Honor
Satisfaction	Penal substitution

85. Church condemnation was not a new thing in medieval theology. Other prominent theologians were at least temporarily repudiated by the established church: Origen was condemned at the Synod of Constantinople in 543 and by the Fifth Ecumenical Council in 553. Erigena's *On the Divisions of Nature* was condemned by the Council of Sens in 1225. In 1142, another Council at Sens condemned Abelard. In 1270 and 1277, a French bishop condemned the works of Thomas Aquinas. Occam was excommunicated by Pope John XXII, but his writings were never condemned.

Supererogation
Sic et Non
Sentences
Natural reason (Aquinas)
Theology (Aquinas)
Five ways (Aquinas)
Efficient cause
Final cause
E contingentia mundi
Criteriological argument
Way of eminence
Simplicity of God
Nature
Genus
Accidents
Active intellect
Principle of sufficient reason
Equivocal
Analogy of proper proportionality
Analogy of resemblance
Will
Universals
Nominalism
Ante rem
Post rem
Empiricism
A German Theology
Scholasticism
Moral-influence theory
Sacred doctrine (Aquinas)
Philosophy (Aquinas)
Nature-grace scheme
Cosmological argument
Formal cause
Material cause
Teleological argument
Way of causality
Way of remotion
Essence
Esse (as divine attribute)
Substance
Passive intellect
Illumination
Univocal
Analogical
Analogy of attribution
Intellect
Voluntarism
Particulars
Conceptualism
In re
Occam's razor
Fecundity

STUDY QUESTIONS

1. "The medieval period, then, represented a parenthesis—an interlude in history—between two eras." What two eras? Explain and evaluate Frame's summary.
2. Frame calls Boethius's *Consolation* "a curious volume." In what respect? What is Boethius's view there of man's highest good?
3. Frame says that Boethius "anticipates Aquinas's doctrine of *natural reason*." How? Is this a good thing?
4. Why does Frame criticize Dionysius's *via negativa* and mysticism? Evaluate.
5. Summarize Erigena's four divisions of nature. Show how his positions reflect those described in Frame's rectangle.
6. Contrast the views of faith and reason taught by Anselm and Abelard.

7. What does it mean to describe Anselm as a *presuppositionalist*? What is the case *against* such a description? Evaluate Frame's response to that objection.
8. Summarize and evaluate Anselm's arguments for the existence of God in the *Monologium*.
9. Same for the argument of the *Proslogium*. Describe and respond to Gaunilo's objections, as well as presenting your own response. Is it ever legitimate to reason from concept to reality? How does the definition of *perfection* affect the argument?
10. Berkhof says that the position of Anselm's *Cur Deus Homo* is "the Roman Catholic doctrine of penance applied to the work of Christ." Explain; evaluate.
11. Mention one idea of importance from each of Avicenna, Al Ghazali, Averroes, and Maimonides.
12. Compare and evaluate Anselm's and Abelard's theories of the atonement.
13. How did Aquinas deal with the controversy over faith and reason? How did he distinguish the proper spheres of faith and of natural reason? Evaluate.
14. Describe and evaluate Aquinas's *five ways*.
15. Describe and evaluate Aquinas's epistemology.
16. Frame says that the main problem in Aquinas's epistemology is "autonomy itself." Explain; evaluate.
17. Explain and evaluate Aquinas's doctrine of analogy. Discuss Frame's response.
18. Compare Duns Scotus's view of the will with that of Aquinas. What consequences does Duns Scotus draw from his formulation?
19. How does Frame argue that Duns Scotus's view of the divine will is unscriptural? Evaluate.
20. What is the "debate over universals"? Discuss the views of Abelard, Aquinas, Occam. What do you think?
21. How did Occam and Eckhart anticipate Luther? Discuss.
22. Describe and evaluate Frame's summary of medieval philosophy.

BIBLIOGRAPHY: MEDIEVAL PHILOSOPHY AND THEOLOGY

Print

Abelard, Peter. *Abelard & Heloise: The Letters and Other Writings*. Edited by William Levitan. Indianapolis: Hackett Publishing, 2007.

Anselm of Canterbury. *St. Anselm's Basic Writings*. Edited by S. N. Deane. Chicago: Open Court, 1998.

Aquinas, Thomas. *Summa Theologiae: Complete Set Latin-English Edition.* Rochester, NY: Aquinas Institute, 2012.

Boethius, Ancius. *The Consolation of Philosophy.* New York: Empire Books, 2012.

Dionysius the Areopagite. *Pseudo-Dionysius: The Complete Works.* Mahwah, NJ: Paulist Press, 1988.

Duns Scotus, John. *Duns Scotus—Philosophical Writings: A Selection.* Translated by Allan Wolter. Indianapolis: Hackett Publishing, 1987.

Erigena, John Scotus. *Treatise on Divine Predestination.* Notrc Dame, IN: University of Notre Dame Press, 2003.

Fairweather, Eugene R., ed. *A Scholastic Miscellany: Anselm to Ockham.* Louisville, KY: Westminster John Knox Press, 1956.

Gilson, Étienne. *The Spirit of Medieval Philosophy.* Notre Dame, IN: University of Notre Dame Press, 1991. Classic analysis by great neo-Thomist scholar.

Gyula, Klima, ed., with Fritz Allhof and Arnand Jayprakash Vaidya. *Medieval Philosophy: Essential Readings with Commentary.* Hoboken, NJ: Wiley Blackwell, 2007.

Hyman, Arthur, James J. Walsh, and Thomas Williams, eds. *Philosophy in the Middle Ages: The Christian, Islamic, and Jewish Traditions.* 3rd ed. Indianapolis: Hackett Publishing, 2010. Readings and commentary.

Kenny, Anthony. *A New History of Western Philosophy.* Vol. 2, *Medieval Philosophy.* New York: Oxford University Press, 2007.

McKeon, Richard, ed. *Selections from Medieval Philosophers II from Roger Bacon to William of Occam.* New York: Charles Scribner's Sons, 1930.

Ross, James B., and Mary M. McLaughlin, eds. *The Portable Medieval Reader.* London: Penguin, 1977. Over a hundred selections of medieval writers.

Schroedinger, Andrew B. *Readings in Medieval Philosophy.* New York: Oxford University Press, 1996. Fifty-four readings; comprehensive collection.

Online

Aquinas, Thomas. *On Being and Essence.* Available at http://faculty.fordham.edu/klima/Blackwell-proofs/MP_C30.pdf.

Christian Classics Ethereal Library. Site hosts writings of Boethius, Abelard, Anselm, Aquinas, and others. http://www.ccel.org.

READ FOR YOURSELF

I don't recommend Boethius's *Consolation of Philosophy* as an edifying text, but it might be a good idea for you to look through it here and there to get the feeling and the gist.

Anselm's *Proslogium* is important. Read the first five chapters carefully; skim the rest. *Cur Deus Homo* is very important to those studying theology, less so for philosophers.

I recommend that philosophy students read Aquinas's small book *On Being and Essence*, to orient themselves into Aquinas's terminology. Then in Aquinas's *Summa Theologica*, carefully read the First Part, Questions 1–5, and then look at what interests you in the rest of the book.

LISTEN ONLINE

Link: http://itunes.apple.com/us/course/legacy-history-philosophy/id694658914

- Christian Neoplatonism and Anselm of Canterbury: 44:59
- Thomas Aquinas—Faith, Reason, and Epistemology: 36:14
- Thomas Aquinas Continued and Late Medieval Developments: 57:10

FAMOUS QUOTES

- **Boethius:** http://en.wikiquote.org/wiki/Anicius_Manlius_Severinus_Boethius
- **John Scotus Erigena:** http://en.wikiquote.org/wiki/Johannes_Scotus_Eriugena
- **Aquinas:** http://en.wikiquote.org/wiki/Thomas_Aquinas
- **Occam:** http://en.wikiquote.org/wiki/William_of_Ockham

5

EARLY MODERN THOUGHT

DURING THE MEDIEVAL PERIOD, Western philosophers try to combine, with greater or lesser success, the biblical worldview with Greek philosophy. In the postmedieval period, thinkers lose confidence in the attempt to synthesize these traditions. Eventually there is a sharp split between some thinkers (such as Luther and Calvin), who advocate a more consistently biblical position, and others (such as Hobbes, Descartes, and Locke), who revert to a purer secularism like that of the early Greeks, with an even more explicit claim of intellectual autonomy.

During the medieval period, Western philosophers try to combine, with greater or less success, the biblical worldview with Greek philosophy. In the postmedieval period, thinkers lose confidence in the attempt to synthesize these traditions.

THE RENAISSANCE

The Renaissance was a period of major cultural change in Europe, roughly from 1350 to 1650. It was a time of impressive achievement in literature and the arts, including such figures as Dante,[1] Boccaccio, Petrarch, Chaucer, Leonardo, Michelangelo, and Raphael, and, toward the end of the period, Cervantes and Shakespeare. This era also marked the beginning of modern empirical science (Copernicus, Galileo, Brahe, Bruno, Kepler, Francis Bacon). It was also the first great period of European world exploration (Columbus, Magellan, da Gama, Polo, Cabot, Champlain, Drake).

It was not, however, a time of notable achievement in philosophy. Although people continued to practice the discipline, none of them

1. Dante's dates, 1265–1321, challenge my general chronology, but that's why I added the qualification "roughly." Dante is sometimes seen as the poetic expression of Thomas Aquinas's *medieval synthesis*, and that is a helpful parallel. But it seems to me that Dante's work is more an anticipation of the Renaissance than a product of the Middle Ages.

stand out as having the kind of influence that Aquinas, Duns Scotus, and Occam had earlier, or that Hobbes, Locke, and Descartes would later have. Most philosophers of the time were traditional Catholic Christians (only a few, including the logician Petrus Ramus, identified with the Reformation toward the end of this period).

A few, nevertheless, are worth noting: Marsilio Ficino (1433–99) became the first head of a Platonic Academy in Florence and translated a number of Plato's dialogues into Latin. Pico Della Mirandola (1463–94) tried to bring all human knowledge together into a large Neoplatonic system. Pietro Pomponazzi (1462–1525) lectured on Aristotle, adopting the position of some Averroists that a proposition could be true in philosophy, but false in theology. Michel de Montaigne (1533–92) was also something of a skeptic, wondering aloud whether we can be sure of anything. He rejected the model of the formal philosophic treatise in favor of a kind of stream-of-consciousness self-description, which makes him sound remarkably modern.

A number of Renaissance thinkers took an interest in political philosophy, moved by the intrigues of the empires and city-states of the period. The most famous of these was Niccolo Machiavelli (1469–1527), who denied the role of absolute morality in the administration of the state and said that a prince should be prepared to deceive and otherwise violate moral standards in order to preserve order (and, of course, to preserve his own power). In holding that in politics the ends justify the means, he revived the position of the Greek Sophists and anticipated Marx, Lenin, Hitler, Mao, together with many other thinkers and politicians.

Machiavelli regarded religion as a tool at the disposal of the political ruler. This was a fairly extreme position in the church-state debates of the time, but it echoed the Erastianism[2] of Ficino and others (including John Wycliffe, 1320–84) who protested the special privileges of the church and thought the church should be subordinate to the state.

It is not easy to find common themes to analyze this lively intellectual era. But students of the period tend to settle on two distinctive emphases: antiquarianism and humanism.

It is not easy to find common themes to analyze this lively intellectual era. But students of the period tend to settle on two distinctive emphases: antiquarianism and humanism. Antiquarianism is suggested by the slogan *ad fontes*, "to the sources." The Renaissance thinkers put a great emphasis on recovering ancient (primarily Greek and Roman) culture: not only philosophic and literary texts, but also styles of architecture and art, and forms of government. There were many fresh translations of ancient texts, including Scripture, and many exposures of ancient forgeries. Lorenzo Valla (1407–57), Nicholas of Cusa (1401–64), and Desiderius Erasmus (1466–1536) argued convincingly that Pseudo-Dionysius (see chapter 4) was not a convert of Paul.

2. Named after Thomas Erastus (1524–83), who thought the state, not the church, should punish the sins of Christians. Of course, in my narrative there were Erastians before Erastus.

Valla also denied the authenticity of the "Donation of Constantine" in which the emperor Constantine supposedly bequeathed his authority to the pope. Erasmus also produced one of the earliest published editions of the NT in Greek.

The invention of movable-type printing by Johannes Gutenberg, around 1450, facilitated the distribution of these scholarly works to an extent unimaginable in the ancient and medieval periods. This technology radically changed human civilization, enabling rapid communication of knowledge, both literature from the past and new discoveries.

The invention of movable-type printing by Johannes Gutenberg, around 1450, facilitated the distribution of these scholarly works to an extent unimaginable in the ancient and medieval periods. This technology radically changed human civilization.

The other major theme of the Renaissance is humanism—not the secular humanism of the modern period, which is in effect a deification of man, but a serious Christian preoccupation with man as God's image. In the Middle Ages, earthly life was typically considered only a prelude to heavenly existence. But the Renaissance had a more intense concern with earthly life for its own sake. Renaissance art, for example, presents the human body with vividness, accuracy, and admiration unprecedented in the medieval period. Renaissance science was not content to place the world among the various spheres of Aristotle's cosmology, but used various instruments to look and see what the world was really like, connecting our worldview with our actual experience. And Renaissance philosophy also sought to get beyond traditional abstractions to understand the world in which we live: political realities (Machiavelli) and existential subjectivity (Pomponazzi, Montaigne).

The Renaissance was not a time of unbelief. All the thinkers I have mentioned professed Christianity. But the Bible did not play a central role in their thinking (except as an object for textual scholars to analyze). In the famous encounter between Galileo and the church over Copernicus's heliocentrism, neither party referred much to Scripture. The conflict was not so much between science and the Bible as between science and the Aristotelian cosmology that the church had imposed on the Bible. Although the Renaissance thinkers had new linguistic and textual tools for understanding Scripture, none of them (until the Reformation; see below) challenged philosophical and cultural assumptions with the worldview of the Bible.

The two Renaissance themes, antiquarianism and humanism, were never well integrated. They tended to press thinkers in opposite directions: antiquarianism toward the past, and humanism toward the present and future.

So the two Renaissance themes, antiquarianism and humanism, were never well integrated. They tended to press thinkers in opposite directions: antiquarianism toward the past, and humanism toward the present and future. This tension also had epistemological consequences, raising the question: do we gain knowledge primarily from revisiting the past, or from analyzing our present existence?

To correlate these with a distinction I employed in chapter 1, Renaissance antiquarianism could not resist the rationalism of the ancient philosophers, and Renaissance humanism could not make sense of the irrational confusion of human subjectivity, leaving room for skepticism to develop. The resulting rationalist-irrationalist dialectic prevented these brilliant Renaissance thinkers from achieving progress in philosophy, as their colleagues certainly made progress in astronomy, in the arts, and in world exploration; see fig. 5.1.

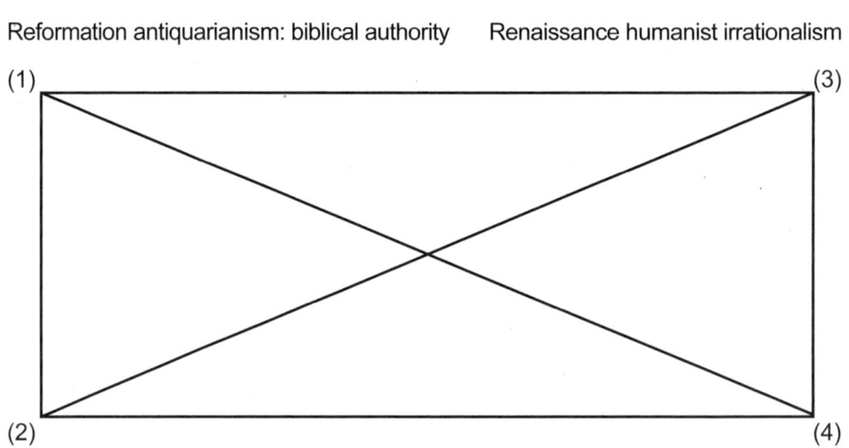

Fig. 5.1. Polarities in the Reformation and Renaissance

THE REFORMATION

The Reformers did not consider themselves philosophers, but what they taught was extremely significant for philosophy. They presented alternatives in metaphysics, epistemology, and ethics that had not been seriously considered by the previous philosophical communities.

The Protestant Reformation came toward the end of the Renaissance period, so the two movements were partially contemporary. But the Reformation moved in a radically different intellectual direction from the Renaissance philosophers that we have considered, and from medieval philosophy as well. The Reformers did not consider themselves philosophers, but what they taught was extremely significant for philosophy. They presented alternatives in metaphysics, epistemology, and ethics that had not been seriously considered by the previous philosophical communities. And despite the newness of their proposals, they made progress toward the old biblical goal of taking "every thought captive to obey Christ" (2 Cor. 10:5).

For all its newness, we can understand the Reformation as a Renaissance phenomenon. It is antiquarian in the sense that it returns *ad fontes*, to the Scriptures and the older church fathers, particularly Augustine, bypassing much, but not all, of medieval scholasticism. It is humanistic in that it is concerned in a fresh way with the individual's relation to God. It arises out of previous movements (led by John Wycliffe, John Huss, and Peter Waldo) that sought a more biblical theology and were critical of the corruption of the church. Humanists such as Erasmus, too, prefigured the Reformation in their complaints against Roman luxury and their desire for a simpler Christianity, as well as their greater sophistication in biblical languages and manuscripts. The Reformers also made much use of the new biblical scholarship and the transformative technology of the printing press.

Martin Luther (1483–1546)

Martin Luther

The first Protestant was the German priest and university professor Martin Luther. Luther went through personal agony, trying to gain an assurance of divine forgiveness through moral and spiritual exertions. He was appalled when John Tetzel offered divine forgiveness—swifter entrance to heaven for departed souls—for money.

Eventually Luther came to a new interpretation of Paul's concept of "righteousness" in passages such as Romans 1:16–17:

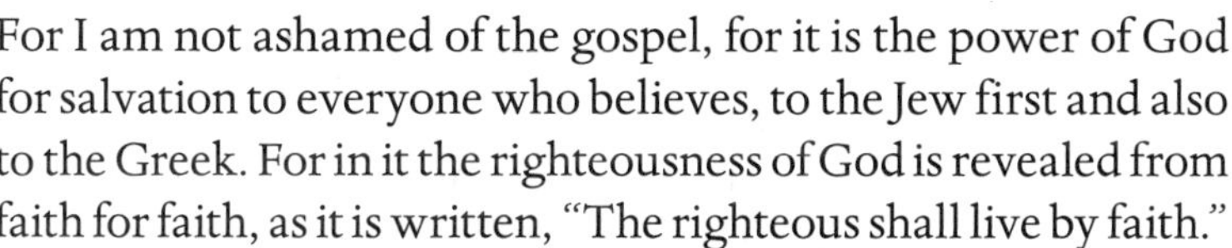

> For I am not ashamed of the gospel, for it is the power of God for salvation to everyone who believes, to the Jew first and also to the Greek. For in it the righteousness of God is revealed from faith for faith, as it is written, "The righteous shall live by faith."

Luther believed that the "righteousness" of this passage was not the righteousness of God's condemnation that had so terrorized Luther's earlier life. Rather, it was the righteousness proclaimed in the *gospel*, the good news: the righteousness of Christ himself imputed by God to us and received by faith. By this righteousness, God forgives our sins for Christ's sake and declares that Christ has borne their punishment in our place. In him, therefore, we are justified, righteous by faith in Christ alone. Salvation is God's gift ("by grace alone") apart from our works. Only thus, Luther believed, could the gospel be the power of God "for salvation." Later, these assertions were summarized by the five *solas* of the Reformation: by grace alone (*sola gratia*), by faith alone (*sola fide*), through Christ alone (*solo Christo*), on the basis of Scripture alone (*sola Scriptura*), to the glory of God alone (*soli Deo gloria*).

These assertions were summarized by the five solas *of the Reformation: by grace alone* (sola gratia)*, by faith alone* (sola fide)*, through Christ alone* (solo Christo)*, on the basis of Scripture alone* (sola Scriptura)*, to the glory of God alone* (soli Deo gloria)*.*

The theological implications of Luther's insight filled volumes. I won't deal with Lutheran dogmatics here, but I would like to make some observations of philosophical importance. First, in his metaphysics, we see Luther here turning away from the nameless *One* of Gnosticism and Neoplatonism, which so captivated most of medieval theology. Luther's God, as in the biblical model I sketched in chapter 1, is both absolute and personal. Luther does not approach God as a finite being trying to ascend to the infinite, but (understandably in the light of his personal experience) as a sinner seeking forgiveness for disobeying the Great King.

Grace, too, is not an impersonal, metaphysical substance that trickles down to people through the sacraments, as in much popular Catholicism. Grace is an irreducibly personal category, first, in that it is a personal attitude of favor from God's heart, bringing us into relationship with him as our Savior, Friend, and Father. Only persons give gifts to one another. Second, and implicitly, grace is a choice. When we give gifts to one another, we choose whom to give to, and we choose what gifts to give. An impersonal force does not make a choice as to whom it will affect and how. Put your finger into an electrical outlet, and it will automatically shock you. It will shock anyone who is foolish enough to put his finger there. The outlet does not choose whether or not to shock you. But a gift always results from a personal choice. And God's gift of salvation presupposes his personal intention to save an individual person. So impersonalist concepts of the absolute tend to lead to doctrines of salvation by works, and ultimately to universalism. Salvation by grace is inseparable from a supreme being who is personal.

Luther's individualism is somewhat related to his training in the tradition of the nominalism of William of Occam (see chapter 4). He thinks mainly in specifics rather than generalities, more about the individual than the group,[3] more about the Bible than church tradition.

So epistemologically, going beyond Occam, Luther bases his whole theology on divine revelation, *sola Scriptura*. Convinced of his understanding of Scripture, he is prepared to overturn the whole body of medieval tradition in favor of what he believed to be the Word of God.[4] The role of reason is not independent of Scripture, for Luther. Luther sometimes said negative things about reason, in the context of his general critique of scholastic theology. But at the Diet of Worms, on trial for heresy, he said that he would not recant his writings unless convinced by "Scripture and right reason"—that is, Scripture rightly interpreted and applied by godly thinking.

Epistemologically, going beyond Occam, Luther bases his whole theology on divine revelation, sola Scriptura. *Convinced of his understanding of Scripture, he is prepared to overturn the whole body of medieval tradition in favor of what he believed to be the Word of God.*

Ethically, too, Luther draws from Scripture (often in defiance of tradition) the requirements of God for our lives and his authoritative promises to those who believe.

In chapter 3, I noted a four-stage historical pattern in the church's defense of the doctrine of the Trinity: (1) a *synthesis* of Scripture with non-Christian philosophy dominates the church; (2) a *heresy* indicates the urgency of dealing with this issue; (3) a *reformer* emerges to lead

3. Nevetheless, the Occamists under whom Luther was trained followed Gabriel Biel, who said that God had determined to give his grace to those who first do as well as they can do. That principle was the source of the huge moral burden Luther felt in his early adulthood. How could he do his best when even his righteous deeds were "like a polluted garment" (Isa. 64:6)? Luther's theology of grace rejected Biel's scheme. So Luther accepted parts of the Occamist approach and rejected others.

4. Luther did, of course, respect and treasure much of that tradition, particularly the early church fathers and Augustine.

the orthodox in combatting the heresy by setting forth fundamental truths of Scripture; and (4) a *consolidator* appears after the controversy to rethink the whole body of theology according to the knowledge acquired through the battle. In the fourth-century context, I identified these four stages with (1) Origen's Christian Platonism; (2) Arius's view that the Son of God is a created being; (3) Athanasius's historic struggle against an Arianized empire; and (4) Augustine's theological reconstruction.

The sixteenth-century parallel: (1) medieval scholasticism as a synthesis between the Bible, Plato, and Aristotle; (2) the heresy of works-salvation, perhaps with Tetzel as an extreme case; (3) Luther the Reformer, who like Athanasius pushes hard for the fundamental principle of justification by faith alone; and (4) Calvin the consolidator, who rethinks the whole of theology in the light of the knowledge gained in the Reformation.

Luther's ideas took root principally in Germany and in Scandinavia. Christians in Switzerland and France also appreciated his work, but the Reformation in these countries took a somewhat different direction.

Parallel Histories of Reformation			
Synthesis	*Heresy*	*Reformer*	*Consolidator*
Origen	Arius	Athanasius	Augustine
Thomas Aquinas	Tetzel	Luther	Calvin

For both Athanasius and Luther, the fundamental issue was the acknowledgment of God: in Athanasius, the fully divine nature of Jesus; in Luther, salvation as an act of God alone.

John Calvin (1509–64)

Luther's ideas took root principally in Germany and in Scandinavia. Christians in Switzerland and France also appreciated his work, but the Reformation in these countries took a somewhat different direction, under such leaders as Ulrich Zwingli (1484–1531) and Martin Bucer (1491–1551).[5] The most prominent of these was John Calvin, who served as a "pastor of pastors" in Geneva for many years.[6] Those who followed Luther most closely were called *evangelicals* and, later, *Lutherans*. Protestants in the Swiss branch of the Reformation were called *Reformed*, and sometimes *Calvinists*.[7]

Those who followed Luther most closely were called evangelicals *and, later,* Lutherans. *Protestants in the Swiss branch of the Reformation were called* Reformed, *and sometimes* Calvinists.

5. English Protestantism included both Lutheran and Calvinistic influences. In addition, the separation of the Church of England from Rome under Henry VIII brought some unique features to the English movement, not least a conflict between conservative and liberal revisions to the existing theology, government, and liturgy.

6. Calvin was exiled from Geneva in 1538 and labored in Strasbourg (with Martin Bucer) before returning to Geneva in 1541.

7. There is no etymological reason why *evangelical* should primarily designate Lutherans or why *Reformed* should designate Calvinists. So far as the words themselves are concerned, the designations could have as easily been reversed. For in the literal senses of the terms, the Lutherans were certainly reformed and the Calvinists were certainly evangelical.

Like Luther, Calvin did not consider himself a philosopher, but his theology is even more directly relevant to philosophy than Luther's. Metaphysically, Calvin, like Luther, stresses that the supreme being is absolute and tripersonal, quite distinct from the created world.[8]

Calvin's epistemology is a remarkable departure from medieval and Renaissance thought, and it dominates the opening chapters of his systematic theology, his *Institutes*. Remarkably, Calvin does not begin this summary of Christian doctrine by setting forth the doctrine of God (existence, attributes, Trinity), as did the medievals and post-Reformation theologians. Rather, he begins the *Institutes* with a description of the *knowledge* of God: an epistemological and personal, rather than a metaphysical, focus.

Calvin does not define the knowledge of God as intellectual assent to the proposition that God exists. Certainly such assent is indispensable in his view. But he insists that knowledge of God does not exist without "reverence and love"[9] for him. So for Calvin, the path to knowing God does not proceed through rational demonstration, as in Aquinas, but through repentance and faith. Calvin follows the argument of the apostle Paul in the first chapter of the Letter to the Romans: All human beings have a knowledge of God and his moral standards from his revelation in the natural world[10] and in their own consciences.[11] But they repress this knowledge,[12] worship false gods, and violate his moral standards, sins for which they have no excuse.

So although this natural revelation is competent to take away excuses for sin, it is not sufficient to give the knowledge of salvation. For that, people need to hear the gospel of grace, found in Scripture.[13] But a person will repress the truth of Scripture, too, unless he receives as well the testimony of the Holy Spirit to the truth of Scripture.[14]

So for Calvin, the knowledge of God is a wholly personal relationship. We cannot know God without the personal assistance of God's

John Calvin

8. Lutherans and Calvinists debated their respective views of the Creator-creature distinction, especially in regard to the divine and human natures of Christ. Lutherans believed that since Jesus' human nature was influenced by his divine nature, it took on divine attributes. So, for example, Lutherans regarded Christ's human nature as "ubiquitous," and therefore capable of being physically present in the bread of the Lord's Supper. Calvinists thought this notion resulted in an unbiblical confusion of deity and humanity. In the language of the fifth-century Christological controversy, Calvinists accused Lutherans of affinity with the Monophysite position (in which Jesus' two natures were melded into one), and Lutherans accused Calvinists of being Nestorian (dividing Christ into two persons, one divine and one human).

9. *Institutes*, 1.2.1.

10. Ibid., 1.5, 8.

11. Ibid., 1.3.

12. Ibid., 1.4.

13. Ibid., 1.6–9.

14. Ibid., 1.7.

own Spirit. And when the Spirit reveals God, he also reveals our sin to us and our need of salvation from sin in Christ. Indeed, Calvin begins the *Institutes* by saying that the knowledge of God and of ourselves is mutually connected—connected so that we cannot know ourselves without knowing God, or know God without knowing ourselves.[15] And Calvin testifies that he does not know which comes first.[16]

Calvin's doctrine of the knowledge of God, therefore, has three perspectives.[17] Normative perspective: the knowledge of God is based on God's own revelation of himself. Situational perspective: God's revelation is evident in the created world as well as in Scripture.[18] Existential perspective: to know God, we must know ourselves, especially our sinful condition and need for redemption. And our knowledge is a person-to-person encounter between ourselves and the Holy Spirit; see fig. 5.2.

Calvin begins the Institutes *by saying that the knowledge of God and of ourselves is mutually connected—connected so that we cannot know ourselves without knowing God, or know God without knowing ourselves. And Calvin testifies that he does not know which comes first.*

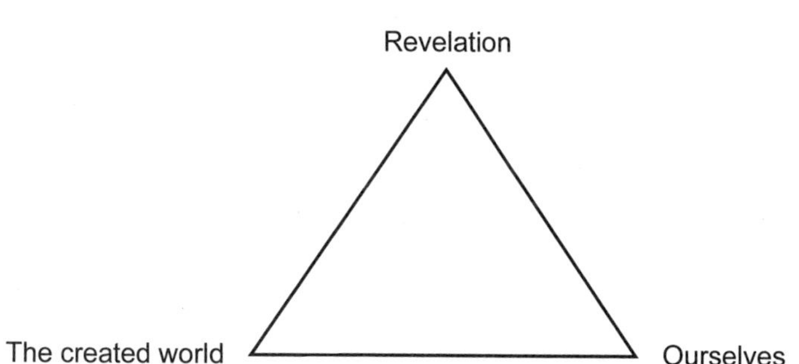

Fig. 5.2. Calvin's Perspectives on the Knowledge of God

Calvin's position is significant for Christian apologetics. If an apologist seeks to follow Calvin, he must present the gospel (normatively) as something based on God's revelation, not autonomous reason.

Calvin's position is significant for Christian apologetics. If an apologist seeks to follow Calvin, he must present the gospel (normatively) as something based on God's revelation, not autonomous reason.

15. Ibid., 1.1.

16. Calvin rarely confessed ignorance. That he did in this case indicates philosophical insight. It is common enough for preachers and theologians to say that we cannot really know ourselves without knowing God. But Calvin recognizes that in some sense the opposite relation must also obtain. For how can we imagine knowing anything without knowing ourselves, that is, knowing our knowing? Augustine made use of this insight (as Descartes would later do) in his argument from thinking to self-knowledge, and in his *Confessions*, which present his knowledge of God in terms of an autobiography.

17. Compare the triperspectival epistemology set forth in this volume, chapter 1.

18. Calvin is, of course, famous for his view of predestination: his view that God foreordains everything that comes to pass. So for him, *everything* is providence; every event, therefore, is a revelation of the nature and plan of God. Apologists following Calvin will not be limited to showing God in unique events and facts such as miracles. They will, rather, be able to point to every fact in creation as evidence of God. The very factuality of every fact presupposes God. This is the *transcendental argument* of Cornelius Van Til.

Situationally, he must present the evidences of the creation as something supplied by divine providence and interpreted by revelation, expecting the non-Christian to repress them. Existentially, he must appeal to an inquirer as a whole person, not as an isolated thinking machine: a whole person who is lost in sin and in need of salvation. He must seek to bring the Bible's saving message, not just a bare notion of divine existence. And he must pray that his witness will be visited by the power and love of the Holy Spirit, driving the Word of God into the heart of the inquirer.

The personalism of Calvin's thought is reflected in the style and tone of his writings. Although Calvin was a classical scholar, he rarely writes recognizably academic treatises. He refers to himself often in the first person and makes personal criticisms of his opponents (too many for some modern readers). *Stupid* and *silly* are frequent epithets. Precedents for this style are few, of which Augustine's *Confessions* and Anselm's *Proslogium* are the most notable. Luther's writings are, if anything, even more personal than Calvin's.[19]

Calvin's triperspectival epistemology follows from his theistic metaphysics. Because God determines the norms for knowledge, human knowers must presuppose them. Because God foreordains all the facts, all the facts presuppose God's interpretations of them. And because God has made human beings in his image, we must understand ourselves (and our knowing) in relation to God.

Calvin's triperspectival epistemology follows from his theistic metaphysics. Because God determines the norms for knowledge, human knowers must presuppose them. Because God foreordains all the facts, all the facts presuppose God's interpretations of them. And because God has made human beings in his image, we must understand ourselves (and our knowing) in relation to God.

Calvin's epistemology represents a sharp departure from the patterns of medieval and Renaissance philosophy. These previous movements all made some compromises with the doctrine of intellectual autonomy. Such compromises were inevitable, given the influence of Greek philosophy on these thinkers, and given the doctrine of libertarian freedom that allows the human mind and will to operate independently of God. Calvin himself was a classical scholar, a Renaissance intellectual, and he admired ancient philosophers (especially Plato). But the epistemology of the *Institutes* makes no accommodation to Greek philosophical views, or to intellectual autonomy, on which those views depend. For Calvin, the human mind works only as God has ordained it to work.

Calvin's absolute-personality theism presented a new opportunity to philosophers: the opportunity to find a sure road to truth through divine revelation. This was the opportunity that had been missed by the medieval and Renaissance Christian thinkers, who to one extent or another compromised with Greek thought. Calvin's thought presents a clear challenge to the next generations, indeed to us today: which of these two paths will we follow?

19. These thinkers rebut the common notion that theology ought to be written in an impersonal, academic style.

POST-REFORMATION PROTESTANTISM

Protestant Scholasticism

Successors of Calvin and Luther[20] worked out the Reformation insights into systematic form. In the early to mid-twentieth century, much was said about the differences between the Reformers and the post-Reformation thinkers, often positing sharp differences, for example, between "Calvin and the Calvinists." The claims of a great chasm between Reformation and post-Reformation were extremely overblown. In general, the teaching of Calvin's successors was not much different from that of Calvin, and the successors of Luther were not much different from Luther himself.[21]

The writings of Luther and Calvin are highly personal, existential responses to the theological and ecclesiastical crises they faced. The post-Reformation theology is more academic, more detailed, more argumentative.

But the *feeling* one gets from the post-Reformation literature is very different from the atmosphere generated by the original Reformers. The writings of Luther and Calvin are highly personal, existential responses to the theological and ecclesiastical crises they faced. The post-Reformation theology is more academic, more detailed, more argumentative. It makes more use of philosophy and therefore is often described by the phrase *Protestant Scholasticism*.[22] That is appropriate in a way, because one of their main interests was to present a version of Protestant theology suitable for academic study and therefore academically respectable. This is not wrong in itself, and it has not been proved that this drive for academic respectability led the Protestant scholastics into any specific departure from the teaching of Luther and Calvin. But as we have seen in our studies of earlier periods, the quest for academic respectability has sometimes led theology into compromise with non-Christian thought, at least over the course of several generations. The reader will have to decide whether the later declension of the churches into liberalism is to some extent the result of this academic movement.

As we have seen in our studies of earlier periods, the quest for academic respectability has sometimes led theology into compromise with non-Christian thought, at least over the course of several generations.

20. Luther's colleague Philipp Melanchthon (1497–1560) was the founder of Lutheran dogmatics. Others in this tradition were Martin Chemnitz (1522–86) and Johann Gerhard (1582–1637). On the Reformed side, the dogmatic tradition continued with Peter Martyr Vermigli (1499–1562), Theodore Beza (1519–1605), Gisbertus Voetius (1589–1676), Girolamo Zanchi (Zanchius) (1516–90), John Owen (1616–83), Francis Turretin (1623–87), and many others. Owen was the chief theologian of the Puritan movement. Turretin's *Institutes of Elenctic Theology* was the chief textbook for ministerial students at Princeton Theological Seminary in the United States until the publication of Charles Hodge's *Systematic Theology*.

21. One exception: it is difficult to find among Luther's successors a doctrine of predestination as strong as that of Luther's *Bondage of the Will*.

22. The confessions of Lutheran churches (Augsburg Confession, Formula of Concord) and Reformed churches (Belgic Confession, Heidelberg Catechism, Canons of Dort, Westminster Confession of Faith, Westminster Larger and Shorter Catechisms, and others) attempted to summarize their churches' doctrines in a concise and systematic fashion. So they became a central focus of Protestant scholastic theology, much of which was devoted to examining and defending them.

Pietism

In any case, the scholastic pattern of theology and church generated a reaction in the opposite direction. Philipp Jakob Spener (1635–1705) wrote in his *Pia Desideria* that the emphasis on theological orthodoxy within Lutheranism had a deadening effect on the practical Christian life. To restore the life of the church, Spener made these proposals:

1. The earnest and thorough study of the Bible in private meetings, *ecclesiolae in ecclesia* ("*little churches within the church*").
2. The Christian priesthood being universal, the laity should share in the spiritual government of the Church.
3. A knowledge of Christianity must be attended by the practice of it as its indispensable sign and supplement.
4. Instead of merely didactic, and often bitter, attacks on the heterodox and unbelievers, a sympathetic and kindly treatment of them.
5. A reorganization of the theological training of the universities, giving more prominence to the devotional life.
6. A different style of preaching, namely, in the place of pleasing rhetoric, the implanting of Christianity in the inner or new man, the soul of which is faith, and its effects the fruits of life.[23]

Spener's movement was called *pietism*, which like many other group designations began as a derogatory expression. Another early leader was August Herrmann Francke (1663–1727), founder of an orphanage in Halle, Germany. Pietism was the subject of fierce attacks by orthodox theologians. The pietists saw themselves, however, as orthodox Protestants, seeking to emphasize principles of spiritual living that were neglected by the academics.

Pietism was the subject of fierce attacks by orthodox theologians. The pietists saw themselves, however, as orthodox Protestants, seeking to emphasize principles of spiritual living that were neglected by the academics.

Although I admire the work of the Protestant scholastics, I also agree with all of Spener's six points above, and I don't see any conflict between these and Protestant theology at its best. The conflict seems to be one of emphasis: an overemphasis on doctrinal precision, giving rise to an overemphasis on Christian practice and inner piety. Or, in terms of the epistemology I presented in chapter 1, an overemphasis on the normative perspective generating overemphases on the situational and existential. It is too bad that Christians at the time could not see that their differences were in fact reconcilable.

Still, even today, some groups of Christians use *pietism* as a derogatory expression, implying a nondogmatic or subjectivist kind of faith, while others complain that a concern for doctrinal soundness leads to *dead orthodoxy*.

23. *Encyclopaedia Britannica*, 11th ed., s.v. "pietism."

REBIRTH OF SECULAR PHILOSOPHY

The Reformation marked a rebirth of biblical Christian thought, emphasizing as had not been done in many centuries the biblical metaphysic (absolute-personality theism, creation), biblical epistemology (based on revelation and the working of the Spirit), and biblical ethics (God's law applied to God's creation by redeemed subjects). This is essentially the biblical philosophy that I outlined in chapter 1 of this book.

The Reformation marked a rebirth of biblical Christian thought, emphasizing as had not been done in many centuries the biblical metaphysic (absolute-personality theism, creation), biblical epistemology (based on revelation and the working of the Spirit), and biblical ethics (God's law applied to God's creation by redeemed subjects).

But in the seventeenth century there was a similar rebirth in non-Christian thought, in which secular thinkers renewed and pressed the claim of autonomous knowledge more consistently than anyone since the Greeks. Indeed, this rebirth echoes strikingly the beginning of philosophy itself in Greek Asia Minor. In chapter 2, I indicated how Greek philosophy was intended to be a replacement for religious and traditional ways of thinking. The philosophers sought for the first time to understand the world by reason alone. The same may be said of the seventeenth-century revival of secular philosophy. Although these philosophers were unavoidably influenced by past philosophical and religious movements, they resolved not to regard any of these as authoritative. They saw human reason as autonomous, as self-authenticating, and as the chief arbiter of all philosophical controversies.

Thus was born the movement known as *modern philosophy*. Modern philosophy in this sense has dominated the philosophical conversation to the present day, though thinkers have arisen from time to time who have gone against the grain, trying to do philosophical work on a Christian foundation. So from a present-day perspective, the Christian dominance of philosophy of the Middle Ages and the Renaissance must be seen as a parenthesis between two periods (the ancient and the modern) in which philosophy is dominated by unbelief.

In the seventeenth century there was a similar rebirth in non-Christian thought, in which secular thinkers renewed and pressed the claim of autonomous knowledge more consistently than anyone since the Greeks.

CONTINENTAL RATIONALISM

Rationalism and Empiricism

The earliest period of modern philosophy featured a contrast between two epistemological positions. Earlier in this book, especially in chapter 1, I have used the term *rationalism* to designate a view common to all non-Christian philosophers, namely, the view that human reason is the ultimate authority of truth and falsehood, right and wrong. In that sense, I contrast rationalism with irrationalism, the view that there is no objective truth or right, and I maintain, following Van Til, that non-Christian thought is such that its rationalism always degenerates into irrationalism and vice versa: the *rationalist-irrationalist dialectic*. In this sense, every non-Christian philosopher is both a rationalist and an irrationalist.

But the term *rationalism* is also used in a narrower sense, and this is the sense more commonly used among philosophers themselves. It distinguishes between two human faculties: reason and sense experience. Sense experience is what we see, hear, taste, feel, smell. Perhaps there are other senses, but there are at least these. Reason is the work of the mind to classify, order, categorize, and understand our knowledge from the senses and whatever other sources of knowledge there may be.

Now, philosophers have differed as to the importance, workings, relationships, and functions of these two human capacities. Plato, for example, thought that the data of our senses was confused and unreliable. He thought that true knowledge came only from beholding the Forms, a knowledge of the reason, not the senses. Locke, on the other hand, thought that even though sense knowledge is not absolutely certain, it is the absolute starting point of knowledge. If reason does not base its thinking on the deliverances of the senses, it becomes speculative, useless, and sometimes bizarre. In my broader uses of the terms, both Plato and Locke are rationalists and irrationalists. But in a narrower sense, Plato is called a *rationalist* and Locke an *empiricist*, for Plato believes in the primacy of reason, Locke the primacy of sense experience.

When there is apparent conflict between these two capacities, a rationalist will resolve it in favor of reason, and an empiricist will resolve it in favor of sense experience. For empiricists, knowledge is primarily inductive, an accumulation of sensory experience. For rationalists, it is primarily a deductive process, drawing inferences from supposedly self-evident axioms. For empiricists, knowledge is mainly *a posteriori*, information gained by means of an empirical inquiry. For rationalists, knowledge is mainly *a priori*, a knowledge of principles known before, and governing any inquiry. Rationalists often regard their *a priori* principles as innate, while empiricists are skeptical about claims to innate knowledge and tend rather to see (as Locke) the mind as an "empty slate" (*tabula rasa*) to be written on by sense experience.

For empiricists, knowledge is mainly a posteriori, *information gained by means of an empirical inquiry. For rationalists, knowledge is mainly* a priori, *a knowledge of principles known before, and governing any inquiry.*

In the period that we consider below, approximately 1600–1800, philosophers are grouped according to their views on this issue. On the continent of Europe, the main tradition of philosophy is rationalist (Descartes, Spinoza, Leibniz). In the British Isles, the main tradition is empiricist (Locke, Berkeley, Hume).[24] We will consider the rationalists first, partly because the rationalist thinkers appeared a bit earlier chronologically, but also because the first rationalist, Descartes, is also known as the first truly "modern" philosopher.

24. It is interesting that even down to the present day the English Channel serves as a general boundary between philosophical schools. But when a thinker such as Immanuel Kant or Ludwig Wittgenstein bridges this boundary, it often creates a major new philosophic conversation.

René Descartes (1596–1650)

My earlier account of the origins of modern philosophy closely parallels Descartes' own search for knowledge. Descartes searched for truth through his travels and his studies of history, philosophy, and theology. He was intent on finding knowledge that was absolutely certain, knowledge that he "clearly and distinctly perceived to be true." So he resolved to doubt everything of which he was not absolutely certain, everything that could possibly be doubtful. But none of his fields of study yielded a certainty that satisfied him.

Descartes was intent on finding knowledge that was absolutely certain, knowledge that he "clearly and distinctly perceived to be true." So he resolved to doubt everything of which he was not absolutely certain, everything that could possibly be doubtful.

Even the knowledge of everyday experience, such as the knowledge that "I am now sitting by the fire," or that "I have two hands," was not absolutely certain, for Descartes reasoned that it was always possible that these experiences were part of a dream. He could never be absolutely certain whether he was dreaming or whether he was awake.

Descartes did have a unique respect for mathematics (he was the inventor of analytic geometry), but during his skeptical experiment, he regarded even mathematics as doubtful. For it was at least possible that a malevolent demon, an "evil genius," was deceiving him into thinking falsely, for example, that $1 + 3 = 4$.

What could deliver him from the skepticism of radical doubt? Ultimately, doubt itself. The one thing that he could not doubt was that he was doubting. Even if he was the victim of an evil genius, and the evil genius was causing him to doubt, he could not doubt that he was doubting. The doubt was real, from whatever cause it came. And even if he was dreaming, he could not doubt that as a participant in the dream he was in a state of doubt. So he "clearly and distinctly perceived" that he was doubting, and he perceived that his doubt itself could not be doubted.

René Descartes

But what is *doubt*? It is an activity of a mind, a thought process. So doubt proves the existence of thought, and that in turn proves the existence of a thinking subject. Hence Descartes' most famous observation: "I think, therefore I am": *cogito, ergo sum*. Here he reproduces an argument from Augustine's *Contra Academicos*, but in a very different context. For Descartes, this argument has a centrality in human knowledge that Augustine attributed only to divine revelation. For Augustine, the argument had some value in refuting skepticism, but it was not his ultimate ground for believing in God and in the possibility of knowledge.

So this one man's intellectual biography tells the story of the rebirth of autonomous reasoning. During the medieval and Renaissance periods, philosophers sought to accumulate knowledge for themselves by comparing and contrasting authorities: Scripture, church tradition, Greek philosophy. Descartes and his successors swept all that aside and began afresh, just as the Greeks around 600 B.C. swept aside all the old religious ideas and the myths of Olympus to seek knowledge by reason alone.

It is not as though Descartes simply rejected God and the church. He always considered himself a faithful Catholic. Indeed, he hoped that the Roman Catholic Church would one day adopt his philosophy as its official philosophy, in place of that of Thomas Aquinas.[25]

Further, he believed that his own argument provided the only possible certainty of the existence of God. Having proved the existence of himself as a thinking being, he presents two arguments for God's existence. The first is a cosmological argument based on the existence in our minds of an *idea* of God. Descartes believes that only a really existing God could have caused us to have that idea.[26] Second, he presents an ontological argument similar to that of Anselm's *Proslogium*: existence is part of the *concept* of God, just as having three angles is part of the concept of a triangle. Since we have a concept of God, therefore, God must exist.

But if God exists, then he bears all perfections. In that way, Descartes sets aside the possibility of an evil genius. For God is not a deceiver, and he would not permit an evil demon to deceive us, at least as to the basic principles of knowledge. Thus Descartes rehabilitates much of the knowledge that he had earlier resolved to doubt. We can, after all, trust much of our sense experience and most of our mental intuitions.

But we should notice that in all this argumentation, Descartes ultimately appeals to his own subjective consciousness as the ultimate criterion of truth. Here there is no role for Scripture or church tradition. As in 600 B.C., tradition is cast aside. Descartes makes a new beginning. His appeal is to *reason*, as with the Greek philosophers. But what is reason in this context? For Descartes, the beginning of reason, its presupposition, is a subjective certainty: that we think. That self-consciousness is an innate idea. And we will see that he acknowledges three other innate ideas: sameness, substance, and God.

We should notice that in all this argumentation, Descartes ultimately appeals to his own subjective consciousness as the ultimate criterion of truth. Here there is no role for Scripture or church tradition.

25. Descartes agreed with Galileo in his controversy with the church over Copernicus's heliocentric theory. He expressed these views in some writings, but subtly, so as not to incur the wrath of the church authorities.

26. The parallel between knowledge of God and knowledge of self is an important one in philosophy. In Scripture and Christian thought, man is the image of God. Recall Augustine's statement that "God and the soul" were the only things he wanted to know. Recall also Calvin's statement that knowledge of God and knowledge of self are interdependent. This parallel continues into more recent philosophical works. Thinkers such as David Hume who are skeptical about the human soul tend also to be skeptical about God. Immanuel Kant, who dismissed the concept of God to the unknowable *noumenal* world, did the same thing to the metaphysical soul. Alvin Plantinga, in his book *God and Other Minds: A Study of the Rational Justification of Belief in God* (Ithaca, NY: Cornell University Press, 1990), argued that the problems of affirming God's existence and the problems of affirming the existence of souls are parallel, equally difficult and equally manageable.

Descartes acknowledges two types of substance. Recall from Aristotle that a substance is a subject of predication—a reality that we can talk and reason about. Substances are expressed in language by nouns, and nouns fit into the subject place in sentences. The substance is "that which is in itself," not an attribute of something else. Descartes distinguished infinite substances and finite ones. The only infinite substance is God. Finite substances include minds and bodies. As we have seen, for Descartes people are essentially minds, beings that think. But we also have intuitions of things other than mind: things such as chairs, tables, and bricks. These are not thinking beings, but extended objects. What is their nature? Descartes uses the example of a piece of wax. As we hold a piece of wax in the hand, we may note that it has such properties as a distinctive color, odor, temperature, and shape. But when we bring the wax close to the fire, all these sense data may change. But the wax remains the same wax.[27] The *real* wax is not red, or round, or sweet-smelling. It is a mere quantity of solid stuff, moving at one velocity or other.[28] The colors, sounds, and tastes are in the mind, caused by material substances, but they are not qualities of the material substance itself.

For Descartes, then, there are mental substances (minds, selves, souls) and material substances (things, objects). Mental substances are thinking beings; material substances are extended beings.

For Descartes, then, there are mental substances (minds, selves, souls) and material substances (things, objects).[29] Mental substances are thinking beings; material substances are extended beings. Material substances do not think, and mental substances have no extension (they are *incorporeal*). Mental substances are free in a libertarian sense, material substances determined by a mechanistic causality.

How can mental and material substances have any effect on each other? Specifically, how can the human mind (an incorporeal thinking being) have any effect on the body (an extended thing)?

This distinction creates a major problem in Descartes' system: how can mental and material substances have any effect on each other? Specifically, how can the human mind (an incorporeal thinking being) have any effect on the body (an extended thing)? An unextended substance such as the mind, it would seem, is weightless and powerless. It cannot move an extended object such as the body. Yet it seems obvious that, for example, a mental intention can cause my arm to rise.

Descartes' answer to this problem has become a long-standing philosophical joke: He says that the body and mind can affect each other *just a little bit* in the body's pineal gland.[30] The mind creates a tiny movement

27. For Descartes, sameness, like substance, is an innate mental intuition. The other two innate mental intuitions are self and God.

28. Conveniently, the reduction of material substances to extension in motion makes it easier to analyze them by mathematics alone and renders sense experience less important.

29. Note the echo here of the Greek distinction between form and matter. Descartes' distinction is not the same as that of either Plato or Aristotle, but he is trying to interpret some of the same data that led the Greeks to this distinction.

30. At the time, medical scientists were unaware that this gland had any actual functions. So it was a suitable object of philosophical speculation.

in the gland, which creates a larger movement, and so on. But if these substances are defined so that they cannot affect each other in principle, how can Descartes say that they can affect each other just a little bit?[31]

This issue is known as the *mind-body problem* in modern philosophy. We will see several solutions to it by other philosophers.[32] It should not be surprising that they have not found Descartes' solution to be adequate.

Such was the rebirth of philosophy based on would-be autonomous reasoning. This is a major turning point in the history of philosophy, and it has governed the mainstream of academic philosophy down to the present day. Many have disagreed with Descartes on this matter or that, but most respectable philosophers have agreed that the problems of philosophy must be resolved by autonomous thought, not by submission of the mind to divine revelation.

Baruch (Benedict) Spinoza (1634–77)

Spinoza's parents were Portuguese Jews who lived in Spain but were expelled because of their religion. They settled in Amsterdam, Holland, which was one of the most tolerant cultures of the world in those days. Baruch ground lenses for a living, and gave attention to philosophy. In time, he was expelled from the synagogue because of his heretical view of God.

Spinoza admired Descartes and joined his project of reconstructing philosophy on a rationalistic basis. He said at one point that "the order and connection of ideas is the same as the order and connection of things." This is a rationalistic slogan, similar to that of Parmenides that "it is the same thing to be and to be thought."[33] The implication is that true human thought is so perfectly attuned to the real world that it not only corresponds with the world, but is *identical* with the world. A true rationalist can be satisfied with nothing less than identity between thought and thing. As we will see below, this epistemological principle is connected with Spinoza's pantheism.

Such was the rebirth of philosophy based on would-be autonomous reasoning. This is a major turning point in the history of philosophy, and it has governed the mainstream of academic philosophy down to the present day.

Descartes, as I noted, was an admirer of mathematical reasoning and hoped to organize his philosophy as a kind of mathematical system. He never accomplished the axiomatization of his philosophy, but Spinoza

31. So Gilbert Ryle, in his book *The Concept of Mind* (New York: Barnes and Noble, 1949), famously described Descartes' view as "the ghost in the machine."

32. Nicolas Malebranche (1638–1715), following Arnold Geulincx, responds to the problem this way: minds do not cause effects in bodies, or vice versa, but God causes effects in both, making it appear that minds cause effects in bodies and the reverse. Malebranche's solution is called *occasionalism*, and it echoes Spinoza's view that God is, in the end, the only true cause.

33. Plotinus quoted this statement favorably. Later, we will note Hegel's similar slogan: "the real is the rational and the rational is the real."

attempted that in his early work *The Principles of Cartesian Philosophy*. Later, his own magnum opus, *Ethics Geometrically Demonstrated*, presented his philosophy in a form similar to Euclid's geometry: with axioms, propositions deduced from them, corollaries, lemmas, and so on.

Spinoza intended to be more God-centered than Descartes. For Descartes, the existence of God was a logical implication of our own idea of God. But Spinoza intended to *start* with God. His proof of God's existence, however, was an ontological argument similar to that of Descartes.[34]

Baruch (Benedict) Spinoza

Like Descartes, Spinoza identifies God as a substance. His definition of *substance* is similar to the common definition, but adds a rationalistic twist: substance is that which is in itself *and is conceived through itself*. On this understanding, substance is not only self-existent (*a se*) but also self-attesting or self-authenticating. It is the supreme criterion of truth and falsity, right and wrong. Note the connection between metaphysics (self-existence) and epistemology (self-authentication).[35] If God is the first principle of being, he is also the first presupposition of knowledge.

Understood thus, God is the only substance. Only one being can be truly self-existent, dependent on nothing else for his existence and maintenance. If there were another such being, then it would have properties that belong to God, and the two beings would be mutually limited. Also, only one being can be the first principle of knowledge. Spinoza thought Descartes was inconsistent for allowing mental and material substances to exist alongside the divine substance.

Spinoza, therefore, is a monist, one who believes that the universe consists of only one being. In this regard he follows the tradition of the Milesian nature philosophers and especially of Parmenides and Plotinus. Epistemological rationalism tends to beget metaphysical monism.

Spinoza, therefore, is a monist, one who believes that the universe consists of only one being. In this regard he follows the tradition of the Milesian nature philosophers and especially of Parmenides and Plotinus. Epistemological rationalism tends to beget metaphysical monism. For the rationalist wants to find one comprehensive explanation for everything in the universe. The explanation that he claims to find becomes the ultimate reality, which reduces all other phenomena to illusion or, in Spinoza's case, to attributes of the one reality. Of course, monism is antithetical to Christianity, because it denies the fundamental distinction between Creator and creature. Indeed, biblical Christianity denies the rationalist quest altogether. For the rationalist seeks

34. It might seem contradictory to say that we should "start with" God and at the same time prove his existence by an argument. But the reader should recall from my treatment of Anselm's argument that the ontological argument is often a way of setting forth one's ultimate presupposition. Spinoza and Descartes, like Anselm, indicate by their argument that the highest being in their thought must bear the attribute of existence, or else it would not be the highest being.

35. This connection between metaphysics and epistemology is one that presuppositional Christians should embrace. The biblical God is very different from the god of Spinoza, but like Spinoza's god he is self-attesting because he is self-existent.

an *ultimate* rational understanding of the world, an understanding that Scripture attributes only to God.

But to continue with Spinoza's argument: For Spinoza, God has infinite attributes. An attribute is what the intellect perceives to be the essence of an object.[36] Everything in the world around us is an attribute of God. Therefore, God and the world are one. God is the world and the world is God. The whole may be called either *God* or *nature*: *Deus sive natura*. God is "nature naturing itself" (*natura naturans*), and the world is "nature receiving its nature from God" (*natura naturata*).

The two attributes of God most knowable to man, among the infinity of others, are mind and body. Descartes had defined these as substances with properties so opposite that their interaction was virtually impossible. Spinoza says, rather, that these are both attributes of God, ways by which we perceive him. As such, they are not separate from each other. Rather, they are perspectives on God and on each other. To Spinoza, the mind is "the idea of the body."[37] And on his basis we should also say that the body is the extension of the mind. So the mind-body problem disappears. Recall that for Spinoza the order and connection of ideas (mind) is the same as the order and connection of things (body).[38] So ideas and bodies are the same realities, seen from different perspectives. It is not that ideas or volitions *cause* the motions of bodies, or vice versa; rather, they *are* the motions of bodies, seen from a different perspective.

For Spinoza, there is an important analogy between the necessity of logical conclusions deduced from their premises and the necessity of effects generated by causes. So Spinoza is a determinist.

For Spinoza, there is an important analogy between the necessity of logical conclusions deduced from their premises and the necessity of effects generated by causes. So Spinoza is a determinist. Just as in his philosophy each proposition is a necessary logical deduction from an axiom, so in the world each event is a necessary consequence of an antecedent cause, with God as the First Cause. Again, the structure of the world corresponds to the structure of reason; indeed, the two are identical. There is no free will in the libertarian sense, no chance or randomness. Human thought, in its best form (i.e., geometrically axiomatized), is a system of propositions that necessarily follow from one another. The reality of the world is a system of things that follow from necessary causes, ultimately from God.

Nevertheless, Spinoza denied that this causal system has a goal. Aristotle had distinguished efficient cause from final cause, the latter

36. Spinoza's reference to the human intellect here may suggest that these attributes are only apparent—existing in our perceptions rather than in reality. But we should remind ourselves that for Spinoza the rationalist, what the intellect perceives is what really is.

37. Compare Aristotle's view that the mind is the *form* of the body.

38. Another point of connection between epistemology and metaphysics in Spinoza's system.

being the goal for which something exists.[39] Spinoza denied the final cause and affirmed only efficient cause. So in Spinoza's view, God does not seek a particular outcome to history.

Spinoza's main work is called *Ethics Geometrically Demonstrated*, in which all the above metaphysics and epistemology are intended to lay a foundation for human behavior. After all the ingenious, creative reasoning early in the book, his ethical conclusions are a bit disappointing. He starts with a crude egoism, like the Greek Cyrenaics: Good is what we perceive as pleasure; bad is what brings pain. But eventually Spinoza's egoism blossoms with altruistic implications, as with Epicurus: our highest pleasure is found in the pleasure of others and ultimately in the well-being of all nature, that is, the well-being of God. As in Stoicism, which also denied libertarian free choice, Spinoza urges us to gain higher levels of knowledge (= goodness) by understanding the causes of events. As in Plato (but not in Scripture), knowledge necessarily leads to virtue. The more we understand the interconnections of things, the more we will understand the value of doing good to all beings.

Spinoza denied the final cause and affirmed only efficient cause. So in Spinoza's view, God does not seek a particular outcome to history.

The end of this ethical quest, then, is knowledge of everything, that is, the knowledge of God. To know God is to love him. So Spinoza commends to his readers as their highest goal in life what he calls the "intellectual love of God."

Gottfried Wilhelm Leibniz (1646–1716)

Leibniz, the third[40] of the great rationalists, was the first important philosopher of Germany. Like Descartes and Spinoza, he was a mathematician. He published the first formulation of the infinitesimal calculus, before Isaac Newton, but many argued that Newton had discovered it first, and Leibniz's claim remains controversial.

In rationalistic philosophy, a major goal is to discover the ultimate character of the things and forces in the universe. In metaphysics, this is a quest for what is most fundamental to everything else in the world (to Thales, water; to Plato, Form; etc.). In epistemology, it is a quest for the ultimate criterion of truth and falsity, right and wrong. Often this study seeks to identify what objects are *substances*, for substances are thought to be fundamental to other realities.

In rationalistic philosophy, a major goal is to discover the ultimate character of the things and forces in the universe. In metaphysics, this is a quest for what is most fundamental to everything else in the world . . . . In epistemology, it is a quest for the ultimate criterion of truth and falsity, right and wrong.

39. In addition, Aristotle spoke of the formal cause (which makes something what it is) and the material cause (what something is made of).

40. It is interesting that in many of the famous philosophical schools there are three major representatives. Among early Protestants: Lutherans, Calvinists, Anabaptists. British empiricists: Locke, Berkeley, Hume. Among German idealists: Fichte, Schelling, Hegel. British idealists: Green, Bradley, Bosanquet. American pragmatists: Peirce, James, Dewey. I won't speculate here as to how this phenomenon may or may not reflect the threenesses mentioned in chapter 1 of this book.

Gottfried Wilhelm Leibniz

We recall that for Descartes there are two substances, mind and matter, which govern the realms of epistemology and metaphysics, respectively, but which, perplexingly, do not interact with each other except in the pineal gland. There is also for Descartes the divine substance. But Descartes does little with the concepts of creation (metaphysics) and revelation (epistemology) that define God's involvement in creation according to traditional Christian thought. For Spinoza, there is one substance, God, and mind and matter are two perspectives on that substance. But Spinoza, too, fails to explain how God informs us of the nature of truth, and he appears to deny the doctrine of creation, making the world and God coeternal. So neither God nor nature explains the other.

But historically there has been another way of seeking the ultimate nature of being. If Thales, Parmenides, Plotinus, and Spinoza have essentially identified the whole universe as the metaphysical ultimate, others such as Democritus and Epicurus (like many modern scientists) have tried to identify the smallest components of the world. They have assumed, of course, that once you chop everything down to its smallest constituents, you will discover that the universe is made up of essentially the same kind of stuff. These smallest constituents of the universe are likely to be the most ultimate, those that provide the most significant explanations of everything else. This is the procedure of *atomism*, and Leibniz is essentially an atomist, though he has a very different view of atoms from Democritus. Atomists are usually materialists. But Leibniz, interestingly, argues that the smallest things in the world are actually *minds*. One who believes that everything is essentially mind is called an *idealist*. So Leibniz is an atomistic idealist.

It makes some sense, I suppose, to assume that if you try to identify the smallest reality, you will eventually find something that cannot be chopped up any further. You will perhaps discover elements, molecules, atoms, protons, neutrons, electrons, quarks, bosons, superstrings. Perhaps even superstrings can be further divided. But eventually you will discover something that cannot be chopped any more. If not, then you have failed to find what you are looking for: a principle that explains everything else.

When you do reach your goal, a smallest point, it cannot be chopped any more. The reason is not only that we lack small enough instruments and sufficient dexterity, but that it is *in principle* unchoppable. It can be argued that matter, however small, can always be chopped smaller. For in the rationalism of the seventeenth and eighteenth centuries, matter is, by definition, extension; and where there is extension, there can be less extension. But if you discover something that cannot be chopped any further in principle, the particle must be unextended, and therefore something other than matter. And what else is there, besides matter? In the seventeenth century, the only alternative is mind. Hence atomistic idealism.[41]

These mental atoms Leibniz calls *monads*. And he has a number of things to say about them that are both interesting and a bit bizarre. Monads are units of psychic *force*. They are not passive or inert like Descartes' *matter*, or like Descartes' unextended (therefore impotent) minds. Leibniz's monads make things happen. Still, they don't have free will in the libertarian sense. They are, rather, preprogrammed by God.

All things and people are made of monads. They are clustered together to form larger objects. So Leibniz is a *panpsychist*, one who believes that everything thinks, from rocks and clouds to human beings to God. My body is a society of monads, every one of which engages in thought and exercises force. But that society is ruled by a *queen monad*, what I call my *mind*, which sets forth the larger direction of the whole society.

Leibniz is a panpsychist, one who believes that everything thinks, from rocks and clouds to human beings to God. My body is a society of monads, every one of which engages in thought and exercises force. But that society is ruled by a queen monad, *what I call my* mind, *which sets forth the larger direction of the whole society.*

God is the queen monad of the whole universe, the supreme monad. Leibniz proves the existence of God by a cosmological argument with a rationalistic twist:[42] He formulates what he calls the *principle of sufficient reason*, which means that nothing ever exists or does anything without a reason. God must exist, because only he can be the sufficient reason of the universe. Similarly, everything that a monad thinks or does requires a sufficient reason—and the only sufficient reason is divine foreordination.

Leibniz's philosophy of language merges with his monadological metaphysics. Leibniz is one of the first important thinkers to use the distinction between *analytic* and *synthetic* sentences. An analytic statement is true by definition, for in such a statement the predicate is part of the subject, as in "All bachelors are unmarried." Analytic statements are necessarily true; they cannot possibly be false. And they are a priori in the sense that they can be known by knowing the meaning of the terms alone, without observation or experience of anything beyond the language.

Leibniz's philosophy of language merges with his monadological metaphysics. Leibniz is one of the first important thinkers to use the distinction between analytic *and* synthetic *sentences.*

Synthetic sentences, such as "the cat is on the mat," are not true or false by definition. To determine their truth, we must investigate the world of experience. Thus, they are *a posteriori*, that is, based on an empirical inquiry.

Leibniz grants this distinction as a starting point. But then he argues that all sentences, once all is said and done, are analytic. For everything we are and do is foreordained by God. When God determines to create

41. It is interesting to compare Leibniz's thinking here with that of twentieth-century process thought. See chapter 11.

42. Recall the "rationalistic twist" in Spinoza's definition of *substance*.

Charlie, the name *Charlie* means, for God, everything that Charlie will ever be or do. We might think "Charlie learned how to play the oboe" is a synthetic statement. But Charlie's learning to play the oboe is simply what God planned for him to do. To God, it is part of Charlie's nature, his essence. So "learning to play the oboe" is part of the meaning of *Charlie*. "Charlie learned to play the oboe" is therefore an analytic statement, a statement about the *nature* of Charlie as seen by the divine mind.[43]

Similarly, everything that every monad thinks or does is part of its nature. It exists only to carry out the mission that God has inscribed on its nature. Monads do not act because other monads cause them to act. They act only by their own natures, as God has created them. So there is no monad-to-monad causality. A monad will not act in response to another monad, but only according to its own nature. The monad is "pregnant with its own future states." So, Leibniz says, the monads "have no windows."

But why, then, do things appear to work together, to be coordinated in their actions? Why does it *appear* that one monad causes changes in another? Evidently, God makes them work together. Leibniz speaks of a divinely "pre-established harmony." So that even though each monad is merely acting out its internal nature, its actions are perfectly coordinated with everything else. It is like each member of an orchestra playing his own instrument from its own piece of music, but contributing to the greater harmony of the whole.

Leibniz speaks of a divinely "pre-established harmony." So that even though each monad is merely acting out its internal nature, its actions are perfectly coordinated with everything else.

Although the monads have no windows, they do have mirrors. For God makes each monad to reflect the entire universe from its own perspective. Monads on planet Earth are fairly isolated from those, say, on Jupiter. But Leibniz believed that each monad hears and sees everything in the universe, however faintly, by *tiny perceptions* (*petite perceptions*).

God does not choose to actualize monads at random. He has sufficient reason for everything. Among those is his purpose to actualize monads of all kinds and levels, of all different degrees of power. Given that general purpose, he creates the largest number of monads that are logically compatible with one another (*compossible*). He makes the

43. Here Leibniz does something that would have seemed very radical to medieval thinkers. Aristotle distinguished between substances, attributes (some necessary, some accidental), and actions. For him, definitions denote the substance, what something *is*. They state the kind of substance (in a man, "rational animal") and perhaps some of his necessary attributes. But for Aristotle, accidental predications (snub-nosed, five feet ten) were not part of the substance or definition. Nor, certainly, were his actions (e.g., that he went to college). Statements about a person's accidental properties and actions are, for Aristotle, never part of the person's definition, and are synthetic, not analytic. But Leibniz boldly asks: how can we actually prove where that line should be drawn, between substance, necessary attribute, accidental attribute, and action? Essentially he says there is no way to do it. So all of these form aspects of the definition of the person in God's mind. And to God, statements of all these types are analytic.

best world that he can. But not all goods are compossible. So some evils are necessary. Leibniz says that this is the best possible world. It would not have been possible for God to create a world without evil. But in God's world, the evils will certainly be overcome by good. This is Leibniz's solution to the problem of evil: evil is logically necessary to the achievement of a good world. Many, such as Voltaire in *Candide*, have found this solution inadequate: can we really believe, in the midst of terrible suffering, that a good God could not have made a better world than this?[44]

Leibniz says that this is the best possible world. It would not have been possible for God to create a world without evil. But in God's world, the evils will certainly be overcome by good. This is Leibniz's solution to the problem of evil: evil is logically necessary to the achievement of a good world.

At times, Leibniz appears to be a conventional theist, for he believes that God is the One who has established the preexisting harmony. But at other times, God seems himself to be constricted by the implacable force of logic. Leibniz's "best possible world" argument seems to suppose that logic is a force that constrains God—in this case, constraining him from making a perfect world. The point is not merely that God observes logic, which he does in many other philosophical and theological systems.[45] The problem, rather, is that Leibniz seems to think that the structure of the universe is exhaustively dictated by logic, so that God's activity is superfluous. At most, God is a "cosmic accountant," one who makes the kind of world that logic dictates to him. That is a serious issue in discussions of Leibniz, but I will not be able to enter further into it now.

BRITISH EMPIRICISM

Thomas Hobbes (1588–1679)

As I indicated earlier in this chapter, philosophers between 1600 and 1800 are usually grouped under the categories *rationalists* and *empiricists*. In this configuration, Hobbes is something of an anomaly, fitting neither category very comfortably. I choose to discuss him in this location because he was British, he antedated and influenced the main British empiricists, and there are at least some empirical elements in his thinking.

Thomas Hobbes

Hobbes did, however, travel extensively in Europe, and he studied and interacted with the philosophy of Descartes. Later, he engaged in a careful, detailed critique of Descartes' *Meditations*. Like the Continental rationalists, he was convinced that the certainty of geometry was the model that philosophers should follow.

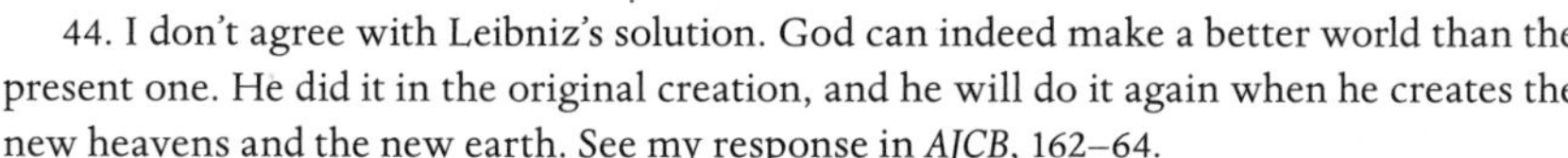

44. I don't agree with Leibniz's solution. God can indeed make a better world than the present one. He did it in the original creation, and he will do it again when he creates the new heavens and the new earth. See my response in *AJCB*, 162–64.

45. In Christian thought, it is typical to say that God *is* logic or rationality and that therefore his actions will always be logical, however much there may be *apparent* contradictions in his actions and words from human points of view.

But if his admiration of mathematics turned him toward the Continental rationalists, his love of science pushed him in a more empirical direction. Francis Bacon (1561–1626) befriended him. Bacon's scientific method featured induction and experiment. Hobbes was also a nominalist, also in the British tradition, following William of Occam. Nominalism also inclines thinkers toward empiricism, since it demands that they study the particulars of the world, rather than trying to deduce them from the general principles of nature.

I think that in the final analysis Hobbes is an empiricist, but one dominated in a fairly obvious way[46] by some dogmatic presuppositions. He is a materialist, believing that all reality consists of matter in motion.[47] For him, no reality—not the soul, nor even God—is incorporeal. He acknowledges the existence of God by traditional arguments, but God plays little role in his philosophy except First Cause. For Hobbes, the world is a deterministic sequence of material causes and effects. Hobbes does not argue any of these propositions from any kind of empirical evidence. He seems to think (in a way more like rationalism) that materialism is an *axiom*, a self-attesting truth. He seems to think that to say that something exists is sufficient to say that it is material and that it is part of the deterministic causal order.[48]

For Hobbes, the world is a deterministic sequence of material causes and effects. Hobbes does not argue any of these propositions from any kind of empirical evidence. He seems to think (in a way more like rationalism) that materialism is an axiom, *a self-attesting truth.*

Indeed, these presuppositions underlie his epistemology, rather than the other way around. Hobbes regards knowledge as a particular kind of material causation. It begins when something outside us moves and causes a motion inside us. The result is an image within the mind (what Hobbes called a *phantasm*). The phantasm has some lingering effects. Although it fades away, we are able in many cases to retrieve it (memory) or to combine it with other phantasms (imagination). We are able to think about them later, because thinking of one leads us to think of the next: we recall not only the phantasms, but their order as well.

This theory of knowledge is certainly empiricist in the sense that it is sensationalist: all knowledge begins in the sensory process, and we know what we know by tracing a set of causes and effects back to their sensory source. At the same time, as we saw earlier, Hobbes's determinism is not warranted by any empirical argument. How could we *sense* that all reality is corporeal and that all events are mechanistically determined?

Hobbes is of interest today mainly because of his social and political philosophy. He is one of the major authors of the *social-contract* theory

46. That is, more obvious than with most empiricists.

47. In this regard, he resembles the ancient Stoics, and also the atomists, such as Democritus and Epicurus.

48. Recall my similar remark about Stoic "materialism" in Chapter 2.

of political obligation,[49] primarily in his major work, *Leviathan*. He believes that apart from government, human beings have "the right of all to all," the right to anything we desire. That naturally leads to conflict—as he puts it, "the war of all against all." In an anarchic world, there are "no arts; no letters; no society; and which is worst of all, continual fear, and danger of violent death; and the life of man solitary, poor, nasty, brutish, and short."[50] But there are "laws of nature" that motivate people to avoid or escape this kind of existence, which require us to give up our "right to all" and enter into a contract with others to create an artificial person, the commonwealth or state, Leviathan, which has totalitarian power.

Hobbes believes that apart from government, human beings have "the right of all to all," the right to anything we desire. That naturally leads to conflict—as he puts it, "the war of all against all."

In this book, I am not able to give much attention to social theory. But it is interesting to know here how many questions Hobbes leaves unanswered. For one thing, if the world consists entirely of matter and motion, on what basis does Hobbes speak of *rights*, *laws*, and *obligations*?[51]

Although it is not clear whether we should call Hobbes a rationalist or an empiricist, it is clear that he is an example of the *new* philosophy based on a renewal of secularism. Hobbes no more than Descartes made explicit use of Scripture or religious tradition in formulating his views, and he had no regard for the authority of Plato or Aristotle, though he follows the Stoics in important ways. His fundamental principle, like that of Descartes and Locke, is the autonomy of human reason.

John Locke (1632–1704)

One of the best arguments for regarding Hobbes as a rationalist rather than an empiricist is this: Empiricists typically begin with epistemology and work their way from there to metaphysics and ethics. Rationalists, rather, begin with metaphysical *axioms* and deduce from them what knowledge and ethics must be. So Descartes begins with his own existence as a thinking being separate from all matter, deduces

Empiricists typically begin with epistemology and work their way from there to metaphysics and ethics. Rationalists, rather, begin with metaphysical axioms *and deduce from them what knowledge and ethics must be.*

49. As Samuel Rutherford, in *Lex, Rex* (1644), pointed out, there are contractual elements in the Israelite kingship. Rutherford was a theologian and member of the Westminster Assembly. Recall that although David was anointed king in early life (1 Sam. 16:13), he did not begin to rule until he was accepted by the nation's elders, first in Judah (2 Sam. 2:4) and then in Israel (2 Sam. 5:1–5). But in Scripture, God's choice was determinative. The idea of a social contract can be found among Greek philosophers (Epicurus), and later in Hugo Grotius (1625), John Locke (1689), and Jean-Jacques Rousseau (1752). But these could not agree with one another or with Hobbes about the character of the state of nature, the nature of human rights (either within or beyond the state of nature), or the elements of the social contract. In this book, I have decided not to give much attention to ethics or to social and political philosophy. For a summary analysis of philosophic thought on these subjects, see *DCL*, 54–125, 603–4.

50. Hobbes, *Leviathan*, 13.

51. The argument from facts to obligations is what G. E. Moore later called the *naturalistic fallacy*. Empiricist David Hume was one of the first to identify the problem.

John Locke

from that the existence of God, and then deduces from these propositions his concepts of epistemology and ethics. Spinoza begins with a metaphysic of the existence of God, Leibniz with a metaphysical monadology that supposedly explains how we have knowledge. Hobbes is rationalistic in that he begins with a materialistic determinism, and then analyzes knowledge as a process through which the mechanism of the cosmos determines changes in our sense organs.

Locke, however, refuses to comment on the nature of the universe until he describes how it is possible for us to know the universe. He puts epistemology before metaphysics, a pattern that we will find repeated in the other major representatives of the empirical tradition, Berkeley and Hume. Seen from this perspective, Locke would seem to be, rather than Hobbes, the first representative of the empirical tradition.

The biblical philosophy that I advocate in this book would take a third option: neither metaphysics nor epistemology is prior to the other. Both these disciplines have legitimate implications for each other. The biblical epistemology presupposes the biblical metaphysics, and vice versa. But their unity is evident only through divine revelation, which stands above human life and presents a complete worldview.

Let us, however, follow Locke's epistemological argument. For Locke, and for others in the empiricist tradition, knowledge is primarily a knowledge of our *ideas*, the contents of our minds.[52] This is important. People sometimes talk as though an empiricist were someone who sets aside the restraints of human thought and who goes out to look at the *world*, to investigate the *facts*. That model would seem to bring empiricist philosophy close to the natural sciences. But empiricists do not hold that kind of "direct realism," and for that matter, neither do most scientists (see chapter 12). They understand that our knowledge of the world is *mediated* by our mental equipment.[53] In terms of the triangular diagram I expounded in chapter 1, knowledge is existential (a knowledge of ourselves), not directly situational (a knowledge of the world). Metaphysics, therefore (a knowledge of the world), presupposes epistemology (a knowledge of our own epistemic equipment).

Locke begins his study of ideas negatively: he denies that there are any *innate* ideas, thus taking issue with Plato, Descartes, Leibniz, and many others. Plato, for example, thought we should judge experience by comparing it with certain ideas we have independent of experience. For example, the concept of perfect virtue is independent of experience, for we have never experienced it on earth. But we do have the *idea* of perfect virtue, and it serves as a criterion for the virtues we experience.

52. Locke's "ideas" are essentially the "phantasms" of Hobbes.

53. Of course, in science and to some extent in ordinary life, we supplement our mental equipment by devices of various kinds: eyeglasses, telescopes, microscopes, and so forth.

Such ideas, distinct as they are from experience, are often regarded as innate. The necessity of such criteria is one common argument for the existence of innate ideas. Recall, then,[54] that many philosophers have affirmed *a priori* knowledge—knowledge that exists before any inquiry, and that governs the process of inquiry.[55] Examples of claims to *a priori* knowledge are, besides Plato's recollection of Forms, laws of logic and mathematics, and moral standards. All of these would seem to be innate, for it is difficult to account for them otherwise.

Many philosophers have affirmed a priori *knowledge—knowledge that exists before any inquiry, and that governs the process of inquiry. Examples of claims to* a priori *knowledge are, besides Plato's recollection of Forms, laws of logic and mathematics, and moral standards. All of these would seem to be innate, for it is difficult to account for them otherwise.*

Locke seems to reject all these contentions. But let us look more closely at the laws of logic. Locke says that these are not innate, but that they are "immediately persuasive." Yet what is there in us that enables us to see these as immediately persuasive? It is not plausible to say that this conviction comes from sensation;[56] rather, it would seem to be part of the equipment of the mind itself. Locke would say that this is not innate, for very young children are not able to formulate logical principles. But that is to take innateness in a fairly trivial sense. Tiny babies cannot formulate any propositions at all. The more interesting question is whether the human mind naturally, as it matures, forms beliefs that are *a priori* in the sense of governing experience rather than arising from it.

Locke suggests that we imagine the mind as something altogether devoid of knowledge:[57] a clean slate, a *tabula rasa*. What, then, might fill up that tablet? *Experience*, Locke says, setting forth the charter of the empirical tradition in philosophy.

Locke suggests that we imagine the mind as something altogether devoid of knowledge: a clean slate, a tabula rasa. *What, then, might fill up that tablet?* Experience, *Locke says, setting forth the charter of the empirical tradition in philosophy.*

Locke's thought-experiment is worth pondering. What is this *experience* that constitutes and underlies the whole content of the mind? It is not the facts of the world itself, but some sort of relation between the facts and our own thought about them, our ideas. But what sort of relation? Locke says that although experience does not present to us the actual world (i.e., the world apart from experience[58]), it does present to us a distinction between *ideas of sensation* and *ideas of reflection*:

> Sensation is "the great source of most of the ideas we have." The other facet of experience is reflection, an activity of the

54. We discussed this in the earlier section on Leibniz.

55. Since it "governs" inquiry, it stands as a *normative perspective* in terms of my triangular diagram.

56. The empiricists of this period did not try to derive laws of logic from sense experience. John Stuart Mill (1806–73) did try to make this derivation, but his attempt has been largely rejected, even by other empiricists.

57. A little bit like Descartes' *radical doubt*. Both Locke and Descartes are looking for something that they can clearly and distinctly believe to be true. Descartes finds it in the intuition of self-existence, Locke in ideas based on sense experience.

58. That is, what Kant called the *noumenal*. See chapter 7.

> mind that produces ideas by taking notice of previous ideas furnished by the senses. Reflection involves perception, thinking, doubting, believing, reasoning, knowing, willing, and all those activities of the mind that produce ideas by taking notice of previous ideas furnished by the senses.[59]

But if the mind has a capacity to reflect on the data of its senses, that capacity is innate, at least in the sense that it is not acquired through sense experience. It would seem that Locke's *experience* is something more than mere sensation. Indeed, he may well be importing into his concept of experience some content that others would rather ascribe to *a priori* knowledge—content, indeed, that others would describe as innate. Such considerations make it less clear, then, that Locke's epistemology is radically different from that of the rationalists.

If the mind has a capacity to reflect on the data of its senses, that capacity is innate, at least in the sense that it is not acquired through sense experience.

But we should follow Locke's argument further. He makes much of two further distinctions: between simple and complex ideas and between primary and secondary qualities. First, the distinction between simple and complex ideas. Simple ideas come passively into our minds through the senses, or through the reflective process: whiteness, sweetness, bitterness, and so on. Complex ideas are the result of the mind's actively bringing simple ideas into various relationships to one another: combining, separating, or abstracting one from another.[60]

The distinction between primary and secondary qualities is not a distinction between different classes of our ideas, but a distinction between the different kinds of objects to which our ideas correspond. To Locke, a *quality* is "the power [in an object] to produce any idea in our mind."[61] Now, *primary* qualities are those that "really do exist in the bodies themselves."[62] So our ideas of them "resemble exactly" the qualities of the object itself.

> Secondary qualities, on the other hand, produce ideas in our mind that have no exact counterpart in the object. We have the idea of *cold* when we touch the snowball and the idea of *white* when we see it. But there is no whiteness or coldness in the snowball. What *is* in the snowball is the quality, the power to create in us the ideas of cold and white. Primary qualities, then, refer to solidity, extension, figure, motion or rest, and number—or qualities which belong to the object. Secondary

59. Samuel Enoch Stumpf and James Fieser, *Socrates to Sartre and Beyond: A History of Philosophy* (Boston: McGraw-Hill, 2003), 254.

60. This is reminiscent of Aristotle's distinction between the passive and the active intellect.

61. Stumpf and Fieser, *Socrates to Sartre and Beyond*, 255.

62. Ibid.

> qualities, such as colors, sounds, tastes, and odors, do not belong to or constitute bodies except as powers to produce these ideas in us.[63]

We may recall that by a similar argument Descartes had reduced all qualities of material objects to *extension*. All other qualities, he thought, could be changed while the substance remained. In Newtonian science, which both Descartes and Locke respected, colors are understood as the effects of objects on the eye, rather than as qualities of the objects themselves.[64] This understanding of material objects makes it easier to analyze them by mathematics and physics. If objects are essentially extended bodies in motion, then the scientist-philosopher need not be preoccupied with all the colors, tastes, and sounds that make the world interesting to us. He needs only to consider volume, weight, location, acceleration, and the like.

Both Descartes and Locke invoke the concept of substance, for traditionally substance is what bears qualities; it is the subject of which qualities are predicates.

But is it possible to further describe these objects? Both Descartes and Locke invoke the concept of *substance*, for traditionally substance is what bears qualities; it is the subject of which qualities are predicates. So Locke says that we can give the name *substance* to the objects that have the power to give us ideas of simple predicates. But here he admits some perplexity:

> If anyone will examine himself concerning his notion of pure substance in general, he will find he has no other idea of it at all, but only a supposition of he knows not what support of such qualities which are capable of producing simple ideas in us.[65]

In the end, for Locke, substance is "something, I know not what." We know it not from experience, but from a causal argument: we must posit substance as a cause of our ideas.

In the end, for Locke, substance is "something, I know not what." We know it not from experience, but from a causal argument: we must posit substance as a cause of our ideas.[66] This raises questions about the consistency of Locke's empiricism. It also raises questions about whether empiricism can give us knowledge about the real world. For, as everybody understood the term, *substance* is what the world consists of, the subject of all predicates. If we cannot know substances, what can we know? This perplexity suggests that empiricism is vulnerable to skepticism, a skepticism made acute by the later arguments of David Hume.

63. Ibid.

64. Democritus used a similar argument to show that the basic substances of the universe, the atoms, have only the characteristics of matter and motion.

65. Stumpf and Fieser, *Socrates to Sartre and Beyond*, 256.

66. In this respect, Locke's *substance* is like Kant's *noumenal*, which I will discuss in chapter 7.

Locke is known today mainly for his political theory. Like Hobbes, he is part of the social-contract tradition: government emerges from an agreement among people living in a "state of nature" where no government exists. But Hobbes and Locke present the state of nature in very different terms. For Hobbes it is horrible: a war of all against all; "solitary, poor, nasty, brutish, and short." But for Locke it is not nearly so bad. It is a society in which people live by moral law. But there are no objective ways of resolving disputes, so political society is needed.

Locke speaks about the "inalienable character of human rights," well known to students of the founding of the United States of America. Government rests on the consent of the governed, who always retain their right to life, liberty, and property. Contrary to Hobbes, Locke believes that there are a number of circumstances in which the people have the right to rebel against their sovereigns. Indeed, the American Revolution was defended chiefly on Lockean grounds.

As an American, I am grateful to Locke for the role he played in the establishment of American freedoms. But I am not convinced that all this talk of "rights," let alone "inalienable rights," can be justified by Locke's epistemology. Among the dark substances ("something, I know not what") of Locke's philosophy, what is there exactly that gives us the right to political liberty? The American Declaration of Independence attributes these rights not to experience, but to God.

Locke is known today mainly for his political theory. Like Hobbes, he is part of the social-contract tradition: government emerges from an agreement among people living in a "state of nature" where no government exists.

George Berkeley (1685–1753)

Berkeley,[67] the second of the major empiricists, taught at Trinity College in Dublin, and later became the Anglican Bishop of Cloyne. From 1728 to 1731 he lived in Rhode Island, seeking to raise funds for a college that he hoped to build in Bermuda. During that time he had conversations with Jonathan Edwards. But after it was evident that there were not sufficient funds to build the college, he returned to London.

Berkeley followed Locke's project of seeking knowledge by an examination of our ideas. But he was unable to accept Locke's supposition of substance as a source of our ideas. Locke himself admitted ignorance as to what substances might be, and as we have seen, affirming them was inconsistent with his empiricism. Berkeley applied Occam's razor: to him, material substances were unnecessary entities. We should not suppose the existence of such things, but rather be content to explore what we actually know: our ideas, and our minds.

Like Occam, Berkeley was a nominalist. He believed that only individual objects existed. As Locke had rejected innate ideas, Berkeley

67. Sometimes pronounced BAHR-klee, sometimes BURR-klee. The former seems to be preferred by speakers of British English.

rejected "abstract" ideas, such as Platonic Forms. In Berkeley's view, we have no idea of *house in general* or *virtue in general* or *man in general*. Our ideas of houses, and even virtues, are particular. To Berkeley, Locke's substance is one of those abstract ideas, and on that account dispensable. Similarly, Berkeley rejects notions such as *forces*, *gravity*, and *attraction*, if they are taken to denote things that lie behind (and explain) the behavior of particular objects. Same for *cause*: when event B follows A, what we see is a particular sequence that might or might not help us to predict future sequences of the same kind. But we do not perceive a mysterious *causality* flowing from A to B. As we will see, David Hume would use a similar argument to deny any *necessary connection* between cause and effect. But unlike Hume, Berkeley believed that we can understand causality by reflecting on our own mind. Causality is not something we can perceive in the relations between things in the world. But we do perceive it when by our own mental activity we make things happen.

George Berkeley

So Berkeley did accept a distinction in the mind between sense data and interpretation, a distinction (similar to Aristotle's) between the mind as passive and the mind as active. The mind recognizes and understands not only its sense experience, but also its own activity.[68] Part of the active work of the mind is to recognize resemblances between particular objects, and this sort of reflection leads us to use general language. But in Berkeley's view, this use of language should not lead us to believe that general or abstract terms denote objects distinct from particulars.

Unlike Hume, Berkeley believed that we can understand causality by reflecting on our own mind. Causality is not something we can perceive in the relations between things in the world. But we do perceive it when by our own mental activity we make things happen.

Since for Berkeley there are no Lockean substances, we also have no need to distinguish, as Locke did, between primary and secondary qualities. For Locke, the *primary qualities* were qualities of substance, the qualities that belonged to the substances themselves, as opposed to our experience of them. But we know the primary qualities only by inference from the secondary qualities (colors, tastes, smells, etc.). So Berkeley, sticking to sense experience and Occam's razor, denied the distinction altogether.

But without substance and its primary qualities, what is there? For Aristotle, substances were literally the contents of the world. For Berkeley, there is no substance, only sense experience. So for him, the world is nothing more than perception. Hence his slogan, *esse est percipi*: "to be is to be perceived."

This conceptual move commits Berkeley to idealism, the belief that the world is nothing but mind. In this regard, he is similar to Leibniz. But of course, the two philosophers came to their conclusions in rather

68. Berkeley said that we have *ideas* of our sense data, but *notions* of the functioning of our mind.

different ways: Leibniz by a logical deduction from the nature of matter, Berkeley by rejecting the notion of matter altogether. Leibniz is sometimes called a *metaphysical* or *atomistic idealist*. Berkeley is often described as a *subjective idealist*. For to him, reality is the content of our perceptions, our mind's experience.

As a Christian and bishop, Berkeley also believes in God. But one wonders how he can affirm an invisible God in an epistemology limited to sense perception. What he does is to prove God's existence by cosmological arguments with idealist modifications. Our sense experience, he says, is orderly, regular, and predictable. We cannot explain this in terms of abstract substances and forces. So what might account for it? The only thing we know that has the power to order reality is mind. So the First Cause must be, like us, a mind.

That mind must have powers beyond ours. For if *esse est percipi*, what happens to the being of a room when there is no human being there to perceive it? Must we say that it disappears? No, says Berkeley. The important thing is that *someone* perceives it, and the One who is always able to perceive it is God. So God keeps all the being of ideal reality in place. He is therefore omnipresent, omnipotent, and omniscient. In this way, Berkeley offers his idealistic philosophy as a Christian apologetic.

Of all the philosophers discussed in this chapter (from Descartes on), Berkeley is the most Christian. His concept of God is essentially biblical. Berkeley recognizes that the functioning of the world requires not only a First Cause (Locke), a guarantor of truth (Descartes), an impersonal world system (Spinoza), or a "cosmic accountant" (Leibniz), but a *person* who communicates with us mind-to-mind.

There is no place for an authoritative word from God in Berkeley's theory of knowledge. In effect, Berkeley, like other rationalists and empiricists of the period, sees the philosopher as someone who is locked up in himself, trying to figure things out by his own autonomous reason, introspection, and sensation.

But Berkeley's philosophy does not *begin* with God. It begins, as with Descartes and Locke, with the human being shut up within himself to consider his ideas autonomously. Eventually Berkeley confesses God as an implication of his sensation and reflection. But if he consults the Scriptures, that happens after the basic argument is complete. Of course, I have no doubt that Bishop Berkeley knew the Bible before he even began to study empiricist philosophy. No doubt some of that biblical content influenced his formulation. But there is no place for an authoritative word from God in Berkeley's theory of knowledge. In effect, Berkeley, like other rationalists and empiricists of the period, sees the philosopher as someone who is locked up in himself, trying to figure things out by his own autonomous reason, introspection, and sensation.

I'm inclined to agree with Berkeley that there is no reason for a Christian to accept the spirit-matter dualism of Descartes and Locke. Contrary to the view of some theologians, Scripture does not tell us that spirit and matter are contrary to each other. But neither does it say that one of these should be rejected in favor of the other, as in Berkeley's idealism or in Hobbes's materialism. Scripture makes different kinds of distinctions: God as Lord, man as his image, the earth as their domain. Man is made of God's breath and also of the earth. *Earth* is not the inert "extension" that Descartes meant by *matter* and Locke by *substance*, and man's soul is not quite what these philosophers meant by *mind*. A biblical epistemology might have opened these philosophers to other ways of understanding such concepts.

In Hume's philosophy, the empiricist tradition devolves into skepticism. Hume reaches this conclusion by developing the empiricist epistemology more rigorously than his predecessors.

David Hume (1711–76)

In Hume's philosophy, the empiricist tradition devolves into skepticism. Hume reaches this conclusion by developing the empiricist epistemology more rigorously than his predecessors.

Like Locke and Berkeley, Hume believes that epistemology must be essentially introspective, an examination of our own ideas and perceptions. He begins by distinguishing within our experience between *impressions* and *ideas*. The former include sense perceptions as well as the immediate feelings and volitions within the mind itself. These are the original source of all knowledge, and we distinguish them by their "liveliness" and "vividness." Ideas are fainter copies of impressions, such as we have in memory. But of course, the *having* of an idea is a new impression, which may itself be reflected in further ideas. So in Hume's thought, there is give-and-take between impressions and ideas.

Hume distinguishes, as did Leibniz, between analytic and synthetic statements, which he called relations of ideas *and* relations of fact, *respectively. This distinction is sometimes called* Hume's fork.

Ideas aren't always reliable. For example, we might have an idea of a flying horse, but that is not proof that there are such things in reality. In order to determine whether such ideas are veridical, we must trace them back to the impressions from which they originate. We have impressions of horses and of flying creatures, but no impressions of flying horses. So the idea of a flying horse does not commend belief that such animals exist.

Hume distinguishes, as did Leibniz, between analytic and synthetic statements, which he called *relations of ideas* and *relations of fact*, respectively.[69] This distinction is sometimes called *Hume's fork*. Analytic statements are true by virtue of the fact that their predicate is included in the subject, for example, "every unmarried man is a bachelor." These are not based on evidence or empirical verification. They are true by

69. Recall that Leibniz also made use of this distinction. In the end, Leibniz concluded that the distinction between analytic and synthetic collapses, because from God's point of view (*sub specie aeternitatis*) every fact about an object is part of its concept or definition. So that for Leibniz, all statements are analytic. Hume, rather, believes that there is no way of relativizing this distinction, contrary to the paper of Quine cited in the following note.

virtue of the meanings of the words.[70] For him, statements of mathematics and logic are analytic in this way, and therefore certainly true. So for Hume, it is not necessary for us to verify them by tracing them back to impressions. Synthetic truths, however, require sensory verification if we are to affirm them as true. This is the work of science. Hence Hume's famous saying:

> If we take in our hand any volume; of divinity or school metaphysics, for instance; let us ask, Does it contain any abstract reasoning concerning quantity or number? No. Does it contain any experimental reasoning concerning matter of fact and existence? No. Commit it then to the flames: for it can contain nothing but sophistry and illusion.[71]

Clearly, though, "experimental reasoning concerning matter of fact and existence" (e.g., Newton's law of gravitation) cannot be certain in the way that "abstract reasoning concerning quantity or number" (e.g., $2 + 2 = 4$) can be. As Locke said, empirical knowledge, knowledge of matters of fact, can be no more than probably certain, although in some cases that probability is very high.

So when Hume applies this method to the traditional problems of philosophy, certainty is very hard to come by, indeed. His main approach is to sort out our impressions by noting *associations* among them: resemblances, contiguity (the nearness of one object to another), and causality. He puts particular emphasis on causality; the very nature of science is to determine the causes of different effects. But in Hume's method, the very idea of *cause* is problematic.

Hume's main approach is to sort out our impressions by noting associations *among them: resemblances, contiguity (the nearness of one object to another), and causality.*

Hume states that when we say that event A is the "cause" of event B, we mean that (1) A occurs prior to B, (2) A and B are contiguous in time and place, and (3) there is a *necessary connection* between A and B, so that A *makes* B to take place. So Hume tries to trace each of these three elements back to sense impressions. He has no problem with the first two, priority and contiguity. But as he surveys the impressions in his experience, he does not find any that correspond to the idea of necessary connection.[72] In the classic case in which A is the motion of one

70. Of course, determining the meanings of words is itself an empirical exercise, and not always easy. That issue calls the sharpness of the analytic-synthetic distinction into question, but I will not discuss that complication here. For a recent analysis of this issue, see Willard Van Orman Quine's paper, "Two Dogmas of Empiricism," *Philosophical Review* 60 (1951): 20–43, reprinted in Willard Van Orman Quine, *From a Logical Point of View: Nine Logico-Philosophical Essays*, 2nd rev. ed. (Cambridge, MA: Harvard University Press, 1961), available at http://www.ditext.com/quine/quine.html. I discuss Quine briefly in chapter 12 of this volume.

71. Hume, *An Enquiry concerning Human Understanding*, 12.3.

72. Recall that Berkeley made the same argument. But unlike Hume, he appealed to God as the One who imparted efficacy to all causes.

billiard ball and B is the motion of the second, Hume acknowledges that A moves first, and that B moves when A strikes it. But he does not perceive any power in A that *necessitates* the movement of B.

This conclusion, then, requires a new understanding of causality. Hume states that to say "A caused B" is to say that (1) A was prior to B, (2) A and B were contiguous, and (3) we are *accustomed* to seeing B-type movements following A-type movements. Condition (3), *constant conjunction*, replaces the traditional notion of necessary connection. Here as elsewhere, Hume replaces metaphysics with psychology. Causation is not something that we directly perceive in nature. It is the expectation of the human observer, reinforced by many such observations of many observers over time. It is a mental *custom*.

Hume replaces metaphysics with psychology. Causation is not something that we directly perceive in nature. It is the expectation of the human observer, reinforced by many such observations of many observers over time. It is a mental custom.

Berkeley had also argued that we cannot observe necessary connection in nature. But he said that we gain the notion of necessary connection by observing the workings of our own minds. By executing our intentions, we are able to make things happen. So he taught that we should understand causality by analogy with our own thought, and for him this analogy leads us to ascribe causality ultimately to God.

But that course was not available to Hume. He was not only skeptical about necessary connection, but also skeptical about the existence of the *mind* or *soul* in the traditional metaphysical sense. He agreed with Berkeley that an examination of experience does not reveal any such thing as material substance.[73] But what of immaterial substance? What of the soul, self, or mind? Hume said that whenever he focused on himself, he encountered some perception or other. He had no perception of a self or soul that brought these perceptions together into a single consciousness. So he defined *soul* minimally, to agree with his experience, as a *bundle* of perceptions.[74] So my soul differs from yours in that my bundle of perceptions is different from yours.[75]

David Hume

And of course, God is also imperceptible, so that for a consistent empiricist such as Hume, God cannot play the sort of role in philosophy that he played for Berkeley. Hume was very careful on the subject of God. Though accused of atheism during his life, he often took pains to express his theology in traditional terms. In his posthumously

73. Locke, too, we recall, had problems with material substance. He described it as "something, I know not what."

74. The bundle has a kind of compatibilist freedom, he argues elsewhere. In fact, it is questionable how a bundle of perceptions can be either free or unfree, in any sense.

75. In one commonsense view, knowledge consists of a relation between a subject and an object. But in empiricism, Berkeley absorbs the object into the subject. Hume does the reverse: the subject vanishes into the objects of its perception. In my proposed Christian philosophy (chapter 1), we need a third factor besides the subject (existential) and the object (situational). That third factor is the *norm*, God's revelation, which provides rules to distinguish object from subject (in other words, to distinguish truth from illusion).

published *Dialogues concerning Natural Religion*, he claims kinship with the moderate Christian character Cleanthes, not the skeptic Philo. And he claims there that the force of his argument is not to refute religion but to underscore the fact that it is based on faith rather than reason. Elsewhere, he says that though the existence of God is certain, we cannot prove *what* he is, that is, his nature.[76]

In the *Dialogues*, Hume (in the voice of Philo) attacks in detail the teleological argument, the fifth of Aquinas's five proofs, which says that the world shows evidence of design, and that the designer can be no one other than God. Hume notes the following: (1) Although we have seen many products of human design, such as houses, there is very slight analogy between those and the whole universe. (2) Similarly, the analogy between the human mind and the divine mind is rather weak. God's mind is thought to be eternal, immutable, omniscient, and so forth. (3) Even if it can be proved that God designed and made the world, that does not prove in turn that God is infinite, perfect, and the like. The world is imperfect and finite. (4) Most significantly, there is evil in the world, which raises the question whether it could have been designed and made by a perfectly good being. (5) The teleological argument cannot prove that the world was made by one God rather than many. (6) The order and structure to which the teleological argument appeals can be explained by other means. Perhaps the world is more like an animal or vegetable, which gets its structure from its inner nature, not from an external designer.

Alternatively, Christians have sometimes appealed to miracles as evidence for God and for the claims of Christ. In section 10 of his *Enquiry concerning Human Understanding*, Hume argues that there can never be sufficient evidence to affirm that a miracle has taken place. He begins by defining *miracle* as a violation of a law of nature. But that definition makes it impossible for us to believe that any event was a miracle. We always have more evidence, says Hume, for the normal course of nature than we have for any claimed exception to it. So when confronted with a strange event, we should always prefer natural explanations of it to supernatural explanations. Says Hume, it is always more likely that the witnesses misunderstood or misrepresented the event than that it was a violation of the laws of nature.

Hume argues that there can never be sufficient evidence to affirm that a miracle has taken place. He begins by defining miracle *as a violation of a law of nature. But that definition makes it impossible for us to believe that any event was a miracle.*

In the rest of the essay, Hume discusses the character of testimony concerning miracles. He says that no miracle has had witnesses of sufficient character, education, and intelligence to warrant our belief. Further, he says that miracle stories tend to arise in nations that are credulous about such things. Finally, he points out that the miracle

76. Of course, this distinction is impossible. Nobody can prove that anything exists without having any knowledge of what it is.

claims of one religion cancel out those of all the others. For religions contradict one another; so if one set of claims is true, all the others must be false.

In the field of ethics as well, Hume is known as a skeptic. He is skeptical, first, about the *is-ought* argument: arguments of the form "A is the case; therefore, we ought to do B." Such arguments are common in ethics and politics—for example:

In the field of ethics as well, Hume is known as a skeptic. He is skeptical, first, about the is-ought *argument: arguments of the form "A is the case; therefore, we ought to do B." Such arguments are common in ethics and politics.*

Vaccinations prevent polio.
Therefore, everyone ought to be vaccinated for polio.

Or:

Many murders are committed with guns.
Therefore, guns ought to be be prohibited.

Such arguments often give us good advice, and they are sometimes shortcut ways of making better arguments. But, Hume pointed out, these arguments as they stand are fallacies.[77] The fact that vaccinations prevent polio does not *obligate* us to be vaccinated. Without an *ought* in the premise, there cannot be an *ought* in the conclusion. The first argument, however, can be amended to make a valid argument:

Everyone ought to avail himself of anything that prevents polio.
Vaccinations prevent polio.
Therefore, I ought to be vaccinated for polio.

One of Hume's most famous sayings is: "Reason is, and ought only to be the slave of the passions, and can never pretend to any other office than to serve and obey them."

Hume also expressed skepticism about the *social-contract* theory that we noted in Hobbes and Locke. A historian, he asked when and how such a contract was ever made. There is no evidence of such a contract among savage societies, or more generally in history. Rather, the evidence indicates a gradual accumulation of power by the chiefs of tribes.

In general, Hume's ethics, like that of the Greek Sophists, is a form of subjectivism, based on feelings of approval and disapproval.

Hume was aware of the subjectivist and skeptical implications of his philosophical work. He had set his method explicitly over against the rationalism of Descartes and the Continental thinkers. One of his most famous sayings is: "Reason is, and ought only to be the slave of the passions, and can never pretend to any other office than to serve and obey them."[78] He remarked that sometimes he became personally troubled by the skeptical results of his philosophy:

77. G. E. Moore (1873–1958) later called this form of argument the *naturalistic fallacy*, because it tries to derive obligations from natural facts.

78. Hume, *Treatise of Human Nature*, 3.

> The intense view of these manifold contradictions and imperfections in human reason has so wrought upon me, and heated my brain, that I am ready to reject all belief and reasoning, and can look upon no opinion even as more probable or likely than another. Where am I, or what? From what causes do I derive my existence, and to what condition shall I return? Whose favour shall I court, and whose anger must I dread? What beings surround me? and on whom have I any influence, or who have any influence on me? I am confounded with all these questions, and begin to fancy myself in the most deplorable condition imaginable, inironed with the deepest darkness, and utterly deprived of the use of every member and faculty.
>
> Most fortunately it happens, that since reason is incapable of dispelling these clouds, nature herself suffices to that purpose, and cures me of this philosophical melancholy and delirium, either by relaxing this bent of mind, or by some avocation, and lively impression of my senses, which obliterate all these chimeras. I dine, I play a game of backgammon, I converse, and am merry with my friends; and when after three or four hours' amusement, I would return to these speculations, they appear so cold, and strained, and ridiculous, that I cannot find in my heart to enter into them any farther.[79]

But, he continues, he also has a personal inclination to indulge in philosophical questions, and he sees no reason not to satisfy that appetite.

I think Hume's best contribution to philosophy is his refutation of the is-ought *fallacy. Among the modern philosophers considered in this chapter, I consider Hume to be the clearest and the most cogent.*

Hume raises a number of good questions. I think his best contribution to philosophy is his refutation of the *is-ought* fallacy.[80] Among the modern philosophers considered in this chapter, I consider Hume to be the clearest and the most cogent. But in the end I must concur with Hume's own judgment that his work is nothing more than an expression of his own subjective feeling.

Of all the thinkers mentioned in this chapter, Hume is the one by whom Christians have often felt most threatened. Hume's refutations of the teleological argument and of the argument from miracle have often seemed devastating. I have dealt with these elsewhere.[81] Here, I want to indicate that the problem is not so much with Hume's conclusions as with his starting point, his presuppositions.

79. Ibid., 7.

80. For more discussion of this, see my *DCL*, 57–63. I argue that moral obligation can come only from the biblical God, the personal absolute (chapter 1 of this book), and that therefore all attempts to derive morality from other sources commit the *is-ought* fallacy.

81. On the teleological argument (and other theistic proofs), see *AJCB*, 95-123; on miracles, *DG*, 241–73.

Hume's subjectivism and skepticism are unavoidable if, like him, we begin in solitary dialogue with our own perceptions. To make our "impressions" the only source of factual certainty guarantees that we will not find certainty about anything else. As Hume knew, we do not have impressions of causality, of God, or even of ourselves. Nor do we have impressions of moral obligation or of freedom.

So the problem with Hume's critique of the teleological argument is not his acute analysis of the analogy between the universe and products of design. The problem is rather how one can talk about analogies or disanalogies at all. Is there an impression, or a group of impressions, that certifies how A must be analogous to B to justify assertions of analogous origin? And in the discussion over miracle, what impressions authorize us to judge what sorts of events are possible, impossible, or probable?

Hume's subjectivism and skepticism are unavoidable if, like him, we begin in solitary dialogue with our own perceptions. To make our "impressions" the only source of factual certainty guarantees that we will not find certainty about anything else.

But what if we are not, in fact, trapped within the subjectivity of our impressions and ideas? What if we live not only with ourselves, but also in the presence of our Creator? If so, then we will need to take account of him, of who he is, and of what he says. We will need then to interpret our subjectivity (existential perspective) by his Word (normative perspective), which gives us access to an environment far larger than our own minds, the created world (situational perspective).

We will listen to God's Word, which will tell us that indeed there is an (imperfect, but cogent) analogy between the created world and products of human design. And it will be very easy for us to believe that God can perform miracles, mighty works, in the world that he has made and continues to rule; see fig. 5.3.

We will listen to God's Word, which will tell us that indeed there is an (imperfect, but cogent) analogy between the created world and products of human design.

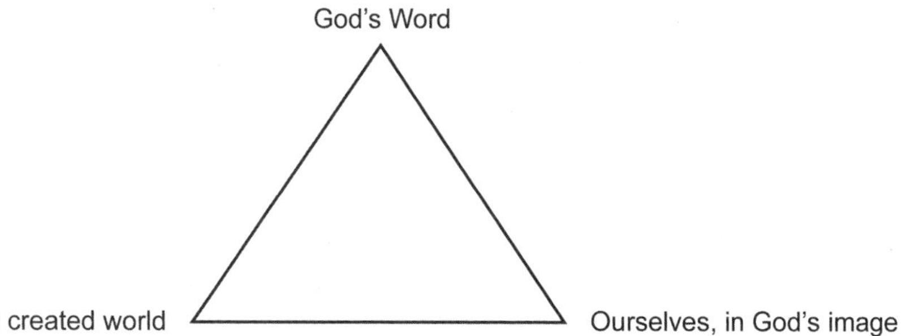

Fig. 5.3. Perspectives in Christian Epistemology

SUMMARY

From the beginning of the Renaissance (around 1350) to the death of Hume (1776), the philosophic world experienced several convulsions. The Renaissance was a time of cultural change more than of philosophical change, though the developments in scholarship and the arts were a major impetus to the subsequent developments in philosophy and theology.

The Protestant Reformation was a major turning point, radically different in philosophy and theology from the medieval traditions. In the Reformation, the biblical worldview came into its own. Luther and Calvin, for the first time in the history of Christian thought, admitted no obligation to Greek philosophy and were able to set forth in relative purity the biblical metaphysic, epistemology, and ethic.

But then another convulsion struck the Western intellectual world. The Continental rationalists and British empiricists sought a new beginning in philosophy. This event was analogous to the beginnings of Greek philosophy around 600 B.C. Like the Greeks, the Europeans determined to set aside everything they had inherited by religious tradition and to seek knowledge of the world by autonomous reason alone.

The term *reason*, of course, had to be further nuanced. For Descartes, Spinoza, and Leibniz, reason was opposed to sense experience. To Locke, Berkeley, and Hume, reason was based on sense experience. But in either case, human thought was considered autonomous, not under the authority of God's Word.

For both rationalists and empiricists, reasoning had a radically subjective foundation. For Descartes, that foundation was the intuition of my own thought. For Spinoza, it was a concept of substance, accepted as an intuited self-evident axiom, from which all else could be deduced. For Leibniz, it was a rationality carried on in the privacy of my windowless monad. For the British, it was my ideas.

Rationalism seeks the norms or rules for knowledge (particularly in logic and mathematics) and . . . empiricism seeks to connect our knowledge with the situation of the real world: what I earlier called normative *and* situational *perspectives, respectively.*

It might seem, then, that rationalism seeks the norms or rules for knowledge (particularly in logic and mathematics) and that empiricism seeks to connect our knowledge with the situation of the real world: what I earlier called *normative* and *situational* perspectives, respectively. But both reduce to subjectivism, the project of trying to gain knowledge from inspection of our own consciousness. Descartes looked within to try to find an idea that was "clear and distinct." Locke tried to gain knowledge from his own ideas. But in both traditions, the quest for knowledge reduced to subjectivism and thus skepticism; see fig. 5.4.

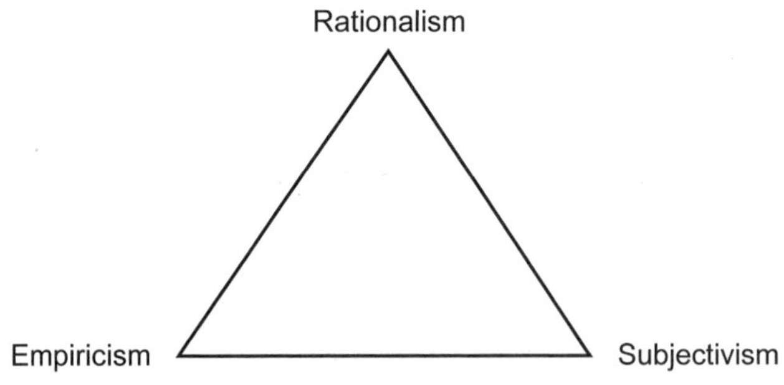

Fig. 5.4. Enlightenment Epistemologies as Perspectives

But from such foundations, what knowledge do we gain? Rationalism culminates in Leibniz's monadology, which seems to his critics to be a rather bizarre sort of speculation. Empiricism culminates in Hume's skepticism. So from all the brilliant arguments of this period, it is not clear what have we actually learned.

The period 1650–1800 (more or less) is sometimes called the *Enlightenment* or the *age of reason*. It is a period in which mainstream philosophy radically rejected the worldview of the Bible and embraced the autonomy of the human mind. But *Enlightenment* suggests at least some progress in the discovery of knowledge. During this period, there were discoveries in the sciences. But in philosophy during these years, it is impossible to speak of progress. The Enlightenment in this respect is like the period of Greek philosophy. The questions discussed at the beginning were still open questions at the end, without any answers' being found, with a continuing sense of futility. And yet many people have the impression that the Enlightenment was a great intellectual watershed, in which mankind divested itself of superstition and awoke to the vast potential of reason. Those people need to be more aware of the facts.

The period 1650–1800 (more or less) is sometimes called the Enlightenment *or the* age of reason. *It is a period in which mainstream philosophy radically rejected the worldview of the Bible and embraced the autonomy of the human mind.*

Later, we will see how Immanuel Kant and others sought to bring together elements of rationalism and empiricism, and to restore confidence in what can be learned from philosophy. But first we will need to consider a convulsion in Christian thought itself.

KEY TERMS

Renaissance	Erastianism
Ad fontes	Antiquarianism
Donation of Constantine	Humanism
Righteousness (Luther)	Five *solas*
Ubiquitous	Nestorian
Monophysite	Protestant scholasticism
Pietism	*Ecclesiolae in ecclesia*
Dead orthodoxy	Rationalism (two senses)
Sense experience	Reason
Empiricism	*Tabula rasa*
Clear and distinct ideas	Evil genius
Radical doubt	Substance
Material substance (Descartes)	Mental substance (Descartes)
Extension (Descartes)	Pineal gland (Descartes)
Mind-body problem	Occasionalism
Substance (Spinoza)	Monism
Deus sive natura	*Natura naturans*
Natura naturata	Determinism

Intellectual love of God
Idealism
Panpsychism
Supreme monad
Analytic
Pre-established harmony
Compossible
Materialism
State of nature
Innate ideas
Ideas of sensation
Simple and complex ideas (Locke)
Primary and secondary qualities (Locke)
State of nature (Locke)
Abstract ideas (Berkeley)
Necessary connection (Berkeley, Hume)
Esse est percipi
Impressions
Cause (Hume)
Bundle (Hume)
Naturalistic fallacy
Enlightenment
Atomism
Monads
Queen monad
Principle of sufficient reason
Synthetic
Tiny perceptions
Cosmic accountant
Social contract
Rights
A priori knowledge
Ideas of reflection
Inalienable rights
Subjective idealism
Ideas (Hume)
Necessary connection (Hume)
Is-ought argument
Age of reason

STUDY QUESTIONS

1. What is notable about Michel de Montaigne? Niccolo Machiavelli? Lorenzo Valla?
2. "This technology radically changed human civilization, enabling rapid communication of knowledge, both literature from the past and new discoveries." What technology? Explain; evaluate.
3. "In the famous encounter between Galileo and the church over Copernicus's heliocentrism, neither party referred much to Scripture." What did they refer to? What larger point is Frame trying to make in this context?
4. "So the two Renaissance themes, antiquarianism and humanism, were never well integrated. They tended to press thinkers in opposite directions." Explain; evaluate.
5. "The Reformers did not consider themselves philosophers, but what they taught was extremely significant for philosophy." Discuss the implications of Reformation doctrine for philosophy, both in Luther and in Calvin.
6. "Grace is an irreducibly personal category." Frame draws two implications from this statement. Name them and discuss.

7. Discuss Frame's four-stage historical pattern as it applies to the Reformation period.
8. "Calvin's epistemology is a remarkable departure from medieval and Renaissance thought, and it dominates the opening chapters of his systematic theology, his *Institutes*." Describe that epistemology and discuss its significance.
9. "Calvin's doctrine of the knowledge of God, therefore, has three perspectives." Elaborate; explain.
10. "Calvin's position is significant for Christian apologetics." How?
11. "But the *feeling* one gets from the post-Reformation literature is very different from the atmosphere generated by the original Reformers." How is that feeling different? Evaluate the significance of this.
12. Summarize Spener's pietism and Frame's evaluation. What do you think?
13. Frame says that in the seventeenth century there was a "rebirth [of] non-Christian thought." Describe this and discuss.
14. Describe in general the differences between rationalists and empiricists.
15. Describe Descartes' radical doubt, and his proposed escape from it. What role does God play in Descartes' epistemology?
16. "But we should notice that in all this argumentation, Descartes ultimately appeals to his own subjective consciousness as the ultimate criterion of truth." Explain; evaluate.
17. For Descartes, what is a material substance? A mental substance? Discuss his arguments for these definitions. Discuss the mind-body problem that these definitions produce.
18. Compare Spinoza's rationalistic slogan to that of Parmenides.
19. Why did Spinoza think God was the only substance?
20. How does Spinoza solve Descartes' mind-body problem? Discuss.
21. Discuss Leibniz as an idealistic atomist. Why does he think that all things are made of mindlike entities?
22. Why does Leibniz think that all sentences are analytic? Evaluate.
23. "The monads have no windows." Explain.
24. Describe Leibniz's solution to the problem of evil. Evaluate.
25. Is Leibniz's God a "cosmic accountant"? Why might someone think so? Reply.
26. Was Hobbes an empiricist or a rationalist? Discuss.
27. Summarize Hobbes's epistemology. Evaluate.
28. Summarize Hobbes's social philosophy. Evaluate.

29. "Empiricists typically begin with epistemology and work their way from there to metaphysics and ethics. Rationalists, rather, begin with metaphysical *axioms* and deduce from them what knowledge and ethics must be." Explain and evaluate, using an example. How does Frame's "biblical philosophy" deal with this issue?
30. Discuss Locke's rejection of innate ideas. Is it consistent?
31. Compare Descartes and Locke on material substance.
32. What does Locke say about substance? Why? Is this consistent with his empiricism?
33. How does Berkeley respond to Locke's view of material substance? Evaluate.
34. Discuss Berkeley's view of abstract ideas. How does this affect his view of causation?
35. Describe Berkeley's response to Locke's view of primary qualities.
36. Describe and evaluate Berkeley's apologetic for God's existence.
37. Is Berkeley's philosophy Christian?
38. "In Hume's philosophy, the empiricist tradition devolves into skepticism." How? Explain; evaluate.
39. Compare Hume's view of the *analytic-synthetic* distinction with that of Leibniz.
40. Discuss Hume's view of causality and his arguments for it. Compare it with those of Locke and Berkeley.
41. Describe and evaluate Hume's account of mental substance.
42. Describe and evaluate Hume's view of the teleological argument.
43. Same for his argument about miracles.
44. Present and evaluate Hume's discussion of the *is-ought* argument.
45. Hume was troubled by his own skepticism. Discuss his resolution of it.
46. "Of all the thinkers mentioned in this chapter, Hume is the one by whom Christians have often felt most threatened." How? Respond to their fears.
47. Summarize the "convulsions" discussed in this chapter, and Frame's evaluation.
48. Describe and evaluate Frame's triperspectival analysis of the philosophical schools of this period.

BIBLIOGRAPHY: EARLY MODERN THOUGHT

Print

Calvin, John. *Institutes of the Christian Religion*. Edited by John T. McNeill. Translated by Ford Lewis Battles. 2 vols. Philadelphia: Westminster Press, 1960.

Descartes, René. *The Philosophical Writings ofDescartes*. 3 vols. Cambridge: Cambridge University Press, 1985.

Hobbes, Thomas. *Leviathan*. New York: Empire Books, 2013.

Kramnick, Isaac, ed. *The Portable Enlightenment Reader.* London: Penguin, 1995. Over a hundred selections from the period 1650–1800. Focuses on political and economic thought more than on the issues I have highlighted.

Leibniz, G. W. *Philosophical Essays*. Indianapolis: Hackett Publishing, 1989.

Locke, John, George Berkeley, and David Hume. *The Empiricists*. New York: Anchor Books, 1960. Contains the chief works of the three major empiricists.

Luther, Martin. *The Martin Luther Collection: 15 Classic Works*. Kindle ed. Waxkeep Publications, 2012.

———. *Works of Martin Luther, with Introductions and Notes*. Vol. 1. Bel Air, CA: FQ Books, 2010.

Ross, James B., and Mary M. McLaughlin, eds. *The Portable Medieval Reader.* London: Penguin, 1977. Over a hundred selections of Renaissance authors.

Spinoza, Baruch (Benedict de Spinoza). *Spinoza: Complete Works*. Edited by Michael L. Morgan. Translated by Samuel Shirley. Indianapolis: Hackett Publishing, 2002.

Online

Berkeley, George. *Three Dialogues between Hylas and Philonous*. Available at http://www.sacred-texts.com/phi/berkeley/three.txt.

———. *A Treatise concerning the Principles of Human Knowledge*. Available at http://www.gutenberg.org/catalog/world/readfile?fk_files=1983609&pageno=1.

Descartes, René. *Discourse on the Method of Rightly Conducting One's Reason and of Seeking Truth in the Sciences*. Available at http://www.literature.org/authors/descartes-rene/reason-discourse/.

———. *Meditations on First Philosophy*. Available at http://faculty.ycp.edu/~dweiss/phl321_epistemology/descartes%20meditations.pdf.

Early Modern Philosophy. Some texts of the secular philosophers of this period are available at http://www.earlymoderntexts.com, in addition to the locations in this bibliography.

Hobbes, Thomas. *The Leviathan*. Available at http://oregonstate.edu/instruct/phl302/texts/hobbes/leviathan-contents.html.

Hume, David. *Dialogues concerning Natural Religion*. Available at http://latourgifford2013.wikispaces.com/Hume%27s+Dialogues+Concerning+Natural+Religion.

———. *An Enquiry concerning Human Understanding*. Available at http://ebooks.adelaide.edu.au/h/hume/david/h92e/index.html.

———. *An Enquiry concerning the Principles of Morals*. Available at http://www.gutenberg.org/files/4320/4320-h/4320-h.htm.

———. *A Treatise of Human Nature*. Available at http://www.gutenberg.org/files/4705/4705-h/4705-h.htm. His tract "Concerning the Eternal Predestination of God" is a striking summary of his controversial doctrine of predestination.

Leibniz, G. W. *Theodicy* and *Monadology*. Available at http://www.gutenberg.org/ebooks/author/7168.

Locke, John. *An Essay concerning Human Understanding*. Available at http://oregonstate.edu/instruct/phl302/texts/locke/locke1/Essay_contents.html.

———. *The Works of John Locke in Nine Volumes*. 12th ed. Vol. 6, *The Reasonableness of Christianity*. London: Rivington, 1824. Available at http://oll.libertyfund.org/?option=com_staticxt&staticfile=show.php%3Ftitle=1438&Itemid=27.

———. *The Works of John Locke in Ten Volumes*. New ed. Vol. 5, *Two Treatises of Government*. London: Printed for Thomas Tegg, 1823. Available at http://www.efm.bris.ac.uk/het/locke/government.pdf.

Luther, Martin. Many of Luther's and Calvin's writings (including Calvin's *Institutes* and *Commentaries*) are available at http://www.ccel.org.

Spinoza, Baruch (Benedict de Spinoza). *Ethics*. Available as free e-book at http://www.gutenberg.org/ebooks/3800.

———. *A Theologico-Political Treatise*. Translated by R. H. M. Elwes. New York: Dover, 1951. Available at http://www.spinozacsack.net78.net/Theologico-Political%20Treatise,%20Benedict%20de%20Spinoza.pdf.

READ FOR YOURSELF

Read Luther's Ninety-five Theses, and then his major works on the Reformation, *To the German Nobility*, *On Christian Liberty*, and *The Babylonian Captivity of the Church*. His *Bondage of the Will* is a major theological treatise that he considered to be his best work. His commentaries on Galatians and Romans, two catechisms, and *Treatise on Good Works* are also among his most important writings.

Calvin's *Institutes* is a concise, systematic summary of his teaching and the basis of Reformed doctrine. His tract *On the Necessity of Reforming the Church*, his sermons, and his commentaries amplify his contribution.

Read Descartes' *Discourse on Method*, supplemented by his *Meditations* and *Principles of Philosophy*. Spinoza's *Ethics Geometrically Demonstrated* sets forth his philosophy systematically. His *Theologico-Political Treatise* introduces his liberal views of biblical criticism. In Leibniz, look at the *Monadology*, *Theodicy*, and *Discourse on Metaphysics*. He never wrote up a summary of his whole philosophy in a single place.

Hobbes's *Leviathan* is his main work. In Locke, read his *Essay concerning Human Understanding* to understand his epistemology. His important political theory can be found in *Two Treatises on Government*. Berkeley expounds his idealism in *Three Dialogues between Hylas and Philonous*, and *A Treatise concerning the Principles of Human Knowledge*. Hume presents his philosophy comprehensively in *A Treatise of Human Nature*, but he rewrote parts of that for easier comprehension, resulting in the two "Enquiries." Read the *Enquiry concerning Human Understanding* for his epistemology, especially chapter 10, which presents his critique of miracles. More of his religious skepticism appears in his posthumous *Dialogues concerning Natural Religion*.

LISTEN ONLINE

Link: http://itunes.apple.com/us/course/legacy-history-philosophy/id694658914

- John Calvin and Seventeenth-Century Orthodoxy: 20:39
- Continental Rationalism and British Empiricism: 1:06:08

FAMOUS QUOTES

- **Luther:** http://en.wikiquote.org/wiki/Martin_Luther
- **Calvin:** http://en.wikiquote.org/wiki/John_Calvin
- **Descartes:** http://en.wikiquote.org/wiki/Ren%C3%A9_Descartes
- **Spinoza:** http://en.wikiquote.org/wiki/Baruch_Spinoza
- **Leibniz:** http://en.wikiquote.org/wiki/Gottfried_Leibniz
- **Hobbes:** http://en.wikiquote.org/wiki/Thomas_Hobbes
- **Locke:** http://en.wikiquote.org/wiki/John_Locke
- **Hume:** http://en.wikiquote.org/wiki/David_Hume

6

THEOLOGY IN THE ENLIGHTENMENT

TO REVIEW THE STORY so far: God revealed in Scripture not only a way of salvation, but a worldview capable of philosophical articulation. The way of salvation presupposes the worldview. In that worldview, the supreme being, distinct from all other beings, is a tripersonal absolute, who rules over his creation as Lord in his control, authority, and presence. This metaphysic dictates an epistemology and ethic in which divine revelation is the supreme authority, and the worst error is the denial of revelation, that is, the claim of human autonomy. But in the fall human beings embraced intellectual autonomy, so that in their thought and practice they lived by their own wisdom rather than God's. To atone for that sin, God sent his Son, Jesus Christ, who died to suffer the penalty we deserved and to regenerate the hearts and minds of his elect people. Those who believed renounced their claim to autonomy and sought, however inconsistently, to live and think as followers of Jesus.

The problem, then, in the Greek view, was with the world, the object of knowledge—that it was not an entirely rational place. So the problem for Greek philosophy was to impose a rational intellectual scheme (form) on an irrational world (matter), a task doomed to failure.

But around 600 B.C., some thinkers in ancient Greece set aside religions and traditions so that they might understand the world, as much as possible, by human reason alone. They made a determined attempt to develop ideas consistent with the claim of intellectual autonomy. Autonomy, the belief that the human mind, unassisted, is sufficient to understand the workings of nature, led Greek philosophy to a rationalistic emphasis. The Greeks did note that human rationality was not perfect. But the errors of human thought did not lead them to scale back their claim of autonomy. They could not bring themselves to deny that human reason was the very criterion of truth. The problem, then, in their view, was with the world, the *object* of knowledge—that it was not an entirely rational place. So the problem for Greek philosophy was to impose a rational intellectual scheme (*form*) on an irrational world (*matter*), a task doomed to failure.

After Jesus ascended to heaven, he sent his disciples to preach the gospel throughout the world. Some of those disciples tried to bring the gospel to the intellectuals of their day, who were dominated by the worldview of Greek philosophy. Sometimes (as in Augustine's work) they brought a meaningful challenge to Greek thought, based on the biblical worldview. But too often they sought to accommodate, seeking intellectual approval from the Greek philosophical establishment, and compromising the biblical philosophy with Greek philosophical movements such as Neoplatonism and Aristotelianism. This happened even after God removed the governments that persecuted the Christians. That is the story of medieval philosophy.

The Protestant Reformation raised the possibility of a more consistently biblical way of thinking. But before that could get much under way, a convulsion in the intellectual world occurred that every thinker needed to take account of.

The Protestant Reformation raised the possibility of a more consistently biblical way of thinking. But before that could get much under way, a convulsion in the intellectual world occurred that every thinker needed to take account of. That event, in the mid-seventeenth century, was the rebirth of a pure form of secular thought, similar to the birth of Greek philosophy in 600 B.C. It began in Descartes' determination to doubt everything that he had been taught, everything that he had thought he knew. That included Scripture and church tradition. Like the early Greek thinkers, Descartes sought to replace that tradition with a new system of knowledge based on human autonomous reason alone. His project, and that of the other "modern" philosophers, was not like that of the medievals, to combine the Christian and Greek ways of thinking, but rather to embrace a completely new, consistently autonomous system of philosophy.

To be sure, the modern philosophers did claim to be religious in various ways. Frequently their systems incorporated a concept of god. But even in the more religious systems, that god did not reveal himself in such a way as to govern their thinking about the world.

The modern philosophers found it no easier than the Greeks to impose autonomous rational thought on a world of recalcitrant fact.

The modern philosophers found it no easier than the Greeks to impose autonomous rational thought on a world of recalcitrant fact. They disagreed over many things, particularly the relative roles of reason and sense. But even when (as in Hume) modern philosophers veered toward skepticism, they grasped tightly to the claim of autonomy and showed no interest in compromising that fundamental point. They did not call out to God for intellectual salvation.

Such was the period from 1600 to 1800, often called the *Enlightenment* or the *age of reason*.[1] From a Christian view, it was a time of darkness

1. Often the Enlightenment is identified with the eighteenth century. I believe, however, that the spirit of autonomous rationality that we identify with the Enlightenment goes back much further, to the origins of *modern philosophy* that we discussed in the previous chapter. Of course, there were many thinkers during the seventeenth century, notably the Protestant scholastics, who could not be described as "Enlightenment" thinkers. But that is true of the eighteenth century as well, as we will see later in this chapter.

rather than enlightenment, but these names have become conventional labels for this period in history.

Of course, there is more to be said about this period. As I noted, the Protestant Reformation was still gaining converts at this time. And Roman Catholics were maintaining the medieval traditions of philosophy. So it might have seemed as though the two approaches could carry on concurrently: modern secularism and Christian philosophy. That happened to some extent. But something else also happened: another convulsive intellectual change, after which Christian thought would never be the same.

THE BIRTH OF LIBERAL THEOLOGY

That change was that in the late seventeenth century, many professing Christians adopted the modern style of philosophizing and reconstructed their whole theology so as to agree with its assumptions. The movement began with a new way of reading the Bible, not as the revealed Word of God, but as a merely human document containing errors as well as religious wisdom. This was very much a part of the modern approach to philosophy that we explored in the previous chapter. Both Hobbes and Spinoza (in his *Tractatus Theologico-Politicus*), like the French writer Richard Simon (1638–1712), denied the Mosaic authorship of the Pentateuch and questioned much that Scripture said about God and the world. With them was a group of Bible scholars devoted to criticizing the claims of Scripture, such as H. S. Reimarus (1694–1768) and Baron D'Holbach (1723–89), who wrote a biography of Jesus divested of anything supernatural. Thomas Jefferson's Bible, in which he tried to exise everything supernatural, was part of this development.

This naturalistic view of Scripture led eventually to a total abandonment of traditional theology (both Protestant and Catholic). These thinkers did not, however, want to reject Christianity entirely. They were moved by ideas of God and Jesus.

This naturalistic view of Scripture led eventually to a total abandonment of traditional theology (both Protestant and Catholic). These thinkers did not, however, want to reject Christianity entirely. They were moved by ideas of God and Jesus. But the gospel of the Bible, as we have seen, presupposes a thoroughly supernaturalist worldview. If the supernatural view of biblical inspiration was incredible to these thinkers, how could they accept stories of creation, of miracles, of incarnation, virgin birth, atonement, and resurrection? They came to believe that they must reject not only the authority of Scripture, but also its supernatural content, its gospel. But after this drastic criticism, what of biblical Christianity could remain?

The tradition of liberal theology, born in the seventeenth century and stretching into the present, came into existence for the purpose of answering this question. I use the term *liberal* to describe any kind of theology that does not submit to the infallible authority of Scripture.[2]

Liberalism in this sense is distinct from previous forms of heresy within the Christian community, such as Sabellianism, Arianism, Eutychianism, and Arianism. In the sixteenth century, there was a conflict with Socinianism, which rejected the Nicene doctrine of the Trinity, and there were various doctrinal battles between Calvinists, Arminians, Lutherans, and Catholics. But all parties to these conflicts, even the Socinians, appealed to the final authority of Scripture. Eventually, some groups such as the "Cambridge Platonists" of the early seventeenth century[3] advocated appealing to human reason as a kind of neutral arbiter in such disagreements. They were sometimes called *latitudinarian* because of their tendency to avoid taking clearly defined positions. Latitudinarians, certainly, were edging toward liberalism. But they did not deny the authority of Scripture, which is the mark of *liberalism* as I define it.[4]

Some groups such as the "Cambridge Platonists" of the early seventeenth century advocated appealing to human reason as a kind of neutral arbiter in such disagreements.

Deism

The first form of theological liberalism is called *deism*. This word refers to the view that God created the world and established in that world a system of natural laws (causal and ethical), but does not thereafter enter into nature or history. *Pantheism* (as in Spinoza) refers to the view that God is the world and the world is God, and that is often described as the polar opposite of deism. People are inclined to say that in pantheism God is too immanent, but in deism God is too transcendent. But of course, these concepts of transcendence and immanence are the "nonbiblical" concepts that I described in chapter 1. Neither pantheist nor deist accepts biblical transcendence (that God rules his creation as covenant Lord) or biblical immanence (that as Lord, God is present with, though distinct from, his created work); see fig. 6.1.

The first form of theological liberalism is called deism. *This word refers to the view that God created the world and established in that world a system of natural laws (causal and ethical), but does not thereafter enter into nature or history.*

2. Many prefer different terminology. The main difficulty with my terminological choice is that *liberal theology* is often understood as a technical term for the theology of Albrecht Ritschl and his disciples in the late nineteenth and early twentieth centuries. Opponents of Ritschlianism prefer not to be called *liberal*, even when they agree with the Ritschlians on the nature of Scripture. And to use *liberal* to designate seventeenth-century thinkers sounds anachronistic to many. But we do need a single term to designate all theologians who reject the authority of Scripture and embrace intellectual autonomy. Although there have been other suggestions (such as *modernist*, *neo-Protestant*, and *historical-critical*), *liberal* seems to me to be the best choice.

3. Two examples: Ralph Cudworth (1617–88), and Benjamin Whichcote (1609–83).

4. The clearest general account of liberal theology is J. Gresham Machen, *Christianity and Liberalism* (New York: Macmillan, 1923). Machen's target is the specific form of liberalism represented by Albrecht Ritschl and his disciples. But in general, his account well represents all forms of liberalism, and shows especially the sharp antithesis between liberalism and biblical Christianity.

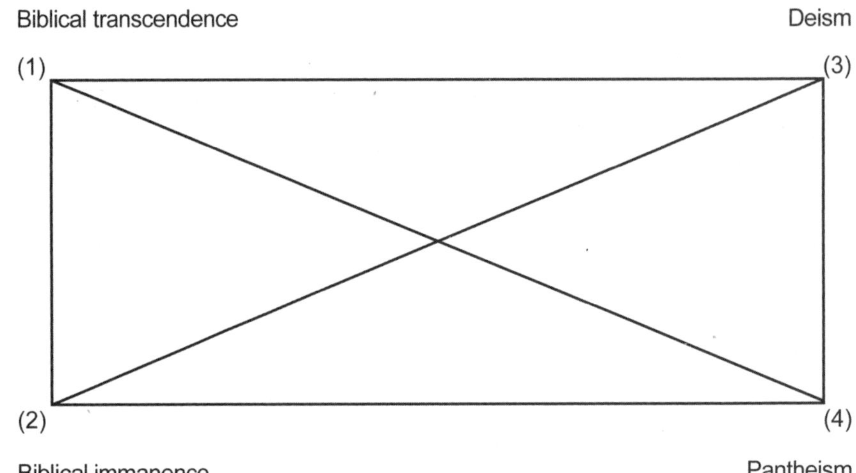

Fig. 6.1. Transcendence and Immanence in Deism

John Locke, whom I discussed in the previous chapter, is sometimes called the *father of deism*. That title is not entirely accurate, for Locke's beliefs were more orthodox than those of the more typical deists such as Cherbury and Toland (discussed below). But Locke was much interested in bridging the religious differences of his time in the interest of religious tolerance. In 1695 he published anonymously a book called *The Reasonableness of Christianity*. This book actually defends the notion of special revelation, which Cherbury and others rejected. Locke believed that God is able to reveal himself in word as well as in the world, and that God's verbal revelation is fully authoritative. But he also said that human reason is the test that enables us to judge among purported revelations. When we apply that test, we discover that Christ's teachings are essentially the fulfillment of the moral law of nature, discovered by reason. Anyone should be considered a Christian, then, who believes in God and in Jesus as Messiah. The essence of Christianity, therefore, is *reasonable*, that is, simple and accessible to everyone. It is not an abstruse system for theologians and politicians to battle one another about. Yet Locke did believe that Christians also have an obligation to go beyond the simplicities, to understand and believe all the other doctrines of Scripture.

Edward, Lord Herbert of Cherbury

But the first "textbook" representative of deism is **Edward, Lord Herbert of Cherbury** (1583–1648). In his *De Veritate* (1624), he proposes to discuss "Truth, as Distinguished from Revelation." In *De Religions Gentilum* (1645), he lists five principles by which we can recognize truth in the religions of the world: (1) God exists. (2) We are obligated to worship him. (3) The essence of worship is practical morality. (4) When we sin, we should repent of it and abandon it. (5) God will reward and/or punish our misdeeds in this world and/or the next.

This minimalistic theology is echoed by other writers, such as **John Toland** (1670–1722) (*Christianity Not Mysterious*, 1695) and **Matthew Tindal** (1657–1733) (*Christianity as Old as Creation*, 1730). The subtitle of Tindal's work: *The Gospel a Republication of the Religion of Nature.*

These deist authors flatly rejected the claim of the Scriptures to be the infallible written Word of God. For them, God's revelation is located in the natural world, not in a book. It is general revelation, not special revelation. Thus, all revelation is accessible to reason alone.

These deist authors flatly rejected the claim of the Scriptures to be the infallible written Word of God. For them, God's revelation is located in the natural world, not in a book. It is general revelation, not special revelation. Thus, all revelation is accessible to reason alone.

That reason is *autonomous* in the sense in which I have been using the term. Previous Christian writers, such as Thomas Aquinas and John Locke, have given some space to autonomous rationality. But among the deists, not only is it *permissible* to claim rational autonomy, but autonomous reason is *sufficient* as an authority for theology, just as for the rationalist and empiricist philosophers autonomous reason is sufficient for our understanding of the world. For the deists, Scripture has no divine authority at all.

Such an epistemology necessarily leads to a theology radically different from the creeds of the churches. A rational examination of natural revelation leads to doctrines such as the five principles of Cherbury. To the deists, then, Christianity is a "republication of the religion of nature."

This natural religion essentially removes the gospel from the Christian catechism. God exists, says Cherbury, and he will reward our goodness and punish our wickedness. But what of forgiveness? No news of divine forgiveness can be discovered through a rational analysis of nature. Nor evidence of miracle, nor prophecy. There is no reason to believe that God has sent his Son to die for sinners and be raised from the dead. It is hard to imagine a more drastic alteration of the Christian system of belief. There is no gospel here, and no grace. Cherbury's theology is works-righteousness, no less so than the theology of modern Judaism or Islam.

Such an epistemology necessarily leads to a theology radically different from the creeds of the churches. . . . To the deists, then, Christianity is a "republication of the religion of nature."

A God who is transcendent in the deist sense cannot reach out to individual sinners. There can be no personal relationship with such a God. The deist God, indeed, has very few personal characteristics.

One would have expected the Christian community to have immediately risen up to repudiate deism in the strongest terms. This heresy is certainly more serious than any heresy of the past. For deism does not merely question individual doctrines. It repudiates Christ himself and denies that there is any gospel of salvation. Many individual Christians did recognize the seriousness of these denials. But in the academic-intellectual establishments, deism became a popular, even flourishing position. And since pastors were trained in universities, these ideas were accepted even in some churches. That is hard to believe, but true.

What amazes me most is this: Deism in particular and liberalism in general are the most serious doctrinal deviations that the church has ever experienced. Deism is certainly worse than Arianism, or Sabellianism, or any of the other heresies. But the churches fought pitched battles over those heresies. They denounced, they excommunicated. At the extreme they held church councils and formulated creeds and confessions to repudiate ("anathematize") these false doctrines. But when deism and other forms of liberalism appeared, the churches did nothing comparable. There were no church councils, no new confessions, no anathemas. The churches were asleep, powerless. They seemed to take for granted that the universities would be in the hands of liberals, and that their pastoral candidates would be educated in that intellectual climate. But they seemed to assume that it would all work out in the end. They seemed to have no idea of the horrible consequences of this tolerance.

So again, we must take account of a convulsion in the history of philosophy that continues to afflict Christianity in our own time. In the rest of this book, I will trace the history of liberal theology along with other philosophical developments and themes. If anyone wonders why I discuss liberal theology in a philosophy text, I hope it will be plain to readers from this discussion that liberal theology is a philosophical movement. It is a product of the rebirth of secular philosophy in the seventeenth century and an extension of the claim of autonomy from philosophers to theologians. It is the imposition of a radically non-Christian philosophy on the theology of the Christian church. And it is a surrender of professing Christian thinkers to the demands of intellectual autonomy.

The churches were asleep, powerless. They seemed to take for granted that the universities would be in the hands of liberals, and that their pastoral candidates would be educated in that intellectual climate. But they seemed to assume that it would all work out in the end.

Gotthold E. Lessing (1729–81)

Lessing was and is better known as a literary figure (a playwright, poet, stage director) than as a philosopher or theologian. But he developed a line of argument that had an immense influence on the later debates about religion.

Lessing was, like Locke, an advocate of religious toleration. In his blank-verse play *Nathan the Wise*, he presents three main characters: Saladin, a Muslim; Nathan,[5] a Jew; and "Knight Templar," a Christian. At one point, Nathan presents a story from Boccaccio's *Decameron*. In the story, a father possesses a ring that is said to bring God's extraordinary favor to the possessor. Which of his three sons will inherit this great blessing? At the distribution, they find that the father has three

5. Nathan is a surrogate for the Jewish philosopher Moses Mendelssohn, a friend of Lessing. Mendelssohn was the grandfather of the composer Felix Mendelssohn, whose father had converted to Christianity.

rings, humanly indistinguishable, and gives one to each son. They argue among themselves as to which one has the authentic ring. But the only way they can prove which ring is authentic is to live in a way that befits one who is in favor with God.

Nathan's point, and Lessing's, was that nobody can prove which of the great religions is God's truth. The only way to establish the truth of a religion is by the character of its disciples, as in Jesus' saying, "You will recognize them by their fruits" (Matt. 7:20).

Gotthold E. Lessing

This viewpoint freed Lessing, in his view, from the necessity of historical apologetics, from the need to establish the truth of Christianity (or any other religion) from historical evidence. He was therefore free to encourage the development of radical biblical criticism. To that end, he published some writings of H. S. Reimarus (1694–1768), without revealing the author, as the "Wolfenbüttel Fragment."[6]

But Lessing's most famous work was a pamphlet he published in 1777 called "On the Proof of the Spirit and of Power." Here he notes that Origen, in *Contra Celsum*, commended Christianity because of the abundance of miracles that attended it. Lessing comments, however, that there is a difference between miracles themselves and mere reports of miracles. The former might constitute impressive proof, but not the latter. For the latter themselves require proof of authenticity. He generalizes the point with his most famous saying, "The accidental truths of history can never become the proof of necessary truths of reason."

Lessing comments . . . that there is a difference between miracles themselves and mere reports of miracles. The former might constitute impressive proof, but not the latter. For the latter themselves require proof of authenticity. He generalizes the point with his most famous saying, "The accidental truths of history can never become the proof of necessary truths of reason."

Now, by "necessary truths of reason" Lessing is not referring to truths of logic or mathematics, or what Leibniz and Hume described as *analytic* truths. He is, rather, referring to the fundamental truths of metaphysics and morals, by which we govern our lives. One of his examples is "the nature of the Godhead." Hume would have called that a body of synthetic propositions. But it is certainly a truth that cannot be discovered by autonomous historical study alone.

Lessing claims to believe in the historical accounts of Jesus, including his miracles and his resurrection. But he denies that those historical propositions, even if we accept them as fact, can justify claims about the deity of Christ and the Trinity.

Now, the deists were arguably more negative than Lessing toward traditional theology, because they rejected miracles altogether. Lessing's position is more subtle than theirs, because his objection is epistemological: that from miracles, even if they do take place, we cannot deduce theological truths. But on the whole, Lessing's position is not different from theirs. In neither view do historical events serve as proof of the nature of Christ and the nature of salvation. And Lessing goes beyond the deists in an important respect. For them, the issue is the

6. *Wolfenbüttel* was the name of the library in which Lessing worked at the time.

authority of special revelation in general. For Lessing, the issue is a particular form of special revelation: the authority and significance of historical events. From this point on, the concept of *history*, as both a philosophical and theological category, will receive attention.

Christians have always claimed that their faith is rooted in history. In this respect (as in the respects discussed in chapter 1), Christianity is different from all other religions. The substance of Hinduism, Buddhism, and even Islam is not found in their historical claims. What is important about these religions is certain general truths that they propose for belief. These truths do not depend on any historical events, even though they were supposedly discovered or revealed in historical situations. If these religions are true, they are true in all times and places, indeed timelessly. But Christianity is different. It is essentially a story about certain things that happened in geographic places and historic times: creation, fall, the history of Israel, the incarnation of Christ through the virgin birth, his miracles, his atonement, his resurrection, ascension, and return. One may be skeptical about the Buddha's reported enlightenment under the Bodhi Tree and still be a good Buddhist. But one may not be skeptical about Jesus' resurrection and be a good Christian. Indeed, Paul says that "if Christ has not been raised, then our preaching is in vain and your faith is in vain" (1 Cor. 15:14). In orthodox Christianity, our entire salvation comes through acts of God in history.

But for Lessing, as an epistemological necessity, faith *cannot* be based on historical events. He considers the objection that possibly the proof of these events comes through divinely inspired writers. But, he replies, that claim, too, is subject to the relativity of history; there is no reliable proof of it. So there is, he says, an "ugly, broad ditch" between history and faith—a ditch "which I cannot get across, however often and however earnestly I have tried to make the leap."

For Lessing, as an epistemological necessity, faith cannot be based on historical events. . . . There is, he says, an "ugly, broad ditch" between history and faith—a ditch "which I cannot get across, however often and however earnestly I have tried to make the leap."

The deists simply rejected Scripture because they thought only natural revelation was credible. Lessing is more specific. He rejects any foundation of Christian faith based on historical events. But of course, this means that he, like the deists, rejects the gospel, a message of good news about historical events.

Later generations of theologians would talk much about "Lessing's ditch" and would try to reply to it. Orthodox theologians did not admit to a problem here. For them, our faith is based on history, but not on an *autonomous* analysis of history. God has spoken to us in Scripture, and we authenticate the Scripture not by an autonomous analysis of its history, but by Scripture's self-testimony illumined by the Holy Spirit.

But liberal theologians generally found Lessing's argument to be unanswerable. So they scrambled to try to find a plausible basis for faith other than history. For Kant (as in Lessing's *Nathan*), that basis was ethics; for Schleiermacher, feeling; for Ritschl, value judgments; for Barth, *Geschichte*, a special kind of history beyond geographical place and calendar time; and so on. I will discuss these alternatives in later chapters.

BIBLICAL CHRISTIANITY IN THE ENLIGHTENMENT

Like J. Gresham Machen in *Christianity and Liberalism*, I consider liberalism to be something very different from, and antithetical to, biblical Christianity. But we should note here that in addition to the early advocates of liberalism during the Enlightenment, there were also thinkers who articulated authentic forms of biblical Christianity. This is not to say that all of them were perfectly orthodox or perfectly consistent with their biblical commitment. But certainly the thinkers whom we will discuss in the remainder of this chapter were committed to Christ, and their theology was more biblical than unbiblical. Certainly they did not agree with the true Enlightenment thinkers that autonomous reason was sufficient for human knowledge. I will disagree with them on some matters, but I will also commend their important insights.

We should note here that in addition to the early advocates of liberalism during the Enlightenment, there were also thinkers who articulated authentic forms of biblical Christianity.

Blaise Pascal (1623–62)

Pascal's dates and viewpoint might lead some to question whether he should be considered an "Enlightenment" thinker. Of course, anyone may draw lines where he wishes. But it is significant that Pascal met Descartes and interacted with his thought. In 1647, Descartes visited the family when Pascal, then twenty-four, was ill. They disagreed on philosophical and scientific matters, but the next day Descartes returned and ministered to Pascal as a physician. Pascal got better, but the disagreements remained. Later, Pascal would write:

> I cannot forgive Descartes. In all his philosophy he would have been quite willing to dispense with God. But he had to make Him give a fillip to set the world in motion; beyond this, he has no further need of God.[7]

In 1647, Descartes visited the family when Pascal, then twenty-four, was ill. They disagreed on philosophical and scientific matters, but the next day Descartes returned and ministered to Pascal as a physician. Pascal got better, but the disagreements remained.

More significantly, Pascal is profoundly concerned with issues that became prominent in the Enlightenment, particularly science and the role of human reason.

Like Descartes and Leibniz, Pascal was a mathematician and scientist. At sixteen, he wrote an essay on conic sections. He later developed

7. Blaise Pascal, *Pensées*, 77. 76–79 all mention Descartes.

ideas foundational to the infinitesimal and integral calculus and presented influential ideas about probability. He built one of the first adding machines. He followed empirical observations of Galileo and Evangelista Torricelli in rebutting Aristotle's view that "nature abhors a vacuum." And he made important discoveries in hydraulics. A principle called Pascal's Law states, "When there is an increase in pressure at any point in a confined fluid, there is an equal increase at every other point in the container."[8]

But several incidents led Pascal to focus his interests on religion. In 1646, two doctors who attended his father after a hip injury turned out to be followers of the Dutch theologian Cornelius Jansen (1585–1643). Jansen was a Roman Catholic thinker who promoted an Augustinian theology, emphasizing original sin, predestination, and God's unconditional grace.[9] Pascal's discussions with these doctors led to an interest in religion sometimes called his *first conversion*. But in the three years following his father's death in 1651, he entered a "worldly" period, preoccupied by mathematical, cultural, even hedonistic pursuits. In 1654, however, he experienced a carriage accident in which he narrowly escaped with his life. Later that year, his niece Marguerite was healed from a serious sinus infection by the application of a thorn supposedly taken from Christ's crown of thorns. He thankfully saw the hand of God in both these events, and they led to what is called the *second conversion*. The *third conversion*, however, is the most famous: a private experience in the night of November 23, 1654. He recorded the experience in a "Memorial," which he sewed into his clothes. The text follows:

The third conversion, however, is the most famous: a private experience in the night of November 23, 1654. Pascal recorded the experience in a "Memorial," which he sewed into his clothes.

> Monday, 23 November, feast of St. Clement, pope and martyr, and others in the martyrology.
> Vigil of St. Chrysogonus, martyr, and others.
> From about half past ten at night until about half past midnight,
>
> FIRE.
> GOD of Abraham, GOD of Isaac, GOD of Jacob not of the philosophers and of the learned.

8. Carol Hodanbosi, "Pascal's Principle and Hydraulics," National Aeronautics and Space Administration, http://www.grc.nasa.gov/WWW/k-12/WindTunnel/Activities/Pascals_principle.html.

9. It is interesting to speculate about the possible influence of the Protestant Reformers on Jansen, particularly Calvin, whose followers established many churches in the Netherlands. The three emphases mentioned above are tempting points of comparison, as are the emphasis on Scripture in the movement and the questioning of reason and tradition. Later I will call attention to Pascal's emphasis on the *existential perspective* of epistemology, which I noted in Calvin in the previous chapter. We can understand, then, why Pascal was later criticized as Calvinistic. But he denied that influence and wrote some critical words about Calvin, though it is not clear that he had actually read the Reformer's works.

> Certitude. Certitude. Feeling. Joy. Peace.
> GOD of Jesus Christ.
> My God and your God.
> Your GOD will be my God.
> Forgetfulness of the world and of everything, except GOD.
> He is only found by the ways taught in the Gospel.
> Grandeur of the human soul.
> Righteous Father, the world has not known you, but I have known you.
> Joy, joy, joy, tears of joy.
> I have departed from him:
> They have forsaken me, the fount of living water.
> My God, will you leave me?
> Let me not be separated from him forever.
> This is eternal life, that they know you, the one true God, and the one that you sent, Jesus Christ.
> Jesus Christ.
> Jesus Christ.
> I left him; I fled him, renounced, crucified.
> Let me never be separated from him.
> He is only kept securely by the ways taught in the Gospel:
> Renunciation, total and sweet.
> Complete submission to Jesus Christ and to my director.
> Eternally in joy for a day's exercise on the earth.
> May I not forget your words. Amen.[10]

Pascal's greatest work, begun while he was writing the Letters, was a collection of sayings (some just a few words or phrases, some one sentence long, some going on for many pages) that he intended to bring together as an apology for Christianity.

From that time on, he gave himself completely to the service of God. He moved to Port Royal, the Jansenist convent that his sister Jacqueline had entered in 1651. In 1656–57, he wrote the *Provincial Letters*, a defense of Port Royal and Jansenism against the criticisms of the Jesuits. These established Pascal's reputation as a witty, ironic, and insightful writer, but they did not accomplish their purpose, to bring acceptance of Jansenism in the church. There were papal condemnations of Jansenist writers (Saint-Cyran and Arnaud, but not Pascal himself), and in 1660 the school at Port Royal was closed down.

Blaise Pascal

But Pascal's greatest work, begun while he was writing the *Letters*, was a collection of sayings (some just a few words or phrases, some one sentence long, some going on for many pages) that he intended to bring together as an apology for Christianity. His death in 1662 prevented him from completing the book, but after his death various editors assembled and published the fragments. These sayings have been published as the book *Pensées* (*Thoughts*).

10. Translation from Pascal's "Memorial," available at http://www.users.csbsju.edu/~eknuth/pascal.html.

Although scholarly editors have given some thought to the order of the remarks, the progress of Pascal's argument is not always easy to follow. Themes appear, then disappear, and then reappear pages later. But there is a consensus as to the main structure of Pascal's argument. After some apparently miscellaneous "Thoughts on Mind and on Style," he discusses "The Misery of Man without God."[11] In the second half of the book, he discusses "The Happiness of Man with God." In the first half, he condemns the hedonism and the casual attitude toward religious questions that he finds characteristic of his age. These are matters of life and death, he says, and deserve the most passionate attention.

To stimulate his readers to ask these ultimate questions, he appeals to science. There are two infinites: the incomparable greatness of the universe discovered by the new astronomy, and the incredible smallness of the microscopic world. Man is midway between the two: both small and large.[12] But the paradox is one not only of size, but of competence. Pascal says that man is a mere reed, bending in the wind. But he is a reed that transcends the whole universe by his power to think about it. A "thinking reed."[13] This paradox should convince people to ask about their nature, purpose, and destiny.

But the greatness of the universe, both macro- and microscopic, should caution us. We are thinking beings, as Descartes said, but the capacity of reason in eternal matters is more limited than Descartes imagined. Pascal has little confidence in the traditional "demonstrations" of the existence of God, whether by Aquinas or by Descartes. As in his "Memorial," he is interested in the God of Abraham, Isaac, and Jacob, not the god of the philosophers and the learned. At some point, rational demonstration ends, and we must "wager."[14] In all of life, we act on uncertainties, probabilities. We cannot always be sure of the results of our decisions. Yet we must make them, if we are to live.

At some point, rational demonstration ends, and we must "wager." In all of life, we act on uncertainties, probabilities. We cannot always be sure of the results of our decisions. Yet we must make them, if we are to live.

Pascal does believe that although the Christian faith cannot be demonstrated, it can be shown to be probable by various evidences.[15] These include the success of the Christian church against impossible odds, the character of Christ and the biblical writers, the character of Christian believers,[16] the preservation of the Jews, the arguments from prophecy

11. His programmatic statement is in number 60:
—*First part*: Misery of man without God.
—*Second part*: Happiness of man with God.
—Or, *First part*: That nature is corrupt. Proved by nature itself.
—*Second part*: That there is a Redeemer. Proved by Scripture.

12. Pascal, *Pensées*, 72.

13. Ibid., 347–8.

14. Ibid., 233–34.

15. Ibid., 425–924.

16. I wish it were possible today to point to the character of believers as evidence for the truth of Christianity. Unfortunately, today the case is not so evident.

and miracle, the ring of truth in the biblical accounts, the evidences for Jesus' resurrection. These evidences have been repeated and elaborated often in books of apologetics down to the present day. Pascal also deals with comparative religion: the non-Christian religions of the world lead to either pride (that I can please God on my own) or despair (that I can never hope to win God's favor), while Christianity rebukes both of these views; see fig. 6.2.[17]

For Pascal, our fundamental decision as to faith or unbelief is importantly analogous to a wager. . . . It is like a wager in that we must make a commitment, though we lack perfect rational certainty.

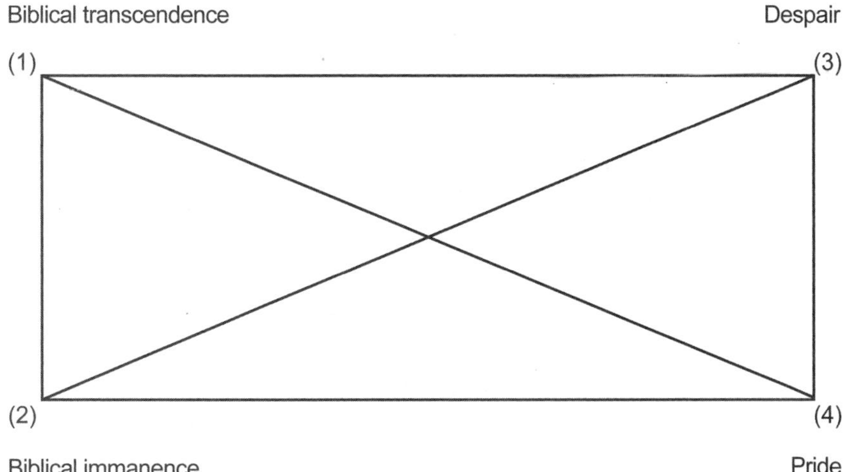

Fig. 6.2. Pascal's Critique of Non-Christian Religion

But the end of these arguments does not result in what Pascal would call rational demonstration. He believes he has shown Christianity to be highly probable, however. How, then, should people respond to the probable evidence?

If Christianity is true and we bet against it (by resolving to live and think as unbelievers), we lose everything. But if Christianity is not true and we bet in favor of it, we lose nothing. Prudence therefore dictates a decision to follow Christ.

For Pascal, our fundamental decision as to faith or unbelief is importantly analogous to a wager. Of course, it is uniquely important, compared to other wagers. The stakes are our earthly lifestyle and our eternal destiny. But it is like a wager in that we must make a commitment, though we lack perfect rational certainty. The terms are these: If Christianity is true and we bet against it (by resolving to live and think as unbelievers), we lose everything. But if Christianity is not true and we bet in favor of it, we lose nothing. Prudence therefore dictates a decision to follow Christ.

Pascal's Wager is somewhat like Anselm's argument in the *Proslogium*. On first hearing, it almost certainly appears that there must be something wrong with it. But it is terribly difficult to show where the

17. In terms of the rectangular diagram presented in chapter 1, despair is a form of nonbiblical transcendence (God is too far from us, so we cannot hope to please him) and pride is nonbiblical immanence (I can please God because he is not very much different from me); see fig. 1.5.

error lies. So down to the present day, as with the ontological argument, there are serious philosophers who reject the Wager and others who defend it.[18]

Many of the arguments against Pascal's Wager are easily refuted. Some have objected, for example, to the very suggestion that faith is a kind of wager. The very analogy seems to do injustice to the dignity of faith. But no analogy is perfect.[19] The most we can ask of an analogy is that it illumine some important matters. Faith is, of course, much more than a wager, and it is not, like most wagers, only a game. But Pascal understood that fact more completely than most other writers. He spoke eloquently about the enormous consequences of the decision we must make. And of course, as we will see below, this wager is a heart-commitment, not a mere intellectual assent.

Others argue that the Wager is an appeal to self-interest, which is inappropriate in our relation to God. But Scripture itself often appeals to human self-interest in motivating our repentance and faith (as, e.g., Luke 13:3, 5). Scripture discourages selfishness, which is a *short-term* self-interest, but in the same contexts where it discourages selfishness it often points to our *long-term* self-interest in the kingdom of God (Mark 10:29–30).

Some, like Cornelius Van Til, object to all arguments for Christianity based on probability. They say that since God's revelation is clear, Christianity is *certainly* true, not merely probable, and that we should make that claim in every apologetic argument. But many people do not acknowledge the certainty of God's revealed evidence. Some of these, however, might admit that the evidence is probable, and Pascal's argument is addressed to them.[20] Pascal says, in effect, that if someone recognizes even the probable truth of the Christian faith, he has an obligation to act on that probability, as we all act on probabilities in

Pascal says, in effect, that if someone recognizes even the probable truth of the Christian faith, he has an obligation to act on that probability, as we all act on probabilities in everyday life.

18. See, for example, the articles in the section titled "Prudential Accounts of Religious Belief," in *Contemporary Perspectives on Religious Epistemology*, ed. R. Douglas Geivett and Brendan Sweetman (New York: Oxford University Press, 1992), 257–92.

19. In my judgment, theologians, philosophers, and politicians could save valuable time by skipping the familiar argument "how dare you compare X to Y?" It is important for us to remember that (1) in some ways, everything is like (and therefore analogous to) everything else, and (2) in some ways, nothing is exactly the same as anything else (and therefore every analogy is imperfect). So we ought to be generous with people who compare us to undignified objects and gently point out where their analogies break down.

20. I agree with Thomas V. Morris, "Pascalian Wagering," in *Contemporary Perspectives on Religious Epistemology*, ed. R. Douglas Geivett and Brendan Sweetman (New York: Oxford University Press, 1992), 257–69, that Pascal did not intend the Wager to influence people who think that Christianity is absurd or highly improbable. Rather, the Wager is for those who, after considering the evidences such as those offered in the *Pensées*, agree that Christianity has a high probability of being true, but are unwilling to make a final commitment.

everyday life.[21] Of course, once someone makes that wager, his epistemology will be renewed so that he recognizes God's revelation as certain.[22]

The most serious argument against the Wager is that Pascal does not consider other possibilities. He considers only the possibilities (1) that Christianity is true and (2) that Christianity is false. But perhaps there are others, such as (3) that Islam is true, and Allah will punish in hell anyone who worships Christ as God. Given the number of religions and worldviews, one can contemplate many other possibilities as well. But if (3) or one of the others is true, then prudence does not dictate commitment to Christianity.

Pascal's intended audience consisted of people who, by exposure to Christian culture and to other parts of the Pensées, *described here earlier, were convinced that the case for Christianity was at least highly probable.*

In defense of the Wager against this argument, we should note that Pascal is addressing a somewhat narrow audience: not people who are exploring the entire field of comparative religions and worldviews, but those who are considering Christianity in a very specific way. For them, the question is not "which, if any, of all the religions of the world should I embrace?" but specifically "should I become a Christian or not?" Further, Pascal's intended audience consisted of people who, by exposure to Christian culture and to other parts of the *Pensées*, described here earlier, were convinced that the case for Christianity was at least highly probable.

And although Pascal doesn't stress this point, Scripture itself presents the nature of religious decision in just this way. Since the fall of man, the basic issue for each human being is whether I will worship the true God or an idol. The alternatives are no more than two: obedience or sin; faith or unbelief; the wisdom of God or the wisdom of the world.

Since the fall of man, the basic issue for each human being is whether I will worship the true God or an idol. The alternatives are no more than two: obedience or sin; faith or unbelief; the wisdom of God or the wisdom of the world.

As for those who want to consider many more alternatives, Pascal's Wager is not for them. They are not ready for it. If they were to ask Pascal for help, he would offer them, as we have seen, many other kinds of evidence that set Christianity off against its rivals.

But what if, having heard the Wager argument, someone says that he is not ready to make this commitment? Should Pascal simply break off the conversation with him? Or are there other things the inquirer can do to draw near to faith? In the same context in which he describes the Wager, Pascal says:

21. "Christianity is probable" is a partial truth. In an apologetic conversation, it sometimes leads people toward more complete truth (for probability itself presupposes Christian theism), and sometimes leads people away from it (for if Christianity is *only* probable, it is also in some measure improbable). The direction of the apologetic conversation will depend on the decision of the Holy Spirit. But the apologist cannot share the truth *exhaustively*. So partial truths are legitimate in the apologetic enterprise, even unavoidable.

22. The point of this sentence is mine, not Pascal's, though I suspect that Pascal would agree with it.

> But at least learn your inability to believe, since reason brings you to this, and yet you cannot believe. Endeavour, then, to convince yourself, not by increase of proofs of God, but by the abatement of your passions. You would like to attain faith and do not know the way; you would like to cure yourself of unbelief and ask the remedy for it. Learn of those who have been bound like you, and who now stake all their possessions. These are people who know the way which you would follow, and who are cured of an ill of which you would be cured. Follow the way by which they began; by acting as if they believed, taking the holy water, having masses said, etc. Even this will naturally make you believe, and deaden your acuteness. "But this is what I am afraid of." And why? What have you to lose?—But to show you that this leads you there, it is this which will lessen the passions, which are your stumbling-blocks.[23]

Act as if you believe, and eventually you will, he says. Is Pascal here recommending a hypocritical observance? I think not. He is not telling his reader to deceive anybody, let alone God.

Rather, he is trying to show us that the issue of faith and unbelief is not just intellectual. It is also a matter of the passions. Contrary to Descartes and some other Enlightenment thinkers,[24] Pascal believed that discussions of belief and unbelief must take the passions into account. To a large extent, we believe what we want to believe, what we feel like believing. So if we want to wager our souls, we must discipline our emotions to go along with the Wager.

For Pascal, the way to knowledge is not deduction from axioms, as in rationalism (though he deeply respects mathematics), nor from introspection into our ideas, as in empiricism (though he deeply respects scientific observation and experimentation).

So Pascal's epistemology includes illuminating nuances that take us beyond the conventional wisdom of the age of reason. For Pascal, the way to knowledge is not deduction from axioms, as in rationalism (though he deeply respects mathematics), nor from introspection into our *ideas*, as in empiricism (though he deeply respects scientific observation and experimentation). Rather, there are three *orders* that are irreducible to one another.

These orders are the body, the mind, and the heart (sometimes called *charity*). As lines, squares, and cubes cannot be added together in mathematics, so the three orders are not commensurate. Epistemologically, we may think of the body as the realm of sensation and the mind as the realm of reason. Empiricism focuses on the senses and rationalism on reason. But what interests Pascal the most is the knowledge of the heart, as in his most famous saying, "The heart has its reasons which reason does not know."[25]

23. Pascal, *Pensées*, 233.
24. But recall that Hume said that reason should be the slave of the passions.
25. *Pensées*, 277.

Pascal does not define precisely what he means by *heart*, but in the following context he interchanges it with love, feeling, deciding, faith, intuitions, knowledge of first principles.[26] This kind of knowledge is a gift of God, a revelation. He would probably agree to align his concept with the biblical use of *heart* to designate the core of human existence, that which determines the basic direction of our thinking and decisions (cf. Matt. 15:8, 18, 19; 22:37; Luke 6:45; 12:34). By God's revelation to the heart, accepted by faith, we intuit the general nature of things, a worldview and way of life that could not be deduced from senses or reason alone. Philosophers have been known to say that appeals to feeling and intuition stand in the way of a disciplined epistemology. Pascal believes, on the contrary, that without the right heart-commitment, no knowledge is possible.

Pascal is one of the first philosophers to take into account sophisticated concepts of mathematical probability. He is one of the first thinkers to take seriously the subjective or existential dimension of knowledge, not as a barrier to understanding, but as a necessary basis for it.

Of course, in Scripture the heart can also be wicked, rejecting and repressing the truth. Pascal surely understood this reality as well.

In the context of this epistemology, we can understand Pascal's Wager and his advice to act "as if," not as concessions to irrationalism, but as legitimate forms of thought, necessary if we are to think rightly about God or anything else. As in his "Memorial," he practices a philosophy that thinks of God not as a mere concept, but as a real person, who speaks to men out of the holy fire. In the *Pensées*, he addresses our psychology and feelings as much as our reason and senses. That is, he understands how people really do come to make decisions (intellectual and practical), and he deals with us where we are.

In these remarkable *Pensées*, Pascal introduces themes that are new to the history of philosophy and will be taken up by others: (1) He is one of the first Christian thinkers to take seriously the implications of modern science. (2) He is one of the first philosophers to take into account sophisticated concepts of mathematical probability. (3) He is one of the first thinkers to take seriously the subjective or existential dimension of knowledge, not as a barrier to understanding, but as a necessary basis for it.[27]

Joseph Butler

Joseph Butler (1692–1752)

Butler was born in Berkshire, England, to Presbyterian parents, but converted to the Church of England. In 1738 he became Bishop of Bristol, and in 1751 Bishop of Durham. Theologically he was Arminian, philosophically indebted to Locke's empiricism. The character of Cleanthes in Hume's *Dialogues concerning Natural Religion* may have been patterned after Butler.

26. We recall Aristotle's comment that the first principles of philosophy cannot be proved.

27. See my discussion of the existential perspective in chapter 1. Note also the parallel here with the epistemology of John Calvin as I presented it in chapter 5.

He is remembered today for his moral philosophy and as a Christian apologist. I will deal here only with his apologetics, set forth in *Analogy of Religion*. The *Analogy* has had much influence on later generations of apologists. Cornelius Van Til opposed Butler, finding in Butler the roots of much that has been wrong in the history of apologetics since his time. Van Til thought that Butler, like Aquinas, appealed to autonomous thinking in his argumentation. So he spoke of the apologetic method he opposed as the *Aquinas-Butler Method*.

Like Pascal, Butler rejected the rationalistic apologetics of Descartes[28] and embraced probabilistic argumentation. He discusses probability at great length and explains how probability in many cases confers moral obligation, that is, *moral certainty*. In many situations of life, it is not right to wait for a conclusive demonstration of what is right before we act. Most of the choices we make each day, such as getting out of bed and choosing food to eat for breakfast, are based on judgments of probability, not rational demonstration. So Butler says, "Probability is the very guide to life."[29] For Butler, probability is also the very guide to religious belief. Faith, too, should act on probable evidence.

So when Butler speaks of *reason*, he doesn't mean a quasi-mathematical deductive system as in Descartes and Spinoza, but rather a careful analysis of the probabilities of experience, what he calls "the reasonable use of reason." Given that qualification, however, he agrees with Locke that any claim of revelation must be subject to the test of reason:

> Let reason be kept to: and if any part of the Scripture account of the redemption of the world by Christ can be shown to be really contrary to it, let the Scripture, in the name of God, be given up.[30]

When Butler speaks of reason, *he doesn't mean a quasi-mathematical deductive system as in Descartes and Spinoza, but rather a careful analysis of the probabilities of experience, what he calls "the reasonable use of reason."*

Of course, as a bishop and a convinced Christian, Butler didn't believe that any part of Scripture's message could be shown to be really contrary to reason, even given his qualified definition of *reason*. But it is significant that he gives to this somewhat minimal concept of reason the prerogative of judging whether a revelation is true. At this point, of course, Butler violates the principle I argued in chapter 1, that in a Christian philosophy God's Word must take precedence over any other authority.

28. Butler was aware of the work of Samuel Clarke (1675–1729), who upheld a form of the principle of sufficient reason (compare our discussion of Leibniz in chapter 4). (Hume might have had Clarke in mind when he developed the character of Demea in his *Dialogues*.) Butler appreciated some of Clarke's argumentation, but in general favored a more empirical method.

29. Joseph Butler, *Analogy of Religion* (Philadelphia: J. B. Lippincott, 1865), introduction.

30. Ibid., 245.

Like most other apologists of his time, Butler deals with the general problem of religious skepticism. So he discusses the existence of God and the various arguments from miracle, prophecy, and testimony. But his distinctive contributions to apologetics are directed against deists. This emphasis becomes explicit in Part Two of the *Analogy*. Deists, we recall, believe there is evidence in the "course and constitution of nature" for the existence of God and for his moral standards. But they reject special revelation, or any notion of divine interference in the course of nature. So deism is a moralistic, nonredemptive theology.

Butler tries to show the deists that there is an analogy (hence the title of his major work) between the teaching of Scripture and natural revelation as the deists understand it.

Butler tries to show the deists that there is an analogy (hence the title of his major work) between the teaching of Scripture and natural revelation as the deists understand it. Scripture includes much of the same content as nature, and what it adds is not contrary to nature but an appropriate supplement. So the rationality of natural revelation acknowledged by the deists also supports the rationality of special revelation. On the other hand, Butler argues, if there are problems in Scripture, there are similar problems in the deist account of nature. The deists had argued that nature is simple and easy to understand, but that Scripture is obscure and complicated. Butler seeks to show that there are mysteries in nature, too, and that these mysteries are analogous to those of Scripture.

We know that the powers of the self can persist through apparent inactivity. Sleep is a bit like death, coma even more so. Yet through such times of inactivity, life and personal identity continue. Indeed, it is likely that they continue even through that inactivity we call death.

For example, in the debate over immortality, some[31] argue that death is a simple event in which all consciousness and action is extinguished, a change from life to nonlife. But Butler points out that we undergo many analogous changes during life itself, as we grow from embryo to child to adult to old age. Despite these changes, life and personal identity continue. Further, we know that the powers of the self can persist through apparent inactivity. Sleep is a bit like death, coma even more so. Yet through such times of inactivity, life and personal identity continue. Indeed, it is *likely* that they continue even through that inactivity we call death, for natural things and human powers have a certain momentum when pursuing a certain course. We should therefore assume that when a being has been living for a time, it has a tendency to go on living, even when there is evidence to the contrary.

Butler also points out that bodily changes do not necessarily affect our ability to think. So it may be that when the body dies, the mind continues to exist and to act.

There is, in other words, an analogy between natural realities (growth, sleep, thought) and the Christian doctrine of the future life. But, someone might object, is there not also an analogy between body and soul, so that when the body dies we should assume that the soul

31. Some deists believed in immortality; some did not.

dies as well? Here, Butler invokes mystery, that is, *dis*analogy. We do not know enough about the soul's powers to say that it expires along with the body.

Arguments from analogy are by nature slippery. No analogy is perfect, so when there is analogy, there is also disanalogy. If one arguer advances an analogy, his opponent can point to disanalogy. What is the conclusion? For Butler, that merely implies that the conclusion can be no more than probable (and therefore will always be somewhat improbable). Butler would not be embarrassed at this fact, for probability is at the heart of his epistemology. But then each argument requires calibration. Butler must assure his reader that the argument is sufficiently probable to make the conclusion a moral certainty, and that the disanalogies, the contrary probabilities, are insufficient to invalidate it. And the reader may wonder: how much probability should he demand, and how much has Butler provided?

Consideration of analogy arguments is a way of reminding ourselves how often we (Christians and non-Christians alike) manipulate our rational demands. We tend to press an analogy when its conclusion is congenial to our worldview, and to press disanalogies when the conclusion of the analogy violates our presuppositions. This manipulation also appears in larger debates over metaphysics or epistemology. To pick up the language of chapter 1 of this book, often a rationalist will press an analogy and an irrationalist will insist on disanalogy—or sometimes the reverse.

Arguments from analogy are by nature slippery. No analogy is perfect, so when there is analogy, there is also disanalogy. If one arguer advances an analogy, his opponent can point to disanalogy.

My conclusion is that arguments from analogy (or disanalogy) never settle anything by themselves. They are useful, mostly, in loosening dogmatism. Why, we might ask a skeptic, are you so sure that death ends everything, when you routinely expect your wife to awaken from sleep? When a skeptic considers closely the phenomena of sleep and coma, he might come out of that study less sure of the proposition that death ends it all. But of course, the Christian is in the same boat. When he considers the disanalogy between coma and death, he might be somewhat shaken in his faith, unless his faith is built on something more sturdy than analogy. At best, it seems that the argument about analogy comes out a draw.

To reach an assured conclusion, we often need to know *how* analogous A is to B. An objector may well put pressure on us to evaluate the strength of the analogy in a precise way. But if we could show precisely the degree to which, say, sleep resembles (and does not resemble) death, then we would not need to talk about analogies at all. We would have a precise, mathematical point of comparison.

But of course, we do not have such precise points of comparison between nature and Scripture, life and eternal life, human beings and

God. There is always some mystery, some vagueness, in the analogies between earth and heaven. That is necessarily the case because of the Creator-creature distinction. Creatures are like God, but they are not God. If we could understand in a precise way how much we are like God, we would be God.

If we are to have assured knowledge, rather than guesswork, about eternal life, then we need to have a standpoint beyond the probabilities of sense experience. My suggestion in chapter 1 was that God's Word must interpret nature for us if we are to interpret nature rightly. God alone knows precisely how analogous and disanalogous everything is to everything else. That entails that special revelation has a certain primacy over natural revelation, contrary to the viewpoints of both the deists and Bishop Butler. We must not judge God's revelation by autonomous reason, as Butler would like us to do.[32]

Jonathan Edwards (1703–58)

Two Christian thinkers could hardly differ more in their epistemology than Butler and Edwards. Edwards is an heir of Puritanism, and in Puritan fashion he seeks to bring all his thinking under the authority of Scripture. He does not see the Bible as a problematic text, awaiting the vindication of human reason. While Butler is trying as a Christian to meet the demands of the Enlightenment, Edwards stands against those demands and challenges them.

Edwards is an heir of Puritanism, and in Puritan fashion he seeks to bring all his thinking under the authority of Scripture. He does not see the Bible as a problematic text, awaiting the vindication of human reason.

He does not resist the Enlightenment in ignorance. As a college student he read Locke's *Essay concerning Human Understanding* and professed to take great enjoyment in it. During his student years, he also wrote a paper in response to Newton's *Opticks* and wrote papers on the habits of spiders and the colors of the rainbow. Before 1720 he wrote highly regarded papers on "Being" and "Mind." His precocity in science and philosophy was similar to that of the Enlightenment thinkers whom we have considered.

Jonathan Edwards

He devoted his life, however, not primarily to the academic world, but to the pastorate. He was pastor of a Presbyterian congregation in New York from 1722 to 1724, and then took a position as a senior tutor at Yale. In 1727 he became assistant minister to his grandfather Solomon Stoddard in Northampton, Massachusetts. When Stoddard died in 1729, Edwards became the senior minister there. In 1748 he left there amid controversy[33] and went to Stockbridge, Massachusetts, to

32. Van Til attributed Butler's reliance on autonomous reason to his Arminian theology. If man has free will in the libertarian-Arminian sense, then God has not interpreted man's free choices in advance. So God does not have the final word on what happens and does not happen in the world.

33. I have decided that it would not fit the purposes of this book to describe the nature and course of the controversy.

minister to a largely Indian congregation. In 1757, he was appointed president of Princeton University. He died in Princeton, New Jersey, the next year, following a smallpox inoculation.

For all his work in the Christian ministry, however, Edwards also produced philosophical work of the highest order. Edwards has often been described as the greatest philosopher-theologian that America has produced. From his student days through his years in ministry, he had a regular practice of jotting down observations about a wide range of subjects (his *Miscellanies*) that were later published in collections of his works. He published a number of large books as well.

The main emphasis of his philosophy, theology, and preaching is the Calvinist teaching of absolute divine sovereignty and the inability of man to resist God's will or to save himself from sin. But Edwards develops these ideas in an atmosphere of Enlightenment ideas, with considerable originality.

In his student notes "Of Being," he agrees with Parmenides that absolute nothingness is impossible: contradictory and inconceivable. So being, the opposite of nothingness, is necessary, eternal, and omnipresent. Further, being is immaterial, because the main characteristic of material, "solid" things is their ability to resist other solid things. But since being is everywhere, there is nothing outside of being that might resist it.

But though Parmenides regarded being as an impersonal reality, Edwards recognized in these descriptions attributes of the God of Scripture. So for Edwards, God is being. He is also space, for as it is impossible to conceive the nonexistence of being, or anything outside of being, it is similarly impossible to conceive the nonexistence of space.

The main emphasis of Edwards's philosophy, theology, and preaching is the Calvinist teaching of absolute divine sovereignty and the inability of man to resist God's will or to save himself from sin.

Edwards also wrote notes on "The Mind." Like Locke, he distinguishes the mental faculties of understanding and will. Understanding begins in sensation, yet the objects of sensation are not qualities of bodies, but impressions and ideas given to us by God. This includes, for Edwards, not only what Locke called "secondary" qualities (colors, tastes, smells), but "primary" qualities as well (extension, motion, solidity). So in Edwards's view, all objects are mental in character. They begin in God's mind, and God communicates ideas of them to us. This is an idealistic view, similar to that of Berkeley.[34] Minds alone are, properly, beings. Bodies are only "shadows of being."[35]

34. Although Edwards evidently met Berkeley when Berkeley spent some years in Rhode Island, scholars differ as to whether he actually interacted with Berkeley's ideas, or whether he came to his idealism independently.

35. This language reminds us of Plato's. Edwards was acquainted with Plato's work and with the Cambridge Platonists.

For Edwards, then, God is the only true substance, the only true being, the only true cause. His view of the divine cause behind every finite cause (influenced by the occasionalism of Malebranche) animates his critique of libertarian freedom in *Freedom of the Will*. His view of God as the only true being has led some to charge him with pantheism. For if God is the only true being, then it would seem that finite beings must be identical with God. But Edwards, outside this metaphysical context, does make a distinction between Creator and creature, a distinction between cause and effect. Clearly, Edwards recognizes a distinction between God and those responsible to him, between God and sinners. Edwards's most famous sermon, "Sinners in the Hands of an Angry God," for example, would be nonsense if Edwards did not recognize a distinction between God and man. Scholars continue to debate where, exactly, Edwards drew the line between Creator and creature, but clearly he intended to draw one.[36]

For Edwards, then, God is the only true substance, the only true being, the only true cause. His view of the divine cause behind every finite cause . . . animates his critique of libertarian freedom in Freedom of the Will.

We have been looking at Edwards's view of the mind's faculty of understanding. For him, understanding comes as God supplies us with impressions and ideas. The other mental faculty that Edwards discusses is the will. The will is particularly the seat of passions and affections, the highest of which is love. The will, of course, is also our capacity of choice. But our choices arise from affection. Knowledge itself includes both right understanding and right affections. The knowledge of God is no exception to this principle. The essence of religion is a holy love of God. The elect enjoy a "sweetness" in their experience of God that transcends rational knowledge.[37] Edwards therefore opposes the notion that emotion must be excluded from faith. As with Calvin and Pascal, Edwards has an affirmative view of religious feeling. He doesn't believe that anyone can claim to know God unless he loves God, worships him, and senses the sweetness of his reality. So he doesn't believe that people are fully converted unless their emotions are changed by the Holy Spirit.

The other mental faculty that Edwards discusses is the will. The will is particularly the seat of passions and affections, the highest of which is love.

This issue was central to the controversies over revival throughout Edwards's life. Under his preaching, Northampton experienced revival in 1733–35 and in 1740–42, and multitudes also heard the gospel then under the preaching of George Whitefield and others. This time became known as the *Great Awakening*.[38] In revival settings, people

36. The technical debate over pantheism in Edwards tends to focus not on the naive distinction between God and the world, but on philosophical questions about the nature of being, substance, identity, and so on. Those, I think, are too subtle to make any serious theological or religious difference.

37. John Piper, a modern student of Edwards, has restored "delight in God" to the evangelical religious vocabulary. He argues for a "Christian hedonism," that our highest duty is to find our highest pleasure in God, as God seeks his own highest pleasure in himself. See John Piper, *Desiring God* (Sisters, OR: Multnomah, 1986, 2003), and many other books.

38. Do not confuse the Great Awakening with the Enlightenment. The two movements influenced culture in opposite ways.

OUTLINE

frequently displayed great emotion and sometimes bizarre behavior. Edwards, in *A Faithful Narrative* (1737), described the events surrounding the revival at Northampton. In later years, he analyzed revival in the books *The Distinguishing Marks of a Work of the Spirit of God* (1741), *Thoughts on the Revival in New England* (1742), and *A Treatise concerning Religious Affections* (1746). He defended the revivals, including their emotional component. But he recognized that not all the emotional behavior was the authentic work of the Spirit. He made suggestions as to how we should distinguish between authentic and inauthentic responses to divine grace.

I will not defend Edwards's quasi-Parmenidean speculations on being. For his idealism and occasionalism, the reader should compare my earlier discussion of Berkeley. Edwards, like most Christian philosophers, was not always able to resist the temptation to accommodate his views to respectable academic thought. On the whole, however, his philosophy and theology represent a welcome challenge to the prevailing ideas of the Enlightenment. Clearly, the highest authority for Edwards was the Word of God in Scripture, and he presented God as One who is absolute, personal, real, and active.

William Paley (1743–1805)

Pascal, Butler, and Edwards advocated Christianity in the context of various broad philosophical discussions. So in their work as a whole they contributed much to the general history of metaphysics, epistemology, and axiology. Paley's thought was often philosophical in its precision and clarity, and he did make some contributions to philosophical ethics.[39] But he is remembered today almost exclusively as a Christian apologist. And as an apologist he is known chiefly for one illustration of one argument for God's existence:

William Paley

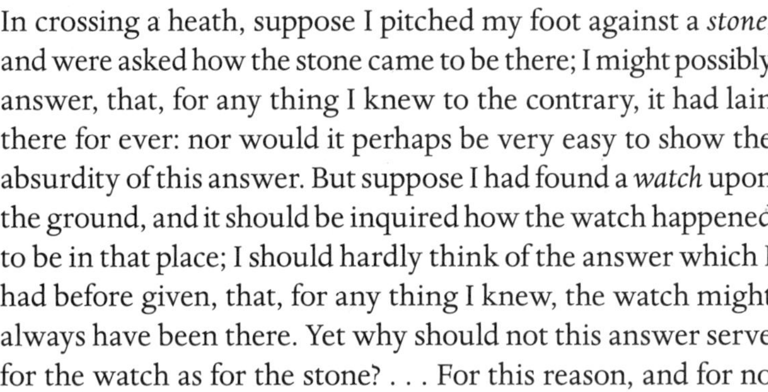

> In crossing a heath, suppose I pitched my foot against a *stone*, and were asked how the stone came to be there; I might possibly answer, that, for any thing I knew to the contrary, it had lain there for ever: nor would it perhaps be very easy to show the absurdity of this answer. But suppose I had found a *watch* upon the ground, and it should be inquired how the watch happened to be in that place; I should hardly think of the answer which I had before given, that, for any thing I knew, the watch might always have been there. Yet why should not this answer serve for the watch as for the stone? . . . For this reason, and for no

39. See his *Principles of Moral and Political Philosophy* (1785), which somewhat anticipates the utilitarianism of Bentham and Mill, but taking into account God's judgment on our moral choices. See *DCL*, 91–100.

> other, viz. that, when we come to inspect the watch, we perceive (what we could not discover in the stone) that its several parts are framed and put together for a purpose.[40]

This is Paley's famous "watchmaker" illustration of the teleological argument, which, we may recall, was the fifth of Aquinas's *five ways* of demonstrating the existence of God. Aquinas presents the argument in a brief paragraph, but Paley presents it in a large book, containing many illustrations of things in nature that have the appearance of design. He goes into great detail about the human eye, for example, noting how the many parts of it are brought together for the evident purpose of sight.

Paley's books were part of the course of study at Cambridge for many years later. Among many who read them with interest and pleasure was Charles Darwin, in 1831.

As Paley illustrated, applied, and developed the argument, it became central to Christian apologetics and remains so down to the present time. Paley taught at Cambridge University from 1767 to 1776, and his books were part of the course of study at Cambridge for many years later. Among many who read them with interest and pleasure was Charles Darwin, in 1831. Darwin later wrote that "I did not at the time trouble myself about Paley's premises, and taking these on trust I was charmed and convinced of the long line of argumentation."[41] Of course, Darwin later developed the theory of evolution, which is often thought to show, contrary to the teleological argument, that it is possible to explain life without reference to God. But more recent thinkers, such as F. R. Tennant and the writers of the "intelligent design" movement (Phillip Johnson, William Dembski, Michael Behe, and others), maintain Paley's view that the adaptation of means to ends in the natural world cannot be explained apart from God.

More recent thinkers, such as F. R. Tennant and the writers of the "intelligent design" movement . . . , maintain Paley's view that the adaptation of means to ends in the natural world cannot be explained apart from God.

Many otherwise skeptical thinkers (including Hume and Kant) have remarked about the naive sense of wonder evoked by the natural world. But formulating this awesomeness into a cogent argument for God's existence has not always been easy. Paley has perhaps taken a cue from Butler: the teleological argument is an argument from analogy. At one level, we seem to have a natural aptitude to recognize similarities between things that are in some degree different. We seem to be able to distinguish between things that are products of design and things that are not. Watches, refrigerators, oil paintings, and palaces are products of design; stones are not. All products of design are analogous to one another in some important ways. Our ability to recognize that analogy, to distinguish between things that are designed and things that are not designed, seems important to the argument.

40. William Paley, *Natural Theology* (Chillicothe, OH: DeWard Publishing, 2010), chap. 1.
41. Frances Darwin, ed., *Autobiography of Charles Darwin* (n.p., n.d.), 24.

But the odd thing about the teleological argument is that at some point this distinction breaks down. For Paley wants us to eventually see that even the *stones* are part of the design. In the end, *everything* is designed. But if everything is designed, then we must abandon the insight with which Paley's argument began, namely, that there are some things (stones) that are clearly *not* designed.

In Paley's Christian worldview, the relevant distinction is not between some things that are designed and others that are not. Rather, it is between things of human design and things of divine design.[42] So there is a discrepancy between the things being compared. The watch is a product of *human* design. But that is not the case with the universe. If there is an analogy between human and divine design, there is also disanalogy.[43] If there were no disanalogy, then Paley would have proved that the world was designed by a human being, and that would be contrary to the Christian faith.

So Paley needs to show (1) that there is both analogy and disanalogy between the world and products of human design, and (2) that the disanalogy is sufficient to show that the designer of the world is divine. Certainly he tries to show the disanalogy in various ways, as by citing the sheer size of the universe and the complexity of the world order. But this sort of distinction is merely quantitative. Hume's reaction is understandable: if the teleological argument is sound, then it proves only the existence of a god who is a little bigger than the universe, not one who is infinite, eternal, and unchangeable.

So I draw the same conclusion that I drew in regard to Bishop Butler's arguments from analogy:[44] To reach an assured conclusion, we often need to know *how* analogous A is to B (in this case, A is the universe, and B is a product of human design). An objector may well put pressure on us to evaluate the strength of the analogy in a precise way. But if we could precisely show the degree to which, say, sleep resembles (and does not resemble) death, then we would not need to talk about analogies at all. We would have a precise, mathematical point of comparison.

There is always some mystery, some vagueness, in the analogies between earth and heaven. That is necessarily the case because of the Creator-creature distinction.

But of course, we do not have such precise points of comparison between nature and Scripture, life and eternal life, human beings and God. There is always some mystery, some vagueness, in the analogies between earth and heaven. That is necessarily the case because of the Creator-creature distinction. Creatures are like God, but they are not God. If we could understand in a precise way how much we are like God, we would be God.

42. Of course, the latter category includes the former.

43. Recall that Hume's refutation of the teleological argument suggested many differences between human and divine designs.

44. I have copied the next three paragraphs, with some revision, from the end of the section in this chapter dealing with Bishop Butler.

If we are to have assured knowledge, rather than guesswork, of God's existence, then we need to have a standpoint beyond the probabilities of sense experience. My suggestion in chapter 1 was that God's Word must interpret nature for us if we are to interpret nature rightly. God, and God alone, knows precisely how analogous and disanalogous everything is to everything else. That entails that special revelation have a certain primacy over natural revelation, contrary to the viewpoints of the deists, Bishop Butler, and William Paley. We must not judge God's revelation by autonomous reason, as Butler maintains, and as Paley seems to ask us to do with the teleological argument.

Thomas Reid

Paley does suggest another way in which we can show that the designer of the universe is infinite and eternal, rather than finite but large. That is by supplementing the teleological argument with the cosmological argument. Like Aquinas, he denies that there could be an infinite series of causes for the universe. As with his watchmaker analogy, he makes the case against infinite series with a vivid illustration: "A chain, composed of an infinite number of links, can no more support itself, than a chain composed of a finite number of links."[45] He believes this argument eliminates the possibility that the chain of designers can go on without end. To account for the links in the chain, there must be someone at the other end holding up the chain, not just more chain.

But this, too, as Aquinas would agree, is an argument from analogy. To what extent is God a cause like earthly causes? To what extent is he like a man holding a chain? To assess the analogy and disanalogy, I believe we need to be able to look at the relation from God's point of view. And that requires revelation.

If we are to have assured knowledge, rather than guesswork, of God's existence, then we need to have a standpoint beyond the probabilities of sense experience.

Thomas Reid (1710–96)

Reid served as a pastor in the Church of Scotland from 1737 to 1751, and then held teaching positions at the University of Aberdeen (1751–64) and the University of Glasgow (1764–96). He was the dominant figure in the "Scottish Common Sense Philosophy" or "Common Sense Realism" (which I will abbreviate as *CSR*). Other members of that school were James Beattie (1735–1803), Dugald Stewart (1753–1828), and William Hamilton (1788–1856).[46] The Scottish school took root in France (Victor Cousin, 1792–1867) and in the New World as well. Noah Porter (1811–92)[47] taught this philosophy at Yale. James McCosh, president of

45. Paley, *Natural Theology*, chap. 2.

46. Hamilton published an annotated edition of Reid's works, but his personal philosophy was influenced by Kant as well as by the Scottish school.

47. There is a Noah Porter chair of philosophy at Yale, recently occupied by Nicholas Wolterstorff (see chapter 13), who has much appreciation for Reid.

Princeton University from 1868 to 1888, advocated CSR, and Reid's influence also extended to Princeton Theological Seminary under such thinkers as Charles Hodge, B. B. Warfield, and J. Gresham Machen. Through them, CSR still has considerable influence, especially on American evangelicals.[48]

Reid's influence on American thought did decline following the death of McCosh and the liberalization of Princeton Seminary in 1929. When I studied philosophy at Princeton University from 1957 to 1961, Reid was not mentioned. The history-of-philosophy textbook that we used at the time gives Reid only two paragraphs.[49] But in the revival of Christian philosophy that began in the 1970s (chapter 13), led by such figures as Alvin Plantinga, Nicholas Wolterstorff, and Paul Helm, Reid played a major role.[50] So CSR is a movement that still carries significant influence today.

Reid takes on the challenge to turn back the skepticism of David Hume. To do this, he challenges a premise that Hume held in common with Locke and Berkeley, that our knowledge is essentially a knowledge of our own perceptions. For empiricism in the eighteenth century, *experience* is experience of the contents of our own minds: sensation, impressions, ideas. On that basis, we do not know the world directly. Our ideas *represent* the world to us. By close introspection, we can learn about the world by studying our ideas. But the question arose: What is the relationship between these ideas and the "real world"? Indeed, is there any world out there? Locke worried that he had no clear idea of what constituted *substance*. It was, as he said, "something, I know not what." But to modern philosophers, both rationalist and empiricist, substance is what *is*, the real world. Berkeley simply rejected the notion of material substance: for him, the world consists entirely of ideas in the mind. But for Hume, the mind was also suspect. If there is no material substance, there is no mental substance either, just a bundle of perceptions.

Reid takes on the challenge to turn back the skepticism of David Hume. To do this, he challenges a premise that Hume held in common with Locke and Berkeley, that our knowledge is essentially a knowledge of our own perceptions.

Reid rejects the fundamental premise of empiricism that all we know is our own perceptions. To Reid, what we know is the real world—

48. There has been a controversy over whether and to what extent the evangelical doctrine of biblical inerrancy is based on CSR. I agree with A. T. B. McGowan, *The Divine Authenticity of Scripture: Retrieving an Evangelical Heritage* (Downers Grove, IL: IVP Academic, 2008), that CSR is not the source of this doctrine, but contra McGowan, I believe that the doctrine comes from Scripture itself. See my review of McGowan, Appendix L in my *DWG*.

49. Frank Thilly and Ledger Wood, *A History of Philosophy* (New York: Henry Holt, 1957), 382–83.

50. See the essays on Reid in Hendrik Hart, Johan van der Hoeven, and Nicholas Wolterstorff, eds., *Rationality in the Calvinian Tradition* (Lanham, MD: University Press of America, 1983). Reid also plays a major role in the *Classical Apologetics* of R. C. Sproul, John H. Gerstner, and Arthur Lindsley (Grand Rapids: Zondervan, 1984).

hence "common sense *realism*." We are able to know the real world because our minds are not mere bundles of perceptions. Rather, our minds have innate powers that give rise in us to concepts of qualities and of sensed objects.[51] These concepts are not mere sensations, as in Hume. Concepts, as opposed to sensations, have objects: they are always concepts *of* something. So to have a concept of a tree is to know a tree, not just to know a mental idea of a tree.[52] This process creates immediate, irresistible convictions, which are justified beliefs.

We are able to know the real world because our minds are not mere bundles of perceptions. Rather, our minds have innate powers that give rise in us to concepts of qualities and of sensed objects. These concepts are not mere sensations.

The first of these beliefs presented to us by our mental faculties is called the *deliverances of "common sense."* These are principles accepted by people in everyday conversation and business. They cannot be justified by Cartesian arguments or reduced to sensations as in empiricism. But they do not need that kind of justification. They are *first* principles, the principles that we assume when we seek to gain additional knowledge. We have the right to believe these principles even if we cannot justify them, even if we cannot demonstrate that they belong to common sense. The fact is that common-sense principles are better known than any of the claims that people might use to refute them. If, for example, Hume tries to argue that there is no such thing as a soul or mind, Reid can reply that our intuition of selfhood is far more persuasive than any of the philosophical principles by which Hume might try to cast doubt on it.[53]

Here are some of the principles that Reid lists as belonging to common sense:

1. Consciousness is reliable in showing us what exists.
2. Conscious thoughts reveal a self, mind, or person.
3. Memory is generally reliable.
4. Personal identity continues through the course of remembered events.
5. Sense perception is generally reliable.
6. People intuit that they have free will.
7. All natural faculties (*reason*) are generally reliable.
8. Others have life and intelligence similar to ours.
9. Physical expressions and actions of people reveal their minds.
10. Human testimony is generally reliable.
11. People's actions are more or less regular.
12. The future will be generally like the past.

The fact is that common-sense principles are better known than any of the claims that people might use to refute them.

51. The idea of innate mental powers, of course, rejects the *tabula rasa* theory of Locke and is in some ways more like the views of the rationalists than the empiricists.

52. This insight is similar to the views of later phenomenologists such as Husserl and Heidegger. See chapter 9.

53. Certainly at this point Reid is closer to Descartes than to any empiricist.

In my view, point 6 is the most questionable of these. Reid holds to a view of libertarian freedom similar to many of the church fathers and later theologians such as Molina and Arminius, though this view is inconsistent with the confessions to which he subscribed as a Presbyterian minister. This doctrine of free will is often based on intuition, but I question whether it is possible to know by intuition that your choices have no causes.

Point 8 deals with the so-called problem of other minds, often debated by philosophers. The question is: how can we know that other people have minds like ours? Reid concedes that some evidence is relevant in justifying a positive answer: the words and actions of other people indicate powers of understanding such as we are conscious of in ourselves. But that evidence doesn't amount to demonstration. It leaves open the possibility that other people are automatons, robots, illusions, without actual minds or souls. But Reid says that in the end we must regard point 8 as a first principle.

He extrapolates somewhat from point 8 to prove that God exists. The existence of God is not itself a common-sense principle, but it can be derived from other such principles. Many have noted the analogy between the knowledge of God and the knowledge of human beings. (Recall Augustine's "God and the soul" and Descartes' argument from soul to God.) Alvin Plantinga, a contemporary philosopher much influenced by Reid, wrote *God and Other Minds: A Study of the Rational Justification of Belief in God*,[54] arguing that whatever problems there are in knowing God, there are similar problems in knowing other minds. Plantinga's argument is in the spirit of Reid (and also of Bishop Butler). (See further in chapter 13.)

Many have noted the analogy between the knowledge of God and the knowledge of human beings. . . . Alvin Plantinga, a contemporary philosopher much influenced by Reid, [argues] . . . that whatever problems there are in knowing God, there are similar problems in knowing other minds.

Point 12 deals with the so-called problem of induction. It is not possible to *demonstrate* that, say, the law of gravity will continue to be in effect tomorrow, or five minutes from now. But to deny the inference from present to past would violate common sense in the way that Reid opposes.

There is no way to prove that a principle belongs to common sense, for common-sense principles are prior to proof. But Reid indicates several "marks" of common-sense principles: (1) They appear early in human life. They do not take long to learn, and we find ourselves, from childhood, assuming them and making use of them. (2) They are universal among mankind. People at all times and places, for example, rely on memory (point 3). (3) They are irresistible; they "force assent." If I tried to deny, say, the reliability of my consciousness (point 1), I would not be able to deny it for long. We need to presuppose these principles in order to accomplish things in everyday life. (4) Significantly, at one

54. Ithaca, NY: Cornell University Press, 1990.

point, Reid attributes this common-sense knowledge to "the inspiration of the Almighty."

Reid's approach had a great appeal to people who, at the end of the age of reason, were tired of abstruse philosophical attempts to prove and attack the common beliefs of human beings. It is a fitting obituary to the Enlightenment that at the end of it all we should just fall back on our common sense. Indeed, if we look closely, we can find the same trends in earlier thinkers. Descartes, frustrated by the complexity of medieval philosophy, sought a practical summation, asking: what, after all this, do I really know for sure? Locke's philosophy strikes many as an attempt to reproduce common sense in philosophical terms (a mind, seeking to understand things in the world through its ideas). Berkeley rejected material substance, what seemed to be an occult idea, and urged us to trust the contents of our own minds. That seemed to him to be the common-sense thing to do. And David Hume, once he was done refuting everyone else's philosophy, often remarked about the frustration of it all, in contrast with the simple pleasures of farming and backgammon. For him, in the end, causality was a matter of *custom*. We judge causality because we are in the habit of expecting B when we see A.

Reid's approach had a great appeal to people who, at the end of the age of reason, were tired of abstruse philosophical attempts to prove and attack the common beliefs of human beings. It is a fitting obituary to the Enlightenment that at the end of it all we should just fall back on our common sense.

Reid's philosophy can be understood not as a straightforward attack on Hume, but as an analysis of what it means to live by *custom*. If we take seriously our customary thinking, says Reid, we will follow a philosophy very different from that of Hume.

Reid's philosophy is Christian in an important way, because he believes that our common-sense principles are in some sense given by God.[55] Scripture does teach that people know God from nature as well as special revelation (Rom. 1:20–21), and that even though people repress this revelation, it does influence their behavior through their lives. But Reid doesn't show that these principles lose their coherence if we fail to presuppose the reality of God. If this world is governed not by an absolute person, but by impersonal principles, why should we think that our common sense is a reliable guide?

Reid's philosophy can be understood not as a straightforward attack on Hume, but as an analysis of what it means to live by custom.

SUMMARY

In this chapter, we have considered the beginning of liberal theology, which applies to theology the same claim of autonomous thinking that animates philosophical rationalism and empiricism. On the other hand, we have also looked at Christian thinkers who have seriously attempted to practice philosophy in a way that is faithful to the biblical revelation. For these, too, the claim of autonomy is a temptation.

55. I don't think *inspired* is the best term to describe God's relation to these principles.

Pascal and Edwards resist that temptation with a full understanding of what the temptation would entail. Reid at least resists the fashionable philosophies with a remarkable creative alternative. But Reid, like Butler and Paley, does not embrace a distinctly biblical epistemology.

Some of the trends of this period are worth noting:

1. During this period, philosophers are deeply interested in *science* and are often, like Descartes, Leibniz, and Pascal, practicing scientists themselves. Edwards is at least a learned layman in several scientific fields. The relationship of science, philosophy, and theology will be a major theme in the coming centuries.
2. Philosophers are also interested in mathematics, and *probability* becomes a central consideration. Philosophers are less inclined to try to demonstrate their conclusions; it is sufficient to present them as "highly probable."
3. As philosophy is increasingly related to science and mathematics, it is also increasingly integrated with *everyday life*. Philosophers are increasingly interested in ethics and politics. But philosophical epistemology, too, is more sensitive to the ways in which we seek to gain knowledge in practical life. We note this theme in Pascal's Wager, Hume's *custom*, and Reid's common-sense principles.
4. Philosophers are attending more and more to the *presuppositions* of knowledge, the *a priori*, what we assume at the outset of philosophical inquiry. We noted this theme earlier in Augustine and Anselm. But in the modern period, it takes on more importance. The *axioms* of the Continental rationalists serve as presuppositions of knowledge. In empiricism, Locke's *tabula rasa* and the view that our *ideas* serve as a foundation of knowledge are presuppositional. For Pascal and Edwards, the presupposition is Scripture, as it is, at least nominally, for all other Christian thinkers. But Butler and Paley seem intent to appear "neutral" to the non-Christian and deist opponents they engage. Reid, however, raises the question at a deeper level, and he claims that a great many of our most important beliefs are presuppositions rather than the conclusions of inquiry.

Reid at least resists the fashionable philosophies with a remarkable creative alternative. But Reid, like Butler and Paley, does not embrace a distinctly biblical epistemology.

KEY TERMS

Enlightenment	Age of reason
Liberal theology	Latitudinarianism
Deism	Pantheism
Wolfenbüttel Fragment	Accidental truths of history
Necessary truths of reason	history

Lessing's ditch	Pascal's third conversion
Pascal's "Memorial"	Jansenism
Port Royal*Pensées*	*Provincial Letters*
Thinking reed	Pascal's Wager
Pascal's three orders	Heart (for Pascal)
Aquinas-Butler Method	Reason (Butler)
Course and constitution of nature	Analogy (Butler)
Disanalogy	*Miscellanies*
Sweetness	Idealism
Occasionalism	Great Awakening
Watchmaker illustration	Common Sense Realism
Problem of other minds	Problem of induction

STUDY QUESTIONS

1. Summarize the main events of the history of philosophy up until the Enlightenment, and show how the Enlightenment developed out of them.
2. Explain how liberal theology differs from orthodoxy.
3. Describe Locke's relation to deism. How did he show that Christianity was reasonable?
4. List the five principles of Herbert of Cherbury. Evaluate them.
5. "But among the deists, not only is it *permissible* to claim rational autonomy, but autonomous reason is *sufficient* as an authority for theology." Explain; evaluate. What did it mean to say that Christianity is "a republication of the religion of nature"?
6. "Cherbury's theology is works-righteousness, no less so than the theology of modern Judaism or Islam." Explain; evaluate.
7. Frame says, "What amazes me most is this." What amazes him and why?
8. Narrate Lessing's parable of the three rings. Evaluate its theological point.
9. Recite Lessing's most famous statement and evaluate it.
10. Pascal: "I cannot forgive Descartes." Why? Evaluate.
11. How did Pascal's *third conversion* influence his thought?
12. How is Pascal's God different from the "god of the philosophers"?
13. Describe Pascal's Wager and evaluate. Reply to the argument that there are more alternatives than two.
14. Is it wrong to appeal to probable evidence for the truth of Christian theism? Explain.
15. What does Pascal mean in teaching that you should act "as if" Christianity were true? Evaluate.

OUTLINE

The Birth of Liberal Theology
- Deism
- Gotthold E. Lessing (1729–81)

Biblical Christianity in the Enlightenment
- Blaise Pascal (1623–62)
- Joseph Butler (1692–1752)
- Jonathan Edwards (1703–58)
- William Paley (1743–1805)
- Thomas Reid (1710–96)

Summary

16. Explain and evaluate Pascal's statement that "the heart has its reasons which reason does not know."
17. Frame says of Pascal, "He is one of the first thinkers to take seriously the subjective or existential dimension of knowledge, not as a barrier to understanding, but as a necessary basis for it." Explain; evaluate.
18. Explain Butler's statement that "probability is the very guide to life." How is this statement relevant to his apologetic?
19. What does Butler mean by the "reasonable use of reason"? How does that bear on the use of reason in apologetic argument?
20. Explain and evaluate how Butler uses reason to challenge deists.
21. Describe and evaluate Butler's argument for immortality.
22. Describe Butler's use of analogy and evaluate. Frame says, "My conclusion is that arguments from analogy (or disanalogy) never settle anything by themselves." Explain; evaluate.
23. "Two Christian thinkers could hardly differ more in their epistemology than Butler and Edwards." Explain.
24. Frame compares Edwards's account of *being* to Parmenides. What do you think of this comparison?
25. Compare Edwards's concept of the mind with that of Berkeley.
26. Is Edwards a pantheist? Why or why not?
27. Compare Edwards and Pascal on the place of emotion in faith.
28. Frame says that Paley's teleological argument is an argument from analogy. Explain; evaluate. How does that affect the cogency of Paley's argument?
29. Frame: "Our ability to recognize that analogy, to distinguish between things that are designed and things that are not designed, seems important to the argument. But the odd thing about the teleological argument is that at some point this distinction breaks down." Explain. How does this observation affect the teleological argument?
30. What illustration does Paley use to justify the cosmological argument? Evaluate.
31. How does Reid attempt to refute the skepticism of Hume? To what extent is he successful?
32. "Concepts, as opposed to sensations, have objects: they are always concepts *of* something." Explain; evaluate.
33. List some principles that Reid ascribes to common sense. Evaluate.
34. How does Reid propose to solve the problem of other minds? Evaluate.
35. What role does God play in Reid's philosophy? Evaluate.
36. Summarize some of the themes that are common to the philosophers considered in this chapter.

BIBLIOGRAPHY: THEOLOGY IN THE ENLIGHTENMENT

Print

Butler, Joseph. *The Works of Joseph Butler.* Chestnut Hill, MA: Adamant Media Corp., 2000.

Edwards, Jonathan. *The Works of Jonathan Edwards.* Edited by Edward Hickman. 2 vols. Amazon Digital Services, 2011.

Israel, Jonathan I. *Radical Enlightenment: Philosophy and the Meaning of Modernity, 1650–1750.* New York: Oxford University Press, 2002. Begins with Spinoza.

Kreeft, Peter. *Christianity for Modern Pagans: Pascal's* Pensées *Edited, Outlined, and Explained.* San Francisco: Ignatius Press, 1993.

Mackenzie, Charles S. *Blaise Pascal: Apologist to Skeptics.* Lanham, MD: University Press of America, 2008.

———. *Pascal's Anguish and Joy.* New York: Philosophical Library, 1973.

Marsden, George M. *Jonathan Edwards: A Life.* New Haven, CT: Yale University Press, 2004.

Paley, William. *Natural Theology.* Chillicothe, OH: DeWard Publishing, 2010.

Pascal, Blaise. *Pensées and Other Writings.* New York: Oxford University Press, 2008.

Reid, Thomas. *Thomas Reid's Inquiry and Essays.* Long Beach, CA: Lexico Publishing, 2012.

Wolterstorff, Nicholas. *Thomas Reid and the Story of Epistemology.* Cambridge: Cambridge University Press, 2001.

Online

Butler, Joseph. *Analogy of Religion.* Philadelphia: J. B. Lippincott, 1865. Available at http://www.ccel.org/ccel/butler/analogy.html.

Edwards, Jonathan. *Works of Jonathan Edwards.* 2 vols. Available at http://www.ccel.org/ccel/edwards/works1.html; http://www.ccel.org/ccel/edwards/works2.html.

Lessing, G. E. *The Dramatic Works of G. E. Lessing.* Edited by Ernest Bell. London: George Bell and Sons, 1878. Available at http://www.gutenberg.org/files/33435/33435-h/33435-h.htm.

———. "On the Proof of the Spirit and of Power." In *Lessing's Theological Writings,* edited by Henry Chadwick. Stanford, CA: Stanford University Press, 1956. Available at http://faculty.tcu.edu/grant/hhit/Lessing.pdf.

Paley, William. *Natural Theology.* Available at http://naturaltheology.us/table-of-contents/209.html.

Pascal, Blaise. *Pensées.* Translated by W. F. Trotter. Available at http://www.ccel.org/ccel/pascal/pensees.html.

Reid, Thomas. "Thomas Reid." Some Texts in Early Modern Philosophy. http://www.earlymoderntexts.com/authors/reid.html.

READ FOR YOURSELF

Lessing's "On the Proof of the Spirit and of Power" is very short and hugely influential. Pascal's *Pensées* deserves long attention, both as an apologetic and as a devotional text. Read Butler and Paley only to get the main ideas. Jonathan Edwards's most important works are *Freedom of the Will*, *The Nature of True Virtue*, *The Religious Affections*, and *Charity and Its Fruits*. Read here and there in Reid's *Inquiry* and *Essays*.

LISTEN ONLINE

Link: http://itunes.apple.com/us/course/legacy-history-philosophy/id694658914

- Blaise Pascal and Joseph Butler: 1:09:56
- Joseph Butler Continued, William Paley, and Thomas Reid: 44:21
- Introduction to Liberal Theology, Enlightenment Rationalism, and Gotthold Lessing: 36:40

FAMOUS QUOTES

- **Lessing:** http://en.wikiquote.org/wiki/Gotthold_Ephraim_Lessing
- **Pascal:** http://en.wikiquote.org/wiki/Blaise_Pascal
- **Edwards:** http://en.wikiquote.org/wiki/Jonathan_Edwards_%28theologian%29

OUTLINE

7

KANT AND HIS SUCCESSORS

OUR NARRATIVE so far has been dramatic, describing a number of historical convulsions and their consequences. The initial convulsion, of course, was God's creation of the world out of nothing, bringing into being a creature in God's image who could think about philosophy. Then the fall of man, in which human thought and behavior turned violently from the divinely revealed worldview to a variety of human fantasies, suppressing God's truth and claiming intellectual autonomy. The third convulsion was the beginning of Western philosophy among the Greeks in around 600 B.C., pushing aside all traditional and religious ways of thinking, trying to explain the world by reason alone. But then there was the earthshaking event in around A.D. 33, the death, resurrection, and ascension of Jesus, which brought forth a torrent of God's grace, bringing radical changes to hearts and minds. The dominance of Christian thought, however, came to an end in the early seventeenth century, with a convulsion initiating "modern" philosophy and the period of its initial dominance, otherwise known as the *Enlightenment*. Again, the main body of Western philosophers cast aside the restraints of tradition and Christian theology and sought to understand the world by autonomous thinking, sometimes emphasizing reason, sometimes sense experience. And at almost the same time the convulsion spread to theologians in liberal theology, which sought to accommodate Christian doctrine to the presuppositions of the Enlightenment.

The dominance of Christian thought, however, came to an end in the early seventeenth century, with a convulsion initiating "modern" philosophy and the period of its initial dominance, otherwise known as the Enlightenment.

IMMANUEL KANT (1724–1804)

But the thought of Immanuel Kant was another convulsion all by itself. Descartes, Locke, and their followers had tried to reason

Immanuel Kant

autonomously, without the constraints of divine revelation. But it was Kant who developed a comprehensive *rationale* for autonomous reasoning. It was Kant who argued that we *must* reason autonomously and must never reason in any other way. These arguments so persuaded mainstream philosophers and theologians as to transform those disciplines in radical ways. Those arguments are still with us; we deal with them all the time. And many philosophies and theologies after Kant mirror elements of his philosophical system. His distinction between *phenomena* and *noumena*, for example, reappears in Schopenhauer's distinction between *idea* and *will*, Wittgenstein's distinction between *fact* and *the Mystical*, Heidegger's distinction between *technology* and *poetry*, Gadamer's between *techne* and *phronesis*, Barth's between *Historie* and *Geschichte*, the distinction Buber and Brunner made between the *I-it* and the *I-thou*, and in the various neo-Gnostic and neopagan[1] distinctions between *the many* and *the one*. So Kant is arguably the most influential philosopher from his time to our own; see fig. 7.1.

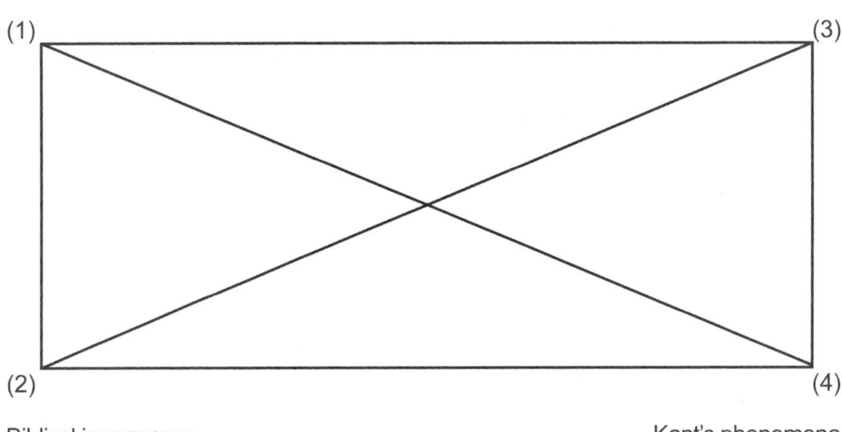

Fig. 7.1. Kant's Noumena and Phenomena

Kant studied, and later taught for most of his life, at the University of Königsberg. At the time, German universities were dominated by the thought of Christian Wolff, a disciple of Leibniz. Kant's major teacher, whom he later replaced on the Königsberg faculty, was Martin Kuntzen, who shared Wolff's desire to apply to philosophy the rigor of science and mathematics. Kant's early work reflected these rationalist emphases, which he later described as *dogmatic* speculation. At some point, however, Kant read David Hume, who, he said, roused him from

1. See, e.g., Peter R. Jones, *One or Two: Seeing a World of Difference* (Escondido, CA: Main Entry Editions, 2010).

his dogmatic slumbers. Hume's skepticism was a frontal challenge to Continental rationalism. No longer could philosophers simply assume that logical deduction from carefully chosen axioms would lead them to certainty about the structure of the world. Hume moved Kant, then, to a more careful and detailed analysis of the rational process itself, to a "critique of reason."[2] Kant set out to discover what we can learn from reason and what we cannot, and of course *how* we can gain the knowledge that we need to have.

Hume's skepticism was a frontal challenge to Continental rationalism. No longer could philosophers simply assume that logical deduction from carefully chosen axioms would lead them to certainty about the structure of the world. Hume moved Kant, then, to a more careful and detailed analysis of the rational process itself, to a "critique of reason."

Phenomena and Noumena

I have remarked earlier in this book that the greatest philosophers are those who are not satisfied with a narrow range of insights, but who try to bring together ideas that initially seem irreconcilable. So Plato brought together the changeless Being of Parmenides and the ever-changing world of Heraclitus. Thomas Aquinas brought together the ideas of Plato, those of Aristotle, and those of Christian tradition. The method of such synthesis is often to distinguish different realms of being and thought, so that one set of ideas predominates in one realm, another in another. So for Plato, the ideas of Parmenides prevail in his world of Forms, those of Heraclitus in his world of matter. For Aquinas, the ideas of Aristotle predominate in the realm of natural reason, the teachings of Scripture in the realm of faith. For both Plato and Aquinas, however, the relationship between the two realms is a continuing difficulty.

Similarly, Kant distinguishes between the noumenal world, the world of things as they are apart from our experience (the world of the *Ding an Sich*, the "thing in itself"), and the phenomenal world, the world of our experience, the world as it appears to us. As for the noumenal world, Kant follows Hume's skepticism: We know that there is such a world, because there must be a source for our experience. But otherwise, we know nothing about it.[3] The phenomenal world, however, is accessible to our senses and our reason, and in this realm the methods of German rationalism are helpful. But Kant is not merely a follower of rationalism or empiricism, nor does he mechanically bring the two together. His synthesis, like that of Plato and of Aquinas, is highly creative.[4]

Kant distinguishes between the noumenal world, the world of things as they are apart from our experience . . . , and the phenomenal world, the world of our experience, the world as it appears to us.

2. His chief works: *Critique of Pure Reason*, *Critique of Practical Reason*, and *Critique of Judgment*.

3. To say that the noumenal world is unknown and unknowable to us is virtually tautological. If we knew anything about it, it would be part of our experience, and therefore phenomenal.

4. Most of the following discussion is based on Kant's first and most influential work, the *Critique of Pure Reason*.

The Transcendental Method

Kant's rationalist and empiricist predecessors saw philosophy essentially as an exploration of discovery: starting with one landmark and following a trail to the next. The starting point, the foundation,[5] was self-evident axioms (rationalism) or sense experience (empiricism). The method was to follow the axioms or the sense data wherever they seemed to lead. Kant (and again, this is typical of greater philosophers) backs away from both of these methods to ask a larger question: Granted that knowledge is possible (and if it isn't, why be a philosopher at all?), what are the conditions that make it possible? That is, if we are capable of knowing the world, what must the world (including ourselves) be like? This is what Kant called the *transcendental* method: not following the impressions of the senses or the steps of a deduction, but asking what such activities *presuppose*.[6]

Note that Kant does not try to prove that knowledge is possible. Rather, he assumes that it is, and then asks what follows from that assumption.

The Synthetic A Priori

Kant's answer to the transcendental question begins with the claim that if knowledge is possible at all, it must be possible for us to know synthetic a priori truths.

Kant's answer to the transcendental question begins with the claim that if knowledge is possible at all, it must be possible for us to know *synthetic a priori truths*. Recall here our earlier discussion (under Leibniz and Hume) of the distinctions between *a priori* and *a posteriori* and between *analytic* and *synthetic*.[7] Hume believed that all *a priori* statements[8] were analytic and that all synthetic statements were *a posteriori*, that is, derived from experience.[9] But analytic statements convey no information, no knowledge, except about the meanings of words.[10] The

5. These systems are sometimes described as forms of *classical foundationalism*.

6. Those familiar with the apologetics of Cornelius Van Til can understand why he described his apologetic method as *transcendental*, in Van Til's vocabulary synonymous with *presuppositional*.

7. To review: *A priori* knowledge is knowledge that precedes an inquiry, knowledge that we *bring to* an inquiry. *A posteriori* knowledge is knowledge that we *gain from* the inquiry. In an *absolute* sense, *a priori* knowledge is knowledge that we possess before any inquiry at all. *Analytic* and *synthetic* are terms applied to propositions or statements. An *analytic* statement is a statement in which the meaning of the predicate is included in the meaning of the subject: for example, "this triangle has three sides." A *synthetic* statement is a statement in which that is not the case: for example, "this apple is red." Today, philosophers sometimes regard the analytic-synthetic distinction as a continuum. Compare my discussion of Willard Quine in chapter 12.

8. That is, *a priori* in the *absolute* sense described in the preceding footnote.

9. Leibniz believed that in the deepest sense all statements were analytic, but that position appeared untenable to most philosophers. Among other problems, Leibniz's view assumed that God foreknew and foreordained all things.

10. This exception is perhaps more significant than many philosophers (including both Hume and Kant) understood.

conclusion is that we have no *knowledge* in advance of experience, no knowledge that we can *bring to* experience, no knowledge that *governs* experience.[11]

But this in turn implies that we have no general knowledge *about* experience, no knowledge of its universal or necessary structure. Experience becomes just a random collection of data, with no organizing principles. That is, experience becomes a bundle of Humean *impressions.*[12] To Kant, this view was intolerable. He, like all other philosophers of the time, was committed to Newtonian physics. But Newton believed that there were universal and necessary principles such as the law of gravity that governed all physical things and events in the universe. Kant insists that if such knowledge is possible (remember again that he does not question its possibility), then it must be possible to gain genuine knowledge (i.e., synthetic propositions) about the universe as a whole. Such knowledge cannot be grounded in sense experience, because we do not have sense experience of the entire universe. So some part of this knowledge must be *a priori*. There must, then, be knowledge that is both synthetic and *a priori*. Otherwise, science is impossible.

Such knowledge cannot be grounded in sense experience, because we do not have sense experience of the entire universe. So some part of this knowledge must be a priori. *There must, then, be knowledge that is both synthetic and* a priori. *Otherwise, science is impossible.*

Kant offered a number of examples of synthetic, *a priori* statements. He believed, as implied in the previous paragraph, that scientific laws, formulated as universal and necessary propositions, were synthetic and *a priori*. The same is true for the propositions of geometry—for example, that a straight line is the shortest distance between two points. To argue that this proposition is analytic, one would have to argue that "shortest distance between two points" is part of the *meaning* of *straight line*. Some philosophers have held that view, but it is by no means obvious.

Kant also believed (contrary to Hume and to many twentieth-century thinkers) that all mathematical equations were synthetic and *a priori*. He used the example $7 + 5 = 12$. Here the argument is whether the meaning of *12* is contained in the meanings of *7*, *5*, and +. It is at least plausible for someone to argue that such equations, using small quantities of objects, are analytic.[13] But is it plausible to believe that *45026* is part of the meaning of 958×47, so that if one understands 958×47, one will understand *45026*? It is more natural, or at least Kant would argue that it is, to believe that working out this problem gives us information we didn't have before, so that this multiplication equation is a synthetic statement.

Kant also believed (contrary to Hume and to many twentieth-century thinkers) that all mathematical equations were synthetic and a priori.

11. This point was alarming to Kant. But a philosopher committed to empiricism could see it as an obvious truth. Indeed, it is essentially a definition of empiricism, Locke's *tabula rasa*.

12. A different bundle, of course, from the bundles that Hume identified as our souls.

13. Such was the view of Hume and of logical positivists in the twentieth century.

OUTLINE

The Mind Structures Experience

Kant believed, then, that to rescue science and mathematics from Hume's skepticism, it is necessary for us to affirm synthetic *a priori* knowledge. But that raises a further question. If science and mathematics are based on synthetic *a priori* knowledge, how does that knowledge come to us? Is it innate? Kant believes, like Aristotle, Reid, and many others, that the mind is not a Lockean *tabula rasa*. Rather, it is an active faculty that contributes something to its experience. But Kant's view of this activity is different from the traditional concept of innate ideas.

Both the rationalists and the empiricists believed that knowledge was a matter of conforming the mind to the data of the world outside the mind. The rationalists tried to achieve this conformity by logical deduction from selected axioms, the empiricists by observation of impressions and ideas within the mind. But both of these methods, in Kant's view, became untenable after Hume's critique.

So Kant proposed a breathtakingly radical alternative: Our most basic knowledge comes about not by the world's impressing it on the mind, but by the mind's impressing it on the world. Experience is the result of the mind's imposing various concepts on the raw data given to it by the noumenal world. Gordon Clark[14] illustrated this idea by a parable: imagine that there is a shelf in the pantry filled with intelligent jelly jars. These jars are philosophers, and they argue among themselves why it is that the jelly inside them always takes a cylindrical shape. They try to answer the question by studying the chemical and physical properties of the jelly, but none of those studies produces an adequate reason why *all* the jelly in *all*[15] the jars has a cylindrical shape. But then one exceptionally brilliant jar makes a stunning proposal: What if the shape of the jelly is caused not by anything in the jelly, but by the shape of the jars, our own shape? See fig. 7.2.

Kant proposed a breathtakingly radical alternative: Our most basic knowledge comes about not by the world's impressing it on the mind, but by the mind's impressing it on the world. Experience is the result of the mind's imposing various concepts on the raw data given to it by the noumenal world.

Fig. 7.2. Intelligent Jelly Jars

We may compare Kant's proposal to this one. He understood how radical it was. Indeed, he called it a *Copernican revolution* in philosophy.

14. Gordon H. Clark, *Thales to Dewey: A History of Philosophy* (Boston: Houghton Mifflin, 1957), 400–401.

15. Note that the jelly jars, like Kant, are seeking universal and necessary knowledge.

As Copernicus argued that the earth revolves around the sun, reversing centuries of geocentric astronomy from such great thinkers as Aristotle and Ptolemy, so Kant now argues that man, not nature, is the source of the synthetic *a priori* truths that constitute genuine knowledge.[16]

How does this happen, specifically? Kant distinguished, as his predecessors had, between sense perception and rational operations. The empiricists thought that philosophy was the analysis of sense perception; the rationalists thought that it was the analysis of our rational operations. But Kant saw that the two were inseparable: "concepts without percepts are empty; percepts without concepts are blind."[17] A concept without sense perception is a concept of nothing; a perception without rational understanding is just a random *impression*, with no meaning. Sense perception and rational understanding coincide, because the mind organizes both into an intelligible field of experience. And neither sense nor reason is intelligible until this happens.

As Copernicus argued that the earth revolves around the sun, reversing centuries of geocentric astronomy from such great thinkers as Aristotle and Ptolemy, so Kant now argues that man, not nature, is the source of the synthetic a priori *truths that constitute genuine knowledge.*

Kant's Assembly Line

It happens in three ways. One may imagine an assembly line, such as one that produces candy bars, or automobiles, or pork chops, in which raw materials come in from one entrance and pass through several stations, each of which performs an operation on the material. In Kant's system, think of the raw material as the data of the noumenal world. The assembly line is the mind. That assembly line performs three operations on everything that comes through: in Kant's terminology, the transcendental aesthetic, the transcendental analytic, and the transcendental unity of the apperception. The assembly-line illustration could mislead, because Kant might not have thought of these three steps as temporally successive; see fig. 7.3.

"Concepts without percepts are empty; percepts without concepts are blind." A concept without sense perception is a concept of nothing; a perception without rational understanding is just a random impression, *with no meaning.*

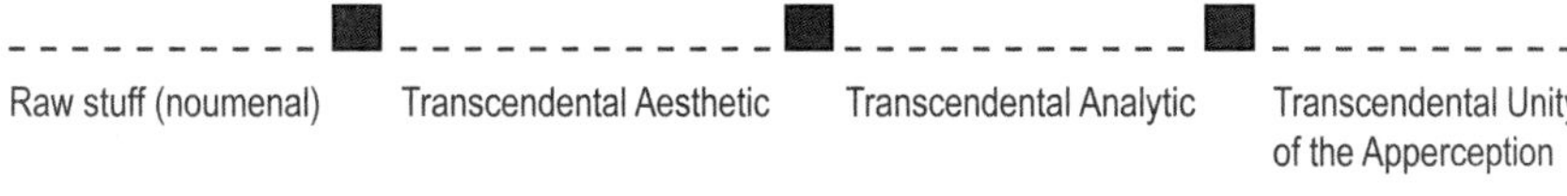

Fig. 7.3. Kant's Assembly Line

The Transcendental Aesthetic

The *transcendental aesthetic* adds to the raw data the ingredients that make it suitable for sense perception. In Kant's view, our sense

16. Of course, the reader may note that the Copernican and Kantian revolutions move in opposite directions. Copernicus's theory rebuked the anthropocentrism of his predecessors, while Kant's theory was far more anthropocentric than those of previous philosophers.

17. Kant, *Critique of Pure Reason*, A 51.

experience is not isolated and meaningless *impressions* as in Hume. Rather, actual perceptions are already intelligible. What we perceive are *things* located in time and space. Now, time and space are themselves not visible objects. Where do they come from? The answer is that the mind *imposes* a spatiotemporal order on everything that it perceives. That order comes from the mind itself, imposing a shape on the data that comes before it.

Actual perceptions are already intelligible. What we perceive are things *located in time and space. Now, time and space are themselves not visible objects. Where do they come from? The answer is that the mind* imposes *a spatiotemporal order on everything that it perceives.*

The Transcendental Analytic

The second step on the assembly line is the *transcendental analytic,* which enables us to develop a rational understanding of those spatiotemporal objects. Here, Kant begins by listing twelve types of *judgments*, statements that we may choose to make about things in our experience, grouped into four general types:

1. Quantity
   a. Universal
   b. Particular
   c. Singular
2. Quality
   a. Affirmative
   b. Negative
   c. Infinite
3. Relation
   a. Categorical
   b. Hypothetical
   c. Disjunctive
4. Modality
   a. Problematic
   b. Assertoric
   c. Apodeictic

Kant thought that this list expresses every judgment we might ever choose to make about anything presented to us by the senses. So "All men are mortal" is an instance of class 1.a; "Fish are not mammals" is a judgment of class 2.b; "If it rains, the picnic is canceled" is an instance of 3.b; and so on.

This list corresponds to twelve *categories,*[18] ways in which the mind comes to understand experience:

18. This list is somewhat modified from Aristotle's list of categories.

1. Categories of quantity
   a. Unity
   b. Plurality
   c. Totality
2. Categories of quality
   a. Reality
   b. Negation
   c. Limitation
3. Categories of relation
   a. Inherence and subsistence (substance and accident)
   b. Causality and dependence (cause and effect)
   c. Community (reciprocity between agent and patient)
4. Categories of modality
   a. Possibility-impossibility
   b. Existence-nonexistence
   c. Necessity-contingency

Kant is astonishingly nontraditional in his belief that these categories are essentially imposed on reality by the mind. The world exhibits these patterns because that is the structure of our thinking.

Note that this list contains a number of subjects asserted and debated by past philosophers: Under "categories of quantity," recall the debates over the *one* and the *many*, between monists (such as Parmenides, Plotinus, and Spinoza) and pluralists (such as Democritus, Leibniz, and the early Wittgenstein). Under "categories of quality," recall the confusion over being and nonbeing.[19] Under "categories of relation," note especially the questions of substance and of cause and effect. And under "modality," recall our earlier discussions about necessary and contingent being, for example, in connection with the third of Aquinas's *five ways*.

These categories . . . are like the divider in an ice-cube tray that governs the shape of the ice after water is poured into it.

So in the transcendental analytic, Kant presents a system for dealing with the issues raised by earlier philosophers. In that respect, Kant is traditional. But he is astonishingly nontraditional in his belief that these categories are essentially imposed on reality by the mind. The world exhibits these patterns because that is the structure of our thinking. These categories are like the cylindric shape of the jelly jar in our previous illustration. To use another common illustration, they are like the divider in an ice-cube tray that governs the shape of the ice after water is poured into it.

Remember Hume's famous argument that from sense experience we cannot derive anything like a necessary connection between cause and effect. Kant's reply is that cause and effect is category 3.b. Hume was wrong to try to find the necessary connection by inspecting his

19. And of course the related discussions of existence and nonexistence, 4.b in Kant's list.

impressions and ideas. Rather, he should have understood that cause and effect is a structure that the mind *imposes* on its experiences. It is therefore a transcendental *presupposition* of knowledge. Without it, science is not possible. But science is possible, so that necessary connection exists. Yet it is not a kind of force that exists in the world itself; it is part of the mind's structure.

Students sometimes ask, given today's emphasis on the sociology of knowledge and the diversity of ways in which people think: why did Kant think that everyone reasoned with these same categories? Kant would have answered, I think, that these categories define the nature of rational thought. If someone claims to think using different categories, then to that extent he is not thinking rationally. That is to say that in one sense he is not thinking.

The Transcendental Unity of the Apperception

The third station in Kant's assembly line is the *transcendental unity of the apperception*. Kant's argument at this point sounds a bit like traditional proofs of the existence of the soul, but again we must be careful lest we misunderstand Kant's distinctive, "Copernican" position. Kant's argument is that experience, even submitted to the operations of stations 1 and 2, is meaningless unless it is held together as a *unified* experience. It won't do to have a miscellaneous spatial object here and there (disappearing into the past), a bit of unity, a bit of plurality, a bit of causality here and there. Rather, there needs to be something like a "unity of consciousness" beholding it all as a single field (or, as we like to say today, a single "story"), putting everything into a context relevant to that consciousness. But (and here is Kant's distinctive qualification) this consciousness is a *presupposition* of experience, not an item of experience. (That is why Hume failed to locate the soul despite considerable searching.) So Kant does not believe that he has discovered a metaphysical self or soul, nor does he think it possible for anyone else to discover it. The unity of apperception is *transcendental*, not empirical or metaphysical. It is a *condition* of experience, not an item we find in our experience. So much for Descartes' "I am."

Kant does not believe that he has discovered a metaphysical self or soul, nor does he think it possible for anyone else to discover it. The unity of apperception is transcendental, *not empirical or metaphysical. It is a* condition *of experience, not an item we find in our experience.*

The Transcendental Dialectic

Now, in Kant's philosophy, there is also a fourth aspect of thinking, expressed in parallel terms with the three stations outlined above. He calls it the *transcendental dialectic*. But this one is significantly different from the other three. The others are necessary aspects of knowledge. But the transcendental dialectic is primarily a source of error, though there is a positive use for it.

The dialectic arises because many, perhaps most, human beings are not satisfied with finding a transcendental basis for knowledge as outlined above. They are interested, rather, in metaphysics, which means, for Kant, the fruitless quest for realities beyond the realm of any possible experience. So they use the transcendental analytic and transcendental apperception as arguments to prove the existence of things beyond experience.

1. Paralogisms

Kant distinguished three general types of errors under the heading of *transcendental dialectic*. First, *paralogisms*. These are arguments that try to prove the existence of a substantial, immaterial, immortal soul. As I said above, it is tempting to turn Kant's argument for the transcendental unity of the apperception into an argument for an immortal soul; but Kant will not permit that logical move. The transcendental unity is a description of the unity of experience, not a proof of an immortal soul. Kant faults such arguments by saying that they confuse different senses of *self* and *soul*. The temptation to misconstrue these terms comes from the human desire to discover something beyond possible experience. Our experience does exhibit a unity, but we cannot prove that unity is substantial, immaterial, or immortal.

The dialectic arises because many, perhaps most, human beings are not satisfied with finding a transcendental basis for knowledge as outlined above.

2. Antinomies

The second kind of error that Kant describes under *transcendental dialectic* is *antinomies*. In an antinomy, it is possible to argue either one of two contradictory propositions with equal cogency. Kant particularly notes the following antinomies:

1. The universe is limited in space and time vs. the universe is unlimited (infinite) in space and time.
2. The world is infinitely divisible vs. the world is composed of indivisible atoms.
3. Everything has a cause vs. the human will is free from causation.
4. There is a necessary being (God) vs. there is no necessary being.

The transcendental unity is a description of the unity of experience, not a proof of an immortal soul.

Kant believes that in each pair, the two opposites are equally defensible. You can prove that the universe is limited and, equally well, that the universe is unlimited. Same for the others. The reason why we find ourselves in this trouble is that we are trying to use categories from the transcendental analytic (such as limitation and causality) to prove the existence of things beyond possible experience.

3. Ideals

Finally, Kant, under the label *transcendental dialectic*, speaks of the *ideals* of reason, namely, self, world (understood as a totality of things), and God. Kant has already discussed these entities under paralogisms (the self), and the antinomies (world in 1 and 2, self in 3, God in 4). But here he underscores his belief that none of these objects can be proved to exist on the basis of experience. I will confine my discussion here to his refutations of the traditional theistic proofs. In the fourth antinomy, Kant already dealt with Aquinas's third way, the argument that the universe requires an absolutely necessary being. But here Kant deals with the more conventional arguments for God's existence, which he reduces to three: the ontological, the cosmological, and the teleological.

Kant says that the ontological argument (the argument from Anselm's *Proslogium*) makes the mistake of reasoning from concept (the concept of a perfect being) to reality (the real existence of the perfect being). Anselm himself would admit that he reasons here from concept to reality, but he would claim that such an argument is justified in this one case, as I argued in chapter 4. But this violates the most fundamental principle of Kant's philosophy: that we cannot reason from ideas in our minds to anything beyond experience (that is, that we cannot reason from phenomena to noumena). Once we grant Kant's point, we cannot accept Anselm's argument. But then the issue is whether we accept Kant's system as proved.[20]

The cosmological argument, as Kant understands it, says that the whole universe requires a cause, and that cause can be nothing less than a being who has all perfections. Kant argues that this argument reduces to the ontological. Like the ontological, the cosmological makes the claim that a being corresponding to our mental concept of perfection must exist. Introducing the idea that there must be a cause for the universe doesn't help, in Kant's view, for as Hume pointed out, we have no experience of such a universal cause.

For Kant, then, all these proofs make the same mistake. They begin with the contents of the mind and try to deduce from those the existence of a being beyond all possible experience.

Similarly the teleological argument, which Kant calls *physico-theological*. He is more impressed with this argument than with the others, but he believes that it yields at best only a probable conclusion. To demonstrate God's existence, it must be supplemented by the cosmological argument (the designer must be the cause of everything and must possess all perfections), which in turn reduces to the ontological.

For Kant, then, all these proofs make the same mistake. They begin with the contents of the mind and try to deduce from those the existence of a being beyond all possible experience.

So far, it seems that Kant is entirely skeptical about God, the world, and the self. But that is not quite the case. Remember my

20. Kant also opposes Anselm's idea that existence is a perfection, arguing that it is not even a proper predicate. I find that argument rather confused, but I cannot take the time to unravel the confusions here.

earlier remark that for Kant the transcendental dialectic, though primarily a source of error, has a positive use. So we should note Kant's further distinction about the *ideals*, a distinction between the *constitutive* and *regulative* uses of these ideals. To use a concept *constitutively* is to regard it as a designation of something that actually exists in the world, one of the constituents of experience. But as we have seen, Kant thinks it is impossible to prove the existence of God (or, similarly, the existence of self or world). So the concepts of God, self, and world cannot be constitutive. Nevertheless, these concepts have important *regulative* uses. A regulative concept is one that is useful for our lives. In Kant's view, even though we cannot prove that God or the other ideals really exist, we ought to behave *as if* they really existed.

A regulative concept is one that is useful for our lives. In Kant's view, even though we cannot prove that God or the other ideals really exist, we ought to behave as if *they really existed.*

These regulative ideas are useful, for example, in science. Someone who believes that the universe is ordered by God, that it operates in its totality as a system of laws, and that it can be understood by the mind will, other things being equal, make a better scientist than somebody who does not believe in God, the world, or the self. Kant also believed that the concept of God is important to regulating our moral behavior. He said that one is likely to take morality more seriously if he believes that moral standards are divine commands and that God will reward obedience and punish disobedience. So even if God does not exist, it is better to believe in him than not to believe in him.

Kant's Ethics

Kant is an emphatic deontologist, believing that there are absolute duties, and that ethical rightness is to do one's duty for duty's sake.

I will not here go into much detail about Kant's ethical system, though it is as important historically as his epistemology and metaphysics.[21] Given Kant's emphasis on the limitations of reason, one might expect him to be an ethical relativist. In fact, however, he is an emphatic deontologist, believing that there are absolute duties, and that ethical rightness is to do one's duty for duty's sake. Ethical judgments, like statements of mathematics and physics, are synthetic *a priori*, and they are imposed on experience by the mind. The mind determines that our duty, for example, is to treat others as ends, not as means. To contradict such ethical principles, says Kant, creates contradictions so as to invalidate ethical discourse entirely. But we cannot doubt that ethics is possible, any more than we can doubt that knowledge is possible. The Kantian system of duties results from a transcendental analysis of the conditions of moral choice (i.e., universal and necessary duties), just as the Kantian system of categories results from a transcendental analysis of the conditions of knowledge (universal and necessary propositions).

21. I discuss Kant's ethics in *DCL*, 109–16.

Kant's Theology

We should also note that Kant is a theologian of some importance. Theology is important to him. At one point he said that he had limited reason to make room for faith. But the faith he makes room for is a liberal faith. His book *Religion within the Limits of Reason Alone* is a milestone in the liberal theological tradition—the tradition that I began to describe in the preceding chapter in the sections on deism and Lessing.

Kant's *Religion* is really the first liberal systematic theology. The deists had advocated natural theology, denying the redemptive message of Scripture. Lessing had also presented an influential argument against any religion based on historical claims. Kant, however, takes an interest not only in general theism (as above) but in the traditional doctrines of sin, Christ, and redemption. In that way, Kant sounds more conservative than Lessing or the deists. But the content of Kant's theology is profoundly opposed to that of traditional Christianity.

Kant is a theologian of some importance. Theology is important to him. At one point he said that he had limited reason to make room for faith. . . . His book Religion within the Limits of Reason Alone *is a milestone in the liberal theological tradition.*

In my treatments of liberal theology, I will sometimes note that there is a tendency in the movement to get more and more conservative in language, but not in the content of its doctrine. Kant sounds more conservative than Cherbury and Lessing, Schleiermacher more conservative than Kant, Ritschl more than Schleiermacher, Barth more than Ritschl, and so on. I call this historical pattern the *conservative drift.*[22] It has been discernible down to the present day, though there is an occasional glitch: Bultmann and Tillich, for example, are not more conservative than their predecessors either in language or in doctrine. The conservative drift may be explained by a desire of liberal theologians to gain acceptance in the church. During the Enlightenment, the liberal tradition quickly took control of the centers of academic theology, but it did not find it as easy to gain dominance in the church. It was more successful when it used more conservative language, the language of the creeds, confessions, hymns, and orthodox theologies. Each generation of liberal theologians (with a few exceptions, as I noted) has been more successful than the last in credibly using the language of the tradition and in gaining the allegiance of churches and denominations.

All of this is to indicate at this point that Kant's *Religion* is the first instance of the conservative drift—more traditional in its approach than deism. So Kant speaks not only of the existence and providence of God, but also of traditional Christian doctrines that deal with sin and redemption. Still, we will have to note that although Kant addresses these topics, he evacuates them of their traditional meaning, even reverses them, turning the gospel of grace into a doctrine of works-

22. I described this progression briefly in chapter 6.

righteousness. And even worse, we will see that in his theology, man replaces God.

For Kant, religion is performing our ethical duties as if they were divine commands. So as with Lessing, the whole content of religion is ethics. And as we recall, Kant's ethics is a rational imposition of synthetic *a priori* duties: man imposing duties on himself. As with the rest of Kant's philosophy, ethics is an exercise in intellectual autonomy. The book *Religion* begins here, with the will of man confronted by his ethical duties. The human will has a natural inclination toward what is right (Kant's equivalent of the image of God), and it may freely choose to do the good.[23] Nevertheless, it often mysteriously chooses to abuse its freedom and violate the moral law. Kant calls this *radical evil*. It is Kant's equivalent to the traditional doctrine of sin. Yet he denies "original" sin. The tendency to radical evil is found in every human being. It did not originate in the sin of a particular person in a historical event. Each person is responsible only for his own sin, not the sin of a first ancestor. For Kant, we are morally responsible only for the things that we ourselves have done, not for the actions of anyone else.

Jesus of Nazareth is a moral archetype—a symbol of our ability to overcome the radical evil within us and to advance toward moral perfection.

Jesus of Nazareth is a moral archetype—a symbol of our ability to overcome the radical evil within us and to advance toward moral perfection. Kant does not affirm Jesus' historical existence, his miracles, or his deity. As with original sin, our moral restoration comes about through our free will, not through any events in the past. But as an ideal of morality, Jesus dwells in each of us (Kant's equivalent of incarnation) and suffers within us as our bad choices offend him (cf. the traditional concept of Jesus' redemptive sufferings). Kant urges us to have "practical faith in the Son of God"—that is, confidence that the moral archetype points us in the right direction.

Kant does accept the possibility of divine revelation, but he insists that it be subject to our autonomous rationality. Indeed, this is the main theme of the book. It is Religion's *main conclusion and is presupposed throughout.*

This theology is the result of autonomous rational thought. Kant does accept the possibility of divine revelation, but he insists that it be subject to our autonomous rationality. Indeed, this is the main theme of the book. It is *Religion*'s main conclusion and is presupposed throughout.

We recall that for Kant religion is about morality, and that for him morality is determined by autonomous rationality, not by revelation from a source external to us. Indeed, for him it is immoral to accept an ethical principle on any ground except its rationality. If someone claims to have a revelation from God, that claim must be assessed by our reason. But revelation is unnecessary, he says, because it cannot tell

23. Free choice, for Kant, is the libertarian concept that we have seen in Epicurus and in many of the church fathers. Augustine opposed Pelagius's use of it, but later medieval (as Duns Scotus) and more recent (Arminius, Molina) thinkers embraced it. But recall from our earlier discussion that Kant rejected any proof of freedom. Freedom, like God and immortality, is a *regulative*, not *constitutive*, concept. Kant recommends that for our moral health we should act "as if" we had libertarian freedom.

us anything that we cannot discover by our own ("practical") reason. Reason, further, knows the moral law directly, while revelation is at best an indirect source, a record of the reasonings of others. At best, revelation is a means to rational faith, but rational faith is an end in itself. Further, revelation is limited in space and time, given only to some people. So it cannot be the source of morality or religion, which must, in the nature of the case, be universal and necessary. A revelation must be verified and interpreted by scholars, but rational faith is available to everyone. It is self-authenticating and self-interpreting. Rational faith is complete, revelation only partial, and so on.

So Kant's theology transforms the biblical gospel of grace into a message of works-righteousness. He says, "True religion is to consist not in the knowing or considering of what God does or has done for our salvation but in what we must do to become worthy of it."[24]

Kant's theology transforms the biblical gospel of grace into a message of works-righteousness. He says, "True religion is to consist not in the knowing or considering of what God does or has done for our salvation but in what we must do to become worthy of it."

Conclusions on Kant

Kant is the most consequential philosopher of the modern period. We will see his tracks everywhere as we explore the thinking of his successors down to the present. Essentially his contribution is a radical application of human intellectual autonomy. Descartes and those others who started "modern" philosophy adopted rational autonomy as their working method. But Kant does more: he works this method with a passionate consistency and defends it explicitly in every area of philosophy. Yet Kant also exemplifies the failures of autonomous thought, in several areas:

1. As we recall, Kant taught that the ideals of reason, God, the soul, and the world as a whole are to be used *regulatively*, not *constitutively*. That means that we are not to regard these as actually existing, but that we should resolve to act "as if" they existed in our experience. But (to use the example of God) Kant's "as if" is an anemic "as if." If I were an atheist, and Kant told me to act as if God existed, this would mean some pretty radical changes in my life. Kant himself would want me to change my moral habits: to keep promises, not to steal or cheat. But acting as if God exists certainly means more than this. It means, for example (assuming that we are talking about the God of Scripture), attending worship, joining a church, receiving sacraments. It means urging others to trust Christ as Lord. And it also means, certainly, *believing that God exists* and that the Bible is true. Epistemology is part of ethics, believing

24. Kant, *Religion within the Limits of Reason Alone*, division 2.

part of life. Acting as if God exists requires us to change our morality, but part of that is changing our belief system.[25] So we cannot use the idea of God regulatively unless we also use it constitutively. *Regulative* and *constitutive* cannot be separated as Kant tries to separate them.

2. Nevertheless, Kant's *intention* to separate these puts him in a tradition that has been gaining influence through the Enlightenment. That is the tradition of employing prudence as a philosophical principle—a tradition that will later be called *pragmatism*. We recall that Hume relegated the "necessary connection of cause and effect" to the category of custom or habit. Kant was, as we know, very disturbed by this position of Hume. But by saying that this necessary connection is imposed by the mind on experience rather than the reverse, Kant in effect ratified Hume's contention. Further, Kant's relegation of God, the self, and the world (all of being, in other words) to "as if" status put them also in the category of habit—habits of thought and action that we form for our practical benefit. So even though Kant's philosophy looks like a series of logical demonstrations, rigorous and technical as it is, it is, in the end, a practical recommendation to think in a certain way so as to live a happy life. So there are important comparisons to be made between Kant's philosophy, Pascal's Wager, Butler's moral certainty, Reid's common-sense assumptions, and the pragmatists (Peirce, James, and Dewey), whom we will look at in chapter 9, not to mention the phenomenologists and existentialists (also in chapter 9), who distinguish sharply between the scientific viewpoint and the viewpoint of everyday life.

Kant's relegation of God, the self, and the world (all of being, in other words) to "as if" status put them also in the category of habit—habits of thought and action that we form for our practical benefit.

3. It is also interesting to compare Kant and Plato. Both these great thinkers distinguish two aspects of reality, one knowable, the other unknowable. In Plato's two worlds, the "higher" one is supremely knowable, the "lower" one confused, incoherent, and essentially unknowable. For Kant it is the lower world, the phenomena, that is knowable, the higher world, the noumena, unknown and unknowable. So Kant in one sense reverses Plato, but both equally seek to correlate one realm that is unknowable and unintelligible with another that promises clear and certain knowledge. Note also that for Plato the intelligibility of the universe comes from the Forms. But for Kant,

For Kant it is the lower world, the phenomena, that is knowable, the higher world, the noumena, unknown and unknowable.

25. Many would object that changing our beliefs cannot be done by an act of will. I disagree. We regularly suppress truths that we do not want to believe (Rom. 1:18), and we often choose to believe what we want to believe, so that it is meaningful to command a person to believe (as Acts 16:31). See *DKG*, 343–44, for more discussion.

the intelligibility of the universe comes from the categories imposed on reality by the mind. In effect, the human mind replaces Plato's Forms. That shows something of the extent to which Kant's intellectual autonomy reaches. Man's autonomous mind, for Kant, not only *knows* the world, but makes the world intelligible.

4. The comparison between Kant and Plato extends further. For Plato, the world of change is the world that *reflects* the Forms, *bears* the Forms, but has no Form of its own. In itself, then, it is nothing, for Plato equates being with Form. This is even more obvious with Aristotle's prime matter. As I argued in chapter 2, prime matter bears form, but in itself it is without form and therefore nothing. But in another sense it must be something, for Plato and Aristotle give it an important role in their metaphysics. Kant faces a similar problem with his noumenal world. We may not ascribe any structure to the noumenal world, before it takes on the structures of the transcendental aesthetic, analytic, and unity of apperception. To us, the noumenal world is indistinguishable from nothing. But it must be something if Kant's system is to work.[26]
5. In chapter 2, I applied Van Til's analysis to Plato and Aristotle: they are rationalistic in their view of form, irrationalistic in their view of matter. Form is supremely knowable, matter not knowable at all. So the Greeks faced the impossible task of using supremely rational categories to interpret a supremely irrational world. The unchanging, perfect forms were not adequate to account for a changing, imperfect ("mud, hair, and filth") world. Similarly, Kant seeks to interpret an unknowable, unstructured world (the noumena) by applying a knowable structure of categories supplied by autonomous reason (the phenomena). On the one hand, Kant is a skeptic worse than Hume: we cannot know the world as it really is. On the other hand, he claims that autonomous reasoning can determine everything in our experience, including what God may and may not do.
6. In the end, then, Kant's knowledge (which he thought enabled him to rescue science and mathematics from skepticism) is not a knowledge of the real world. It is a knowledge of its own structure, a knowledge of the categories that it imposes on experience. It is therefore in an important sense tautological. It is the knowledge of Aristotle's Prime Mover: thought thinking thought, thinking thought. But it is not thought *of* anything,

Kant's knowledge (which he thought enabled him to rescue science and mathematics from skepticism) is not a knowledge of the real world. It is a knowledge of its own structure, a knowledge of the categories that it imposes on experience.

26. Here we are back to Locke's description of *material substance*: "something, I know not what."

and therefore not thought at all. So Kant is far more deeply skeptical than Hume, both in regard to the noumenal world and in regard to the phenomenal. There is no knowledge of the noumenal, and knowledge of the phenomenal is an empty thought of thought.

7. But if we presuppose that there must be something like a real world for Kant, then it is man's creation. The noumenal world is nothing, as I indicated above. What being there is consists of the categories supplied by the mind. So it is the human mind that creates the world out of nothing. Man plays the role of God. This conclusion fits the picture that Kant supplies of the autonomous human mind as the criterion of intelligibility, truth, and moral rightness. All these functions of the Kantian mind are traditionally and biblically ascribed to God.

Kant is far more deeply skeptical than Hume, both in regard to the noumenal world and in regard to the phenomenal. There is no knowledge of the noumenal, and knowledge of the phenomenal is an empty thought of thought.

8. Earlier in the book I mentioned Dooyeweerd's understanding of the history of philosophy as a series of *ground-motives*. The ground-motive of Scripture is *creation-fall-redemption*. That of Greek philosophy is the *form-matter scheme*. In medieval philosophy, the *form-matter scheme* becomes *natural reason* in Aquinas, which he supplements by a realm of *grace*, so *form-matter* becomes *nature-grace*. But in the modern period, best exemplified by Kant, the *grace* of Aquinas becomes secularized into the concept of *freedom*. So *nature-grace* becomes *nature-freedom*. This analysis shows us something of the logical development by which Kant replaces the grace of God with its virtual opposite, the freedom of autonomous man. In Kant's religion, it is the freedom of man, not the grace of God, that saves us.[27] For Kant, man replaces God: in metaphysics, epistemology, ethics, and religion. In this, he anticipates, unfortunately, the main currents of philosophy since his time. This is, finally, the meaning of Kant's *Copernican revolution*.

In Kant's religion, it is the freedom of man, not the grace of God, that saves us. For Kant, man replaces God: in metaphysics, epistemology, ethics, and religion. In this, he anticipates, unfortunately, the main currents of philosophy since his time.

9. For all this, the Kantian revolution was anything but necessary. Kant thought that the attempt to find reality through sense experience or reason was a hopeless quest, and that therefore a Copernican shift was called for: the mind imposing order on the world rather than the reverse. But who is to say that the quest was so desperate? In the years after Kant, others thought there was still, despite Hume, some potential in empiricism (John Stuart Mill) and rationalism (Georg W. F. Hegel). Reid's common-sense philosophy remained popular for over a hundred years. To my knowledge, Kant never showed that these approaches could

27. Kant wrote that if we seek to obey God, we may expect that he will give us some assistance; but our works come first, then God's grace.

never bear fruit. And most seriously, what about the philosophy of Scripture (chapter 1 of this book)? Would we not have more certainty of knowledge if it turned out that God revealed the truth to us in nature, Scripture, and ourselves, and equipped our minds to apply the categories that were his in the first place? Wouldn't it make a difference if that revelation taught us about things that we could not otherwise experience? What if our reason is not the ultimate standard of truth, but a student of God, seeking to think his thoughts after him? Consider, then, that perhaps Kant's philosophy is not the discovery of a grand new truth, but rather the suppression of some old truths.

GEORG W. F. HEGEL (1770–1831)

Hegel was not the first member of the school of German idealism that followed Kant. It was Johann Gottlieb Fichte (1762–1814) who first suggested that Kant's noumenal world was superfluous: if we cannot know anything about it, then on what ground should we affirm its existence?[28] But if we remove the noumenal from Kant's system, what is left is the phenomenal. But then the phenomenal world is no longer a mere phenomenon (i.e., an appearance of something else). It is itself reality. So then we can know the real world after all. On that basis, we can return to rationalism of a sort.

These rationalist slogans call for a radical confidence in human reason: the concepts of our reason do not merely correspond to the realities of the world; they are those realities. The goal is not to achieve an idea that corresponds with the object of thought; it is to be that object of thought.

So the radical skepticism of Hume and Kant devolves into the equally radical rationalism of idealism. As Hegel said, "the real is the rational and the rational is the real." This slogan is essentially the same as Parmenides' "to be is the same as to be thought," a slogan with which Plotinus agreed, and Spinoza's "the order and connection of ideas is the same as the order and connection of things." Recall that these rationalist slogans call for a radical confidence in human reason: the concepts of our reason do not merely correspond to the realities of the world; they *are* those realities. The goal is not to achieve an idea that corresponds with the object of thought; it is to *be* that object of thought. This could, of course, mean either that the concepts of the mind are material objects or that the objects of thought are themselves thought.

Idealism refers generally to the second alternative, views in which all reality is mind. We have seen variations of this position in Berkeley, Leibniz, and, with less consistency, Jonathan Edwards. Kant himself is sometimes called an idealist, for, as I pointed out earlier, he limits knowledge to subjective experience, including, of course, the concepts imposed on that experience by the mind. But from the early nineteenth

28. Kant sometimes said that the noumenal was the source or cause of the phenomenal. But *cause* is one of the categories of the understanding (3.b on the earlier chart). Kant insisted that those categories could not be applied to the noumenal.

century on, *idealism* becomes a name for a particular philosophical movement. It begins with the German idealists, Fichte, Hegel, and Friedrich Wilhelm Schelling (1775–1854). Later in the nineteenth century a related movement develops in Britain, led by T. H. Green (1836–82), F. H. Bradley (1846–1924), and Bernard Bosanquet (1848–1923). In the United States, idealism was represented especially by Josiah Royce (1855–1916), Archibald A. Bowman (1883–1936),[29] and Brand Blanshard (1892–1987). Note that the movement continued a long time. And although few philosophers today would claim to follow this school of thought, it continues to attract interest. In theology we detect its influence especially in Paul Tillich (1886–1965) and Wolfhart Pannenberg (1928–2014), to say nothing of Hegel's indirect influence on the many followers of Karl Marx. If Hegelians are few today, Hegel scholars and Hegel citations are many. So our study of German idealism will introduce us to a movement with continuing relevance down to our own time.

Georg W. F. Hegel

There are differences among the many idealists mentioned above, but I will refer to Hegel, the most prominent of them, as the spokesman for the school. First, we should ask how a rationalist philosophy can operate credibly, following Kant's critiques of reason. Hegel's answer is "dialectic." Kant's transcendental dialectic described the errors that people make when they use the categories of the understanding to prove the existence of entities beyond possible experience. But to Hegel, reasoning from the categories of the understanding to the nature of the real world is not an error.[30] Reason is a dependable guide to the world; in fact, reason at its best *is* the world.

[According] to Hegel, reasoning from the categories of the understanding to the nature of the real world is not an error. Reason is a dependable guide to the world; in fact, reason at its best is the world.

But in carrying out this project, he thought, we should not revert back to the older rationalists such as Descartes, Spinoza, and Leibniz. Hegel's rationalism is a rationalism chastened by Kant's critique. Hegel agrees with Kant that the actual practice of reason often goes into false paths and needs to be corrected. But he also believes, contrary to Kant, that these very missteps are the key to discovering truth. Recall that Kant's dialectic referred to *antinomies*—arguments in which two opposite conclusions can be proved with equal cogency. For example, the universe is infinitely divisible and the universe is not infinitely divisible. For Kant, the antinomy is a warning that our reason is seeking to

29. It may be of interest to readers of this book that Bowman was the adviser for Cornelius Van Til's doctoral dissertation, "God and the Absolute," which compared the idealist absolute with the biblical God. Van Til rejected idealism, but his writing often reflected its vocabulary, as *concrete universal* and *presupposition*. He emphasized that in apologetics we should not try to understand individual facts apart from the worldview or system that bound those facts together, an idealist insight shared by other evangelicals such as James Orr (1844–1913) and Gordon H. Clark (1902–85). See discussion of Clark in chapter 13.

30. So, contrary to Kant, Hegel affirms the ontological argument. It is of the very nature of reason to argue from concept to reality.

enter a forbidden place. But for Hegel, the antinomy tells us something about the world (in this case about infinite divisibility). If we back away from the formal contradiction, we can see the whole issue in a broader context—that is, more truly.

It is a common experience in life that when we consider contrary arguments, a broader truth sometimes emerges. For example, consider the parable of the blind men and the elephant. One blind man, feeling the elephant's leg, thinks the animal is like a tree. Another, feeling the elephant's trunk, thinks he is like a snake. These assertions seem to be contradictory: how can an animal be both like a tree and like a snake? But if we look at the creature from a broader vantage point (and especially with the gift of sight), the contradiction dissolves, we know the truth in a broader context, and we can better assess the truth that was available to the more limited perspectives. So antinomy can actually be a means to greater truth, contrary to Kant.

Often a greater insight arises when we combine different points of view. So Plato developed his ideas using the dialogue form. (Plato's dialogues are often called *dialectic*.) Plato's dialogues don't always reach conclusions on the subjects they explore. But Plato seems to have felt that just asking the question and opening it to discussion was a means of learning. We find ourselves persuaded by one idea, but then we hear a case for the contrary idea and we are persuaded by that (cf. Prov. 18:17). But the first idea was a means by which we heard of the second. And by such experiences, we are prepared for the realization that we might have to abandon even the second idea to embrace a third, more adequate idea.

The essence of Hegel's dialectic is a pursuit of truth by way of negation and higher synthesis. Like other human activities, knowledge proceeds by trial and error—by questioning what we think we know, in order to reach a higher level of insight.

So the essence of Hegel's dialectic is a pursuit of truth by way of negation and higher synthesis. Like other human activities, knowledge proceeds by trial and error—by questioning what we think we know, in order to reach a higher level of insight. Interpreters commonly identify three stages in Hegel's dialectical reasoning:[31] *thesis, antithesis, synthesis*. The thesis is a proposition up for discussion. The antithesis is an assertion that seems to arise from the thesis, but is in fact contrary to it. The synthesis is a view that dismisses the errors of the thesis and the antithesis, but presents a larger picture that affirms what is true in these earlier steps. Then that synthesis, in turn, is negated, and the dialectic moves on to higher and higher levels, until we reach comprehensive knowledge of the world. For this process, Hegel uses the German verb *aufheben* (passive participle *aufgehoben*), which has three meanings: "preserve," "cancel," and "lift up."[32] At every stage of the

31. Hegel himself used these terms occasionally, but not regularly.

32. Appropriately, these multiple meanings themselves embody an apparent contradiction—such as the English word *cleave*, which means both "cut apart" and "cling to." And Hegel finds that the three meanings of *aufheben* can be combined to express a single, higher concept.

dialectic, the earlier stages are simultaneously preserved, canceled, and raised to a higher level of understanding.

We can better understand Hegel's method by looking at the substantive content of his philosophy. He begins his exploration of the world by analyzing the concept of being. Like Parmenides before him and Heidegger after him, he believes that the nature of being is the fundamental question of philosophy. Being includes everything. So if we can understand being, we are in sight of exhaustive knowledge.[33]

Hegel begins his exploration of the world by analyzing the concept of being. . . . Being includes everything. So if we can understand being, we are in sight of exhaustive knowledge.

Philosophers have sought exhaustive knowledge in one of two ways: either by mastering the general nature of the universe (such as Parmenides, Plotinus, Spinoza, Hegel) or by isolating its smallest constituents (Democritus, Epicurus, Leibniz, Wittgenstein [early]). The former group are monists, the latter group pluralists. From a Christian perspective, either of these methods is bound to fail, because (1) only God has exhaustive knowledge, and (2) God has made the world to reflect his Trinitarian nature: that is, there is no unity without plurality, and no plurality without unity. Hegel is a monist, and he seeks to understand the world by understanding being in general.

But being initially disappoints us. Certainly if we are to know being, the first item on the agenda is to distinguish being from nonbeing. How can we know being if we don't know what being is not? It seems that being must be defined in terms of nonbeing.

But that seems impossible. Is there anything that really has no being? Unicorns, we say, do not exist; but they do have a kind of being—in literature, and in fantasy. What is *nonbeing*, anyway? If you try to define it, you've made it into something, and nonbeing then becomes a kind of being. Recall from chapter 2 that Parmenides tried to eliminate all nonbeing from his view of the world, by eliminating the words *not* and *no* from all descriptions of that world. But his attempt was a complete failure. Parmenides' world was precisely a world in which there is *no* change, *no* beginnings, *no* endings, *no* plurality, and the like. So being and nonbeing are inseparable, mutually defining. We are told that Hegel suggested a thought-experiment for his students: Close your eyes, and think *being*. Now, close your eyes again, and think *nonbeing*. What difference is there?

Close your eyes, and think being. *Now, close your eyes again, and think* nonbeing. *What difference is there? So we cannot think of pure being or pure nonbeing. The idea of pure being (thesis) devolves into the idea of pure nonbeing (antithesis).*

So we cannot think of pure being or pure nonbeing. The idea of pure being (thesis) devolves into the idea of pure nonbeing (antithesis). Is there a higher synthesis that would represent a real advance in

33. Note that Hegel starts with being in general, not with a distinction between the being of the creator and that of the creature. Eventually he affirms a kind of god. But that god is the being of the world, and the rationalist philosopher is perfectly competent to scrutinize him. Already we can see that Hegel's god (the Absolute) is radically different from the God of Scripture.

knowledge? Yes, says Hegel. The synthesis is *becoming*. The being of the universe is becoming. Becoming is something real, a kind of being, but it incorporates change—movement from what something is to what it is *not*. So becoming contains all we were seeking to find both in being and in nonbeing. In becoming, being and nonbeing are *aufgehoben*.

Being, *nonbeing*, and *becoming* seem to be mere abstract ideas. But in fact, Hegel's dialectic ties them to concrete reality. These ideas cannot be understood in themselves. What is *becoming* apart from changing things? And how can the idea of becoming be meaningful unless it is the becoming of an objective universe? So the next step in the dialectic is for us to recognize the ideas as ideas of the material world, which Hegel calls *nature*. Nature is the antithesis of ideas, an antithesis that led Descartes to posit his sharp mind-body distinction. But as Descartes failed to realize, the two define each other. Nature *is* an idea of ours, and our ideas are not true if they are not ideas of something real, something objective, namely, nature.

But Descartes is not entirely wrong. There is a difference between our thoughts and the natural world. But this idea-nature antithesis leads to a further synthesis, namely, *spirit*. Spirit is a mind, either human or, as we will see, divine. Spirit thinks the ideas and employs them in nature. So ideas and nature are nothing in themselves. They find their reality only in spirit. Ideas are ideas of spirit, and nature exists only for spirit.

The being of the universe is becoming. Becoming is something real, a kind of being, but it incorporates change—movement from what something is to what it is not. So becoming contains all we were seeking to find both in being and in nonbeing.

But as we reflect further, we see that spirit, too, is a complex reality, undergoing dialectical evolution. When we look at spirit in itself, we notice first an inward consciousness like the "I am" of Descartes. This is *subjective spirit*. But that is an insufficient description of what is there. Mind or spirit does not hide out by itself, but it by its nature is part of a society of spirits, and it prescribes ideas for the whole society.[34] This world of spirits under the authority of its corporate mind is the *objective spirit*. Objective spirit includes law (which governs individual spirits from outside themselves), morality (which governs spirit from within), and ethics (a synthesis between law and morality). Ethics, in turn, governs three spheres, namely, family, society, and state.

All of this in turn presupposes[35] and manifests God, or the Absolute spirit. The Absolute manifests itself in three areas: art, religion, and philosophy. Art reveals a divine depth in reality, expressing it in images. Religion the same, using symbols. Philosophy, by which Hegel meant the philosophy of Hegel, is the highest manifestation of the

34. Kant said that to observe the moral law is to be able to prescribe the principle of your action as a duty for every other ethical agent.

35. Notice that the whole dialectical process is presuppositional or transcendental. At each stage, we ask: What are the conditions that make this possible? What are its presuppositions? Thus Hegel's method perpetuates Kant's.

Absolute. It reveals the full meaning of art and the literal meaning of the religious symbols.[36]

Recall, though, that for Hegel the real is the rational and the rational is the real. In our survey of Hegel's dialectic, we have been focusing on the dialectic that goes on in the philosopher's mind as he tries to understand reality. But for Hegel, the dialectic is not something that occurs only in our subjectivity. It is the very nature of reality. The dialectical movement of human thought is at the same time the dialectical movement of history and the dialectical nature of God.

For Hegel, the dialectic is not something that occurs only in our subjectivity. It is the very nature of reality. The dialectical movement of human thought is at the same time the dialectical movement of history and the dialectical nature of God.

So just as human thought progresses through negation and synthesis, so human history progresses through conflict and resolution. One tribe fights another, leading to a nation. Nations fight and create empires. One empire fights another, leading to a greater civilization.[37]

And the progress of the dialectic is nothing less than God's coming to self-consciousness. God himself is being. When he seeks to think about himself, he negates himself, for like us he cannot think *being* without thinking *nonbeing*. So God's thought inevitably is a kind of *self-alienation*. And when God announces who he is (the "I am," but also his attributes such as eternity and omniscience), he divides his subjectivity from his objectivity. The dialectic of God's being shows that his positive and negative sides are necessary to each other.

God's dialectical movement is not only parallel to the movement of history and the movement of individual human thought. It is *identical* to these. Human thought and history are God as he comes to self-consciousness. So Hegel's philosophy is a dialectical idealistic pantheism.

The progress of the dialectic is nothing less than God's coming to self-consciousness. God himself is being. When he seeks to think about himself, he negates himself, for like us he cannot think being *without thinking* nonbeing. *So God's thought inevitably is a kind of* self-alienation.

This bare-bones summary gives only the faintest suggestion of the palpable brilliance of Hegel's thought. In his analysis of concepts, there is a rare depth of insight.[38] He explains remarkably well how things that appear to be opposite really depend on each other, even define each other. For example, according to Hegel, slavery and democracy seem to be opposed, but it was slavery that gave leisure to the Greek upper classes to think about and implement democracy. But eventually the contradiction destroyed the slave-leisure society and created a higher kind of civilization, feudalism. But that, too, embodied social tension, in this case between nobles and serfs. In general, Hegel antici-

36. Don't neglect to notice that for Hegel the point of religion is to set forth Hegelian philosophy using symbols. Similar to Tillich's later theology, for Hegel the cross of Jesus is a symbol of dialectical self-negation.

37. Hegel thought that just as his philosophy had reached a kind of consummation that would not again be negated, so the Prussian state had achieved a consummation of political history.

38. I am often impressed with the accuracy of Hegel's dialectic as a description of how we learn things in ordinary life: postulating, backtracking, looking at facts from a broader context.

pates Marx as he presents history as deterministic class struggle: The master dominates the slave, but in doing so he becomes dependent on the slave so that the slave in effect masters him.

It is thus that for Hegel any fact, any thing, becomes a perspective on all reality.[39] To know A is to know B, and in turn the whole universe. But the converse is that one cannot fully know A, unless one knows B and in turn the whole universe. As the idealist slogan put it, the truth is in the whole.

We should also note that in the debate between realists and nominalists (see chapters 1 and 4), this is a fairly extreme realist position. The dialectic is a parade of abstract concepts that barely hints at any particulars that might exemplify those concepts. Hegel does have a place in his system for what others call *material reality*, the place where spirit posits the world of its experience. But that, too, is mind. And Hegel's critics regularly observed that he had no place in his system for the pen with which he wrote his great tomes. We will see that Marx and especially Kierkegaard[40] thought that Hegel's system had no room for concrete reality. Worse, as both Schopenhauer and Kierkegaard complained, Hegel gave no account of individual choice. He assumed

Marx and especially Kierkegaard thought that Hegel's system had no room for concrete reality. Worse, as both Schopenhauer and Kierkegaard complained, Hegel gave no account of individual choice.

39. It is interesting to compare Hegel's triadic perspectivalism with that of Frame and Poythress described in chapter 1 of this book as a form of Christian philosophy. (1) In that view, too, apparent opposites can be seen as identical. In the epistemological triangle, for example, the normative perspective seems to be opposed to the situational, for the normative supplies rules to govern our understanding of situations. Nevertheless, since God reveals himself in situations, and since the norms are themselves facts of the situation, the normative and the situational are identical. (2) In the triangular sets, the third angle can be seen as a *synthesis* of the other two. Considering again the epistemological triangle: the normative and the situational perspectives come together in the mind of a thinking subject, turning them into real knowledge. Thus the existential perspective fulfills the normative and the situational. But we can also understand the situational and the existential as opposite poles (object and subject) that are clearly identified and distinguished in the normative. Similarly, the normative and the existential find their proper places in the situation (which embraces all reality).

In Christian perspectivalism, however, the same-opposite pairs do not form (as in Hegel) a system that includes the mind of God himself. Christian perspectivalism seeks to consistently honor the Creator-creature distinction of the Bible. The perspectival triangles are *images* of the Trinitarian mind of God, but they are not identical with it. Nor are the triads even linked together in such a way as to yield exhaustive knowledge of the creation, as in Hegel's philosophy. Such exhaustive knowledge is not possible for man.

More should be said about the relation between Hegel's triads and the Christian doctrine of the Trinity. Hegel recognized the similarity between his triads and the biblical *one* and *many*. Typically, he regarded the latter as a symbol of the former. I think that Hegel's triadic analysis of the world shows that God created the world indeed as an image of his own unity and plurality. I disagree, of course, with Hegel's pantheistic belief that the triadic structure of the universe is *identical* with the divine Trinity.

40. I have chosen to discuss Kierkegaard in chapter 8, though chronologically he would fit into this one. His chief influence can better be understood in the context of twentieth-century thought.

that the human will would passively follow the dialectical course of reason until the consummation. But to Schopenhauer and Kierkegaard, that squeezed all the life out of human experience.

Hegel's rationalism, furthermore, entails irrationalism. If one must be omniscient in order to know the book on the table, or the pen with which one is writing, then knowledge is impossible, for none of us is omniscient. Further, Hegel's dialectic implies that whenever we think we have knowledge, we can expect that knowledge to be negated, resulting in a "higher" view. So we never know for sure when we have truth, until the Absolute has completed his (its?) path to self-consciousness and our own minds are completely in union with that Absolute. Sensing this difficulty, Hegel sometimes bars the door to further dialectical development. He is convinced, for example, that his own philosophy will never be negated and yield to another kind of philosophy.[41]

Hegel's rationalism, furthermore, entails irrationalism. If one must be omniscient in order to know the book on the table, or the pen with which one is writing, then knowledge is impossible, for none of us is omniscient.

But this assurance is arbitrary, with no basis in the dialectic. The dialectic gives us no reason to think that it will ever stop, even with Hegel. So Hegel's rationalism devolves into irrationalism, like other forms of non-Christian philosophy.

ARTHUR SCHOPENHAUER (1788–1860)

Schopenhauer came of age during the heyday of Hegel and had little respect for the great idealist. Schopenhauer scheduled his classes at the University of Berlin to be held at the same time as Hegel's (incidentally, limiting the number of students he had to teach), and he expressed the following opinion:

> Hegel, installed from above by the powers that be as the certified Great Philosopher, was a flat-headed, insipid, nauseating, illiterate charlatan, who reached the pinnacle of audacity in scribbling together and dishing up the craziest mystifying nonsense.[42]

Arthur Schopenhauer

Indeed, Schopenhauer revered few previous philosophers, except for Plato, Kant, and the writers of the Hindu Upanishads. In his own philosophical context, he saw himself as the champion of Kant, swimming against the Hegelian tide.

In Schopenhauer, Kant's *phenomenal-noumenal* distinction reappears, undeterred by Fichte's and Hegel's rejection of the noumenal. At the

41. Hegel's authoritarian stance here is ironic, for in his *Early Theological Writings* (the article on "The Positivity of Christianity") he objects to traditional Christianity on the ground that it makes authoritarian demands. He objects to the fact that the OT contains commands concerning what we should believe and do, and he claims that the NT is even worse, because it presumes to tell us what to feel, as in "do not be anxious" (Phil. 4:6).

42. Quoted in Karl R. Popper, *The Open Society and Its Enemies*, vol. 2, *Hegel and Marx* (Princeton, NJ: Princeton University Press, 1966), 32–33.

OUTLINE

beginning of his most famous work, *The World as Will and Idea*, he states, "The world is my idea," a statement that Kant might have made. For Schopenhauer as for Kant, all we know is phenomena, appearances, experience structured by the mind's imposition of time and space and the categories of the understanding. That is, what we know is our own ideas. To know the world, then, is to know my own ideas.

The first part of this book, then, essentially repeats the argument of Kant's *Critique of Pure Reason*, explaining how our concepts of time and space and of the categories of the understanding shape our experience.

But as it turns out, Schopenhauer is less agnostic about the noumenal world than was Kant. Of course, even Kant spoke of God, freedom, and immortality as noumenal ideals that are regulative, not constitutive, ideas. For Kant, we should act and think "as if" these ideals were real. As I noted, one of the problems in Kant is his notion that we can think "as if" these ideals were real, structuring our lives, thoughts, and methods around them, while claiming ignorance as to their real existence.

But Schopenhauer has his own ideas about the contents of the noumenal, very different from Kant's. Kant admitted an admiration for "the starry heavens above and the moral law within" that stimulated his attraction to the concept of God. But Schopenhauer's preoccupations were darker: violence, death, illicit sex. He came to think that these preoccupations were a clue to the nature of the noumenal world:

> a wild, seething, inexorable, meaningless force that he called "will." This force creates all and destroys all in its insatiable demand for "More!" (More of what it does not know—it only knows that it wants more.)[43]

Schopenhauer's preoccupations were darker: violence, death, illicit sex. He came to think that these preoccupations were a clue to the nature of the noumenal world.

It is this blind force that rules the world and human actions.[44] At heart, we care not for anybody or anything except to procreate and to destroy. For all of that, Schopenhauer also thinks that we have a desire to escape the bondage of this awful force, and that we can do this in a partial way by attending to certain kinds of Baroque music—music that he considered to be "formal" rather than sensuous.[45]

As an argument for the nature of the world, Schopenhauer's philosophy is laughable. His projection of the noumenal is not one whit

43. Donald Palmer, *Looking at Philosophy: The Unbearable Heaviness of Philosophy Made Lighter* (New York: McGraw-Hill, 2010), 248.

44. Palmer points out that Sigmund Freud found in Schopenhauer's blind will the model for his concept *id*, the lustful force beneath the ego and the superego. Certainly, however, Schopenhauer's will is not what Calvinist theology calls *total depravity*. Sin in this theology is not a blind force, but a personal decision to disobey God's law.

45. Nietzsche was somewhat amused by this recommendation. He thought that this "formal" music was in fact highly sensuous. Was Schopenhauer deceiving himself as he believed the will impels us all to self-deception?

more persuasive than Kant's, only more revealing of Schopenhauer's own pessimistic disposition. And his vision is highly inconsistent: an all-conquering, all-determining will that we can nevertheless resist by playing Baroque music! And why would we want to resist it in any case, being what we are? And why *ought* we to resist it?

Schopenhauer therefore, in my opinion, does not offer any answers to the questions of philosophy or insight into its subject matter. In that regard, most of his philosophical successors would agree with me. But he does inject *themes* into the history of philosophy—themes neglected by Kant and Hegel—which influence profoundly the thought of the later nineteenth and twentieth centuries:

Schopenhauer's vision is highly inconsistent: an all-conquering, all-determining will that we can nevertheless resist by playing Baroque music!

1. *The will*: During the Enlightenment, philosophy was mainly concerned with examining the contents of the mind, its impressions, ideas, concepts, and so on. It had largely neglected the discussion about choice, decision, and will that had been so lively during the medieval period and that had distinguished the philosophy of John Duns Scotus. Surely the human being is not propelled through life by rational cogitation alone. He must *choose* to behave rationally, and often chooses otherwise. In Feuerbach, Kierkegaard (*either-or*) (anticipated by Pascal), and especially Nietzsche (the *will to power*), the will again becomes the central matter, and also in the forms of twentieth-century existentialism and postmodernism that proceed from this root.[46]
2. *The irrational*: In Schopenhauer's *will* we see the return of Aristotle's prime matter, the primordial ooze without any meaningful structure, and therefore no possibility of restraint. Duns Scotus had regarded will as a human psychological faculty that at times resisted and went beyond the alternatives proposed by the intellect. But Schopenhauer's will is a transhuman, metaphysical force that mocks the intellect and overwhelms us. Our intellectual concepts are only manifestations of this all-consuming will. Schopenhauer's principles of idea and will are an example of what Van Til described as the rationalist-irrationalist dialectic: the futile attempt to project rational categories over a meaningless existence. In that respect, Schopenhauer is like Plato and Aristotle. But unlike these, in Schopenhauer's philosophy it is the irrationalist principle that prevails. Indeed, it is so powerful that one wonders what Schopenhauer thinks he can accomplish by arguing for it rationally.

Schopenhauer does inject themes *into the history of philosophy—themes neglected by Kant and Hegel—which influence profoundly the thought of the later nineteenth and twentieth centuries.*

46. As I indicated in my discussion of Duns Scotus (chapter 4), I believe that intellect, will, and emotions are not sharply distinguishable faculties, but perspectives on the actions and thoughts of the whole person. See also *DKG*, 319–46; *DCL*, 361–82.

3. *The romantic*: The notion of sex as a dark, wild, destructive, untamable force comes into its own during the romantic period of the late eighteenth and early nineteenth centuries. Romanticism is a broad cultural movement, embracing art, literature, and music. It was not primarily a philosophical movement, though it influenced philosophy, as in the work of Jean-Jacques Rousseau (1712–78). We will see its influence in theology when we consider Friedrich Schleiermacher in chapter 8 (1768–1834). Schopenhauer is perhaps the best example of a philosopher who embraces the romantic spirit and allows its intense emotionalism to influence his work. To anticipate distinctions emphasized by Nietzsche, Schopenhauer embraces the *Dionysiac* as opposed to the *Apollonian* spirit of the old Greek religion (see chapter 2), the will to throw off boundaries. Later generations would disavow the influence of romanticism, but would develop their own ways of resisting structure and order.

LUDWIG FEUERBACH (1804–72)

Despite Schopenhauer's efforts to debunk him, Hegel gained a large number of disciples, large enough to divide into factions. *Right-wing* Hegelians gravitated toward conservative politics and traditional religion, using Hegel's dialectic as apologetic. Feuerbach was one of the *left-wing* or *young* Hegelians who developed a secular, materialistic interpretation of Hegel that led to Karl Marx.

Feuerbach diverged very radically from Hegel by rejecting idealism and embracing materialism. Although materialism was common among the Greeks (the Milesians, the atomists, and the Stoics), only Hobbes in the modern period had espoused it. Most other philosophers were either mind-matter dualists (as Descartes)[47] or idealists (as Berkeley, Leibniz, Kant, and Hegel).

Feuerbach rejected Hegel's Absolute as well as the God of Christianity and maintained that the idea of God was essentially a projection of man's ideals for himself. . . . So man creates God in his image, not the other way around. Theology becomes anthropology. God is what we wish we were.

Most radically yet, he rejected Hegel's Absolute as well as the God of Christianity and maintained that the idea of God was essentially a projection of man's ideals for himself. In his most famous work, translated *The Essence of Christianity*,[48] Feuerbach claimed that all traditional statements about God attribute to him qualities of human beings: either qualities possessed by humans or qualities that humans wish they had. Human beings come to value consciousness, morality, and love in themselves and in one another. But if these are desirable qualities among people, they surely cannot be denied to mankind's object of worship. So man creates God in his image, not the other way around. Theology becomes anthropology.[49] God is what we wish we were.

47. Spinoza was a mind-body perspectivalist.

48. Recently republished: New York: Dover, 2008.

49. We will see later that Karl Barth accused the liberal theological tradition of substituting anthropology for theology. He said that liberalism could not escape "the smile on Feuerbach's face."

In the second part of the book, Feuerbach identifies what he considers to be the most serious errors of traditional theology. First is the idea of God as a real, existing being, having an existence separate from man (i.e., what I called in chapter 1 the *Creator-creature distinction*). Second is the concept of revelation in which God tells us what to believe and to do. Like Kant, Feuerbach insists that such authoritarianism injures our moral sense, which cannot function as it should without autonomous freedom. Third, he thinks that the traditional Christian sacraments encourage superstition and immorality.

Ludwig Feuerbach

During the Enlightenment, many criticized the traditional arguments for the existence of God and the allegedly historical basis for biblical redemption. But how, then, did Christianity gain such a large following? Feuerbach begins a new line of criticism: The success of Christianity can be explained without presupposing its truth, on a purely naturalistic and materialistic basis. People came to embrace faith, he said, because it matched what they hoped was true. *God* is simply a wish-projection of idealized humanity. Marx followed Feuerbach in declaring that religion was the "opiate" of the people, and Freud's *Future of an Illusion* claimed that religion is a kind of wish-fulfillment.

Christians, however, have nothing to fear from this kind of argument. The fact that God and man share traits in common does not prove that God is a projection of ideal human nature, unless we presuppose at the outset that God does not exist. If we presuppose on the contrary that the God of Scripture does exist, these common traits only validate the biblical claim that God has made us in his image. And on biblical presuppositions we should affirm what Feuerbach emphatically denies: that our belief in God comes not by extrapolating from ourselves, but by divine revelation in nature, Scripture, and ourselves.

Feuerbach identifies what he considers to be the most serious errors of traditional theology. First is the idea of God as a real, existing being, having an existence separate from man . . . . Second is the concept of revelation in which God tells us what to believe and to do.

Further, even if it can be shown that people come to believe in God by contemplating ideal humanity, that does not prove that God does not exist. Anselm's ontological argument suggests the reverse: that ideas of perfection in our mind actually entail the real existence of God. But short of Anselm's view, certainly it cannot be argued that ideas of perfection entail the *nonexistence* of God.

Feuerbach in effect says that belief in God is based on a questionable psychological process and should therefore be rejected. But Feuerbach's contention is a *genetic fallacy*: A comes from an inferior source; therefore, A is inferior. In fact, the psychological process generating a belief has no bearing on the validity of the belief. Someone (A) might believe that Senator B is dishonest because A has a psychological hatred of all senators. But that does not prove that Senator B is or is not honest.

The same conclusion follows if we put Feuerbach's point in terms of argument, rather than psychological process: belief in God is the conclusion of a bad argument; therefore, we should not believe in God. But that, too, is a genetic fallacy. Some people once believed the earth was round because they thought circularity was a metaphysically superior shape. Their argument was bad, but their conclusion was right. In fact, as Thomas Reid[50] and more recently Alvin Plantinga have pointed out, it is often legitimate to believe something with no argument or evidence at all. The belief that other people have minds like mine, for example, is not a belief for which I have conclusive argument. But like the rest of us, I have the right to believe it.

KARL MARX (1818–83)

Marx was another of the young or left-wing Hegelians who applied Hegel's dialectic to a materialistic worldview. He is sometimes quoted as saying that he had "turned Hegel on his head." Rather, he compared Hegel to a man standing on his head, trying to manage the awkwardness of that position. Marx's intention was to turn Hegel right side up, so that he could stand on his feet. Translation: Hegel, the idealist, believed that mind was the foundation of human life. Marx would show (or perhaps presuppose) that human life is based on material reality, and that mind is the outcome of material processes. Marx was an admirer of Charles Darwin (1809–82), and it is interesting during this period to see how Hegel's philosophical theories intertwine with Darwin's biological ones.[51]

Marx was a determinist like Hegel, and he believed that the laws of being progressed in the form of a Hegelian dialectic. But he believed that the ultimate causes of events were material, not mental. So he was a dialectical materialist. *Further, in his view, those ultimate causes were economic.*

Marx was a determinist like Hegel, and he believed that the laws of being progressed in the form of a Hegelian dialectic. But he believed that the ultimate causes of events were material, not mental. So he was a *dialectical materialist*. Further, in his view, those ultimate causes were economic. The attempts of people to achieve material well-being are what motivate the events of history. In his analysis of the production of goods, Marx distinguished between factors of production (food, clothing, shelter, work skills) and relations of production (master-slave, owner-worker, etc.). It was the relations of production Marx thought to be the more important in understanding historical change.

50. Recall my discussion of him in chapter 6.

51. It is important to remember that Darwin was not the first evolutionist. Hegel's philosophy is every bit as "evolutionary" as Darwin's science. Darwin's grandfather Erasmus Darwin (1731–1802) had advocated evolution of life-forms in his *Zoonomia* (1796). Indeed, evolution is the de facto position of every thinker who does not affirm the biblical doctrine of creation. The earliest Greek philosophers, Thales, Anaximander, and Anaximenes, believed that the earth and all the life in it developed by natural causes from a primeval element or elements. Same for later Greek and secular thinkers. The importance of Darwin, then, is not that he was the first evolutionist, but that he posited a plausible naturalistic mechanism (natural selection) to *explain* the development of life.

So in his understanding, all past history has been determined by class conflict. There is always an upper class and a lower class, haves and have-nots. In ancient times, the haves were the slave-owners and the have-nots the slaves.[52] The interests of these two groups were entirely opposed. Any increase in the prosperity of the owner is at the expense of the slave, and vice versa. It is a *zero-sum* relationship. So conflict is an unavoidable consequence. There is no possibility of reconciling the two parties so that they can live together in peace. They can only jostle for position until a full-scale class war breaks out. In time it is inevitable that the conflict will dissolve the whole social order that is dependent on slavery and bring a new economic arrangement into play.

In Marx's understanding, all past history has been determined by class conflict. There is always an upper class and a lower class, haves and have-nots. . . . The interests of these two groups were entirely opposed. Any increase in the prosperity of the owner is at the expense of the slave, and vice versa. It is a zero-sum *relationship.*

In Marx's analysis, this arrangement amounted to an "alienation" of the slave from the fruits of his labor.[53] Marx advocated the "labor theory of value," in which the value of something is based on the labor used to produce it.[54] So when the master takes from the slave what he has labored to produce, the slave's interest has been violated, and the stage is set for conflict.

This talk about alienation suggests that Marx is thinking in ethical categories. Alienation occurs when someone robs a person of what he *ought* to keep. But Marx does not understand his analysis as an ethical one. It is not based on the unfairness of slavery, but on Marx's claim to have discovered scientific laws governing history. To him, indeed, there is no objective right or wrong. There is only what is right for the advancement of one's class. So the ethics of one class will be opposite to the ethics of the rival class.[55]

So we continue to follow Marx's account of history: with the fall of the Roman Empire, the master-slave economic structure yielded

Karl Marx

52. Recall that Hegel had also discussed the master-slave relationship as a significant element of the overall dialectic.

53. Recall that in Hegel's dialectic, God (the Absolute) experiences self-alienation when the dialectic moves from thesis to antithesis. Marx, too, describes the dialectic as self-alienation. But, translating Hegel's idea into an atheistic materialism, he transfers the self-alienation to man.

54. The chief alternative is to value objects by the market: the worth of something is whatever someone else is willing to pay for it. That is the theory of value generally accepted among capitalists, and of course, it does not lead to Marx's conclusions about self-alienation.

55. Often when young people become Marxists, they claim, unlike Marx himself, to be following conscience. They become socialists or communists because they think that only Marxists "care" about the poor. In this discussion it is important to point out that Marx and his philosophically sophisticated followers carry out their program not out of moral conviction, but out of a conviction that class warfare is scientifically inevitable, and their desire to be on the winning side. For example, the American Communist Party praised Hitler when he made a pact with Stalin. But when Hitler violated that pact and attacked the Soviet Union, the party changed its ethical judgment of Hitler. The ethics of Marx are essentially relativistic, though relative to class rather than to individual preference.

to a new order: feudalism.[56] In that order, the haves are the nobles, the have-nots the serfs. The serfs were better off than the slaves were because they had some freedom. But they lived and worked on the land of someone else, the nobility. The nobles received a large share of the profit of the serfs' labors, alienating them, as in the case of the slaves, from the fruit of their labors.

The next stage in Marx's dialectic is the one he faced in his own time, the industrial revolution of the nineteenth century. In this stage, the haves are the *bourgeois*, the owners of the factories; the have-nots are the *proletariat*, the factory workers. Again, Marx understands the profit of the owners to entail the poverty of the workers[57] and therefore their self-alienation.[58] Therefore, the poor are driven to revolt. Again, Marx anticipates that this will bring a radical change in the social order, a revolution. Marx believes that in this particular revolution the proletariat will be the winner. So society will be governed for a time by a *dictatorship of the proletariat* under the administration of a state representing the worker class, which takes ownership of all the means of production.

People have often asked whether violent revolution is really necessary. Peaceful social movements, particularly religions, have brought great improvements in the condition of the poor. Christians were in the vanguard in abolishing the slave trade and slavery itself, also in the care of orphans and widows, improving education, encouraging science and art. But Marx thought that religions and liberal social movements should not be encouraged. In his view, they were counterproductive because they waste precious time and energy and do not get to the root of the problems. The real problems, he and later Marxists argued, are *structural*. They cannot be solved until there is a radical change in the very nature of society. The means of production must be taken from the rich capitalists and given to the representatives of the poor. So Marx described religion (particularly Christianity) as an "opiate," a kind of drug given to the poor by the rich to persuade them that revolution is not needed. Under the influence of the opiate, they come to think that they will get their due reward through normal social change and, eventually, a reward "in the sky, by and by." So Marxists

Marx described religion (particularly Christianity) as an "opiate," a kind of drug given to the poor by the rich to persuade them that revolution is not needed.

56. Marx's analysis would lead us to think that this change came about because of violent rebellions of slaves against masters. Historically, however, that does not appear to be the main cause of this cultural transition. Similar criticisms can be made of Marx's analysis of feudalism and industrial society.

57. Apologists for capitalistic free enterprise regularly take issue with Marx's zero-sum view that the profit of the upper class necessarily leads to the impoverishment of the lower. They argue that a strong economy benefits both rich and poor: "a rising tide lifts all boats."

58. He maintains that the situation brings alienation of the poor from nature, from themselves, from other people.

regard religion as a barrier to revolution and therefore a barrier to truly radical social change.[59]

But Marx thought that after the dictatorship of the proletariat has continued for a while, people will somehow be cured of the profit motive and will work for the benefit of society as a whole. People will then live according to the principle "from each according to his ability, to each according to his need." When that happens, the state will no longer be needed; it will "wither away." People will live together in peace, without resentment, without using force against one another. This consummate existence is sometimes called the *Marxist utopia* or the *Marxist eschatology*, a secularized version of the new heavens and new earth of Revelation 21:1.

Marx thought that after the dictatorship of the proletariat has continued for a while, people will somehow be cured of the profit motive and will work for the benefit of society as a whole.

Although "Communist revolutions" actually took place in several countries, Marx's analysis turned out to be faulty in a number of ways:

1. Communist revolution did not happen worldwide, or even throughout the industrialized world, but only in several countries, because of local conditions.
2. In these revolutions, the proletariat (factory workers) was never the leading revolutionary force. In Russia, the spearhead was a group of professional revolutionaries led by Vladimir Lenin, who led a political *coup d'état*. In China's revolution, the vanguard was the peasants.
3. In western Europe and America, there was a Marxist revolutionary faction in the labor unions, but that element did not prevail. The unions came to support nonrevolutionary socialism and in some cases even capitalism.
4. When the *dictatorship of the proletariat* was installed in Russia, China, Cuba, and elsewhere, it did not seek to achieve the stateless utopia, but rather did everything it could do to maintain and strengthen its own power. Communist governments became indistinguishable from other tyrannies.
5. Like Hegel, therefore, Marx erred in his judgment about the end of the dialectic. It did not end with the Communist revolution. Ironically, indeed, the dialectic continued in a way that paralleled Marx's analysis of past relations of production. For the revolution brought about a new arrangement of haves and have-nots: the haves were the government and their political allies, and the have-nots were everybody else. The arrangement was economically intolerable. It yielded to more capitalistic social orders, both in Russia and in China. In remaining Communist dictatorships such as North Korea and Cuba, there is

When the dictatorship of the proletariat *was installed in Russia, China, Cuba, and elsewhere, it did not seek to achieve the stateless utopia, but rather did everything it could do to maintain and strengthen its own power.*

59. But compare the alternative of the later Marxist Ernst Bloch that I discuss in chapter 11.

not much promise of economic prosperity or even continuing stability, let alone the withering of the state. Even the milder socialisms of western Europe, also indebted to Marx, appear at this writing to be leading those societies to financial ruin.

6. Contemporary Marxists generally dismiss Marx's eschatology as idealistic. But without the promise of such a goal to history, one wonders, why would anybody choose to be a Marxist?
7. Marx said, "Philosophers have hitherto only interpreted the world in various ways; the point is to change it."[60] Few philosophies have changed the world as much as Marx's. But that change has been almost entirely for the worse. Indeed, it has been the source of monstrous evils. In the name of Marxism, socialism,[61] and Communism, millions of people have been killed and imprisoned in horrible conditions. Marx himself did not intend for his philosophy to cause such atrocious levels of death and suffering. But he certainly bears some responsibility for the results of his philosophizing. Consider: (a) he refused to evaluate his system in moral terms, insisting that he was presenting only an objective scientific account. (b) He placed no limits on the powers of the *dictatorship of the proletariat*, having an eye only for the progress of the dialectic, not for the actual well-being of people. (c) He had no conception of the depth of human sin and the extent to which that sin leads rulers to abuse their power.

Marx said, "Philosophers have hitherto only interpreted the world in various ways; the point is to change it."

KEY TERMS

Critique of reason
Phenomena
Ding an Sich
Presuppose
Universal
Copernican revolution (Kant)
Transcendental aesthetic
Transcendental unity of the apperception
Transcendental dialectic (Kant)
Types of judgments
Paralogisms
Ideals
Dogmatic slumbers
Noumena
Transcendental method
Synthetic *a priori*
Necessary
Jelly-jar analogy (Kant)
Transcendental analytic
Categories of the understanding
Antinomies
Physico-theological argument
Constitutive use
Religion (for Kant)
Moral archetype
Nature-freedom

60. Karl Marx with Friedrich Engels, *The German Ideology* (Amherst, NY: Prometheus Books, 1998), 11. Includes *Theses on Feuerbach* and *Introduction to the Critique of Political Economy.*

61. Let us not forget the "national" socialism of Hitler's Germany, which was also deeply indebted to Marx.

Dialectic (Hegel)	Practical faith
Antithesis	Idealism
Aufheben, aufgehoben	Thesis
Subjective spirit	Synthesis
Absolute spirit	Spirit (Hegel)
Divine self-alienation	Objective spirit
Will (Schopenhauer)	Religion (Hegel)
Apollonian	Idea (Schopenhauer)
Left-wing Hegelians	Dionysiac
Genetic fallacy	Right-wing Hegelians
Relations of production	Wish-projection
Zero-sum	Dialectical materialism
Dictatorship of the proletariat	Class conflict
Marxist eschatology	Alienation (Marx)
Regulative use	Withering of the state
Radical evil	Marxist utopia

STUDY QUESTIONS

1. How did Kant respond to the philosophical schools of his predecessors? How does his method differ from theirs? Evaluate.
2. Why did Kant think it important that we have synthetic *a priori* knowledge? Mention some of his examples. Why does he think synthetic *a priori* knowledge is necessary for mathematics? Science? Ethics?
3. Expound the parable of the intelligent jelly jars. Why does Kant say that his proposal has "Copernican" significance?
4. "Concepts without percepts are empty; percepts without concepts are blind." Explain; evaluate.
5. Describe what Frame calls *Kant's assembly line*. What happens at each station?
6. "These apples are not red." From Kant's list, what type of judgment is this?
7. How does Kant reply to Hume's contention that there is no necessary connection between cause and effect? Evaluate Kant's view.
8. Why did Kant think that everyone reasons with the same categories? Evaluate his answer.
9. Describe Kant's view of the self or soul, mentioning (a) the transcendental unity of the apperception, (b) paralogisms, (c) the noumenal self, and (d) the self as a regulative concept. Contrast his view with that of Hume.

OUTLINE

Immanuel Kant (1724–1804)
- Phenomena and Noumena
- The Transcendental Method
- The Synthetic *A Priori*
- The Mind Structures Experience
- Kant's Assembly Line
- Kant's Ethics
- Kant's Theology
- Conclusions on Kant

Georg W. F. Hegel (1770–1831)

Arthur Schopenhauer (1788–1860)

Ludwig Feuerbach (1804–72)

Karl Marx (1818–83)

10. Describe Kant's refutations of the traditional theistic proofs, and evaluate.
11. Describe Kant's regulative use of the concept of God. Evaluate. Consider, at the end of the Kant section, Frame's statement that Kant's "as if" is "anemic."
12. Describe Kant's view of general revelation, special revelation, free will, sin, Christ, incarnation, atonement, and redemption.
13. Frame: "So Kant's theology transforms the biblical gospel of grace into a message of works-righteousness." Explain; evaluate.
14. Describe elements of pragmatism in Kant and his predecessors.
15. Compare Kant and Plato and Aristotle.
16. Frame: "So Kant is far more deeply skeptical than Hume, both in regard to the noumenal world and in regard to the phenomenal." Explain; evaluate.
17. Why does Frame think that in Kant man is made to play the role of God? Evaluate Frame's argument and Kant's view.
18. Frame: Elimination of the noumenal leads back to rationalism. How?
19. Compare Hegel's rationalist slogan with those of Parmenides and Spinoza.
20. Describe Hegel's dialectic and his justification for this kind of reasoning. Evaluate.
21. Show how Hegel's dialectic analyzes *being*. What was the point of Hegel's thought-experiment? Evaluate.
22. "The progress of the dialectic is nothing less than God's coming to self-consciousness." Explain; evaluate. In what sense is this process a divine self-alienation?
23. "So Hegel's philosophy is a dialectical idealistic pantheism." Explain; evaluate.
24. "In general, Hegel anticipates Marx as he presents history as deterministic class struggle." How? Discuss.
25. "It is thus that for Hegel any fact, any thing, becomes a perspective on all reality." Explain; evaluate.
26. "The truth is in the whole." Explain; evaluate. Does this view justify any criticisms of Hegel?
27. Discuss the criticisms that Hegel is an extreme realist, that he is too abstract, and that he is both rationalist and irrationalist.
28. How does Schopenhauer differ from Kant? From Hegel?
29. Describe the influence of Schopenhauer on his nineteenth-century successors.

30. What does it mean to say that in Feuerbach "theology becomes anthropology"? Why did Barth say that liberal theology could not escape "the smile on Feuerbach's face"?
31. Reply to a Christian who begins to worry that his faith might be only a wish-projection.
32. Frame: "But Feuerbach's contention is a *genetic fallacy*." Explain; evaluate.
33. Describe the relation of Marx to Hegel.
34. Describe Marx's employment of ethical categories.
35. Outline Marx's analysis of economic history. Do you find it persuasive? Evaluate.
36. What if someone objects to Marx that religions and other social services are able to meet the needs of the poor without violent revolution? Describe Marx's reply, and evaluate.
37. In what ways did Marx fail to accurately predict the future, according to Frame? Evaluate.
38. Discuss some of the atrocities justified by Marx's doctrine. Should these be blamed on Marx? To what extent?

BIBLIOGRAPHY: KANT AND HIS SUCCESSORS

Print

Feuerbach, Ludwig. *The Essence of Christianity*. Seattle: CreateSpace, 2013.

Gay, Peter. *The Enlightenment: The Rise of Modern Paganism*. New York: W. W. Norton, 1995.

Guyer, Paul. *The Cambridge Companion to Kant's Critique of Pure Reason*. Cambridge: Cambridge University Press, 2010.

Hegel, G. W. F. *Early Theological Writings*. Translated by T. M. Knox and Richard Kroner. Philadelphia: University of Pennsylvania Press, 1971.

———. *The Phenomenology of Spirit*. Translated by A. V. Miller. New York: Oxford University Press, 1976.

Kant, Immanuel. *Critique of Pure Reason*. Edited and translated by Paul Guyer and Allen W. Wood. Cambridge: Cambridge University Press, 1999.

———. *Prolegomena to Any Future Metaphysics*. Translated by James W. Ellington. 2nd ed. Indianapolis: Hackett Publishing, 2002.

———. *Religion within the Boundaries of Mere Reason: And Other Writings*. Edited by Allen Wood and George di Giovani. Cambridge Texts in the History of Philosophy. Cambridge: Cambridge University Press, 1999.

Kaufmann, Walter. *Hegel: A Reinterpretation*. Notre Dame, IN: University of Notre Dame Press, 1988.

———. *Hegel: Texts and Commentary*. Notre Dame, IN: University of Notre Dame Press, 1989.

Marx, Karl. *Karl Marx: Selected Writings*. Edited by David McLellan. 2nd ed. Oxford: Oxford University Press, 2000.

Marx, Karl, with Friedrich Engels. *The Communist Manifesto*. Seattle: CreateSpace, 2013.

Schopenhauer, Arthur. *The World as Will and Representation*. Translated by E. F. J. Payne. 2 vols. Mineola, NY: Dover, 1966.

Online

Feuerbach, Ludwig. Ludwig Feuerbach Archive. His works and significant essays about him are available at http://www.marxists.org/reference/archive/feuerbach/.

Hegel, G. W. F. His main works are available at http://www.hegel.net/en/etexts.htm and http://www.hegel.org/links.html#texts.

Kant, Immanuel. Kant on the Web. English translations of many of Kant's works are available at http://staffweb.hkbu.edu.hk/ppp/K2texts.html; http://ebooks.adelaide.edu.au/k/kant/immanuel/.

Marx, Karl. Marx/Engels Library. Marx's writings are available at http://www.marxists.org/archive/marx/works/.

Schopenhauer, Arthur. Many of his works are available at http://ebooks.adelaide.edu.au/s/schopenhauer/arthur/.

READ FOR YOURSELF

Kant's *Critique of Pure Reason* is very difficult, but it is the main statement of his philosophy. His other two critiques, of *Practical Reason* and *Judgment*, extend his thought to ethical and aesthetic matters. His *Prolegomena to Any Future Metaphysics* is a shorter, less formal exposition of the ideas of the first critique, but some readers think you have to understand the first critique before you can understand the *Prolegomena*.

Kant's *Religion within the Limits of Reason Alone* is his theology, and it is absolutely crucial to understanding his impact on the liberal religious movement.

Hegel's *Early Theological Writings* indicate his early commitment to a liberal understanding of the Bible. His philosophical system runs through many volumes, but probably *The Phenomenology of Spirit* is the best place to get the main thrust of it. Kaufmann's commentary on it is helpful. Hegel's *Lectures on the Philosophy of Religion*, transcribed from student notes, is of some interest to Christians, if only to show how far Hegel wandered from Christian orthodoxy.

Schopenhauer is a significant bridge between Kant and Nietzsche. Feuerbach was a major influence on Marx, and those who, like Marx and Freud, criticize Christianity as a wish-fulfillment often refer to him.

In Marx himself, read the *Communist Manifesto*; then look at *Capital*. *Capital* is in three volumes, but the first gives the main thrust of his teaching.

LISTEN ONLINE

Link: http://itunes.apple.com/us/course/legacy-history-philosophy/id694658914

- Immanuel Kant: Transcendental Method, Phenomena, Noumena, and Critique: 1:07:39
- Immanuel Kant Continued and Idealism: 57:39
- Karl Marx: 17:57

FAMOUS QUOTES

- **Kant:** http://en.wikiquote.org/wiki/Immanuel_Kant
- **Hegel:** http://en.wikiquote.org/wiki/Georg_Wilhelm_Friedrich_Hegel
- **Schopenhauer:** http://en.wikiquote.org/wiki/Arthur_Schopenhauer
- **Feuerbach:** http://en.wikiquote.org/wiki/Ludwig_Andreas_Feuerbach
- **Marx:** http://en.wikiquote.org/wiki/Karl_Marx

8

NINETEENTH-CENTURY THEOLOGY

AS I INDICATED in chapter 6, liberal theology first appeared at the beginning of the Enlightenment, when some theologians decided to follow the example of rationalist philosophers. Thinkers such as the deists and Lessing treated the Bible as a purely human book, denying its divine inspiration. The deists developed a worldview that excluded the supernatural; and Lessing, though he personally believed in miracles, denied that there was any historical foundation for the Christian faith.

In chapter 7, I said that Kant followed a similar course. Like the deists, he rejected the idea of special revelation, insisting that any claim to revelation must be tested by autonomous reason. Unlike the deists, he also rejected general revelation: the traditional proofs for God's existence, he said, ventured beyond the proper limits of reason. What basis remains, then, for religion? Kant thought that reason dictated our moral duties, and that religion could function well as an incentive to moral living. We should act "as if" God exists.

Feuerbach and Marx dismissed religion entirely as an illusion devised by man himself. But others thought that even in this intellectual climate there was still an important place for religion, even for theology.

Hegel also found religion useful, but only within the limits of a worldview provided by Hegelian reason. For him, religion provided symbols of his philosophical dialectic.

Feuerbach and Marx dismissed religion entirely as an illusion devised by man himself. But others thought that even in this intellectual climate there was still an important place for religion, even for theology. In this chapter, I will consider the development of this theology. In the twentieth century it would be called the *older liberalism*. This is the theology criticized in J. Gresham Machen's great book *Christianity and Liberalism*.[1] Later, this theology would be presented

1. Grand Rapids: Eerdmans, 1923.

as something antiquated, even though theologians such as Barth and Bultmann maintained many of the same ideas using different terminology. In my judgment, the newer vocabulary did nothing to overcome Machen's basic analysis and critique. But that is a subject for later chapters.

I will also consider, later in this chapter, the thought of Søren Kierkegaard. Kierkegaard may not fairly be described as part of the older liberalism, but rather pointed forward to developments of a different sort in the twentieth century. Barth, Bultmann, and other "neoorthodox" theologians appropriated some of Kierkegaard's ideas, as we will see in chapter 10.

FRIEDRICH D. E. SCHLEIERMACHER (1768–1834)

Friedrich D. E. Schleiermacher

Schleiermacher is often called the *father of modern theology*. Of course, that means "father of modern liberal theology." As we have seen, he was not the first liberal theologian, as I define *liberal*. But his book *The Christian Faith* is more like a classical systematic theology than any other book from a liberal theologian up to this time. The deists had discussed many theological issues, and Kant's *Religion* actually attempts to cover most of the traditional theological topics. But Schleiermacher's book is much longer and much more detailed in its treatment of the theological *loci*. In that sense, it is an example of the *conservative drift* that I mentioned in chapter 6. His book contains extensive discussions of the attributes of God, the three offices of Christ, his person and work, his role as the second Adam, his sinlessness, human sin and grace, justification by faith, repentance, election, the church, the sacraments, and the Trinity. But it is very different from the works of the seventeenth-century Protestant scholasticism that it formally resembles.

Schleiermacher is often called the father of modern theology. *Of course, that means "father of modern liberal theology."*

Schleiermacher was the son of a Reformed minister, but like Kant, his early religious influences were among pietists.[2] He had a very broad range of interests other than theology, including psychology, philosophical dialectics, philosophy of mind, philosophy of language, aesthetics, ethics, and political and social philosophy. He was one of the first to comment systematically on hermeneutics as a science of interpretation.

2. Schleiermacher's pietistic background might partly explain his later subjectivism. But lest anyone employ the connections between pietism and liberalism in Kant and Schleiermacher to condemn the whole pietist movement, I point out that liberalism also came to infest the movement that competed with pietism: academic Protestant scholasticism. In the latter movement, one may compare, for example, the orthodox Francis Turretin with his more liberal son, J. A. Turretin. And we should note the wider context, that liberalism eventually came to pervade all traditions and branches of the Christian church. I discussed pietism and academic Protestant scholasticism briefly in chapter 5.

When he moved to Berlin in 1796, he became friends with Friedrich and August W. Schlegel, along with other literary figures of the romantic movement. His major book *Speeches on Religion to Its Cultured Despisers* (1799) was aimed to dispel the objections offered against religion within this society. Like other apologetic works since the church fathers, *On Religion* was so intent on finding common ground with the despisers of Christianity that it compromised biblical teachings. In this book, Schleiermacher begins to develop his theory that the essence of religion is a "feeling of absolute dependence" rather than any particular doctrinal convictions. Even the existence of God and immortality are not essential to the religion of this book.

Still, Schleiermacher is not happy with previous forms of liberalism. His settled view, in *The Christian Faith* (1821–22, revised 1830–31), comes out sounding more conservative than the formulations of the deists, Lessing, Kant, and Hegel. Schleiermacher does not believe that religion should be derived from natural theology or philosophical reasoning (as with the deists and Hegel). Nor does he agree with Lessing and Kant that religion can be reduced to morality. Rather, he is convinced that there is something distinctive about religion. He is concerned to uphold its uniqueness. That uniqueness is the feeling of absolute dependence, the *Gefühl des schlechtinnigen Abhängigkeit*.

Schleiermacher does not believe that religion should be derived from natural theology or philosophical reasoning . . . . Rather, he is convinced that there is something distinctive about religion. He is concerned to uphold its uniqueness. That uniqueness is the feeling of absolute dependence.

Gefühl is usually translated "feeling," but Schleiermacher also refers to this feeling by the term *intuition*. He also speaks of it using such terms as *religious consciousness*. He understands it to be a sense of the unity (ultimately God) that underlies all the diversities of experience. Like his contemporary Hegel, he believes that all diversities in experience are diversities within unity, and that seeking that unity is the most important task of human thought. This feeling is experienced in culture, art, poetry, and all thought. But religion is the discipline that explores it most directly.

In 1817 there took place a union in Prussia of Lutheran and Reformed churches under Friedrich Wilhelm III. Schleiermacher saw that as an opportunity to develop Protestant theology in a new direction, moving beyond the old antitheses to a synthesis. The synthesis comes by examining the feeling that lies behind the dogmas. All religions seek to articulate the religious feeling in their own ways. None of these are false, but they are more or less incomplete. Schleiermacher thought, however, that Christianity did it best. It is "the religion in which the sense of dependence is defined by faith in Jesus Christ as savior."[3] In

3. Friedrich Schleiermacher, *The Christian Faith*, trans. H. R. Mackintosh and J. S. Stewart (Edinburgh: T&T Clark, 1928), 52.

Christianity, "everything is related to the redemption accomplished by Jesus of Nazareth."[4]

So for Schleiermacher, "Christian doctrines are accounts of the Christian religious affections set forth in speech."[5] Notice that the immediate source of theology is not the Scriptures or doctrines or church traditions, but religious feelings. Scripture is important in that it records the original "impression"[6] that Jesus made on his disciples, the original feelings they had about him, set forth in speech. But Scripture is not the foundation of faith; rather, faith is the foundation of Scripture.[7] Scripture records[8] the faith of the first disciples of Jesus and therefore communicates that faith, that religious feeling, to us. So when we run into a contradiction between Reformed and Lutheran views, or Catholic and Protestant, or orthodox and Enlightenment, we should deal with the contradiction by appealing to the feeling that all these groups share. Whereas doctrines divide, feelings unite. Revelation, Schleiermacher says, does not operate on man primarily as a cognitive being, "for that would make the revelation to be originally and essentially *doctrine*."[9]

For Schleiermacher, "Christian doctrines are accounts of the Christian religious affections set forth in speech." Notice that the immediate source of theology is not the Scriptures or doctrines or church traditions, but religious feelings.

This principle is common to liberal theologians: that divine revelation cannot take the form of *propositions, information*, or *doctrine*. Doctrines are created by human beings out of reflection on their religious feelings. Liberal theologians have characterized revelation in various ways: for Cherbury, it was nature and natural reason; for Lessing and Kant, ethical reason. Later we will discuss other ways of understanding revelation within the liberal tradition. But all liberal theologians agree that revelation cannot be *propositional* or *doctrinal*. Why? Because that would mean that in revelation God tells us what to believe and what to do, and that would contradict the most fundamental principle of liberal epistemology, that human autonomous thought has the final word.

This principle is common to liberal theologians: that divine revelation cannot take the form of propositions, information, *or* doctrine. *Doctrines are created by human beings out of reflection on their religious feelings.*

Like other liberal theologians, Schleiermacher uses various arguments to show that revelation *cannot* be propositional, such as: (1) God is beyond all concepts, though he is presupposed by them.[10] (2) Revelation is never given "in the abstract" (and therefore objectively), but is

4. Ibid. Schleiermacher often stresses what we would call today the Christocentric nature of theology.

5. Ibid., 76.

6. Ibid., 125.

7. Ibid., 591–97.

8. For Schleiermacher, Scripture is fallible, not inerrant. But it is our primary source to access the original faith of the disciples.

9. Schleiermacher, *Christian Faith*, 50 (emphasis his).

10. If "beyond all concepts" means that God cannot be truly represented by conceptual thoughts and language, then this position is patently unscriptural.

always "for us."[11] (3) Revelation may never be "directly given," for it is always subject to counterinfluence by the recipient. The hearer always affects what he hears to some degree.[12] (4) Revelation may never be external. Only what I accept inwardly can be revelation to me.[13]

This is the earliest historical example I know of what I call the *subjective turn* in the doctrine of revelation. In liberal theology, beginning with Schleiermacher, revelation is an inward illumination, rather than an external or objective display of God's Word. In the Bible, the term *revelation* (with other forms of *reveal*) is used of God's communication with human beings both objectively and subjectively. The revelation of God's wrath in Romans 1:18 is an objective communication of God's judgment. Some people accept it; others "suppress" it. Its character as revelation does not depend on the subjective response of its recipients. But in Matthew 11:27 and Ephesians 1:17, the concept of *revelation* refers to inward illumination, communication that inevitably produces a godly subjective response. Liberal theologians, however, tend to neglect or deny revelation in the objective sense and accept the concept only in the subjective sense. Schleiermacher makes this move in statement (4) above. This implies that those who have not "accepted inwardly" what God says have not received revelation at all and therefore cannot be held responsible for their rejection of it.

This is the earliest historical example I know of what I call the subjective turn *in the doctrine of revelation. In liberal theology, beginning with Schleiermacher, revelation is an inward illumination, rather than an external or objective display of God's Word.*

Schleiermacher does believe that the Scriptures, confessions, and creeds of the church are important to theology:

> All propositions which claim to place in an epitome of Evangelical doctrines must approve themselves both by appeal to Evangelical confessional documents, or, in default of these, to the New Testament Scriptures, and by exhibition of their homogeneity with other propositions already recognized.[14]

But of course, on Schleiermacher's view, none of these documents can be called *revelation*.

If there is no propositional revelation, then the content of theology must be derived from Christian religious feeling. This view of theology

11. Reply: (a) All language is abstract in some degree. (b) If revelation is not objectively true, it is unclear how it could benefit us.

12. This argument concerns communication between human beings, not only between God and man. If it invalidates the latter, it invalidates the former as well, so that no communication is possible.

13. It is interesting to see what Schleiermacher said about revelation in his earlier, more radical book *On Religion*: "What is revelation? Every original and new communication of the Universe to man is a revelation. . . . What is inspiration? It is simply the general expression for the feeling of true morality and freedom." Friedrich Schleiermacher, *On Religion: Speeches to Its Cultured Despisers*, trans. John Oman (New York: Harper and Brothers, 1958), 89.

14. Schleiermacher, *Christian Faith*, 112.

is highly problematic. Though it is often hard to do, we can understand what it would mean to derive theological propositions by means of deduction or application from verbal documents. But for Schleiermacher, the propositions of theology must be derived from nonpropositions, from feelings. Since people feel differently about different things, it is difficult to imagine how any level of theological agreement could be reached on this basis, or how anyone could even argue one theological position against another. And as a matter of fact, Schleiermacher, in *The Christian Faith*, rarely argues from feelings as such. Like most other theologians, he exegetes the Scriptures and the documents of the church. But he often skews his discussion in the direction of what feels best to him. I cannot recognize this as a cogent theological method.

Schleiermacher's doctrine of God is, first of all, the "co-determinant" of the "feeling of absolute dependence." That is, God is the name of whatever it is we feel absolutely dependent on.

But, however he arrives at it, we should consider the specific theological content of Schleiermacher's system. When he seeks to express his religious affections in speech, it comes out something like this. His doctrine of God is, first of all, the "co-determinant" of the "feeling of absolute dependence." That is, *God* is the name of whatever it is we feel absolutely dependent on. In his earlier book *Religion*, some of his descriptions of God are criticized as pantheistic or panentheistic.[15] Schleiermacher also hesitates to clearly affirm God's personality.

The attributes of God are expressions of our relationships to him, for everything we know about God is "for us." (But that raises the question of how God transcends our existence and has a life independent of the world.) The doctrine of the Trinity, for Schleiermacher, derives from the doctrines of providence and salvation. He describes it at the end of *The Christian Faith*[16] as the "coping stone of Christian doctrine." For him, the main point of the Trinity is that it is the same God who works in providence (the Father), in redemption (Christ), and in the Spirit who is in the church.

Schleiermacher calls the traditional doctrine of original sin "external" and "legalist." He . . . defines sin *differently: it is "sensuous consciousness."*

For Schleiermacher, the image of God in man is the religious feeling, our inalienable God-consciousness. Sin is not the violation of a particular command in history. Schleiermacher calls the traditional doctrine of original sin "external" and "legalist." He thinks (feels?) it arbitrary that man's eternal life or destruction could be made contingent on one decision of one man at one moment of time. So he defines *sin* differently: it is "sensuous consciousness." That is the opposite of

15. *Pantheism* = God is everything and everything is God. *Panentheism* = God is *in* everything, and everything is *in* God. For the panentheist, the universe is divine, but God is more than just the universe.

16. Some people criticize Schleiermacher for considering the Trinity at the end of his book rather than at the beginning. I myself do not think Scripture gives us a normative order in which to consider the topics of systematic theology. (Full disclosure: I discuss the doctrine of the Trinity at the end of my own *DG*.) But to the extent that Schleiermacher neglects the Trinitarian character of the other doctrines of the faith, that criticism could be illuminating.

the feeling of absolute dependence: a preoccupation with the world rather than God.

Sensuous consciousness is part of the nature of man.[17] So it is universal and unavoidable. Man's biological and intellectual development progresses more rapidly than his spiritual and moral development. The discrepancy between these is sin. But sin can be understood only as a privation[18] of good, so our basic goodness (God-consciousness) continues, despite sin.

Schleiermacher values Jesus especially because Jesus had religious feeling in unique measure. As for the Bible's teachings about Jesus' crucifixion, resurrection, ascension, and return, Schleiermacher says that he believes them. But for him they are important for the doctrine of Scripture, not for our understanding of the person of Christ. Scripture teaches these occurrences, and we should confess that Scripture does, in fact, teach them. But one can believe in Christ (i.e., one can share his religious feeling) without believing in these historical claims. Schleiermacher maintains that redemption does not come through such "accidental" historical events (so he affirms the "ugly, broad ditch" that Lessing said he could not cross). The traditional Christian belief in these events implies, for Schleiermacher, that we are saved by something "external" to us. For Schleiermacher, that is inadequate: we are saved only by an enhancement of religious feeling, something *within* us. The traditional theories, therefore, are "artificial."

Then how does Christ save us from sensuous consciousness? We recall that in Kant's *Religion*, Christ was a moral archetype, which we seek to emulate. Schleiermacher's view is similar, but for him Christ is the archetype specifically of God-consciousness, of religious feeling.

The traditional Christian belief in these events implies, for Schleiermacher, that we are saved by something "external" to us. For Schleiermacher, that is inadequate: we are saved only by an enhancement of religious feeling, something within *us.*

Now, to say that Christ is true man is to say that he embodies possibilities inherent in human nature. Christ shows us the God-consciousness that already exists in us. He shows us that we are like him, and that we can become more like him. So the person of Christ is not something different from our own persons. It is "for us."

But sensuous consciousness is also part of human nature. How can we confess the sinlessness of Christ without diminishing the union between him and ourselves? Schleiermacher does not claim to have historical evidence of Jesus' sinlessness. But he confesses it as a consequence of Jesus' God-consciousness. There is no sin in essential God-

17. This would seem to imply that man cannot be redeemed without becoming something other than human. On the other hand, if sin came in "through one man [Adam]" (Rom. 5:12; cf. vv. 16–19) (which Schleiermacher denies), then our sin is not necessary to our humanity, and it is possible for man to be redeemed through one man (Christ) in a historical event, without becoming other than human.

18. For the concept of evil as a privation, review the discussion of Augustine in chapter 3, and my critique of the privation concept.

consciousness. And our feeling about Jesus is that he possesses that God-consciousness without any defect. Schleiermacher believed that eventually we, too, will know this perfect God-consciousness. So even in his sinlessness, Jesus is one with us. Specifically, he anticipates our future state.

This concept of salvation renders unnecessary what Schleiermacher considers the "artificial theory" that we obtain forgiveness through the suffering of another. That view of the atonement he dismisses as "external" and "artificial." Again, Lessing's ditch forbids us to seek salvation on the basis of a historical occurrence.

This concept of salvation renders unnecessary what Schleiermacher considers the "artificial theory" that we obtain forgiveness through the suffering of another. That view of the atonement he dismisses as "external" and "artificial."

So liberal theology, following Lessing, denies any doctrinal significance to the events of history. For Schleiermacher, redemption takes place in the present: in our inner subjectivity, our feelings. But he also tries to do justice, within his framework, to the biblical idea of *redemption* as a cosmic process, for example, in Colossians 1:15–20. He says that God's election in Christ is a decree that ordains the development of religious consciousness from potential to actual. Creation itself begins the fulfillment of this decree in time. So grace ordains the development of human potential. Man is free to accept or reject that advancement, but the purpose of God's redemptive decree will certainly be fulfilled. Ultimately, Schleiermacher's vision is universalistic. Eventually, everyone will enjoy the fulfillment of religious consciousness.

That fulfillment coincides with the consummation of man's cultural aspirations. We can trace its progress as human beings achieve unity of various sorts: between rich and poor, spirit and flesh, ideal and real, reason and nature, individual and universal, production and appropriation. So the actualization of religious consciousness is the same as the fulfillment of love.[19]

Grace ordains the development of human potential. Man is free to accept or reject that advancement, but the purpose of God's redemptive decree will certainly be fulfilled. Ultimately, Schleiermacher's vision is universalistic.

To summarize, Schleiermacher exemplifies many themes and principles in the liberal theological tradition; indeed, many of them originate in his work.

1. *The Principle of Rational Autonomy*: Schleiermacher's work does not contain the adulation of reason characteristic of Kant and

19. Schleiermacher's ethics introduce another common theme of liberal theology: that love and law are opposed. Law, he says, does not "pierce behind the outward act." So it cannot deal with inner motives. Therefore, in his view, the two great commandments, the commandments of love in Matthew 22:36–40, are not laws at all! I take the argument in the other direction: since love is obviously a law, a commandment, that proves that law does in fact pierce behind the outward act. That was Jesus' position in his exposition of the law in the Sermon on the Mount. Schleiermacher's argument, however, is taken for granted in many liberal treatments of religious ethics, as Emil Brunner, *The Divine Imperative* (Louisville, KY: Westminster John Knox Press, 1979), and Joseph Fletcher, *Situation Ethics: The New Morality* (Louisville, KY: Westminster John Knox Press, 1966).

Hegel. He prefers to speak of autonomous feeling rather than of autonomous reasoning. But in the end, there is not much difference between these.[20] And of course, Schleiermacher's writings are not mere expressions of feeling. They are rational analyses of feeling. And because of Schleiermacher's understanding of revelation, these analyses are immune to the authority of divine revelation.

2. *Nonpropositional Revelation*: Schleiermacher finds revelation in the broad course of history and in our private subjectivity, but not in any form that would threaten our autonomous rationality.
3. *Nonbiblical Transcendence and Immanence*: For Schleiermacher, God is so far beyond us that he cannot be described in concepts. But he can be found in our inner feelings, and the person of Christ is essentially an archetype of religious feeling. Everything he is is "for us"; see fig. 8.1.

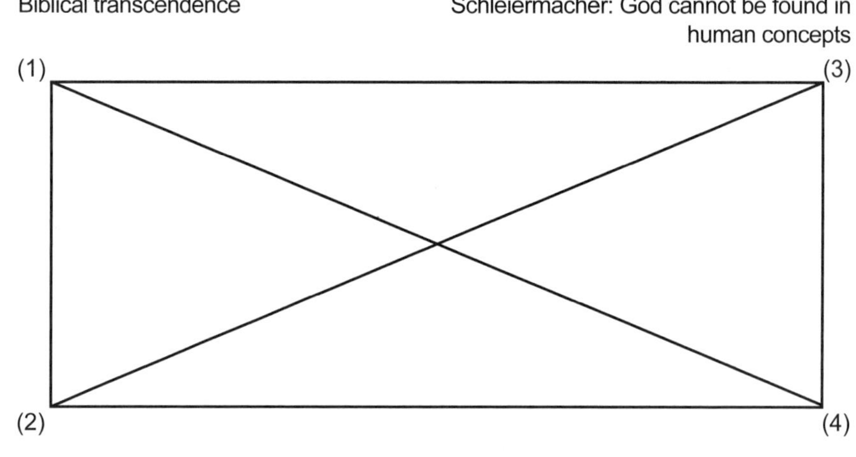

Fig. 8.1. Schleiermacher's Transcendence and Immanence

To escape Lessing's "ugly, broad ditch," Schleiermacher describes redemption not as an accomplishment of divine acts in history, but as (a) a universal process through which all people are raised to their highest potential of religious consciousness, and (b) a subjective, individual process wherein that religious consciousness progresses to perfection in each individual.

4. *Nonhistorical Redemption*: To escape Lessing's "ugly, broad ditch," Schleiermacher describes redemption not as an accomplishment of divine acts in history, but as (a) a universal process through which all people are raised to their highest potential of religious consciousness, and (b) a subjective, individual process wherein that religious consciousness progresses to perfection in

20. For my account of the relation between reason and emotion, see *DKG*, 335–40, and *DCL*, 370–82.

each individual. So the history of redemption becomes a mere metaphor for the development of man's religious sensibility. And the grace of God becomes synonymous with man's best efforts.

5. *Conservative Drift*: Schleiermacher shows a remarkably detailed knowledge of the content of traditional theology, and he takes every concept, distinction, and argument very seriously. To a superficial reader, his theology (compared with Hegel, Kant, and Cherbury) seems like a return to orthodox Protestantism, formulated with a much higher level of philosophical and biblical sophistication. But in fact, there is no gospel here. Schleiermacher's message is that our problem is not sin in the traditional sense, but our preoccupation with earthly matters. We have the power in ourselves to seek better objects of concentration, and in time we will.

What Ritschl finds in his quest is not the supernatural being of the ancient creeds. Ritschl dismisses the traditional doctrines about Jesus—his virgin birth, his two natures, his deity and eternity—as impositions of Greek philosophical speculation.

ALBRECHT RITSCHL (1822–89)

Ritschl, who taught at the University of Bonn, then Göttingen, was influenced early by Hegelian teachers, particularly Ferdinand Christian Baur,[21] but by 1850 he was working against Hegelian influence in theology. More prominent then in his thought was the influence of Kant, whose critiques of reason emboldened Ritschl to reject attempts to reduce Christian faith to a philosophical system.

To Ritschl, "all theological propositions have for their aim the explanation of the phenomena of the Christian life."[22] Although Ritschl appreciates the work of Schleiermacher, he does not interpret *Christian life* primarily as inner feeling. For Ritschl, theology has two foci: the historical Jesus and the present-day life of the believer.

Albrecht Ritschl

Like many other theologians and Bible scholars of his time, he seeks the historical Jesus by the means of historical scholarship—scholarship that is *autonomous* in the sense in which I have been using the term. What he finds in his quest is not the supernatural being of the ancient creeds. Ritschl dismisses the traditional doctrines about Jesus—his virgin birth, his two natures, his deity and eternity—as impositions of Greek philosophical speculation.

For Ritschl, however, Jesus is indeed divine, in the sense that he is fully and truly human. He exemplifies every quality that we ascribe to ideal humanity. This conclusion is not based on logical proof, or even on conclusive historical study. It is, rather, a *value judgment* that

21. Baur developed a Hegelian triad in which Peter was the thesis, Paul the antithesis, and Luke the synthesis.

22. Albrecht Ritschl, *The Christian Doctrine of Justification and Reconciliation*, ed. and trans. H. R. Mackintosh and A. B. Macaulay (Edinburgh: T&T Clark, 1900), 49.

we make as we examine the life of Jesus. In that study, we discover a Jesus who helps us to become more truly human. So Jesus' righteousness is not an attribute of a divine nature. For truly human righteousness requires an effort to maintain it from moment to moment. Like Schleiermacher, Ritschl rejects the Protestant orthodox teaching that Jesus' righteousness is imputed to us. In fact, Ritschl considers that teaching a symptom of a "legal world order." Rather, Jesus' righteousness is purely human, and therefore we are able to imitate it.

In place of the legal world order, Ritschl promotes a concept of the kingdom of God based on the fatherhood of God and all mankind as God's family. *Redemption, justification, regeneration, adoption, forgiveness,* and *reconciliation* are all essentially synonyms,[23] referring to God's action in restoring the broken family relationship. He does it through Jesus, who maintains that family relationship to the end, faithful always to his Father. The kingdom for Ritschl, then, is the common moral end of God and man, a union of men for mutual, common action, for the motive of love. It is not limited to the end of this age, but is found in the present world, and Christian believers are called to expand the divine family and its influence. People have commonly summarized Ritschlian liberalism as "the fatherhood of God and the brotherhood of man." That phrase at least states accurately Ritschl's view of the kingdom's goal.

In place of the legal world order, Ritschl promotes a concept of the kingdom of God based on the fatherhood of God and all mankind as God's family.

Rightly understood, therefore, Jesus' deity is an ethical value judgment. Jesus receives the divine title because he has been supremely faithful to the task given him by God. Thus, his saving work is more valuable to us, Ritschl thinks, than in traditional Protestant orthodoxy. For on Ritschl's basis, we are capable of doing the same thing that Jesus does, and therefore of sharing Jesus' divine nature.

Ritschl's theology is an example of the conservative drift. Its emphasis on history, indeed the historical Jesus, seems more orthodox than Kant's moralism, Hegel's speculation, or Schleiermacher's subjectivism. Ritschl's emphasis on the practical Christian life, on following Jesus, would seem to restore some of the vitality of evangelical religion. But what Ritschl has actually done has been to present a theology devoid of the supernatural, a purely human Jesus, and a gospel of works-righteousness, based on a merely human Scripture.

23. It is interesting that liberal theology tends to equate such concepts. The reason is that since its adherents regard God as beyond all human discourse (nonbiblical transcendence), they cannot distinguish one of his acts from another. Also, they reject propositional revelation, so that on their basis God cannot explain to us the difference between these aspects of salvation.

WILHELM HERRMANN (1846–1922)

Herrmann is a member of the "Ritschlian school" and would probably not have disagreed much with the points of Ritschl's theology mentioned above. But his emphasis is significantly different. He stresses even more than Ritschl the personalistic nature of the Christian message and the possibility of a present-day relationship between the believer and God.

He was a teacher of both Barth and Bultmann. We will see that both reacted against him in various ways, but his positive influence on both is quite discernible, even in the development of their distinctive views. His personalism contributes importantly to the *personal-encounter* theology of Brunner, to the existentialist theology of Bultmann, and to other twentieth-century movements. Apparently his influence came not only through his ideas, but also through his manner of teaching and life. J. Gresham Machen, who would later be a strong critic of Ritschlianism, studied with Herrmann in his earlier years, and it is remarkable to consider his reaction to Herrmann as a person. He wrote to his mother:

Wilhelm Herrmann

> The first time that I heard Herrmann may almost be described as an epoch in my life. Such an overpowering personality I think I almost never before encountered—overpowering in the sincerity of religious devotion.
>
> My chief feeling with reference to him is already one of the deepest reverence. . . . I have been thrown all into confusion by what he says—so much deeper is his devotion to Christ than anything I have known in myself during the past few years. . . . Herrmann affirms very little of that which I have been accustomed to regard as essential to Christianity; yet there is no doubt in my mind but that he is a Christian, and a Christian of a peculiarly earnest type. He is a Christian not because he follows Christ as a moral teacher; but because his trust in Christ is (practically, if anything even more truly than theoretically) unbounded.
>
> Herrmann represents the dominant Ritschlian school. . . . Herrmann has shown me something of the *religious* power which lies back of this great movement, which is now making a fight even for the control of the Northern Presbyterian Church in America. In New England those who do not believe in the bodily Resurrection of Jesus are, generally speaking, religiously dead; in Germany, Herrmann has taught me that is by no means the case. He believes that Jesus is the one thing in all the world that inspires *absolute* confidence, and an *absolute*, joyful subjection; that through Jesus we come into communion with

Herrmann stresses even more than Ritschl the personalistic nature of the Christian message and the possibility of a present-day relationship between the believer and God.

> the living God and are made free from the world. It is the faith that is a real experience, a real revelation of God that saves us, not the faith that consists in accepting as true a lot of dogmas on the basis merely of what others have said. . . . *Das Verkehr des Christen mit Gott* is one of the greatest religious books I ever read. Perhaps Herrmann does not give the whole truth—I certainly hope he does not—at any rate he has gotten hold of something that has been sadly neglected in the church and in the orthodox theology. Perhaps he is something like the devout mystics of the middle ages—they were one-sided enough, but they raised a mighty protest against the coldness and deadness of the church and were forerunners of the Reformation.[24]

Later, Machen went to teach at Princeton Theological Seminary, at the time a very non-Ritschlian school, and he wrote *Christianity and Liberalism*, which I earlier mentioned as a powerful critique of liberalism especially in its Ritschlian form. But Machen's critique of liberalism was all the stronger because he understood the movement so well, particularly because he had felt its spiritual power.

Herrmann's view of revelation follows the *subjective turn* that I earlier ascribed to Schleiermacher, with which Ritschl concurred:

> According to the traditionalist view revelation is a tradition which communicates to us the forms in which the faith of religious men once expressed itself. That this definition is not satisfactory follows from the fact that we can give the name of revelation only to that which is the foundation of our own faith. The way in which others have expressed their faith cannot possibly provide a foundation for our own faith.[25]

On this view, I cannot acknowledge anything as revelation unless it is revelation to me, that is, unless I appropriate it in faith. There is no such thing as objective revelation—revelation that I am obligated to accept whether I actually do or not.

On this view, I cannot acknowledge anything as revelation unless it is revelation to me, that is, unless I appropriate it in faith. There is no such thing as objective revelation—revelation that I am *obligated* to accept whether I actually do or not.[26] True faith, then, does not require intellectual assent to Scripture or doctrine. To make faith depend on such assent, furthermore, is to compromise our freedom, to make faith a matter of compulsion.[27]

24. Quoted in Ned Bernard Stonehouse, *J. Gresham Machen: A Biographical Memoir* (Edinburgh: Banner of Truth, 1987), 106–8.

25. Wilhelm Herrmann, *Systematic Theology* (New York: Macmillan, 1927), 39.

26. Recall that I earlier indicated that Scripture itself speaks of revelation in both objective and subjective senses. But Herrmann, like Schleiermacher and Ritschl, denies the possibility of objective revelation.

27. Herrmann, *Systematic Theology*, 91.

Herrmann senses a contradiction between God's omnipotence and his personality. Nevertheless, he says that full confidence in God requires both these ideas.[28] So our knowledge of God is paradoxical: "God remains hidden to us even when he is near us."[29]

Ritschlian theology seeks to maintain a balance between a historical foundation and the personal value judgment (to Herrmann, the present experience).[30] But as we saw in Ritschl, the latter tends to diminish the former. This is even more true of Herrmann. When he speaks of the resurrection of Christ, he says that we cannot tell what actually happened, and that this does not matter. Scripture records resurrection *appearances*, and we today have our own appearances to go on:

Ritschlian theology seeks to maintain a balance between a historical foundation and the personal value judgment (to Herrmann, the present experience). But as we saw in Ritschl, the latter tends to diminish the former.

> Our assurance that Jesus is alive and is not separated from us is not primarily based on a report of events such as these; for it is already implicit in the faith created and maintained in us by the power of Jesus, under whose influence we stand. For a firm faith it would, of course, be self-evident that Jesus cannot have perished in death and departed from us; but in our own case also we observe that which occurred with the first disciples.[31]

So according to Herrmann, our faith is not based on the study of history, but on our inner religious experience.[32] This is essentially the Kantian distinction between the phenomenal and the noumenal, between nature and freedom. Herrmann says in *The Communion of the Christian with God*:

According to Herrmann, our faith is not based on the study of history, but on our inner religious experience.

> The decision which we reach that these things are facts, proceeds from our own independent activity, and is based upon that which we regard as real in the present rather than on any decisions of historical criticism.[33]

He adds that our conviction that Jesus is "the present revelation of God to us" "has nothing to do with the judgment of the historian."[34]

Van Til expresses these conclusions about the Christ of Herrmann:

28. Ibid., 98. I don't understand why he thinks these are contradictory.

29. Ibid. Note the dialectic of transcendence and immanence that I have often referred to in this book.

30. Or, as in my discussion in chapter 1, between the situational and existential perspectives.

31. Herrmann, *Systematic Theology*, 129.

32. Here Herrmann veers toward Schleiermacher and away from Ritschl.

33. Wilhelm Herrmann, *The Communion of the Christian with God* (London: Williams and Norgate, 1906), 60.

34. Ibid.

> When [Herrmann's Christ] is historical he tends to disappear in the unknown past. To the extent that he is more than historical we have to reach him by perpendicular procedure, by a "religious concept" which passes over the historical in the way an airplane passes over the rough, mountainous terrain.[35]

Herrmann exemplifies the conservative drift of modern theology in his protest against mere formalism and academic objectivism. He is right in his attempt to integrate the truths of our historic faith with our present experience of God. In my understanding (chapter 1), Herrmann seeks to do justice to the situational (history) and existential (experience) perspectives. But he lacks any idea of a revealed *normative* perspective, which is needed if we are not to vacillate between subjectivism and objectivism, between supertranscendence and superimmanence; see fig. 8.2.

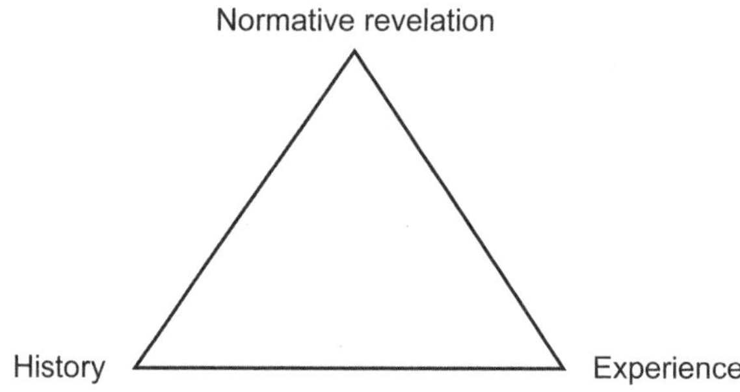

Fig. 8.2. Elements of Herrmann's View of Revelation

Herrmann exemplifies the conservative drift of modern theology in his protest against mere formalism and academic objectivism.

ADOLF VON HARNACK (1851–1930)

Harnack, the third of the most prominent Ritschlians, was known not primarily as a systematic theologian (as Ritschl and Herrmann), but as a NT scholar and a historian of doctrine. Like Ritschl, he rejected the metaphysics of the early church dogmas because he thought they were an imposition of Greek philosophy on Christianity.

Harnack attained great prominence as a public scholar, so there was great demand for his testimony. People asked what this great scholar's personal religious beliefs were. In the academic term 1899–1900, Harnack delivered his response to a large audience at the University of Berlin, the lectures later published as *Das Wesen Des Christentums*, and in English as *What Is Christianity?*[36]

35. Cornelius Van Til, *The Triumph of Grace: The Heidelberg Catechism* (Philadelphia: Westminster Theological Seminary, 1958), 69. I have followed Van Til's argument at a number of points in this chapter.

36. London: Williams and Norgate, 1901.

Harnack's view of the essence of Christianity requires him to do some critical sifting among the contents of the Bible, removing the *kernel* from the *husk*. He will have nothing to do with nature miracles, with angels and devils, or with apocalyptic expectations: "It is not a question of angels and devils, thrones and principalities, but of God and the soul, the soul and its God."[37] But the idea of miracle is of some value: it expresses the power of man to "escape from the power and service of transitory things."[38] That experience is found not only in religion, but everywhere in human life. But the greatness of Jesus is that he was "the first to bring the value of the human soul to light, and what he did no one can any more undo."[39]

Harnack's view of the essence of Christianity requires him to do some critical sifting among the contents of the Bible, removing the kernel *from the* husk. *He will have nothing to do with nature miracles, with angels and devils, or with apocalyptic expectations.*

Harnack summarizes Jesus' teaching under three heads:

> Firstly, the kingdom of God and its coming.
> Secondly, God the Father and the infinite value of the human soul.
> Thirdly, the higher righteousness and the commandment of love.[40]

Each of these, he says, is "of such a nature as to contain the whole, and hence it can be exhibited in its entirety under any one of them."[41] The first takes Jesus' eschatology in a "realized" sense, as Ritschl did: the development and dissemination of social justice and high culture through the world.

The second principle emphasizes Harnack's view that "the gospel, as Jesus proclaimed it, has to do with the Father only and not with the Son."[42] This assertion is singularly unpersuasive to most readers of the NT. Jesus there certainly seeks to draw attention to himself. But we must remember that Harnack feels free to reconstruct the NT according to his historical-critical understanding.

Adolf von Harnack

To Harnack, Jesus is not a supernatural being, only the first man to bring the gospel (seen in terms of the three points above) to light. Jesus dissociates the concept of messiahship from its external, legal Jewish associations, Harnack says, and teaches us to imitate his filial piety. This relation to the Father (not a bodily resurrection) is what survives death and gives us victory over death. It teaches us not to serve transient, external things, but to seek the higher righteousness, the kingdom of God.

37. Ibid., 55. The "God and the soul" language recalls that of Augustine; recall our discussion of that in chapter 3. Note also that of Calvin (chapter 5).

38. Ibid., 29.

39. Ibid., 73.

40. Ibid., 55.

41. Ibid. That is to say, in my terminology, that they are perspectivally related.

42. Ibid., 154.

The third principle encourages the social gospel as the work of the church, and as a measure of the church's faithfulness to its task.

But note how much is missing here: prophecy, incarnation, miracle, atonement, resurrection, ascension, session, return in glory. Everything supernatural is gone. So in Harnack, as in Ritschl and Herrmann, we see a theology without gospel. The teaching of Jesus, according to Harnack, is finally an admonition to be like him, seeking social justice, nothing more.

THE RISE AND FALL OF RITSCHLIANISM

During the late nineteenth and early twentieth centuries, Ritschlian liberalism attained some prominence in the European and American religious scene. It became much more than an academic theological movement, coming to dominate many theological seminaries, colleges, denominations, and congregations. This was an exciting time for religious liberals. They faced the new twentieth century with ambition and excitement. The liberal magazine *Christian Oracle* changed its name to *Christian Century* to express its belief that the new century would mark the success of the kingdom of God, measured in terms of the Ritschlian social gospel. To Ritschlians, a great era was beginning. Following Jesus, the world was on the verge of renouncing war and entering into the new family of the fatherhood of God and the brotherhood of man. The excitement of it shines through in liberal hymns such as James Russell Lowell's "Once to Every Man and Nation," William Merrill's "Rise Up, O Men of God," Harry Emerson Fosdick's "God of Grace and God of Glory," and Henry Van Dyke's "Joyful, Joyful, We Adore Thee."[43]

There was opposition to Ritschlianism, but initially the Ritschlians won most of the battles. Their opponents in America were called fundamentalists, *from the book series* The Fundamentals.

There was opposition to Ritschlianism, but initially the Ritschlians won most of the battles. Their opponents in America were called *fundamentalists*, from the book series *The Fundamentals*. The articles in these books were written by pastors and evangelists, but sometimes also by serious scholars such as B. B. Warfield, defending the supernatural doctrines of the Scriptures.[44] Eventually, however, the term *fundamentalist* came to be used as a derogatory name for those who believed and defended these doctrines. *Fundamentalist* eventually came to connote not only orthodox beliefs, but also anti-intellectualism. Thus was launched the *fundamentalist-modernist controversy*.

This Protestant debate parallels the *modernist controversy* in the Roman Catholic Church. Pope Pius X in 1907 condemned the modernist

43. These hymns are powerful exhortations to seek the kingdom of God. I do not object to their use in evangelical worship, but sometimes the words need to be changed a bit, such as the reference to "God's new Messiah" in "Once to Every Man and Nation."

44. These books are available in a single volume, *The Fundamentals*, ed. R. A. Torrey and Charles Feinberg (Grand Rapids: Kregel, 1990).

faction, stifling somewhat (but not extinguishing) the development of liberal theology in that communion until the Second Vatican Council in the 1960s.

In 1924, a document called the *Auburn Affirmation* circulated at the General Assembly of the Presbyterian Church in the United States of America. Several times earlier (in 1910, 1916, and 1923), the Assembly had listed five doctrines as the *fundamentals* of the Christian faith:

1. The inerrancy of Scripture.
2. The virgin birth and deity of Jesus.
3. The doctrine of substitutionary atonement.
4. The bodily resurrection of Jesus.
5. The authenticity of Christ's miracles.

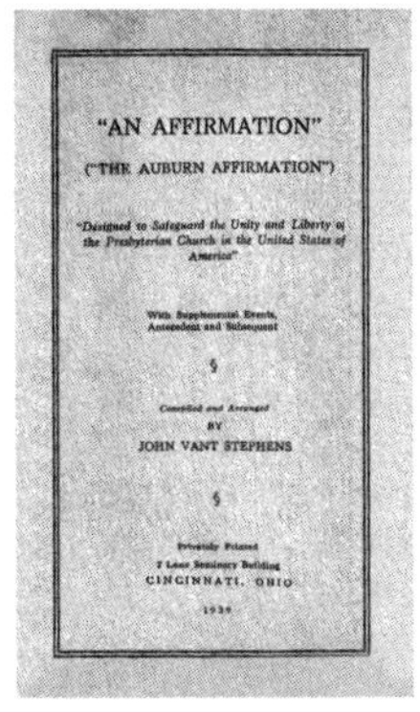

"AN AFFIRMATION"

("THE AUBURN AFFIRMATION")

"Designed to Safeguard the Unity and Liberty of the Presbyterian Church in the United States of America"

With Supplemental Events, Antecedent and Subsequent

§

Compiled and Arranged
BY
JOHN VANT STEPHENS

§

Privately Printed

CINCINNATI, OHIO

The Auburn Affirmation

But the *Affirmation* protested these past statements. Wikipedia summarizes:

> The *Affirmation* has six sections that can be summarized as:
> 1. The Bible is not inerrant. The supreme guide of scripture interpretation is the Spirit of God to the individual believer and not ecclesiastical authority. Thus, "liberty of conscience" is elevated.
> 2. The General Assembly has no power to dictate doctrine to the Presbyteries.
> 3. The General Assembly's condemnation of those asserting "doctrines contrary to the standards of the Presbyterian Church" circumvented the due process set forth in the Book of Discipline.
> 4. None of the five essential doctrines should be used as a test of ordination. Alternate "theories" of these doctrines are permissible.
> 5. Liberty of thought and teaching, within the bounds of evangelical Christianity is necessary.
> 6. Division is deplored, unity and freedom are commended.

In 1924, a document called the Auburn Affirmation *circulated at the General Assembly of the Presbyterian Church in the United States of America.*

Referring to the Five Fundamentals as "particular theories," the *Affirmation*'s argument is succinctly summarized in two sentences:

> Some of us regard the particular theories contained in the deliverance of the General Assembly of 1923 as satisfactory explanations of these facts and doctrines. But we are united in believing that these are not the only theories allowed by the Scriptures and our standards as explanations of these facts and doctrines of our religion, and that all who hold to these facts

> and doctrines, whatever theories they may employ to explain them, are worthy of all confidence and fellowship.[45]

The Assembly itself did not adopt the *Affirmation*, but the document bore the signatures of 1,274 Presbyterian ministers and claimed to represent the convictions of many more. Denying these fundamentals or regarding them as mere theories reflects the influence of Ritschlian liberalism. And the *Auburn Affirmation* indicates the extent in the Presbyterian Church USA of support for this movement.

Another episode in the controversy took place in 1925, the so-called *Scopes* Monkey Trial. John Thomas Scopes was then accused of teaching the theory of evolution to high school students in Dayton, Tennessee, contrary to state law. The trial was a publicity circus, with famous atheist attorney Clarence Darrow defending Scopes and former presidential candidate and fundamentalist William Jennings Bryan prosecuting for the state. Although Bryan and Tennessee won the verdict, the media, led by H. L. Mencken, concluded that the case against evolution, like fundamentalism in general, was ignorant and stupid.

At that point, Ritschlianism was riding high. It dominated Protestant denominations and academies and was well regarded by the press. Its opponents appeared to be powerless factions. But its victory turned out to be short-lived. A number of developments had already been working against it.

Most significant was a new development in Jesus scholarship. Scholars such as Johannes Weiss (1863–1914) and Albert Schweitzer (1875–1965) showed that it was not possible to present Jesus as the advocate of a liberal social gospel. On the contrary, Jesus was an apocalyptic visionary, and his message *consistently eschatological*. According to Weiss and Schweitzer, Jesus (mistakenly) believed that the world was going to end soon and that he would himself be the central figure in God's devastating universal judgment. The ethic of the Sermon on the Mount, therefore, is not a practical social program. It is a temporary expedient. It explains the way people should live while they await the soon end of everything. On this basis, liberals could not point to Jesus as the inspiration for a program of unending social progress. Indeed, it was very difficult to know what to do with Jesus. The concluding paragraph of Schweitzer's *The Quest of the Historical Jesus* reads:

Scholars such as Johannes Weiss (1863–1914) and Albert Schweitzer (1875–1965) showed that it was not possible to present Jesus as the advocate of a liberal social gospel. On the contrary, Jesus was an apocalyptic visionary, and his message consistently eschatological.

> He comes to us as One unknown, without a name, as of old, by the lake side, He came to those men who knew Him not. He speaks to us the same word: "Follow thou me!" and sets us to

45. Jack B. Rogers, Donald K. McKim, *The Authority and Interpretation of the Bible: An Historical Approach* (Eugene, OR: Wipf & Stock, 1999), 365.

> the tasks which He has to fulfill for our time. He commands. And to those who obey Him, whether they be wise or simple, He will reveal Himself in the toils, the conflicts, the sufferings which they shall pass through in His fellowship, and, as an ineffable mystery, they shall learn in their own experience Who He is.[46] (See fig. 8.3.)

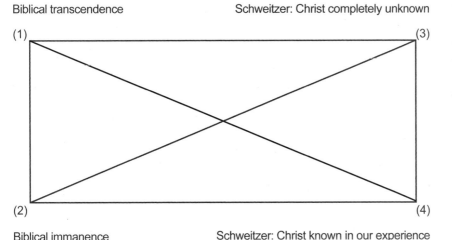

The consistently eschatological view of Jesus would in time overcome the Ritschlian view of Jesus as a social reformer.

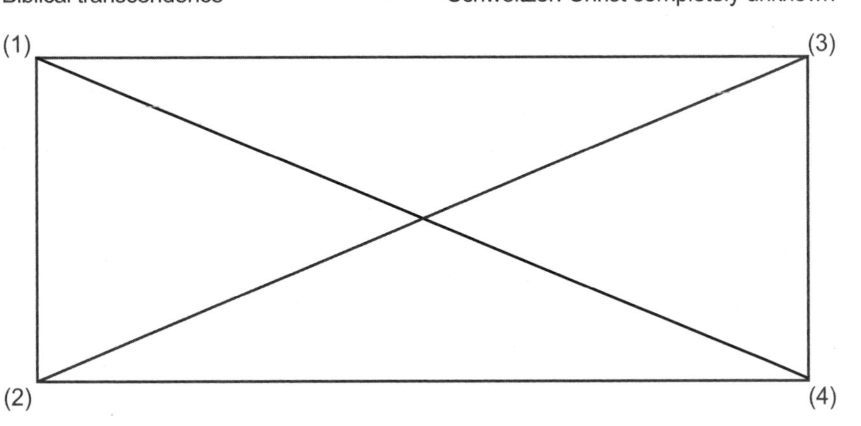

Fig. 8.3. Schweitzer's Transcendence and Immanence

Albert Schweitzer

Schweitzer himself chose to largely abandon his study of academic theology. He gained a medical degree[47] and became a jungle doctor in the village of Lambaréné in Gabon, Africa.[48]

The *consistently eschatological* view of Jesus would in time overcome the Ritschlian view of Jesus as a social reformer.

There were also new developments in the philosophy of history. As Schweitzer had attacked the "quest of the historical Jesus," so Ernst Troeltsch (1865–1923) called into question the very idea of ascertaining what had actually happened in a historical setting and applying such knowledge to our lives today. The *Encyclopedia Britannica* summarizes:

> He was both fascinated and troubled by "historicism" (historical relativism): the view that whatever is valued, pursued, conceived, or achieved at any given time or place is relative to, and only understandable in the context of, the conditions of that

46. Albert Schweitzer, *The Quest of the Historical Jesus: A Critical Study of Its Progress from Reimarus to Wrede*, trans. W. Montgomery (London: A. and C. Black, 1910), 403.

47. His dissertation: "The Psychiatric Study of Jesus."

48. Schweitzer was also a classical organist and musicologist specializing in the interpretation of Bach.

> time or place. Although the view seemed to him in important respects inescapable, he surmised that it applied inadequately to the norms—whether legal, religious, or ethical—that govern human conduct. If consistently applied, the historicist view would, he thought, make any present understanding of past ages impossible. The polymorphous, historically changing dogmas of the Christian church had to be reconciled with the absolute aspects of revealed truth interpreted anew by every generation.[49]

In effect, Troeltsch added sophistication to Lessing's argument that history is never a sufficient ground of faith. In the present context, we would have to draw the conclusion that whether Jesus was a social reformer or an apocalyptic visionary doesn't really matter for our current faith and life.[50]

So the scholarship of Weiss, Schweitzer, and Troeltsch attacked the heart of the Ritschlian theology. These developments made more plausible the arguments of those who attacked Ritschlianism directly, such as James Orr[51] and J. Gresham Machen.[52] Orr and Machen attacked Ritschlianism from the standpoint of orthodox, evangelical theology. We will see in chapter 10 that eventually Ritschlian liberalism was also attacked by Barth and Brunner, theologians nurtured within the Ritschlian movement itself. These more recent movements dismantled the prestige that Ritschlianism had accumulated and supplanted its role in theology.

Orr and Machen attacked Ritschlianism from the standpoint of orthodox, evangelical theology. . . . Eventually Ritschlian liberalism was also attacked by Barth and Brunner, theologians nurtured within the Ritschlian movement itself.

And there were also events outside the academic community that worked against Ritschlian liberalism, chiefly war. The Ritschlians had hoped that the natural goodness of man, nurtured by the example of Jesus, would lead the nations to treat one another as brothers. That did not happen. Indeed, the new "Christian Century" turned out to be the bloodiest ever, as technology joined man's native power of brutality. The Ritschlians were helpless to deal with the new situation. Barth and his colleagues never forgave Harnack for supporting the Kaiser in

49. Eva Schaper, "Ernst Troeltsch," *Encyclopedia Britannica*, available at http://www.britannica.com/EBchecked/topic/606217/Ernst-Troeltsch.

50. I note the following: (1) Troeltsch's philosophy itself is grounded in detailed analysis of many historical events. To conclude that historical events cannot govern present values is therefore self-refuting. (2) Historical relativism is, in the end, a presupposition, rather than a conclusion of Troeltsch's study. He assumes that historical study must proceed *autonomously*, as I have used the term. If instead we presuppose that God has spoken and identified to us his historical intentions, then Troeltsch's generalizations need not trouble us.

51. James Orr, *Ritschlianism: Expository and Critical Essays* (London: Hodder and Stoughton, 1903).

52. Machen, *Christianity and Liberalism*.

Germany's war preparations. And the advent of Hitler and the Second World War destroyed all hope of a pacifist utopia.

SØREN KIERKEGAARD (1813–55)

I am treating Kierkegaard somewhat out of chronological order because his thought was not well appreciated during his own time, but became very influential in the next century.

As I mentioned earlier, Kierkegaard is not a Ritschlian, but it is not easy to define positively what he is. He anticipates and greatly influences twentieth-century neoorthodox theology and philosophical existentialism, but it would be misleading to say that he is a member of either of these movements, even by anticipation.

He would be pleased to find that he is difficult for interpreters to categorize. In his view, one of the great errors in philosophy is to imagine that we can sum up a person's existence under some label or other. He wanted his gravestone to carry the inscription "that individual." Prepare, then, for a good dose of philosophical nominalism.[53]

Kierkegaard's thought is very different from anything that has come before. . . . He meditates on dread, anxiety, despair, choice, decision, stages of life, communication, and many other subjects that have become part of philosophy in later eras.

Kierkegaard's thought is very different from anything that has come before. He does not line up philosophical treatises on the traditional topics of metaphysics, epistemology, and ethics, nor does he present systematic views on theological matters such as divine attributes, the Trinity, Christ, atonement, and the sacraments. Rather, he meditates on dread, anxiety, despair, choice, decision, stages of life, communication, and many other subjects that have become part of philosophy in later eras. These have implications both for philosophy and for theology, but those implications have to be teased out from between the lines of Kierkegaard's writing, rather than read off the surface of it.

Kierkegaard blamed Hegel for the loss of the individual in philosophy, for Hegel's dialectic swallowed up all concrete objects into its abstract categories.

Kierkegaard is fascinating to read. He seems to be living in the real world, as opposed to the abstractions of Kant and Hegel. His personal life enters his arguments often, or lies behind them: his melancholy father, his broken engagement to Regina Olsen, his feud with the periodical *The Corsair.*

It is easier to identify what Kierkegaard is not than what he is. Kierkegaard faces two main opponents. One is Hegelian philosophy, and the other (especially later in his life) is the "Danish People's Church," the state Lutheran church. Kierkegaard blamed Hegel for the loss of the individual in philosophy, for Hegel's dialectic swallowed up all concrete objects into its abstract categories. And Kierkegaard blamed the Danish People's Church in large part for the formalism and deadness of Christianity in Denmark. So he posed the question: how does one become a Christian in Christendom?

53. Review my account of Occam in chapter 4 and my discussion of universals in chapter 1.

Of course, these two problems were closely related in Kierkegaard's mind. Hegel's philosophy reinforced the ungodly tendency of Danish Christians to think that true beliefs were the sum total of religion, and the spiritual corruption of the church weakened the church's witness to the sanctity of the individual and (as we will see) the paradox of the eternal entering time.

Recall Hegel's principle that the real is the rational and the rational is the real. This implies that all of reality is thought, mind; hence we describe Hegel as an idealist. But what of the will? What of our choices and decisions? Hegel thought (or so Kierkegaard understood him) that to choose is to take the next step in the rational dialectic, from thesis to antithesis to synthesis.[54] For Hegel, choice of a thesis will eventually pass into its antithesis. If you choose A, you will eventually find yourself embracing not-A. For A and not-A are really the same thing as aspects of (and perspectives on) a great reality embracing them both.

But for Kierkegaard, this picture destroys the essence of choice. A choice, in Kierkegaard's understanding, is always a choice between two genuinely different alternatives. We choose "either" A "or" not-A. Hence the title of Kierkegaard's early work, *Either/Or.* And to Kierkegaard, rational thought never determines a choice. We may gather rational considerations and arguments as to whether, say, we should live in Atlanta or New York, but in the end we must *decide*. The rational analysis won't force us to choose in one way or another. Even if the best reasons favor one alternative, we are still able to choose the other. And there is no justification for Hegel's view that these two choices are, in the end, somehow equivalent.

Søren Kierkegaard

For Kierkegaard, human *existence* consists of free[55] choices, of decisions. Each choice is unique, and so none of them can be described by a general term. We know our decisions as we make them, but we cannot analyze them by rational concepts. Existence is a "surd." You can live through it, observe it, but you cannot capture it in labels.

So in the area of human existence, Kierkegaard is something of an extreme nominalist, though in other matters he is not. Hence his sharp distinction between thought and existence. For him, human existence is a kind of pure particularity that cannot be incorporated under general concepts. On that score, I am not persuaded. It seems to me that human choices are different from one another in some respects, but the same in other respects. In that way, human choices are no different from anything else: apples, planets, virtues. They are particulars describable by general terms.[56] Choices are of different types that can

54. Hegel's view is like that of Plato, who taught that virtue is knowledge: that if you know the right, you will inevitably do the right.

55. *Free* in the libertarian sense, as I discussed in chapter 3 and elsewhere.

56. Compare my account in chapter 1 on universals and particulars.

be labeled: choices of what to eat, choices of where to live, choices of right and wrong, and, as Kierkegaard describes at great length, choices of lifestyle (the *stages*; see below).

In my view, therefore, rational analysis is capable of *describing* choice, but I think Kierkegaard is right in saying that rational analysis does not *determine* choice. Plato thought that if you know the right, you will do the right. Kierkegaard, with his understanding of the biblical doctrine of sin, knew that wasn't true. And he sensed here the major problem of the Danish state church: people had heard true doctrine all their lives, but they weren't taught to choose the good.

Kierkegaard's question of how one can become a Christian in Christendom is the question of how one's will can be changed.

So Kierkegaard's question of how one can become a Christian in Christendom is the question of how one's will can be changed. In line with his nominalism and his sense that rational analysis does not determine choice, Kierkegaard doesn't address the will directly, by explaining the process of change in propositional belief. Rather, he communicates *indirectly*, by telling stories, giving examples of different lifestyles.[57] Sometimes he writes under a pseudonym, leaving the reader uncertain whether the views are Kierkegaard's own, or whether they are views that Kierkegaard proposes only for consideration. One important feature of indirect communication is that unlike the communication of propositional information, the personality and character of the communicator, his own lifestyle, is a necessary element in the transaction.

Human life, he believes, typically moves through three stages, though it can sometimes be stalled at one of them, and though often our lives display features of more than one. These are the aesthetic, *the* ethical, *and the* religious.

Three case studies of lifestyle choices appear several places in Kierkegaard's writings. Human life, he believes, typically moves through three stages, though it can sometimes be stalled at one of them, and though often our lives display features of more than one. These are the *aesthetic*, the *ethical*, and the *religious*.

In the *aesthetic* stage, a person seeks what is immediately pleasurable. He is uncommitted, often irresponsible and selfish, dedicated to pure enjoyment. In his relationships to others, he might be manipulative, even diabolical. He acknowledges no principle or person capable of limiting and governing his behavior. His life is governed by the present moment, rather than deliberate choice. There is no *either-or* in his life.

57. I have often thought of Nathan's parable in 2 Samuel 12:1–15 as a good illustration of indirect communication. David had committed adultery and had arranged the death of Bathsheba's husband to hide his sin. Nathan the prophet did not begin by condemning David directly from the law of God, or by reviewing David's actions. Rather, he told David a story about a rich man who took a poor man's ewe lamb to entertain a guest. David grew angry, and Nathan said to him, "You are the man!" David already knew, surely, what the law of God said about his actions (normative perspective) and the circumstances of his actions (situational). What he needed was a word that shattered his complacency and addressed his heart (existential). The law of God (normative), circumstances (situational), and the heart (existential) are three epistemological perspectives on David's repentance.

But this lifestyle yields a low quality of existence, leading to boredom, weariness, self-disgust, despair. Kierkegaard's chief example of the aesthetic spirit is the seducer Don Juan from Mozart's *Don Giovanni*.

You may well have had a college roommate like this—trapped in the aesthetic. Perhaps you have tried to intervene, to get him to change his ways. But that is very difficult. The aesthetic is his very life, almost his very nature. Likely he has no interest in the kind of radical change he needs. If you tell him that he needs to invest his life in some great cause, he is likely to laugh at you, to pity you, to brush you aside. Your arguments might have no effect, because the aesthetic lifestyle sets his very criteria for truth.[58] Your argument cannot be right, because the lifestyle you propose is not aesthetically pleasing. In fact, you yourself, with your arguments, are becoming a bore. Clearly, if he is to change from the aesthetic lifestyle to a different one, something other than your rational argument is needed.

But people do sometimes change. The causes and reasons are mysterious, but it does happen. Kierkegaard describes this change as a *leap*.

The second stage is the *ethical*, in which we govern our lives by the rules given us by society. In the aesthetic, one avoids taking a principled stand; but principled standing is what the ethical stage is all about. Kierkegaard sees this stage in Kantian terms: obedience to an absolute moral law. Further, as with Kant, the moral law is *universal*, an obligation to do what is right for *all* men, refusing to follow one's individual inclination. The ethical person recognizes that he has an obligation to others; he cannot live as a mere spectator. He plans his life into the future, rather than living by impulse. As Don Juan is the exemplar of the aesthetic, Kierkegaard's chief model of ethical living is Socrates.

Our strongest resolutions are insufficient to maintain our ethical purity. We are easily overwhelmed with a sense of sin and guilt, resulting in a condition that Kierkegaard calls anxiety.

In many ways, the ethical is the opposite of the aesthetic, though often our lives exhibit both tendencies simultaneously. Sometimes the coexistence of these tendencies means inconsistency. But in some ways, the ethical affirms the aesthetic. There is pleasure in sacrificing one's own interests for a higher cause. But in a case of conflict, ethical considerations must prevail over aesthetic, if the ethical life is to be fulfilled.

But there is a downside to the ethical stage as to the aesthetic. For our strongest resolutions are insufficient to maintain our ethical purity. We are easily overwhelmed with a sense of sin and guilt, resulting in a condition that Kierkegaard calls *anxiety*. Somehow, there must be something better, another radical change of life and thinking.

That third stage is what Kierkegaard calls *religious*. In the religious stage, we govern our lives on the basis of an intimate, individual rela-

58. So Kierkegaard's stages supply their own concepts of rationality. That is to say, they serve as *presuppositions* in the sense used in chapter 1 of this book and elsewhere.

tionship to God. The transition from the ethical to the religious is what Kierkegaard calls the *leap of faith*. This relationship is by faith alone, not by reason. God's existence cannot be proved; it will always be uncertain. But faith by its very nature is uncertain, for God is beyond our understanding. The object of faith is the *absurdity* of incarnation, that the eternal God has entered time in Christ and therefore is able to enter a relationship with each individual.

The religious stage combines the immediacy of the aesthetic with the principled personal commitment of the ethical, but it transforms both into a higher life. These three stages are actually very much like a Hegelian triad: the aesthetic as the thesis, the ethical as the antithesis, the religious as the synthesis. With each new stage, the previous stage is canceled, affirmed, raised to a higher level (*aufgehoben*). But unlike Hegel's dialectic, this process is not a rational necessity. There is no *reason* that requires us to abandon one stage for another. The change is a leap.

The religious stage combines the immediacy of the aesthetic with the principled personal commitment of the ethical, but it transforms both into a higher life.

Typically, the religious stage affirms the ethical. But there are exceptions. In *Fear and Trembling*, Kierkegaard presents the Genesis 22 story of Abraham, who receives a divine command to kill his son Isaac. Abraham knows that obeying this command is contrary to ethics, but after much agony he agrees to follow God's command rather than his own ethical standards. Kierkegaard says that in this command God ordains a "teleological suspension of the ethical," a temporary lifting of the ethical law, to ascertain whether Abraham's highest commitment is to God (his personal religious obligation) or to ethical law. Abraham's response is religious. He becomes the *knight of infinite resignation*, because he has given up everything, even his ethical standards, to follow God. But positively, because he does indeed follow God, Kierkegaard also gives him the title *knight of faith*.

But the religious stage can suffer corruption. In *Concluding Unscientific Postscript*, Kierkegaard distinguishes two religious stages, A and B. Religion A is the religion of the Danish state church. In that religion, the believer tries to find forgiveness by relating to God out of his own resources. He maintains an essentially passive relation to God. He is baptized, married, and buried in the church; he might even attend services, because he knows he is supposed to. But he experiences nothing like a vital relationship with Christ. The characteristics of Religion A include resignation (renouncing relative goals), suffering (sorrow over resignation, need for transformation), and continued guilt (a partially severed fellowship with God).

Kierkegaard distinguishes two religious stages, A and B. Religion A is the religion of the Danish state church. In that religion, the believer tries to find forgiveness by relating to God out of his own resources. He maintains an essentially passive relation to God.

Religion B is what Kierkegaard considers to be true religion, *transcendent* religion, governed by faith alone. It comes from God himself—his paradoxical act of bridging the "infinite qualitative difference between time and eternity."[59] By God's grace,[60] eternal truth comes into relation with an existing individual. We come into this relation not just by going beyond the evidence (which we also do in Religion A), but by believing in something beyond our understanding, in the context of a new life. God himself, for Kierkegaard, is wholly other, incognito. He cannot be reached through science or philosophy, but can be grasped only in passionate inwardness.

The result is not that we come to believe new doctrines, but that we receive an *existence communication* from God, by which we are actually transformed. This new existence cannot be learned from direct communication, but indirect communication (recall our reference to that concept earlier in this section) can be a tool of God in bringing about this new state. In this new existence, we feel sin not as abstract guilt for failure to perform religious duties as in Religion A, but as an offense against the personal God, breaking fellowship with him. This sense of sin is far more radical, and therefore the sense of forgiveness as well. Radical forgiveness, then, sends us forth to life in the spirit, rather than in the flesh. The new life does not consist in formal duties, but in a living fellowship with Christ. In this existence communication, we become "contemporaneous with Christ." This new existence, then, provides the answer to Kierkegaard's question, "How may I become a Christian within Christendom?"

Kierkegaard's distinction between the communication of doctrines and the communication of life has more implications, which have raised controversy. Generally, Kierkegaard is orthodox concerning the traditional doctrines of the church,[61] and he makes statements about the authority of Scripture that are surprisingly orthodox, given the intellectual atmosphere of his day.[62] But in *Concluding Unscientific Postscript* he shows considerable appreciation of Lessing, who as we saw in chapter 6 denied that there was a historical foundation for Christianity. Kierkegaard agrees with him that Christian faith is not based on history, but not for the same reasons. Lessing had said that history is too doubtful to be a basis for "necessary truths of reason," which are

Generally, Kierkegaard is orthodox concerning the traditional doctrines of the church, and he makes statements about the authority of Scripture that are surprisingly orthodox, given the intellectual atmosphere of his day.

59. Although Kierkegaard often spoke of *paradox* and *the absurd*, he did not believe that God's entry into time was logically contradictory. He defended Aristotelian logic against the Hegelians in his *either-or*. For him, A really is A, and not not-A. God, therefore, understands the paradoxes of time and eternity, but they are beyond the power of *human* reason to understand.

60. From God's point of view, the change comes by grace. From ours, it comes by a leap of faith. Since Kierkegaard typically focuses on the human side, since his view of freedom is libertarian, and since he denies the historicity of the story of the fall in Genesis 3, he is often accused of Pelagianism (recall my account of Augustine and Pelagius in chapter 3). But he understands that there is a mystery here that cannot be reduced to human reasoning or choice.

61. I mentioned earlier his skepticism about the account of the fall of man in Genesis 3.

62. See his *On Authority and Revelation* (New York: Joanna Cotler Books, 1967).

in turn the only basis for religious faith. Kierkegaard disagrees with Lessing, for he does not believe that religious faith is based on reason. But he agrees with Lessing that faith is not based on history either. It is, rather, based on the paradox of the eternal entering time.

This view, along with Kierkegaard's other hesitations about the role of propositional belief in religion, raises questions about his view of the *content* of Christian faith. Consider this famous passage:

> If one who lives in the midst of Christendom goes up to the house of God, the house of the true God, with the true conception of God in his knowledge, and prays, but prays in a false spirit; and one who lives in an idolatrous community prays with the entire passion of the infinite, although his eyes rest upon the image of an idol: where is there most truth? The one prays in truth to God though he worships an idol; the other prays falsely to the true God, and hence worships in fact an idol.[63]

[For Kierkegaard, religious faith is] based on the paradox of the eternal entering time. This view, along with Kierkegaard's other hesitations about the role of propositional belief in religion, raises questions about his view of the content *of Christian faith.*

Many on the basis of this quotation have thought that for Kierkegaard the content of religion is indifferent, that it doesn't matter whom you pray to as long as you pray with passion. This would be an extreme relativist position. But the terms *true* and *truth* in this quotation are highly problematic and, doubtless, ironic. Kierkegaard puts some emphasis on them (note repetitions of them in the first sentence).

Note that he does speak twice of the God of Christianity as the "true" God and the traditional Christian view of God as a "true conception." So he is not indifferent about truth in the normal sense, Aristotelian truth in contrast with falsity.[64] The object of the pagan worshiper is "an idol," which is certainly something other than the "true God." But Kierkegaard also ascribes truth to the pagan worshiper. The pagan prays "in truth" to God, "though he worships an idol."

Subjective truth, for Kierkegaard, is first a quality of the knower, rather than of the object of knowledge.

Evidently, Kierkegaard is speaking of *truth* in two senses. The first sense is Aristotelian, in which a true proposition is contrasted with a false one. We might call that *objective truth*. The second sense is what Kierkegaard sometimes calls *subjective truth*. Note that in the quoted material Kierkegaard's question has to do not with the truth of the object of knowledge, but with the truth that is "in" the subject: It is not "which God is true," but "where (i.e., in which of the two situations) is there most truth?"

Subjective truth, for Kierkegaard, is first a quality of the knower, rather than of the object of knowledge. It is not so much concerned

63. Søren Kierkegaard, *Concluding Unscientific Postscript* (Princeton, NJ: Princeton University Press, 1941, 1968), 179–80.

64. Remember Kierkegaard's defense of traditional truth over against Hegel.

with *what* is believed as *how*. Subjective truth is truth that we believe with an attitude of passionate dedication, a truth that establishes the right relationship between the object and the knower. Subjective truth is something that we apply in depth to our whole selves in all situations. Subjective truth determines a new lifestyle. This is the kind of truth appropriate to Religion B.

In the controversial quotation, Kierkegaard evidently wants to say that the pagan has subjective truth, though objectively his conception is false. The Christendom worshiper prays to an objectively true God, but without subjective truth. Kierkegaard is not a relativist, because he does distinguish an objectively true belief from a false one.

He does seem to sense the genuine complications in the relationship between the object of knowledge and the application of knowledge—the what and the how. We are inclined to draw a sharp distinction between our beliefs and our behavior, or in worship between the object of worship and the way we worship. But Scripture speaks of idolatry both as worshiping a false god and as worshiping the true God in a way he forbids.[65] God is not an abstract supreme being, but a real, personal Lord who cares about how he is worshiped and how his worshipers behave. It is not easy to pinpoint the difference between behaving wrongly toward the true God and worshiping a different god (a god with different demands). So there is something of a continuum between objective and subjective truth. Our subjective response to God might become so ungodly as to call into question whether we believe in him objectively. That could be the problem of the one who prays in Christendom, in Kierkegaard's thought-experiment. The Christendom worshiper might be praying so formally, without passion, that his prayer is in a "false spirit," even a prayer to a false god.

Kierkegaard does seem to sense the genuine complications in the relationship between the object of knowledge and the application of knowledge—the what and the how.

But the real question about the quotation from Kierkegaard is whether the pagan can pray "in truth to God though he worships an idol." The only thing in his favor is that he prays with "the entire passion of the infinite." But elsewhere Kierkegaard has said that such passion comes only by the grace of the true God. It is Religion B, a saving relationship with Christ. But if the pagan has received from Christ this new passion, how can he still be a pagan? Kierkegaard might believe that there could be some interval between the conversion of the pagan's passions and the conversion of his ideas. But the impression we get from the Kierkegaard quotation is that this man's paganism is settled and permanent, and that his failure to believe in the true God—that is, in Jesus Christ—is consistent with regeneration.

From this we cannot conclude that Kierkegaard is indifferent as to which god we pray to. Yet we can see here a level of confusion that

65. See my *DCL*, 405–20, 454–56.

should not be present in a theologian or philosopher, but that has certainly affected many of Kierkegaard's successors.

Some general comments on Kierkegaard's thought:

1. Kierkegaard is helpful in his descriptions of the psychology of belief. Changing one's beliefs is not simply a matter of hearing good arguments and logically following them to their conclusions. Such change is the product of many factors, including feelings, habits, lifestyles, and indeed divine grace. Often it is not clear why someone has changed his beliefs, his attitudes, his priorities, his preferences, his faith. In my judgment, this analysis is especially important when we try to understand someone's change from one fundamental presupposition to another.
2. But, contrary to Kierkegaard, none of this implies that the evidence for God's existence or the truth of the gospel is insufficient. Scripture tells us that God's revelation of himself is clear, both in the creation and in Christ. If we refuse to bow to that revelation, it is our fault. As Paul says in Romans 1:18, unbelief "by . . . unrighteousness suppress[es] the truth."
3. Kierkegaard's emphasis on the existence communication correlates somewhat with what I have called the *existential perspective* (see chapter 1). In Reformed theology, salvation has three dimensions: God's authoritative gospel (normative perspective), his acts in history in Christ to redeem his people (situational perspective), and the work of the Spirit in the heart to transform us, applying the Word of Christ (existential perspective). It seems to me that the existential perspective contains everything that Kierkegaard legitimately calls for. One wonders whether the existential perspective, the doctrines of regeneration and sanctification, was largely missing in the churches that Kierkegaard attended; see fig. 8.4.

Kierkegaard is helpful in his descriptions of the psychology of belief. Changing one's beliefs is not simply a matter of hearing good arguments and logically following them to their conclusions.

One wonders whether the existential perspective, the doctrines of regeneration and sanctification, was largely missing in the churches that Kierkegaard attended.

Fig. 8.4. An Evangelical View of How We Come to Faith

4. But Kierkegaard neglects the other two perspectives. Although he speaks well of the Bible and refers to it frequently, he is reluctant to describe the new life as a life of obedience to the written Word. And his tribute to Lessing creates huge confusion as to the relevance of Jesus' work in history, his cross and resurrection.
5. Kierkegaard rarely considers—perhaps he actually denies—God's involvement in the space-time world, the world of ordinary existence. Existence in Religion B is a transcendent world, in which we rise up to a relationship with God impossible in ordinary life. Note:
   a. Kierkegaard believes that God's command to Abraham in Genesis 22 is something other than ethics, a suspension of ethics, substituting a direct personal relationship between himself and Abraham. But in Scripture, ethics, the law, is also the Word of God. Its source is just as personal as that of God's command in Genesis 22.
   b. Kierkegaard concedes to Lessing that the world of history is autonomous. God's saving action must come from above history. But that is to disparage the intensively historical narrative of the Bible's own account of salvation.
   c. The transcendent world is a world above reason. The ordinary world is a world in which reason is perfectly competent. So we see in Kierkegaard the *transcendence-immanence dialectic* that I described in chapter 1 and mentioned in other parts of this book; see fig. 8.5.

Although Kierkegaard speaks well of the Bible and refers to it frequently, he is reluctant to describe the new life as a life of obedience to the written Word. And his tribute to Lessing creates huge confusion as to the relevance of Jesus' work in history, his cross and resurrection.

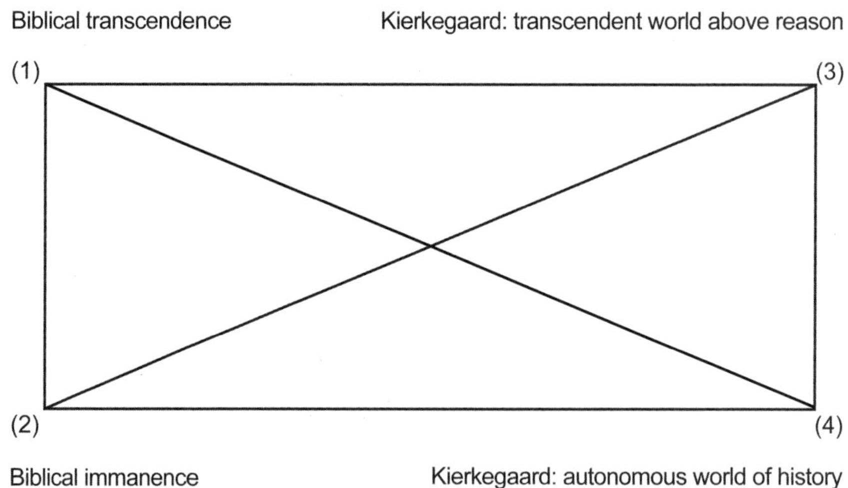

Fig. 8.5. Transcendence and Immanence in Kierkegaard

6. Kierkegaard draws far too sharp a distinction between propositional assent and passionate commitment. In the parable of the pagan, he seems to imply that one can have a passionate commitment to God without propositional belief in him. The Bible denies this (Heb. 11:6). In fact, a passionate commitment to God presupposes belief that God exists. And passionate commitment to someone typically rises out of beliefs about the person that arouse feelings of passion and intensity of commitment. Indeed, passionate commitment is in many cases proportional to the strength of assent.[66]

In the parable of the pagan, Kierkegaard seems to imply that one can have a passionate commitment to God without propositional belief in him. The Bible denies this (Heb. 11:6). In fact, a passionate commitment to God presupposes belief that God exists.

KEY TERMS

Gefühl
Doctrines (for Schleiermacher)
Subjective turn (in doctrine of revelation)
Feeling of absolute dependence
Pantheism
Sensuous consciousness
Essential God-consciousness
Legal world order
Fundamentalists
Auburn Affirmation
The *Scopes* trial
Johannes Weiss
Ernst Troeltsch
Regina Olsen
Indirect communication
Ethical stage
Religious stage B
The absurd (in Kierkegaard)
Subjective truth (Kierkegaard)
Knight of faith
Existence communication
Religious consciousness
Propositional revelation
Panentheism
External (in Schleiermacher)
Value judgment (Ritschl)
Kernel and husk
Modernists
The Five Fundamentals
Consistently eschatological
Albert Schweitzer
J. Gresham Machen
The Corsair
Aesthetic stage
Religious stage A
Leap
Teleological suspension of the ethical
Knight of infinite resignation
God incognito

STUDY QUESTIONS

1. Why is Schleiermacher called the *father of modern theology*? Is that designation appropriate? Why or why not?
2. Describe the content of Schleiermacher's *Speeches on Religion*. What do you think of it?
3. Explain and evaluate Schleiermacher's view of the religious consciousness.

66. See *DKG*, 54–57.

OUTLINE

Friedrich D. E. Schleiermacher (1768–1834)

Albrecht Ritschl (1822–89)

Wilhelm Herrmann (1846–1922)

Adolf von Harnack (1851–1930)

The Rise and Fall of Ritschlianism

Søren Kierkegaard (1813–55)

4. State and evaluate Schleiermacher's view of theological doctrines.
5. Frame argues that the whole liberal tradition seeks to refute propositional revelation. State and evaluate the objections to it by Cherbury, Lessing, Kant, Hegel, and Schleiermacher.
6. Describe and evaluate the *subjective turn* in the liberal view of revelation and Scripture.
7. Is it possible to derive theological propositions from feelings? Respond to some of the problems with this idea.
8. Why does Schleiermacher think the traditional doctrine of original sin is legalist? Comment.
9. Outline Schleiermacher's view of sin, Christ, and atonement.
10. Schleiermacher criticizes traditional soteriology as *external*, *artificial*, and *legalist*. Explain; evaluate.
11. Frame: "So liberal theology, following Lessing, denies any doctrinal significance to the events of history." Explain; evaluate. Do Ritschl and Kierkegaard improve on Schleiermacher in this regard?
12. For Schleiermacher, "grace ordains the development of human potential." How? Explain; evaluate.
13. How does Schleiermacher's theology illustrate Frame's dialectic of transcendence and immanence?
14. Is history important for Ritschl? If so, how? Evaluate.
15. To Ritschl, "all theological propositions have for their aim the explanation of the phenomena of the Christian life." Explain; evaluate.
16. Outline Ritschl's view of Christ and what Christ does to save us. Evaluate.
17. "*Redemption*, *justification*, *regeneration*, *adoption*, *forgiveness*, and *reconciliation* are all essentially synonyms." Explain. Why does liberal theology often treat these terms as synonymous?
18. Summarize Machen's evaluation of Herrmann. What is surprising about it? How do you evaluate this exchange?
19. Describe and evaluate Herrmann's view of salvation.
20. What is Harnack's view of the essence of Christianity? Evaluate. Is Frame right to say that in Harnack's theology "everything supernatural is gone"?
21. Describe the "rise and fall of Ritschlianism."
22. Describe Schweitzer's conclusions about Jesus.
23. "In effect, Troeltsch added sophistication to Lessing's argument that history is never a sufficient ground of faith." How? Evaluate.
24. How did political developments affect the success of Ritschlianism?

25. Summarize and evaluate Kierkegaard's critique of Hegel, using some examples.
26. How does Kierkegaard reply to his own question, "How may I become a Christian within Christendom?" Evaluate.
27. How does Kierkegaard differ from Hegel on the nature of human decision?
28. Frame cites Nathan's parable to David as an example of indirect communication. Explain.
29. How are Kierkegaard's three stages of life similar to a Hegelian triad? Different?
30. Distinguish Kierkegaard's two concepts of religion. Evaluate.
31. Is Kierkegaard indifferent to the nature of the object of faith? Explore pros and cons.
32. How is Kierkegaard's view of history like Lessing's? How different?
33. Does Kierkegaard fall into the *transcendence-immanence dialectic*? Explain.

BIBLIOGRAPHY: NINETEENTH-CENTURY THEOLOGY

Print

Harnack, Adolf von. *What Is Christianity?* Eastford, CT: Martino Fine Books, 2011.

Herrmann, Wilhelm. *The Communion of the Christian with God*. Charleston, SC: BiblioBazaar, 2009.

Kierkegaard, Søren. *Attack upon Christendom*. Princeton, NJ: Princeton University Press, 1968.

———. *Concluding Unscientific Postscript*. Princeton, NJ: Princeton University Press, 1992.

———. *Either/Or*. New York, Penguin, 1992.

———. *The Essential Kierkegaard*. Princeton, NJ: Princeton University Press, 2000.

———. *Fear and Trembling*. New York: Penguin, 1986.

———. *On Authority and Revelation*. New York: Joanna Cotler Books, 1967.

———. *Philosophical Fragments*. Princeton, NJ: Princeton University Press, 1985.

———. *The Sickness unto Death*. Princeton, NJ: Princeton University Press, 1983.

———. *Stages on Life's Way*. Princeton, NJ: Princeton University Press, 1988.

Ritschl, Albrecht. *The Christian Doctrine of Justification and Reconciliation*. Edited and translated by H. R. Mackintosh and A. B. Macaulay. Edinburgh: T&T Clark, 1900.

Schleiermacher, Friedrich. *The Christian Faith*. Translated by H. R. Mackintosh and J. S. Stewart. Edinburgh: T&T Clark, 1928.

———. *On Religion: Speeches to Its Cultured Despisers*. Edited by Richard Crouter. Cambridge Texts in the History of Philosophy. Cambridge: Cambridge University Press, 1996.

Online

Harnack, Adolf von. *Works*. Includes *What Is Christianity?* and his six-volume *History of Dogma*. Available at http://www.ccel.org/ccel/harnack.

Herrmann, Wilhelm. *The Communion of the Christian with God*. Translated by J. Sandys Stanyon. Revised by R. W. Stewart. London: Williams & Norgate and New York: G. P. Putnam's Sons, 1906. Available at http://archive.org/details/communionofchris00herrrich.

Kierkegaard, Søren. *Attack upon Christendom*. Translated, with an introduction, by Walter Lowrie. Princeton, NJ: Princeton University Press, 1946. Available at http://www.christianebooks.com/pdf_files/kierkegaard-satta00kier.pdf.

———. *Concluding Unscientific Postscript*. Edited and translated by Alastair Hannay. Cambridge: Cambridge University Press, 2009. Available at http://www.clas.ufl.edu/users/burt/KierkegaardConcludingUnscientificPostscript.pdf.

———. *Either/Or*. Edited and translated by Howard V. Hong and Edna H. Hong. Princeton, NJ: Princeton University Press, 1987. Available at http://sqapo.com/CompleteText-Kierkegaard-EitherOr.htm.

———. *Fear and Trembling*. Translated by Walter Lowrie. Princeton, NJ: Princeton University Press, 1941. Available at http://sqapo.com/CompleteText-Kierkegaard-FearandTrembling.htm.

———. Kierkegaard's writings as e-books, from Princeton University Press, http://press.princeton.edu/titles/1335.html#evendors.

———. *Philosophical Fragments*. Available at http://pol-ts.com/Research_files/Source%20Material/Kierkegaard/Philosophical%20Fragments.pdf.

———. Selections from the writings of Kierkegaard, including *Fear and Trembling*. Available at http://www.ccel.org/ccel/kierkegaard/selections.

———. *The Sickness unto Death*. Princeton, NJ: Princeton University Press, 1941. Available at http://www.naturalthinker.net/trl/texts/Kierkegaard,Soren/TheSicknessUntoDeath.pdf.

———. *Works of Love*. Translated by Howard and Edna Hong. New York: Harper and Row, 1964. Pages 58–98 only (out of 378 pages). Available at http://moe.machighway.com/~cliffor1/Site/EXSupplementalReadings_files/kierkegaard_works.pdf.

Ritschl, Albrecht. *The Christian Doctrine of Justification and Reconciliation.* Translated and edited by H. R. Mackintosh and A. B. Macaulay. 2nd ed. Edinburgh: T&T Clark, 1902. Available at http://archive.org/details/christiandoctri00edgoog.

Schleiermacher, Friedrich. Christian Classics Ethereal Library. http://www.ccel.org/ccel/schleiermach. Includes his *On Religion: Speeches to Its Cultured Despisers* and *Selected Sermons of Schleiermacher.* Translated by Mary F. Wilson. Some other English translations of Schleiermacher (but not *The Christian Faith*) are available at http://en.wikipedia.org/wiki/Friedrich_Schleiermacher#Works.

———. *The Christian Faith.* New York: Bloomsbury Academic, 1999. Available at http://books.google.com/books/about/The_Christian_Faith.html?id=8JiQhmLykAYC.

LISTEN ONLINE

Link: http://itunes.apple.com/us/course/legacy-history-philosophy/id694658914

- Friedrich Schleiermacher and Albrecht Ritschl: 56:28
- Albrecht Ritschl Continued, Wilhelm Herrmann, Adolf Harnack, and Søren Kierkegaard: 58:29
- Søren Kierkegaard Continued: 20:40

READ FOR YOURSELF

Schleiermacher's *On Religion* will show you how radical his thinking was early in his career. Look here and there in *The Christian Faith* to see how he carried out and modified this early vision. Harnack's *What Is Christianity?* is sufficient to give you the essence of Ritschlianism, but you can supplement it with readings from Herrmann and Ritschl himself. Read Herrmann's *The Communion of the Christian with God* to understand the spiritual force of the Ritschlian movement—for example, what attracted Machen to it in his early years.

Kierkegaard's writings are difficult and profound. Start with *Fear and Trembling* and *The Sickness unto Death.* Then look at *Either/Or* and *Stages along Life's Way* to understand Kierkegaard's three-stage spiritual typology. The *Philosophical Fragments, Concluding Unscientific Postscript,* and *Attack upon Christendom* focus on his distinction between objectivity and subjectivity, and what is required to be a Christian within Christendom.

FAMOUS QUOTES

- **Schleiermacher:** http://en.wikiquote.org/w/index.php?title=Friedrich_Schleiermacher
- **Kierkegaard:** http://en.wikiquote.org/wiki/S%C3%B8ren_Kierkegaard

9

NIETZSCHE, PRAGMATISM, PHENOMENOLOGY, AND EXISTENTIALISM

THE REST OF THIS BOOK will deal with thinkers of the twentieth century and a bit of the twenty-first. We begin with Nietzsche, however, mainly a nineteenth-century figure. He barely makes it into the twentieth century, dying in 1900.[1] But his thought seems to me to be far more typical of the twentieth century than the nineteenth.[2] His writing feels modern—even postmodern (see chapter 12). For what we call *postmodernism* today is remarkably congruent with Nietzsche's main ideas.

Nietzsche's early interest in philology set the stage for some of his distinctive ideas. As we will see, the twentieth century is the century of language philosophy.

FRIEDRICH W. NIETZSCHE (1844–1900)

Nietzsche's father and grandfather were Lutheran ministers, but his father died when Nietzsche was four years old. He grew up in an all-female household, with his mother, sister, grandmother, and two maiden aunts. At the University of Basel, he was appointed a professor of classical philology in 1869 at the unheard-of age of twenty-four. Poor health and his growing distaste for academic work led him to resign this position ten years later. He then wandered through Europe, seeking healing, and wrote a number of books. But he collapsed on a street in Turin, Italy, in 1888 and spent the rest of his life in dementia, possibly because of a syphilis infection.

His early interest in philology set the stage for some of his distinctive ideas. As we will see, the twentieth century is the century of *language philosophy*. At that time, every school of thought seeks in one way or

1. Some might, however, quibble that the twentieth century did not begin until 1901.
2. I would make the same point about Kierkegaard.

Friedrich W. Nietzsche

another to gain philosophical insight through the study of language. One can argue that this trend begins with Nietzsche's inferences from his studies in ancient languages.

At the time, it was common for scholars to devote their efforts to finding the "original text" of classical documents (including, of course, the Bible). But Nietzsche broke radically with the consensus, as he would do on many other matters. As Nietzsche saw it, scholars are faced with fragments of documents. They choose (for no adequate reason) to regard a particular manuscript as the end product of a textual tradition, and then work back from that to posit an original source for that tradition. Nietzsche thought it would be better just to recognize the empirical fact that what we have is fragments, and leave it at that.

Indeed, language itself is just a "copy in sound of a nerve stimulus."[3] We may not infer a cause of that stimulus from anything outside ourselves. So language does not refer to objects in the world, in any straightforward sense. And language is essentially metaphorical, since the same word is applied to things that are very different from one another. (Note that Nietzsche, like Kierkegaard, is an extreme nominalist.) Even logic is not a reliable guide to the nature of things. It is a kind of prison, Nietzsche said. If we were different kinds of beings, we would use different logics.

From this skepticism about language and logic follows some consequences for philosophy. Like philologists studying ancient texts, philosophers have typically seized on some data—sense data, supposedly self-evident axioms, things in themselves, substances, pure being, atoms, and the like—and from that data have tried to reconstruct the nature of reality. But Nietzsche claimed that no datum given to us enables us to determine the nature of everything. Rather, the world is a flux, a chaos, upon which we impose our will, in order to achieve our purposes. We overhear in this Nietzsche's fascination with Schopenhauer. For both men, *will* is a powerful motive in our behavior. Nietzsche famously called it the *will to power.*

So Kant was right to abandon traditional metaphysics. But Nietzsche went beyond Kant: Not only have we no knowledge of the "thing in itself," we cannot even find universal (synthetic *a priori*) categories within experience. Traditional religion, too, has lost its power, according to Nietzsche, to give modern people a comprehensive view of the world. Nietzsche proclaimed this as the *death of God*.

What we call *knowing* is, in the end, an invention of the will. It is a tool to achieve our interests and to get along with other people. The honored *desire for truth* is never disinterested. We do not desire

3. Friedrich Nietzsche, "On Truth and Lies in a Nonmoral Sense" (unpublished essay, 1873).

knowledge for the sake of knowledge, only for our own success, for a pleasant life, for an aesthetically pleasing way to look at the world. So claims to knowledge are self-serving lies, illusions. Those lies are not necessarily bad; indeed, we can scarcely avoid telling them to ourselves and to others. We should use the imagination self-consciously in order to create metaphors of mythology and art, good deceptions, to enhance the quality of life.

Nietzsche is quick to point out that truth *and* falsity *do apply to everyday facts, but not to general theories . . . . Postmodernists today make the same distinction—in their language: we need not be skeptical in everyday life, but we must be incredulous about* metanarratives.

In *The Gay Science*, Nietzsche says that there is no human organ to detect truth or knowledge, in the way that the eye detects light and the ear detects sound.[4] We know, or believe, or imagine, as much as may be *useful* in the interests of the human "herd," the species.[5] And even the idea of what is useful is also no more than a mere belief, which could lead us to perish someday. Nietzsche's language here clearly anticipates the language of the American pragmatists, whom we will consider next: truth is what is useful. But as we can see, Nietzsche is skeptical of the idea of utility as well.

So for Nietzsche there are no facts, only interpretations. He describes his position as *perspectivism*.[6] Some have asked whether his thought is not self-refuting: is his own thought, in the end, just one more perspectival interpretation? Nietzsche does not fear to accept that consequence, but he adds that interpretations are not necessarily false. And (like contemporary postmodernists) Nietzsche is quick to point out that *truth* and *falsity* do apply to everyday facts, but not to general theories such as those of traditional philosophy and religion. Postmodernists today make the same distinction—in their language: we need not be skeptical in everyday life, but we must be incredulous about *metanarratives*.[7] Still, Nietzsche insists, irresolvable disagreement should be accepted as a fundamental fact of human existence.

For Nietzsche, God is dead. What do we have left? . . . Nietzsche urges us to respond more positively. For him, we should accept the death of God joyfully, as a kind of freedom.

Some might take a grim view of Nietzsche's conclusions. He seems to deny what we are inclined to call the *meaning of life*. He has ruled all traditional philosophy and religion out of court. For him, God is dead. What do we have left? Schopenhauer responded in pessimism, able to escape the horrifying power of will only by listening to certain kinds of Baroque music. But Nietzsche urges us to respond more positively. For him, we should accept the death of God joyfully, as a kind of freedom. We should acknowledge nihilism and press beyond

4. Friedrich Nietzsche, *The Gay Science: With a Prelude in Rhymes and an Appendix of Songs*, trans., with commentary, Walter Kaufmann (New York: Random House, 1974), 300.

5. Nietzsche is a confirmed follower of Darwin's theory of evolution, and of course a materialist.

6. Note: *perspectivism*, not *perspectivalism*. I have preferred the latter term, to distinguish my view from Nietzsche's relativism.

7. Of course, neither Nietzsche nor contemporary postmodernists offer clear criteria to distinguish between everyday life and metanarratives.

it. We should be excited and eager to participate in a "transvaluation of all values."

For Nietzsche, traditional philosophy, ethics, and religion have been barriers to the full exercise of our will to power. Christianity, particularly, has shackled human beings to a *slave morality*. To Nietzsche, Christian ethics favors the poor and weak. It discourages wealth and earthly accomplishment. It tells the poor to view the rich with *ressentiment*, a term that combines the ideas of envying someone's goods and hating him for his success. Interestingly, Marx viewed Christianity in the opposite way: as a rich man's religion designed to keep the poor in their place, comforting the poor with thoughts of heavenly rewards so that they would not revolt. So Marx and Nietzsche both rejected Christianity, though they interpreted it in opposite ways.[8]

To Nietzsche, the death of the Christian God means that we are free to seek our own greatness, to pursue excellence. We should reject moral and religious ideas that restrict the full expression of our will to power. To the contrary, we should aspire to be *Übermenschen* ("supermen," sometimes translated "overmen") who achieve more than the "herd" through superior creativity.

This notion appealed to the Nazis, who appeared on the scene some years later and claimed that the Aryan race was superior to all others. But Nietzsche himself was neither a racist nor an admirer of all things German. He broke off a close friendship with the composer Richard Wagner because of Wagner's anti-Semitism.[9]

The *Übermensch*, in Nietzsche's mind, is not a national dictator, but one who understands far more than the herd how to find joy without the crutches of religion and ideology. Borrowing from classical writers, Nietzsche cites the *eternal recurrence*, the idea that given infinite time and finite combinations of things, every event is destined to be repeated over and over again. The *Übermensch* will live in such a way as to take joy in this repetition.

For Nietzsche, traditional philosophy, ethics, and religion have been barriers to the full exercise of our will to power. Christianity, particularly, has shackled human beings to a slave morality.

But I think most readers will not find much joy in the thought that their conduct might be repeated again in 7 million years or so, or in the "freedom" of living in a world that, in the end, is a total chaos. It is not possible to derive values of any kind from a world grounded in impersonal chance.

CHARLES SANDERS PEIRCE (1839–1914)

Recall from the previous section Nietzsche's belief that our quest for knowledge is really a quest for the *useful*. Of course, he backed away

8. Perhaps it speaks well for a viewpoint that it is attacked both from the right and from the left.

9. And because of Wagner's opera *Parsifal*, which Nietzsche took to be an insincere tribute to Christianity.

from that statement somewhat, realizing that even the concept *useful* is problematic in his very skeptical viewpoint. But we will now be looking at a group of thinkers, Peirce, James, and Dewey, who focus even more on the idea of *usefulness* as an epistemological category. Hence *pragmatism*. Nietzsche is, of course, much more than a pragmatist, given his grandiose visions of the death of God, eternal recurrence, and the *Übermensch*. But if one simply seeks to use the data of mind and the senses as Nietzsche intended, the term *pragmatism* may express what it all comes down to.

Charles Sanders Peirce

Pragmatism would not have been appealing to ancient and medieval philosophers, who drew a very sharp distinction between what is true and what is useful. But we have seen in the modern period that a number of thinkers have given roles to human prudence, aesthetic beauty, and practical success in their epistemology, beyond *pure reason*. Recall Pascal's Wager, Edwards's sweetness of God, Butler's moral certainty, Hume's custom, Reid's common sense, Kant's regulative ideas, Kierkegaard's leap of faith, Schleiermacher's feeling, Ritschl's value judgment. Challenged by the skepticism of the modern period, these thinkers have emphasized that reason is at most a tool by which we make our way in the practical world, and epistemology draws a map to help us make the proper turns.

Pragmatism, therefore, represents strains of philosophical thinking from many historical periods and nationalities. The movement that we consider here is, however, American and, some would say, distinctively so, the first distinctly American contribution to the history of philosophy since Jonathan Edwards. People have often noted that it reflects the spirit of American culture, oriented toward practice rather than theory, preoccupied with "what works" rather than abstract truth, and so with technological progress.

Like other philosophers before him, Peirce was impressed with the success of science in finding truth, compared with the relative inability of philosophers to achieve consensus. His goal was for philosophy to become more like science.

Peirce,[10] son of a Harvard professor of mathematics, studied mathematics and chemistry at Harvard and worked as a scientist for the U.S. Coast and Geodetic Survey for thirty years. But he became more concerned with philosophical issues through that period, and in 1887 he retired to Milford, Pennsylvania, to devote more attention to them. He lectured in philosophy at various universities, but was unable to find a permanent teaching job in that field. Nevertheless, he influenced many philosophers, and the Harvard philosopher William James, whom we will discuss in the next section, befriended Peirce and helped him to meet his expenses.

Like other philosophers before him, Peirce was impressed with the success of science in finding truth, compared with the relative inability of philosophers to achieve consensus. His goal was for philosophy to become more like science.

10. Pronounced "purse."

In a sense, that was also the intention of Descartes. But according to Peirce, Descartes had gotten off on the wrong foot,[11] in these ways:

1. His starting point was to doubt everything he thought it possible to doubt. But Peirce thought Descartes went too far. Philosophy, like science, should deal only with *real* doubts, propositions that we honestly doubt and want to try to resolve. If we try to doubt everything, said Peirce, much of that doubt will be insincere, and when we develop our philosophic method, we might be too eager to reinstate those beliefs that we really never did doubt.[12]
2. Descartes found his ultimate certainty in the individual consciousness ("I think"). But scientists typically reason together as part of a community. Peirce said that people tend to let their speculative imaginations run wild when their ideas are not monitored by others.
3. Descartes rested all knowledge on a single thread of inference. Peirce replied that it is better to use many mutually reinforcing arguments, like threads of a cable.[13]
4. Descartes supposed that some things were inexplicable apart from God. But Peirce replied that we can never make such an assumption. No one can ever prove that there is only one possible explanation of a piece of evidence.
5. Descartes thought he needed to base his cognition on absolutely certain premises. Peirce replied that no proposition (even, presumably, "I think") can be identified as absolutely certain. Better to base one's reasoning on propositions that are, for now, free from *actual* doubt, recognizing that they in turn might have to be eventually revised.

According to Peirce, beliefs are objectively true or false. But acquiring them is a subjective, psychological process. Doubt is an uneasy state of mind; belief is a corresponding calm or satisfaction. The struggle to move from doubt to belief Peirce calls inquiry.

So Peirce thought Descartes had taken a wrong path to philosophical knowledge. But he acknowledged the legitimacy of the task. To find better methods than those of Descartes, Peirce sought to examine the psychology of belief formation, the mental process by which one moves from a state of doubt to a state of belief.

According to Peirce, beliefs are objectively true or false. But acquiring them is a subjective, psychological process. Doubt is an uneasy state of mind; belief is a corresponding calm or satisfaction.[14] The struggle

11. Recall my account of him in chapter 5.

12. Here, Peirce anticipates the argument of Wittgenstein in *On Certainty*.

13. In Christian apologetics, this is sometimes called the *cumulative case* method.

14. I call this state of calm "cognitive rest" in *DKG*, 152–62, and provide there an analysis in terms of the existential perspective of knowledge.

to move from doubt to belief Peirce calls *inquiry*. Sometimes we move from one belief to another, unable to be sure what belief to hold. We are tossed back and forth, without solid grounds to keep us in one place. Peirce identifies this difficulty as the problem of the *fixation* of belief. He lists the following methods that people use to achieve fixation:

No serious philosopher holds to a blind tenacity, *refusing in principle ever to change.*

1. *Tenacity*, simply to continue to hold our present beliefs against all challenges.
2. *Authority*, to accept the beliefs imposed on us by society, state, or church.
3. *A priori*, to affirm what our past beliefs incline us to believe. Often we choose beliefs that produce aesthetic symmetry, as when Plato argued that the distances of the celestial spheres were proportional to the different lengths of strings that produce musical chords, or when Hegel argued that all true ideas fit a pattern of thesis, antithesis, and synthesis. Peirce says that such methods are not reliable because they are not based on observed facts.
4. *Science*. Peirce says that this is the only method based on facts that we can check objectively. Tongue-in-cheek, he says that other methods have some value: for achieving comfort, ruling the masses, or producing strong character. But if one wants to achieve a legitimate true belief, science is the only way.[15]

Peirce's conclusion raises the further question of how we go about reasoning scientifically. Peirce outlines a method called critical commonsensism: *inquiry guided by common-sense principles.*

The first three alternatives listed here are, in my view, caricatures rather than careful descriptions of actual alternatives to Peirce's scientism. No serious philosopher holds to a blind *tenacity*, refusing in principle ever to change. Nor do I know any who are as blindly deferential to human authority as Peirce's number 2 suggests. The *a priori* category is more interesting, and it does describe what is wrong with Plato's theory of cosmic vibrations and Hegel's dialectic. But Hegel's dialectic is backed up by some serious reasoning that Peirce never undertakes to refute. And we have seen in our survey of the history of philosophy that there are many alternatives to scientism that Peirce doesn't even acknowledge, such as Aristotelianism, Thomism, and Kantianism.

In any case, Peirce's conclusion raises the further question of how we go about reasoning scientifically. Peirce outlines a method called *critical commonsensism*: inquiry guided by common-sense principles. These principles are fallible, and it's good to question them occasionally.

15. Here Peirce anticipates the verification principle of logical positivism, which I will discuss in chapter 12.

But they are the best starting points we have. He identifies the steps of scientific method as follows:

1. *Abduction or retroduction*: formulating a relevant hypothesis.
2. *Deduction*: determining testable consequences that would follow if the hypothesis were true.
3. *Induction*: actually testing the hypothesis by its practical effects.[16]

The hypothesis must be a *clear* one, if the scientist is to devise experiments that accurately measure its truth. In an essay called "How to Make Our Ideas Clear," Peirce recalls that Descartes resolved to believe only what he "clearly and distinctly believed to be true."[17] Peirce believed a third criterion was necessary in addition to clarity and distinctness: practical consequences. Two ideas differ, he argued, as they entail different practical consequences.

So Peirce formulated his famous *pragmatic maxim*:

> To ascertain the meaning of an intellectual conception one should consider what practical consequences might result from the truth of that conception—and the sum of these consequences constitute the entire meaning of the conception.[18]

Descartes had written as if intuition were sufficient to ensure the meaningfulness of our ideas. But Peirce says that we would have no idea of the meaning of, say, *hard* without knowing how a hard object actually behaves, as opposed to a soft object. This reinforces Peirce's argument for the primacy of scientific method. We don't even know the meaning of a term, he says, until we see how its concept functions in experiments.

We don't even know the meaning of a term, Peirce says, until we see how its concept functions in experiments. But this implies that concepts that cannot be tested through scientific methods are without meaning.

But this implies that concepts that cannot be tested through scientific methods are without meaning. Peirce did not extensively discuss concepts of metaphysics (mind, matter, oneness, manyness, form, matter, substance), ethics (right, wrong, virtue, good, evil), and theology (regeneration, kingdom of God, etc.), but we will see how the early Wittgenstein and the logical positivists, who held views similar to Peirce's, found these concepts highly problematic.

As we will see, William James and John Dewey went beyond Peirce's pragmatic philosophy of meaning to develop a pragmatic theory of

16. In my analysis, (1) is existential (a use of imagination), (2) normative (focused on the rules of logic), and (3) situational (examining the facts of the world).

17. Charles S. Peirce, "How to Make Our Ideas Clear," *Popular Science Monthly* 12 (January 1878): 286–302.

18. Charles S. Peirce, *Collected Papers of Charles Sanders Peirce*, ed. Charles Hartshorne and Paul Weiss, 6 vols. (Cambridge, MA: Harvard University Press, 1931–35), 5:9.

truth (the truth is what works). Peirce repudiated that development. To him, the truth was objective, independent of our thoughts or aspirations. For that and other reasons, he renamed his own position *pragmaticism*, which he called "a term ugly enough to keep it from kidnappers."[19]

Peirce also wrote extensively about semiotics (the theory of signs), another example of late-nineteenth- and twentieth-century philosophical preoccupation with language. Another movement that Peirce anticipates is phenomenology, which I will discuss later in this chapter. Peirce argues that only three categories are necessary to describe all the phenomena of experience; see fig. 9.1.

To Peirce, the truth was objective, independent of our thoughts or aspirations. For that and other reasons, he renamed his own position pragmaticism.

1. *Firstness*: qualities such as color and shape.
2. *Secondness*: "brute factitity," the objects that bear these qualities.
3. *Thirdness*: laws of nature.

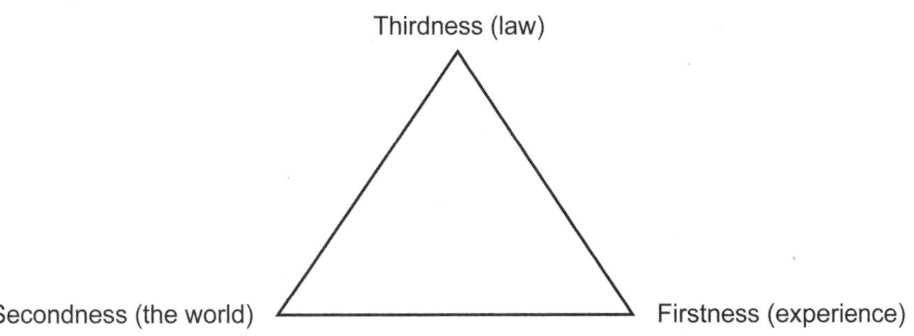

Fig. 9.1. Peirce's Phenomenology and Biblical Perspectives

Scientism, *the belief in science as the ultimate way of knowing, is what chiefly distinguishes Peirce's philosophy.*

Peirce's firstness recalls the Greek concept of *form*, secondness of *matter*. Secondness also represents Locke's *primary qualities* and firstness Locke's *secondary qualities*.[20] We should note here, as in Peirce's scientistic pragmatism, an affirmation of empiricist epistemology.[21] And as earlier, it is clear that in his account of experience there is no place for metaphysics, ethics, or God.

Scientism, the belief in science as the ultimate way of knowing, is what chiefly distinguishes Peirce's philosophy. Since the Enlighten-

19. Ibid., 5:414.

20. Triperspectivally, (1) is existential (what we experience), (2) situational (the actual structure of the world), and (3) normative (what governs the behavior of objects); see fig. 9.1.

21. Kant's critical appropriation of empiricism did not bring the empirical tradition to an end. Notably, Jeremy Bentham (1748–1832) and John Stuart Mill (1806–73) carried that tradition forward in the nineteenth century. Mill was somewhat extreme in his empiricism, arguing that even mathematics is the result of inductive arguments from sense experience. Bentham and Mill are chiefly known for their development of utilitarian ethics, and I discuss them in *DCL*, 96–99. The pragmatists and many language analysts (particularly the logical positivists) held to forms of empiricist epistemologies.

OUTLINE

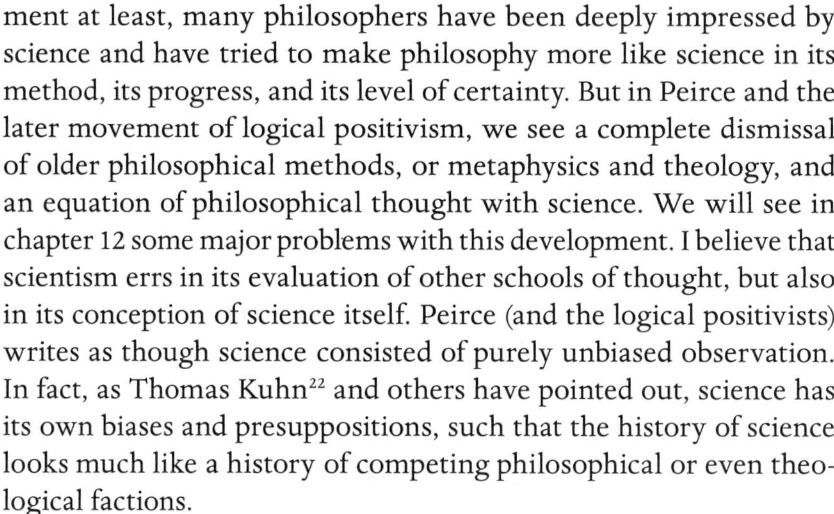

ment at least, many philosophers have been deeply impressed by science and have tried to make philosophy more like science in its method, its progress, and its level of certainty. But in Peirce and the later movement of logical positivism, we see a complete dismissal of older philosophical methods, or metaphysics and theology, and an equation of philosophical thought with science. We will see in chapter 12 some major problems with this development. I believe that scientism errs in its evaluation of other schools of thought, but also in its conception of science itself. Peirce (and the logical positivists) writes as though science consisted of purely unbiased observation. In fact, as Thomas Kuhn[22] and others have pointed out, science has its own biases and presuppositions, such that the history of science looks much like a history of competing philosophical or even theological factions.

WILLIAM JAMES (1842–1910)

William James earned a medical degree at Harvard in 1869 and in 1872 became an instructor there in physiology. But he moved on from these disciplines to the relatively new science of psychology, and then to Harvard's department of philosophy. His brother was the famous novelist Henry James. Some have opined that Henry should have been the psychologist (given his deep insight into human character) and William should have been the novelist (given his remarkable ability to speak clearly and vividly).

William James developed the pragmatism of Peirce into a theory of truth. As I mentioned earlier, Peirce was not pleased by this use of his ideas, but it seems to me that James's pragmatism was a logical implication of Peirce's. I see nothing in the following paragraph of James that Peirce could not himself have said:

William James

> Is the world one or many?—fated or free?—material or spiritual?—here are notions either of which may or may not hold good of the world; and disputes over such notions are unending. The pragmatic method in such cases is to try to interpret each notion by tracing its respective practical consequences. What difference would it practically make to anyone if this notion rather than that notion were true? If no practical difference whatever can be traced, then the alternatives mean practically the same thing, and all dispute is idle.[23]

22. Thomas S. Kuhn, *The Structure of Scientific Revolutions*, 3rd ed. (Chicago: University of Chicago Press, 1996). See chapter 12 of the present book.

23. William James, *Pragmatism and the Meaning of Truth* (Cambridge, MA: Harvard University Press, 1979), 28.

We see here how Peirce's theory of meaning enables us to resolve questions about truth. The paragraph is entirely about determining the meanings of terms. But it shows how discovering these meanings can be the key to determining whether one view is true or false, or whether the dispute is "idle." So James says that true ideas are those that *work*, that *lead somewhere*, that have *cash value*, that *succeed*. He prefers such functional terms to static ones such as that a true idea should be a *copy* of reality or should *agree* with it.

So he says:

> The truth of an idea is not a stagnant property inherent in it. Truth *happens* to an idea. It *becomes* true, is *made* true by events.[24]

James says that true ideas are those that work, *that* lead somewhere, *that have* cash value, *that* succeed.

Ideas "made true by events" can certainly happen in the context of Peircean scientific experiments. But James wants to carry it further. He thinks that our beliefs are justified in many ways, not limited to clearly defined experiments. Sometimes an intense emotion is sufficient to deserve our commitment. Here James goes beyond Peirce into territory that we have explored in Pascal and Kierkegaard.

In his essay "The Will to Believe," James defends Pascal's Wager (see our chapter 6) in which Pascal urges commitment to Christ based on the odds of greatest benefit. James says that we can neither prove nor disprove the existence of God. But under three conditions it is legitimate to go beyond reason and believe on emotion alone: (1) The belief must be a *live option*—one that we are genuinely tempted to hold in our present cultural context. (2) The choice must be *forced*—such that I cannot choose to withhold judgment. (3) It must be *momentous*—an urgent, important decision. As Pascal said, in such a situation the choice would be a risk, but the risk of commitment might be more rewarding than the risk of missing out. Obviously, this is true of religious decision. James also points out a secular application: a young man does not know whether or not a woman loves him, but he chooses to act as if she does, and thereby creates a situation in which the evidence of her love can become visible. So the will plays a legitimate role in belief.

Many more (from Thomas Reid to Alvin Plantinga) have acknowledged the legitimacy in some cases of believing propositions in the absence of compelling argument—or even in the absence of any argument at all.

Many have criticized "The Will to Believe." James's colleague George Santayana has been quoted as saying that "[James] wished the intellectual cripples and hunchbacks not to be jeered at."[25] But many continue to defend the essay and its source in Pascal. And many more (from Thomas Reid to Alvin Plantinga) have acknowledged the legitimacy

24. Ibid., 97.

25. Quoted in Walter Kaufmann, ed., *Critique of Religion and Philosophy* (Princeton, NJ: Princeton University Press, 1979), 119. I could not locate Kaufmann's source for the Santayana quote.

in some cases of believing propositions in the absence of compelling argument—or even in the absence of any argument at all.

We should not assume, however, the general orthodoxy of James's religious views. He was a major defender of libertarian free will, which I have often criticized in this book. He also wrote a significant book[26] surveying the religious experiences of many individuals. The book concluded that the existence of a finite god would be sufficient to account for the testimonies narrated.

James and Peirce have certainly persuaded me that *practical consequences* is an important factor in determining the meanings of terms and the truth of propositions. But there are problems with this criterion:

1. Although the pragmatist arguments establish the importance of practical consequences, they do not show that practical consequences are *sufficient* for determining meaning or truth. Ptolemaic astronomy is still useful as a guide to ocean navigation. But most astronomers have concluded that where it differs from Copernican astronomy it is false. In this case, practical consequences need to be supplemented by the more traditional tests of truth, coherence, and correspondence; see fig. 9.2.[27]

James and Peirce have certainly persuaded me that practical consequences *is an important factor in determining the meanings of terms and the truth of propositions.*

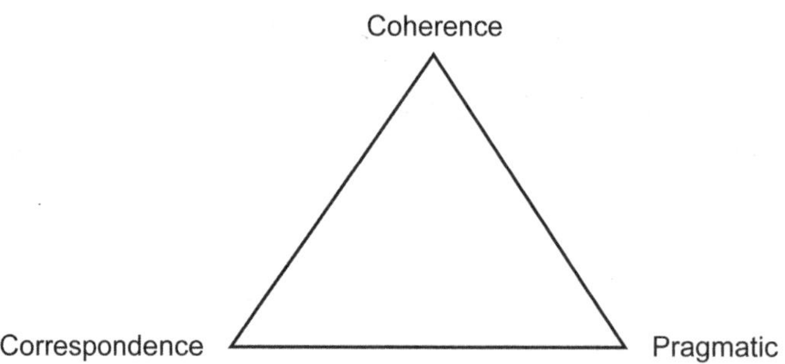

Fig. 9.2. Theories of Truth

2. That raises a further concern as to what counts as a *practical consequence*. James, for example, seemed to think that whether the world is material or spiritual makes no practical difference and is therefore a meaningless distinction. But the Gnostics, for example, thought this distinction vitally important for human well-being. As the pragmatists themselves emphasize, beliefs

26. William James, *Varieties of Religious Experience: A Study of Human Nature* (London: Longmans Green, 1902).

27. *Coherence* is normative, *correspondence* situational, *pragmatic* existential. In my view, testing for truth, under biblical presuppositions, includes all these methods; see fig. 9.2.

> are found in contexts of life situations, but it is possible for people to differ as to the nature of these contexts. A Gnostic, an orthodox Christian, and a materialist, for example, would have very different ideas about the roles of the material and the spiritual in human life, and therefore about the practical consequences of the two concepts. But the pragmatists offer no analysis to show which context (in the end, which worldview) is correct. And if a pragmatist tried to show that one context was "true," he could do that only by setting forth its practical consequences, a circular argument.

For Dewey, then, thought is a tool given by natural selection, adapted to the survival of the species.

JOHN DEWEY (1859–1952)

Dewey's first philosophical training was in the Hegelian idealist tradition, but he came under the influence of James. Like the other pragmatists, he was also enthusiastic about Darwinian evolution.

For Dewey, then, thought is a tool given by natural selection, adapted to the survival of the species. He therefore rejected the *spectator* model of knowledge, in which the mind stands outside of nature, observing and analyzing facts for its edification. The mind, rather, is part of nature, a capacity for solving problems, surmounting obstacles to human survival and flourishing.

The mind encounters situations that it does not understand and seeks to clarify them, either by clarifying its own thought patterns or by changing the world. The goal is always action. Thought, Dewey said, is deferred action. That leads Dewey to a pragmatic understanding of philosophy:

John Dewey

> There is a first-rate test of the value of any philosophy which is offered us: Does it end in conclusions which, when they are referred back to ordinary life-experiences and their predicaments, render them more significant, more luminous to us, and make our dealing with them more fruitful? Or does it terminate in rendering the things of ordinary experience more opaque than they were before and depriving them of having in "reality" even the significance that they seemed to have?[28]

Universals (as in philosophic rationalism) and sense data (as in empiricism) are not, according to Dewey, *objects* of knowledge, but they are *instruments* for solving problems in life. Hence, Dewey called his philosophy *instrumentalism*. The world is not a collection of substances (as in Aristotle), but a field in which man seeks to make his way.

28. John Dewey, *Experience and Nature* (New York: Dover, 1958), 7.

Like Peirce and James, Dewey sees his method of knowledge as being governed by the scientific model. He recognizes the existence of knowledge outside the scientific field, but he believes that the scientific model is sufficient to govern and explain all kinds of knowledge, practiced in all walks of life.

One can see some leftover Hegelian influence in Dewey's view of a world in which there are no sharp separations between one thing and another. Spirit and matter, mind and body, universals and particulars, thought and action interpenetrate in his philosophy. Same with facts and values. For Dewey, value is what we achieve when thought leads to action and a problem is solved, for now.[29] But on this theory there are no eternal, normative values. Values change with our situations—our problems and solutions.

Certainly he is right in saying that we must relate to changing situations by changing responses. That is not problematic if these changing responses are applications of fundamental values. But Dewey believes that our most fundamental values are also changeable, determined by situation and resources. Yet Dewey does not make sufficient distinction between values in general and those that establish *obligations*. Here I would make the argument that although situations call for different responses, they cannot *obligate*. Moral obligation must come from a personal source, not an impersonal environment, as Dewey thinks.[30]

Dewey is best known today for his work in education. He encourages schools to teach in an interactive way, giving students training and experience in problem-solving, teaching them good habits through experimentation. He is a strong advocate of public schooling, seeing it as an important means of liberal social change. He believes that the public schools should turn children away from the traditional ideas of their families and toward views he considered better for society. Dewey's politics were *progressive*, under the influence of Marx. Though he often commended democracy, he also praised the Soviet Union in glowing terms after a visit there.

Dewey is a strong advocate of public schooling, seeing it as an important means of liberal social change. He believes that the public schools should turn children away from the traditional ideas of their families and toward views he considered better for society.

In my view, Dewey's influence in the public schools continues to pose a major problem for Christians. Scripture calls us to educate our children in an atmosphere saturated by the Word of God (Deut. 6:4–9).

29. In ethics, Dewey begins with utilitarianism, but goes beyond Bentham and Mill in noticing that our goals cannot be defined in any static way. They constantly change according to our changing needs, and then we must find new means to reach the new goals. See my discussion of Dewey's ethics in *DCL*, 99–100. He advocates self-realization, the process of bringing together all our incompatible impulses into "an orderly release in action." But he adds that even self-realization should not be considered a fixed goal, but only a criterion for evaluating other goals.

30. I have developed this argument in *AJCB*, 95–123, and in *DCL*, 54–71.

We should not be comfortable with a school system that seeks to indoctrinate children in a secular progressive mind-set.

Pragmatism has continued to be an influential philosophical movement in America since the death of Dewey. Associated with it have been the names of C. I. Lewis, Willard Quine, Hilary Putnam, Richard Rorty, and many others. But we must move on.

EDMUND HUSSERL (1859–1938)

Edmund Husserl

During the Enlightenment, the English Channel served as a barrier between schools of philosophy, as well as between nations: rationalists in Continental Europe, empiricists in the British Isles. I noted that one of Kant's substantial accomplishments was to bridge that gap by taking into account the concerns of both schools. Thereafter, Kant, Hegel, and Marx had disciples in both geographic areas. But in the twentieth century the gap opened up again, with pragmatism and language analysis (see chapter 12) predominating on the British-American side and rather different concepts of philosophy on the Continent. I will look at Continental philosophy first, beginning with Edmund Husserl, the founder of phenomenology.

Although there are some common concerns between pragmatists and phenomenologists, the two movements begin by facing in opposite directions. The pragmatists want our ordinary thinking to become more like science. Phenomenologists, too, admire the rigor and clarity of science, and they hope to make philosophy more like science in those respects. But they see the prevailing methods of science as something of a barrier to our understanding of human life and experience. Science in Husserl's time (as often in our own) was largely naturalistic, assuming that all reality could be reduced to the physical. Husserl and his successors, however, say that the world described by science is somehow different from the world we know in everyday life. To say this is not to oppose science, but to recognize that it describes only part of reality. Everyday life includes the vast integration of nature, art, culture, food, drink, social relationships, conversations, feelings, dreams, and so on that we constantly experience. Science abstracts some aspects of this experience that can be quantified, measured, and experimented with. But it has no right to say that this quantifiable, physical world is "all there is," as naturalists claim.

Husserl, then, believes that to understand the world of actual experience, the natural standpoint *or* life-world (Lebenswelt)*, we need different methods from those of science.*

Husserl, then, believes that to understand the world of actual experience, the *natural standpoint* or *life-world* (*Lebenswelt*), we need different methods from those of science. Of course, we cannot confine ourselves to the life-world either. Philosophy is a technical discipline and requires specialized methods of observation. To find an appropriate method, he explores the idea of human consciousness in the philosophy of Descartes, the "I am." Descartes began with consciousness as an axiom for a series of deductions leading to mind, matter, and God. But Husserl says, in effect, "not so fast." He pauses to examine human consciousness itself, the experience of being a conscious individual. In experience, consciousness itself is what we are first confronted with. So our first priority is to gain an understanding of that. But to understand consciousness itself, we might have to move beyond the natural standpoint.

Consciousness includes everything that goes on in our minds: beliefs, thoughts, ideas, feelings, and the like. These are the *phenomena* of consciousness, and according to Husserl, the work of philosophy is to carefully describe these phenomena.[31] These data are *given* to consciousness. The empiricists and Kant were troubled as to whether and to what extent the *ideas* of the mind were related to the real world. The usual conception was that ideas were copies or images of things in the world external to us.[32] Locke thought that the extramental material world contained *substances*, but he found the idea of a material substance very mysterious. Kant thought that *phenomena* were the appearances, or representatives, of realities in the *noumenal* world. But for him, the noumenal world, the world of things as they really are, was unknown and unknowable.

But for Husserl, the real world is not something behind the phenomena. It is right there, in the phenomena, the things that the phenomena are of. For Husserl, the most important thing about our data of consciousness is that they are all "of" something. An idea is never just an idea; it is an idea "of" a chair, or a horse, or a virtue. He expressed this fact by saying that phenomena are *intentional* or *referential*.[33] The intentionality of an idea is not something outside the idea, as in empiricism and Kantianism.

For Husserl, the real world is not something behind the phenomena. It is right there, in the phenomena, the things that the phenomena are of. For Husserl, the most important thing about our data of consciousness is that they are all "of" something. An idea is never just an idea.

My mental idea of a horse is not an image of a horse that exists somewhere outside my mind. It is helpful, I think, as one of my correspondents suggested to me in a letter, to regard Husserl's phenomena not as images, but as *windows*. The idea of a horse is a *window* through which we look at the horse. My correspondent elaborates:

> So, instead of worrying about whether there are any things behind the images you experience, Husserl would say, "You're

31. Kierkegaard's philosophy anticipates Husserl's in this regard.

32. But Berkeley, whose ideas in some respects resemble Husserl's, rejected the notion that our ideas refer to anything outside the mind.

33. Husserl inherited the concept of intentionality from his teacher, Franz Brentano (1838–1917). See also my discussion of Thomas Reid in chapter 6.

> not experiencing images at all, you're experiencing windows." And you don't look *at* windows (unless they're made of stained glass and are in a cathedral), you look *through* windows.
>
> Furthermore, there's no question about whether there's anything behind these phenomena/windows. Whatever's "behind" the window (i.e., the thing in itself) appears through the window. (Who, after all, ever argues about what's "behind" a window? All you have to do is look.)[34]

It would be better for philosophers simply to describe *the phenomenon, for the phenomenon is the only reality that we are acquainted with. And it is the only reality that we know with certainty.*

But someone philosophically inclined might ask whether the horse, which we see in the window, is itself an appearance of some higher reality. Something like a Platonic Form or a Kantian noumenon? Certainly it is hard to imagine any way of resolving this question. (It would not meet Peirce's criterion of *genuine doubt*.) Husserl thought that philosophers of the past had largely wasted their time on questions such as this one. It would be better for philosophers simply to *describe* the phenomenon, for the phenomenon is the only reality that we are acquainted with. And it is the only reality that we know with certainty. This certain knowledge is the only way to determine the *essence* of what we are contemplating. So for Husserl, the phenomenon *is* the "thing in itself," contrary to Kant, who considers it a mere appearance.

Phenomenology restricts its attention to what we can know for sure, what is given to consciousness, the mental acts themselves, and it emerges with certain, essential truths.

It is difficult for us to say what lies "behind appearances." But we can never be wrong about what we directly experience. We can be uncertain about our body temperature, for example, but we cannot be uncertain that we *feel* hot. So phenomenology restricts its attention to what we can know for sure, what is *given* to consciousness, the mental acts themselves, and it emerges with certain, essential truths.

It is at this point that Husserl asks us to *bracket*[35] the relation of the phenomenon to realities that are not part of the phenomenon itself. At this point we must turn away from the natural standpoint. Donald Palmer explains:

> This method brackets any experience whatsoever and describes it while suspending all presuppositions and assumptions

34. E-mail letter to me, dated March 3, 2009. Thanks to this correspondent for suggesting this metaphor and some other ideas in this section. Of course, I take full responsibility for the formulation here. My friend also shared his view that Husserl was something of a multiperspectivalist: For him, every perspective on an object implies others, fulfills others, corrects others. But to look at an object from even one perspective is to look at the object itself. Our perspectives as finite beings are limited, but not on that account false.

35. He refers to this *bracketing* also by the Greek term *epoché* and by the phrase *phenomenological reduction*. He also draws an analogy between this reduction and the *radical doubt* of Descartes.

> normally made about that experience. Bracketing the experience of looking at a coffee cup, for instance, requires suspending the belief that the cup is for holding coffee and that its handle is for grasping. Bracketing reveals the way the cup presents itself to consciousness as a number of possible structures. (I can't see the front and the back at the same time, nor the top and the bottom, nor see more than one of its possible presentations at any given moment.)[36]

We should not ask, for example, whether a unicorn is fictional or "real." It is sufficient just to explore our own thoughts about the unicorn, to describe it as a phenomenon.

So Husserl tells us to contemplate other things in the same way, even relatively abstract things, such as the nature of time. Husserl calls us to consider time apart from such things as clocks and schedules, concluding that "lived time" is the consciousness of an "eternal now," somewhat tempered by memory of earlier nows and anticipating future nows.[37]

Husserl seeks a kind of absolute, incorrigible truth, truth about the essences *of reality, by trying to think apart from any assumptions or presuppositions.*

I have only hinted at the complications of Husserl's phenomenology, expounded at length in eight books and forty-five thousand manuscript pages.[38] I confess that I find Husserl more difficult to understand than almost any other philosopher. But the following may serve as a summary, my conception of what it all seems to boil down to: Husserl seeks a kind of absolute, incorrigible truth, truth about the *essences* of reality, by trying to think apart from any assumptions or presuppositions. He finds that truth in the most fundamental human experience, which he considers to be self-attesting and self-validating. This is his rationalism. But the more he gazes at himself, the less he knows about the context of his experience. To know the coffee cup in this fundamental way, we must ignore its uses in culture, its place in human life. To know the phenomenon of time, we must place ourselves in a (mystical?) realm outside any kind of normal time. To know time, we must turn away from time as we know it in everyday life. And yet he claims that such knowledge brings us closer to the life-world. This is irrationalism; see fig. 9.3.

36. Donald Palmer, *Looking at Philosophy: The Unbearable Heaviness of Philosophy Made Lighter* (New York: McGraw-Hill, 2010), 360–61.

37. Ibid., 361. Readers of Wittgenstein's *Philosophical Investigations* (see my account in chapter 12 of this book) will see Husserl here as the anti-Wittgenstein. For Wittgenstein, in analyzing concepts including time (and at one point Wittgenstein calls his own work *phenomenology*), insists on precisely what Husserl here rules out: connecting each concept with its practical functions in human life. The pragmatists, too, are on the side of Wittgenstein.

38. Richard Schmitt, "Husserl, Edmund," in *The Encyclopedia of Philosophy*, ed. Paul Edwards (New York: Macmillan/Free Press, 1967), 3:97.

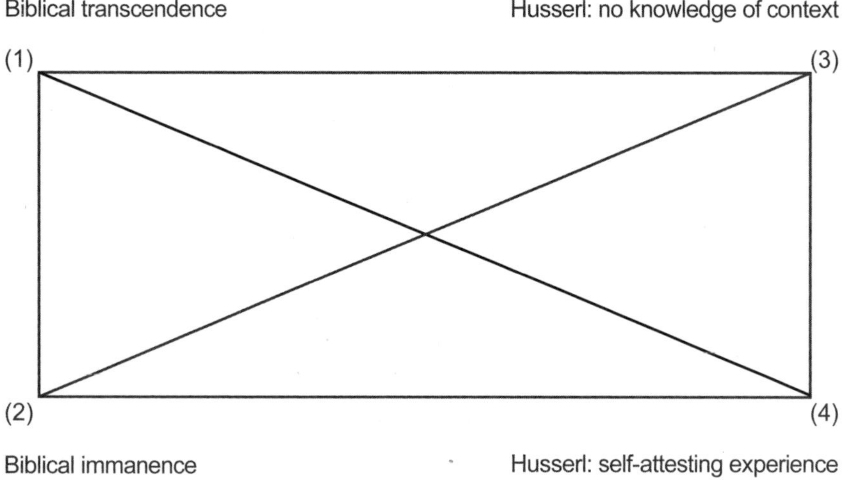

Fig. 9.3. Transcendence and Immanence in Husserl

For the most part, we gain knowledge of our world precisely by taking account of all the connections between things in our experience and by recognizing the role that each thing plays in human life.

In the real life-world, we come to understand the coffee cup in the context of its uses. The same for time and the other realities that Husserl explores. There might sometimes be some value in standing back from our cultural context and asking, "Just what do I actually see?"[39] But for the most part, we gain knowledge of our world precisely by taking account of all the connections between things in our experience and by recognizing the role that each thing plays in human life. This knowledge of the ordinary world is not absolute or incorrigible. God has reserved that kind of knowledge for himself and for his Word. The best knowledge we can have of the world we live in comes not by setting aside all assumptions and presuppositions, not by looking for "brute," uninterpreted facts, but by embracing the revelation of God as our fundamental presupposition.

Martin Heidegger

MARTIN HEIDEGGER (1889–1976)

Heidegger studied with Husserl at the University of Freiburg. After a time at the University of Marburg, where one of his colleagues was Rudolf Bultmann (see chapter 10), he received an appointment to succeed Husserl at Freiburg. He was appointed Rector of the University in 1933, and joined the Nazi party briefly, commending Hitler on occasion. But in 1934 he resigned and became critical of Nazism at times, though accounts differ as to the extent of his cooperation with the regime. He was drafted into the "People's Militia" in 1944, and after Germany's defeat was not permitted to return to teaching until 1951. He retired the next year and published several works before his death in

39. Like Wittgenstein's advice: "don't think; look."

Freiburg at eighty-six. Many philosophers, especially in Europe, never forgave him for his dalliance with Nazism, and they connect that with deficiencies in his philosophy. Others consider him a major thinker in the development of phenomenology and existentialism.

Heidegger, as we will see, used a method resembling that of phenomenology. But his deepest concern was to understand Being itself, as the Greek philosophers had investigated the concept. To him, the deepest question is: "Why is there something rather than nothing?"[40] We may recall from chapter 2 the difficulties Parmenides experienced in trying to describe Being exclusively, without any admixture of nonbeing. And we may recall from chapter 7 Hegel's dialectical attempt to resolve the problem.

Heidegger believed that the study of Being (*Sein*) had been obscured by all sorts of confusions, since the time of the Greek thinkers. He thought the only way to get back toward a study of Being was to approach it from the standpoint of *human* being, a part of Being that we are actually acquainted with. *Human being* he called *Dasein* ("being there").[41] *Dasein* inhabits the life-world of Husserl, the world of everyday experiences and decisions. It is our *existence*, the course of our choices and decisions. For it is in those decisions that we are most truly human, as in Kierkegaard's thought. *Dasein* is not an essence, something that might limit our freedom to choose.

Dasein is *being-in-the-world*,[42] but it is not defined by anything else in its environment. To exist as *Dasein* is not only to be in the world, but to *have* a world. Other beings *are*, but we *ek-sist* (= stand out from among them).[43]

The world is *my* world. Things in my environment, such as cars and screwdrivers, are extensions of myself, since they are tools of mine, to fulfill my plans.[44] When one breaks, however, it becomes a mere object, to be treated as something other than myself. What is important, though, is always the relation that something sustains to me as *Dasein*. And the fundamental relation is *Sorge*—the *care* that I have for my world.

Heidegger's deepest concern was to understand Being itself, as the Greek philosophers had investigated the concept. To him, the deepest question is: "Why is there something rather than nothing?"

40. Leibniz had originally posed this question, but in a more theological context.

41. It is interesting to consider possible connections between Heidegger's thought and the Peter Sellers film *Being There*. Chance, the Sellers character, is a kind of intellectual Forrest Gump, who always just happens to be in the right place at the right time. Perhaps that represents Heidegger's notion that we are all "thrown" into the world.

42. There are a great number of hyphenated terms in English translations of Heidegger, owing partly to the nature of the German language and partly to Heidegger's penchant for coining neologisms. Heidegger often thought that philosophical problems required new terminology, because the old terminology obscured what he thought was important. He often expressed this concern by reference to etymologies in a way quite contrary to that of present-day linguistics. James Barr criticized definitively this kind of reliance on etymologies in *The Semantics of Biblical Language* (London: Oxford University Press, 1961), 107–60.

43. Another of Heidegger's fanciful etymologies.

44. Note that this understanding is rather far from Husserl's *epoché*. Husserl urges the phenomenologist to look at things apart from their uses. Heidegger, like the pragmatists, thinks that to know a thing is initially to know its use in my life.

Care has three aspects: (1) My *thrownness* into the world by chance, creating relations to many other things, which Heidegger calls *facticity*. (2) But I have freedom of choice,[45] to determine how I will respond to this situation and its elements. (3) But I am tempted to simply accept thrownness as my fate, rather than acknowledging my freedom to transcend it. Heidegger calls this our *fallenness*, and the corresponding life choices *inauthentic existence*.

My world consists not only of things, but of other people. To *be-within-the-world* is to *be-with-others*. But others make demands of me. Giving in to these demands too much is especially inauthentic. It denies my own uniqueness and makes me into an extension of other people. We should[46] rather make choices that justify our own worth. (Here, Nietzsche's *Übermensch* seems to enter Heidegger's thought.)

Others make demands of me. Giving in to these demands too much is especially inauthentic. It denies my own uniqueness and makes me into an extension of other people.

Nevertheless, we will all die, Heidegger tells us. We are *being-toward-death*. On that account, we are *anxious*. Anxiety is like fear, but fear is directed to something or someone else, such as an enemy. Anxiety, rather, is directed against death, against the fact that we will one day become nothing, nonbeing. Everything we think or do is in the shadow of death. Time is always the time before death. So our being, our *being-in-the-world*, is inseparable from nonbeing.

We can transcend this anxiety only through *risk*. As with Kierkegaard, we are most fully human when we are making hard choices. We may transcend the world not just by knowing it, as many philosophers have said, but by direct participation in it. (Heidegger emphasizes that we should not be bound by the subject-object distinction.) We may achieve transcendence in our relationships with others through *rapport* (direct involvement, not just communication). And we may transcend time by risking death to care for the future.

Everything we think or do is in the shadow of death. Time is always the time before death. So our being, our being-in-the-world, *is inseparable from nonbeing.*

Such is Heidegger's teaching in his influential (and unfinished[47]) early work, *Being and Time* (1927). It is sometimes described as the thought of the "early Heidegger."[48]

The "later Heidegger," in his writings after this period, urges on his readers a more passive stance toward the world as a more fruitful

45. Libertarian, of course.

46. Heidegger's *shoulds* and *oughts* are essentially naturalistic fallacies. That is the fallacy of reasoning from nonmoral facts to moral obligation. Heidegger teaches that the world is essentially a world of chance. In that, what basis is there for determining our moral obligations, or for judging some choices as authentic or inauthentic? Why shouldn't I live in a way that Heidegger calls inauthentic if I choose to?

47. *Being and Time* consists of two parts, ending in a series of questions that Heidegger promised to answer in part 3. But he never wrote part 3. George Steiner, in *Martin Heidegger* (New York: Viking, 1979), says that for Heidegger the path toward Being had "come to a dead end" (114).

48. Bultmann's theology seems to be more influenced by the early than by the later Heidegger. But some of his disciples drew on the later Heidegger for their *new hermeneutic* (chapter 10).

way to communion with Being. We cannot master or comprehend the world. Rather, all our attempts to master and comprehend are responses to something greater than we are.

In the later Heidegger, language comes to the fore: "Language is the house of Being in which man ek-sists by dwelling."[49] Through language, Heidegger believes, Being addresses us. We should not seek to grasp Being, but should listen as Being speaks to us through language. That is not, of course, limited to philosophical language. Poetry tends to be more revealing. The silences, especially, between words are significant.[50]

In the later Heidegger, language comes to the fore: "Language is the house of Being in which man ek-sists by dwelling." Through language, Heidegger believes, Being addresses us.

In *Being and Time*, Heidegger avoids the artificial and abstract meditation of Husserl, seeing that the context of human consciousness is all-important. His *being-in-the-world* keeps him from Husserl's attempts to isolate the individual consciousness. But in the end, he is as mystical as Husserl, as much alone in his linguistic silence as Husserl in his *eternal now*. Much of what he says is true enough: we are indeed placed in a world not of our making, called to make responsible choices in a situation that tempts us to do otherwise. And yes, our ultimate limit is death, and that affects everything we think, say, and do.

But Heidegger secularizes these ideas, leaving one wondering why he thought they needed to be said. How much better it would have been if he had drawn on biblical revelation, which shows us the true importance of these insights: We are created (not *thrown*, for that suggests chance) into a world in which indeed we are called by God to make responsible choices. If you secularize this point and leave God out of it, it turns into something trivial and obvious. And yes, we are *beings-unto-death*. But death is really the wages of sin. To secularize death is to rob human life of meaning, regardless of how much Heidegger attempts to inject significance into it. He does no better than Nietzsche in trying to make his nihilistic worldview a joyful existence. And like Nietzsche, Heidegger eliminates all possibility of grace, salvation, and resurrection.

Heidegger makes a determined attempt to find answers to the hardest questions by a highly technical terminology and sophisticated argument. That is his rationalism. But in the end, we are all, including Heidegger, thrown into the world by pure chance, deprived of significance by the inevitability of death, so that in the end nothing really matters. That is his irrationalism.

49. Martin Heidegger, "Letter on Humanism," in *Martin Heidegger: Basic Writings*, ed. David F. Krell (New York: Harper and Row, 1977), 213.

50. One is reminded of the ending of Wittgenstein's *Tractatus*: "Whereof one cannot speak, thereof must one be silent."

JEAN-PAUL SARTRE (1905–80)

Sartre's existentialism is not very different from Heidegger's, but it introduces new terminology,[51] illustrations, and arguments. Like Heidegger, he was influenced by Kierkegaard, Nietzsche, and Husserl, and indeed by Heidegger himself. He accepts Nietzsche's proclamation of the death of God, and determines that his philosophy will be consistently atheistic. He succeeds in formulating an atheistic philosophy, but he fails in one other major goal: to provide a basis for human responsibility and morality.

Jean-Paul Sartre

If there is no God, he reasons, then man has no essence. Aristotle said that the essence of man is to be a *rational animal*. So human happiness is a life dictated by that essence, a life lived according to reason. Christian theologians have said that man's essence is to be the "image of God," so that human life must be essentially the imitation of God (as 1 Peter 1:15–16). But, Sartre argued, such an essence can exist only if a higher intelligence has designed us and determined what we ought to be. If there is no God, then we have no designer or determination. Sartre criticizes some past philosophers who, though atheists, maintain the concept of a *human nature*.

Rather, says Sartre, we simply appeared on the scene, without definition, without purpose. So we have no essence that we need to live up to. We have only existence. *Existence*[52] is simply our daily sequence of choices and decisions.

At the end of life, it will be possible for people to evaluate those decisions and thereby to describe what kind of person we have been. We may call that *essence*. So essence comes at the end of life, not the beginning.[53] Existence precedes essence, not the reverse as in traditional philosophy and theology. This is why Sartre describes his philosophy as *existentialism*, rather than *essentialism*.

[According to Sartre,] essence comes at the end of life, not the beginning. Existence precedes essence, not the reverse as in traditional philosophy and theology.

But it gets worse. If we have no essence, there is one sense in which we have no being, either. Many philosophers, from Parmenides to Heidegger, have struggled over the meaning of being and its relation to nonbeing. It seems impossible to define *nonbeing* without making it part of *being*, a something. But Sartre proposes, in his *Being and Nothingness*, that nonbeing is part of human life and experience. A great part of human life is dealing with what is not. When we look for someone

51. Sartre writes in French, in contrast with the German of Heidegger and Husserl. One of my professors in graduate school said that he always read Heidegger in French translations because, in his view, "you can't say anything unclearly in French." However that may be, Sartre brings to his work not only the French language, but great literary gifts, as a novelist and playwright, as well as a philosopher.

52. Remember Heidegger's *ek-sistence*? Kierkegaard also made much of the centrality of choice as what is most distinctive of man.

53. Compare the Greek proverb, "Call no man happy until he is dead."

and don't find him, his not-being-here is a kind of nonbeing. Further, we cannot live in the present without remembering the past; but the past *is not*. Nor can we live without anticipating the future; but the future, also, *is not*.[54]

Sartre says:

> I await myself in the future. Anguish is the fear of not finding myself there, of no longer even wanting to be there.[55]

In this quote, the future is unpredictable because the self is unpredictable. We have no idea what we will be in the future, and we have no reason to think we will like what we become then.

When we study consciousness phenomenologically, we discover a chaos, a "monstrous . . . impersonal spontaneity."[56] It seems that thoughts come and go without our making an effort to think them. They are free, even free of us. We try to impose order on this deluge, but we cannot. In the mind, anything can happen, it seems, including the most bizarre behavior that we can think of. We can commit murder, or suicide. That is our dreadful freedom.

We are never forced, then, by our past to choose a certain way. At every moment, we choose to be what we are. There are limits, of course. But those limits themselves are chosen. If I choose to go to medical school and the admissions requirements are too high, that is a limit. But it is a limit because it frustrates my desire, which I have freely chosen. Even death is a limit only insofar as I choose to value life.

It might seem that Sartre's radical view of libertarian freedom would lead to an equally radical relativism in ethics. We would expect Sartre to debunk the whole notion of ethical responsibility as a relic of theism. But in fact, Sartre argues that existentialism is the best defender of responsibility.

Now, it might seem that Sartre's radical view of libertarian freedom would lead to an equally radical relativism in ethics. We would expect Sartre to debunk the whole notion of ethical responsibility as a relic of theism. But in fact, Sartre argues that existentialism is the best defender of responsibility.[57] (1) First, Sartre tells us that on an existentialist basis we have no excuses. Because of our radical freedom, we are never forced to make a particular choice. Our heredity, occupation, race,

54. And what is the present? A knife-edge between past and future, which we cannot even talk about until it becomes at least slightly past. That would seem to lead to the conclusion that all our experience is of nonbeing, though I don't know of any text in Sartre that carries the argument that far.

55. Jean-Paul Sartre, *Being and Nothingness: An Essay on Phenomenological Ontology*, trans. Hazel Estella Barnes (New York: Washington Square Press, 1984), 73.

56. Jean-Paul Sartre, *The Transcendence of the Ego: An Existentialist Theory of Consciousness*, trans. Forest Williams and Robert Kirkpatrick (New York: Noonday Press, 1957), 98–99.

57. Recall that Kant, for all his skepticism about the real world, developed an ethic that stressed absolute and universal duty. Human responsibility is often the last assurance that secular philosophers are willing to dispense with—but it is human responsibility that points (in my view) most definitively to God.

sex, or age never relieves us of the responsibility of choice. At every moment, we choose to be what we are.

(2) Further, Sartre says, in every choice, I choose a certain image of man. This is a principle of Kant's ethics, that ethical principles are necessarily universal. If a certain choice is obligatory for me in a certain situation, then it is obligatory for everyone in the same situation. If I choose to rob a bank, I'm saying that it is legitimate for any human being to rob a bank. I am therefore contributing something to the essence of mankind.

Sartre distinguishes between human beings and inanimate reality. Inanimate reality is en soi, *"in itself," that is, solid, definable, constant. Human reality is* pour soi, *"for itself," that is, indefinable and free.*

I don't find either of Sartre's arguments cogent. (1) Excuses presuppose the existence of normative rules. When Billy gives Mom an excuse for failing to clean his room, that presupposes that there is a rule obligating him to clean his room. But in Sartre's philosophy, where do the moral rules come from?

(2) Sartre's second principle also presupposes the existence of universal, obligatory moral rules, as in Kant's ethics. If there is no such rule, say, against theft, then whether I steal or not does not reflect one way or another on the whole human race. It doesn't matter whether everybody steals or does not.

There is, however, one ethical rule in Sartre's philosophy that he considers an important guide to life: as Heidegger said, we should live *authentically*. Sartre's argument for this principle is actually metaphysical. He distinguishes between human beings and inanimate reality. Inanimate reality is *en soi*, "in itself," that is, solid, definable, constant. Human reality is *pour soi*, "for itself," that is, indefinable and free.[58] Now, we are afraid of our freedom. We wish we were predictable, definable. Not that we would set aside the power of free choice; we want that, too. We would like to be both *en soi* and *pour soi*; we would like to have both essence and existence. But in classical theology, God is the One who is both essence and existence. And Sartre is convinced that this classical concept of God is contradictory for precisely this reason. In his view, you cannot have essence and existence in the same being.

What we seek is to be God; and that goal is impossible, Sartre says. This ambition leads only to anguish. To avoid that anguish, we deny our freedom.

So what we seek is to be God; and that goal is impossible, Sartre says. This ambition leads only to anguish. To avoid that anguish, we deny our freedom. We pretend that we are mere objects, determined by our past or our station in life. We deceive ourselves into thinking that we have excuses for what we do. But to live that way, says Sartre, is *inauthentic existence*.

We should, rather, live authentically: in such a way as to display our freedom, to display our nonbeing for all to see. That might entail behaving in bizarre ways, like some of the characters in Sartre's novels.

58. The distinction is Hegel's, but Sartre will not resolve the contrast in a dialectical unity.

To live inauthentically is *mauvaise foi*, "bad faith" (sometimes translated "self-deception").

A philosophy so much concerned with ethics inevitably deals with social relationships. Sartre wrestles with the question of how I can be perfectly free and still live in a world of other people. For others are free, too. Sartre talks about *the gaze*, of *the look*, when someone else looks at me and transforms me into an object of *his* consciousness. The only way to counter this is to reverse the relationship, for me to turn the other person into an object of *my* consciousness.[59] This mutual objectification, this making of mutual demands, is painful for Sartre to contemplate, provoking the famous statement in his play *No Exit*: "Hell is other people."[60]

Nevertheless, Sartre is sensitive to the plight of the poor and, like most other secular philosophers in the twentieth century, favors Marxism as the best recipe for social justice. He never joined the Communist Party, however, for he was not able to escape the contradiction between Communism and freedom. Later in life, he modified somewhat his view of radical freedom, noting that the poor did not have as many choices available to them as the bourgeois and the rich.[61] But he continued to believe that his original view of freedom was essentially right.

To evaluate: Sartre is perceptive about moral choice. His view of libertarian freedom is not biblical, but he agrees with Scripture that our moral responsibility is pervasive, and that we have no excuses for the wrong that we do. But his concept of responsibility is opposite to that of Christianity. For him, responsibility is an attribute of autonomy. In Scripture, however, autonomy is the virtual definition of irresponsibility. It is interesting that Sartre says that our main problem is our desire and attempt to be God. That is profoundly right, at one level. But autonomy is precisely the attempt to take over God's prerogatives. Sartre's ethic is based on human autonomy more explicitly, perhaps, than any other ethic. The Christian must attack that assumption head-on.

It is interesting that Sartre says that our main problem is our desire and attempt to be God. That is profoundly right, at one level. But autonomy is precisely the attempt to take over God's prerogatives. Sartre's ethic is based on human autonomy more explicitly, perhaps, than any other ethic.

On the one hand, Sartre claims to set us free from all ethical rules (irrationalism). Yet on the other, he stigmatizes a certain kind of behavior as inauthentic and claims for his philosophy the authority to legislate our behavior (rationalism). All of this is supposedly based on a system that reduces ethics to metaphysics, the relation of being to nonbeing.

59. This recalls Hegel's argument about masters and slaves: the master becomes a slave of the slave, in the dialectic. For him, the tension is resolved at higher syntheses within the dialectic—new social orders in which slavery doesn't exist. But there is no such synthesis for Sartre.

60. Jean-Paul Sartre, *No Exit (Huis Clos) and The Flies (Les Mouches)*, trans. Stuart Gilbert (New York: Alfred A. Knopf, 1948), 61.

61. See his *Critique of Dialectical Reason*, ed. Jonathan Rée and Arlette Elkaïm-Sartre, trans. Alan Sheridan and Quintin Hoare, new ed., 2 vols. (London: Verso, 2004).

But it is a naturalistic fallacy to try to derive the *oughts* of ethics from the *being* of metaphysics; see fig. 9.4.

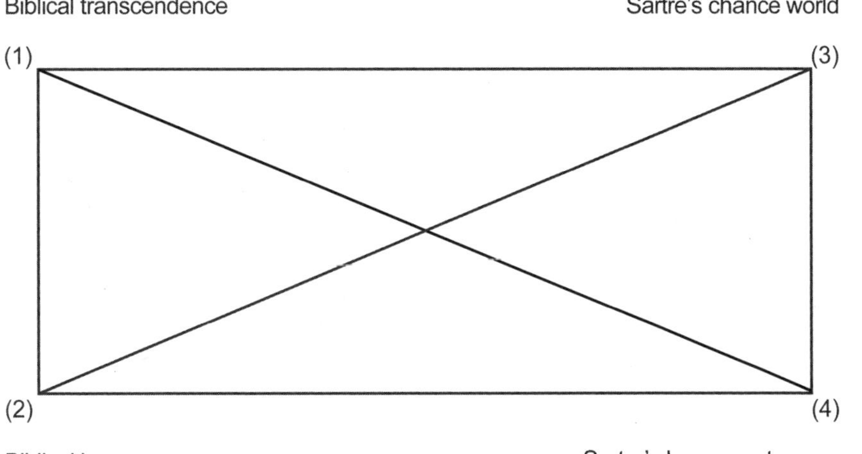

Fig. 9.4. Transcendence and Immanence in Sartre

Jaspers sounded the familiar warning that science and technology, valuable as they are, stand in the way of understanding human existence.

OTHER EXISTENTIALISTS

The ideas of Husserl, Heidegger, and Sartre represented a way of thinking common to many in Europe in the early to mid-twentieth century. **Karl Jaspers** (1883–1969), who rejected the term *existentialism*,[62] nevertheless was deeply influenced by Kierkegaard, Nietzsche, and Husserl. He sounded the familiar warning that science and technology, valuable as they are, stand in the way of understanding human existence. Existence can never be an object of thought,[63] can be known only through inner experience. Self-knowledge reaches a higher level in *limiting situations* such as recognizing the possibility of one's own death, as Heidegger emphasized. Understanding of our finitude, however, opens a still higher dimension, namely, the opposite of finitude—transcendence or God. Authentic existence is to affirm this not by proof, or by a Hegelian dialectical play, but by a Kierkegaardian leap of faith. So in Jaspers, existentialism leads to a kind of religion.

Karl Jaspers

Maurice Merleau-Ponty (1908–61) put a special emphasis on the body, and perception through the body as the beginning of knowledge.

62. In an essentially nominalist movement, one expects resistance to any general labels. But for purposes of teaching, labels are indispensable.

63. Many philosophers say this sort of thing, but what does it actually mean? Normally, an *object of thought* is anything that you can think about. Certainly Jaspers has thought about existence more often than most of us. I grant that there is a difference between gathering data about something and the feeling we get when we are directly experiencing it. But I see no reason why we should not incorporate that feeling into the process of *thinking about*.

He is famous for saying, "I am my body." The body is not an object[64] but rather the subject's point of view. The presence of the body in a particular place gives to each person a distinct perspective or point of view. In some respects, the human race shares a perspective (the "*a priori* of species") due to the position of the human species in the universe, enabling human beings to converse with one another. We can expect that others will at least be open to hear the same truths that we do. Merleau-Ponty, like Sartre (his friend and sometimes opponent), was inclined toward Marxism, but (also like Sartre) was at times disillusioned by its violence.

Gabriel Marcel (1889–1973) is sometimes called a *religious existentialist*, since he converted to Catholicism at the age of thirty-nine. Although atheism was at the center of the philosophies of Heidegger and Sartre, it should not be too surprising that religion sometimes enters the existential community, given the origin of so many of its ideas in Kierkegaard's search for Christianity in Christendom.

Marcel begins with Husserl's project, to understand human consciousness, the "I" in "I am." The question "who am I?" cannot be answered by *objective* methods,[65] that is, dividing it into parts, surveying lines of evidence. That would be to treat the question as a *problem*. The body, Marcel thinks, can be considered an object, and the self is closely connected with it, but the self is not a *mere* object. So the quest for the meaning of the self is not a *problem*, but a *mystery*.

We come to a higher understanding of the mystery in interpersonal relations. As Nietzsche said, man is the only being who can make promises. By exercising friendship and love, we understand people in a higher way than by treating them as objects. But what of Sartre's *gaze*? What of Heidegger's warnings about accepting too easily the demands of others? Since people are free, we never know certainly what to expect of them. That uncertainty leads us to put our faith in a being of a higher order. Hence Marcel's religion.

Albert Camus

Albert Camus (1913–60) is, like Marcel and Sartre, as well known for his novels as his philosophy, but his *Myth of Sisyphus* (1943) is taken seriously as a philosophical essay. Camus emphasizes the absurdity of man, with his demand for rationality and justice, confronting a universe that is entirely indifferent to these demands. In *The Stranger* (1942), Camus' anti-hero accepts that indifference and becomes indifferent himself. But in *The Myth of Sisyphus*, Sisyphus defies the gods and, like Nietzsche, takes some pleasure in it. Here are two responses to the absurdity of the human condition. But unlike Marcel and Jaspers, Camus never thought he could transcend that absurdity.

64. See previous footnote.
65. See previous two footnotes.

EVALUATION

Existentialism, springing out of Kierkegaard and Nietzsche by way of Husserl, begins with the conviction that human consciousness, particularly the experience of choice, gives the philosopher access to levels of understanding unavailable to previous thinkers. Certainly we can appreciate the conviction of Husserl and others that the methods of science (autonomous science, particularly naturalistic science) are insufficient to account for everything important to us. But Husserl got off on the wrong foot by urging his colleagues to carry out this study without presuppositions, something that cannot be done. And in fact, the movement largely dispensed with Kierkegaard's Christian presuppositions and adopted the presupposition of human autonomy, even its *radical freedom*.

What the study yields, in the end, is nothing more than Nietzsche's nihilism, whether or not one adopts Nietzsche's cheerful attitude toward it. We see in ourselves a dreadful kind of freedom in which anything can happen. We find in other people hellish challenges to our freedom. Sartre and Marcel challenge us with ethics of *authenticity* and *fidelity*, respectively, but they offer us no authoritative norm that makes them obligatory. Jaspers and Marcel think this quest leads us to some kind of dimension of transcendence. But that is so vague, and the way so vague, that the promise of it does nothing to curb Camus' hopelessness.

What the study [of existentialism] yields, in the end, is nothing more than Nietzsche's nihilism, whether or not one adopts Nietzsche's cheerful attitude toward it. We see in ourselves a dreadful kind of freedom in which anything can happen. We find in other people hellish challenges to our freedom.

We were not made to think or live without presuppositions, but to think with the presupposition that God's revelation is true, that we are his image, and that his redemption alone saves us from the nihilistic kingdom of Satan. Kierkegaard, with some inconsistency, pointed the way to a deep understanding of the mind of a believer in a nihilistic intellectual environment. But the existentialists, claiming to be his heirs, surrendered to that environment. Sartre sought to make existentialism the most consistently atheistic philosophy ever, and he largely succeeded. So existentialism's best service to us is to show the horror of life without Jesus.

KEY TERMS

Will to power	Perspectivism
Transvaluation of all values	*Ressentiment*
Slave morality	*Übermensch*
Eternal recurrence	Pragmatism (Peirce)
Pragmatism (James)	Pragmaticism
Inquiry	Fixation of belief
Method of tenacity	Method of authority
Critical commonsensism	Abduction
Retroduction	Deduction (Peirce)

OUTLINE

Induction (Peirce)
Pragmatic maxim
Scientism
The will to believe
Spectator model of knowledge
Instrumentalism
Naturalism
Consciousness
Lebenswelt
Natural standpoint
Phenomena
Given
Bracket
Epoché
Dasein
Being-in-the-world
Ek-sistence
Care (Heidegger)
Inauthentic existence (Heidegger)
Thrownness
Being-toward-death
Anxiety
Risk
Rapport
Essence (Sartre)
Existence (Sartre)
Authentic existence
En soi
Pour soi
Mauvaise foi
The gaze
Limiting situations (Jaspers)
Transcendence (Jaspers)
Mystery (Marcel)

STUDY QUESTIONS

1. Summarize Nietzsche's view of language and logic. Why is it important?
2. Nietzsche: "What we call *knowing* is, in the end, an invention of the will." Explain. Why is this important?
3. Distinguish Nietzsche's *perspectivism* from Frame's *perspectivalism*.
4. Describe Nietzsche's plan for transvaluing all values.
5. Contrast the critiques of Christianity by Nietzsche and Marx.
6. Describe and evaluate Nietzsche's concepts of the death of God, *Übermensch*, and eternal recurrence.
7. "But we have seen in the modern period that a number of thinkers have given roles to human prudence, aesthetic beauty, and practical success in their epistemology, beyond *pure reason*." Give some examples and discuss.
8. Describe and evaluate Peirce's critique of Descartes.
9. Describe and discuss Peirce's methods of belief fixation.
10. Describe and evaluate Peirce's critical commonsensism.
11. How should we make our ideas clear, according to Peirce? Evaluate.
12. Summarize and analyze Peirce's phenomenology.
13. "William James developed the pragmatism of Peirce into a theory of truth." Explain; evaluate.
14. Summarize and evaluate the argument of James's "The Will to Believe."

15. Describe Dewey's "first-rate test of the value of any philosophy." Evaluate.
16. Describe and discuss Dewey's view of the relation of fact to value. Does he do justice to values that *obligate*?
17. Frame: "Dewey's influence in the public schools continues to pose a major problem for Christians." Why does he say this? What do you think?
18. Why does Husserl think that to understand consciousness, we need methods other than those of science? What methods does he propose?
19. "It is helpful, I think, . . . to regard Husserl's phenomena not as images, but as *windows*." Explain; evaluate.
20. "So for Husserl, the phenomenon *is* the 'thing in itself.'" Explain. Compare with Kant. How can we be *certain* about the phenomena, according to Husserl?
21. Explain Husserl's *bracketing* of the phenomena. Evaluate.
22. What is *Dasein* for Heidegger? How is it related to the world?
23. Distinguish the early from the late Heidegger. What does he mean by saying that "language is the house of Being"?
24. Frame: "To secularize death is to rob human life of meaning." How does this apply to Heidegger?
25. Sartre defines *existentialism* as the view in which "existence precedes essence." Explain.
26. Summarize the relation of being to nothingness in human nature, according to Sartre.
27. Sartre: "We are never forced, then, by our past to choose a certain way." Why not? Explain.
28. Is Sartre an ethical relativist? Why or why not?
29. Describe Sartre's account of how we come to live an *inauthentic existence*.
30. Why was Sartre unable to join the Communist Party? What does that say about his philosophy?
31. Merleau-Ponty: "I am my body." Explain; evaluate.
32. Explain how Jaspers and Marcel bring God into their philosophies. Evaluate.

BIBLIOGRAPHY: NIETZSCHE, PRAGMATISM, PHENOMENOLOGY, AND EXISTENTIALISM

Print

Dewey, John. *A Common Faith*. New Haven, CT: Yale University Press, 1991. Dewey's suggestions to rescue religion from dogmatism and superstition.

———. *The Philosophy of John Dewey: Two Volumes in One*. Edited by John J. McDermott. Chicago: University of Chicago Press, 1981.

Heidegger, Martin. *Basic Writings*. Edited by David Farrell Krell. New York: Harper Perennial Modern Classics, 2008.

———. *Being and Time*. Translated by John MacQuarrie and Edward Robinson. New York: Harper Perennial Modern Classics, 2008.

Husserl, Edmund. *The Essential Husserl: Basic Writings in Transcendental Phenomenology*. Indianapolis: Indiana University Press, 1999.

———. *Ideas: General Introduction to Pure Phenomenology*. New York: Routledge, 2012.

James, William. *Pragmatism*. Seattle: CreateSpace, 2013.

———. *The Writings of William James: A Comprehensive Edition*. Chicago: University of Chicago Press, 2011.

Kaufmann, Walter, ed. *Basic Writings of Nietzsche*. New York: Modern Library, 2000. Six books of Nietzsche plus a large collection of aphorisms.

———. *Existentialism from Dostoevsky to Sartre*. New York: New American Library, 1975. Many primary sources with illuminating commentary.

———, ed. *Nietzsche: Philosopher, Psychologist, Antichrist*. Princeton, NJ: Princeton University Press, 1975.

Mooney, Timothy, and Dermot Moran, eds. *The Phenomenology Reader*. New York: Routledge, 2002. Writings of Husserl and Heidegger, and many others, including recent postmodernists.

Peirce, Charles S. *Philosophical Writings of Peirce*. Edited by Justus Buchler. New York: Dover, 2011.

Sartre, Jean-Paul. *Being and Nothingness: An Essay on Phenomenological Ontology*. Translated by Hazel Estella Barnes. New York: Washington Square Press, 1984.

———. *Existentialism Is a Humanism*. Translated by Carol Macomber. New Haven, CT: Yale University Press, 2007. Includes Sartre's commentary on Camus' *The Stranger*.

Talisse, Robert B., and Scott Akin, eds. *The Pragmatism Reader: From Peirce to the Present*. Princeton, NJ: Princeton University Press, 2011.

Online

Dewey, John. The Online Books Page. Numerous books by John Dewey. http://onlinebooks.library.upenn.edu/webbin/book/lookupname?key=Dewey%2C%20John%2C%201859-1952.

Heidegger, Martin. His shorter articles and letters are available at http://archive.org/search.php?query=creator%3A%22Martin%20Heidegger%22.

Husserl, Edmund. Online Texts. http://www.husserlpage.com/hus_online.html.

James, William. The Online Books Page. Numerous books by William James. http://onlinebooks.library.upenn.edu/webbin/book/lookupname?key=James%2C%20William%2C%201842-1910.

———. *Pragmatism: A New Name for Some Old Ways of Thinking.* Available at http://www.gutenberg.org/ebooks/5116.

Nietzsche, Friedrich. *The Complete Works of Friedrich Nietzsche.* Edited by Oscar Levy. Vol. 10, *The Joyful Wisdom.* New York: Macmillan, 1924. Available at http://www.archive.org/stream/completenietasch10nietuoft/completenietasch10nietuoft_djvu.txt.

———. *A Contemporary Nietzsche Reader.* Available at http://nietzsche.holtof.com/reader/index.html. Additional Nietzsche texts are available at http://nietzsche.holtof.com/.

———. The Online Books Page. Numerous books by Friedrich Wilhelm Nietzsche. http://onlinebooks.library.upenn.edu/webbin/book/search?amode=start&author=Nietzsche%2C%20Friedrich%20Wilhelm%2C%201844-1900.

Peirce, Charles S. Peirce's Writings On Line. http://www.peirce.org/writings.html.

Sartre, Jean-Paul. "Existentialism Is a Humanism." In *Existentialism from Dostoevsky to Sartre*, edited by Walter Kaufman. Translated by Philip Mairet. Meridian Publishing Company, 1989. Available at http://www.marxists.org/reference/archive/sartre/works/exist/sartre.htm.

———. Jean-Paul Sartre Archive. http://www.marxists.org/reference/archive/sartre/.

READ FOR YOURSELF

Explore Nietzsche's philosophical analysis of philology in his *Birth of Tragedy* and *Genealogy of Morals*. For his view of truth, read "On Truth and Lies in a Non-Moral Sense" from *Beyond Good and Evil*. Then look at his more confrontational works such as *The Cheerful Science, Thus Spake Zarathustra*, and *Twilight of the Idols. Ecce Homo* is his autobiography.

In the pragmatist school, you will enjoy reading James better than either Peirce or Dewey. Read James, *Pragmatism* and "The Will to Believe." Peirce's "How to Make Our Ideas Clear" is not, ironically, very clearly written, but it makes its point. In Dewey, *Reconstruction in Philosophy* and *Experience and Nature* will present well his philosophical position.

Phenomenology is especially hard to manage for nonspecialists, but I think the introductions of Mooney and others in *The Phenomenology Reader* are helpful. Existentialism similarly, but Kaufmann in *Existentialism from Dostoevsky to Sartre* makes it intelligible and interesting. Sartre's *Existentialism Is a Humanism* has been criticized by many (including

Sartre himself) as not being true to the basic existentialist vision, but it is a fascinating position in its own right. And as Kaufmann says, you can almost hear Sartre talk.

LISTEN ONLINE

Link: http://itunes.apple.com/us/course/legacy-history-philosophy/id694658914

- Friedrich Nietzsche, Charles Sanders Peirce, and William James: 53:23
- Edmund Husserl, Martin Heidegger, and Jean-Paul Sartre: 41:06

FAMOUS QUOTES

- **Nietzsche:** http://en.wikiquote.org/wiki/Friedrich_Nietzsche
- **Peirce:** http://en.wikiquote.org/wiki/Charles_Sanders_Peirce
- **James:** http://en.wikiquote.org/wiki/William_James
- **Dewey:** http://en.wikiquote.org/wiki/John_Dewey
- **Husserl:** http://en.wikiquote.org/wiki/Edmund_Husserl
- **Heidegger:** http://en.wikiquote.org/wiki/Martin_Heidegger
- **Sartre:** http://en.wikiquote.org/wiki/Jean-Paul_Sartre

10

TWENTIETH-CENTURY LIBERAL THEOLOGY, PART I

IN CHAPTER 8 we ended our survey of nineteenth-century theology by observing the undoing of the Ritschlian consensus in the early twentieth century. The Jesus-scholarship of Weiss and Schweitzer, the historicism of Troeltsch, and the coming of world war combined to squelch the academic assurance and the spiritual idealism of the Ritschlians. But I only alluded there to another factor that is arguably the most important: new theological developments that would almost suddenly replace this consensus and relegate it to the status of "the older liberalism." An intellectual movement is never entirely set aside until the next movement renders it passé, and that is what happened to Ritschlian theology.

The new movement went by various names. Barth called it crisis theology *and the* theology of the word. *Others, noting its resemblance in language to post-Reformation scholasticism, called it* neoorthodoxy.

The new movement went by various names. Barth called it *crisis theology*[1] and the *theology of the word*. Others, noting its resemblance in language to post-Reformation scholasticism, called it *neoorthodoxy*. Still others, noting its tendency to affirm, yet also deeply qualify, orthodox doctrine, were reminded of Hegel and called it *dialectical theology*.[2] Its more obvious philosophical influences (especially, but not exclusively, in Bultmann) were from the existentialists. But that provoked Barth to say, in the preface to his *Church Dogmatics*:

1. That is, theology of the judgment of God, using the Greek word *krisis*.

2. It also reveled, like Hegel, in the apparent contradictions of the faith: divine judgment and grace, God's love and evil, Christ as God and man, transcendence and immanence, revelation and hiddenness, and so on.

> To the best of my ability I have cut out in this second issue of the book[3] everything that in the first issue might give the slightest appearance of giving to theology a basis, support, or even a mere justification in the way of existential philosophy.[4]

Whatever we may call it (it is now commonly called *Barthianism*), it was easily distinguishable from what had gone before. When Barth published his *The Epistle to the Romans*[5] in 1919, Karl Adam, the Roman Catholic scholar, later remarked that it "fell like a bombshell in the playground of the theologians."[6] It began a new era in the history of theology.

KARL BARTH (1886–1968)

Barth was unquestionably the leader of the new movement and became the most influential theologian of the twentieth century. He is also, arguably, the most influential so far in the twenty-first. Barth established a paradigm for preachers and theologians who want to be considered conservative, but who also want to remain part of the community of mainstream intellectual society, in the universities and the liberal denominations. This is a prime example of what I called in chapter 6 the *conservative drift*, the tendency of liberal thinkers to advance their cause through the use of conservative terminology. Almost inevitably today, this kind of "conservatism" takes on a Barthian shape.

Karl Barth

Barth's teachers were Ritschlians, including Wilhelm Herrmann and Adolf Harnack. He served as a Reformed pastor in the Swiss village of Safenwil from 1911 to 1921. He reacted against Ritschlianism during that time for various reasons. For one thing, he was disappointed that Harnack signed a statement in 1914 supporting the German war policy. He believed that the Christians who signed this statement had put the defense of German culture above the kingdom of God. And gradually there dawned on him the conviction that the old liberal theology offered no comfort to those who were suffering the losses of war. He turned back to the Bible, and to "biblical realist" thinkers such as Johann and Christoph Blumhardt, Martin Kähler, Adolf Schlatter, and Søren Kierkegaard. Then in 1919, he dropped his bombshell.

He served as professor of theology at the universities of Göttingen

3. Barth had previously begun work on a *Christian Dogmatics*. But after publishing a very large first volume, he had discontinued that and replaced it with the *Church Dogmatics*, which would extend for many volumes and would become his magnum opus.

4. Karl Barth, *Church Dogmatics* (New York: Charles Scribner's Sons, 1936) (henceforth *CD*), 1.1.9; cf. 141–47. The main comparison between existentialism and this new theological movement is that in the latter the events of salvation occur in a realm sharply distinct from any realm accessible to science or "objective" thought.

5. English translation: London: Oxford University Press, 1933.

6. Karl Adam, "Die Theologie der Krises," *Das Hochland* 23 (June 1926): 276–77.

(1921–25), Münster (1925–30), and Bonn (1930–35). While at Bonn, he was instrumental in the founding of the Confessing Church, which (contrary to the "German Christians" of the major denominations) resisted Hitler. He was the chief author of the *Barmen Declaration*, the founding document of the Confessing Church, which insisted that only Christ was Lord, and the church could not yield any part of that lordship to another. Barth lost his professorship in 1935 because he refused to swear an oath to Hitler, and he returned to his native Switzerland to serve from 1935 to his death as a professor at the University of Basel.[7]

Barth's theology is highly critical of neo-Protestantism, *or* modernism . . . . *It is, he says, subjectivistic, psychologistic. It confuses God's voice with man's, theology with anthropology. It identifies Christianity with culture and treats sin lightly.*

His theology is highly critical of *neo-Protestantism*, or *modernism*, which includes Schleiermacher and the Ritschlian school.[8] It is, he says, subjectivistic, psychologistic. It confuses God's voice with man's, theology with anthropology.[9] It identifies Christianity with culture and treats sin lightly. Barth responds warmly, however, to Luther and Calvin, and to others of the Reformed tradition. He quotes Kuyper, Bavinck, and Berkouwer with approval, and he even says that the post-Reformation doctrine of biblical inspiration, which he opposes, was preferable to the neo-Protestant view of Scripture. Further, his massive *CD* aims to present serious analyses of every traditional doctrine. He claims throughout that his theology is governed by Scripture rather than philosophy or human feeling. These emphases have led many to think of Barth as conservative, neoorthodox, even a paradigm for authentic Reformed Christianity today.

Some others have held that Barth is far from orthodox, indeed a substantial threat to traditional Christianity, concealing heretical beliefs beneath orthodox language.

Nevertheless, some others have held that Barth is far from orthodox, indeed a substantial threat to traditional Christianity, concealing heretical beliefs beneath orthodox language. G. C. Berkouwer's first book on Barth, *Karl Barth*,[10] was harshly critical of him.[11] Other Dutch and Dutch-American thinkers shared Berkouwer's criticisms and went beyond. Cornelius Van Til's *The New Modernism*[12] argues by its very title that the theology of Barth (and that of Brunner, also treated there)

7. Barth is thus one of the true Christian heroes of World War II. That he did not take a similar stance against the Soviet advance (and its impositions on the church) following the war is somewhat perplexing. For his rationale, see Karl Barth, "Nazism and Communism," *Christianity and Crisis* (February 5, 1951). In the article he raises some valid considerations, but I don't find his overall case persuasive, nor his stance heroic. He is critical of Communism, but one wonders whether his early Socialist associations have distorted his sense of proportion.

8. In his important *Protestant Theology in the Nineteenth Century*, eleven chapters of which are translated into English as *Protestant Thought: From Rousseau to Ritschl* (New York: Simon and Schuster, 1969), Barth gives Schleiermacher's work a serious, respectful, almost admiring (though critical) analysis. He gives Ritschl, however, short shrift.

9. "Modernism hears man answer without anyone having called him. It hears him talk to himself." Barth, *CD*, 1.1, 68.

10. Kampen: Kok, 1936.

11. His second book on Barth, *The Triumph of Grace in the Theology of Karl Barth* (Grand Rapids: Eerdmans, 1956), was more favorable, but also made serious criticisms.

12. Nutley, NJ: Presbyterian and Reformed, 1973 (originally published 1946).

is no different from Ritschlianism, except in vocabulary. The title of his *Christianity and Barthianism*,[13] intentionally parallel to Machen's *Christianity and Liberalism*, also argues that Barth is not much different from the neo-Protestants that he so disparages.

Some liberals, such as Bultmann, as we will see, have criticized Barth for being too orthodox. But others, including Richard R. Niebuhr, Langdon Gilkey, Alan Richardson, Paul Tillich, and Jürgen Moltmann, have argued that for all his efforts Barth has not escaped the limitations of the older liberalism.[14]

The wide differences among scholars on the evaluation of Barth arise partly through the difficulty of interpreting him. Because of the huge volume and complexity of his writings, there has been much controversy over what Barth "really means." This is true of his individual sentences as well as his books. Barth is a master of the complicated sentence, which goes on and on, dangling subordinate clauses right and left. It is possible to argue a wide variety of interpretations from the *CD*. Almost any thesis about Barth can be supported somewhere in his writings, opposed from somewhere else. My own view of him is generally negative, but I confess that I can spend hours reading page after page of Barth and finding nothing wrong, and much that edifies me. Any interpreter of Barth is sure to find a critic who insists that the interpreter "doesn't understand Barth," and who advances multiple quotations from Barth's writings supporting the opposite thesis. So the secondary literature, favorable and unfavorable, is often passionately partisan.

The wide differences among scholars on the evaluation of Barth arise partly through the difficulty of interpreting him. Because of the huge volume and complexity of his writings, there has been much controversy over what Barth "really means."

In the following discussion, I intend to document my statements carefully from Barth's writing, realizing that that intention will not be sufficient to silence critics. But the critics will face the task of explaining, or explaining away, what Barth appears to say in my quotations.

Early in the *CD*, Barth presents a theme that he will repeat often in his theology:

> Revelation has its truth in the free decision of God made once for all in Jesus Christ, and for that very reason and in that way strictly future for us, and must become true in the Church from time to time in the intractable reality of faith. Truth of revelation is the freely acting God, Himself and quite alone.[15]

Why, we must ask, does the freedom of God in Christ to reveal himself render that revelation "strictly future"? Over and over in Scripture, we are told to attend to the *permanent* revelations of God

13. Philadelphia: Presbyterian and Reformed, 1962.

14. For documentation, see *CVT*, 365–66.

15. Barth, *CD*, 1.1, 16.

given in the *past*, such as God's covenant document, written by his very finger (Ex. 31:18), kept in the holiest part of the tabernacle and the temple.[16] Revival came in Israel when King Josiah discovered that neglected volume in the temple (2 Kings 22:8–23:20). Jude also points his readers to God's revelation in the past, telling them "to contend for the faith that was once for all delivered to the saints" (Jude 3), indicating that in his time the content of the gospel was fixed. Paul (2 Tim. 3:16–17) and Peter (2 Peter 1:19–21) tell their readers to use the "breathed out by God" OT to deal with their needs in the present.

[The Scriptures] do not "become true in the church from time to time," as Barth says. They are true for all times, and the church must attend to them.

These documents do not "become true in the church from time to time," as Barth says. They are true for all times, and the church must attend to them. We do not have to wait for his revelation to become true. It is always true, because God the revealer is Jesus Christ, who is "the same yesterday and today and forever" (Heb. 13:8). His promises are sure (Pss. 19:7; 132:11; 2 Cor. 1:20).

It is the case, of course, that the church's understanding, assurance, and application of revelation rises and falls. Traditional theology has always understood that. Sin affects our willingness to accept God's revelation, and the Holy Spirit renews our appropriation of it. But in biblical terms, that process cannot be described as God's revelation becoming true, then untrue, and then true again. Traditional Reformed theology has described this process as the illumination of the Holy Spirit opposing the noetic effects of sin.[17] Barth has often been accused of confusing this illumination with revelation. Scripture does, on at least two occasions (Matt. 11:27; Eph. 1:17), describe illumination as a kind of revelation. But this is not Scripture's usual practice. And Scripture never uses this teaching to deny the objectivity of revelation. The illumination is precisely the illumination of an objective revelation. So Scripture never suggests that revelations of God "become true in the Church from time to time," that is, being true, then untrue, and then true again.

Barth has often been accused of confusing . . . illumination with revelation. Scripture does, on at least two occasions (Matt. 11:27; Eph. 1:17), describe illumination as a kind of revelation. But this is not Scripture's usual practice. And Scripture never uses this teaching to deny the objectivity of revelation.

Why, then, does Barth not only believe but take it as axiomatic that God's revelation is not true permanently, but becomes true only from time to time? In the quotation, what he appeals to is the freedom of God. Evidently, for Barth, the freedom of God is so erratic that God can at will make his Word false, and then true again. This is what we have described in chapter 4 and elsewhere as an extreme nominalism.[18] In

16. See chap. 16, "The Permanence of God's Written Word," in my *DWG*, 101–4.

17. That is, the repression of truth described in Romans 1:18–32.

18. In chapter 8, I discussed the nominalism of Kierkegaard. Kierkegaard also stressed "the moment" in which eternity, paradoxically, enters time. That moment is essentially what Barth calls *revelation*, belying his claim that his theology is not influenced at all by existentialist philosophy. He also describes this moment as the *event* that takes place when we hear God speaking in Scripture (see following discussion). I believe this is essentially the nonbiblical view of transcendence diagrammed in the rectangular figure in chapter 1.

the Bible and traditional theology, although God is sovereign, he is not free in every way. He cannot lie, cannot do evil, cannot make another God, and so on.[19] He lacks these freedoms not because of weakness, but because of his nature and character. Goodness, truthfulness, and faithfulness are his permanent, necessary attributes, his nature. He cannot be otherwise. If he could be, he would be a monster, not the God of Scripture. So his Word is truth (Ps. 119:160; John 17:17). God is not free to make it become untruth, then truth, and then untruth again. But that seems to be the kind of freedom that Barth ascribes to God.

Barth's nominalist concept of divine freedom is similar to the Kierkegaardian-existentialist idea that persons are not essences but series of free choices. Barth translates all the concepts of traditional Christianity into the language of *event*. His critics describe this as *activism* or *actualism*. But whatever it is, it is not biblical Christianity. In Scripture, God redeems his people in space-time events that are permanently recorded in prophecy and in written words. It is precisely these permanent revelations that express God's sovereign freedom to rule his people as he sees fit.

Barth discusses revelation under three categories: the Word as preached, the Word written, and the Word as Christ himself. Only Christ *is* revelation as such; the written Word is revelation insofar as it bears witness to him. And the preached Word is revelation insofar as it bears witness to Christ by appeal to the written Word.[20] In each of these, God speaks to us, and his speech becomes true to us from time to time as God determines.

Barth's nominalist concept of divine freedom is similar to the Kierkegaardian-existentialist idea that persons are not essences but series of free choices. Barth translates all the concepts of traditional Christianity into the language of event.

Although Barth said in a previous quotation that revelation (presumably in all three forms) is "strictly future for us,"[21] he does admit to a past dimension of revelation in his doctrine of Scripture:

> We said that Church proclamation must be ventured upon in recollection of past, and in expectation of future revelation.[22]

That "recollection" takes place as we consult Scripture. But Barth denies that the biblical text is in itself the Word of God. Rather, it is the locus for an event (which I earlier described as *illumination*) in which God speaks *through* the Bible to us:

> The Bible therefore becomes God's Word in this event, and it is to this being in this becoming that the tiny word "is" relates

19. See my *DG*, 513–23.
20. Barth, *CD*, 1.1, 98.
21. Here he anticipates the "future-oriented" theologies of Jürgen Moltmann and Wolfhart Pannenberg. See chapter 11.
22. Barth, *CD*, 1.1, 111.

> in the statement that the Bible is God's Word. . . .[23] But its becoming the word of revelation for us . . . [is] precisely not in abstraction from the act of God, in virtue of which the Bible must from time to time become his Word to us.[24]

So the pastness of the Bible, its place in "recollection," is not an exception to Barth's principle expressed earlier, that revelation is strictly future. For even as we read the Bible, God speaks to us only "from time to time." Recollection, he says, must always be accompanied by expectation. The past revelation is not a settled revelation, but the promise of future revelation:

The pastness of the Bible, its place in "recollection," is not an exception to Barth's principle expressed earlier, that revelation is strictly future. For even as we read the Bible, God speaks to us only "from time to time."

> The Bible is, therefore, not itself and in itself God's past revelation, just as Church proclamation also is not itself and in itself the expected future revelation. But the Bible speaking to us and heard by us as God's Word attests the past revelation.[25]

So the Bible, he says, claims no authority for itself. It is like John the Baptist, pointing away from himself to Christ.[26]

> Therefore we do the Bible a poor honour, and one unwelcome to itself, when we directly identify it with this something else, with revelation itself.[27]

That happens when we accept "the doctrine of the general, equal, and permanent inspiration of the Bible."[28] That doctrine, that "fatal doctrine of inspiration"[29] in seventeenth-century orthodox Protestantism, is one that Barth entirely rejects.[30] Nevertheless, "where the Word of God is an event, revelation and the Bible are one in fact, and word for word one at that."[31] But, he adds, they are also not one, because their unity is an event.[32] Elsewhere, Barth expresses this idea by saying that the Bible in this event is "indirectly identical" with the Word of God.[33]

The Bible, he says, claims no authority for itself. It is like John the Baptist, pointing away from himself to Christ.

23. Recall the coalescence between *being* and *becoming* in Hegel's dialectic.

24. Barth, *CD*, 1.1, 124.

25. Ibid., 125. In 1.2, 457–72, Barth expounds his understanding of Scripture as "witness" to revelation.

26. Barth, *CD*, 1.1, 126.

27. Ibid.

28. Ibid.

29. Ibid., 128.

30. See his discussion in *CD*, 1.2, 524–26. He claims that the Bible contains errors, not only in the areas of nature and history but also "in respect of religion and theology." Ibid., 510.

31. Barth, *CD*, 1.1., 127.

32. Ibid.

33. Compare Kierkegaard's concept of *indirect communication* (chapter 8).

OUTLINE

Karl Barth (1886–1968)

Emil Brunner (1889–1966)

Rudolf Bultmann (1884–1976)

Form Criticism
Demythologization
Existential Analysis

Paul Tillich (1886–1965)

Dietrich Bonhoeffer (1906–45)

The New Hermeneutic

New Quests

Heilsgeschichte

Christian Atheism

Secular Theology

The *Hartford Declaration*

We can now understand why Barth's theology is sometimes called *dialectical.* The Bible is the Word of God, but only because it might *become* the Word of God.[34] It becomes the Word in an event on which we may not presume. Anytime we read the Bible, God may decide to speak or not to speak. So the Bible's inspiration is not "general, equal, and permanent."

This view of Scripture encourages us to hear the Bible tentatively, selectively, critically. But this is not the attitude that believers should have, according to the Bible itself.[35] To Paul in 2 Timothy 3:16–17, the Bible is a permanent canon, breathed out by God (i.e., spoken by God), that we can turn to in any situation. Its inspiration is "general" and "equal" because it pertains to "all" Scripture.[36] And Isaiah 40:8 formulates the view of all biblical writers, that the Word of God given by the prophets will stand "forever," a permanent revelation.

Barth continues by announcing:

> Revelation in fact does not differ from the Person of Jesus Christ, and again does not differ from the reconciliation that took place in Him. To say revelation is to say "The Word became flesh."[37]

So Barth recognizes Christ as the supreme revelation of God. But he is, like all revelation, revelation in hiddenness, revelation in mystery. We might think that Barth here (as certainly in John 1:1–14, to which he alludes) is identifying the historical Jesus of Nazareth with the Word of God, jumping Lessing's ditch and abandoning the Enlightenment biblical criticism. But Barth says this:

We can now understand why Barth's theology is sometimes called dialectical. *The Bible is the Word of God, but only because it might* become *the Word of God. It becomes the Word in an event on which we may not presume. Anytime we read the Bible, God may decide to speak or not to speak.*

> Jesus Christ in fact is also the Rabbi of Nazareth, historically so difficult to get information about, and when it is got, one

34. Recall Hegel's philosophical play on the relation of *being* to *becoming.*

35. The biblical writers' own view of biblical inspiration, following the view of Jesus himself, has been expounded in a huge literature by evangelical writers. For my summary, see *DWG.*

36. Barth's account of 2 Timothy 3:14–17 is one of the least persuasive discussions in the whole *CD.* See *CD,* 1.2, 504. On 505 he claims that *theopneustia* (the "God-breathed" quality of Scripture in 2 Timothy 3:16) "in the bounds of biblical thinking cannot mean anything but the special attitude of obedience in those who are elected and called to this obviously special service." But the passage ascribes *theopneustia* to the text, not to the authors.

37. Barth, *CD,* 1.1, 134. Cf. 155–56, 174. Cf. "This reconciling action of God is the being of God in Christ, but this reconciling *action* of *God* is the being of God in Christ" (372 [emphasis his]). Note also 380, where he says, "What is involved at Whitsuntide [Pentecost] is no wise different from the event of Good Friday and Easter." On 372, he treats these three events as a kind of dialectic: Good Friday is the "veiling," Easter the "unveiling," Pentecost the "impartation," corresponding to the Father, the Son, and the Spirit, respectively. For Barth, it seems, all the events of the redemptive-historical sequence presented in Scripture get absorbed into "the being of God in Christ."

> whose activity is so easily a little commonplace alongside more than one other founder of a religion and even alongside many later representatives of his own "religion."[38]

So God's revelation enters into "worldliness." Barth doesn't say that the skeptical historical-Jesus scholars are wrong. Here and elsewhere, he affirms them, allowing even the most radical biblical criticism to take its course. What he is saying is that we may even grant the findings of these skeptics, but affirm nonetheless that God reveals himself in Jesus. Here we must doubt whether the Christ whom Barth identifies with revelation is the same as the historical Jesus. Barth's description of the latter is radically different from, even inconsistent with, his description of the former.

Barth doesn't say that the skeptical historical-Jesus scholars are wrong. Here and elsewhere, he affirms them, allowing even the most radical biblical criticism to take its course.

But this inconsistency does not trouble Barth as he presents "Jesus Christ" as God's revelation. For like all other revelation, the revelation in Jesus is "the veiling of God in his unveiling, equally with the unveiling of God in his veiling."[39] So *believing* means

> hearing the divine content of the Word of God, although absolutely nothing but worldly form is discernible by us. And faith now means hearing the worldly form of the Word of God, although nothing but its divine content is discernible by us.[40]

The same dialectical paradox appears as we try to relate biblical declarations of judgment to biblical declarations of God's saving grace. Despair and triumph are not successive revelations, but each is found in the other.[41] That is Barth's interpretation of Luther's *theology of the cross*. We know about God's wrath and judgment only when we know his grace, and vice versa.[42]

The same dialectical paradox appears as we try to relate biblical declarations of judgment to biblical declarations of God's saving grace. Despair and triumph are not successive revelations, but each is found in the other.

How, then, can human beings gain a knowledge of this paradoxical revelation? Barth says:

38. Ibid., 188. The quotation marks anticipate a later theme in *CD*, a long section attacking the idea of *religion*, *CD*, 1.2, 280–361. Barth defines *religion* as "self-will," "self-salvation," and the like. I regard this as an unbiblical definition. The word *religion* is not often found in English translations of Scripture, but in James 1:26–27 it means simply the outworking of faith in practical service. Theologians and preachers should not redefine good terms in order to make points. I would say the same about Bonhoeffer's repetition of this polemic, and about recent "I hate religion but I love Jesus" videos. Such language has a cool feel about it, and I agree with its intent—to rebuke formalism and traditionalism. But I don't appreciate the loss of a good term because of lexical dishonesty.

39. *CD*, 1.1, 200.

40. Ibid., 201.

41. Ibid., 204.

42. Ibid., 205.

> The reality of the Word of God in all its three forms is based only upon itself. So, too, knowledge of it by men can consist only in acknowledgement of it, and this acknowledgement can only become real through the Word itself, and can only become comprehensible if we start with itself.[43]

This epistemology recalls the *presuppositional* approach that I defended in chapter 1, discussed in Anselm[44] (chapter 4), and will discuss later in connection with Gordon H. Clark and Cornelius Van Til (chapter 13). To know and understand God's Word, we must begin with God's Word, not with thoughts or ideas that are contrary to it. I believe this is essentially right. But what can this mean for Barth? Barth believes that revelation is an occasional event, not a permanent deposit of truth. And even when we experience such an event, that event veils God as much as it unveils him. Agreeing with Barth that our knowledge of God's Word must be ruled by God's Word, we need to know the difference between being ruled by the Word and being ruled by something else. But the paradoxical, mysterious nature of revelation allows no answer to this question.

Traditional theology does, of course, recognize that God's revelation is mysterious in the sense that it does not give us an exhaustive transcript of God's mind. But it confesses also that God's revelation is knowable as well as incomprehensible. So the revelation of Scripture communicates genuine knowledge, teaching that we can identify as true. That truth we can presuppose as we seek to understand more about God through his revelation. It is clear how this process of knowledge differs from the knowledge sought by unbelievers. But in Barth's scheme, we do not have anything clear to presuppose. For Barth, the process of trying to understand God's Word, starting with God's Word, is grasping at the wind.

Traditional theology does, of course, recognize that God's revelation is mysterious in the sense that it does not give us an exhaustive transcript of God's mind. But it confesses also that God's revelation is knowable as well as incomprehensible.

The traditional approach, however, is a specific target of Barth's criticism:

> The man, the Church, the Church proclamation, the dogmatics which claimed to be able to work with the Word and with faith as with a capital sum standing at their disposal, would simply prove thereby that they possessed neither the Word nor faith. Where there is possession of them, we simply do not take it for granted as such, we strain after it hungering and thirsting, the only way to blessedness.[45]

43. Ibid., 213.

44. Barth often spoke very favorably about Anselm, particularly in his book *Anselm: Fides Quaerens Intellectum* (Eugene, OR: Wipf and Stock, 1975). See also his comment on Anselm in *CD*, 1.1, 263. I benefited greatly from Barth's presuppositional interpretation of Anselm.

45. *CD*, 1.1, 258. Cf. 309–10.

Most traditional theologians would not accept Barth's characterization of their relation to revelation as to "a capital sum standing at their disposal," but clearly Barth thinks this is the attitude of orthodox Protestant theologians or *fundamentalists*. This becomes a pervasive theme of Barth's writings: that the orthodox think God's revelation (and therefore God himself!) is "at their disposal," so that they can "possess," "control," "preserve," "manipulate," "depersonalize," "master" (etc.) the Word of God. The only way to avoid such an attitude is to regard revelation as Barth does, that is, as an "event" that "becomes true from time to time." That way, Barth thinks, we will recognize that we cannot master the Word; it must master us.

Most traditional theologians would not accept Barth's characterization of their relation to revelation as to "a capital sum standing at their disposal," but clearly Barth thinks this is the attitude of orthodox Protestant theologians or fundamentalists.

We can acknowledge that this sinful attempt to master God's Word does happen. Most of us who have studied theology have run across theological writings that are far too arrogant for their divine subject matter, by writers who never question their own expertise. Some of us have even written theology of this type. Such writers grant theoretically that God is incomprehensible, but they never cite any instances of it, and they never agree to any tentativeness in their own theories that might indicate understanding of their own limits. Nor do they hesitate to throw condemnations at believers who disagree with them, as if their own theories were beyond question. We all need to examine ourselves for indications of this syndrome.

But: (1) This sin is not limited to fundamentalists or orthodox theologians. It is also found in the liberal scholar who looks down on his fundamentalist opponents, sneering about "the assured results of modern biblical criticism." And it is also found among Barthians who think their dialectical subtlety is oh-so-profound compared to the simplistic views of traditional Christians. (2) This arrogance is a moral and spiritual issue, and it is hard to imagine how Barth's dialectical concept of revelation could even discourage it, let alone eliminate it. The solution is the work of the Spirit, not the Barthian dialectic. And since the Spirit testifies to the Word, the theologian must compare his behavior and attitudes with what God commands in Scripture. (3) The Barthian dialectic makes the Word evanescent, an event that disappears immediately after it happens, leaving us with only recollection and expectation. So if one is inclined to the sin of trying to possess God's Word, there is no continuing Word of God in Scripture to convict him of this sin.

What, then, of theology? How can we move from evanescent revelatory events to the verbal analyses and conclusions of books such as Barth's CD?

What, then, of theology? How can we move from evanescent revelatory events to the verbal analyses and conclusions of books such as Barth's *CD*? Dogmatics, Barth would say, must be based on revelation. But how can a propositional dogmatics be based on a nonpropositional revelation? How can a sentence be based on an event?

Later in *CD*, he argues against the Roman Catholic[46] definition of *dogma* as a group of "revealed truths."[47]

> Is the truth of revelation—so we must ask . . .—like other truths in that it may be fixed as *aletheia*, i.e., as the unveiled state of a hidden characteristic in human thoughts, concepts, and judgments and in this form thus limited and minted, held in preserve, so to speak, quite apart from the event of its becoming revealed as truth? Such obviously is the case with the truth of a doctrinal proposition. But will the truth of revelation submit to such materialization and depersonalization? Can it be possessed in abstraction from the person of Him who reveals it, and from the revealing act of this person, in which it is given to another person to perceive?[48]

Barth says here that if theology (dogmatics) is understood to consist of revealed truths expressed in propositions, then it violates the very nature of revelation. Propositions are subject to human possession, manipulation, preservation, and so on. As we saw earlier, Barth offered his doctrine of revelation as event to discourage human beings from attempting to treat the Word of God this way. Now he is saying that if dogmatics is to be true to revelation, it, too, must be put into a form that is immune to such human corruption.

Barth's argument is different: for him, propositional revelation is impossible not because it violates the freedom of men, but because it violates the freedom of God.

So Barth places a vast gap between revelation and propositions. We have seen that this has been a major theme in the history of liberal theology: that the truth about God cannot be stated in propositional form. Spinoza, Cherbury, Lessing, Kant, Hegel, Schleiermacher, and Ritschl all developed arguments as to why there can be no revealed propositions. This one is Barth's. The earlier thinkers typically rejected propositional revelation because they did not want the autonomous human intellect to be bound by any authority outside itself. Barth's argument is different: for him, propositional revelation is impossible not because it violates the freedom of men, but because it violates the freedom of God. But of course, the result is the same. For Barth, too, there are no revealed propositions, and so the human thinker is not bound to divine dictates as to what he should believe and do. Human beings are bound only to God's revelation as event. And nobody knows

46. But his critique, if valid, certainly bears against traditional Protestants and Eastern Orthodox as well, and every other branch of the church except the liberal.

47. In context, he prefers to say that dogma consists of divine "behest" or "command" rather than "doctrinal propositions." That makes some biblical sense. But it seems to me that Barth's criticisms of theology as proposition would entail the same criticisms against theology as "behest."

48. *CD*, 1.1, 309–10. Cf. 1.2, 507.

when such an event has taken place or what its content might be. So for Barth as for Ritschl, God's revelation places no limits on the work of the autonomous historical scholar. Barth affirms the freedom of God, and also the freedom of biblical criticism. So in the end, Barth's complaint against neo-Protestantism stands against his own approach to theology. For in the end, the "voice of God" turns out to be man's own voice. For Barth as for Schleiermacher, man listens to himself. He confuses God's voice with man's.

For Barth as for Ritschl, God's revelation places no limits on the work of the autonomous historical scholar. Barth affirms the freedom of God, and also the freedom of biblical criticism. . . . In the end, the "voice of God" turns out to be man's own voice.

In the later part of *CD*, 1.1, Barth develops the doctrine of revelation by correlating it with the doctrine of the Trinity. This accords with his earlier identification of revelation with Christ. Here he tries to reverse the program of Schleiermacher, who regarded revelation primarily from the standpoint of its human recipients. Revelation itself, says Barth, "insists on being regarded from the side of its subject, God."[49] But then:

> If we wish really to regard the revelation from the side of its subject, God, then above all we must understand that the subject, God, the Revealer, is identical with His act in revelation, identical also with its effect.[50]

So Barth expounds his doctrine of the Trinity as an elaboration of the claim "God reveals himself as the Lord."[51] The Father is the Revealer (*God* reveals himself). The Son is the Revelation (God *reveals* himself). The Spirit is the "Revealedness," the "effect" of the act (God reveals *himself*).[52] The three are the same God, but they are distinct in ways similar to those formulated by the Nicene Council. Some writers have questioned whether these distinctions within the concept of revelation are sufficient. It is not clear that Barth's formulation allows sufficient distinctions between the three *persons* to acquit him of the charge of Sabellianism. But it is more relevant to note how Barth's doctrine of God is radically different from anything that has gone before. Neither Sabellius nor Athanasius (chapter 3) imagined anything quite like Barth's view, his "activist" equation[53] of God's Trinitarian being with his act of revealing himself to human beings.

Barth's doctrine of God is radically different from anything that has gone before.

> According to Scripture God's revelation is God's own immediate speaking, not to be distinguished from the act of this speaking, therefore not to be distinguished from God Himself,

49. Ibid., 339. But one still wonders how such an "insistence" can be derived from a nonpropositional event.

50. Ibid., 340.

51. Ibid., 351, 353.

52. Ibid. 340.

53. But on ibid., 357, he says that he does not intend to "confuse" or "equate" revelation with the Trinity, but only to assert between them a "genuine and truly found correlation."

> from the divine I which confronts man in this act in which it addresses him as "thou." Revelation is *Dei loquentis persona*. . . . God's Word is identical with God Himself.[54]

Barth recognizes, however, that revelation is not only an event in the divine being. It is also an event of human history. History is the "destination" of revelation.[55] But he has a unique understanding of that aspect of revelation as well:

> Historical does not mean fixable as historical or fixed as historical. Historical does not have its usual meaning of "historical" . . . i.e., as apprehensible by a neutral observer or as apprehended by such an one.[56]

A neutral observer, he says, could observe the *form* of revelation, as a passer-by looking at the temple or listening to Jesus. But to such observers these experiences are not revelation. This is true even of the resurrection of Jesus:

> Even the historical element of the resurrection of Christ, the empty grave regarded as an element of this event, that might possibly be fixed, was certainly not revelation. This historical element, like everything historical, is admittedly susceptible of an even highly trivial interpretation. . . . The neutral observer who understood the events narrated in it as revelation, ceased by that very fact to be a neutral observer.[57]

Neutral historians, that is, historians without faith, can neither confirm nor deny the existence of revelation.

Barth recognizes, however, that revelation is not only an event in the divine being. It is also an event of human history. History is the "destination" of revelation.

In this context, Barth says that the revelation in Scripture may contain saga, but not myth.[58] The distinction is not terribly clear, but Barth seems to use *saga* to refer to a temporally sequenced "story" or "narrative,"[59] as in Genesis 1–3, while to him *myth* is the attempt to set forth timeless truths in temporal language, as in Gnosticism, or the Greek stories of the Olympic gods. Neither saga nor myth, according to Barth, is inerrant in its description of what happened. But the distinction enables Barth to stress that revelation comes through historical events, rather than through timeless knowledge, as in Gnosticism.[60]

54. Ibid., 349.
55. Ibid., 373.
56. Ibid.
57. Ibid. Cf. the discussion of resurrection in 1.2, 113–21.
58. Ibid., 1.1, 376–78.
59. A *Geschichte* in the sense discussed below.
60. But we saw earlier that for Barth the historical sequence of redemptive events seems to be erased when he equates revelation with reconciliation, Good Friday, Easter, Pentecost, the Trinity, and the "being of God in Christ."

Later he deals more generally with the relation between revelation and history: *"Revelation is not a predicate of history, but history is a predicate of revelation."*[61] This somewhat obscure statement seems to mean that we cannot discover revelation from a "neutral" historical examination (as, for example, the Ritschlians tried to do), but that when God chooses to reveal himself, his revelation takes place in a historical situation, and we must take account of that situation in order to respond properly to the revelation.[62] In this connection Barth discusses the "times" of revelation, the relation between OT and NT, and so on.

Later Barth deals more generally with the relation between revelation and history: "Revelation is not a predicate of history, but history is a predicate of revelation."

Elsewhere in *CD*, Barth discusses the historicity of Scripture in terms of the concepts *Historie* and *Geschichte*. Both these terms can be translated into English as "history," but in recent German theology[63] they have different connotations. *Historie* is the discipline of academic history, controlled by scholarly professionals with a claim of religious "neutrality." Most theologians and philosophers agree that this discipline determines what happened in the past, where, and when. Most European scholars of *Historie*, however, were convinced that miracles cannot take place, that historical explanations must exclude the supernatural.[64] Obviously, *Historie*, so defined, could not be the basis for religious conviction. On that definition, Lessing was entirely correct to place an ugly, broad ditch between history and faith.

Geschichte is a looser concept. It can be translated "story," and it refers to a narrative thought to have some human significance. But a *Geschichte* does not require the verification of professional historians. It functions on its own terms. To employ Husserl's expression, a *Geschichte* "brackets" the kinds of questions that naturalistic scholars ask about date, time, detailed accuracy, and so on. A *Geschichte* may incorporate miracle or religious significance. But it need not be entirely true. It may incorporate erroneous fact claims, but that does not necessarily impair its validity.

A Geschichte *may incorporate miracle or religious significance. But it need not be entirely true. It may incorporate erroneous fact claims, but that does not necessarily impair its validity.*

In Barth's view, *Historie* is irrelevant to determining the truth of revelation. God's Word will not be subject to the judgment of

61. *CD*, 1.2, 58.

62. The statement also reinforces Barth's denial (over against Brunner) of the existence of *natural revelation*. He argues elsewhere that Brunner's position implies a *point of contact* in man's nature for divine revelation, so that man can discover it for himself. In Barth's view, revelation creates its own point of contact. See *CD*, 1.1, 29, 218–26, 271, and his various critiques of the Roman Catholic *analogy of being*.

63. Martin Kähler, *The So-Called Historical [Historische] Jesus and the Historic [Geschichtliche] Biblical Christ*, trans. Carl E. Braaten (1896; repr., Philadelphia: Fortress Press, 1964), is often considered the beginning of this discussion. On page 46, he says, "I regard the entire Life-of-Jesus movement as a blind alley."

64. Hardly a "neutral" position!

unbelieving "neutral" historians. But God's Word does enter into history and does make historical claims. For Barth, these should be understood as *Geschichte.*

In the famous debate between Barth and Bultmann as to the historicity of Jesus' resurrection,[65] Bultmann took the position that if the resurrection took place in space and time, it must be subject to the criteria of professional historians (*Historie*). Since it is miraculous, it does not measure up to those criteria, and so it cannot have happened. Barth argued that it was arbitrary to assume that nothing can happen in time and space without the verification of historical science. The Word of God says that the resurrection happened in space and time, and so it did, regardless of what the historical professionals say.[66]

Now, part of the problem here is that both Barth and Bultmann have evidently conceded the profession of historical scholarship to partisans of post-Enlightenment naturalism. So if Barth is to argue against Bultmann that the resurrection actually took place, which he certainly intends to do, he must argue that it has a very odd relationship with historical scholarship. I agree with Barth that to identify the resurrection in history requires faith. But I would go further and say that to identify any historical event at all requires faith.[67] Barth and Bultmann should never have conceded the field of historical scholarship to naturalistic, "neutral" scholars. But having done that, Barth must find a location for the events of revelation and salvation that is separate from the realm interpreted by naturalistic scholarship. For that purpose, *Geschichte* becomes something more than a designation of an informal kind of storytelling.

For Barth, Geschichte *is the realm of divine revelation, which, as we saw earlier, "must become true in the Church from time to time in the intractable reality of faith." That revelation Barth identifies with Christ himself, and therefore with all the work of Christ.*

For Barth, *Geschichte* is the realm of divine revelation, which, as we saw earlier, "must become true in the Church from time to time in the intractable reality of faith."[68] That revelation Barth identifies with Christ himself, and therefore with all the work of Christ: incarnation, reconciliation, and resurrection. He also identifies revelation-*Geschichte* more generally with God himself: "Truth of revelation is the freely acting God, Himself and quite alone."[69] So *Geschichte* is the sphere in which the whole story of redemption takes place. It is the

65. *CD*, 3.2, 446–47; 4.1, 336.

66. Here, as often, Barth is assuming that revelation makes propositional truth claims, something that he elsewhere denies.

67. This is in the broad sense that whatever we do must be done to the glory of God (1 Cor. 10:31). Unbelievers can gain some knowledge by God's general revelation and common grace, as I have argued in *DKG*, but they will miss what is most important about their discipline, its relation to God, if they persist in unbelief.

68. *CD*, 1.1.16.

69. Ibid.

moment of Kierkegaard in which, paradoxically, the eternal becomes temporal. It also resembles, uncomfortably, the noumenal world of Kant (which we can access practically, but not theoretically).[70] Thus it risks identification with what I called in chapter 1 the *nonbiblical* view of transcendence.

Unlike Kant's noumenal, however, *Geschichte* is not completely separate from the world of our experience. As I mentioned, Barth insists against Bultmann that the resurrection, a *geschichtlich* event, took place in space and time. Still, Barth's proposal is radically different from the theology of Scripture and of historic Christianity. Not only is revelation, for him, a momentary event, but everything else of religious importance is reduced to this event: Christ, reconciliation, redemption, resurrection, even God himself.[71] Each of these touches our historical experience, but it quickly vanishes from that experience, leaving us with only "recollection and expectation." As we have seen, the reality of the *geschichtlich* Christ is compatible with radically negative conclusions about the historical Jesus. And the union of the Word of God with Scripture as event is compatible with errors of all kinds in the Bible. For Barth, revelation takes place in history in the sense that it occurs in the experience of historical people. But it does not necessarily give any reliable information about what happened in space and time.

Barth's proposal is radically different from the theology of Scripture and of historic Christianity. Not only is revelation, for him, a momentary event, but everything else of religious importance is reduced to this event.

So God, though he reveals himself, remains "wholly hidden" or "wholly other," as in the nonbiblical view of transcendence. Like any momentary event, God, for Barth, cannot be captured, possessed, manipulated, and so forth. But because in that event he is one with Christ, he is also "wholly revealed."[72] There is no mysterious, secret decree behind the revelation of Christ that could put his promises of salvation in question.[73] Indeed, human beings are not only elected

God, though he reveals himself, remains "wholly hidden" or "wholly other," as in the nonbiblical view of transcendence. Like any momentary event, God, for Barth, cannot be captured, possessed, manipulated, and so forth. But because in that event he is one with Christ, he is also "wholly revealed."

70. It might be of some interest that Barth's brother Heinrich was a philosopher who was known as a neo-Kantian.

71. Barth identifies all these events with one another, because in the *geschichtlich* world of momentary events, there is no way to tell them apart. So similarly Barth identifies the person of Christ with his work, contrary to the theological tradition. As in existentialist philosophy, God's acts are his essence. I said earlier that Barth embraces a nonbiblical view of transcendence (chapter 1) by putting God and his redemptive acts in a sphere only evanescently accessible to man. But he also adopts a nonbiblical view of immanence by identifying our history with God's being.

72. In Barth's formal discussion of the doctrine of God, *hiddenness* and *revealedness* become God's *freedom* and *love*, respectively, which Barth considers his fundamental attributes. See *CD*, 2.1, 257–636.

73. *CD*, 2.2, 3–508. Calvin and his successors taught that God's choice of individuals to salvation is the result of a decree executed in eternity, "before the foundation of the world." Barth here rejects that notion. He focuses on Paul's statement in Ephesians 1:4 that God chose us in Christ. If election is in Christ, says Barth, nothing can threaten that election, not even a "secret decree."

in Christ, but created in Christ.[74, 75] Nevertheless, in his revelation, God remains hidden to us, because of his freedom to become what he chooses to be,[76] and because

> the pictures in which we view God, the thoughts in which we think Him, the words with which we can define Him, are in themselves unfitted to this object and thus inappropriate to express and affirm the knowledge of Him.[77]

The apparent contradiction is part of Barth's dialectic. But we can understand it better if we consider that our knowledge of God coincides with the event of revelation, so it exists only "from time to time"; see fig. 10.1.[78]

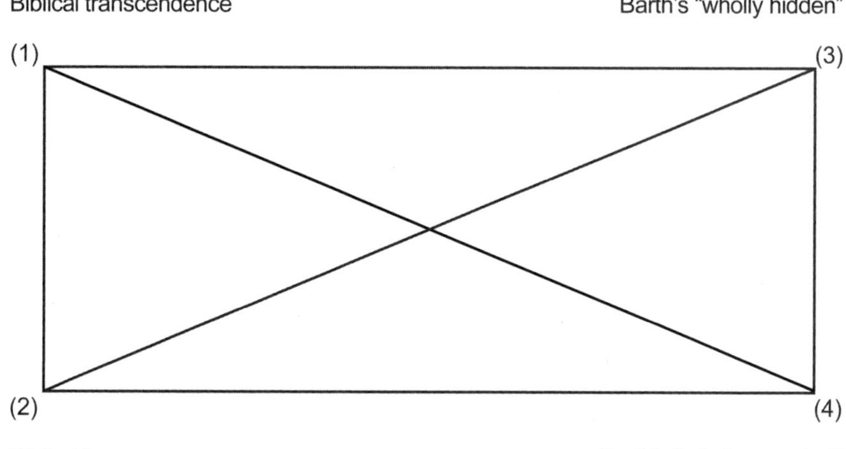

Fig. 10.1. Transcendence and Immanence in Barth

The apparent contradiction is part of Barth's dialectic. But we can understand it better if we consider that our knowledge of God coincides with the event of revelation, so it exists only "from time to time."

The place of sin in creation is problematic for Barth. He follows a pattern that I criticized in my account of Augustine (chapter 3), namely,

74. *CD*, 3.1, 42–350. When he speaks about our creation and election in Christ, he typically speaks of *all* people, unlike traditional Reformed theology, which distinguishes between elect and reprobate. For Barth, since election is in Christ, we should regard Christ as the elect man and the only reprobate man as well (because he bore God's wrath). So all human beings are reprobate in Christ, but also elect in him. That formulation suggests universalism, the doctrine that all people will be finally saved. Barth resists this accusation by saying that universalism neglects the freedom of God. See also 1.1, 175–76.

75. Because we are created in Christ, we, too, are included in *Geschichte*. *Geschichte* is in effect the place where God, Christ, and man are together. One wonders, though, how they can be distinguished from one another in the momentary event.

76. *CD*, 2.1, 179–203.

77. Ibid., 188.

78. Ibid., 204–54.

that sin is an abuse of metaphysical nonbeing. Evil, then, is a privation of being, and sin is a misuse of human freedom to align oneself with evil. This idea can be found in many medieval thinkers, including Aquinas, but I reject it because it seeks to provide a metaphysical explanation of an ethical matter. In Scripture, sin is personal disobedience, and to claim a metaphysical origin for it is to offer an excuse.

Barth's concept is also fundamentally metaphysical. Barth believes that the good creation has a "shadowside,"[79] what Augustine called *nonbeing*. The shadowside is not evil, but part of the good creation. In every created being, there must be "not only a height but an abyss, not only clarity but obscurity; . . . yet it is irrefutable that creation and creature are good even in the fact that all exist in contrast and antitheses."[80] Jesus participated in the shadowside by taking finitude and weakness upon himself. But the shadowside makes it possible for human beings to fall into real evil, which Barth calls *Das Nichtige*, "nothingness."[81] *Das Nichtige* is what God *refused* to create when he made the good creation. He said yes to the good, no to evil. But as God's yes is a powerful yes, his no is a powerful no, and it, too, had a result.[82] Man fell into *Das Nichtige*, and Jesus conquered it in his reconciling work.[83]

[According to Barth, evil] is a privation of being, and sin is a misuse of human freedom to align oneself with evil. . . . I reject [this] because it seeks to provide a metaphysical explanation of an ethical matter.

As an account of the origin of evil, Barth's formulation is not persuasive. Does it help us understand evil, does it even make sense, to say that evil exists as the result of God's powerful prohibition? One would have thought that if God's prohibition were truly powerful, evil would not have existed. But even worse, it would seem that for Barth evil, too, is part of the revelatory event, *Geschichte*. And the "triumph of grace" means that grace (which is also a *geschichtlich* event) predominates in *Geschichte* over *Das Nichtige*, the negative *geschichtlich* event.

As an account of the origin of evil, Barth's formulation is not persuasive. Does it help us understand evil, does it even make sense, to say that evil exists as the result of God's powerful prohibition?

Geschichte is a moment in which eternity enters time. Wrapped up in that moment is all the theology of Christianity: God, creation, man, evil, the fall, Christ, the incarnation, reconciliation, resurrection, and parousia. Occasionally some element of this complex will touch down in ordinary time and space, as Barth asserts of the resurrection. But that time-and-space happening is never to be identified with the saving event of *Geschichte*. Barth describes these happenings as "pointers" to the real salvation that comes through the momentary revelatory *Geschichte*.

79. *CD*, 3.3, 351–52.

80. Ibid., 296–97.

81. That is, it would make it possible to fall into real evil, except that Barth also talks about the "ontological impossibility of sin."

82. *CD*, 3.3, 311.

83. Barth does not affirm Adam's fall as an event in space-time. But in view of Paul's parallel between the work of Christ and that of Adam (Rom. 5:12–20), it would seem equally difficult to affirm the atonement of Christ as an event in space-time. Fall and redemption both are, for Barth, part of the *Geschichte* event.

OUTLINE

Karl Barth (1886–1968)

Emil Brunner (1889–1966)

Rudolf Bultmann (1884–1976)

Form Criticism
Demythologization
Existential Analysis

Paul Tillich (1886–1965)

Dietrich Bonhoeffer (1906–45)

The New Hermeneutic

New Quests

Heilsgeschichte

Christian Atheism

Secular Theology

The *Hartford Declaration*

Many evangelicals have recently suggested that we should give Barth a "second look." I am not averse to that. We should be open to new evidence and arguments as we seek to evaluate past theologians. In preparing this section of my book, I have tried to hear Barth with fresh ears. But I have not come to view him more sympathetically. Essentially, I don't recognize Barth's theology as the gospel of Scripture. To summarize:

1. When God reveals himself in Scripture, he expects us to obey his commands and trust his promises without question. He does not allow us to dither, waiting for them to become true from time to time.
2. In Scripture, the gospel story is not the story of a momentary event that comes to an individual. It is the story of definite actions of God in the created world over years and centuries.
3. The biblical text is not a mere "locus of recollection and expectation." It is the very speech of God (2 Tim. 3:16) written down, to which we can reliably turn to find out what God says to us.
4. As such, it is, though written by human beings, infallible and inerrant, because it is also God's speech.
5. The infallible Bible does not allow us to "possess" or "manipulate" the Word of God. Scripture's infallible inspiration is precisely what prevents us from doing that.
6. Because Scripture is the infallible Word of God, it contains propositional truth that should govern the church's theology.
7. The gospel story (point 2 above) narrates events that take place in time and space. It presents these events truly, despite the skepticism of historical critics. We can trust the Bible's own account, because it speaks with God's authority.
8. Mankind became sinful in the past action of our first parents. Through Jesus' atonement in space and time, his people were redeemed.

Barth clearly fits the definition of liberalism *that I presented in chapter 6: "any kind of theology that does not submit to the infallible authority of Scripture."*

Many would resist my inclusion of Barth in the school of liberal theology dating from Spinoza and Cherbury. Barth seems far too serious about the content of Scripture to be compared with such thinkers. But he clearly fits the definition of *liberalism* that I presented in chapter 6: "any kind of theology that does not submit to the infallible authority of Scripture." And his presentation of the actual content of Scripture, for all its orthodox terminology, is very far from what the Bible teaches.

Still, Barth is something of a climax to the trend that I have described as *conservative drift*. (With Bultmann, we will see, that trend is interrupted.) My theological evaluation of Barth, furthermore, is not a judgment of his heart. As I said, large amounts of Barth's writings are edifying to me, and I think they would be edifying to anyone who loves Jesus. I have often asked whether his heart lies with his edifying observations or with his existentialized theology. It is possible that God did a work of grace in his heart, but when he tried to formulate his new thoughts into academic theological form he had to rely on his theological education, no matter how much he sought to rethink it.

Certainly I am moved by his answer to the question, "What is the deepest theological truth you know?"—"Jesus loves me, this I know, for the Bible tells me so."

Certainly I am moved by Barth's answer to the question, "What is the deepest theological truth you know?"—"Jesus loves me, this I know, for the Bible tells me so."

And I smile at his frequently quoted aphorism, recognizing its application to theologians of all schools:

> The angels laugh at old Karl. They laugh at him because he tries to grasp the truth about God in a book of Dogmatics. They laugh at the fact that volume follows volume, and each is thicker than the previous ones. As they laugh, they say to one another, "Look! Here he comes now with his little pushcart full of volumes of the Dogmatics!"—and they laugh about the persons who write so much about Karl Barth instead of writing about the things he is trying to write about. Truly, the angels laugh.[84]

EMIL BRUNNER (1889–1966)[85]

Brunner traveled more than Barth. After having earned his doctorate at the University of Zurich (1913), he spent one year (1919–20) studying at Union Theological Seminary, New York. (From 1916 to 1924, he was pastor in a small Swiss village, Obstalden.) From 1922 to 1953, he taught at the University of Zurich, but lectured around the world, including a visiting professorship at Princeton Theological Seminary (1937–38). From 1953 to 1955, he taught at the International Christian University of Tokyo, Japan. He also wrote many books and articles, and because of this exposure he was better known than Barth in many parts of the world.

Emil Brunner

Still, he acknowledged that Barth's achievements were greater. He said that Barth was the only theological genius of the twentieth century, and despite the Barth-Brunner dispute on natural theology (below), he told inquirers that he had always been a Barthian. In effect, his achievement was to spread the Barthian theology outside Switzerland and Germany. His writing is much easier to read than Barth's, his reasoning more oriented toward common sense.

For the most part, then, Brunner's theology does not differ from that of Barth. But he does have a distinctive emphasis or perspective,

84. Quoted in Stephen H. Webb, *Re-Figuring Theology: The Rhetoric of Karl Barth* (New York: State University of New York Press, 1991), 164.

85. Actually, *H.* Emil Brunner, the *H* standing for *Heinrich*.

which we may call *personalism*. As I said in chapter 1, the Bible emphasizes that the supreme being of the universe is an absolute person, and that teaching is unique among religions and philosophies. This confession has important implications for philosophy and ethics, but in the twentieth century it received a new twist. Others with Brunner emphasized the personal character of God, particularly **Ferdinand Ebner** (1882–1931), **John W. Oman** (1860–1939), and the Jewish thinker **Martin Buber** (1878–1965). These are sometimes called *dialogical* thinkers. Buber famously distinguished between *I-it* and *I-thou* relationships in his book *I and Thou* (1923).[86] Barth also developed this theme, but it doesn't play as central a role in Barth's work as in Brunner's.[87]

Revelation, to Brunner, is a personal encounter with God himself. In an impersonal relationship, he says, I can contemplate my object and thereby master it. (Recall Sartre's account of "the gaze" in chapter 9.) But in a truly personal relationship, I cannot contemplate or master the other. I can speak only *to* him, not *about* him. Afterward, I can think about the relationship. But the more I think objectively about the other person, the less personal the relationship becomes. Divine revelation, however, always remains personal, nonobjective. We can never master it. So in revelation, God never reveals information; he reveals only himself, though he is "wholly other." This occurs only in the momentary present, and is never apart from my response. This is the event of salvation; see fig. 10.2.

Revelation, to Brunner, is a personal encounter with God himself. In an impersonal relationship, he says, I can contemplate my object and thereby master it. But in a truly personal relationship, I cannot contemplate or master the other.

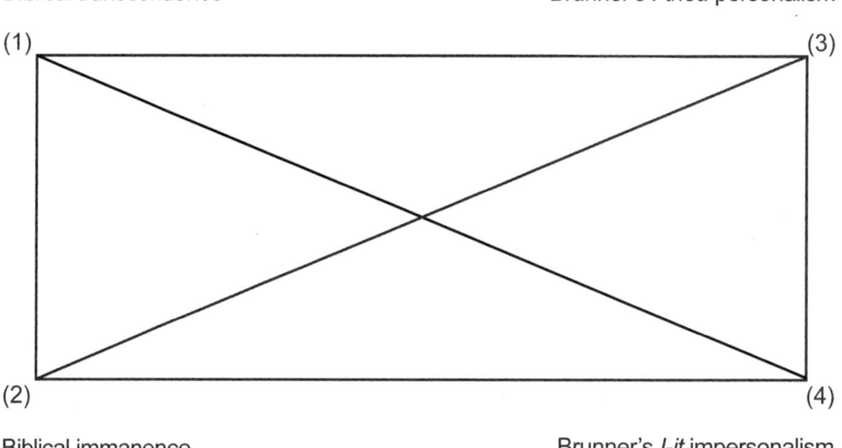

Fig. 10.2. Transcendence and Immanence in Brunner

86. There are several English translations. One, by Walter Kaufmann, is Eastford, CT: Martino Fine Books, 2010.

87. See Barth, *CD*, 1.1, 77, 155, 309–10, 349.

To readers of this book, my description of Brunner's doctrine will strike many familiar notes: the subject-object dilemma of existentialism; the instantaneous present salvation event (= Barth's *Geschichte*); the opposition to anything that tries to "master" revelation (such as Barth's polemic against trying to "possess," "control," "manipulate," etc.); the denial of propositional revelation ("revelation of information"); the identification of the event of revelation with God himself, as in Barth; Barth's concept of God as the "wholly other" who is totally free.

But in Brunner, this collection of points is even more implausible than the similar collection in Barth. Is it really true that gaining information about another person makes the relationship less truly personal? I have often found that learning something new about a friend deepens that relationship, opens greater areas of commonness and intimacy. Is it true that knowing "about" somebody is an attempt to "master" the other person? That point is no more persuasive in Brunner than it is in Sartre.

Is it really true that gaining information about another person makes the relationship less truly personal? I have often found that learning something new about a friend deepens that relationship, opens greater areas of commonness and intimacy.

Brunner here is trying to develop still another argument for the traditional liberal conclusion, that revelation is not propositional in character, even a little bit. If God reveals propositions, then we lose the main motivation for the liberal movement: theological rationale for human intellectual autonomy. But of course, according to the Bible, God reveals propositions all the time, from Genesis 1:1 to John 14:6. In fact, that is the primary meaning of *revelation* in the Bible. It rarely if ever speaks of God's revealing "himself" (mystically, as it were) without a propositional context.[88] And when God reveals propositions, this revelation deepens, rather than detracts from, the personal character of our relation to God.

Brunner speaks of revelation in nature, history, and Scripture. His view of natural revelation provoked the sharp condemnation of Barth. Brunner maintained that despite sin, fallen man has some ability (a *point of contact*, as it was called) to understand God's revelation in the natural world and in the human heart. Barth's article in reply was titled simply "*Nein*" ("No"). Barth denied any such point of contact as a limit on the freedom of God. To him, God creates his own point of contact, only in the moment of revelation (*Geschichte*). Barth seemed to think that God's grace was at stake.

Brunner speaks of revelation in nature, history, and Scripture. His view of natural revelation provoked the sharp condemnation of Barth.

Brunner affirms (somewhat more clearly than Barth) that faith rests on objective events that took place thousands of years ago. So unlike Barth, he affirms the importance of the historical Jesus, over against the historical relativism of Troeltsch. But, he says, we know these events only by the revelation of God in the present, by faith. So in Brunner's view as in Barth's, historical criticism is no barrier to faith. Brunner

88. See my *DWG* for argument to this effect.

tends to be more skeptical than Barth about the supernatural, particularly the virgin birth and the miracles of Jesus (including his physical resurrection). So for Brunner, as for Barth, revelation may never be identified with anything historical.

Like Barth, Brunner describes Scripture as a witness to revelation. It is not itself revelation, but points away from itself to Christ. It is like the crib in which Mary and Joseph placed the baby Jesus. It is normative witness because it is our primary historical source for the gospel events. But it is a fully human book, a human word about a divine Word. But besides being a witness to revelation in the past, Scripture is an instrument of revelation in the present. It brings God's Word to me in the moment of faith. Brunner's writings contain a severe polemic against the orthodox doctrine of verbal inspiration.[89] He says that it is idolatry, trusting a book rather than Christ. But Brunner's honesty undercuts his argument. Unlike Barth, he admits that the doctrine of verbal inspiration is taught, in effect, in Scripture itself, particularly in the later epistles (2 Tim. 3:16), in some of Jesus' sayings, and in the OT regard for God's law. But given Brunner's view of Scripture, he feels free to charge Scripture with inconsistency on that and other points. He believes that the critique of law in the NT goes against the idea of verbal inspiration, as do the nonliteral NT quotations of the OT. (Odd, certainly, to say that authoritative quotations, literal or not, are inconsistent with verbal inspiration.)

In Brunner's work, there is a fairly pervasive polemic against orthodoxy in general, in what I regard as a bitter tone. He says that orthodox or *fundamentalist* Christians are opposed to science, are motivated by fear,[90] lack any true fellowship or spiritual power.

Brunner's writings contain a severe polemic against the orthodox doctrine of verbal inspiration. He says that it is idolatry, trusting a book rather than Christ. But Brunner's honesty undercuts his argument. Unlike Barth, he admits that the doctrine of verbal inspiration is taught, in effect, in Scripture itself.

RUDOLF BULTMANN (1884–1976)

We take our leave, for now, from my thesis of the *conservative drift*. In that thesis I maintained that each generation of liberal theologians tends to state its views in more conservative-traditional language than the generation before. That thesis has held for the most part, I believe, from Spinoza and Cherbury to Barth and Brunner. Liberals during that time felt that they needed to speak the language of the church in order

89. Barth, too, objected strongly to the seventeenth-century/fundamentalist doctrine of inspiration. But he equivocated on the verbal aspect of inspiration. Usually, *verbal inspiration* means that the words of the Bible are words of God. But Barth affirmed a kind of verbal inspiration in which the event of revelation (*Geschichte*) employs words in the Bible so that they "become" the Word of God to us. In my judgment, this is obfuscation; Brunner is clearer to simply deny verbal inspiration altogether. Clearly, he and Barth both deny what the term has meant historically.

90. I am impressed at how often liberals criticize orthodox Christians by imputing bad motives to them. Of course, the reverse is sometimes true, but in my experience less often.

to gain wide influence in the Christian world. But the conservative drift is not a straight line; it has a number of glitches in it. Every now and then, theologians arise who are more interested in parading their unbelief than in displaying their allegiance to the tradition.[91] Typically this happens more often with biblical scholars than with systematic theologians. In past centuries, H. S. Reimarus (1694–1768), David F. Strauss (1808–74), and Bruno Bauer (1809–82) (who denied that Jesus ever existed) defied all that the church ever said about Jesus. In the twentieth century, Rudolf Bultmann, a leading NT scholar, is the most conspicuous exception to the conservative drift. I could have ignored Bultmann in this book as I ignored Reimarus and Strauss, for this book is not primarily about NT scholarship. But although Bultmann never wrote a systematic theology, he became the largest influence on liberal theology in all forms after the heyday of Barth.

Although Bultmann never wrote a systematic theology, he became the largest influence on liberal theology in all forms after the heyday of Barth.

Bultmann studied with Hermann Gunkel, the founder of form criticism, and with Harnack, Herrmann, and Weiss. From 1922 to 1928, he was a colleague of Martin Heidegger at the University of Marburg. He was close to Barth in the early years of *crisis theology*, emphasizing that the Word of God is something that comes from beyond ourselves and speaks with power from above. He maintained that emphasis through his life, but he was more liberal than Barth on matters of biblical criticism and, importantly, in his formulation of the gospel.

Passing over the details of Bultmann's prolific writings in biblical scholarship, we should note three areas in which he had the greatest influence on the larger theological scene.

Rudolf Bultmann

Form Criticism

Bultmann provided great momentum to the application of form-critical methods to the NT. Form criticism[92] presupposes a liberal view of Scripture, to the extent that the Bible is generally presumed unreliable unless proved otherwise. Particularly, form critics assume that the stories told, for example in the Gospels, did not originate in the settings described in the text. On this view, the early church had collections of sayings of Jesus and stories of Jesus. They arranged these sayings and stories into a framework that was largely their own invention. The form critic seeks to reconstruct the *actual* settings in which the sayings and stories originated. To this end, he seeks to classify the material

91. One example: For some reason, it always seems that some Anglican bishop regularly gains headlines by proclaiming how little he believes: in my lifetime, James Pike, John Robinson, Shelby Spong.

92. Form criticism is one of several methods used among modern scholars to analyze and reconstruct the Bible. *Source-criticism* attempts to identify the literary sources that lie behind books of the Bible. *Redaction-criticism* tries to identify the supposed motives and patterns of thought among those who first edited the raw materials that became Scripture.

into different categories: miracle story, prophecy, parable, and the like. This categorization feeds theories of what is earlier, what later, in the tradition. Some form critics allow that a portion of that tradition, often a very small portion, brings us close to the actual teachings of Jesus.

Bultmann's conclusion from this study is that nothing much can be known about the historical Jesus. But Bultmann (unlike, say, Bruno Bauer) did believe that Jesus was a historical man, a teacher who was born and died in Palestine. He said that we could know *that* Jesus was, but not *what* he was.[93] Bultmann follows the *consistent eschatology* of his teacher Weiss, that Jesus proclaimed (erroneously) the imminence of the apocalypse.

Demythologization

In 1941, Bultmann published an essay called "The NT and Mythology"[94] that powerfully influenced the course of subsequent theology. Myth, he says there, describes the eternal in terms of the temporal, the divine in terms of the human, and so on. Much of Scripture is myth in this sense. Not only are supernatural-miraculous events mythological, according to Bultmann, but also the larger worldview in which the events of the narrative take place is mythological: a three-story universe with heaven above, the earth below, and the underworld below the earth.

Not only are supernatural-miraculous events mythological, according to Bultmann, but also the larger worldview in which the events of the narrative take place is mythological: a three-story universe with heaven above, the earth below, and the underworld below the earth.

Now, modern man cannot believe in these myths, literally understood, Bultmann says. Modern man believes in a world system governed entirely by scientific law, with no possibility of supernatural interference.[95] How can we believe in angels and demons, Bultmann asks rhetorically, when we listen to the radio, ride in airplanes, and take medicine for our illnesses?[96] He qualifies his point, however: he is not saying that people are *obligated* to believe the modern worldview. He is saying only that this is what modern people *in fact* believe.

The problem that this poses for the church is one of communication.[97] Whether or not the modern view is right, the fact that people believe it makes it difficult for them to understand the world of the

93. As it was sometimes put, the *dass*, but not the *was*.

94. Available in many places, such as Hans Werner Bartsch, ed., *Kerygma and Myth: A Theological Debate*, trans. Reginald H. Fuller, 2 vols. (New York: Harper and Row, 1961), 1:1–44.

95. This is a scientific determinism that reflects some older forms of science, but not twentieth-century science after the development of relativity theory and quantum mechanics. Bultmann, the quintessential "modern man," here actually appears rather old-fashioned.

96. I wonder whether anybody is able to take this kind of argument seriously. I see no reason why modern technology should be thought to exclude all supernatural causation.

97. Bultmann emphasizes that demythologization is not reconstructing or rewriting the NT message, but presenting it in a form that communicates clearly to our time. It is not *eliminating* myth so much as *reinterpreting* it.

Bible. Bultmann's solution is that it is possible to preach the Bible *without* myth. He says that the purpose of myth in the Bible is not to impose the mythical worldview on readers. Faith according to Scripture, he says, is independent of any worldview at all. So the biblical writers do not seek to inculcate irrational belief in a supernatural realm, but to express and recommend a certain *self-understanding*.[98] That self-understanding can in fact be better expressed in our time without the mythological trappings of the biblical worldview. According to Bultmann, the gospel of the NT does not require belief in any worldview, whether first-century or modern. In fact, it rejects *any* attempt to find security through a worldview.

The process of demythologizing (expressing the gospel without myth) begins in the NT itself, according to Bultmann.

The process of demythologizing (expressing the gospel without myth) begins in the NT itself, according to Bultmann. In Paul's writings, there is realized eschatology, the view that the end-time is in some sense present now. And John's writings, Bultmann says, have no interest in literal eschatology.

Existential Analysis

What, then, is the gospel, once we have demythologized it? What message emerges once we have seen past the myths to the real concerns of the NT? Well, it turns out to be essentially the message of existentialist philosophy! This should not be too surprising, considering the nature of the school of thought that Bultmann is part of, and considering that he was a friend and colleague of Heidegger at Marburg University. Barth and Brunner were also influenced by existentialism, but Barth went to great lengths to deny it. Bultmann is quite forthright about it.

To Bultmann, both Scripture and existentialism forbid us to understand human existence by "general" categories (philosophical or ethical categories) because these take inadequate account of human freedom.

Bultmann says that exegesis without presuppositions is impossible.[99] We ask about God, he says, because we are moved by the question of our own existence. We should recognize that existential philosophy is also concerned with that question (Heidegger's *Dasein*). And that question will influence the answer we will find in Scripture.

To Bultmann, both Scripture and existentialism forbid us to understand human existence by "general" categories (philosophical or ethical categories) because these take inadequate account of human freedom. We should recognize that man exists in and through his decisions, not by some sort of abiding "nature." (Cf. Sartre's "existence precedes

98. Barth made a little joke in the title of his essay "Rudolf Bultmann: An Attempt to Understand Him," in *Kerygma and Myth*, ed. Hans Werner Bartsch, trans. Reginald H. Fuller, 2 vols. (London: SPCK, 1962), 2:83–132. He concludes that Bultmann's distinctive approach comes from his Lutheranism.

99. Rudolf Bultmann, "Is Exegesis without Presuppositions Possible?," in *Existence and Faith: Shorter Writings of Rudolf Bultmann*, ed. and trans. Schubert M. Ogden (New York: Meridian Books, 1960), 289–96. This is one proposition on which he and I agree. But of course, Bultmann's presuppositions are very different from those of Van Til.

essence.") Nevertheless, human beings often seek to avoid living by decision and seek security through objective guarantees based on the past, "objective truth," rational proofs, and so on. This is what the Bible means when it warns us against seeking satisfaction in what is visible and tangible—the "world" and the "flesh." In existential philosophy and Bultmann's theology, this is called *inauthentic existence.*

Authentic existence is renouncing man-made security, and being open to the future, trusting God in the absence of evidence validating our decision. Thus Scripture calls us to a life of faith and love. Once we renounce security for ourselves, we are able to live for others.

So far, Bultmann acknowledges his agreement with Heidegger. But how do we gain the power to live authentically? For Heidegger and other secular existentialists, authenticity comes through human resolve. But here Bultmann finds something in the NT that goes beyond Heidegger: we can receive the power to live authentically as a gift of God when we hear the preached Word in faith. We cannot save ourselves, but God enables.

That experience is revelation.[100] Bultmann says that the concept of revelation can be

> differentiated in two ways: (1) Revelation is the *communication of knowledge by the word*, i.e., it is information through which we become acquainted with something that we were previously unacquainted with so that henceforth it is known. . . . (2) Revelation is *an occurrence that puts me in a new situation as a self*, in which, to be sure, there is also given the possibility of knowledge . . . but without regard for whether or not this knowledge becomes explicit.[101]

Authentic existence *is renouncing man-made security, and being open to the future, trusting God in the absence of evidence validating our decision. Thus Scripture calls us to a life of faith and love. Once we renounce security for ourselves, we are able to live for others.*

Revelation in the NT, Bultmann claims, is of the second sort. So the importance of it is not its content, but the fact that God speaks it. It is always an event in the present, not the past. And it is the presence of God himself. For me to receive it is for me to exist authentically.

Revelation in this sense is *Geschichte*, a saving event that happens again and again in the present. For Bultmann, Jesus' crucifixion, resurrection, and second coming are not events that literally occurred in the past and brought salvation. Rather, they happen in the present as I respond to preaching in faith. So Paul's words in Galatians 2:20 can become true: "I am crucified with Christ" (KJV).

Historie is, as with Barth, the field of past events that are understood by historians. Bultmann does say that Christianity has some *historisch*

100. See Bultmann, "The Concept of Revelation in the NT," in ibid., 58–91.
101. Ibid., 59.

basis, but not much. The earthly life of Jesus, he says, is the *presupposition* of the preaching (*kerygma*). But we know very little about him. We know *that* (*dass*) he existed, but not *what* (*was*) he is. The *what*, however, is not important. What is important is what he means to faith; and that is expressed in the *kerygma*, regardless of its historical basis.

The traditional doctrine of the atonement, therefore, is mythological in Bultmann's view. But he allows a special role for the preaching of the cross in the present. In preaching (i.e., as *Geschichte*) it symbolizes our renouncing (dying to) the world (inauthentic existence). It is God's judgment on the world and therefore his act, which sets us free for the future. It is the cross of *Christ* because of its saving efficacy, not vice versa. The resurrection is mythological, in Bultmann's view, but it plays an important role in preaching.[102] The preaching of the resurrection only spells out the meaning of the cross. The resurrection is not a miraculous proof of the efficacy of the cross. To trust such a miraculous proof would be inauthentic, though Paul mistakenly uses the resurrection that way in 1 Corinthians 15. The resurrection shows that the power of death (= the world, the tangible) is overcome, but in Bultmann's view we already know that through the preaching of the cross.

The traditional doctrine of the atonement, therefore, is mythological in Bultmann's view.

Bultmann applies this understanding to the doctrine of justification by faith alone. Inauthentic existence, he says, is the attempt to find salvation through the works of the law. Authentic existence receives the future as God's gift. Bultmann applies this doctrine to the intellect as well: Belief in verbal inspiration or any other ultimately authoritative revelation is an attempt to achieve justification by works. It seeks favor with God through intellectual orthodoxy.[103]

Bultmann's theology is very similar to that of Barth and Brunner, but with a far greater level of admitted historical skepticism.

By way of evaluation: Bultmann's theology is very similar to that of Barth and Brunner, but with a far greater level of admitted historical skepticism. For all three thinkers, salvation comes not from events in time and space as such, but through a divine communication in the present, the *Geschichte*, which comes through preaching. That makes it

102. There was a famous discussion between Bultmann and Karl Jaspers, the existentialist philosopher. Jaspers there expresses puzzlement as to why Bultmann—who, like Jaspers, takes a modern skeptical attitude to the resurrection—still gives it a positive role in his theology. Bultmann replies that both he and Jaspers know that a man dead for three days does not come out of the grave. But, he asks, what do you do if you're a pastor and must preach on the Easter texts? Many have claimed that Bultmann comes out of this exchange looking very dishonest. Maybe even inauthentic. See Karl Jaspers and Rudolf Bultmann, *Myth and Christianity: An Inquiry into the Possibility of Religion without Myth*, trans. Norbert Gutermann (New York: Noonday Press, 1958).

103. Barth made a similar argument. But Scripture never suggests that to believe the Word of God as our supreme authority is works-righteousness. What, after all, do we have faith *in* when we are justified by faith? Abraham, the great exemplar of saving faith, trusted the objective promise given him by the Word of God (Rom. 4:20–22).

irrelevant what actually happened in history (apart from the *that*), and we can thank Bultmann for being honest about that. His point bears on Barth and Brunner, too. Once you locate salvation in a *Geschichte* event (Barth) or a divine-human encounter (Brunner) or a preached Word in the present (Bultmann), it doesn't matter whether Christ actually died an atoning death in time and space or rose from the dead for our justification. Barth and Brunner are very hesitant to acknowledge that fact; Bultmann is not. But the price of that honesty is that Bultmann must dismiss Paul's argument in 1 Corinthians 15 as a mistake. To those who embrace the Christ of Scripture, that is too high a price.

Unwilling to pay that price, we embrace Jesus' resurrection in the biblical context of redemptive events. That opens to us the vast riches of the kingdom of God, far more than an empty "openness to the future." And to embrace the resurrection kingdom is to reject the whole movement of existentialist theology, including Barth and Brunner as well as Bultmann. And that includes Tillich as well.

PAUL TILLICH (1886–1965)

Tillich continues the pattern of reformulating Christian theology in terms of existentialist philosophy, but in Tillich there is also a fairly heavy dose of Hegelian dialectic.[104] While Barth and Brunner state their theology in the traditional language of dogmatics, and Bultmann in the language of NT scholarship (with some admixture of Heideggerian existentialism), Tillich's formulations are highly philosophical, which has led some critics to charge that he has converted the biblical gospel into an abstract philosophical system.[105]

Tillich's formulations are highly philosophical, which has led some critics to charge that he has converted the biblical gospel into an abstract philosophical system.

Tillich taught at the University of Berlin from 1919 to 1924, and then for a year at the University of Marburg, where he was acquainted with Heidegger and Bultmann. (Later he would refer to Bultmann as his esteemed teacher.[106]) He taught at the University of Leipzig from 1925 to 1929 and at the University of Frankfurt from 1929 to 1933. In Frankfurt, Tillich expressed criticism of Nazism, and when Hitler came to power in 1933, Tillich lost his teaching position. Through the mediation of Reinhold Niebuhr, Tillich then joined the faculty of Union Theological

104. Thus Tillich marks a transition from the Kantian structure (noumenal-phenomenal = *Geschichte-Historie*) of Barth, Brunner, and Bultmann to a more Hegelian understanding.

105. See, e.g., Kenneth Hamilton, *The System and the Gospel: A Critique of Paul Tillich* (New York: Macmillan, 1963). Hamilton sharply contrasts Tillich with Kierkegaard in this respect.

106. Although his theology is much more philosophical in tone than Bultmann's, it is conceptually more congruent with Bultmann's thought than with that of Barth or Brunner. And we should not forget that Bultmann identified the content of the biblical *kerygma* with the message of authentic existence in existential philosophy. So the two were at least equally subservient to philosophical trends.

Seminary of New York, and remained in the United States, becoming a citizen in 1940. From 1955 to 1962, Tillich taught with the prestigious title of "University Professor" at Harvard University, and from 1962 at the University of Chicago until his death in 1965.

Tillich published a great many books, both in German and in English, but his specific approach is most clearly expressed in his three-volume *Systematic Theology*.[107] At the beginning of that work he describes two *formal criteria* of theology:

> The object of theology is what concerns us ultimately. Only those propositions are theological which deal with their object in so far as it can become a matter of ultimate concern for us.[108]

> Our ultimate concern is that which determines our being or not-being. Only those statements are theological which deal with their object in so far as it can become a matter of being or not-being for us.[109]

Paul Tillich

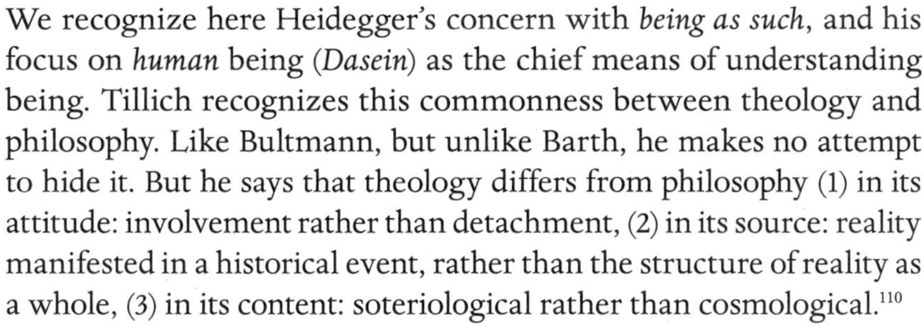

We recognize here Heidegger's concern with *being as such*, and his focus on *human* being (*Dasein*) as the chief means of understanding being. Tillich recognizes this commonness between theology and philosophy. Like Bultmann, but unlike Barth, he makes no attempt to hide it. But he says that theology differs from philosophy (1) in its attitude: involvement rather than detachment, (2) in its source: reality manifested in a historical event, rather than the structure of reality as a whole, (3) in its content: soteriological rather than cosmological.[110]

The sources for theology, according to Tillich, are Scripture, church history, and the history of religion and culture.[111] Scripture is fundamental because it is the original document on which the church is founded. But it is not ultimately authoritative. The material norm of theology is "the New Being in Jesus as the Christ as our ultimate concern."[112]

Scripture is fundamental because it is the original document on which the church is founded. But it is not ultimately authoritative. The material norm of theology is "the New Being in Jesus as the Christ as our ultimate concern."

The method of theology, Tillich says, is the *method of correlation*. That is to say, theology "makes an analysis of the human situation out of which the existential questions arise, and it demonstrates that the symbols used in the Christian message are the answers to those questions."[113] I am actually sympathetic with Tillich's method of correlation, because it resembles somewhat my own definition of *theology*

107. Chicago: University of Chicago Press, 1951–63.
108. Ibid., 1:12.
109. Ibid., 1:14.
110. Ibid., 1:22–24.
111. Ibid., 1:34–40.
112. Ibid., 1:50.
113. Ibid., 1:62.

as "the application of the Word of God by persons to all areas of life."[114] Both these definitions imply a twofold concern: the revelation of God and the data of human life. I differ with Tillich in a couple of ways: (1) "Existential questions" suggests that the questions arise out of existential philosophy. I think the theologian should be willing to tackle questions arising from philosophy, but he should not confine himself to those. Perhaps Tillich does not intend to limit theology in this way, but his formulation and theological practice suggest that he does. (2) It is unclear how "symbols" are able to answer questions, apart from propositions and arguments that make use of those symbols. Tillich's appeal to symbols reflects the aversion to propositional revelation that characterizes his thought as well as that of his liberal predecessors.

Tillich contrasts his method of correlation with "inadequate methods."

1. The *supranaturalist* method "takes the Christian message to be a sum of revealed truths which have fallen into the human situation like strange bodies from a strange world."[115] Tillich, like Brunner, seems to have an emotional, as well as intellectual, aversion to Christian orthodoxy.[116] He tends to formulate the orthodox position in ways that no orthodox Christian would select. For the record, I know of no evangelical theologian who thinks (a) that the Christian message consists exclusively of revealed propositions, (b) that revealed truth has no connection with earthly history, the two beliefs by which Tillich defines their position here.
2. But Tillich also opposes the *naturalist* or *humanist* method, which, he says, develops the theological answer out of the human situation itself, identifying the existential with the essential. In this method, there is no revelation: everything is said by, not to, man.[117] Here Tillich reflects Barth's criticism of Schleiermacher and the Ritschlians.
3. And he also rejects the *dualist* method, which he describes using the example of traditional Roman Catholicism: erecting a supranatural superstructure on top of a natural foundation.[118] He credits such dualists with a better understanding of complexity of the theological task, but he thinks the Thomist theistic

Tillich's appeal to symbols reflects the aversion to propositional revelation that characterizes his thought as well as that of his liberal predecessors.

114. Frame, *DKG*, 81–85; *DWG*, 272–79. Cf. the opening chapter of my *ST*.

115. Tillich, *Systematic Theology*, 1:64.

116. I take it that Tillich uses the terms *supranaturalism*, *orthodoxy*, and *fundamentalism* more or less synonymously.

117. Tillich, *Systematic Theology*, 1:65.

118. Ibid.

proofs (like the naturalists) derive a theological answer from the form of the question.

Now, the main structure of Tillich's *Systematic Theology* is in five parts:

1. Reason and Revelation
2. Being and God
3. Existence and the Christ
4. Life and the Spirit
5. History and the Kingdom of God

These are examples of Tillich's method of correlation. In each pair, the first member represents a question (or group of questions) derived from existential philosophy, and the second represents the Christian "symbol" that Tillich proposes to answer it. Otherwise, the five parts represent a fairly traditional pattern: Epistemological prolegomena at the beginning, eschatology at the end, and a Trinitarian pattern between the two.

Autonomy is reason affirming itself without recognizing its depth. Heteronomy is the imposition of an external authority in the name of the depth, such as myth or cult. Tillich thinks that supranaturalism *does this. Theonomy resolves the conflict, somewhat in the manner of a Hegelian synthesis. Theonomy is autonomous reason united with its own depth.*

In Part 1, "Reason and Revelation," Tillich begins by making some distinctions within the concept of reason: ontological and technical, objective and subjective. He is particularly concerned to emphasize the "depth" of reason, which can be called "substance," "being itself," "truth itself," "ground," "abyss," the reality behind limited and partial truths. I suppose these expressions refer to those "Aha" moments when we feel that our reason has really penetrated to something significant and illuminating, rather than just solving everyday problems.

Naturally, reason points to its own depth, but myth and cult offer a false depth that separates reason from its true depth. That separation is the "fallenness" of reason, which creates ambiguities in our thinking. He refers to three ambiguities in particular.

(1) Autonomy and heteronomy. Autonomy is reason affirming itself without recognizing its depth. Heteronomy is the imposition of an external authority in the name of the depth, such as myth or cult. Tillich thinks that *supranaturalism* does this. Theonomy resolves the conflict, somewhat in the manner of a Hegelian synthesis. Theonomy[119] is autonomous reason united with its own depth. It is never complete under the conditions of existence, but this is our quest. That quest may also be called the quest for revelation.

(2) Relativism and absolutism. Absolutism elevates the static element in reason, relativism the dynamic element to the point of removing

119. Obviously, a very different concept from the "theonomy" advocated by Rousas Rushdoony and Greg Bahnsen.

any stability at all. The *concrete absolute* (a phrase that Hegel used to describe his Absolute[120]) somehow provides resolution.

(3) Formalism and emotionalism. Formalism (Nietzsche's *Apollonian spirit*) stresses the laws of logic, art, law, and social tradition without considering adequately their bearing on actual lived experience (the *Lebenswelt* of Husserl and Heidegger). Emotionalism (Nietzsche's *Dionysiac*) reacts against this, but becomes irrational because it resists structure. Revelation provides a working union of form and emotion.[121]

Notice how in all of this, revelation is not revelation of the gospel in any traditional Christian sense. It is, rather, a secular enlightenment, a moment of "real understanding" about anything at all. But Tillich does argue that there is a "final" revelation, a revelation that resolves these problems in a definitive way. The criteria for this revelation are: (1) It must be united to the ground of being without separation or disruption, and therefore transparent to the mystery. (2) So it must be able to negate itself without losing itself. The problem with myth, cult, heteronomy, formalism, and absolutism (in short, supranaturalism), according to Tillich, is that these pretend to be absolute and never acknowledge their limitations. A final revelation will acknowledge those limitations without losing itself.

So the content of final revelation is this: the revelation of Jesus as the Christ. Jesus, according to Tillich, renounced all claims to ultimacy.[122] He sacrificed himself on the cross, negating himself.[123] Thus he liberates us from the authority of everything finite in him, such as his conditioned worldview. He sacrifices what is merely "Jesus" in him. (Tillich here takes the occasion to criticize "Jesus centered" religion.[124]) To know the

Revelation is not revelation of the gospel in any traditional Christian sense. It is, rather, a secular enlightenment, a moment of "real understanding" about anything at all.

120. Van Til also used this phrase to indicate that in Christianity, ultimate truth is found in a personal, concrete reality, rather than in abstract forms such as those of Plato and Aristotle.

121. Here Tillich shows an understanding of what Van Til and I have called the *rationalist-irrationalist dialectic*. In all three "ambiguities," Tillich describes contrasts that I characterize in these terms. Heteronomy, relativism, and emotionalism can be described as forms of irrationalism, and autonomy, absolutism, and formalism as forms of rationalism.

122. This will come as a surprise to readers of the NT.

123. Tillich's doctrine of the resurrection: after Jesus' death, the disciples had ecstatic experiences in which the picture of Jesus of Nazareth (see the following note) became united to the reality of the New Being.

124. When Tillich refers to *Jesus* or *Christ*, it is not always clear what he is referring to. His Christology is a mixture of three different concepts: (1) The actual historical man Jesus of Nazareth. About this man, Tillich, like Barth, is quite skeptical. He rejects the "quest of the historical Jesus." (2) The "picture" of Jesus in the Gospels. That picture might or might not be true, but it is the foundation, he thinks, of Christology. (3) "The New Being in Jesus as the Christ." This is Tillich's concept of the salvation supposedly brought about through Christ. Elsewhere he defines the "basic Christian assertion" this way: "Essential God-manhood has appeared within existence and subjected itself to the conditions of existence without being conquered by them." Tillich, *Systematic Theology*, 2:98. So Christ conquers the gap between essence and existence.

depth of reason, then, is ultimately the same as receiving salvation. Here Tillich formally agrees with Barth's equation of revelation and salvation.

This revelation is not propositional, because propositions lack the "sound of ultimacy."[125] Here Tillich joins the scores of liberal theologians who have developed arguments against propositional revelation, or, in other words, arguments in favor of autonomous reason (with or without its "depth"). There are no revealed words or revealed doctrines. These are heteronomous distortions. Revelation must begin with autonomous reason, seeking to join that reason to its depth.

Tillich joins the scores of liberal theologians who have developed arguments against propositional revelation, or, in other words, arguments in favor of autonomous reason.

The second part of Tillich's system, "Being and God," develops the doctrine of God in a way similar to his development of the doctrine of revelation in part 1. The symbol *God* is the solution to various antitheses, this time on the much-discussed subject of *being*.[126] We need to understand being because of our own limits (cf. Heidegger's *being-toward-death*). Like the existentialists, Tillich feels a need to transcend the subject-object distinction, specifically as it affects certain antitheses. The antitheses in this case are (1) individualization and participation, (2) dynamics and form, and (3) freedom and destiny. As with the antitheses of part 1, these are overcome as they are grounded in a reality deeper than both alternatives.

That reality is *God*, whom Tillich defines as "being itself," or the "ground of being." In volume 1 of his *Systematic Theology*, he says that "God is being itself" is the only nonsymbolic statement that we can make about God; but in volume 2 he says that even this statement is symbolic.[127] God, he says, is not "a" being, or else God would be subordinate to being. Nor should we say that he "exists," for he is beyond essence and existence. He is neither universal essence (the totality of finite possibilities) nor an existent being (for existence involves some estrangement from essence).[128]

God, he says, is not "a" being, or else God would be subordinate to being. Nor should we say that he "exists," for he is beyond essence and existence.

For Tillich, God unites individualization and participation, dynamics and form, freedom and destiny, because of his Trinitarian[129] unity and particularity. He is not "a" person, but rather is the ground of

125. Ibid., 2:124. The "ultimacy" here is the "depth" in his earlier discussion.

126. The immediate background of this concern of Tillich's is Heidegger's *Sein* and *Dasein*. But the "question of being" stretches back to Greek philosophy, particularly Parmenides.

127. Tillich says that symbols (as opposed to signs) participate in the reality to which they point. God infinitely transcends the finite world of which our language speaks, so symbols of him must affirm and negate their assertions simultaneously. But symbolic statements are possible because, though God transcends the finite world, everything participates in being itself.

128. Of course, with this statement the popular press raced to bring the news that according to Tillich, God did not exist. As we will see, the later *Christian atheists* claimed Tillich as a mentor—but also Barth, Bultmann, and Bonhoeffer.

129. Tillich identifies the Trinity as (1) ground of being, (2) creative self-actualization (*logos*), and (3) uniting of objectifications with himself (Spirit). In my opinion, there is biblical insight here.

everything personal and the ontological power of personality.[130] To the idea of God as "a heavenly, completely perfect person who resides above the world and mankind," Tillich replies, "the protest of atheism is correct."[131]

Creation, he says, is not an event in time, but a basic description of the God-world relationship. Creation *ex nihilo* shows that nonbeing is involved in the existence (but not the essence) of finite reality. For this reason, creation and fall are simultaneous.[132] Self-actualization through freedom, he says, inevitably involves separation from the ground of being. God does, however, participate in the negativities of creaturely life, but in him these negativities are eternally conquered.[133]

But there is another formulation of the nature of God, for which Tillich is better known and perhaps more influential. It is not clearly developed in the *Systematic Theology*, but in his *The Courage to Be*.[134] Tillich defines *faith* as "ultimate concern," a concern with something that is a matter of life or death to the person.[135] A *god* is any object of ultimate concern, whether appropriate or not. Faith is inseparable from doubt. Since it seeks the depth of being, it renounces all objective certainty (cf. Bultmann). Therefore, true faith can be discerned in a really passionate doubt, an "unbelief" that is serious, ultimately concerned about what it doubts.[136] Now, true faith, perhaps the most profound faith, exists as the "courage to be," the courage to affirm being "without seeing anything concrete which could conquer the nonbeing in fate and death."[137] This faith, therefore, does not overcome anxiety and meaninglessness, but it is "the courage to take the anxiety of meaninglessness upon oneself."[138] The object of such faith is a God "above the God of theism" who emerges "when the traditional symbols . . . have lost their power." So "*the courage to be is rooted in the God who appears when God has disappeared in the anxiety of doubt.*"[139]

Tillich defines faith as "ultimate concern," a concern with something that is a matter of life or death to the person. A god is any object of ultimate concern, whether appropriate or not.

130. We recall that Plotinus (chapter 2) also denied all attributes to God because God was the "ground" of those qualities and therefore beyond them. But that line of argument led to a God about whom nothing could be said.

131. Tillich, *Systematic Theology*, 2:245.

132. So Tillich rejects the history of Genesis 3. He says that there was no time of "dreaming innocence" in which mankind was unfallen.

133. This is Tillich's theodicy—his answer to the problem of evil.

134. New Haven, CT and London: Yale University Press, 1952.

135. Here, note especially his *Dynamics of Faith* (New York: Harper and Brothers, 1957).

136. So the most profound faith is found in the most passionate unbelief. One is reminded of Kierkegaard's story of the pagan who prays to his idol with "infinite passion," thereby excelling the truth (i.e., subjective truth) of a Danish church member engaged in formalistic worship.

137. Tillich, *Courage*, 189. Or it is "accepting of the acceptance without somebody or something that accepts" (185).

138. Ibid., 190.

139. Ibid. (emphasis his).

I will not continue through the remaining three parts of Tillich's system, or through the large number of other books he has written. The basic picture should now be clear. Like Barth, Brunner, and Bultmann, Tillich renounces the inerrancy of Scripture and past historical events as the location of salvation. Positively, salvation consists in a nonpropositional *Geschichte*, an event in which we are impressed with the "depth" of reason,[140] which is identical with God as "being itself" or the "ground of being." This salvation comes through a symbolic Christ who can be said to have negated himself and therefore entered the conditions of existence without being conquered by them. The historical Jesus plays no role in any of this. So one wonders, when did it happen that Christ entered the conditions of existence without being conquered by them? Why should anybody believe that this has actually happened?

Like Barth, Brunner, and Bultmann, Tillich renounces the inerrancy of Scripture and past historical events as the location of salvation.

In any case, it should not require much astuteness for the reader to see that this is not the biblical gospel. It is a philosophical mythology that gains its persuasive power by its parallelism with the true gospel of Scripture. Its structure is fundamentally Kantian (*Geschichte-Historie*, like *noumenal-phenomenal*) with some Hegelian triads and existentialist meditations on *being*.

As "mere philosophy," Tillich's system has some value. It is true, for example, that either mere autonomous reason or mere heteronomous reason (in bondage to a false claim of authority) invariably leads to confusion rather than truth. Yet even amid such confusion there are occasions when we feel struck by a "depth" of insight, for the true God has made us to know his world and himself, and although we subdue that knowledge, it often breaks through our consciousness in spite of ourselves.[141] That sense of depth explodes to wonderful proportions when we bow (in our thinking and in all aspects of life) to the true God in Jesus Christ. But the God who remedies the triviality of our workaday knowing is the God of the Bible, not the God-beyond-god of Tillich, which we meet in passionate unbelief.

Even amid such confusion there are occasions when we feel struck by a "depth" of insight, for the true God has made us to know his world and himself, and although we subdue that knowledge, it often breaks through our consciousness in spite of ourselves.

DIETRICH BONHOEFFER (1906–45)

We have seen how profoundly twentieth-century philosophy and theology was influenced by the political developments of the Hitler period and World War II. Germany, of course, was the center of most of the philosophical and theological discussion at the time. So I noted that Karl Barth, especially, played a heroic role in his authorship of the

140. An event that, doubtless, conveys the "sound of ultimacy."

141. I argued in *DKG* (152–62) that our ground for saying "I know" is typically something like a feeling, something that might be called *cognitive rest*.

Barmen Declaration and his encouragement to the Confessing Church. Bonhoeffer was an important disciple of Barth who, unlike Barth, remained in Germany through most of these hard times. He did cross the ocean to accept an appointment to teach at Union Theological Seminary, New York,[142] in 1939, but he decided soon afterward that he had made a mistake. He returned to Germany on the last commercial passenger ship to cross the Atlantic.

From 1935 to 1940, he taught at an "underground seminary," which was first located at Finkenwalde, but which moved from place to place as the authorities sought to eliminate it. After it was finally closed by the Gestapo, Bonhoeffer became involved in various resistance efforts, eventually in a plot to kill Hitler, which failed in 1944. He was hanged in 1945, at the Flossenbürg concentration camp, two weeks before the camp was liberated by U.S. forces.

Bonhoeffer's writings of the 1930s, particularly *The Cost of Discipleship*[143] and *Life Together*,[144] were later treasured by all branches of Christianity. The first criticizes the notion of *cheap grace*, that since salvation is by grace, we have no more obligations. Bonhoeffer insists that grace is in fact costly, in the response that God expects of his disciples. When Christ calls disciples, Bonhoeffer said, he bids them come and die. The book contains an extended treatment on the Sermon on the Mount. *Life Together* comes out of the setting of the underground seminary, where, under pressure from the regime, faculty and students frequently lived in a communal way. The fact that these books emerged out of the Nazi persecution gave them all the more credibility.

Dietrich Bonhoeffer

Theological controversy, however, arose from Bonhoeffer's *Letters and Papers from Prison*.[145] That controversy was somewhat unfair, of course, because Bonhoeffer's prison writing was done under extreme duress. But there have been intensive discussions of how Bonhoeffer would have developed some of the ideas expressed there. As in all his other writings, Bonhoeffer affirms here that Christ is the center of all things and ought to be the center of human life, not a "religious" figure on the periphery. Christ is not the answer to our unanswered questions on the periphery of knowledge, but is involved in all we know. Bonhoeffer fully accepts Barth's attack on *religion*[146] and opposes the tendency of professing Christians to isolate their faith to Sunday worship.[147] God is best seen in the everyday world, where he suffers

142. He had studied there in 1930, where he taught Sunday school at Harlem's Abyssinian Baptist Church. He was deeply affected by African-American Christianity.

143. New York: Touchstone, 1995.

144. New York: Harper, 2009.

145. Ed. Eberhard Bethge (New York: Touchstone, 1997).

146. Recall that I criticized Barth for this in an earlier footnote. I think *religion* represents something good (James 1:26–27) and should not be redefined as Barth does to refer to self-will.

147. He blames this tendency somewhat on Luther's distinction between the "two kingdoms."

the persecution of his people and calls his people to suffer with him as they seek justice where they are.

But in *Letters and Papers* he goes further, observing as Nietzsche and Bultmann did that modern men have "come of age," and so have no place for God in their lives. He writes that it might be necessary to find a way to practice our faith without religion. At one point, he identifies religion with the concepts of metaphysics and inwardness and says that we might have to learn to speak and live without those. At other points, he insists that God is not the answer to the unanswered questions of philosophy and science, but is present in all our earthly knowledge. We should not, he says, try to impose a theistic religion on modern people, trying to win them over to an ideology that they have renounced. Rather, we should serve them as they are, suffer with them as Jesus did.

Bonhoeffer said, "Before God and with God we live without God." Of course, this statement is ironic . . . . But if God is real, and if he lives in this world, particularly at the "center" of it, in what sense can we live without him?

Bonhoeffer said, "Before God and with God we live without God."[148] Of course, this statement is ironic, for it affirms God while saying that we live without him. But if God is real, and if he lives in this world, particularly at the "center" of it, in what sense can we live without him?

I suspect that at this point something like the Barthian dialectic comes to the fore. God is present in his absence, absent in his presence, present with us in *Geschichte* and therefore only "from time to time." Unlike Barth, Bonhoeffer does not generally stress this sort of language. But his view of Scripture and the miraculous dimension of biblical events is not different from Barth. And so for Bonhoeffer, as for Barth, theological substance can arise only in a paradoxical way.

But his view of Scripture and the miraculous dimension of biblical events is not different from Barth. And so for Bonhoeffer, as for Barth, theological substance can arise only in a paradoxical way.

The paradox seems to be that of nonbiblical transcendence and immanence, as I described those concepts in chapter 1. God is "absent" from modern culture (transcendence), but "present" in the secular world (immanence). Christians should be committed, then, to the secular world, in which we embrace man as man and (together with modern man) renounce the traditional supernatural gospel.

THE NEW HERMENEUTIC

The phrase *new hermeneutic* has been used to designate various liberal movements in denominational controversies.[149] But in the history of recent theology, the phrase generally refers to a movement of Bultmann disciples impressed with the writings of the later Heidegger. Bultmann himself, we recall, patterned his theology after Heidegger's early work, *Being and Time*. But the post-Bultmannians pressed beyond this. Names of theologians associated with this movement are **Gerhard Ebeling**

148. Bonhoeffer, *Letters and Papers*, 360.

149. See, e.g., http://www.burlingtonurc.org/new_hermeneutic.html; http://www.christiancourier.com/articles/228-new-hermeneutic-an-abandonment-of-reason.

(1912–2001), **Ernst Fuchs** (1903–83), **Heinrich Ott** (1929–2013),[150] **James M. Robinson** (1924–), and **Robert O. Funk** (1926–2005).

Traditionally, *hermeneutics* teaches the rules and techniques for interpreting texts, biblical texts being of crucial importance to theology. Heidegger (building on suggestions of Schleiermacher and Dilthey) suggests a more comprehensive notion: hermeneutics is not just the interpretation *of* language, but the interpretation of reality *through* language. On this basis, hermeneutics and philosophy become virtually identical. Recall, then, from chapter 9 how Heidegger developed in his later writings the idea that language is "the house of Being," that is, that being speaks to us through language.[151]

The advocates of the new hermeneutic argued, then, that language is rightly understood only when by means of language there is an existential encounter between the hearer and reality. This encounter is sometimes called a *language event*. This approach abandoned the older notion that interpretation should be "objective" or "neutral." As Bultmann said, we should approach each text with our preunderstanding and expect to encounter its power. This slogan came into vogue: "We don't interpret the Word; the Word interprets us."

The advocates of the new hermeneutic argued, then, that language is rightly understood only when by means of language there is an existential encounter between the hearer and reality. This encounter is sometimes called a language event.

The language event communicates not information, but God himself as a person.[152] It is not so much meaning as power. The result is that in this event the Word opens the future to us.

The new element in the new hermeneutic is the reference to the later Heidegger. There are some useful emphases in this literature. In Funk's *Language, Hermeneutic, and Word of God: The Problem of Language in the New Testament and Contemporary Theology*,[153] for example, there are several studies of parables, which focus not on what each element symbolizes, but on how the parable forces us to reconsider our self-images. That can be valuable.[154]

But in fact, I see no substantial difference in the doctrine of revelation between this movement and the teaching of the five thinkers presented

150. Ott, Barth's successor at Basel, was closer to Barth than the others, but he, too, was attracted to the formulations of the later Heidegger.

151. I will not in this book be able to discuss the movement of hermeneutical philosophy associated with figures such as **Hans-Georg Gadamer** (1900–2002) and **Paul Ricoeur** (1913–2005). They are particularly concerned with how contexts affect knowledge—the environment ("horizon," Gadamer) of the knower and that of what he knows. For Gadamer, interpretation occurs in a fusion of the "two horizons." For him, this fact makes interpretation more dependent on practical life (cf. Husserl's life-world) than on science and technology.

152. As we've seen, every liberal theological movement has its own argument against propositional revelation. This is the argument of the *new hermeneuts*.

153. New York: Harper and Row, 1966.

154. But it is unclear how this is consistent with the denial of propositional revelation. When Jesus recommends a new self-image to his hearers, that teaching certainly has propositional aspects: self-image A is bad; self-image B is good.

earlier in this chapter. In all these thinkers, revelation is a *Geschichte* that comes upon us from time to time, with no propositional content. The same problem exists for all of them. They deny the biblical claim that salvation comes through events in space-time history,[155] and they make it impossible to construct theology from the data of revelation. So in the final analysis, there is no gospel here.

NEW QUESTS

None of these quests has produced a consensus among scholars as to a portrait of Jesus. This result might have been expected, since among the various criteria of authenticity the authority of Scripture itself was not included.

Still, there were at the same time some who took a lively interest in the history of Jesus. We recall that Bultmann was very skeptical about the old "quest of the historical Jesus." He said that we knew *that* he existed (*dass*), but not *what* (*was*) he was. But some of his disciples, especially **Ernst Käsemann** (1906–98) and **Günther Bornkamm** (1905–90), were not satisfied with that. They asked, "Why Jesus?" Why should we discover the powerful language event in the preaching of Jesus, rather than in preaching about some other figure? Trying to answer that question, they investigated the historical data again, with more modern techniques. They said they were not seeking to write a biography of Jesus, but to see how Jesus can be understood in faith. Like Heidegger, they renounced the goal of "objective" historiography. Later, in the 1980s, after a few years' lapse of interest in the historical Jesus, there was another movement that N. T. Wright called the *third quest*. But none of these quests has produced a consensus among scholars as to a portrait of Jesus. This result might have been expected, since among the various criteria of authenticity the authority of Scripture itself was not included.

HEILSGESCHICHTE

Protestant scholastics and pietists, as well as Roman Catholic thinkers, maintained traditions that acknowledged the supernatural and the authority of the Bible.

By the emphasis of these chapters, I might have given the false impression that liberal presuppositions govern all academic theology from the seventeenth century to the present. Of course, as we saw in chapter 5, both Protestant scholastics and pietists, as well as Roman Catholic thinkers, maintained traditions that acknowledged the supernatural and the authority of the Bible. I considered Jonathan Edwards briefly in the context of Puritanism. And the tradition of such orthodox theology continued through the eighteenth century down to the present, though it gained little respect in the secular academy. So in the Protestant tradition, we could have discussed E. W. Hengstenberg,

155. If anything, their position on biblical history is even more skeptical than Bultmann's. They practiced *Sachkritic*: not just demythologization, but a radical skepticism about all the contents of Scripture. They practiced biblical scholarship with sharply anti-supernaturalistic assumptions. Bultmann had warned against any defense of biblical history, lest that be used as an "external grounding for faith." These disciples of Bultmann took the same position.

Archibald Alexander, Charles Hodge, and B. B. Warfield, though their substantive theological thought does not go much beyond the various Protestant confessional standards. In the last chapter of this book, I will discuss Abraham Kuyper, Herman Dooyeweerd, and others who seek to do philosophical theology in accord with Scripture.

But I would say just a few words here about a relatively orthodox movement in the academic world of the mid-twentieth century. If we look at the Bible more or less on its surface, it appears to set forth as a central matter a historical sequence of divine actions. God creates the world, deals with the fall of man, and then makes covenants with selected people: Adam, Noah, Abraham, Israel under Moses, David, Christ. All these covenants anticipate the coming of Jesus Christ, who comes into the world to die for the sins of his people, to be buried, to rise again, to ascend to the throne of God. Then the Spirit descends to empower the church to bring the news of Jesus to the whole world. What remains to come is the return of Jesus to judge the world and to bring a new heavens and new earth.

Read as such a history, the Bible can be called a *Heilsgeschichte*, "salvation-history" or "redemptive history." Some theologians, often called *biblical theologians*, have used this story as the focus of their theology. They have stressed the coming of Christ as the center of the biblical timeline, the event that inaugurates the "age to come." But the "present evil age" will nevertheless continue until the final judgment. So the time in which we live is a portion of both ages, the old and the new. Our time is therefore "semi-eschatological," a time in which redemption is accomplished, but not entirely fulfilled. In Cullmann's figure, it is like World War II, when "D-Day" marked the beginning of the end for Hitler's Germany, but "V-Day" marked the final end. Our time is like the period between D-Day and V-Day: Jesus is raised victorious, but Satan continues his wicked work until Jesus returns on the clouds.

Read as such a history, the Bible can be called a Heilsgeschichte, *"salvation-history" or "redemptive history." Some theologians, often called* biblical theologians, *have used this story as the focus of their theology.*

This redemptive-historical structure was emphasized by a number of Dutch theologians of the 1920s and '30s. **Geerhardus Vos** (1862–1949), a Dutch-American theologian who taught at Princeton Theological Seminary, influenced many conservative Protestants in the United States, as did **Richard B. Gaffin Jr.** (1936–). **Herman N. Ridderbos** (1909–2007), a Dutch theologian, wrote major works developing the details of redemptive history, such as *The Coming of the Kingdom*[156] and *Paul: An Outline of His Theology*.[157] In Germany, **Hans Conzelmann** (1915–89) and **Oscar Cullmann** (1902–99) adopted similar programs. Vos and Gaffin believed that Scripture was inerrant; the Europeans

156. Ed. Raymond O. Zorn, trans. H. de Jongste (Philadelphia: Presbyterian and Reformed, 1962).

157. Trans. John Richard de Witt (Grand Rapids: Eerdmans, 1975).

did not. But all of these were fairly conservative on questions of biblical history, and they took seriously the Bible's claim that these events really happened and stand as the basis of our relation with God.[158] In this respect, *Heilsgeschichte* should not be confused with *Geschichte*. The *Heilsgeschichte* of Vos and Cullmann occurred in space and time; the *Geschichte* of Barth and Bultmann enters space and time only in a word of proclamation, a word that becomes true for the church only "from time to time."

Heilsgeschichte is one of the more conservative academic theological movements of the twentieth century. Christian atheism is the most radical—so much so that it is often called simply radical theology.

CHRISTIAN ATHEISM

Heilsgeschichte is one of the more conservative academic theological movements of the twentieth century. Christian atheism is the most radical—so much so that it is often called simply *radical theology*, as if everyone would know which of the many liberal theologies is most radical. Many of us will never forget the black cover of *TIME* magazine on April 8, 1966, with the question "Is God dead?" We also remember Nietzsche's startling pronouncement, "God is dead."

But the remarkable thing about radical theology is that the death of God was embraced by several professedly Christian theologians.

As it turned out, it was not an important movement. I often joke with my students that it was famous for about fifteen minutes in 1967 or so. But it is an important instruction to us as to where the main movements of theology had led us by this time.

[Radical theology] was not an important movement. I often joke with my students that it was famous for about fifteen minutes in 1967 or so. But it is an important instruction to us as to where the main movements of theology had led us by this time.

There were three main figures in the movement. **Thomas J. J. Altizer** (1927–) worked from a dialectical view of the incarnation: When God became man in Christ, he relinquished his divine attributes. Altizer called this a *fully kenotic* Christology. But without his attributes, God existed no more. As with Nietzsche, however, there is a bright side to this event: the death of God frees mankind to seek his fulfillment. **William Hamilton** (1924–2012) followed Nietzsche's, Bultmann's, and Bonhoeffer's argument that modern man has "come of age" and, living in modern culture, has no place for God in his life. **Paul Van Buren** (1924–98) argued from the logical-positivist verification principle (see chapter 12): since there is no (scientific) means of verifying or falsifying God's existence, the proposition "God exists" is meaningless. But the story of Jesus opens the future to us (as Bultmann).

These figures, of course, did not arise from nowhere. They were deeply impacted by the classical liberal theologians, specifically by the

158. Within this general movement, some took mediating positions. For example, **G. Ernest Wright** (1909–74), in *God Who Acts* (London: SCM Press, 1964), argued that revelation in the Bible consists of divine acts, not words. The divine acts are not miraculous, but natural events interpreted by faith. In fact, revelation in the Bible is very much by word as well as deed, and God's deeds cannot be restricted to the range of "natural" events.

movement of twentieth-century existential theology. Van Buren began as a Barthian. He and the others were deeply influenced as well by Bultmann, Tillich, and Bonhoeffer. It is important that we understand the themes in the earlier theologians that led to atheism and that were already implicitly atheistic. Barth, Brunner, Bultmann, and Tillich all presupposed a Kantian two-realm structure. Kant's *noumenal* was the *Geschichte* of the theologians, an area devoid of any propositional truth. Kant's *phenomenal* was the theologians' *Historie*, an area where not God but human reason was autonomous. These theologians, whatever their intentions, banished God from both *Geschichte* and *Historie*, from the whole world. To them, God was too transcendent to be known (*Geschichte*) and too immanent to be sovereign (*Historie*). The logical conclusion is that there is no God. Add to this Bultmann's view that modern man cannot believe in the supernatural,[159] Tillich's view that the true God is discovered through passionate disbelief, and Bonhoeffer's view that modern man has "come of age" and must learn to live before God as if God didn't exist. Christian atheism is the inevitable fruit of the once-promising movement of existential theology.

These theologians, whatever their intentions, banished God from both Geschichte *and* Historie, *from the whole world. . . . Christian atheism is the inevitable fruit of the once-promising movement of existential theology.*

SECULAR THEOLOGY

During and after the outbreak of Christian atheism, some writers impressed with Bonhoeffer's later teachings tried to broaden, defend, and apply his affirmation of secularism. **John A. T. Robinson** (1919–83) was the Anglican Bishop of Woolich, England. As a NT scholar, he took a very conservative position on the dates of the Gospels. He believed that all four Gospels had been written before A.D. 64, because they contain no reference to the destruction of Jerusalem in A.D. 70.[160] But in his theological writings he was an extreme liberal. His *Honest to God*[161] caused a great stir in the popular religious press. There he opposed the idea of a "God up there" or "out there," but endorsed Paul Tillich's idea of a *ground of being* and affirmed that *God* is essentially a synonym of *love*. Amid this was considerable Bonhoeffer rhetoric about how we must accept the values of the world come of age.

Harvey Cox (1929–) in *The Secular City*[162] argues that God is present in the secular world as much as in the "sacred." He makes the case that the history of redemption is the history of secularization: In creation, God affirms the world. The exodus is a desacralization of the Egyptian

159. The Swiss theologian **Fritz Buri** (1907–95) noted that Bultmann's demythologization was inconsistent. Why should we eliminate everything supernatural in the Bible and retain God? Buri, therefore, should be added to our list of "radical theologians."

160. John A. T. Robinson, *Redating the New Testament* (Eugene, OR: Wipf and Stock, 1976).

161. Philadelphia: Westminster Press, 1963.

162. New York: Collier Books, 1965.

pharaoh and nature gods. At Sinai, God teaches Israel that the way to God is through morality, not religious rites. And in the incarnation, God saves us in the arena of secularity. Cox adapts a *kenotic* Christology to affirm that Jesus redeems us only as a secular man.

Secular is an ambiguous term. Clearly, we must distinguish between the world as God's creation and the world as a society of fallen men in rebellion against God. There is all the difference in the world between "affirming" the original creation and "affirming" a culture of sinful rebellion. Further, there is a difference between a "sacred" realm consecrated to false gods and a sacred realm consecrated to the true God, as the temple in Israel. God himself establishes sacred space in Israel, and he also ordains other "religious" institutions, such as the Sabbath and the Lord's Supper. When God says that he desires mercy and not sacrifice, this is a relative contrast. If we take seriously all the relevant biblical texts, he wants both, but mercy most of all.

The Hartford Declaration *is a kind of exasperation on the part of mainstream theologians (liberals among them) with the radical and secular theologies.*

THE HARTFORD DECLARATION

On January 26, 1975, "An Appeal for Theological Affirmation" was issued by a group of theologians meeting at the Hartford Seminary Foundation in Hartford, Connecticut. The group included Roman Catholic, Eastern Orthodox, and Protestant clergy and covered a remarkably wide theological spectrum. Christian Reformed scholars Richard Mouw and Lewis Smedes signed the document, but also the very liberal William Sloane Coffin, then chaplain at Yale. Other well-known names: sociologist Peter Berger, Richard John Neuhaus,[163] George Lindbeck,[164] Roman Catholic scholars Avery Dulles and George Tavard—eighteen in all.

Harvey Cox

What is interesting in the *Hartford Declaration* is a kind of exasperation on the part of mainstream theologians (liberals among them) with the radical and secular theologies. Liberals almost never criticize one another as being false to the gospel; even the Christian atheists got a largely sympathetic hearing. But I guess there always comes a time when enough is enough. This is an example of the *conservative drift* at work. Bultmann, Tillich, and the radical and secular theologians represented a "glitch" in the conservative drift. Instead of seeking the allegiance of the traditional church, they defied it. But except for headlines in the press, these thinkers (unlike Barth and Brunner) got little respect among the churches.

The *Hartford Declaration* is a rejection of these movements by the leaders of the academic theological community, a return to the

163. Then a Lutheran, later Roman Catholic.

164. Sometimes called the *father of postliberalism* for his book *The Nature of Doctrine: Religion and Theology in a Postliberal Age* (Philadelphia: Westminster Press, 1984).

rhetoric of traditional conservative theology. I could be exaggerating the historical importance of this particular document and the conference that produced it. But it does seem to me that since 1975 the radical movements have quieted down somewhat.

The *Declaration* lists thirteen "false themes" with attached explanations. In my judgment, many of the false themes are overstated. It is often difficult to imagine anyone literally holding them, let alone defending them. But the document certainly succeeds in setting forth clearly a theological direction in which the authors do not want to go. Here are the themes:[165]

The Declaration *lists thirteen "false themes" with attached explanations. . . . The document certainly succeeds in setting forth clearly a theological direction in which the authors do not want to go.*

1. Modern thought is superior to all past forms of understanding reality, and is therefore normative for Christian faith and life.
2. Religious statements are totally independent of reasonable discourse.
3. Religious language refers to human experience and nothing else, God being humanity's noblest creation.
4. Jesus can only be understood in terms of contemporary models of humanity.
5. All religions are equally valid; the choice among them is not a matter of conviction about truth but only personal preference or life-style.
6. To realize one's potential and to be true to oneself is the whole meaning of salvation.
7. Since what is human is good, evil can adequately be understood as failure to reach human potential.
8. The sole purpose of worship is to promote individual self-realization and human community.
9. Institutions and historical traditions are oppressive and inimical to our being truly human; liberation from them is required for authentic existence and authentic religion.
10. The world must set the agenda for the Church. Social, political and economic programs to improve the quality of life are ultimately normative for the Church's mission in the world.
11. An emphasis on God's transcendence is at least a hindrance to, and perhaps incompatible with, Christian social concern and action.
12. The struggle for a better humanity will bring about the Kingdom of God.
13. The question of hope beyond death is irrelevant or at best marginal to the Christian understanding of human fulfillment.

165. Text taken from http://www.philosophy-religion.org/handouts/pdfs/Hartford-Affirmation.pdf.

KEY TERMS

Crisis theology
Neoorthodoxy
Dialectical theology
German Christians
Neo-Protestantism
Illumination
Nominalism (in Barth)
Three forms of revelation (in Barth)
Recollection and expectation
Dialectical (as applied to Barth)
Capital sum (Barth)
Myth (Barth)
Geschichte
Wholly other
Shadowside
Personalism (Brunner)
I-thou relation
Point of contact
Demythologization
Self-understanding
Inauthentic existence (Bultmann)
Authentic existence (Bultmann)
Openness to the future
Ultimate concern
Method of correlation
Supranaturalism (Tillich)
Autonomy (Tillich)
Theonomy (Tillich)
Being itself (Tillich)
The God-beyond-God (Tillich)
World come of age
Religionless Christianity
Language event
Third quest

Two ages
Christian atheism
Secular theology
Theology of the word
Conservative drift
Confessing Church
Barmen Declaration
Modernism
Freedom of God (Barth)
Activism
Indirect identity
Religion (in Barth)
Saga (Barth)
Historie
Wholly hidden
Wholly revealed
Das Nichtige
Dialogical
I-it relation
Form criticism
Myth (Bultmann)
Existential analysis
Formal criteria of theology (Tillich)
Material norm of theology (Tillich)
Symbols (Tillich)
Depth of reason
Heteronomy (Tillich)
Final revelation (Tillich)
Ground of being (Tillich)
Cheap grace (Bonhoeffer)
Religion (Barth, Bonhoeffer)
New hermeneutic
New quest
Heilsgeschichte
D-Day (Cullmann)
Radical theology
Hartford Declaration

STUDY QUESTIONS

1. Why do you think Barth considers the post-Reformation doctrine of biblical inspiration to be superior to the neo-Protestant doctrine? Discuss.

OUTLINE

2. Barth says that revelation "must become true in the Church from time to time." Explain and evaluate, taking into account Frame's comments about the *permanence* of revelation in Scripture, and the traditional doctrine of illumination.
3. Why does Frame say that Barth's view of divine freedom is nominalistic? Evaluate.
4. Frame says that Barth's "view of Scripture encourages us to hear the Bible tentatively, selectively, critically." Explain; evaluate.
5. Barth says that Jesus is an obscure historical figure, but also that he is identical with God's revelation. Explain; evaluate.
6. Barth regards redemptive events as identical with each other and with God himself. Explain; evaluate.
7. Is Barth a presuppositionalist? Explain.
8. Barth is determined to avoid a view of Scripture that allows us to "possess," "control," and "manipulate" it, and so forth. Explain the sin that Barth condemns here, and evaluate his suggestion as to how to eliminate that sin.
9. Describe and evaluate Barth's argument against "revealed truths" and "propositional revelation."
10. Frame: "So in the end, Barth's complaint against neo-Protestantism stands against his own approach to theology." Explain; evaluate.
11. Explain how Barth correlates the doctrine of revelation with the doctrine of the Trinity. Evaluate.
12. Is the resurrection historical for Barth? In what sense? Discuss.
13. Compare Barth's *Historie-Geschichte* with Kant's *phenomenal-noumenal*.
14. Is Barth a universalist? Discuss.
15. What is sin, according to Barth? Explain; evaluate.
16. How do you value Barth's theology, from what you know about it?
17. Compare Brunner to Barth.
18. Define and evaluate Brunner's concept of a personal (*I-thou*) relationship.
19. Compare Brunner's argument against propositional revelation to Barth's.
20. Describe the Barth-Brunner debate over natural theology. Evaluate the two positions.
21. Describe and evaluate Brunner's view of inspiration. How does it differ from Barth's?
22. Frame: "the conservative drift is not a straight line; it has a number of glitches in it." Explain; evaluate.
23. How does the modern worldview affect the need for demythologizing, according to Bultmann? Discuss.

24. Bultmann: "exegesis without presuppositions is impossible." Explain; evaluate.
25. What does Bultmann mean by *authentic existence*, and how does he relate it to the biblical gospel?
26. Describe Bultmann's view of revelation. Why in his view can revelation not be propositional? Describe and evaluate his argument from the doctrine of justification by faith.
27. What can we know of Christ, according to Bultmann? What does it mean to preach the cross of Christ? The resurrection?
28. Enumerate the five parts of Tillich's *Systematic Theology* and explain them.
29. How does Christ answer our epistemological quest, according to Tillich?
30. Why does Tillich think that revelation cannot be propositional? Discuss.
31. Describe Tillich's view of God: (a) being itself, (b) the God beyond God.
32. Frame on Tillich: "In any case, it should not require much astuteness for the reader to see that this is not the biblical gospel." Show how he reaches this conclusion and evaluate it.
33. Outline Bonhoeffer's role in the struggle against Nazism. Show how these events influenced his theology.
34. Describe Bonhoeffer's "religionless Christianity." Relate this concept to other aspects of his theology and evaluate.
35. "We don't interpret the Word; the Word interprets us." Explain; evaluate.
36. Compare *Heilsgeschichte* to *Geschichte*.
37. Frame says that Christian atheism is a natural development from the major existential theologies of the twentieth century. Explain and examine this thesis.
38. How does Harvey Cox defend "secular theology"? Evaluate.
39. Frame thinks the themes of the *Hartford Declaration* overstate the theses of radical and secular theologians. What do you think?

BIBLIOGRAPHY: TWENTIETH-CENTURY LIBERAL THEOLOGY, PART I

Print

Altizer, Thomas J. J. *The New Gospel of Christian Atheism*. Aurora, CO: Davies Group, 2002. Rewritten version of Altizer's original *Gospel*.

Barth, Karl. *Anselm: Fides Quaerens Intellectum*. Eugene, OR: Wipf and Stock, 1975. One of Barth's own favorites among his writings. Insightful on Anselm, with interesting parallels to Barth's own thought.

———. *Church Dogmatics*. Edinburgh: T&T Clark, 2004. Barth's major work, in many volumes.

———. *Church Dogmatics: A Selection*. Edited by Helmut Gollwitzer. Louisville, KY: Westminster John Knox Press, 1994.

———. *Dogmatics in Outline*. New York: Harper, 1959.

———. *The Epistle to the Romans*. New York: Oxford University Press, 1968. This was the commentary that Karl Adam described as a "bombshell in the playground of the theologians."

———. *Evangelical Theology: An Introduction*. Grand Rapids: Eerdmans, 1992.

Berkouwer, G. C. *The Triumph of Grace in the Theology of Karl Barth*. Grand Rapids: Eerdmans, 1956. Generally favorable account of Barth from a Dutch Reformed thinker. Barth commended Berkouwer's account.

Bonhoeffer, Dietrich. *The Cost of Discipleship*. New York: Touchstone, 1995.

———. *Letters and Papers from Prison*. Edited by Eberhard Bethge. New York: Touchstone, 1997.

———. *Life Together*. New York: Harper, 2009.

Brunner, Emil. *Dogmatics I: The Christian Doctrine of God*. Library of Theological Translations. Cambridge: James Clarke and Co., 2002.

———. *Dogmatics II: The Christian Doctrine of Creation and Redemption*. Library of Theological Translations. Cambridge: James Clarke and Co., 2002.

———. *Dogmatics III: The Christian Doctrine of the Church, Faith and the Consummation*. Library of Theological Translations. Cambridge: James Clarke and Co., 2002.

———. *Natural Theology: Comprising Nature and Grace by Professor Dr. Emil Brunner and the Reply No! by Dr. Karl Barth*. Eugene, OR: Wipf and Stock, 2002.

Buber, Martin. *I and Thou*. Translated by Walter Kaufmann. New York: Touchstone, 1971. Buber is the Jewish theologian who deeply influenced the personal-encounter theology of Emil Brunner and many others.

Bultmann, Rudolf. *Existence and Faith: Shorter Writings of Rudolf Bultmann*. Edited and translated by Schubert M. Ogden. New York: Meridian Books, 1960. Important shorter writings.

———. *New Testament and Mythology and Other Basic Writings*. Edited and translated by Schubert M. Ogden. Philadelphia: Fortress, 1984.

———. *Theology of the New Testament*. Translated by Kendrick Grobel. Waco, TX: Baylor University Press, 2007.

Cox, Harvey. *The Secular City*. Princeton, NJ: Princeton University Press, 2013.

Funk, Robert W. *Language, Hermeneutic, and Word of God: The Problem of Language in the New Testament and Contemporary Theology*. New York: Harper and Row, 1966. The *new hermeneutic* of Ebeling and Fuchs.

Hamilton, Kenneth. *The System and the Gospel: A Critique of Paul Tillich*. Charleston, SC: Nabu Press, 2011. Argues that Tillich turns the gospel into a mere philosophical system.

Kelsey, David H. *The Fabric of Paul Tillich's Theology*. Eugene, OR: Wipf and Stock, 2011. Excellent analysis.

McCormack, Bruce L. *Karl Barth's Critically Realistic Dialectical Theology*. New York: Oxford University Press, 1997. Analysis by a recent follower of Barth.

Metaxas, Eric. *Bonhoeffer: Pastor, Martyr, Prophet, Spy*. Nashville, TN: Thomas Nelson, 2011.

Tillich, Paul. *The Courage to Be*. New Haven, CT: Yale University Press, 2000.

———. *Dynamics of Faith*. New York: HarperOne, 2009. Faith as ultimate concern, always mixed with doubt.

———. *Systematic Theology*. 3 vols. Chicago: University of Chicago Press, 1973.

Van Til, Cornelius. *Christianity and Barthianism*. Phillipsburg, NJ: P&R Publishing, 2004. A very negative evaluation of Barth from an orthodox Calvinist.

Online

Many twentieth-century books are still under copyright, and so few titles are available in complete editions on the Internet. There are a few exceptions. There are also many articles *about* the figures of this period, which you may find useful. This note applies to chapters 10–13 of this book.

Barth, Karl. The Digital Karl Barth Library. http://solomon.dkbl.alexanderstreet.com/. Includes Barth's *Church Dogmatics* complete in both German and English, with other writings. Requires subscription.

Bonhoeffer, Dietrich. Dietrich Bonhoeffer Reading Room. http://www.tyndale.ca/seminary/mtsmodular/reading-rooms/theology/bonhoeffer. Most of these online versions are incomplete.

———. "Who Am I?" 1944. Available at http://neilwillard.com/2015/04/09/dietrich-bonhoeffer-who-am-i/.

Brunner, Emil. *Dogmatics I: The Christian Doctrine of God*. Translated by Olive Wyon. Philadelphia: Westminster Press, 1950. Available at http://archive.org/details/dogmatics01brun.

Bultmann, Rudolf. *History and Eschatology: The Presence of Eternity.* 1954–55 Gifford Lectures. Harper, 1962. Available at http://www.giffordlectures.org/books/history-and-eschatology.

———. "The Mythological Element in the Message of the New Testament and the Problem of Its Re-interpretation" (also known as "New Testament and Mythology"). In *Kerygma and Myth: A Theological Debate*, edited by Hans Werner Bartsch. Translated by Reginald H. Fuller. London: SPCK, 1953. Available at http://www.sunysuffolk.edu/About/search.asp?cx=018295863947272962766%3An8erqd-hxfk&cof=FORID%3A9&ie=UTF-8&q=bultmann&x=0&y=0.

Bultmann, Rudolf, Ernst Lohmeyer, Julius Schniewind, Helmut Thielicke, and Austin Farrer. *Kerygma and Myth: A Theological Debate.* Edited by Hans Werner Bartsch. Translated by Reginald H. Fuller. London: SPCK, 1953. Available at http://www.sunysuffolk.edu/About/search.asp?cx=018295863947272962766%3An8erqd-hxfk&cof=FORID%3A9&ie=UTF-8&q=bultmann&x=0&y=0.

Tillich, Paul. Articles by and about Paul Tillich are available at www.archive.org. Search "Paul Tillich."

READ FOR YOURSELF

The shorter works of Barth, such as *Dogmatics in Outline* and *Evangelical Theology: An Introduction*, are useful in getting a toehold on Barth's formidable system. The trouble is that these shorter works don't give a very good impression of the more controversial aspects of Barth's thought, particularly his activism and *Geschichte.* So students who have read mainly Barth's shorter works tend to have a more favorable impression of Barth than would be warranted by serious study of the *CD.* I suggest that the serious student get into the *CD.* One helpful feature of these volumes is that there are one-paragraph summaries at the beginning of each chapter. Read each summary, and when you find something notable, questionable, or interesting, then read the actual chapter.

Instead of reading Brunner, I suggest that you look at Martin Buber's short work, *I and Thou*, which will give you much of the spirit and the rationale for the personal-encounter theology of Brunner and others.

Read Bultmann's article "The New Testament and Mythology," and then his thoughts about existentialist theology in articles such as those in *Existence and Faith.*

In Tillich, read *The Courage to Be* and *Dynamics of Faith.* Then if you're still interested, look into his *Systematic Theology.*

In Bonhoeffer, read *The Cost of Discipleship* and *Life Together* for edification, and then *Letters and Papers from Prison* to explore the theological controversy over his work.

Harvey Cox's *The Secular City* will present an argument that is still with us, to the effect that theology in the modern world needs to follow a secular course.

LISTEN ONLINE

Link: http://itunes.apple.com/us/course/legacy-history-philosophy/id694658914

- Karl Barth: Direction and Fundamental Structure of Thought: 55:29
- Karl Barth Continued, Emil Brunner, and Rudolf Bultmann: 1:09:49
- Rudolf Bultmann Continued, Paul Tillich, the New Hermeneutic, and Christian Atheism: 57:07
- Christian Atheism Continued and Dietrich Bonhoeffer: 27:48

FAMOUS QUOTES

- **Barth:** http://en.wikiquote.org/wiki/Karl_Barth
- **Buber:** http://en.wikiquote.org/wiki/Martin_Buber
- **Bultmann:** http://en.wikiquote.org/wiki/Rudolf_Bultmann
- **Tillich:** http://en.wikiquote.org/wiki/Paul_Tillich
- **Bonhoeffer:** http://en.wikiquote.org/wiki/Dietrich_Bonhoeffer
- **Cox:** http://en.wikiquote.org/wiki/Decisions

11

TWENTIETH-CENTURY LIBERAL THEOLOGY, PART 2

THE THINKERS I will describe in this chapter have been influential especially since 1960. Besides the chronological difference, the main difference between these theologians and those discussed in the previous chapter is their philosophical orientation. The theologies described in the previous chapter operated from a Kantian framework: *Geschichte-Historie = noumenal-phenomenal*. (The secular theologians are something of an exception.) Those described in this chapter (except for the process theologians, a breed apart) are more greatly influenced by Hegel and Marx.[1] In the present group, there is also less influence of Heidegger and other existentialists.

The theologies described in the previous chapter operated from a Kantian framework: Geschichte-Historie = noumenal-phenomenal. . . . *Those described in this chapter (except for the process theologians, a breed apart) are more greatly influenced by Hegel and Marx.*

JÜRGEN MOLTMANN (1926–)

Moltmann came to profess Christ as a prisoner of war. He studied then at the University of Göttingen under professors who had been influenced especially by Karl Barth and who had been part of the Confessing Church. After some time in the pastorate and in various teaching posts, he became professor of systematic theology at the University of Tübingen, where he taught from 1967 to 1994.

At Tübingen, he became acquainted with the Marxist philosopher **Ernst Bloch** (1885–1977), author of *The Principle of Hope*.[2] Bloch rejects

1. Of course, the influence of Hegel is already seen in the *dialectic* of Barth and in Tillich's resolution of antinomies.

2. Trans. Neville Plaice, Stephen Plaice, and Paul Knight, 3 vols. (Cambridge, MA: MIT Press, 1986).

the traditional Marxist eschatology (the dictatorship of the proletariat and the classless society) in favor of an "open" future. He agrees with Marx that matter ultimately determines the course of history, but he rejects the notion that the direction of this process is predetermined. As the existentialists denied that human beings have a fixed essence or nature, Bloch said the same about history. Only the future will disclose what something "is," and that future will never arrive. So our thought and action should not seek to conform to the way things are (*being*), as in traditional philosophy, but should rather be governed by hope for the future. Present reality is incomplete, therefore, both ontologically and epistemologically. Present and past have value only as they are valued by the future. So there are no normative, fixed categories that human thought must observe.

Ernst Bloch

Bloch suggests that on this basis one may view religion in a more favorable light than in traditional Marxism. In Scripture, Bloch says, man is oriented toward God's *promises*, and therefore toward the future. Yahweh is the One who "will be what he will be."[3] Sometimes, however, in Bloch's view, it is good and necessary to oppose God. Sin is a kind of creativity, which enables us to "be as gods."[4] We ought to engage in such creativity, which rejects the "structures of creation" for an unstructured future. Thus Bloch rejects the God of creation in favor of the god of the future. So he uses Genesis to support his view of the autonomy of human thought. Clearly, his new appreciation of Scripture has not led him into anything like orthodox Christianity.

Moltmann became famous initially for his book *Theology of Hope: On the Ground and the Implications of a Christian Eschatology*.[5] This book makes much use of Bloch's argumentation, but its terminology, at least, is more distinctively Christian. So with Moltmann, we return to what I have called the *conservative drift*, the tendency of liberal theology to use traditional language in order to gain a hearing in the traditional church.

Bloch rejects the God of creation in favor of the god of the future. So he uses Genesis to support his view of the autonomy of human thought.

In *Theology of Hope*, Moltmann refers often to Scripture. Like Bloch, he points out that in the Bible, God is the God who *promises*. Man is related to him through the promise. God's people are strangers and pilgrims (1 Peter 2:11), wanderers in the world, who seek a future kingdom (Heb. 11). Prophecy intensifies this expectation. But the fulfillment of prophecy does not bring an end to the expectation, only an enlargement of it. Whenever a prophecy is "fulfilled," it reveals unanticipated aspects

3. The Hebrew verb *I am* that underlies the divine name in Exodus 3:14–15 can indeed be translated by a future tense, but it is not at all clear that the context necessitates or prefers such a translation. See my *DG*, 37–42.

4. Bloch here refers to Genesis 3:5, taking *elohim* as a plural form, though the original passage clearly operates with a monotheistic worldview.

5. Trans. James W. Leitch (New York: Harper and Row, 1967).

that are yet to be fulfilled. So what God does cannot be anticipated on the basis of past expectations, even prophecy. His acts are enormously *surprising*. Creation is *ex nihilo*, that is, not to be expected on the basis of a previous state of affairs. Same for the resurrection of Christ from the dead, for death gives no reason for expecting life.

For Moltmann, these facts explain something that puzzled his predecessors: the pervasively eschatological nature of Jesus' teaching and ministry. Jesus was indeed an apocalyptic visionary, and his disciples were caught up in eschatological hope.

In his book, Moltmann compares his recent predecessors' views of this eschatology with his own, a comparison that will help us to review some important points from chapter 10 about the earlier twentieth-century theologians. The Ritschlians, he says, simply suppressed the eschatological element in order to regard Jesus as primarily a moral teacher. Schweitzer and Weiss, however, demonstrated that the NT was pervasively eschatological, but they made no positive theological use of this discovery. Barth sought to make use of it, hence his *crisis theology*. Moltmann comments:

> In the second edition of his *Römerbrief*, Karl Barth in 1921 makes the programmatic announcement: "If Christianity be not altogether and unreservedly eschatology, there remains in it no relationship whatever to Christ."[6] Yet what is the meaning of "eschatology" here? It is not history, moving silently and interminably onwards, that brings a crisis upon man's eschatological hopes for the future, as Albert Schweitzer said, but on the contrary it is now the *eschaton*, breaking transcendentally into history, that brings all human history to its final crisis. This, however, makes the *eschaton* into a transcendental eternity, the transcendental meaning of all ages, equally near to all the ages of history and equally far from all of them.[7]

Jürgen Moltmann

Barth's *Eschaton* is what he elsewhere calls *Geschichte*, a revelational occurrence that comes upon people "from time to time." It is an intersection of time and eternity, and so not locatable in calendar time and geographic space. So it is not much like the eschatological expectation of the NT.

> Now these forms of thinking [in Barth—JF], in which the real language of eschatology is still obscured today, are entirely the

6. *Der Römerbrief*, 2nd ed. (1922), 298 (English translation: *The Epistle to the Romans* [New York: Oxford University Press, 1968], 314).

7. Moltmann, *Theology of Hope*, 39–40.

> thought forms of the Greek mind, which sees in the *logos* the epiphany of the eternal present of being and finds the truth in that.[8]

Bultmann is no better, says Moltmann. He did emphasize, as Moltmann, the *open future*. And he does come close to identifying God with the open future, as Moltmann also does. But as with Barth, Bultmann's existentialism allows no relevance for the passing of calendar time. Our relation with God is wholly in the present. Secular theology adds the theme of *this worldliness*, a useful corrective to Barth and Bultmann, for whom the movement of secular history was irrelevant. But secular theology loses any sense of transcendence. Moltmann believes he can restore this by placing transcendence in the future. Moltmann intends to formulate for the twentieth century a *realistic* eschatology: not epiphany, but apocalypse; not *logos*, but promise.

Eschatology, Moltmann says, "means the doctrine of the Christian hope." And hope, he says, ought to be the central category of theology, not merely one topic within it.

Eschatology, he says, "means the doctrine of the Christian hope."[9] And hope, he says, ought to be the central category of theology, not merely one topic within it.

> From first to last, and not merely in the epilogue, Christianity is eschatology, is hope, revolutionizing and transforming the present. The eschatological is not one element of Christianity, but it is the medium of Christian faith as such, the key in which everything in it is set, the glow that suffuses everything here in the dawn of an expected new day.[10]

Hope is not knowing the future, but accepting it as a gift, being open to whatever happens. The future, Moltmann says, is genuinely open.

Hope is not knowing the future, but accepting it as a gift, being open to whatever happens. The future, Moltmann says, is genuinely open.

8. Ibid., 40.

9. Ibid.

10. Ibid., 16. Inspiring language, certainly, until one remembers that Schleiermacher said the same thing about religious feeling, Ritschl about love, Barth about the Word of God, Brunner about personal relationships, Bultmann about existential self-understanding, and so forth. Many concepts in Scripture can arguably be presented as the *center* of Christian faith. Think of covenant, Trinity, history, holiness, and freedom, for example. For they all entail one another and point to Christ, who is the only true center. It is typical of liberal theology, however, to take one concept, such as *eschatology* or *hope*, and expound the rest of the Bible in terms of this specific concept, discarding biblical elements that do not easily fit the pattern. Liberal theology does not believe that Scripture (actually a complexity of many overlapping concepts) is fully true in all it says. Its adherents want nothing of *propositional revelation*, the authority of biblical *teachings*. So they retreat from biblical teachings to biblical *concepts*, choose the one they find most appealing, and expound that. This introduces a profound implausibility into their formulations. And in general: is it likely, after two thousand years of Bible study in the church, that some academic in 1967 has finally discovered what the Bible is really all about?

OUTLINE

Jürgen Moltmann (1926–)
The Theology of Liberation
Wolfhart Pannenberg (1928–2014)
Process Thought
Open Theism
Postliberal Theology

So hope is optimistic, not fearful. Since God acts in surprising ways, we should never despair at the difficulties of our present situation. Moltmann opposes the pessimism of the existential theologies, their *being-toward-death*.[11]

Revelation, then, has the character of *promise*, according to Moltmann. It is apocalyptic, not epiphany: not an illumination of present reality, but a revelation of what God is *doing* from the perspective of the end. Thus it carries us beyond our rational expectations.[12]

Since the future is open, he continues, revelation does not give us propositional information about the future.[13] Therefore, all our thinking about God is provisional. The future is open, and the past is no sure guide. So there can be no "static" norms for thought or life, nor any certainty about historical events. Yet we can think of the future in hope, courageously expecting it to be better than the present.

God is present only in his promises, that is, in hope, according to Moltmann. Therefore, "future is his essential nature."[14] So he agrees with Barth that we can never "have" or "possess" God, but his grounds for saying this are somewhat different from Barth's. Further, for Moltmann, as for Tillich, the "existence" of God is problematic. God does not fully exist in the present, because the future is not here yet. Today we experience an anticipation of God, but not "God himself" as with Brunner. This explains the dialectic between God's "presence" and "absence" as we consider the nature of evil.

For Moltmann, there is no transcendent sphere of reality in the present in which God may be found. But God is transcendent over us as the future is transcendent over the present. He is also immanent in that he is the future of human history. The story of God is the story of human history.[15]

For Moltmann, there is no transcendent sphere of reality in the present in which God may be found. But God is transcendent over us as the future is transcendent over the present. He is also immanent in that he is the future of human history. The story of God is the story of human history.

In that history, God participates in the story of our humiliation and

11. But in *The Crucified God: The Cross of Christ as the Foundation and Criticism of Christian Theology*, trans. R. A. Wilson and John Bowden (Minneapolis: Fortress, 1993), Moltmann insists that Christian hope is not the hope for social progress as defined by capitalism. It is, rather, realistic about oppression and suffering.

12. So Moltmann thinks that Pannenberg is too rationalistic. See later in this chapter for a discussion of Pannenberg.

13. As we have seen, every liberal theologian produces his own argument as to why propositional revelation is impossible. This is Moltmann's.

14. Moltmann, *Theology of Hope*, 16, 30. Moltmann here continues the trend in twentieth-century liberalism to identify God with revelation and then to derive the nature of God from the nature of revelation.

15. In *The Trinity and the Kingdom: The Doctrine of God*, trans. Margaret Kohl (San Francisco: HarperCollins, 1981), Moltmann has more to say about the inner life of God in the Trinity. There he makes a case for *social Trinitarianism*, which emphasizes the distinctness of the Trinitarian persons from one another at the expense of the unity of the Godhead. See my critique in *DG*, 724–26.

oppression.[16] Jesus is true humanity in the midst of inhumanity. Moltmann's Christology is *kenotic*, Christ divesting himself of any power that would compromise his suffering and humility. His deity is that he embodies the future of man. His resurrection is not a past event, but the beginning of the future. Therefore, it is not "in" history, but is rather the *basis* of history and of hope.

As in existentialism, *man* has no fixed definition in Moltmann's theology. He is *becoming* rather than *being*, and thus he can be understood only from the end of time. He is the image of God in his ability to transcend the past and freely anticipate the future. Sin is hopelessness. It is *presumption*—seeking to bring future change in one's own strength, without hope in God (works-righteousness). But it is also *desperation*: apathy, indifference, unbelief.

As in existentialism, man *has no fixed definition in Moltmann's theology. He is* becoming *rather than* being, *and thus he can be understood only from the end of time.*

In his ecclesiology, Moltmann opposes the *Constantinian model*, in which the church seeks to rule the world in the present, as though the end of history had arrived and the church were fit to impose its will on others. Rather, we should see the church as *servant* to the world. It should seek no favored position. It is not qualitatively different from the world, but that vanguard of a new humanity, the promise of humanity's future.[17] The sacraments proclaim future hope. The church should directly confront the evils of society, not merely leave this up to individual Christians.

In his ethics, he follows Brunner and others who reject the idea of a fixed ethical norm. Moltmann's argument is that only the future is ethically normative, and we don't know what form the future will take. So the standard for our actions is the anticipated result. In effect, the end justifies the means, as in Marx.

The future frees us to love those who are not presently attractive or appealing (*agape*). So we are called to identify ourselves with the oppressed, as God does in Christ. We cannot accept the status quo; that would be "desperation." Rather, we must challenge "what is" in the interest of "what will be." Revolution is *one* appropriate means for accomplishing change. No revolution will bring in utopia, as Marx thought. Still, it might in some cases be necessary. He says:

We cannot accept the status quo; that would be "desperation." Rather, we must challenge "what is" in the interest of "what will be." Revolution is one *appropriate means for accomplishing change.*

> The problem of violence and non-violence is an illusory problem. There is only the question of the justified and unjustified

16. In *The Crucified God*, Moltmann stresses that God the Father suffers with the oppressed. In *The Trinity and the Kingdom*, he actually opposes "monotheism," because he thinks it entails the "idea of the almighty ruler of the universe everywhere," which makes creatures completely dependent on him (192). So Moltmann actually opposes the central biblical idea of God's lordship. See my *DG*, 627–31. He offers his social Trinitarianism (previous footnote) as an egalitarian model of society, in which nobody has supreme power.

17. Here, Moltmann recapitulates the argument of the secular theologians.

use of force and the question of whether the means are proportionate to the ends.[18]

Moltmann has certainly provided a service to the church in stressing the pervasiveness of eschatology in Scripture and in his insistence on giving eschatology a major role in his theology, contrary to his predecessors. *Hope* is a legitimate vantage point from which to view the Bible's teaching. But he is surely wrong to insist that it is the only perspective on Scripture, or the best for all purposes.

In Scripture, the future does play a major role. But so does the past: we are to "remember" God's past deliverances, most of all the cross and resurrection of Christ. And we must understand "the times," our present situation in the light of God's Word. God is the God of promises, but he is also the God who did mighty works in the past and who is with his people today. Without the past and present dimensions of experience, it is impossible to make sense of the promises, let alone rely on them.

It is not clear how we can make any decisions about the future unless we have knowledge of the present and past. And to deny, as Moltmann does, what "is" is to rob ourselves of any even provisional means of preparing for the future. If the future is as "open" as Moltmann claims, then why should we think our actions can affect it? Indeed, why should we *hope* when we are confronted by an open future? Why should we think the future will be better rather than worse? Often in our experience (and in biblical history), it is worse. Much of Moltmann's argumentation makes the case for surprise, rather than hope itself. I've often thought that it might be more appropriate to call Moltmann's first book *Theology of Surprise* rather than *Theology of Hope*.

On Moltmann's nonpropositional view of revelation, it's hard to know what to do. He renounces absolute ethical norms and embraces a form of ethical utilitarianism (the end justifies the means).

What about Moltmann's justification for human action, even revolution, to relieve the burdens of the oppressed? Theologians of liberation (next section of this chapter) sometimes criticize Moltmann for his confusion as to man's role in initiating social change. Sometimes Moltmann seems to be urging us to act, but at other times he says that the future is unknown to us and so we should wait to be surprised by some divine action. Otherwise, we might be guilty of "presumption." But how can we know when to act and when to wait? On Moltmann's nonpropositional view of revelation, it's hard to know what to do. He renounces absolute ethical norms and embraces a form of ethical utilitarianism (the end justifies the means). But how do we determine what end to embrace? How do we know what constitutes oppression or liberation?

18. Jürgen Moltmann, *Religion, Revolution and the Future*, trans. Meeks M. Douglas (New York: Scribner's, 1969).

Moltmann responds to the liberation theologians by distinguishing the "foreseeable" future from the "unforeseeable," and advocating social action based on the foreseeable. But the whole dynamic of Moltmann's theology is that our lives should be governed by the unforeseeable.

The source of Moltmann's confusion is what I described in chapter 1 as the transcendence-immanence and irrationalist-rationalist dialectics. Moltmann's God is hypertranscendent (he is the future and therefore does not fully exist in the present) and hyperimmanent (suffering with humanity in all ages so that his story is the story of afflicted humanity). God's immanence dictates our participation in social change along Marxist lines (rationalism). But his transcendence takes away any assurance we may have about how this will work out (irrationalism); see fig. 11.1.

Moltmann's God is hypertranscendent (he is the future and therefore does not fully exist in the present) and hyperimmanent (suffering with humanity in all ages so that his story is the story of afflicted humanity).

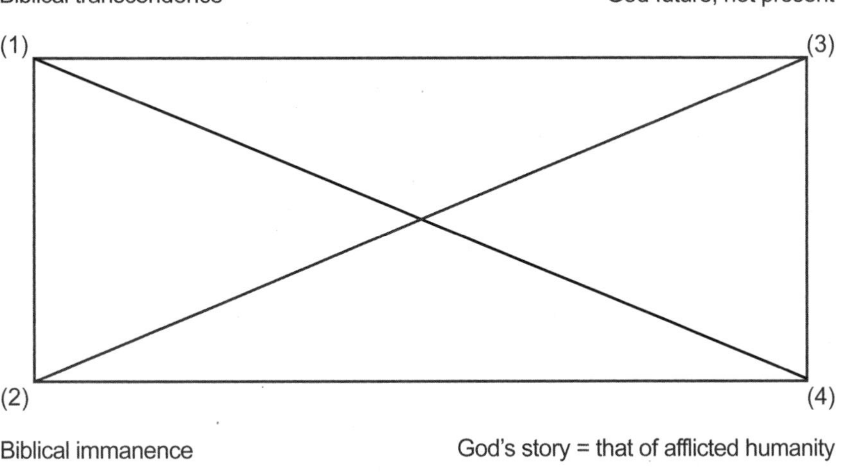

Fig. 11.1. Transcendence and Immanence in Moltmann

The theology of liberation became quite pervasive in the second half of the twentieth century.

THE THEOLOGY OF LIBERATION

The theology of liberation became quite pervasive in the second half of the twentieth century. To illustrate: Deane W. Ferm's *Contemporary American Theologies*[19] contains eight chapters, five of which discuss currently fashionable theological positions. Of these five, one is evangelical theology, one is Roman Catholic theology, and three are various forms of liberation theology: Latin American, black, and feminist. Slogans, concepts, and arguments from liberation theologians have been appearing in Roman Catholic and evangelical theologies as well,

19. San Francisco: Harper and Row, 1990.

and there has been much commonality between liberation theology and the others mentioned in this chapter: Moltmann, Pannenberg, and process thought.

As Ferm indicates, *liberation theology* has become a general name for several different movements: *Latin American, African American, feminist.*[20] Latin American thinkers include Rubem Alves, Gustavo Gutierrez, Hugo Assmann, Jose Miranda, Juan Luis Segundo, Jon Sobrino, Leonardo Boff, Jose Miguez-Bonino. James Cone is considered to be the founder of *black theology*, with other writers Albert B. Cleage, J. Deotis Roberts, Major J. Jones, and W. R. Jones.[21] Feminist theological writers include Mary Daly, Rosemary Reuther, Letty Russell, Sheila Collins, Penelope Washbourn, Elizabeth Johnson, Letha Scanzoni, Virginia Mollenkott, and Helen Longino. In this discussion, I will focus on the Latin American form of liberation theology, and in particular Gustavo Gutierrez's *A Theology of Liberation*, considered by many to be the leading text of the movement.[22]

The theology of **Gutierrez** (1928–) deals primarily with the relations of rich and poor. Black theology, of course, focuses more closely on race, and feminism more closely on gender. But for all these groups, it is a question of relations between one group considered oppressive and another considered oppressed. They argue that the Bible should be read from the perspective of the oppressed.

For all these groups, it is a question of relations between one group considered oppressive and another considered oppressed. They argue that the Bible should be read from the perspective of the oppressed.

Liberation theology agrees with Bultmann that exegesis without presuppositions is not possible. Specifically, the liberationists focus on presuppositions derived from the socioeconomic, race, and gender status of the exegete. The Bible looks different to the poor and to the rich, to black and to white, to female and to male. Those who are relatively prosperous often fail to note what the Bible says about poverty. So no exegesis is socially, racially, economically, or politically neutral. We should not assume, for instance, that European or North American theology provides adequate categories for theology in the Third World.

Understanding Scripture, for the liberationists, presupposes not only ideas, but practical involvement—*praxis*, as they say. We need contact and experience with reality if we are to think rightly about it. So truth itself is something practical, as theory is part of practice. It is an event,

20. The Minjung theology of Korea has some kinship with liberation theology, but also some differences.

21. At this point in history, we should not ignore the Rev. Jeremiah Wright, pastor for many years to now-President Barack Obama and his family at Trinity United Church of Christ in Chicago. Wright's sermons became controversial in the 2008 campaign, leading to the Obamas' leaving the membership of the church. Wright explained his sermons by citing Cone's *black theology*.

22. Maryknoll, NY: Orbis Books, 1973.

something that happens.[23] To know God is to do justice (Jer. 22:16).[24] Praxis is the only way by which truth can be verified: ideas for social improvement should be judged by how they actually work.

Even more specifically, the liberationists emphasize that we must be involved in *sociopolitical* action if we are to rightly understand the Scriptures. Christ must be heard in every area of life, and here, too, neutrality is impossible. Everyone already has some social agenda. The only question is which one it will be. But sociopolitical action is, they say, necessarily "conflictual"[25] in character. For the interests of the poor and the rich inevitably conflict.[26] In this matter, we must choose sides.

Gutierrez considers the objection that such militancy is inconsistent with the Bible's teaching that we should love our enemies. He replies that combat with one's enemies does not necessarily involve hatred. It might be for the enemy's good. In any case, one cannot love his enemies until he has identified them *as* enemies. Cheap conciliation helps no one.

So Gutierrez insists that all theology must take its bearings from the *axis* of oppression and liberation. In the Bible, such an emphasis will focus on the exodus, God's delivering his people from slavery, and on the laws and prophecies that call Israel to have compassion for the poor. Jesus' redemption is a second exodus in which God again brings down the proud and exalts the humble.

Gutierrez says that Marxism presents the best analysis of the oppression-liberation conflict in terms of class struggle. So the liberation theologian must be committed to Marxism at least as an "analytical tool," at most to socialist revolution as such.

Gutierrez says that Marxism presents the best analysis of the oppression-liberation conflict in terms of class struggle. So the liberation theologian must be committed to Marxism at least as an "analytical tool,"[27] at most to socialist revolution as such. So theology is the critical reflection on praxis, from within praxis.

Its ultimate goal is that of Marx: not to understand the world, but to change it. Particularly, its goal is not to protect and defend a tradition. The theologian should venture beyond the traditional historical models, making use of sociological analysis to understand the culture for whom he is writing.

Gustavo Gutierrez

23. Note here overtones of Barth's activist theology, and before that the pragmatist epistemologies of Charles Peirce and William James.

24. I have some sympathy with the liberation theologies up to this point. Compare my triperspectival theory of knowledge and truth in *DKG*.

25. This word seems to occur almost exclusively in contexts dealing with Marx or with liberation theology.

26. This is, of course, a Marxist assumption. On the contrary, I believe that it is possible for a just and godly social order to improve the prosperity of all.

27. Here Gutierrez chooses his words carefully. He is Roman Catholic, and Marxism as an ideology has been condemned by the Vatican. Through the history of liberation theology, there has been trouble between the theologians and the bishops, including the pope. I do not personally understand the difference between being a Marxist and using Marxism as an analytical tool. But Gutierrez evidently chooses this phrase as indicating something less than a total commitment to Marxist philosophy.

But most of all, the theologian should be involved in the social conflicts of his time. He should not seek theological permission for this involvement. Rather, the involvement is the presupposition of theology itself. Hugo Assmann says that commitment to revolution is independent of and prior to any theological rationale. In my judgment, this is wrong. It limits the scope of God's Word, forbidding it to judge whether a revolution is legitimate.

Liberation theology borrows many concepts and much rhetoric from the theology of secularization; compare our discussion of Cox in the previous chapter. Gutierrez says that we should accept the modern development toward secularization.[28] It coincides with a Christian vision of man: that redemption makes us more fully human. And it affirms creation as something distinct from God, and man as its lord. So, he says, the church should be understood in terms of the world, religion in terms of the profane, rather than vice versa.[29] The church should not try to use the world for its own ends, but should be a servant.

So history is one. There is no ultimate distinction between the profane and the sacred.[30] Creation is a saving act, and political liberation (as in the exodus) is a self-creative act. Salvation is re-creation, fulfillment, in which man is an active participant, in response to grace. The incarnation of Christ underscores the sacredness of the profane.[31]

Gutierrez follows Moltmann's argument that theology ought to be "future oriented,"[32] but he puts more importance than Moltmann on the *present* situation, citing biblical and historical examples. There is an *already*, as well as a *not yet*. He says:

Gutierrez says that we should accept the modern development toward secularization. It coincides with a Christian vision of man: that redemption makes us more fully human.

> The hope which overcomes death must be rooted in the heart of historical *praxis*; if this hope does not take shape in the present to lead it forward, it will be only an evasion, a futuristic illusion. One must be extremely careful not to replace a Christianity of the Beyond [like Barth and Bultmann—JF] with a Christianity of the Future; if the former tended to forget the world, the latter runs the risk of neglecting a miserable and unjust present and the struggle for liberation.[33]

I will now summarize how Gutierrez treats the familiar theological *loci*. In his doctrine of God, he affirms God's transcendence and

28. Gutierrez, *A Theology of Liberation*, 66–68.

29. As with Moltmann, the liberationists are deeply influenced by secular theology.

30. Gutierrez, *A Theology of Liberation*, 153–60.

31. Ibid., 189–94.

32. Ibid., 14–15, 160–68, 213–20.

33. Ibid., 218. At 241n33, Gutierrez says that Moltmann is moving closer to a liberationist position.

immanence, but in both cases with a liberationist accent: God is transcendent, for the first commandment brings judgment against all false gods, including those forms of Christianity that accept injustice. He is immanent in that he acts in history to deliver the oppressed,[34] and he continually exists in and with mankind.[35] His presence is universal: in Gentiles as well as Jews, and in non-Christians as well as Christians. Particularly, he dwells in the "neighbor,"[36] which includes all people. To be united to God, we must be "converted to the neighbor," and vice versa.[37]

Gutierrez says that within human nature there is an infinite openness to God.[38] So there is no antagonism between the natural and the supernatural. Because of God's "infinite salvific will," therefore, all are affected by grace and effectually called to communion with God. They are all in Christ.[39] So the boundaries between church and world are fluid. "Some even ask if they are really two different things."[40] So participation in liberation is a saving work. Sin is a selfish turning in on oneself, refusing to love neighbors and therefore to love God.[41] Ultimately, man is therefore the source of poverty, injustice, and oppression, both individually and by way of "structures" of collective society. Individual and corporate sin feed on each other. In a footnote, Gutierrez mentions Marx's correlation between private ownership and sin. Because of private ownership, in Marx's view, the worker is alienated from the fruit of his work. Gutierrez, however, warns us against "overestimating" the importance of this correlation.[42]

There is no antagonism between the natural and the supernatural. Because of God's "infinite salvific will," therefore, all are affected by grace and effectually called to communion with God.

Most liberationists accept the biblical history in its main outlines, though some among them are skeptical, such as Leonardo Boff. They do not, however, put much emphasis on the miracles, atonement, and resurrection of Christ, except, like Moltmann, as incentives to expect God to work surprises in the future.

Liberationists do not, however, put much emphasis on the miracles, atonement, and resurrection of Christ, except, like Moltmann, as incentives to expect God to work surprises in the future.

The liberation theologians do devote considerable energy to the question why Jesus himself did not engage in political action during his earthly ministry. Gutierrez points out that Jesus had friends among the Zealot revolutionaries.[43] He agreed with them on the soon coming of

34. Like Moltmann, he takes the name *Yahweh* as "I will be who will be"—not an ahistorical being, but a force in our future, ready to act in power. Ibid., 165.

35. Ibid., 189–212.

36. Ibid., 194–203.

37. Ibid., 207.

38. Ibid., 69. Cf. 149–52.

39. Gutierrez here goes somewhat beyond Karl Rahner's thoughts about "anonymous Christians" who are saved, but outside the Catholic Church. Gutierrez is clearly a universalist.

40. Gutierrez, *A Theology of Liberation*, 72. Cf. 258.

41. Ibid., 36–37.

42. Ibid., 187n98.

43. Ibid., 226–27.

the kingdom, his role in it, and the seizing of that kingdom by violent men (Matt. 11:12). But Jesus nevertheless kept his distance from them, because: (1) His was a universal mission, not a narrow nationalism. (2) His attitude toward the law was different from that of the Zealots. (3) He saw the kingdom coming as a gift of God, not from man's own effort. (4) He saw the root of the political problems in a lack of brotherhood. (5) He respected the autonomy of political action. Thus, says Gutierrez, Jesus' revolution was more radical than that of the Zealots. His message is directed to the heart, and it is heart-change that best leads to structural change. Saving grace, therefore, destroys the root of the problems of society. But all human attempts to overcome oppression are also opposed to selfishness and sin, and are therefore liberating. So again, sacred and secular work together.

The church is the "universal sacrament of salvation,"[44] a community oriented toward the future promised by the Lord. It should be preoccupied with the world, not itself. Indeed, as a part of the world it must be inhabited and evangelized by the world. So it reveals the world's true nature as being in Christ.

Like Moltmann, Gutierrez opposes the *Constantinian model* and prefers the concept of secular theology, that the church exists to serve the world and should take its agenda from the world. Thus the church must be mobilized to fight poverty. He is convinced that capitalism is no solution to the poverty of Latin America and that Christians should encourage their societies on a socialist path.[45] The establishment of socialism might require violence. But Gutierrez insists that economic oppression is itself the result of violence, so that removing that oppression can justify "counter-violence."[46]

The liberationists demand that commitment to Marxist revolution is the presupposition *of the theological task, so it requires no "theological permission."*

Like many other philosophical and theological movements, liberation theology makes serious mistakes at the beginning of its thinking process (epistemology) that infect everything else it says. The liberationists demand that commitment to Marxist revolution is the *presupposition* of the theological task, so it requires no "theological permission." Thus the Word of God is silenced on the central tenets of liberation theology, where it ought to speak the loudest.

44. Ibid., 258–62.

45. Ibid., 111–13. As indicated in my discussion of Marx, chapter 7, I disagree with the socialist theory and program. Capitalism is not perfect, but it has done more to combat poverty than any other economic system. Scripture endorses the principle of private property in the eighth commandment, while urging God's people to deal generously with the needs of the poor. For more discussion of this, see my *DCL*, 796–829. Every year, however, brings more proof of the economic unsoundness of socialism and its connection with governmental tyranny and class warfare. I find it hard to take seriously the liberationists' talk of *humanization* as a goal of socialism.

46. Gutierrez, *A Theology of Liberation*, 22, 88–92, 108.

Nevertheless, the liberationists (I think inconsistently) provide a lot of insight into biblical social and individual ethics. God does care especially for the poor, and those who have contempt for the poor will bear special judgment. But the liberationists, by presupposing Marxism, cut themselves off from serious discussion about the best way to aid those trapped in poverty, leaving only violence as the means of settling the question. That so many Christians have fallen into this trap is a major part of the tragedy of the church in Latin America. And those liberationists who are concerned about the state of women, or of African Americans, should beware of encouraging similar results.

Wolfhart Pannenberg

WOLFHART PANNENBERG (1928–2014)

Throughout his long career, Pannenberg was, in my judgment, the most impressive individual thinker in Protestant systematic theology. The breadth of his knowledge and quality of his argumentation were not matched, in my view, by anyone else in the field. Which is not to say, of course, that I agree with his positions.

Pannenberg marks a rationalist turn in modern theology. I have argued that all liberal theologians are rationalist and irrationalist at the same time, and that is also true of Pannenberg. But twentieth-century theology up until Pannenberg has tended to disparage reason as a guide in religious matters. Barth's *Geschichte*, for example, is an attempt to escape from Lessing's ditch, to place redemptive history in a realm that is inaccessible to the autonomous rationality of scholars.[47] But Pannenberg, though a student of Barth, maintains that autonomous rationality is the only way to determine truth in any sphere of life, including history and religion. His relation to Barth and Bultmann is somewhat similar, then, to the relation of Hegel to Kant. In fact, Hegel is a major influence in Pannenberg's thought, and I encourage readers to revisit the discussion of Hegel in chapter 7 of this book so as to better understand Pannenberg's proposals.

Pannenberg is probably the most impressive individual thinker today in Protestant systematic theology.

The other major theme in Pannenberg's thought is resurrection. Pannenberg believes he can prove rationally that Jesus' resurrection (or something else worthy of the name—see below) occurred in space and time, and serves as the key to history. This is the Barthian side of Pannenberg: an event from out of the blue that comes dramatically into our history. Often Pannenberg's arguments for the historicity of the resurrection parallel those of traditional evangelical apologetics, and many evangelicals were initially excited about the appearance of these arguments in the work of a German theologian. We will see,

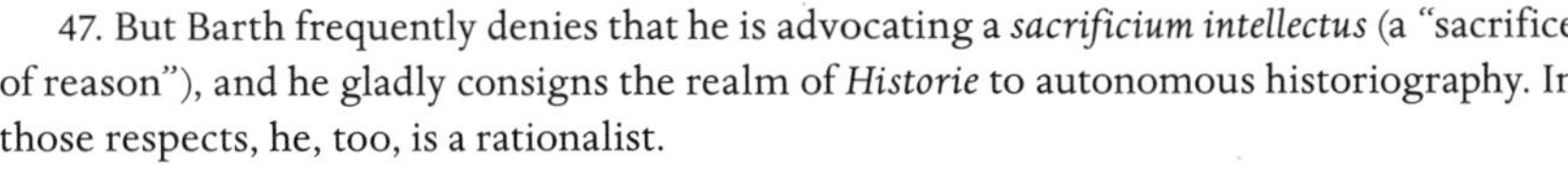

47. But Barth frequently denies that he is advocating a *sacrificium intellectus* (a "sacrifice of reason"), and he gladly consigns the realm of *Historie* to autonomous historiography. In those respects, he, too, is a rationalist.

OUTLINE

Jürgen Moltmann (1926–)

The Theology of Liberation

Wolfhart Pannenberg (1928–2014)

Process Thought

Open Theism

Postliberal Theology

however, that Pannenberg's views of Scripture, of faith and history, and even of resurrection are far removed from those of evangelicalism.

Pannenberg says that faith is a commitment that depends on the truth of its object.[48] It is not "theoretical cognizance," but it does involve "believing certain things to be true."[49] Based on the creation and the events of the life of Jesus, it makes a commitment to the reality of God, and rests on the truth of his promises. But all knowledge, including the knowledge of faith, is incomplete, provisional. God is an *invisible* reality,[50] and statements of the creed are "subject to considerable doubt."[51] And this is true also of our knowledge of the world in general. Our experience of the world is constantly changing. What was certain yesterday is not necessarily certain today.[52] There are no absolute laws or similarities in nature.[53] Final answers will not be known until the consummation of history.[54] Only the future will show the essence of things.[55] So our understanding of Christ, like our general response to him, will always be "capable of improvement."[56] The Spirit helps us, but he doesn't give us "theoretical certainty."[57] Indeed, part of the work of the church is to remind the world and itself of the provisional character of all finite reality.[58]

Therefore, the claims of faith must be subject to rational verification. The alternative is to leave these claims undecided—but their truth is crucial.[59] The truth of these claims is not established by our decision to believe them: that is *blind* faith, which is inevitably an attempt to redeem ourselves.[60] We can test assertions about the resurrection and other factual claims

Pannenberg says that faith is a commitment that depends on the truth of its object. It is not "theoretical cognizance," but it does involve "believing certain things to be true."

> solely and exclusively by the methods of historical research. There is no other way of testing assertions about happenings

48. Wolfhart Pannenberg, *The Apostles' Creed in the Light of Today's Questions*, trans. Margaret Kohl (London: SCM Press, 1972), 6. Although Pannenberg has published many other books, including his three-volume *Systematic Theology*, trans. Geoffrey W. Bromiley (Grand Rapids: Eerdmans, 1991–98), I will refer most often to his smaller work *The Apostles' Creed*, which clearly summarizes the basic thrust of his theology.

49. Here Pannenberg rejects the theory of Brunner and others that faith as a personal relationship is opposed to a knowledge of factual information.

50. Pannenberg, *The Apostles' Creed*, 8.

51. Ibid., 10.

52. Ibid., 25–26.

53. Ibid., 40–41.

54. Ibid., 35–36.

55. Here Pannenberg echoes the existentialists and the approach of Bloch and Moltmann.

56. Pannenberg, *The Apostles' Creed*, 127.

57. Ibid., 131–32, 140.

58. Ibid., 156–57.

59. Ibid., 10.

60. Ibid.

that are supposed to have once taken place in the past; see fig. 11.2.[61]

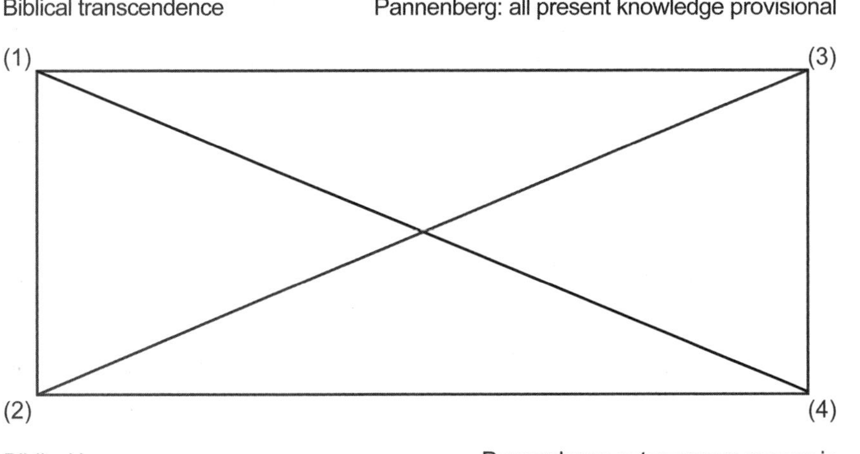

Fig. 11.2. Transcendence and Immanence in Pannenberg

[According to Pannenberg,] people who try to make Christianity independent of historical research are trying to escape the vulnerability of Christianity—its susceptibility to falsification.

Not every Christian need be involved in this verification process, but every Christian ought to know that *somewhere* in the church this process is going on.[62] Pannenberg adds that people who try to make Christianity independent of historical research are trying to escape the *vulnerability* of Christianity—its susceptibility to falsification. But that vulnerability is central to the very nature of the gospel, as opposed to the other religions of the world.[63] Historical facts, therefore historical research, are indispensable to Christianity.

Is it not the case that many professional historians adopt presuppositions that rule out the Christian gospel from the outset? Pannenberg gives some recognition to the role of presuppositions in historical study.

Here Pannenberg departs from predecessors such as Barth, Brunner, and Bultmann, who (in order to escape from Lessing's ditch) adopt theological constructions (as *Geschichte*) that make historical research irrelevant to Christian faith. I applaud this departure in general. But I must ask whether *historical research* is religiously neutral. Is it not the case that many professional historians adopt presuppositions that rule out the Christian gospel from the outset? Pannenberg gives some recognition to the role of presuppositions in historical study:

> In every historical judgment the valuator's whole experience of the world and himself plays a part. What this or that historian

61. Ibid., 108–9.
62. Ibid., 11.
63. Ibid., 45–46.

> believes to be in any way possible depends on his own picture of reality.[64]

He adds, however, that the historian is not justified in assuming that nature is absolutely uniform. Science itself denies that.[65] So the historian must "keep an open mind" when faced with possible events that are not fully explicable according to normal rules.[66]

What place does divine revelation play in our examination of history? Pannenberg doesn't speak directly of revelation in *The Apostles' Creed*, but he deals with the topic extensively elsewhere.[67] For him, there are several kinds of revelation mentioned in Scripture: torah, prophecy, *logos*, and so on. At times, God does convey information to and through prophets. Pannenberg does not, however, affirm "propositional revelation" from God to us today.[68] Rather, he insists that God gives revelation to us "indirectly," that is, through our own rational analysis of historical events. Direct revelation occurs only at the end of history. But the event of Christ in his incarnation, resurrection, and ascension has brought the end-time into our time, in a manner of speaking (see below), and so this event serves as the criterion for our thinking about God.

Among Pannenberg's predecessors, it was fashionable to deny the legitimacy of rational arguments for the existence of God. Obviously, that was the case for the Christian atheists, secular theologians, Paul Tillich, and Jürgen Moltmann, who raised questions about God's very existence. But it was also the case with Barth, Brunner, and Bultmann, who believed that we come to know God by revelation through faith alone. Pannenberg, however, says that the message of Jesus presupposes the real existence of God, and that only his relation to God gives his message universal significance.[69] So Pannenberg deals with the existence of God as a rational question, as he has done the same with the study of history. He argues that the old causal arguments are no longer cogent, because infinite regress is no longer considered absurd, and it is no longer assumed that motion always requires an explanation.[70]

Pannenberg does not, however, affirm "propositional revelation" from God to us today. Rather, he insists that God gives revelation to us "indirectly," that is, through our own rational analysis of historical events.

64. Ibid., 109.

65. Ibid., 111–12; cf. 40–43.

66. Ibid., 112–13.

67. Wolfhart Pannenberg, ed., *Revelation as History*, trans. David Granskou and Edward Quinn (New York: Sheed and Ward, 1969); Pannenberg, *Systematic Theology*, 1:189–257.

68. Recall from our previous studies that to affirm propositional revelation from God is to deny the autonomy of human reason, the heart of liberalism as a distinct form of theology. Although he differs much from his predecessors, Pannenberg is still firmly in the liberal tradition. He does not believe in an inerrant Bible, but rather a Bible that we examine through autonomous reason to evaluate its truth.

69. Pannenberg, *The Apostles' Creed*, 16.

70. Ibid., 21–22.

But he believes there are rational routes to God acceptable even to modern people. Even today we recognize that we are limited beings. But consideration of our limits presupposes knowledge of something beyond those limits and therefore something without limit. This is not, he says, a deductively certain conclusion. Each person must judge for himself whether the concept of God illumines reality for him.[71]

Pannenberg then proceeds to discuss the divine nature and attributes, as they arise out of the history of redemption.[72] Essentially, we know God by Jesus Christ, and vice versa.[73] So we are not free to renounce research into the "historical Jesus" as the existential theologies did. Now, Pannenberg accepts the thesis of Schweitzer and Weiss that Jesus' life and message were determined by his expectation of the immediately impending end of the world. To Schweitzer and Weiss, that thesis made the message of Jesus unbelievable to modern man. Later theologians, including Bultmann, took that eschatology as mythology that had to be reinterpreted in terms of existential self-understanding. But Pannenberg looks for a more historical explanation: Jesus was right. The kingdom *did* indeed appear in the lifetime of Jesus and his disciples, in the resurrection.

The kingdom did indeed appear in the lifetime of Jesus and his disciples, in the resurrection. For Pannenberg, the resurrection, then, is the key to NT Christology.

For Pannenberg, the resurrection, then, is the key to NT Christology. The titles of Jesus—Son of Man, Suffering Servant, Messiah (Christ), Son of God—were appropriate only in the light of the resurrection. Although the Gospels say that Jesus (and others) applied these names to himself through his earthly ministry, Pannenberg believes that this is unhistorical: the church applied these titles to him only after the resurrection and inserted them into the Gospel narratives. The same can be said of events narrated in the Gospels. The virgin birth, Pannenberg says, is a legend presented as a retrospective justification of Jesus' divine sonship. But that sonship was affirmed by the church only after the resurrection, on the basis of the resurrection.

The virgin birth, Pannenberg says, is a legend presented as a retrospective justification of Jesus' divine sonship. But that sonship was affirmed by the church only after the resurrection, on the basis of the resurrection.

What of Jesus' atoning death? Of course, there is no historical problem here; all agree that Jesus did die. But was his death vicarious in some sense? How can historical research answer that question one way or another? Pannenberg attempts to answer this question, and again the resurrection is central to his answer.

Jesus was declared guilty on two charges. The charge of blasphemy was prosecuted by the Jews: Jesus claimed to be God. But the Jews could not execute Jesus on their own authority. So they took him to the Romans. The Romans cared little about the Jews' religion, so the Jews suggested another charge: sedition. Jesus claimed to be a king,

71. Ibid., 22–25.
72. Ibid., 27–178.
73. Ibid., 44–45.

therefore a rival to Caesar. In effect, then, Jesus' death was punishment for blasphemy and for sedition.

But the resurrection proves that both charges were false. In fact, the Jews were the blasphemers, since they denied Jesus' claim. And the Romans were guilty of sedition against God. So Jesus died in the place of both Jews and Gentiles. Together, the officers of the Jews and Gentiles represented the whole human race, so Jesus died for all. His death is vicarious. And not only did he die in the place of his accusers; he took away their guilt by forgiving their sin.[74]

Modern men might say that substitutionary atonement is incredible, even immoral. But in fact, even today there is a corporate dimension to our moral responsibility. Each of us is answerable in some degree for the groups of which we are parts. And the NT is right that each of us does, in fact, live a blasphemous existence apart from grace. So God rightly established the Jews and Pilate as our representatives.[75] As we live and die in faith, we live in solidarity with Jesus' death and its meaning.

Bultmann is said to have remarked that Pannenberg was "clever," and his argument for the vicariousness of the atonement is certainly that. He does not use the traditional argument based on Romans 5 about our solidarity with Adam in sin and our solidarity with Christ in his atonement. For Pannenberg knows that such an appeal to Genesis 3 and Romans 5 could not be validated by autonomous historical scholarship. Instead, he has come up with a different argument that he thinks can be established by historical scholarship alone. But in order to do this, he must appeal to concepts of representation (the Jews and Romans as representatives of the race) and forgiveness of sins that could certainly never be verified by historical scholarship.[76] Like all other liberal theologians, Pannenberg picks and chooses this and that in the Bible, deciding what he can accept and what he (in the name of modern man) must reject. But his choices leave him with less than a plausible case.

Like all other liberal theologians, Pannenberg picks and chooses this and that in the Bible, deciding what he can accept and what he (in the name of modern man) must reject.

The same is true of Pannenberg's account of the resurrection itself, especially important since it is the linchpin of his whole theology. Here we receive a great letdown. Pannenberg has been saying that all depends on the resurrection, and that the resurrection can be established only by historical research. Pannenberg's great level of knowledge and

74. Ibid., 79–87.

75. Ibid., 88–89.

76. At the very least, this is a naturalistic fallacy, an argument from *is* to *ought*. Pannenberg argues that Jesus *ought* to have been released and that we *ought* to accept representation by the Jewish and Gentile leaders, without presenting any *moral* premises to establish his conclusion. This problem is fairly common in Pannenberg, since his whole project is to establish spiritual obligation by means of historical research.

philosophical sophistication leads us to expect that he will produce a historical proof of the resurrection like no other. But his discussion of resurrection leaves us so short of certainty that he leaves his whole theological structure hanging in the air.

First, he tries to clarify what Jesus' resurrection is. It is not "a mere revivification of his body,"[77] but rather a "radical transformation."[78] Revivification would be like the raising of Lazarus, "a temporary return to this life by someone already dead."[79] Radical transformation, however, is a metaphor for a change

> into a reality which is entirely unknown to us—if we have to talk about it at all. For this reality is as such unknown to us; it quite obviously does not belong to the constantly recurring events of our everyday lives.[80]

Pannenberg's discussion of resurrection leaves us so short of certainty that he leaves his whole theological structure hanging in the air.

Though this reality is "entirely unknown to us," Pannenberg does give it some further description. The resurrection body is the "spiritual body" of 1 Corinthians 15:43–44. He explains:

> In Paul's sense God's "Spirit" is the creative origin of all life, and a spiritual body is a living being which, instead of being separated from this origin—as we are in our present existence—remains united with it; so that it is a life which no death can end any more.[81]

*Pannenberg says that Paul's concept of resurrection comes from the Jewish tradition of a general resurrection at the end of the age. In effect, Paul believed that the end of the age had already come in advance—*proleptically*—in Jesus.*

But why did Jesus' disciples come to the conclusion that Jesus' body had been transformed in this way? Pannenberg says that Paul's concept of resurrection comes from the Jewish tradition of a general resurrection at the end of the age.[82] In effect, Paul believed that the end of the age had already come in advance—*proleptically*—in Jesus.

Pannenberg argues that resurrection, so understood, is a meaningful concept. He repeats his earlier argument that since we recognize the limitations of life, we implicitly recognize some knowledge of what lies beyond this limit.[83] We can describe this reality only by analogy with what we know—hence "life after death."[84]

77. Pannenberg, *The Apostles' Creed*, 99.

78. Ibid.

79. Ibid., 100. Pannenberg thinks the accounts of Jesus' raising people from the dead are less credible than the account of his own resurrection.

80. Ibid., 98.

81. Ibid., 98–99. He connects this with Paul's distinction between the perishable and the imperishable in 1 Corinthians 15:50.

82. Ibid., 100–104.

83. Ibid., 105. Cf. 22–24.

84. Ibid., 106.

But what is the historical *argument* that Jesus was raised from the dead? Pannenberg has lectured us often to the effect that assurance of any historical claim can be had only through historical research. So we await eagerly Pannenberg's historical proof of the resurrection of Jesus.

Some level of skepticism is legitimate, he says, because this claim is a claim to a very unusual event, to say the least. But there can be no scientific objection. Science cannot allow us "to establish without more ado the possibility or impossibility of a single event which is otherwise vouched for."[85] To verify the occurrence of such an event, historical research is necessary. And the resurrection, in particular, escapes scientific objection,

> for the happening which is asserted here is one whose final point lies in a sphere which is otherwise totally inaccessible to human experience and which can consequently only be expressed metaphorically or in other forms of language which cannot yet be completely realized and controlled in empirical terms.[86]

Given, then, that the resurrection is *possible*, how shall we evaluate the evidence?

> The traditions about the resurrection do undoubtedly contain legendary elements. But it is impossible to prove that what is at issue is legend as a whole. On the contrary, the state of the traditions speaks against such an assumption, especially as regards the accounts of the appearances, but also in the tradition of Jesus' empty tomb, although in the latter case opinions are divided. Moreover, all attempts to explain the appearance of the risen Jesus as hallucinations have failed up to now. The necessary indications are lacking, or at least insufficient.[87]

Pannenberg has lectured us often to the effect that assurance of any historical claim can be had only through historical research. So we await eagerly Pannenberg's historical proof of the resurrection of Jesus.

He continues:

> In view of this state of affairs, it is, of course, possible to suspend judgment altogether about the kind of events which may lie behind the traditions of Jesus' resurrection. But this means renouncing the possibility of understanding the origins of Christianity. . . . Moreover it is perfectly possible to arrive at

85. Ibid., 110–11.
86. Ibid., 111.
87. Ibid., 113.

> the opinion that, when one has subjected the early Christian traditions of Jesus' resurrection to a critical examination, the description of the event in the language of the eschatological hope still proves itself to be the most plausible, in the face of all rival explanations. Nobody could call this opinion indisputable. This matter is not historically decided, or decidable, in the sense that all further discussion about it is superfluous.

To say the least, Pannenberg's historical argument here falls far short of certainty, as he readily admits.

He reverts, then, to his previous argument that all human knowledge is fragmentary and provisional in the present age.[88] But to confess the resurrection in this context is not without some legitimate historical basis.[89]

To say the least, Pannenberg's historical argument here falls far short of certainty, as he readily admits. Indeed, the question of what happened and why is very obscure, as he presents it. If the whole body of NT teaching rests on this argument of Pannenberg, then it is very uncertain indeed. He sometimes hints that the proleptic coming of the end-time into history provides a criterion of truth that enables us to escape in some measure the *provisionality* of knowledge in this age. (If as he says the end-time will bring us perfect knowledge, then shouldn't the proleptic entrance of the end-time bring us an anticipation of that?) That would be to recognize the resurrection as a kind of revelation that provides certainty in the place of skepticism. But that seems not to be his view. For him, our study of the resurrection itself is caught up in the relativity and fragmentariness of human knowledge, so that there is no place for certainty at all.

Our knowledge, of course, is not exhaustive. It is partial and incomplete (1 Cor. 13:9–12). But incomplete does not mean "uncertain" or "provisional." Pannenberg regularly confuses these concepts.

But contrary to Pannenberg, the fact that the end of history has not arrived in its consummate form does not imply that our knowledge is all provisional. Scripture never draws that inference; quite the contrary. The new covenant is a time of *completed* revelation (Heb. 1:1–3; 2:1–4; 2 Peter 1:3–4). We have no excuse if we fail to understand or believe (Heb. 2:1–4 and other "warning passages"). Our knowledge, of course, is not exhaustive. It is partial and incomplete (1 Cor. 13:9–12). But *incomplete* does not mean "uncertain" or "provisional." Pannenberg regularly confuses these concepts.[90]

And contrary to Pannenberg, God has not made us to investigate history autonomously. Rather, he has revealed himself in history and has proportioned his revelation to our minds in such a way that certainty

88. This is like Hegel's argument that since the "truth is in the whole," we cannot finally claim to know anything until the consummation of knowledge, when the Absolute becomes fully self-conscious.

89. Pannenberg, *The Apostles' Creed*, 114–15.

90. The equation between completeness and certainty is essentially Hegelian.

is possible.[91] I respond enthusiastically to Pannenberg's defense of propositional truth (though denying propositional revelation) and the role of reason in theology. But like every other liberal theologian, he has relegated the study of history to *autonomous* reason, and that is not biblically acceptable, as I have often argued in this volume.

Pannenberg's general view of the resurrection is evidently as follows: After Jesus was killed, something very extraordinary took place among the disciples. It was the occurrence of something that previously was "entirely unknown." Searching for descriptive terminology, they drew on their Jewish eschatology. The most extraordinary event they could conceive of was the last judgment, which included the "resurrection" of the righteous and the wicked. So they used the name *resurrection* as a metaphor to refer to the entirely unknown event they had experienced. And since they had been convinced that Jesus was the Messiah, they took it that the resurrection was of Jesus himself, and that in him the eschatological kingdom of God had come in advance. But that was all metaphorical description of something beyond human language. What actually happened? Only God knows.

But this is not what the Bible teaches about the resurrection—that it is a metaphorical name for something inexpressible. The Bible teaches that the tomb was really empty, that Jesus walked and talked with disciples after his death, that he taught them for forty days, and that he then ascended visibly to heaven. These events are remarkable and unique, but they were not inexpressible; in fact, they are lavishly expressed on the pages of Scripture. Nor are they expressed only in metaphors.

This is not what the Bible teaches about the resurrection—that it is a metaphorical name for something inexpressible.

Now, Pannenberg says that Jesus' resurrection is *more* than this, *more* than a man who (like Lazarus) meets with people after he has died. I grant that. Pannenberg's references to the spiritual body in 1 Corinthians 15 are appropriate and edifying. And in some sense, the resurrection does mark the entrance of the final judgment into history. But the resurrection is not *less* than a set of literal happenings.

Pannenberg's system is interesting mainly for the differences between it and the existential theologies of the early twentieth century. But in the end, the similarities are more significant than the differences. Unlike the earlier theologies, Pannenberg's theology is based on rational historical research. But like them, his theology accepts the autonomy of reason and is therefore unable to establish the fundamentals of the

91. Paul says that the truth of the resurrection is so certain that it is the foundation of the Christian life, so that if it did not occur, our faith is vain, and we are yet in our sins (1 Cor. 15:14, 17). It is not merely probable (Ps. 93:5; Isa. 53:4; John 6:69; 17:8; Acts 12:11; Rev. 22:20). Certainty is one of the blessings of being in Christ (1 John 5:13–15; cf. Luke 1:4; 2 Tim. 1:12; 3:16–17; Heb. 6:18–19; 1 Peter 1:3–9; 2 Peter 1:19–21). See *DWG*, 297–315, and my article "Certainty," at http://www.frame-poythress.org/certainty/, also available as Appendix A in this book.

Christian faith with any level of certainty. In the end, people are left free to decide for themselves whether to accept or reject the argument for the resurrection. If they do not accept it, they are not culpable. If they accept it, they cannot claim that their decision is grounded in the historical evidence. Rather, it is based in something more like faith.

And what is the object of that faith? An ineffable event to which the church has given the name *resurrection*. In the end, that event is very much like Barth's *Geschichte*: an experience that conveys no definite or clear information about God's nature or intentions. We may choose to interpret it according to Jewish eschatological expectations. Then again, we may also choose not to. The cogency of Pannenberg's whole system depends on this choice, not on rational historical scholarship.

Process philosophy developed in England and America out of a secular metaphysics, and then gradually developed into an approach to theology. It is not built on biblical theology or traditional Christian doctrine.

PROCESS THOUGHT

And now for something very different. Process philosophy and theology are not part of the German theological tradition that we have surveyed in the previous chapter and this. This movement developed in England and America out of a secular metaphysics, and then gradually developed into an approach to theology. It is not built on biblical theology or traditional Christian doctrine. There is not a trace here of *conservative drift*, and there is very little respect in this school for biblical authority or church tradition.

The movement might have begun with **Samuel Alexander** (1859–1938), who wrote *Space, Time, and Deity*.[92] But most people today regard **Alfred North Whitehead** (1861–1947) as the movement's founder, with his *Process and Reality: An Essay in Cosmology*[93] as the main text of the movement. In 1910, Whitehead collaborated with Bertrand Russell on the book *Principia Mathematica*,[94] which I will mention in chapter 12. He was a mathematician and physicist who in 1924 (at sixty-three!) went to teach philosophy at Harvard.

Alfred North Whitehead

Both authors of *Principia Mathematica* became philosophical atomists, but in very different ways. An atomist (chapter 2) is a philosopher who seeks to determine the smallest constituents of reality and analyzes them to determine the nature of reality as a whole. Examples of atomists before Whitehead and Russell are Democritus, Epicurus (chapter 2), and Leibniz (chapter 5).[95] Russell and the early Wittgenstein

92. New York: Macmillan, 1920.

93. Ed. David Ray Griffin and Donald W. Sherbourne, corrected ed. (New York: Free Press, 1979) (originally published: New York: Macmillan, 1929).

94. 3 vols. (Cambridge: Cambridge University Press, 1910–13).

95. The opposite metaphysical strategy is *monism*, in which the philosopher tries to characterize being as a whole, and uses that concept as a key to understanding all lesser segments of being. Examples: Parmenides, Plotinus, Spinoza, Hegel.

understood the world as made up of *atomic facts* (chapter 12), Whitehead *atomic processes*.[96] He thought that individual things and facts were abstractions from processes.

Whitehead complained that many philosophers commit the "fallacy of misplaced concreteness"[97] (sometimes called the *fallacy of reification*), namely, the fallacy of talking about an abstract concept as if it were a concrete reality. Many philosophers have accused Plato of that fallacy in his doctrine of Forms, but of course, the question whether Plato commits that fallacy depends on the question whether Plato's theory is right. Whitehead sometimes speaks also of the "fallacy of simple location." What he opposes here is the idea that reality is made up of things that are sharply definable and separate from one another. So he opposes the mind-matter dualism of Descartes. What Descartes called *mind* is not a concrete reality, according to Whitehead, but an abstraction from a reality (experience) in which mental and physical aspects are distinguishable but never separate. Similarly, Whitehead opposes philosophers who have made sharp distinctions between facts and concepts, and between past, present, and future facts. Whitehead's world is a world of processes in which everything flows together, influencing everything else. The actual object of experience is an event intimately connected with a complex ordered environment.[98]

Whitehead calls this event an "actual occasion" or "actual entity." These are "the final real things of which the world is made up."[99] Actual occasions are spatiotemporal occurrences that enter relationships and transactions with one another. They are all bound together in a unified process. Each is itself a process, so motion and change characterize everything *actual* in Whitehead's metaphysics, like that of Heraclitus.[100]

Whitehead complained that many philosophers commit the "fallacy of misplaced concreteness" (sometimes called the fallacy of reification*), namely, the fallacy of talking about an abstract concept as if it were a concrete reality.*

Nothing reaches a point of stability so that it could be defined as *being* in distinction from other independently existing *beings*. There are no Aristotelian substances. Each actual occasion goes through

96. Aristotle understood the world as made up of individual things (*substances*) (chapter 2). The early Wittgenstein thought the world was the collection of *facts* (chapter 12). Whitehead, like Heraclitus (chapter 2), Hegel (chapter 7), John Dewey (chapter 9), and Henri Bergson, believed that the world was made up of *processes*.

97. Alfred North Whitehead, *Science and the Modern World* (New York: Free Press, 1925), 51.

98. Whitehead's reduction of the world to *events* provides one area of commonness between him and the existential tradition.

99. Alfred North Whitehead, *Process and Reality: An Essay in Cosmology* (New York: Macmillan, 1929), 28.

100. We will see later that in process thought "there are unchanging principles of process and abstract forms." John B. Cobb Jr. and David Ray Griffin, *Process Theology: An Introductory Exposition* (Philadelphia: Westminster Press, 1976), 14. These principles are like the *logos* of Heraclitus, like the Forms of Plato.

a cycle similar to that of human life: birth, action, death.[101] This is a process of *becoming* in which the occasion perishes before it reaches a state of *being*.[102] Then the occasion that perished is replaced by others that continue the universal process.

What takes place during the life of an actual occasion, between its birth and its death? Basically, prehension.[103] To *prehend* is to take account of something. Causal interactions, influence, loving relationships, and knowledge are all different kinds of prehension. Each actual occasion has two poles. One is the *physical pole*. Just as a human being is born with physical qualities inherited from his parents, so the actual occasion receives a certain nature by prehending past occasions.[104] The occasion has no control over its physical pole. That aspect of it (him?) is determined.[105] But the occasion also has a *mental pole*, by which it can change itself in various ways. It makes these changes by free choice, understood as libertarian freedom. In remaking itself, the occasion might prehend other entities. It might prehend past actual occasions (as human beings draw on the past by memory and historical research) and use that knowledge as a model for its own becoming. It might prehend contemporary occasions (as human beings draw on friends, authorities, current news, present experience) and allow those to change it in various ways. Or it might prehend ideals that are possible, though not actually existent (see below), or even God (see below).

What takes place during the life of an actual occasion, between its birth and its death? Basically, prehension. To prehend *is to take account of something. Causal interactions, influence, loving relationships, and knowledge are all different kinds of prehension.*

101. In my judgment, Whitehead's analogy between the actual occasion and human life is really too close, as if Whitehead were reading the former off the latter. Where else does his concept of an actual occasion come from? Certainly, Whitehead never claimed to be able to *see* an actual occasion, even with scientific instruments. The concept seems to be an armchair speculation, based on the intuition that the changing, spontaneous universe is unlikely to be made up of static elements. But why should we assume that the most fundamental elements of the universe have essentially the very attributes that constitute human existence? Why should we not accuse Whitehead of the *fallacy of division*, that is, the fallacy of assuming that the parts of something have the same qualities as the whole? A Chevrolet can travel 60 mph, but it would be foolish on this account to assume that the radio in the car can also travel 60 mph.

102. Whitehead quotes a statement of Plato about the world of changing experience and applies it to his own concept of an actual occasion: "But that which is conceived by opinion with the help of sensation and without reason, is always in the process of becoming and perishing and never really is." *Process*, 129. Here is a point of contact between process thought and existentialism (people have no *essence* until they die), and between process thought and Hegelianism (there is no being, only becoming). But what is *being* in this sort of context? Doesn't everything we can discuss have being in some sense? And doesn't Whitehead discuss the characteristics of the actual occasion, virtually interminably?

103. I am reminded of a remark that I heard George Gobel make many years ago on his TV show: "I wasn't overwhelmed; but I wasn't underwhelmed either. I guess you should just say that I was whelmed." So prehension is not necessarily apprehension or comprehension, but some kind of action underlying those concepts.

104. Again, we note a close analogy between an actual occasion and a human being.

105. Determined by past occasions or, alternatively, by God, as we will see.

The occasion also has a mental pole, *by which it can change itself in various ways. It makes these changes by free choice, understood as libertarian freedom. In remaking itself, the occasion might prehend other entities.*

Because actual entities become what they are by interaction with other realities, process thinkers describe them as *essentially related* to one another. Each entity is a *unification* of past entities into a single experience.[106] Cobb and Griffin see here an analogy of *incarnation*, in which the past *enters* us and thereby influences us.

At some point in this process, the actual occasion will perish. But when it perishes, it will still be available for other occasions to prehend. Thus it will be *objectively immortal*. This means that it will *always* be the case that occasion A existed in one time and place and remains as a previous entity to be prehended. George Washington, for example, is dead; but it will always be the case that he lived from 1732 to 1799 and that we can draw instruction from his life.[107]

There are therefore two kinds of processes among the actual occasions. There is *transition*, which is the change from one actual occasion to another, when one dies and another takes its place. The second kind of process is *concrescence*, the process occurring *within* each occasion, as the occasion prehends other entities and chooses to remake itself. Concrescence begins with the *initial aim* of the occasion, a God-given impulse to actualize the best possibility. It continues as the occasion prehends various realities. The initial aim, together with the prehensions, influences (but does not determine) the occasion's *subjective aim*, its free choice of what to become. That leads to its *creative aim*, by which it re-creates itself and seeks to influence other occasions in the future. Again, one would think that this narrative was a human biography.

John B. Cobb

Now, the actual occasion is not only an event, but a unit of experience, the occasion's experience of itself. So each occasion has a kind of *subjective immediacy* or *enjoyment*. Process thinkers believe that all actual occasions have such experience, which in its highest form is *consciousness*. This is true of occasions in every sphere, at every level—not only human life, but the occasions underlying animals and plants as well, even inanimate objects. So Whitehead is a *panpsychist*, like Berkeley and Leibniz; he believes that mind, or something significantly analogous to mind, exists in all reality.[108]

I have pointed out that Whitehead's descriptions of actual entities are highly analogous to the phenomena of human life: birth, learning, choosing, perishing. But for Whitehead, human beings, animals, objects, molecules, electrons, and so on are not actual entities but

106. So Cobb and Griffin, *Process Theology*, 22, urge that we prehend as many past occasions as possible: "our concrete moments of experience are richer to the extent that they include others and are thereby dependent on them."

107. Obviously, this kind of "objective immortality" falls far short of the biblical doctrine of the resurrection of the body.

108. Ethically, Whitehead takes this to imply that every occasion is an end in itself.

groups of actual entities called *societies*. Persons, therefore, are not "true individuals." Personal human existence is a "serially ordered society" of occasions of experience.[109] Societies have a kind of permanence that actual entities do not have. They persist through time,[110] are capable of definition (up to a point), in some cases have memory, and so forth. But of course, in process thought nothing is changeless. Or rather, nothing *actual* is changeless.

So far, I have been describing the processes that Whitehead calls *actual occasions*. But these are only part of Whitehead's world. There are two other modes of being[111] in his metaphysics: eternal objects and God. Eternal objects, or *essences*, are like Platonic Forms or universals.[112] These represent the element of permanence in process metaphysics. But unlike traditional substances, they are not actual, only *potential*. They are *possibilities*. In themselves they are abstract. But they become manifest in concrete reality when they are prehended in various degrees or ways by actual entities. I mentioned earlier that an actual entity can prehend other actual entities, or it can prehend abstract concepts, such as moral ideals. As in Plato, such qualities as courage, virtue, or goodness, at the level of perfection, cannot be found in the world of experience. But somehow we can think of them and seek to incorporate them into our character. We urge our children to do this when we tell them to "develop their potential." For Whitehead, any actual occasion can make a similar decision. When it does, it is prehending an eternal object.

Eternal objects, or essences, are like Platonic Forms or universals. These represent the element of permanence in process metaphysics. But unlike traditional substances, they are not actual, only potential.

The third mode of being is God. Whitehead invoked God to account for the creativity and newness of the world. God answers the question why every actual occasion is different from all past ones. The eternal objects do not answer that question because they are abstract. There must, Whitehead thought, be a being who makes the world of possibilities (eternal objects) available to the actual entities. In addition to this argument, some process thinkers appeal to traditional (or modified) theistic arguments. Charles Hartshorne, for example, uses the ontological argument to show that God is a necessary being, one who must exist in any possible world.

Whitehead invoked God to account for the creativity and newness of the world. God answers the question why every actual occasion is different from all past ones.

109. Cobb and Griffin, *Process Theology*, 15.

110. Some process thinkers believe that actual occasions have temporal extension, however short that extension may be. They have even argued as to the maximum length of an occasion's life span. But that is an odd argument to make about something that doesn't even possess being. Cobb and Griffin, however, believe that time applies only to the process of transition, not to that of concrescence. "In the process of concrescence itself there is no time. . . . Every moment is a now, which in this sense is timeless." Ibid., 16. Later, Cobb and Griffin correlate this experience of the eternal now with Buddhist "emptiness" or "void" (138–39).

111. To use a phrase of Paul Weiss.

112. Whitehead was fond of Plato. He said that all philosophy was a series of footnotes to Plato.

The process God, however, is very different from the God of the Bible. He has two natures or aspects, *primordial* and *consequent*. These are analogous to the two poles of the actual occasions: the mental pole (primordial) and the physical pole (consequent). God's *primordial* nature consists of qualities that must pertain to God in any possible universe and are therefore not dependent on any particular world. These include some of the traditional attributes of God: eternity, absoluteness, independence, unchangeability. Still, these attributes must not all be taken in their traditional senses. Omniscience, for example, does not mean that God knows all things past, present, and future, for that kind of divine knowledge would negate human libertarian freedom. But the process theologians do say that God knows all things that are "knowable," that is, not contingent on the free choice of actual occasions.[113]

There is a close relationship between the primordial nature of God and the eternal objects. Whitehead usually describes that relationship this way: that God prepares the eternal objects, making them relevant for ingression into actual occasions (i.e., relevant so that actual occasions can prehend them).[114] But like the Demiurge of Plato's *Timaeus*, God does not *create* the eternal objects. Indeed, it is not clear in Whitehead how the eternal objects differ from the divine attributes. What seems to be the case is that God's nature and the eternal objects are mutually dependent.[115]

The *consequent* nature of God is his physical pole, by which he carries out the ideals of his mental pole. That nature includes the qualities that he has by virtue of his interaction with actual occasions in one particular world, such as this one. God himself is changing, in process. He responds, therefore, to the changes in the world and adjusts to them. So although he is an absolutely necessary being, he is dependent on the world for his concrete nature. Without the world, he would be abstract, with no definite character. With the world, he is relative to it. Process theologians say that the nature of love requires relativity, dependence, responsiveness. So God is not changeless or static. He changes as his world changes. He enjoys the world; in fact, his enjoyment *is* the enjoyment of creatures.

God himself is changing, in process. He responds, therefore, to the changes in the world and adjusts to them. So although he is an absolutely necessary being, he is dependent on the world for his concrete nature.

We can see that in process theology, God includes the world, though he is above it in some respects. This is sometimes called *panentheism*. *Pantheism* means that God is the universe and the universe is God.

113. Cobb and Griffin, *Process Theology*, 47.

114. I've never understood why the eternal objects are irrelevant without divine help, that is, what is the inadequacy in the eternal objects that makes God necessary.

115. See, e.g., Norman Geisler, "Process Theology," in *Tensions in Contemporary Theology*, ed. Stanley N. Gundry and Alan F. Johnson (Grand Rapids: Baker, 1976), 244.

Panentheism means that the universe is *in* God. The universe is divine, but it does not exhaust the divine. Clearly, at any rate, God and the world affect and change each other. They are mutually dependent, "correlative," as Van Til put it. God does not control everything that takes place in the world. Many things happen simply by the free will of actual occasions. God simply adjusts to those happenings (prehending them) and in effect remakes himself.

So Cobb and Griffin tell us that God's creative activity[116] is based on his responsiveness to the world.[117] It is therefore *persuasive*, not *coercive*. He provides each actual entity with its initial subjective aim—the impulse to actualize the best possibility available.[118] The actual entity may accept or reject this aim. Its rejection, out of its free will, is the source of evil. We should imitate this divine model: seek to persuade others using coercion only as a last resort. This is, of course, a naturalistic fallacy: God accomplishes his will persuasively, so we should, too. Process theology is riddled with naturalistic fallacies, because it is unclear on the source (or reality) of ethical *norms*. The closest Cobb and Griffin come to discussing that question is a passage in which they say that God is not a "cosmic moralist" as in traditional theology. They grant that morality is important, since we should not seek to harm the enjoyment of others. But enjoyment is the source of morality, not the reverse. Seen in this way, the ethics of process theology is a form

God and the world affect and change each other. . . . God does not control everything that takes place in the world. Many things happen simply by the free will of actual occasions.

This is . . . a naturalistic fallacy: God accomplishes his will persuasively, so we should, too. Process theology is riddled with naturalistic fallacies, because it is unclear on the source (or reality) of ethical norms.

116. There is no such thing as creation out of nothing in process theology. God and the world have both existed eternally, for they are correlative. So when process thinkers talk about God's *creative activity*, their concept is closer to the traditional concept of providence. God's *creativity* is like that of a human artist, who makes beautiful things out of various existing materials, as in Plato's *Timaeus*. But see following note on *creativity*.

117. Cobb and Griffin, *Process Theology*, 52–54. In process thought, there is also a quality of the universe that Whitehead called *creativity*. This quality is defined as the striving of the universe toward novelty and change. It is unclear to me how this is distinct from God's own creativity, which the process thinkers also define as the source of novelty and change in the universe. It is also unclear to me how it is related in general to the three modes of being; should we think of it as a fourth? Whitehead compared it to the receptacle of Plato's *Timaeus* and to Aristotle's prime matter (see chapter 2). But I criticized these concepts as unintelligible and therefore as major problems for Plato and Aristotle. Prime matter, for example, has no form, and so is strictly nothing—but it must be something, since Aristotle needs something to *bear* form. Same for Plato's receptacle. Similarly, Whitehead seems to see creativity as a tendency for the universe to take on many different forms, but without sufficient character to delimit those forms. Perhaps in process thought creativity is a kind of *openness* to novelty and change, which God fulfills by bringing new actual occasions into being, a kind of "canvas" on which he can produce works of divine art. That would create a closer analogy between creativity, prime matter, and the receptacle. But it would make creativity itself a more passive principle than Whitehead seems to want it to be. And it is hard to conceive of how this concept could avoid the criticisms that I made against the corresponding Greek concepts.

118. What is "best" here? Cobb and Griffin tend to identify it as complexity. But they give no reason for preferring complexity to simplicity. This is another area in which process thought is rendered implausible because of its lack of a source of ethical norms.

of utilitarianism, an approach to ethics often criticized for its lack of straightforward ethical norms.[119]

According to Cobb and Griffin, the process God does not favor the status quo, as in their opinion traditional theism does. The process God favors novelty and risks, to achieve the goal of "the enjoyment of intense experience."[120] Though he seeks to persuade us of the best way to live, he doesn't know whether he'll be successful. He sometimes fails, and feels the hurt of failure.[121]

So far, this thought-system is more like philosophy than theology (though I am pretty flexible with this distinction). Whitehead himself was not much interested in Christology, soteriology, or eschatology. But some of his disciples came to see ways in which Whitehead's metaphysics could be developed into a full-scale theology. Among those who pursued that goal: **Charles Hartshorne** (1897–2000), **John B. Cobb** (1925–), **David Ray Griffin** (1939–), **Schubert Ogden** (1928–), **Norman Pittenger** (1905–97), and **Daniel Day Williams** (1910–73).

As an outline for one form of process theology, I will summarize the rest of the book by Cobb and Griffin, *Process Theology: An Introductory Exposition*, to which I have referred often already.

1. Cobb and Griffin seek to do justice to feminist concerns.[122] The assertion that God is persuasive rather than coercive and that he is, in some respects, passive in respect to the world seems to them to encourage the use of female imagery for God. But doesn't this idea rely on images of women (passive, suffering, changeable) that feminists often regard as stereotypical?[123]
2. Cobb and Griffin believe that process theology is capable of reconciling creation and evolution. Indeed, they argue that God could not have brought about the present nature of creation except by small changes occurring over billions of years. For the process God cannot do anything coercively, only persuasively, and therefore over many acts of persuading actual occasions to take on higher forms, leading to higher levels of enjoyment.[124] Of course, as I mentioned before, there is no place in process

The process God favors novelty and risks, to achieve the goal of "the enjoyment of intense experience." Though he seeks to persuade us of the best way to live, he doesn't know whether he'll be successful.

119. Cobb and Griffin, *Process Theology*, 54–57. See my treatment of utilitarianism in *DCL*, 96–100.

120. Cobb and Griffin, *Process Theology*, 59. This is almost like the crude hedonism of the Greek Cyrenaics.

121. Ibid., 60–61. As to whether God has feelings, see my *DG*, 608–11. As to whether he can suffer loss, see the same volume, 611–16.

122. Cobb and Griffin, *Process Theology*, 61–62, 132–36.

123. This same problem invalidates much of what is said about God in feminist circles today. For a more elaborate discussion of God and gender, see my *DG*, 378–86.

124. Cobb and Griffin, *Process Theology*, 63–68.

thought for creation out of nothing. So process thought reconciles creation and evolution by redefining creation.

3. They respond to the problem of evil (how is evil consistent with the goodness of God?) by appealing to human libertarian freedom, as in many previous theological accounts. God is interested, they say, not only in minimizing discord, but in creating increased complexity and therefore greater capacity for enjoyment of different kinds of good.[125] My response: if the suffering of the world is for the sake of more complex prehensions, I doubt if it has been worth it.[126]
4. They encourage an "ecological attitude" by emphasizing (a) the interdependence of all beings, and (b) the striving of all nature for "enjoyment."[127]
5. In regard to human existence, they cite a number of parallels between process thought and existentialism. In both, (a) existence precedes essence, (b) the future is radically open, (c) our being is not apart from the world; we are *being-in-the-world*, and (d) we should seek "authentic existence." But process thinkers differ from some other existentialist views: (a) Life is *being-toward-death*. Cobb and Griffin say that human death is important, but more fundamental is the doctrine of "perpetual perishing," the loss of each actual occasion. (b) For existentialists, persons "share" the world, but in Whitehead, individuality and participation are correlative. (c) For Whitehead, *all* creatures, not only man, have a "being in the world." God also faces a worldly environment. (d) For both process thinkers and existentialists, "decision" is important; but process thinkers are more concerned with "enjoyment" as a goal, rather than moral perfection. (e) Process thinkers seek not mere liberation from the past, as existentialism, but a creative synthesis of elements of the past. (f) For process thinkers, human existence is both *historisch* and *geschichtlich*. The meaning of human life (*Geschichte*) presupposes its evolutionary origin and development (*Historie*). (g) Beyond "authentic existence," which can be a form of self-preoccupation, process thinkers, like the NT, call us to love. (h) We can become more loving through being open to God's creative and responsive love. God gives us assurance that we are accepted despite sin.[128]

Cobb and Griffin respond to the problem of evil (how is evil consistent with the goodness of God?) by appealing to human libertarian freedom, as in many previous theological accounts.

For both process thinkers and existentialists, "decision" is important; but process thinkers are more concerned with "enjoyment" as a goal, rather than moral perfection.

125. Ibid., 69–75.

126. For my response to the problem of evil, see *AJCB*, 155–88; *DG*, 160–82.

127. Cobb and Griffin, *Process Theology*, 76–79, 144–58.

128. Ibid., 80–94. But sin is, according to Cobb and Griffin, an inevitable part of our evolutionary development. It is not clear how we can be held responsible for it.

6. Christ, according to Cobb and Griffin, is the primordial nature of God, present in creatures as their initial aim. He provides creative possibilities in which otherwise discordant elements can be harmoniously united, increasing enjoyment. This is called *creative transformation*. The man Jesus of Nazareth teaches in such a way as to open us to the possibilities of creative transformation. So as in liberal theology generally, Jesus is at best a human teacher, symbolic of a metaphysical principle.[129]
7. Process theologians differ among themselves as to the doctrine of the Trinity.[130] That doctrine is especially difficult to reconcile with the process concept of God, since that concept is dipolar, not tripolar. But for Cobb and Griffin, the Son is the primordial nature of God, the Spirit the consequent nature. What the Cobb-Griffin theology lacks is a coherent concept of God the *Father*. The authors recognize that, with some embarrassment:

> The doctrine of the Trinity is the heart of Christian faith, a source of distortion, and an artificial game that has brought theology into justifiable disrepute.[131]

I will leave Cobb and Griffin at this point, though they do continue on to say various things about the doctrine of the church and eschatology. It should be evident that process theology is a liberal theology, misusing biblical concepts to symbolize a philosophical metaphysics and to press various ethical themes.

OPEN THEISM

Open theism is similar to process theology in some ways, but it emerges from a different background. . . . [Its] arguments are not primarily philosophical, but biblical.

Open theism is similar to process theology in some ways, but it emerges from a different background. Process thought is the development of a secular metaphysics, but the recent exponents of open theism began, for the most part, as evangelical Christians.[132] Their arguments are not primarily philosophical, but biblical. Wikipedia sets forth the following recent history of the movement:

> The term "open theism" was introduced in 1980 with theologian Richard Rice's book *The Openness of God: The Relationship of*

129. Ibid., 95–108.
130. Ibid., 108–10.
131. Ibid., 109.
132. They have drawn on some historical positions. The open-theist view that God does not know the future exhaustively was anticipated by Faustus and Lelio Socinus in the sixteenth century, and a number of theologians of the eighteenth (Samuel Fancourt, Arthur Ramsey) and nineteenth (Isaak August Dorner, Gustav Fechner, Otto Pfleiderer, Jules Lequier, Adam Clarke) centuries.

> *Divine Foreknowledge and Human Free Will*.[133] The broader articulation of open theism was given in 1994, when five essays were published by Evangelical scholars (including Rice) under the title *The Openness of God*.[134] Theologians of note currently espousing this view include: Clark Pinnock (deceased as of 2010), John E. Sanders, Jürgen Moltmann, Richard Rice, Gregory Boyd, Thomas Jay Oord, C. Peter Wagner, John Polkinghorne, Karen Winslow, Hendrikus Berkhof, Alan Rhoda, Adrio Konig, Harry Boer, Thomas Finger (Mennonite), W. Norris Clarke (Roman Catholic), Brian Hebblethwaite, Robert Ellis, Kenneth Archer (Pentecostal), Barry Callen (Church of God), Henry Knight III, Gordon Olson, and Winkie Pratney. A significant number of philosophers of religion affirm it: William Hasker, David Basinger, Nicholas Wolterstorff, Dean Zimmerman, Timothy O'Connor, Richard Swinburne, Peter Van Inwagen, James D. Rissler, Robin Collins (philosopher/theologian/physicist), J. R. Lucas, Vincent Brümmer, Peter Geach, Richard Purtill, A. N. Prior, Dale Tuggy, and Keith Ward. Biblical scholars Terence E. Fretheim and John Goldingay affirm it. Others include writers Madeleine L'Engle and Paul C. Borgman, mathematician D. J. Bartholomew and biochemist Arthur Peacocke.[135]

A number of these writers (not all) come out of the Arminian theological tradition, and their open theism is a response to a problem in Arminian theology.

A number of these writers (not all) come out of the Arminian theological tradition, and their open theism is a response to a problem in Arminian theology. Traditional Arminianism teaches (1) that man has libertarian freedom, so God does not control all things, and (2) that God nevertheless *foreknows* everything that comes to pass. Arminians think (2) is important in the doctrine of salvation. They do not want to maintain, with Calvinists, that God chooses (elects) people to salvation merely by his own power. Rather, they want to affirm that God *foreknows* how each person will respond (freely) to his offers of grace and prepares his blessings accordingly.

If God foreknows everything that happens, he thereby renders every event certain. If God knew in 1931 that I would publish this book in 2015, then it would certainly happen. I would not be free to avoid writing and publishing it.

But if God foreknows everything that happens, he thereby renders every event certain. If God knew in 1931 that I would publish this book in 2015, then it would certainly happen. I would not be free to avoid

133. Originally published by the Seventh-Day Adventist publishing house Review and Herald, but withdrawn because of controversy. Republished as *God's Foreknowledge and Man's Free Will* (Grand Rapids: Baker/Bethany House, 1994).

134. Downers Grove, IL: InterVarsity Press, 1994.

135. Wikipedia, s.v. "Open Theism," http://en.wikipedia.org/wiki/Open_theism. I regret that in my book *NOG* I included the name of Steven T. Davis in a list of advocates of open theism. In fact, he was a critic of the movement. I have asked Prof. Davis's forgiveness for this error. I repent of my foolish carelessness and consequent failure to protect a brother's reputation.

writing and publishing it. So if God foreknows everything, everything that happens must happen, and there can be no libertarian free will.[136] There are two possible solutions to this dilemma: either deny libertarian free will (as in Calvinism) or deny exhaustive divine foreknowledge. Open theists choose the second alternative.

This choice leads to a theology that differs from traditional evangelicalism in a number of ways. Richard Rice summarizes the open-theist view of God in the following propositions.[137] I paraphrase and summarize them here, using much of Rice's own language:

1. Love is God's most important quality.
2. Love is not only care and commitment, but also being sensitive and responsive.
3. Creatures exert an influence on God.
4. God's will is not the ultimate explanation of everything. History is the combined result of what God and his creatures decide to do.
5. God does not know everything timelessly, but learns from events as they take place.
6. So God is dependent on the world in some ways.

Of course, the most pervasive and significant proposition of the open theists is one that Rice does not include on his list:

7. Human beings are free in the libertarian sense.

If God foreknows everything, everything that happens must happen, and there can be no libertarian free will. There are two possible solutions to this dilemma: either deny libertarian free will (as in Calvinism) or deny exhaustive divine foreknowledge. Open theists choose the second alternative.

I have defined *libertarian freedom* elsewhere in this volume, but for our present discussion it will be useful to have before us the definition of William Hasker, an open theist:

> An agent is free with respect to a given action at a given time if at that time it is within the agent's power to perform the action and also in the agent's power to refrain from the action.[138]

On this view, our free choices are absolutely undetermined and uncaused. They are not foreordained by God, or by circumstances,

136. This is true even if we reject the notion that God makes everything happen. The relevant point is the *certain occurrence of all events*, whether by divine action or some other determining factor(s). In our example, if God did not make me write the book, then someone or something else did, and it is on the basis of that causality that God foreknew my writing of the book. So exhaustive divine foreknowledge implies determinism, whether or not that determinism is the result of divine causality.

137. Richard Rice, "Biblical Support," in *The Openness of God*, 15–16.

138. Hasker, "A Philosophical Perspective," in ibid., 136–37.

or even by our own character or desires. In open theism, this view of freedom not only is maintained and defended, but becomes a kind of "grid" that tests every other theological statement. It is bad enough when a theologian affirms an erroneous view, but much worse when he makes it a fundamental principle, using it as a presupposition governing the whole structure of his theology.

Libertarian freedom was, arguably, the chief view of freedom among the church fathers (chapter 3), following suggestions of Greek philosophers such as Epicurus (chapter 2). The medieval thinkers were somewhat inconsistent or ambiguous in their views of freedom (chapter 4), but Luther and Calvin rejected libertarianism, as did Calvin's successors.[139] The Socinians and Arminians, however, embraced libertarian free will.

In open theism, this view of freedom not only is maintained and defended, but becomes a kind of "grid" that tests every other theological statement.

Now, I have interacted extensively with the assertion and arguments of the open theists. My *NOG* deals specifically with the open-theist literature, and my *DG* treats in various locations the theological issues of the debate. Here I will respond briefly to the seven chief assertions of the open theists.

1. *Love is God's most important quality.* Scripture does say, "God is love" (1 John 4:8, 16). But it also says, "God is light" (1 John 1:5) and "God is spirit" (John 4:24). It also closely identifies with God's being the attributes of jealousy (Ex. 34:14), holiness (Isa. 6:3), and lordship (Ex. 3:14; Deut. 6:4; Rom. 10:9).[140] All of these and other divine attributes are closely related to one another, so that it is perilous to claim that one attribute is "more important" than another.
2. *Love is not only care and commitment, but also being sensitive and responsive.* Certainly God in Scripture is sensitive. Part of his omniscience is that he knows exactly how his creatures feel. And the biblical doctrine of prayer makes it clear that he responds to our cries.[141] So the open theists are right to think that God's love in Scripture is sensitive and responsive. But many open theists seem to have a further idea about God's love that is more controversial: vulnerability.[142] It is a fairly common idea that someone must be vulnerable in order to love someone else. But is that really true? On the contrary, I think we value in a lover

The open theists are right to think that God's love in Scripture is sensitive and responsive. But many open theists seem to have a further idea about God's love that is more controversial: vulnerability.

139. Luther's successors adopted a view in which fallen man is able to "resist" the power of the gospel.

140. God is called "Lord" in Scripture over seven thousand times.

141. How can God be responsive to our prayers if God controls the outcome of our prayers before we utter them? Because his eternal plan has established that many events on earth take place because of prayer.

142. Clark Pinnock, "Systematic Theology," in *The Openness of God*, 103.

the kind of love that will hold us fast, from which nothing can separate us. And that is the kind of love that Scripture ascribes to God (John 10:28–29; Rom. 8:35).

3. *Creatures exert an influence on God.* As I mentioned under point 2, God's love is responsive in the sense that he responds to the prayers of his creatures. But that responsiveness is by his prior ordination. Creatures do not determine that prior ordination. They do not determine what God is or make him change his eternal plan. He is what he is (Ex. 3:14). And everything that creatures do is itself controlled by God (Lam. 3:37–38; Rom. 8:28; 11:33–36; Eph. 1:11).
4. *God's will is not the ultimate explanation of everything.* History is the combined result of what God and his creatures decide to do. The passages cited under point 3 show that in fact God is the ultimate explanation of everything.[143]
5. *God does not know everything timelessly, but learns from events as they take place.* The *timelessness* of God is a difficult issue, but it is clear in Scripture that God's relation to time is different from ours. He has no beginning or end. In some sense, he does not change (Mal. 3:6). Time never moves too fast for him, or too slow (2 Peter 3:8). He has complete sovereignty, then, over the timing of events. These differences from human experience justify the metaphor that God is "above time." But open theists argue that God is sometimes ignorant of the future and needs to learn as events actually happen. One example is Genesis 22:12, in which, following Abraham's obedient willingness to sacrifice his son Isaac, God says, "Now I know that you fear God." But if God was ignorant here, he was ignorant not only of the future, but of the present—the state of Abraham's heart. And open theists usually say that God knows everything in the present. It is better, I think, to take this and similar passages to describe God's *testing* of human beings. There is, of course, a period of time between the test and the verdict. The verdict is presented in the words "Now I know . . ." But this phrase does not indicate that God was ignorant in advance of what the verdict would be.

Scripture says . . . that God does not need anything, certainly not the support of the things he has made (Acts 17:25). This is because he has created all things (Gen. 1:1) and brings to pass everything that happens (Eph. 1:11).

6. *So God is dependent on the world in some ways.* Scripture says, to the contrary, that God does not need anything, certainly not the support of the things he has made (Acts 17:25). This is because he has created all things (Gen. 1:1) and brings to pass everything that happens (Eph. 1:11).

143. I included many other passages to this effect in *DG* and in *NOG*, citing God's sovereignty in the natural world, human history, individual human lives, human decisions, human sins, faith, and salvation.

7. *Human beings are free in the libertarian sense.* The passages I cited under point 3 above, and many others, show that God is the ultimate cause of everything that happens. So God is the cause of our free decisions, eliminating the possibility that those decisions are free in the libertarian sense. We do make free decisions in the *compatibilist* sense, in the sense that we do what we want to do. But that does not imply that any of our actions have no cause. In the following passages, we read about God's causing the free decisions of certain people, such as Joseph's brothers (Gen. 45:5–8), Cyrus (Isa. 44:28), and Judas (Luke 22:22; Acts 2:23–24; 3:18; 4:27–28; 13:27).

God is the cause of our free decisions, eliminating the possibility that those decisions are free in the libertarian sense. We do make free decisions in the compatibilist *sense, in the sense that we do what we want to do. But that does not imply that any of our actions have no cause.*

POSTLIBERAL THEOLOGY

In the previous chapter I cited the *Hartford Declaration*, which rejected radical and secular types of theology. But what would replace those movements in the American theological dialogue? **George Lindbeck** (1923–), one of the signers of the *Declaration*, in 1984 published a book called *The Nature of Doctrine: Religion and Theology in a Postliberal Age*.[144] In that book, he says that we need not new doctrines, but a new understanding of what doctrines are. What he offers is what is sometimes called *metatheology*, a study of theological method, structure, purpose. In the past, he says, doctrine has been understood as propositional truth (as in orthodoxy) or as the articulation of religious experience (liberalism, especially Schleiermacher). There is, however, a third alternative: doctrine is a kind of *language*. Language is a system of symbols that we use to do different jobs in our common life.[145]

So, says Lindbeck, doctrine provides the religious community with a way of talking, and hence, as in all language, a set of "rules" by which many things can be done and said. In that way he is able to reject propositional revelation and theology (following the liberal tradition), but also to reject certain theological formulations as "out of order" (as in orthodoxy), as he did by signing the *Hartford Declaration*. Creeds, he thinks, are not simply to be repeated, but to be used as tools for saying other things, as when we study grammatical principles. For example, we learn the Latin conjugation *amo, amas, amat*, not to repeat it endlessly but so that we may learn to say other things, such as *rogo, rogas, rogat*.

[According to] Lindbeck, doctrine provides the religious community with a way of talking, and hence, as in all language, a set of "rules" by which many things can be done and said.

Lindbeck tries very hard to show that on his theory some doctrines

144. Philadelphia: Westminster Press, 1984. Disclosure: Lindbeck was one of my teachers at Yale, 1964–68. I reviewed the book in my *DKG*, 380–81.

145. This is essentially the view of Ludwig Wittgenstein in his later work (see chapter 12). Postliberalism in general is highly dependent on Wittgenstein's views of language and meaning. In the book, he also appeals to modern anthropologists (as Clifford Geertz), linguists (e.g., Noam Chomsky), and philosophers of science (e.g., Thomas Kuhn).

may be regarded as superior to others, even infallible. I don't think he succeeds. He offers us "rules," but doesn't offer us any means of judging what rules we ought to use.[146] I do think, however, that once we accept (as Lindbeck does not) an orthodox view of Scripture, then we can learn much from his theory. Doctrine, I believe, is all three things: propositional truth claims, expressions of the inner experiences of regeneration and sanctification, and rules for the speech and conduct of God's people. In terms of my triperspectival understanding (chapter 1), we may call these *existential*, *situational*, and *normative*, respectively. None of them needs to be considered prior to the others if all three are determined by the content of Scripture. And I do also appreciate the implication of Lindbeck's theory that the work of theology can be described as the application of God's norms to all the different situations of life; see fig. 11.3.

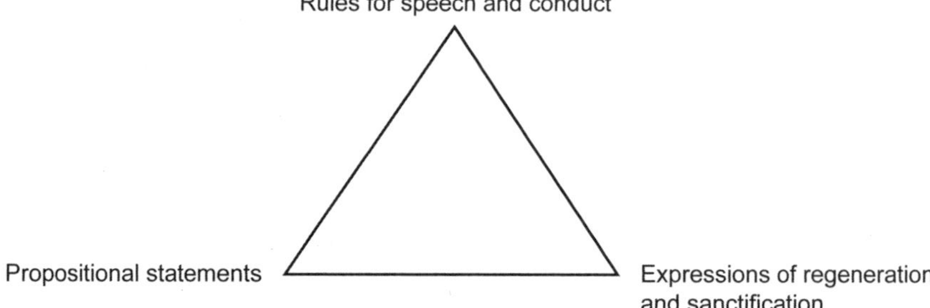

Fig. 11.3. Lindbeck's Perspectives for Theological Speech

Doctrine, I believe, is all three things: propositional truth claims, expressions of the inner experiences of regeneration and sanctification, and rules for the speech and conduct of God's people.

But Lindbeck believes that his construal of Scripture as rules of speech *excludes* the other two historical methods of reading the Bible. I think, rather, that it ought to *include* them, so that each of the three defines the other two.

The postliberal movement has also appealed to other writers who have gone into more detail on the nature of the rules of theology, especially as they pertain to biblical exegesis. An important milestone was *The Eclipse of Biblical Narrative: A Study in Eighteenth and Nineteenth Century Hermeneutics*[147] by **Hans W. Frei** (1922–88). Frei argued that the theologians of the Enlightenment had distorted Scripture by trying to adjust it to models that it did not fit: either a textbook of eternal truths or a set of data for critical historians. On the contrary, Frei said: the Bible is *narrative*, a *story* of the dramatic events from creation to consummation.[148]

146. His metatheology seems to require a meta-metatheology.

147. New Haven, CT: Yale University Press, 1974.

148. Here Frei's concern has much in common with that of the *Heilsgeschichte* theologians (see chapter 10) and the conservative redemptive-history movement.

Frei, like Lindbeck, was setting forth "rules" for doing theology, rather than making theological claims as such: metatheology rather than theology. His book set in motion a movement sometimes called *narrative theology* or *story theology* (David Kelsey, Stanley Hauerwas, Michael Novak, Sam Keen, Harvey Cox,[149] Michael Goldberg, George Stroup), in which many advocated "telling the story" with varying views on whether and in what way the story was true. Because Lindbeck, Frei, Childs (below), and David Kelsey taught at Yale and Hauerwas studied there, the movement is sometimes called the *Yale theology*.

Frei, like Lindbeck, was setting forth "rules" for doing theology, rather than making theological claims as such: metatheology rather than theology.

The OT scholar **Brevard Childs** (1923–2007) also contributed to this project, with two important books.[150] Childs, like Frei, was concerned that the historical-critical method, the method of determining the real history behind Scripture by autonomous historical study, had reduced the meaning of Scripture in the church. When the church received Scripture as its canon, it was not as a good source of historical information. It was because they believed the "story" and received it as the Word of God. So the projects of biblical critics were largely irrelevant to the theological role of Scripture. The church is not interested in the supposed real history behind the biblical writers' representations, those facts that the source critics and form critics labored to find. The church was moved not by some precanonical form of Scripture (such as the supposed sources of the Pentateuch, or the "Q" sayings of Jesus), but by the canonical documents we have today. We should be focusing on those canonical documents when we tell the story through preaching and teaching.

Childs' approach became known as canon criticism, in parallel with source criticism, form criticism, and redaction criticism. But it merges very easily into the concerns of narrative theology, and it fills in some "rules" of Lindbeck's metatheology.

Childs' approach became known as *canon criticism*, in parallel with *source criticism*, *form criticism*, and *redaction criticism*. But it merges very easily into the concerns of narrative theology, and it fills in some "rules" of Lindbeck's metatheology: to summarize, Bible students should give priority to the canonical form of Scripture (i.e., the narrative) over any historical reconstruction of the canonical text.

Postliberal theology is a good example of what I have called the *conservative drift*. The postliberal scholars have a passionate desire to develop a theology that can be preached, one that sounds very much like the gospel of traditional orthodoxy. A postliberal preacher may expound Israel's crossing of the Red Sea, for example without even posing the question whether it "really happened," using the story to draw our attention to God's covenant faithfulness in our lives today. What can be wrong with that?

149. Yes, the same one I listed in chapter 10 as a secular theologian. He was both.

150. *Biblical Theology in Crisis* (Philadelphia: Westminster Press, 1970) and *Introduction to the Old Testament as Scripture* (Philadelphia: Fortress, 1979). See also his *Biblical Theology of the Old and New Testaments: Theological Reflection on the Christian Bible* (Philadelphia: Fortress, 1993).

But in fact, it is often very important whether a Bible story "really happened," as Paul says about the resurrection of Christ (1 Cor. 15:12–19). In Jesus' parables, reference to real history is not a relevant consideration. But when careful exegesis reveals that a Bible passage intends to describe a literal happening, then the authority of the Bible requires us to believe that it describes that happening truly.

As with Barth and others, the postliberal theologians are trying to allow complete freedom to would-be autonomous historical critics of the Bible, while accepting the biblical narrative as something other than real history. The former purpose is rationalist, the latter irrationalist. The result, unfortunately, is that postliberalism does not take us beyond liberalism in any substantive way; see fig. 11.4.

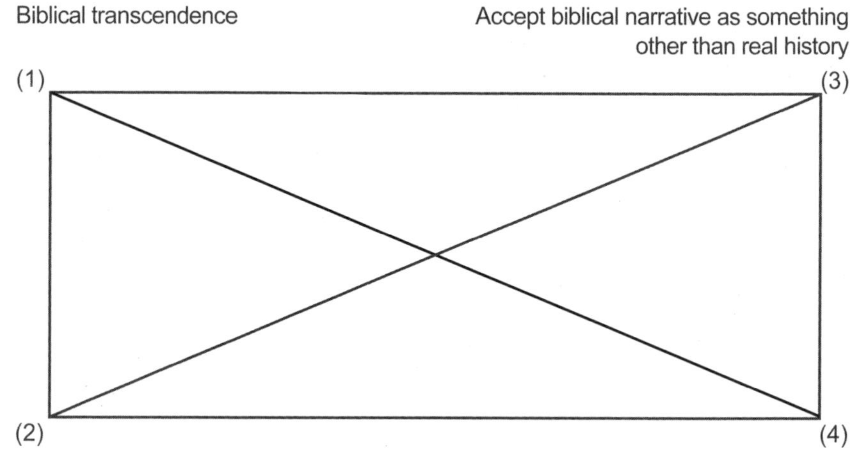

Fig. 11.4. Rationalism and Irrationalism in Postliberalism

When careful exegesis reveals that a Bible passage intends to describe a literal happening, then the authority of the Bible requires us to believe that it describes that happening truly.

KEY TERMS

- Ernst Bloch
- Epiphany (Moltmann)
- Kenotic Christology (Moltmann)
- Constantinian model
- Desperation
- Praxis
- Analytical tool
- Conversion to the neighbor
- Zealots
- Vulnerability of Christianity (Pannenberg)
- Open future
- Apocalypse (Moltmann)
- Sin (Moltmann)
- Presumption
- Black theology
- Conflictual
- Theology (Gutierrez)
- God's infinite salvific will
- Universal sacrament of salvation
- Indirect revelation (Pannenberg)
- Revivification

Provisionality
Atomic processes
Fallacy of reification
Actual occasion
Prehension
Mental pole
Incarnation (Whitehead)
Transition
Initial aim
Subjective immediacy
Consciousness (Whitehead)
True individuals
God (Whitehead)
Consequent nature
Correlative
Coercive
Creativity (Whitehead)
Open theism
Metatheology
Narrative theology
Proleptic
Fallacy of misplaced concreteness
Fallacy of simple location
Fallacy of division
Physical pole
Essentially related
Objectively immortal
Concrescence
Creative aim
Enjoyment
Societies (Whitehead)
Eternal objects
Primordial nature
Panentheism
Persuasive
Cosmic moralist
Creative transformation
Postliberalism
Rules (Lindbeck)
Canon criticism

STUDY QUESTIONS

1. Frame says that the thinkers discussed in this chapter are less influenced by Kant and more influenced by Hegel and Marx. Discuss this thesis in regard to Moltmann, Gutierrez, Pannenberg, Whitehead.
2. How does Moltmann agree with Bloch? Disagree? Comment.
3. Evaluate Moltmann's criticisms of Schweitzer, Barth, Bultmann, secular theology.
4. Evaluate Frame's critique of Moltmann's theology of hope, and state your own.
5. How do the thinkers in this chapter oppose propositional revelation? Consider Moltmann, Gutierrez, Pannenberg, Whitehead, postliberalism.
6. Is Moltmann rationalist? Irrationalist? Both? Neither? Discuss.
7. According to liberation theologians, what are the conditions of rightly understanding the Bible?
8. "All theology must take its bearings from the *axis* of oppression and liberation." Explain; evaluate.
9. "So theology is the critical reflection on praxis, from within praxis." Explain; evaluate. How does Assmann expand this principle? Evaluate that as well.

OUTLINE

Jürgen Moltmann (1926–)
The Theology of Liberation
Wolfhart Pannenberg (1928–2014)
Process Thought
Open Theism
Postliberal Theology

10. Is Gutierrez a Marxist? Discuss.
11. How does Gutierrez question Moltmann's "future-oriented" theology? Evaluate.
12. Describe and discuss Jesus' relation to the Zealots.
13. Describe and evaluate Pannenberg's view of reason and its role in theology. How does he differ from Barth in that respect? Does he recognize any deficiencies in or limitations to human reason?
14. Describe and evaluate Pannenberg's view of the role of presuppositions in historical study.
15. Describe and evaluate Pannenberg's argument for the existence of God.
16. How does Pannenberg evaluate the thesis of Schweitzer and Weiss that Jesus' teaching was consistently eschatological?
17. Describe and evaluate Pannenberg's views of the virgin birth and the vicarious atonement.
18. Same in regard to his view of Jesus' resurrection. Evaluate Frame's response.
19. Compare Pannenberg with the existential theologians. Do you agree with Frame's evaluation? Why or why not?
20. Describe an actual entity according to Whitehead, including its birth, action, and death. Frame says, "In my judgment, Whitehead's analogy between the actual occasion and human life is really too close, as if Whitehead were reading the former off the latter." Explain; evaluate.
21. How does Whitehead reconcile determinism and freedom? Evaluate.
22. Is Whitehead a panpsychist? Discuss.
23. Why are human beings not "true individuals," according to Whitehead? Discuss.
24. Describe Whitehead's concept of God. Evaluate.
25. Compare Cobb and Griffin's doctrine of human existence with existentialism.
26. Describe and evaluate the Christology of Cobb and Griffin.
27. Same for their doctrine of the Trinity.
28. How does open theism differ from traditional Arminianism? Why does it make that move?
29. Summarize the distinctive position of open theism. Evaluate.
30. Describe and evaluate the theses of George Lindbeck.
31. Same for Hans Frei, Brevard Childs.

BIBLIOGRAPHY: TWENTIETH-CENTURY LIBERAL THEOLOGY, PART 2

Print

Boff, Leonardo. *Introducing Liberation Theology.* Maryknoll, NY: Orbis Books, 1987.

Bonino, José Miguez. *Doing Theology in a Revolutionary Situation.* Minneapolis: Fortress, 1975. One of the few Protestants in the movement of liberation theology. Particularly interesting in his epistemological reflections.

Boyd, Gregory. *God of the Possible: A Biblical Introduction to the Open View of God.* Grand Rapids: Baker, 2000.

Childs, Brevard S. *Biblical Theology in Crisis.* Philadelphia: Westminster Press, 1970.

———. *Biblical Theology of the Old and New Testaments: Theological Reflection on the Christian Bible.* Minneapolis: Fortress, 2012.

Cobb, John B., Jr., and David Ray Griffin. *Process Theology: An Introductory Exposition.* Louisville, KY: Westminster John Knox Press, 1996.

Cone, James H. *A Black Theology of Liberation.* Maryknoll, NY: Orbis Books, 2011.

Frame, John M. *No Other God: A Response to Open Theism.* Phillipsburg, NJ: P&R Publishing, 2001.

Frei, Hans W. *The Eclipse of Biblical Narrative: A Study in Eighteenth and Nineteenth Century Hermeneutics.* New Haven, CT: Yale University Press, 1980.

Gutierrez, Gustavo. *A Theology of Liberation.* Maryknoll, NY: Orbis Books, 1988.

Hartshorne, Charles. *The Divine Relativity.* New Haven, CT: Yale University Press, 1982.

Johnson, Elizabeth A. *She Who Is: The Mystery of God in Feminist Theological Discourse.* New York: Crossroad Publishing, 2002.

Lacugna, Catherine Mowry, ed. *Freeing Theology: The Essentials of Theology in Feminist Perspective.* New York: HarperOne, 1993.

Lindbeck, George A. *The Nature of Doctrine: Religion and Theology in a Postliberal Age.* Louisville, KY: Westminster John Knox Press, 2009.

Moltmann, Jürgen. *The Crucified God: The Cross of Christ as the Foundation and Criticism of Christian Theology.* Translated by R. A. Wilson and John Bowden. Minneapolis: Fortress, 1993.

———. *Theology of Hope: On the Ground and the Implications of a Christian Eschatology.* Translated by James W. Leitch. Minneapolis: Fortress, 1993.

———. *The Trinity and the Kingdom: The Doctrine of God.* Translated by Margaret Kohl. Minneapolis: Fortress, 1993.

Pannenberg, Wolfhart. *The Apostles' Creed in the Light of Today's Questions.* Translated by Margaret Kohl. London: SCM Press, 1972.

———. *Jesus, God and Man.* Translated by Lewis L. Wilkins and Duane A. Priebe. Philadelphia: Westminster Press, 1977.

———. *Systematic Theology.* Translated by Geoffrey W. Bromiley. 3 vols. Grand Rapids: Eerdmans, 1991–98.

———. *Theology and the Kingdom of God.* Edited by Richard John Neuhaus. Philadelphia: Westminster Press, 1969.

Ware, Bruce A. *God's Lesser Glory: The Diminished God of Open Theism.* Wheaton, IL: Crossway, 2000.

Whitehead, Alfred North. *Process and Reality: An Essay in Cosmology.* Edited by David Ray Griffin and Donald W. Sherbourne. Corrected ed. New York: Free Press, 1979.

———. *Religion in the Making: Lowell Lectures, 1926.* Cambridge: Cambridge University Press, 2011.

———. *Science and the Modern World: Lowell Lectures, 1925.* New York: Free Press, 1997.

Online

Boyd, Gregory. "What Is Open Theism?" Video. http://www.youtube.com/watch?v=gApXDGjyksw.

Frame, John M. "Open Theism and Divine Foreknowledge." In *Bound Only Once*, edited by Douglas Wilson, 83–94. Moscow, ID: Canon Press, 2001. Available at http://www.frame-poythress.org/open-theism-and-divine-foreknowledge/.

———. Review of *The Nature of Doctrine*, by George A. Lindbeck. *Presbyterian Journal* 43 (February 27, 1985): 11–12. Available at http://www.frame-poythress.org/review-of-lindbecks-the-nature-of-doctrine/.

Moltmann, Jürgen. *Theology of Hope: On the Ground and the Implications of a Christian Eschatology.* New York: Harper and Row, 1967. Concluding chapter available at http://www.pubtheo.com/page.asp?pid=1036.

Pannenberg, Wolfhart. "God of the Philosophers." Available at http://www.firstthings.com/article/2007/06/002-god-of-the-philosophers.

Postliberalism. Olson, Roger E. "Back to the Bible (Almost): Why Yale's Postliberal Theologians Deserve an Evangelical Hearing." *Christianity Today* 40, 6 (May 20, 1996). Available at http://www.christianitytoday.com/ct/1996/may20/6t6031.html. Requires subscription to read full article.

Process Thought. The Center for Process Studies. Various basic articles, including "What Is Process Thought?" Available at http://www.ctr4process.org/about/process/.

Whitehead, Alfred North. "God and the World." In *Process and Reality: An Essay in Cosmology.* Edited by David Ray Griffin and Donald W.

Sherburne. Corrected ed. New York: Free Press, 1978. Available at http://www.anthonyflood.com/whiteheadgodandtheworld.htm.

READ FOR YOURSELF

Moltmann's early *Theology of Hope* is the most accessible of his writings. Some critics found in it an inadequate doctrine of the Trinity, and that issue became central to the rest of his writings. In liberation theology, first read (or skim) Gutierrez's *Theology of Liberation*, and then look at other expressions of this movement. Miguez Bonino's *Doing Theology in a Revolutionary Situation* is particularly interesting to me.

Read Pannenberg's *The Apostles' Creed* as an introduction to his work; then dig into his *Systematic Theology*.

Read the first few chapters of Cobb and Griffin, *Process Theology: An Introductory Exposition*; then move on to what interests you. In open theism, read the Boyd book and Frame's critique.

Then read Lindbeck, *The Nature of Doctrine*, and Childs, *The Eclipse of Biblical Narrative*. My review at http://www.frame-poythress.org/review-of-lindbecks-the-nature-of-doctrine/ responds to Lindbeck's book.

LISTEN ONLINE

Link: http://itunes.apple.com/us/course/legacy-history-philosophy/id694658914

- Jürgen Moltmann and the Theology of Liberation: 1:01:11
- The Theology of Liberation Continued and Wolfhart Pannenberg: 1:08:28
- Process Philosophy, Process Theology, and Open Theism: 52:38

FAMOUS QUOTES

- **Moltmann:** http://www.goodreads.com/author/quotes/52217.J_rgen_Moltmann
- **Gutierrez:** http://en.wikiquote.org/wiki/Gustavo_Gutierrez
- **Whitehead:** http://en.wikiquote.org/wiki/Alfred_North_Whitehead

12

TWENTIETH-CENTURY LANGUAGE PHILOSOPHY

IN CHAPTER 9, I indicated that the twentieth century was the "century of 'language'" among philosophers. Participating in this interest were philosophers and theologians of many types. We may recall Nietzsche's observations about philology, the enigmatic statement of the later Heidegger that language is the "house of Being," and the *new hermeneutic* disciples of Bultmann who sought to unpack that insight in their concept of a *language event*. This discussion occurred in the context of new researches into hermeneutics by people such as Hans-Georg Gadamer and Paul Ricoeur, which, unfortunately, I was able to refer to only in passing. We should also not forget the strong emphasis on *Word of God* and *revelation* among Barth and other existential theologians. In this chapter, however, I will deal with other movements—schools of thought that urged certain kinds of language analysis as the fundamental method for approaching philosophical issues.

Invoking language to answer philosophical questions is not new. When Socrates, in Plato's dialogues, investigated the nature of virtue, or courage, or goodness, he did not do empirical research . . . , looking for people bearing these attributes. Rather, he discussed language. *He discussed the meaning of virtue by discussing the meaning of the term* virtue.

Invoking language to answer philosophical questions is not new. When Socrates, in Plato's dialogues, investigated the nature of virtue, or courage, or goodness, he did not do empirical research (as Diogenes, with his fabled lantern), looking for people bearing these attributes. Rather, he discussed *language*. He discussed the meaning of virtue by discussing the meaning of the term *virtue*. If someone were to do this, he would ask, would we *call* him virtuous? The ontological and moral questions reduce to questions about the meaning of language.

Aristotle's metaphysics is evidently patterned after the grammar of sentences. A *substance* is something that can be denoted by a noun and placed in the subject slot of a sentence. An *attribute* or *property* fits into the predicate slot. Aquinas's doctrine of analogy begins, at least, as a doctrine of linguistic predication. The *analytic-synthetic* distinction, much discussed by Hume, Leibniz, Kant, and many others, is a distinction between two kinds of sentences.

The twentieth century carries this interest to a higher level, explicitly making the study of language the whole subject matter of philosophy, the road to answering all philosophical questions. It might be interesting to pause for a moment to try to understand this development. I think the new emphasis on language has at least two motivations: (1) Compared to other disciplines, philosophy has been very slow to achieve consensus on its chief questions. Such persistent failure provokes questions about communication: to what extent have philosophers simply failed to understand one another? So in the twentieth century there have been appropriate new attempts to clarify the language in which we state and argue philosophical proposals. (2) Some thinkers have felt that language is a tantalizing new gateway to the knowledge that philosophy seeks. Is it possible, for example, that we can better discover "what is" by asking "what can be said?" Certainly the minimal requirement of a theory of being is that it be expressible in language. Philosophy, for better or worse, is among other things a conversation in language. So if being transcends language, to that extent it cannot be part of a philosophical theory. Philosophy can assert only what it can say, what it can talk about. That is a tautology. So perhaps Hegel's statement "the real is the rational and the rational is the real" can be converted (with a similar rationale) to "the real is the sayable and the sayable is the real."

G. E. Moore

In this chapter, I will consider two broad forms of twentieth-century language analysis (with several subdivisions of each one). As with philosophical movements in the past, these two forms are divided somewhat by the English Channel. In the English-speaking world, the tradition begun by Moore, Russell, and Wittgenstein[1] is dominant. But the continent of Europe, after (and overlapping) the heyday of existentialism, was more interested in structuralism and then deconstruction.

The twentieth century carries this interest to a higher level, explicitly making the study of language the whole subject matter of philosophy, the road to answering all philosophical questions.

G. E. MOORE (1873–1958)

First, the English movement. In the late nineteenth century, there was a strong influence of Hegelian idealism[2] in Britain: T. H. Green, F. H. Bradley, B. Bosanquet, J. M. E. McTaggart. G. E. Moore studied with McTaggart but found himself asking many common-sense ques-

1. Russell, however, was influenced by the German Gottlob Frege, and Wittgenstein was an Austrian who studied and taught in England for many years. The logical positivists were largely Austrian and German thinkers who fled west to escape Hitler. So, as when Kant read David Hume, international cross-pollination often leads to significant results.

2. See chapter 7.

tions. By a complicated argument, for example, McTaggart had tried to show that time and space did not exist. But Moore professed not to understand what McTaggart was saying. If time were not real, did this mean that the philosophy class would not end at noon? Moore became known as a "philosopher of common sense," like Thomas Reid (chapter 6), and for reasons similar to Reid's. Moore maintained in a 1925 essay, "In Defense of Common Sense,"[3] that certain statements such as "There exists at present a living human body, which is my body" are known with certainty by common sense. These cannot be refuted by philosophical arguments, for these common-sense statements are more certain than any philosophical principles that could be used to refute them.

Philosophers such as Hegel and McTaggart had thought that the purpose of philosophy was to construct grand systems of thought. Moore, on the contrary, came to believe that the purpose of philosophy was to remove confusions, many produced by philosophy itself. Moore got into the habit of responding to any technical expression with "what *exactly* do you mean by that?" Moore and others repeated this question many times, informally and in print, and it came to characterize a new kind of philosophy. These thinkers held that the most important thing in philosophy was clarity about the meaning of expressions. This kind of philosophizing was called *language analysis*, *language philosophy*, or *analytic philosophy*, to distinguish it from the traditional system-building.

BERTRAND RUSSELL (1872–1970)

These thinkers held that the most important thing in philosophy was clarity about the meaning of expressions. This kind of philosophizing was called language analysis, language philosophy, *or* analytic philosophy, *to distinguish it from the traditional system-building.*

Russell was a friend of Moore and shared much of Moore's thinking. But he also brought to analytic philosophy strong interests and abilities in mathematics, logic, and science. He read and became acquainted with Gottlob Frege (1848–1925), a German mathematician, who developed a number of ideas that Russell considered important for philosophy. One was a derivation of mathematics from logic, which Russell defended in the book *Principia Mathematica*,[4] cowritten with Alfred North Whitehead.

In chapter 11, we saw that Whitehead later developed a kind of atomistic metaphysics, isolating as *actual occasions* the fundamental entities out of which all other entities are made. Russell also developed a kind of atomistic philosophy, which he called *logical atomism*. Russell's atomism can be understood as reaction against the monism of British Hegelianism, the idea that you cannot really understand one

3. In G. E. Moore, *Philosophical Papers* (London: Allen and Unwin, 1959).
4. 3 vols. (Cambridge: Cambridge University Press, 1910–13).

thing unless you understand the whole of reality.[5] Russell wanted to believe that some entities could be understood in themselves, so that we could have some genuine knowledge without being omniscient.

Whitehead's atoms were processes, *atomic events*, but Russell's were *atomic facts*. Facts are not things. Things, like Aristotelian substances, can be designated by nouns, such as *car, house, planet, Bill*. Facts, rather, are designated in language by statements or clauses, for example, "the car is red," "the house is large," "Bill is a grocer." A fact, then, is a state of affairs, that which "is the case." Often when we refer to facts, we use the word *that*: e.g., the fact *that* there are caribou in Alaska.

In Russell's worldview, as his student Ludwig Wittgenstein put it, "the world is the totality of facts, not of things."

Aristotle's metaphysics held that the world was a collection of things—substances. His logic reflected that metaphysics: "All men are mortal," for Aristotle, ascribes an attribute to the substances that we call *men*. But in Russell's worldview, as his student Ludwig Wittgenstein put it, "the world is the totality of facts, not of things."[6] Let's say that you were asked to list all the components in the world, and you began listing things: *the car, the house, the planet, Bill, Jane*. Even if you could list all the things in the world, that list would be incomplete. For the *components* of the world include not only the things, but also the properties of the things (red, blue, large, talented), and the relationships between the things (Bill is in the car, Jane is sitting to the right of Bill).

Bertrand Russell

As Aristotle's logic reflected his metaphysics, so Russell's logic reflected his. In *Principia Mathematica*, the premise "all men are mortal" is translated into logical symbolism that reads: "for all X, if X is a man, then X is mortal." Aristotle's interpretation of the premise clearly assumes that there are such beings as men. (So logicians say that in Aristotle's logic, universal affirmative statements have *existential import*.) But Russell's interpretation does not presuppose the existence of men. The existence of men is only hypothetical: *if* there are men, then they are mortal. Although both formulations state facts, only Aristotle's presupposes belief in things or substances. To say that "men exist" in Russell's logic, we would have to say that "there exists at least one X, such that X has the property of manhood." Even when Russell is plainly talking about things, his logic stresses *facts* about variables having properties. In that respect he is more Platonic than Aristotelian. For Aristotle, the world is a collection of things; for Plato, it is a world in which bits of our experience participate in properties that exist in the

5. Whitehead's system is something of a middle way between monism and atomism, since he believes that each actual occasion is *internally related* to many others, incorporating other realities within itself, and that God includes all actuality within himself.

6. Ludwig Wittgenstein, *Tractatus Logico-Philosophicus*, 1.1, available at http://people.umass.edu/phil335-klement-2/tlp/tlp.pdf.

world of Forms. For Plato, properties are more real than things; so Plato could have said that the world is a collection of properties.

Russell does allow for the existence of things, but only as elements of facts. In his view, a fact consists of two or more of three types of entities: things, properties, and relations. "The car is red" includes a thing and a property, ascribing the property to the thing. "Jane is to the right of Bill" includes two things (people are in the category of things) and the relation between them.

But what, then, is an *atomic fact*? For Democritus and Epicurus, atoms are the fundamental material things of which all other reality is composed. But if, as on Russell's view, the world is made of facts, then atomic facts are the fundamental facts of which all other facts are composed. Russell believes that if we can identify these atomic facts, through them we can understand the world.

Facts, of course, are stated and expressed in language. So the variety of language gives us some indication of what kinds of facts there are. Some sentences are *compound*, expressing more than one fact at once, for example, "This morning it was sunny, but this afternoon it is raining." This sentence, if true, states a fact, but not an *atomic* fact, since it can be divided into two simpler statements of fact.

Some sentences include *general terms*, such as *happiness* and *green*. But Russell (displaying his nominalism) believed that statements about general concepts were reducible to statements about particulars—in this case, individual happy people and individual green things. So statements about general concepts cannot be atomic facts. Sometimes generality can be hidden under expressions that sound particular. "England declared war" appears to be a particular statement, but in fact it is a shorthand, referring to a great many things done by individual members of Parliament, the Prime Minister, the King, and so on. So the search for atomic facts must translate statements about generalities to statements about particulars.

It is not easy to find atomic facts. Some logical positivists (below) later said that atomic facts (or, as they put it, protocol sentences*) can be experiences only of momentary sense data, such as "this red here, now."*

Even "Billy went out to play" is a general statement that, for Russell's philosophical purposes, must be reduced to particular statements about Billy's opening the door, taking one step, then another, and so on. And if a philosopher wants to be really rigorous, he would need to refer to everything going on in Billy's body: the breaths he takes, the neural events in his brain, and on and on.

So it is not easy to find atomic facts. Some logical positivists (below) later said that atomic facts (or, as they put it, *protocol sentences*) can be experiences only of momentary sense data, such as "this red here, now." That reflects Russell's inclination to empiricism, that all our knowledge must be reducible to perceptions in some way. It is as if all our experience and all our thinking is built up out of what Hume called *impressions*. But is that true? Critics noted that they had never seen a red patch per se. Our concept of a red patch is, in fact, an abstraction!—a generalization from all our experiences of red clothing, red lights, red beets, red cars, red flags, and so forth. As I have argued throughout this book, we never, in fact, experience particularity without generality, or generality without particularity. We never experience the one without the many, because in God one and many are inseparable, and he has made the universe to reflect his Trinitarian mystery.

We never, in fact, experience particularity without generality, or generality without particularity. We never experience the one without the many, because in God one and many are inseparable, and he has made the universe to reflect his Trinitarian mystery.

None of these considerations, however, deterred Russell from his pursuit of atomic facts. The atomic fact was an important element in his overall philosophy. His goal was to develop a perfect language, one that perfectly reflects the nature of the world. (This is sometimes called the *picture theory of language*.) Of course, the perfect language has one function, that of stating facts. And only atomic facts are true facts.

So in the perfect language, each sentence states one, and only one, fact. If a fact has three elements (things, properties, relations), then the corresponding sentence has three words: a word for each element. Thus language corresponds precisely to the world. The perfect language consists of atomic sentences, stating atomic facts, reflecting the fact-oriented logic of *Principia Mathematica*.

I will leave Russell at this point, though I will take up his ideas again in my discussion of Wittgenstein. It is difficult, in this time period, to tell where Russell leaves off and where Wittgenstein begins. Since Russell lived for ninety-eight years, however, I should point out that his interests in technical philosophical matters declined over his lifetime. After 1918, he did not defend logical atomism. Generally, he defended *realist* positions—that there really is a world external to our own minds.[7] In that respect, he follows Moore's conception of common sense. But more significantly, he became a sort of "public atheist" (like Richard Dawkins and Christopher Hitchens in later years), criticizing legal and social limits on sex, opposing religion, standing with the far-left antiwar movements. In 1966, he published *War Crimes in Vietnam*[8] and soon afterward organized a simulated war-crimes trial ("The Russell Tribunal") of Americans who had played roles in the war. His legacy is most often expressed not by the theory of logical atomism, but by statements such as the following:

In the perfect language, each sentence states one, and only one, fact. . . . The perfect language consists of atomic sentences, stating atomic facts.

> That Man is the product of causes which had no prevision of the end they were achieving; that his origin, his growth, his hopes and fears, his loves and his beliefs, are but the outcome of accidental collocations of atoms; that no fire, no heroism, no

7. *Realism* here should not, of course, be confused with Plato's realism, by which we refer to Plato's view of universals.

8. London: Monthly Review Press, 1966.

intensity of thought and feeling, can preserve an individual life beyond the grave; that all the labours of the ages, all the devotion, all the inspiration, all the noonday brightness of human genius, are destined to extinction in the vast death of the solar system, and that the whole temple of Man's achievement must inevitably be buried beneath the débris of a universe in ruins—all these things, if not quite beyond dispute, are yet so nearly certain, that no philosophy which rejects them can hope to stand. Only within the scaffolding of these truths, only on the firm foundation of unyielding despair, can the soul's habitation henceforth be safely built.[9]

LUDWIG WITTGENSTEIN (1889–1951)

Wittgenstein's family was the second-wealthiest in Austria, after the Rothschilds, but also a tragic one. Three of his brothers committed suicide, and he contemplated doing so himself. His remaining brother, Paul, lost his right arm in World War I, but returned to become a concert pianist.[10] Ludwig was never comfortable with the life of a philosopher, but other experiences were even less rewarding, so although he left the academic field on several occasions, he kept returning to philosophical work.

He came to England in 1908, originally to study aeronautical engineering, but he had written some philosophical material, and in 1911, at the suggestion of Gottlob Frege, he asked Bertrand Russell to look at it. Russell came to be astounded at Wittgenstein's brilliance and took him under his wing. Wittgenstein left Cambridge to fight for Austria in World War I, but he carried with him through the war a set of papers on which he wrote the only book published during his lifetime, the *Tractatus Logico-Philosophicus*,[11] a book that comes to 111 pages in the Internet edition, including introductions, but not indices.

Ludwig Wittgenstein

The *Tractatus* basically followed Russell's logical atomism, but worked it out in an apparently rigorous set of definitions, explanations, and deductions. It is arranged in seven numbered propositions, each defined, applied, and defended by subpropositions numbered in decimal fashion. To illustrate, the first proposition, with its subpoints, is as follows:

1 The world is all that is the case.

1.1 The world is the totality of facts, not of things.

9. Bertrand Russell, "A Free Man's Worship" (1903), available at http://www.philosophicalsociety.com/archives/a%20free%20man's%20worship.htm.

10. Ravel's "Piano Concerto for the Left Hand" was commissioned for Paul Wittgenstein.

11. References same as citation in footnote 6, using the Pears-McGuinness translation. Wittgenstein had considered other titles, but he accepted this one, suggested by G. E. Moore, parallel to Spinoza's *Tractatus Theologico-Politicus*.

1.11 The world is determined by the facts, and by their being all the facts.
1.12 For the totality of facts determine what is the case, and also whatever is not the case.
1.13 The facts in logical space are the world.
1.2 The world divides into facts.
1.21 Each item can be the case or not the case, while everything else remains the same.

The other propositions, without subpoints, are as follows:

2 What is the case—a fact—is the existence of states of affairs.
3 A logical picture of facts is a thought.
4 A thought is a proposition with a sense.
5 A proposition is a truth-function of elementary propositions.[12]
6 The general form of a truth-function is $\left[\bar{p}, \bar{\xi}, N(\bar{\xi})\right]$.[13] This is the general form of a proposition.
7 What we cannot speak about we must pass over in silence.

Elementary propositions are statements of what Russell called atomic facts. *In effect, what this meant is that meaningful propositions must be reducible to reports of immediate sense experience.*

The *Tractatus* attempts to establish rigorous limits to meaningful language. Language, in this book, consists of propositions, that is, assertions of fact. Only propositions can be true or false. Language that fails to measure up to Wittgenstein's criteria is neither true nor false, but meaningless, *nonsense*, in a certain technical sense. (The logical positivists used the term *cognitively meaningless.*) A meaningful proposition is either an *elementary proposition* or one that can be reduced to one. Elementary propositions are statements of what Russell called *atomic facts*. In effect, what this meant is that meaningful propositions must be reducible to reports of immediate sense experience.

On the criteria of the Tractatus, *ethical statements are cognitively meaningless. Wittgenstein says, "It is impossible for there to be propositions of ethics."*

But that criterion rules out great amounts of language as cognitively meaningless. For example, ethical statements, statements of ethical obligation, clearly cannot be reduced to statements of empirical fact. This is merely to restate Hume's argument that you cannot derive *ought* from *is*—you cannot derive ethical obligations from statements of facts.[14] So on the criteria of the *Tractatus*, ethical statements are cognitively meaningless. Wittgenstein says, "It is impossible for there to be propositions of ethics."[15] Wittgenstein,

12. That is to say that the truth-value (truth or falsity) of a proposition depends on the truth-value of the elementary propositions of which it is composed.

13. What he is trying to do is to establish a general rule by which complex propositions can be derived from elementary propositions.

14. Wittgenstein's friend G. E. Moore described this inference as the *naturalistic fallacy*.

15. *Tractatus*, 6.42.

however, was an ethically concerned person, and he could not accept a view that made ethical obligation appear to be meaningless. So he also said[16] that apparent ethical propositions fall into a special category. "It is clear that ethics cannot be put into words. Ethics is transcendental."[17] Their truth cannot be *stated*, but it can be *shown*.[18] Statements of this sort fall into a category that Wittgenstein called *the Mystical*.

The same is true of religious statements. Wittgenstein says in the *Tractatus*:

> 6.432 How things are in the world is a matter of complete indifference for what is higher. God does not reveal himself in the world.
>
> 6.44 It is not how things are in the world that is mystical, but that it exists.[19]
>
> 6.45 To view the world sub specie aeternis[20] is to view it as a whole—a limited whole. Feeling the world as a limited whole—it is this that is mystical.

Sentences about God, in other words, are not meaningful by Wittgenstein's criteria. The same is true of the human soul, at least as religions and metaphycians have discussed it.[21] Also creation, or any other metaphysical or religious doctrine dealing with the world as a whole (quotation above).

The Mystical of Wittgenstein is similar to the noumenal world of Kant. Kant addresses directly the limits of reason, Wittgenstein the limits of language and therefore the limits of reason. But both find it necessary to define the limits of reason so as to exclude metaphysical or religious discussions of morality, God, the soul, and the world as a whole. It never occurs to either Kant or Wittgenstein that we must *presuppose* God and his revelation if we are to make complete sense of these. But they have done us the favor of showing us that God and revelation make no sense at all in a philosophical scheme presupposing human autonomy.

The Mystical of Wittgenstein is similar to the noumenal world of Kant. . . . Both find it necessary to define the limits of reason so as to exclude metaphysical or religious discussions of morality, God, the soul, and the world as a whole.

But Wittgenstein is too honest to let the discussion end here. The *Tractatus* ends as follows:

16. In *Tractatus*, 6.41–6.422, and in his "Lecture on Ethics," given around 1929–30, published in *Philosophical Review* 74, 1 (January 1965): 3–12.

17. *Tractatus*, 6.421.

18. Ibid., 6.522.

19. Wittgenstein, like Heidegger, could be referring to the classical *problem of being*: why should there be being, and not rather nothing?

20. *Sub specie aeternis* (or *aeternitatis*) was Spinoza's description of a view of the world from God's perspective.

21. *Tractatus*, 6.4312. See also his remarks about the "subject" in 5.632–33.

6.54 My propositions serve as elucidations in the following way: anyone who understands me eventually recognizes them as nonsensical, when he has used them—as steps—to climb up beyond them. (He must, so to speak, throw away the ladder after he has climbed up it.) He must transcend these propositions, and then he will see the world aright.

7 What we cannot speak about we must pass over in silence.

Here, Wittgenstein recognizes that his own book falls prey to the same criticisms he has made of ethical, metaphysical, and religious language. The *Tractatus* aims to show the relation between language and the world. But as we have seen, *world* has a problematic status in this book. Further, if Wittgenstein accurately describes a relation R between proposition p and atomic fact A, his description amounts to a proposition p2, which itself is related to R by, say, relation R2. If Wittgenstein accurately describes R2, that description requires another relation, R3, ad infinitum. The infinite regress refutes itself.

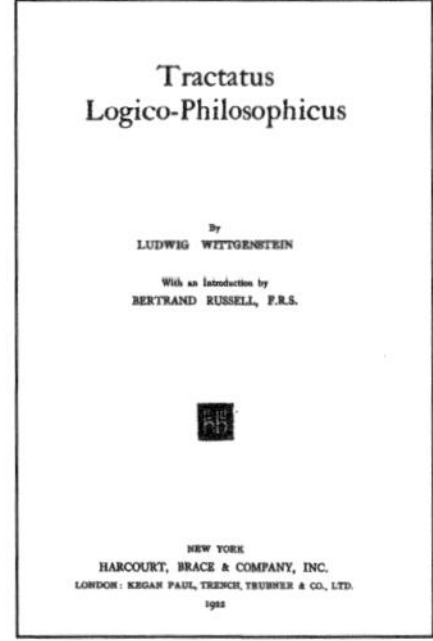
Tractatus
Logico-Philosophicus
By
LUDWIG WITTGENSTEIN
With an Introduction by
BERTRAND RUSSELL, F.R.S.
NEW YORK
HARCOURT, BRACE & COMPANY, INC.
LONDON: KEGAN PAUL, TRENCH, TRUBNER & CO., LTD.
1922

Tractatus Logico-Philosophicus

So Wittgenstein's special language, his perfect language, not only excludes ethical, religious, and metaphysical language, but also excludes attempts to show the relation between language and reality. Yet that exclusion applies to the *Tractatus* itself.

That is to say, in Wittgenstein's view the perfect language can only state facts. It cannot refer to relations between language and fact, even though those relations are indeed facts of a higher order. But the *Tractatus* is precisely an attempt to state in language the relationships between language and fact. Wittgenstein's final claim is that the book *shows* these relationships, but it fails to state these in language, for they really cannot be stated. So in his technical sense, his book is "nonsensical" and belongs to the "mystical." Wittgenstein admits that what he has tried to do violates his own criteria for meaningful language. But it is a tool to enable people to *see* the relationships from some (unspeakable) transcendent vantage point.

Wittgenstein's special language, his perfect language, not only excludes ethical, religious, and metaphysical language, but also excludes attempts to show the relation between language and reality.

And that is precisely the claim that mystics (such as Plotinus and Eckhart—chapters 2 and 4) have made for their use of reason. It is a tool to achieve a vision that in the end transcends reason. Once we have reached the goal of reason, we may dispense with it, throw away the ladder.[22]

Indeed, Wittgenstein himself threw away the ladder for a time. He believed that he had sufficiently dealt with all philosophical problems:

22. *Tractatus*, 6.521, puts this point in a fascinating way: "The solution of the problem of life is seen in the vanishing of the problem. (Is not this the reason why those who have found after a long period of doubt that the sense of life became clear to them have then been unable to say what constituted that sense?)"

OUTLINE

> The correct method in philosophy would really be the following: to say nothing except what can be said, i.e., propositions of natural science[23]—i.e., something that has nothing to do with philosophy—and then, whenever someone else wanted to say something metaphysical, to demonstrate to him that he had failed to give a meaning to certain signs in his propositions. Although it would not be satisfying to the other person—he would not have the feeling that we were teaching him philosophy—this method would be the only strictly correct one.[24]

On that criterion, the *Tractatus* had solved all philosophical problems. The rationalism of this claim correlates with the irrationalist claim that answers to foundational questions are mystical; see fig. 12.1.[25]

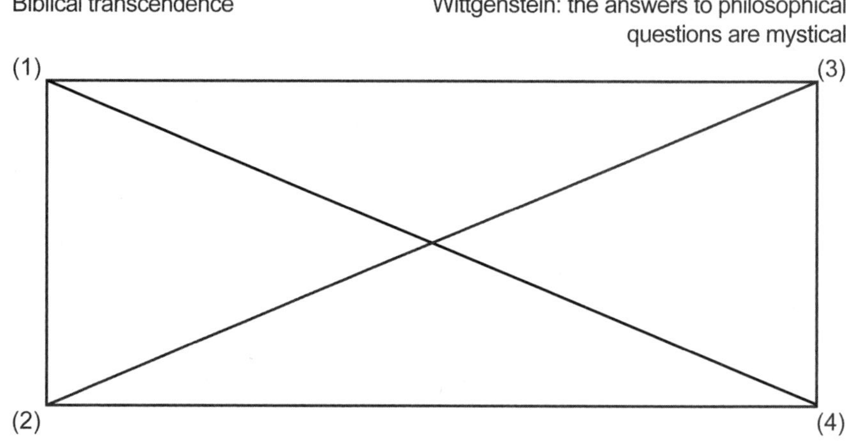

Fig. 12.1. Transcendence and Immanence in Wittgenstein's *Tractatus*

Wittgenstein for several years took his own advice ("what we cannot speak about we must pass over in silence"). He returned to Austria, where he worked as a gardener in a monastery in 1920, and then taught in elementary schools until 1926.

Wittgenstein for several years took his own advice ("what we cannot speak about we must pass over in silence"). He returned to Austria, where he worked as a gardener in a monastery in 1920, and then taught in elementary schools until 1926, an unpleasant experience, we are told, for him and for his students. He returned to gardening for several months at another monastery, where he inquired about becoming a monk. But instead he accepted an invitation from his sister to help

23. This *scientism*, the view that only scientific method can warrant claims to factual knowledge, is similar to that which we noted earlier in Charles S. Peirce (chapter 9). Bertrand Russell shared it, and we will see that it is the chief assertion of logical positivism.

24. *Tractatus*, 6.53.

25. And of course, it parallels Kant's similar claims about the phenomenal and the noumenal.

design her new townhouse in Vienna with a team of architects. The result was "a spare, modernist house."[26]

But in the meantime, the *Tractatus* had been published and had aroused considerable interest in the philosophical community. The philosopher Frank P. Ramsey[27] had visited Wittgenstein in 1923, during his schoolteacher days, to discuss the *Tractatus* for a review he was writing. Over the next years, Ramsey, the economist John Maynard Keynes, and others urged Wittgenstein to return to Cambridge to teach philosophy. Russell and Moore arranged to have the *Tractatus* accepted as a dissertation, and in 1929 Wittgenstein became a fellow of Trinity College, Cambridge. I will discuss the second phase of his philosophical work later in this chapter.

Russell and Moore arranged to have the Tractatus *accepted as a dissertation, and in 1929 Wittgenstein became a fellow of Trinity College, Cambridge.*

LOGICAL POSITIVISM

Among those who took much interest in the *Tractatus* while Wittgenstein was absent from the academic philosophical world was a group of scientists and philosophers who met together at the University of Vienna and thus became known as the Vienna Circle. It was later reconstituted as the Ernst Mach Society, named for the influence Mach had on their thinking. The group was chaired by Moritz Schlick, and included Gustav Bergmann, Rudolf Carnap, Philipp Frank, Richard Von Mises,[28] Otto Neurath, Friedrich Waismann, and others. Herbert Feigl and Kurt Gödel attended the meetings as students, but were not considered members of the group.[29] Wittgenstein himself met with them beginning in 1926, but he thought they had misunderstood his work. He mocked them by reading poetry aloud when he found a meeting to be tiresome.

Among those who took much interest in the Tractatus *while Wittgenstein was absent from the academic philosophical world was a group of scientists and philosophers who met together at the University of Vienna and thus became known as the Vienna Circle.*

26. David Egan, Stephen Reynolds, and Aaron Wendland, *Wittgenstein and Heidegger*, Routledge Studies in Twentieth Century Philosophy (New York: Routledge, 2013), 4.

27. Ramsey was a brilliant philosopher and mathematician who, we are told, learned German in a little over a week and, with Wittgenstein's help, translated the *Tractatus*. Ramsey died at the age of twenty-six from complications following abdominal surgery. In his short career, he published a very large number of influential papers.

28. His older brother, the economist Ludwig Von Mises, disagreed sharply with the Vienna Circle approach and defended free-market economics.

29. There was also the "Berlin Circle" with similar interests and goals; it included Hans Reichenbach, Carl Hempel, and David Hilbert. They shared with the Vienna Circle the journal *Erkenntnis*. They preferred to be called *logical empiricists* rather than *logical positivists*, but over time the names became interchangeable. I should also mention the name of A. J. Ayer, author of *Language, Truth and Logic* (London: Gollancz, 1936; many editions since), who popularized logical positivism in the English-speaking world. Many of the European logical positivists fled to England and America with the rise of Hitler. Like Wittgenstein, many of them had some Jewish ancestry. (Three of Wittgenstein's grandparents were Jewish, but he was baptized as a Roman Catholic. His writings do not indicate any faith in God, but a certain longing for something "higher.") So logical positivism gained more adherents in the English-speaking world than on the continent of Europe.

The word *positivist* attached to these thinkers comes from the thought of Auguste Comte (1798–1857), whom some consider to be the founder of the discipline of sociology. Comte divided history into (1) the theological stage, (2) the metaphysical stage, and (3) the positive stage. In the positive stage, science prevails over theology and metaphysics and the "religion of humanity" prevails over Christianity. The term *positivism* came to refer to what I have called *scientism*, the belief that scientific method is the only reliable means of establishing truth. The Vienna Circle described themselves as "logical" positivists, to indicate that (in place of Comte's speculative history) they had developed a logical rationale for their scientistic philosophy.

The logical positivists found the *Tractatus* to be fascinating and formative, but they rejected its metaphysics and its mysticism. Of course, the *Tractatus* itself is an antimetaphysical book, for it claims that metaphysical statements arise from misunderstandings of language.[30] But it should be noted that proposition 1.1 of the *Tractatus*, "The world is the totality of facts, not of things," is a bona fide metaphysical statement. It presents an alternative, for example, to Aristotle's metaphysics of substances and Whitehead's metaphysics of processes. Further, the *Tractatus* presents a very elaborate metaphysical view of the universe as divided into atomic facts, which correspond so precisely to the sentences of a perfect language that the language can serve as a picture of the universe. The logical positivists set aside this picture theory of language, with Wittgenstein's general description of the world, as metaphysical relics.

They also sought to evade the mystical side of the *Tractatus*. They liked Wittgenstein's arguments to the effect that God, religion, and metaphysics were nonsense.[31] But Wittgenstein treated these as a special, important kind of nonsense, which should be regarded as belonging to a transcendent realm. To the positivists, that was speculative foolishness.

The logical positivists liked Wittgenstein's arguments to the effect that God, religion, and metaphysics were nonsense. But Wittgenstein treated these as a special, important kind of nonsense, which should be regarded as belonging to a transcendent realm.

Then what is left of the *Tractatus*, denuded of metaphysics and mysticism? Well, essentially, scientism: "The correct method in philosophy would really be the following: to say nothing except what can be said, i.e., propositions of natural science."[32] Truth is to be found through scientific method, and anything else is nonsense—including metaphysics and mysticism. The only legitimate work of philosophy is to analyze and clarify the language of science.

So, like Wittgenstein and Russell, the logical positivists approached their task by way of an analysis of language. They divided language into four categories:

30. Note especially 6.53.

31. The positivists did avoid rejecting ethics altogether, by interpreting ethical injunctions as disguised imperatives or expressions of feeling. See below.

32. *Tractatus*, 6.53.

1. Tautologies, such as "these bachelors are unmarried."[33] In tautologies, the predicate is included in the meaning of the subject. They are all necessarily true, and we know that they are true by knowing the meanings of the words. So they are known *a priori*, and they are analytic rather than synthetic.[34]
2. Contradictions, such as "these bachelors are married." These are all necessarily false, and we know that they are false by knowing the meanings of the words. Their falsehood, therefore, is known *a priori*.
3. Empirical propositions, such as "the back fence is white." These may be either true or false. We cannot determine their truth or falsity merely by the meanings of the terms. Rather, we must have empirical knowledge of the fact in question. So these propositions are synthetic and *a posteriori*.
4. *Emotive language*, a catchall category for every kind of language not covered by categories 1–3, including commands, questions, and poetic expressions. The term is a misnomer, for language in this category does not necessarily communicate emotion, and that is not necessarily its purpose.

The logical positivists believed that only propositions in category 3 above were capable of conveying factual information. Hence they often described themselves as logical empiricists.

The logical positivists believed that only propositions in category 3 above were capable of conveying factual information. Hence they often described themselves as *logical empiricists*. They held (with Comte, Peirce, and Russell) that only scientific method could yield knowledge and that scientific method was a radically empirical discipline. They developed a sharp distinction in science between *theoretical* statements and *observation* statements. In their view, the former were to be verified by the latter. The most fundamental observation statement was the *protocol* statement, a statement of a simple sense datum—what Russell called an *atomic fact*.

The term verification *became an important concept for logical positivism. The logical positivists developed the* verification principle, *which stated that only propositions of class are "cognitively meaningful" or "empirically meaningful," and therefore capable of stating truth or falsity.*

So the term *verification* became an important concept for logical positivism. The logical positivists developed the *verification principle*, which stated that only propositions of class are "cognitively meaningful" or "empirically meaningful," and therefore capable of stating truth or falsity. On the contrary, forms of language that cannot be verified by something like the methods of empirical science are not cognitively meaningful. Such forms of language cannot be true, and

33. In all these examples, of course, the relevant terms must be taken literally and must retain their literal sense in both subject and predicate.

34. Review this terminology in the discussions of Hume and Leibniz (chapter 5) and of Kant (chapter 7).

they cannot be false either. They are cognitively meaningless.[35] They may, to be sure, have some value in conveying emotion, commanding obedience, or some other function (category 4), but they cannot convey any factual information; they cannot state what is or is not the case. So cognitively meaningful language is verifiable language, and the meaning of a statement is the method of its verification.

This verification principle had consequences for ethical, metaphysical, and religious language similar to the consequences of the *Tractatus*, though not exactly the same. None of the assertions of these kinds of language were scientifically verifiable, so the positivists maintained that they were not propositions at all. They were neither true nor false. They were cognitively meaningless, though they might have some "emotive" uses.[36]

Many Christians felt terrorized by the positivists' verification principle. It was more radical than the atheisms of Nietzsche, Russell, and Sartre. The positivists not only refused to acknowledge God's existence, but also argued that the very question of God's existence was a meaningless question. "God exists" was neither true nor false, but nonsense.

But the Christians' sense of terror was short-lived. The secular philosophical community itself made devastating criticisms of the verification principle, so that by 1970 nobody defended it anymore. In the first place, many found the principle to be vague. The positivists tried to formulate it in various precise ways, but none of those ways could accomplish what the positivists wanted.

The secular philosophical community itself made devastating criticisms of the verification principle, so that by 1970 nobody defended it anymore. In the first place, many found the principle to be vague.

(1) An early formulation was that a statement is cognitively meaningful if it is *conclusively verifiable* through empirical evidence. But this version of the principle ruled out as meaningless all general statements, since none of our senses or scientific instruments gives us access to the entire universe. Now, since scientific laws themselves ($E = MC^2$, $F = MA$) are expressed as general statements, and the positivists thought of themselves as vindicating science as the sole road to truth, this version of the verification principle could not stand.

35. Compare David Hume's words about "committing to the flames" any volume that did not meet his specifications for meaningful discourse (quoted in chapter 5). The positivists were a bit more open to emotive language than Hume was in his statement. But Hume was also open to such language in other contexts. Compare also Charles S. Peirce's view of "how to make our ideas clear" in chapter 9, in which, like the later positivists, he connects practical verification with the determination of meaning.

36. The positivists had little interest in rehabilitating the language of metaphysics and religion, but they did hesitate (especially given the evils of the Hitler regime) to discard entirely the language of ethics. Carnap said that ethical statements were disguised imperatives. Schlick said that they were rules for behavior, analogous to rules for procedure in science. Charles L. Stevenson developed a more elaborate account, in his *Ethics and Language* (New Haven, CT: Yale University Press, 1944): ethical statements are (1) expressions of emotion, and (2) recommendations that others feel the same way. So "stealing is wrong" means "I don't like stealing, and you should not like it either." This position was called *emotivism* and became the most popular ethical position among the positivists. For more discussion, see *DCL*, 82–84.

(2) An alternative, suggested by Karl Popper: a statement is cognitively meaningful if it is *conclusively falsifiable*, that is, if there are empirical means of showing conclusively that it is false if indeed it is false. But as the previous version ruled out all general assertions, this version ruled out all particular assertions, such as "Black holes exist." One cannot prove empirically that something does not exist (cf. the saying "you can't prove a negative"), so there can be no scientific proof that black holes do *not* exist. Such a proof would have to take into account all the facts in the universe. Since science requires particular assertions, Popper's principle also proved intolerable to science and was therefore abandoned.

(3) Some thought they could rescue the verification principle by weakening it: a statement is cognitively meaningful if there is some empirical evidence *relevant* to its truth or falsity. But this formulation provoked replies from all sorts of metaphysicians and theologians who said that certainly there was evidence *relevant to* the truth of their own positions, even if those positions could not be proved.

Such wavering over versions of the verification principle suggested a broader criticism of the positivist attempt to define cognitive meaning*: it is* arbitrary*.*

Such wavering over versions of the verification principle suggested a broader criticism of the positivist attempt to define *cognitive meaning*: it is *arbitrary*. Initial readings of this literature suggest that the goal of the positivists was to discover a responsible definition of *cognitive meaning*, much as writers of dictionaries formulate definitions of other terms, based on common usage. But of course, *cognitive meaning* is not a phrase in common usage. Furthermore, what the positivists seem to have attempted to do was to draw up a concept that admitted all scientific language but rejected all ethical, metaphysical, and religious language. They failed in their purpose, because their definitions of *cognitive meaning* were either too narrow to accommodate all the language of science or too broad to exclude all the language of metaphysics and religion. Clearly, none of their definitions reflected any common usage, but rather were intended to promote an ideology, as often in political speech (e.g., defining *compassion* as including governmental welfare, or *women's reproductive health* as including abortion).[37]

What the positivists seem to have attempted to do was to draw up a concept that admitted all scientific language but rejected all ethical, metaphysical, and religious language.

Further, the positivists were unable to come to an agreement on the *nature of verification*. In general, they were empiricists, believing that every hypothesis or theory had to be verified by protocol sentences, stating elementary facts. But (1) the positivists' concept of "protocols"

37. Later, Ayer responded to these criticisms of the verification principle by saying that the principle was a kind of *convention*, that is, the positivists agreed implicitly to use this definition of *cognitive meaning* among themselves, even though it did not reflect broader social usage. That being the case, of course, the verification principle needed no verification. People can define terms to use among themselves in any way they want to. In saying this, however, Ayer was admitting that nobody outside the positivist circle was under any obligation to recognize their private conventional definition of *meaning*, or its alleged implications.

faces the same difficulties as Russell's *atomic facts* (see earlier discussion of Russell). It is not at all clear that reality is divided into such tiny components and that we have access to them. More likely, the concept of an atomic fact is an abstraction or extrapolation from facts of a more common-sense type. (2) Further, even given that elementary facts exist, how do we determine them? Carnap and Neurath thought these could be identified either as self-evident axioms or by coherence with an existing body of knowledge. Schlick followed Hume and Russell more closely: protocol statements arise from psychological experiences of sensation, pain, and so on. In other words, positivism does not give us a new alternative way of discovering truth; rather, it brings back all the traditional difficulties of past epistemologies.

Finally, the verification principle turned out to be *self-refuting*. As it turns out, the verification principle itself, that cognitive meaning depends on verification, cannot be verified under any of its various broad or narrow formulations. That is to say that if the principle were true, the principle itself would have to be rejected as cognitively meaningless. In other words, like metaphysics and religion, the verification principle belongs to category 4, not category 3, of the language functions I distinguished earlier. So as Wittgenstein admitted concerning his *Tractatus*, positivism was self-refuting.

These criticisms essentially show that positivism, like other non-Christian philosophies, is caught up in the rationalist-irrationalist dialectic. Positivism is militantly rationalistic, believing that it can limit not only truth and falsity but even meaningfulness to its criteria. But upon examination, its rationality turns out to be vacuous, arbitrary, and self-refuting—that is, irrational; see fig. 12.2.

The verification principle turned out to be self-refuting. As it turns out, the verification principle itself, that cognitive meaning depends on verification, cannot be verified under any of its various broad or narrow formulations.

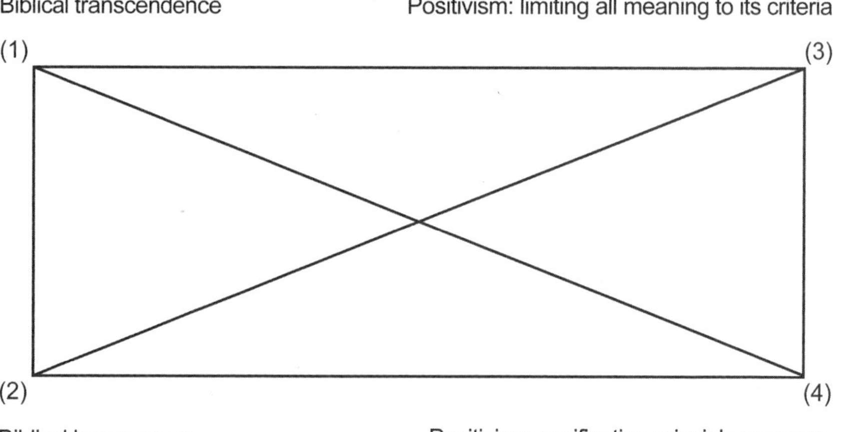

Fig. 12.2. Transcendence and Immanence in Logical Positivism

Some years after the heyday of positivism, Antony Flew[38] developed a similar argument against Christianity that many tried to refute.[39] He presented a parable as follows:

> Once upon a time two explorers came upon a clearing in the jungle. In the clearing were growing many flowers and many weeds. One explorer says, "Some gardener must tend this plot." So they pitch their tents and set a watch. No gardener is ever seen. "But perhaps he is an invisible gardener." So they set up a barbed-wire fence. They electrify it. They patrol with bloodhounds. (For they remember how H. G. Wells's *The Invisible Man* could be both smelt and touched though he could not be seen.) But no shrieks ever suggest that some intruder has received a shock. No movements of the wire ever betray an invisible climber. The bloodhounds never give cry. Yet still the Believer is not convinced. "But there is a gardener, invisible, intangible, insensible to electric shocks, a gardener who has no scent and makes no sound, a gardener who comes secretly to look after the garden which he loves." At last the Sceptic despairs, "But what remains of your original assertion? Just how does what you call an invisible, intangible, eternally elusive gardener differ from an imaginary gardener or even from no gardener at all?"[40]

Flew's parable raises the positivist challenge in a new form: How does a God whose existence cannot be verified or falsified empirically differ from no God at all?

Flew's parable raises the positivist challenge in a new form: How does a God whose existence cannot be verified or falsified empirically differ from no God at all? Doesn't this parable raise again the question whether the existence of God is a "meaningful" proposition? But this question presupposes an epistemology, a form of empiricism, and that epistemology is open to the same objections as those of Hume, Russell, and Carnap that we have considered. Consider, then:

Given Christian presuppositions, Christianity is indeed verifiable. All facts speak of God. Christianity is also falsifiable: if Christ is not risen, then our hope is vain. If God's promises fail, God is not true.

1. Given Christian presuppositions, Christianity is indeed verifiable. All facts speak of God. Christianity is also falsifiable: if Christ is not risen, then our hope is vain. If God's promises fail, God is not true.
2. But Christianity resists arguments that purport to falsify Christianity from a non-Christian presupposition.

38. Much later, Flew became a deist, convinced by the literature of the intelligent-design movement.

39. Antony Flew et al., "Theology and Falsification," in *New Essays in Philosophical Theology*, ed. Antony Flew and Alasdair C. MacIntyre (London: SCM Press, 1955), 96–130. For my response, see my "God and Biblical Language: Transcendence and Immanence," Appendix E in *DWG* and Appendix H in this book.

40. Flew, "Theology and Falsification," 96.

3. Christianity resists falsification from non-Christian assumptions because, like every other worldview, including positivism, it is itself a presupposition; it claims the right to judge evidence.[41]
4. Flew's verification principle is also a presupposition, and should be evaluated like other presuppositions.
5. But Flew's verification principle, like those discussed earlier, is incoherent as an attempt to define the limits of meaningful discourse.

As I mentioned, hardly anyone defended the program of logical positivism after 1970. Jon Wheatley was not too far off the mark when he said, "Logical positivism is one of the very few philosophical positions which can easily be shown to be dead wrong, and that is its principal claim to fame."[42]

OTHER PHILOSOPHIES OF SCIENCE

This chapter is mainly devoted to twentieth-century philosophies of language analysis. But it should be evident from our discussions so far that many twentieth-century philosophers focused more closely on science than on language per se. As we have seen, many philosophers in the Enlightenment were deeply interested in science, and that has continued since. Karl Marx (chapter 7) claimed scientific status for his theory of economic determinism. Charles S. Peirce (chapter 9) argued a kind of *scientism*, the view that scientific method is ultimately the only method of determining truth. The phenomenologists and existentialists, however, warned against confusing the life-world with the world of science and technology. The logical positivists, however, as we have seen, were not embarrassed at all by their militant scientism and contempt for metaphysics and theology. But I would not want to leave readers with the impression that the logical positivists were right about anything, even about science. Therefore, I will argue here that the main traditions of twentieth-century philosophy of science in fact opposed scientism and the views of science held by the logical positivists.

Jon Wheatley was not too far off the mark when he said, "Logical positivism is one of the very few philosophical positions which can easily be shown to be dead wrong, and that is its principal claim to fame."

The positivists' view of science reminds me of a letter to the editor I found in my local newspaper some years ago, from a Mr. Angel Sanchez:

> Ever wonder why most people refuse to discuss religion and politics? I suspect it's because they are both so ambiguous. Isn't it time we built our beliefs on a firm foundation, something

41. In my response to Flew ("God and Biblical Language," cited earlier), I deal with this argument at greater length.

42. Jon Wheatley, *Prolegomena to Philosophy* (Belmont, CA: Wadsworth, 1970), 103.

> which most of us can understand, something which affects our lives every day and we can control? SCIENCE. Think about it.[43]

I thought about it, and often asked my students to critique this statement on their exams. As often, what the positivists said more precisely and elegantly is similar to what many people consider to be common sense. Science is objective and reliable, religion and politics subjective and ambiguous. Science is the firm foundation on which all other knowledge must be built. Scientists gather *facts*, while metaphysicians and theologians merely accumulate legends, myths, and fantasies.

Although philosophers no longer defend positivism, the scientistic notion that science is objective *while metaphysics and theology are* subjective *is routinely assumed in much contemporary discourse in politics, religion, and popular culture.*

Although philosophers no longer defend positivism, the scientistic notion that science is *objective* while metaphysics and theology are *subjective* is routinely assumed in much contemporary discourse in politics, religion, and popular culture. This picture of science assumes that scientists merely go out and look at the world and record what they see. They gather the objective, uninterpreted, "brute" facts, free of bias, prejudice, or presupposition.

But this popular picture is very rare among scientists themselves and among postpositivist philosophers who analyze scientific method and discourse. Indeed, the consensus among twentieth-century philosophers of science is decidedly contrary to the picture presented in Mr. Sanchez's letter. For one thing, the problems of epistemology—from the Greeks, through the Enlightenment and Kant, down to the present—pertain to science as much as to any other area of knowledge. Questions about the relation of sense to reason, the *a priori* to the *a posteriori*, the roles of testimony and authority, bear on science as much as they bear on history or religion. And it cannot be said that the philosophical community has achieved any solid consensus on any of these issues.

Questions about the relation of sense to reason, the a priori *to the* a posteriori, *the roles of testimony and authority, bear on science as much as they bear on history or religion.*

So twentieth-century philosophers of science, for the most part, have held much more modest views of science than the positivists or Angel Sanchez. One view of science was *conventionalism*, the view that scientific assertions are not assertions of objective fact, but agreements of scientists to construe data one way rather than another. This approach was developed by **Henri Poincaré** (1854–1912), who thought that given the usefulness of non-Euclidean geometries, we should think of geometry as a convention, rather than a body of *a priori* truths as in positivism. The physicist and philosopher **Pierre Duhem** (1861–1916) broadened this principle to include all science. Duhem argued a *holistic view*,[44] that scientific conclusions are never simply based on observations (as in positivism), because every observation can be accounted

43. Angel Sanchez, letter to the editor, *Escondido Times-Advocate*, April 28, 1983 (emphasis his).

44. Somewhat like Hegel and Willard Quine, whom I discuss later in this chapter.

OUTLINE

for by many explanations. So experiments in physics are not simple observations, but interpretations of observations within a theoretical framework. One cannot submit a single hypothesis to a single experimental test, for every experiment actually tests a whole complexity of hypotheses, background assumptions, and theories. Our reasons for accepting one hypothesis over another are often complex, sometimes having to do with aesthetic simplicity and symmetry.

John Dewey (chapter 9) and others developed the view of *instrumentalism*, which held that scientific theories are not descriptions of the world at all. Rather, they are instruments, tools, by which we can manipulate nature. We can understand how this view arose from the pragmatic view of truth that Dewey shared with William James.

Still another view of science was known as *operationalism*. On this view, scientific theories do not describe the world, but summarize research programs. The physicist **Percy Bridgman** (1882–1961), concerned about paradoxes related to the theory of relativity and quantum mechanics, suggested that the meaning of any concept is nothing more than a set of operations.[45] The astrophysicist **Arthur Eddington**, who tried to show that science and Christianity were compatible, told Christians not to worry: scientific theories are nothing but instrumental readouts, "pointer readings." The Christian philosopher and apologist **Gordon H. Clark** (1902–85) (chapter 13) appealed to Bridgman's theory in his quest to show that empirical science gives us no knowledge of the world.[46]

Conventionalism, instrumentalism, and operationalism overlapped and influenced one another, but their net effect was to dismantle the claims of positivists and others that science is an exclusive road to the discovery of fundamental, bedrock fact.

Conventionalism, instrumentalism, and operationalism overlapped and influenced one another, but their net effect was to dismantle the claims of positivists and others that science is an exclusive road to the discovery of fundamental, bedrock fact.

Other thinkers exposed even more fully and clearly the complicated nature of scientific inquiry. **Michael Polanyi** (1889–1976) made important discoveries in physical chemistry and later became a defender of free-market economics. He rejected the positivist notion of objective scientific knowledge, arguing that personal commitments are necessary to scientific discovery.[47] We cannot gain knowledge without personally seeking it. We choose questions and hypotheses that we think are likely to yield discoveries, and we commit ourselves to the means necessary to find what we are looking for, risking our resources and reputations for the chance to learn about the universe. So scientific knowledge presupposes personal knowledge.

45. Percy Bridgman, *The Logic of Modern Physics* (New York: Macmillan, 1927).

46. Gordon H. Clark, *The Philosophy of Science and Belief in God* (Nutley, NJ: Craig Press, 1964).

47. See his *Science, Faith and Society*, Riddle Memorial Lectures (London: Oxford University Press, 1946), and especially *Personal Knowledge: Towards a Post-Critical Philosophy* (Chicago: University of Chicago Press, 1958).

Often we are unable to specify formally, or even clearly, what it is that motivates us to seek truth. But that inability to describe our motivations does not invalidate our search. Polanyi says that these inexpressible motivations themselves grasp the truth at some level. We believe more than we can prove and know more than we can say. Polanyi describes those subsidiary beliefs and understandings as *tacit knowledge*. For example, Copernicus, he says, was motivated to risk his reputation on the heliocentric hypothesis not because heliocentrism was the automatic result of an empirical or rationalistic method, but because the new worldview captured his imagination and his sense of beauty. Success in science, therefore, results from integrating our tacit knowledge with our focal knowledge.

Thomas Kuhn (1922–96) was motivated by Polanyi and others to look beyond common descriptions of scientific method and to make a serious historical study of how science is actually practiced.

Thomas Kuhn (1922–96) was motivated by Polanyi and others to look beyond common descriptions of scientific method and to make a serious historical study of how science is actually practiced. The result of his study was a book, *The Structure of Scientific Revolutions*,[48] which has been the starting point of all subsequent discussions of the nature of science. Kuhn denies the common picture (as in the Sanchez letter quoted earlier), reinforced by logical positivism, that scientific progress is simply an accumulation of factual discoveries over the years. Rather, Kuhn's study of the major turning points in science associated with the names of Copernicus, Newton, Lavoisier, and Einstein leads him to conclude:

> Each produced a consequent shift in the problems available for scientific scrutiny and in the standards by which the profession determined what should count as an admissible problem or as a legitimate problem-solution. And each transformed the scientific imagination in ways that we shall ultimately need to describe as a transformation of the world within which scientific work was done. Such changes, together with the controversies that almost always accompany them, are the defining characteristics of scientific revolutions.[49]

Thomas Kuhn

"Normal science," says Kuhn, occurs within one of these traditions:

> In this essay, "normal science" means research firmly based upon one or more past scientific achievements, achievements that some particular scientific community acknowledges for a time as supplying the foundation for its further practice.[50]

48. Chicago: University of Chicago Press, 1962.
49. Ibid., 6.
50. Ibid., 10.

Those achievements create *paradigms*, a term that Kuhn's book contributed to the general language of our time:

> By choosing [the term *paradigm*], I mean to suggest that some accepted examples of actual scientific practice—examples which include law, theory, application, and instrumentation together—provide models from which spring particular coherent traditions of scientific research.[51]

Examples of these are *Ptolemaic astronomy*, *Copernican astronomy*, *Aristotelian dynamics*, and *corpuscular optics* (or *wave optics*). Normal science presupposes and operates within one or more of these paradigms. It aims to extend the paradigm to additional phenomena, to discover new facts that apply and illustrate the paradigm. It is possible, of course, to do science of a sort without a paradigm. But:

> In the absence of a paradigm or some candidate for paradigm, all of the facts that could possibly pertain to the development of a given science are likely to seem equally relevant. As a result, fact-gathering is a far more nearly random activity than the one that subsequent scientific development makes familiar.[52]

That science is somewhat random, marked by arguments against competing schools of thought, each scientist seeking to build the fundamentals of his discipline from the ground up. But once a foundational paradigm gains acceptance by a community, scientists can agree on a common effort. Generally it is at that point that research becomes most fruitful. Under a paradigm, scientists can agree on what experiments are likely to be most helpful, and the methods and instrumentation necessary to carry out those experiments successfully. They "solve puzzles," phenomena seeming to require explanation, by assimilating those phenomena to the paradigm.

Once a foundational paradigm gains acceptance by a community, scientists can agree on a common effort. . . . Under a paradigm, scientists can agree on what experiments are likely to be most helpful, and the methods and instrumentation necessary to carry out those experiments successfully.

But occasionally scientists will detect an especially difficult problem that Kuhn calls an *anomaly*:

> Discovery commences with the awareness of anomaly, i.e., with the recognition that nature has somehow violated the paradigm-induced expectations that govern normal science.[53]

Scientists resolve anomalies in different ways: sometimes by eventually showing that an anomaly can after all be accommodated to the existing

51. Ibid.
52. Ibid., 15.
53. Ibid., 52–53.

paradigm. Or the anomaly can be set aside, in effect, awaiting resolution by future scientists.[54] But sometimes anomalies multiply, leading to *crisis*, that is, "the persistent failure of the puzzles of normal science to come out as they should."[55] As one of his examples, he cites the ferment among Ptolemaic astronomers before Copernicus: "astronomy's complexity was increasing far more rapidly than its accuracy and . . . a discrepancy corrected in one place was likely to show up in another."[56]

Crises "begin with the blurring of a paradigm and the consequent loosening of the rules for normal research."[57] If the scientists cannot accommodate the phenomena to the existent paradigm, or set it aside for future resolution, "the crisis may end with the emergence of a new candidate for paradigm and with the ensuing battle over its acceptance."[58] The battle over the acceptance of a new paradigm is what Kuhn calls a *scientific revolution*: "scientific revolutions are here taken to be those non-cumulative developmental episodes in which an older paradigm is replaced in whole or in part by an incompatible new one."[59]

Crises "begin with the blurring of a paradigm and the consequent loosening of the rules for normal research."

The issue between two competing paradigms cannot be resolved by observation, as the positivists imagined, for observation itself is relative to one's paradigm. Kuhn refers to experiments with anomalous playing cards. The experimenter replaces the black 6 of spades with a red one and asks the subject to identify a series of cards. When the subject reaches the anomalous card, at first he identifies it according to his normal expectations, "black 6 of spades." After several rounds of this, however, the subject might become uncertain and confused, until he is told the nature of the anomaly. But until then, his expectations, not his visual experience, determined his responses.[60] Kuhn comments:

The battle over the acceptance of a new paradigm is what Kuhn calls a scientific revolution*: "scientific revolutions are here taken to be those non-cumulative developmental episodes in which an older paradigm is replaced in whole or in part by an incompatible new one."*

> That psychological experiment provides a wonderfully simple and cogent schema for the process of scientific discovery. In science, as with the playing card experiment, novelty emerges only with difficulty, manifested by resistance, against a background provided by expectation.[61]

54. This is a perfectly respectable strategy, even in theology. There are difficult problems in Christian theology, dealing with evil, the Trinity, divine sovereignty and human freedom. But contrary to the notions of many nonbelievers, the nature of the Christian faith is such that none of these problems needs to be resolved right away. Christians have ample reason to believe God's revelation in the absence of such resolutions. Indeed, if God is as Christians describe him, it would be unreasonable to believe in him if there were no unsolved problems.

55. Kuhn, *Revolutions*, 68.

56. Ibid. He cites J. L. E. Dreyer, *A History of Astronomy from Thales to Kepler*, 2nd ed. (New York: Dover, 1953), chaps. 11–12.

57. Kuhn, *Revolutions*, 84.

58. Ibid.

59. Ibid., 92.

60. Ibid., 62–64.

61. Ibid., 64.

Nor, in an argument over paradigms, is there some neutral court of appeal by which we can evaluate one paradigm against another. Rather:

> When paradigms enter, as they must, into a debate about paradigm choice, their role is necessarily circular. Each group uses its own paradigms to argue in that paradigm's defense.
>
> The resulting circularity does not, of course, make the argument wrong or even ineffectual. The man who premises a paradigm when arguing in its defense can nevertheless provide a clear exhibit of what scientific practice will be like for those who adopt the new view of nature. That exhibit can be immensely persuasive, often compellingly so. Yet whatever its force, the status of the circular argument is only that of persuasion. It cannot be made logically or even probabilistically compelling for those who refuse to step into the circle. . . . This issue of paradigm choice can never be unequivocally settled by logic and experiment alone.[62]

Recall that for Kuhn, paradigms create *coherent traditions*. He has much to say about the community structure of science, the communities that gather around these paradigm traditions. When one is trying to choose between one paradigm and a rival one, and the circular arguments aren't persuasive, often the most relevant issue is the character of the communities that hold the paradigms in question. This is part of the *personal knowledge*, the *tacit knowledge*, that Polanyi said was so important to scientific discovery.

When one is trying to choose between one paradigm and a rival one, and the circular arguments aren't persuasive, often the most relevant issue is the character of the communities that hold the paradigms in question.

Still, Kuhn argues that there is a vast gulf between scientists who hold different paradigms. This leads him to his most controversial position:

> In so far as their only recourse to that world [i.e., the world of their research-engagement—JF] is through what they see and do, we may want to say that after a revolution scientists are responding to a different world.[63]

Kuhn hesitates at this point, but he is inclined to say that moving from one paradigm to another is far more than a change in interpretation. Interpretation is paradigm-dependent. When two people differ on the interpretation of something, they share agreement on the existence of the thing that they are trying to interpret. But in a paradigm conflict, even that agreement can be lost. Kuhn gives many instances of objects (such as *phlogiston*) that exist under one paradigm, but not in another.

62. Ibid., 94.
63. Ibid., 111.

Interpretation occurs in the work of normal science, but the term *interpretation* does not accurately describe the change that takes place in the adoption of a new paradigm. So in one sense, to accept a new paradigm is more than to accept a new interpretation of something; it is to live in a different world.

This and other aspects of the book suggest an analogy with theology, as a discipline developed in religious communities. In a postscript written seven years after the initial publication of *Revolutions*, Kuhn addresses the question whether similar analyses can be made of fields other than science, such as art, literature, music, and politics. Kuhn replies, in effect, "Of course"—because *Revolutions* aims to take patterns that are obviously true of these other disciplines and apply them to science, which is often thought to have a very different structure.[64] But because of the frequent tendency in Christian theology to try to accommodate itself to the sciences, we should perhaps note again a point I made in chapter 1: living under the lordship of Christ leads us to see the world very differently from those who do not trust Christ in that way. We presuppose the truth of God's revelation, and that presupposition constrains us to a worldview very different from that of any non-Christian philosophy. Arguing for that worldview is, as Kuhn says about paradigms, circular in a sense. But to display the Christian world and life view, as it is lived within the Christian community, is a sufficient argument.

In one sense, to accept a new paradigm is more than to accept a new interpretation of something; it is to live in a different world.

Kuhn's book produced a torrent of criticism. The chief criticism was that *Revolutions* was relativist. Kuhn qualified his position in various ways, but never quite satisfied his critics. Others, like Norwood Hanson[65] and Paul Feyerabend,[66] developed models similar to, or even more radical than, Kuhn's. What is certain is that the positivist verificationist model of science is no longer assumed among scientists or philosophers of science, however much it may persist in the popular mind. Kuhn's work has provided a new starting point for discussions of the philosophy of science.

What is certain is that the positivist verificationist model of science is no longer assumed among scientists or philosophers of science, however much it may persist in the popular mind.

ORDINARY-LANGUAGE PHILOSOPHY

We now return to the subject of twentieth-century language analysis, and to the story of Ludwig Wittgenstein. When Wittgenstein returned to Cambridge in 1929, the word soon got out that his thinking had changed from that of the *Tractatus*. The "later Wittgenstein" is evident

64. Ibid., 208–9.

65. Norwood Russell Hanson, *Patterns of Discovery: An Inquiry into the Conceptual Foundations of Science* (Cambridge: Cambridge University Press, 1958).

66. Paul Feyerabend, *Against Method: Outline of an Anarchistic Theory of Knowledge* (London: Verso, 1975).

in the *Blue and Brown Books*,[67] which he dictated to his students from 1933 to 1935. The standard text, however, is considered to be the posthumously published *Philosophical Investigations*.[68] Actually, Wittgenstein's basic argument is easier to follow in the *Blue and Brown Books*, which presents a continuous text. The *Investigations*, however, is a numbered series of aphorisms (resembling Pascal's *Pensées*) that are not always easy to relate to one another. After Wittgenstein's death in 1951, his disciples and friends gathered together his notes on many topics, which led eventually to the publication of over twenty books under Wittgenstein's name, many of these further collections of aphorisms, which he had written, kept, and refined over the years.

The "later Wittgenstein" is most famous for his thoughts about the meaning of language, a major concern for all language-analysis philosophers. The *Investigations* begin with a long quote from Augustine's *Confessions*, 1.8, explaining how Augustine had learned language from his elders. Wittgenstein replies:

> These words, it seems to me, give us a particular picture of the essence of human language. It is this: the individual words in language name objects—sentences are combinations of such names.—In this picture of language we find the roots of the following idea: Every word has a meaning. This meaning is correlated with the word. It is the object for which the word stands.[69]

The "later Wittgenstein" is most famous for his thoughts about the meaning of language, a major concern for all language-analysis philosophers.

The view that Wittgenstein attributes to Augustine is sometimes called the *referential theory of meaning*. This means that every word "refers to" or "denotes" something, and its meaning is its referent, what it refers to. The meaning of *tree* is the set of actual trees in the world. But there are problems with this view. Gottlob Frege's famous paper "On Sense and Reference"[70] argued that "the morning star," "the evening star," and "the planet Venus" all had the same reference, but they did not have the same meaning, because they could not be freely substituted for one another. So meaning must include something other than merely word and reference. He called that additional factor *sense* (*Sinn*). But Frege left the concept of *sense* somewhat mysterious.

Nevertheless, Russell's logical atomism and Wittgenstein's *Tractatus* had followed essentially the referential view of meaning. In Russell's

67. Ludwig Wittgenstein, *Preliminary Studies for the "Philosophical Investigation": Generally Known as the Blue and Brown Books*, 2nd ed., Harper Torchbooks (New York: Harper and Row, 1965).

68. Trans. G. E. M. Anscombe (New York: Macmillan, 1968).

69. Ibid., 1. In references to this book, I will use numbers to refer to aphorisms, not pages.

70. Written 1892; translation by Max Black available at http://en.wikisource.org/wiki/On_Sense_and_Reference.

perfect language, every sentence states, refers to, an atomic fact, and every word refers to an *element* of the fact—a thing, property, or relation. The meaning of the sentence is the fact to which it refers, and the meaning of each word is the element to which it refers. But we should remind ourselves that this kind of meaning was restricted to Russell's perfect language. It was not true of ordinary language. Ordinary language had to be reworked, reconstructed, so that these meanings could become evident. In this respect, Wittgenstein's *Tractatus* followed Russell.

Philosophical Investigations

This bent toward language reconstruction was typical of Russell and the early Wittgenstein. In Russell's famous article "On Denoting,"[71] he discussed denoting phrases, or "definite descriptions," that attribute predicates to nonexistent subjects, such as "The present king of France is bald." We would like to say that this sentence is false, since there is no present king of France. But then the contradictory "The present king of France is not bald" would be true (by the law of the excluded middle), and that seems an undesirable result. So Russell claimed that when we utter "The present king of France is bald," what we are *really* saying is, "There is an entity C, such that 'X is kingly, French, and bald' is true if and only if X = C." That reconstructed sentence is certainly false. But does the reconstruction actually reproduce the *meaning*, the sense, of the original sentence? Does Russell's complicated formulation actually describe what people who use this sentence are trying to say?

The Wittgenstein of the *Tractatus* attempted a large-scale reconstruction of ordinary language, believing that ordinary language was full of confusions that mislead us about the nature of the world. Only in the perfect language would meaning show through clearly. But the restatement of language in complicated logical formulae and supposed atomic-fact metaphysics took away from language its ability as a tool of communication between ordinary persons.[72]

The later Wittgenstein now thinks ordinary language is sufficient to perform its function. But we should listen and try to understand what it says. It is for this reason that the philosophical movement following the later Wittgenstein is often called ordinary-language philosophy.

So one important difference between the earlier and later Wittgenstein is that the later Wittgenstein no longer tries to reconstruct ordinary language. He now thinks ordinary language is sufficient to perform its function. But we should listen and try to understand what it says. It is for this reason that the philosophical movement following the later Wittgenstein is often called *ordinary-language philosophy*. Analytic philosophy continues to reflect this difference. Some thinkers,

71. *Mind* 14 (1905): 479–93.

72. So Wittgenstein's student Peter Strawson writes in "On Referring," *Mind*, n.s., 59, 235 (July 1950): 320–44, that reference, contrary to Russell, is not the inadequate statement of a complicated logical formula. When someone says, "The present king of France is bald," he is not making a complicated false assertion, but is merely expressing his own confusion, not saying anything either true or false. The sentence in question is not a proposition at all.

such as Russell, seek to clarify the meanings of expressions by reconstructing them into other terms or logical symbols, alleging that the reconstruction tells us what the original expression "really means." Others, like the later Wittgenstein, seek to find the "proper use" of ordinary expressions themselves.[73]

But how does ordinary-language philosophy deal with the question of the meaning of *meaning*? After identifying the view that he attributes to Augustine, Wittgenstein points out that not all words function as names ("five" is his example).[74] Further, even words that designate or refer to objects do so only in the context of certain human practices. To learn a word is to associate it not merely with an object (or a mental picture),[75] but with patterns of human life. "Slab," to use one of his examples,[76] is a word associated not only with certain objects, but also with things that we *do* with objects: carrying them, using them to build, and so forth. The human practices that make use of words Wittgenstein calls "language games."[77] He says:

> Think of the tools in a tool-box: there is a hammer, pliers, a saw, a screw-driver, a rule, a glue-pot, glue, nails and screws.—The functions of words are as diverse as the functions of these objects. (And in both cases there are similarities.)
>
> Of course, what confuses us is the uniform appearance of words when we hear them spoken or meet them in script and print. For their *application* is not presented to us so clearly. Especially when we are doing philosophy![78]

To learn a word is to associate it not merely with an object (or a mental picture), but with patterns of human life.

On the differences between uses of words:

> But how many kinds of sentence are there? Say assertion, question, and command? There are *countless* different kinds of use of what we call "symbols", "words", "sentences". And that multiplicity is not something fixed, given once for all; but new types

73. In recent philosophy of religion, the impulse to reconstruct religious language in logical terms can be found in Joseph M. Bochenski, *The Logic of Religion* (New York: New York University Press, 1965), and William A. Christian, *Meaning and Truth in Religion* (Princeton, NJ: Princeton University Press, 1964). The impulse to treat religious language as ordinary language can be found in Paul L. Holmer, *The Grammar of Faith* (San Francisco: Harper and Row, 1978), and Ian T. Ramsey, *Religious Language: An Empirical Placing of Theological Phrases* (New York: Macmillan, 1957). For Wittgenstein's approach, see later discussion in this section.

74. Wittgenstein, *Investigations*, 1.

75. Ibid., 6.

76. Ibid., 2.

77. Ibid., 7.

78. Ibid., 11.

of language, new language-games, as we may say, come into existence, and others become obsolete and get forgotten. . . .

Here the term "language-*game*" is meant to bring into prominence the fact that the *speaking* of language is part of an activity, or of a form of life.

Review the multiplicity of language-games in the following examples, and in others:

Giving orders, and obeying them—

Describing the appearance of an object, or giving its measurements—

Constructing an object from a description (a drawing)—

Reporting an event—

Speculating about an event— . . .[79]

Asking, thanking, cursing, greeting, praying.

—It is interesting to compare the multiplicity of the tools in language and of the ways they are used, the multiplicity of kinds of word and sentence, with what logicians have said about the structure of language. (Including the author of the *Tractatus Logico-Philosophicus*.)[80]

The Wittgenstein of the Investigations *rejects such reductionism. Words have many uses, and their uses cannot be described apart from the tasks they perform in human activities, language games.*

The *Tractatus*, following Russell's logical atomism, had tried to reduce all words to one use: naming or referring to objects, "picturing facts." Words that proved inadequate to that task were considered nonsensical or relegated to various kinds of linguistic limbo: Wittgenstein's *Mystical*, the positivists' *emotive language*. But the Wittgenstein of the *Investigations* rejects such reductionism. Words have many uses, and their uses cannot be described apart from the tasks they perform in human activities, language games. Is it possible, then, to formulate a general definition of *meaning*? We might expect Wittgenstein to give a negative answer to that question. But he does provide the following: "For a *large* class of cases—though not for all—in which we employ the word 'meaning' it can be defined thus: the meaning of a word is its use in the language."[81]

[According to Wittgenstein]: "For a large class of cases—though not for all—in which we employ the word 'meaning' it can be defined thus: the meaning of a word is its use in the language."

79. This ellipsis covers nine other examples.

80. Wittgenstein, *Investigations*, 23.

81. Ibid., 43. This definition of *meaning* has influenced my own definition of "theology as application" (see *DWG*, 272–79, and *ST*, chap. 1). Vern S. Poythress, however, has developed a more sophisticated account of meaning from his linguistic study and our shared triperspectival model. He distinguishes classificational, instantiational, and associational aspects of language, which leads to a view of meaning that balances sense, application, and import. See his *God-Centered Biblical Interpretation* (Phillipsburg, NJ: P&R Publishing, 1999), 72–74. Also his general treatment of language, *In the Beginning Was the Word: Language: A God-Centered Approach* (Wheaton, IL: Crossway, 2009), 24–28 and passim.

OUTLINE

This concept of *meaning* makes the later Wittgenstein far more liberal than the early Wittgenstein in acknowledging the legitimacy of different kinds of language. He now rejects the notion of a perfect language, for language has many functions, and no language is perfect for all of them. Further, the later Wittgenstein rejects the program of trying to reduce complex facts to simple, or atomic, ones.[82] There is no reason for preferring logical simplicity, and indeed the very concept of simplicity is complicated. No fact is simple in every respect, and complex facts have many kinds of complexity at once.[83]

The earlier Wittgenstein tried to make his perfect language absolutely precise. But the later Wittgenstein recognizes that much language is not meant to be precise. When a photographer says, "Stand roughly there," the phrase is not shorthand for a precise location. "Stand roughly there" might be exactly what he intends to say.[84]

The later Wittgenstein is still somewhat nominalist in his approach to the question of *universals*, but for different reasons from those in the *Tractatus*:

> 65. Here we come up against the great question that lies behind all these considerations.—For someone might object against me: "You take the easy way out! You talk about all sorts of language-games, but have nowhere said what the essence of a language-game, and hence of language, is: what is common to all these activities, and what makes them into language or parts of language. So you let yourself off the very part of the investigation that once gave you yourself most headache, the part about the *general form of propositions*[85] and of language."
>
> And this is true.—Instead of producing something common to all that we call language, I am saying that these phenomena have no one thing in common which makes us use the same word for all,—but that they are *related* to one another in many different ways. And it is because of this relationship, or these relationships, that we call them all "language". I will try to explain this.

This concept of meaning *makes the later Wittgenstein far more liberal than the early Wittgenstein in acknowledging the legitimacy of different kinds of language.*

82. Wittgenstein, *Investigations*, 39.

83. A rug, for example, is complex in its shape, its composition, the materials of its construction, its colors, its purposes, and the like.

84. Wittgenstein, *Investigations*, 71. Inspired by Wittgenstein's point, I have sometimes said that the evangelical doctrine of Scripture does not assert that Scripture is maximally precise, only that it is completely true. Scripture often uses approximate numbers and figures as we use them in ordinary language, and these are exactly what God wants to say to us. That is to say that God in Scripture speaks *ordinary* language.

85. Cf. *Tractatus*, 6.0, referred to earlier in the present chapter.

> 66. Consider for example the proceedings that we call "games". I mean board-games, card-games, ball-games, Olympic games, and so on. What is common to them all?—Don't say: "There *must* be something common, or they would not be called 'games' "—but *look and see* whether there is anything common to all . . . .
>
> And the result of this examination is: we see a complicated network of similarities, overlapping and criss-crossing: sometimes overall similarities, sometimes similarities of detail.
>
> 67. I can think of no better expression to characterize these similarities than "family resemblances"; for the various resemblances between members of a family: build, features, colour of eyes, gait, temperament, etc. etc. overlap and criss-cross in the same way—And I shall say: "games" form a family.[86]

Wittgenstein is still suspicious of metaphysics, as in Tractatus, *6.53, and for the same reason: that metaphysics misuses language. But the* Investigations *locates this misuse in a different place.*

He illustrates: "The strength of a thread does not reside in the fact that some one fibre runs through its whole length, but in the overlapping of many fibres."[87]

So much for Plato's essences.

These examples illustrate the concept of philosophy that Wittgenstein practices in the second phase of his thought. He is still suspicious of metaphysics, as in *Tractatus*, 6.53, and for the same reason: that metaphysics misuses language. But the *Investigations* locates this misuse in a different place. Wittgenstein quotes Augustine again, who in the *Confessions* asks, "What is time? If nobody asks me, I know; but if somebody asks me, I don't know." For Wittgenstein, this question describes the typical origin of a metaphysical problem.[88] Time is a common concept in ordinary life. We measure how much time we have for a task, how much time we have before the next appointment, and so on. Yet if someone asks, "But what *is* time, anyway?" we draw a blank. Imagine someone asking you the time, and when you say, "3:45 P.M." he replies with the further question, "Yes, but what *is* time?" And when you express puzzlement, he says, "But how can you claim to know the time, if you don't know what time *is*?" At that point, an ordinary question becomes a metaphysical one, a question about the *essence* of time.[89] For Wittgenstein, metaphysical questions arise when we take terms of ordinary language and try to make them do jobs that they were not made to do. *Time, substance, form, simplicity, truth, mind*

For Wittgenstein, metaphysical questions arise when we take terms of ordinary language and try to make them do jobs that they were not made to do.

86. Wittgenstein, *Investigations*, 65–67.

87. Ibid., 67.

88. Ibid., 89.

89. I am assuming, of course, that our interlocutor will not be satisfied with definitions of time taken from physics.

are examples, and many others. Wittgenstein applies this analysis to the concept of *naming*:

> This is connected with the conception of naming as, so to speak, an occult process. Naming appears as a *queer* connection of a word with an object.—And you really get such a queer connection when the philosopher tries to bring out *the* relation between name and thing by staring at an object in front of him and repeating a name or even the word "this" innumerable times. For philosophical problems arise when language *goes on holiday*. And *here* we may indeed fancy naming to be some remarkable act of mind, as it were a baptism of an object. And we can also say the word "this" *to* the object, as it were *address* the object as "this"—a queer use of this word, which doubtless only occurs in doing philosophy.[90]

So what is the work of philosophy? It is *therapeutic*. Philosophy should not seek to find occult entities, or to build big systems of truth like Hegel, said Wittgenstein, but rather to help people who are caught in confusions over the use of language. "What is your aim in philosophy?—To shew the fly the way out of the fly-bottle."[91] Recall that Russell and the positivists had said that the work of philosophy was simply to clarify the language of science, since philosophers had no means of finding truth that scientists lacked. The later Wittgenstein also limits the work of philosophy to clarification—not only of science, but of all language—but clarification of certain kinds of confusion.

What is the work of philosophy? It is therapeutic. *Philosophy should not seek to find occult entities, or to build big systems of truth like Hegel, said Wittgenstein, but rather to help people who are caught in confusions over the use of language.*

Apart from metaphysics, the later Wittgenstein appears to be fairly liberal in evaluating types of language. No longer does he try to reduce all discourse to the one function of stating facts. Rather, he recognizes a vast variety of language games, of things that people do with language. If meaning is use, of course, there is no possibility of restricting meaning to one narrow kind of language and dismissing others as "cognitively meaningless." Any kind of language that people actually use in their communication with one another, any genuine language game, is on that account meaningful. The relevant response to such language is, as Wittgenstein puts it, "*this language-game is played*."[92]

90. Ibid., 38. In logical atomism, the word *this* was often thought to be the only true proper name, the only way in which one could name a truly atomic fact, as in "this red, now."

91. Ibid., 309. See also 109: "Philosophy is a battle against the bewitchment of our intelligence by means of language."

92. Ibid., 654 (emphasis his).

It is, therefore, interesting (especially for readers of the present volume) to compare his later views of religious language with those he held earlier. We recall that in the *Tractatus* Wittgenstein concluded that talk about God did not measure up to Wittgenstein's criteria for meaningful language, so he relegated it to *the Mystical*. He does not take up that question in the *Investigations* (so far as I can tell), but he does discuss religion elsewhere. I note his discussion with some students in 1938. Student notes of these discussions were published in the small book *Lectures and Conversations on Aesthetics, Psychology, and Religious Belief*.[93]

Wittgenstein's main point in the discussion of religion concerns the uniqueness of religious language.

Wittgenstein's main point in the discussion of religion concerns the *uniqueness* of religious language. He says:

> Suppose someone were a believer and said, "I believe in a Last Judgment," and I said: "Well, I'm not so sure. Possibly." You would say that there is an enormous gulf between us. If he said, "There is a German aeroplane overhead," and I said "Possibly; I'm not so sure," you'd say we were fairly near.[94]

In this book, Wittgenstein concedes the meaningfulness of religious language. But what, in fact, does it mean? Clearly, at least, it is different from the language in which we report observation of airplanes. One thing that seems to distinguish Wittgenstein's view of religious language is that it plays a role in *regulating* one's life.[95]

Wittgenstein concedes the meaningfulness of religious language. But what, in fact, does it mean? . . . One thing that seems to distinguish Wittgenstein's view of religious language is that it plays a role in regulating one's life.

> Suppose somebody made this guidance for this life: believing in the Last Judgment. Whenever he does anything, this is before his mind. In a way, how are we to know whether to say he believes this will happen or not?
>
> Asking him is not enough. He will probably say he has proof. But he has what you might call an unshakeable belief. It will show, not by reasoning or by appeal to ordinary grounds for belief, but rather by regulating for in all his life.
>
> This is a very much stronger fact—foregoing pleasures, always appealing to this picture. This in one sense must be called the firmest of all beliefs, because the man risks things

93. Ed. Cyril Barrett, comp. from notes by Yorick Smythies, Rush Rhees, and James Taylor (Oxford: Blackwell, 1966).

94. Wittgenstein, *Investigations*, 53. Cf. 56, where Wittgenstein applies the same reasoning to belief in the resurrection.

95. Interestingly, this was also Kant's view of religious language. He listed the concept of God among his "regulative concepts." Wittgenstein here also reflects some ideas of Kierkegaard. Wittgenstein actually learned Danish in order to read Kierkegaard, at a time before it was fashionable to read Kierkegaard.

> on account of it which he would not do on things which are far better established for him.[96]

When a religious belief regulates life, says Wittgenstein, it often has a large emotive component: "Terror. That is, as it were, part of the substance of the belief."[97]

Wittgenstein says that the function of a belief in regulating one's life is independent of whether or not one has evidence or proof. Even if people had certain evidence for the coming of a judgment day, their belief in it would not necessarily be religious; that is, they could hold that belief without using it to regulate their lives and without any emotional response to it.[98]

And, Wittgenstein says, when religious people appeal to historical evidence for their faith, they don't

> apply the doubt which would ordinarily apply to *any* historical propositions. . . . They base things on evidence which taken in one way would seem exceedingly flimsy. They base enormous things on this evidence. Am I to say they are unreasonable? I wouldn't call them unreasonable.
>
> I would say, they are certainly not *reasonable*, that's obvious.
>
> "Unreasonable" implies, with everyone, rebuke.
>
> I want to say: they don't treat this as a matter of reasonability.
>
> Anyone who reads the Epistles will find it said: not only that it is not reasonable, but that it is folly.[99]
>
> Not only is it not reasonable, but it doesn't pretend to be.[100]

Wittgenstein presents religion . . . as a language game governing a form of life *different from the various games (science, history, observation) that make rational judgments. Religious believers claim knowledge, in the absence of the kind of reasons or evidence that Wittgenstein would consider adequate.*

So Wittgenstein presents religion here as a language game governing a *form of life* different from the various games (science, history, observation) that make rational judgments. Religious believers claim knowledge, in the absence of the kind of reasons or evidence that Wittgenstein would consider adequate. Typically they even claim certainty (not mere probability or possibility), so that they regard unbelief as a sin.

96. Wittgenstein, *Investigations*, 53–54.

97. Ibid. We recall Kierkegaard's emphasis on the importance of passion in true faith.

98. Ibid., 56.

99. This is what the apostle Paul says in 1 Corinthians 1:18: "For the word of the cross is folly *to those who are perishing*, but to us who are being saved it is the power of God." The gospel is not simply folly, as Wittgenstein thinks, but folly to unbelievers. Wittgenstein assumes here (as did Barth and Bultmann) that rationality should be defined by unbelieving thought, which implies that the gospel must be something other than rational. But given God's criteria of rationality, it is possible for him to say through Isaiah, "Come now, let us reason together" (Isa. 1:18).

100. Wittgenstein, *Investigations*, 57–58.

In my opinion, Wittgenstein's account of religion is insightful up to a point. It is true that true faith in Christ regulates all of life including the emotions, that believers typically do claim certainty for their faith, and that this faith is not dependent on what Wittgenstein would consider adequate visual, scientific, or historical evidence. What Wittgenstein misses is the actual objective basis of Christian faith, namely, the revelation of God. That revelation incorporates historical and rational data, but it may not be reduced to those. Scripture, too, is important, and the internal testimony of the Holy Spirit. By ignoring revelation, Wittgenstein is able to present faith as having no rational or historical basis at all.

It is true that true faith in Christ regulates all of life including the emotions, that believers typically do claim certainty for their faith, and that this faith is not dependent on what Wittgenstein would consider adequate visual, scientific, or historical evidence.

We wonder, as we read these arguments, why Wittgenstein, a professing nonbeliever, thinks he has the authority to tell believers what their faith consists of. In the context he ridicules a Catholic priest for saying that his religious faith is reasonable.[101] I conclude that the later Wittgenstein is not nearly as liberal as he claims to be. On the one hand, he seems to say that we can freely believe in Christ, since "that language-game is played."[102] On the other hand, he is quite ready to make judgments about the "proper use" of language, even in games in which he does not himself participate. On the one hand, he seems to say that anything goes (irrationalism), but on the other, he claims the authority to declare the "proper use" of words in any language game (rationalism).

Wittgenstein is like many other critics of religion who try to say that religion is fine if kept within certain limits.[103] So religion is fine as a lifestyle within a worshiping community, but it should not be brought up in discussions of science, the arts, philosophy, or politics. In such discussions, it evades its limits, its proper use. But God's Word in Scripture is "odd" in a different way from the ways that Wittgenstein mentions. It is odd because it claims the right to rule over all aspects of human life, including science, history, the arts, philosophy, and politics. Its evidence is certain, because it maintains the right to determine the grounds for certainty.[104] And so no human being, only Scripture itself, can limit its proper use; see fig. 12.3.

Wittgenstein is like many other critics of religion who try to say that religion is fine if kept within certain limits.

101. Ibid., 58.

102. He should actually be more friendly to metaphysics, for that language game is also played. He believes he can show that all metaphysicians are misusing language. But again, that presupposes that he has some access to the criteria for "proper use."

103. He is quoted as saying in a letter, "Make sure that your religion is a matter between you and God only." Comment to Maurice O'Connor Drury, as quoted in Jacques Bouveresse, *Wittgenstein Reads Freud: The Myth of the Unconscious*, trans. Carol Cosman (Princeton, NJ: Princeton University Press, 1996), 14.

104. Cf. my article "God and Biblical Language," Appendix E in *DWG*, 422–39, and Appendix H in this book.

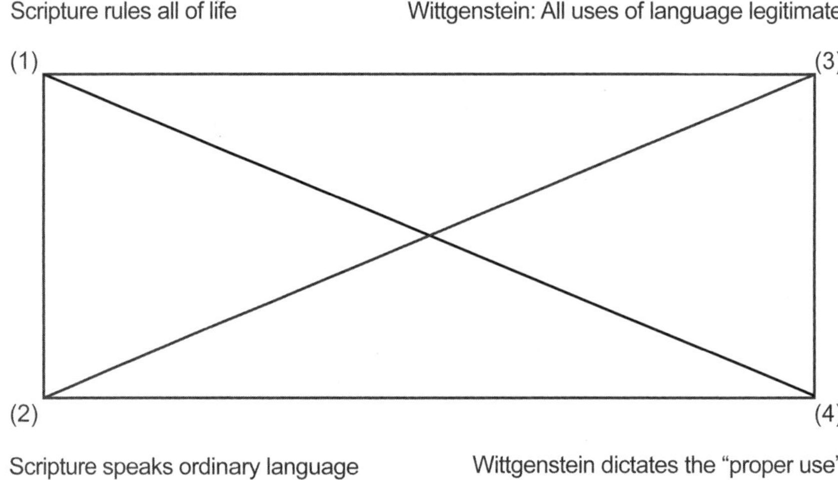

Fig. 12.3. Rationalism and Irrationalism in the Later Wittgenstein

OTHER ANALYTIC PHILOSOPHERS

Wittgenstein's disciples and many others continued the tradition of philosophy as language analysis.

Gilbert Ryle (1900–1976) wrote *The Concept of Mind*,[105] which famously ridiculed Descartes' mind-body distinction as "the ghost in the machine." Ryle argued, following hints in Wittgenstein, that language about thinking, willing, and so on was not about an independent, incorporeal soul, but rather about physical actions, seen from certain perspectives.

Peter Strawson (1919–2006) wrote *Individuals: An Essay in Descriptive Metaphysics*.[106] Wittgenstein himself had written almost entirely negatively about metaphysics, but occasionally he suggested that his language analysis yielded positive insight about the world. For example, he said, "The limits of my language mean the limits of my world,"[107] and his statement about the world being facts, not things, is a clearly metaphysical commitment. Strawson, in any case, seeks to show that when careful analysis of language strips away confusions, it necessarily leaves us with a clearer vision of what the world is really like.

J. L. Austin (1911–60) developed in great detail the theory of speech acts, *the things that we do with words. In* How to Do Things with Words, *he distinguishes three kinds of actions that we perform with speech.*

J. L. Austin (1911–60) developed in great detail the theory of *speech acts*, the things that we do with words. In *How to Do Things with Words*,[108] he distinguishes three kinds of actions that we perform with speech: *locutionary acts*, the acts of speech themselves; *illocutionary acts*, acts

105. Chicago: University of Chicago Press, 1949.

106. London: Methuen, 1959.

107. *Tractatus*, 5.6.

108. Oxford: Oxford University Press, 1976. After his death, Austin's *Sense and Sensibilia* (Oxford: Oxford University Press, 1962) was published. The allusion to Jane Austen's novel brought some chuckles to the philosophical community.

that we perform *in* speaking (questioning, commanding, promising, and the like); and *perlocutionary acts*, acts that we perform *through* speaking (informing, amusing, boring). He pointed out that promising (an illocutionary act) is not the same thing as making an assertion, but is rather a self-involving, or *performative*, utterance. By uttering it, a person does not merely predict that something will happen, but makes a personal commitment to ensure that something will happen.

Austin pointed out that promising (an illocutionary act) is not the same thing as making an assertion, but is rather a self-involving, or performative, utterance. By uttering it, a person does not merely predict that something will happen, but makes a personal commitment to ensure that something will happen.

John Searle (1932–) carried on Austin's program with his *Speech Acts: An Essay in the Philosophy of Language*[109] and many other writings. He focuses on many aspects of the illocutionary act, including *indirect speech acts*. When I remark that you are standing on my foot, I appear to be making a simple assertion. But indirectly I am also expressing pain and commanding you to move.

Willard Van Orman Quine (1908–2000) was not known as a disciple of Wittgenstein, but rather emerged from the circle of logical positivism. But his most famous article, "Two Dogmas of Empiricism,"[110] attacks notions very central to logical positivism, indeed to the whole empiricist tradition since Locke. The first "dogma" is *reductionism*, the view that all synthetic sentences can be reduced to reports of basic sense data. Quine points out that this attempt presupposes a verification principle such as we considered earlier in this chapter—and of course, the positivists never overcame the problems with the verification principle. The other "dogma of empiricism" is the *analytic-synthetic* distinction.[111] Quine sees *analytic* and *synthetic* as opposite ends of a continuum. At the extremes, some statements are clearly analytic (such as "bachelors are male") and others clearly synthetic (such as "the back fence is white"). But both types of statements depend on the definitions of subjects and predicates, and definitions have a flexibility not always recognized by philosophers. The status of "dogs bark," for example, depends on whether or not we choose to include "barking" in our definition of *dog*. Quine also points out that philosophers have defined *analyticity*, *synonymy*, and *meaning* in terms of one another, creating a vicious circle.

Quine replaces verificationism with a *holist* theory of knowledge.[112]

Willard V. Quine

109. Cambridge: Cambridge University Press, 1969.

110. *Philosophical Review* 60 (1951): 20–43. Reprinted in Willard Van Orman Quine, *From a Logical Point of View* (Cambridge, MA: Harvard University Press, 1953).

111. I have discussed this earlier in the book in connection with Hume, Leibniz, Kant, and (in this chapter) logical positivism.

112. Compare the view of Duhem, discussed earlier in this chapter. This contradicts a premise that was very important to Russell and the early Wittgenstein. In *Tractatus*, 1.21, Wittgenstein says of atomic facts that "each item can be the case or not the case, while everything else remains the same." Quine suggests, on the contrary, that the truth of one proposition depends on the truth of others and ultimately on the entire system of ideas in our minds. Quine's view is actually more like Hegel's than like that of the *Tractatus*.

Each of us has a body of beliefs that we hold with different degrees of certainty. Those that are least certain we often let go of, in response to new evidence. We are inclined to think of these as synthetic propositions. Others are more certain, and we are more reluctant to let go of them when they are challenged. These resist falsification. At the extreme (as statements of mathematics), we regard them as analytic and resolve to hold on to them, regardless of would-be defeaters to those beliefs. So questions about verification do not concern only "simple" facts, but rather the whole web of beliefs that we hold. When a belief is challenged, we are faced with the question whether that challenge requires us to change anything in that web and, if so, what we must change. For example, were we to experience what looks like a dragon in the woods, we might consider several revisions of beliefs we currently hold, such as the belief that giant lizards have been extinct for many years, the belief that we are of sound mind, or the belief that our sense experience is veridical. Or we might simply add the belief that dragons exist to our catalogue of beliefs. What change, if any, we make in that catalogue depends on various circumstances and considerations.

STRUCTURALISM

At the beginning of this chapter, I mentioned that there were two broad traditions of language philosophy in the twentieth century, based on opposite sides of the English Channel. We have so far been looking at the English side, the tradition begun by Moore, Russell, and Wittgenstein (an Austrian, to be sure!). Now we should look at the other tradition, that of structuralism, and then deconstruction.

Structuralism began with Ferdinand de Saussure (1857–1913), often regarded as the father of modern linguistics. For him, the meaning of a word or sentence is defined by its position in a system of signs.

Structuralism began with **Ferdinand de Saussure** (1857–1913), often regarded as the father of modern linguistics. For him, the meaning of a word or sentence is defined by its position in a system of signs.[113] A *sign* is a sound, image, or written expression, correlated with an idea (concept). The former is called a *signifier*, the latter a *signified*. Note that what is signified is not external to the mind, as in the referential theory of Russell and the early Wittgenstein, but rather a concept in the mind.[114] The signified is like the *ideas* of Locke and Hume, but they did not see their ideas as direct correlates of linguistic expressions.

The linguistic signs, however, are not *necessarily* correlated with the signified. Their correlation is the result of human convention, and therefore arbitrary. Nothing about the word *window* makes it more suitable than *fenêtre* to designate "an opening in a wall for the

113. Compare the other definitions of *meaning* that we have considered in this chapter: "reference," "verification," "use."

114. Nevertheless, it seems to me that the arguments of the later Wittgenstein against referential theories of meaning would also apply to this view.

admission of air or light."[115] Neither conveys anything that could be called the *essence* of the object. But the arbitrary, conventional connections between signifiers and signifieds are what create a language.

Languages change over time. New signifiers emerge, and new signifieds; and old ones perish. Different languages yield different concepts as they cut the "pie of reality" into different shapes. One language might divide the color spectrum into twenty shades, another into only four. The language of one northern tribe might have twenty words for different kinds of snow, but many of those concepts might be incomprehensible to another tribe. So a concept can exist in one language but not in another. So Saussure sets aside the Platonic ideal of absolute, eternal essences, as Wittgenstein did with his theory of "family resemblances."

Ferdinand de Saussure

The meaning of a term is defined by its position in the system of language of which it is a part.[116] Usually that meaning is defined negatively: we understand *cat* when we see that it is not *bat, fat, hat, vat, cot, cage, cake, can, car,* and so forth.[117] The negative focus is important, for if we try to determine meaning from the positive qualities of a word, then we are denying the arbitrariness of the word's association with a signified, or so Saussure believed.

Now, **Claude Lévi-Strauss** (1908–2009) extended Saussure's structural linguistics to the field of anthropology. Lévi-Strauss looks at societies the way Saussure looks at languages. For Lévi-Strauss, the phenomena of societies cannot be completely understood by their utilitarian value. Rather, they are *signifiers* that correlate with other elements of the society. They are understood in relation to those elements, as Saussure's signifiers are understood in distinction from one another. Furthermore, the features of individual societies correlate with something larger. Human beings are sufficiently similar that the practices of different cultures can be expected to reflect needs and

Claude Lévi-Strauss (1908–2009) extended Saussure's structural linguistics to the field of anthropology. Lévi-Strauss looks at societies the way Saussure looks at languages.

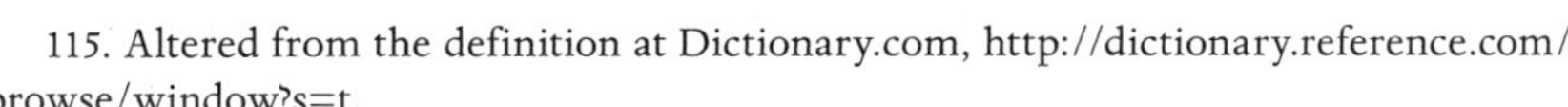

115. Altered from the definition at Dictionary.com, http://dictionary.reference.com/browse/window?s=t.

116. Another famous distinction of Saussure is between *langue* (the systematic structure of language) and *parole* (the actual speech of people). He might also have been the first to make the distinction commonly made today between *diachronic* analysis of language (charting the history through time of a linguistic expression) and *synchronic* analysis (analysis of the current usage of a linguistic expression). James Barr, in *The Semantics of Biblical Language* (London: Oxford University Press, 1961), rebuked biblical exegetes for their tendency to ascertain the meanings of terms through diachronic analysis (e.g., etymology) rather than synchronic.

117. In the triperspectival linguistics of Kenneth Pike and Vern Poythress (see chapter 13), words are identified by *particle, wave,* and *field* criteria = *contrast, variation,* and *distribution*. Saussure's negative criterion is Pike's *contrast*. But a word can also be understood by its *variation* (i.e., in what ways its expression can change while it remains the same word) and *distribution* (i.e., the contexts in which it is typically found). See Vern S. Poythress, *Philosophy, Science, and the Sovereignty of God* (Nutley, NJ: Presbyterian and Reformed, 1976), and his *In the Beginning Was the Word*.

desires that are universal. So like Saussure's accounts of languages, Lévi-Strauss defines every cultural practice as relations between two or more terms, and seeks to chart all the possible relations between those terms (e.g., mother to son, nephew, husband). Then he describes a particular society by noting the choices made by the people among the possible relations. "Human societies," he says, "like individual human beings . . . , never create absolutely; all they do is choose certain combinations from a repertory of ideas."[118]

POSTSTRUCTURALISM, DECONSTRUCTION, POSTMODERNISM

Some features of structuralism could have developed in the service of a new rationalism. **Noam Chomsky** (1928–), the inventor of *generative grammar,* wrote *Cartesian Linguistics,*[119] in which (following Descartes' sharp separation between mind and body) he distinguishes the *surface structure* of language from the *deep structure,* associated with body and mind, respectively. The deep structures of language are common to speakers of different actual languages and might be universal. This, of course, approaches a theory of innate ideas, certainly far from the philosophies of the English-speaking world. The idea that signs are meaningful only in a system might well have been given a Hegelian interpretation.

On the other hand, the arbitrariness of the relation between signifier and signified, and the consequent general rejection of essences in structuralism, is, like philosophical nominalism, a traditional path to irrationalism. And indeed, as structuralism developed, that is the theme that prevailed.

Noam Chomsky (1928–), the inventor of generative grammar, *wrote* Cartesian Linguistics, *in which . . . he distinguishes the* surface structure *of language from the* deep structure, *associated with body and mind, respectively.*

Saussure held that signs refer to concepts, and that concepts are, in the end, the signified. But as I mentioned earlier, that view places both signifiers and signifieds in the mind, rather than associating signifiers with the objective world.[120] And what is a concept? What can it be but itself a complex of signs? So this approach implies that signs refer only to other signs. That makes some sense, of course. When someone asks me what a window is, I might show him a window (sometimes called *ostensive definition*), but more likely I will give him something like a dictionary definition, replacing one term with other terms.[121] So as **Roland Barthes** (1915–80) pointed out, we do not have access

118. Claude Lévi-Strauss, *Tristes Tropiques* (New York: Atheneum, 1964), 160.

119. New York: Harper and Row, 1966.

120. We will see below that this restriction does not lead to subjectivism, but to a public system of language. But this is a world of more signs, not of anything like objective facts.

121. If I give him an ostensive definition, I might have to reassure him that the window I point to is not the only thing that is called *window,* that there are others, and different types. Or he might not need to be told these things. But in any case, ostensive definition itself presupposes facts that can be explained only in verbal concepts.

to an objective system of truth. We can only describe the relations of signs to one another. **Jacques Derrida** (1930–2004) pointed out that for Saussure, the meaning of every sign involves every other. So no meaning is ever fully available to us.

But can't we understand the meaning of the signs by consulting the author of them? No. When we discuss Shakespeare's *Macbeth*, for example, Shakespeare is not present to describe his intentions or to explain his meanings. And even if he were, he would not have the authority to settle questions about the meanings of his words. For once words are published, they become public property. The meanings of the words are determined by cultural usage (summarized in dictionaries), not by what might have been in an author's mind.[122] Hence poststructuralists urge us to reject the *myth of presence*, the myth that we should read texts as if the author were there to help us understand them.[123]

The poststructuralists regularly interpret these submeanings in Marxist terms. To them, we use our words to oppress others, especially by expressing prejudice against other races, gender, sexual orientations, and so forth.

The determination of meaning is even more difficult, however. For language often has meanings that *contradict* the author's apparent intention. Language is not only an instrument of communication, but an instrument of *power.* When we speak, we are seeking not only to express thoughts, but to "do things with words" (as J. L. Austin said). As Nietzsche and **Michel Foucault** (1926–84) emphasized, knowledge is power, and everyone uses his speech to dominate others. The power of language (divine and human) is, of course, a biblical theme (cf. Gen. 11:6; Ps. 33:6; Rom. 1:17; Heb. 4:12), and the poststructuralists are right to emphasize that, along with our frequent self-deception about it. For often what we say, with apparently innocent intentions, actually conveys evil designs.

The poststructuralists regularly interpret these submeanings in Marxist terms. To them, we use our words to oppress others, especially by expressing prejudice against other races, gender, sexual orientations, and so forth. Like the liberation theologians, these philosophers try to see everything according to the axes of oppression and liberation.

Michel Foucault

All of this makes for interesting discussions in literary salons, but it gives us little hope of ever being able to understand objective meanings in language, and through it objective truth about the world. So decon-

122. Cf. Roland Barthes, "The Death of the Author," *Aspen* 5–6 (1967). I once reviewed a book in which the author intended to speak of the "noetic influence of sin," but because of a typo spoke instead of the "poetic influence of sin." Should we say in that context that *poetic* meant *noetic*? No. *Poetic* meant *poetic*, in the normal dictionary meaning. The author's intentions could not change the meaning of the word. Of course, wise readers would take into account that the author used the wrong word, and therefore communicated the wrong meaning.

123. As a technical point, this is certainly true. But (contrary to the *new criticism* of the 1950s, in which this argument developed) it is hard to believe that the presence of Shakespeare in a seminar on *Macbeth* would be no help at all, unless we renounce all distinctions between "right" and "wrong" interpretations, or interpretations that are more or less helpful, illuminating, and so on.

structionists often express skepticism on a large scale. Typically, they believe that language and thought are serviceable enough for everyday life (the *small narratives*), but they reject talk about worldview or *great narrative* (also called *metanarrative*). So **Jean-François Lyotard** (1924–98) defines the *postmodern* as "incredulity toward metanarratives."

At this point, poststructuralism and deconstruction (the gradual reduction of Saussure's linguistics into a form of skepticism) join forces with *postmodernism*, a broad cultural trend. Postmodernism began as a movement in architecture in the 1930s and distinguishes itself from *modernism*. In modernism, truth is discovered through rational and scientific exploration (think positivism). Ultimate reality is the physical world, and whatever can be reduced to the physical. Seekers of truth are urged to be objective and independent of the community. History is progressing through technology toward a utopia in which people will have all the goods they can desire. In postmodernism, however, truth is discovered through both rational means and spiritual or traditional means. Myth and tradition again receive respect. There is no certainty of the future,[124] but overlapping and crisscrossing visions, metanarratives, and myths continue to speak to us.[125]

As to what they say, however, there is no consensus.

The struggle between modernism and postmodernism is one contemporary form of the struggle between rationalism and irrationalism; see fig. 12.4.

Poststructuralism and deconstruction (the gradual reduction of Saussure's linguistics into a form of skepticism) join forces with postmodernism, *a broad cultural trend.*

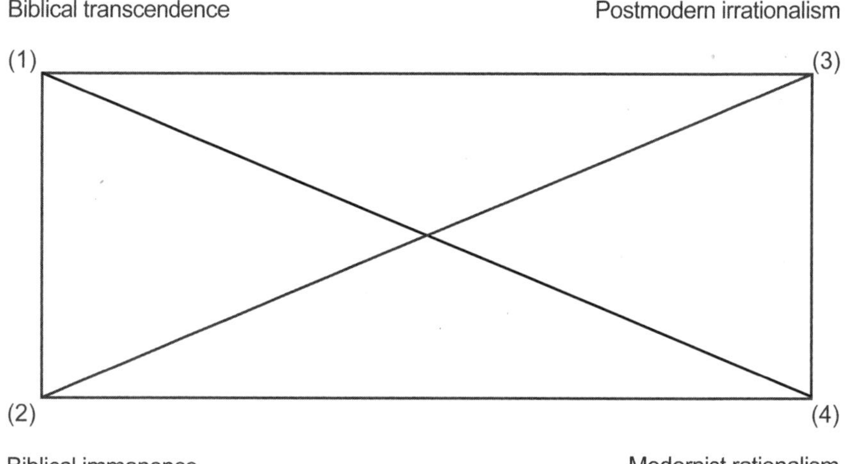

Fig. 12.4. Rationalism and Irrationalism in Contemporary Options

124. Postmodernists resemble Marxists in many ways, but their view of history seems to be more like Bloch's (chapter 11) than like that of Marx himself.

125. See Jean-François Lyotard, *The Postmodern Condition: A Report on Knowledge* (Minneapolis: University of Minnesota Press, 1984).

KEY TERMS

Language-analysis philosophy	Metanarrative
Atomic fact	Fact
Public atheist	Picture theory of language
Proposition	Russell Tribunal
Elementary proposition	Cognitive meaning
Logical positivism	The Mystical (Wittgenstein)
Scientism	Auguste Comte
Contradiction	Tautology
Logical empiricism	Empirical proposition
Theoretical statements (same)	Emotive language (logical positivism)
Protocol statement	Observation statements (same)
Cognitively meaningful	Verification principle
Brute facts	Falsifiable
Holism	Conventionalism
Operationalism	Instrumentalism
Normal science (Kuhn)	Personal commitments (Polanyi)
Puzzles	Paradigm
Crisis (Kuhn)	Anomaly
Anomalous playing cards	Scientific revolution
Referential theory of meaning	Ordinary-language philosophy
Meaning as use	Sense (Frege)
Family resemblances (Wittgenstein)	Language game
Therapeutic (Wittgenstein)	Structuralism
Signifier	Signified
Arbitrariness (Saussure)	Surface structure
Deep structure	*Langue*
Parole	Diachronic
Synchronic	Ostensive definition
Poststructuralism	Deconstruction
Postmodern	Myth of presence

STUDY QUESTIONS

1. "Invoking language to answer philosophical questions is not new." Review the history of this practice before the twentieth century.
2. Why does language take on such a central importance in twentieth-century philosophy? Cite Frame's answers, and your own.
3. "The real is the sayable and the sayable is the real." Explain; evaluate.
4. After Russell and Whitehead wrote *Principia Mathematica*, they went on to develop metaphysical systems. Describe these and compare them.

OUTLINE

G. E. Moore (1873–1958)

Bertrand Russell (1872–1970)

Ludwig Wittgenstein (1889–1951)

Logical Positivism

Other Philosophies of Science

Ordinary-Language Philosophy

Other Analytic Philosophers

Structuralism

Poststructuralism, Deconstruction, Postmodernism

5. Explain the distinction between facts and things. What are the metaphysical implications of this distinction? Its implications for logic?
6. Describe Russell's attempts to reduce complex facts to simple ones. Why is this important for him?
7. Describe the relation of Russell and Wittgenstein to the epistemology of empiricism.
8. Describe the program of logical atomism.
9. How does Wittgenstein deal with ethical, metaphysical, and religious propositions in the *Tractatus*?
10. Frame: "The Mystical of Wittgenstein is similar to the noumenal world of Kant." Explain; evaluate.
11. In what way does the *Tractatus* contradict itself? Explain. Discuss whether and how Van Til's rationalist-irrationalist critique applies to the *Tractatus*.
12. How did the logical positivists depend on the *Tractatus*? What did they reject in it? Why?
13. Describe the categories of language admitted by logical positivists.
14. What is the verification principle? Discuss its importance to logical positivism and the criticisms that made it untenable. Why did some say that it was self-refuting?
15. Discuss how the logical positivists dealt with religious language.
16. Describe Flew's parable of the gardener. How should Christians respond to it?
17. Respond to Angel Sanchez.
18. Distinguish conventionalism, instrumentalism, operationalism.
19. Describe and evaluate Michael Polanyi's view of science.
20. Same for that of Thomas Kuhn.
21. Kuhn says that arguments between those holding competing paradigms are "circular." Explain; evaluate. Is it legitimate to say that people holding different paradigms live in different worlds? Why not say merely that they hold different interpretations of the same reality?
22. How does Wittgenstein interpret Augustine's theory of meaning? Explain; evaluate.
23. How did the later Wittgenstein deal with "the meaning of *meaning*"?
24. How did Wittgenstein's new view of meaning affect his views of simplicity and vagueness? Evaluate.
25. How did the later Wittgenstein deal with the problem of universals? Evaluate.

26. How did the later Wittgenstein understand the work of philosophy? Evaluate.
27. Describe and evaluate the treatment of religious language in the later Wittgenstein. Compare Wittgenstein and Kant.
28. Summarize the distinctive positions of Ryle, Strawson, Austin, Searle.
29. Discuss Quine's treatment of the *analytic-synthetic* distinction. Also his holism.
30. Describe some significant features of Saussure's view of language. How does this bear on the nature of universals?
31. How did Lévi-Strauss apply Saussurean linguistics to anthropology? Evaluate.
32. How is structuralism rationalistic? Irrationalistic?
33. Describe and discuss the poststructural rejection of the *myth of presence*. Relate this to the notion of *language as power.*
34. Lyotard defines the *postmodern* as "incredulity toward metanarratives." Explain; evaluate.
35. Frame correlates the conflict between modern and postmodern with the categories of rationalism and irrationalism. Explain; evaluate.

BIBLIOGRAPHY: TWENTIETH-CENTURY LANGUAGE PHILOSOPHY

Print

Austin, J. L. *How to Do Things with Words.* Cambridge, MA: Harvard University Press, 1975.

———. *Philosophical Papers.* Oxford: Clarendon, 1990.

Ayer, A. J. *Language, Truth and Logic.* New York: Dover, 1952. Influential formulation and defense of logical positivism.

Flew, Antony, and Alasdair C. MacIntyre, eds. *New Essays in Philosophical Theology.* London: Macmillan, 2012. Essays by believers and unbelievers responding to British analytic philosophy. Includes Flew's parable of the gardener.

Kuhn, Thomas S. *The Structure of Scientific Revolutions.* 50th anniversary ed. Chicago: University of Chicago Press, 2012.

Lévi-Strauss, Claude. *Structural Anthropology.* New York: Basic Books, 1974.

Lyotard, Jean-François. *The Postmodern Condition: A Report on Knowledge.* Minneapolis: University of Minnesota Press, 1984.

Moore, G. E. *Principia Ethica.* New York: Dover, 2004. Discusses the naturalistic fallacy and other ethical issues.

———. *Selected Writings*. Edited by Thomas Baldwin. New York: Routledge, 1993. Includes his most famous essays, including "A Defense of Common Sense" and "Proof of an External World."

Polanyi, Michael. *Personal Knowledge: Towards a Post-Critical Philosophy*. Chicago: University of Chicago Press, 1974.

Quine, Willard Van Orman. *From a Logical Point of View: Nine Logico-Philosophical Essays*. 2nd rev. ed. Cambridge, MA: Harvard University Press, 1980. Includes "Two Dogmas of Empiricism" and "On What There Is."

Russell, Bertrand. *The Basic Writings of Bertrand Russell*. Edited by Robert E. Egner and Lester E. Denonn. New York: Routledge, 2009.

———. *The Problems of Philosophy*. Hollywood, FL: Simon and Brown, 2013.

———. *Why I Am Not a Christian and Other Essays on Related Subjects*. New York: Touchstone, 1967. Includes "A Free Man's Worship," as well as the titular essay.

Russell, Bertrand, and Alfred North Whitehead. *Principia Mathematica*. 3 vols. Cambridge: Cambridge University Press, 1910–13.

Ryle, Gilbert. *The Concept of Mind*. Chicago: University of Chicago Press, 2000.

Saussure, Ferdinand de. *Course in General Linguistics*. Edited by Charles Bally and Albert Sechehaye. Translated by Roy Harris. Chicago: Open Court, 1998.

Urmson, J. O. *Philosophical Analysis: Its Development between the Two World Wars*. New York: Oxford University Press, 1956.

Wittgenstein, Ludwig. *Lectures and Conversations on Aesthetics, Psychology, and Religious Belief*. Edited by Cyril Barrett. Compiled from notes by Yorick Smythies, Rush Rhees, and James Taylor. Berkeley, CA: University of California Press, 2007.

———. *On Certainty*. Translated by Denis Paul and G. E. M. Anscombe. New York: Harper and Row, 1972.

———. *Philosophical Investigations*. Translated by G. E. M. Anscombe, P. M. S. Hacker, and Joachim Schulte. Rev. 4th ed. Oxford: Blackwell, 2009.

———. *Preliminary Studies for the "Philosophical Investigations": Generally Known as the Blue and Brown Books*. 2nd ed. Harper Torchbooks. New York: Harper and Row, 1965.

———. *Tractatus Logico-Philosophicus*. New York: Dover, 1998.

Online

Austin, J. L. *How to Do Things with Words*. Cambridge, MA: Harvard University Press, 1975. Available at http://www.ling.upenn.edu/~rnoyer/courses/103/Austin.pdf.

Ayer, A. J. *Language, Truth and Logic*. New York: Dover, 1952. Available at http://archive.org/stream/AlfredAyer/LanguageTruthAndLogic_djvu.txt.

Kuhn, Thomas S. *The Structure of Scientific Revolutions*. 3rd ed. Chicago: University of Chicago Press, 1996. Available at http://moodle.eosmith.org/pluginfile.php/3436/mod_resource/content/1/The%20Structure%20OF%20Scientific%20Revolutions%203rd%20ed%20-%20Thomas%20Kuhn.pdf.

Moore, G. E. "A Defence of Common Sense." In *Contemporary British Philosophy*, edited by J. H. Muirhead. 2nd ser. 1925. Reprinted in G. E. Moore, *Philosophical Papers*, 32–45. London: George Allen & Unwin, 1959. Available at http://www.ditext.com/moore/common-sense.html.

———. *Principia Ethica*. Amherst, NY: Prometheus Books, 1988. Available at http://fair-use.org/g-e-moore/principia-ethica/.

———. "Proof of an External World." In *Philosophical Papers*, 126–48. New York: Collier Books, 1962. Available at http://www.hist-analytic.com/MooreExternalWorld.pdf.

———. "The Refutation of Idealism." *Mind*, n.s., 12, 48 (October 1903): 433–45. Available at http://www.ditext.com/moore/refute.html.

Quine, Willard Van Orman. "Two Dogmas of Empiricism." *Philosophical Review* 60 (1951): 20–43. Reprinted in Willard Van Orman Quine, *From a Logical Point of View: Nine Logico-Philosophical Essays*. 2nd rev. ed. Cambridge, MA: Harvard University Press, 1961. Available at http://www.ditext.com/quine/quine.html.

Russell, Bertrand. "Has Religion Made Useful Contributions to Civilization?" Available at http://www.positiveatheism.org/hist/russell2.htm.

———. *Mysticism and Logic and Other Essays*. London: George Allen & Unwin, 1917. Available at http://en.wikisource.org/wiki/Mysticism_and_Logic_and_Other_Essays.

———. *Our Knowledge of an External World as a Field for Scientific Method in Philosophy*. London: George Allen & Unwin, 1914. Available at http://archive.org/details/ourknowledgeofth005200mbp.

———. *The Philosophy of Logical Atomism*. Oxford: Taylor & Francis e-Library, 2009. Available at http://www.ualberta.ca/~francisp/NewPhil448/RussellPhilLogicalAtomismPears.pdf.

———. *The Problems of Philosophy*. Oxford: Oxford University Press, 1959. Available at http://www.ditext.com/russell/russell.html.

Urmson, J. O. *Philosophical Analysis: Its Development between the Two World Wars*. Oxford: Clarendon, 1958. Available at http://www.questia.com/library/465525/philosophical-analysis-its-development-between-the. Membership required for full texts.

Wittgenstein, Ludwig. *The Blue Book*. Available at http://www.geocities.jp/mickindex/wittgenstein/witt_blue_en.html.

———. *On Certainty (Uber Gewissheit)*. Edited by G. E. M. Anscombe and G. H. von Wright. Translated by Denis Paul and G. E. M. Anscombe. Oxford: Basil Blackwell, 1969–75. Available at http://web.archive.org/web/20051210213153/http://budni.by.ru/oncertainty.html.

———. *Tractatus Logico-Philosophicus (Logisch-philosophische Abhandlung)*. Side-by-side-by-side ed. Version 0.41. February 11, 2014. Available at http://people.umass.edu/phil335-klement-2/tlp/tlp.pdf. Contains the original German, alongside both the Ogden-Ramsey and the Pears-McGuinness English translations. First published: London: Kegan Paul, 1922.

READ FOR YOURSELF

Read Moore's "Defense of Common Sense" to get a feel of the early analytic philosophical discussions. Russell's article "Logical Atomism" describes the position later formalized by Wittgenstein's *Tractatus*. You might also want to look at Russell's "Why I Am Not a Christian" and "A Free Man's Worship" to understand the intense secularism of this movement.

Wittgenstein's *Tractatus* is very difficult for beginning philosophers. Urmson's *Philosophical Analysis* and other commentaries might help. Read Ayer's *Language, Truth and Logic* as your primary text in logical positivism; then look at the Flew and MacIntyre *New Essays* (especially "Theology and Falsification") to understand the religious impact of the movement.

The later Wittgenstein is easiest to understand in the *Blue and Brown Books*, but eventually you will want to get into his *Philosophical Investigations*. His *Lectures on Aesthetics, Psychology, and Religious Belief* will show you one way in which Wittgenstein and his students discussed religious issues during this period.

In philosophy of science, Polanyi's *Personal Knowledge* and Kuhn's *Structure of Scientific Revolutions* will introduce you to the issues.

Look at Lyotard for the issues surrounding deconstruction-postmodernism.

LISTEN ONLINE

Link: http://itunes.apple.com/us/course/legacy-history-philosophy/id694658914

- Hans-Georg Gadamer, Ferdinand de Saussure, Claude Lévi-Strauss, and Deconstruction: 36:30

- Introduction to Language Analysis, Logical Atomism, and Logical Positivism: 1:01:26
- Logical Positivism Continued and Ordinary-Language Philosophy: 57:50
- Ordinary-Language Philosophy Continued and Contemporary Epistemology: 55:07

FAMOUS QUOTES

- **Moore:** http://en.wikiquote.org/wiki/G._E._Moore
- **Russell:** http://en.wikiquote.org/wiki/Bertrand_Russell
- **Wittgenstein:** http://en.wikiquote.org/wiki/Ludwig_Wittgenstein
- **Polanyi:** http://en.wikiquote.org/wiki/Michael_Polanyi
- **Kuhn:** http://en.wikiquote.org/wiki/Thomas_Kuhn
- **Quine:** http://en.wikiquote.org/wiki/Willard_van_Orman_Quine
- **Lévi-Strauss:** http://en.wikiquote.org/wiki/Claude_L%C3%A9vi-Strauss
- **Lyotard:** http://en.wikiquote.org/wiki/Jean-Fran%C3%A7ois_Lyotard

13

RECENT CHRISTIAN PHILOSOPHY

THE NARRATIVE OF THIS BOOK so far will be discouraging to many. To review: fallen thinkers have sought to conceptualize the world autonomously. Even Christian thinkers who have sought to be faithful in their philosophical and theological work have often compromised with nonbiblical philosophies. And some who have claimed to be Christian, in the liberal tradition, have essentially advocated these nonbiblical philosophies, in Christian terminology.

[The] reformational line of thinking has produced a long line of writers down to the present who have set forth the biblical worldview by expounding a biblical theology.

But God has not abandoned the world of thought. Through all this time, faithful pastors, church teachers, evangelists, theologians, and fathers and mothers have maintained the authentic biblical gospel. Hearts have been transformed, and Christian people have spread abroad the love of Christ. At times, as in the thought of Augustine and in the Protestant Reformation, there has been a turn even in the philosophical world toward a more consistently biblical outlook. And this reformational line of thinking has produced a long line of writers down to the present who have set forth the biblical worldview by expounding a biblical theology. I have not had space in this book to describe the long succession of orthodox Christian theologians. The list would have included Francis Turretin, John Owen, Archibald Alexander, E. W. Hengstenberg, Charles Hodge, A. A. Hodge, B. B. Warfield, Geerhardus Vos, Herman Bavinck, Louis Berkhof, Carl F. H. Henry, John Murray, James I. Packer, Roger Nicole, Norman Shepherd, Wayne Grudem, and many others. In this book, I have focused on those who have influenced the history of philosophical thought, and the men I have just listed here have not done that to any substantial extent. But they have performed the immensely valuable task of keeping the authentic Christian faith alive and passing it on to new generations.

Yet there have also been Christian philosophers, and their number is increasing. By "Christian philosophers," I refer to philosophers committed to the biblical worldview more or less as I described it in chapter 1.[1] There have been many more of these in the twentieth century than in the nineteenth or eighteenth, and I do not hesitate to say that this is a movement of God. I intend to describe this movement in this, the final chapter of the book. So I intend to conclude the book on a note of hope.

Abraham Kuyper

I do not agree with everything that these Christian philosophers have said. Even given the presupposition of the Christian worldview, there is room for brotherly disagreement. But I do believe that each of the people discussed in this chapter is on the right track and is making valuable contributions to the work of philosophy.

ABRAHAM KUYPER (1837–1920)

Living in the Netherlands of the late nineteenth and early twentieth centuries, Kuyper was gifted and prominent in theology, church leadership, philosophy, education, politics, journalism, and the analysis of culture. For several decades he was the best-known figure in the Netherlands, and from 1901 to 1905 he was Prime Minister of the country. He was so prominent that he was commonly called "Father Abraham" and "Abraham the Mighty."

Kuyper was gifted and prominent in theology, church leadership, philosophy, education, politics, journalism, and the analysis of culture. For several decades he was the best-known figure in the Netherlands, and from 1901 to 1905 he was Prime Minister of the country.

He trained at the University of Leiden, particularly under J. H. Scholten, an influential liberal theologian. But he was also introduced to the thought of Reformed orthodoxy, particularly as he wrote a doctoral paper comparing Calvin's ecclesiology with that of the Polish Reformer John à Lasko. From 1863 to 1867 he was pastor of a church in the town of Beesd, where he was deeply impressed with the faith of the people in the congregation. At that time, he also corresponded with Guillaume Groen Van Prinsterer (1801–76), a major figure in the Anti-revolutionary political party.[2] In time, he came to believe that the simple faith of the historical Calvinists had more truth in it than any of the speculations of the academic liberals.

1. In this chapter, I will therefore be focusing on thinkers who are largely orthodox in their theology, since we have considered liberalism in earlier contexts. I will also be omitting (with one or two exceptions) philosophers in the Roman Catholic and Eastern Orthodox traditions, though there are many of them and they have often made worthwhile contributions. I am not personally well equipped to deal with these groups, and I think to do justice to them would take more space than I am able to give. I will tend to focus on thinkers in the Calvinistic tradition, because of my judgment that in that tradition there is more hope to be found. But I will not complain if others refer to that judgment as bias.

2. *Anti-revolutionary* indicates rejection of the atheistic, rationalistic, and tyrannical principles of the French Revolution.

In 1867 Kuyper was called to a pastorate in Utrecht. In 1870 he moved to Amsterdam, where he wrote articles for the religious newspaper *De Heraut*. In 1872 he founded his own paper, *De Standaard*. In these journals he articulated and refined his vision for the church and politics, and for all areas of human life under the lordship of Christ. He even founded a university that would articulate his vision, free from interference by the state: the Free University of Amsterdam. In his inaugural address there as professor of theology (1880), he summarized his philosophy in a nutshell:

> Oh, no single piece of our mental world is to be hermetically sealed off from the rest, and there is not a square inch in the whole domain of our human existence over which Christ, who is Sovereign over *all*, does not cry: "Mine!"[3]

In this regard, Kuyper followed Calvin. In Kuyper's *Lectures on Calvinism*,[4] he describes the history of Calvinism and its influence in various areas of human life. The chapter titles are "Calvinism a Life-system," "Calvinism and Religion," "Calvinism and Politics," "Calvinism and Science," "Calvinism and Art," and "Calvinism and the Future." In Kuyper there is none of the tendency that we have seen in liberal theology to set religious knowledge over against the knowledge of science (*phenomenal-noumenal*, *Historie-Geschichte*), or of the tendency of the later Wittgenstein to set religious language sharply over against the language of science and historical evidence. Religion is rather a foundation for all human enterprises and disciplines.[5]

Ecclesiastical issues concerned Kuyper much during the 1880s and '90s. The Reformed Church suspended him and others from the ministry in 1886 for insisting on confessional subscription for all ministers and members.

Ecclesiastical issues concerned him much during the 1880s and '90s. The Reformed Church suspended him and others from the ministry in 1886 for insisting on confessional subscription for all ministers and members.[6] Kuyper did not accept his suspension, but preached to his supporters, who became known as the *Doleantie*, the "grieving ones." The *Doleantie* joined in 1892 with another group, the Christian Reformed Church, that had separated from the main Reformed Church in 1834. The union was called the Reformed[7] Churches in the Netherlands.

3. James D. Bratt, *Abraham Kuyper, A Centennial Reader* (Grand Rapids: Eerdmans, 1988), 488.

4. Grand Rapids: Eerdmans, 1931, originally presented as the Stone Foundation Lectures at Princeton Theological Seminary in 1898, a book that everyone should read.

5. Compare my discussion of religion in chapter 1.

6. My views on confessional subscription differ from Kuyper's. See *DWG*, 280–88. But my general sympathies are entirely on the side of the *Doleantie* and against the liberalism of the state church.

7. Both *Hervormde* and *Gereformeerde* are translated "Reformed" in English. The large, liberal denomination was called *Hervormde*, Kuyper's separatists *Gereformeerde*. Sad to say, the *Gereformeerde Kerken* also, through the twentieth century, succumbed to liberalizing influences.

While all this was going on, Kuyper continued as a writer, professor, journalist, and politician, advancing through the ranks of the Anti-revolutionary Party to become Prime Minister in 1901. His main issue as a politician was *sphere sovereignty*. He rejected the popular sovereignty of the French Revolution, in which all rights come from the individual, and the state sovereignty of Germany, in which all rights come from the state (prefiguring the Fascist and Communist regimes of the twentieth century). Rights come from God, said Kuyper, and God apportions rights and responsibilities not only to individuals and the state, but also to *intermediate bodies*, such as families, the schools, the press, business, and the arts. Each of these has a particular *sphere* of life with which it is concerned, and in which it should be free from the encroachments of other spheres, including the state. During the medieval period, there were extended debates about whether the church was superior to the state or inferior. Kuyper's view is that neither of these is the case—that church and state are equal, but each subject to the Word of God, which determines the sphere of their respective competence. Of course, determining the precise extent of each sphere is a difficult problem, and not one to which Kuyper gave a final, definitive analysis; see fig. 13.1 and fig. 13.2.

Rights come from God, said Kuyper, and God apportions rights and responsibilities not only to individuals and the state, but also to intermediate bodies, *such as families, the schools, the press, business, and the arts.*

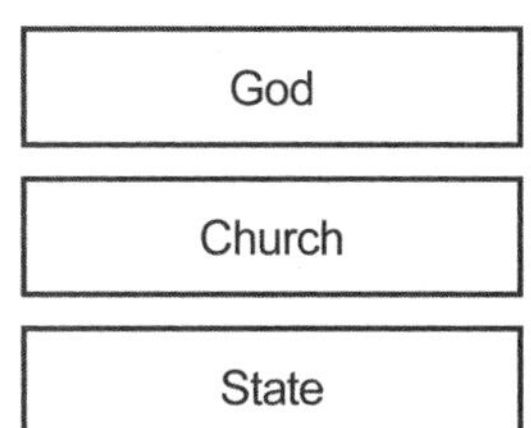

Fig. 13.1. The Roman Catholic View

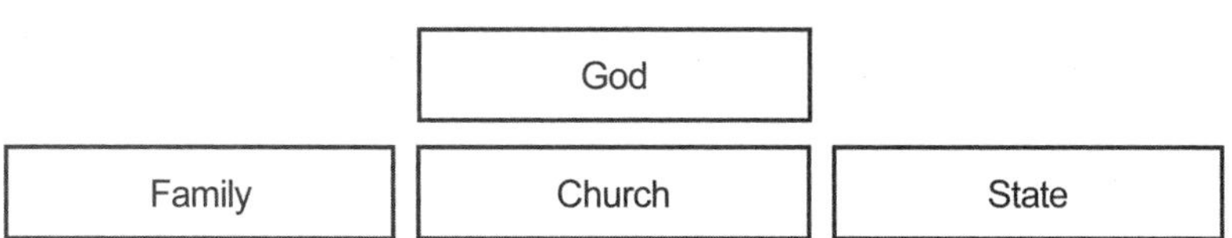

Fig. 13.2. Kuyper's Sphere Sovereignty

In his view, every faith community (not only churches and synagogues, but also such groups as humanists and socialists) should have equal rights, including the right to have their own schools, newspapers, hospitals, and so forth.

In his view, every faith community (not only churches and synagogues, but also such groups as humanists and socialists) should have equal rights, including the right to have their own schools, newspapers, hospitals, and so forth. The government should support each group equally. Today in the United States, all citizens must support by their taxes state-sponsored "public" schools, which inculcate secular humanistic values. If someone wants to send his children instead to Christian schools, for example, he must pay for that on top of his taxes. A Kuyperian policy would remove that double taxation and would give equal government support to every school system.[8] Of course, a Kuyperian policy, like Kuyper himself, would reject the notions that religion can be separated from education and that state-sponsored schools are somehow religiously neutral.

Nor is any other human endeavor or discipline religiously neutral. That includes science. In his three-volume *Encyclopedia of Sacred Theology*, Kuyper expounds at length his view that science must take into account "the fact of sin."[9] The fact of the fall, together with God's regeneration of some people, necessarily leads to the view that there are "two kinds of people,"[10] and that there are "two kinds of science."[11] Both sciences are "universal"[12] in that they claim validity for all facts, and they make a claim to the allegiance of all people. On that understanding, theology, the knowledge of God, plays a central role in all the sciences. Sciences dealing with man—namely, natural sciences, medical, philological, and juridical studies—are subject to the work of theology.[13] Theology, in turn, "finds its object of investigation *in the revealed, ectypal knowledge of God*."[14] He later goes into great detail, showing that that knowledge must be based on the infallible Scriptures.[15]

Nor is any other human endeavor or discipline religiously neutral. That includes science. In his three-volume Encyclopedia of Sacred Theology, *Kuyper expounds at length his view that science must take into account "the fact of sin."*

Of course, non-Christian scientists will not accept the revelation of the Christian God as the basis of their scientific work. For that reason, there is an *antithesis* between the two kinds of science. Christian scientists seek to do all their work in agreement with Scripture and to the glory of God. Non-Christian scientists avoid that methodology at all costs.

Is it, then, impossible for Christians and non-Christians to cooperate in scientific inquiries? Kuyper says no, it is possible, but he finds it difficult to show why and how this is possible, given the restraints of his view of antithesis. He speaks of *formal faith* as something that

8. Kuyper did not question the legitimacy of government support for education. That, too, however, is a subject for discussion.

9. Abraham Kuyper, *Principles of Sacred Theology* (Grand Rapids: Eerdmans, 1965), 106–49. This volume is a translation by J. Hendrik De Vries of large parts, but not the entirety, of Kuyper's *Encyclopedia*.

10. Ibid., 150–54.

11. Ibid., 155–76. Kuyper points out, however, that in another sense there is only one science. Where the two kinds of sciences contradict each other, the believer must reject unbelieving science as "science falsely so-called."

12. Ibid., 181–82.

13. Ibid., 190, 192–210.

14. Ibid., 215 (emphasis his). *Ectypal* is opposed to *archetypal*. It refers to man's knowledge of God, while *archetypal* refers to God's knowledge of himself.

15. Ibid., 257–91, 341–563.

Christians and non-Christians share: a faith that assures us of the trustworthiness of our senses, the axioms of logic, and the universality of scientific law. But he insists that formal faith is not saving faith, nor even faith in the true God. It has, in fact, no "content." So he thinks that Christians and non-Christians share common ground in natural sciences, but not in spiritual sciences. They can agree on weighing and measuring, but not on the nature of God.[16]

Cornelius Van Til believes that Kuyper here contradicts himself, for Kuyper had said on other occasions, following Calvin, that "man always confronts God in every fact that he meets."[17] But of course, part of that confrontation is that the non-Christian, despite himself, finds that he must acknowledge the trustworthiness of the senses, the axioms of logic, and the universality of scientific law—principles that make sense only in the Christian worldview. *Formal faith* is certainly not the best name for this confrontation, for it is full of content, and it is a confrontation with the true God. But as we will see, Van Til, like Kuyper, also has problems in defining what *antithesis* means.

Part of that confrontation is that the non-Christian, despite himself, finds that he must acknowledge the trustworthiness of the senses, the axioms of logic, and the universality of scientific law—principles that make sense only in the Christian worldview.

As for Kuyper, though he never quite satisfies himself as to *how* Christians and non-Christians can cooperate in science, he is sure that they can, and that this ability is due to God's common grace, God's non-saving favor to the nonelect. So Kuyper devoted another three-volume work (translation in progress[18]) to the subject of common grace.[19]

HERMAN DOOYEWEERD (1894–1977)

Dooyeweerd sought to apply Kuyper's vision first to law, and then to philosophy. He found that his legal studies led to philosophical implications, so he developed the *Philosophy of the Idea of Law*, sometimes called *cosmonomic philosophy* or *reformational philosophy*. Together with him on this project was a large group of Dutch scholars, including S. U. Zuidema, K. Popma, J. P. A. Mekkes, and H. Van Riessen, and Americans Robert D. Knudsen, H. Evan Runner, and Calvin Seerveld. Dooyeweerd's brother-in-law Dirk Vollenhoven worked closely with him, especially in historical matters. H. G. Stoker, of the University of Potchefstroom in South Africa, developed a *Philosophy of the Creation Idea*—somewhat different from Dooyeweerd's proposal, but influenced by it. Cornelius Van Til of Westminster Seminary in Philadelphia, whom I discuss later in this chapter, was associated with Dooyeweerd early on (listed, for example, as a contributing editor on the masthead

Herman Dooyeweerd

16. Cornelius Van Til, *The Defense of the Faith*, ed. K. Scott Oliphint, 4th ed. (Phillipsburg, NJ: P&R Publishing, 2008), 369–74.

17. Ibid., 370.

18. See http://www.acton.org/research/kuyper-translation-project.

19. For my biblical analysis of the doctrine, see *DG*, 429–37.

of the cosmonomic journal *Philosophia Reformata*), but later dissociated himself from the group.[20] A second generation of this movement (James Olthuis, John Olthuis, Hendrik Hart, Paul Marshall, and others) set up the Institute for Christian Studies in Toronto. A group of reformational scholars somewhat more conservative (theologically and politically) joined the faculty of Redeemer University in Hamilton, Ontario.[21]

Dooyeweerd makes a sharp distinction, reminiscent of the phenomenology of Husserl and Heidegger, between pretheoretical (sometimes called *naive*) experience and theoretical thought.[22] Pretheoretical experience sees the world as a whole. Theory abstracts various aspects of this world for close study, but it is in danger of losing connections, the sense of coherence and wholeness. Further, theory is in danger of considering itself *autonomous*. In this book, I have often criticized non-Christian thought for believing that human thought may proceed autonomously, in the sense of claiming independence from God's revelation. Dooyeweerd's argument is similar. But instead of referring directly to divine revelation, he sees apostate theoretical thought as claiming independence from pretheoretical experience and from the commitments of the heart, and therefore losing its roots in reality as a whole.

Pretheoretical experience reveals that human thinking is based on a heart-orientation, either for or against God. Dooyeweerd says, cryptically, that the human heart is "super-temporal," citing Ecclesiastes 3:11, "Also, he has put eternity into man's heart." It would seem that Dooyeweerd believes that if the human heart is to be oriented toward God, it must somehow share God's eternity. But that is a stretch exegetically, and it introduces unclarity into the Creator-creature distinction.

God's Word, in Dooyeweerd's view, also transcends the temporal order. It is not identical with either God or the cosmos, so it forms a kind of third reality, intermediate between the two.

God's Word, in Dooyeweerd's view, also transcends the temporal order. It is not identical with either God or the cosmos, so it forms a kind of third reality, intermediate between the two.[23] The Word in this sense provides direction to the heart, but no theoretical or conceptual knowledge. It provides, however, fundamental knowledge of God and the self.[24]

Our heart-direction in the area of thought may be described in

20. He said that he preferred Stoker's *creation idea* to Dooyeweerd's *law idea*.

21. Of course, there are many differences within the movement. I will here focus on Dooyeweerd himself.

22. I have never understood why Dooyeweerd and others insist on a sharp distinction between pretheoretical and theoretical. To me, it is fairly obvious that this distinction is a difference in degree, and that there is a continuum between these two categories.

23. This is inconsistent with the Creator-creature distinction as I presented it in chapter 1.

24. On the pairing of "God and the self," see my comments on Augustine (chapter 3) and Calvin (chapter 5). Descartes, Kant, Wittgenstein, and other modern philosophers frequently give to God and the self (the "soul") similar status. Later, I will discuss Alvin Plantinga's arguments about "God and other minds." The frequent pairing of God and the self in philosophical discussions bears testimony to the biblical doctrine that man is in the image of God.

terms of "ground-motives," Dooyeweerd says. The Christian heart is governed by the ground-motive of creation, fall, and redemption, which summarizes the story of Scripture. But fallen thinkers embrace other alternatives. I have mentioned several times in this book Dooyeweerd's useful summary of the history of thought in terms of four ground-motives: (1) Form and matter—the chief division of the world in Greek philosophy. (2) Nature and grace—the chief division in medieval philosophy. In this ground-motive, form and matter are combined as *nature*, and *grace* (God's salvation) is added as a supplement. This, then, is an inconsistent merger of non-Christian and Christian motifs. (3) Nature and freedom—the chief division in modern philosophy, in which medieval *grace* is secularized into *freedom*, as in Kant's noumenal. Christian thought, when consistent, rejects all of these in favor of (4) creation, fall, and redemption.

The Christian heart is governed by the ground-motive of creation, fall, and redemption, which summarizes the story of Scripture. But fallen thinkers embrace other alternatives.

Now, when we abstract data from pretheoretical experience in order to construct theories, our theoretical thought distinguishes fifteen *modal aspects* or *law spheres* in the world. Dooyeweerd groups these from higher to lower as follows:

- Faith (*pistical*)
- Moral
- Judicial
- Aesthetic
- Economic
- Social rules
- Linguistic
- History
- Logical
- Feeling
- Biotic
- Energy
- Kinetic
- Spatial
- Numerical

To some extent, then, each sphere is mirrored in all the others. It is possible to describe the whole world under each aspect, for example, as a kinetic, biotic, historical, or aesthetic whole.

These spheres interpenetrate in some ways. The lower spheres "anticipate" the higher ones, presenting features that are normally found in higher spheres. So, for example, life (the biotic sphere) has features analogous to works of art (the aesthetic). Similarly, the higher spheres "retrocipate" the lower ones. For example, works of art (aesthetic) display economy of line, color, and so on (economic) in what we call *aesthetic economy*. To some extent, then, each sphere is mirrored in all the others. It is possible to describe the whole world under each aspect, for example, as a kinetic, biotic, historical, or aesthetic whole.[25] But it

25. I am therefore inclined to call these aspects *perspectives* on reality.

is wrong to claim that the world is *only* kinetic, or biotic, or the like, or that all the other spheres are reducible to one of them.

Dooyeweerd uses this framework as an apologetic tool against non-Christian philosophies and religions. Typically, he says, philosophers fall to the temptation of reducing the diversity of experience to a single aspect. Marx, for example, absolutizes the economic sphere, Pythagoras the numerical, Bergson and Whitehead the biotic, Schleiermacher the feeling, Heraclitus the kinetic, Parmenides logic, and so on. Biblically speaking, these are idolatries, absolutizing or deifying something in the world. And Dooyeweerd seeks to show that none of these idols can do the job of the true God.

Each modal sphere defines a particular science: mathematics the science of number, physics the science of kinetics, biology the science of life, and so forth. Theology is the science of faith.

Things, including persons, exist in all modal spheres, but each is specially "qualified by" a particular sphere: numbers are numerical objects, animals biotic, money economic, symphonies aesthetic, human beings faith. Things are *subjects* in all spheres up to the sphere that qualifies them, *objects* to the spheres above that one. So human beings, qualified by faith, are subjects in all spheres. Animals are qualified by the biotic sphere and are subjects in that and all spheres beneath it. But they are objects of spheres above: that is, they have economic value, aesthetic beauty, and so forth.

This is the sort of big metaphysical[26] system that generally lost its popularity in the nineteenth and twentieth centuries. One can imagine the response of G. E. Moore to the complicated technical terminology ("What *exactly* do you mean by this?") or the incredulity of Jean-François Lyotard to this massive metanarrative. But Dooyeweerd argues these ideas in great detail, in his three-volume *A New Critique of Theoretical Thought*,[27] his three-volume *Reformation and Scholasticism*, and many other works.

One can imagine the response of G. E. Moore to the complicated technical terminology ("What exactly do you mean by this?") or the incredulity of Jean-François Lyotard to this massive metanarrative.

Though I hesitate to criticize this undoubtedly impressive intellectual structure, I have found fault with it in detail, and particularly in the doctrine of revelation that emerges from the project.[28] As I mentioned,

26. The Dooyeweerdians, like most other twentieth-century philosophers, do not want to admit that they are doing metephysics. One way that they avoid this label is by saying that the created world consists of *meaning* rather than *being*.

27. Philadelphia: Presbyterian and Reformed, 1953. The translators added a fourth volume to include indices.

28. See my booklet *The Amsterdam Philosophy: A Preliminary Critique* (Phillipsburg, NJ: Pilgrim Press, 1972), available at http://www.frame-poythress.org/wp-content/uploads/2012/08/FrameJohnAmsterdamPhilosophy1972.pdf, and my short papers on "Dooyeweerd and the Word of God," available at http://www.frame-poythress.org and as Appendix D in *DWG*, 392–421. I was involved in controversy with some of Dooyeweerd's followers in the early 1970s, when some of them criticized traditional Reformed theology as being "scholastic" and "dualistic." These criticisms presupposed what I considered to be erroneous views of Scripture.

for Dooyeweerd the Word of God is a supertemporal reality that speaks to the human heart in a realm beyond all theory and concept. Scripture, however, is a temporal book. It is directed toward the faith aspect, studied by the science of theology. Now, Dooyeweerd might have argued (in the spirit of Kuyper) that since the faith aspect retrocipates all other spheres and all other spheres anticipate it, Scripture addresses all areas of human life, though it deals focally with faith. Dooyeweerd chose, rather, to say that Scripture's focus on faith is exclusive, so that Scripture may not address the concerns of other spheres. So disciples of Dooyeweerd have argued that Scripture does not teach morality, the difference between right and wrong. Dooyeweerd himself taught that the "days" of Genesis 1 cannot be literal, since Scripture is about only faith, not numbers. The days of Genesis are faith numbers, not numerical numbers.[29]

The disturbing conclusion that I reach from all of this is that for Dooyeweerd, revelation in the highest sense is a supertemporal, nonconceptual reality that transforms the heart, but does not direct the philosopher or scientist in any propositional way.

The disturbing conclusion that I reach from all of this is that for Dooyeweerd, revelation in the highest sense is a supertemporal, nonconceptual reality that transforms the heart, but does not direct the philosopher or scientist in any propositional way.[30] The Bible, on the other hand, contains propositional revelation in the sphere of faith (theology), but does not direct us in every area of human life. Further, Dooyeweerd insists that our reading of Scripture must be directed by his philosophical system, which I cannot help but regard as a philosophical imperialism.

Certainly his work is a great help in criticizing the idolatries of would-be autonomous philosophy. But Dooyeweerd never thought through in a theologically responsible way what Scripture teaches about itself. So his philosophy has not succeeded in avoiding the dangers of autonomy. In fact, it has been something of a regression from Kuyper's vision of God's Word embracing all of life.

Dooyeweerd insists that our reading of Scripture must be directed by his philosophical system, which I cannot help but regard as a philosophical imperialism.

GORDON H. CLARK (1902–85)

Clark was an American Presbyterian theologian, apologist, and philosopher. He stood firmly on the Bible as the inerrant Word of God, and he was one of the first thinkers to be called a *presuppositionalist*.[31]

29. I once visited a disciple of Dooyeweerd at his hotel. He needed to return to his room to find something, and I went with him. But we got lost, because there was a problem with the numbering of the rooms. They didn't seem to proceed in sequence; at least we couldn't figure out how the sequence progressed. I turned to my friend and suggested, "Maybe these are faith numbers rather than numerical numbers." As I recall, he was not amused.

30. Something like Barth's *Geschichte* (chapter 10).

31. The term *presuppositionalist* was likely invented by James Oliver Buswell Jr., a Christian empiricist who used the term to disparage Clark and Van Til. Clark rather liked it and applied it to himself. Van Til was not pleased with it, but sometimes used it of himself in deference to the usage of others. The reason, I think, is that Clark had a systematic preference for the *a priori*; Van Til did not, but rather saw the *a priori* and the *a posteriori* as correlative aspects of human knowledge.

He presented his philosophical approach in sharp opposition to the empiricist tradition. He used standard rationalistic, Humean, and Kantian arguments to show that from sense experience alone one can derive no universal or necessary principles. But universal and necessary knowledge are necessary for logic, science, and ethics. And without logic, Clark said, nothing can be known.

But isn't science, inevitably, an empirical discipline? Clark replies in the negative: scientific laws do not describe the actual universe, but only summarize a set of experimental operations. So he signs on to the *operationalism* of Percy Bridgman (see chapter 12). If science merely records operations (science recording science), then attempts to criticize Christianity on scientific grounds are fallacious.[32]

On the other hand, we are also unable to use empirical knowledge for positive purposes. From sense experience it is impossible to prove the existence of God or the truth of Christianity. For example, the cosmological argument, Clark says, is invalid. Aquinas, Clark points out, insisted that in the sentence "God is cause of the world" the word *cause* must be taken analogously rather than literally. But the cosmological argument requires that God be the *literal* cause of the world, or it is of no use. Further, Clark agrees with Hume and Kant that empirical proofs can prove only, at most, the existence of things within experience; but the God of the Bible transcends experience. If the theistic proofs are limited to their proper sphere, then they prove at most a god within experience, that is, a finite god.

Gordon H. Clark

Clark also rejects historical arguments for the truth of Christianity, even arguments based on the resurrection of Christ. Such evidence proves nothing in itself, he says. *Bare facts* are of no theological interest. Even if it could be shown that a Jewish man rose from the dead two thousand years ago, that would not prove anything relevant to the truth of Christianity. For the Christian confession is not of a bare fact that someone rose from the dead. Rather, it is the fact that the Son of God, according to the Scriptures, died to bear the wrath of God for sinners and rose with them that they might have newness of life. It is, then, a fact with theological significance. But the theological significance cannot be proved by historical arguments alone.

I remember hearing a student ask Clark how he would deal with 1 John 1:1–3:

> That which was from the beginning, which we have heard, which we have seen with our eyes, which we looked upon and have touched with our hands, concerning the word of life—the

32. Gordon H. Clark, *The Philosophy of Science and Belief in God* (Unicoi, TN: Trinity Foundation, 1996).

> life was made manifest, and we have seen it, and testify to it and proclaim to you the eternal life, which was with the Father and was made manifest to us—that which we have seen and heard we proclaim also to you, so that you too may have fellowship with us; and indeed our fellowship is with the Father and with his Son Jesus Christ.

Clark, as he sometimes did, answered the question with a question: "What did they *see*?" I think the answer he wanted was that they saw colors and shapes, heard sounds, touched a solid-feeling object. That was all there was to empirical data, in Clark's view. But those empirical data were not good news in themselves, just bare facts again. The disciples didn't *see* that Jesus was the Son of God and that he had redeemed his people from sin. That good news came when the empirical data were combined with divine propositional revelation (as Matt. 16:16–17). It was through the revelation that they understood who it was they were seeing, hearing, touching, and because of that revelation those experiences became precious to them.

Facts, . . . in Clark's view, have no meaning in themselves, but only in relation to others and ultimately to a whole system of thought. Clark's epistemology, therefore, is holistic, based on apprehension of a whole system of truth.

Facts, therefore, in Clark's view, have no meaning in themselves, but only in relation to others and ultimately to a whole *system* of thought. Clark's epistemology, therefore, is *holistic*, based on apprehension of a whole system of truth (Hegel, Duhem, Quine), rather than building up knowledge one fact after another (Locke, Hume, Russell, early Wittgenstein). Clark sees these systems in an analogy to geometric systems. Geometric systems are based on *axioms*, which serve as the ultimate tests of truth within the system. Similarly, systems of philosophy and theology are governed by *presuppositions*. These presuppositions are not themselves demonstrable, for they are the basis of demonstration. For Christianity, the ultimate presupposition is the propositional truth of Scripture.

If we start with the traditional philosophical definition of knowledge as "justified, true belief," it would seem that we cannot accept any proposition as knowledge unless we are assured of its truth. To the extent that we doubt the truth of a proposition, we must doubt that we know it.

Indeed, in the Christian system, Clark tells us, only the content of Scripture constitutes genuine knowledge. If we start with the traditional philosophical definition of *knowledge* as "justified, true belief,"[33] it would seem that we cannot accept any proposition as knowledge unless we are assured of its truth. To the extent that we doubt the truth of a proposition, we must doubt that we know it. So knowledge requires certainty. Sense experience, as we've seen, is too uncertain, for Clark, to deserve the name of *knowledge*. But Scripture is God's Word, and therefore Scripture, and only Scripture, provides truth with absolute certainty. Clark calls this view *scripturalism*.

The problem here is that our access to Scripture is at least partly empirical. We read it with our eyes, hear it with our ears. That would

33. This is, by the way, a perspectival triad. *Justified* deals with norms, *true* with the facts of a situation, and *belief* with the state of the knower's mind. Normative, situational, existential.

seem to make sense experience equal in authority to Scripture, or even higher in authority. I don't know where, if anywhere, Clark deals with this question. I would guess, however, that his best answer would be to say that although the senses figure in our knowledge of Scripture, we can still resolve to reject any empirical claims that contradict our firm convictions of what Scripture says, recognizing in that way that Scripture is higher in authority than sense experience.

But what now becomes of apologetics? Clark has rejected traditional theistic proofs as invalid and historical evidence as irrelevant. What is left? Clark insists that we must defend the faith holistically, as a system of truth analogous to geometry. That means that apologetic arguments are essentially arguments between competing presuppositions (= axioms). Ultimately, says Clark, no demonstration is possible, since presuppositions are prior to demonstrations and govern them.[34] But as in geometry, it is possible to choose one set of presuppositions over another on the criteria of logical consistency and richness of content. I will consider these criteria in turn.

Clark puts great emphasis on logic as a system containing universal and necessary knowledge. Because it is universal and necessary, it cannot be based on sense experience. It can be nothing less than the structure of the divine thought itself, implanted into man's mind at creation. Violating logic leads you to contradict yourself and therefore reduces your thought and words to nonsense. So the first test of an intellectual system is whether it is *logically consistent*. In Clark's many books, he exposes contradictions in non-Christian thought: materialism reduces its own thought to matter and motion and thereby invalidates itself (cf. our chapter 2); the positivist verification principle is unverifiable (chapter 12). In general, non-Christian thought ends up in "skeptical futility."

Clark . . . believes he can show that there are no logical contradictions at all in the Christian faith. Some Christians have said that there are "apparent" contradictions or "paradoxes" in Christian theology. But Clark is contemptuous of those alternatives.

Of course, people sometimes accuse Christian thought of logical contradiction as well. The doctrine of the Trinity seems to say that God is three and not-three. God's goodness appears to contradict the reality of evil. Clark, however, believes he can show that there are no logical contradictions at all in the Christian faith. Some Christians have said that there are "apparent" contradictions or "paradoxes" in Christian theology. But Clark is contemptuous of those alternatives. He is reported to have said, "A paradox is a charley-horse between the ears." So he argues that the Trinity is perfectly consistent and that any apparent contradiction can be resolved. The doctrine of the Trinity does

34. Van Til, on the contrary, said that presuppositions could prove themselves, in a way that is circular in a sense. Clark was not willing to take that step. But his unwillingness to take it led him to say that logical consistency and richness of content are standards for judging Scripture—and that compromises Clark's presuppositionalism.

not teach that God is one and three in the same respect, but rather one *substance* and three *persons*. As for evil, we can say that God is "ex-lex,"[35] not subject to the moral laws that he has ordained for human beings. So "God is not responsible for sin, even though he decrees it."[36]

Clark's resolution of the question of the Trinity is traditional, and adequate on the whole. But the Bible and the Christian traditions do not tell us the precise difference between *substance* and *person*, so as to assure us that the singularity of the first is compatible with the plurality of the second. As for his resolution of the problem of evil, I certainly concur with his affirmation that God decrees evil, but I don't think it is biblical to describe him as simply "ex-lex." The laws that God ordains for human beings are for the most part reflections of his own attributes: In Leviticus 19:2, the Lord says, "You shall be holy, for I the LORD your God am holy."[37] Our first responsibility is to image God. So we should assume that God values human life as he tells us to. Therefore, when he decrees a terrible tragedy, we naturally have questions as to how this is consistent with God's good nature.[38]

I think it is right to believe that God is a logical being, since he speaks truth, and that truth excludes falsehood. That fact is the root of the law of noncontradiction.

I think it is right to believe that God is a logical being, since he speaks truth, and that truth excludes falsehood. That fact is the root of the law of noncontradiction. In addition, there are logical arguments in the Bible, sometimes indicating their conclusion with *therefore*. Such arguments render normative the logical process, not only the arguments' conclusions.

Clark assumes that God's perfect logic is identical with some system of human logic. This assumption, however, is unreasonable. Human beings make mistakes in logic as in many other things.

But Clark assumes that God's perfect logic is identical with some system of human logic. This assumption, however, is unreasonable. Human beings make mistakes in logic as in many other things. Is it not likely that they will also make mistakes in formulating the principles of logic itself? Given the differences between Aristotle's and Russell's logics, it is evident that either Aristotle or Russell or both made a mistake somewhere. Clark admitted that this was a legitimate question. He believed that God's mind included not merely logic in general or the law of noncontradiction, but a specific system of logic. But who was right? Aristotle or Russell? Or is there a third alternative? In a postlecture discussion, Clark did not hesitate to answer the question: Aristotle was right and Russell was wrong. But how can we be sure of that? Clark said he had written a paper that established Aristotle's position. But how can we be sure that Clark's paper is correct? Clark said, in effect, well, if my paper is not correct, then there is no possibility of coherent thought or intelligible discourse.

35. Gordon H. Clark, *Religion, Reason, and Revelation* (Philadelphia: Presbyterian and Reformed, 1961), 240.

36. Ibid.

37. Cf. Matt. 5:48; 1 Peter 1:15–16.

38. For my approach to the problem of evil, see *AJCB*, 155-88; *DG*, 160–84.

Some have accused Clark, therefore, of adding logic to the canon, attributing to it the certainty that belongs to Scripture alone. But in the dialogue above, he attributes infallibility not only to logic, but to Aristotle, and not only to Aristotle, but to Clark's paper about Aristotle.

Logic is a wonderful gift of God. Clark is right to say that it is universal, necessary, certain. But everyone who has studied logic in college knows that there are things that it cannot do. Logic cannot give us empirical fact unless we provide it with empirical premises, premises that must be obtained from outside logic itself. Further, the infallibility of logic cannot guarantee that logicians will not make mistakes. A syllogism will not work, for example, if an operative word has one sense in one premise and a different sense in another premise. This point shows in another way that logic is in a way dependent on empirical knowledge, because determining the sense of words inevitably requires some empirical investigation. And of course, the logician's own fallibility, which infects all attempts to know reality, also frequently prevents logical investigation from yielding truth.

The comments in the previous paragraph may be called comments about the *limitations of logic.*[39] But even though these limitations are obvious, admitted in every logic textbook, Clark (and even more his disciples) does not seem to want to admit any limitations to logic at all. They regularly accuse anyone who makes such observations of "belittling logic." To those who said that logic was an idol for Clark, Clark would reply that it could not be an idol, because on his view it is nothing less than a divine attribute, the divine *logos.*[40] One cannot make an idol of something that is already divine.

Some have accused Clark . . . of adding logic to the canon, attributing to it the certainty that belongs to Scripture alone. But in the dialogue above, he attributes infallibility not only to logic, but to Aristotle, and not only to Aristotle, but to Clark's paper about Aristotle.

The second criterion that Clark presents for judging systems of propositions is the criterion of *richness.* Clark is less explicit about this, but it is an important element in the evaluation of geometric systems, and it is certainly necessary if one is to develop an apologetic along Clark's lines. It is, of course, possible for two different systems to be equal in their logical consistency. To use a trivial example, the system

- $1 + 1 = 2$
- $2 + 2 = 4$

contains no contradiction, and so would be equal to the Bible in its logical consistency. But this system of two equations would not be

39. Cf. my more elaborate discussion in *DKG,* 254–60.

40. See Gordon H. Clark, *The Johannine Logos* (Nutley, NJ: Presbyterian and Reformed, 1972).

equally useful. It could not be used, for example, to resolve questions about the doctrine of the Trinity. So Clark recommends Christianity not only for its logical consistency, but also for the breadth of its applications to different kinds of human questions. That is the thrust of Clark's first (and I think his best) apologetic work, *A Christian View of Men and Things*.[41] A subtitle describes it as *A Treatise Showing that Social Stability Demands a Christian Society*. To demonstrate this broad thesis, Clark includes chapters on history, politics, ethics, science, religion, and (which he says is most fundamental) epistemology.[42] In these chapters, he attempts to show that prevalent non-Christian views of the subjects are either contradictory or otherwise inadequate, and that the Christian Scriptures present viable alternatives. The quality of Clark's argument and the clarity of his writing are very impressive to me.

Clark recommends Christianity not only for its logical consistency, but also for the breadth of its applications to different kinds of human questions.

Clark is sometimes called a *rationalist* because of his confidence in logic and his general rejection of paradox. His critique of empiricism is certainly in the rationalist tradition. He makes some of the same mistakes that rationalists have made before him in minimizing the value of sense experience. Often, as in his treatment of 1 John 1:1–3 above, he, like earlier rationalists, seems to have the idea that empiricists rely on sense experience *alone*. And of course, nothing much can be learned from mere visual and auditory signals, for example. But most empiricists understood that we cannot even describe sense experience without rational categories. Actual empiricist theories ascribe epistemological primacy to *perception* (sense data organized by the mind into objects and facts), not to *sensation* alone.

Clark believes . . . that all truth is propositional: we can have knowledge of propositions—that is, of facts—but not of things. So his view of revelation is opposite to those of the liberal theologians.

But of course, more fundamentally, Clark is not a rationalist but a Christian. He recognizes that if one cannot learn truth through the senses alone, no more can he learn it through reason alone, or even from a combination of the two. Clark's argument is that we learn truth by placing our reason and senses under the authority of God's revelation in Scripture.

Yet his conception of that revelation is unnecessarily intellectualist, in my view. Clark believes, as Russell and the early Wittgenstein, that all truth is propositional: we can have knowledge of propositions—that is, of facts—but not of things.[43] So his view of revelation is opposite to those of the liberal theologians. For him, revelation is entirely propositional, and it is learned through the intellect. In his early work *A*

41. Grand Rapids: Eerdmans, 1952.

42. Compare the list of topics in Kuyper's *Lectures on Calvinism*.

43. On this matter, Clark sides with Russell over against Aristotle, contrary to the stance he took on the issue I previously discussed.

Christian Philosophy of Education,[44] Clark cites in his preface J. Gresham Machen's *What Is Faith?*[45] which defends the "primacy of the intellect," the view that truth enters human life through the intellect and thence spreads to other faculties and actions. Clark states that his own book will advance Machen's position.[46]

Similarly, Clark argues that faith is essentially assent to propositions, rejecting at least formally the traditional Reformed understanding of faith as including knowledge and trust as well as assent. I have argued that Clark's view of faith can be maintained if his view of assent is sufficiently robust.[47] If our assent to the proposition that Jesus is Lord is strong and confident, then it will produce the trust, the *fiducia*, that Reformed theology ascribes to faith. But there are levels of assent much less strong than that, as when we recite the creed on Sunday and then go out and forget it.

Clark argues that faith is essentially assent to propositions, rejecting at least formally the traditional Reformed understanding of faith as including knowledge and trust as well as assent.

I have often wondered, though, why it is that Clark always found it necessary to praise the intellect (and despise the emotions, for example), to adopt a rhetoric in which nothing disparaging can be said about the mind, or about logic. My guess is this: Clark lived his formative years in the environment of American evangelicalism, which, in the years following the *Scopes* Monkey Trial, had developed a bitterness toward experts, scholars, intellectualism, and the academic world generally. It was typical then for Christians to elevate "heart knowledge" over "head knowledge" and to exalt feelings over doctrines. Clark was alarmed at this anti-intellectualism, and he rightly thought it alien to true evangelical and Reformed theology. So he adopted a vocabulary and persona that constantly elevated the intellectual and downplayed the emotional. He found a colleague in J. Gresham Machen. It is significant that after World War II, a number of men who had been students of Clark at Wheaton College[48] became leaders of a "new evangelicalism," which sought to undo the anti-intellectualism of the 1920s and '30s and to restore to evangelicalism the academic and intellectual accomplishment, and respectability, that it often had before 1920. To a great extent, we have Clark to thank for the postwar scholarly successes (and, alas, pretensions) of evangelicals.[49]

In the next section, I will consider the Van Til-Clark controversy over the incomprehensibility of God.

44. Unicoi, TN: Trinity Foundation, 2000.

45. New York: Macmillan, 1925.

46. I have expressed disagreement with this position in *DKG*, 78–79, 331, and in *DCL*, 318–20, 353–55, 366–69.

47. *DKG*, 54–57.

48. Among them: Edmund Clowney, Carl F. H. Henry, Edward John Carnell.

49. For a discussion of the upsides and downsides of this development, see my *The Academic Captivity of Theology* (Lakeland, FL: Whitefield Publishers, 2012), available at http://whitefieldmedia.com/product/the-academic-captivity-of-theology/.

CORNELIUS VAN TIL (1895–1987)

Van Til came to the United States from Grootegast, Holland, with his family at the age of ten. He attended schools of the Christian Reformed denomination: Calvin Preparatory School, Calvin College (where he studied philosophy under W. Henry Jellema and others), and, for one year, Calvin Theological Seminary, when Louis Berkhof was on the faculty. He then transferred to Princeton Theological Seminary, earning a Th.M. there in 1925 and in 1927 a Ph.D. in philosophy at nearby Princeton University. At the seminary, he studied with J. Gresham Machen, Geerhardus Vos, William Brenton Greene, Caspar Wistar Hodge, and others[50] who were known for their stand against theological liberalism. His doctoral dissertation adviser was Archibald Allan Bowman, an idealist philosopher. Van Til's dissertation was a comparison between the God of the Bible and the Absolute of philosophical idealism.[51]

Cornelius Van Til

Through his education, Van Til grew in his appreciation for the concept of *antithesis* that we noted in Kuyper's work. Already an admirer of Kuyper, Van Til arrived at Princeton in the midst of the fundamentalist-modernist controversy, in which liberals in the Presbyterian Church USA were trying to eliminate Princeton Seminary's stand for Reformed orthodoxy. Machen's teaching sharpened the sense of antithesis between these two parties, as illustrated by the title of his important book *Christianity and Liberalism*.[52] Van Til developed a kind of apologetic that stressed the antithesis between belief and unbelief.

Despite the antithesis, however, Van Til believed with Warfield that objective truth about God was available to all through revelation. So he believed that a cogent case could be made for the truth of Christianity. Kuyper had stressed antithesis, Princeton objective rationality. Van Til sought to combine both emphases.

Van Til believed with Warfield that objective truth about God was available to all through revelation. So he believed that a cogent case could be made for the truth of Christianity.

Van Til stressed the Creator-creature distinction as fundamental to the biblical worldview. As implied in the *Chalcedonian Declaration*, God may never be confused with anything in the creation. Nor is there anything intermediate between Creator and creature. The Son of God, Jesus, is not an intermediate being, not a divine-human mixture. Rather,

50. B. B. Warfield, one of Princeton's greatest scholars, had died in 1921, two years before Van Til came to Princeton. But Warfield's influence had not diminished. So he should also be regarded as one of the major influences on Van Til.

51. Van Til's Ph.D. and his highly philosophical approach to theology and apologetics ought to provoke retraction of William Lane Craig's statement that "Van Til, for all his insights, was not a philosopher." Steven B. Cowan, ed., *Five Views on Apologetics* (Grand Rapids: Zondervan, 2000), 235. I note, however, that because Van Til's philosophical vocabulary was idealist, rather than analytic or existentialist, twentieth-century philosophers such as Craig always had a hard time understanding him and appreciating the quality of his thought.

52. Grand Rapids: Eerdmans, 1923.

he has two distinct natures, fully God and fully man. Even in Christ, where God and man are most intimately related, Creator and creature are distinct. Therefore, everything divine is distinct from everything in creation. Importantly for epistemology, God's *thoughts* are not our thoughts (Isa. 55:8–9). At best, our thoughts are analogical reflections of God's original thoughts. That is to say, God's thoughts are original, ours derivative. His thoughts have divine attributes (eternity, infinity, omniscience, etc.), while ours do not. God's subjective experience of thinking is very different from ours—an *eternal intuition*. He thinks as Lord, as the supremely authoritative criterion of truth. We, on the contrary, are called to think as servants, honoring that criterion. As Van Til often says, we are to "think God's thoughts after him."

The distinction between God's thoughts and man's provoked Van Til's controversy with Gordon H. Clark.[53] I am told that Van Til and Clark were friends in the early 1930s, when Clark taught at the University of Pennsylvania, and Van Til at Westminster Seminary, then in downtown Philadelphia. They used to take long walks, discussing theological and philosophical issues. And on a number of important matters, they came out in agreement. Edmund Clowney told me that Clark, when teaching at Wheaton, advised him to come to Westminster to study with Van Til.

But after leaving Wheaton College, Clark sought ordination in the Orthodox Presbyterian Church, the denomination founded by Machen's supporters when they left the Presbyterian Church USA in 1936. Philadelphia Presbytery sustained Clark's theological examination in 1944, but a group of twelve elders, including Van Til, presented a "complaint" against that action. It took the denomination about five years to resolve the controversy. Clark remained a minister in good standing, but later Clark and some of his supporters left because they thought the denomination was discriminating against them in General Assembly committee assignments.

At best, our thoughts are analogical reflections of God's original thoughts. That is to say, God's thoughts are original, ours derivative. His thoughts have divine attributes (eternity, infinity, omniscience, etc.), while ours do not.

There were a number of issues in the controversy, but the main one concerned what was called the *incomprehensibility of God*. Actually, that phrase was something of a misnomer. The real issue was whether any human thought could be identical to any divine thought. Van Til denied that such an identity was possible, based on his understanding of the Creator-creature distinction. For him, man's thoughts at best were only "analogous" to God's. Clark said that at best man's thoughts are not analogous to God's, but identical. Such an identity is not only possible, but necessary. For Clark, truth is identity between man's thoughts (= propositions) and God's. If there is no such identity, we have no access to truth.

53. I discuss the Van Til-Clark controversy at length in *CVT*, 97–113.

I think that Clark in effect conceded Van Til's point when he said that the thoughts of God differed from man's in "mode," God's being an eternal intuition. And I think that Van Til conceded Clark's essential point that God and man can know the same propositions: Van Til wrote, "That two times two are four is a well-known fact. God knows it. Man knows it."[54] But the two men never admitted any common ground on these matters, and still today their most fervent disciples fight the same battle. In my view, that battle was completely unnecessary, and neither man was at his best. The fervent disciples, for the most part, are in over their heads.

Van Til always urged the Creator-creature distinction as fundamental not only to Christian metaphysics, but to epistemology as well. For him, all facts are preinterpreted by God.

In any case, Van Til always urged the Creator-creature distinction as fundamental not only to Christian metaphysics, but to epistemology as well. For him, all facts are preinterpreted by God; there are no brute facts. Human knowledge is essentially a reinterpretation of God's interpretations. Therefore, human knowledge must be subordinate to God's revelation; it must *presuppose* that revelation. In this context, a *presupposition* may be defined as a belief that takes precedence over another belief, and an *ultimate* presupposition (for Christians, divine revelation) is one that takes precedence over *all* beliefs. It is therefore a basic commitment of the heart.

We must hold our presupposition firmly in every area of life, including our philosophical work. We should even hold it in our evangelistic and apologetic approach to non-Christians. Some have said that since the non-Christian does not grant Christian presuppositions, apologists should set those presuppositions aside and assume only what the non-Christian himself assumes: the "common ground" of logic, science, causality, rationality, sense experience, and the like. But to assume common ground in this sense implies that the world makes sense even if God did not create it. Yet that is not really common ground; it is capitulation to a non-Christian worldview. And if the apologist begins by assuming a non-Christian worldview, he has lost the battle from the outset.

Since Van Til puts such emphasis on presuppositions in human knowledge, many have criticized him for denying a role for evidence in arguing for the truth of Christianity.

Since Van Til puts such emphasis on presuppositions in human knowledge, many have criticized him for denying a role for evidence in arguing for the truth of Christianity. But he said over and over again that evidence is an important aspect of apologetics. It is right for the apologist to appeal to facts, but not brute facts. The facts are created, directed, and therefore interpreted by God. That raises, however, another point of frequent criticism: if we reason from God-created facts to the existence of God, based on the presupposition of God's revelation, is not our argument circular in a sense? Clark avoided the

54. Cornelius Van Til, *An Introduction to Systematic Theology* (Nutley, NJ: Presbyterian and Reformed, 1974), 172.

charge of circularity by pointing to logic and richness as standards that revelation would have to meet.[55] But Van Til agreed that his approach was circular in one sense.

Van Til insisted (1) that all systems are circular in this way when they seek to vindicate their fundamental presuppositions. The rationalist can prove that reason is the ultimate standard only by appealing to reason. The Muslim can prove that the Qur'an is the ultimate standard only by appealing to reasons supported by the Qur'an. And Van Til showed (2) that arguments that are circular in this way can be enriched with factual material so that they can be made more persuasive. For example, "the Bible says it is the Word of God; therefore, it is the Word of God" is a narrowly circular argument, not very persuasive.[56] But that argument can be broadened and made more persuasive with subarguments concluding that, for example, "the Bible is consistent," "the Bible reveals our true needs," "the Bible answers our deepest questions." These conclusions are also based on biblical presuppositions, so these arguments are equally circular. But they broaden the circle and make the overall argument more persuasive. We can also appeal to evidences such as "archaeological discoveries support the reliability of the book of Acts," as long as the methodology of the archaeology in question is consistent with the biblical worldview and epistemology. Such an argument directed by the biblical worldview is still circular, but more persuasive, since it brings more facts to the table.

Van Til appeals to the biblical metaphysic in his philosophical apologetic. God is a Trinity, one God in three persons. That means, Van Til says, that in God the one and the many are correlative.

In still another way, Van Til appeals to the biblical metaphysic in his philosophical apologetic. God is a Trinity, one God in three persons. That means, Van Til says, that in God the one and the many are correlative. There is no oneness without manyness, and vice versa. Now, the world is not a unity or a diversity in the same way that God is. It is not a second unity of persons, for it introduces impersonal realities into reality: stones, air, planets, stars. But the creation does in important ways reflect God's unity and diversity. So human philosophers will never discover in the world a unity without plurality (like Parmenides' *Being* or Plotinus's *One*). Nor will they discover a plurality without a oneness that defines its nature, like Aristotelian formless prime matter.

Now, when philosophers seek a perfect unity or a perfect plural-

55. Clark validated this procedure from Scripture itself, however. So arguably he was doing the same thing as Van Til: verifying the Scriptures by a scripturally understood logic.

56. Narrowly circular arguments for Christianity are logically valid (the premise implies the conclusion) and sound (to a Christian, the premises are true). But they lack the third characteristic of a good argument: persuasiveness. (Validity is normative, soundness situational, persuasiveness existential.)

ity, they are usually seeking ultimate and final enlightenment as to the nature of reality. They are seeking a oneness that explains all the plurality in the world, or a plurality that lies behind all the oneness. They are seeking exhaustive knowledge, a kind of knowledge available only to God. But, Van Til says, God has made the world in such a way that no man will ever have that kind of knowledge. Whenever man thinks he has discovered a perfect unity, such as *Being*, he cannot speak of it without referring to plural attributes, emanations, and so forth. And whenever he thinks he has discovered something radically plural, such as prime matter, he cannot speak of it except in abstract terms derived from (and uniting it to) other items of experience.

Van Til's apologetic, however, also emphasizes an ethical-historical reality, the fall of man. Even if the fall had not occurred, it would be necessary for us to think presuppositionally, to think in accordance with God's revelation.

So Van Til sometimes claims that the doctrine of the Trinity "solves the problem of the one and the many."[57] Actually, what his argument shows is that the relation of unity and diversity in the world is in fact *not* solvable, not definable, because God has made the world in such a way as to reflect his own mystery and to keep that relation secret.

So far, I have been describing the metaphysical position that Van Til derives from Scripture: the Creator-creature distinction, divinely interpreted facts, and the one and many of Creator and creation. Van Til's apologetic, however, also emphasizes an ethical-historical reality, the fall of man. Even if the fall had not occurred, it would be necessary for us to think presuppositionally, to think in accordance with God's revelation. But the fact that we are fallen adds another dimension to Van Til's argument: we must think presuppositionally because otherwise we sinfully distort the truth. This is Van Til's doctrine of the noetic effects of sin.

Van Til puts much emphasis on Romans 1:18–32: All human beings know God clearly from creation. (Note verse 21: they not only know facts about God; they know God.) But fallen men "by their unrighteousness suppress the truth" (v. 18).

Van Til puts much emphasis on Romans 1:18–32: All human beings know God clearly from creation. (Note verse 21: they not only know facts about God; they know God.) But fallen men "by their unrighteousness suppress the truth" (v. 18). So (as in 1 Cor. 1–3) there is an antithesis (n.b.) between the wisdom of the world and the truth of God, between the mind of the flesh and that of the Spirit, and so on. Satan

57. Van Til often refers to this problem, defining it only sketchily. I think the problem is something like this: When philosophers seek a single principle to explain everything in the world, such as the *One* of Plotinus, they discover that they cannot define it except in terms of plural realities. In that way, the one reduces to the many. But when they seek to explain the world by its constituents, the plurality of objects that make up the world (such as the atoms of Democritus), they cannot describe these except by general concepts that unite them to other objects (e.g., the atoms are small, hard, moving). So the one disappears into the many, and the many into the one. This is related to the dynamic to which I have often referred (beginning in chapter 1) by which rationalism becomes irrationalism and vice versa. But it is ultimately destructive of any epistemology whatsoever. For it implies that neither oneness nor manyness can be identified.

and his unbelieving servants oppose the truth of God, though they know it is true. This is almost the definition of irrationalism.

For Van Til, the antithesis is absolute "in principle." But in fact, Satan and human unbelievers do often utter true statements, even about God. The devils admit that God is one (James 2:19), and that Jesus is "the Holy One of God" (Mark 1:24). The Pharisees were relatively orthodox OT believers, but Jesus identifies them as children of the devil. Somehow, God's common grace keeps unbelievers from speaking falsely all the time. So Van Til, like Kuyper before him, admits to some difficulty in formulating the relation between antithesis and common grace. Some of his formulations seem to me to lack cogency and even to contradict one another.[58] At times, he seems to be saying that the non-Christian doesn't know anything at all, because he reasons on a false presupposition. But he doesn't say that often or consistently. Rather, he admits that this is "a difficult point."[59]

To formulate the concept of antithesis for myself, I would say that there is no truth that the non-Christian is incapable of uttering. He lives in God's world, and to thoroughly deny that reality would be to plunge his thinking and existence into total chaos. So as Van Til says, he admits the truth "in spite of himself." But the antithesis can be seen (1) in the unbeliever's overall project of joining Satan to overthrow God's sovereignty—a project so irrational that it infects his thinking in profound ways; (2) in the unbeliever's consistent purpose of opposing and attacking the truth of God—in his own consciousness, in others, and in society. When he speaks truth (as when Satan quotes Scripture), he speaks it for this purpose.

To formulate the concept of antithesis for myself, I would say that there is no truth that the non-Christian is incapable of uttering. He lives in God's world, and to thoroughly deny that reality would be to plunge his thinking and existence into total chaos.

I said that for Van Til the unbelieving position is irrational. And as we have seen in this book, many non-Christian thinkers have adopted positions that have undermined reason: Aristotle's prime matter, Kant's noumenal, Wittgenstein's Mystical, for example, are asylums of irrationality. But that irrationalism is correlative to rationalism. Non-Christian thought, as we've seen from many examples, is not only irrationalist, but also rationalist in the sense that it maintains the ultimate authority of human reason. I have therefore appealed to the *rationalist-irrationalist dialectic* in criticizing many philosophers in this book. That form of criticism is one of Van Til's many contributions to apologetics; see fig. 13.3.

58. See my chapter "Antithesis," in *CVT*, 187–213.

59. Van Til, *Introduction to Systematic Theology*, 26. Recall that Kuyper had to write a three-volume work to deal with that difficult point. Alvin Plantinga and his followers have sometimes said that for Van Til, non-Christians "don't know anything." Although they are responding to some of Van Til's expressions, their knowledge of Van Til is evidently very superficial. They think Van Til advocated a simple answer to what he (and Kuyper) admitted was a difficult point.

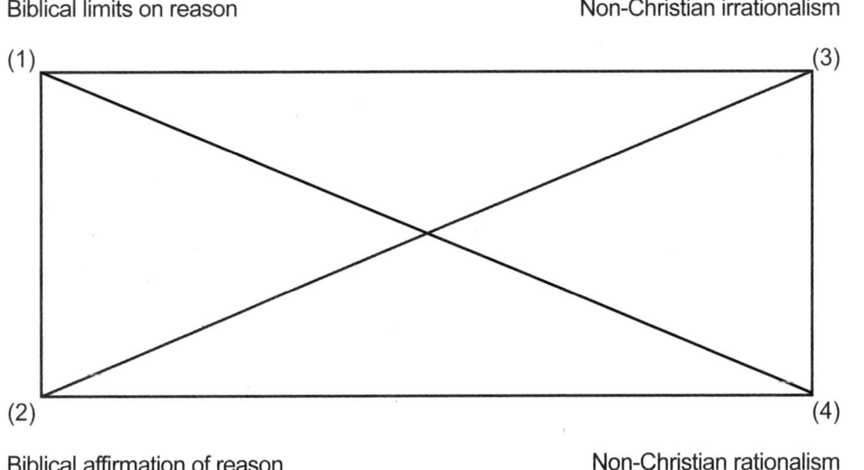

Fig. 13.3. Van Til's Rationalist-Irrationalist Dialectic

We should insist that God's revelation is the only source of meaning and rationality in the world. To deny this revelation leads to chaos and irrationality.

When Van Til discusses apologetic method specifically, he contrasts his own approach with what he called the *traditional method*. He associates that method especially with Aquinas (chapter 4) and Butler (chapter 6). Van Til criticizes these apologists for (1) leaving room for human autonomy, (2) hesitating to presuppose God's revelation (sometimes from fear of circularity), (3) assuming that the world is somehow intelligible without God, (4) assuming that the world as known without God can be a source of evidence for God, (5) arguing that Christianity is only *probably* true, not certainly true.[60]

Then we should evaluate the two systems [the Christian and non-Christian worldviews], each on its own terms, to discover which system (if either) validates rationality, coherence, and meaning.

Positively, Van Til describes his own apologetic approach as follows: We should frankly deny the premise of intellectual autonomy and presuppose God's revelation. Indeed, we should insist that God's revelation is the only source of meaning and rationality in the world. To deny this revelation leads to chaos and irrationality. Van Til proposes that in an apologetic conversation we should place both sets of presuppositions before the non-Christian: the Christian and non-Christian worldviews together with their associated epistemological and ethical consequences. Then we should evaluate the two systems, each on its own terms, to discover which system (if either) validates rationality, coherence, and meaning.

This type of argument Van Til calls *transcendental*, following Kant

60. I am more friendly than Van Til to the concept of probability in apologetics. Van Til says that to claim only probability for apologetic argument is to deny that God's revelation is fully clear (Ps. 19:1; Rom. 1:18–21). But it seems to me that we can grant the clarity of God's revelation while being modest about the logical force of our own arguments. An apologetic argument aims to capture the clarity of God's revelation in words. Some arguments do this well, some less well. Those that capture it less well might nevertheless have some value, and we may call that *probability*.

(see chapter 7). Van Til also calls it *presuppositional*. Kant defined *transcendental argument* as an argument that tries to show the ultimate conditions of rationality. He concluded that his own philosophy provided those conditions, but his successors have not been so sure of that. Van Til argued that only the God of the Bible can account for meaning and rationality. Any other worldview will necessarily lapse into incoherence. This is a very strong claim to make for an apologetic. But Van Til believes that any lesser claim dishonors the prior claim of God himself to universal lordship. As the sovereign Lord of all, God claims to be the Creator of all meaning, rationality, and truth in the world.

Van Til's philosophy, theology, and apologetics deeply influenced a number of younger thinkers, pastors, writers, and evangelists. **Greg L. Bahnsen** (1948–95) died young, of complications from surgery for a congenital heart problem. But he was a powerful writer and debater, and still stands out among the successors of Van Til. He studied with Van Til at Westminster Seminary (Philadelphia), earned a doctorate at the University of Southern California,[61] and wrote *Van Til's Apologetic*,[62] *Presuppositional Apologetics*,[63] and *Always Ready*,[64] with many articles and lectures on philosophical and apologetic subjects. He was also the chief advocate of *theonomy*, the thesis that OT biblical laws are normative for civil governments in the NT age. He was vigorous in defending both Van Til and theonomy, and those who disagreed with him over one position tended to overlook the cogency of his arguments for the other. He was not much involved in the discussions of *Reformed epistemology* because of his short life. But he made a strong case for the Van Tillian alternative. His debate with atheist Gordon Stein, advocating a transcendental argument for the existence of God, is considered a classic among Van Tillians.[65]

Greg L. Bahnsen

Other students of Van Til were influential, but he did not often accept them as legitimate disciples. **John H. Gerstner** (1914–96) went on to a doctorate in Harvard's program in history, philosophy, and religion. He taught at Pittsburgh-Xenia and Pittsburgh Seminaries for many years. He was a critic of Van Til, rather than a disciple, but he was much indebted to Van Til's interactive style of pedagogy and was one of the most impressive teachers of theology I have ever encountered. He

61. His dissertation, written under the direction of Dallas Willard, was on self-deception.

62. Phillipsburg, NJ: P&R Publishing, 1998.

63. Atlanta: American Vision, 2008. For my review of this volume, see my *John Frame's Selected Shorter Writings, Volume 1* (Phillipsburg, NJ: P&R Publishing, 2014), 174–86.

64. Atlanta: American Vision, 1996.

65. Transcript available at http://www.brianauten.com/Apologetics/apol_bahnsen_stein_debate_transcript.pdf. For the audio, see http://vimeo.com/34998731 and http://www.cmfnow.com/thegreatdebatedoesgodexistbahnsenstein-1.aspx.

was the main intellectual influence on **R. C. Sproul** (1939–), founder of Ligonier Ministries.

Edward John Carnell (1919–67) studied with both Clark and Van Til and went on to teach apologetics for some years at Fuller Theological Seminary. He wrote several books, each taking a somewhat different approach to apologetics. Van Til, however, thought he made too many concessions to "traditional" apologetics.

Francis Schaeffer

Another important student of Van Til was **Francis Schaeffer** (1912–84), who established the L'Abri ministry in Switzerland, where many young intellectuals found hospitality and "honest answers to honest questions." Through that ministry, many of Schaeffer's guests embraced Christianity. Schaeffer was an evangelist, rather than a professional philosopher, but he had a broad knowledge of philosophy, art history, music, literature, culture, and modern theology. He endorsed presuppositional apologetics, but as with Carnell, Van Til did not think that Schaeffer's allegiance to presuppositionalism was pure. Still, Schaeffer led to Christ a number of younger thinkers, such as William Edgar (below), who applied his insights to the academic disciplines.

Schaeffer was an evangelist, rather than a professional philosopher, but he had a broad knowledge of philosophy, art history, music, literature, culture, and modern theology. He endorsed presuppositional apologetics.

Another one converted through L'Abri was **Andrée Seu Peterson** (1951–), Faith & Inspiration columnist for *WORLD* magazine. (Disclosure: Peterson was a student of mine at Westminster Seminary in the late 1970s, and she and I have corresponded on a number of subjects.) Peterson is not an academic theologian or philosopher, but I have sometimes said that she is the best theologian writing today. I define *theology* as "the application of the Word of God by persons to all areas of life." Peterson does not apply Scripture to the big philosophical questions that have been the main subject matter of the present volume. Rather, she applies it to the events of everyday life.[66] But she does it extremely well, and often in surprising ways. She has a knowledge of Scripture that dwarfs that of most theologians and philosophers, and she has a nuanced understanding of every life situation she deals with. Her columns draw me into the Lord's presence more than any other writing (outside of Scripture) that I know of.

ALVIN PLANTINGA (1932–)

Plantinga, like Van Til, was raised in the Dutch-American Reformed community, and attended, among other schools, Calvin College, the college of the Christian Reformed Church. He studied there under W. Henry Jellema, who had also taught Van Til a generation earlier, and one of his classmates in Jellema's classes was Nicholas Wolterstorff

66. It is a pity that this focus stereotypes her in the category of *women writers*.

OUTLINE

(see next section).[67] After graduate study at the University of Michigan and a doctorate at Yale, Plantinga taught briefly at Yale and Wayne State University, and then taught for longer periods at Calvin College and the University of Notre Dame.

He is known especially for his *Reformed epistemology*, a name based on Calvin's view that the knowledge of God begins not with reasoning, but with a divinely implanted "sense of deity." For Calvin, further, although there is a wealth of evidence for the reality of God, our full persuasion comes through the inner witness of the Holy Spirit.

Plantinga sometimes refers[68] to the essay of W. K. Clifford, "The Ethics of Belief,"[69] in which the author reiterates an argument of John Locke and David Hume to the effect that it is wrong to believe anything without sufficient evidence. Plantinga replies that there are all sorts of things that we believe, and ought to believe, without evidence or argument.[70] We cannot prove that the sun will rise tomorrow, that the earth is more than five minutes old, or, significantly, that other people have minds like ours. We are naturally certain of these beliefs, more certain than we are (at present) of any arguments that could be used to refute them. So Plantinga calls them *basic* or *foundational*: that is, we believe them not on the basis of other beliefs, but as the foundation for other beliefs.

Now, the term *foundation* might suggest comparisons to the *presuppositions* of Clark and Van Til. Actually, Plantinga's *basic beliefs* are very different from these. A *presupposition*, in the vocabulary of Clark and Van Til, establishes the criteria of rationality in a particular system. So one who holds a Christian presupposition may, simply on the ground of that presupposition, dismiss any competing presupposition as irrational. A presupposition, once accepted, cannot be defeated, because it establishes its own criteria of rationality and truth. (Of course, Van Til and Clark recognized, even emphasized, that presuppositions can be

Alvin Plantinga

67. The process philosopher Paul Weiss once told me that Henry Jellema was the best teacher of philosophy in the world. Plantinga himself said that Jellema was "by all odds . . . the most gifted teacher of philosophy I have ever encountered." Wikipedia, s.v. "William Harry Jellema," http://en.wikipedia.org/wiki/William_Harry_Jellema#cite_note-2. But it helped Jellema to have been blessed by such gifted students. I forget whether it was Plantinga or Wolterstorff who mused about what Jellema would have thought to know that he had two future Gifford lecturers in his classroom. (The Gifford Lectures are among the most prestigious lectures in philosophical theology.)

68. As in "Reason and Belief in God," in *Faith and Rationality: Reason and Belief in God*, ed. Alvin Plantinga and Nicholas Wolterstorff (Notre Dame, IN: University of Notre Dame Press, 1983), 16–93.

69. Originally published 1877; now available in *The Ethics of Belief and Other Essays* (New York: Prometheus Books, 1999) and at http://www.infidels.org/library/historical/w_k_clifford/ethics_of_belief.html. I am pleased that at least Clifford saw a relation between epistemology and ethics.

70. Here he acknowledges his debt to the similar argument of Thomas Reid (chapter 6).

defeated by nonlogical factors, such as Satan's temptations or the testimony of the Holy Spirit. These nonlogical factors may be combined with assertions and arguments based on a competing presupposition.) But for Plantinga, basic beliefs do not establish standards of rationality. Rather, they share with all other human beliefs the quality of *defeasibility*: they can be overcome by competing beliefs, evidence, and argument, even though they are not held on the basis of evidence and argument.[71]

For example, if you are raised in a community of sun-worshipers, you are within your epistemic rights[72] to believe in the deity of the sun, and even to make that belief foundational in your consideration of other beliefs. You don't need to have arguments on which to base your position. But it is possible that someone will present to you arguments that defeat your belief. You have no right to claim that this is impossible. Your basic belief does not carry with it its own standards of rationality or the right to dismiss all other views as irrational. So if you are wise, you will carefully consider the arguments of those who question your basic beliefs.

For Plantinga, basic beliefs do not establish standards of rationality. Rather, they share with all other human beliefs the quality of defeasibility: *they can be overcome by competing beliefs, evidence, and argument.*

In *God and Other Minds: A Study of the Rational Justification of Belief in God*,[73] Plantinga reviews the philosophical controversy over how we can know that other people have minds like ours. On his view, there is no evidence that conclusively proves this proposition. Yet we all believe it, and we should. It is a basic belief. But belief in God, Plantinga argues, is similar. In fact, whatever difficulties attend belief in God are parallel to the difficulties in believing in other minds. Similarly, the justification for believing in God is similar to the justification for believing in other minds.

[Plantinga argues that] whatever difficulties attend belief in God are parallel to the difficulties in believing in other minds. Similarly, the justification for believing in God is similar to the justification for believing in other minds.

In his later writing,[74] he develops a significant epistemology, which supports theism as basic belief. Some philosophers have defined

71. That raises the question, of course, of the grounds for sound evidence and argument. If these grounds aren't established by the foundational beliefs, then where do they come from? And if they are established by, say, principle A, then doesn't A become the *actual* foundation for the thought of the person in question? And if that actual foundation turns out to be some principles of logic or experience, that would suggest that Plantinga is doing what the philosophical tradition has regularly done—making his Christian beliefs subject to general standards of logic and experience.

72. Plantinga and his colleagues often refer to *knowledge* in ethical terms. I am enthusiastic about those interconnections. But I wish Plantinga and his disciples would speak of epistemic *obligations*, not just of epistemic *rights*. If it turns out that belief in God is a moral obligation (and the Bible in Romans 1 and elsewhere suggests that it is: Prov. 1:7; 1 Cor. 1–3; Col. 3:10; etc.), then that would require changes in Reformed epistemology.

73. Ithaca, NY: Cornell University Press, 1967.

74. His magnum opus is a three-volume series called *Warrant*. (What is it about Dutch writers and three-volume masterworks? See on Kuyper, earlier in this chapter.) These are *Warrant: The Current Debate* (New York: Oxford University Press, 1993), *Warrant and Proper Function* (New York: Oxford University Press, 1993), and *Warranted Christian Belief* (New York: Oxford University Press, 2000).

knowledge as "justified, true belief."[75] But others have had difficulty with this definition. In 1963, Edmund Gettier (significantly, then a colleague of Plantinga at Wayne State University) published a short paper called "Is Justified True Belief Knowledge?"[76] Gettier proposed two cases in which someone (S) has a justified, true belief, but in which most readers would not concede that S has knowledge. What happens is that S has a belief, and a justification for his belief, but the belief merely *happens* to be true, so that the justification turns out not to be relevant. Gettier's essay provoked much discussion among philosophers, including reexamination of the concept of *justification*.[77]

Plantinga drops the concept *justification* as too confused and replaces it with what he calls *warrant*. He says that a belief, B, is warranted if

> (1) the cognitive faculties involved in the production of B are functioning properly . . . ; (2) your cognitive environment is sufficiently similar to the one for which your cognitive faculties are designed; (3) . . . the design plan governing the production of the belief in question involves, as purpose or function, the production of true beliefs . . . ; and (4) the design plan is a good one: that is, there is a high statistical or objective probability that a belief produced in accordance with the relevant segment of the design plan in that sort of environment is true.[78]

Discussions of *justification* have sometimes distinguished *internalist* and *externalist* concepts. An internalist view says that I may justify belief B by appealing to other beliefs that I hold. The justification of B, then, is internal to my own thinking. An externalist view, however, says that the justification of B is its relation to things beyond the thinker himself.[79] Plantinga's view of justification, or rather warrant, is externalist. To him, the beliefs of a subject S are not warranted by other beliefs, but by their production, environment, and design plan[80]—in short, by their connection to the real world beyond S's own subjectivity; see fig. 13.4.

Plantinga's view of justification, or rather warrant, is externalist. To him, the beliefs of a subject S are not warranted by other beliefs, but by their production, environment, and design plan—in short, by their connection to the real world beyond S's own subjectivity.

75. Note the three perspectives: *justified* = normative, *true* = situational, *belief* = existential.

76. *Analysis* 23 (1966): 121–23, available at http://philosophyfaculty.ucsd.edu/faculty/rarneson/Courses/gettierphilreading.pdf.

77. In my view, the problem with justification—or, for that matter, warrant—is that these are ultimately based on God's revelation. But the philosophers debating the nature of justification and warrant, including Plantinga, do not give attention to this alternative.

78. Plantinga, *Warrant and Proper Function*, 194.

79. For what it's worth, I think we need justifications in both senses. I need an internal justification to justify my own beliefs to myself, but it takes an external justification to make them objectively true. Without an external justification, my beliefs may not connect with the real world. Without an internal justification, I would not know what that connection is.

80. Forgive, please, one more triangular analysis: the design plan is normative, the environment is situational, and the actual production of beliefs within my consciousness is existential; see fig. 13.4.

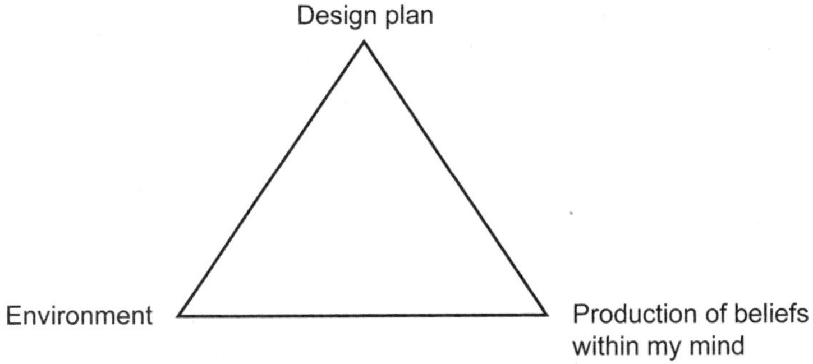

Fig. 13.4. Perspectives on Plantinga's Epistemology

Christians may defend their belief as rational by claiming that their cognitive equipment is working properly, and that this equipment is designed so that in a certain environment it will generate true beliefs.

On this basis, belief in God does not require evidence or argument, but may be held as a foundational or basic belief. Christians may defend their belief as rational by claiming that their cognitive equipment is working properly, and that this equipment is designed[81] so that in a certain environment it will generate true beliefs.[82] What happens, perhaps, is that when looking at the sky on a clear, starry night, a person finds himself believing that this great complexity was intelligently designed. So without evidence or argument,[83] he finds himself believing in God.

So far, Plantinga has defended the *rationality* of belief in God, but not the truth of that belief. If the argument above is sound, Plantinga has shown that one can believe in God without being mentally deranged. But many such rational beliefs, as Plantinga has said, can be defeated and thus can turn out to be false.

Plantinga has defended the rationality *of belief in God, but not the truth of that belief. If the argument above is sound, Plantinga has shown that one can believe in God without being mentally deranged.*

But Plantinga also takes an interest in the question of truth. In his books *The Nature of Necessity*[84] and *God, Freedom, and Evil*,[85] Plantinga develops a modal version of the ontological argument for God's existence that he certifies as being sound. He also defends theism against the argument that evil is inconsistent with God's goodness, by appealing to libertarian free will.[86] Further, Plantinga has supported the intelligent-design movement of Phillip Johnson, Michael Behe, William

81. Designed, that is, by a "good" plan.

82. But how can we actually know that these conditions have been fulfilled? At this point, it would seem that we need an internalist warrant as well as an externalist one. We need, that is, an internal reason for believing that the external conditions have been met.

83. In my hypothetical example, I am assuming that the person's belief in God arises *not* from a cosmological or teleological argument based on the data of the stars, but directly from the experience itself. Arguably, this is the source of the knowledge of God in Romans 1:18–21.

84. Clarendon Library of Logic and Philosophy (Oxford: Clarendon, 1974).

85. Grand Rapids: Eerdmans, 1974.

86. Compare my negative response to this view of freedom in chapters 2 and 3, and in *DG*, 119–84. Here Plantinga departs from Calvin and from the Reformed theological tradition.

Dembski, and others, without committing to the idea that design can be scientifically proved.

He has also become known for his *evolutionary argument against naturalism*: If evolution and naturalism[87] are both true, then the cognitive faculties of human beings have evolved for survival, not for achieving truth. Truth is not always conducive to survival, and vice versa. So if the theory of evolution claims to give us the complete purpose of the human mind, there is reason to doubt the products of the mind, including the theories of evolution and naturalism. On the other hand, if the human mind is designed by God,[88] then there is reason to trust the ideas generated in the mind.

Indeed, we should recall that Plantinga's externalist epistemology relies on the concept of a *design plan*. What could have been the source of such a plan? He sometimes concedes that evolution itself could be the source of that plan.[89] But elsewhere he says that the model of a personal designer is the best way of accounting for this design.[90, 91]

My own view is closer to Van Til than to Plantinga, for Van Til, like Kuyper, and indeed like Calvin,[92] insists that Christian faith is firmly based on the presupposition of God's revelation. Plantinga, like most of the other recent analytic Christian philosophers, rarely mentions revelation or Scripture, and he writes as if revelation, particularly Scripture, were irrelevant to philosophical discourse. But without the presupposition of Scripture, it seems to me that Plantinga's philosophy lacks a crucial element for a Christian epistemology.

Plantinga, like most of the other recent analytic Christian philosophers, rarely mentions revelation or Scripture, and he writes as if revelation, particularly Scripture, were irrelevant to philosophical discourse.

Nevertheless, Plantinga's contribution to Christian philosophy is certainly very substantial. When I first studied philosophy, from 1957 to 1961, it was rare to hear any Christian positions expressed in lectures or seminars. When someone took a distinctively Christian view, he was regularly laughed out of the classroom. But in the years since that time, there has developed a substantial presence of Christians in the philosophical field. Plantinga's work is deeply respected

87. *Naturalism* = belief that there is no God and that therefore nature is all there is.

88. Plantinga always assumes that divine design is consistent with an evolutionary process.

89. Plantinga, *Warrant and Proper Function*, 21. I myself do not understand how an exclusively impersonal process could generate a normative plan, a purpose for an object or person.

90. Ibid., 237.

91. For more of Plantinga's thoughts about the existence of God, see "Two Dozen (or So) Theistic Arguments," available at http://www.calvin.edu/academic/philosophy/virtual_library/articles/plantinga_alvin/two_dozen_or_so_theistic_arguments.pdf.

92. Remember Calvin's statement that we cannot understand God's natural revelation properly without the "spectacles" supplied by Scripture (Calvin, *Institutes*, 1.6). Those spectacles are part of our "cognitive equipment" that Plantinga fails to discuss.

by non-Christian as well as Christian thinkers, and in this he has been joined by a great many others, some of whom I discuss below.[93] There is a Society for Christian Philosophers that publishes a serious academic journal, *Faith and Philosophy*. Plantinga and his colleagues are largely responsible for all of this. Because of their labors, it is a good time to be a Christian philosopher.

My favorite of Plantinga's publications is his "Advice to Christian Philosophers."[94] In that paper, he urges Christians to take their faith into account in their philosophical work: their choice of mentors, models, methods, and so on. Christians should be suspicious of claims that this or that approach is necessary for philosophical or scientific respectability, and they should be alert for proposals that emerge out of and/or support their Christian faith. That advice is the same as that which I would offer to readers as we draw near to the end of this book.

My favorite of Plantinga's publications is his "Advice to Christian Philosophers." In that paper, he urges Christians to take their faith into account in their philosophical work: their choice of mentors, models, methods, and so on.

OTHER CHRISTIAN LANGUAGE-ANALYSIS PHILOSOPHERS IN NORTH AMERICA

Other philosophers of distinction have been associated with the new philosophical movement connected with Plantinga and the Society of Christian Philosophers. Special mention should be given to **Nicholas Wolterstorff** (1932–), arguably as prominent as Plantinga in the philosophical community. Wolterstorff and Plantinga were classmates at Calvin College, under Henry Jellema among others. Wolterstorff doctored at Harvard (Plantinga at Yale). Wolterstorff taught many years at Yale, while Plantinga taught at Notre Dame. Wolterstorff and Plantinga were essentially partners in the development of Reformed epistemology. So for me to discuss Wolterstorff's religious epistemology would be unnecessarily repetitious. But I confess that my initial enthusiasm for this project was kindled and has been often renewed by Wolterstorff's early *Reason within the Bounds of Religion*.[95]

Nicholas Wolterstorff

But Wolterstorff also wrote on ontology (*On Universals: An Essay in Ontology*[96]). In this book, he argues (contrary to the modern nominalistic spirit) that universals really exist, and that they can be characterized as *kinds*. He has also published two books on aesthetics,[97] as well as

93. Significantly, these Christian philosophers are generally more orthodox in their Christian beliefs than those who call themselves theologians.

94. *Faith and Philosophy* 1 (October 1984): 1–19, available at http://www.calvin.edu/academic/philosophy/virtual_library/articles/plantinga_alvin/advice_to_christian_philosophers.pdf.

95. Grand Rapids: Eerdmans, 1976. Note the inversion in the title from Kant's *Religion within the Limits of Reason Alone*.

96. Chicago: University of Chicago Press, 1970.

97. *Works and Worlds of Art* (Oxford: Clarendon, 1980); *Art in Action: Toward a Christian Aesthetic* (Grand Rapids: Eerdmans, 1980).

many more on justice, political issues, education, and theology. His *Lament for a Son*,[98] dealing with the death of his own son, is deeply moving.

William P. Alston (1921–2009), having already made a considerable reputation as a philosopher of language and epistemology, "went back to church," as he put it, became deeply involved in the Society of Christian Philosophers, and was a close ally of Plantinga and Wolterstorff in the development of Reformed epistemology.[99] Within that movement, he focused particularly on the issue of religious experience. He defended it as a means of knowledge in his *Perceiving God: The Epistemology of Religious Experience*.[100] He also published a number of other books and many articles on epistemology and philosophy of language.

George Mavrodes (1926–) wrote, with Plantinga, Wolterstorff, and Alston, several articles in the seminal presentation of Reformed epistemology, *Faith and Rationality*, cited in footnote 68 above.[101] I have found him to be a remarkably stimulating thinker, as one can tell from the fourteen references to his *Belief in God: A Study in the Epistemology of Religion*[102] in my *DKG*. Often, I have been moved by brief arguments in his writing, even more than by his broader theses. For example, in *Belief in God*,[103] he points out (contrary to logical positivism) that typically we must know the meaning of an expression *before* we can learn how to verify it. And we often cannot tell whether a statement is verifiable unless we first ascertain that it is true. That means that on the basis of the verification principle, every claim to verification must be verified ad infinitum.[104]

Mavrodes points out (contrary to logical positivism) that typically we must know the meaning of an expression before *we can learn how to verify it. And we often cannot tell whether a statement is verifiable unless we first ascertain that it is true.*

Similarly, Mavrodes makes the case that we must often answer substantive questions (such as "does God exist?") before we can answer epistemological questions ("how can I know God?").[105] He makes the important distinction between *having* a reason and *being able to give* a reason.[106] So, as Plantinga says, we have a right to believe some things without being able to verify them with evidence and argument.

So a person "cannot learn everything he knows from proofs."[107] At some point, we must have knowledge that we have not proved by

98. Grand Rapids: Eerdmans, 1987.

99. An Anglican, he wasn't entirely pleased with the *Reformed epistemology* label.

100. Ithaca, NY: Cornell University Press, 1991.

101. I will refer to his article, "Jerusalem and Athens Revisited," 192–218.

102. New York: Random House, 1970.

103. Ibid., 47–48.

104. Ibid., 75.

105. Ibid., 41–50. Cf. 72, 76, 95, 112.

106. Ibid., 11–13.

107. Ibid., 41.

evidence or argument, and of course, that is precisely the claim of Reformed epistemology.

Mavrodes also frequently stresses that proofs of propositions are "person-variable,"[108] a point of great importance to apologetics. An argument, no matter how valid or sound, may be persuasive to one person, but not to another; the second person might need a different kind of proof, if he needs one at all.

Mavrodes also frequently stresses that proofs of propositions are "person-variable," a point of great importance to apologetics. An argument, no matter how valid or sound, may be persuasive to one person, but not to another.

In "Jerusalem and Athens Revisited," Mavrodes counsels Plantinga and Wolterstorff to give more attention to the *truth* of our beliefs and correspondingly less to their *rationality*. As time went on, however, I think that Plantinga and the others heeded that counsel, as they developed their arguments for the existence of God, the veridical nature of religious experience, the design of the universe, and the relation between God and evil.

But another of Mavrodes's suggestions deserves further exploration. The whole idea of Reformed epistemology is to distinguish between *basic* and *nonbasic* beliefs, and to argue that belief in God belongs to the former category. Recall that a basic belief is one that we hold without basing it on another belief. But Mavrodes raises a significant question about that distinction:

> Readers of this volume who are theists might usefully try the following experiment on themselves. Pause for a moment and consider your own belief that God exists, just as it stands right now. . . . Is that belief . . . based on some other beliefs that you hold? And if so, what are those other beliefs, and *how* is the belief in God's existence based on them? (Do they entail it, for example, or render it probable, or what?)[109]

The whole idea of Reformed epistemology is to distinguish between basic *and* nonbasic *beliefs, and to argue that belief in God belongs to the former category. . . . Mavrodes raises a significant question about that distinction.*

Mavrodes suspects (and I think rightly so) that for most of us there will be no clear answer to these questions, or that perhaps our answers will change from time to time.[110] That fact suggests that the contrast between basic and nonbasic beliefs oversimplifies the epistemic situation.[111]

108. Ibid., 7–8, 17–48, 80–89, 101–11.

109. Mavrodes, "Jerusalem and Athens Revisited," 203.

110. In this respect, I think that presuppositionalism, in which people commit all their thought and lives to the presupposition, allows for a clearer distinction between the foundation and the beliefs that are built on it. As I point out in *DKG*, however, there is a similar problem in presuppositionalism: since the normative perspective encompasses all of reality, it cannot be finally separated from situational and existential perspectives. I think that objection can be answered, but it takes all of *DKG* to present that answer clearly.

111. This discussion is adapted from my review of *Faith and Rationality*, Appendix I in *DKG* (382–400).

Kevin J. Vanhoozer

Kevin J. Vanhoozer (1957–) is somewhat more removed from the Plantinga circle than the figures recently mentioned. Having earned his doctorate at Cambridge University, he has taught mostly at Trinity Evangelical Divinity School (Deerfield, Illinois), with periods of teaching at the New College, Edinburgh, Scotland, and Wheaton College.[112] He is more commonly described as a theologian than a philosopher, but he combines both disciplines most intimately and effectively. Evangelical and Reformed in conviction, he has developed models of theology in interaction with the speech-act theories of Wittgenstein, Austin, and Searle (chapter 12 of this book). This has equipped him to discuss hermeneutical issues in Paul Ricoeur, Hans-Georg Gadamer, and others. Contrary to deconstructionists (chapter 12), he argues that the intention of a text's author does indeed carry weight in its interpretation. But author, text, and reader form a community analogous to that of biblical covenants, and so the interpretation of a text has multiple dimensions.

Others associated with this North American flowering of Christian analytic philosophy are Robert and Marilyn Adams, Kelly James Clark, William Lane Craig, Stephen T. Davis, C. Stephen Evans, John Feinberg, Gary Habermas, William Hasker, Peter Van Inwagen, J. P. Moreland, Nancey Murphy, and Linda Zagzebski. Somewhat removed from the analytic tradition have been Ronald Nash, who was close to Gordon Clark, historian and educator Arthur Holmes, and Norman Geisler, an evangelical Thomist.

Younger philosophers and apologists include:

- James Anderson,[113]
- John Barber,[114]
- Bruce Baugus,[115]

112. Disclosure: Vanhoozer was a student of mine at Westminster Seminary in the late 1970s. He dedicated to me his book *Remythologizing Theology: Divine Action, Passion, and Authorship*, Cambridge Studies in Christian Doctrine (Cambridge: Cambridge University Press, 2010). Of all my students, he has probably made the greatest impression in the contemporary theological world.

113. http://www.proginosko.com/. He wrote *Paradox in Christian Theology* (Eugene, OR: Wipf and Stock, 2007) and *What's Your Worldview? An Interactive Approach to Life's Big Questions* (Wheaton, IL: Crossway, 2014). Anderson also moderates a website with information about Cornelius Van Til, http://www.vantil.info.

114. Barber is one of the best theologians of culture now writing. His *The Road from Eden: Studies in Christianity and Culture* (Lakeland, FL: Whitefield Media Publications, 2008) is a wonderfully full and nuanced critique of Western culture. In an endorsement, I wrote, "Barber has mastered and/or referenced a huge amount of literature. His book is a great resource, . . . his arguments careful, cogent and revealing. I hope his argument has a great deal of influence on the church. . . . It is like a mighty force for reformation, revival and cultural renewal. There has never been anything like it (as a single volume) in Reformed literature."

115. Baugus received his doctorate from Calvin Theological Seminary and has recently begun to teach apologetics at Reformed Theological Seminary in Jackson, Mississippi.

- William Edgar,[116]
- William Davis,[117]
- Paul Manata,[118]
- K. Scott Oliphint,[119]
- James K. A. Smith,[120] and
- Greg Welty.[121]

BRITISH CHRISTIAN PHILOSOPHERS

C. S. Lewis

C. S. Lewis (1898–1963) is often considered more a popular writer than a true philosopher. But he did study philosophy and in 1924 worked as a philosophy tutor at University College of Oxford University. The following year, however, he was elected a Fellow and Tutor of English at Magdalen College, establishing his main vocation as a scholar of medieval and Renaissance literature. We know him now, however,

C. S. Lewis (1898–1963) is often considered more a popular writer than a true philosopher. But he did study philosophy and in 1924 worked as a philosophy tutor at University College of Oxford University.

116. A jazz pianist and musicologist, Edgar came to faith through Francis Schaeffer's ministry and studied with Cornelius Van Til. Like Schaeffer's, his apologetic work is sensitive to the milieu of contemporary culture. Note his *The Face of Truth: Lifting the Veil* (Phillipsburg, NJ: P&R Publishing, 2001) and *Truth in All Its Glory: Commending the Reformed Faith* (Phillipsburg, NJ: P&R Publishing, 2004). He also edited, with K. Scott Oliphint, two volumes of primary source readings in apologetics: *Christian Apologetics Past and Present: A Primary Source Reader*, vol. 1, *To 1500* (Wheaton, IL: Crossway, 2009), and vol. 2, *From 1500* (Wheaton, IL: Crossway, 2011). He now teaches at Westminster Theological Seminary, Philadelphia.

117. Known as an excellent teacher of philosophy at Covenant College and other institutions, Davis studied with Gordon Clark earlier at Covenant, and earned his doctorate at the University of Notre Dame. He has written on C. S. Lewis, J. R. R. Tolkien, and open theism.

118. At my most recent glance, Manata is still a "student of philosophy" at Calvin College (serving as a teaching assistant for Christian philosopher Kevin Corcoran). But he has written a great many blog pieces and has entered many debates, with considerable cogency. One example is "Free Will, Moral Responsibility, and Reformed Theology: A Contemporary Introduction," available at http://analytictheologye4c5.files.wordpress.com/2011/07/free-will-and-moral-responsibility-intro11.pdf. I am expecting great things from him, as from all the other younger men listed here.

119. Oliphint teaches at Westminster Theological Seminary, and has reedited several volumes of Van Til's works. His most recent book is *Covenantal Apologetics* (Wheaton, IL: Crossway, 2013).

120. Smith is one of the most cogent writers today in relating philosophy to culture. Two of his recent books are *Desiring the Kingdom: Worship, Worldview, and Cultural Formation* (Grand Rapids: Baker, 2009) and *Imagining the Kingdom: How Worship Works* (Grand Rapids: Baker, 2013), dealing with culture and the liturgy in a Kuyperian spirit.

121. Welty, who did his doctoral work under Richard Swinburne at Oxford, now teaches philosophy at Southeastern Baptist Theological Seminary. Disclosure: he was my teaching assistant at Westminster Seminary (California) for four years: http://sebts.academia.edu/GregWelty lists his current and past projects. His doctoral dissertation (2006, University of Oxford) argues the Augustinian thesis that abstract objects are thoughts in the mind of God, rather than created objects as some have maintained. He recently defended this view in *Beyond the Control of God? Six Views on the Problem of God and Abstract Objects* (London: Bloomsbury Academic, 2014), and developed it into a theistic argument in an article: "The Lord of Non-Contradiction: An Argument for God from Logic" (*Philosophia Christi* 13, 2 [2011], co-written with RTS-Charlotte professor James Anderson). Welty has also written on transcendental argument, Molinism, baptism, and new covenant theology.

principally as "the most dejected and reluctant convert in all England,"[122] who wrote many books on apologetics and many less obvious apologetics in the form of novels and essays. I have many testimonies of people who have turned toward Christ in some measure after reading Lewis's *Mere Christianity*.[123] This book was helpful to me as well, when I was seeking help amid the complications of university philosophy classes. Readers can evaluate my revision of Lewis's moral argument for God in my *AJCB*.[124] But the book of Lewis that moved me most was his *Miracles: A Preliminary Study*,[125] in which he brilliantly and clearly showed that the controversy over miracles was a controversy over two worldviews: naturalism and supernaturalism.[126] In that respect, it was C. S. Lewis who prepared me for Van Til. Van Til didn't like Lewis's work very much, aligning him with Aquinas and Butler as one who sought a "neutral" starting point. But at the point of miracle, Van Til and Lewis converged in my mind.

Alasdair MacIntyre (1929–) is a Scotsman who has taught at many universities in Britain and the United States. His first well-known book, *After Virtue: A Study in Moral Theory*,[127] influenced by Thomas Kuhn (chapter 12), Imre Lakatos, and others, seeks for a new paradigm of ethics, grounded in Aristotle's teleological ethic of virtue. He thinks this paradigm will defend local communities against the corrosive effects of wider cultures. In *Whose Justice? Which Rationality?*[128] he grounds ethical decisions in traditions of *practical rationality* that, like Kuhnian paradigms, might be incommensurate with one another. Still, there can be dialogue between these traditions that can benefit all of them and even lead to "crisis" and revolution analogous to Kuhn's scientific revolutions.

Alasdair MacIntyre

Richard Swinburne (1934–) taught at Keele University from 1972 to 1985, and then was a professor at Oxford University from 1985 until his retirement in 2002. He wrote over ten books on philosophical theology. His approach is probabilistic, accommodating. He advocates

122. C. S. Lewis, "Surprised by Joy," in *The Inspirational Writings of C. S. Lewis* (New York: Harcourt Brace Jovanovich, 1987), 118.

123. San Francisco: HarperCollins, 2001.

124. Chapter 4, 95–123.

125. San Francisco: Harper One, 2009.

126. There was a famous debate between Lewis and Wittgensteinian philosopher Elizabeth Anscombe about the third chapter of *Miracles*, which tries to show that naturalism is self-defeating. Some have written that Lewis lost that debate, even that Anscombe humiliated him. But Anscombe herself remembered the debate as a cordial exchange, and she mentions that Lewis rewrote the chapter in question to deal with her objections. See G. E. M. Anscombe, *The Collected Philosophical Papers of G. E. M. Anscombe*, 3 vols. (Oxford: Blackwell, 1981), introduction to vol. 2, *Metaphysics and the Philosophy of Mind*.

127. Notre Dame, IN: University of Notre Dame Press, 1981.

128. Notre Dame, IN: University of Notre Dame Press, 1988.

an open-theist view of God's eternity and omnipresence (see Chapter 12 of this book).

Paul Helm (1940–) taught at the University of Liverpool, King's College of the University of London, Regent College (Vancouver, B.C.), and Highlands Theological College in Scotland. He is certainly the most consistent Calvinist[129] of all the analytic philosophers mentioned so far in this chapter, including the Reformed epistemologists. A former editor of the neo-Puritan *Banner of Truth* magazine, he has done impressive work in the history of theology as well as in philosophy. He has published three books on Calvin and his intellectual environment. In philosophy, he has published *Belief Policies*,[130] *Faith and Understanding*,[131] and *Faith with Reason*.[132] He has developed the best recent arguments for God's existing outside time, *Eternal God*,[133] and for a Calvinist understanding of divine providence, *The Providence of God*.[134] For some discussion of Helm's ideas, methods, and arguments, see my review of *Belief Policies*, Appendix O of this book, and my review of *The Providence of God*, Appendix E in my *DG*.

Paul Helm

EUGEN ROSENSTOCK-HUESSY (1888–1973)

Now for someone rather different.[135] Rosenstock-Huessy was born in Germany of Jewish parents, but was baptized as a Lutheran in his late teens. Unlike many Jews who converted to Christianity at that time, however, Rosenstock-Huessy was passionately devoted to Christ in life and doctrine.[136] During World War I, he was a close friend and correspondent of the Jewish thinker Franz Rosenzweig. He led Rosenzweig to take his faith more seriously, but did not succeed in leading him to Christianity.

Helm has developed the best recent arguments for God's existing outside time, Eternal God, *and for a Calvinist understanding of divine providence,* The Providence of God.

Like so many other thinkers in this book, he emigrated to the United States during the rise of Hitler. Then he taught, first at Harvard, and then at Dartmouth.

His work is not easy to classify. He wrote forty books and around five hundred articles, covering linguistics, sociology (especially labor issues), philosophy, jurisprudence, theology, and history, but he always insisted that the God of Scripture was at the center of it.[137] His central

129. But he is not, alas, a presuppositionalist.

130. Cambridge: Cambridge University Press, 1994.

131. Grand Rapids: Eerdmans, 1997.

132. Oxford: Clarendon, 2000.

133. Oxford: Clarendon, 1988.

134. Downers Grove, IL: InterVarsity Press, 1993.

135. Not "completely different," because no two things, or two people, are completely different from each other.

136. G. K. Chesterton's *Orthodoxy* was one of his favorite books.

137. Peter Leithart says, "Harvard didn't know what to do with him. Since he talked a lot about God, they sent him to the divinity school." Peter J. Leithart, "The Relevance of Eugen Rosenstock-Huessy," *First Things*, June 28, 2007, available at http://www.firstthings.com/onthesquare/2007/06/the-relevance-of-eugen-rosenst.

Eugen Rosenstock-Huessy

thought, perhaps, is that God is a *speaking* God.[138] Language, even more than religion, certainly more than philosophy, is the greatest power behind historical change, and it is the great events of historical change (rather than mere ideas) that have the most power to transform our thinking and institutions. So Rosenstock-Huessy, though he did not interact much with the philosophical movements of language analysis and structuralism, contributes to the twentieth-century philosophical preoccupation with language.

For him, language is not primarily a means of expressing propositions (as with Russell and the early Wittgenstein), nor a way of breaking up reality into elements (as structuralism), but a social medium. It is a way of offering up ourselves to other people. In conversation, two persons remake each other. The various purposes of language,[139] further, determine various cultural endeavors such as poetry, science, history, and ethics. Philosophers' preoccupation with *being* narrows the variety and dynamism of the world. Rosenstock-Huessy prefers Homer's prephilosophical interest in names to the later Greek philosophical interest in essences. He prefers polytheism to deism and atheism. Among philosophers, he prefers Heraclitus to Parmenides.

So philosophers, he thinks, have been too preoccupied with timeless logic, insufficiently interested in historical events. Christianity, too, has been misunderstood even by many Christians as a religion of transcendence, easily merged with a spiritualistic Platonism. Rather, said Rosenstock-Huessy, it is a force for changing history. In Christianity, as opposed to Gnosticism, the body leads the mind. One article summarizes Rosenstock-Huessy's epistemology with Goethe's aphorism, "What is fruitful, that alone is true."[140] Fruitfulness, however, does not mean material prosperity. Historical catastrophes, provoking great suffering, are the events most historically significant. The Christian church is called to change history through suffering love. Much of its suffering is by divine ordination. The wars of the last millennium have been miniature "last judgments" through which the church is refined and new words are spoken, directing the future into new paths. Rosenstock-Huessy hopes these will teach the human race the need to deal with problems through local conversations, not by trying to devise a new world order.[141]

138. Cf. my discussion in *DG*, 469–79; *DWG*, 47–49.

139. He made the same discovery as the later Wittgenstein, that language not only is descriptive, but has many other functions and should be free to perform those.

140. Wayne Cristaudo, "Eugen Rosenstock-Huessy," *Stanford Encyclopedia of Philosophy* (June 14, 2012), http://plato.stanford.edu/entries/rosenstock-huessy/. We can make useful comparison between Huessy's view here and the views of Charles S. Peirce and William James (chapter 9).

141. In this respect, he echoes the postmodern rejection of metanarrative.

RADICAL ORTHODOXY[142]

The movement bearing this name started with the book *Theology and Social Theory: Beyond Secular Reason*[143] by **John Milbank** (1952–), but it got its name from the book of essays by Milbank, Catherine Pickstock, and Graham Ward, called *Radical Orthodoxy: A New Theology.*[144] These three authors are Anglicans, with strong Anglo-Catholic sympathies, but in the wider RO group there are Christians from other backgrounds. Reformed philosopher James K. A. Smith wrote a standard introduction to the movement, *Introducing Radical Orthodoxy: Mapping a Post-Secular Theology.*[145]

John Milbank

Like the work of Kuyper, Dooyeweerd, Van Til, and Rosenstock-Huessy, RO seeks to rethink not only theology, but all of life from a Christian perspective: "RO interventions can be found in academic disciplines such as politics, economics, linguistics, poetics, history, social and cultural theory, and even the natural sciences."[146]

Their opponent is secularism, the movement called *modernism* by the postmodern writers (chapter 12). The RO writers draw on postmodernism's critique of the modernist mentality, but their main standpoint is the Christian orthodoxy of the ecumenical creeds.[147] They believe the old claim that theology is queen of the sciences, and that orthodoxy has the intellectual power to overcome the inflated claims of the secularists and to provide a more intellectually rigorous basis for modern life.

RO's opponent is secularism, the movement called modernism *by the postmodern writers (chapter 12). The RO writers draw on post-modernism's critique of the modernist mentality, but their main standpoint is the Christian orthodoxy of the ecumenical creeds.*

I have some enthusiasm for this movement, as for any that seeks to rethink all areas of life from a Christian point of view. Christ claims rule over all of life, and the fall has corrupted all of life. So a Christian theology or philosophy that would make a major difference needs to have a broad vision. But it must enter into detailed discussions as well, and here I find RO hard to follow, and not always edifying. It spends a lot of time untangling this postmodernist philosopher and that, giving the deconstruction movement (chapter 12) more credit than it deserves. Postmodernism is an important movement, but if possible, RO exaggerates its importance.

142. Henceforth RO.

143. Oxford: Blackwell, 2006; originally published 1990.

144. London: Routledge, 1999.

145. Grand Rapids: Baker, 2004.

146. Ashley Woodiwiss, "What's So Radical about Orthodoxy?," *Christianity Today*, May 2005, available at http://www.christianitytoday.com/ct/2005/mayweb-only/22.0c.html?start=1.

147. Milbank once described his approach as "postmodern critical Augustinianism." John Milbank, "Postmodern Critical Augustinianism: A Short Summa in Forty-two Responses to Unasked Questions," in *The Postmodern God: A Theological Reader*, ed. Graham Ward (Oxford: Blackwell, 2005).

One line of discussion that seems to get close to the center of RO's concerns is formulated thus by R. R. Reno:

> However deeply invested Radical Orthodoxy might be in the vocabulary, thought forms, and literature of postmodernism, it rests on a different foundational assumption about what we might call *the glue that holds the world together.* It is Augustine's vision of heavenly peace, made effective in the dynamic and binding power of divine purpose, that shapes Radical Orthodoxy's reflections, not Nietzsche's violence wrought by an omnipotent will-to-power.[148]

RO's understanding of Augustine's vision of heavenly peace is mediated through Neoplatonism, as it was to some extent by Augustine himself. So ultimately the glue that holds things together is not the oppressiveness of human language, but God, who brings things together while properly differentiating them from one another.

Ultimately the glue that holds things together is not the oppressiveness of human language, but God, who brings things together while properly differentiating them from one another.

> Christian theology counters the Nietzschean nihilism of foundational violence (in the language Radical Orthodoxy borrows from postmodernism) by advancing a participatory framework, an analogical poetics, a *semiosis* of peace, a metanarrative that does not require the postulate of original violence. Put more simply, Radical Orthodoxy hopes to recover Neoplatonic metaphysics as an explanation for the glue that holds the world together. Something can be what it is—a unit of semantic identity or meaning, a person, a social practice—and at the same time depend upon and reach toward something else. Or more strongly, something is real only in and through this constitutive dependence and fecundity. For the Neoplatonist, you, or I, or the value of my moral acts, or the meaning of this essay, *are* as emanating from and returning to the One.[149]

This metaphysics of peacefulness is reflected in the nature of sacrament:

> We need not become "not selves" in order to receive the body and blood of Jesus Christ, nor can we remain simply "ourselves," unchanged and unaltered. (The Neoplatonic note is struck.) Christian liturgical practice assumes that we can be ourselves *and* be enrolled in the drama of redemption. We can participate,

148. R. R. Reno, "The Radical Orthodoxy Project," *First Things* 100 (February 2000), available at http://www.firstthings.com/article/2000/02/the-radical-orthodoxy-project.

149. Ibid.

> without either abandoning our identities or guarding them against divine dominion.[150]

And all of this in turn becomes a model for the state and society, a harmony in which people can be themselves but also participate together toward a common good.

Reno appreciates all of this, but he speaks of RO's "slide toward the standard moves of modern theology,"[151] namely, the tendency to think of redemption (especially the atonement) in terms of ideas rather than actual historical events.[152] Reno doesn't think this slide is generated by the usual motivations that lead people into liberal theology. Rather, he attributes this drift to a general disorganization, attending to too many things, without bringing them together in a consistent picture. Anglo-Catholicism, he says, for all its love of tradition, finds itself in presently liberal denominations in which the formulation of an authentic Christian tradition requires some creativity. That entails some improvising, some absence of rigor.

Anglo-Catholicism, Reno says, for all its love of tradition, finds itself in presently liberal denominations in which the formulation of an authentic Christian tradition requires some creativity.

So Reno concludes:

> To escape the patterns of theological modernism, therefore, the first task is not to imagine and invent. Instead, we must train ourselves in that which modernity rejects most thoroughly and fatally: the discipline of receiving that which has been given. We must eat the scrolls that the Lord has given us, and dwell amidst his people. Only then will the scope of an Augustinian ambition recover the intense, concrete, and particular Christ-centered focus that gives it the power of good news. Only there can we taste God's peace.[153]

I am not comfortable in the conceptual world of Anglo-Catholicism, and I have little initial sympathy for a movement that seeks to draw inspiration from Plotinus.

I have chosen Reno to be my spokesman, because he says the things that I think most need to be said, better than I can say them, and in a style that RO people will probably understand better than mine. I am not comfortable in the conceptual world of Anglo-Catholicism, and I have little initial sympathy for a movement that seeks to draw inspiration from Plotinus. As I indicated in chapters 2–4, I believe Neoplatonism (with a worldview similar to Gnosticism) was one of the factors that corrupted theology and philosophy in the medieval period. Its doctrine of a wholly other God with various kinds of emanations and mediations confuses the biblical Creator-creature distinction, which I believe is utterly central to a biblical view of reality. With Reno, I call RO away

150. Ibid.
151. Ibid.
152. Rosenstock-Huessy, of course, would have something to say about this.
153. Reno, "The Radical Orthodoxy Project."

from this kind of spiritualist monism to a more historical, concrete understanding of biblical events. And the way to gain this understanding is by a closer focus on the biblical text itself as God's inerrant Word.

ESTHER LIGHTCAP MEEK (1953–)

Esther Meek is another Christian philosopher of substantial importance. (Disclosure: Meek was a student of mine at Westminster Philadelphia in the late 1970s, and I have corresponded with her about her book projects. I reviewed the first one favorably,[154] and in the second she wrote a chapter interacting with my work.) She is a professor of philosophy at Geneva College, near Pittsburgh, which, as she notes at one point, is my hometown. She is also Visiting Professor of Apologetics at Redeemer Seminary.

Her work focuses on epistemology, unpacking the implications of the work of Michael Polanyi (chapter 12). Although her books abound in Polanyian themes, they are not analyses of Polanyi's writings, but Meek's original work, employing the insights of Polanyi and others. Her first book, *Longing to Know*,[155] is subtitled *The Philosophy of Knowledge for Ordinary People*. She notes the paradox that the epistemologies of professional philosophers make truth (and therefore certainty) a condition of knowledge, making knowledge something rare, difficult, or nonexistent. But in fact, ordinary people seek and claim to have knowledge in all sorts of ordinary situations, even in cases in which we would not claim to have certainty.[156]

Esther Lightcap Meek

The "ordinary" view of knowledge, she says, is person-centered. There is a close analogy between knowing the world (and, significantly, knowing God) and knowing one's auto mechanic. So she defines *knowing* not as attaining justified (or warranted) true belief, but as "the responsible human struggle to rely on clues to focus on a coherent pattern and submit to its reality."[157] The book takes up each clause of that definition consecutively.

Her second book, *Loving to Know*,[158] is longer and more ambitious.[159] The subtitle is *Introducing Covenant Epistemology*, an idea that she calls

> an innovative, biblically compatible, holistic, embodied, life-shaping epistemological vision in which all knowing

154. Reproduced here as Appendix P.

155. Grand Rapids: Brazos Press, 2003.

156. She advocates *confidence* rather than *certainty*. But my review, noting some biblical passages about certainty, takes issue with her on this point.

157. In terms of my three perspectives, the *struggle* is existential, the *clues* and *pattern* are situational, and the *submitting* is normative.

158. Eugene, OR: Cascade Books, 2011.

159. Though she characterizes it, like the first, as a "popular philosophy book." Ibid., xii.

> takes the shape of the interpersonal, covenantally shaped, relationship.[160]

As in *Longing to Know*, personal relationships are fundamental to the process of knowing everything, from rocks to God:

> Knowing is less about information and more about transformation; less about comprehension and more about being apprehended. Rather than knowing in order to love, we love in order to know. I want to show that all knowing is like knowing God—a transformative encounter.[161]

As in Longing to Know, *personal relationships are fundamental to the process of knowing everything, from rocks to God.*

The structure of *Loving to Know* mirrors its thesis. Meek engages in "conversations" that she envisions between Michael Polanyi, James Loder, me, Mike Williams, John Macmurray, Martin Buber, David Schnarch, Colin Gunton, Philip Rolnick. In between, the conversations are "textures":

> A texture is an excursus, a foray; it goes at the matter from a different direction, or from it to venture in a fresh direction. I want there to be interweaving, but not so tightly as to create a homogeneously smooth product.[162]

At the end of the book, Meek sums up what she has learned in more formal philosophical categories: Covenant epistemology accesses the real world, though not by "an exact representational correspondence of knowledge to reality."

At the end of the book, she sums up what she has learned in more formal philosophical categories: Covenant epistemology accesses the real world, though not by "an exact representational correspondence of knowledge to reality."[163] But such a correspondence would be possible "only if the world were two-dimensionally wooden—actually, *less* real."[164] The personal dimension of reality exposes it as "far deeper and richer . . . than we have given it the credit of being."[165] That leads her to speak of "covenant realism,"[166] "covenant ontology,"[167] and various interpersonal understandings of the knower, the known, and the act of knowing.[168] Some further theses: "Knowing is variably personal,"[169] "All knowing is coming to know,"[170] "Knowing is covenantally

160. Her description at http://www.longingtoknow.com/loving-to-know-l2k.html.
161. Ibid.
162. Meek, *Loving to Know*, xiii.
163. Ibid., 399.
164. Ibid.
165. Ibid.
166. Ibid., 400.
167. Ibid., 401.
168. Ibid., 402–3.
169. Ibid., 403.
170. Ibid., 405.

constituted,"[171] "Knowing is perichoretically rhythmical,"[172] "Knowing is subsidiary-focal transformative integration,"[173] "Knowing transforms the known and the knower."[174] She then explores various "corollaries of covenant epistemology,"[175] puts in order traditional dichotomies such as knowledge and belief, knowledge and opinion, fact and value,[176] lists "sources" of knowledge,[177] and discusses what may be said about the "justification" of knowledge.[178]

The next chapter, 15, is "Inviting the Real: An Epistemological Etiquette."[179] This is the chapter that she "most longed to write."[180] Here she discusses practices conducive to knowing, beginning with a personal invitation, seeking the "freely-initiated response of someone else." "Inviting the real implies that the real is there, and self-discloses."[181] That self-disclosure often takes the form of "surprising recognition." Ways of inviting the real include desire,[182] longing,[183] love,[184] composure[185] before God and other people, comportment (the virtues),[186] strategy (listening, looking, etc.),[187] and "consummation" (friendship, sacramental worship).[188]

The final chapter, "Knowing for *Shalom*,"[189] relates the process to the goal, wholeness in relation to God and others.

Clearly, Meek's epistemology is holistic (as I have used this term of Hegel, Duhem, Quine, and Gordon Clark), trying to understand knowledge as part of a large complex of experience and interpersonal relationships, rather than trying to build it up out of discrete elements, bit by bit. But most distinctively, it is seriously Christian. Philosophy is at its best when it relates its data and experiences to the reality of

Meek's epistemology is holistic . . . , trying to understand knowledge as part of a large complex of experience and interpersonal relationships, rather than trying to build it up out of discrete elements, bit by bit. But most distinctively, it is seriously Christian.

171. Ibid., 406.

172. Ibid., 407. *Perichoresis* is dance, and is a word applied to the communion of the persons of the Trinity. Meek applies it to epistemological concepts such as relationality and particularity, love and covenant, knower and known, overture and response.

173. Polanyi explained how knowledge proceeds from interaction of what we focus on and what we know peripherally (subsidiarily, tacitly).

174. Meek, *Loving to Know*, 408.

175. Ibid., 408–11.

176. Ibid., 411–15.

177. Ibid., 415–19.

178. Ibid., 419–23.

179. Ibid., 425.

180. Ibid.

181. Ibid.

182. Ibid., 428–30.

183. Ibid., 431–32.

184. Ibid., 432–36.

185. Ibid., 436–46.

186. Ibid., 446–53.

187. Ibid., 453–65.

188. Ibid., 465–68.

189. Ibid., 469–80.

God. Certainly Meek's epistemology does that, and thereby shows great insight into God's creation as well.

VERN S. POYTHRESS (1946–)

Finally, I wish to commend the work of my longtime colleague in the work of philosophy and theology. My disclosure is that we have been close friends and collaborators for nearly forty years. He came to study with us at Westminster Seminary in the early 1970s, after having earned a Ph.D. in mathematics at Harvard. Since then, I have learned at least as much from him as he learned from me. He joined the faculty in 1976, and in years since we have shared the website http://www.frame-poythress.org.

Vern S. Poythress

Through the early 1970s, Poythress also studied linguistics with Kenneth Pike and taught the subject at the Summer Institute of Linguistics.[190] Later, he earned degrees in NT studies, an M.Litt. from the University of Cambridge, and a Th.D. from the University of Stellenbosch in South Africa. So he combines knowledge of a great variety of subjects: theology, Bible and Bible scholarship, linguistics, philosophy (especially Van Til and Dooyeweerd), mathematics, and science.

When Poythress came to Westminster as a student, he noted a certain correspondence between the Tagmemic linguistic system of Kenneth Pike and the multiperspectival analysis that we were starting to explore at the seminary. Pike's linguistics also made much use of threefold distinctions, including *particle*, *wave*, and *field* as aspects of word-meanings. The *particle view* identifies the characteristics of each word that distinguish it from others. The *wave view* describes the changes that a word can undergo while remaining the same word. The *field view* describes the contexts in which a word normally functions. Poythress noticed that *particle* is parallel to my normative perspective,[191] since it serves as a normative identification of an expression. *Wave* is parallel to the existential perspective, because it narrates our changing experience of that expression. *Field* is situational, because it surveys a range of other objects that help to identify the expression. These apply not only to words, but also to any "item" of experience. In Poythress's later *In the Beginning Was the Word*,[192] these aspects become *features*,[193] *variation*, and *context*. In *God-Centered Biblical Interpretation*[194] Poythress

The particle view *identifies the characteristics of each word that distinguish it from others. The* wave view *describes the changes that a word can undergo while remaining the same word. The* field view *describes the contexts in which a word normally functions.*

190. So his work opens still another chapter in the philosophical emphasis on language characteristic of the twentieth century.

191. See chapter 1 on the meaning of these perspectives.

192. Vern S. Poythress, *In the Beginning Was the Word: Language: A God-Centered Approach* (Wheaton, IL: Crossway, 2009), 272–73, 24–28, passim.

193. *Features* replaces the term *contrast*, which he used in earlier writings.

194. Vern S. Poythress, *God-Centered Biblical Interpretation* (Phillipsburg, NJ: P&R Publishing, 1999), 72–74.

distinguishes classificational, instantiational, and associational aspects of language, which leads to a view of meaning that balances sense, application, and import.

Poythress's first book, *Philosophy, Science, and the Sovereignty of God*[195] combines insights of Pike with those of theological multiperspectivalism. So the book abounds in threefold distinctions: ontology, axiology, methodology; vocative, dynamic, appraisive; modality, temporality, structurality; aggregative, quantitative, spatial. In each of the triads, the terms are perspectivally related: each can serve as a perspective on the others. The book seeks nothing less than to classify and describe all the features of experience and the disciplines of human study.[196]

Poythress's second book, an introduction to multiperspectivalism, was called *Symphonic Theology: The Validity of Multiple Perspectives in Theology*.[197] And so it went. Often, I would get an idea, only to find that Poythress had had the same one, and was able to formulate it better than I. But in some disciplines, especially science, mathematics, and linguistics, Poythress conceived ideas far beyond anything that I could have come up with.

He has written on biblical theology,[198] hermeneutics,[199] language,[200] gender-neutral Bible translations (he opposes them),[201] the sciences,

Philosophy, Science, and the Sovereignty of God *combines insights of Pike with those of theological multiperspectivalism.*

195. Nutley, NJ: Presbyterian and Reformed, 1976. The book is arranged in decimal subsections, similar to Wittgenstein's *Tractatus*.

196. Needless to say, I was overwhelmed. There is a story about how Wittgenstein (come to England to study aeronautical engineering) approached Bertrand Russell with some philosophical materials that he had written. He said to Russell something like this: "Sir, if I am a complete idiot, I will become an aeronaut; but if I am not a complete idiot, I should like to be a philosopher." After reading a bit, Russell replied, "Young man, you must not become an aeronaut." I must have felt a bit like Russell when I first encountered Poythress and his work.

197. Phillipsburg, NJ: P&R Publishing, 2001. It followed by several months the publication of my *DKG*, which sought to achieve the same purpose, albeit more awkwardly.

198. Vern S. Poythress, *Understanding Dispensationalists* (Phillipsburg, NJ: P&R Publishing, 1993); Vern S. Poythress, *The Shadow of Christ in the Law of Moses* (Phillipsburg, NJ: P&R Publishing, 1995) (this is the best response to the issues raised by theonomy—JF); Vern S. Poythress, *The Returning King: A Guide to the Book of Revelation* (Phillipsburg, NJ: P&R Publishing, 2000); Vern S. Poythress, *What Are Spiritual Gifts?* (Phillipsburg, NJ: P&R Publishing, 2010). The last title breaks new ground in the theological discussion of the "cessation of the charismatic gifts."

199. Vern S. Poythress, *Science and Hermeneutics: Implications of Scientific Method for Biblical Interpretation* (Grand Rapids: Zondervan, 1988); Vern S. Poythress, *God-Centered Biblical Interpretation* (Phillipsburg, NJ: P&R Publishing, 1999).

200. Poythress, *In the Beginning Was the Word*.

201. Vern S. Poythress and Wayne A. Grudem, *The Gender-Neutral Bible Controversy: Muting the Masculinity of God's Words* (Nashville, TN: Broadman and Holman, 2000); Vern S. Poythress and Wayne A. Grudem, *The TNIV and the Gender-Neutral Bible Controversy* (Nashville, TN: Broadman and Holman, 2004).

logic, and mathematics,[202] and biblical inerrancy.[203] He has also written many valuable articles and shorter studies.[204] He writes with great academic sophistication, but always with faithfulness to Scripture as God's Word and with a heart of compassion for his audience. I have sometimes said that whatever Poythress writes always turns out to be the best book in its field.

I do not have nearly the space I would need to expound Poythress's many creative (yet biblically faithful) contributions to Christian thought. I have lately been particularly impressed by Poythress's argument in the first chapter of *Redeeming Science*[205] to the effect that scientists *must* believe in God. Poythress points out that the characteristics of scientific law are the same as what theologians describe as the attributes of God: truthfulness, power, personality (law implies a lawgiver), incomprehensibility, goodness, beauty, and, indeed, Trinitarianism. The second chapter, then, deals with the relation of the Bible to science, one of the most cogent and nuanced explorations of this old issue that I know.

[Poythress argues] that scientists must believe in God. He points out that the characteristics of scientific law are the same as what theologians describe as the attributes of God.

One of his most important theological-philosophical writings is "Reforming Ontology and Logic in the Light of the Trinity: An Application of Van Til's Idea of Analogy."[206] I made use of this article in my *DG*.[207] There he relates the instantiational, associational, and classificational categories to the nature of God and illustrates the oneness in manyness of the Trinity. That God is one and three is the root of all the triadic distinctions in both Poythress's work and mine. And these distinctions are philosophically important. As I summarized in *DG*:

> Poythress reiterates Van Til's critique of realism and nominalism by showing that realism (both Platonic and Aristotelian) exalts the classificational aspect above the others, trying to find "pure categories" untainted by particular instantiations and contextual associations. Empiricism absolutizes the instantiational; subjectivism absolutizes the associational. These types of reductionism are plausible, because the aspects coinhere: each encompasses the other two. But in fact there are no pure

That God is one and three is the root of all the triadic distinctions in both Poythress's work and mine. And these distinctions are philosophically important.

202. Vern S. Poythress, *Redeeming Science: A God-Centered Approach* (Wheaton, IL: Crossway, 2006); Vern S. Poythress, *Redeeming Sociology: A God-Centered Approach* (Wheaton, IL: Crossway, 2011); Vern S. Poythress, *Logic: A God-Centered Approach to the Foundation of Western Thought* (Wheaton, IL: Crossway, 2013).

203. Vern S. Poythress, *Inerrancy and Worldview: Answering Modern Challenges to the Bible* (Wheaton, IL: Crossway, 2012); Vern S. Poythress, *Inerrancy and the Gospels: A God-Centered Approach to the Challenges of Harmonization* (Wheaton, IL: Crossway, 2012).

204. Many of these, and some of his books, can be found on http://www.frame-poythress.org.

205. Poythress, *Redeeming Science*, 13–31.

206. *WTJ* 57, 1 (Spring 1995): 187–219.

207. *DG*, 730–32.

> universals, pure particulars, or pure relationships. Trying to reduce knowledge to one aspect is idolatrous. It is trying to find an absolute starting point in creation, rather than in God's triune existence.[208]

Poythress also relates these categories to divine communication (the Word of God), the distinction between univocal, equivocal, and analogical, and the limitations of logic (pace Clark), as he later discussed these issues at greater length in *Logic*.

On the more popular level, I appreciate Poythress's attempts to deal with issues in the church such as the continuation or cessation of the gifts of tongues and prophecy. Rather than taking a militant position on either alternative, he has developed a thoughtful approach based on a careful treatment of Scripture and the historical discussion.[209]

Poythress has developed the vision of Kuyper and Van Til: that when human study begins with God and seeks to see everything in the light of God's revelation, that study leads us to the greatest level of understanding and the most satisfying resolutions of problems. Poythress is the best contemporary example of the approach that I pray that more Christian thinkers will share: bringing every thought captive to the obedience of Christ.

EPILOGUE

As this book draws to a close, I hope I've been able to present a true, responsible account of the history of Western philosophy and theology. Of course, *true* and *responsible* don't mean "unbiased." I make no apologies for writing this book from a Christian point of view. As I have indicated at many points, I don't think it's possible to write history, or anything else, from a religiously neutral standpoint. Our presuppositions inevitably play a major role in the selection and the evaluation of facts.

Poythress has developed the vision of Kuyper and Van Til: that when human study begins with God and seeks to see everything in the light of God's revelation, that study leads us to the greatest level of understanding and the most satisfying resolutions of problems.

So this book is not only description, but also advocacy. In the preface, I mentioned that Van Til saw his historical work as a form of apologetic. He believed that the best apologetic would carry weight not only with the man on the street, but also with the opinion-makers of the academy and society. So he tried to show in his historical writing that thought-systems denying biblical presuppositions fall into incoherence.

208. Ibid., 731.

209. See his "Modern Spiritual Gifts as Analogous to Apostolic Gifts," *JETS* 39, 1 (1996): 71–101, available at http://www.frame-poythress.org/modern-spiritual-gifts-as-analogous-to-apostolic-gifts-affirming-extraordinary-works-of-the-spirit-within-cessationist-theology/. See also his booklet *What Are Spiritual Gifts?* (Phillipsburg, NJ: P&R Publishing, 2010), available at http://www.frame-poythress.org/wp-content/uploads/2012/08/PoythressVernWhatAreSpiritualGifts.pdf.

I have tried to write this book so that readers can see that a biblical philosophy and theology can prevail against even the most intelligent among its detractors. And an apologetic that does that can be made to prevail against unbelief also in the man on the street.

So I do hope God will use this book in the lives of some, to give them a new level of respect for evangelical Christianity, for the Bible, and indeed for Christ himself. And here is his invitation: if you find yourself sympathetic to the arguments of this book, you should take this action: Recognize that you have sinned against God and deserve his wrath. Turn from that sin, and trust Jesus, believing that his self-sacrifice on the cross bore the punishment you deserve, and believing that he is Lord of all. Trust him, then, not only as your sin-bearer, but as the One who will turn your life around, as you obey his Word. And as he turns your life around, he will turn your mind around as well.

I do hope God will use this book in the lives of some, to give them a new level of respect for evangelical Christianity, for the Bible, and indeed for Christ himself.

KEY TERMS

Christian philosophers	Abraham the Mighty
De Standaard	Free University of Amsterdam
Doleantie	*Gereformeerde Kerken*
Anti-revolutionary Party	Sphere sovereignty
Intermediate bodies	Two kinds of people
Two kinds of science	Revealed, ectypal knowledge of God
Antithesis	Formal faith
Common grace	Cosmonomic
Creation idea	*Philosophia Reformata*
Institute for Christian Studies	Pretheoretical experience
Autonomy (Dooyeweerd)	Supertemporal heart
Ground-motives	Modal aspects
Law spheres	Anticipate
Retrocipate	Subjects (Dooyeweerd)
Objects (Dooyeweerd)	Presuppositionalism (Clark)
Operationalism	Bare facts
Axioms	Scripturalism
Logic (Clark)	Paradox
Ex-lex	Limitations of logic
Richness	Primacy of the intellect
Knowledge	Assent
Trust	*Fiducia*
Van Til-Clark controversy	Mode of God's thoughts
Eternal intuition	Presupposition (Van Til)
Common ground	Circularity
One and many (Van Til)	Noetic effects of sin (Van Til)
Traditional method (Van Til)	Transcendental argument (Van Til)

OUTLINE

Reformed epistemology (Plantinga)
Basic beliefs (Plantinga)
Defeasible
Internalist
Evolutionary argument against naturalism
Design plan
Radical Orthodoxy
Covenant epistemology
Foundational beliefs (Plantinga)
Warrant (Plantinga)
Externalist
Person-variable (Mavrodes)
Knowledge (Meek)

STUDY QUESTIONS

1. Frame expresses hope for the future of philosophy and theology. What is his ground for that? Discuss.
2. Memorize the quote from Kuyper's inaugural address. What does it mean to you?
3. Expound Kuyper's *sphere sovereignty*. What does it mean? With what did Kuyper contrast it?
4. How did Kuyper seek to support Christian schools? Evaluate.
5. Van Til thought Kuyper contradicted himself on the question of antithesis and common grace. Explain both views, and your own.
6. Frame thinks that Dooyeweerd's *pretheoretical* and *theoretical* categories should be seen as a continuum rather than as a sharp distinction. Explain these concepts and your own point of view.
7. Describe and evaluate Dooyeweerd's concept of the Word of God and Scripture. Evaluate Frame's critique.
8. Describe and evaluate Dooyeweerd's four "ground-motives."
9. Describe Dooyeweerd's system of modal spheres. How does this system have apologetic value?
10. Describe and evaluate Clark's critique of empiricism. Why does he object to the cosmological argument? To historical evidences? Does sense experience play any role in the knowledge of the Christian? Discuss.
11. Describe and evaluate Clark's *scripturalism*.
12. Describe and evaluate Clark's apologetic.
13. Describe and evaluate Clark's view of logic.
14. "But in the dialogue above, he attributes infallibility not only to logic, but to Aristotle, and not only to Aristotle, but to Clark's paper about Aristotle." How did this happen? Describe and evaluate.
15. Does logic have any limitations? Interact with Clark's view.
16. Is Clark a rationalist? Why or why not? What historical circumstances might help us to understand his rhetoric on these matters?

17. Describe and evaluate Clark's view of faith.
18. Tell us how Van Til combined emphases of Kuyper with emphases of Warfield.
19. What was at issue in the Van Til-Clark controversy? Can that disagreement be resolved?
20. Describe Van Til's apologetic method. Is there any place in it for evidences? Facts? Explain.
21. Is Van Til's apologetic circular? If so, in what sense? Discuss.
22. What is the "problem of the one and the many"? How does Van Til believe the problem can be resolved?
23. How does the fall of man bear on the necessity of reasoning presuppositionally?
24. For Van Til, does the non-Christian know or say anything truly? Discuss.
25. How do the noetic effects of sin generate the rationalist-irrationalist dialectic, according to Van Til?
26. What is the *traditional method*? Describe some philosopher who advocated something like it. Are Van Til's criticisms of it accurate?
27. What is *transcendental argument* for Van Til? Compare it with Kant.
28. W. K. Clifford argues that we should never claim knowledge of something without evidence or argument. Present Plantinga's response and evaluate.
29. How do Plantinga's *basic beliefs* differ from the *presuppositions* of Van Til and Clark? Discuss.
30. Summarize and evaluate the argument of Plantinga's *God and Other Minds*.
31. Discuss Edmund Gettier's problem with *justification* as an element of knowledge. How did Plantinga respond?
32. How does Plantinga show that belief in God is rational? Evaluate.
33. In what ways does Plantinga try to show that belief in God is not only rational, but true? Evaluate.
34. Describe Plantinga's influence in the philosophical community.
35. Describe something important about (a) Nicholas Wolterstorff, (b) William Alston, (c) George Mavrodes, (d) Kevin Vanhoozer, (e) C. S. Lewis, (f) Alasdair MacIntyre, (g) Paul Helm.
36. What does Mavrodes say about basic vs. nonbasic beliefs? Evaluate the significance of this.
37. Summarize what you can about Rosenstock-Huessy.
38. Same for "Radical Orthodoxy." Evaluate its adherents' critique of secularism.

39. Describe Esther Meek's *covenant epistemology*. What does she mean by "inviting the real"?
40. Summarize some of the value of Vern Poythress's work. How is his work on linguistics relevant to theology?
41. Frame says in the "Epilogue" that this book constitutes an apologetic. Evaluate it in this respect.

BIBLIOGRAPHY: RECENT CHRISTIAN PHILOSOPHY

Print

Alston, William. *Perceiving God: The Epistemology of Religious Experience.* Ithaca, NY: Cornell University Press, 1993.

Anderson, James N. and Greg Welty. "The Lord of Non-Contradiction: An Argument for God from Logic." *Philosophia Christi* 13, 2 (2011): 321–38. http://goo.gl/5Xn0w.

Bahnsen, Greg L. *Van Til's Apologetic.* Phillipsburg, NJ: P&R Publishing, 1998.

Bratt, James. *Abraham Kuyper: Modern Calvinist, Christian Democrat.* Grand Rapids: Eerdmans, 2013.

Clark, Gordon H. *A Christian View of Men and Things.* Unicoi, TN: Trinity Foundation, 1998.

———. *Religion, Reason, and Revelation.* Philadelphia: Presbyterian and Reformed, 1961.

Crampton, W. Gary. *The Scripturalism of Gordon H. Clark.* Unicoi, TN: Trinity Foundation, 1997.

Dooyeweerd, Herman. *In the Twilight of Western Thought.* Grand Rapids: Paideia Press, 2012.

———. *A New Critique of Theoretical Thought.* 4 vols. Philadelphia: Presbyterian and Reformed, 1953.

Frame, John M. *Cornelius Van Til: An Analysis of His Thought.* Phillipsburg, NJ: P&R Publishing, 1995.

Helm, Paul. *Belief Policies.* Cambridge: Cambridge University Press, 2007.

———. *Eternal God: A Study of God without Time.* New York: Oxford University Press, 2011.

———. *Faith and Understanding.* Grand Rapids: Eerdmans, 1997.

———. *The Providence of God.* Downers Grove, IL: IVP Academic, 1994.

Kuyper, Abraham. *Abraham Kuyper: A Centennial Reader.* Edited by James Bratt. Grand Rapids: Eerdmans, 1998.

———. *Encyclopedia of Sacred Theology.* London: Forgotten Books, 2012.

———. *Lectures on Calvinism.* Edited by James D. Bratt. Grand Rapids: Eerdmans, 1943.

———. *To Be Near unto God*. London: Forgotten Books, 2012. Devotional work.

———. *Wisdom and Wonder: Common Grace in Science and Art*. Grand Rapids: Christian's Library Press, 2011. Part of the recent Kuyper translation project.

Lewis, C. S. *Mere Christianity*. San Francisco: HarperCollins, 2009.

———. *Miracles: A Preliminary Study*. San Francisco: HarperOne, 2009.

———. *The Problem of Pain*. San Francisco: HarperOne, 2009.

MacIntyre, Alasdair C. *After Virtue: A Study in Moral Theory*. 3rd ed. Notre Dame, IN: University of Notre Dame Press, 2007.

———. *Whose Justice? Which Rationality?* Notre Dame, IN: University of Notre Dame Press, 1988.

Mavrodes, George I. *Belief in God: A Study in the Epistemology of Religion*. New York: Random House, 1970.

Meek, Esther Lightcap. *A Little Manual for Knowing*. Eugene, OR: Wipf and Stock, 2013.

———. *Longing to Know: The Philosophy of Knowledge for Ordinary People*. Grand Rapids: Brazos Press, 2003.

———. *Loving to Know: Introducing Covenant Epistemology*. Eugene, OR: Cascade Books, 2011.

Milbank, John, ed. *The Radical Orthodoxy Reader* (London: Routledge, 2009).

———. *The Word Made Strange: Theology, Language, Culture*. London: Wiley-Blackwell, 1997.

Milbank, John, Catherine Pickstock, and Graham Ward, eds. *Radical Orthodoxy: A New Theology*. London: Routledge, 1999.

Mouw, Richard. *Abraham Kuyper: A Short and Personal Introduction*. Grand Rapids: Eerdmans, 2011.

Plantinga, Alvin. *God, Freedom, and Evil*. Grand Rapids: Eerdmans, 1977.

———. *God and Other Minds: A Study of the Rational Justification of Belief in God*. Ithaca, NY: Cornell University Press, 1990.

———. *Warrant and Proper Function*. New York: Oxford University Press, 1993.

———. *Warranted Christian Belief*. New York: Oxford University Press, 2000.

———. *Warrant: The Current Debate*. New York: Oxford University Press, 1993.

———. *Where the Conflict Really Lies: Science, Religion, and Naturalism*. New York: Oxford University Press, 2011.

Plantinga, Alvin, and Nicholas Wolterstorff, eds. *Faith and Rationality: Reason and Belief in God*. Notre Dame, IN: University of Notre Dame Press, 1991.

Poythress, Vern S. *Chance and the Sovereignty of God*. Wheaton, IL: Crossway, 2014.

———. *In the Beginning Was the Word: Language: A God-Centered Approach*. Wheaton, IL: Crossway, 2009.

———. *Logic: A God-Centered Approach to the Foundation of Western Thought*. Wheaton, IL: Crossway, 2013.

———. *Philosophy, Science, and the Sovereignty of God*. Phillipsburg, NJ: P&R Publishing, 2004.

———. *Redeeming Science: A God-Centered Approach*. Wheaton, IL: Crossway, 2006.

———. *Symphonic Theology: The Validity of Multiple Perspectives in Theology*. Phillipsburg, NJ: P&R Publishing, 2001.

Rosenstock-Huessy, Eugen. *I Am an Impure Thinker*. Essex, VT: Argo Books, 2001.

———. *The Origin of Speech*. Essex, VT: Argo Books, 1981.

———. *Out of Revolution: The Autobiography of a Western Man*. Essex, VT: Argo Books, 1969.

———. *Speech and Reality*. Eugene, OR: Wipf and Stock, 2013.

Smith, James K. A. *Introducing Radical Orthodoxy: Mapping a Post-Secular Theology*. Grand Rapids: Baker, 2004.

Swinburne, Richard. *The Coherence of Theism*. Rev. ed. Clarendon Library of Logic and Philosophy. New York: Oxford University Press, 1993.

———. *The Existence of God*. 2nd ed. New York: Oxford University Press, 2004.

Troost, Andree. *What Is Reformational Philosophy?* Grand Rapids: Paideia Press, 2012.

Vanhoozer, Kevin J. *The Drama of Doctrine: A Canonical-Linguistic Approach to Christian Doctrine*. Louisville, KY: Westminster John Knox Press, 2005.

———. *First Theology: God, Scripture, and Hermeneutics*. Downers Grove, IL: IVP Academic, 2002.

———. *Is There a Meaning in This Text?* Grand Rapids: Zondervan, 2009.

———. *Remythologizing Theology: Divine Action, Passion, and Authorship*. Cambridge Studies in Christian Doctrine. Cambridge: Cambridge University Press, 2012.

Van Til, Cornelius. *Christian Apologetics*. Phillipsburg, NJ: P&R Publishing, 2003.

———. *The Defense of the Faith*. Edited by K. Scott Oliphint. 4th ed. Phillipsburg, NJ: P&R Publishing, 2008.

———. *An Introduction to Systematic Theology*. Phillipsburg, NJ: P&R Publishing, 2007.

Welty, Greg. "Theistic Conceptual Realism: The Case for Interpreting Abstract Objects as Divine Ideas." DPhil dissertation (2006), University of Oxford. http://goo.gl/nrCP5o.

———. "Theistic Conceptual Realism." In Paul Gould, ed. *Beyond the Control of God? Six Views on the Problem of God and Abstract Objects.* London: Bloomsbury Academic, 2014. http://goo.gl/0Ahgdl.

Wolterstorff, Nicholas. *Divine Discourse: Philosophical Reflections on the Claim That God Speaks.* Cambridge: Cambridge University Press, 1995.

———. *Lament for a Son.* Grand Rapids: Eerdmans, 1987.

———. *Reason within the Bounds of Religion.* 2nd ed. Grand Rapids: Eerdmans, 1988.

Online

Alston, William. *Perceiving God: The Epistemology of Religious Experience.* Ithaca, NY: Cornell University Press, 1993. Available at http://www.questia.com/library/103762715/perceiving-god-the-epistemology-of-religious-experience. Requires subscription for full text.

Clark, Gordon H. A number of Clark's works and works about Clark are available at http://www.trinityfoundation.org/.

Dooyeweerd, Herman. A number of his works are published online. See the list at http://www.allofliferedeemed.co.uk/dooyeweerd.htm. See also http://reformatorische.blogspot.com/2009/11/herman-dooyeweerd.html. My critique of him can be found at http://www.frame-poythress.org/wp-content/uploads/2012/08/FrameJohnAmsterdamPhilosophy1972.pdf, developed further at http://www.frame-poythress.org/dooyeweerd-and-the-word-of-god/.

Dorrien, Gary. "The Origins of Postliberalism." *Christian Century* (July 4–11, 2001): 16–21. Available at http://thinkerkang.blogspot.com/2014/04/the-origins-of-postliberalism-by-gary.html.

Helm, Paul. Articles on many subjects are available at http://paulhelmsdeep.blogspot.com/.

Kuyper, Abraham. Abraham Kuyper Translation Society. http://www.acton.org/research/kuyper-translation-project.

———. Six books by Kuyper, including his *Lectures on Calvinism* (the Stone Lectures), are available at http://www.ccel.org/ccel/kuyper. See also the Kuyper Digital Library at http://kuyper.ptsem.edu/. It contains most of his published works along with an archive of unpublished writings.

Lewis, C. S. The C. S. Lewis Reading Room. Articles by and about Lewis. http://www.tyndale.ca/seminary/mtsmodular/reading-rooms/theology/lewis.

OUTLINE

Abraham Kuyper (1837–1920)
Herman Dooyeweerd (1894–1977)
Gordon H. Clark (1902–85)
Cornelius Van Til (1895–1987)
Alvin Plantinga (1932–)
Other Christian Language-Analysis Philosophers in North America
British Christian Philosophers
Eugen Rosenstock-Huessy (1888–1973)
Radical Orthodoxy
Esther Lightcap Meek (1953–)
Vern S. Poythress (1946–)
Epilogue

———. *Mere Christianity*. London: Fontana, 1952. Available at http://lib.ru/LEWISCL/mere_engl.txt.

MacIntyre, Alasdair C. "Prologue" to *After Virtue: A Study in Moral Theology*. 3rd ed. Notre Dame, IN: University of Notre Dame Press, 2007. Available at http://www3.undpress.nd.edu/excerpts/P01162-ex.pdf.

Meek, Esther Lightcap. *Loving to Know: Introducing Covenant Epistemology*. Eugene, OR: Wipf and Stock, 2011. Synopsis available at http://www.longingtoknow.com/loving-to-know-l2k.html.

———. Various resources are available on her website, http://www.longingtoknow.com/. Conversations with others on *Longing to Know* are available at http://www.missouriwestern.edu/orgs/polanyi/TAD%20WEB%20ARCHIVE/TAD31-3/TAD31-3-fnl-pg29-44-pdf. Her blog is available at http://www.longingtoknow.com/blog.

Milbank, John, et al. *Radical Orthodoxy: Theology, Philosophy, Politics*. Online journal, with many articles on RO. http://journal.radicalorthodoxy.org/index.php/ROTPP. See also Radical Orthodoxy Online. http://www.calvin.edu/~jks4/ro/.

Olson, Roger E. "Back to the Bible (Almost): Why Yale's Postliberal Theologians Deserve an Evangelical Hearing." *Christianity Today* 40, 6 (May 20, 1996). Available at http://www.christianitytoday.com/ct/1996/may20/6t6031.html. Requires subscription to read full article.

Plantinga, Alvin. "Advice to Christian Philosophers." *Faith and Philosophy* 1 (October 1984): 1–19. Available at http://www.calvin.edu/academic/philosophy/virtual_library/articles/plantinga_alvin/advice_to_christian_philosophers.pdf.

———. His thoughts about the existence of God are expressed in his "Two Dozen (or So) Theistic Arguments." Available at http://www.calvin.edu/academic/philosophy/virtual_library/articles/plantinga_alvin/two_dozen_or_so_theistic_arguments.pdf.

———. Many of Plantinga's papers are available under "Alvin Plantinga" at the Virtual Library of Christian Philosophy. http://www.calvin.edu/academic/philosophy/virtual_library/plantinga_alvin.htm. One of my favorites, quite accessible to beginners, is his "Advice to Christian Philosophers." His "Two Dozen (or So) Theistic Arguments" is fascinating.

Poythress, Vern S. Most of Poythress's books and articles are available at http://www.frame-poythress.org.

Rosenstock-Huessy, Eugen. Guide to the Papers of Eugen Rosenstock-Huessy, 1870–2001. http://ead.dartmouth.edu/html/ms522.html. See also Eugen Rosenstock-Huessy Society of North America. http://www.erhsociety.org/, with many resources available at http://www.erhsociety.org/documents/.

Swinburne, Richard. Selected full-text books and articles are available at http://www.questia.com/library/religion/philosophy-of-religion/richard-swinburne. Membership required for full texts.

Vanhoozer, Kevin J., ed. *The Cambridge Companion to Postmodern Theology*. Cambridge: Cambridge University Press, 2003. Available at http://docs.google.com/viewer?url=http://assets.cambridge.org//052179/062X/sample/052179062Xws.pdf. Requires (free) Google account.

———. "The Inerrancy of Scripture." Available at http://www.theologynetwork.org/biblical-studies/getting-stuck-in/the-inerrancy-of-scripture.htm.

———. "Lost in Interpretation? Truth, Scripture, and Hermeneutics." *JETS* 48, 1 (March 2005): 89–114. Available at http://www.etsjets.org/files/JETS-PDFs/48/48-1/48-1-pp089-114_JETS.pdf.

———. Vanhoozer on the Net. Various articles, lectures, reviews. http://achorusofehoes.wordpress.com/2010/08/10/vanhoozer-on-the-net/.

Van Til, Cornelius. A number of works by and about Van Til are available at http://www.vantil.info/byauthor.html; http://presupp101.wordpress.com/2011/10/03/why-i-believe-in-god-by-cornelius-van-til/. Forty volumes of Van Til's works are available on CD-ROM at http://www.logos.com/product/3994/the-works-of-cornelius-van-til. His *Survey of Christian Epistemology* is available in a free PDF at http://veritasdomain.wordpress.com/2011/10/08/free-pdf-book-a-survey-of-christian-epistemology-by-cornelius-van-til/. His *Christianity and Idealism* is available at http://presupp101.wordpress.com/. Make sure that you read his brief, and tantalizing, "Why I Believe in God." Available at http://www.the-highway.com/why_I_believe_cvt.html.

———. Van Til Info. "A comprehensive catalogue of online resources explicitly related to the theology, philosophy, and apologetics of Cornelius Van Til." http://www.vantil.info/.

———. "Why I Believe in God." Available at http://www.the-highway.com/why_I_believe_cvt.html.

Wolterstorff, Nicholas. "The Grace That Shaped My Life." In *Philosophers Who Believe: The Spiritual Journeys of 11 Leading Thinkers*, edited by Kelly James Clark, 259–75. Downers Grove, IL: IVP Academic, 1997. Available at http://www.calvin.edu/125th/wolterst/w_bio.pdf.

READ FOR YOURSELF

There are far too many titles in the Bibliography above for anyone to deal with in, say, a college or seminary course. But I hope the list will intrigue you. Begin with Kuyper's *Lectures in Calvinism*, the Stone Lectures. Every Christian should read these and take them very seriously. To get more deeply into Kuyper's philosophy, dip into his *Encyclopedia*, or at least the table of contents.

Dooyeweerd is best approached through secondary sources. Troost will serve as an introduction. Then try to follow his shorter book, *In the Twilight of Western Thought*, and ask whether my critical approach holds water. Then dig into his *New Critique*, if you can manage it.

Among Gordon Clark's writings, I think *A Christian View of Men and Things* is the best apologetic, and the easiest to follow. Allow Gary Crampton to try to explain Clark's scripturalism.

Van Til's books are being rereleased in new formats, with new introductions and notes by William Edgar and Scott Oliphint. Read his *Why I Believe in God* to get the flavor of his work, an excellent appetizer for his larger works. His *Christian Apologetics* is probably the best place to begin serious study.

Plantinga's "Advice to Christian Philosophers" is an excellent article and a good introduction to his philosophical work. Among his longer works, *God and Other Minds* is the most accessible. Eventually you will need to get into the *Warrant* trilogy.

Wolterstorff's *Reason within the Limits of Religion* is a great introduction to Christian thinking in philosophy, as is Mavrodes's *Belief in God*.

Vanhoozer's recent *Remythologizing Theology* is difficult, but perhaps the best introduction to his theology and his theological style.

The most famous work of C. S. Lewis, beyond his children's series *The Chronicles of Narnia*, is his *Mere Christianity*. I found his *Miracles* even more helpful; it introduced to me the importance of worldview in theology and philosophy.

When you can, look at Swinburne's *The Existence of God*, Helm's *The Providence of God*, and Huessy's *I Am an Impure Thinker*. I think the best way to enter the RO discussion is through James K. A. Smith's *Introducing Radical Orthodoxy*.

Esther Meek's *Longing to Know* is very clearly written and illustrated, and will whet your appetite for *Loving to Know*.

Poythress's books present, I think, a general way of doing Christian philosophy that encompasses all the issues in principle. You should get into the habit of thinking the way he does.

LISTEN ONLINE

Link: http://itunes.apple.com/us/course/legacy-history-philosophy/id694658914

- Abraham Kuyper, Herman Dooyeweerd, and Alvin Plantinga: 1:08:02

- Gordon Clark and Cornelius Van Til: 56:59
- Cornelius Van Til Continued: 34:45

FAMOUS QUOTES

- **Kuyper:** http://www.goodreads.com/author/quotes/385896.Abraham_Kuyper

- **Dooyeweerd:** [In naive experience] we . . . experience concrete things and events in the typical structures, of individual totalities which in principle function in all the modal aspects of our temporal horizon in their continuous mutual coherence. Our logical mode of distinction is entirely embedded in this integral experience. Our pre-theoretical logical concepts are only related to things and events as individual wholes, and not to the abstract modal aspects of their empirical reality. . . . These aspects are only experienced implicitly in the things and events themselves, and not explicitly in their analytical dissociation and opposition to the logical function of thought. (*In the Twilight of Western Thought* [Nutley, NJ: Presbyterian and Reformed, 1960], 13–14)

- **Dooyeweerd:** All conceptual knowledge in its analytical and inter-modal synthetical character *presupposes* the human ego as its central reference-point, which consequently must be of a super-modal nature and is not capable of logical analysis. ("Cornelius Van Til and the Transcendental Critique of Theoretical Thought," in E. R. Geehan, ed., *Jerusalem and Athens* [Philadelphia: Presbyterian and Reformed, 1971], 85 [emphasis his])

- **Dooyeweerd:** In the process of directing my philosophical thought in the idea towards the totality of meaning, I must be able to ascend a lookout-tower above all the modal speciality of meaning that functions within the coherence of the modal aspects. (*A New Critique of Theoretical Thought* [4 vols. Philadelphia: Presbyterian and Reformed, 1953], 1:8)

- **Dooyeweerd:** The genuine *conceptual* contents of these transcendental limiting ideas do not transcend the modal dimension of our temporal horizon of experience. The same applies to the theological limiting concepts relating to the so-called attributes of God. (*Jerusalem and Athens*, 87)

OUTLINE

Abraham Kuyper (1837–1920)

Herman Dooyeweerd (1894–1977)

Gordon H. Clark (1902–85)

Cornelius Van Til (1895–1987)

Alvin Plantinga (1932–)

Other Christian Language-Analysis Philosophers in North America

British Christian Philosophers

Eugen Rosenstock-Huessy (1888–1973)

Radical Orthodoxy

Esther Lightcap Meek (1953–)

Vern S. Poythress (1946–)

Epilogue

- **Dooyeweerd:** Our temporal empirical horizon has a numerical aspect, a spatial aspect, an aspect of extensive movement, an aspect of energy in which we experience the physico-chemical relations of empirical reality, a biotic aspect, or that of organic life, an aspect of feeling and sensation, a logical aspect, i.e., the analytical manner of distinction in our temporal experience which lies at the foundation of all our concepts and logical judgments. Then there is a historical aspect in which we experience the cultural manner of development of our societal life. This is followed by the aspect of symbolical signification, lying at the foundation of all empirical linguistic phenomena. Furthermore there is also the aspect of social intercourse, with its rules of courtesy, politeness, good breeding, fashion, and so forth. This experiential mode is followed by the economic, aesthetic, juridical and moral aspects, and, finally, by the aspect of faith or belief. (*In the Twilight of Western Thought*, 7)

- **Dooyeweerd:** So long as this central meaning of the Word-revelation is at issue we are beyond the scientific problems both of theology and philosophy. Its acceptance or rejection is a matter of life or death to us, and not a question of theoretical reflection. (*In the Twilight of Western Thought*, 125)

- **Clark:** http://www.goodreads.com/author/quotes/73852.Gordon_H_Clark

- **Van Til:** Anti-theism presupposes Theism. (*The Defense of the Faith*, ed. K. Scott Oliphint, 4th ed. [Phillipsburg, NJ: P&R Publishing, 2008])

- **Van Til:** [The intellect of fallen man] may be compared to a buzz-saw that is sharp and shining, ready to cut the boards that come to it. Let us say that a carpenter wishes to cut fifty boards for the purpose of laying the floor of a house. He has marked his boards. He has set his saw. He begins at one end of the mark on the board. But he does not know that his seven-year-old son has tampered with the saw and changed its set. The result is that every board he saws is cut slantwise and thus unusable because too short except at the point where the saw made its first contact with the wood. As long as the set of the saw is not changed, the result will always be the same. So also whenever the teachings of Christianity are presented to the natural man, they will be cut according to the set of sinful human personality. (*The Defense of the Faith*)

- **Van Til:** Now, in fact, I feel that the whole of history and civilization would be unintelligible to me if it were not for my belief in God. So true is this, that I propose to argue that unless God is back of everything, you cannot find meaning in anything. I cannot even argue for belief in Him, without already having taken Him for granted. And similarly I contend that you cannot argue against belief in Him unless you also first take Him for granted. Arguing about God's existence, I hold, is like arguing about air. You may affirm that air exists, and I that it does not. But as we debate the point, we are both breathing air all the time. (*Why I Believe in God* [Chestnut Hill, PA: Westminster Theological Seminary, 1976], 3)

- **Van Til:** Deep down in his mind every man knows that he is the creature of God and responsible to God. Every man, at bottom, knows that he is a covenant-breaker. But every man acts and talks as though this were not so. It is the one point that cannot bear mentioning in his presence. . . .

  Romanism and evangelicalism, by failing to appeal exclusively to that which is within man but is also suppressed by every man, virtually allow the legitimacy of the natural man's [1 Cor. 2:14] view of himself. They do not seek to explode the last stronghold to which the natural man always flees and where he always makes his final stand. . . . The truly Biblical view, on the other hand, applies atomic power and flame-throwers to the very presupposition of the natural man's ideas with respect to himself. . . .

  Only by thus finding the point of contact in man's sense of deity that lies underneath his own conception of self-consciousness as ultimate can we be both true to Scripture and effective in reasoning with the natural man. Man, knowing God, refuses to keep God in remembrance (Rom. 1:28). (*The Defense of the Faith*)

- **Van Til:** If the facts of the world are not created and redeemed by God in Christ, then they are like beads that have no holes in them and therefore cannot be strung into a string of beads. If the laws of the world are not what they are as relating the facts that are created and redeemed by Christ, these laws are like a string of infinite length, neither end of which can be found. Seeking to string beads that cannot be strung because they have no holes in them, with string of infinite length neither end of which you can find; such is the task of the educator who seeks to educate without presupposing the truth of what the self-attesting Christ has spoken in the Scriptures. (*Essays on Christian Education* [Nutley, NJ: Presbyterian and Reformed, 1971])

- **Van Til:** We cannot *prove* the existence of beams underneath a floor if by proof we mean that they must be ascertainable in the way that we can see the chairs and tables of the room. But the very idea of a floor as the support of tables and chairs requires the idea of beams that are underneath. But there would be no floor if no beams were underneath. Thus there is absolutely certain proof for the existence of God and the truth of Christian theism. Even non-Christians presuppose its truth while they verbally reject it. They need to presuppose the truth of Christian theism in order to account for their own accomplishments. (*The Defense of the Faith*, 103)

- **Plantinga:** http://www.calvin.edu/academic/philosophy/virtual_library/articles/plantinga_alvin/advice_to_christian_philosophers.pdf and http://en.wikiquote.org/wiki/Alvin_Plantinga

- **Vanhoozer:** http://www.goodreads.com/author/quotes/194641.Kevin_J_Vanhoozer

- **Lewis:** http://en.wikiquote.org/wiki/C._S._Lewis

- **MacIntyre:** http://en.wikiquote.org/wiki/Alasdair_MacIntyre

- **Rosenstock-Huessy:** http://en.wikipedia.org/wiki/Eugen_Rosenstock-Huessy#Quotations

- **Milbank:** http://ortusmemoria.wordpress.com/2011/05/31/no-ethics-outside-the-church-or-how-milbank-has-influenced-my-theology/

- **Meek:** *Knowing* is the responsible human struggle to rely on clues to focus on a coherent pattern and submit to its reality. (*Longing to Know: The Philosophy of Knowledge for Ordinary People* [Grand Rapids: Brazos Press, 2003], 13)

- **Meek:** Our Western heritage has, generally speaking, had it backwards: obedience does not require truth; truth requires obedience. Obedience, I like to say, is *lived* truth. Do you want to know my auto mechanic? Live my words. Do you want to know God? Live his words. (*Longing to Know*, 140)
- **Meek:** http://quoteswithreferences.blogspot.com/2013/11/esther-lightcap-meek_28.html (*Longing to Know*)
- **Meek:** Readers of my former book, *Longing to Know*, will find *Loving to Know* different and similar. This book represents the further development of my covenant epistemology promised in a footnote in that one. It takes the epistemic proposal that drives *Longing to Know* and advances it into the personal—the interpersoned, as I will call it. Knowing works the way I have described it in that book because its telltale features are fraught with the interpersoned. (*Loving to Know: Introducing Covenant Epistemology* [Eugene, OR: Cascade Books, 2011], xiv)
- **Meek:** The false ideal of certainty itself leads us to approach reality in a certain way, and to see reality in a certain way. It leads us to see reality as impersonal objects or disembodied rationality, and to see knowing as a passive, dispassionate, registering of data. (*Loving to Know*, 22)
- **Poythress:** Human speech is possible because God made man in his image, in his likeness. Human speech imitates divine speech and is analogous to it. Not only so, but speech in human language can be used and actually is used by both God and man to speak to one another (note the interchanges in Gen 3:9–19). In fact, language is a principal mode through which God and human beings bring to expression and promote the personal, spiritual, and responsible relationship that they enjoy with one another. (*God-Centered Biblical Interpretation* [Phillipsburg, NJ: P&R Publishing, 1999], 23–24)
- **Poythress:** Understanding the Bible involves understanding God's covenant with us. And that understanding is inexhaustible. (*God-Centered Biblical Interpretation*, 31)
- **Poythress:** But the whole of the Old Testament is about God working out salvation. And salvation is to be found only in Christ. So the whole Old Testament, not just a few isolated verses, speaks of Christ. (*God-Centered Biblical Interpretation*, 59)

- **Poythress:** We need, then, to head off the idea that only one kind of speech, such as "Thus says the Lord," constitutes the real divine speaking. Within Scripture the genres of speaking are quite diverse. (*God-Centered Biblical Interpretation*, 81)

- **Poythress:** We must not construe heaven simply as a static otherness, but as a power source that will transform the whole. (*Understanding Dispensationalists* [Phillipsburg, NJ: P&R Publishing, 1993], 44)

- **Poythress:** Although one analogy may be the main point in a particular passage, the Bible as a whole uses a multitude of analogies, each of which makes a contribution. No one analogy tells the whole story. In short, the Bible does not use a single dominant perspective. (*Symphonic Theology: The Validity of Multiple Perspectives in Theology* [Phillipsburg, NJ: P&R Publishing, 2001], 17)

- **Poythress:** I claim that no single category, theme, or concept and no system of categories can furnish us with an infinitely deep analysis of the world. (*Symphonic Theology*, 82)

- **Poythress:** God uses ordinary human language rather than a technically precise jargon. He does not include all the technical, pedantic details that would interest a scholar. (*Symphonic Theology*, 69)

- **Poythress:** We are to strive through the gospel to bring genuine reconciliation to people groups through cultural unity in diversity and diversity in unity. We replicate in human beings the glory of the unity and diversity in the Godhead. This unity in diversity offers an answer that differs from other common answers abroad today. Our answer differs from forced uniformity, which some people think they can attain through autonomous reason. That hope for uniformity is the answer associated with what has been called modernism. Our answer also differs from the popular recipe of tolerance, which celebrates diversity but gives up on universal truth. (*Redeeming Sociology: A God-Centered Approach* [Wheaton, IL: Crossway, 2011], 142)

- **Poythress:** Without God, it is difficult for human beings even to articulate where moral obligations come from. . . . If there is no transcendent source for moral standards, what are moral ideas except subjective preferences thrown up by our glands?

Instinctively we know better than this. But the attempt systematically to exclude God leads to suppressing these God-given instincts. (*Redeeming Sociology*, 39)

- **Poythress:** All scientists—including agnostics and atheists—believe in God. They have to in order to do their work. (*Redeeming Science: A God-Centered Approach* [Wheaton, IL: Crossway, 2006], 13)

APPENDICES

AS IN MY PREVIOUS BOOKS, I have decided to supplement the main text by republishing shorter articles and reviews that bear on the subject matter of the book. In this case, however, there are a great many of these, and quite a few of them have already been used as appendices in previous volumes. So rather than trying to include all of them here, with some exceptions, I will include only those that have not appeared in other books. The others are shown in the following lists, with the locations where they can be found. Besides the locations mentioned here, many of these articles can be found at http://www.frame-poythress.org.

The Doctrine of the Knowledge of God

1. *DKG*.

- Review of George Lindbeck, *The Nature of Doctrine* (supplements my discussion of Lindbeck in chapter 11).

2. *DG*.

- Review of Benjamin Wirt Farley, *The Providence of God* (supplements the discussion of liberal theology in chapters 10–11).
- Review of Paul Helm, *The Providence of God* (see brief discussion of Helm in chapter 13).
- Review of David Ray Griffin, *Evil Revisited* (supplements discussion of process theology in chapter 11).

The Doctrine of God

3. *DWG*.

- Lecture, "Antithesis and the Doctrine of Scripture" (supplements discussions of liberal theology in chapters 10–11).
- "Rationality and Scripture" (same; also interacts with some of the Christian views noted in chapter 13).
- "Dooyeweerd and the Word of God" (supplements the account of Dooyeweerd in chapter 13).

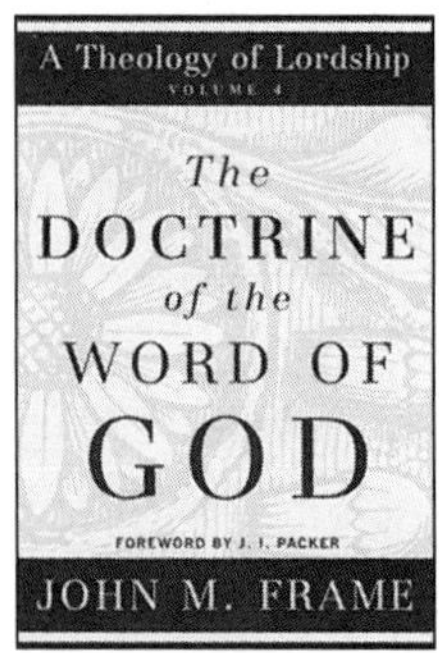

The Doctrine of the Word of God

- Review of David Kelsey, *The Uses of Scripture in Recent Theology* (supplements discussions of liberal theology from chapters 5–12).
- Other appendices in *DWG* provide thoughts on current evangelical thought (chapter 13) as it relates to the doctrine of Scripture.

4. *John Frame's Selected Shorter Writings, Volume 1* (Phillipsburg, NJ: P&R Publishing, 2014).

- "A Primer on Perspectivalism" (relevant to chapter 1 of the present volume, and much else).
- "Review of Greg Bahnsen, *Presuppositional Apologetics*" (relevant to the discussions in chapter 13 of Clark, Van Til, and Bahnsen).
- "The Picture Theory of Theology" (supplements the discussion of the picture theory of language in chapter 12).
- "Narrative and the Picture Theory of Theology" (same).
- "Intellectual Repentance" (relevant to the general approach of the present book).
- "Intellectual Discipleship" (same).
- "Meditation on Romans 11:33–36" (same).

John Frame's Selected Shorter Writings, Volume 1

5. Articles published in W. C. Campbell-Jack and Gavin J. McGrath, eds., *New Dictionary of Christian Apologetics*, consulting ed. C. Stephen Evans (Downers Grove, IL: InterVarsity Press, 2006). These articles are also available at http://www.frame-poythress.org, by permission from InterVarsity Press.

- "Cornelius Van Til"
- "Presuppositional Apologetics"

New Dictionary of Christian Apologetics

The following articles and reviews I have chosen for inclusion in this present volume. The first nine, Appendices A through I, are my own treatments of philosophical and theological problems that are treated more briefly in the text. The next four, reviews of books by Achinstein and Barker (J), Dallas High (K), Paul Van Buren (L), and Paul Holmer (M), deal with analytic philosophy and particularly with its relationship to Christian theology (chapters 12 and 13 of the present volume). The next (N) reviews a work of Schubert Ogden, a Bultmannian (and later a process theologian, though his process theology does not show forth clearly in this particular book; see chapters 10–11 of the present volume). O–Q deal with epistemology. O is a review of a book on epistemology by Paul Helm, whom I mentioned in chapter 13. P reviews Esther Meek's first book, *Longing to Know* (also chapter 13). Q deals with the epistemology of John Pollock, an alternative to that of Alvin Plantinga (chapters 12–13). R is my reply to criticisms of me and Van Til by Gordon H. Clark, published here for the first time (chapter 13), and S reviews a substantive cultural critique by Herbert Schlossberg. T is a treatment of some problems in the work of Van Til.

APPENDIX A

"CERTAINTY"

Originally published in W. C. Campbell-Jack and Gavin J. McGrath, eds., *New Dictionary of Christian Apologetics*, consulting ed. C. Stephen Evans (Downers Grove, IL: InterVarsity Press, 2006), 141–45. Used by permission. Note: Many philosophers have sought certainty or denied its possibility. In my view, we do have certainty about God and about many things in creation. This article summarizes my argument. (For stylistic purposes, this appendix has been copyedited for inclusion in this volume.)

Certainty admits of degrees, just as doubt admits of degrees. Absolute certainty is the lack of any doubt at all. Short of that, there are various levels of relative certainty.

CERTAINTY IS A lack of doubt about some state of affairs. For example, if I have no doubt that the earth is the third planet from the sun, then I can be said to be certain of that fact. Certainty admits of degrees, just as doubt admits of degrees. Absolute certainty is the lack of any doubt at all. Short of that, there are various levels of relative certainty.

Philosophers have sometimes distinguished between *psychological certainty*, which I have described above, and another kind of certainty that is called *epistemic*, *logical*, or *propositional*. There is no universally accepted definition of this second kind of certainty, but it usually has something to do with the justification or warrant for believing a proposition: a proposition is epistemically certain if it has, let us say, a maximal warrant. The nature of a maximal warrant is defined differently in different epistemological systems. Descartes thought that propositions, to be certain, must be warranted such as to exclude all grounds for doubt. For Chisholm, a proposition is epistemically certain if no proposition has greater warrant than it does. And different philosophers give different weight to logic, sense experience, intuition, and so on in determining what constitutes adequate warrant.

In my judgment, *epistemic certainty*, however defined, is not something sharply different from *psychological certainty*. Whatever level of warrant is required for epistemic certainty, it must be a level that gives us psychological confidence. Indeed, if we are to accept some technical definition of *warrant*, we must also have psychological confidence that that definition actually represents what we call *certainty*. So it may be said that epistemic certainty is reducible to psychological certainty. But it is also true that we should try to conform our psychological feelings of certainty to objective principles of knowledge, so that our doubts and feelings of certainty are reasonable, rather than arbitrary or pathological. So perhaps it is best to say that psychological and epistemic certainty are mutually dependent. In *DKG*, I have tried to describe and defend the mutual reducibility of feelings and knowledge.

In my judgment, epistemic certainty, *however defined, is not something sharply different from* psychological certainty. *Whatever level of warrant is required for epistemic certainty, it must be a level that gives us psychological confidence.*

Philosophers have also differed as to the extent to which certainty is possible, some being relatively skeptical, others claiming certainty in some measure. Some have distinguished different levels of knowledge and have relegated certainty to the higher levels. Plato, for example, in the *Republic*, distinguished between conjecture, belief, understanding, and direct intuition, conjecture being the most uncertain, and direct intuition (a pure knowledge of the basic Forms of reality) warranting absolute certainty.

Is it possible to be absolutely certain about anything? Ancient and modern skeptics have said no. According to Descartes, however, we cannot doubt that we are thinking, and from the proposition "I think," he derived a number of other propositions that he thought were certain: our existence, the existence of God, and so on. Empiricists, such as Locke and Hume, have argued that we cannot be mistaken about the basic contents of our own minds, about the way that things *appear* to us. But in their view, our knowledge of the world beyond our minds is never certain, never more than probable. Kant added that we can also be certain of those propositions that describe the necessary conditions for knowledge itself. And Thomas Reid and G. E. Moore argued that certain deliverances of common sense are beyond doubt, because they are in some sense the foundation of knowledge, better known than any principles by which they can be challenged.

Ludwig Wittgenstein distinguished between merely theoretical doubt and real, practical doubt. In everyday life, when we doubt something, there is a way of resolving that doubt.

Ludwig Wittgenstein distinguished between merely theoretical doubt and real, practical doubt. In everyday life, when we doubt something, there is a way of resolving that doubt. For example, when we doubt how much money we have in a checking account, we may resolve that doubt by looking at a check register or bank statement. But theoretical, or philosophical, doubts are doubts for which there is no standard means of resolution. What would it be like, Wittgenstein asks, to doubt that I have two hands, and then to try to relieve that doubt? Similarly for doubts as to whether the world has existed more than five minutes, or whether other people have minds.

The language of doubt and certainty, Wittgenstein argues, belongs to the context of practical life. When it is removed from that context, it is no longer meaningful—for meaning, to Wittgenstein, is the use of words in their ordinary, practical contexts, in what he calls their *language game*. To raise such philosophical questions is to question our whole way of life. Thus, for Wittgenstein, relative certainty is possible in ordinary life through standard methods. But the traditional philosophical questions are not proper subjects either of doubt or of certainty.

So the questions concerning certainty remain open among secular philosophers. Since Wittgenstein, these questions have been raised in terms of foundationalism, the view that all human knowledge is based on certain "basic" propositions.

So in the context of ordinary life, Wittgenstein allows for certainty of a relative kind. His argument evidently excludes absolute certainty, but he does recognize some beliefs of ours (e.g., that the universe has existed for more than five minutes) about which there can be no doubt. He excludes doubt not by proposing an extraordinary way to know such matters, but rather by removing such questions from the language game in which *doubt* and *certainty* have meaning.

But philosophy is also a language game, and doubts about the reality of the experienced world have troubled people for many centuries. Philosophers have not hesitated to propose ways of resolving those doubts. So it might be arbitrary to restrict the meanings of *doubt* and *certainty* to the realm of the practical, even given the possibility of a sharp distinction between theoretical and practical. At least it is difficult to distinguish between questions that are improper in Wittgenstein's sense and questions that are merely difficult to answer.

The philosophical trend today is opposed to the idea of absolute certainty, and that opposition is rampant among deconstructionists and postmodernists.

So the questions concerning certainty remain open among secular philosophers. Since Wittgenstein, these questions have been raised in terms of foundationalism, the view that all human knowledge is based on certain "basic" propositions. Descartes is the chief example of classical foundationalism, because of his view that the basic propositions are absolutely certain. Many recent thinkers have rejected foundationalism in this sense, but Alvin Plantinga and others have developed a revised foundationalism in which the basic propositions are defeasible, capable of being refuted by additional knowledge. In general, then, the philosophical trend today is opposed to the idea of *absolute* certainty, and that opposition is rampant among deconstructionists and postmodernists.

The question also arises in the religious context: can we know God with certainty? The Bible often tells us that Christians can, should, and do know God and the truths of revelation (Matt. 9:6; 11:27; 13:11;

John 7:17; 8:32; 10:4–5; 14:17; 17:3; many other passages). Such passages present this knowledge not as something tentative, but as a firm basis for life and hope.

Scripture uses the language of certainty more sparingly, but that is also present. Luke wants his correspondent Theophilus to know the "certainty" (*asphaleia*) of the things he has been taught (Luke 1:4) and the "proofs" (*tekmeria*) by which Jesus showed himself alive after his death (Acts 1:3). The centurion at the cross says, "Certainly [*ontos*] this man was innocent" (Luke 23:47).

Scripture uses the language of certainty more sparingly, but that is also present. Luke wants his correspondent Theophilus to know the "certainty" (asphaleia) *of the things he has been taught (Luke 1:4) and the "proofs"* (tekmeria) *by which Jesus showed himself alive after his death (Acts 1:3).*

The letter to the Hebrews says that God made a promise to Abraham, swearing by himself, for there was no one greater (Heb. 6:13). So God both made a promise and confirmed it with an oath, "two unchangeable things, in which it is impossible for God to lie" (v. 18). This is "a sure and steadfast anchor of the soul" (v. 19). Similarly, Paul (2 Tim. 3:16–17) and Peter (2 Peter 1:19–21) speak of Scripture as God's own words, which provide sure guidance in a world where false teaching abounds. God's special revelation is certain, and we ought to be certain about it.

On the other hand, the Bible presents doubt largely negatively. It is a spiritual impediment, an obstacle to doing God's work (Matt. 14:31; 21:21; 28:17; Acts 10:20; 11:12; Rom. 14:23; 1 Tim. 2:8; James 1:6). In Matthew 14:31 and Romans 14:23, it is the opposite of faith and therefore a sin. Of course, this sin, like other sins, may remain with us through our earthly life. But we should not be complacent about it. Just as the ideal for the Christian life is perfect holiness, the ideal for the Christian mind is absolute certainty about God's revelation.

We should not conclude that doubt is always sinful. Matthew 14:31 and Romans 14:23 (and indeed the others I have listed) speak of doubt in the face of clear special revelation. To doubt what God has clearly spoken to us is wrong. But in other situations, it is not wrong to doubt. In many cases, in fact, it is wrong for us to claim knowledge, much less certainty. Indeed, often the best course is to admit our ignorance (Deut. 29:29; Rom. 11:33–36). Paul is not wrong to express uncertainty about the number of people he baptized (1 Cor. 1:16). Indeed, James tells us, we are always ignorant of the future to some extent, and we ought not to pretend that we know more about it than we do (James 4:13–16). Job's friends were wrong to think that they knew the reasons for his torment, and Job himself had to be humbled as God reminded him of his ignorance (Job 38–42).

Matthew 14:31 and Romans 14:23 (and indeed the others I have listed) speak of doubt in the face of clear special revelation. To doubt what God has clearly spoken to us is wrong.

So Christian epistemologist Esther Meek points out that the process of knowing through our earthly lives is a quest: following clues, noticing patterns, making commitments, respecting honest doubt. In much of life, she says, confidence, not certainty, should be our goal.

But I have said that absolute certainty is the appropriate (if ideal) response to God's special revelation. How can that be, given our finitude and fallibility? How is that possible when we consider the skepticism that pervades secular thought? How is it humanly possible to know anything with certainty?

First, it is impossible to exclude absolute certainty in all cases. Any argument purporting to show that there is no such certainty must admit that it is itself uncertain. Further, any such argument must presuppose that argument itself is a means of finding truth. If someone uses an argument to test the certainty of propositions, he is claiming certainty at least for that argument. And he is claiming that by such an argument he can test the legitimacy of claims to certainty. But such a test of certainty, a would-be criterion of certainty, must itself be certain. And an argument that would test absolute certainty must itself be absolutely certain.

In Christian epistemology, God's Word is the ultimate criterion of certainty. What God says must be true, for, as the letter to the Hebrews says, it is impossible for God to lie (Heb. 6:18; cf. Titus 1:2; 1 John 2:27). His Word is truth (John 17:17; cf. Pss. 33:4; 119:160). So God's Word is the criterion by which we can measure all other sources of knowledge.

In Christian epistemology, God's Word is the ultimate criterion of certainty. What God says *must* be true, for, as the letter to the Hebrews says, it is impossible for God to lie (Heb. 6:18; cf. Titus 1:2; 1 John 2:27). His Word is truth (John 17:17; cf. Pss. 33:4; 119:160). So God's Word is the criterion by which we can measure all other sources of knowledge.

When God promised Abraham a multitude of descendants and an inheritance in the land of Canaan, many things might have caused him to doubt. He reached the age of one hundred without having any children, and his wife Sarah was far beyond the normal age of childbearing. And though he sojourned in the land of Canaan, he didn't own title to any land there at all. But Paul says of Abraham that "no distrust made him waver concerning the promise of God, but he grew strong in his faith as he gave glory to God, fully convinced that God was able to do what he had promised" (Rom. 4:20–21). God's Word, for Abraham, took precedence over all other evidence in forming Abraham's belief. So important is this principle that Paul defines justifying faith in terms of it: "That is why [Abraham's] faith was counted to him as righteousness" (v. 22).

It is the responsibility of the Christian to regard God's Word as absolutely certain, and to make that Word the criterion of all other sources of knowledge.

Thus Abraham stands in contrast to Eve, who, in Genesis 3:6, allowed the evidence of her eyes to take precedence over the command of God. Abraham is one of the heroes of the faith who, according to Hebrews 11, "died in faith, not having received the things promised, but having seen them and greeted them from afar" (v. 13). They had God's promise, and that was enough to motivate them to endure terrible sufferings and deprivations through their earthly lives.

I conclude that it is the responsibility of the Christian to regard God's Word as absolutely certain, and to make that Word the criterion of all other sources of knowledge. Our certainty of the truth of God ultimately comes not through rational demonstration or empirical verification, useful as these may often be, but from the authority of God's own Word.

God's Word does often testify to itself by means of human testimony and historical evidence: the "proofs" of Acts 1:3, the centurion's witness in Luke 23:47, the many witnesses to the resurrection of Jesus in 1 Corinthians 15:1–11. But we should never forget that these evidences come to us with God's own authority. In 1 Corinthians 15, Paul asks the church to believe the evidence because it is part of the authoritative apostolic preaching: "so we preach and so you believed" (v. 11; cf. vv. 1–3).

Certainty comes ultimately through God's Word and Spirit. The Lord calls us to build our life and thought on the certainties of his Word, that we "will not walk in darkness, but will have the light of life" (John 8:12).

But how does that Word give us psychological certainty? People sometimes make great intellectual and emotional exertions, trying to force themselves to believe the Bible. But we cannot make ourselves believe. Certainty comes upon us by an act of God, through the testimony of his Spirit (1 Cor. 2:4, 9–16; 1 Thess. 1:5; 2 Thess. 2:13). The Spirit's witness often accompanies a human process of reasoning. Scripture never rebukes people who honestly seek to think through the questions of faith. But unless our reason is empowered by the Spirit, it will not give full assurance.

So certainty comes ultimately through God's Word and Spirit. The Lord calls us to build our life and thought on the certainties of his Word, that we "will not walk in darkness, but will have the light of life" (John 8:12). The process of building, furthermore, is not only academic, but ethical and spiritual. It is those who are willing to do God's will who know the truth of Jesus' words (John 7:17), and those who love their neighbors who are able to know as they ought to know (1 Cor. 8:1–3).

Secular philosophy rejects absolute certainty, then, because absolute certainty is essentially supernatural, and because the secularist is unwilling to accept a supernatural foundation for knowledge.

Secular philosophy rejects absolute certainty, then, because absolute certainty is essentially supernatural, and because the secularist is unwilling to accept a supernatural foundation for knowledge. But the Christian regards God's Word as the ultimate criterion of truth and falsity, right and wrong, and therefore as the standard of certainty. Insofar as we consistently hold the Bible as our standard of certainty, we may and must regard it as itself absolutely certain. So in God's revelation, the Christian has a wonderful treasure, one that saves the soul from sin and the mind from skepticism.

BIBLIOGRAPHY

Frame, John M. *The Doctrine of the Knowledge of God*. Phillipsburg, NJ: Presbyterian and Reformed, 1987.

Meek, Esther Lightcap. *Longing to Know: The Philosophy of Knowledge for Ordinary People*. Grand Rapids: Brazos Press, 2003.

Plantinga, Alvin. *Warranted Christian Belief.* New York: Oxford University Press, 2000. A profound Christian reflection on the nature of knowledge and its warrant.

Wittgenstein, Ludwig. *On Certainty.* Translated by Denis Paul and G. E. M. Anscombe. New York: Harper and Row, 1972.

Wood, W. Jay. *Epistemology: Becoming Intellectually Virtuous.* Downers Grove, IL: InterVarsity Press, 1998. Christian philosopher shows how knowledge is related to virtues and to the emotions.

APPENDIX B

"INFINITE SERIES"

Originally published in W. C. Campbell-Jack and Gavin J. McGrath, eds., *New Dictionary of Christian Apologetics*, consulting ed. C. Stephen Evans (Downers Grove, IL: InterVarsity Press, 2006), 353–54. Used by permission. Aristotle (chapter 2), Aquinas (chapter 4), and others have been interested in the concept of infinity: whether, for example, it is possible to prove God's existence by denying an infinite series of causes. In this article, I address this problem, taking account of some more recent thinkers. (For stylistic purposes, this appendix has been copyedited for inclusion in this volume.)

CONCEPT AND DISTINCTIONS

In general, an infinite series is a series without an ending term, such as the series of natural numbers, 1, 2, 3 . . . Mathematician and logician Georg Cantor defined it more precisely as a series that has the same number of terms as one of its subseries. For example, the series 1, 2, 3 . . . , the series of natural numbers, has a subseries 2, 4, 6 . . . , the series of even numbers. Yet there are just as many even numbers as there are natural numbers, paradoxical as that might sound. That paradox identifies the series as infinite.

Among infinite series, we may distinguish between actual *and* potential *infinites.*

Among infinite series, we may distinguish between *actual* and *potential* infinites. The set of natural numbers is an actual infinite: that set actually contains an infinite number of members. A potential infinite, however, is a series that approaches an infinite number but never reaches that point, as when we try to list all the natural numbers, one by one, or when we divide an object by half, and then by half again, and so on. In those cases we never reach an ending point, a last member of the series. We never reach a number that we could call *infinity.*

APOLOGETIC IMPORTANCE

William Lane Craig

Some forms of the cosmological argument for the existence of God deny the existence of certain kinds of infinite series. Thomas Aquinas, in the first three of his *five ways,* denied that chains of causes (causes of motion, being, and necessity, respectively) can go back forever. He argued that every causal chain has a beginning: a first mover, a First Cause of being, and a first necessary being, namely, God. (See Aquinas, *Summa Theologica,* part 1, question 2, article 3.) The *Kalam* argument of Al-Ghazali, recently expounded by William Lane Craig, denies that there can be an actually infinite series of events succeeding one another in time. Therefore, the universe had a beginning, which must be explained by a divine cause.

Craig argues, first, that there cannot be an actually infinite collection of *things* (though there can be actually infinite sets of numbers), and second, that even if such a collection were possible, it could not be achieved by adding one member after another, as must happen in a temporal succession of events.

To show that there cannot be an actually infinite collection of things, he refers to the paradoxes noted by Cantor: (1) In an infinite series, the whole is equivalent to some of its parts. (2) One can add members to an infinite set without increasing the number of members in the set. (The number remains at infinity.) (3) One can remove members from the set without decreasing its membership. Such is the case in the abstract world of numbers. But, Craig says, it would be impossible to have a set of concrete objects or a series of events that had these properties. He uses the illustration of "Hilbert's Hotel" from George Gamow, *One, Two, Three, Infinity,* 17: If a hotel had an infinite number of rooms filled with guests, additional guests could check in without anyone moving out, and the number of guests would be the same as before. The sign could read: "NO VACANCY—GUESTS WELCOME" (Craig, *Reasonable Faith,* 96).

Craig argues that even if we grant the possibility of an actually infinite collection of things, we cannot form such a collection by adding one member after another.

Then Craig argues that even if we grant the possibility of an actually infinite collection of things, we cannot form such a collection by adding one member after another. It is impossible, for example, to count an infinite collection one by one, for "no matter how many numbers you count, you can always add one more before arriving at infinity" (98). The same must be said of an infinite series of events in time. If the process of nature and history extends infinitely far into the past, then it is an infinite succession of events, and that succession has proceeded one by one, ending precisely at the present moment. But why did it end now, rather than yesterday, or a thousand years ago? For on this hypothesis, yesterday was also the end of an infinite chain of events, and so was the moment a thousand years before the present one. But in fact, there can be no end at all, for an infinite series never ends. So, Craig concludes, the series of past events is finite. Therefore, the universe had a beginning, and therefore a cause, because "whatever begins to exist has a cause" (92).

In fact, there can be no end at all, for an infinite series never ends. So, Craig concludes, the series of past events is finite. Therefore, the universe had a beginning, and therefore a cause, because "whatever begins to exist has a cause."

EVALUATION

Certainly it is difficult to conceive of an actually infinite collection of things. Hilbert's Hotel is counterintuitive, but many find the Cantor paradoxes themselves hard to believe at first hearing. After we learn to work with infinite sets of numbers, we tend to accept the Cantor definitions as a matter of course. We have not, however, encountered infinite sets of material objects. But if we ever do, might we not eventually get used to the strange properties of such sets? Here, images are important. The idea of an infinite hotel is somewhat ridiculous, as is, say, the idea of a hotel with the hiccups. But how about the idea of an infinitely extended chain of beads? Might we not one day get used to the idea of adding or subtracting beads without changing the number in the infinite collection?

Part of the problem is that when we try to picture in our minds an infinite hotel, we tend to think of it as a finite hotel with very odd properties: people being squeezed into it without others being squeezed out. But if the hotel were truly infinite, those properties would not be odd, but expected, hard as it might be to imagine these properties in a mental picture. It is also hard to imagine such properties in a series of numbers, but Cantor proved that they exist.

If we could go backward in time from the present, then we could visit yesterday, the day before yesterday, and the day before that, much as we now move from today, to tomorrow, to the day after.

Similarly, the notion of an infinite series of events continuing through time is hard to comprehend, but is it impossible? I agree with Craig that it is impossible to count through an infinite series and end with a final number. But (1) if time itself were subjective, rather than objective, then an infinite set of past events might exist simultaneously (like the series 1, 2, 3 . . .), rather than existing by a temporal process of addition. (2) The same would be the case if time were an objective dimension of n-dimensional space, and all events of past, present, and future could be viewed together by a being of a higher dimension. And (3) if we could go backward in time from the present, then we could visit yesterday, the day before yesterday, and the day before that, much as we now move from today, to tomorrow, to the day after. In that case, we would perceive the days of past history much as we now perceive the days of the future: as a potential infinity, rather than an actual infinity.

Of course, these three suppositions are contrary to Craig's own theory of time. See his *Time and Eternity: Exploring God's Relationship to Time* (Wheaton, IL: Crossway, 2001). So I am not here challenging the consistency of Craig's view. But these considerations indicate that our present questions about infinite series do not have obvious answers. Indeed, they are linked to other issues that deserve book-length treatment.

Aquinas argues that the universe has a cause; therefore, there cannot be an infinite series of causes. Craig argues the reverse: there cannot be an infinite series of causes; therefore, the universe must have one cause.

Thomas Aquinas would object to supposition (3) that even a potentially infinite series of natural events in the past is insufficient to account for the world as we know it. For on this supposition, each event is caused by a previous one; no event actually begins the series. Therefore, no event (or group of events, by the same logic) serves as the cause of the rest. So the universe is uncaused, unexplained. Aquinas believes the universe must have a cause, so the chain of causal explanation cannot be infinite, even potentially infinite.

Aquinas argues that the universe has a cause; therefore, there cannot be an infinite series of causes. Craig argues the reverse: there cannot be an infinite series of causes; therefore, the universe must have one cause. I confess that I find Aquinas more persuasive: it seems more obvious to me that the universe requires a cause than that an infinite series of events is impossible. But even Aquinas's view requires assumptions, namely, that nothing exists or happens without a sufficient cause, and that causes (including the cause of the universe) are accessible to human reason. Many skeptics of the past and present would not grant those assumptions.

Our concepts of cause, reason, and infinite series depend on worldviews, on ontological and epistemological assumptions. They are insufficient in themselves to serve as grounds for worldviews.

My conclusion is that our concepts of cause, reason, and infinite series depend on worldviews, on ontological and epistemological assumptions. They are insufficient in themselves to serve as grounds for worldviews. A Christian theist will think differently from a skeptic about these matters. His Christian theism will govern his concepts of cause, reason, and infinity, rather than the reverse.

BIBLIOGRAPHY

Cantor, Georg. *Contributions to the Foundations of the Theory of Transfinite Numbers.* Translated by Philip E. B. Jourdain. Chicago: Open Court, 1915.

Craig, William Lane. *The Kalām Cosmological Argument.* New York: Barnes and Noble Books, 1979.

———. *Reasonable Faith: Christian Truth and Apologetics.* Wheaton, IL: Crossway, 1994.

Gamow, George. *One, Two Three . . . Infinity: Facts and Speculations of Science.* London: Macmillan, 1946.

APPENDIX C

"ONTOLOGICAL ARGUMENT"

Originally published in W. C. Campbell-Jack and Gavin J. McGrath, eds., *New Dictionary of Christian Apologetics*, consulting ed. C. Stephen Evans (Downers Grove, IL: InterVarsity Press, 2006), *513–16*. Used by permission. We have seen in the book that many philosophers have supported this argument for God's existence (Augustine, Anselm, Descartes, Spinoza, Leibniz, Plantinga, Hartshorne), and that others have rejected it (Aquinas, Kant, Russell). This article sums up my own view. (For stylistic purposes, this appendix has been copyedited for inclusion in this volume.)

THE MOST INFLUENTIAL formulation of this argument (though he did not use the term *ontological*) is found in the first three chapters of the *Proslogium* of Anselm of Canterbury (1033–1109). He had earlier written a *Monologium* in which he considered many arguments for God's existence. But then, he says, "I began to ask myself whether there might be found a single argument which would require no other for its proof than itself alone; and alone would suffice to demonstrate that God truly exists . . . ; and whatever we believe regarding the divine being" (Preface, 1). He says that he made an extensive search for such an argument and that, when he was almost ready to discontinue his quest, that argument "began to force itself on me, with a kind of importunity" (2).

The Proslogium, *unlike the* Monologium, *is a prayer. In the first chapter, Anselm invokes God's presence, confessing God's incomprehensibility and his own sin.*

The *Proslogium*, unlike the *Monologium*, is a prayer. In the first chapter, Anselm invokes God's presence, confessing God's incomprehensibility and his own sin. He concludes with these famous words: "I do not endeavor, O Lord, to penetrate thy sublimity, for in no wise do I compare my understanding with that; but I long to understand in some degree thy truth, which my heart believes and loves. For I do not seek to understand that I may believe, but I believe in order to understand [*credo ut intelligam*]. For this also I believe, — that unless I believed, I should not understand" (6–7).

The second chapter begins the argument that seemed to force itself on Anselm. In accord with the resolution of his prayer, that he seeks to believe in order to understand, he begins with a Christian belief: "And, indeed, we believe that thou art a being than which no greater can be conceived" (7).

A being that truly meets Anselm's definition of God, a being than which no greater can be conceived, must exist not only in the understanding, but also in reality. Therefore, God must exist, by virtue of his very definition.

Now, Anselm recognizes that some do not believe in such a God, like the fool in Psalm 14:1 who "says in his heart, 'There is no God.'" Nevertheless, this fool at least understands the words "a being than which no greater can be conceived," so we may say that in a sense this being "exists in the [fool's] understanding" (8). But if it exists in the fool's understanding alone, and not in reality, then we can imagine a greater being, namely, one that exists not only in the understanding, but in reality. So then the being in the fool's understanding is not really a being than which no greater can be conceived. So a being that truly meets Anselm's definition of God, a being than which no greater can be conceived, must exist not only in the understanding, but also in reality. Therefore, God must exist, by virtue of his very definition.

In chapter 3, Anselm draws the further implication that this God "cannot be conceived not to exist" (8). That is, if God can be conceived not to exist, it would be possible for us to conceive of a still greater God, one that cannot be conceived not to exist. So God not only exists, but exists *necessarily*, as some later philosophers and theologians would put it. He doesn't just happen to exist; he must exist. Once we know the meaning of *God*, as Anselm has defined it, we *cannot* conceive of his not existing. For it is greater, better for him to exist than not to exist, and to exist necessarily rather than contingently.

Anselm of Canterbury

Then through the rest of the book, Anselm seeks to prove the traditional attributes of God using the same method: God is "just, truthful, blessed, and whatever it is better to be than not to be" (11).

We can simplify Anselm's argument, for ease of reference: (1) God has all perfections; (2) existence is a perfection; (3) therefore, God exists.

At first glance, many immediately suspect a fallacy. I recall a party game in which one friend produced a proof that 1 = 2 and challenged us all to find out what was wrong with it. (Turned out that there was a concealed division by zero.) Similarly, one suspects a bit of conceptual legerdemain in Anselm's argument. Can it really be this easy to prove the existence of God? But it has not been easy for philosophers and theologians to show where the fallacy is located, if indeed there is one. Anselm's contemporary Gaunilo, Thomas Aquinas, David Hume,

Immanuel Kant, J. L. Mackie, and others have rejected the argument, but many philosophers down to the present have accepted versions of it: Descartes, Spinoza, Leibniz, Hegel and his followers, and twentieth-century thinkers Charles Hartshorne, Norman Malcolm, and Alvin Plantinga.

The *Proslogium* includes an appendix "In Behalf of the Fool" by the monk Gaunilo, with a response by Anselm. Gaunilo points out that it is doubtful that we can even conceive of God in our minds according to Anselm's definition: for who can conceive of a being than which no greater can exist? And if we can reason from concept to reality as Anselm does, we could as easily prove the existence of a perfect island. "For if it does not exist, any land which really exists will be more excellent than it" (151).

In Kant's view, existence is not a perfection, not even a property. It is not, indeed, a "real" predicate, though it can occupy the predicate position in a sentence such as "God exists."

Anselm answers Gaunilo at considerable length. Although Gaunilo speaks "In Behalf of the Fool," Anselm knows that he is "by no means a fool, and is a Catholic." So, he says, "I think it sufficient that I answer the Catholic" (153). In response to Gaunilo's first point, Anselm replies that Gaunilo, being a Catholic, cannot deny that God is conceivable, for he himself conceives of God. Anselm rather brushes off Gaunilo's analogous proof of a perfect island, but his basic reply is that such an island could not fit his definition of God, that than which no greater can be conceived. Only one being meets the terms of that definition, namely, the God of Christianity. The rest of Anselm's reply discusses various senses of *conceiving*, *understanding*, and *existing*, and relations among these concepts.

Kant admits, however, that his financial position is better with real dollars than with possible ones. And we know that a real car is different from an imaginary one, and that a real unicorn, if it existed, would be different from an imaginary one.

Immanuel Kant thought that Anselm misunderstood the nature of existence, by treating it as a perfection of God. In Kant's view, existence is not a perfection, not even a property. It is not, indeed, a "real" predicate, though it can occupy the predicate position in a sentence such as "God exists." For existence, Kant said, doesn't add anything to our concept of something. If you conceive of a nondescript car and add to it the color blue, your concept changes. But if you conceive of a car and then conceive that same car as existing, nothing changes, Kant argued, for it is, after all, the same car. As Kant puts it, "a hundred real dollars do not contain a penny more than a hundred possible dollars" (Kant, *Critique of Pure Reason*, 282). So Kant thinks Anselm has erred by making existence one of God's attributes or properties.

Kant admits, however, that his financial position is better with real dollars than with possible ones. And we know that a real car is different from an imaginary one, and that a real unicorn, if it existed, would be different from an imaginary one. The real car might look the same as the one in our heads, but it is certainly something different. Existence is therefore different from other properties and predicates in some ways, but not in the sense that it makes no difference to the objects that have it. Thus, it seems that Kant's objection to the ontological argument fails, though it has generated and continues to generate much discussion.

The most common objection to the argument, voiced by Aquinas, followed by many others, is that concepts in the mind imply only mental existence, never existence in reality. There can be no "leap" from mind to reality. This argument invokes our intuition that we can think of many things, such as unicorns and leprechauns, that do not exist in reality, and it is hard to conceive of anything in such mental concepts that in itself could prove that these objects exist in the real world. Anselm, however, does not say that it is generally valid to infer realities from concepts. For him, this inference is valid in only one case—the case of God. It is not valid for our concepts of unicorns or perfect islands, only for that being than which no greater can be conceived.

The most common objection to the argument, voiced by Aquinas, followed by many others, is that concepts in the mind imply only mental existence, never existence in reality. There can be no "leap" from mind to reality.

Now, if it is *never* possible to argue from the contents of the mind to the nature of reality, then we are in a bad way. In one sense, the contents of our minds (including the experience of our senses, our rational reflection, our memories, imaginations, and concepts) are all that we are directly acquainted with. If we are never able to reason from any of these to conclusions about the real world, then we cannot know the real world at all; we are shut up to skepticism. Empiricists, rationalists, idealists, and others propose various ways of drawing this inference. (Insofar as Kant denied its possibility, he implicated himself of the charge of skepticism.) But the inference must be drawn.

Anselm's own inference may owe something to Plato, for whom objects of our experience are reflections of more perfect objects, Forms or Ideas. We have a concept of goodness, for example, though nothing in our experience is perfectly good. Therefore, Plato believed, there must be a Perfect Good in the real world that serves as a model, criterion, or standard of goodness. Although we may well reject Plato's idea that we know the Perfect Good from having experienced it in a past life, it still makes sense to assert that the highest criteria of truth, beauty, and goodness must exist in reality, not only in our minds. Otherwise, we could not measure these qualities except by a subjective (and therefore arbitrary) standard. If goodness, truth, and beauty exist, there must be an objective standard by which to measure them.

To say with Anselm that God is that than which no greater can be conceived is to identify God as the highest perfection, the standard and exemplar of all greatness, and therefore of all goodness, truth, and beauty, and whatever other perfections there may be.

To say with Anselm that God is that than which no greater can be conceived is to identify God as the highest perfection, the standard and exemplar of all greatness, and therefore of all goodness, truth, and beauty, and whatever other perfections there may be. Without such a standard or exemplar, there could be no goodness, truth, or beauty in the world; that is, the world would be a chaos. So there is a kinship between the ontological argument and the transcendental argument.

Both argue that if God exists only in our minds, there is no truth or meaning—indeed, no being at all. The greatness of God, therefore, must necessarily exist.

The ontological argument, therefore, expresses for Anselm the heart of the Christian worldview. God is the source of all value, so his existence must be presupposed if we are to accept the existence of anything else. It is not surprising, then, that this argument arises in answer to prayer and is expressed in the language of prayer, and it is not surprising that when Gaunilo raises objections, Anselm responds not to the fool, but to the Catholic. As he says in his preface, he is not trying to understand in order to believe, but to believe in order to understand. When he discovers in a deeper way who the God of the Bible really is, that than which no greater can be conceived, he sees an important reason why he *must* exist.

The ontological argument, therefore, expresses for Anselm the heart of the Christian worldview. God is the source of all value, so his existence must be presupposed if we are to accept the existence of anything else.

The trouble with the argument is that people with other worldviews try to use it, too. The God proved by Spinoza's version of the argument is very different from Anselm's, a God identical with nature, *Deus sive natura*. The same may be said of the Absolute of Hegel and the process God of Hartshorne. In part, the differences lie in the fact that different worldviews differ as to what is great or perfect. For Anselm, it is a perfection for God to create all things from nothing (*Proslogium*, 10–11), but not for Spinoza. For Anselm, it is a perfection for God to be passionless (11), but not for Hartshorne. The ontological argument necessarily presupposes a system of values. For Anselm, that system comes from his understanding of the Christian faith. In that sense, the argument presupposes the Christian revelation, which, again, should not be surprising in view of Anselm's prayers and the *credo ut intelligam*.

As Thomas Aquinas says, not everybody would acknowledge God to be "that than which nothing greater can be conceived," for some, he says, have thought that God has a body (*Summa Theologiae*, First Part, Q. 2, Art. 1, Obj. and Ans. 2). Nor would some acknowledge that existence is a perfection, even given that it is a "real predicate": to many Buddhists, for example, annihilation is preferable to existence.

The cogency of the ontological argument as an apologetic for the Christian faith depends on the cogency of the biblical system of values, its notion of perfection. It is not a religiously neutral argument, but one that immediately assumes the truth that it seeks to validate.

So the cogency of the ontological argument as an apologetic for the Christian faith depends on the cogency of the biblical system of values, its notion of perfection. It is not a religiously neutral argument, but one that immediately assumes the truth that it seeks to validate. Presuppositional apologists frankly acknowledge and defend that kind of circularity in apologetics. Others might reject the ontological argument for this reason. But they must ask whether other arguments are not circular in similar ways. Does the cosmological argument not presuppose a causal order such as we find in Scripture, but not in David

Hume? Does the teleological argument work if it does not understand purpose to be personal, rather than impersonal?

BIBLIOGRAPHY

Anselm of Canterbury. *St. Anselm: Basic Writings*. Edited by S. N. Deane. La Salle, IL: Open Court, 1962.

Aquinas, Thomas. *Summa Theologica*. In *Introduction to St. Thomas Aquinas*, edited by Anton C. Pegis. New York: Modern Library, 1948.

Barth, Karl. *Anselm: Fides Quaerens Intellectum*. Richmond, VA: John Knox Press, 1960. Expounds the theological presuppositions of Anselm's argument.

Frame, John M. *Apologetics to the Glory of God*. Phillipsburg, NJ: P&R Publishing, 1994.

Kant, Immanuel. *Critique of Pure Reason*. Abridged, edited, translated, and with an introduction by Norman Kemp Smith. New York: Modern Library, 1958.

Plantinga, Alvin. *God, Freedom and Evil*. New York: Harper and Row, 1974. Includes a contemporary reconstruction of the argument according to modal logic and possible worlds.

APPENDIX D

"TRANSCENDENTAL ARGUMENTS"

Originally published in W. C. Campbell-Jack and Gavin J. McGrath, eds., *New Dictionary of Christian Apologetics*, consulting ed. C. Stephen Evans (Downers Grove, IL: InterVarsity Press, 2006), 716–17. Used by permission. Kant (chapter 7) introduced to philosophy the concept of a transcendental argument. Others, such as Cornelius Van Til (chapter 13), have applied it to Christian apologetics. This article presents my thoughts about it. (For stylistic purposes, this appendix has been copyedited for inclusion in this volume.)

IMMANUEL KANT (1724–1804) is responsible for introducing the term *transcendental* to philosophical discussion. Seeking to repel the skepticism of David Hume, but unable to accept the rationalist methods of Christian Wolff, Kant came to advocate transcendental argument as a new means of grounding the certainty of mathematics, science, and philosophy.

All of us, he argued, must concede that knowledge is possible. Otherwise, there is no point to any discussion or inquiry. Now, given that knowledge is possible, said Kant, we should ask what the conditions are that make knowledge possible. What must the world be like, and what must the workings of our minds be like, if human knowledge is to be possible?

Given that knowledge is possible, said Kant, we should ask what the conditions are that make knowledge possible. What must the world be like, and what must the workings of our minds be like, if human knowledge is to be possible?

Kant argued that among the conditions of knowledge are the transcendental aesthetic, in which the mind orders sense experience into a spatiotemporal sequence, and the transcendental analytic, in which the mind imposes categories such as substance and cause upon experience. So we know by transcendental argument that the world (more precisely, the world of appearances, the phenomena, not the world "in itself") is a collection of substances located in space and time, with causal relationships to one another. We do not get this knowledge from sense experience alone (Hume) or from rational deduction alone (Leibniz, Wolff), but from an argument assuming the reality of knowledge and showing the necessary presuppositions of that assumption.

Traditional methodologies applied to apologetics, said Van Til, assume that human sense experience and/or human reason can function adequately without God, that is, autonomously *or* neutrally. *So at the very outset of an apologetic argument, they concede the whole game.*

Transcendental argument became a staple of the writings of the idealist school that followed Kant, and from there it made its way into Christian apologetics. James Orr (1844–1913) employed it. But the twentieth-century apologist who placed the most weight on the transcendental argument (which he sometimes called *reasoning by presupposition*) was Cornelius Van Til (1895–1987).

Like Kant, Van Til was unhappy with empiricism and rationalism, and with traditional ways of combining reason and sense experience such as that of Aquinas. Kant found these approaches to knowledge logically invalid. But for Van Til, they were also wrong in a distinctively theological way. Traditional methodologies applied to apologetics, said Van Til, assume that human sense experience and/or human reason can function adequately without God, that is, *autonomously* or *neutrally*. So at the very outset of an apologetic argument, they concede the whole game. They adopt a presupposition contrary to the conclusion that they wish to argue. They seek to gain knowledge of God by adopting a nontheistic epistemology.

Van Til answered the charge of circularity in these ways: (1) Every system of thought is circular when arguing its most fundamental presuppositions (e.g., a rationalist can defend the authority of reason only by using reason). (2) The Christian circle is the only one that renders reality intelligible on its own terms.

The only alternative, Van Til argued, is to adopt a theistic epistemology when arguing for the existence of God. But that approach seems to be viciously circular: presupposing God in our epistemology and then using that epistemology to prove his existence.

Van Til answered the charge of circularity in these ways: (1) Every system of thought is circular when arguing its most fundamental presuppositions (e.g., a rationalist can defend the authority of reason only by using reason). (2) The Christian circle is the only one that renders reality intelligible on its own terms.

In defense of (2), Van Til developed his own transcendental argument. He maintained that Christian theism is the presupposition of all meaning, all rational significance, all intelligible discourse. Even when someone argues against Christian theism, Van Til said, he presupposes it, for he presupposes that rational argument is possible and that truth can be conveyed through language. The non-Christian, then, in Van Til's famous illustration, is like a child sitting on her father's lap, slapping his face. She could not slap him unless he supported her. Similarly, the non-Christian cannot carry out his rebellion against God unless God makes that rebellion possible. Contradicting God assumes an intelligible universe and therefore a theistic one.

But how can we defend the logical move from *intelligible universe* to *theistic universe*? Van Til rarely articulated his reason for that move; he seemed to think it was self-evident. But in effect, he reverted at this point to apologetics of a more traditional type. Apologists have often noted that we could not know the world at all unless it had been designed for knowledge. If the world were nothing but matter, motion, time, and chance, we would have no reason to think that the ideas in our heads told us anything about the real world. Only if a person had designed the world to be known, and the human mind to know it, could knowledge be possible. So Van Til at this point reverted to a traditional teleological argument. He never admitted to doing this, and he could not have admitted it, because he thought the traditional teleological arguments (like the other traditional arguments) were autonomous and neutral.

How can we defend the logical move from intelligible universe *to* theistic universe? *Van Til rarely articulated his reason for that move; he seemed to think it was self-evident. But in effect, he reverted at this point to apologetics of a more traditional type.*

If Van Til's transcendental approach is to succeed, however, it must abandon the assumption that traditional arguments are necessarily autonomous and welcome the assistance of such arguments to complete the transcendental argument. The traditional arguments are in fact necessary to establish the existence of God as a transcendental conclusion. And there is no reason to assume, as Van Til does, that anyone who uses an argument from design or causality is presupposing a nontheistic epistemology. On the contrary, people who use these traditional arguments show precisely that without God the data of our experience suggesting order and causality are unintelligible.

What, then, does transcendental argument add to the apologist's arsenal, beyond the traditional arguments? First, it presents a goal for apologetics. The goal of the apologist is to show not only that God exists, but also who he is: that he is the source of all meaning and intelligibility in the universe.

What, then, does transcendental argument add to the apologist's arsenal, beyond the traditional arguments? First, it presents a goal for apologetics. The goal of the apologist is to show not only that God exists, but also who he is: that he is the source of all meaning and intelligibility in the universe.

Further, it suggests apologetic strategies somewhat neglected in the tradition. Traditional apologists have often argued that causality (for example) *implies* God. A transcendental argument makes a stronger claim: that causality *presupposes* God. The difference between *implies* and *presupposes*, according to Peter Strawson and Bas Van Fraasen, is that in the latter case God's existence is implied by either the assertion *or the denial* of causality. That is, not only does the existence of causality imply the existence of God, but even to deny (intelligibly, if it were possible) the existence of causality would be to invoke a framework of meaning that presupposes God's existence. Don Collett argues that the Strawson-Van Fraasen kind of presupposition is identical with Van Til's. So if creation presupposes God, even the denial of creation presupposes him, and the atheist is like the little girl slapping her father while sitting on his lap.

The Bible does make this kind of radical claim, that creation not only implies but presupposes God. For God is the Creator of all, and therefore the source of all meaning, order, and intelligibility. It is in Christ that all things hold together (Col. 1:17). So without him everything falls apart; nothing makes sense. Thus Scripture teaches that unbelief is foolish (Ps. 14:1; 1 Cor. 1:20). There are many arguments to be made on the way to that conclusion. Not every individual apologetic argument needs to go that far. But the apologist's work is not done until he reaches that conclusion, until he persuades the objector that God is everything that the Bible says he is. That is to say that a complete argument for Christian theism, however many subarguments it contains, will be transcendental in character.

The apologist's work is not done until he reaches that conclusion, until he persuades the objector that God is everything that the Bible says he is. That is to say that a complete argument for Christian theism, however many subarguments it contains, will be transcendental in character.

BIBLIOGRAPHY

Collett, Don. "Van Til and Transcendental Argument." *WTJ* 65, 2 (Fall 2003): 289–306.

———. "Van Til and Transcendental Argument," in *Revelation and Reason: New Essays in Reformed Apologetics*, ed. K. Scott Oliphint and Lane G. Tipton (Phillipsburg, NJ: P&R Publishing, 2007), 258–78.

Frame, John M. *Cornelius Van Til: An Analysis of His Thought*. Phillipsburg, NJ: P&R Publishing, 1995.

Kant, Immanuel. *Critique of Pure Reason*. Abridged, edited, translated, and with an introduction by Norman Kemp Smith. New York: Modern Library, 1958.

Oliphint, K. Scott, and Lane G. Tipton, eds., *Revelation and Reason: New Essays in Reformed Apologetics* (Phillipsburg, NJ: P&R Publishing, 2007), 258–78.

Strawson, Peter F. *An Introduction to Logical Theory*. London: Methuen, 1952.

Van Fraassen, Bas C. "Presupposition, Implication, and Self-Reference." *Journal of Philosophy* 65, 5 (1968): 136–52.

Van Til, Cornelius. *The Defense of the Faith*. Philadelphia: Presbyterian and Reformed, 1963.

APPENDIX E

"DETERMINISM, CHANCE, AND FREEDOM"

Originally published in W. C. Campbell-Jack and Gavin J. McGrath, eds., *New Dictionary of Christian Apologetics*, consulting ed. C. Stephen Evans (Downers Grove, IL: InterVarsity Press, 2006), 218–20. Used by permission. In this book, we have seen examples of determinists (Democritus, the Stoics, Spinoza) and those who argue different kinds of free will (Epicurus, Whitehead, open theism). In this article, I analyze some of the concepts at work in the discussion. (For stylistic purposes, this appendix has been copyedited for inclusion in this volume.)

DETERMINISTS BELIEVE THAT every event (or every event in a certain category) has a cause that makes it happen exactly as it happens. Among the varieties of determinism are the views of (1) Plato, who held that one's ethical choices are determined by his view of what is good, (2) B. F. Skinner, who believed that stimuli, dispositions, and motives govern all human behavior, (3) Democritus, Hobbes, Spinoza, and many others, who have held that every event in the universe is determined by a physical cause. Of special interest to us are (4) theological determinists, who hold that all events occur exactly as God has foreordained them. These include Calvin and others in his tradition. The classic exposition of theological determinism is Jonathan Edwards's *Freedom of the Will*. Note that it is possible to be a determinist in sense (4) without being a determinist in sense (3). That seems to be the position of the *WCF*, which says in 3.1 that "God . . . did . . . ordain whatsoever comes to pass," but also says in 9.1 that man's will "is neither forced, nor, by any absolute necessity of nature, determined to good, or evil" (cf. 5.2).

Determinists believe that every event . . . has a cause that makes it happen exactly as it happens. . . . Of special interest to us are theological determinists, who hold that all events occur exactly as God has foreordained them.

William James, in his article "The Dilemma of Determinism," distinguished between *hard* and *soft* determinism. On his view, soft determinists hold that all events, including human decisions, are determined, but that some kind of freedom and moral responsibility also exists. Hard determinists hold (what James thought was the more consistent position) that the determination of human decisions requires us to reject the concept of moral responsibility. Other writers, however, have used the *hard-soft* distinction differently, defining *soft determinism* as a view that is largely deterministic but that allows for some uncaused or self-caused human choices.

Soft determinists hold that all events, including human decisions, are determined, but that some kind of freedom and moral responsibility also exists. Hard determinists hold . . . that the determination of human decisions requires us to reject the concept of moral responsibility.

Chance can refer (1) to uncaused events, or (2) to events of which the causes are uncertain and normally uncontrollable. When we throw dice, we often say that the result is "by chance"; but we then don't usually mean that the result is uncaused, only that the causes are hard to ascertain or control. Laws of probability enable us to predict the results of such chance events over the long term (for example, 50 percent of coin flips come out tails), but not in individual cases. *Chance* can also be (3) a synonym of *fate*, conceived as an impersonal force that makes everything happen as it happens. In the first sense, chance is incompatible with determinism. In the second sense, it is compatible with determinism. In the third sense, it presupposes determinism.

Freedom is a more complicated notion. Generally speaking, a person is free when (1) he has the ability to do something, (2) there is some obstacle or barrier that might have prevented him from exercising that ability but is not now preventing him. Someone is "set free" from prison, for example, when he can go where he likes without the barriers of prison walls, bars, guards, and so on. People have political freedom when they are able to do such things as to publish political opinions and organize political parties without government interference. So freedom is always "freedom to" and "freedom from": freedom to do something, and freedom from some obstacle.

Generally speaking, a person is free when (1) he has the ability to do something, (2) there is some obstacle or barrier that might have prevented him from exercising that ability but is not now preventing him.

On this account, there are many different kinds of freedom, since there are many different things that we can be free to do, and many obstacles that we can be free from. So we speak of economic freedom, political freedom, religious freedom, freedom from illness, and many others.

The following kinds of freedom are of particular interest to theologians and apologists: (1) *Moral* freedom, or the ability to do good, despite the barrier of our sinful condition. God gives us this freedom by his grace (John 8:32–36; Rom. 6:7, 18–23; 8:2). When Scripture speaks of human freedom, it is almost always in this sense.

(2) The freedom to act according to our own desires. This kind of freedom is sometimes called *compatibilism*, because it is compatible with determinism. Scripture doesn't describe this capacity as *freedom*,

but it does ascribe this capacity to all human beings. Jesus teaches, for example, that the good person acts out of the desires of his good heart, the wicked person out of his wicked heart (Matt. 12:35). There are times, of course, when we are unable to do what we "want" to do, at some level of wanting (as Rom. 7:15). But in most of the decisions of life, we do what we want, in the face of potential obstacles.

(3) Freedom *from natural necessity*, the freedom to act without the constraint of natural causes. This is the freedom mentioned in my earlier reference to the WCF. Its theological importance is its implication that human choice is not necessarily or always the result of natural causes. As image of God, we have dominion over the earth and in some ways transcend the world process. And we may not excuse our sins by saying that they were forced upon us by heredity or environment.

Freedom from natural necessity *[is] the freedom to act without the constraint of natural causes. . . . Its theological importance is its implication that human choice is not necessarily or always the result of natural causes.*

(4) Freedom from all causation, sometimes called *libertarianism*. I have freedom in the libertarian sense when, no matter what I choose to do, I might equally have chosen the opposite. So my choices are free not only from natural causes (as in [3]) but also from divine causation. Indeed, my libertarian choices are also free from myself in a way, for they are not determined by my character, dispositions, or desires. These inner motives may *influence* a free decision in this sense, but they never *determine* it. So a libertarian free decision is entirely indeterminate, uncaused. Thus libertarianism is sometimes called *incompatibilism*, since it is incompatible with determinism.

Libertarianism has been taught by a number of philosophers from ancient Greece (Epicurus) to the present (Alvin Plantinga). It was the position of some church fathers, including Justin Martyr and Tertullian; Pelagius, the opponent of Augustine; the Jesuit Luis Molina; Fausto and Lelio Socinus; Jacob Arminius; and present-day Arminians, open theists, and process theologians.

Freedom from all causation [is] sometimes called libertarianism. *I have freedom in the libertarian sense when, no matter what I choose to do, I might equally have chosen the opposite. So my choices are free not only from natural causes . . . but also from divine causation.*

Libertarians argue that we must have this kind of freedom because (1) our intuition reveals that we have it, and (2) it is necessary for moral responsibility, for we cannot be held responsible for anything that we are determined to do.

Opponents of libertarianism, however, reply: (1) Human intuition reveals that we choose among various alternatives, but it never reveals to us that any of our choices are absolutely uncaused. Intuition cannot prove a universal negative. (2) Far from teaching that libertarian freedom is essential to moral responsibility, Scripture never mentions libertarian freedom. (3) This doctrine would make it impossible for us to judge anyone's guilt in a court of law. For to prove someone responsible for a crime and therefore guilty, the prosecution would have to take on the impossible burden of proof of showing that the decision of the accused had no cause whatsoever. (4) Law courts, indeed, assume the opposite of libertarianism, namely, that people are responsible only for actions that they are *sufficiently motivated* to perform. If it could be shown that an accused person committed a crime without any sufficient cause or motivation at all, he would most likely be judged insane rather than guilty. (5) Scripture contradicts libertarianism, by ascribing divine causes to human decisions (Ex. 34:24; Isa. 44:28; Dan. 1:9; John 19:24; Acts 13:48; 16:14), even sinful ones (Gen. 45:5–8; Ps. 105:24; Luke 22:22; Acts 2:23–24; 3:18; 4:27–28; Rom. 9:17). In none of these (or many other) cases does divine causation eliminate human responsibility. In fact, these texts often mention human responsibility in the same context. (6) Scripture also contradicts libertarianism by teaching that human decisions are governed by the heart (Luke 6:45), and by teaching that the human heart itself is under God's control (Ps. 33:15; Prov. 21:1). (7) In Scripture, the basis of human responsibility is not libertarian freedom, but (a) God's sovereign right to evaluate the conduct of his creatures (Rom. 9:19–21), and (b) the knowledge (Luke 12:47–48; Rom. 1:18–32) and resources (Matt. 25:14–29) that God has given to each person. As (b) shows, Scripture contains an important relation between responsibility and ability, but the abilities in view here do not include the absolute ability to choose opposite courses of action.

The Bible teaches theistic determinism, one that is soft in James's sense. Scripture renounces chance in the first and third senses above, but not in the second. And it teaches that human beings sometimes have moral freedom, usually have compatibilist freedom, never have libertarian freedom.

These considerations lead to the conclusion that the Bible teaches theistic determinism, one that is *soft* in James's sense. Scripture renounces chance in the first and third senses above, but not in the second. And it teaches that human beings sometimes have moral freedom, usually have compatibilist freedom, never have libertarian freedom. Scripture might imply that we have freedom from natural causation as well. Certainly it doesn't deny that, but I don't know of any passage that clearly affirms it.

BIBLIOGRAPHY

Edwards, Jonathan. *Freedom of the Will*. Edited by Paul Ramsey. New Haven, CT: Yale University Press, 1973.

Frame, John M. *The Doctrine of God*. Phillipsburg, NJ: P&R Publishing, 2002.

———. *No Other God: A Response to Open Theism*. Phillipsburg, NJ: P&R Publishing, 2001.

James, William. "The Dilemma of Determinism." In *Essays in Pragmatism*, edited by Alburey Castell, 37–64. New York: Hafner Publishing, 1954. Also in many other editions of James's works.

Poythress, Vern S., *Chance and the Sovereignty of God: A God-centered Approach to Probability and Random Events* (Wheaton, IL: Crossway, 2014).

APPENDIX F

"SELF-REFUTING STATEMENTS"

Originally published in W. C. Campbell-Jack and Gavin J. McGrath, eds., *New Dictionary of Christian Apologetics*, consulting ed. C. Stephen Evans (Downers Grove, IL: InterVarsity Press, 2006), 660–62. Used by permission. (For stylistic purposes, this appendix has been copyedited for inclusion in this volume.)

SEVERAL KINDS OF statements have been described as *self-refuting*:

(1) Logical contradictions, such as "Socrates is mortal and Socrates is not mortal." If the two occurrences of *mortal* in this sentence are predicated of Socrates at the same time and in the same respect, then the sentence cannot be true. The first clause refutes the second, and vice versa.

(2) Some self-referential statements, that is, statements that refer to themselves, such as "All statements are false." If that statement is true, then it is false.

(3) Some statements that refute themselves not because of their explicit content, but because of the one who utters them. An example is "I am lying now." Generally, there is no contradiction involved in saying that someone is lying. Replace the first person with the third, "He is lying now," and the contradiction disappears. But in the first person the statement is self-refuting, because the very act of asserting something involves a claim to be telling the truth. So "I am lying now" means, in effect, "I am telling the truth, and I am also lying now," which is a contradiction.

Some statements . . . refute themselves not because of their explicit content, but because of the one who utters them. An example is "I am lying now." . . . The statement is self-refuting, because the very act of asserting something involves a claim to be telling the truth.

(4) Other "practical" forms of self-refutation, which pertain more

to the speaker than to the actual words he utters. If a person says that he hates beans, but he gorges himself with large helpings of them, observers may well claim that his behavior refutes his statement. His statement itself is not self-refuting, but in an important sense the person has refuted himself. To argue against such practical self-contradictions is, of course, to argue ad hominem.

Some philosophical theories . . . set up conditions of meaning, rationality, or truth that they themselves are unable to meet. Ludwig Wittgenstein . . . candidly admitted at the end that the propositions of his book did not measure up to his own criteria of meaning, so he suggested that those propositions were a kind of ladder that one throws away after using it to reach a higher vantage point.

(5) Some philosophical theories that set up conditions of meaning, rationality, or truth that they themselves are unable to meet. Ludwig Wittgenstein in his *Tractatus Logico-Philosophicus*, for example, candidly admitted at the end that the propositions of his book did not measure up to his own criteria of meaning, so he suggested that those propositions were a kind of ladder that one throws away after using it to reach a higher vantage point. Later, the logical positivists insisted that a piece of language cannot meaningfully state an empirical fact (either truly or falsely) unless it is empirically verifiable by methods akin to those of natural science. But many observed that this *verification principle* itself could not be empirically verified in that way. That argument led to the demise of logical positivism as an influential philosophical movement.

(6) The philosophical view known as the *general form of skepticism*, which claims that there are no truths or that nothing can be known. The antiskeptic accuses the skeptic of making the error noted above under (2): trying to state truly that there are no truths or claiming to know that nothing can be known. In response, skeptics might (a) abandon their skepticism, (b) modify it to exclude their own claim (a move that can easily be criticized as arbitrary or self-serving), or (c) modify their view to allow for a few knowable truths. Alternative (c) might involve some sort of distinction between first-order truths and second-order truths (i.e., truths about truths), limiting skepticism to truth claims of the first order. But it is hard to imagine any reason for first-order skepticism that would not apply equally to second-order skepticism. In any case, such a distinction naturally invites further arguments.

Christian apologists have often employed the concept of self-refutation against alternatives to Christian theism.

(7) The view that, as Immanuel Kant argued, the truth of mathematics and science cannot be proved by rational deduction (as Leibniz) or by sense experience alone (Hume), but rather by a transcendental argument that shows the conditions under which alone knowledge is possible. To deny this theory, Kant believed, is to deny the necessary conditions of knowledge while claiming to have knowledge, a self-refuting position. Similar claims, however, have been made for many other epistemological theories, some very different from Kant's.

Christian apologists have often employed the concept of self-refutation against alternatives to Christian theism. Gordon H. Clark, in *A Christian View of Men and Things* and other writings, is one of many apologists who emphasize the logical contradictions of non-Christian thinkers, particularly those that entail skepticism. Stuart Hackett's *The Resurrection of Theism*, which develops a modification of Kant's transcendental argument, is another example of an apologetic work in which this approach is prominent.

Francis Schaeffer frequently employed the "practical" sense of self-refutation (4). In *The God Who Is There* (72–74), he refers to John Cage, who wrote "random" music expressing his view that pure chance governs reality. But Cage also collected mushrooms as a hobby, and he came to realize that he would die if he applied his philosophy of chance to the gathering of mushrooms. In Schaeffer's view, Cage refuted himself in that his practice was inconsistent with his theory.

Cage also collected mushrooms as a hobby, and he came to realize that he would die if he applied his philosophy of chance to the gathering of mushrooms.

Cornelius Van Til mentions often in his writings (such as *Essays on Christian Education*, 89) a man he saw on a train whose little daughter was slapping his face. But she could not have reached him if he had not kept her on his lap. Van Til uses this incident to illustrate his view that the non-Christian cannot even argue against Christian theism without depending on it. To argue at all, even against Christianity, presupposes that the world is meaningful, knowable, and expressible in language. In Van Til's view, only Christian theism provides the conditions that make such rational discourse possible. Therefore, the unbeliever's very decision to argue against God refutes his position. This type of self-refutation is akin to (3) and (4) above, because the self-refutation is found not directly in the content of the assertion, but in the decision of a speaker to state that assertion.

To argue at all, even against Christianity, presupposes that the world is meaningful, knowable, and expressible in language. In Van Til's view, only Christian theism provides the conditions that make such rational discourse possible.

BIBLIOGRAPHY

Clark, Gordon H. *A Christian View of Men and Things*. Grand Rapids: Eerdmans, 1952.

Hackett, Stuart C. *The Resurrection of Theism: Prolegomena to Christian Apology*. Chicago: Moody Press, 1957.

Hasker, William. "Self-Referential Incoherence." In *The Cambridge Dictionary of Philosophy*, edited by Robert Audi, 721. Cambridge: Cambridge University Press, 1995.

Schaeffer, Francis A. *The God Who Is There*. Chicago: InterVarsity Press, 1968.

Van Til, Cornelius. *Essays on Christian Education*. Nutley, NJ: Presbyterian and Reformed, 1974.

Wittgenstein, Ludwig. *Tractatus Logico-Philosophicus*. London: Routledge and Kegan Paul, 1963.

APPENDIX G

"UNREGENERATE KNOWLEDGE OF GOD"

Originally published in W. C. Campbell-Jack and Gavin J. McGrath, eds., *New Dictionary of Christian Apologetics*, consulting ed. C. Stephen Evans (Downers Grove, IL: InterVarsity Press, 2006), 732–35. Used by permission. This article discusses the effects of sin upon human knowledge, supplementing my treatment in chapter 1 of this book and my discussion of Van Til in chapter 13. (For stylistic purposes, this appendix has been copyedited for inclusion in this volume.)

A good apologist will want to have some idea of what an inquirer already knows about God. Do non-Christians have any knowledge of the true God? If so, what do they know? In what ways does that knowledge manifest itself?

GOOD TEACHING PROCEEDS from the known to the unknown. So a good apologist will want to have some idea of what an inquirer already knows about God. Do non-Christians have any knowledge of the true God? If so, what do they know? In what ways does that knowledge manifest itself?

Scripture says that unbelievers know God (Rom. 1:21), but it also says that they do not know him (1 Cor. 2:14; 15:34; 1 Thess. 4:5; 2 Thess. 1:8; cf. 2 Tim. 3:7; Titus 1:16; 1 John 4:8). Evidently, then, we must make some distinctions, for in some sense or senses, knowledge of God is universal, and otherwise it is not.

Romans 1:18–32 is the classic text on this question. Here Paul stresses the clarity of God's revelation to the unrighteous. God reveals his wrath to them (v. 18), and makes truth about himself "plain to them" (v. 19), "clearly perceived" (v. 20). That revealed truth includes his "eternal power and divine nature" (v. 20). It also contains moral content, the knowledge of "God's decree that those who practice [wicked] things deserve to die" (v. 32). Significantly, the text does not state that this revelation in nature communicates the way of salvation. Paul evidently believes that this additional content must come through the preaching of the gospel (10:13–17). Thus, he warrants the traditional theological distinction between general revelation (God's revelation of himself through the created world) and special revelation (his revelation through prophecy, preaching, and Scripture).

The knowledge given by general revelation is not only a knowledge *about* God, a knowledge of propositions. It is a knowledge of God himself, a *personal* knowledge. For Paul says not only that the wicked have information about God, but that "they knew God" (Rom. 1:21).

The knowledge given by general revelation is not only a knowledge about God, a knowledge of propositions. It is a knowledge of God himself, a personal *knowledge. For Paul says not only that the wicked have information about God, but that "they knew God" (Rom. 1:21).*

Nevertheless, according to Paul, the wicked do not make proper use of this revealed knowledge. Rather, they "by their unrighteousness suppress the truth" (Rom. 1:18). He continues, "Although they knew God, they did not honor him as God or give thanks to him, but they became futile in their thinking, and their foolish hearts were darkened. Claiming to be wise, they became fools" (vv. 21–22). Paul describes their foolishness as idolatry (vv. 22–23). In his view, idolatry is not an innocent search for the divine or the result of honest ignorance. It is, rather, willfully and culpably turning away from clear revelation of the true God. So it is "exchang[ing] the glory of the immortal God for images" (v. 23), exchanging "the truth about God for a lie" (v. 25).

Because the wicked willfully turned from God's clear revelation, God "gave them up" (Rom. 1:24, 26, 28) to serious sin, particularly sexual. Even then, however, the original clear revelation continues to function, for it serves as a standard of judgment. As Paul says, it leaves them "without excuse" (v. 20).

From this passage, we can understand the senses in which the unregenerate do and do not know God. They know God as they are confronted by his revelation. Other Scriptures tell us that this revelation is found not only in the natural world, but in their own persons, for we are all made in God's image (Gen. 1:27). So God's revelation is inescapable. But apart from the special revelation and saving grace of God, people exchange this truth for lies and engage in such wickedness that they become enemies of God, not friends.

The unregenerate know God as they are confronted by his revelation. Other Scriptures tell us that this revelation is found not only in the natural world, but in their own persons, for we are all made in God's image (Gen. 1:27). So God's revelation is inescapable.

It is the grace of God that turns this enmity into friendship, so that people come to know God in a higher sense than the knowledge of Romans 1:21. This is the knowledge of God that Jesus equates with eternal life in John 17:3. Many other passages, too, describe various kinds of knowledge that presuppose saving grace (e.g., Rom. 15:14; 1 Cor. 1:5; 2:12; 2 Cor. 2:14; 4:6; 6:6; 8:7; Eph. 1:17; Phil. 1:9; 3:8, 10; Col. 1:10; 1 Tim. 2:4; 2 Tim. 1:12; Heb. 8:11; 2 Peter 3:18; 1 John 2:3–5, 13, 20–21; 3:14, 19, 24; 4:2, 4, 6, 7, 13, 16; 5:2, 13, 19–20; 2 John 1:1). The unregenerate do not have this kind of knowledge. In this sense we should understand the passages saying that they do not know God.

There have been two different accounts of unregenerate knowledge of God in the theological traditions. One, advocated by Thomas Aquinas, says that this knowledge comes through man's natural reason. In Aquinas's view, natural reason is sufficient to accomplish our earthly happiness, but a higher, supernatural knowledge is required for eternal life. Natural reason operates apart from divine revelation, but supernatural knowledge is based on revelation, which functions as a supplement to what we know naturally.

Reformed theologians have objected to this view that God never intended our natural reason to function autonomously, or apart from his revelation. For one thing. all human knowledge comes through revelation, either general or special or both.

Reformed theologians have objected to this view that God never intended our natural reason to function autonomously, or apart from his revelation. For one thing. all human knowledge comes through revelation, either general or special or both. Further, even before the fall, God supplemented Adam's natural knowledge with verbal revelation. And after the fall, our natural knowledge requires both general and special revelation for its proper functioning. Left to our own devices, as Romans 1 teaches, we suppress and distort the truth of general revelation. Only God's grace, operating through the gospel given in special revelation, can enable us to see general revelation rightly. So Calvin spoke of special revelation as the "spectacles" by which we understand general revelation.

Calvinists, therefore, have been more pessimistic than Aquinas about the unbeliever's knowledge of God. Aquinas regarded the pagan Aristotle as a paradigm of natural reason, and he followed Aristotle closely in his proofs for God and in other philosophical and theological matters. Followers of Calvin, however, have generally not thought that we can learn much about God from non-Christians. And since the knowledge of God is integral to all human knowledge, some Calvinists, such as Abraham Kuyper and Cornelius Van Til, have argued that non-Christian thought is radically distorted even in relatively nontheological subject matter. Yet the Reformed tradition (with significant exceptions) has generally also accepted the doctrine of *common grace*, in which God restrains non-Christians from the full implications of their rebellion against him and thus preserves in them some inclination toward civic virtue and true beliefs.

On the Reformed view, unregenerate knowledge of God needs more than supplementation. It needs a radical reorientation. The work of the apologist is not merely to add information to what the unbeliever already knows. It is, rather, to "take every thought captive to obey Christ" (2 Cor. 10:5).

On the Reformed view, unregenerate knowledge of God needs more than supplementation. It needs a radical reorientation. The work of the apologist is not merely to add information to what the unbeliever already knows. It is, rather, to "take every thought captive to obey Christ" (2 Cor. 10:5). This will involve questioning the unbeliever's basic worldview, the most basic presuppositions of his thinking. So Reformed presuppositional apologists have spoken of an *antithesis* between believing and unbelieving thought, corresponding to the biblical distinction between God's wisdom and the world's foolishness. But it has been difficult for them to reconcile and balance their doctrine of antithesis with the doctrine of common grace. If there is such an antithesis, so that the non-Christian opposes the truth of God at every point, how can we ascribe to the non-Christian any knowledge at all?

I have tried to address this question in my book *CVT*. To summarize, agreements between believers and unbelievers are never perfect agreements; they are always agreements with a difference. Believer and unbeliever can agree that the sky is blue, but the unbeliever tries to see this fact as a product of matter, energy, and chance. Christian and Pharisee may agree that God requires Sabbath observance, but the Pharisee will fail to see the mercy of God in the commandment and therefore the appropriateness of healing. Non-Christians, in other words, might agree with Christians on various matters, but seen as a whole their understanding of God is seriously distorted, and apologists must deal with that distortion.

Non-Christians . . . might agree with Christians on various matters, but seen as a whole their understanding of God is seriously distorted, and apologists must deal with that distortion.

The remainder of this article will consider three questions about unregenerate knowledge of God: (1) How is it obtained? (2) How is it suppressed? (3) In what ways does it continue to function, despite its suppression?

(1) Romans 1 tells us that this knowledge is gained from God's revelation "in the things that have been made," that is, the entire created world, including human beings themselves. But how do people obtain this knowledge from creation? Some apologists have thought that this knowledge comes about through rational activity, particularly through theistic proofs and evidences. But this understanding would limit the knowledge of Romans 1 only to those competent to understand and be persuaded by those arguments and evidences. Paul, however, sees this knowledge as universal. Romans 1 begins the argument that leads into Romans 3:10–20, 23, to the conclusion that all have sinned and stand in need of God's grace. So the knowledge of Romans 1 renders all human beings inexcusable (v. 20).

Evidently we discern the general revelation of God by some form of intuition, an intuition that some are able to articulate and defend by proofs and evidences, but that does not depend on them.

If that knowledge were less than universal, the conclusion of Romans 3 would not follow from it.

So the knowledge of God by creation evidently reaches all, even those who are not competent to formulate or evaluate proofs and evidences. Evidently we discern the general revelation of God by some form of intuition, an intuition that some are able to articulate and defend by proofs and evidences, but that does not depend on them. Alvin Plantinga says that we come to believe in God when our rational faculties are operating as God intended, and when they are placed in an environment naturally conducive to the formation of theistic belief. No better explanation of the process has been offered to date.

The difference between unregenerate and regenerate knowledge of God may be described as ethical. The unregenerate represses his knowledge of God by disobeying God. This disobedience could lead in some cases to psychological repression, or explicit atheism, but it does not always.

(2) How do people suppress the truth of this revelation? It is tempting to think of *suppression* in psychological terms, as when someone relegates an unwelcome truth to his subconscious or unconscious. But that is not the biblical picture. The enemies of God in the Bible, from the Egyptians (Ex. 14:4), to the Pharisees, to Satan himself, often acknowledge consciously the existence of God. In Romans 1, the suppression is seen in idolatrous worship and illicit sexual behavior. The unregenerate deny their knowledge of God by their ethical rebellion.

When Scripture describes the knowledge of God that comes by grace, that knowledge is always accompanied by obedience and holiness. John says, "And by this we know that we have come to know him, if we keep his commandments" (1 John 2:3). Thus, Scripture closely relates epistemology to ethics.

So the difference between unregenerate and regenerate knowledge of God may be described as ethical. The unregenerate represses his knowledge of God by disobeying God. This disobedience could lead in some cases to psychological repression, or explicit atheism, but it does not always. The apologist should recognize, therefore, that the unbeliever's problem is primarily ethical, not intellectual. He rejects the truth because he disobeys God's ethical standards, not the other way around.

This ethical rebellion does, however, always inject an element of irrationality into the thinking of the unregenerate. To know God and his commandments, even his "eternal power" (Rom. 1:20), and yet to rebel against him, is supremely futile. In this sense, unbelief is foolishness (Ps. 14:1). Consider Satan, who knows God in some respects better than we do, yet who seeks to replace God on the throne. In some ways, Satan is highly intelligent and knowledgeable. But in the most important sense, he is supremely irrational. It is important for the apologist to understand that in the final analysis, the position of the non-Christian is like this: often intellectually impressive, but at a deeper level ludicrous.

The non-Christian's suppression of the truth is never complete. He can never completely eradicate the truth from his consciousness. If he could, he could not live at all. For this is God's world, and all the world's structure, order, and meaning is God's work.

(3) The non-Christian's suppression of the truth is never complete. He can never completely eradicate the truth from his consciousness. If he could, he could not live at all. For this is God's world, and all the world's structure, order, and meaning is God's work. Further, as we have seen, God's common grace restrains the non-Christian's distortions of the truth. So even Satan uses the truth for his own purpose, and there are some unregenerate human beings, such as the Pharisees, who are relatively orthodox.

Therefore, we can expect the unbeliever's knowledge of God to bubble up at times through his consciousness, despite his attempts to repress that knowledge. How does that happen? In several ways: (a) Unbelievers might sometimes display explicitly quite a lot of knowledge of the true God, as the Pharisees did. (b) The non-Christian must assume that the world is not a chaos, but that it is orderly and relatively predictable, even though this assumption in turn presupposes God. (c) In ethics, non-Christians often reveal a knowledge of God's law. Apologists such as C. S. Lewis and J. Budziszewski have pointed out that principles such as "Play fair," "Don't murder," "Be faithful to your spouse," and "Take care of your family" are universally recognized. Although many people violate these principles, they show that they know them by making excuses or rationalizations, and by accusing others of violating the same principles.

Although some theorize that moral principles are mere feelings, conventions, or instincts, no one really believes that, especially when injustice is done to him. When someone treats him unfairly, he regards that unfairness as an objective wrong.

In other words, they treat the moral law as law. Although some theorize that moral principles are mere feelings, conventions, or instincts, no one really believes that, especially when injustice is done to him. When someone treats him unfairly, he regards that unfairness as an objective wrong. But objective wrongs cannot be derived from mere instincts, feelings, conventions, evolutionary defense mechanisms, and the like. Moral rights and wrongs are based on personal relationships, specifically relationships of allegiance and love. And that means that absolute moral standards must be derived from an absolute person. So develops the "moral argument for the existence of God." But that argument is based on conscience, a sense of objective right and wrong that is universal, that exists even in those who do not formulate it as an argument. Budziszewski also points out the terrible consequences that result from violating one's conscience. Apologists should draw on the data of the unbeliever's conscience to lead him to that greater knowledge of God, which is eternal life in Christ.

Moral rights and wrongs are based on personal relationships, specifically relationships of allegiance and love. And that means that absolute moral standards must be derived from an absolute person. So develops the "moral argument for the existence of God."

BIBLIOGRAPHY

Budziszewski, J. *The Revenge of Conscience.* Dallas: Spence Publishing, 1999.

———. *What We Can't Not Know.* Dallas: Spence Publishing, 2003.

Frame, John M. *Apologetics to the Glory of God.* Phillipsburg, NJ: P&R Publishing, 1994. Develops the moral argument for God's existence.

———. *Cornelius Van Til: An Analysis of His Thought.* Phillipsburg, NJ: P&R Publishing, 1995. See chapters 15 and 16 on the antithesis between believing and unbelieving knowledge of God.

———. *The Doctrine of the Knowledge of God.* Phillipsburg, NJ: Presbyterian and Reformed, 1987. Seeks to show that epistemology can be regarded as a branch of ethics, showing why the two are so closely united in Scripture.

Lewis, C. S. *Mere Christianity.* London: Bles, 1952.

Plantinga, Alvin. *Warranted Christian Belief.* New York: Oxford University Press, 2000.

Sproul, R. C. *If There's a God, Why Are There Atheists?* Wheaton, IL: Tyndale, 1988. A good treatment of the psychology of atheism according to Romans 1.

APPENDIX H

"GOD AND BIBLICAL LANGUAGE: TRANSCENDENCE AND IMMANENCE"

Originally published in John W. Montgomery, ed., *God's Inerrant Word* (Grand Rapids: Bethany House Publishers [a division of Baker Publishing Group], 1974), 159–77. Used by permission. Reprinted as Appendix E in John M. Frame, *The Doctrine of the Word of God*, A Theology of Lordship (Phillipsburg, NJ: P&R Publishing, 2010), 422–38. We saw in chapter 12 that some philosophers of language analysis have dismissed belief in God on the ground that statements about him are not verifiable or falsifiable, and therefore convey no *cognitive meaning*. This article discusses the matter in more detail than in chapter 12. It also discusses Karl Barth's view of revelation, supplementing my discussion in chapter 10. (For stylistic purposes, this appendix has been copyedited for inclusion in this volume.)

ONE OF THE MOST PERSUASIVE and frequent contemporary objections to the orthodox view of biblical authority goes like this: the Bible cannot be the Word of God because no human language can be the Word of God. On this view, not only the Bible but human language *in general* is an unfit vehicle—unfit to infallibly convey a message from God to man.

One of the most persuasive and frequent contemporary objections to the orthodox view of biblical authority goes like this: the Bible cannot be the Word of God because no human language can be the Word of God.

This objection takes various forms, three of which I will discuss.

1. Some linguists and philosophers of language have suggested that language is never completely true—that the undeniable discrepancy that always exists between symbol and reality (the word *desk* is not a desk, for instance) injects falsehood into every utterance. This contention is sometimes buttressed by the further assertion that all language is metaphorical, figurative, and thus can never convey the "literal"

truth. There is, however, something odd about any view that attributes falsehood to all language. For one thing, the assertion that "all sentences are false" is self-refuting if taken literally; and if we don't take it literally, what does it mean? Perhaps the real point is that language never conveys the "*whole* truth"—that it never conveys the truth with absolute precision or absolute comprehensiveness. But consider the following: (a) Some sentences are, in one sense, perfectly precise and comprehensive. Take "Washington is the capital of the United States"; could that fact be stated more precisely? more comprehensively? (b) Of course, even the aforementioned sentence is not comprehensive in the sense of "saying everything there is to say" about Washington and the United States. But no human being ever *tries* to say all that. Nor does the Bible claim to say "everything" about God. The claim to infallibility does not entail a claim to comprehensiveness in this sense. And where no claim to comprehensiveness is made, lack of comprehensiveness does not refute infallibility. (c) Nor is imprecision necessarily a fault. "Pittsburgh is about three hundred miles from Philadelphia" is imprecise in a sense, but it is a perfectly good sentence and is in no usual sense untrue. An "infallible" book might contain many imprecise-but-true statements of this sort. Granting, then, that there is a sense in which language never conveys the "whole truth," we need not renounce on that account any element of the orthodox view of biblical authority.

The claim to infallibility does not entail a claim to comprehensiveness in this sense. And where no claim to comprehensiveness is made, lack of comprehensiveness does not refute infallibility.

An "infallible" book might contain many imprecise-but-true statements of this sort. Granting, then, that there is a sense in which language never conveys the "whole truth," we need not renounce on that account any element of the orthodox view of biblical authority.

More might be said about this first form of the objection that we are discussing—its reliance on the discredited referential theory of meaning, its strangely generalized concept of *metaphor*, its dubious presuppositions about the origin and development of language, its ultimate theological roots. These topics, however, have been adequately discussed elsewhere,[1] and my own interests and aptitudes demand that I press on immediately to other aspects of the problem. The following discussion will raise some basic issues that I trust will shed further light on this first area of concern.

2. If the first form of our objection was raised primarily by linguists, philosophers of language, and their entourage, the second form (though similarly focused on language) arises out of broader epistemological and metaphysical concerns. In the 1920s and 1930s, the philosophy of logical positivism attempted to divide all philosophically important language into three categories: (a) tautologies ("A book is a book"; "Either it is raining or it is not raining"), (b) contradictions ("It is raining and it is not raining"; "The table is square and it is not square"), and (c) assertions of empirical fact ("There is a bird on the roof"; "The

1. One helpful discussion of these matters from an orthodox Christian perspective can be found in Gordon H. Clark, *Religion, Reason and Revelation* (Philadelphia: Presbyterian and Reformed, 1961), 111–50.

President has put price controls on beef"). Tautologies, on this view, were said to be true purely by virtue of the meanings of the terms, and contradictions false on the same account. Empirical assertions could be either true or false, and their truth or falsity was said to be ascertainable by something like the methods of natural science. When someone claims to state a fact, but upon examination it turns out that this "fact" cannot be verified or falsified by such methods, then, said the positivists, this utterance is not a statement of fact at all; it is not an "empirical assertion," so it is neither true nor false. Such an unverifiable utterance may have a use as poetry, expression of feeling, or the like, but it does not state any fact about the world; it is (to use the positivists' technical term) "cognitively meaningless"; it does not measure up to the "verification criterion of meaning." On such grounds, the positivists dismissed metaphysical statements ("Mind is the absolute coming to self-consciousness") and theological statements ("God is love") as cognitively meaningless. Ethical statements ("Stealing is wrong") were also seen not as statements of fact but as expressions of attitude, commands, or some other noninformative type of language.[2]

The positivists dismissed metaphysical statements ("Mind is the absolute coming to self-consciousness") and theological statements ("God is love") as cognitively meaningless.

As a general theory of meaningfulness, logical positivism was too crude to last very long. Disputes quickly arose over what methods of verification were to be tolerated, how conclusive the verification or falsification must be, and other matters too technical to discuss here. Many felt that the whole project was to some extent a rationalization of prejudice—not an objective analysis of what constitutes "meaningfulness," but an attempt to get rid of language distasteful to various philosophers by constructing a "principle" arbitrarily designed for that purpose.[3]

No thinker of any consequence today subscribes to the *verification principle* as a general criterion of meaningfulness. One aspect of the positivists' concern, however, is very much with us. Although we do not buy the whole logical-positivist theory, many of us are quite impressed with the basic notion that *a fact ought to make a difference*. This concern is vividly presented in the oft-quoted parable of Antony Flew:

No thinker of any consequence today subscribes to the verification principle *as a general criterion of meaningfulness. . . . Although we do not buy the whole logical-positivist theory, many of us are quite impressed with the basic notion that* a fact ought to make a difference.

> Once upon a time two explorers came upon a clearing in the jungle. In the clearing were growing many flowers and many

2. The classical exposition of logical positivism in the English language is A. J. Ayer, *Language, Truth and Logic* (New York: Dover, 1946).

3. One of the sharpest debates was over the status of the verification principle itself. Surely it was not to be regarded as a tautology, but it did not seem to be "verifiable" either in any quasi-scientific sense. Was it then to be dismissed as "cognitively meaningless"? Ayer himself (see previous note) came to the view that the verification principle was a "convention" (see his introduction to the anthology *Logical Positivism* [Glencoe, IL: Free Press, 1959], 15). He maintained that this convention had some basis in ordinary usage, but admitted that it went beyond ordinary usage in crucial respects.

> weeds. One explorer says, "Some gardener must tend this plot." So they pitch their tents and set a watch. No gardener is ever seen. "But perhaps he is an invisible gardener." So they set up a barbed-wire fence. They electrify it. They patrol with bloodhounds. (For they remember how H. G. Wells's *The Invisible Man* could be both smelt and touched though he could not be seen.) But no shrieks ever suggest that some intruder has received a shock. No movements of the wire ever betray an invisible climber. The bloodhounds never give cry. Yet still the Believer is not convinced. "But there is a gardener, invisible, intangible, insensible to electric shocks, a gardener who has no scent and makes no sound, a gardener who comes secretly to look after the garden which he loves." At last the Sceptic despairs, "But what remains of your original assertion? Just how does what you call an invisible, intangible, eternally elusive gardener differ from an imaginary gardener or even from no gardener at all?"[4]

Anthony Flew

If there is *no difference* between "invisible gardener" and "no gardener," then surely the dispute between the Believer and the Sceptic is not about facts. If there is no difference, then talk of an "invisible gardener" may be a useful way of expressing an attitude toward the world, but it cannot make any empirical assertion about the world. Flew is not asking the Believer to verify his view in some quasi-scientific way (although one suspects that this is what would make him most happy); he is simply asking him to state what *difference* his belief makes.

As we might suspect, Flew thinks that much language about God makes "no difference." Believers say that "God is love," even though the world is full of cruelty and hatred. How does such a God differ from a devil or from no God at all?

As we might suspect, Flew thinks that much language about God makes "no difference." Believers say that "God is love," even though the world is full of cruelty and hatred. How does such a God differ from a devil or from no God at all? And if "God is love" makes no difference, how can it be a fact? How can it be, as the positivists liked to say, "cognitively meaningful"?

Flew does not suggest that *all* religious language succumbs to this difficulty, or even that all language about God is in jeopardy. He seems to be thinking mainly of what "often" happens in the thought of "sophisticated religious people."[5] Still, his knife cuts deep. Can any Christian believer offer a straightforward answer to Flew's concluding question, "What would have to occur or to have occurred to constitute for you a

4. Antony Flew et al., "Theology and Falsification," in *New Essays in Philosophical Theology*, ed. Antony Flew and Alasdair C. MacIntyre (London: SCM Press, 1955), 96. [**Editor's Note:** As the title of Antony Flew's 2008 book *There Is a God: How the World's Most Notorious Atheist Changed His Mind* (New York: HarperOne, 2008) suggests, since the publication of his article "Theology and Falsification" (1955), Flew (d. 2010) changed from championing atheism to advocating deism.]

5. Flew et al., "Theology and Falsification," 98.

disproof of the love of, or of the existence of, God?"[6] Our first impulse is to say with the apostle Paul, "If Christ be not risen, then is our preaching vain, and your faith is also vain."[7] The resurrection shows that God does make a difference! Disprove the resurrection, and you disprove God. The resurrection (but of course, not only the resurrection!) demonstrates the great difference between God and no-God.

But push the argument back another step: what would have to occur or to have occurred to constitute for you a disproof of the *resurrection*? Do we have a clear idea of how the resurrection may be falsified? Paul appeals to witnesses,[8] but the witnesses are dead. What if a collection of manuscripts were unearthed containing refutations of the Christian message by first-century Palestinian Jews? And what if these manuscripts contained elaborate critiques of the Pauline claim in 1 Corinthians 15, critiques backed up with massive documentation, interviews with alleged witnesses, and so on? And then: what if the twenty-five most important NT scholars claimed on the basis of this discovery that belief in the physical resurrection of Christ was untenable? Would that be sufficient to destroy our faith in the resurrection? It would be hard to imagine any stronger sort of "falsification" for any event of past history. And I don't doubt that many would be swayed by it. But many would not be. I for one would entertain all sorts of questions about the biases of these documents and those of the scholars who interpreted them. I would want to check out the whole question myself before conceding the point of doctrine. And what if I did check it out and found no way of refuting the antiresurrection position? Would that constitute a disproof? Not for me, and I think not for very many other professing Christians. We all know how abstruse scholarly argument can be; there are so many things that can go wrong. In such a situation, it is not difficult to say, "Well, I can't prove the scholars wrong, but they may be wrong nonetheless." And if the love of Christ has become precious to me, and if I have been strongly convinced that the Bible is his Word, I am more likely to believe what he says in 1 Corinthians 15 than to believe what a lot of scholars say on the basis of extrabiblical evidence. Could we *ever* be persuaded that the resurrection was a hoax? Perhaps—but such a change would be more than a change in opinion; it would be a loss of faith. In terms of Scripture, such a change would be a yielding to temptation. For our God calls us to believe his Word even when the evidence appears against it. Sarah will bear a son, even though she is ninety and her husband is a hundred![9] God is just, even

The resurrection shows that God does make a difference! Disprove the resurrection, and you disprove God. The resurrection (but of course, not only the resurrection!) demonstrates the great difference between God and no-God.

Could we ever *be persuaded that the resurrection was a hoax? Perhaps—but such a change would be more than a change in opinion; it would be a loss of faith.*

6. Ibid., 99.

7. 1 Cor. 15:14. All quotations of Scripture in this appendix are from the KJV.

8. 1 Cor. 15:5–8.

9. Gen. 17:16–17.

though righteous Job must suffer! The heroes of the faith believed the Word of God *without* the corroboration of other evidence: they walked by faith, not by sight.[10] As long as we remain faithful, God's Word takes precedence over other evidence.

God-language resists falsification. It is difficult to say what would refute a faith assertion, for faith requires us to resist all temptation to doubt.

Flew's objection, therefore, is not to be lightly dismissed. There is a sense in which not only the language of "sophisticated religious people" but even the language of simple Christian believers fails to measure up to his challenge. God-language *resists* falsification. It is difficult to say what would refute a faith assertion, for faith requires us to resist all temptation to doubt. Within the faith language, no terms can be specified for renouncing faith assertions, for faith *excludes*, *prohibits*, such renouncement.

Does this, then, mean that the resurrection "makes no difference"? We hope not! We certainly want to say that it *does* make a difference. Yet we find it difficult to say what would refute our belief in the resurrection. We find it difficult to conceive of any state of affairs in which we would abandon our belief. We find it difficult to say what the resurrection rules out. And thus we find it difficult to state *what difference it makes*. Perhaps, then, talk of the resurrection does not really concern any empirical fact. Perhaps all God talk is cognitively meaningless. And perhaps, then, God cannot be spoken of at all in human language. And if that is true, all talk of Scripture as the Word of God is clearly nonsense.

The third form of our objection is more distinctively theological. Karl Barth, for example, suggests on theological grounds that human language is unfit to convey truth about God.

This, then, is the second form of the objection that I stated at the beginning of the paper, the second way in which human language is said to be disqualified as a medium of divine speech. Let us briefly examine the third form of the objection before I present my response:

3. The third form of our objection is more distinctively theological. Karl Barth, for example, suggests on theological grounds that human language is unfit to convey truth about God:

> The pictures in which we view God, the thoughts in which we think Him, the words with which we can define Him, are in themselves unfitted to this object and thus inappropriate to express and affirm the knowledge of Him.[11]
>
> The Bible, further is not itself and in itself God's past revelation, but by becoming God's Word it attests God's past revelation and is God's past revelation in the form of attestation. . . .

10. Heb. 11. The contrast between faith and sight alludes to 2 Corinthians 5:7.

11. Karl Barth, *Church Dogmatics*, vol. 2, *The Doctrine of God*, ed. G. W. Bromiley and T. F. Torrance, trans. T. H. L. Parker, W. B. Johnston, H. Knight, and J. L. M. Haire (New York: Scribner, 1957), 1:188.

> Attestation is, therefore, the service of this something else, in which the witness answers for the truth of this something else.[12]

This sort of point, which is very common in twentieth-century theology, is essentially a religious appeal to the divine transcendence. God is the Lord, the Creator, the Redeemer. To him belong all praise and glory. How can any human language ever be "fitted" to the conveyance of his Word? Surely human language, like everything else human and finite, can be only a servant, confessing its own unfitness, its own inadequacy. The Bible cannot *be* revelation; it can only *serve* revelation. To claim anything more for human language, for the Bible, is to dishonor God—to elevate something finite and human to divine status. To claim anything more is to think of revelation "in abstraction from" God himself and from Jesus Christ.[13] It is not just a mistake; it is an impiety.

This sort of point, which is very common in twentieth-century theology, is essentially a religious appeal to the divine transcendence. God is the Lord, the Creator, the Redeemer. To him belong all praise and glory. How can any human language ever be "fitted" to the conveyance of his Word?

At the same time, Barth does insist that the words of revelation have an importance:

> Thus God reveals Himself in propositions by means of language, and human language at that, to the effect that from time to time such and such a word, spoken by the prophets and apostles and proclaimed in the Church, becomes His Word. Thus the personality of the Word of God is not to be played off against its verbal character and spirituality.
>
> The personification of the concept of the Word of God . . . does not signify any lessening of its verbal character.[14]

The words are still unfit; they are not themselves revelation; they are not necessarily true themselves, but they witness to the truth of "something else." Nevertheless, the words are important, because from time to time God may use them to communicate with man. Even when they are false, they are God's instruments. God uses them, however, not as true propositional representations of his message, but as the instruments for an encounter that no human language is fit to describe.

Barth, therefore, like Flew, argues that God cannot be truly spoken of in human language. Here, it would seem, the resemblance between Barth and Flew ceases, for Barth argues "from above," Flew "from below." Barth argues that God is too great for language; Flew argues that language cannot speak meaningfully of God. But are the two positions really that far apart? Thomas McPherson suggests that an alliance

Barth, therefore, like Flew, argues that God cannot be truly spoken of in human language. . . . Barth argues "from above," Flew "from below." Barth argues that God is too great for language; Flew argues that language cannot speak meaningfully of God.

12. Karl Barth, *Church Dogmatics*, vol. 1, *The Doctrine of the Word of God*, ed. G. W. Bromiley and T. F. Torrance, trans. G. T. Thomson (New York: Scribner, 1936), 1:125.

13. Ibid., 1:155ff.

14. Ibid., 1:156f.

is possible between the logical-positivist philosophers and theologians such as Rudolph Otto (McPherson might also have cited Karl Barth in this connection) who stress the transcendence of God over language:

> Perhaps positivistic philosophy has done a service to religion. By showing, in their own way, the absurdity of what theologians try to utter, positivists have helped to suggest that religion belongs to the sphere of the unutterable. And this may be true. And it is what Otto, too, in his way, wanted to point out. Positivists may be the enemies of theology, but the friends of religion.[15]

In positivism and in these modern theologies, God belongs to the sphere of the unutterable, and human language (when "cognitively meaningful") belongs to the sphere of the humanly verifiable.

Enemies of *some* theology—not of Otto's theology, nor of Barth's, nor of Buber's (to which McPherson refers in a footnote), nor (I would judge) of the broad tradition of dialectical and existential theologies of the twentieth century. In positivism and in these modern theologies, God belongs to the sphere of the unutterable, and human language (when "cognitively meaningful") belongs to the sphere of the humanly verifiable. Let us then consider the Flew problem and the Barth problem as one.

RESPONSE

Religious language is "odd" in a great number of ways. Not only does it tend to resist falsification, as Flew has pointed out, it also tends to claim certainty for itself, as opposed to mere possibility or probability. It also tends to be connected with moral *predicates—as if disbelief in it were a* sin*, rather than a mere mistake.*

Religious language is "odd" in a great number of ways. Not only does it tend to resist falsification, as Flew has pointed out, it also tends to claim certainty for itself, as opposed to mere possibility or probability.[16] It also tends to be connected with *moral* predicates—as if disbelief in it were a *sin*, rather than a mere mistake.[17] It is frequently spoken with great passion; with Kierkegaard, we tend to be suspicious of allegedly religious language that seems detached or uncommitted.

On the other hand, religious language is in some respects very "ordinary," very similar to other language. It is not a technical, academic language like that of physics or philosophy; it is the language of ordinary people. It is not restricted to some limited and distinctive compartment

15. Thomas McPherson, "Religion as the Inexpressible," in *New Essays in Philosophical Theology*, ed. Antony Flew and Alasdair C. MacIntyre (London: SCM Press, 1955), 140f. In a footnote, McPherson notes a similar view in Martin Buber, *I and Thou*, trans. Ronald Gregor Smith, 2nd ed. (New York: Scribner, 1958).

16. Note Ludwig Wittgenstein's interesting discussion of this point in *Lectures and Conversations on Aesthetics, Psychology, and Religious Belief*, ed. Cyril Barrett, comp. from notes by Yorick Smythies, Rush Rhees, and James Taylor (Oxford: Blackwell, 1966), 53–59. Wittgenstein seems to make the extreme suggestion that religious belief is *never* "probable" in character. Wittgenstein obviously never spent much time around seminary students and academic theologians.

17. Cf. ibid., 59.

of human life; rather, it enters into all human activities and concerns. We pray for the healing of a loved one, for help in a business crisis; we seek to eat and drink to the glory of God.[18] We believe that our faith "makes a difference" in the real world, that God can enter into all the affairs of our life and make his presence felt. In this respect, the "action of God in history" is like the action of *anyone* in history. God can change things, can make them different. And what he does does not occur unless he chooses to do it. God makes a difference, and in that sense he is *verifiable*—much as the existence of any other person is verifiable (or so, at least, it appears to the simple believer!). Few religious people would claim that their faith is a blind leap in the dark. They have "reasons for faith." These reasons might be the technical theistic arguments of the philosophers, or simply the childlike appeal to experience—"He lives within my heart." One who really believes (as opposed to one who merely drifts along in a religious tradition) believes for a *reason*, because he thinks God has somehow made his presence felt, because God now *makes a difference*—to him.

Religious language, then, is "odd" and it is "ordinary." If an analysis of religious language is to be adequate, it must take both *features into account, not just one of them.*

Religious language, then, is "odd" and it is "ordinary." If an analysis of religious language is to be adequate, it must take *both* features into account, not just one of them. Flew and Barth do not reflect very much on the "ordinariness" of religious language. They seem to imply that it is a sort of delusion, for it makes a claim to verifiability that cannot upon analysis be sustained, or because it betrays a spirit of human pride, bringing God down to man's level. For Barth at least, we gather that the "ordinariness" of religious language is a mark of its *humanity*, a mark of its *unfitness* to convey the word of God. There is, however, another interpretation of the data—one that does not write off the "ordinariness" of religious language as a delusion, one that accounts both for the verifiability of religious statements and for their tendency to resist verification, one that illumines the ways in which Scripture itself speaks of God.

Religious language is language of basic conviction. *It is the language by which we state, invoke, honor, and advocate (and otherwise "bring to bear") those things of which we are most certain, those things that are most important to us, those things that we will cling to even though we must lose all else.*

Religious language is language of *basic conviction*. It is the language by which we state, invoke, honor, and advocate (and otherwise "bring to bear") those things of which we are most certain, those things that are most important to us, those things that we will cling to even though we must lose all else. Not all language of basic conviction is religious in the usual sense. Many people who consider themselves irreligious have basic convictions of some sort. In fact, it may well be disputed whether anyone can avoid having *some* basic conviction—whether it be a faith in reason, in material success, in a philosophical absolute, or in a god. But all language that is religious in the usual sense is language of basic conviction.

18. 1 Cor. 10:31.

Someone might object that for many people their religion is *not* their most basic commitment. A man might mumble through the church liturgy every Sunday while devoting his existence almost exclusively to acquiring political power. For him, surely, the liturgy does not express his "basic commitment." True, but that is because there is something wrong. We call such a man a hypocrite, for the liturgy is *intended* to express basic conviction, and our fanatical politician utters the words deceitfully. He does not *really* "believe in God, the Father almighty" in the sense of biblical faith, though he says he does. His real faith is in something else. The man is a liar. But his lying use of the language does not change the meaning of it, which is to confess true faith in God.

All of us have basic convictions, unless possibly we are just confused. Positivists do, too—and Barthians. And insofar as we try to be consistent, we try to bring all of life and thought into accord with our basic conviction.[19] Nothing inconsistent with that conviction is to be tolerated. An inconsistency of that sort amounts to a divided loyalty, a confusion of life direction. Most of us, at least, try to avoid such confusion. The conviction becomes the paradigm of reality, of truth, and of right, to which all other examples of reality, truth, and right must measure up. As such, it is the cornerstone of our metaphysics, epistemology, and ethics. It is not, be it noted, the *only* factor in the development of a system of thought. Two people may have virtually identical basic commitments while differing greatly in their systems of thought. The two will both try to develop systems according to their common presupposition, but because of differences in experience, ability, secondary commitments, and the like, they may seek such consistency in opposite directions. But though the basic commitment is not the only factor in the development of thought (and life), it is (by definition) the most important factor.

All of us have basic convictions, unless possibly we are just confused. Positivists do, too—and Barthians. And insofar as we try to be consistent, we try to bring all of life and thought into accord with our basic conviction. Nothing inconsistent with that conviction is to be tolerated.

The conviction becomes the paradigm of reality, of truth, and of right, to which all other examples of reality, truth, and right must measure up. As such, it is the cornerstone of our metaphysics, epistemology, and ethics.

19. Some readers might be helped here by the observation that there are many different degrees of "basicness" among our convictions. All our convictions govern life to some degree. When someone disagrees with one of our opinions, we naturally tend to try to defend it—either to refute our opponent's argument or to show that his position is compatible with ours. The learning process is such that we always try to interpret new knowledge in such a way as to minimize disturbance to past opinions. Some opinions we hold more tenaciously than others. It is fairly easy to convince me that I am wrong about, say, the team batting average of the Pittsburgh Pirates. It is much more difficult to persuade me that the earth is flat. In the first instance, citation of one presumably competent authority is enough. In the second instance, the intrinsic unlikelihood of a flat earth would bring into question the competence of any "presumably competent authority" who held such a position. Nevertheless, if there were a full-scale revolution among scientists over systems of measurement, and cogent reasons could be given for reverting to a flat-earth view, I might be persuaded to reconsider. Some convictions, then, we relinquish less easily than others, and the "most basic convictions" (which we focus on in the text of the article) are relinquished least easily of all. In fact, we never relinquish those unless at the same time we change our basic concept of rationality.

We have suggested that religious language is a subdivision of "basic-commitment language." The next point is that basic-commitment language in general displays the same kinds of "oddness" and "ordinariness" that we have noted in religious language. We state our basic commitments as certainties, not merely as possibilities or probabilities, because our basic commitments are the things of which we are most sure—the paradigms of certainty against which all other certainties are measured. Basic commitments are paradigms, too, of *righteousness*; challenges to those commitments invariably seem to us unjust because such challenges, if successful, will deny our whole reason for living. And basic-commitment language is (almost tautologically) the language of *commitment*, not of detached objectivity. And to these "oddnesses" we must add the oddness of resistance to falsification.

Basic-commitment language in general displays the same kinds of "oddness" and "ordinariness" that we have noted in religious language. We state our basic commitments as certainties, not merely as possibilities or probabilities, because our basic commitments are the things of which we are most sure—the paradigms of certainty against which all other certainties are measured.

Take a man whose basic commitment in life is the earning of money. To him, the legitimacy of that goal is a *certainty* beyond all question. When that goal conflicts with other goals, the basic goal must prevail. Questions and doubts, indeed, may enter his mind, but these questions and doubts are much like religious temptations. Insofar as he takes them seriously, he compromises his commitment; he becomes to that extent double-minded, unstable. He faces then a crisis wherein he is challenged to change his basic commitment. Under such pressure he may do so. But then the new commitment will demand the same kind of loyalty as the old one. Challenges *must* be resisted. Evidence against the legitimacy of the commitment must somehow be ignored, suppressed, or accounted for in a way that leaves the commitment intact. "Are people starving in India? We must be compassionate, of course, but the best means of helping the poor is by teaching them the virtues of free enterprise and self-help. If everyone were truly dedicated to earning money, there would be no poverty. We do them no favor by compromising our commitment!" A rationalization? It might not seem so to one so committed, especially if no other answer to the poverty question lies close at hand.

Basic commitments are paradigms, too, of righteousness*; challenges to those commitments invariably seem to us unjust because such challenges, if successful, will deny our whole reason for living.*

Let us rephrase Flew's question as it might be addressed to the mammon-worshiper: What would have to occur or to have occurred to constitute for you a disproof of the primacy of moneymaking? What would have to happen to cause him to abandon his faith? Well, one simply cannot say in advance. Committed as he is, he devoutly hopes that *nothing* will bring about such a change. He not only hopes, but *knows* (or so he thinks), because he interprets all reality so as to accord with that commitment. Some event, indeed (we can't say what), could cause him to change—if he yields to the temptation of regarding that event from a nonmammon perspective. He changes then because he has already compromised; it is like a change in religious faith.

The basic-commitment language is "odd," indeed, but it is also "ordinary." It is not something strange or esoteric; we use it all the time. It enters into every area of life, simply because it is so basic, so important. It is important because it "makes a difference"—more difference than anything else. Without it, nothing would make sense. All of experience, then, "verifies" the validity of the commitment. We can "prove" our commitment true in any number of ways. The evidence is there.

But how can a commitment be verifiable and nonverifiable at the same time? How can it present proof, and at the same time resist falsification by contrary evidence? The resolution of this paradox gets us to the heart of the matter.

But how can a commitment be verifiable and nonverifiable at the same time? How can it present proof, and at the same time resist falsification by contrary evidence? The resolution of this paradox gets us to the heart of the matter. Think of a philosopher who is committed to establishing all truth by the evidence of his senses. Sense experience is his criterion of truth. What evidence would disprove that criterion? In one sense, none, for if sense experience is truly his criterion, then all objections to the criterion will have to be verified through sense experience. They will have to be tested by the criterion they oppose. "Disproof," as with other basic commitments, will come only when there is something like a crisis of faith. At the same time, all evidence proves the criterion. The philosopher will argue very learnedly to establish his conviction. He will refute contrary claims; he will produce carefully constructed arguments.

When we are arguing on behalf of an absolute authority, then our final appeal must be to that authority and to no other. A proof of the primacy of reason must appeal to reason; a proof of the necessity of logic must appeal to logic.

The arguments, of course, will be "circular." Arguments for the sense criterion must be verified by the sense criterion itself. The philosopher must argue for sense experience by appealing to sense experience. What choice does he have? If he appeals to something else as his final authority, he is simply being inconsistent. But this is the case with any basic commitment. When we are arguing on behalf of an absolute authority, then our final appeal must be to that authority and to no other. A proof of the primacy of reason must appeal to reason; a proof of the necessity of logic must appeal to logic; a proof of the primacy of mammon must itself be part of an attempt to earn more money; and a proof of the existence of God must appeal in the final analysis to God.

Such arguments are circular, but they are also arguments. A "proof" of, say, the primacy of reason can be highly persuasive and logically sound, even though, at one level, circular. The circularity is rarely blatant; it lurks in the background. One never says, "Reason is true because reason says it is." One says instead, "Reason is true because one must presuppose it even to deny it." The second argument is just as circular as the first. Both presuppose the validity of reason. But in the second argument, the presupposition is implicit rather than explicit. And the second one is highly persuasive. The irrationalist cannot help but note that he is (in many cases) presenting his irrationalism in a highly rational way. He is trying to be more rational than the rationalists—a contradictory way to be. He must decide either to be a more consistent irrationalist (but note the paradox of that!) or to abandon his irrationalism. Of course, he might renounce consistency altogether, thus renouncing the presupposition of the argument. But the argument shows him vividly how *hard* it is to live without rationality. The argument is circular, but it draws some important facts to his attention. The argument is persuasive, though circular, because down deep in our hearts we know that we cannot live without reason.[20]

Some circular arguments are persuasive to us, others not. Those circular arguments that verify the most basic commitments of our lives are by definition the *most* persuasive to us. And because we believe those commitments true, we believe that those arguments ought to be persuasive to others, too. A Christian theist, while conceding that the argument for God's existence is circular, will nevertheless claim that the argument is sound and persuasive. For he devoutly believes

Some circular arguments are persuasive to us, others not. Those circular arguments that verify the most basic commitments of our lives are by definition the most persuasive to us.

20. *How* do we know? That's hard to say, but we do. Some circular arguments are simply more plausible than others. "Truth is a giant onion, for all true statements are onion shoots in disguise." That argument is best interpreted as a circular one, the conclusion being presupposed in the reason offered. But there is something *absurd* about it. "Reason is necessary, for one must use reason even in order to deny it." That, too, is circular, but it seems much more plausible. A skeptic might say that the second argument seems plausible because it is our argument, while the first is not.

Knowledge itself is dreadfully hard to define. Logicians, epistemologists, and scientists have devoted countless hours to the task of finding criteria for genuine knowledge. Yet *knowledge* may not be defined as the observance of any such criteria. Knowledge occurred in human life long before there was any science of logic or epistemology or biology, and people still gain knowledge without referring to such disciplines. These disciplines try to conceptualize, define, and understand a phenomenon that exists independently of those disciplines. They do not make knowledge possible. And their concepts of knowledge change rather frequently. It would be presumptuous indeed to suppose that these disciplines have succeeded at last in defining everything that constitutes knowledge. Thus, if the recognition of plausibility in a circular argument does not fit any existing technical criteria of knowledge, then so much the worse for those criteria.

The fact is that recognition of such plausibility is a type of knowledge that epistemologists are obligated to note and account for. "Basic convictions" cannot be avoided, and such convictions may be proved only through circular argument. Therefore, circular argument is unavoidable at the level of basic conviction. This sort of circularity is not a defect in one system as opposed to others. It is an element of all systems. It is part of the human condition. It is altogether natural, then, that the term *knowledge* be applied to basic convictions, and if no technical account has yet been given of this sort of knowledge, then such an account is overdue.

Within a particular system, the basic convictions are not only truths, but the most certain of truths—the criteria of other truths. If we deny the term *knowledge* to these greatest of all certainties, then no lesser certainty can be called *knowledge* either. And no epistemologist may adopt a view that doing away with all knowledge does away with his job. Knowledge is not an ideal; it is not something that we strive for and never attain. It is a commonplace of everyday life. It is the job of epistemologists to account for that commonplace, not to define it out of existence. One may not define *knowledge* in such a way as to require us to transcend our humanity in order to know. One must defer to the commonplace. And knowledge of basic principles is part of that commonplace.

Because we believe those commitments true, we believe that those arguments ought to be persuasive to others, too. A Christian theist, while conceding that the argument for God's existence is circular, will nevertheless claim that the argument is sound and persuasive.

that his position is true, and he believes that it can be clearly recognized as such. He believes that God made men to think in terms of *this* circularity, rather than in terms of some competing circularity.[21]

Basic-commitment language, therefore, is both "odd" and "ordinary." It resists falsification; it refuses to be judged by some antithetical commitment; yet it accepts the responsibility to verify itself. It accepts the responsibility of displaying whatever rationality and consistency it may claim.

Basic-commitment language, therefore, is both "odd" and "ordinary." It resists falsification; it refuses to be judged by some antithetical commitment; yet it accepts the responsibility to verify itself. It accepts the responsibility of displaying whatever rationality and consistency it may claim.

What is Antony Flew's basic commitment? To reason? To "academic integrity" of some sort? To a secular ethic? To religious agnosticism? I don't know, but I assume that he has one, since he does not seem like the sort of person who accepts values unreflectively. And more can be said: if with the Bible we divide the human race into Christian and non-Christian, those who know God and those who don't, those who love God and those who oppose him, clearly Flew by his writings has identified himself with the God-opposing group. If this self-identification truly represents his heart-commitment, then according to Scripture Flew is committed to "hindering the truth" of God, exchanging the truth of God for a lie.[22] According to Scripture, he is committed at a basic level to opposing, contradicting, and resisting the truth of God that in some sense he nevertheless "knows."[23] This commitment, too, will be unfalsifiable and yet self-verifying, for it is a basic commitment; and for all its irreligiosity, it is logically like a religious commitment. Let us illustrate by a parody on Flew's parable:

According to Scripture, Flew is committed at a basic level to opposing, contradicting, and resisting the truth of God that in some sense he nevertheless "knows." This commitment, too, will be unfalsifiable and yet self-verifying, for it is a basic commitment; and for all its irreligiosity, it is logically like a religious commitment.

> Once upon a time two explorers came upon a clearing in the jungle. A man was there, pulling weeds, applying fertilizer, trimming branches. The man turned to the explorers and introduced himself as the royal gardener. One explorer shook his hand and exchanged pleasantries. The other ignored the gardener and turned away: "There can be no gardener in this part of the jungle," he said; "this must be some trick. Someone is trying to discredit our previous findings." They pitch camp. Every day the gardener arrives and tends the plot. Soon the plot is bursting with perfectly arranged blooms. "He's only doing it because we're here—to fool us into thinking that this is a royal garden." The gardener takes them to a royal palace and introduces the explorers to a score of officials who verify the gardener's status. Then the skeptic tries a last resort: "Our

21. These are the terms in which the matter must be phrased. The controversy is between competing circularities, not between circularity and noncircularity.

22. Rom. 1:18–25.

23. Rom. 1:19–21a; note the phrase *gnontes ton theon*, "knowing God."

> senses are deceiving us. There is no gardener, no blooms, no palace, no officials. It's still a hoax!" Finally the believer despairs: "But what remains of your original assertion? Just how does this mirage, as you call it, differ from a real gardener?"

God is verifiable, knowable, "clearly seen" in his works; but men still—"irrationally" because sinfully—deny him. To the Christian, the denials lapse into cognitive meaninglessness—an attempt to evade God by using atheistic language to describe a patently theistic world.

A garden indeed! How convenient that we should be talking about gardens—for that is where the Bible's own story begins. Adam and Eve lived in a garden, and they knew the divine Gardener. He talked to them, worked with them, lived with them, until one day Eve—and Adam—denied that he was there. Irrational it was, for sin is at its root irrational. And Scripture tells us that ever since that day, sinners have been guilty of the same irrationality. God is verifiable, knowable, "clearly seen" in his works;[24] but men still—"irrationally" because sinfully—deny him. To the Christian, the denials lapse into cognitive meaninglessness—an attempt to evade God by using atheistic language to describe a patently theistic world.

From a "neutral" point of view, both Flew and the Christian are in the same boat. Both have beliefs that are "odd" and "ordinary"—resistant to falsification, yet verifiable on their own terms. But of course, there is no "neutral" point of view. You are either for God or against him. You must place yourself in one circle or the other. Logically, both systems face the difficulties of circularity. But one is true and the other is false. And if man is made to know such things, then you can tell the difference. You *know* you can!

Both [Flew and Christians] have beliefs that are "odd" and "ordinary"—resistant to falsification, yet verifiable on their own terms. But of course, there is no "neutral" point of view. You are either for God or against him. You must place yourself in one circle or the other.

Our response to Flew, in short, is as follows: (1) He has told only half the story—religious language does resist falsification, as he says, but it also often claims to be verifiable in terms of its own presuppositions. (2) These epistemological peculiarities attach to all basic-commitment language, not just to religious or Christian language, and thus they attach to unbelieving language as well. Therefore, these considerations may not be urged as a criticism of Christianity. They are simply descriptive of the human epistemological condition. (3) Scripture pictures the *unbeliever* as the truly ridiculous figure, who ignores patent evidence and makes mockery of reason, on whose basis no knowledge is possible. To the Christian, the unbelieving circle is, or ought to be, absurd: something like "Truth is a giant onion; therefore, truth is a giant onion."

Flew, therefore, does not succeed in showing religious language to be "cognitively meaningless," and therefore he fails to show that human language cannot speak of God. But what of the third form of our objection? What of Karl Barth? Should we simply leave him behind?

Let us go back to the "oddness" and "ordinariness" of religious language, and Christian language in particular. The oddness of Christian

24. Rom. 1:20.

language derives from the transcendence of God, and the ordinariness of it derives from God's immanence. Christian language is odd because it is the language of basic commitment, and the transcendence of God's lordship demands that our commitment be basic. This language is odd because it expresses our most ultimate presuppositions, and these presuppositions are the demands that God makes upon us—nothing less. It is odd because it attempts to convey God's demands—his demands for all of life. It will not be "falsified" by some secular philosophical criterion, because God will not be judged by such a criterion. "Let God be true, but every man a liar."[25] God's own Word, the paradigm of all Christian language, is therefore *supremely* odd.

Christian language is odd because it is the language of basic commitment, and the transcendence of God's lordship demands that our commitment be basic. This language is odd because it expresses our most ultimate presuppositions, and these presuppositions are the demands that God makes upon us—nothing less.

Christian language is "ordinary," verifiable, because not only is God the transcendent Lord, he is also "with us," close to us. These two attributes do not conflict with each other. God is close to us *because* he is Lord. He is Lord, and thus free to make his power felt everywhere we go. He is Lord, and thus able to reveal himself clearly to us, distinguishing himself from all mere creatures. He is Lord, and therefore the most central fact of our experience—the least avoidable, the most verifiable.

And because God's own Word is supremely odd, it is supremely ordinary. Because it is supremely authoritative, it is supremely verifiable. Because it furnishes the ultimate presuppositions of thought, it furnishes the ultimate *truths* of thought.

Barth's argument essentially reverses this picture (derived from Scripture) of God's transcendence and immanence. To Barth, God's transcendence implies that he *cannot* be clearly revealed to men, clearly represented by human words and concepts. This view of God's transcendence contradicts the view of God's immanence that we presented. Similarly, Barth has a view of God's immanence that contradicts the view of transcendence that we presented. To Barth, the immanence of God implies that words of merely human authority, words that are fallible, may from time to time "become" the Word of God. Thus, the only authority we have, in the final analysis, is a fallible one. The only "Word of God" we have is a fallible human word. God does not make authoritative demands that require unconditional belief; he does not determine the presuppositions of our thought; he does not resist all falsification—rather, he endorses falsehood and sanctifies it.

Christian language is "ordinary," verifiable, because not only is God the transcendent Lord, he is also "with us," close to us.

Well, who is right? Does God's transcendence include or exclude an authoritative verbal revelation of himself to men? Note that this question must be faced squarely. It is not enough to say that revelation must be seen in the context of God's transcendence, for that transcendence has been understood in different ways, and one must therefore defend

25. Rom. 3:4.

his particular view of it. One does not get into the heart of the matter by saying that one view sees revelation "in abstraction from" God's lordship, for the two sides do not agree on the nature of this lordship or the relation that revelation is supposed to sustain to that lordship.

Both views claim scriptural support. Barth can appeal to the basic Creator-creature relationship as presented in Scripture: man is a creature; his ultimate trust must rest solely in God. To put ultimate confidence in something finite is idolatry. Human words are finite. Therefore, to put ultimate confidence in Scripture is idolatry. And in a fallen world, such confidence is all the more foolish, for human words are sinful as well as finite. Sinful speech can never perfectly honor God. The gospel precisely requires us to *disown* any claim to perfection, to confess the *inadequacy* of all human works, to cast all our hope on the mercy of God. How can we put ultimate trust in human words and in God's mercy at the same time?

Barth's view can be stated very persuasively, as long as it focuses on the general facts of creation and redemption. . . . But when this view turns specifically to the concept of revelation, its unbiblical character becomes obvious. For Scripture itself never deduces from God's transcendence the inadequacy and fallibility of all verbal revelation.

Barth's view can be stated very persuasively, as long as it focuses on the general facts of creation and redemption. Scripture *does* condemn idolatry; it *does* condemn reliance on merely human means of salvation. But when this view turns specifically to the concept of revelation, its unbiblical character becomes obvious. For Scripture itself never deduces from God's transcendence the inadequacy and fallibility of all verbal revelation. Quite to the contrary: in Scripture, verbal revelation is to be obeyed without question, *because* of the divine transcendence:

> Hear, O Israel: the LORD our God is one LORD: and thou shalt love the LORD thy God with all thine heart, and with all thy soul, and with all thy might. And these words, which I command thee this day, shall be in thine heart: and thou shalt teach them diligently unto thy children, and shalt talk of them when thou sittest in thine house, and when thou walkest by the way, and when thou liest down, and when thou risest up. . . . Ye shall diligently keep the commandments of the LORD your God, and his testimonies, and his statutes, which he hath commanded thee.[26]

One who serves God as Lord will obey his verbal revelation without question. One who loves Christ as Lord will keep his commandments. God's lordship—transcendence—demands unconditional belief in and obedience to the words of revelation; it never relativizes or softens the authority of these words.

One who serves God as Lord will obey his verbal revelation without question. One who loves Christ as Lord will keep his commandments.[27] God's lordship—transcendence—demands unconditional belief in and obedience to the words of revelation; it *never* relativizes or softens the authority of these words. But how can that be? Is Scripture itself

26. Deut. 6:4–7, 17.

27. John 14:15, 21, 23; 15:10. On these matters, compare my essay "Scripture Speaks for Itself," Appendix I in this volume.

guilty of idolizing human words? The answer is simply that Scripture does not regard verbal revelation as merely human words. Verbal revelation, according to Scripture, is the Word of *God*, as well as the word of man. As with the incarnate Christ, verbal revelation has divine qualities as well as human qualities. Most particularly, it is divine as to its *authority*. To obey God's Word is to obey *him*; to disobey God's Word is to disobey *him*. Unconditional obedience to verbal revelation is not idolatry of human words; it is simply a recognition of the divinity of God's own words. It is the deference that we owe to God as our Creator and Redeemer.

Scripture does not regard verbal revelation as merely human words. Verbal revelation, according to Scripture, is the Word of God, *as well as the word of man.*

Dishonoring the divine is just as sinful as idolizing the creature. The two are inseparable. To disobey God is to obey something less than God. When we turn from God's words, we idolize human words. If Scripture is right, if verbal revelation does have divine authority, then it is Barth's view that encourages idolatry. For Barth's view would turn us away from proper deference to God's words, and would have us instead make a basic commitment to the truth of some other words—our own, perhaps, or those of scientists, or those of theologians.

Scripture is divine as to its authority. *To obey God's Word is to obey* him; *to disobey God's Word is to disobey* him.

These considerations do not prove that Scripture is the Word of God. They do show, however, that the biblical doctrine of divine transcendence does not compromise the authority of verbal revelation. One may, indeed, prefer Barth's concept of transcendence to the biblical one, but such a view may not be paraded and displayed as the authentic Christian position.

We conclude, then, that the "objection" before us is unsound in all its three forms. Human language may convey the infallible Word of God, because God is *Lord*—even of human language.

APPENDIX I

"SCRIPTURE SPEAKS FOR ITSELF"

Originally published in John W. Montgomery, ed., *God's Inerrant Word* (Grand Rapids: Bethany House Publishers [a division of Baker Publishing Group], 1974), 178–200. Used by permission. Reprinted as Appendix F in John M. Frame, *The Doctrine of the Word of God*, A Theology of Lordship (Phillipsburg, NJ: P&R Publishing, 2010), 440–62. Often in this book I have asserted that the authority of Scripture is fundamental to a Christian epistemology. In this article, I argue that this concept of biblical authority is itself warranted by Scripture. And toward the end of this essay I deal with Barth's alternative. (For stylistic purposes, this appendix has been copyedited for inclusion in this volume.)

WHAT DOES SCRIPTURE say about itself? The question is both momentous and commonplace.

It is momentous: the self-witness of Scripture has been for centuries the cornerstone of the orthodox Christian argument for biblical authority. For one thing, there would never be any such argument unless there were reason to believe that Scripture *claimed* authority. If Scripture renounced all claim to authority, or even remained neutral on the subject, there would not be much reason for Christians today to claim authority *for* Scripture. But if Scripture *does* claim authority over us, then we are faced with a momentous challenge indeed. Acceptance or rejection of that claim will influence every aspect of Christian doctrine and life.

If Scripture renounced all claim to authority, or even remained neutral on the subject, there would not be much reason for Christians today to claim authority for Scripture.

Furthermore, the authority of Scripture is a doctrine of the Christian faith, a doctrine like other doctrines—like the deity of Christ, justification by faith, and sacrificial atonement. To prove such doctrines,

Christians go to Scripture. Where else can we find information on God's redemptive purposes? But what of the doctrine of the authority of Scripture? Must we not, to be consistent, also prove that doctrine by Scripture? If so, then the self-witness of Scripture not only must be the *first* consideration in the argument, but must also be the final and decisive consideration.

It is impossible to avoid circularity of a sort when one is arguing on behalf of an ultimate criterion. One may not argue for one ultimate criterion by appealing to another. And the argument over scriptural authority is precisely an argument over ultimate criterion.

Now, of course, someone might object that that claim is not competent to establish itself. If the Bible *claims* to be God's Word, that does not prove that it is God's Word. That is true in a sense. Many documents claim to be the word of some god or other. The Qur'an, the Book of Mormon, and countless other books have made such claims. In no case does the claim in itself establish the authority of the book. The claim must be compared with the evidence—evidence furnished through the presuppositions that come from, among other things, our religious convictions. A Christian must look at the evidence with Christian assumptions; a rationalist must look at the evidence with rationalistic assumptions. And the Christian finds his most basic assumptions in the Bible.

As I have argued elsewhere,[1] it is impossible to avoid circularity of a sort when one is arguing on behalf of an *ultimate criterion*. One may not argue for one ultimate criterion by appealing to another. And the argument over scriptural authority is precisely an argument over ultimate criterion.

The non-Christian must learn that even the evidentiary procedures he uses to establish biblical authority must be reformed by the Bible. He must learn that evidence is at bottom an elaboration of God's self-witness, that proving God is the same as hearing and obeying him.

We must not, of course, simply urge non-Christians to accept the Bible because the Bible says so. Although there is much truth in that simplicity, it can be misleading if stated in that form without further explanation. A non-Christian must start where he is. Perhaps he believes that Scripture is a fairly reliable source, though not infallible. He should then be urged to study Scripture as a historical source for Christian doctrine, as the *original* "source." He will be confronted with the claims of Scripture—about God, about Christ, about man, about itself. He will compare the biblical way of looking at things with his own way. And if God wills, he will see the wisdom of looking at things Scripture's way. But we must not mislead him about the demand of Scripture. He must not be allowed to think that he can become a Christian and go on thinking the same old way. He must be told that Christ demands a *total* repentance—of heart, mind, will, emotions: the whole man. He must learn that Christ demands a change in *ultimate criterion*. And thus he must learn that even the evidentiary procedures he uses to establish biblical authority must be reformed by the Bible. He must learn that *evidence* is at bottom an elaboration of God's self-witness, that *proving* God is the same as hearing and obeying him.

1. See Appendix H, "God and Biblical Language," in this volume.

So the question[2] of the biblical self-witness is a momentous one indeed. In a sense, it is the *only* question. If by *self-witness* we mean not merely the texts in which the Bible explicitly claims authority but the whole character of the Bible as it confronts us, then the question of biblical authority is purely and simply the question of biblical self-witness.

The question of the biblical self-witness is a momentous one indeed. In a sense, it is the only *question. If by* self-witness *we mean not merely the texts in which the Bible explicitly claims authority but the whole character of the Bible as it confronts us, then the question of biblical authority is purely and simply the question of biblical self-witness.*

On the other hand, the question is also commonplace: simply because it is so important, the question has been discussed over and over again by theologians. Although I feel greatly honored by the invitation to speak and write on such a basic question, I must confess also to a slight feeling of numbness. What can I say that hasn't been said already? What can I say that Gaussen, Warfield, Kuyper, Murray, Young, Van Til, Kline, Ridderbos, Pache, Wenham, Packer, Montgomery, Pinnock, and Gerstner haven't said? Even in this collection,[3] some of the other papers will overlap this topic. No doubt, in a collection of papers of this sort, someone ought to summarize the basic material. But I can't help thinking that it might be best just to quote snatches from other authors whose scholarship and eloquence are far superior to my own. It *might* be, but I won't follow that course here, because I do have a few reasons for attempting an individual, if not independent, study.

Past orthodox Christian discussions of this matter have, in my opinion, done a very adequate job, on the whole. As in all other human

2. We will cite some of the most helpful sources, in these questions. The classic nineteenth-century work on the subject, still useful, is Louis Gaussen, *The Inspiration of the Holy Scriptures*, trans. D. D. Scott (Chicago: Moody Press, 1949). The most impressive piece of scholarly work in this area to date remains Benjamin Breckinridge Warfield, *The Inspiration and Authority of the Bible*, ed. S. G. Craig (Philadelphia: Presbyterian and Reformed, 1948). In relating the doctrine of inspiration to a comprehensive Christian world and life view, Abraham Kuyper's *Principles of Sacred Theology*, trans. J. H. De Vries (Grand Rapids: Eerdmans, 1965) is unsurpassed. Almost the only new things that have been said in the last few years about the doctrine have been said by Meredith G. Kline in his *Structure of Biblical Authority* (Grand Rapids: Eerdmans, 1972). A helpful guide through the issues raised by NT biblical scholarship is Herman N. Ridderbos, *The Authority of the New Testament Scriptures*, ed. J. M. Kik, trans. H. de Jongste (Philadelphia: Presbyterian and Reformed, 1963). The soundest overall guide to the theological controversies (in my opinion) is Cornelius Van Til, *A Christian Theory of Knowledge* (Nutley, NJ: Presbyterian and Reformed, 1969); cf. his "unpublished" syllabus, *The Doctrine of Scripture* (Ripon, CA: Den Dulk Foundation, 1967). For general summaries of the issues, see: Ned Bernard Stonehouse and Paul Woolley, eds., *The Infallible Word*, 3rd rev. ed. (Philadelphia: Presbyterian and Reformed, 1967)—the article by John Murray is especially helpful; Carl F. H. Henry, ed., *Revelation and the Bible* (Grand Rapids: Baker, 1958); and, on the more popular level, but most eloquent and cogent, Edward J. Young, *Thy Word Is Truth* (Grand Rapids: Eerdmans, 1957). Other recent works useful to resolving the question of the Bible's self-witness are René Pache, *The Inspiration and Authority of Scripture*, trans. Helen I. Needham (Chicago: Moody Press, 1969); Clark H. Pinnock, *Biblical Revelation: The Foundation of Christian Theology* (Chicago: Moody Press, 1971); and John William Wenham, *Christ and the Bible* (Downers Grove, IL: InterVarsity Press, 1973).

3. The collection in which this paper was originally published. See introductory note.

endeavors, however, there is room for improvement here. The improvements I have in mind are chiefly two.

There needs to be a greater emphasis on the pervasiveness *throughout Scripture of the biblical self-witness. As we suggested earlier, there is a sense in which the entire Bible is self-witness.*

1. There needs to be a greater emphasis on the *pervasiveness* throughout Scripture of the biblical self-witness. As we suggested earlier, there is a sense in which the entire Bible is self-witness. Whatever the Bible says, in a sense, it says about itself. Even the genealogies of the kings tell us about the content, and therefore the character, of Scripture. The way in which the Bible speaks of kings and vineyards and wilderness journeys and God and man and Christ—its *manner* is a testimony to its character. More specifically, the overall doctrinal structure of Scripture is an important element of the biblical self-witness. For when the Bible speaks of atonement, reconciliation, justification, and glorification, it speaks of these in such a way as to presuppose a crucial role for itself. Or, to look at redemption from a more historical perspective, from the beginning of God's dealings with men, God has taught them to give his words a particular role in their lives—a lesson that is taught again and again throughout the thousands of years of redemptive history. Now, when we neglect this emphasis on the pervasiveness of the biblical self-witness, at least two bad things happen. (a) People can get the idea that the concept of biblical authority is based largely on a few texts scattered throughout the Bible, texts that might not be very important in the overall biblical scheme of things. They might even get the idea that the doctrine of inspiration is based largely on a *couple* of texts (2 Tim. 3:16; 2 Peter 1:21), which liberal scholars dismiss as being late and legalistic. Thus, it might seem as though the doctrine of biblical authority is a rather peripheral doctrine, rather easily dispensable for anyone who has even the slightest inclination to dispense with unpalatable doctrines. (b) People can get the idea that Christ and the Bible are separable, that you can believe in and obey Christ without believing in and obeying the Bible. They might think that Scripture is unimportant to the Christian message of redemption.

From the beginning of God's dealings with men, God has taught them to give his words a particular role in their lives—a lesson that is taught again and again throughout the thousands of years of redemptive history.

2. If, as orthodox people maintain, the biblical self-witness to its authority and infallibility is *obvious* and *clear*—and certainly if it is "pervasive"!—then we must face more squarely the question why not-so-orthodox people see the matter differently. At one level, of course, it is legitimate to say that they fail to see the truth because of their unbelief: the god of this world has blinded their minds.[4] Sin is "irrational"—it turns away from the obvious. But sinners, when they are scholars, at least, generally do things for a *reason*, perverse as that reason may be. And perverse or not, such reasoning is often highly plausible. If orthodox people can identify that reasoning, explain its

4. 2 Cor. 4:4.

surface plausibility, and expose its deeper error, then the orthodox view of the biblical self-witness will be stated much more cogently.

In the remaining portion of this essay, I will present an essentially traditional argument concerning the character of the biblical self-witness, but I will structure the discussion in such a way as to implement the two concerns above—not comprehensively, to be sure, probably not adequately, but to a greater degree than one might expect in a paper of this length.[5] The first section will examine the role of verbal revelation in the biblical understanding of salvation. The second will discuss the relationship of that verbal revelation to Scripture, and the third will analyze what I take to be the most common and plausible objection to the previous line of reasoning.

The whole Bible is self-witness, but the Bible is not only *or* primarily *self-witness. It is first and foremost not a book about a book, but a book about God, about Christ, about the salvation of man from sin.*

REVEALED WORDS AND SALVATION

We have suggested that the whole Bible is self-witness, but the Bible is not *only* or *primarily* self-witness. It is first and foremost not a book about a book, but a book about God, about Christ, about the salvation of man from sin. But that message of salvation includes a message about the Bible. For this salvation requires *verbal revelation*. In saving man, God *speaks* to him.

Lord and Servant

God spoke to man even *before* man fell into sin. The first human experience mentioned in Scripture is the hearing of God's word. Immediately after the account of man's creation, we read:

God spoke to man even before *man fell into sin. The first human experience mentioned in Scripture is the hearing of God's word.*

> And God blessed them, and God said unto them, Be fruitful, and multiply, and replenish the earth, and subdue it: and have dominion over the fish of the sea, and over the fowl of the air, and over every living thing that moveth upon the earth.[6]

It is appropriate that the hearing of these words be presented in Scripture as man's first experience. For this was the experience by which the whole course of man's life was determined. When man heard these words of God, he heard God's own definition of man. God was telling man who man was, what his task was. Everything else that man did was to be in obedience to this command. Whether a shepherd, a farmer, a miner, a businessman, a teacher, or a homemaker, his main job was to replenish and subdue the earth in obedience to this command. The command

5. Therefore, the paper will also *fail* to do justice to other legitimate concerns.

6. Gen. 1:28. All quotations of Scripture in this appendix are from the KJV, unless otherwise noted.

covered *all* of life, not just some compartments of it. The command was not to be questioned; it was God's sovereign determination of man's responsibility. The command asserted God's claim to *ultimate* authority, for, paradoxically, while the command declared man to have dominion over the earth, it also declared God's dominion over man. Whatever dominion man enjoys, he receives from God; he enjoys it at God's pleasure; he enjoys it out of obedience to God's command.

God's command asserted God's claim to ultimate *authority, for, paradoxically, while the command declared man to have dominion over the earth, it also declared God's dominion over man.*

Why? Simply because God is God, and man is man. God is Lord; man is servant. God commands; man must obey. To have a Lord is to be under authority. A servant is responsible to obey the *commands* of another. What kind of lordship would there be without commands? The very idea is absurd. Without commands, no obedience; without obedience, no responsibility; without responsibility, no authority; without authority, no lordship.

Man was created in obedience; he fell through disobedience—disobedience to another command, this time the command concerning the forbidden tree.[7] The simplest biblical definition of *sin* is "lawlessness"[8]—rejection of, disobedience to God's commands. Therefore, just as the Word of God defines our status as God's creatures and servants, it also defines our status as *fallen* creatures, as sinners.

Redemption, according to Scripture, involves a reassertion of God's lordship. The fall, of course, did not annul God's lordship; God's lordship over fallen man is vividly expressed in divine judgment against sin.

Redemption, according to Scripture, involves a reassertion of God's lordship. The fall, of course, did not annul God's lordship; God's lordship over fallen man is vividly expressed in divine judgment against sin. But if man is to be saved, he must be brought to realize again that God is Lord and demands man's unconditional obedience. When God saved Israel from Egypt, he called himself by the mysterious name *Jehovah*, which, although its exact meaning is uncertain, clearly asserts his claim to unconditional lordship.[9] And throughout the history of redemption, God continually asserted this claim by making *absolute demands* on his people.

God's demands are absolute in at least three senses. (1) They *cannot be questioned*. The Lord God has the right to demand unwavering, unflinching obedience. God blessed Abraham because he "obeyed my voice, and kept my charge, my commandments, my statutes, and my laws."[10] He did not waver,[11] even when God commanded him to sacrifice his son Isaac, the son of the promise.[12] To waver—even in that horrible situation—would have been sin. (2) God's demand is also absolute in

7. Gen. 2:17; 3:6, 11f.

8. 1 John 3:4 NASB.

9. Ex. 3:14; note context. In later years, when this sacred name was considered too sacred to be pronounced, the Jews read the word *Adonai*, "Lord," in its place.

10. Gen. 26:5.

11. Rom. 4:20.

12. Gen. 22:18.

the sense that it *transcends all other loyalties*, all other demands. The Lord God will not tolerate competition; he demands *exclusive* loyalty.[13] The servant must love his Lord with all his heart, soul, and strength.[14] One cannot serve two masters.[15] One of the most remarkable proofs of the deity of Christ in the NT is that there Jesus Christ demands—and receives—precisely this kind of loyalty from his followers, the same sort of loyalty that Jehovah demanded of Israel.[16] The Lord demands *first* place. (3) God's demand is also absolute in that it *governs all areas of life*. In the OT period, God regulated not only Israel's worship but also the diet, political life, sex life, economic life, family life, travel, and calendar of his people. No area of life was immune to God's involvement. To be sure, the NT gives us more freedom in a certain sense: the detailed dietary restrictions, uncleanness rituals, animal sacrifices, and other elements of the old order are no longer literally binding. But the NT, if anything, is *more* explicit than the OT on the comprehensiveness of God's demand: *whatsoever* we do, even eating and drinking, must be done to the glory of God.[17] We must never shut the Lord out of any compartment of our lives; there must be no areas kept to ourselves. God's lordship involves such *absolute demands*.

Whatsoever we do, even eating and drinking, must be done to the glory of God. We must never shut the Lord out of any compartment of our lives; there must be no areas kept to ourselves. God's lordship involves such absolute demands.

Savior and Sinner

But salvation is more than a reassertion of God's lordship. If God merely reasserted his lordship, we would be without hope, for we have turned against him and deserve death at his hand.[18] If God merely spoke to us absolute demands, we would perish, for we have not obeyed these demands. Yet our God is not only Lord, but also *Savior*. And he speaks to us not only demands, not only law, but also *gospel*—the good news of Jesus Christ. But we must emphasize that he *speaks* the gospel. The gospel is a *message*, a revelation in words. How can we know that the death of Christ is sufficient to save us from sin? No human wisdom could have figured that out. Only God can declare sinners to be forgiven; only God has the right to promise salvation to those who believe. The same Lord who speaks to demand obedience also speaks to promise salvation. As Abraham,[19] we are called to believe the gospel simply because it is God's own promise. We know that believers in Christ are saved because Jesus has told us they are.[20] Only the Lord

The same Lord who speaks to demand obedience also speaks to promise salvation. As Abraham, we are called to believe the gospel simply because it is God's own promise.

13. "Thou shalt have no other gods before me" (Ex. 20:3).
14. Deut. 6:4f.; cf. Matt. 22:37ff. and parallels in the other Gospels.
15. Matt. 6:22ff.
16. Matt. 19:16–30; cf. 8:19–22; 10:37; Phil. 3:8.
17. 1 Cor. 10:31—an NT dietary law! Cf. Rom. 14:23; 2 Cor. 10:5; Col. 3:17.
18. Rom. 3:23; 6:23.
19. Rom. 4:19f.
20. John 5:24.

can speak the word of forgiveness, the word that declares sinners to be forgiven and that promises eternal life.

Just as there can be no lordship without an absolute demand, so there is no salvation without a gracious and certain promise. Therefore, the whole biblical message presupposes the *necessity of verbal revelation*. Without revealed words, there is neither lordship nor salvation. To "accept Christ as Savior and Lord" is to accept from the heart Christ's demand and promise. Let there be no misunderstanding: you *cannot* "accept Christ" without accepting his words. Christ himself emphasizes this point over and over again.[21] If we set aside the words of Christ in favor of a vague, undefined "personal relationship" to Christ, we simply lose the biblical Christ and substitute a Christ of our own imagination.

Just as there can be no lordship without an absolute demand, so there is no salvation without a gracious and certain promise. Therefore, the whole biblical message presupposes the necessity of verbal revelation.

And not just any words will do. They must be *God's* words—words of divine (not merely human) authority, words that cannot be questioned, that transcend all other loyalties, and that govern all areas of life. They must be words that cannot be contradicted by human philosophies or theologies—or even by the "assured results of modern scholarship." Without words like *that*, we have no Lord and we have no Savior.

But where can we find words like *that*? No mere philosopher or theologian or scholar speaks such words. Many religions, indeed, claim to have such words, but how are we to judge among these many claims? How do we distinguish the voice of God from the voice of devils and the imaginations of our own hearts?

If we set aside the words of Christ in favor of a vague, undefined "personal relationship" to Christ, we simply lose the biblical Christ and substitute a Christ of our own imagination.

REVEALED WORDS AND SCRIPTURE

Scripture tells us to go to Scripture. Or, rather, the God of Scripture tells us in Scripture to go to Scripture.

Of course, we must note at the outset that the Bible is not the *only* word that God has spoken. God has spoken words to and by his apostles and prophets that are not recorded in the Bible. He has also spoken, in a sense, to the earth, to the storms, to the winds and waves.[22] And in a mysterious sense, the word of God may also be identified with God himself[23] and particularly with Jesus Christ.[24] But God does not always tell us what he says to the winds and waves, and he has not always provided us with prophets at a handy distance. Rather, he has directed us to a *book*. That is where we are to go for daily, regular guidance.

21. Matt. 7:24–29; Mark 8:38; Luke 8:21; 9:26; John 8:31, 47, 51; 10:27; 12:47–50; 14:15, 21, 23f.; 15:7, 10, 14; 17:6, 8, 17. The relationship between Christ and his words is essentially the same as that between God and his words in the OT.

22. Gen. 1:3; Pss. 33:6, 9; 119:90f.; 147:15–18; 148:5f.; cf. Matt. 8:27.

23. John 1:1.

24. John 1:14.

That is where we may always find the demands of the Lord and the promise of the Savior.

Writing goes back a long way in the history of redemption. The book of Genesis appears to be derived largely from books of "generations."[25] We don't know much about the origin of these books, but it is significant that (1) they include inspired prophecies,[26] and (2) they were eventually included among Israel's authoritative writings. From a very early time, God's people began to *record* the history of redemption for their posterity. It was important from the beginning that God's covenants, his demands and his promises, be written down, lest they be forgotten. The first explicit reference, however, to a divinely authorized book occurs in connection with the war between Israel and Amalek shortly after the exodus:

From a very early time, God's people began to record *the history of redemption for their posterity. It was important from the beginning that God's covenants, his demands and his promises, be written down, lest they be forgotten.*

> And Joshua discomfited Amalek and his people with the edge of the sword. And the LORD said unto Moses, Write this for a memorial in a book, and rehearse it in the ears of Joshua: for I will utterly put out the remembrance of Amalek from under heaven. And Moses built an altar, and called the name of it Jehovah-nissi: For he said, Because the LORD hath sworn that the LORD will have war with Amalek from generation to generation.[27]

Not only does the Lord authorize the writing of the book, the content of it is God's own oath, his pledge. It is the Word of God, a word of absolute authority and sure promise. Because God has spoken it, it will surely happen.

Not only does the Lord authorize the writing of the book, the content of it is God's own oath, his pledge. It is the Word of God, a word of absolute authority and sure promise. Because God has spoken it, it will surely happen.

But an even more important example of divine writing occurs a few chapters later. In Exodus 20, God speaks the Ten Commandments to the people of Israel. The people are terrified, and they ask Moses to act as mediator between themselves and God. From Exodus 20:22 to 23:33, God presents to Moses further commandments, in addition to the ten, that Moses is to convey to the people. In Exodus 24:4, we learn that Moses wrote down all these words, and in verse 7 that he read them to the people. The people received these words as the word of God himself: "All that the LORD hath said will we do, and be

25. Gen. 5:1; cf. 2:4; 6:9; 10:1; 11:10, 27; 25:12, 19; 36:9; 37:2.

26. Gen. 9:25–27. Though Noah is speaking, he is administering covenantal blessing and curse, which can take effect only under divine sanction. The fulfillment of these words at a much later period shows that these words were in essence the words of God. Cf. Gen. 25:23; 27:27–29; etc.

27. Ex. 17:13–16. The language here suggests a parallel with the divine "book of life," as though this earthly book were a kind of copy of the divine original.

obedient."[28] They accepted these *written* words as words of absolute demand. But something even more remarkable occurs a few verses later. The Lord calls Moses alone to ascend the mountain, "and I will give thee tables of stone, and a law, and commandments which I have written; that thou mayest teach them."[29] Note the pronouns in the first-person singular. *God* did the writing! In fact, the implication of the tenses is that God had completed the writing before Moses ascended the mountain. Moses was to go up the mountain to receive a completed, divinely written manuscript. Nor is this the only passage that stresses divine authorship of the law. Elsewhere, too, we learn that the tables were "written with the finger of God";[30] they were "the work of God, and the writing was the writing of God, graven upon the tables."[31]

Meredith G. Kline

What was going on here? Why the sustained emphasis on divine writing? Meredith G. Kline[32] suggests that this emphasis arises out of the nature of covenant-making in the ancient Near East. When a great king entered a "suzerainty covenant relation" with a lesser king, the great king would produce *a document* setting forth the terms of the covenant. The great king was the author because he was the lord, the sovereign. He set the terms. The lesser king was to read and obey, for he was the servant, the vassal. The covenant document was the law; it set forth the commands of the great king, and the servant was bound to obey. To disobey the document was to disobey the great king; to obey it was to obey him. Now, in Exodus 20 and succeeding chapters, God is making a kind of "suzerainty treaty" with Israel. As part of the treaty relation, he authors a document that is to serve as the official record of his absolute demand. Without the document, there would be no covenant.

When a great king entered a "suzerainty covenant relation" with a lesser king, the great king would produce a document *setting forth the terms of the covenant. The great king was the author because he was the lord, the sovereign. He set the terms. The lesser king was to read and obey, for he was the servant, the vassal. The covenant document was the law; it set forth the commands of the great king, and the servant was bound to obey.*

Later, more words were added to the document. We read in Deuteronomy that Moses put all these words in the ark of the covenant, the dwelling place of God, the holiest place in Israel, "that it may be there for a witness against thee."[33] The covenant document is not man's

28. Ex. 24:7.

29. Ex. 24:12.

30. Ex. 31:18.

31. Ex. 32:16; cf. also 34:1; Deut. 4:13; 9:10f.; 10:2–4. In Exodus 34:27f., Moses, too, is said to have done some writing—probably portions of the law other than the Ten Commandments. And yet the written work of Moses is no less authoritative than that of the Lord himself (cf. Ex. 34:32). Moses was the mediator of the covenant, and as such was a prophet conveying God's word to the people. Cf. Ex. 4:10–17; Deut. 18:15–19. Therefore, the unique "finger of God" writing is not necessary to the authority of the documents; humanly *written* documents may be equally authoritative, as long as the words are God's. But the "finger of God" picture places awesome emphasis on the authority of the words.

32. Kline, *Structure of Biblical Authority*.

33. Deut. 31:26.

witness concerning God; it is God's witness *against* man. Man may not add to or subtract anything from the document,[34] for the document is God's Word, and must not be confused with any mere human authority.

This divine authority takes many forms. In the extrabiblical suzerainty covenants, certain distinct elements have been discovered:[35] the self-identification of the lord (the giving of his name), the *historical prologue* (proclaiming the benevolent acts of the lord to the vassal), the basic demand for exclusive loyalty (called *love*), the detailed demands of the lord, the curses on the disobedient, the blessings on the obedient, and finally the details of covenant administration, use of the document, and so on. In the law of God, all these elements are present. God tells who he is;[36] he proclaims his grace through his acts in history;[37] he demands love;[38] he sets forth his detailed demands;[39] he declares the curses and blessings contingent on covenant obedience;[40] and he sets up the machinery for continuing covenant administration, laying particular emphasis on the use of the covenant book.[41] All these elements of the covenant are authoritative; all are words of God.

Man may not add to or subtract anything from the document, for the document is God's Word, and must not be confused with any mere human authority.

Theologians generally oversimplify the concept of biblical authority. To some theologians, it is God's personal self-manifestation (as in the giving of the divine name) that is authoritative. To others, it is the account of historical events. To others, the demand for love is the central thing. To others, it is the divine self-commitment to bless. But the covenantal structure of revelation has room for all these elements—and, what's more, places them in proper relation to one another.

Theologians generally oversimplify the concept of biblical authority. To some theologians, it is God's personal self-manifestation (as in the giving of the divine name) that is authoritative. To others, it is the account of historical events. To others, the demand for love is the central thing. To others, it is the divine self-commitment to bless.

34. Deut. 4:2; 12:32; cf. Prov. 30:6; Rev. 22:18f. How, then, could any additions be made to the document? For some additions were clearly made (Josh. 24:26; etc.). Since no man could add or subtract, the addition of a book to the covenant canon carries with it the claim that the addition has *divine* sanction.

35. Kline, *Structure of Biblical Authority*; we are listing the elements that Kline finds in treaties of the second millennium B.C. He regards the Decalogue and the book of Deuteronomy as having this basic structure (thus implying a second-millennium date for Deuteronomy!), and he regards the entire OT canon as an outgrowth of these "treaties."

36. "I am the LORD thy God" (Ex. 20:2; cf. 3:14; etc.).

37. "Which have brought thee out of the land of Egypt, out of the house of bondage" (Ex. 20:2).

38. "Thou shalt have no other gods before me" (Ex. 20:3). Compare Deuteronomy 6:4f., where "love" is actually used to denote this exclusive covenant loyalty. The demand for love follows the account of God's gracious acts in history, and is regarded as the vassal's response of gratitude for the Lord's benevolence. Compare the NT emphasis, "We love him, because he first loved us" (1 John 4:19).

39. Ex. 20:12–17. Though the division cannot be sharply made, the first four commandments might be said to represent the fundamental love requirement, while the last six describe some of its detailed outworkings.

40. Ex. 20:5f., 12. We have been tracing these covenant elements through the Decalogue, but we could have used many other parts of Scripture as well.

41. This emphasis is not found in the Decalogue, but it is a major emphasis of Deuteronomy (see 31:24–29), which Kline also identifies as a covenant document.

There is both love and law, both grace and demand, both *kerygma* and *didache*, both personal disclosure (stated in *I-thou* form) and objective declarations of facts, both a concept of history and a concept of inspired words. The covenant document contains authoritative *propositions* about history (the servant has no right to contradict the lord's account of the history of the covenant), authoritative commands to be obeyed, authoritative *questions* (demanding the vassal's pledge to covenant allegiance), and authoritative *performatives* (God's self-commitment to bless and curse).[42] The propositions are infallible, but infallibility is only part of biblical authority. This authority includes the authority of nonpropositional language as well.

There is both love and law, both grace and demand, both kerygma *and* didache, *both personal disclosure (stated in* I-thou *form) and objective declarations of facts, both a concept of history and a concept of inspired words.*

We have seen that the idea of a *canon*, an authoritative written Word of God, goes back to the very beginning of Israel's history, back to its very creation as a nation. The Scripture is the constitution of Israel, the basis for its existence. The idea of a written Word of God did *not* arise in twentieth-century fundamentalism, nor in seventeenth-century orthodoxy, nor in the postapostolic church, nor in 2 Timothy, nor in postexilic Judaism. The idea of a written Word of God is at the very foundation of biblical faith. Throughout the history of redemption, therefore, God continually calls his people back to the written Word. Over and over again, he calls them to keep "the commandments of the LORD your God, and his testimonies, and his statutes, which he hath commanded thee."[43] These are the words of absolute demand and sure promise, the words of the Lord. These were the words that made the difference between life and death. These were the words that could not be questioned, which transcended all other demands, which governed all areas of life. When Israel sinned and returned to the Lord, she also returned to the law of God.[44]

The idea of a canon, *an authoritative written Word of God, goes back to the very beginning of Israel's history, back to its very creation as a nation. The Scripture is the constitution of Israel, the basis for its existence.*

From time to time there were new words of God. Joshua added to

42. Performatives ("I pronounce you man and wife"; "You are under arrest"; "Cursed be all who do not obey") do not merely state facts, but "perform" various sorts of actions. When spoken by one in authority, they "accomplish" what they set out to do. Performatives of the Lord in Scripture are uniquely authoritative, but their authority is not adequately characterized by the term *infallibility*. Infallibility is important, but it is only part of the meaning of biblical authority. *Infallibility* is not too strong, but too *weak* a term to adequately characterize biblical authority.

43. Deut. 6:17; cf. 4:1–8; 5:29–33; 6:24f.; 7:9–11; 8:11; 10:12f.; 11:1, 13, 18ff., 27f.; 12:1, 28; 13:4. In Deuteronomy, almost every page contains exhortations to obey God's commandments and statutes and ordinances. But not only in Deuteronomy. Cf. Josh. 1:8; 8:25–28; 2 Kings 18:6; Pss. 1:1–3; 12:6f.; 19:7–11; 33:4, 11; 119:1–176; Isa. 8:16–20; Dan. 9:3ff. Read over these and the many similar passages and let the message sink into your heart. The conclusion concerning the authority of the written Word is simply inescapable.

44. 2 Kings 23:2f., 21, 25; Neh. 8. The whole OT history is a history of obedience and disobedience: obedience and disobedience to what? To God's commands—and, after Exodus 20, to God's written Word. The self-witness of the OT is therefore present on every page. *Pervasive*, as we said.

the words that Moses had placed in the ark.[45] How could a mere man add to the words of God, in view of the command of Deuteronomy 4:2? The only answer can be that Joshua's words were also recognized as God's words. The prophets also came speaking God's words,[46] and some of them were written down.[47]

Thus the "Old Testament" grew. By the time of Jesus, there was a well-defined body of writings that was generally recognized as God's Word, and that was quoted as supreme authority, as Holy Scripture. Jesus and the apostles did not challenge but rather accepted this view. Not only did they accept it, they actively testified to it by word and deed. The role of Scripture in the life of Jesus is really remarkable: although Jesus was and is the Son of God, the second person of the Trinity, during his earthly ministry he subjected himself completely to the OT Scripture. Over and over again, he performed various actions, "that the scripture might be fulfilled."[48] The whole point of his life—his sacrificial death and resurrection—was determined beforehand by Scripture.[49] Jesus' testimony to Scripture, then, is not occasional but pervasive. His whole life was a witness to biblical authority. But listen particularly to what Christ and the apostles say concerning the OT. Listen to the way in which they quote Scripture, even in the face of Satan, to "clinch" an argument, to silence objections.[50] Listen to the titles by which they describe the OT: "Scripture," "holy Scripture," "law," "prophets," "royal law of liberty . . . the oracles of God."[51] Listen to the formulae by which they quote Scripture: "It is written"; "it says"; "the Holy Spirit says"; "Scripture says."[52] All these phrases and titles denoted to the people of Jesus' day something far more than a mere human document. These terms denoted nothing less than inspired, authoritative words of God. As Warfield pointed out, "Scripture says" and "God says" are interchangeable.[53]

By the time of Jesus, there was a well-defined body of writings that was generally recognized as God's Word, and that was quoted as supreme authority, as Holy Scripture. Jesus and the apostles did not challenge but rather accepted this view.

The whole point of Jesus' life—his sacrificial death and resurrection—was determined beforehand by Scripture. Jesus' testimony to Scripture, then, is not occasional but pervasive. His whole life was a witness to biblical authority.

And consider further the explicit *teaching* of Jesus and the apostles concerning biblical authority.

45. Josh. 24:26.

46. Deut. 18:15–19; Isa. 59:21; Jer. 1:6–19; Ezek. 13:2f., 17. The mark of the prophet was the phrase "Thus saith the Lord," which is found over and over again in the prophetic literature. Many theologians hostile to the orthodox view of biblical authority recognize that the prophets *claimed* an identity between their words and God's. See, e.g., Emil Brunner, *Dogmatics*, vol. 1, *The Christian Doctrine of God*, trans. Olive Wyon (Philadelphia: Westminster Press, 1950), 18, 27, 31f.

47. Isa. 8:1; 34:16ff.; Jer. 25:13; 30:2; 36:1–32; 51:60ff.; Dan. 9:1f.

48. John 19:28; see also Matt. 4:14; 5:17; 8:17; 12:17; 13:35; 21:4; 26:54–56; Luke 21:22; 24:44.

49. "*Was it not necessary that?*" (Luke 24:26 ESV). Scripture imposes a *necessity* upon Christ!

50. Matt. 4; 22:29–33; etc.

51. See Warfield, *The Inspiration and Authority of the Bible*, esp. 229–41, 361–407.

52. Ibid., 229–348.

53. Ibid.

> 1. Think not that I am come to destroy the law, or the prophets: I am not come to destroy, but to fulfil. For verily I say unto you, Till heaven and earth pass, one jot or one tittle shall in no wise pass from the law, till all be fulfilled. Whosoever therefore shall break one of these least commandments, and shall teach men so, he shall be called the least in the kingdom of heaven: but whosoever shall do and teach them, the same shall be called great in the kingdom of heaven.[54]

Jesus is saying that everything in the Law and the Prophets (equals the OT) carries divine authority. And obedience to that law is the criterion of greatness in the kingdom of heaven.

Jots and tittles were among the smallest marks used in the written Hebrew language. Jesus is saying that *everything* in the Law and the Prophets (equals the OT) carries divine authority. And obedience to that law is the criterion of greatness in the kingdom of heaven.

> 2. Do not think that I will accuse you to the Father: there is one that accuseth you, even Moses, in whom ye trust. For had ye believed Moses, ye would have believed me: for he wrote of me. But if ye believe not his writings, how shall ye believe my words?[55]

The Jews claimed to believe Moses' writings, but they rejected Christ. Jesus replies that they do not really believe Moses, and he urges them to a greater trust in the OT. He urges them to believe all the law and thus come to accept his messiahship.

The Jews claimed to believe Moses' writings, but they rejected Christ. Jesus replies that they do not *really* believe Moses, and he urges them to a *greater* trust in the OT. He urges them to believe *all* the law and thus come to accept his messiahship. We see here that Jesus did not merely quote Scripture because it was customary among the Jews. Rather, he *criticized* the prevailing custom because it was insufficiently loyal to Scripture. Jesus' view of Scripture was *stronger* than that of the Pharisees and scribes. Jesus sees Moses as justly accusing the Jews because of their unbelief in Scripture. Believing Moses is the prerequisite to believing Christ.

> 3. The Jews answered him, saying, For a good work we stone thee not; but for blasphemy; and because that thou, being a man, makest thyself God. Jesus answered them, Is it not written in your law, I said, Ye are gods? If he called them gods, unto whom the word of God came, and the scripture cannot be broken; say ye of him, whom the Father hath sanctified, and sent into the world, Thou blasphemest; because I said, I am the Son of God?[56]

54. Matt. 5:17–19. For detailed exegesis, see John Murray, *Principles of Conduct* (Grand Rapids: Eerdmans, 1957), 149–57. Cf. also his essay "The Attestation of Scripture," in Stonehouse and Woolley, *The Infallible Word*, 15–17, 20–24.

55. John 5:45–47.

56. John 10:33–36; cf. Warfield, *The Inspiration and Authority of the Bible*, 138–41.

A difficult passage, this, but note the parenthetical language. Concerning a fairly obscure psalm, Jesus says that "the scripture cannot be broken." It cannot be wrong; it cannot fail; it cannot be rejected as we reject human words.

> 4. For whatsoever things were written aforetime were written for our learning, that we through patience and comfort of the scriptures might have hope.[57]

Concerning a fairly obscure psalm, Jesus says that "the scripture cannot be broken." It cannot be wrong; it cannot fail; it cannot be rejected as we reject human words.

Here, the apostle Paul tells us that the OT is relevant not only for the people of the OT period but for us as well. It teaches us, and gives us patience, comfort, and hope. And most remarkably, the *whole* OT is relevant. None of it is dated; none of it is invalidated by more recent thought. Of what human documents may *that* be said?

> 5. We have also a more sure word of prophecy; whereunto ye do well that ye take heed, as unto a light that shineth in a dark place, until the day dawn, and the day star arise in your hearts: knowing this first, that no prophecy of the scripture is of any private interpretation. For the prophecy came not in old time by the will of man: but holy men of God spake as they were moved by the Holy Ghost.[58]

Note the context of this passage: Peter expects to die soon, and he wishes to assure his readers of the truth of the gospel.[59] He knows that false teachers will attack the church, deceiving the flock.[60] He insists that the gospel is not myth or legend, but the account of events that he himself had witnessed.[61] Yet even when the eyewitnesses have left the scene, the believers will still have a source of sure truth. They have the "word of prophecy"—the OT Scriptures—a word that is "more sure."[62] They are to "take heed" to that Word, and forsake all conflicting teaching, for the Word is light, and all the rest is darkness. Moreover, it did not originate through the human interpretive process; it is not a set of human opinions about God, nor did it originate in any human volition. Rather, the Holy Spirit carried the biblical writers along as

The apostle Paul tells us that the OT is relevant not only for the people of the OT period but for us as well. It teaches us, and gives us patience, comfort, and hope.

57. Rom. 15:4.

58. 2 Peter 1:19–21; cf. Warfield, *The Inspiration and Authority of the Bible*, 135–38.

59. 2 Peter 1:12–15.

60. 2 Peter 2.

61. 2 Peter 1:16–18. In the current theological scene, it is worth noting that Peter denies any mythological character to the message. It is not *mythos*.

62. Is the Word "more sure" in the sense of being confirmed by eyewitness testimony? Or is it, as Warfield suggests (above reference), "more sure" than eyewitness testimony? In either case, the passage places a strong emphasis on the *certainty* of the Word.

they spoke for him. The Holy Spirit determined their course and their destination. The Bible consists of human writings, but its authority is no mere human authority.

> 6. All scripture is given by inspiration of God, and is profitable for doctrine, for reproof, for correction, for instruction in righteousness: that the man of God may be perfect, thoroughly furnished unto all good works.[63]

Both Testaments, then, pervasively claim authority for the OT Scriptures. But what about the NT Scriptures? Can we say that they, also, are the Word of God?

Note again the context, for it is similar to that of the previous passage. Paul in this chapter paints a gloomy picture of deceivers' leading people astray. How can we know the truth in all this confusion? Paul tells Timothy to hang on to the truth as he learned it from Paul,[64] but also to the "holy scriptures"[65] (which, we note, are available even to us who have not been taught personally by Paul). This Scripture is "given by inspiration of God," as the KJV says,[66] or more literally "God-breathed"—*breathed out by God*. In less picturesque language, we might say simply "spoken by God"; but the more picturesque language also suggests the activity of the Holy Spirit in the process, the words for "spirit" and "breath" being closely related in the original Greek. Scripture is *spoken* by God; it is *his Word*; and as such it is *all* profitable, and it is *all* that we need to be equipped for good works.

Jesus told his disciples over and over again that obedience to his words was an absolute necessity for kingdom service and a criterion for true discipleship.

Both Testaments, then, pervasively claim authority for the OT Scriptures. But what about the NT Scriptures? Can we say that they, also, are the Word of God?

We have seen the importance of verbal revelation in both OT and NT. Both Testaments insist over and over again that such words are a necessity of God's plan of salvation. As we have seen, the concepts of lordship and salvation presuppose the existence of revealed words. And in the NT, Jesus Christ is Lord and Savior. It would be surprising indeed if Jehovah, the Lord of the OT people of God, gave a written record of his demand and promise, while Jesus, the Lord incarnate of whom the NT speaks, left no such record. Jesus told his disciples over and over again that obedience to *his words* was an absolute necessity for kingdom service and a criterion for true discipleship.[67] We *need*

63. 2 Tim. 3:16f. For detailed exegesis, see Warfield, *The Inspiration and Authority of the Bible*, 133–35, and also 245–96 (a comprehensive treatment of the meaning of "God-breathed," another translation of "given by inspiration of God").

64. 2 Tim. 3:14.

65. 2 Tim. 3:15.

66. 2 Tim. 3:16.

67. Matt. 7:21ff., 24, 28f.; Mark 8:38; Luke 8:21; 9:26; John 8:47; 10:27; 12:47; 14:15, 21, 23f.; 15:7, 10, 14; 17:6, 8, 17; 18:37; cf. 1 Tim. 6:3; 1 John 2:3–5; 3:22; 5:2f.; 2 John 6; Rev. 12:17; 14:12. Again, look these up, and allow yourself to be impressed by the *pervasiveness* of this emphasis.

the words of Jesus. But where are they? If there is no written record, no NT "covenant document," then has Jesus simply left us to grope in the dark?

Praise God that he has not. Jesus promised to send the Holy Spirit to lead his disciples into all truth.[68] After the Holy Spirit was poured out on the day of Pentecost, the disciples began to preach with great power and conviction.[69] The pattern remains remarkably consistent throughout the book of Acts: the disciples are filled with the Spirit, and *then* they speak of Jesus.[70] They do not speak in their own strength. Further, they constantly insist that the source of their message is God, not man.[71] Their words have absolute, not merely relative, authority.[72] And this authority attaches not only to their spoken words but also to their written words.[73] Peter classes the letters of Paul together with the "other scriptures."[74] Paul's letters are "Scripture," and we recall that "Scripture" is "God-breathed."[75]

The pattern remains remarkably consistent throughout the book of Acts: the disciples are filled with the Spirit, and then they speak of Jesus. They do not speak in their own strength. Further, they constantly insist that the source of their message is God, not man. Their words have absolute, not merely relative, authority.

We conclude, then, that the witness of Scripture to its own authority is *pervasive.* (1) The whole biblical message of salvation presupposes and necessitates the existence of revealed words—words of absolute demand and sure promise; without such words, we have no Lord, no Savior, no hope. (2) Throughout the history of redemption, God directs his people to find these words in written form, in those books that we know as the OT and NT.

The witness of Scripture to its own authority is pervasive. The whole biblical message of salvation presupposes and necessitates the existence of revealed words—words of absolute demand and sure promise; without such words, we have no Lord, no Savior, no hope.

68. John 16:13; cf. Acts 1:8.

69. Acts 2.

70. Acts 2:4; 4:8, 31; 6:10 (cf. vv. 3, 5); 7:55; 9:17–20; 13:9f., 52ff.

71. Rom. 16:25; 1 Cor. 2:10–13; 4:1; 7:40; 2 Cor. 4:1–6; 12:1, 7; Gal. 1:1, 11f., 16; 2:2; Eph. 3:3; 2 Thess. 2:2.

72. Rom. 2:16; 1 Thess. 4:2; Jude 17f.; cf. the passages listed in the preceding and following notes.

73. 1 Cor. 14:37; Col. 4:16; 1 Thess. 5:27; 2 Thess. 3:14.

74. 2 Peter 3:16. Compare 1 Timothy 5:18, which appears to couple a quotation from Luke with a quotation from the law of Moses under the heading "Scripture."

75. The question of what books are to be regarded as NT Scripture is beyond the scope of this paper, since no actual list can be found as part of the NT's self-witness. We may certainly assume, however, on the basis of what has been said, that if revealed words are a *necessary* ingredient of biblical salvation, and if specifically the words of the incarnate Christ and his apostles have such necessity, our sovereign God will "somehow" find a way to enable us to find those words. And surely he has. Although there have been disputes among different churches concerning the *OT* canon, there have never been any church-dividing disputes over the *NT* canon. Through history, of course, some NT books have been questioned. But once all the facts have gotten before the Christian public, it seems, the questions have always melted away. This is rather amazing, for the Christian church has always been, to its shame, a very contentious body. And yet no serious contentions have ever arisen over the matter of canonicity, a matter that many have found baffling. Try an experiment: read Paul's letter to the Corinthians (canonical), and then read Clement's (noncanonical) letter. *Think* about it; *pray* about it. Is there not an *obvious* difference? Christ's sheep hear his voice.

REVEALED WORDS AND MODERN THEOLOGIANS

Our conclusion, however, raises a serious problem. If the witness of Scripture to its own authority is *pervasive*, then why have so many biblical scholars and theologians failed to see it?

Our conclusion, however, raises a serious problem. If the witness of Scripture to its own authority is pervasive, *then why have so many biblical scholars and theologians failed to see it?*

We are not asking why these theologians fail to *believe* the claim of Scripture. The unbelief of theologians is at bottom rather uninteresting; it is not much different from the unbelief of anyone else. Yet it is surely possible to disbelieve Scripture's claim while at the same time admitting that Scripture makes such a claim. And some liberal theologians have indeed accepted this option: the Bible *claims* inspiration and authority, but modern men cannot accept such a claim.[76] But others have refused to admit even that Scripture makes that claim. Or more often, they have recognized this claim in some parts of Scripture, but they have judged this claim to be inconsistent with other, more important scriptural teachings, and thus have felt that Scripture "as a whole" opposes the notion of authoritative Scripture in our sense.

Putting the same question differently: is it possible to construct a sound *biblical* argument for biblical *fallibility*? Some theologians, amazingly enough, have said yes, despite the evidence to the contrary that we and others have adduced. Is this simply a wresting of Scripture in the interest of a heresy? Is it at bottom simply another form of modern unbelief (and therefore as "uninteresting" as the unbelief alluded to earlier)? In the final analysis, I would say that the answer is yes. But some analysis, final or not, is called for. The argument must be scrutinized, lest we miss something important in the biblical self-witness.

Is it possible to construct a sound biblical *argument for biblical* fallibility? *Some theologians, amazingly enough, have said yes, despite the evidence to the contrary that we and others have adduced.*

We are not here going to argue specific points of exegesis. Some thinkers would question our interpretation of Matthew 5:17–19, arguing that in the Sermon on the Mount and elsewhere, Jesus makes "critical distinctions" among the OT precepts. Some, too, would question our reading of the phrase "inspiration of God" or "God-breathed" in 2 Timothy 3:16. And indeed, some would argue from 2 Peter 1:21 (but in defiance of 2 Timothy 3:16) that inspiration pertains only to the writers of Scripture and not to the books that they have written. For enlightenment on these controversies, see the references in the footnotes. In general, we may say that even if it is possible to question a few points of our exegesis, the evidence is so *massive* that the general conclusion is still difficult to avoid:

> The effort to explain away the Bible's witness to its plenary inspiration reminds one of a man standing safely in his laboratory

76. Cf. Warfield, *The Inspiration and Authority of the Bible*, 115, 175ff., 423f. More recently, Frederick C. Grant admits that the NT writers assume Scripture to be "trustworthy, infallible, and inerrant." *An Introduction to New Testament Thought* (Nashville, TN: Abingdon Press, 1950), 75.

> and elaborately expounding—possibly by the aid of diagrams and mathematical formulae—how every stone in an avalanche has a defined pathway and may easily be dodged by one of some presence of mind. We may fancy such an elaborate trifler's triumph as he would analyze the avalanche into its constituent stones, and demonstrate of stone after stone that its pathway is definite, limited, and may easily be avoided. But avalanches, unfortunately, do not come upon us, stone by stone, one at a time, courteously leaving us opportunity to withdraw from the pathway of each in turn, but all at once, in a roaring mass of destruction. Just so we may explain away a text or two which teach plenary inspiration, to our own closet satisfaction, dealing with them each without reference to the others: but these texts of ours, again, unfortunately do not come upon us in this artificial isolation; neither are they few in number. There are scores, hundreds, of them, and they come bursting upon us in one solid mass. Explain them away? We should have to explain away the whole New Testament. What a pity it is that we cannot see and feel the avalanche of texts beneath which we may lie hopelessly buried, as clearly as we may see and feel an avalanche of stones![77]

Not even the cleverest exegete can "explain away" the biblical concepts of lordship and salvation and the necessary connection of these concepts with the revealed words of Scripture.

Not even the cleverest exegete can "explain away" the biblical concepts of lordship and salvation and the necessary connection of these concepts with the revealed words of Scripture. No exegete can explain away *all* the verses that call God's people to obey "the commandments, statutes, testimonies, ordinances" of the Lord; *all* the "it is written" formulae; *all* the commands delivered by apostles and prophets in authoritative tone.

Just as we have argued that the biblical concepts of lordship and salvation require *the existence of revealed words, so others have argued that certain basic biblical concepts* exclude the possibility of *such words.*

Rather than such detailed questions, therefore, we will confine our attention to broader considerations that have carried considerable weight in contemporary theological discussion. For just as we have argued that the biblical concepts of lordship and salvation *require* the existence of revealed words, so others have argued that certain basic biblical concepts *exclude the possibility of* such words.

The primary appeal of these theological views is to the divine transcendence, as the following quotes from Karl Barth and Emil Brunner, respectively, will indicate:

> Again it is quite impossible that there should be a direct identity between the human word of Holy Scripture and the Word of God, and therefore between the creaturely reality in itself and as such and the reality of God the creator.[78]

77. Warfield, *The Inspiration and Authority of the Bible*, 119f.

78. Karl Barth, *Church Dogmatics*, vol. 1, *The Doctrine of the Word of God*, ed. G. W. Bromiley and T. F. Torrance, trans. G. T. Thomson and Harold Knight (New York: Scribner, 1956), 2:499.

> It is therefore impossible to equate any human words, any "speech-about-Him" with the divine self-communication.[79]

Such statements have a kind of primitive religious appeal. God alone is God, and nothing else may be "equated with him." To "equate" or "directly identify" something else with God is idolatry. Now, surely we must agree that Scripture endorses this sentiment, for Scripture clearly opposes idolatry and exalts God above all other things. And if this is the case, then it seems that Scripture requires us to distinguish sharply between God himself on the one hand and language about him on the other; the transcendence of God is surely a central biblical concept. And if transcendence requires us to eliminate all thought of "revealed words," even though other biblical doctrines suggest otherwise, then perhaps we ought to give serious thought to this issue.

Such statements have a kind of primitive religious appeal. God alone is God, and nothing else may be "equated with him." To "equate" or "directly identify" something else with God is idolatry.

But Barth's concept of "direct identity" is a difficult one, as is Brunner's reference to "equating." What does it mean to assert—or deny—a "direct identity" or "equation" between God and language? Clearly, no one wants to say that *God* and *language about God* are synonymous terms. Nor has anyone in recent memory suggested that we bow down before words and sentences. Even the most orthodox defenders of biblical infallibility maintain that there is *some* distinction to be made between God and language. Further, even the most orthodox agree that the words of Scripture are in some sense creaturely, and thus specifically because of their creatureliness to be distinguished from God. On the other hand, if such words are *God's* words, and not *merely* human, then they are closely related to him, at least as closely as in words that are related to me. If God has spoken them, then their truth is his truth; their authority is his authority; their power is his power. Barth is willing to say that from time to time Scripture *becomes* the Word of God; therefore, he admits that some close relation between God and Scripture is essential. The question then becomes: in what way is God "distinct" from this language, and in what way is he "related" to it? A pious appeal to God's transcendence, eloquent though it may be, does not really answer this sort of question. Both the orthodox and the Barthian would like to avoid being charged with idolatry. But *what kind* of distinction between God and language is required by the divine transcendence?

In what way is God "distinct" from this language, and in what way is he "related" to it? A pious appeal to God's transcendence, eloquent though it may be, does not really answer this sort of question.

Barth is most reluctant to give any positive description of this relationship. Commenting on 2 Timothy 3:16, he says:

> At the centre of the passage a statement is made about the relationship between God and Scripture, which can be understood

79. Brunner, *The Christian Doctrine of God*, 15.

> only as a disposing act and decision of God Himself, which cannot therefore be expanded but to which only a—necessarily brief—reference can be made. At the decisive point all that we have to say about it can consist only in an underlining and delimiting of the inaccessible mystery of the free grace in which the Spirit of God is present and active before and above and in the Bible.[80]

Inspiration, says Barth, is a mystery, because it is an act of God's grace. We cannot define what it is; we can only assert the graciousness of the process. At another point, however, he does venture to describe inspiration, alluding to the term used in 2 Timothy 3:16:

Inspiration, says Barth, is a mystery, because it is an act of God's grace. We cannot define what it is; we can only assert the graciousness of the process.

> *Theopneustia* in the bounds of biblical thinking cannot mean anything but the special attitude of obedience in those [biblical writers] who are elected and called to this obviously special service. . . . But in nature and bearing their attitude of obedience was of itself—both outwardly and inwardly—only that of true and upright men.[81]

Inspiration is an act of God to create in men a special attitude of human obedience. It does not give them more than ordinary human powers. Therefore:

[According to Barth,] inspiration is an act of God to create in men a special attitude of human obedience. It does not give them more than ordinary human powers.

> The Bible is not a book of oracles; it is not an instrument of direct impartation. It is genuine witness. And how can it be witness of divine revelation, if the actual purpose, act and decision of God in His only-begotten Son, as seen and heard by the prophets and apostles in that Son, is dissolved in the Bible into a sum total of truths abstracted from that decision and those truths are then propounded to us as truths of faith, salvation and revelation? If it tries to be more than witness, to be direct impartation, will it not keep from us the best, the one real thing, which God intends to tell and give us and which we ourselves need?[82]

The question, of course, is rhetorical. Barth is appealing to something that he thinks his reader will concede as obvious. And this much we will concede: that if the Bible tries to be more than it is, if it exceeds

80. Barth, *The Doctrine of the Word of God*, 2:504.

81. Ibid., 2:505. In my view and Warfield's, Barth offers here a most inadequate exegesis of the "God-breathed" of 2 Timothy 3:16.

82. Barth, *The Doctrine of the Word of God*, 2:507.

its rightful prerogatives and usurps those of God himself, then it will indeed hide from us the real message of God's transcendence. But what *are* the "rightful prerogatives" of Scripture? That must be established before the rhetoric of divine transcendence can have force. The rhetoric of transcendence does not itself determine what those prerogatives are.

It is clear from the last quoted section, at least, that Barth denies to Scripture one particular prerogative—the prerogative of presenting "truths of revelation in abstraction from" God's saving act in Christ. But what does "in abstraction from" mean in this context? An abstraction is always some sort of distinction or separation, but what kind of distinction or separation? An orthodox theologian will insist that the biblical "truths of revelation" are *not* "in abstraction from" God's act in Christ. On the contrary, we learn about this act, we come to adore this act, because the Bible gives us a true account of it.

An abstraction is always some sort of distinction or separation, but what kind of distinction or separation? An orthodox theologian will insist that the biblical "truths of revelation" are not *"in abstraction from" God's act in Christ.*

I think that in the back of Barth's mind—perhaps in the front of it—is a concern of many academic people. When we teachers see students cramming for theological exams, stuffing truths into their heads, we sometimes wonder what all of this has to do with the kingdom of God. And the students wonder, too. The whole business of "mastering truths" somehow seems "abstract." It almost trivializes the message. Often there is here no real sense of the presence of God, no real spirit of prayer and thankfulness; it seems as though we are taking God's Word and making a *game* of it.

Well, theology examinations, theological study, *can* be a spiritual trial. But surely if we lose touch with God in studying his truths, it is our fault, not his for providing the truths. And sometimes, at least, the study of truths can be downright inspiring; sometimes, even in the academy, the law of the Lord purifies the soul. The evil in Barth's mind (as I understand him) is not an evil that can be remedied by eliminating the concept of revealed truth. It would be nice if such personal sinfulness could be eliminated by such a conceptual shift. But the sin of trivializing God's Word is one of which we are all guilty—Barthians as much as anyone. We cannot eliminate that in Barth's way, nor ought we try to construct a doctrine of Scripture that will make such trivialization impossible. That is the wrong way to go about constructing doctrinal formulations. Doctrines must not be arbitrarily constructed to counteract current abuses; they must be constructed on the basis of God's revelation.

Abstraction, then, can't be avoided by renouncing the idea of revealed truths or revealed words. Nor can it be avoided by renouncing biblical infallibility. And in the absence of any other clearly stated threat to God's transcendence in the doctrine that we have advocated, we are compelled to stand our ground. The orthodox view does *not* "abstract

Abstraction, *then, can't be avoided by renouncing the idea of revealed truths or revealed words. Nor can it be avoided by renouncing biblical infallibility.*

revelation from God's act," and it does not compromise the greatness and majesty of God. On the contrary, the true greatness of God, his lordship and saviorhood as described in Scripture, *requires* the existence of revealed truths. Without such truths, we have no Lord, no Savior, no basis for piety. Without such truths, all that we say, think, and do will be hopelessly "abstracted" from the reality of God. Without such truths, we have no hope. A Barthian or liberal or "neoliberal" theology can provide no such words; it can locate no words of absolute demands and sure promise. Rather, such a theology retains the right to judge the truth or falsity of *all* words with no divinely authorized criterion. Such theologies must be decisively rejected by the church of Christ if she is to have any power, any saving message for our time. When Scripture speaks for itself, it claims to be no less than God's own Word, and the claim is pervasive and unavoidable. Insofar as we deny that claim, we deny the Lord.[83] Insofar as we honor that Word, we honor Christ.[84]

The true greatness of God, his lordship and saviorhood as described in Scripture, requires *the existence of revealed truths. Without such truths, we have no Lord, no Savior, no basis for piety.*

83. Mark 8:38.
84. John 8:31, and those passages cited above in note 66.

APPENDIX J

REVIEW OF *THE LEGACY OF LOGICAL POSITIVISM*

Review of Peter Achinstein and Stephen F. Barker, eds., *The Legacy of Logical Positivism* (Baltimore: Johns Hopkins Press, 1969). This review originally appeared in *WTJ* 34, 2 (May 1972): 199–201. Used by permission of Westminster Theological Seminary. Here it supplements my treatment of logical positivism in chapter 12. (For stylistic purposes, this appendix has been copyedited for inclusion in this volume.)

In its classical phase, the logical-positivist ideology was structured around a few fairly straightforward theses: the analytic-synthetic *distinction, the tautological character of logic and mathematics, the verification criterion of meaning, the elimination of metaphysics, the unity of science, and the reducibility of all science to physics.*

OF ALL THE PHILOSOPHICAL APPROACHES that have been loosely grouped together under the label *analytic philosophy*, logical positivism is perhaps the easiest for nonphilosophers and beginning philosophers to understand. In its classical phase, the logical-positivist ideology was structured around a few fairly straightforward theses: the *analytic-synthetic* distinction, the tautological character of logic and mathematics, the verification criterion of meaning, the elimination of metaphysics, the unity of science, and the reducibility of all science to physics. Over the years, these theses have been considerably modified, and others have been added (particularly a concept of the relation between *theoretical* and *observational* language in science), but to this day most discussions of the movement begin with the simple theses and go on from there.

The volume before us shares that kind of simplicity. The same themes keep recurring. Three of the ten essays are devoted largely to the *theoretical-observational* distinction, and three others devote considerable space to it. The other familiar themes receive frequent treatment also. A reading of this book should make one clear about the nature of the problems, even if he can't accept the answers given. Further, there is little use of symbolic logic, and (especially in the essays of Feigl, Toulmin, and Hempel) there is valuable historical background given. There is no reason, therefore, why, for example, a theologically trained reader could not make use of this book.

And there are many reasons why he *should*. The writers of these essays are first-rate: Feigl and Hempel were among the original positivists and are still doing respected work in a generally positivistic tradition, and the other authors include some of the movement's most distinguished critics. Furthermore, there are reasons for theologians to study logical positivism, apart from the general values of studying analytic philosophy on which I have commented elsewhere. Surely in our day it is important to come to grips with science, to develop an understanding of its structure from a Christian point of view. Of all the secular philosophies, none has expended more concentrated effort on analyzing scientific method than has logical positivism. And what of theology itself? Is theology a scientific or "theoretical" discipline in some sense? If so, how are its "theories" to be compared with those of the other sciences? If not, why not? If theology develops theories "on the basis of" the "data" of Scripture, what is the precise relation between the theory and the data? Is exegesis without presuppositions possible? Or do theological theories inevitably control what counts as legitimate exegesis? Or is there some relationship between *observations* and *theory* that avoids these two extremes? I must say that on such issues I get more help from the clarity of the positivists, for all their patent anti-Christian bias, than from the rather murky formulations of professing Christian philosophers. Not that I am inclined to accept the positivists' conclusions, or even their formulation of the problems as *de*cisive; but their incisiveness is a genuine stimulus to one's own thinking. (Unbelieving philosophers are bad because of sin, but not necessarily stupid.)

There are reasons for theologians to study logical positivism, apart from the general values of studying analytic philosophy on which I have commented elsewhere. Surely in our day it is important to come to grips with science, to develop an understanding of its structure from a Christian point of view.

In a review of this length, no real critical analysis of a book like this is possible, but a general impression may be registered. That impression is one of surprise at finding how solidly logical positivism is rooted *in the concerns of traditional philosophy*. Why surprise? It is because the early positivist manifestos were issued in an apocalyptic spirit: logical positivism was to be the end of all philosophy as traditionally understood; it was to rid us of all "distinctively philosophical" problems at once; it was to remake philosophy into a metascience. Yet as the years go by (and this book is only one example), the positivists are coming to look more and more like the philosophers before them, and not least in their apocalyptic.

The early positivist manifestos were issued in an apocalyptic spirit: logical positivism was to be the end of all philosophy as traditionally understood; it was to rid us of all "distinctively philosophical" problems at once; it was to remake philosophy into a metascience.

For instance, in our volume Putnam finds an inconsistency between the positivists' "idealistic" notion of fact and their "materialistic" concept of mind. Shapere finds that the positivists' *theory-observation* dichotomy is essentially the *impressions-ideas* schema of Hume, with modifications. Toulmin argues that the positivists' main deficiency was that they failed to show how a purely analytic, tautological, formal system can have any application to purely synthetic, empirical, *a posteriori* statements by which we communicate about the real world; or (a broader problem) the positivists failed to show how language can be "connected with" the world in any sense. But is this not a very old philosophical problem—the problem of *laws and facts*, of *one and many*?

Stephen Toulmin

Toulmin shows how Wittgenstein chose a Kantian solution to the problem: the connection between language and the world is to be found not in a theoretical, logical relation, but in the concrete, practical decisions of human beings to use language in a certain way. Toulmin himself feels that we should go beyond Wittgenstein to determine what rules of usage have grown up in our particular culture and hence to determine what can and cannot "be said." But alas! How can a neutral historical, psychological, or sociological study such as Toulmin proposes yield binding linguistic *norms*? Whose "use" of language is the normative use? Wittgenstein failed to answer this question, and I feel that Toulmin will, too. Unless the God of Scripture exists, the God who *speaks*, first to himself and then clearly to men, no answer to this question can be given at all.

How can a neutral historical, psychological, or sociological study such as Toulmin proposes yield binding linguistic norms? Whose "use" of language is the normative use?

Logical positivism, therefore, is in the final analysis just another of many philosophical attempts to achieve an integration of fact and meaning without a surrender of human autonomy. Not even the utmost in intellectual clarity and incisiveness can achieve such a goal. But the positivists' failure to achieve it does not in itself call their clarity and incisiveness—and hence helpfulness—into doubt.

APPENDIX K

REVIEW OF *NEW ESSAYS ON RELIGIOUS LANGUAGE*

Review of Dallas M. High, ed., *New Essays on Religious Language* (New York: Oxford University Press, 1969). This review first appeared in *WTJ* 33, 1 (November 1970): 126–31. Used by permission of Westminster Theological Seminary. I republish it here to supplement my treatment of ordinary-language philosophy in chapter 12. (For stylistic purposes, this appendix has been copyedited for inclusion in this volume.)

SINCE THE FALL of Adam, many men have expressed doubts concerning God's existence; others have gone further and have questioned the very *possibility* of God's existence. In our own century, however, unbelief has reached a still more radical level: learned men have now come to question the very *meaningfulness* of the *sentence* "God exists" and, by implication, the meaningfulness of all Christian language. Others, somewhat less radical, have granted that "God exists" is *somehow* meaningful, but have insisted that the sentence does not state a fact; rather, they propose, this sentence makes a moral resolution, expresses an attitude, makes an aesthetic judgment, or performs some mysterious function not clearly specifiable.

In our own century, . . . unbelief has reached a still more radical level: learned men have now come to question the very meaningfulness *of the* sentence *"God exists" and, by implication, the meaningfulness of all Christian language.*

Such is the challenge of *analytic philosophy* to Christianity. Not all "analysts" are that radical, to be sure, but those with religious interests are characteristically absorbed by that sort of problem—and the problem is indeed a radical one. Furthermore, this challenge is all the more significant in view of the fact that analytic philosophy is *the* dominant philosophical approach today in British and American universities. And in those universities the challenge is most effectively articulated. The analysts present their case with a refreshing straightforwardness, and with higher standards of clarity and logical rigor than any theology of which I know. It is therefore about time that orthodox Christian scholars came to grips with analytic philosophy. Why is it that even in those orthodox circles where "epistemological self-consciousness" is most highly prized there has never (in my opinion) been any really thoroughgoing critical appraisal of this movement? We have totally failed to meet the most significant philosophical challenge of our day to the gospel, while we have squandered our intellectual skills on movements of far less substance. We have, unlike Dr. Robert Dick Wilson, "shirked the difficult questions."

Not one of [the writers] argues that religious language is generally meaningless or even that religious affirmations are generally nonfactual. Yet all feel to some extent the force of the "left-wing" attack on the meaningfulness of language about God and are constrained to reply to it.

Well, if anyone at this late date wants to do something toward remedying this deplorable situation, he will find Professor High's collection of essays an excellent place to start. The articles are written by some of the most prominent analysts of religious language, and the quality of thought (no pun intended) is high indeed (though in my view the contributions of Poteat and McPherson fall somewhat below the overall standard). The first two essays introduce us to Ludwig Wittgenstein, one of the guiding spirits of the movement, perhaps the most important philosopher of our century, and surely the most fascinating philosophical *personality* since Kierkegaard. The other papers make various proposals for the settlement of the "religious-language question" and incidentally provide the reader with a valuable survey of current thinking on the subject. The contributors all represent the "right wing" of the movement. Not one of them argues that religious language is generally meaningless or even that religious affirmations are generally nonfactual. Yet all feel to some extent the force of the "left-wing" attack on the meaningfulness of language about God and are constrained to reply to it. All agree that there is something "odd" (a favorite term in the analytic vocabulary) about sentences containing the term *God*.

Take the sentence "God exists." Clearly, as the logical positivists pointed out earlier in our century, that statement is not verified in the way that scientific theories are verified (at least on the positivist account of verification).

Take the sentence "God exists." Clearly, as the logical positivists pointed out earlier in our century, that statement is not verified in the way that scientific theories are verified (at least on the positivist account of *verification*). Further, as John Wisdom and Antony Flew later observed, religious people are strangely reluctant even to *conceive* of some empirical fact that *possibly* falsifies such a sentence. Since, therefore, this sentence behaves very differently in these respects from other statements of fact, we are tempted to ask what kind of "odd" fact this sentence can be used to state—if indeed it can state any fact at all.

All the essays in the present volume may be read as responses to this problem. One approach is to consider more closely the relationships between religion and science (particularly scientific verification). Ian Ramsey argues that science is not as unreligious as it sometimes seems to be, and that it requires a religious metaphysic to achieve its goal of a comprehensive conceptual scheme. Frederick Ferré gives us the other side of the coin: as Ramsey's scientists are religious, so Ferré's religious people are in important respects scientific—especially in their use of conceptual models (Ferré incidentally includes a valuable catalogue of information on this much-discussed subject). Basil Mitchell takes the discipline of history (sort of a borderline between science and something else) and argues that the historian's treatment of evidence is not so different from the theologian's. Of course, there are differences between religion and the sciences, and Ramsey, Ferré, and Mitchell do point these out. All argue, however, that the sense in which religious statements are "unverifiable" does not disqualify them as meaningless, or even as *scientifically* meaningless.

What are some of the differences between science and religion? The writers in this volume address this question also, and their answers are in part a further justification for the "unverifiability" of religious affirmations.

But now, what are some of the *differences* between science and religion? The writers in this volume address this question also, and their answers are in part a further justification for the "unverifiability" of religious affirmations. Ramsey and Ferré, to be sure, come close to saying that religion and the sciences are so necessary to each other that they should be amalgamated into one embracive discipline. Still, they would argue that such an embracive discipline must contain elements that are in narrower senses either religious or scientific. Religion provides the insight necessary to formulate hypotheses, while science provides the techniques for testing and applying them, though at the higher levels of generality conclusive verification is not possible. Mitchell, in an article especially important for those of us concerned about presuppositions, adds the point that even at the highest levels of generality, *evidence* still has a role to play, but he seems to agree with the others that that role is not one of conclusive verification. Ramsey, in a second essay, discusses what is involved in saying that religious language is *paradoxical*, and Thomas McPherson explores the concepts of *analogy* and *symbol*, thus setting religious language off yet more distinctly from the "straightforward" language of science. Still more interesting is the thought that intrigues several of the essayists, that narrowly scientific language is unable to adequately account for *persons*—human and, *a fortiori*, divine. It is particularly unable to analyze statements containing the first-person singular pronoun. William H. Poteat in his two essays formulates the distinction between *objective, scientific* language and the language of *personal involvement* so crassly that only the poetic prose of a Martin Buber could make it plausible. And Poteat is no Buber. Ramsey, however, along with Robert C. Coburn and C. B. Daly, offers some fascinating "analytic"

Still more interesting is the thought that intrigues several of the essayists, that narrowly scientific language is unable to adequately account for persons—human and, a fortiori, divine. It is particularly unable to analyze statements containing the first-person singular pronoun.

variants on Calvin's theme, that knowledge of God and knowledge of self are interdependent. Daly's article is especially interesting, for to him the analysis of human selfhood is one of many tunnels leading us from Wittgensteinian analysis back to a traditional—or even Heideggerian—sort of metaphysics. He suggests that Wittgenstein's concept of *family resemblances* is virtually a return to the medieval *analogy of being*, but fails to respond to Wittgenstein's explicit strictures against such interpretations.

The reason why a Christian resists conceiving of a "possible falsification" of God's existence is simply that to him God's existence is a presupposition. Nothing can "disconfirm" God's existence because all confirmation and disconfirmation presuppose it.

According to Coburn and Paul L. Holmer, however, the kind of self-knowledge requisite for knowing God is far more than a sharp analysis of a personal pronoun. Coburn tells us that statements such as "God exists" serve to give "logically complete answers" to "religious limiting questions" such as "What is the meaning of life?" When such questions are answered, the personal distress that produced the question is cured, so that the questioner's life is changed in highly practical ways. Holmer argues that theology should not think of itself as endlessly pursuing a set of highly esoteric and elusive facts, as though the facts about God were inadequately presented in Scripture and the creeds, but that rather theology should aim at curing the ills of men—the confusions of thought and the complacencies of life that keep men from feeling the force of the Christian gospel (cf. Daly on 120 for an interesting parallel, with a stress considerably different from that of Ramsey et al.).

There can be no "possible falsification" of God's existence just because it is God who determines what is possible and what is not. At the same time, the existence of God does have a positive relation to evidence; for since all facts presuppose God, all facts are evidence of his reality.

How shall we as Christians respond to all of this? Let us look first for a moment at the central problem, the verifiability of God-language. The reason why a Christian resists conceiving of a "possible falsification" of God's existence is simply that to him God's existence is a *presupposition*. Nothing can "disconfirm" God's existence because all confirmation and disconfirmation presuppose it. There can be no "possible falsification" of God's existence just because it is God who determines what is possible and what is not. At the same time, the existence of God does have a positive relation to *evidence*; for since all facts presuppose God, all facts are evidence of his reality. God's existence, therefore, is verifiable; but because of its logically unique presuppositional status there is a kind of "oddness" in this particular sort of verification. The Christian resists submitting God to human criteria, for he is under orders to "take every thought captive to obey Christ" (2 Cor 10:5). But for that same reason, he must acknowledge *God's own* criterion, his self-attestation! And *self-attestation* is something "odd" indeed, for only God can attest himself.

Now, Ramsey, Daly, and others in the present volume acknowledge that religious statements are terribly basic, that they provide a conceptual scheme for interpreting the whole of reality. Yet at every point, the writers assume that in some realm (generally what we have called the *narrowly scientific*) men can go about their business without listening to God's voice. The religious "conceptual scheme" does not, after all, interpret the *whole* of reality; not *every* thought is to be brought captive to Christ. Mitchell, for instance, argues that it is possible for me to accept arguments against my own faith without even implicitly and incipiently accepting a rival one; my doubts might cause me simply to *modify* my own system in some way. At one level, this is a valid point. There are times when I *should* recognize inadequacies in my own system in order to make it more congruent with that of Scripture. But as Mitchell fails to realize, the Christian is not free to "modify" Scripture itself; and when he "accepts arguments against" Scripture, he is in fact accepting a non-Christian standard of reference. Mitchell, like the other authors, assumes that men have an open-ended right to autonomously shape their own systems; and that assumption the Christian cannot abide. Erich Heller, not a philosopher but a professor of German, in his heretofore unmentioned lead essay in our volume, presents this point strikingly. His remarkable paper attempts to place Wittgenstein in the context of *Continental* philosophy and literature and points up some rather striking parallels between Wittgenstein and Nietzsche! He argues that Nietzsche's "death of God" is parallel to Wittgenstein's loss of faith in the power of language to "mirror" reality and his subsequent insistence that man himself must confer meaning upon language and upon the world through his "form of life." We have seen similar autonomous pretensions in Wittgenstein's followers in this volume. No wonder that "left-wing" analysts have denied the very meaningfulness of Christian language. For how can it be meaningful on such criteria? Clearly, an orthodox Christian can make no compromise with such idolatry.

As Mitchell fails to realize, the Christian is not free to "modify" Scripture itself; and when he "accepts arguments against" Scripture, he is in fact accepting a non-Christian standard of reference.

And yet we can learn so much from the analysts. Yes, theology *does* make use of models. Yes, there is paradox in theology, and we had better learn to distinguish one type of paradox from another. Yes, we have much to learn about the function of signs and symbols. Yes, there are important analogies between *I* and *God* that we have left unexplored. Yes, our standards of clarity and logical rigor have been sinfully shoddy. Yes, we have too often ignored in our theology what is painfully obvious in Scripture, that practical obedience is a *constitutive aspect* of the knowledge of God (1 John 2:3–6), and that therefore any theology worthy of the name will aim, by the power of God, to *cure* men of those ills of thoughts and life that inhibit their grasp of God's Word, even the ills of autonomous "analysis."

Yes, theology does make use of models. Yes, there is paradox in theology, and we had better learn to distinguish one type of paradox from another. Yes, we have much to learn about the function of signs and symbols. Yes, there are important analogies between I and God that we have left unexplored.

APPENDIX L

REVIEW OF PAUL M. VAN BUREN, *THE EDGES OF LANGUAGE*

Review of Paul M. Van Buren, *The Edges of Language* (New York: Macmillan, 1972). This review originally appeared in *WTJ* 36, 1 (Fall 1973): 106–11. Used by permission of Westminster Theological Seminary. Van Buren has followed different philosophical schools of thought during his career. This book of essays presents him as an "ordinary-language" philosopher, a disciple of the later Wittgenstein (chapter 12). (For stylistic purposes, this appendix has been copyedited for inclusion in this volume.)

Van Buren [did not] gain any academic plaudits from his first venture into the philosophy of language analysis, the notorious Secular Meaning of the Gospel, *a book that, though it cashed in handsomely on the "God is dead" fad, won fairly unanimous scorn from philosophically trained critics.*

THIS BOOK GIVES some indication that Paul Van Buren is growing up philosophically. This reviewer still wishes, however, that this author were a bit less eager to share his growing pains with the reading public.

Van Buren received his A.B. from Harvard—*cum laude* in government, the book jacket informs us—and his theological doctorate from the University of Basel for work with Karl Barth (*summa cum laude!*), work that is reflected in an early (and thoroughly Barthian) book by Van Buren called *Christ in Our Place*. The jacket, however, does not claim that Van Buren acquitted himself *cum laude* in the field of philosophy. Nor did he gain any academic plaudits from his first venture into the philosophy of language analysis, the notorious *Secular Meaning of the Gospel*, a book that, though it cashed in handsomely on the "God is dead" fad, won fairly unanimous scorn from philosophically trained critics. Apart from the more theologically focused criticisms against the book, it was urged by many that as philosophy the book was a collection of bits and pieces—a bit of 1930s-style positivism here, a bit of "use-analysis" there, plus a lot of dogmatic secularist metaphysics of a type that few analytically minded philosophers of any school would tolerate. Well, Van Buren kept at it. His next book, *Theological Explorations*, had at least the merit of being modest in scope—a collection of essays, some of which showed real promise. Promising novices in philosophy, however, are best advised not to rush into print until the promise shows more fulfillment than did that of *Theological Explorations*.

So now we come to *The Edges of Language*, the result of the author's attempt "to work out . . . the implications for Christian theology of Wittgenstein's *Philosophical Investigations*" (ix). We are initially amazed at the extent to which this proposal amounts to a confession of earlier irresponsibility. Granting the universally recognized importance of Wittgenstein's book, how could Van Buren, in clear conscience, *not* have worked out its implications *before* writing a book such as *Secular Meaning*? That, however, is in the past. We can be thankful that *The Edges of Language*, unlike *Secular Meaning*, is fairly consistent in its choice of principles. Almost too consistent, for *Edges* leaves the reader with the distinct impression that Wittgenstein's *Investigations* contain nothing wrong whatsoever! Van Buren here turns out to be as slavish a follower of Wittgenstein as he has been previously (and to some extent still is) of the verification principle and of the modern secular metaphysics. (Readers will understand that last sentence; they should be reminded, however, that "slavish follower of Wittgenstein" is almost as much a contradiction in terms as "slavish follower of Socrates.") *Edges*, then, considered as philosophy, is another basically adolescent work. It ranks high in consistency and in the basic soundness of its interpretation of Wittgenstein, but it is weak in that crucial quality that separates philosophers from mere students of philosophy, namely, the ability to present a cogent and clear critical stance over against one's sources.

Van Buren here turns out to be as slavish a follower of Wittgenstein as he has been previously (and to some extent still is) of the verification principle and of the modern secular metaphysics.

Journal readers, therefore, who wish to heed my admonition (often made on these pages) to study language analysis will probably find more challenging and interesting works in the field than Van Buren's. Yet *Edges is* easy to read, contains many interesting examples and illustrations, and in general is probably as good as anything else as an introduction to Wittgenstein's later thought as it bears on religious subjects, at least if its reader keeps in mind the caveats of this review! A few more specific caveats—and appreciations—are therefore in order.

As a phenomenology of some aspects of religious language, the book makes some points that, though not new, deserve more consideration from theologians, especially orthodox ones. Van Buren points out that language has a vast variety of functions alongside the more generally recognized ones of referring to and describing objects. Not all words are names, and not all sentences "state facts" or "communicate thoughts." Language is used in many ways, to accomplish many human tasks. In fact, everything we do is affected by our linguistic capacity; thus, in a sense human existence is "linguistic" (though not only linguistic).

Van Buren points out that language has a vast variety of functions alongside the more generally recognized ones of referring to and describing objects. Not all words are names, and not all sentences "state facts" or "communicate thoughts." Language is used in many ways, to accomplish many human tasks.

Further, in an important sense, there is nothing "supralinguistic"; for we admit nothing to exist unless such an admission can be made in language. Language also contains the predicates that we ascribe to objects. Therefore, the real is the sayable and the sayable is the real! Van Buren does admit that there might be something "unsayable"; but if there is, he reminds us, we had best be silent about it. "Something unsayable," if it is truly, completely beyond language, may not even be called *something*. Thus, when language changes, the world changes; to the extent that we differ in our language, the worlds we live in also differ.

Religion, on Van Buren's view, is a type of human linguistic activity; we can therefore learn about its purpose, its point, by studying its language, of course in its life-context. His discussion focuses on Christianity.

Christians oriented to the cosmonomic school of philosophy are likely to object at this point that Van Buren's view amounts to an "absolutization of the lingual aspect" of reality. Against that sort of criticism, however, I am inclined to defend Van Buren. Note again: Van Buren does not say that human existence *is merely* linguistic, as if it could not also be characterized in other ways. I think also that Van Buren is right to say that there is no supralinguistic Archimedean point by which we can account for language, if by that is meant something that cannot itself be spoken of. Discussion of language is always circular at least in the sense that we must *use* language in order to *understand* it; and it is the attempt to avoid such circularity (and other related types of circularity) that in my view partly accounts for some of the confusions in the cosmonomic philosophy.

Back to Van Buren. Religion, on his view, is a type of human linguistic activity; we can therefore learn about its purpose, its point, by studying its language, of course in its life-context. His discussion focuses on Christianity. Christianity, he says, contains much straightforward "literal" language (e.g., "Moses was born in Egypt"), but also some language of a philosophically perplexing kind (particularly, Christian language about miracles, eternal life, God, etc.). With regard to God-language, Van Buren is still worried (as he was in *Secular Meaning*) about the verification question: why is it that Christian statements about God seem to resist the processes of verification and falsification that we apply to other sorts of sentences about persons?

Van Buren's Christianity is that of "educated Christians in the West in this last third of the twentieth century," those who have among other things fallen under the sway of Bultmann, Bonhoeffer, and the verification principle and have therefore gone beyond "literal theism."

Theological optimists in the orthodox camp may be happy to know that whereas in *Secular Meaning* Van Buren considered the verification problem insoluble and therefore as an invalidation of all God-language, he has now changed his view. The word *God* is no longer "dead"; rather, it is very much alive! Those optimists should be informed in no uncertain terms, however, that Van Buren has not changed one whit in his attitude toward the God of the Bible and of historic Christianity. He makes quite clear that such a God does *not* exist in his view, although he finds some support for his own view in the Christian sources. His Christianity is that of "educated Christians in the West in this last third of the twentieth century" (1), those who have among other things fallen under the sway of Bultmann, Bonhoeffer, and the verification principle and have therefore gone beyond "literal theism."

What, then, is the function of God-talk and other problematic forms of Christian language? Van Buren does not want to say that such language is literal description of persons, events, and so on, but neither does he want to make of such language a merely arbitrary marker for something "wholly other" and therefore "unsayable." This dilemma of literalism vs. unsayability is one that in his view traditional theism (and also the nontraditional theism of Paul Tillich, 1–74) has been unable to avoid. Van Buren's alternative: such talk is to be located at the "edges of language."

Van Buren explains that language is at the "edges" when it is neither straightforwardly literal nor utter nonsense. He gives many examples of metaphors, puns, jokes, and poetry to illustrate this concept.

Van Buren explains that language is at the "edges" when it is neither straightforwardly literal nor utter nonsense. He gives many examples of metaphors, puns, jokes, and poetry to illustrate this concept. Poetry, for example, often stretches the dictionary definitions of terms, using them in unusual ways, yet in ways sufficiently analogous to our usual talk to be understood with some effort. By "stretching" the rules in this way, it risks abandoning them altogether—that is, it risks falling into nonsense, nonlanguage. But it also makes it possible for us to express things that could not be expressed through the ordinary conventions. And in stretching our language, poetry stretches our world, for it opens to us new ways of seeing, of experiencing that world. Problematic Christian language, says Van Buren, is a kind of word-stretching activity that focuses particularly on "history"—that is, it tries to say more about certain historical events than can be said through straightforward literal sentences. "God led his people out of Egypt" is not a statement about the (unverified) activity of some mysterious supranatural person, in Van Buren's view; in fact, he says, in such a sentence, it is wrong to view the word *God* as a name. Rather, such a sentence takes an ordinary (verifiable) event (the departure of the Jews from Egypt) and attributes a significance to that event that is almost more than words can convey. One uses such a sentence—as one uses poetry—when he wants to say what cannot be said by "ordinary language." And though Van Buren doesn't quite say this, it is hard to avoid the conclusion that for him this Christian language is a kind of poetry, a poetry that need not express any of the dogmas of orthodox theism.

Paul M. Van Buren

But this is, after all, only half an answer to the verification question, and unless more can be said, it risks not being an answer at all. Granting that such sentences are a type of poetry, we must then ask what it is that distinguishes good poetry from bad poetry, and what distinguishes poetry itself from nonsense. We cannot expect to have cut-and-dried criteria for every poem, yet for poetry in general there are means of answering such questions. What sort of answers fit the religious case? When a poet tries to say more than can be said in ordinary language, we often evaluate his work in part by asking, "Was there something to be said?" If the poet's "message" turns out to be trivial or dull or incomprehensible or false, we may still give him high marks for aesthetic craftsmanship, but we would be less impressed with the poem as a whole. In religious "poetry," *message* becomes even more important and aesthetic craftsmanship less so; thus, it becomes all the more important to evaluate *what the religion is saying.* As Van Buren points out, of course, we must not demand a precise translation into more prosaic language, but we must have some criteria for determining whether the statements in question are nonsense and, if they are meaningful, what statements tell the truth and which ones don't! On these crucial questions, Van Buren gives no guidance that I can see; at times he almost seems to make the choice of statement a matter of taste (though at other times he does insist that these statements say something about the world and thus can apparently be true or false). But even poetry is not purely a matter of taste. There are all-around bad poets, there are merely skillful poets, and then there are poets worth listening to. Van Buren's scheme displays an arbitrariness characteristic of thought that is not bound to God's self-revelation: In defending the meaningfulness of God-language, he appeals to the fact that God-language is *language*—that is, it is *ruled* and therefore is not nonsense. But when asked to specify what those rules are, he replies that God-language is at the "edge" of language, and therefore *stretches* the rules. But one never learns what the rules are, or how the stretching of those rules differs from breaking them. One finds, therefore, an uneasy balance between what Dr. Van Til has called a *principle of irrationalism* (the *edge*) and a *principle of rationalism* (the *language* with its *rules*). Van Buren therefore fails to stake out a firm middle ground between literalism and unsayability; see fig. L.1.

In religious "poetry," message *becomes even more important and aesthetic craftsmanship less so; thus, it becomes all the more important to evaluate* what the religion is saying.

In defending the meaningfulness of God-language, Van Buren appeals to the fact that God-language is language*—that is, it is* ruled *and therefore is not nonsense. But when asked to specify what those rules are, he replies that God-language is at the "edge" of language, and therefore* stretches *the rules.*

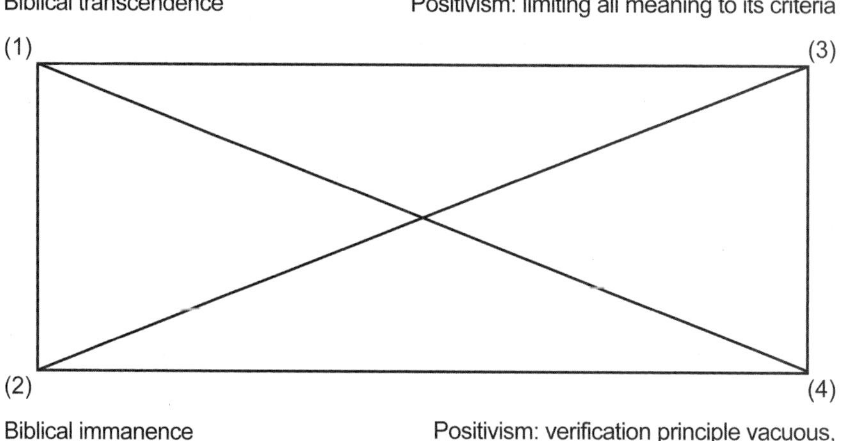

Fig. L.1. Transcendence and Immanence in Van Buren

Van Buren is right to say that talk about God is not just like talk of tables and chairs. There are many ways in which God-talk differs from ordinary language, among them the much-discussed tendency of God-sentences to resist the kind of verification and falsification that we require of some other sentences. He is also right to suggest that there is a sort of tension between *transcendence* and *immanence* in God-sentences: we do want to avoid either making God too much like us or making him too different from us. *Biblical* concepts of *transcendence* and *immanence* could have helped him here, however. The transcendence of the biblical God is not a Wittgensteinian "unsayability," but is rather God's *lordship*—his sovereign control of and authority over the universe. Similarly, the immanence of the biblical God is not a tendency for him to become indistinguishable from man; rather, it is his sovereign freedom to enter man's life and to reveal himself clearly and distinctly. Van Buren rejects both of these biblical concepts, but his acceptance of them could have greatly eased the "God-talk" problem for him. God-sentences resist ordinary sorts of verification and falsification, because they are based on God's sovereign revelation of himself, clearly presented to man in history, not because they are indeterminate as to their meaning and truth.

There are many ways in which God-talk differs from ordinary language, among them the much-discussed tendency of God-sentences to resist the kind of verification and falsification that we require of some other sentences.

And the tension between *transcendence* and *immanence* is also relieved when alleged analogies and disanalogies between God and ourselves are subjected to the supreme test of God's own self-witness in Scripture. We are not shut up to the alternatives of literalism and nonsense, for God's revelation to us is both adequate to our understanding and adequate to its divine message—it is neither obscure nor prosaic.

We are not shut up to the alternatives of literalism and nonsense, for God's revelation to us is both adequate to our understanding and adequate to its divine message—it is neither obscure nor prosaic.

In general, Van Buren has a lot of homework to do on the Bible. His use of it is highly selective, terribly dogmatic on disputed issues (as the use of the divine name in Exodus 3), terribly unpersuasive on controversial points (is it really true that narratives contain no propositions? [17] or that believing in God is "in no way like believing a statement to be true" [76]?). And while we're at it, there are also a number of minor blunders on extrabiblical matters. Is it really true, for instance, that "the test for the proper use of 'intend' lies in what people *say* they intend" (94 [emphasis his])? If that were true, then no one could ever falsely declare an intention. Much about the book needs to be rethought. Most of all, however, Van Buren will have to come to terms with his own dogmatic and uncritical awe of modern secular thought and to see how *diferent* all of this is from the biblical message of creation, fall, and redemption. Then he will have to make a choice—between an arbitrary amalgam of dogmatism and silence on the one hand, and on the other that service of Christ that opens the mouth in true freedom of speech (*parrhesia*).

APPENDIX M

REVIEW OF PAUL L. HOLMER, *THE GRAMMAR OF FAITH*

Review of Paul L. Holmer, *The Grammar of Faith* (San Francisco: Harper and Row, 1978). This review first appeared in *WTJ* 42, 1 (Fall 1979): 219–31. Used by permission of Westminster Theological Seminary. Holmer comes from an evangelical background, and is sympathetic with Kierkegaard (chapter 8) and the later Wittgenstein (chapter 12). (For stylistic purposes, this appendix has been copyedited for inclusion in this volume.)

This book deals in very basic terms with what theology is, what it can and cannot do for people, and how it ought to be done. It presents a genuinely new perspective on these matters that deserves close attention, especially by evangelicals.

THIS BOOK DEALS in very basic terms with what theology is, what it can and cannot do for people, and how it ought to be done. It presents a genuinely new perspective on these matters that deserves close attention, especially by evangelicals. I expect that it will provoke considerable discussion.

Holmer is another of those Yale professors[1] concerned more with the nature of theology itself than with any particular theological theses. He is somewhat older than David Kelsey but has published mostly in scholarly journals to this point. I expect that he will soon be much better known. In 1976 he published a highly regarded volume on C. S. Lewis, and he is currently planning two works called *Logic and the Theologians* and *Philosophy and the Theologians*. The present volume includes essays dating as far back as 1961 (but recently revised) together with some previously unpublished material. Thus it stands as

1. See my article "The Uses of Scripture in Recent Theology," *WTJ* 39, 2 (Spring 1977): 329, for some of the others. I should mention that Holmer was my thesis adviser, so that readers can assess effects of any possible conflict of interest.

a sort of summation of his thought to date, and that makes it especially appropriate for us to give the book some extended attention here.

He is not easy to locate on the theological spectrum. Evangelicalism is certainly one major influence. Once a pianist for Mordecai Hamm (the evangelist through whom Billy Graham was converted), Holmer has lectured at Wheaton on C. S. Lewis, served as faculty adviser to InterVarsity at Yale, and been a good friend to many lonely evangelicals at the latter campus. He acknowledges

> a standing debt to the evangelicals. That debt is not only for childhood nurture which made Christianity vastly momentous and more than a hobby, but also for that stream of reminders that the evangelicals provide which keeps alive the radical breach that the gospel is from the *nous* of the world.[2]

And he speaks of himself, even in later life, as "suffering the angularity of trying to be evangelical and an intellectual" (*Evangelicals*, 69). Yet his work is far from standard evangelical writing, and his critique of the movement might seem to some, at least, to reach a fairly basic level. The thinkers to whom he has devoted the most study and to whom he refers most often, generally with approval, are Kierkegaard and the later Wittgenstein. This might seem an odd combination—the father of existentialism and the father of ordinary-language philosophy. Yet Wittgenstein read Kierkegaard (before it was fashionable to do so) and considered him a highly important figure. And Holmer's Kierkegaard is not quite the one condemned in the familiar evangelical polemics against neoorthodoxy (cf. 182f.).[3] He is not a screaming irrationalist, but one who seeks to make careful distinctions among different kinds of rationality, not unlike Wittgenstein. Wittgensteinian motifs abound in *The Grammar of Faith*. Holmer is always trying to lay to rest "the ghost of those peculiar philosophical longings that grip us ever and anon" (106), to call into question this or that "plausible dogma" (118). He speaks mysteriously of the many confusions or difficulties in this idea or that without bothering to list them or even, sometimes, to give examples. He is suspicious of generalizations, of philosophical schemes, insistent on attention to the particulars of common language and everyday life as the

The thinkers to whom Holmer has devoted the most study and to whom he refers most often, generally with approval, are Kierkegaard and the later Wittgenstein. This might seem an odd combination—the father of existentialism and the father of ordinary-language philosophy.

He is suspicious of generalizations, of philosophical schemes, insistent on attention to the particulars of common language and everyday life as the solution to most really perplexing problems.

2. Holmer, "Contemporary Evangelical Faith: An Assessment and Critique," in *The Evangelicals: What They Believe, Who They Are, Where They Are Changing*, ed. D. F. Wells and J. D. Woodbridge (Nashville, TN: Abingdon, 1975), 68 (henceforth *Evangelicals*). Quotations and references not so labeled will be from the volume under review.

3. It might be possible to state Holmer's theses in a way that would make him sound like a conventional "neoorthodox" thinker: anti-abstractionism, *language about* vs. *language of*, denial of a philosophical grounding for faith, and so on. But one misses in Holmer the dialectical orientation, the suprahistorical salvation event, the Christo-monism, the opposition of propositional to personal encounters. Though he speaks well of Barth (183), his concerns and the structure of his thought are quite different.

solution to most really perplexing problems.[4] Yet unlike Wittgenstein, Holmer is a Christian theologian (Lutheran by confession).

All in all, then, it seems wise to read Holmer as a rather individual thinker, rather than as an instance of some movement or other. His individuality is confirmed by his writing style. The snatches already quoted here provide some examples of his preference for slightly odd word choices and grammatical constructions—not unclear, usually, but almost antagonistic to the traditional academic diction, almost calculated to rouse the reader from dogmatic slumbers. He tells us that "this theological stuff, this news about God and man, helps to redefine the human boundaries, to tame its vagrants" (12); he speaks of "another and wry effect of learning" (72) and of "the foundation, the in *re* point" (95). His *Evangelicals* article, having accused its subjects of unbiblical thinking, concludes with the question, "What could be more dilemmic for evangelicals?" (95). Behind all this, perhaps, is his view that theology in the most edifying sense ought to be in the vernacular (24) and should include "metaphor, figures and stories by way of a necessary projection of imagination" (30). It is Kierkegaard's "indirect communication" (31, 185) that is difficult to achieve, he would admit, when one is speaking of somewhat technical matters as in *Grammar of Faith*; but he seems intent on giving his narrative at least an aura of indirectness.

All in all, then, it seems wise to read Holmer as a rather individual thinker, rather than as an instance of some movement or other. His individuality is confirmed by his writing style.

The main substance of the book is a discussion of the familiar notion that the language of Scripture and the creeds has become meaningless (useless) to modern man because of changes (advances?) in science, technology, philosophy, and so forth. The common remedy for this problem is to try to recover the missing meaning through scholarship in various forms: historians telling us what really happened in ancient Palestine, scientists telling us that there really is room in Einstein's universe for some sort of god, metaphysicians constructing new conceptual schemes by which we can use the old language without intellectual sacrifice, theologians assuring us that such strategies do retain the main drift of the biblical message. This common approach, however, according to Holmer, compounds the problems: First, each

The main substance of the book is a discussion of the familiar notion that the language of Scripture and the creeds has become meaningless (useless) to modern man because of changes (advances?) in science, technology, philosophy, and so forth.

4. At times, Holmer seems almost as much of an uncritical Wittgensteinian as Paul Van Buren in *The Edges of Language* (New York: Macmillan, 1972) (cf. Appendix L in this volume). He writes as though Wittgenstein's equation of meaning and use, for example, were so obvious as to require very little argument, when in fact it is still controversial. Van Buren, however, in *Edges* was going through a phase, dabbling in Wittgenstein a bit as part of his restless pilgrimage from one fashion to another. Holmer, principially opposed to such reverence for the fashionable, has worked hard on Wittgenstein for many years. He seems (and is to an extent) dogmatic because he has gone over the arguments before and is now mainly intent on integrating this work with his now-mature and stable theological outlook. One could nevertheless wish for a bit more consideration of those still suspicious of Wittgenstein for whatever reason, but Holmer's dogmatism ought to be understood in perspective.

of the new schemes is at least initially plausible and thus creates a following, but the nonacademic believer is unable to make judgments among the various schools. Thus, the vital matter of restoring the meaning of Christianity becomes a game for specialists, a conversation-starter for "the talkative bright college set" (48). Second, the history of doctrine turns into a series of short-lived fads, as one new hope for meaning is quickly supplanted by another (2, 195ff.). Third, faddishness begets skepticism: if the most ingenious schemes can be fashionable for only a few years, and if they stand as our only channel to meaning and truth, then who knows what is right? It seems that theology is a "free creation" (1), that one man's idea is as good as another's. Fourth, theology loses its cutting edge. It cannot really *challenge* the spirits of the age, for it is so much in debt to them (12, 14ff.). Fifth, the authority of Scripture gets lost. One's primary allegiance is directed to a scheme in or behind the Bible (46ff.; cf. *Evangelicals*, 77ff., 80ff.) or to a "vague meta-view" (3) about how theology must change with the times. The shift in authority might seem very modern and sophisticated, but Holmer points out how these schemes and metaviews are themselves highly dubious (165, passim). When people recognize that, they might tend to become still more skeptical. Sixth, with the biblical message lost among the ontologies, metatheologies, and the like, the basics of Christianity—faith in Christ, love, obedience—tend to be ignored (162, 172; *Evangelicals*, 74). Thus, the *emphasis* of theology shifts drastically away from that of Scripture.

Paul L. Holmer

Holmer finds this whole approach radically wrong. Religion is *sui generis*—something radically different from the various fields of technical study and needing no foundation in any of them (31, 46ff., etc.).[5] Knowing God is not like knowing anything else. We cannot say that we know God unless we fear and love him (25), rejoice (*Evangelicals*, 94), experience a whole range of godly emotions (34, 64ff., 198ff.), and practice godly virtues (34, 50f.). We find him not by observation (202), but by the practice of the Christian life, in prayer, in church liturgy (198, 202f.). There are no intellectual guarantees; the knowledge of God is not "done on paper" (32). There are "facts" involved, the *consummatum est* of Jesus' work (109; cf. 101f.), but these are facts of a unique sort, not to be measured on criteria used in the technical disciplines. The result is that our knowledge of God is "immediate" (209) and theology is best expressed in the vernacular (24, 30) rather than in any technical language.

Holmer finds this whole approach radically wrong. Religion is sui generis—something radically different from the various fields of technical study and needing no foundation in any of them. Knowing God is not like knowing anything else.

5. Usually by *religion* Holmer means "Christianity." He says that Christian religious concepts are the only ones with which he has "a standing familiarity" (177). We will see that some unclarity develops here, for he sometimes, I think, uses the *religion-science* distinction where the *Christian-non-Christian* distinction would be more appropriate.

There is, to be sure, a kind of theology that is academic—for example, the historical study of biblical texts. Holmer does not wish to discourage or disparage this sort of work (46, 61, 167), but he does insist that such study is not the foundation of faith, nor is it the only kind of theology worthy of the name. There is also a kind of theology that is not scholarly or scientific, but "which is not lesser for all that" (62). This is the sort of theology that we find in Paul, Augustine, Luther (63)—and Kierkegaard. Theology in the first sense is language "about" faith. It is neutral, detached, something that "Christians and non-Christians can share" (64; cf. 58f., 62f., 111ff., 147). The second kind of theology is language "of" faith, not merely "about," though it may speak about many things (31, 50, 63ff., 71ff., 189, 201)—about God, ourselves, "everything else in the world" (73; cf. 12, 22, 189, 201). Yet he denies that the theology of the NT "satisfied also a cognitive interest" (75). The language "of" faith is "passionate, personal, evaluative, and useful for the purposes of being faithful" (64). Theology in this sense "expresses an enthusiasm in virtue of which judgments and beliefs are articulated" (65)—an enthusiasm that would be inappropriate in academic contexts.

Academic theology cannot serve as the basis for faith, cannot produce it in any sense. Intellectual achievements do not make people godly. They can aid faith only "indirectly."

Academic theology cannot serve as the basis for faith, cannot produce it in any sense. Intellectual achievements do not make people godly. They can aid faith only "indirectly" (62). Even theology of the second kind cannot communicate faith "directly" (31, 185), since knowing God is never merely a matter of mastering a certain thought content. But theology in the "of" mood (as Holmer puts it) does seek to set forth the "grammar" of faith, to show what the rules of faith are. And it seeks, through metaphor, parable, exhortation, poetry as well as straightforward prose, to elicit religious enthusiasm, to motivate people to love and obey. It makes true judgments, but makes them "to incite, not merely to inform" (67). Hence, perhaps, Holmer's stylistic oddities noted earlier.

Words become meaningful when people use them to do things, and since we use words in countless different ways, there is no one standard way for words to acquire meaning.

Holmer sees this point as a special instance of a broader one. Language in general cannot be said to derive its meaning from some theoretical scheme or other. Rather, words generally derive their meaning from their use in ordinary life. As Wittgenstein said, meaning is use (154, often elsewhere). Words become meaningful when people use them to do things, and since we use words in countless different ways, there is no one standard way for words to acquire meaning.

Therefore, it is not as though the word *God* derived its original meaning from a cosmology featuring a "three-level universe" and somehow lost its meaning when that cosmology was abandoned. And we are not to try to restore its meaning by finding a new logical home for it within Einstein physics or evolutionary theory or process metaphysics. Its meaning is understood "in use." It takes on life when it is put to work in its natural context of worship and practical godliness. Holmer asks:

> But is there not a great deal of theology that is idle reflection and principally so because there is so little to being faithful? When there is nothing to be, very little to do, and very little to believe that is the way of a Christian, then the burden has to fall upon "understanding" and its correlative, "meaning." (39)

If we were faithful, godly people, he says, we would not have to worry about the "meaning" of Christianity. To be godly is to have the meaning.

The Christian life, as Holmer sees it, and hence the meaning of Christianity, has not changed in its basic character since the first century (12, 112ff., 146ff.). We are still called to love and obey, tempted to despair, anxiety, doubt, unkindness, and so on. When one sees the Christian faith in these terms, the supposed progress of science, philosophy, and so on cannot have any devastating effect on it. And when our faith grows dim, we cannot blame the dimness on our lack of education or scholarly skills.

The Christian life, as Holmer sees it, and hence the meaning of Christianity, has not changed in its basic character since the first century. We are still called to love and obey, tempted to despair, anxiety, doubt, unkindness, and so on.

By way of analysis: it should be evident by now that Holmer's position rests heavily on the force of certain distinctions: between religion and science, knowledge of God and knowledge of other sorts, academic and edifying theology, language "about" and language "of," technical schemes and everyday use of words. Like Wittgenstein, he seeks to cure our philosophical bewitchments by helping us to attend to particulars, to see differences between things, rather than being misled by overstated generalizations. The book exhibits, we may say, a fairly pervasive and emphatic pluralism concerning language. Holmer admits that some concepts are broad enough to function the same way in many different sorts of contexts. Words such as *not, and, if,* particularly, have "meaning in independence of what they are linked to" (148), and also words such as *object, event, hot, cold*. It is important to note these, he says, lest we credit the false notion that all concepts change or become outmoded through historical process (150f.). In general, however, his emphasis is on discontinuity, on the differences between the uses of terms as contexts vary. So he insists that there is no single activity called *interpretation*, but rather *interpretations*—varieties of ways in which we set forth various meanings (6f.; cf. 124ff.). There is no general theory of meaning by which we can judge, for example, scientific language to be more or less "meaningful" than religious: the two are "incommensurable" (68f.).

Like Wittgenstein, he seeks to cure our philosophical bewitchments by helping us to attend to particulars, to see differences between things, rather than being misled by overstated generalizations.

Even logic and rationality escape generalization: the "logic of" science is different from that of religion (68f. again). Rationality is "polymorphic" (74; cf. 183f.). There is no "single and master concept of 'fact'" (102), no "general working concept" of "cause" (171). Same for "knowledge," "objective," "true," "real" (189).

This sort of approach is clearly necessary in the current theological discussion. Holmer is right: there are all sorts of confusions about what constitutes *fact*, *rationality*, and so on, and important distinctions are glossed over. Holmer's argument, however, goes too far and in another sense not far enough. Paradoxically, his pluralism is too generalized; an abstract pluralism such as this will recognize some important distinctions but of its very nature will miss others.

Since Holmer does allow for some field-invariant expressions (not, and, etc.), we naturally look for some justification when he states that such and such an expression is field-variant, and we expect that a thinker so greatly influenced by analytic philosophy would be eager to supply such an argument.

I think he goes too far, first, in that he asserts these discontinuities, often without any argument at all and other times with inadequate argument. Since he does allow for some field-invariant expressions (*not*, *and*, etc.), we naturally look for some justification when he states that such and such an expression is field-variant, and we expect that a thinker so greatly influenced by analytic philosophy would be eager to supply such an argument.[6] Further, the pluralism is often not even adequately defined; for generally the crucial question is not whether a particular expression is field-variant, but *in what respect* it is. Historical facts, scientific facts, religious facts might indeed be different in some ways, but there are also some respects in which they are the same. Holmer himself is willing to submit a definition of *fact* that, though modified by the word *usually*, nevertheless clearly crosses the borders of the disciplines mentioned: "Usually what we call a fact is what we can reason from, what we can take for granted" (105). Thus there is, even for Holmer, some continuity between different kinds of fact. And on the other hand, for all his emphasis on discontinuities, there are *differences* among kinds of facts that he does not explore. If meaning is use, then since two uses of a word are never exactly alike, there is some change in meaning with every use of a word. Thus, the meaning of the word *fact* varies not only from field to field, but even from utterance to utterance. So in a sense, Holmer's pluralism does not go far enough. But the overall point is that more argument is needed to establish the specific kinds of discontinuity needed for his case. Something more needs to be said about how scientific facts differ from religious facts

If meaning is use, then since two uses of a word are never exactly alike, there is some change in meaning with every use of a word. Thus, the meaning of the word fact varies not only from field to field, but even from utterance to utterance.

6. A fairly general weakness in the book is Holmer's frequent use of expressions such as *obviously* and *plainly* precisely where the issue is not obvious or plain, or, on the other hand, his branding alternative views as *absurd* or *silly* where serious discussion might be expected (cf. 103, 111, 121f., 165, 170, 184). He asks, for example, "Is it not madness to interpret the New Testament as though it served the abstract intellectual interests of its authors and readers?" (76). But he has just attributed such a view to Bultmann, and much as we may disagree with Bultmann, do we really want to call him mad? Is the question really that obvious? Holmer is highly critical of some who in his estimation jump to easy answers when problems are difficult. Sometimes, however, I think the shoe is on the other foot.

in *this* way, but not in *that*.[7] That he tends to miss distinctions of this kind suggests an additional and profound sense in which his pluralism does not go far enough. Ironically, he fails precisely to give enough attention to specifics.

I need to get more specific myself. Let us look more closely at Holmer's distinction between language "about" and language "of" faith, and at the related distinction between the knowledge of God and other sorts of knowledge. These distinctions are somewhat reminiscent of Dooyeweerd's distinction between *pretheoretical* and *theoretical*.[8] Like Dooyeweerd, Holmer is concerned (although he does not use this language) about the priesthood of believers and the perspicuity of revelation. Knowledge of God is not reserved for the educated, for the intellectuals. Religious wisdom comes to "conscientious tentmakers, tinkers like Bunyan, lay people like Brother Lawrence" (21). The same is true in other fields: an auto repairman can do his work quite well without a knowledge of atomic physics (174f.); an artist can be first-rate without an academic knowledge of aesthetic philosophy (37). Neither ordinary life in general nor ordinary language in particular gets its meaning from abstract theoretical structures (122ff., 150, etc.), nor can ordinary language be described as "theory-laden" (45). On the contrary, the technical concepts depend on the ordinary ones, and

Holmer is concerned (although he does not use this language) about the priesthood of believers and the perspicuity of revelation. Knowledge of God is not reserved for the educated, for the intellectuals.

> the specialized concepts often mean less rather than more. For such concepts in these abstruse and artificial contexts have very little work to do. Typically it is only the special metaphysical context that keeps such concepts alive. (175)

Neither ordinary life in general nor ordinary language in particular gets its meaning from abstract theoretical structures, nor can ordinary language be described as "theory-laden." On the contrary, the technical concepts depend on the ordinary ones.

Hence the independence of faith from metaphysics, generalized conceptual schemes (120ff., 159ff., 195ff.), scientific theory (68ff., etc.), historical research (7ff., 72ff., 95ff., 109f., 165f.), or even the cogitations of systematic theologians (90; cf. *Evangelicals*, 77, 93). So sharply is faith distinguished from these that Holmer is able to deny that the theology of the NT "among other things . . . satisfied also a cognitive interest" (75). It seems, then, that "the knowledge of God" adds nothing

7. Other examples: Although Holmer thinks *objectivity* is a polymorphic expression, he seems to acknowledge that it can be pretty generally opposed to *whim* (191). *Meaning*, too, is polymorphic, but Holmer is willing to accept Wittgenstein's meaning-use as a fairly general definition. It may be (as Wittgenstein argued) that no single component is present in *all* uses of a particular term, that a word has "sameness of meaning" over a range of use because of a "family" of overlapping likenesses. Still, even on that view, there *are* likenesses; and on that view, it becomes all the more important to sort them out, to map where they begin and end.

8. There are significant differences, too, as we will see. It is interesting to note, however, that despite the rather great differences between Holmer's language analysis and the phenomenology that served as the background for Dooyeweerd's distinctions, Wittgenstein was familiar with phenomenology and at one point was willing to describe his own work with that label.

to our "cognition," and vice versa; that "language about" faith adds nothing to our "language of" faith, and vice versa.

But as we saw in our initial exposition, such is not the case. Faith does depend, for Holmer, on facts of a certain kind (109, 209, 172). Though faith does not have the *primary* purpose of informing, it nevertheless tells "about" all sorts of things, encompassing the whole world.

Faith does depend, for Holmer, on facts of a certain kind. Though faith does not have the primary *purpose of informing, it nevertheless tells "about" all sorts of things, encompassing the whole world.*

> One gets to see as well as understand the world differently. Different feelings about one's tasks develop, and a radically new composure towards the world—a contrasting metaphysics—is also elicited. (158)

Metaphysics! And, he says, Christians do make "ontological commitments," though not as instances of a philosophical scheme (*Evangelicals*, 79; cf. 91). And although in *Grammar* Holmer seems to dismiss *theism* as a needless and harmful sort of philosophizing (159ff.), he tells us in *Evangelicals* that if the notion is understood "in biblical terms," Christians do "become theists" (80). And after all the polemics about technical and theoretical systems, Holmer surprises us all by denying that "the religious life is theory-free" (176). After all this, it even turns out that Christian concepts "depend upon" (!) "the somewhat piecemeal outlook and piecemeal theories that bind them together" (177).

Although he has made faith independent of science and so forth generally, he has not made it independent of those theoretical structures within the language "of" faith. Thus, he goes much too far in saying that faith is independent of all theory.

It seems, then, that there is "language about," even theoretical language, yes, even metaphysical language, within the "language of" faith. But this fact surely demands some modification in the rather strident rhetoric of discontinuity. Once we get the whole picture, it is impossible to see how Holmer can deny "among other things . . . a cognitive interest"[9] to the NT. And although he has made faith independent of science and so forth generally, he has not made it independent of those theoretical structures within the language "of" faith. Thus, he goes much too far in saying that faith is independent of all theory.

The distinction becomes even fuzzier when we look at it from the other side. Academic knowledge is supposed to be "neutral," common to Christians and non-Christians. Occasionally, however, Holmer modifies this principle with "most of the time" (147; cf. 59). He points out that a biblical scholar does use the concepts of faith when seeking "to adequately describe his subject matter" (147), and he mentions the case in which scientific language itself becomes a kind of religious enthusiasm (74). The scientific language "satisfies curiosity first and any other need only indirectly" (62); but this statement leaves the door

9. Or does he want to distinguish between one *sort* of "cognitive interest" and another? Part of the problem is that Holmer uses two incompatible rhetorics—one denying *all* theoretical basis for Christianity and another demanding distinctions between different sorts of theory.

open for science to supply, for example, religious needs "indirectly," which, interestingly, is all that religious language itself can do (31, 185).

What does the distinction, then, amount to, once we strip the discontinuity of rhetorical exaggeration? The scientific language is sometimes, though not always, religiously motivated and sometimes, though not always, accomplishes a religious purpose. The religious language is not *merely*[10] scientific, but it performs scientific functions among others and depends[11] not on any "neutral" science, but on that (piecemeal!) science within itself, the scientific aspect of the "language of faith." The simple twofold distinction might be better seen as a fourfold one: (1) neutral scientific language, (2) scientific language with a religious character or purpose, (3) religious language with a scientific character or purpose, (4) religious language without scientific character or purpose. Items (2) and (3) present, I think, no principial differences, and thus may be taken as identical, or merely as differing in emphasis. Then I have argued elsewhere, contrary to Dooyeweerd, that the distinction between scientific (theoretical) and nonscientific language is a continuum, a relative distinction, not a sharp one. One can be more or less theoretical about something. This argument would somewhat relativize the distinction between (3) and (4) as well.

The distinction between scientific (theoretical) and nonscientific language is a continuum, a relative distinction, not a sharp one. One can be more or less theoretical about something.

Thus, the significant divide would not be between religion and science. Holmer's own qualifications turn that distinction into a relative one. The major distinction is between (1) and the others, between "neutral" language and religious language. This is, indeed, the point where the big issues lie. It is the point where Holmer's main concern—the alleged loss of meaning in Christian language—must be addressed. The main problem is not that people are trying to base religion on science (though Holmer is right to point out confusions when they do), but that they are trying to base it on a (supposedly) *neutral* science. And I have a hunch that this is what Holmer himself cares most about. As we have seen, for instance, he has no quarrel with "ontological commitments" or "the-

The main problem is not that people are trying to base religion on science (though Holmer is right to point out confusions when they do), but that they are trying to base it on a (supposedly) neutral *science.*

10. It has occurred to me lately that a surprising amount of confusion could be avoided if theologians would learn to use this word. So often theological writers say *not* when they mean *not merely*.

11. *Depends* = "is founded on"? The language of foundation, dependence, and so forth is another area in which Holmer's formulations need clarification. There are a number of ways in which something can "depend on" or "be founded on" something else, and by failing to distinguish these, Holmer again compromises his pluralism. *Foundation* and *basis* are architectural metaphors, and their application to concepts is not obvious. They can refer to ontological relations, to causality of different kinds, to logical conditionality (necessary or sufficient), to the psychological preconditions of having certain ideas, and so forth. The work of an auto repairman is not "based on" atomic theory in the sense that the man must take courses in the latter. But this work would indeed be impossible it if were not for certain regularities in the world that we commonly describe in terms of atomic physics. This is a lot like the question whether faith "depends" on the finer points of systematic theology.

ism" as part of Christianity as long as these are understood "in biblical terms." The point is not ontology in general vs. religion, but *unbiblical* ontology vs. religion. Note also his rather odd critique of the doctrine of divine omniscience (103, 173). This is an instance of his assertion that faith is independent of technical schemes even of the systematic theologians. But the force of his argument does not rest on any dichotomy between academic theology and faith: that dichotomy is too unclear to be persuasive, and I have my doubts that even Holmer came to his conclusion on that basis. What seems to generate the critique of omniscience, rather, is Holmer's feeling that the concept is not biblical (cf. his acceptance of a theism in "biblical terms"). "Anyway," he says, "it is very questionable whether most people need to know what God knows in order to become devout" (103). Questionable on what ground? On religious grounds, presumably. He does not find the assumption warranted, as he puts it elsewhere, in Scripture and the creeds. And later he tells us that in Scripture and prayer "we do not find the words of theistic metaphysics at all" (173). Well, I could argue with him here. To be sure, the word *omniscience* is not found in Scripture, but I think the concept clearly is (cf. Ps. 139; Heb. 4:12f.). And it is not a mere speculative notion, as the contexts of those passages indicate; it expresses the very religious conviction that we cannot escape from God or hide anything from him. It promotes fear and worship. There are, perhaps, "merely speculative" concepts of omniscience that deserve Holmer's polemic, but those should be distinguished from the real thing. At this point, too, Holmer could take his pluralism more seriously. But note that the issue for Holmer, as for me, is not whether omniscience is religious or scientific, but whether it is biblical or unbiblical.

If we put the main dividing line not between science and religion, but between neutral and religious language, further issues will have to be faced. Is there any neutral language, or only pretended neutrality?

If we put the main dividing line not between science and religion, but between neutral and religious language, further issues will have to be faced. Is there any neutral language, or only *pretended* neutrality? Holmer opposes *neutrality* in the sense of facts or language without meaning, without context (5, 105), but he does assume that the language of science is neutral in the sense of being "common to Christians and non-Christians," as we have seen. No doubt there are common aspects of scientific language: there are 100 centimeters in a meter for Christians and non-Christians alike. But (again!) there are further distinctions to be made. If we allow (as seems necessary from the discussion above) that religion influences science and vice versa, then every scientist will have to decide not only whether or not to be Christian, but also whether or not he will accept the implications of Christianity for his scientific work. Whatever we say about weights and measures, then, it is clear that science as a whole is not religiously neutral, and that a claim to neutrality amounts to a choice against Christianity.

Whatever we say about weights and measures, then, it is clear that science as a whole is not religiously neutral, and that a claim to neutrality amounts to a choice against Christianity.

The conclusion of our argument is that the great divide is best formulated not as a difference between religion and science, nor between neutral and religious language, but between belief and unbelief. The categories *nonreligious science* and *neutral science* simply do not exist. Thus, if we ask whether some idea is suitable as a "basis" for Christianity in some sense, we must ask not whether it is scientific or religious, nor whether it is neutral or biased, but rather, as we did earlier, whether it is biblical or not.

Putting the matter in this way, we can mount a clear, strong attack on the problems that Holmer addresses in the book. Why has the Christian language become meaningless to many today? Holmer is right: not because of the alleged progress of science and technology, but because people have turned away from the pursuit of biblical godliness. He is right: the situation will not be helped by some new conceptual scheme (although I would say, and I think he would, too, that a *biblically* informed conceptual scheme could be of help), but by people's being moved by grace to obey God instead of their own lusts. On this account, there need be no temptation to faddism or skepticism. Scripture is the authority, the sure Word of God, and it abides forever. On this basis, theology can and must challenge the spirits of the age, including the "vague meta-views." And Scripture must determine our priorities as well. Preoccupation with *being*, *conceptual schemes*, and the like must never be allowed to eclipse our trust in the simplicities of the gospel—that Jesus loved us and gave himself for us. Knowing God is indeed inseparable from fearing and loving (though it involves knowledge of a more pedestrian sort as well). And Christian concepts indeed speak "about" all areas of human life. You can see, then, how much of Holmer's case is reaffirmed and indeed strengthened by our restructuring and clarification of his central distinctions.

Why has the Christian language become meaningless to many today? Holmer is right: not because of the alleged progress of science and technology, but because people have turned away from the pursuit of biblical godliness.

In fact, Holmer of all people ought to recognize that the malaise of our time is not a failure to distinguish one area of life from another—an intellectual mistake after all! It is not a matter of missing information, but a religious disability: a religious disability that, among other things, sets up false intellectual standards and seizes on linguistic confusions to rationalize its unbelief.

The malaise of our time is not a failure to distinguish one area of life from another—an intellectual mistake after all! It is not a matter of missing information, but a religious disability . . . that, among other things, sets up false intellectual standards and seizes on linguistic confusions to rationalize its unbelief.

It will be interesting to read Holmer's next books. At the moment, he seems poised between a radical biblical critique of modern thought and a quasi-neutral analysis of the different areas of human life. It is hard to imagine that he will not move more decisively in one direction or the other. I devoutly hope that he will seize the former alternative. His insight, cogency, and concern to edify could make him a powerful apologist indeed.

APPENDIX N

"OGDEN ON THEOLOGY"

This review article on Schubert M. Ogden's *On Theology* (San Francisco: Harper and Row, 1986) was originally published in *WTJ* 50, 1 (Spring 1988): 157–65. Used by permission of Westminster Theological Seminary. Ogden represents process theology (chapter 11). (For stylistic purposes, this appendix has been copyedited for inclusion in this volume.)

OVER THE YEARS, Schubert Ogden has been a well-known advocate of Bultmann's demythologizing,[1] of process theology,[2] and (despite some metatheological reservations) of liberation theology.[3] In the present volume, he presents his ideas on the nature of theology and some related topics by gathering together eight essays previously published from 1971 to 1982.[4]

Schubert Ogden has been a well-known advocate of Bultmann's demythologizing, of process theology, and (despite some metatheological reservations) of liberation theology.

It is perhaps best to approach Ogden's concept of theology by first taking note of other concepts that, in his view, theology presupposes: existential faith, revelation, religion, religious studies, and philosophy.

1. Ogden, *Christ without Myth: A Study Based on the Theology of Rudolf Bultmann* (New York: Harper and Brothers, 1961).

2. Ogden, *The Reality of God and Other Essays* (New York: Harper and Row, 1966).

3. Ogden, *Faith and Freedom: Toward a Theology of Liberation* (Nashville, TN: Abingdon Press, 1979). See also essay no. 8 of the present volume, 134–50.

4. The titles of these may be of interest, since I do not discuss the articles individually in the review: "What Is Theology?" (1–21), "On Revelation" (22–44), "The Authority of Scripture for Theology" (45–68), "The Task of Philosophical Theology" (69–93), "Prolegomena to Practical Theology" (94–101), "Theology and Religious Studies: Their Difference and the Difference It Makes" (102–20), "Theology in the University" (121–33), "The Concept of a Theology of Liberation: Must Christian Theology Today Be So Conceived?" (134–50).

Existential Faith: Living beings, he says, have a sort of instinctive confidence that their environment is favorable to their struggles to live and reproduce: what Santayana called "animal faith" (70, 106). On the human level, this animal faith becomes "more or less self-conscious." "Thus it has been well said that a human being not only lives his or her life but also leads it" (70). Human existence as such, therefore, is grounded in faith. Reason is "faith seeking understanding." All human reflective thought is ultimately grounded in this existential faith, which itself "neither needs justification nor can ever be justified" (72). To say this, however, is not to say that existential faith is necessarily authentic or true (72, 107f.). While we cannot question our basic confidence that life is worth living, the tragedies of life "drive us beyond any simple understanding" of that faith (108).

Because On Theology *consists of independent essays, it is not always clear how the concepts of one are related to those of another.*

Revelation: Because *On Theology* consists of independent essays, it is not always clear how the concepts of one are related to those of another. There is an essay "On Revelation," but it does not discuss the relation of revelation to existential faith, nor do the essays that deal with existential faith. But I gather that Ogden sees existential faith as a response to a kind of divine revelation (*original* or *natural* revelation): "the original event that is constitutive not only of Christian existence but also of human existence in general or simply as such" (25). God is omnipresent and therefore immanent in all the reality thus constituted. Knowledge of God is thus involved in knowledge of the world and in all self-understanding (22–28), and God is, evidently, the object of existential faith. I would assume, however, that for Ogden one may have existential faith without being *conscious* that God is its object.

Following Bultmann, Ogden construes [the Christian claim to special revelation] as adding no new content to general revelation, but adding only a new event in the life of the individual, creating in him a new authenticity, an "authentic possibility of 'faith working through love.'"

Religion: Various religions, indeed, interpret the object of existential faith in different ways, producing various "answers" to the "question" posed by existential faith. They seek, that is, to make sense of our basic confidence in reality in the context of tragedy. Religions may include symbols, rituals, doctrines, and the like. Significantly, they may also appeal to "special revelations," to various historical events, persons, experiences, rites by which they claim a knowledge of the divine distinctive to that religion. Christianity makes such a claim for Christ. Following Bultmann, Ogden construes that claim as adding no new content to general revelation, but adding only a new event in the life of the individual, creating in him a new authenticity, an "authentic possibility of 'faith working through love' " (44). To Ogden, as to Bultmann, *what* Jesus says is not new, but *that* he says it, and says it *now* (44).

Religious Studies: This discipline reflects on the religions (105ff.). Psychology, sociology, and history also study them, but the religious-studies area studies them specifically as answers to the questions posed by existential faith (114).

Philosophy: The philosopher reflects upon existential faith (73). Its core is metaphysics, which studies being in general and those fundamental forms of being, the self, the world, and God (77). Its "transcendental method" raises to full self-consciousness the "basic beliefs that are the necessary conditions of the possibility of our existing or understanding at all" (77). The question of God is the most fundamental of philosophical questions (81, quoting Hartshorne). Proof of God's existence can come only through metaphysics (82).

Philosophy also has the responsibility of assessing the credentials of purported revelations. It must determine what is true and false about those revelation-claims, including the Christian claims concerning Christ.

Philosophy also has the responsibility of assessing the credentials of purported revelations (84). It must determine what is true and false about those revelation-claims, including the Christian claims concerning Christ.

Theology: Now we come to theology as such, which takes several forms, according to Ogden. There is *philosophical theology*, which is essentially philosophy in its work of reflecting on existential faith, determining whether God exists, assessing the various candidates for revelation. Then there are the theologies of the various religions, one of which is *Christian theology*. Ogden defines *Christian theology* as "the fully reflective understanding of the Christian witness of faith as decisive for human existence" (1).

Christian theology, in turn, is divided into historical (or "descriptive"), systematic (or "constructive") and practical theologies, though each, Ogden says, involves the others (8; cf. 121–28). Historical theology includes exegetical theology as a special case. It asks, "What has the Christian faith already been as decisive for human existence?" (8; cf. 124). As historical theology is oriented toward the past, systematics is oriented toward the present, asking, "What *is* the Christian witness of faith as decisive for human existence?" (10 [emphasis mine]). Practical theology is future-oriented, asking, "What should the Christian witness of faith *now become* as decisive for human existence?" (13 [emphasis mine]). (At this point, Ogden opens some doors toward liberation theology: see 94–101, 134–50.)

Ogden does concede that the Christian revelation has as a historical starting point the sense of a definitive collection of symbols that theology seeks to interpret.

Ogden faces squarely the important question of theology's criteria of truth. Theological statements, he says, may be judged according to their "appropriateness" or according to their "credibility." "Appropriateness" means representing "the same understanding of faith as represented in the 'datum discourse' of normative Christian witness" (4). That "datum discourse" is not the Bible, but the "apostolic witness" determined through historical-critical study of the Bible (45–68). Still, Ogden does concede that the Christian revelation has as a historical starting point the sense of a definitive collection of symbols that theology seeks to interpret (5).

"Credibility," however, is a different issue. It is the question whether the doctrines in question are true. No religious authority, whether the Bible or the "apostolic witness" or whatever, can be the ultimate criterion of credibility. Rather, credibility can be established only by the criteria used by philosophy, history, the sciences. Indeed, the most often repeated point in the book is that theology has no "special criteria" of truth different from philosophy, science, history, and other disciplines. (See 8, 10, 84, 87, 90f., 103f., 140; also the interesting quote from Coleridge on xi.) Some of his arguments:

Schubert M. Ogden

1. Ogden thinks that the early church was correct in using the criterion of apostolicity to determine the extent of the canon, though it made historical errors in applying this criterion. Therefore, the canon is subordinate as an authority to the higher criterion of apostolicity (140; cf. 52–57).
2. All authority in the church is relative except the supreme authority of Christ himself (49–52).
3. Scripture is not identical to the Word of Christ, or even with the apostolic witness. The apostolic witness can be determined only by historical-critical study, by seeking to uncover the earliest form-critical stratum (Marxsen's "Jesus-kerygma"; 62–68).[5]
4. The Christian claim is addressed to all human beings, and thus must appeal to universal norms, not to "special criteria" (87).
5. If Christianity is to make good its claim to be decisively important for all human life, it must appeal not just to the Christian tradition, but to all the evidence available (87).
6. Since Christianity claims to be *true*, it must allow itself to be subject to general criteria of meaningfulness and truth (90–91): "the ultimate criteria for the truth of any claim can only be our common human experience and reason" (140).
7. One cannot establish Christianity as the answer to man's existential question without constructing a theistic metaphysics (92).

The second most frequent point in the book is Ogden's assertion that personal faith is not a condition for theological understanding (17f., 103ff., 115, 130, 138). A theologian must be willing to ask the religious *question*, but not necessarily to accept the Christian *answer* (however difficult it may be to separate the two, 18f., 112).[6] He argues that personal

The second most frequent point in the book is Ogden's assertion that personal faith is not a condition for theological understanding. A theologian must be willing to ask the religious question, but not necessarily to accept the Christian answer (however difficult it may be to separate the two).

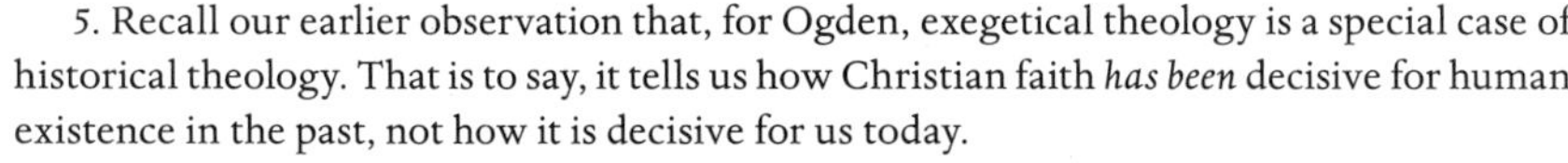

5. Recall our earlier observation that, for Ogden, exegetical theology is a special case of historical theology. That is to say, it tells us how Christian faith *has been* decisive for human existence in the past, not how it is decisive for us today.

6. His qualifications here are rather unclear. He says that in some sense the answer is implicit in the question, yet also insists on separating the two for purposes of the present point. More certainly needs to be said about *how* the two are and are not separable. On 113, his point seems merely to be that the existential question is never *fully* answered. But if that is the point, then all theologians would be in the same boat; there could be no distinction between those who accept and do not accept the Christian answer, because no theologian could be said to accept the answer. There would be no answer to accept! But on 18f., something else seems to be in view.

faith cannot be adequately tested to serve such a function (17f.) and that such a principle would mean that no unbeliever can understand Christianity (18). Liberation theology, with which Ogden is generally sympathetic, errs in demanding a prior commitment to a Christian liberation program before one can properly do theological work (138ff.), though it rightly calls Christians to be involved in such liberating praxis.

Ogden's arguments are tightly constructed and cogent, for the most part, granted his premises. The premises, however, are often questionable, and I suppose my biggest disappointment in the book was that Ogden rarely even seems aware of the most serious kinds of questions that can be raised against them.

Should theology, so conceived, be part of the university curriculum? Philosophical theology yes, says Ogden; also yes to historical or descriptive Christian theology. Constructive or systematic Christian theology, he thinks, has a place in a distinctively Christian university, but not in a non-Christian one (121–33). I confess that I had a hard time following him here, possibly because I tend to lose interest in this topic. But I don't see how on Ogden's basis one can make a meaningful distinction between a Christian and a non-Christian university, since Christianity employs in his view no "special criteria." Further, I do not understand how *systematic theology*, as Ogden defines it, should be *excluded* from a non-Christian university setting. His argument here is that the Christian religion cannot be presupposed "as a necessary condition of the possibility of any but a specifically Christian university." But since when has the university curriculum ever been limited to studies expounding the necessary conditions of the possibility of the university? Does the university presuppose French Literature as a necessary condition of its possibility? I suspect that Ogden has an answer to this question somewhere, but his point does not come out clearly as it stands.

Like Bultmann, he seems to believe that the course of intellectual, cultural, and technological history has made it impossible for twentieth-century man to accept Christian orthodoxy without intellectual ignorance, stupidity, or dishonesty.

Such unclarity is rather exceptional in the book. On the whole, Ogden writes lucidly. His arguments are tightly constructed and cogent, for the most part, granted his premises. The premises, however, are often questionable, and I suppose my biggest disappointment in the book was that Ogden rarely even seems aware of the most serious kinds of questions that can be raised against them. Of course, the questions I have in mind come from the standpoint of orthodox theology, and it is plain that Ogden has so little sympathy with that standpoint that he is entirely out of touch with it. Like Bultmann, he seems to believe that the course of intellectual, cultural, and technological history has made it impossible for twentieth-century man to accept Christian orthodoxy without intellectual ignorance, stupidity, or dishonesty. Well, that view has often been stated dogmatically, but the case has never been made with any cogency. Boiled down, it amounts to the view that one must never believe anything *unfashionable*—a proposition at odds both with Scripture and with the great Socratic tradition of Western rational thought.

To prove that orthodox Christianity should be respected is beyond the scope of this review. But the reader will perhaps permit some responses to the theses of *On Theology*. Ogden's doctrine of existential faith and natural revelation is, I think, insightful. He does insist with Paul in Romans 1 that all people know God, and he does stress with other Scriptures that God is present in every fact of creation and history, including man himself. It is also right to say that everyone lives by faith, however much that faith may be distorted by sin (cf. 107). I am not clear, however, as to what role this concept plays in his overall epistemology. Ogden sometimes gives the impression that existential faith is the "bedrock," the ultimate resort, the presupposition. Yet he also says that existential faith is fallible, that it can be inauthentic and untrue. Apparently his view is that existential faith is incorrigible in its basic optimism, its basic commitment to the value of existence, but that its specific ways of formulating and defending that optimism are corrigible. But then what criteria are available for evaluating those "specific ways"? His answer is that since there are no "special criteria," those criteria must be those of human intellectual disciplines: philosophy, history, science, and the like. But there are no settled criteria of knowledge in those fields. Indeed, matters of epistemology in all areas of knowledge are enormously controversial. Ogden's discussion does nothing to resolve any of these controversies. Surely Ogden himself is aware of them, but one wouldn't know even that from reading *On Theology*. And it is not clear, therefore, what good it does us epistemologically to learn about "existential faith." Apparently that faith is just one more datum to be critically examined by philosophy except that, perhaps, it excludes undue pessimism.[7]

Ogden's doctrine of existential faith and natural revelation is, I think, insightful. He does insist with Paul in Romans 1 that all people know God, and he does stress with other Scriptures that God is present in every fact of creation and history, including man himself.

Moving beyond the concept of existential faith to Ogden's views of philosophy and theology as such, I find the latter to be distorted by a dogmatic adherence to Bultmannian biblical criticism and by some more misconceptions about the nature of authority, criteria, and the relation of these to faith. I will not try here to address the questions about biblical criticism, but only the broader questions about authority.

Moving beyond the concept of existential faith to Ogden's views of philosophy and theology as such, I find the latter to be distorted by a dogmatic adherence to Bultmannian biblical criticism and by some more misconceptions about the nature of authority, criteria, and the relation of these to faith.

First, it is true that Scripture is warranted by Christ and, in one sense, by the apostles. But that fact in itself does not make Scripture a subordinate standard in any meaningful sense. For it may be argued that both Christ and the apostles intended to establish Scripture not as a relative standard, but as an infallible and absolute rule for the church. That is certainly the prima facie intent, at least, of the classic texts on biblical authority such as 2 Timothy 3:16 and 2 Peter 1:19–21, and it is certainly what would be expected on the covenantal understanding of Scripture presented, say, in Deuteronomy 31:24–29.

7. Robert Schuller will doubtless be relieved.

Second, I am sympathetic with Ogden's rejection of "special criteria," but I would establish this rejection on an entirely different basis and thus draw very different conclusions from it. There are no special criteria for theology because God intends not only theology but all human thinking to be governed by his Word. Therefore, to reject special criteria does not necessitate subservience to non-Christian intellectual fashions (without, indeed, any recognition of their problematic character!), as on Ogden's view; rather, it enables the Christian to stand boldly and claim the whole intellectual enterprise, indeed all of human life, for Christ. We can therefore agree with Ogden that we need a metaphysics to prove God's existence; but that metaphysics will have to be a *Christian* metaphysics, itself subject to God's Word and therefore not in bondage to any human fashion. How impoverished this book is, since it does not even consider the possibility that our God is Lord over all human knowledge! Ogden himself is to be pitied, overwhelmed by the modern intellectual fashions to such an extent that he must bow to every wind of doctrine (existentialism, process thought, liberationism) and is entirely unable to speak God's Word into the situation of modern scholarship.

I am sympathetic with Ogden's rejection of "special criteria," but I would establish this rejection on an entirely different basis and thus draw very different conclusions from it. There are no special criteria for theology because God intends not only theology but all human thinking to be governed by his Word.

Third, I would agree with Ogden that personal faith is not a condition for theological understanding, if by that is meant that unbelievers do often state the truth "in spite of themselves," as Van Til used to say. And it is true that one's heart-allegiance to Christ is not something that can be tested objectively. Still, we must reckon, as Ogden does not, with the profound distortions in theological understanding that result from unbelief (cf. 1 Cor. 2:14). And there *are* relatively objective ways, not of testing heart-commitment, but of judging the credibility of a profession (cf. 1 John 4:1–6). It would therefore be foolish for the church (or even the university) to entrust its theological teaching to those who show no evidence of allegiance to Christ.

I would agree with Ogden that personal faith is not a condition for theological understanding, if by that is meant that unbelievers do often state the truth "in spite of themselves," as Van Til used to say.

Ogden's book, therefore, is a book with some insight and some good arguments, granted his dogmatic adherence to the liberal tradition. But for those of us who seek to do theology under the lordship of Christ rather than in bondage to human traditions, it will have to be dismissed as mostly irrelevant.

It was once the case that liberal theologians could simply ignore orthodox scholarship and arguments without much risk, at least without much earthly risk. "Academic respectability" as then understood permitted—indeed, required—such dismissing of the orthodox case. That situation might be changing. Evangelicalism has been gaining numbers and cultural influence, while liberal theology has been losing in both respects. Evangelical scholarship is also improving in amount and quality, on any fair analysis. In time, I believe, economics alone (if not a renewed application of academic fairness) will demand the presence of evangelicals on university religion faculties, perhaps even on now-liberal theological seminary faculties. In such an atmosphere, liberal theology will no longer be able to afford the luxury of ignoring the arguments of those who make the strongest case against their theories. Those liberals who take that challenge seriously could wind up changing their views, or they might be seen by future historians as the founders of a new, revived sort of liberalism that remarkably held its own against the evangelical tide. We don't know what the future will bring, of course. But I am reasonably confident that the sort of liberalism that Ogden represents—self-satisfied, complacent, ignoring its biggest challenges—will be left in the dustbin of history, despite the substantial intelligence and scholarship with which (as in Ogden's case) it is presented. And of course, even if my conjectures about the future of theology prove erroneous, there is still eternity before us. And, Ogden to the contrary, we know that the *eternal* future belongs to those who are faithful to the inerrant Word of God.

I am reasonably confident that the sort of liberalism that Ogden represents—self-satisfied, complacent, ignoring its biggest challenges—will be left in the dustbin of history, despite the substantial intelligence and scholarship with which (as in Ogden's case) it is presented.

APPENDIX O

REVIEW OF PAUL HELM, *BELIEF POLICIES*

Review of Paul Helm, *Belief Policies* (Cambridge: Cambridge University Press, 1994). A shorter version of this review was published in *WTJ* 57, 1 (Spring 1995): 248–51. Used by permission of Westminster Theological Seminary. This is an example of the work of Paul Helm (chapter 13), an orthodox Calvinist who engages in both analytical philosophy (chapter 12) and historical theology. (For stylistic purposes, this appendix has been copyedited for inclusion in this volume.)

Belief Policies plays the philosophers' game as it is played today. It analyzes and evaluates a great many concepts and arguments without digression. The organization is very tight.

PAUL HELM IS PROFESSOR of the history and philosophy of religion at King's College of the University of London. He is also a Calvinistic Christian who has served as associate editor of *The Banner of Truth* magazine. Recently in the *Journal* I reviewed his *The Providence of God*, published by InterVarsity Press. The present volume is very different.

Belief Policies is a philosophy book of a very academic and technical sort. Unlike *Providence*, there is no attempt here to reach a popular audience. Nor is there any indication in this book of Helm's personal religious or theological commitment, although the book does discuss issues of religious epistemology, among other things. *Belief Policies* plays the philosophers' game as it is played today. It analyzes and evaluates a great many concepts and arguments without digression. The organization is very tight; one gets the impression (which one did not get from *Providence*) that every sentence, every discussion, is precisely where it ought to be. Each sentence advances the argument in some way; this is not an easy book to skim. As much as any other philosophy book I have read, *Belief Policies* shows a mastery of the literature relevant to its subject.

For all its philosophical sophistication, however, this book is not only of interest to philosophers. I will focus my attention on its implications, and the questions it raises, for theology and for Christian thought in general.

In the book, Helm explores the role of the will in the formation of human beliefs. This is an important matter for Christian theology, which has always been concerned with the epistemology of knowing God and his world. Specifically, Scripture *commands* people to believe in Christ. Opponents of Christianity have often ridiculed the idea that people can be under obligation to believe something. Belief, they argue, is not under our control, so how can God require us to believe something that we do not in fact believe? In one sense, Reformed theology agrees with the objectors: what we believe is ultimately under God's control rather than our own. But Scripture does assume that we are responsible for beliefs as for actions. Therefore, as secondary causes, we do have control to some extent over what we believe as we have control over what we do. Certainly, Romans 1 presents unbelief as the result of a voluntary decision, to "exchange the truth for a lie." But how can that be?

Helm explores the role of the will in the formation of human beliefs. This is an important matter for Christian theology, which has always been concerned with the epistemology of knowing God and his world. Specifically, Scripture commands *people to believe in Christ.*

At first glance, it seems plausible to argue that the will has no role to play in belief. Obviously, I cannot simply will to believe anything at all. Being American, and believing that I am American, I cannot by fiat will to believe that I am Indonesian. So Bernard Williams argues that one cannot decide to believe something "just like that" (46). Helm, however, who draws many parallels in this book between beliefs and actions, replies that "breaking the smoking habit may involve the will, even though a person cannot break the habit 'just like that'" (46).

Helm points out that, in ways somewhat more subtle than those that Williams has in mind, the will does influence belief. People do, after all, sometimes believe without proper justification. In such cases, we are inclined to say that their belief is "willful." There are, for example, such phenomena as wishful thinking and projection. And often people willfully fail to give proper attention to evidence, or to evaluate it according to proper standards.

Since belief is subject to "standards," to evaluation, there is something like an "ethics of belief." Many writers have commented on the subject of what we are obligated or permitted to believe. Helm says that Locke at one point even "makes epistemology a branch of ethics" (123). (Helm himself does not seem to go that far: see 26–28.) Formulations of the ethics of belief have differed greatly: from W. K. Clifford's view that nothing should be believed without sufficient evidence (90–97) to

Since belief is subject to "standards," to evaluation, there is something like an "ethics of belief." Many writers have commented on the subject of what we are obligated or permitted to believe.

O. K. Bouwsma's view that at least in matters of Christian belief we must "resist any attempt to ground . . . faith in evidence" (207; discussion on 202–7).

Helm gives to such principles the name *belief-policies*. He says, "As I shall use the expression a belief-policy is a strategy or project or programme for accepting, rejecting or suspending judgment as to the truth of propositions in accordance with a set of evidential norms" (58). A belief-policy governs our *use* of evidence in developing our beliefs. In Helm's view, belief-policies are the most important area in which the will influences our beliefs. "We choose to believe by choosing, or choosing to retain, belief-policies for acquiring, retaining, or discarding our beliefs" (58).

A belief-policy governs our use of evidence in developing our beliefs. In Helm's view, belief-policies are the most important area in which the will influences our beliefs. "We choose to believe by choosing, or choosing to retain, belief-policies for acquiring, retaining, or discarding our beliefs."

Not all beliefs are justified by belief-policies, for "there are cases of instinctive and infantile beliefs which are justified" (7). Nor are belief-policies necessarily conscious: they may be "dispositional and tacit, or the result of an overt choice" (58). Belief-policies are of many kinds. In addition to the examples above, Helm discusses the belief-policies of Locke, James, and Plantinga at length and others more briefly. Belief-policies can address questions about the strength of belief, verification, falsification, permission, obligation, the importance or priority of some beliefs over against others, the degree of conservatism in maintaining or revising past beliefs, burden of proof. Some belief-policies seek to maximize the number of true beliefs, others to minimize erroneous ones; others, presumably, seek to balance these concerns in some way.

Helm uses the concept of a belief-policy to illumine the ways in which "weakness of will" and "self-deception" bear upon belief (142–63). As weakness of will can inhibit our actions, so it can hinder the implementation of a belief-policy. The belief-policy specifies the ends we seek to achieve in believing; the will seeks to reach those ends. Failure to carry through one's belief-policy can be seen in actions as well as words.

Helm argues . . . that belief is to a large extent governed by the will, so that people are responsible for their beliefs. Does this view imply the legitimacy of persecuting people for false beliefs?

Sometimes, through weakness of will, we fail to believe as our belief-policy dictates, even though we know what it requires. In Helm's view, this is not self-deception (149). Self-deception enters when "the agent does not recognize the wrongness of his failure to adopt or follow a belief-policy" (150). The "logical form" of self-deception with respect to the belief that proposition p is true "is a person's believing that p, while not believing that p is believed; or more strongly while it is believed that p is not believed" (153). Helm therefore recognizes that a person is able to hold two contradictory beliefs at the same time.

Helm argues, therefore, that belief is to a large extent governed by the will, so that people are responsible for their beliefs. Does this view imply the legitimacy of persecuting people for false beliefs? Helm addresses the question of toleration, pointing out that some classical defenses of toleration are compatible with his doctrine of responsibility for beliefs and belief-policies (164–88).

The last chapter, in which Helm discusses fideism, is the most obviously interesting from a theological point of view. He mentions Popkin's definition of *fideism* as the claim that "truth in religion is ultimately based on faith rather than on reasoning or evidence" (189). But he also presents fideism as something that occurs outside religious discourse narrowly defined: "a fideist is someone who holds that one may justifiably form a belief supported by insufficient evidence for the truth of what is believed or even unsupported by the evidence, or even in the teeth of evidence against; or that one may justifiably give a greater degree of strength to a belief than is warranted by the evidence for the proposition that is believed" (189). Thus, some forms of epistemological skepticism, which recommend the formation of beliefs on nonevidential grounds, may be called fideistic (195–200).

Helm argues that there are many differences within the family of positions called fideisms. *Some are "global," claiming that all knowledge is by faith; others limit fideism to some area(s) of knowledge, such as the knowledge of God.*

On Helm's view, fideism is a belief-policy, but one that paradoxically sets itself against some uses of evidence and reasoning. Nevertheless, some fideists do argue for their positions, using various rational arguments. In religious discussions, for example, the divine transcendence and our obligation to accept revelation on divine authority are used to warrant fideistic epistemologies. Thus, although these thinkers disavow or deemphasize the use of evidence in forming beliefs about God, they nevertheless affirm the use of rational argument in defending their belief-policies. That rational argument is a "second-order" defense of a "first-order" fideism (193).

Helm argues that there are many differences within the family of positions called *fideisms*. Some are "global," claiming that all knowledge is by faith; others limit fideism to some area(s) of knowledge, such as the knowledge of God. Some defend themselves by "second-order" rational arguments; others do not. Some defend their positions on epistemological grounds, others on moral or religious grounds. Fideisms vary as to the specific role of evidence: some seek to go beyond evidence, others to avoid any evidential defense at all. Helm notes Arvin Vos's suggestion that Aquinas, of all people, was in one sense a fideist, because "the transcendent subject-matter of much theology necessarily goes beyond human understanding" (194), although for Aquinas there is "*some* evidence for faith" (195).

Paul Helm

Alvin Plantinga claims that belief in God does not require evidence or argument, but may be placed among the "basic propositions" of one's epistemic system. Nevertheless, he denies that this "Reformed epistemology" is fideistic, because in his view these propositions are "grounded" (e.g., through direct experience) and because, as epistemically basic propositions, they are among the "deliverances of reason."

Helm nevertheless finds some parallels between Plantinga's view and some forms of fideism, particularly his assertion that the grounds for believing that God exists are person-relative or community-relative (216; discussion on 207–16).

At one point I do question Helm's account of Plantinga. Helm thinks that when Plantinga says that "one who takes God as properly basic can also know that God exists," he really should have substituted *does* for *can*, in order to state his view clearly. Helm then points out that when one makes that substitution, a contradiction ensues: for an unbeliever who made the nonexistence of God properly basic would then "know" that God does not exist. Then the believer would know that God exists and the unbeliever would know that God does not exist. But that is impossible. In my view, Helm's argument here raises questions about the legitimacy of his initial substitution of *does* for *can* in Plantinga's statement (212–13).

The notion of a belief-policy is an important one. When Scripture rebukes people for their unbelief in the face of clear revelation (Rom. 1:18–32), it implicitly rebukes their belief-policy, namely, their attempt to avoid proper consideration and evaluation of the evidence given by revelation.

The importance of this book for theology is that Helm has shown some of the important ways in which human belief is influenced by the will. The notion of a belief-policy is an important one. When Scripture rebukes people for their unbelief in the face of clear revelation (Rom. 1:18–32), it implicitly rebukes their belief-policy, namely, their attempt to avoid proper consideration and evaluation of the evidence given by revelation. When people are regenerated by God's Spirit, they receive a new ability to see that revelation for what it truly is. Their new openness to God's revelation may be described as a new belief-policy. When Scripture commands repentance and faith, it implicitly commands people to renounce their old belief-policy and to adopt a new one, one that will generate new beliefs (or, on Van Til's account, formerly repressed beliefs) about God, the world, and themselves.

Helm's account also brings out some of the complexities of human psychology and epistemology that make self-deception possible. That also illuminates the biblical teaching that unbelief is self-deceptive, a repression of what one knows to be true.

Helm's account also brings out some of the complexities of human psychology and epistemology that make self-deception possible. That also illuminates the biblical teaching that unbelief is self-deceptive, a repression of what one knows to be true.

When non-Christians object to the biblical commands to believe on the ground that belief is involuntary, Helm's book provides us with many useful replies. The consideration of belief-policies is especially useful. For to discuss with non-Christian objectors the role of the will in the formation of belief-policies is, in effect, to question what Dooyeweerd called the *autonomy of theoretical thought*. And such a challenge to human autonomy brings us to the central concerns of Christian witness.

Some questions do remain, of course. Helm's account of the justification of belief-policies is somewhat unsatisfying. He lists various factors that should play a role in an individual's determination of what belief-policy to follow (summarized on 140–41). Nevertheless, he insists that there "can be no rationally compelling second-order argument for the superiority of one policy over all others, though there can be fairly compelling arguments for the superiority of one belief-policy over *some* others" (59; cf. 140–41). A belief-policy governs the use of evidence, and so it cannot itself be wholly based on evidence (59, 67). Helm connects the lack of rational compulsion in this matter to the essential role of the will. Since belief-policies are partly voluntary, they cannot be wholly based on rational considerations.

I do not think it is necessary to oppose *will* and *reason* as sharply as Helm seems to suggest. My own inclination would be to say that *will* and *reason* are simply aspects of, perhaps perspectives on, the integrated human personality. On this basis, the will is always rational and reason always acts voluntarily. To be sure, reason is sometimes constrained, and that might seem to separate it from the will; but recall Helm's earlier illustration of breaking the smoking habit: the will may be involved even when it operates under relative constraints. And on the other hand, the "rationality" of the will is sometimes a defective rationality, because human reason itself sometimes functions defectively; but the will does not operate apart from reason.

I do not think it is necessary to oppose will *and* reason *as sharply as Helm seems to suggest. My own inclination would be to say that* will *and* reason *are simply aspects of, perhaps perspectives on, the integrated human personality.*

Helm himself does not define *will* or *reason*, so I am not sure why he finds it necessary to say that the role of the will in belief-policies necessarily excludes a rationally compelling argument for a belief-policy. But I must ask why we cannot say that there are rationally compelling grounds for, say, a Christian belief-policy, and still maintain that people willfully reject that policy. That seems to be the implication of the biblical doctrine of the clarity of revelation in Romans 1:18–21.

As we have seen, Helm also argues that a belief-policy cannot be based on evidence since it governs the use of evidence. Otherwise, circularity ensues. But in my Van Tillian mode, I ask: what's wrong with a little circularity?

Seriously: at this point, we need to define what is meant by *evidence*, as in the discussion above we needed a precise definition of *will*. If *evidence* is limited to what is "self-evident" and "evident to the senses," then I would say that Helm is right. The grounds for adopting a belief-policy are broader than *evidence* in this narrow sense, and the belief-policy governs the use of such evidence without thereby completely controlling its own justification.

But if *evidence* includes everything that legitimately justifies the adoption of a belief, then there is no escape from the circularity in view. The grounds for adopting belief-policies are necessarily evaluated by the belief-policy in effect.

If evidence *includes everything that legitimately justifies the adoption of a belief, then there is no escape from the circularity in view. The grounds for adopting belief-policies are necessarily evaluated by the belief-policy in effect.*

Now, why should we assume, as Helm does, that belief-policies govern evidence in the narrow sense, but not in the broad sense? Is it not the case that human beings adopt policies for dealing with all sorts of rational considerations, not only with *evidence* narrowly defined? And must not those broad belief-policies be, in the nature of the case, self-reflective and, indeed, self-justifying?

Helm's book has an excellent grasp of the fact that voluntary factors enter into human knowledge, and that they enter precisely at the point where people seek to justify their beliefs. The book is therefore a powerful weapon against claims to "neutrality," against claims that knowledge is religiously unproblematic.

Van Til's point, of course, was that a Christian belief-policy, taken as a datum of revelation, is self-attesting, self-justifying. It is self-attesting because it is itself supremely authoritative, not dependent on any other authority for its verification. It does not, therefore, depend for its justification on any *other* belief-policy. In that sense, its justification is "circular." Taken as a datum of the believer's consciousness, however, rather than as a datum of revelation, the Christian belief-policy does have an external justification—in divine revelation itself.

I have defended Van Tillian "circularity" in my *DKG*, 130–33, in *AJCB*, 10–15, and in chapter 22 of *CVT*. I will not, therefore, repeat those arguments here. I do think that circularity of a sort is unavoidable when one is seeking to justify what we might call, in terms of the current discussion, an *ultimate* belief-policy, a policy governing *all* beliefs.

Nevertheless, Helm's book has an excellent grasp of the fact that voluntary factors enter into human knowledge, and that they enter precisely at the point where people seek to justify their beliefs. The book is therefore a powerful weapon against claims to "neutrality," against claims that knowledge is religiously unproblematic. In my view, it takes some large steps in the right direction, even if it has not reached its proper destination.

APPENDIX P

REVIEW OF ESTHER LIGHTCAP MEEK, *LONGING TO KNOW*

Review of Esther Lightcap Meek, *Longing to Know* (Grand Rapids: Brazos Press, 2003). This review originally appeared in *Presbyterion* 29, 2 (Fall 2003). Used by permission of Covenant Theological Seminary. I have discussed Meek's work in chapter 13. Here is my review of her first book. (For stylistic purposes, this appendix has been copyedited for inclusion in this volume.)

IN THIS VOLUME, Esther Meek wrestles with a paradox that has troubled the theory of knowledge since the pre-Socratics. When I say, "I know there is gas in my car," I imply that in fact there is gas in my car. *Knowledge*, classically defined, is "justified, true belief." So for a belief to count as knowledge, it must be true. And if I have any doubt about the truth of that belief, I must doubt that it's really knowledge. So in the history of philosophy, knowledge has come in most circles to imply total certainty and exclude any doubt. Some have thought that through difficult rational exertions we can attain such total certainty (Plato, Descartes); others have thought that since total certainty is not possible, skepticism is our only option (Protagoras, Hume, some postmoderns). In the main traditions of epistemology, then, knowledge either is a rare, difficult achievement or is nonexistent.

In ordinary life we continue to claim knowledge of all sorts of things, such as facts, numbers, people, skills, language, scientific laws, and God. And we claim knowledge even when we do not claim total certainty, even when we admit that we could be wrong.

Nevertheless (and this is the other side of the paradox), in ordinary life we continue to claim knowledge of all sorts of things, such as facts, numbers, people, skills, language, scientific laws, and God. And we claim knowledge even when we do not claim total certainty, even when we admit that we could be wrong.

Meek believes that there is an epistemology implicit in these ordinary claims to knowledge, one significantly different from the rationalist and skeptical options of the philosophical traditions. This epistemology, she believes, saves us both from skepticism and from the fear of falling into skepticism.

As a Christian, Meek sees this skepticism as a source of temptation for people seeking God. So her book has a pastoral function: removing that barrier to faith. She argues that we can know God in the same way in which we come to know other people. Knowing God, she says, is like knowing Jeff, her auto mechanic.

Meek defines knowing *as "the responsible human struggle to rely on clues to focus on a coherent pattern and submit to its reality." The book takes up each clause of that definition consecutively.*

Her epistemology follows that of Michael Polanyi pretty closely, but her book is not a study of his work. She doesn't quote him or analyze his writings. Rather, she applies his basic perspective to a study of how we get to know ourselves, the world, and God in daily life. And her application, I would say, greatly enriches the Polanyian approach.

Meek starts not with *knowledge* as an abstraction, but with concrete acts of knowing, "epistemic acts" that we perform every day. (She hints, but doesn't quite say, that we should jettison the traditional definition of *knowledge* as "justified, true belief.") She defines *knowing* as "the responsible human struggle to rely on clues to focus on a coherent pattern and submit to its reality." The book takes up each clause of that definition consecutively.

We should not expect to achieve complete certainty without any doubt. Meek would like to replace the concept of certainty *(which she thinks connotes exhaustive, inerrant knowledge) with that of* confidence, *the continued reassurance that our acts of knowing are getting us somewhere, leading us in the right direction.*

A good example of knowing, she says, is looking at a newspaper puzzle in such a way as to see a three-dimensional picture. On the surface it appears to be just a blur of shapes and colors. But if you follow the directions, such as by moving the newspaper gradually away from your face, something shifts and the blur becomes a 3-D picture, say, of dolphins. Not everybody sees the pattern right away. For many, the process is a struggle. The surface features give you clues, but many of them serve in the end only as background to the main picture, rather than as parts of that picture. You need to learn to look *through* the clues to see the overall pattern. Then you must submit to that pattern, affirming it, treating it as real.

Similarly for knowing auto mechanics and God. We begin with what data we have, and we seek to make responsible judgments about persons. As we see indications of various qualities, such as trustworthiness, those become a pattern that illumines further experience, and ultimately a pattern to which we must submit in our thoughts and behavior. (Here she has some great things to say about the biblical integration of knowledge and obedience in our relationship to God.)

In these acts of knowing, she says, we should not expect to achieve complete certainty without any doubt. Meek would like to replace the concept of *certainty* (which she thinks connotes exhaustive, inerrant knowledge) with that of *confidence*, the continued reassurance that our acts of knowing are getting us somewhere, leading us in the right direction. Similarly, she thinks, in our knowing we should seek *contact* between our mind and reality, not *correspondence*, which she understands as an exhaustive image of reality.

In my own book *DKG*, I describe several perspectives on knowledge, or knowing. Meek's book operates mainly within what I called there the *existential perspective*, knowledge as a subjective process. Other perspectives are the *normative* (knowledge as following norms or rules) and the *situational* (knowledge as seeking conformity with facts). But since these are perspectives, each involves the other two. As a subjective process, knowing seeks to follow authoritative norms and to bring itself into conformity with the real world. So Meek recognizes normative and situational dimensions as well. The norms are like the newspaper's rules for solving the 3-D puzzle, and the situational facts are both the clues and the patterns we see through the clues. So in the case of knowing God, she makes illuminating comments about the authority of Scripture and God's revelation of himself in the created world.

This is a terrific book. I can't begin in a short review to adequately illustrate the beauty of its writing and the cogency of its reasoning. But let me just say that I have never read a serious philosophical work (and this surely is one) that is as eloquently and delightfully expressed.

This is a terrific book. I can't begin in a short review to adequately illustrate the beauty of its writing and the cogency of its reasoning. But let me just say that I have never read a serious philosophical work (and this surely is one) that is as eloquently and delightfully expressed. Meek has a wonderful gift of illustration. Analogies and pictures fly from her mind like drops of water from a great fountain. Every page contains two or three of them, so there must be hundreds in this book. You'll read about kitchen tables, golf games, copperhead snakes, children, weddings, on and on, as Meek seeks to show us how knowing happens in all the ordinary experiences of life.

Esther Lightcap Meek

I have a few reservations about her critique of certainty and tolerance of doubt. I suppose that, given her definition of *certainty* as exhaustive knowledge, I can go along with her rejection of it. But Scripture says some negative things about doubt (Matt. 14:31; 21:21; 28:17; Acts 10:20; 11:12; Rom. 14:23; James 1:6). In Matthew 14:31 and Romans 14:23, it is the opposite of faith and therefore a sin. Further, knowing God in Scripture often seems to have a sureness about it that may be less than Meek's definition of *certainty*, but is, I think, more than her definition of *confidence*. Note especially the "certainty" of Luke 1:4, the "proofs" of Acts 1:3, and the centurion's words of Luke 23:47. More needs to be said, perhaps, about the nature of submission, the final step in Meek's definition of *knowledge*. If the revelation of God to which we submit is *infallible*, then it must serve as the criterion of all other knowledge.

As such, it is the standard of certitude and must be regarded as itself in some sense maximally certain.

All in all, this is the best book on epistemology (let alone Christian epistemology) to come along in many, many years. It is a must for any serious student of the discipline and, indeed, for ordinary people who are trying to get clear on how to know God.

I agree with Meek that even the certainty of God's Word is not an exhaustive transcript of his mind. And I agree with her that doubt, as an honest admission of our fallibility, is not only tolerable, but even a virtue (James 4:13–16; and note Paul's admission in Romans 11:33–36 concerning our knowledge of God). But *Longing to Know* doesn't help me to distinguish between sinful and justifiable doubt, or to understand fully the sense in which God's revelation leaves us without excuse. Perhaps, in the end, there are differences between knowing God and knowing one's auto mechanic that need to be more fully explored.

But these problems, if they are problems (and not merely my misunderstandings), are errors of omission. And this book includes so much that a few omissions can hardly be ground for complaint. All in all, this is the best book on epistemology (let alone Christian epistemology) to come along in many, many years. It is a must for any serious student of the discipline and, indeed, for ordinary people who are trying to get clear on how to know God.

APPENDIX Q

"CHRISTIANITY AND CONTEMPORARY EPISTEMOLOGY"

An article reviewing John L. Pollock's *Contemporary Theories of Knowledge* (Totowa, NJ: Rowman and Littlefield, 1986). Originally published in *WTJ* 52, 1 (Spring 1990): 131–41. Used by permission of Westminster Theological Seminary. Pollock is a secular analytic philosopher. His epistemology is internalist, and so provides a useful contrast with the externalist epistemology of Plantinga described in chapter 13. (For stylistic purposes, this appendix has been copyedited for inclusion in this volume.)

Theologians have traditionally taken an interest in philosophical epistemology because of their concern with the knowledge of God.

THEOLOGIANS HAVE TRADITIONALLY taken an interest in philosophical epistemology because of their concern with the knowledge of God. Sometimes they have sought to use secular epistemological theories to their advantage; sometimes they have sought to refute such theories. But the interaction has often been vigorous. This history suggests the value to theologians of keeping current in the field. We are still writing quite a bit about the classical epistemologies of Plato and Aristotle (against the background of Parmenides and the Sophists), about traditional rationalism and empiricism, Kant and Hegel. Some theologians have also developed interest in certain twentieth-century developments, particularly those associated with logical positivism, the later Wittgenstein and the existentialists, and especially the movement away from "objective" knowledge represented in different ways by Thomas Kuhn, Michael Polanyi, Norwood Hanson, Paul Feyerabend, Alasdair MacIntyre, D. Z. Phillips, and others.

Like most other theological works, my own *DKG* goes only this far.[1] Of course, its purpose was not to survey secular theories but to set forth some biblical teachings about knowledge. But some comparison between biblical and secular notions was inevitable, and I regret now that I did not in that book refer at greater length to more current developments in the secular field.

Roderick Chisholm, perhaps the best-known contemporary epistemologist, calls the book "a thorough and accurate survey of the present state of the subject, [and Pollock's book] is also an original contribution of first importance. I know of no better introduction to contemporary theories of knowledge."

John Pollock's *Contemporary Theories of Knowledge* is an excellent recent survey of the present-day epistemologies of secular philosophy. Roderick Chisholm, perhaps the best-known contemporary epistemologist, calls the book "a thorough and accurate survey of the present state of the subject, [and Pollock's book] is also an original contribution of first importance. I know of no better introduction to contemporary theories of knowledge" (back cover). I agree with Chisholm's estimate, and I think this book is a very useful tool for bringing theological readers up to date in this area and a good focal point for some Christian evaluations of the contemporary theories.

It is, for the most part, a highly technical book, difficult to read, a book that takes the reader more deeply into the details of its arguments than many of us would prefer to go. At times, however, Pollock wakes us up with vivid illustrations and convenient summaries of his argument. In the former category is the opening of the book, a three-page suspense tale ending with the discovery of Harry. Harry's brain has been surgically removed from his body and placed in a vat of nutrients, where it continues to live. A computer sends impulses over wires attached to the brain, which give Harry the impression that he is living his normal, pre-vat life. As he concludes, the narrator is "racked by the suspicion that I am really a brain in a vat and all this I see around me is just a figment of the computer" (3).

The skeptical conclusion—that we know precisely nothing—is, to Pollock, so implausible, so unlikely, that it actually functions as a reductio. If an argument logically entails skepticism, he maintains, there must be something wrong with the premises.

From this tale, one might anticipate that the book would consist largely of reflection on skepticism. Actually, however, Pollock deals with the skeptic in short fashion. The skeptical conclusion—that we know precisely nothing—is, to Pollock, so implausible, so unlikely, that it actually functions as a reductio. If an argument logically entails skepticism, he maintains, there must be something wrong with the premises. Pure skepticism, of course, is irrefutable, since the skeptic allows his critic no knowledge on the basis of which to debate. But we know that the skeptic is wrong; for if we don't know that, we don't know anything else. And if we do know that, it is evident that we know some things (e.g., that skepticism is false) that we cannot prove.

Skepticism as such, then, is not of much interest to Pollock. But skeptical arguments, he says, are useful, for they alert us to false

1. There is, however, some allusion to more recent developments in the appendix dealing with Plantinga and Wolterstorff.

premises. If a premise leads to skepticism, it cannot be accepted. So skeptical arguments are of considerable negative value (7). From them we can learn various things about what knowledge involves and does not involve.

From here, Pollock takes it for granted not only that we have knowledge, but also that we have various kinds of knowledge: perceptual knowledge, memory knowledge, knowledge by induction and deduction (10ff.). These are the four kinds of knowledge on which the book focuses. Pollock also seems to believe that we may have *a priori* knowledge and moral knowledge, but he notes candidly that these are highly problematic in modern epistemology, and he says nothing more about them through the book. He also ignores, after mentioning it briefly (10), knowledge of other minds. He does not mention the possibility of knowledge coming through the testimony of other persons, which I consider important and sufficiently distinct from the other forms to deserve separate treatment.[2]

John L. Pollock

Nor does he say anything about knowledge through divine revelation. God plays no role in Pollock's epistemology whatsoever, and one gathers that when Pollock describes his position as "naturalistic" (168ff., elsewhere), he means to reject not only the Cartesian ego, the "ghost in [the] machine" (161), but any dependence on religious or supernatural concepts. He claims an advantage to his view in the fact that his concept of knowledge can be applied to a "cognitive machine" (149), and he spends some time speculating on how such a robot might be made to function (149ff.). Pollock's discussion of the cognitive robot is not satisfying to me. He proposes that "Oscar" be given "sense organs" (149), " 'reasoning' faculties, both deductive and inductive" (149), "pain sensors" (150), "a 'language of thought' " (150), "pain-sensor sensors" (151), perceptual organ activation sensors (155), cognitive process sensors (155), mental representations for objects and self (156–61). But he doesn't give us any suggestion as to how these remarkable faculties might be built into a robot. Until he does, the way is open for a critic to argue that such abilities can be performed only by a spirit, even a "Cartesian ego." If Pollock is simply trying to illustrate his epistemological proposal, perhaps Oscar serves a purpose; but if he is presenting this as an argument for naturalism, it certainly does not succeed.

Pollock takes it for granted not only that we have knowledge, but also that we have various kinds of knowledge: perceptual knowledge, memory knowledge, knowledge by induction and deduction. These are the four kinds of knowledge on which the book focuses.

What is *knowledge*? Before 1963, most analytic philosophers defined *knowledge* as "justified, true belief." In 1963, however, there appeared Edmund Gettier's article "Is Justified True Belief Knowledge?"[3] Gettier suggested by counterexamples that not every case of justified true belief

2. Cf. Thomas Reid's *credulity principle.*

3. *Analysis* 23 (1966): 121–23.

was knowledge. Here is one of Gettier's counterexamples, paraphrased by Pollock (180):

> Consider Smith who believes falsely but with good reason that Jones owns a Ford. Smith has no idea where Brown is, but he arbitrarily picks Barcelona and infers from the putative fact that Jones owns a Ford that either Jones owns a Ford or Brown is in Barcelona. It happens by chance that Brown is in Barcelona, so this disjunction is true. Furthermore, as Smith has good reason to believe that Jones owns a Ford, he is justified in believing this disjunction. But as his evidence does not pertain to the true disjunct of the disjunction, we would not regard Smith as *knowing* that either Jones owns a Ford or Brown is in Barcelona.

Many others published articles trying to solve the "Gettier problem," mostly by adding a fourth condition to *knowledge* besides *justification, truth*, and *belief* (9). But still others found counterexamples to those fourth conditions, and so the debate continues to this day.

Many others published articles trying to solve the "Gettier problem," mostly by adding a fourth condition to knowledge *besides* justification, truth, *and* belief. *But still others found counterexamples to those fourth conditions, and so the debate continues to this day.*

Pollock's own solution to the Gettier problem involves some reconstruction of the concept of *justification*, to which we should now turn. "A justified belief," says Pollock, "is one that is 'epistemically permissible' to hold" (7). He distinguishes epistemic permissibility from both prudential and moral permissibility. I am not persuaded by these distinctions. Pollock argues only by giving examples of beliefs that he thinks are prudentially or morally right but epistemically wrong and vice versa. For example, someone promises not to think ill of another; in this case, thinking ill might be morally wrong, though epistemically right. My own analysis of this case, however, is that such a promise is invalid, since it pledges something that cannot be pledged. It is never right to promise someone that I will regard the truth as false or vice versa. Therefore, thinking ill (when epistemically justified) is both epistemically and morally right, and the illustration does nothing to show that the former is not a subset of the latter. Even Pollock's evaluation, however, entails only that epistemic permissibility is not *the only kind* of prudential or moral permissibility, not that epistemic permissibility is outside these two realms. Surely epistemic permissibility is founded on our ethical obligation to believe only the truth. If it is not, then I don't know what basis it might have. (I will discuss Pollock's basis at a later point.)[4]

Pollock distinguishes epistemic permissibility from both prudential and moral permissibility. I am not persuaded by these distinctions. Pollock argues only by giving examples of beliefs that he thinks are prudentially or morally right but epistemically wrong and vice versa.

4. As for prudence, I believe as a Christian that ultimately prudence and morality concur. Pragmatism reduces epistemic norms to prudential ones, which is not, in my view, wrong in itself. But to make this work, one must have a Christian concept of prudence, which was lacking in most forms of pragmatism.

Pollock also distinguishes epistemic permission from any concept of epistemic *obligation*:

> Epistemic norms never tell us that it is *epistemically obligatory* to believe something—only that it is *epistemically* permissible to do so. It is not true, for example, that if I believe both P and "if P then Q" then, in the absence of conflicting reasons, I ought to believe Q. This is because I might not care about Q. (84 [emphasis his]; cf. 124, 185)

My own account of this is that if someone believes P and "if P then Q," in one sense he already believes Q, since Q does not include any information not included in the premises; in another sense, he will believe it if and when he has (at least once) become conscious of the entailment.

Of course, we might be morally obligated to care about Q, which would prevent us from bringing our uncaringness as an excuse. Apart from that, however, Pollock's argument does present a good reason why we would not in this case be obligated to believe Q *consciously*. Most of our beliefs, however, are not being entertained consciously at a particular moment. "Caring" is one reason (among others) why we might consciously attend to a particular belief at a particular time, but it doesn't seem to have much to do with what we believe or don't believe.

My own account of this is that if someone believes P and "if P then Q," in one sense he already believes Q, since Q does not include any information not included in the premises; in another sense, he will believe it if and when he has (at least once) become conscious of the entailment. The element of obligation becomes evident when someone tries to deny what he knows—denying it either to himself or to someone else. At that point, it becomes legitimate to say, "You *ought* to believe Q; and when asked in an appropriate forum, you ought to admit that you believe Q."

One reason that Pollock seems to resist any subjection of reasoning to moral evaluation might be his view that we "do not literally 'decide' what to believe."

One reason that Pollock seems to resist any subjection of reasoning to moral evaluation might be his view that we "do not literally 'decide' what to believe" (22). On page 80, he adds:

> We do not have voluntary control over our beliefs. We cannot just decide to believe that 2 + 2 = 5 and thereby do it. We have at most indirect control over what we believe. We can try to get ourselves to believe something by repeatedly rehearsing the evidence for it, or putting countervailing evidence out of our minds, or by deliberately seeking new evidence for it, but we cannot voluntarily make ourselves believe something in the same sense that we can voluntarily clench our fists.

There is much truth in this. It may be that we simply believe what we believe, and apparent "struggles to decide what to believe" are struggles to form a new belief (by confronting evidence as Pollock outlines above), struggles to determine which of two or more inconsistent beliefs will prevail in our thinking, or introspective struggles to determine what we already believe in our heart of hearts.[5]

Nevertheless, if there is no voluntary decision concerning what to believe as such, there certainly are voluntary decisions to be made as to whether and how a belief is to be confessed, applied, implemented, and so forth. Especially when people refuse to acknowledge what they know to be true ("exchanging the truth for a lie"), the will is obviously active. And there are voluntary decisions concerning the use of evidence, as Pollock mentions in the quote above. Thus, there is plenty of room for moral evaluation in the epistemic sphere. And since epistemology deals not only with the beliefs we actually have but also with the processes by which we confess, defend, implement, apply, resist, or deny our beliefs, it is not wrong to say that there are certain beliefs that we "ought" to hold,[6] beliefs that are justified by a kind of moral rightness.

If there is no voluntary decision concerning what to believe as such, there certainly are voluntary decisions to be made as to whether and how a belief is to be confessed, applied, implemented, and so forth.

The final thing to note about Pollock's view of epistemic justification is that it is subjective, rather than objective (10; cf. 183). He also characterizes this concept as the "belief-guiding" or "reason-guiding" sense of justification (10). It helps us "in determining what to believe."[7] A justification gives us reasons for adopting a particular belief.

Justifications in this sense are person-variable. A good reason for one person to believe P will not necessarily be a good reason for someone else to believe it. A child might believe in the existence of Santa Claus because his mother has testified to that proposition. He has found his mother to be trustworthy, and so he rightly believes he has good reasons for his conclusion. But the child's father, having had much broader experience of Christmas celebrations in their cultural context, would not be right to accept the child's justification for belief.

The final thing to note about Pollock's view of epistemic justification is that it is subjective, rather than objective. He also characterizes this concept as the "belief-guiding" or "reason-guiding" sense of justification.

Now, on this view of justification, one may be justified in believing something, say, P, even though P is false. That fact is illustrated in the previous paragraph. The child has good reasons to believe in Santa and no good reasons to deny that he exists. Therefore, he

5. I say that this "may" be the case. My actual view of the matter is more complicated. I think that there are different *levels* of belief. At the most fundamental level, we know God and we know the world as God made it. We thus have a limited, though adequate, stock of true beliefs. But sin causes us to develop additional beliefs inconsistent with those true beliefs—that is, to "exchange the truth for a lie." Regeneration enables us to resist this process. Belief at the most fundamental level is involuntary; but in the process of belief-substitution in the states both of sin and of regeneration, the will is quite active indeed (though even in those states, the process is not always conscious).

6. Here I take *hold* as a broad term including the possessing, acknowledging, confessing, applying, and implementing of the belief in question.

7. Evidently, as we've seen, we should ignore any moral connotations that we might hear in this phrase.

is justified in believing a proposition that, most of us would say, is objectively false.

The rest of the book focuses on the exploration of this concept of justification. Pollock insists that "the central topic of epistemology is epistemic justification rather than knowledge" (9). He is right as to the importance of this concept in the epistemology literature.[8] I would agree that subjective justification is an important category and therefore deserves study. I don't understand, however, why this concept dominates the literature (including the present volume) to the extent that it does. It is certainly not the only kind of epistemic justification, and it might not even be the most important kind.

Pollock insists that "the central topic of epistemology is epistemic justification rather than knowledge." He is right as to the importance of this concept in the epistemology literature.

Consider again the child who believes in Santa Claus on his mother's testimony. Is he justified in believing in Santa Claus? I have explained how we could answer "yes" to this question, by taking *justified* in the subjective sense. But is it not obvious that in another sense the child's belief is *not* justified? Is it not common for freshmen entering college to be told that beliefs uncritically acquired at Mother's knee are not adequately justified for the purposes of higher education?

Is it not also common for a reviewer of, say, a biography to criticize the author for making "unjustified allegations"? In that context, the reviewer is not referring to whatever private, subjective reasons the author might have had for his disputed beliefs. Rather, the reviewer is expressing disappointment that the author has not *given* reasons in the book sufficient to convince *others* to believe as he does.

I think that *usually* when we[9] speak of justified beliefs, we are speaking of beliefs well enough grounded to stand the scrutiny not only of those holding the beliefs, but of those who know the subject best.[10]

Remarkably, Pollock, in the appendix where he considers the Gettier problem, notes that subjective justification as he has earlier defined it is not the kind of justification necessary for knowledge. In response to the Gettier challenge, Pollock develops a concept of "objective" justification that he thinks will do justice to our intuition that justification is a necessary condition of knowledge. After exploring several possibilities, he settles on this one:

Remarkably, Pollock, in the appendix where he considers the Gettier problem, notes that subjective justification as he has earlier defined it is not the kind of justification necessary for knowledge.

> S knows P if and only if S instantiates some argument A supporting P which is (1) ultimately undefeated relative to the set

8. See my *DKG*, 389–91, 395–98 on Plantinga and Wolterstorff.

9. As indicated earlier, the *we* here will have to exclude professional epistemologists.

10. Another possibility, suggested in *DKG*, 397f., is that there are multiple "levels" of justification corresponding to the kinds of cogency demanded by persons in various contexts (scholarly societies vs. children's Sunday schools). The highest social level on this scale would be our relationship with God, before whom we always stand, and who continually challenges us to be satisfied with nothing less than an absolute justification, a justification based on his Word.

> of all truths, and (2) ultimately undefeated relative to the set of all truths socially sensitive for S. (193)

If Pollock is right that objective, not subjective, justification is the kind of justification necessary to knowledge, and if I am right that objective justification is at least as important to epistemology as subjective, then I cannot understand why Pollock devotes 95 percent of the book to subjective justification!

"Instantiates" here roughly means "accepts," but see page 188 for more precision. "Ultimately undefeated" means that all the potential refutations to the argument can themselves be decisively refuted. "Socially sensitive" truths are truths that S is "expected to know" by others in his social group. If S is expected to know a proposition Q that if true would defeat P, and if he does not know an adequate defeater for Q, then S does not know P even if Q is false. But if S's argument defeats such Qs and all other potential defeaters, then S knows P. This concept of *objective justification* makes more precise the concept that I sketched intuitively in the previous paragraphs.

Well, if Pollock is right that objective, not subjective, justification is the kind of justification necessary to knowledge, and if I am right that objective justification is at least as important to epistemology as subjective, then I cannot understand why Pollock devotes 95 percent of the book to subjective justification! Is it perhaps that, having eliminated any role for God in this epistemology, he is thus unable to give any cogent account of *objective truth*?

Let me try to show how a theistic commitment would modify his perspective and make it more cogent. It is perhaps significant that in describing objective justification, Pollock gives a role to the knower's social group, to what the knower is "expected to know." If Pollock were sufficiently broad-minded to accept the membership of God in such a social group, then "expected to know" would take on moral significance (contrary to Pollock's earlier insistence) and we would have some concrete guidance on how to evaluate claims to objective knowledge: since God is omniscient, anyone who meets condition (2) will automatically meet condition (1). We can then judge A's claim to knowledge on the basis of our knowledge of what God expects A to know = knowledge of God's revelation. (Otherwise, we would need to be omniscient ourselves to judge whether someone had met condition [1].)[11]

The main body of the book is devoted to a survey of contemporary epistemologies in which Pollock defends one type of epistemology and attempts to refute the others.

The main body of the book is devoted to a survey of contemporary epistemologies in which Pollock defends one type of epistemology and attempts to refute the others. By *epistemologies* we are here to understand views of subjective justification, and the term *justification* will henceforth refer to subjective justification unless I indicate otherwise. He first distinguishes between *doxastic* and *nondoxastic* theories. (His taxonomy is found on 19–25.) The former holds that justification of

11. "Knowing what God expects us to know" is, of course, itself problematic. My *DKG* is intended in part to show how we come to know and apply God's revelation.

a belief for S is entirely a function of the other beliefs held by S. On a doxastic view, one justifies his beliefs by relating them (by comparison, deduction, induction, etc.) to other beliefs one holds. On a nondoxastic view, one is not limited to this sort of justification. For example, on one kind of nondoxastic view, a belief derived "directly" from perception is justified because perception is a legitimate cognitive process, whether or not we have beliefs about the origin of the belief and the legitimacy of perception.

Pollock's taxonomy of epistemological views is as follows:

I. Doxastic
   A. Foundationalism
   B. Coherentism
      1. Linear positive
      2. Holistic positive
      3. Negative

II. Nondoxastic
   A. Externalism
      1. Probabilism
      2. Reliabilism
   B. Internalism

On a foundationalist view, beliefs are ultimately justified by reference to "foundational" or "basic" beliefs. Among all the beliefs we hold, some are more fundamental to justification than others.

DIRECT REALISM—POLLOCK'S VIEW

Under the doxastic category are two distinct views: foundationalism and coherentism. On a foundationalist view, beliefs are ultimately justified by reference to "foundational" or "basic" beliefs. Among all the beliefs we hold, some are more fundamental to justification than others. Through the history of philosophy, various sorts of beliefs have been considered foundational: we will recall Descartes' *clear and distinct ideas*, Spinoza's *axioms*, Leibniz's *laws of thought*, Hume's *impressions*,[12] Thomas Reid's *common sense*, and the *logical atoms* of Russell and the early Wittgenstein. We may also recall the recent proposal of Alvin Plantinga and Nicholas Wolterstorff that belief in God be considered "epistemologically basic."[13] The most common view today, however, is a variety of empiricism in which the foundation consists of reports of sense experience, or at least of reports of the "appearances" with which we are acquainted.[14] These beliefs are considered self-justifying,

The most common view today, however, is a variety of empiricism in which the foundation consists of reports of sense experience, or at least of reports of the "appearances" with which we are acquainted.

12. Hume's view might, however, be better understood as nondoxastic, in Pollock's vocabulary.

13. Alvin Plantinga and Nicholas Wolterstorff, eds., *Faith and Rationality: Reason and Belief in God* (Notre Dame, IN: University of Notre Dame Press, 1983). Discussed in *DKG*, 382–402.

14. Chisholm's famous "I am appeared to redly," which Pollock also employs, is a way to avoid prejudicing the question of what reality, if any, the appearance refers to.

and all other beliefs must be justified in relation to them. The nonfoundational beliefs are derived from the foundational by some kind of "reasoning."

Pollock tries very hard to present views that he ultimately rejects in their very best form. His practice in this respect is commendable. J. Gresham Machen was also very good at this, and present-day theologians would do well to follow such examples. I will not, obviously, be able to reproduce Pollock's expositions and arguments in detail, but I will try to summarize accurately.

Pollock tries very hard to present views that he ultimately rejects in their very best form. His practice in this respect is commendable.

The following is a highly condensed summary of Pollock's argument against foundationalism: (1) We do not always know how we are being appeared to; indeed, we can be wrong about that. After an accident, let us say, witnesses often correct their first impressions of how they were appeared to (59–61). Therefore, appearance beliefs are not self-justifying. (2) We rarely have *beliefs* about how we are appeared to. Evidence of our senses does not take the form of beliefs (61). Therefore, if sense perception plays some basic role in justification, it is not by way of *beliefs about* our perceptions, as on a foundationalist theory. (3) Should we say that epistemologically basic beliefs are not incorrigible or self-justifying, but only prima facie justified? To say that is to say that such beliefs are justified until we have reason to disbelieve them, "innocent until proven guilty." But there is no better reason to make this claim for sensory appearance-beliefs than for any other kind of belief; so there is no reason, on this basis, to make any particular kind of belief epistemologically basic. Without "basic" beliefs, what we have is a coherence theory, not a foundations theory (60–66). (This is, I think, what Pollock would say in reply to the type of foundation theory proposed by Plantinga and Wolterstorff.) (4) Even granting the incorrigibility of sense beliefs, we can reason from them to other beliefs only by way of memory, and that requires memory to be an additional source of "basic" beliefs (in which case the problems above recur) or to function nondoxastically (46–57).

It is, of course, normal for us, when questioned about our reason for holding a belief, to derive that belief inductively or deductively from a belief of which we are more sure. This is the intuitive basis for foundationalism.

It is, of course, normal for us, when questioned about our reason for holding a belief, to derive that belief inductively or deductively from a belief of which we are more sure. This is the intuitive basis for foundationalism. But we should keep reminding ourselves of the specific question that Pollock is addressing. That is the question of *subjective* justification. Thus, it is not particularly relevant how we seek to justify our beliefs to other people; that is more in the category of *objective* justification. Rather, he is asking how we gain "epistemic permission" to believe what we believe. And he is arguing, therefore, that whatever role "assured beliefs" may play in our epistemic self-defenses, they are not the reason why, *in general*, our beliefs are subjectively justified. Not every justified belief can be derived from a sensory "basic" belief, and sensory beliefs are not in any meaningful sense self-justifying.

A coherence theory differs from a foundations theory in that for the coherentist there are no "basic" beliefs, no epistemically privileged propositions. A person justifies a belief by relating it somehow to *all* his other beliefs. ("Beliefs" because, like foundationalism, coherentism is doxastic.) If that belief "coheres" with the rest, then it is justified; otherwise, not. Pollock distinguishes *positive* coherence theories, in which positive support is required for all beliefs, and *negative* coherence theories, in which all beliefs are "innocent until proven guilty" and are to be abandoned only by sufficient negative reasons (71ff.). Another distinction is between *linear* and *holistic* coherence theories. In the former, our basic reason for believing a proposition is a small set of beliefs that, to be sure, when we ask reasons for reasons, expands to include our entire stock of beliefs. In the latter, one cannot reduce the justification for a belief to any such linear chain.

A coherence theory differs from a foundations theory in that for the coherentist there are no "basic" beliefs, no epistemically privileged propositions. A person justifies a belief by relating it somehow to all his other beliefs.

Against linear positive coherence theories, Pollock argues that these cannot produce any "plausible candidates for reasons for beliefs that result directly from perception" (77). On a coherence view, all reasoning is by inference—but "perception is not inference. When I believe on the basis of perception that the book is red, I do not infer that belief from something else that I believe. Perception is a causal process that inputs beliefs into our doxastic system without their being inferred from or justified on the basis of other beliefs we already have" (75).

Against linear positive coherence theories, Pollock argues that these cannot produce any "plausible candidates for reasons for beliefs that result directly from perception."

Remember again that Pollock is concerned with subjective justification, with how we acquire epistemic permission to believe, not with how we defend our beliefs to others. In fact, we may always choose to defend our beliefs by inference, but that cannot be the way that our original subjective justification comes about.

Against holistic coherence theories, Pollock objects that in fact we do not derive all our beliefs from beliefs about the coherence of our belief system; in fact, we very rarely have such beliefs about coherence. And if we did, how would we get those beliefs? In order to believe P, we would first have to believe Q, namely, that P coheres with our other beliefs. But to believe Q, we would first have to believe R, namely, that Q coheres. The result is infinite regress.

Against negative coherence theories, Pollock replies that if we consider all beliefs justified until defeated or refuted, then reasons play no positive role in justifying beliefs, only the negative role of rebutting. But this means that no sense can be made out of the notion of believing something for a reason, a notion crucially important to the concept of subjective justification (83–87).

Under nondoxastic theories, Pollock explores externalism and internalism. A nondoxastic theory says that our beliefs are subjectively justified not only by means of other beliefs, but also by some states of affairs about which we may not have beliefs. In an internalist view, those states of affairs are only internal to us. In an externalist view, they might be external to us as well.

Probabilism, the view that beliefs are justified when they have a sufficiently high probability, gets Pollock into some complicated mathematics, from which he concludes that there is "no appropriate kind of probability for use in probabilist theories of knowledge."

He examines two types of externalism: probabilism and reliabilism. Probabilism, the view that beliefs are justified when they have a sufficiently high probability, gets Pollock into some complicated mathematics, from which he concludes that there is "no appropriate kind of probability for use in probabilist theories of knowledge" (113). The more intuitive, ordinary-English concept of epistemological probability, he says, "is defined in terms of epistemic justification, so this provides no analysis of epistemic justification and no support for probabilism" (113).

Reliabilism teaches that "a belief is justified if and only if it is produced by a reliable cognitive process" (114). Pollock rejects this principle also, on the ground that reliability of processes has nothing to do with epistemic (= *subjective*) justification. Poor Harry, the brain-in-the-vat, has unreliable perceptive faculties. But *he* has no reason to think his faculties are unreliable, so he has no alternative but to trust them. In other words, Harry's beliefs about his "normal life" are, in general, subjectively justified, though mostly false. More fundamentally, Pollock argues, most "reliable cognitive processes" (color vision is his example) are reliable only in certain circumstances. But if we narrow the circumstances too far (such as by presupposing the truth-value of the belief under consideration), we reach the conclusion that the belief is justifiable only if it is true, which is not the way that subjective justification is supposed to work.

By process of elimination, then, we are left with a form of internalism. Pollock calls his version of internalism direct realism, *because it is nondoxastic: in it we gain justification for beliefs without the mediating presence of other beliefs. Our reasons for believing, fundamentally, are our mental processes themselves.*

Against all externalism, Pollock insists that in our moment-to-moment belief formation we do not always have access to data concerning the reliability of cognitive processes or concerning the probability of propositions. We do, of course, have access to the cognitive processes themselves, but those are internal rather than external.

By process of elimination, then, we are left with a form of internalism. Pollock calls his version of internalism *direct realism*, because it is nondoxastic: in it we gain justification for beliefs without the mediating presence of other beliefs. Our reasons for believing, fundamentally, are our mental processes themselves. We believe because our mental processes lead us to believe as we do. We do not need to have beliefs *about* our mental processes (e.g., about their reliability) for this to happen. If we sometimes appeal to reliability or probability, or to "basic" ideas or to systematic coherence, that is just the way our mental processes sometimes work. So the fundamental justification is not an appeal to reliability or whatever; it is simply that our mental processes work in this particular way.

But aren't our mental processes sometimes fallible? Yes, but we discover that by means of mental processes themselves, one checking another. And more importantly: don't forget that we are here talking about *subjective* justification. There is often a lack of correlation between subjective justification and truth. So the fallibility of our mental processes is irrelevant to their primacy in subjective justification.

Aren't our mental processes sometimes fallible? Yes, but we discover that by means of mental processes themselves, one checking another.

Consider poor Harry, the brain-in-the-vat. His faculties are supremely unreliable; yet because he himself has no reason to doubt them, his beliefs about his living a normal life are subjectively justified. He is subjectively justified because that is simply the way his faculties work.

This does not mean that all our beliefs are justified. Some of our beliefs are chosen arbitrarily, the result of wishful thinking or the like. They are not the result of the working of our cognitive faculties. (But I wonder how on Pollock's basis one can distinguish properly cognitive faculties from other psychologically actual means of forming beliefs.)

Pollock includes much more exposition and argument in favor of his internalism, but I will stop my exposition here. Internalism appears to be almost the inevitable conclusion of the book, once the reader gains clarity as to the concept of *subjective justification*. Certainly it is true that we use foundationalist, coherentist, reliability, and probabilistic arguments to justify our beliefs to others. Sometimes we use these methods of justifying our beliefs also to ourselves in situations in which we gain some detachment from our own belief commitments. But these are justifications that aim at showing the objective truth of these ideas. They are not the original means by which we acquire such beliefs.

In the original acquiring of beliefs, much is mysterious. Pollock is right; we rarely argue explicitly with ourselves. We rarely appeal to foundations *or* coherence *or* probability *or* reliability. *Rather, we just find ourselves believing.*

In the original acquiring of beliefs, much is mysterious. Pollock is right; we rarely argue explicitly with ourselves. We rarely appeal to *foundations* or *coherence* or *probability* or *reliability*. Rather, we just find ourselves believing. And when we are assured of them, we cannot always say why or how we are assured. Rather, our minds are simply "programmed" to give us assurance in certain situations.

Foundationalism, coherentism, probabilism, and reliabilism therefore really confuse subjective with objective justification to some extent. Internalism is the only fully subjective mechanism available for subjective justification.

Having agreed with Pollock's main point, however, I would like to add something about its *vacuity*. For when I ask, "How am I justified in believing P?" Pollock's answer seems to boil down to this: "You are justified by the justificatory faculties of your mind." That's a bit like the scholastics' explanation of falling bodies by reference to "falling tendencies" within those bodies. Now, Pollock isn't quite as bad as all that. He does present some illuminating psychological description of how we come to make up our minds about beliefs. But most of that description is negative, telling us what we *don't* do. And, we recall, Pollock does no more than to reflect on the general ignorance on such important matters as *a priori* and moral knowledge. (If my arguments in *DKG* are correct, without moral knowledge there is no knowledge of anything.) He says nothing positive about them. What he does say positively is mostly the affirmation of such things as "sensors" (as in the Oscar chapter), but we didn't need him to tell us that we had such faculties. So in general, he leaves our mental processes (and hence subjective justification) under a great veil of mystery. In the end, we think as we do because we think as we do. And as Pollock's main conclusion, that seems too vacuous to be of help.

In general, Pollock leaves our mental processes (and hence subjective justification) under a great veil of mystery. In the end, we think as we do because we think as we do. And as Pollock's main conclusion, that seems too vacuous to be of help.

This reminds me of what some philosophers have called the *paradox of analysis*: Often when someone tries very hard to analyze something and insists on a rigorous equation between the analysis and the analysandum, he comes up with something uninformative. What are black holes? The only way to come up with a perfect equation between analysis and analysandum is to say that a black hole is a black hole. Has Pollock tried to seek too much analytical perfection?

It also reminds me of Cornelius Van Til's point that philosophical rationalism, insofar as it seeks an exhaustive explanation of reality, leads us to see the world in terms of "blank identity," like Parmenides' *Being*, Plato's *Good*, Aristotle's *thought thinking thought*, Plotinus's *One*, and so on.

What might be an alternative, motivated by Christian theism? Well, we can certainly concede that the mind works the way it works! But we should insist that subjective justification is only a small part of the story in epistemology. Objective justification is part of our responsibility to "test all things" and to seek and apply God's truth rightly. That deserves far more analysis than Pollock gives it. And we have epistemic obligations from the living God,[15] not just epistemic permissions, as Pollock insists.

We should insist that subjective justification is only a small part of the story in epistemology. Objective justification is part of our responsibility to "test all things" and to seek and apply God's truth rightly.

As for subjective justification, well, a Christian view would stress that God made man's mind to know him and to know his truth. So in man as originally created, subjective justification and objective justification coincided. Unlike Harry's brain, our mental faculties were reliable. Sin, however, led man to flee from the truth, especially from God. This fact introduced distortions, self-deceptions.

A Christian analysis would have to discuss this process of self-deception[16] and also the restoration of sound thinking as part of God's redemptive grace.

15. See *DKG*.

16. See Greg Bahnsen, "A Conditional Resolution of the Apparent Paradox of Self-Deception" (Ph.D. diss., University of Southern California, 1978).

We can learn much, certainly, from the thoroughness and rigor of Pollock's argument. But clearly we need to learn much more about human knowledge than Pollock (and, I gather, modern philosophical epistemology in general) has to teach us.

We can learn much, certainly, from the thoroughness and rigor of Pollock's argument.

APPENDIX R

"REPLY TO GORDON H. CLARK"

Gordon Clark and I had a brief correspondence in the early 1980s. See chapter 13 for my general assessment of his work. Here, the mail exchange. Note (2005): The first few paragraphs explain the occasion of this paper, written sometime in the early 1980s. I sent copies to Trinity Foundation (John Robbins), who had publicly described my views as neoorthodox, and to Clark, and to a number of friends. Robbins never replied, let alone apologized. Clark, however, did reply. He distanced himself from Robbins somewhat, and we had a cordial correspondence. (For stylistic purposes, this appendix has been copyedited for inclusion in this volume.)

Clark never refers to me or Van Til as neoorthodox. I assume, then, that the term neoorthodoxy *was intended as an attention-grabber by the sellers of the tapes.*

ABOUT SIX DIFFERENT PEOPLE have shown me the recent brochure from the Trinity Foundation advertising Gordon H. Clark's Gordon-Conwell lecture, "The Defense of the Truth." Tape 14, entitled "John Frame and Cornelius Van Til," is described as follows: "Paradox or revelation? Are all the teachings of the Bible apparently contradictory? Neoorthodoxy at Westminster Seminary." That last phrase certainly grabs the eye! Some of my friends have found it rather disturbing and have thought that I really ought to answer Clark, to defend myself and Van Til against the charge of neoorthodoxy.

Well, I listened to the tape, and was reassured on one point at least. In the lecture itself, Clark never refers to me or Van Til as neoorthodox. I assume, then, that the term *neoorthodoxy* was intended as an attention-grabber by the sellers of the tapes. It is not a description of anything in the actual lecture. As an advertising stunt, the idea was a clever one, but ethically somewhat on the level of the *National Enquirer* or the *Christian Beacon*.

If anyone does take it seriously, let me point out that both Van Til and I stand firmly for biblical inspiration, infallibility, and inerrancy, that we believe redemption to be based on literal, datable events in history, that we affirm the reality of the miraculous and insist that the literal incarnation, sacrificial death, bodily resurrection, and bodily return of Jesus are absolutely essential to Christian faith. Anyone, therefore, who calls either of us *neoorthodox* is simply not using language in a responsible way.

Gordon H. Clark

I do recall that in a lecture of some years ago, Gordon Clark expressed considerable irritation with my colleague Harvie Conn because Conn called Clark at one point a *neoevangelical*.[1] Clark replied that the term *neoevangelical* generally denoted a compromising, "limited inerrancy" view of biblical authority, and he vigorously denied that he held any such view. Personally, I do not believe that the term *neoevangelical* necessarily connotes compromise in the area of Scripture authority, although the term itself is so vague that I generally try to avoid it myself. I wish that Harvie had avoided it in the case under discussion, but I don't see that his use of it deserved such a heated response as Clark gave. In any case, if it was misleading for Harvie to call Clark a *neoevangelical*, and if that term provoked, as it did, a sharp response from Clark, then I'm sure that Clark and the Trinity Foundation will understand my taking some offense at the use of *neoorthodox* to describe my position and Van Til's.

Personally, I do not believe that the term neoevangelical *necessarily connotes compromise in the area of Scripture authority, although the term itself is so vague that I generally try to avoid it myself.*

Clark's lecture itself deals with my article "The Problem of Theological Paradox."[2] In the lecture, he simply goes through the article, reading various sections of it, interspersing those readings with his own critical comments. This method of lecturing makes it a bit difficult for me to reply. Clark's comments, all of them very brief, cover a great many areas, and each of them raises a number of issues. If he had spent the whole lecture carefully expounding his criticism of one or two main themes of my article, then I could have replied more easily. As it is, however, an adequate reply to him would require many pages of text, dealing with all sorts of matters, taking up much more of my time than I am now able to give. My reply, then, must be in that sense inadequate. I will keep my comments short (as indeed his comments were), not spelling out all the definitions and arguments. If someone

1. For Van Til's assessment of neoorthodoxy, note his *The New Modernism* (Philadelphia: Presbyterian and Reformed, 1946) and his *Christianity and Barthianism* (Philadelphia: Presbyterian and Reformed, 1962), together with many pamphlets and references in his other writings. Van Til is known as one of the sharpest critics of neoorthodoxy in the evangelical world. I enthusiastically support his position on this matter.

2. In *Foundations of Christian Scholarship: Essays in the Van Til Perspective*, ed. Gary North (Vallecito, CA: Ross House, 1976), 295–330, also published as a pamphlet, *Van Til: The Theologian* (Phillipsburg, NJ: Pilgrim Publishing, 1976).

will read thoughtfully and give me the benefit of the doubt (as all of us Christians should do), then he should see at least the direction that my response to Clark would take, had I the time to spell it out. If the reader is unwilling to make such an intellectual and moral effort, then I simply don't have time to deal with him now.

Let me take Clark's critical comments in the order of the tape:

1. He seems generally to accept my interpretation of Van Til, but early in the tape he accuses me of "diluting" and "trivializing" Van Til's teaching. I really can't reply to this, because he gives no specific examples of such dilution or trivializing. It is true that I don't accept *everything* Van Til says (or that anyone else says, except for Scripture), but I think that what I do say about Van Til can be established from his writings. I have, indeed, been criticized as a "revisionist" by Jim Halsey and others on the Van Tillian "right wing." There is some truth in that, but on the whole I think I am closer to Van Til than they are. See my replies to Halsey in my forthcoming *Doctrine of the Knowledge of God*.[3]

Clark says that Van Til rejects the standard teaching that God is "one in one sense, three in another sense." I disagree. Van Til accepts the standard formulation, but he denies that this standard formulation solves the apparent contradiction.

2. Clark says that Van Til rejects the standard teaching that God is "one in one sense, three in another sense." I disagree. Van Til accepts the standard formulation, but he denies that this standard formulation solves the apparent contradiction. It would solve the apparent contradiction if we knew clearly what a substance (*ousia*) was, what a person (*hypostasis*) was, precisely how the two are related. But we don't. And we are kidding ourselves if we think that by attaching different names to the oneness and threeness, we are resolving the paradox. Attaching different names, of course, is legitimate; it's a way of expressing our faith that there is a solution. But it doesn't tell us what that solution is. Compare my article, page 306f., a section that Clark does not discuss in the lecture, but that he should have discussed in making this point.

To the oneness and threeness, we are resolving the paradox. Attaching different names, of course, is legitimate; it's a way of expressing our faith that there is a solution. But it doesn't tell us what that solution is.

3. Clark quotes me quoting Van Til (301): "We see then that our knowledge of the universe must be true since we are creatures of God who made both us and the universe." Clark replies that this is a non sequitur. Well, it is, if you take that sentence by itself, but clearly it was not intended, either by Van Til or by me, to be a complete argument. The context (both the context in Van Til's book and the context of my article) supplies the missing premises and clarifies the meanings of the terms. As for the context of my article, the thrust of the paragraph is clearly that human thinking can be trusted because of our relationship to God. The Van Til quote expresses that notion in an imprecise way, but this is clearly what he's saying. And I don't think Clark actually disagrees with that point.

4. Clark challenges Van Til to formulate his "absolutely certain proof" for Christian theism. I think it unreasonable to demand one

3. Published in 1987: Phillipsburg, NJ: Presbyterian and Reformed, 1987.

definitive formulation designed to satisfy all people in all situations—see Mavrodes, *Belief in God* on this point. But try this. (a) Consciousness of anything presupposes consciousness of God. (b) I am conscious of something. (c) Therefore, I am conscious of God. (d) If I am conscious of God, God exists. (e) Therefore, God exists. I think that is, in essence, Van Til's "proof." But it is not one whose premises everyone would accept. More to the point: although Van Til does not ever formulate the proof syllogistically, he presents his approach over and over again in his arguments against Plato, Kant, Barth, and many, many others.

Try this. (a) Consciousness of anything presupposes consciousness of God. (b) I am conscious of something. (c) Therefore, I am conscious of God. (d) If I am conscious of God, God exists. (e) Therefore, God exists. I think that is, in essence, Van Til's "proof."

5. Clark discusses Van Til's point that our true ideas are "true because analogical." He finds that point defective because Van Til's notion of analogy contains no "univocal element"! Without such a univocal element, Clark argues, our ideas cannot meaningfully correspond with God's. Strangely, however, at this point in the tape, Clark makes no reference to my discussion of *analogy* on 310f. In that discussion. I argue that Van Til's concept of *analogy* has little or nothing to do with the traditional controversy over literal or figurative theological language, and thus that it is quite compatible with the assertion that some theological language is literal. Now, I realize that my interpretation of Van Til here differs from most conventional interpretations, but I did verify it in an oral conversation with Van Til. It might still be wrong, but if it is, I think Clark is obligated to show that it is wrong, not simply to take the conventional interpretation for granted.

6. On necessity and freedom in God: Clark interprets God's *freedom* simply to mean that nothing external to God controls him. Clearly, in that sense, all of God's acts are free. But theologians have traditionally distinguished another sense of *freedom* in which only those divine acts with reference to creation are free. The point here is that the God of Scripture has certain properties (e.g., justice, eternity, omniscience) and performs certain acts (the Father's generating the Son) without which he would not be God. These properties and actions are "necessary." Other properties and actions, however, are not in this category. God would still be God, even if he had not chosen to create the world or to redeem his people; he would be God even if he were not "God of Israel." This second group of properties and actions is called *free*. Now, on Clark's basis, no such distinction, apparently, is possible. If, as Clark says, God's only freedom is freedom from external constraint, then God's redeeming us is just as necessary to his nature as the eternal generation of the Son from the Father. But anyone trained in theology should be able to see the pantheizing tendency here. Paradoxically, unless we make the distinction in question, we wind up with a Son who is indeed dependent on things external to himself, because his own nature is defined by them. But if we do make this distinction,

If, as Clark says, God's only freedom is freedom from external constraint, then God's redeeming us is just as necessary to his nature as the eternal generation of the Son from the Father. But anyone trained in theology should be able to see the pantheizing tendency here.

then we have to admit some apparent contradiction. Once we grant (as I and Clark think we must) that all of God's acts are rational, then how can we say that *some* of these acts, though rational, are not rationally *necessary*? (You can see that Clark's point about "separating the will and the intellect" is not the issue here. The same problem arises regardless of what psychological model you use.)

Once we grant (as I and Clark think we must) that all of God's acts are rational, then how can we say that some *of these acts, though rational, are not rationally* necessary?

7. On the inclusion of evil in God's plan: First, I disagree with Clark's exegesis of Isaiah 45:7. It seems more natural to me to read it as dealing with those judgments that are the consequences of sin, rather than sin itself. Still, I can agree with Clark that God foreordains evil. On the other hand, Scripture also teaches that God is good, that a good tree does not bring forth evil fruit, that God detests evil. These data are prima facie inconsistent with the notion that God foreordains evil. I don't accept Clark's "solution" to the problem of evil in *Religion, Reason, and Revelation*. It makes some good points, but it veers too close to nominalism for me. Good is not good *merely* because God says so, but also because it comports with his nature. (I'm saying the same thing about goodness that Clark says about *logos* or divine reason.)

8. On the image of God: how can we speak of fallen man as image of God when he is entirely lacking in knowledge, righteousness, and holiness (cf. Eph. 4:23; Col. 3:10)? I think that Clark ought to see an unresolved problem here.

Clark finds a contradiction between my statement that we are to use extrabiblical information "fearlessly, thankfully" and my statement that our knowledge of nature is distorted by sin and finitude.

9. On the "Clark case": I think that the phrase "not coinciding at any point" has precisely the same ambiguities as the phrase "identity of content." Clearly, here the word *coinciding* is a metaphor. It masks all kinds of problems. Van Til rules out all such *coinciding* because he does not see the ambiguities of it. So I'd say the same about this that I said about *content*.

10. Clark has problems with my assertion that we need extrabiblical data to interpret Scripture. I don't understand what his problems are; this need seems to me to be an obvious fact. He asks whether we must hold to discarded theories of gravitation and so on. My answer is no, we don't. So what? I grant that such extrabiblical material introduces fallibility into our thinking. So what? Does Clark really believe that our interpretations of Scripture are infallible?

11. Clark finds a contradiction between my statement that we are to use extrabiblical information "fearlessly, thankfully" and my statement that our knowledge of nature is distorted by sin and finitude. Well, I think we just have to accept the fact that our interpretation of Scripture will be fallible, subject to correction, and then do the best we can. That fact need not inject any fear or thanklessness into the process! Hesitation at times, yes. But at the same time thankfulness

and boldness, because God is using this process to lead his people into more and more truth.

12. Clark asks how, on my view, Scripture can be its own interpreter. I agree that Scripture is the only *infallible* interpreter of Scripture, the hermeneutical tool against which all others must be measured. But if Clark is actually saying that we don't need linguistics, archaeology, and so forth to understand the Bible, then I think he's talking nonsense. God has not only given us Scripture. He has also given us teachers with gifts for understanding and proclaiming Scripture. Scripture assumes that Christians will sometimes have difficulties understanding. God has also given us eyes and ears, for example—and for a reason.

I agree that Scripture is the only infallible *interpreter of Scripture, the hermeneutical tool against which all others must be measured. But if Clark is actually saying that we don't need linguistics, archaeology, and so forth to understand the Bible, then I think he's talking nonsense.*

13. I suppose that in Clark's mind the question of extrabiblical knowledge boils down to the viability of empiricism as a theory of knowledge. I appreciate Clark's critique of empiricism. I think it shows that *mere* sense experience, sense experience without any *a priori* principles, will not yield knowledge. But on the other hand, I don't think *a priori* principles will yield knowledge without sense experience. (Cf. Kant on percepts and concepts.) Thus I think what Clark's argument shows is not that extrabiblical knowledge is unnecessary, but rather that extrabiblical data must be understood in a framework supplied by biblical presuppositions.

14. Clark asks how I can acknowledge some formulations that are nonparadoxical, while agreeing with Van Til that "all teaching of Scripture is apparently contradictory." I agree that this was sloppy of me. The operative word in the Van Til phrase is *teaching*. What I meant to say was that the great biblical teachings that develop the relation of God to the world are apparently contradictory. This would not include statements such as "David was king of Israel." I should have been clearer here. But compare the points made on 326–28, to which Clark does not refer. These raise additional complications.

Thus I think what Clark's argument shows is not that extrabiblical knowledge is unnecessary, but rather that extrabiblical data must be understood in a framework supplied by biblical presuppositions.

15. I disagree with Clark's view that only propositions, not things, are proper objects of thought and knowledge. This idea makes sense only if you define *thought* and *knowledge* very narrowly, in which case it becomes tautological. Further, I see no need to define these terms that narrowly. I see no defect in ordinary language at this point. And using the usual definition of *knowledge*, we know the aroma of coffee, but I think we'd be hard-pressed to reduce that knowledge to propositions.

16. Clark says that on my view you should simply accept apparent contradictions without seeking any solution for them. That this is not my view should be evident from page 325.

Now, the reader will note that although there are some substantial disagreements between Clark and me, they have very little to do with neoorthodoxy. As I indicated earlier, Clark, on the tape, does not even mention the term *neoorthodoxy*, much less accuse me of being neoorthodox. How, then, did neoorthodoxy even enter the discussion, even as an advertising stunt? Well, the ad-writer probably reasoned something like this: neoorthodox theologians defend paradox; Frame defends paradox; therefore, Frame is neoorthodox. If anything like this is going through the reader's mind, let me reply as follows: (a) If you, like Clark, abhor non sequiturs, then please note that the argument under consideration is precisely that. It is logically the same as "Neoorthodox theologians eat roast beef; Gordon Clark eats roast beef; therefore, Gordon Clark is neoorthodox." (b) The defense of paradox is only one element in neoorthodox thought. There are many others with which Van Til and I emphatically disagree, as noted here earlier (one could also mention the neoorthodox doctrine of universal election, the notion that God can reveal truth through false propositions, the odd metaphysicalizing of redemption in Barth, etc.). (c) The concept of paradox in Van Til and Frame is radically different from the concept of paradox in neoorthodoxy. (i) We believe that God is wholly rational and logical, and that therefore his revelation is rational and logical. The neoorthodox do not. (ii) We believe that therefore there are no real contradictions in God's thought, or specifically in Scripture. Neoorthodoxy differs on this point. (iii) We believe that paradox is due therefore to human sin and finitude, contra neoorthodoxy. I gather from the tape that Clark also believes that there are "apparent contradictions" that arise from human misunderstanding. I don't think that Clark and Van Til-Frame differ here.

The major difference in this area between Van Til-Frame on the one hand and Clark on the other has to do with the status of logic. All three of us believe that Scripture is infallible, but Clark also believes that human logic is infallible.

The major difference in this area between Van Til-Frame on the one hand and Clark on the other has to do with the status of logic. All three of us believe that Scripture is infallible, but Clark also believes that human logic is infallible. And Clark not only speaks of the infallibility of the law of noncontradiction as does, for example, John Gerstner. Clark is sophisticated enough to know that the law of noncontradiction will not help you much unless you have a system of methods for determining what is and is not contradictory, what is and is not logically derivable, and so on. Thus, Clark contends for the infallibility of Aristotle's system of logic in toto. Anyone who fails to do this is in Clark's mind an irrationalist and, in the mind of at least one Clark disciple, neoorthodox.

Clark contends for the infallibility of Aristotle's system of logic in toto. Anyone who fails to do this is in Clark's mind an irrationalist and, in the mind of at least one Clark disciple, neoorthodox.

Some years ago in Philadelphia after a lecture by Clark, I asked him how Aristotelian logic could be infallible in the light of our belief in *sola Scriptura*. He answered that if Aristotle is wrong, then there is no basis for intelligibility. I asked him how he knows that Aristotle is right as over against, say, Bertrand Russell, whose system of logic differs significantly from Aristotle's. Clark referred me to a paper of his that, he thought, proves Aristotle right and Russell wrong. I asked Clark how he knows that his paper is right. Clark replied that if it is wrong, then no intelligible communication is possible. It was a remarkable conversation. Here, Gordon Clark, who maintains *sola Scriptura* and *Scriptura ipsius interpres* with a vengeance, even to the distorted extreme of denying any knowledge to us of extrabiblical truth (cf. above, 10–13), maintains the infallibility of Aristotle's logic, and even of Clark's own defense of Aristotle's logic. In my view, that is a *reductio ad absurdum* of his approach.

Clark, who maintains sola Scriptura *and* Scriptura ipsius interpres *with a vengeance, even to the distorted extreme of denying any knowledge to us of extrabiblical truth, maintains the infallibility of Aristotle's logic, and even of Clark's own defense of Aristotle's logic. In my view, that is a* reductio ad absurdum *of his approach.*

For my own view of the competence of logic, see Poythress, *Philosophy, Science, and the Sovereignty of God*, the appendix on the law of noncontradiction, together with my own forthcoming pieces, *Doctrine of the Knowledge of God*[4] and "Rationality and Scripture."[5] In my view, we should follow WCF 1.6 in according authority not only to the explicit statements of Scripture, but also to its logical implications. Nevertheless, the processes of logical reasoning by which we discover these implications are fallible: fallible because of the fallibility of our logical systems, because of the need for extrabiblical knowledge, and so forth. I think logic is simply another of many tools we have for unpacking the *meaning* of Scripture; it is a hermeneutical tool like linguistics, archaeology, history, and literary criticism.

Despite the significant differences between Clark and me, let me emphasize that I have great respect for Clark's work, for the quality of his thought, and for the strong stand that he has always taken for the Reformed faith. I have been his loudest defender, in fact, in Westminster Theological Seminary and Orthodox Presbyterian Church circles, and I will continue to defend him in the many areas where I think he has been misunderstood and wrongly condemned. I take it as something of a compliment that he bothered to spend a whole lecture at Gordon-Conwell discussing my little paper on Van Til. Thus, our differences, though significant, are differences within a more ultimate unity. May God continue to instruct us both until we reach the fullness of unity in Christ.

Despite the significant differences between Clark and me, let me emphasize that I have great respect for Clark's work, for the quality of his thought, and for the strong stand that he has always taken for the Reformed faith.

4. Ibid.
5. *DWG*, 347–70.

APPENDIX S

REVIEW OF HERBERT SCHLOSSBERG, *IDOLS FOR DESTRUCTION*

Review of Herbert Schlossberg, *Idols for Destruction* (Nashville, TN: Thomas Nelson, 1984). This review appeared in *WTJ* 46, 2 (Fall 1984): 438–44, and in the *Presbyterian Journal* 43 (June 6, 1983): 10. Used by permission of Westminster Theological Seminary. Schlossberg is a Christian thinker who develops an incisive critique of modern thought and culture. (For stylistic purposes, this appendix has been copyedited for inclusion in this volume.)

Idols for Destruction is in most respects equal or superior to Guinness's book. And since it is written from a broader historical perspective, it will not so quickly lose its usefulness as an analysis of modern culture.

For some years I (and, I think, others) have been looking for a book that would in effect update Os Guinness's magnificent 1973 volume, *The Dust of Death*. That volume was a wonderfully erudite and persuasive critique of the Western culture of the late 1960s from a thoughtful, balanced Christian perspective. It seemed nearly perfect as a textbook in its field. The only major problem was that, focusing narrowly as it did on a few years in our modern history, the book rapidly became dated. Still, it seemed impossible to hope that any other book would ever do this kind of job so well. But now we have Schlossberg. Amazingly, his *Idols for Destruction* is in most respects equal or superior to Guinness's book. And since it is written from a broader historical perspective, it will not so quickly lose its usefulness as an analysis of modern culture.

Schlossberg might be a new name to many of us, as it was to me. Unfortunately, the book contains no biographical data on the author, but I was able to find the following information in an interview with Schlossberg published in *The Counsel of Chalcedon* 5, 10 (December

1983): 11: He "is a financial planner in the upper midwest. He was educated at Bethel College and the University of Minnesota (Ph.D., 1965). Dr. Schlossberg has been a professor of history at Waterloo University (Ontario, Canada), Academic Dean at Shepherd College (West Virginia), and an employee of the Central Intelligence Agency."

In summarizing the emphases of *Idols for Destruction*, it might be helpful to continue the comparison between this book and that of Guinness. R. J. Rushdoony and Gary North are to Schlossberg what Francis Schaeffer is to Guinness. Schaeffer presented Guinness with a broad Christian worldview, which Guinness expounded and defended in meticulous detail. Similarly, Rushdoony and North are guiding spirits to Schlossberg. But *Idols* is a fully independent work, comprehensively researched, with creative interpretations and applications.

Schlossberg's whole book, indeed, can be read as an extended (and powerful) critique of leftism and its roots (as Schlossberg sees them) in historicism and in hatred of the successful. Why, then, the rhetoric of the "third race"?

The Rushdoony connection (not to mention the CIA connection!) also suggests another difference between Schlossberg and Guinness. Both men use the rhetoric that describes Christians as a "third race," neither liberal nor conservative, neither radical nor establishment. Both men criticize equally the conventional analyses of our times, whether "pessimistic" or "optimistic." But as to the nature of the "third alternative," there is difference between the two writers. Guinness expressed a great deal of sympathy for the radicals of the new left, saying that their critique of the establishment was largely true, though presented from a faulty philosophical base and lacking a credible positive alternative. Guinness's own positive proposals were not entirely clear, but the reader got the impression that these proposals would have transposed much of the leftist rhetoric, somehow, into a Christian key. In Schlossberg, that overtone of sympathy for leftist rhetoric is entirely lacking. His whole book, indeed, can be read as an extended (and powerful) critique of leftism and its roots (as Schlossberg sees them) in historicism and in hatred of the successful. Why, then, the rhetoric of the "third race"? Is Schlossberg not merely siding with one of the existing secular alternatives? Well, his argument is that the secular conservative movement is inadequate because it is itself too socialistic. Only Christianity can, he says, overcome the envious spirit that lies at the root of secular politics and economics. Only Christianity can overcome the socialistic "idols" and produce true free enterprise. It is evident, then, that Schlossberg and Guinness have rather different ideas of where the "third race" will lead us. The reader's preference of one over the other will depend on his prior political and (even more prior) theological commitments. My own view is that Schlossberg has thought through more carefully and profoundly the economic and political implications of Scripture, but that Guinness is more successful in communicating human sympathy for the concerns of those with whom he disagrees.

Only Christianity can, he says, overcome the envious spirit that lies at the root of secular politics and economics. Only Christianity can overcome the socialistic "idols" and produce true free enterprise.

The book begins with an introduction that summarizes the main themes. Schlossberg wishes to survey various "idols" of modern thought and life. The chief errors of our time stem from attempts to deify various aspects of the creation: history, nature, humanity, economics, political power. Only affirmation and application of the Creator-creature distinction can point the way out. The issues, then, are essentially religious and moral: we will not escape our dilemmas by some new form of political organization or a new economic system, even a more "conservative" one. The issues, therefore, may also be described as presuppositional. Schlossberg is very clear (rather more so than Guinness) that no human science or discipline is "neutral," and through the book he frequently exposes false claims to openness and objectivity (see, e.g., 7f., 11, 25ff., 37f., 142ff., 146ff., 210f., 248, 273).

The issues, therefore, may also be described as presuppositional. Schlossberg is very clear (rather more so than Guinness) that no human science or discipline is "neutral," and through the book he frequently exposes false claims to openness and objectivity.

The first chapter deals with history, particularly with historicism, the view that history is "the whole show" (13), all there is. The outcome of historicism is determinism, a sense of helplessness in the face of historical trends. Since we are helpless, it is often said, we "cannot turn back the clock," meaning that we cannot mount any challenge against any fashionable trend. Facts and values, then, become confused: the present state of affairs becomes normative, beyond challenge. No, says Schlossberg. We are not forced to go with the tide. The critique of determinism continues throughout the book, as one of its main themes. Schlossberg attacks talk about the "unbreakable cycle of poverty" (62); he notes the inconsistency of those who relegate some to environment-determined victimhood, while regarding others (the "oppressors") as free and responsible (83, 148ff., 153ff., 274). He argues that supposedly "unbreakable" cycles, historical patterns, have often been reversed, and quite rapidly (16, 25, 33, 260ff.). All of this confirms Schlossberg's initial premise that history is best understood not by spatial or organic metaphors, but by the category of divine judgment (6).

The second chapter attacks humanism, the deification of humanity. Here, Schlossberg introduces another of the book's pervasive themes, that of *ressentiment*, defined by Nietzsche as a hatred for the success of others, occasioned, usually, by envy (51). Modern humanism, dominated by this motive, demands a leveling of distinctions, equalization of wealth, restrictions on economic freedom, not out of concern for the poor, but out of hatred of the rich (102ff., 133). Thus, ironically, the deification of humanity produces strife (283ff.), a distrust of civilization (170), and an indifference to abortion and euthanasia (177ff., 289).

The second chapter attacks humanism, the deification of humanity. Here, Schlossberg introduces another of the book's pervasive themes, that of ressentiment, defined by Nietzsche as a hatred for the success of others, occasioned, usually, by envy.

The third chapter, "Idols of Mammon," deals with economic matters. Schlossberg's ideas on poverty are actually treated earlier in the second chapter. There he denies that the gap between rich and poor is getting larger (70ff.); rather, he says, the politicians and media keep redefining poverty in order to achieve comprehensive socialistic redistribution. In the third chapter, he attacks inflationary policies of government and the use of redistribution to increase state power. He notes the degree to which redistribution policies often benefit the rich, both government bureaucrats and favored businesses.

Chapter 4, "Idols of Nature," attacks the common dogmatic faith in science. The critique of determinism (148ff.) continues from chapter 1. Here there is some kinship between Schlossberg's argument and the arguments of Thomas Kuhn. Unlike Kuhn, however, Schlossberg presents an equally strong critique of irrationalism, particularly the notion (fostered by Kuhn and others) that the sociology of knowledge invalidates any claim to certainty about the nature of the world (153ff.). He rightly points out that such skeptics always claim (implicitly, at least) an exemption for themselves; their ideas, at least, are not invalidated by sociological determinism. Thus, determinism has two faces—rationalistic and irrationalistic. And as scientism and naturalism move from one pole to the other, supposed certainties dissolve in a new onslaught of Eastern religions, spiritualisms, and the like (166ff.). The only solution is a Christian epistemology, which presupposes the Creator-creature distinction and a divinely implanted unity in creation between fact and meaning (175ff.).

Unlike Kuhn, however, Schlossberg presents an equally strong critique of irrationalism, particularly the notion (fostered by Kuhn and others) that the sociology of knowledge invalidates any claim to certainty about the nature of the world.

The next chapter deals with the deification of the state, "Idols of Power." The modern messianic state claims ownership of all things, the right to formulate laws without any reference to transcendent moral standards (205ff.). Therefore, it seeks to reduce other authorities to impotence: local magistrates (212ff.), the family (215ff.). Our only recourse is a renewed faith in the sovereignty of God, which alone justifies resistance to totalitarianism (228ff.).

Herbert Schlossberg

Chapter 6 deals with the impotence of much religion, which has compromised with the earlier-mentioned idolatries. Chapter 7, "Consequences and Expectations," argues that only a return to authentic Christian faith can avert the decline. Chapter 8 summons the church to a consistent witness.

Many of the theses mentioned above are familiar to readers of Rushdoony, North, Van Til, et al. What distinguishes the present book are (1) a systematic account, showing how a great number of these issues are related to one another, (2) an enormous number of illustrations and quotes, as well as much documentary evidence, and (3) a clearer account than is usually found in the reconstructionist literature of the relation between spiritual renewal and social improvement: Schlossberg persuades us of the inadequacies of anything less than a fully biblical reformation.

I do have some problems with the book. The treatment of "multiple causation" in history (21ff.) seems simplistic to me. Schlossberg seems to think that a Christian must regard God as the only cause of world events. While God is the only ultimate cause, I believe that we must do justice to secondary causes as well. No doubt the Babylonian captivity of Israel was God's judgment on the sins of his people (22), but to say this is not to rule out all other causal factors. The glory of God is that he makes all these "multiple causes" work together for his purposes (Rom. 8:28).

Schlossberg sometimes fails to distinguish between those who are guilty of ressentiment and those who are merely misguided in their otherwise laudable desires to help the poor.

I think that Schlossberg also overestimates, somewhat, the role of *ressentiment*. Like Rushdoony, Schlossberg sometimes fails to distinguish between those who are guilty of *ressentiment* and those who are merely misguided in their otherwise laudable desires to help the poor. And I certainly don't think that Scheler's authority is sufficient to force us to define the word *altruism* in terms of *ressentiment* (53). *Altruism* is a good word, and we shouldn't be required on such inadequate grounds to use it in a bad sense.

Schlossberg also leaves me with an unclear impression about state power. It almost seems that any desire for additional state power is sinful. What are the legitimate powers of the state? Much more needs to be said.

I think he ought to give more attention to the workings of common grace in history. The fact is that the unbelief of a nation does not always bring rapid judgment; God often tarries, displaying his long-suffering.

Then, too, I think he ought to give more attention to the workings of common grace in history. The fact is that the unbelief of a nation does not always bring rapid judgment; God often tarries, displaying his long-suffering. And in the short run, at least, the righteous do suffer. One sometimes gets the impression from the book that unless there is mass repentance, the United States will soon be destroyed. But why has judgment already been delayed through eighty years of a very secular century? And why has the Soviet Union continued to gain power since 1917?

I also think Schlossberg gives short shrift to the important matter of the church's divisions. He refers to organizational unity only negatively, saying that some have used it as a substitute for organic unity (332). While his point is right, he should surely have also said that the opposition between organizational and organic unity is unbiblical and that both are required by Scripture.

I would also suggest some format changes for future editions of the book. Certainly the publisher should remedy the present lack of any biographical information on the author. Also, I think there should be a bibliography of works that Schlossberg finds especially helpful to people who wish to improve their understanding of the matters discussed. There is, to be sure, a good index and a multitude of footnotes; but I still think a bibliography is needed, for these reasons: (1) Many of the books quoted and footnoted, even those quoted favorably, are books that represent positions far removed from Schlossberg's Reformed Christianity. Niebuhr, Toynbee, Butterfield, Ellul, and such are quoted often. The reader with only footnotes to guide him could find himself led far from Schlossberg's path. (2) While I appreciate (and share) Schlossberg's desire to avoid party labels (9f.), I do believe that when one is indebted to a particular school of thought, he ought to acknowledge that fact. Those of us familiar with the Rushdoony-North approach can see evidence of its influence on every page of *Idols*, and in the aforementioned issue of *The Counsel of Chalcedon* Schlossberg admits this influence openly. But in *Idols*, Schlossberg quotes Rushdoony and North only rarely and never tells the reader the extent of their influence on him. Thus the reader is not helped to find those sources with closest kinship to Schlossberg (cf. point 1), and Rushdoony and North are not given adequate credit for their rather substantial contribution to the argument of the book. I am not denying Schlossberg's originality; quite the contrary. But I think that originality can be much better appreciated when seen in its intellectual environment.

I do believe the book is a marvelous achievement, the textbook of choice for college and seminary courses in the Christian evaluation of modern culture, "must" reading for thinking Christians, the true successor to Guinness's The Dust of Death.

For all of this, I do believe the book is a marvelous achievement, the textbook of choice for college and seminary courses in the Christian evaluation of modern culture, "must" reading for thinking Christians, the true successor to Guinness's *The Dust of Death*. I have not begun to suggest in this review the breadth of Schlossberg's research or the careful, nuanced development of his argument. Those must be seen to be appreciated. I eagerly await more contributions from this fine author.

APPENDIX T

"VAN TIL RECONSIDERED"

This article, which I wrote for a conference held at Westminster Theological Seminary in 1995, will summarize my own relation to Cornelius Van Til, to whom I have referred often in this book. (See especially chapter 13.) (For stylistic purposes, this appendix has been copyedited for inclusion in this volume.)

I try to dispel the impression that Van Til's thought is a "seamless robe," that it must be either accepted or rejected in its entirety. That impression has, of course, been given by both Van Til's friends and his enemies.

I HAVE WRITTEN a book on Cornelius Van Til, which will be published this year, Lord willing, by Presbyterian and Reformed Publishing Co.[1] The book is a sympathetic, critical analysis of Van Til's thought; it tries to determine what in Van Til is of value for apologists today. Bill Edgar of the Westminster Theological Seminary faculty saw the manuscript, and suggested that I come to the conference and present to you some of its ideas.

In the final chapter, I summarize the approach to Van Til taken in the book, and I address the question of how we contemporary Christians can best use Van Til's ideas in our witness to the world. What I present here will be essentially that final chapter, with some explanatory additions.

In the book, I try to dispel the impression that Van Til's thought is a "seamless robe," that it must be either accepted or rejected in its entirety. That impression has, of course, been given by both Van Til's friends and his enemies. Thus, the literature about Van Til tends to be either uncritical adulation or supercritical debunking. The concept

1. This was published as *Cornelius Van Til: An Analysis of His Thought* (Phillipsburg, NJ: P&R Publishing, 1995).

of a book such as mine that seeks to be both sympathetic and critical seems in this environment to be highly anomalous.

Van Til himself tends to give that same impression. He speaks of proving Christian theism "as a unit." In teaching apologetics, both in class and in print, he tended to throw his whole system at the reader all at once, so to speak, rather than bit by bit. And if the student or reader doesn't grasp it all, well, Van Til throws it all at him a second time. Thus, the reader gets the impression that he cannot pick and choose; it is either all or nothing; Van Til must be thoroughly embraced or totally opposed. All of that is in keeping, of course, with Van Til's background in philosophical idealism and, on the other hand, with his Kuyperian-Machenite "antithetical" mode of thought.

Cornelius Van Til

Yet I have dared to differ with this approach. I have tried to break down Van Til's system into its basic elements, so as to analyze and evaluate each one at a time. I do not deny that Van Til's thought is highly interrelated and systematic; I have tried to bring out those systematic interrelations as best I can. But it seems to me to make more pedagogical sense to move from the simple to the complex, from the known to the unknown.

In this process I have concluded that Van Til's thought is not, after all, a "seamless robe." Some elements of it are unquestionably biblical and fundamental to Christian thought and life. These constitute an indispensable basis for any future apologetic. Other aspects of Van Til's system, however, are not well grounded scripturally and can be forgotten without loss.

Van Til speaks of proving Christian theism "as a unit." In teaching apologetics, both in class and in print, he tended to throw his whole system at the reader all at once, so to speak, rather than bit by bit.

To show this, let me give you my outline of Van Til's system:

I. The Metaphysics of Knowledge
    A. The Self-Contained God
    B. The Trinitarian One and Many
    C. Divine Sovereignty
    D. Analogical Knowledge
    E. Revelation
    F. Presuppositions
    G. Reason, Logic, Evidence

II. The Ethics of Knowledge
    A. Antithesis
    B. Common Grace
    C. Unbelieving Thought: Rationalism and Irrationalism

III. Apologetic Method
    A. The Traditional Method
    B. Spiral or Circular Argument

C. Reasoning by Presupposition
D. Models

IV. Criticism of Other Thinkers
A. Greek Philosophy and Scholasticism
B. Immanuel Kant and Karl Barth
C. Herman Dooyeweerd

The strongest part of Van Til's system is what I have called the metaphysics of knowledge. *In these areas I have very little criticism.*

The strongest part of Van Til's system is what I have called the *metaphysics of knowledge*. In these areas I have very little criticism. It seems to me that in these areas, Van Til is simply reproducing the teaching of Scripture and showing its applications to human thought and life. His view of the Creator-creature distinction is nothing more or less than generic Calvinism. Analogical knowledge simply means that the goal of knowledge is an understanding of reality that images as faithfully as possible on the created level God's own understanding. One who thinks analogously seeks to think in a way that is obedient to God's norms for thought. That means, of course, that all human thought is bound by divine revelation. And in turn, that implies that the truth of divine revelation must be the most fundamental presupposition of human thought.

Van Til does not disparage the use of reason, logic, and evidence, as many critics suppose, though some statements in his writings are a bit confusing in this respect. He merely insists that these be subordinate to God's Word, a limitation to which no Christian should object.

Van Til does not disparage the use of reason, logic, and evidence, as many critics suppose, though some statements in his writings are a bit confusing in this respect. He merely insists that these be subordinate to God's Word, a limitation to which no Christian should object.

I do take issue with his illegitimate *application* of these principles in the Clark controversy. In that controversy, Van Til insisted that there is "not one point of identity" between God's mind and man's. Clark believed that this view had skeptical implications. He insisted that God and man are capable of entertaining and believing the same propositions. Beyond this, the debate went through many complicated twists and turns. But Clark never denied, in my view, the point that God's mind and man's were different in their metaphysical nature. Nor did Van Til deny that God and man could believe the same proposition. Therefore, in my view, the controversy was really unnecessary and largely based on misunderstanding. Van Til in my view was at his worst when he was debating with other Christian apologists.

Van Til's view of the "ethics of knowledge" is an area of both strength and weakness. Certainly he is right to insist that non Christians know, but suppress, the truth of God's revelation. In Romans 1, Scripture makes that assertion quite explicitly. But Van Til seems to search for words in order to express how the unbeliever can in one sense know, and in another sense be ignorant of, the truth of God. In certain moods, he uses the language of "extreme antithesis," suggesting that the unbeliever has no knowledge at all, that he "knows nothing truly," and therefore has no area of agreement with the believer. Other times, however, Van Til describes various senses in which the unbeliever can and does have genuine knowledge. He says, for example, that although the unbeliever seeks to think according to atheistic principles, he is not always successful in thinking according to those principles. At times, "in spite of himself," or by "borrowed capital," he finds himself thinking in terms of Christian principles instead of non-Christian ones. This and other formulations produce a deep tension in Van Til's thought. Uncharacteristically, he did admit that this was a problem in his system, one for which he did not have an adequate answer.

While it is true that all of the unbeliever's actions and thoughts are in service of his would-be autonomy, the language of extreme antithesis is highly misleading and confusing to the practical work of apologetics. It is better to say that the unbeliever's depravity manifests itself in many varied forms, and that the non-Christian can and does utter either truth or falsehood for his purposes.

The language of extreme antithesis is highly misleading and confusing to the practical work of apologetics. It is better to say that the unbeliever's depravity manifests itself in many varied forms, and that the non-Christian can and does utter either truth or falsehood for his purposes.

The doctrine of common grace deals with the question of how God can give good gifts to the nonelect, to the reprobate. More specifically, the question arises of how God can present the promises of the gospel to the reprobate, to those whom he has foreordained not to benefit from those promises. Van Til's doctrine of common grace gets off to a good start, insisting on the importance of historical process. God gives blessings to the reprobate because the final judgment has not arrived. After human beings are assigned to their final destinies, there will be no more common grace. The elect will be blessed; the nonelect will be punished; and there will therefore be no blessings in common between them.

Yet Van Til adds to this account the unhistorical and unbiblical notion that the free offer of the gospel is directed toward a "generality" of people, rather than actual persons. Then Van Til compounds the confusion by postulating, without biblical warrant, a continuous process in which unbelief becomes worse and worse over time.

Van Til adds to this account the unhistorical and unbiblical notion that the free offer of the gospel is directed toward a "generality" of people, rather than actual persons. Then Van Til compounds the confusion by postulating, without biblical warrant, a continuous process in which unbelief becomes worse and worse over time.

On the other hand, he introduces a very helpful apologetic tool in showing that unbelief is inseparably linked to the dialectic of rationalism and irrationalism, which destroys all basis for intelligible predication. Unbelief is rationalistic because it insists on the autonomy of human thought, and therefore insists that human thought is the ultimate criterion of truth and falsity, of right and wrong. On the other hand, unbelief is also irrationalistic because it believes that the apparent order in the universe is ultimately based on disorder, on chance.

Van Til points out how unbelieving thought bounces back and forth, inconsistently, between rationalism and irrationalism. In Parmenides, rationalism generates a doctrine of static "being," while irrationalism generates a mythological explanation of how the illusion of movement can exist. Plato's Forms represent his rationalism; his irrationalism is seen in his view of the empirical world, the world of mere opinion. The enduring problem of Plato's philosophy is the difficulty of achieving any intelligible relationship between the two worlds. In Kant, the same problem recurs in the relation between the irrational noumenal world and the rationalistically conceived phenomenal.

When we seek to prove those presuppositions, we must presuppose them, and that is a kind of circularity. Of course, that is the kind of circularity that always exists when people try to prove the truth of an ultimate standard of rationality.

Now let us look at Van Til's view of apologetic method. He suggests what he calls a "transcendental" method or "reasoning by presupposition." Here he emphasizes that we should seek to show that no meaning, intelligibility, or predication is possible apart from the God of Scripture. He also insists that this argument must be "circular" or "spiral," always resting on the presupposition of God's truth.

I agree that apologetic argument must be circular in one sense, in the sense that a Christian apologist must never abandon his Christian presuppositions when he argues with a non-Christian. We cannot abandon those presuppositions, for we believe that they define the proper way to reason. Therefore, when we seek to prove those presuppositions, we must presuppose them, and that is a *kind* of circularity. Of course, that is the kind of circularity that always exists when people try to prove the truth of an ultimate standard of rationality. To prove that human reason is ultimate, one must presuppose human reason, and so forth. This does not imply that apologetic argument needs to use viciously circular arguments, such as "the Bible is the Word of God because it is the Word of God."

I also agree with the transcendental character of Van Til's apologetic. . . . But Van Til tries to derive from the nature of transcendental argument some additional restrictions on the apologist, restrictions that I consider unnecessary.

I also agree with the transcendental character of Van Til's apologetic. We should seek to establish that the biblical God is the source of all meaning and intelligibility in the world, for indeed he is the source of all meaning and intelligibility in the world. But Van Til tries to derive from the nature of transcendental argument some additional restrictions on the apologist, restrictions that I consider unnecessary. (1) He insists that arguments for Christianity should be indirect rather than direct. Instead of proving the existence of God directly, Van Til insists that we prove it indirectly, by showing the "impossibility of the contrary." He urges us to adopt the unbeliever's presupposition "for the sake of argument" and show that that presupposition leads to incoherence and meaninglessness. (2) He demands that we always claim absolute certainty rather than probability. (3) He occasionally requires that we announce our entire theology "at the outset" of every apologetic encounter. (4) He occasionally requires that the argument conclude by proving the *whole* of Christian theism, rather than merely proving individual doctrines. (5) He insists that we may never present Christian truth as a "supplement" to the unbeliever's knowledge.

In my view, Van Til's own arguments do not always observe these principles, and in any case, I believe that he has failed to make an adequate case for them. I cannot see that any of these five rules can be established from Scripture or as a consequence of the transcendental nature of apologetics. It seems to me (1) that an indirect argument is not necessarily the only kind of argument that can establish the transcendental conclusion, and (2) that although the evidence for God's reality is certain, our verbal formulations of that evidence may be merely probable, and so on.

Van Til is at his worst in his critiques of other thinkers, but even there he provides valuable insight. His critique of the "traditional apologetic method" seems to me often to make unreasonable demands on past thinkers.

Van Til is at his worst in his critiques of other thinkers, but even there he provides valuable insight. His critique of the "traditional apologetic method" seems to me often to make unreasonable demands on past thinkers (such as the illegitimate rules mentioned in the paragraph above). His criticisms are valuable, however, as advice on strategy and clear communication. Certainly, the apologetic tradition has obscured the gospel by failing to make clear (to unbelievers and believers alike) the radical antithesis between Christian and non-Christian thought. It has even used formulae (e.g., "bring on your revelations! let them make peace with the law of contradiction and the facts of experience, and they will deserve a rational man's assent") that, while true in themselves, taken in context encourage unbelievers to continue thinking autonomously. Unfortunately, Van Til sometimes fails to adequately distinguish between (1) issues of communication and strategy, and (2) issues of biblical orthodoxy. He also fails to adequately distinguish between spiritual and procedural issues. For example, he suggests that "direct" arguments, as opposed to "indirect," are unambiguous expressions of an ungodly neutralism.

Unfortunately, Van Til sometimes fails to adequately distinguish between (1) issues of communication and strategy, and (2) issues of biblical orthodoxy. He also fails to adequately distinguish between spiritual and procedural issues.

There are similar problems in Van Til's critiques of scholasticism and of the Amsterdam philosophy, but he does hit upon some genuine and serious errors and confusions in those systems, and even more in the system of Karl Barth. For giving the church such clear warning about these errors, he deserves the commendation of all Christians.

I believe, therefore, that we can learn much that is good and valuable from Van Til, without being slavish devotees. It is not necessary for the Van Tillian movement to maintain a "movement mentality." Nor is it necessary to stand in "antithesis" against all our fellow Christians who have thus far not joined that movement.

A Van Tillian apologetic for the next century should free itself from those Van Tillian restrictions that are illegitimate and then enrich itself by developing a great variety of arguments contextualized for many different sorts of apologetic encounter. Van Til has taught us that every fact of history testifies to the reality of the biblical God. He has only begun to show us how this takes place. It is for us further to implement this vision, by showing how the presuppositions of Scripture reveal everything for what it truly is in relation to God. That is an exciting task indeed.

It is also important for us to move beyond the traditional Van Tillian preoccupation with methodology. . . . More time should be spent on developing actual arguments.

It is also important for us to move beyond the traditional Van Tillian preoccupation with methodology.[2] Van Tillian courses in apologetics, including mine, have focused far too much on methods, especially on distinguishing our methods from those of other schools of thought. More time should be spent on developing actual arguments. We need to spend more time addressing unbelievers, less time arguing with one another over methods. Students of Van Tillian apologetics need to be far better informed about Christian evidences and about the current situations that the apologist must address.

My critical account of Van Til allows us to take a somewhat less apocalyptic view of methodological differences among apologists, so that we can indeed concentrate on fulfilling the Great Commission. If this book can encourage believers in that work, it will have accomplished its purpose.

2. Thanks to Greg Bahnsen, who impressed this truth on me in recent remarks.

GLOSSARY

HERE I BRIEFLY DEFINE some of the philosophical and theological terms used in this book. Most of these come from the list of Key Terms following each chapter, but I have not defined all of those Key Terms here. The numbers in parentheses indicate chapters in the book where these terms are discussed; in a very few instances, if a term is quite general, no chapter reference appears. Most words (or their derivatives) in *italics* are defined elsewhere in the list.

abduction (9). In Peirce, the formulation of a hypothesis suitable for investigation. Correlative with *deduction* and *induction*.

Abraham the Mighty (13). Respectful title given to Abraham Kuyper.

absolute (1). Ultimate, final, eternal.

absolute spirit (7). In Hegel; see *spirit*.

abstract ideas (5). *Ideas* of general qualities or *universals*, such as "red," "horse," or "virtue." Berkeley denied that such *ideas* exist.

absurd (Kierkegaard) (8). The idea of the eternal's entering time; this objective absurdity as the center of Christian faith.

accidental truths of history (6). Lessing's description of the results of scientific historiography. Contrasted with *necessary truths of reason*.

accidents (4). Qualities that do not constitute the *essence* of a *substance*.

account (1). Description of why an assertion constitutes knowledge. (Plato's term for *justification*.)

active intellect (2, 4). In Aristotle, the part of the *intellect* that analyzes and comes to understand the data of the senses. Contrasted with *passive intellect*.

activism, actualism (10). In Barthian theology, the idea that God is constituted by his acts, not by an *essence*. This is similar to the existentialist understanding of human *existence*.

actuality (2). In Aristotle, what something is now, in contrast with its *potentiality*.

actual occasion (11). In process thought, the smallest unit of process.

***ad fontes* (5).** "To the sources," a slogan reflecting the *Renaissance* interest in the earliest literature of learning, especially from Greek culture.

aeons (3). In *Gnosticism*, semidivine beings that *emanate* from *Bythos*.

aesthetic stage (8). The first of Kierkegaard's three or four "stages on life's way." A preoccupation with pleasant appearances and pleasures. Contrasted with *ethical stage* and *religious stage*. See also *knight of faith*.

age of reason (5, 6). Common name for the period called the *Enlightenment*.

alienation (7). In Marx, the estrangement of the worker from the fruits of his labor, because the profit of his work goes to someone else.

analogical (4). Of or relating to a piece of language as it is used on two occasions, in senses that are neither *univocal* nor *equivocal* but have something in common.

analogy (3, 4, 6). Way of knowing God by determining similarities and dissimilarities between God and the universe. Advocated by Origen, Aquinas, Butler, and others. Butler stresses the analogy between God's natural *revelation* in the *course and constitution of nature* and his supernatural *revelation* in Christ. Contrasted with *disanalogy*.

analogy of attribution (4). One form of *analogy*. To speak of God's attributes as analogous to ours, in this understanding, is to say that God is the *cause* of these attributes in us.

analogy of proper proportionality (4). One form of *analogy*. In speaking of the attributes of God, to say that God is "wise" means, under this form of *analogy*, that God's *wisdom* is to God's *nature* as man's *wisdom* is to man's *nature*.

analogy of resemblance (4). One form of *analogy*. In this type of analogy, to say that A is analogous to B is simply to say that A resembles B.

analysis (Origen) (3). Knowing God by knowing what he is not. Same as *via negativa* of Aquinas. Contrasted with *synthesis*.

analytic (5). Of or relating to a sentence in which the meaning of the predicate is part of the meaning of the subject, as in "all bachelors are unmarried." Contrasted with *synthetic*.

analytical tool (11). Phrase used to describe the use of Marxism by liberation theologians: a means of analysis, rather than a substantive commitment.

anomalous playing cards (12). Experiment described by Kuhn in which subjects are presented with cards that they do not expect to see (e.g., a red 6 of spades) and for a while are unable to describe the actual state of affairs by their *sense experience*.

anomaly (12). A *puzzle* within *normal science* that proves especially resistant to resolution.

***ante rem* (4).** "In God's mind, apart from finite things." In Aquinas's view of *universals*, they exist *ante rem*, *in re* (in the things God has made), and *post rem* (in the human mind).

anticipate (13). To reflect a higher *modal aspect*. In Dooyeweerd, lower *modal aspects* reflect higher ones in various ways, called "anticipation." Contrasted with *retrocipate*.

antinomies (7). For Kant, arguments that can prove or disprove the same conclusion with equal persuasiveness. They occur particularly when people try to prove the *existence* of God, the world as a whole, or human freedom as *constitutive* concepts. See *transcendental dialectic*.

antiquarianism (5). Preoccupation with the past.

Anti-revolutionary Party (13). The political party that Abraham Kuyper joined and came to head, so that he became Prime Minister of the Netherlands. Opposed to the *secularist* principles of the French Revolution.

antithesis (1, 7, 13). The opposition between Christian and non-Christian *worldviews*. For Hegel's use of the term, see *dialectic*. See also discussion of Kuyper and Van Til in chapter 13.

anxiety (9). In Heidegger, the particular kind of fear that expresses *being-toward-death*.

***apeiron* (2).** The indefinite *substance* that Anaximander believed to be the ultimate constituent of the world.

apocalypse (11). *Revelation* that discloses the *open future*. Moltmann adopts this view of *revelation*, as opposed to *epiphany*.

***apokatastasis* (3).** View that in the end God will restore all people along with all creation. A form of *universalism*.

Apollonian (7). In Schopenhauer and Nietzsche, of or relating to emulating the Greek god of order, recognizing the rationality of the universe.

***a posteriori* knowledge (5).** Knowledge that results from human inquiry. Contrasted with *a priori knowledge*.

***a priori* knowledge (5).** Knowledge that we have before entering a particular inquiry, and that governs our methods and conclusions from that inquiry. In a more *absolute* sense, knowledge that is independent of any inquiry whatever, and that governs all inquiries. Contrasted with *a posteriori knowledge*.

Aquinas-Butler Method (6). According to Van Til, an apologetic strategy that begins with assumptions held by the unbeliever and tries to deduce from these the *truth* of Scripture. He ascribes this method to many, but thinks that Thomas Aquinas and Joseph Butler are among the most important examples.

argument from gradation (4). Argument for God's *existence* in Anselm and Aquinas holding that degrees of reality, virtue, power, and the like presuppose a maximum, and that must be God.

Arianism (3). The view of Arius that the Son of God was a created being. This view was declared as *heresy* by the Nicene and Constantinopolitan Councils.

aseity (1). God's self-*existence* and self-sufficiency.

assent (13). Acceptance of the *truth* of a *proposition*. In traditional Reformed theology, this is an element of faith, along with *knowledge* and *trust*. But Gordon Clark believes that *assent* is sufficient to define the *nature* of faith.

atomic facts (11). *Facts* that are the constituents of all other *facts*. In Russell's and Wittgenstein's early thought, momentary occurrences of *sense experience*.

atomic processes (11). The processes that make up all other processes, according to process philosophy.

atomism (1, 2, 5). The view that the universe is made of tiny, indivisible objects and is best understood by reference to those. Opposed to *monism* and *dualism*. See also *qualitative atomism* and *quantitative atomism*.

***Auburn Affirmation* (8).** A document signed by 1,274 ministers of the Presbyterian Church USA, denying that the virgin birth, resurrection, and other doctrines were *necessary* for ordination in that denomination. See *Five Fundamentals*.

***aufheben, aufgehoben* (7).** See *dialectic*.

***autexousion* (3).** A Greek word denoting *libertarian freedom* or *incompatibilism*.

authentic existence (9, 10). In Heidegger and Sartre, *existence* in the awareness that our choices are not the result of a design or *fate*, but express our own total (*libertarian*) freedom. In Bultmann, it particularly constitutes *openness to the future*. But to him, authentic existence is a gift of God.

authority (1). God's right to command and to be obeyed in all things. Coordinated with *control* and *presence* as aspects of divine *lordship*.

autonomous reason (1, 5). Human *reason* as the ultimate standard of *truth* and right, having no need to consult divine *revelation*.

autonomy (10, 13). In Tillich, a legitimate type of reasoning that sometimes fails to be united to its own *depth*. Correlated with *heteronomy* and *theonomy*. In Dooyeweerd, the notion that theoretical thought is independent of heart-commitment.

awakening (6). Broad-based revival of Christian religion, as on various occasions in America from the eighteenth century (the Great Awakening) to the present.

axioms (13). The ultimate *presuppositions* in Gordon Clark's view of philosophical systems in a geometrical model.

bare facts (13). Synonymous with *brute facts*.

***Barmen Declaration* (10).** Document largely written by Barth in which the *Confessing Church* repudiated subservience to the Nazi government.

basic beliefs (13). In Plantinga, *beliefs* that we hold without evidence or argument, by which we validate other *beliefs*. See *Reformed epistemology* and *foundational beliefs*.

being (1). What "is" in any sense.

being-in-the-world (9). Synonymous with *Dasein* in Heidegger.

being itself (10). Tillich's term for "God." Synonymous with *ground of being*.

being-toward-death (9). In Heidegger, the chief preoccupation of *Dasein*, recognizing the inevitability of its own nonbeing.

belief (2). An element of knowledge. In Plato, something less than the highest form of knowledge. Contrasted with *conjecture, understanding,* and *intuitive vision*. See also *way of belief* in Parmenides.

biblical theology (3). A method of understanding Scripture, focusing on the *history of redemption*.

black theology (11). A type of liberation theology, from the viewpoint of African Americans, construed as the victims of oppression by whites.

Bloch, Ernst (11). German Marxist whose rejection of traditional *Marxist eschatology* gave him some sympathy for religion unusual among Marxists. A major influence on the thought of Jürgen Moltmann.

bracket (9). In phenomenology, to investigate a phenomenon without asking questions about whether it is an appearance of something else, or about its connections with realities not presented to us in the phenomenon. Husserl calls this procedure the *epoché*.

brute facts (12, 13). *Facts* apart from any interpretation, thought of as the basis of all interpretation. Synonymous with *bare facts*.

bundle (5). In Hume, a term describing the soul. Hume believed that the soul was a bundle of perceptions.

Bythos (3). A name for the supreme being in *Gnosticism*.

canon (3). The books included in Holy Scripture, given by God to rule the church.

canon criticism (11). The approach to Scripture of Brevard Childs and others, regarding it not primarily as a historical source or a set of religious experiences, but as the document adopted by the church as the definitive expression of its faith. Cf. *postliberalism*.

capital sum (Barth) (10). Barth metaphor for the view of Scripture in orthodox theology, which allows the Word of God to be "at their disposal."

care (9). In Heidegger, expresses the inevitable preoccupation of human *Dasein* with other beings.

categories of the understanding (7). See *transcendental analytic*.

cause (4, 5). What makes something happen. That something is called the *effect*. Hume denied the *necessary connection* between cause and *effect*.

cheap grace (Bonhoeffer) (10). Grace without discipleship.

Christian atheism (10). Theology of Altizer, Van Buren, Hamilton attempting to develop a form of Christianity without God. Also termed *radical theology.*

Christian philosophers (1, 13). Philosophers who seek to articulate and defend a Christian *worldview.*

circularity (13). A procedure in which, according to Van Til, when we argue for God and the *truth* of Scripture, we must presuppose it. Van Til admitted that this procedure was circular in a sense, but that all other systems of thought were circular in the same way.

***circumcessio* (1, 3).** The mutual involvement among the persons of the Trinity: the Father is "in" the Son, the Son is "in" the Spirit, and so on. Synonymous with *perichoresis.*

city of God (3). In the book by Augustine, those who are seeking to bring society under Christ's dominion. Contrasted with *earthly city.*

class conflict (7). In Marx, conflict between the rich and poor, the haves and have-nots.

clear and distinct ideas (5). Descartes' criterion of knowledge that could be considered certain.

coercive (11). Or of relating to the view that God coerces, or forces, *actual occasions* to do anything. Process theologians deny this. They rather describe his influence on the world as *persuasive.*

cognitive meaning (12). The capacity of a sentence to make a *truth* claim, whether truly or falsely. *Logical positivists* denied that metaphysical and religious statements have cognitive meaning.

common grace (13). Nonsaving grace common to Christians and non-Christians, enabling them to cooperate in cultural matters.

common ground (13). Something in common between believers and unbelievers. Van Til sometimes denied that there was any such thing. Other times, he said that there was common ground in the knowledge of God that the unbeliever has but suppresses. See also *antithesis.*

Common Sense Realism (6). Philosophical position of Thomas Reid and his school, echoed in later thinkers such as G. E. Moore and Alvin Plantinga. It says that we must begin our thinking with common-sense assumptions, rather than imagining that we can prove everything we believe.

compatibilism (2). A view holding that human choices are free when they are what the person desires. This view of freedom is compatible with *determinism.* Contrasted with *incompatibilism* and *libertarian freedom.*

complex ideas (5). In Locke's *epistemology, ideas* that result from the mind's bringing them into various relationships with one another. Contrasted with *simple ideas.*

compossible (5). Of or relating to the view of Leibniz that two *monads* are capable of existing in the same world.

Comte, Auguste (12). A founder of sociology who believed that the age of religion and the age of metaphysics would be replaced by the "positive" age, in which the methods of natural science prevail. The source for the "positivism" in *logical positivism*.

conceptualism (4). A view holding that *universals* are neither real entities outside the mind (*realism*) nor mere words (*nominalism*), but ideas in the mind.

concrescence (11). One of the two types of processes among *actual occasions* in process thought, the other being *transition*. In concrescence, each *actual occasion prehends* past occasions, *eternal objects*, or God, and freely chooses to change itself.

Confessing Church (10). The churches that refused to support Hitler, supported by Barth, Bonhoeffer, and others. Contrasted with *German Christians*.

conflictual (11). In liberation theology, of or relating to the principle that participation in the struggle for social justice is never without conflict. Reflects Marx's view that in class struggle, benefits to one class always entail losses to another.

conjecture (2). A lower form of knowledge in Plato's account. Contrasted with *belief*, *understanding*, and *intuitive vision*.

consciousness (9, 11). Awareness of the world and the self. In process thought, the highest form of *subjective immediacy*.

consequent nature of God (11). In process thought, distinguished from the *primordial nature of God*. God's consequent nature is dependent on the *actual occasions* of the universe. He changes in response to their free choices.

conservative drift (7, 10). Frame's theory that each generation of *liberal theology* tends to appear more conservative than the previous, in order to gain influence in the church. Not without exceptions.

consistently eschatological (8). Of or relating to the view of Schweitzer, Weiss, and others that Jesus was an apocalyptic visionary, who believed that the end of the world and the final judgment were immediate.

consolidator (3). In Frame's analysis, one who rethinks the corpus of Christian theology in the wake of a triumph over *heresy*. Contrasted with *synthesis*, *heresy*, and *reformer*.

Constantinian model (11). The view that the church should rule over the state and society. Moltmann rejects this. Contrasted with *universal sacrament of salvation*.

constitutive use (7). The principle, in Kant, that when we take *ideals of reason* and use them to try to prove the *existence* of actual entities, we are using these *ideals* constitutively and wrongly. Contrasted with *regulative use*.

contingent being (4). A being whose *existence* is dependent on something other than itself. Contrasted with *necessary being*.

contradiction (12). A form of words that is necessarily false because of logical impossibility, such as "Joe is a married bachelor." Contrasted with *tautology* and *empirical proposition* in *logical positivism*.

control (1). God's comprehensive power over creation, by which everything comes to pass. Coordinated with *authority* and *presence* as aspects of divine *lordship*.

conventionalism (12). The view that science is based not on the *facts* of the world, but on social conventions or agreements to look at reality in a certain way.

conversion to the neighbor (11). In liberation theology, the idea of true conversion as a commitment to serve one's neighbor in the struggle for social justice.

Copernican revolution (7). Kant's description of his philosophy, comparing it with the revolutionary idea of Copernicus. Just as Copernicus forced us to think of the sun as central rather than the earth, so Kant wanted us to think of ourselves as the organizing principle of the world, rather than reality outside us.

correlative (11). Of two things, each relative to the other. In process thought, God and the world are correlative.

***Corsair, The* (8).** Danish periodical that carried on a feud with Kierkegaard for some years.

cosmic accountant (5). Phrase used by Leibniz's critics to disparage his view of God. Their criticism is that Leibniz's God creates the universe that abstract logical possibility tells him to create. So he is merely an accountant of logical possibility.

cosmic moralist (11). Process theologians' description of God in his relation to humans in traditional theology: laying down laws, demanding obedience, cursing disobedience. They believe that their own theology provides a better model.

cosmological argument (4). The argument that the chain of motions, events, or dependencies within the world requires a first member. The first three of Aquinas's *five ways* are cosmological. Contrasted with *ontological argument* and *teleological argument*.

cosmonomic (13). Of or relating to "world-law." Dooyeweerd's "philosophy of the idea of law" is sometimes called "the philosophy of the cosmonomic idea."

Council of Chalcedon (1). Christian council held in 451 to discuss views of the two *natures* of Christ. The council affirmed that he has two *natures*, fully divine and fully human.

course and constitution of nature (6). Butler's characterization of the created world, which serves as a natural *revelation* of God. See *analogy*.

covenant epistemology (13). The *epistemology* developed by Esther Meek, in which personal and interpersonal factors are central. See *knowledge*.

creation *ex nihilo* (1, 3). God's creating the world out of nothing. Contrasted with *emanation*.

creation idea (13). Name for the philosophy of H. G. Stoker, distinguished from Dooyeweerd's philosophy of the "law idea."

creationism (3). The view that every human soul is a special creation of God. Contrasted with *traducianism*.

creative aim (11). In process thought, the decision of each *actual occasion* to change its *initial aim* on the basis of *prehension* of other entities.

creative transformation (11). In process theology, the work of Christ, who provides creative possibilities in which otherwise discordant elements can be harmoniously united, increasing enjoyment.

creativity (11). A general quality of *being* according to process thought, distributed among *actual occasions* and God.

Creator-creature distinction (1). The distinction between God and the world, key concept in a biblical *worldview*.

crede ut intelligas, credo ut intelligam (3, 4). Slogans used by Augustine (in the second person, "believe that you may understand") and Anselm (in the first person, "I believe that I might understand"). Cf. Anselm, *fides quaerens intellectum*, "faith seeking understanding."

crisis (Kuhn) (12). The persistent failure of the *puzzles* of *normal science* to be resolved as they should be.

crisis theology (10). Name given early to the theology of Barth and his school, because of its emphasis on divine judgment.

criteriological argument (4). Frame's name for the fourth of Aquinas's *five ways*, also used by Anselm. It says that qualities that differ in degree presuppose a maximum of that quality, which must be God. Contrasted with *ontological argument*, *cosmological argument*, and *teleological argument*.

critical commonsensism (9). Peirce's name for his *epistemology*: respect common sense, but make good use of critical faculties.

critique of reason (7). Kant's stated purpose for his philosophy. Kant believed that philosophy could not accomplish a rational description of the world until it developed a critique of reason itself. Kant attempted this in his *Critique of Pure Reason*, *Critique of Practical Reason*, and *Critique of Judgment*.

daimon (2). Greek term referring to a supernatural being. Socrates claimed to have gained knowledge from one.

***Dasein* (9).** German word for "being there." Heidegger's term for human *nature*, thrown into its context.

D-Day (10). Cullmann's illustration of redemption in the NT: begun, but not consummated.

dead orthodoxy (5). Subject of the *pietists'* complaint against the established churches.

deconstruction (12). Movement of *poststructuralism* in which ostensible meanings of language are said to be something other than what they appear to be.

deduction (9). Drawing testable logical consequences from one's hypothesis, in order to verify it (Peirce). Coordinated with *abduction* and *induction*.

deep structure (12). In *structuralism*, a *universal* system of language that underlies verbal expressions and human actions.

defeasible (13). Capable of being defeated or refuted. In Plantinga's *Reformed epistemology*, even *basic* or *foundational beliefs* can be refuted by evidence or argument, although they are not themselves based on evidence or argument.

degrees of being (4). The principle in Plato's thought that *being* admits of degrees: only the Forms are fully real. For Dionysius, God is the most real being, and his *emanations* lack *being* to the extent that they are distinct from him.

deification (3). The notion that we are saved either by becoming God (*Gnosticism* and *Neoplatonism*) or by being renewed in God's image (Irenaeus).

deism (1, 6). View that God created the world to run on *natural laws* and is not otherwise involved with the world's *history*. Contrasted with *theism*, *pantheism*, and *panentheism*.

Demiurge (1, 2). Godlike figure in Plato's *Timaeus* who makes the world in imitation of the Forms out of preexisting *matter*.

demythologization (10). Bultmann's attempt to remove mythological elements (see *myth*) from Scripture, to uncover the original existential message of the text.

deontologism (1). The view that ethical standards consist of *universal* and *necessary* duties. Opposed to *teleologism* and *existentialism*.

depth of reason (10). In Tillich, the sense that our reasoning has reached some very significant *truth*, a manifestation of God as *ground of being*.

design plan (13). In Plantinga, an aspect of properly working epistemic equipment. Plantinga believes that one condition of properly working epistemic equipment is that it be working according to a good design plan. But where does that plan come from? This principle suggests that human knowledge presupposes God.

desperation (11). Lack of hope. Part of Moltmann's definition of *sin*.

***De Standaard* (13).** Dutch newspaper founded by Abraham Kuyper.

determinism (1, 2, 5). The view that every event occurs because of a *necessary cause*. Contrasted with *incompatibilism* and *libertarian freedom*. See also *fate*.

***Deus sive natura* (5).** "God or nature," Spinoza's way of characterizing the whole of reality. An expression of *pantheism*.

diachronic (12). In Saussure, of or relating to analysis of language by etymology and other past usage. Contrasted with *synchronic*.

dialectic (2, 7). Method of gaining knowledge by comparing two apparently incompatible views, hoping to rise to a view more adequate than either. The term is applied in different ways to Plato and to Hegel. In Hegel, it often proceeds in a pattern *thesis*, *antithesis*, and *synthesis*. That is, from any piece of presumed knowledge (thesis), one can learn more by considering the *truth* of its opposite (*antithesis*) and then bringing the *truths* together to see the matter in a broader context (*synthesis*). Hegel expresses this pattern by the German word *aufheben*, which means (conveniently) "preserve," "cancel," and "lift up."

dialectical materialism (7). The view of Marx that although *history* proceeds by conflict, it is not fundamentally intellectual conflict (as in Hegel), but conflict over wealth, income, and production.

dialectical theology (10). Name given to the theology of Barth, Brunner, and others, because of their tendency to simultaneously affirm and deny the assertions of Christian theology.

dialogical (10). Of or relating to the emphasis of thinkers such as Brunner, Ebner, Oman, and Buber of *personalism* in our relationships with other people and with God.

dictatorship of the proletariat (7). In Marx, a stage in the Communist revolution in which the means of production are to be placed in the hands of the workers (the proletariat), and they are to govern solely in their own interest. But see *withering of the state*.

***Ding an Sich* (7).** See *noumena*.

Dionysiac (7). In Schopenhauer and Nietzsche, of or relating to thought, emulating the Greek god of debauchery, that seeks to do justice to the chaos behind the rational.

disanalogy (6). The differences between matters of general and special *revelation*. Butler argues that we must do justice both to the *analogy* between these matters and to their disanalogy. Contrasted with *analogy*.

divine self-alienation (7). In Hegel, the principle that God himself confronts and dialectically overcomes his negative side.

Docetism (3). The view that Jesus only appeared to be material and human; influenced by *Gnosticism*.

doctrines (Schleiermacher) (8). Religious affections or feelings expressed in speech.

dogmatic slumbers (7). Kant's description of his condition as a disciple of Leibniz and Wolff before being "awakened" by David Hume.

***Doleantie* (13).** The "grieving" church, formed by the departure of Abraham Kuyper and others from the Dutch *Hervormede Kerk*. Later merged with the Christian Reformed Church to form the *Gereformeerde Kerken*.

Donation of Constantine (5). Document allegedly by the emperor Constantine ceding authority to the Roman church. Shown to be fraudulent by *Renaissance* scholars.

dualism (1). The view that the universe consists of two, and only two, realities. Contrasted with *monism* and *pluralism*.

earthly city (3). Society and culture that is not subject to God's *revelation*. Augustine contrasts this with the *city of God*.

***ecclesiolae in ecclesia* (5).** "Little churches in the church," referring to small-group meetings advocated by *pietism*.

***e contingentia mundi* (4).** "From the contingency of the world." The third of Aquinas's *five ways* of proving God's *existence*. It argues that if everything were *contingent being*, with no *necessary being*, the world could not exist. Contrasted with *cosmological argument*, *ontological argument*, and *teleological argument*.

effect (5). What is made to happen by a *cause*. Hume denied the *necessary connection* between *cause* and effect.

efficient cause (2, 4). One of Aristotle's *four causes*: the *cause* that makes an event take place. Contrasted with *formal cause*, *final cause*, and *material cause*.

ek-sistence (9). Human *existence*, expressed in a faux etymology suggesting "standing out from" in Heidegger.

elementary proposition (12). A *proposition* that can serve as an element of a complex *proposition*. Russell and Wittgenstein in their early work thought that meaningful language was constituted by elementary propositions. For *logical positivists*, elementary propositions were statements of observations on which other statements ought to be based.

emanate, emanation (1, 2). Terms relating to the view of *Gnosticism* and *Neoplatonism* that the world came forth as God's *essence*. This view denies, and is contrasted with, *creation ex nihilo*.

emotion (6, 8, 9). Personal feeling. Coordinated with *intellect* and *will*.

emotive language (12). In *logical positivism*, any piece of language that cannot be qualified as a *tautology*, a *contradiction*, or an *empirical proposition*.

empirical proposition (12). In *logical positivism*, a form of words capable of stating an empirical *fact* because it is capable of being scientifically verified or *falsified*. Distinguished from *tautology* and *contradiction*.

empiricism (1, 4, 5). The view that *sense experience* is the most fundamental ground of knowledge. Contrasted with *rationalism* and *subjectivism*.

enjoyment (11). In process thought, the quality of subjective feeling of each *actual occasion*.

Enlightenment (5, 6). The period of 1650–1800 known as the *age of reason* in which the most important thinkers claimed the ultimacy of *autonomous reason*.

***en soi* (9).** "In itself," according to Sartre, the status of things that are solid and definable as opposed to free persons. Contrasted with *pour soi*.

epiphany (Moltmann) (11). A type of *revelation* that discloses the present *nature* of things. Moltmann rejects this in favor of *apocalypse*.

epistemology (1). The study of human knowledge. Correlated with *metaphysics* and *value theory*.

***epoché* (9).** See *bracket*.

equivocal (4). Of or relating to the state of a piece of language that is used in two very different senses. Contrasted with *univocal* and *analogical*.

Erastianism (5). The view that the church ought to be subject to the state.

***esse* (4).** In Aquinas, the act by which anything is.

***esse est percipi* (5).** "To be is to be perceived." Berkeley's assertion.

essence (4, 9). The fundamental *nature* of anything. Contrasted with *accident*. Sartre denies that human beings have essences, for in his view they are not designed by God.

essential God-consciousness (8). In Schleiermacher, Jesus' religious feeling that made him divine.

essentially related (11). In process thought, of or relating to the state of each *actual occasion*'s entering into the life of all the others, so that each is related to the others in its very *being*.

eternal generation (3). The doctrine that the Son of God is begotten by the Father in eternity as well as in time. Affirmed in the Nicene Creed ("God of God" and so on).

eternal intuition (13). The "mode" of God's thought in the *Van Til-Clark controversy*. See *mode of God's thoughts*.

eternal objects (11). In process thought, possible qualities and states of affairs (analogous to Platonic Forms), capable of *prehension* by *actual occasions*.

eternal procession (3). The doctrine that the Spirit of God proceeds from the Father ("and the Son" in the Western church) as well as in time.

eternal recurrence (9). The idea that since the world is governed by chance, every event will recur, given sufficient time. Nietzsche affirmed this as a good thing.

eternity (Boethius) (4). *Existence* above time.

ethical absolutism (1). The view that some ethical standards apply universally and without exception. Coordinated with *ethical relativism.*

ethical relativism (1). The non-Christian view that no ethical standards are universally applicable and without exception. Coordinated with *ethical absolutism.*

ethical stage (8). The second of Kierkegaard's three or four "stages of life." Characterized by devotion to *universal* and *necessary* ethical principles. Contrasted with *aesthetic stage* and *religious stage.*

evil genius (5). Descartes' term for a being that could deceive us about everything we believed to be true. He rejected the possibility of such a being on the ground that God exists and God is not a deceiver.

evolutionary argument against naturalism (13). Alvin Plantinga's argument that if evolution is true, the mind is programmed for survival, not necessarily for *truth.* So if the theory of evolution claims to give us the complete purpose of the human mind, there is reason to doubt the products of the mind, including the theories of evolution and *naturalism.*

existence (9). Concrete actuality, living. For Sartre, this precedes *essence,* for what we are is not a *design plan* from a supernatural being, but is our own series of choices.

existence communication (8). What God gives to us in true faith, according to Kierkegaard: a new *existence,* rather than mere doctrines or commands.

existential analysis (10). Bultmann's attempt to determine the true (existential) meaning of Scripture beneath its mythological exterior.

existentialism (in ethics) (1). The view that ethical decisions are expressions of the desires of the agent, without reference to *absolute* norms (as in *deontologism*) or *universal* happiness (as in *teleologism*).

existential perspective (1). A way of knowing by understanding one's own personal experience. Coordinated with *normative perspective* and *situational perspective.*

***ex-lex* (13).** Of or relating to Gordon Clark's view that God is not responsible to keep the moral law, and thus he is exempted from moral criticism.

external (8). In Schleiermacher's view, of or relating to anything that is spiritually ineffectual.

externalist (13). In *epistemology,* of or relating to the view that our *beliefs* are justified not by other *beliefs,* but by the connections of those *beliefs* to the world external to us. Alvin Plantinga's *Reformed epistemology* is externalist, as opposed to *internalist*.

fact (12). A state of affairs, expressible by a clause or *proposition*.

fallacy of division (11). The fallacy of supposing that the parts of something have the same characteristics as the whole. Frame's critique of process philosophy.

fallacy of misplaced concreteness (11). Whitehead's term for a view that regards anything as concrete other than Whitehead's *actual occasions*.

fallacy of reification (11). In Whitehead, the idea that reality is made up of things that are sharply definable and separate from one another.

fallacy of simple location (11). Another synonym for the previous two mistakes, stressing the error of regarding *actual occasions* as being precisely located.

falsifiable (12). Of or relating to the idea of Karl Popper that a piece of language can be *cognitively meaningful* if and only if it can be falsified by the methods of natural science. This is an attempt to reformulate the *verification principle* of *logical positivism*.

family resemblances (12). Wittgenstein's equivalent of a doctrine of *universals*. To Wittgenstein, there need not be a single concept conveyed by all uses of a term. Rather, in most cases a term will have a variety of uses (= meanings) that occur, disappear, and reoccur, like resemblances among family members. This is Wittgenstein's contribution to the philosophical discussion of *universals*.

fate (2). An impersonal principle thought to determine all events happening in the world.

feeling of absolute dependence (8). Subjective sense that our very *existence* is dependent on another being (Schleiermacher). See *Gefühl*.

***fides quaerens intellectum* (4).** "Faith seeking understanding." Cf. *crede ut intelligas*.

***fiducia* (13).** "Faith." See *trust*.

final cause (2, 4). One of Aristotle's *four causes*: the *cause* that indicates the purpose or goal of something. Contrasted with *efficient cause*, *formal cause*, and *material cause*.

final revelation (10). In Tillich, a symbol that can negate itself without losing itself; hence the cross of Christ.

first principles (2). In Aristotle, the most basic principles of knowledge, by *nature* unprovable.

Five Fundamentals (8). The inerrancy of Scripture, the virgin birth and miracles of Christ, his substitutionary atonement, his resurrection, and his return in glory. These were the doctrines that the *Auburn Affirmation* denied were *necessary* for ordination in the Presbyterian Church USA.

five *solas* (5). Slogans of the Reformation period: *sola Scriptura*, *sola fide*, *sola gratia*, *solo Christo*, and *soli Deo gloria*. Respectively: "by Scripture alone," "by faith alone," "by grace alone," "by Christ alone," and "to the glory of God alone."

five ways (4). Aquinas's five proofs for the *existence* of God in his *Summa Theologiae*.

fixation of belief (9). In Peirce, the practice of seeking certainty.

form (2). The essential quality that makes something to be what it is.

formal cause (2, 4). One of Aristotle's *four causes*: the *cause* that makes something what it is. Contrasted with *efficient cause*, *final cause*, and *material cause*.

formal criteria of theology (10). In Tillich: (1) *propositions* dealing with their object as a matter of *ultimate concern*; (2) statements dealing with their object insofar as it can be a matter of *being* or nonbeing for us. Correlated with *material norm of theology*.

formal faith (13). In Kuyper, the nonsaving faith common to Christian and non-Christian thinkers, which enables them to trust in such things as the regularity of nature.

form criticism (10). A type of Bible criticism in which the scholar attempts to show the original settings of biblical sayings, for example, those of Jesus. Bultmann was a leading form critic of the NT.

form-matter scheme (2). Philosophies like that of the Greeks that seek to balance *form* with *matter* as the basic constituents of reality (according to Dooyeweerd).

foundational beliefs (13). In Plantinga, *beliefs* that serve as a foundation for others, without themselves needing a foundation in evidence or argument. See also *basic beliefs* and *Reformed epistemology*.

fountain of deity (3). Phrase indicating that the Father is the person of the Trinity from whom the Son is generated and the Spirit proceeds.

four causes (2). In Aristotle, four kinds of causation: *material cause*, *formal cause*, *final cause*, and *efficient cause*.

freedom of God (Barth) (10). Barth's view that God is not bound to his own *nature* or *revelation*. In Frame's analysis, this view is essentially *nominalism*.

Free University of Amsterdam (13). University founded by Abraham Kuyper.

fundamentalists (8). Those who maintained orthodox Christian doctrine during the late-nineteenth- and twentieth-century controversies over liberalism-modernism. See *modernists*.

gaze, the (9). An event in which someone else looks at me and thereby makes me an object in his own life.

Gefühl **(8).** In Schleiermacher, translated "feeling" or "intuition." The feeling of *absolute* dependence that Schleiermacher considers the root of religion.

genetic fallacy (7). A type of argument that argues the goodness of something because it came from a good source, or the badness of something because it came from a bad source.

genus (4). A class of realities, including species. For Aquinas, God is not in a genus.

Gereformeerde Kerken **(13).** See *Doleantie.*

German Christians (10). Those Christians and churches that supported Hitler. Contrasted with *Confessing Church.*

Geschichte **(10).** German word for *history*, but contrasted with *Historie. Geschichte* connotes the *facts* of *history* with their full meaning and significance.

given (9). In phenomenology, what experience presents to consciousness, as opposed to what consciousness makes out of it.

Gnosticism (3). Philosophical-religious movement in the first through third centuries A.D. that sought to dominate the Christian church. It taught that all things *emanated* from a supreme being (sometimes called *Bythos*) and that salvation comes by reabsorption into his *essence.*

God (11). In process thought, a being who includes all other beings, but who creates their *initial aim* and enables them to *prehend* other beings.

God beyond God, the (10). In Tillich, the God who appears when God has disappeared in the anxiety of doubt.

God's infinite salvific will (11). In liberation theology (and in some others, such as Rahner), the doctrine that all *history* reflects God's intention to save all people.

golden mean (2). In Aristotle, the ethical principle that the most desirable course of action is between two extremes.

ground-motives (13). The four basic contrasts by which Dooyeweerd analyzes the *history* of thought: form-matter (Greek philosophy), grace-nature (medieval philosophy), freedom-nature (modern thought), and creation-fall-redemption (Christian thought).

ground of being (10). Tillich's name for God. Synonymous with *being itself.*

ground of knowledge (1). The ultimate basis for believing anything, or for believing a particular thing.

Hartford Declaration **(10).** A 1975 document signed by moderate liberal and conservative theologians that criticized the more extreme statements of the *radical* and *secular theologies.*

heart (6). In Scripture, the fundamental direction of human life. In Pascal, a capacity for knowledge beyond that of *reason.*

hedonism (2). In ethics, the view that pleasure is the *summum bonum*, the highest good. Held by Epicurus and others.

***Heilsgeschichte* (10).** German for "history of salvation." Label given to theologians such as Cullmann and Ridderbos who seek to outline the redemptive-historical narrative of Scripture.

heresy (3). Serious theological error, compromising the fundamentals of the Christian faith. In Frame's analysis, a heretic often provokes a rethinking of the whole of Christian theology. Contrasted with *synthesis*, *reformer*, and *consolidator*.

heteronomy (10). In Tillich, a method of thinking that renounces *autonomy*, but that also loses its own depth in capitulating to an external source of authority. Contrasted and correlated with *autonomy* and *theonomy*.

***Hexapla* (3).** A document in which Origen gathered several versions and translations of Scripture and placed them in parallel columns.

***Historie* (10).** German word for *history*, connoting a scientific discipline under the authority of professional academic historians. Barth and other *dialectical* theologians denied that Scripture contained *Historie*, but acknowledged that it contained *Geschichte*, with which *Historie* is contrasted.

history (6). Sequence of events in past time of importance to human beings. Used both of the actual *facts* constituting that sequence and also of written accounts of that sequence.

history of redemption (3). The events described in Scripture that led to our salvation through Christ. See also *biblical theology*.

holism (12). The view that knowledge must be validated, not one *fact* at a time, but as a function of the thinker's whole rational outlook.

***homoousios* (3).** Greek term meaning "of the same nature." Describes the relation of the Son to the Father in the Nicene Creed.

humanism (5). A cultural tendency emphasizing human *nature* and concerns. Prominent in the *Renaissance* period. Humanism becomes highly *secularized* in the later modern period.

***hypostasis* (3).** The Greek term used in the Nicene formula to designate the three persons of the Trinity in contrast with God's one *being* (*ousia*).

idea (Schopenhauer) (7). Thought, conceived in Kantian fashion.

idealism (1, 5, 6, 7). The view that the universe is fundamentally mental or spiritual. Opposed to *materialism*. *Subjective* idealism is the view of Berkeley, that all reality is found in some individual thinking being. *Objective* idealism is the view of Hegel, which says that the whole universe is characterized by thought.

ideals (7). Attempts, according to Kant, to reason from concepts of the mind to realities that can play a *constitutive use*.

ideals of reason (7)**.** In Kant, *noumenal* realities such as self, world, and God that the mind often mistakenly regards as *constitutive*, rather than *regulative*, concepts.

ideas (5)**.** Contents of the mind. In Hume, contrasted with *impressions*: the faint copies of impressions contained in the mind.

ideas of reflection (5)**.** In Locke's *epistemology*, *ideas* we gain from reflecting on our *ideas of sensation*.

ideas of sensation (5)**.** In Locke's *epistemology*, our most fundamental *ideas*, the sources of our *ideas of reflection*.

***I-it* relation** (10)**.** The sort of relation we have with things, rather than people, opposed to *I-thou relation*. See *personalism*.

illumination (4, 10)**.** Knowledge or understanding given by God.

immanence (**biblical**) (1)**.** God's *presence* with the creation. Coordinated with *transcendence* (biblical).

immanence (**nonbiblical**) (1)**.** The notion that God is so close to the creation that he is indistinguishable from it and therefore cannot be identified as God. Coordinated with *transcendence* (nonbiblical).

impressions (5)**.** In Hume's *epistemology*, the immediate effects of the mind of sensation. Contrasted with *ideas*.

inalienable rights (5)**.** See *rights*.

inauthentic existence (9, 10)**.** In Heidegger, the state of accepting my *thrownness* as my *fate* rather than acknowledging my freedom to transcend it. In Bultmann, similar.

incarnation (**process thought**) (11)**.** The capacity of one *actual occasion* to enter another. Analogously, God's entering into the world-process.

incognito (8)**.** Of or relating to the idea of Kierkegaard that God is *wholly other* and that he cannot be reached through science or philosophy, but can be grasped only in passionate inwardness.

incompatibilism (2)**.** The view that human free choices have no *causes* and are therefore incompatible with *determinism*. Synonymous with *libertarian freedom*. Contrasted with *compatibilism*.

indirect communication (8)**.** In Kierkegaard, the way in which one communicates *existence*. To enable one to become a Christian in Christendom, it is important to use striking methods rather than conventional theological prose.

indirect identity (**Barth**) (10)**.** In Barth, the relation of Scripture and preaching to the Word of God.

indirect revelation (**Pannenberg**) (11)**.** *Revelation* that comes not through verbal communication but through factual evidence that must be evaluated by human *reason*.

induction (9)**.** In Peirce, empirical-scientific observation and experiments to test a hypothesis by its consequences. Coordinated with *abduction* and *deduction*.

initial aim (11). In process thought, the goal of each *actual occasion*, preliminarily given in its *physical pole*. Contrasted with *creative aim*.

innate ideas (5). Mental concepts that people are born with, or concepts that necessarily arise in the mind shortly after birth.

inquiry (9). In Peirce, an activity of trying to discover the *truth* of a matter.

Institute for Christian Studies (13). Graduate-level school in Toronto, staffed by followers of Dooyeweerd's philosophical school.

instrumentalism (9, 12). Dewey's view that gains in knowledge are only tools for advancing human purposes.

intellect (4). The ability of a person to think. Contrasted with *will* and *emotion*.

intellectualism (1). The view that the *intellect* governs, or ought to govern, the *will* and the *emotions*. Contrasted with *voluntarism* and *subjectivism*.

intellectual love of God (5). Spinoza's term for our recognition of the reality and *effects* of God-*nature*.

intermediate bodies (13). Social institutions that have freedom from others. In Abraham Kuyper's thought, freedom belongs not only to the state and the individual, but also to various spheres of association between the two, such as families, churches, and labor associations.

internalist (13). Of or relating to an *epistemology* in which a *belief* is justified by other *beliefs* one holds. Contrasted with *externalist*. Alvin Plantinga is critical of *epistemologies* that are internalist, such as that of John Pollock.

intuitive vision (2). In Plato, the highest form of knowledge. Contrasted with *conjecture*, *belief*, and *understanding*.

irrationalism (1). A view of *epistemology* that emphasizes the deficiencies of human *reason*, at the extreme denying the possibility of rational knowledge. Contrasted with *rationalism*.

***is-ought* argument (5).** An argument in which ethical values ("oughts") are derived from valueless *facts* ("is's"). Hume and G. E. Moore denied the validity of such an argument, and Moore called it the *naturalistic fallacy*.

***I-thou* relation (10).** Person-to-person relation, opposed to *I-it relation*. See *personalism*.

Jansenism (6). Teaching of Cornelius Jansen, defended by Blaise Pascal. Augustinian, predestinarian, biblicist. Taught at *Port Royal*, where Pascal's sister was a nun.

jelly-jar analogy (7). An illustration of Kant's *epistemology*: as jelly jars debate among themselves why their jelly takes on a certain shape, one exceptionally intelligent jar suggests that it is due to the shape of the jars themselves, not due to any ingredient in the jelly.

justification (1). In *epistemology*, the reason why a *belief* constitutes knowledge. Synonymous with Plato's *account*. Coordinated with *truth* and *belief.*

kenotic Christology (Moltmann) (11). The view that Christ divested himself of any power that would compromise his suffering and humility.

kernel and husk (8). In Ritschlianism, the relation between traditional dogma and spiritual reality. Dogma is like a husk that must be pulled away to expose the kernel.

knight of faith (8). Term for Abraham in Kierkegaard's *Fear and Trembling.* God confronts Abraham and commands him to sacrifice his son Isaac. Had Abraham been living in the mere *ethical stage* of Kierkegaard's lifestyles, he might have simply given up all hope for Isaac, becoming a *knight of infinite resignation.* But living by faith, as a *religious* man, he believed not only that God commanded him to kill Isaac, but that he would receive Isaac back. So he becomes a knight of faith, and a model for Christian faith.

knight of infinite resignation (8). See *knight of faith.*

knowledge (13). In the traditional Reformed understanding, one of the elements of faith. The others are *assent* and *trust.* The knowledge in this case is a knowledge of the content of *revelation*, whether or not one chooses to believe it.

knowledge (13) (philosophical definition). In the traditional view of philosophers, something like "justified true belief." Gettier questioned "justified" as a criterion of knowledge, and Plantinga developed in its place the criterion "warranted." Esther Meek developed a rather different definition: "the responsible human struggle to rely on clues to focus on a coherent pattern and submit to its reality."

language-analysis philosophy (12). Philosophy that seeks to analyze and solve philosophical problems by analyzing the language in which they are expressed. Applied particularly to the movement in twentieth-century English-speaking philosophy begun by Moore, Russell, and Wittgenstein.

language event (10). See *new hermeneutic.*

language game (12). In the later Wittgenstein, the human activity in the context of which a piece of language is used and finds its proper meaning.

***langue* (12).** In Saussure, the *deep structure* of language. Contrasted with *parole.*

latitudinarianism (6). Willingness in theology to compromise on traditional doctrinal *beliefs.* Often associated with Cambridge Platonists and others of the seventeenth century.

law (1). Rule or norm. In ethics, the principle to be obeyed. Contrasted with *situation* and *person*.

laws of thought (1). Norms that apply to thinking, such as the laws of logic. In a Christian view, the highest law of thought is divine *revelation*.

law spheres (13). Dooyeweerd's fifteen distinct areas that can be abstracted for theoretical study. See *modal aspects*.

leap (8). In Kierkegaard, a risk. Because it is impossible to make a drastic change in lifestyle by rational argument, at some stage there must be a risk, a "leap."

***Lebenswelt* (9).** "Ordinary life." The world of our everyday lives and perceptions, as opposed to the world described by scientists and philosophers. Correlative with *natural standpoint*.

left-wing Hegelians (7). Thinkers such as Feuerbach, and Marx, who pressed Hegel's *dialectical* method into a justification of radical ideas. Contrasted with *right-wing Hegelians*.

left-wing Origenists (3). Followers of Origen who emphasized his *subordinationist* language about the Trinity. The Arians are often described as left-wing Origenists. Contrasted with *right-wing Origenists*.

legal world order (8). For Ritschl, the principle that we must avoid any assertion in theology that suggests that we are subject to divine laws.

Lessing's ditch (6). Impassable space between the *accidental truths of history* and the *necessary truths of reason*. The discrepancy between these proved to Lessing that Christian faith (based on *necessary truths of reason*) may not be based on historical *facts*.

liberal theology (6). Theology that accepts the principle of *autonomous reason* and will not, therefore, be subject to the Scriptures as the Word of God.

libertarian freedom (1, 3). The state in which a free human decision has no *cause* at all, either outside or within the agent. Synonymous with *incompatibilism*. Contrasted with *determinism* and *compatibilism*.

limitations of logic (13). Purposes for which *logic* is unsuited. Although logicians tell us that *logic* is limited in several ways, for example, in its dependence on the meanings of the words it analyzes, Gordon Clark rejects all talk of limitation as a "belittling" of *logic*.

limiting situations (9). In Jaspers, situations when I become aware of my greatest limitations, particularly the limitation of death (as in Heidegger, Sartre).

logic (13). For Gordon Clark, the very structure of the divine mind, communicated to human beings as an infallible standard of consistency and implication.

logical empiricism (12). Synonymous with *logical positivism*.

logical positivism (12). The view that all *cognitively meaningful* language must be verifiable, by the methods of natural science. Synonymous with *logical empiricism.*

logos **(2).** In Greek, "word," "account," "reason." Thought by Heraclitus to be the principle underlying the changing world that made it intelligible. Later applied to Christ in John 1:1–14.

logos spermatikos **(3).** In Justin Martyr's thought, the Word of God, functioning as a seed, enabling everyone to have rational understanding.

lordship (1). God's sovereignty over all creation, including his *control, authority,* and *presence.*

lordship attributes (1). *Control, authority,* and *presence.*

Machen, J. Gresham (8). Theologian who studied in Germany with Herrmann and others, but returned to America to become one of the most cogent opponents of Ritschlian and other types of liberalism.

Manichaeism (3). *Dualistic* sect that taught the *existence* of two equally ultimate principles: good and evil. Augustine adhered to it before his Christian conversion, and then became one of its strongest critics.

Marcion (3). Second-century *heretic* who rejected most of Scripture out of an aversion to material reality, influenced by *Gnosticism.*

Marxist eschatology (7). A *secularized* view of the last days, in which Communism triumphs, and under the *dictatorship of the proletariat* people learn to work for the common good. Then comes the *withering of the state* in which everyone works on the principle "from each according to his ability, to each according to his need." This is the *Marxist utopia.*

Marxist utopia (7). See *Marxist eschatology.*

material cause (2, 4). One of Aristotle's *four causes*: that which anything is made out of. Contrasted with *formal cause, final cause,* and *efficient cause.*

materialism (1, 5). The view that the universe is fundamentally material, as opposed to *idealism.*

material norm of theology (10). For Tillich, Jesus Christ as the new being. Correlated with *formal criterion of theology.*

material substance (5). In Descartes, a *substance* that has only extension, no thought. Contrasted with *mental substance.*

matter (2). The stuff of which things are made, that bears *form.* In Stoicism, the fundamental reality of everything.

mauvaise foi **(9).** The state of deceiving ourselves into thinking that we are not really free, but controlled by something outside ourselves. Synonymous with *inauthentic existence.*

meaning as use (12). The view of the later Wittgenstein, that in most cases the term "meaning" refers to the use of language.

mental pole (11). In process thought, one of the two poles of each *actual occasion* (the other being the *physical pole*). Unlike the *physical pole*, the mental pole is capable of creative change, by *prehending* other *actual occasions*, *eternal objects*, and God.

mental substance (5). In Descartes, a *substance* that thinks, but has no extension. Contrasted with *material substance*.

***meta logou* (3).** "According to the word." Justin Martyr believed that the Greek philosophers were Christians because they lived according to the Word.

metanarrative (1, 12). A story that expresses one's *worldview*. Postmodern thinkers express suspicion of all such stories.

metaphysical freedom (3). The state of being able to perform acts not foreordained by God. Contrasted with *moral freedom*.

metaphysics (1). The *nature* of *being* in general; the structure of the universe as a whole. Correlated with *epistemology* and *value theory*.

method of authority (9). One of Peirce's methods for *fixation of belief*. In this method, one adopts an authority figure and believes whatever he believes.

method of correlation (10). Tillich's method of theology, which is (1) to determine the existential questions that our culture is asking, and then (2) to show that the *symbols* of the Christian faith provide answers to those questions.

method of tenacity (9). One of Peirce's methods for *fixation of belief*. In this method, one merely continues steadfast in the *beliefs* that he already holds.

Middle Platonism (2). The Platonism of 100 B.C. to A.D. 270.

Milesians (2). The earliest Greek philosophers, Thales, Anaximander, and Anaximenes, living around Miletus in Asia Minor.

mind-body problem (5). The question of how an unextended *mental substance* (the human mind) could cause *effects* in a nonthinking, extended *substance* (the human body). Descartes answered this problem by saying that a slight causal influence takes place in the *pineal gland*.

***Miscellanies* (6).** Jonathan Edwards's notebooks, in which he commented on various thoughts that struck him, philosophical and theological.

modal aspects (13). According to Dooyeweerd, the fifteen *law spheres* into which the world may be divided for purposes of theoretical study: quantitative, spatial, kinematic, and so on.

mode of God's thoughts (13). The way in which God thinks. In the *Van Til-Clark controversy*, the two men agreed that God thought in a different way or mode from man, namely, an *eternal intuition*. But Van Til and his disciples thought that was an insufficient way to describe the difference between God's thoughts and ours.

modernism (8, 10). Liberalism, particularly in its Ritschlian form, in the controversies in the late nineteenth and early twentieth centuries. See also *fundamentalists*.

monads (5). In Leibniz, the tiny mindlike entities that constitute the world.

monism (1, 5). The view that the universe consists of one and only one reality. Contrasted with *dualism* and *pluralism*. See also *Oneism* and *Twoism*.

Monophysite (5). Of or relating to the belief that the incarnate Christ has only one *nature*. Rejected by the church at Chalcedon in 451, but discussed again later between Lutherans and Calvinists. Contrasted with *Nestorian*.

Montanism (3). A third-century sect that claimed to have the gift of prophecy. Tertullian became a member of it.

moral archetype (7). The *nature* of Christ in Kant's *religion*.

moral freedom (3). Ability to do good. Contrasted with *metaphysical freedom*.

moral-influence theory (4). View of Jesus' atonement held by Abelard and modern liberals: that Jesus died to provide a model of and incentive for moral behavior among us.

mystery (Marcel) (9). The view that the self (in its body) cannot be entirely understood by the methods of objective science. It is in that way a mystery, rather than a "problem."

Mystical, the (12). In Wittgenstein's *Tractatus*, the realm in which many things, which can be seen or felt but cannot be expressed in a perfect language, can be said to exist.

mysticism (3, 4). The view that our best knowledge of God consists of union with him, often in transrational experience. At worst, it argues (with *Gnosticism* and *Neoplatonism*) that when we know God best, we become God.

myth (10). A form of literature that expresses earthly *truths* in stories of heavenly beings. Bultmann believed that everything supernatural in Scripture was myth. Barth denied this, but acknowledged that Scripture contained *saga*.

myth of presence (12). In postmodern thought, the myth that the author of a text is entitled to give an authoritative interpretation to the text that he has produced.

nameless God (3). For *Gnostics* and *Neoplatonists*, the supreme being, who they believed could not be known and thus could not be named by human beings. Some church fathers, including Justin, argued the same way.

narrative theology (11). Closely related to *postliberalism*, the attempt to read Scripture as a narrative or story, not as a collection of *propositions* or of religious experiences.

naturalism (9). A *worldview* that eliminates reference to any supernatural entities or forces.

naturalistic fallacy (5). See *is-ought argument.*

natural law (2). Principles governing human conduct derived from the natural world.

natural reason (4). In Aquinas, the type of *reason* used to understand earthly realities. It does not require supernatural *revelation.*

natural standpoint (9). In phenomenology, the standpoint of someone in the *Lebenswelt,* "ordinary life," as opposed to the technical standpoints of scientists and philosophers.

***natura naturans, natura naturata* (5).** Phrases used by Spinoza to describe the world from two different perspectives. The first is the world conceived as the *cause* of everything within it. The second is the world conceived as the *effect* of this causal activity.

nature (4). The *essence* of anything.

nature-freedom scheme (7). Dooyeweerd's description of modern thought as opposed to ancient (*form-matter*) and medieval (*nature-grace*). In the nature-freedom scheme (of which Kant is exemplary), the medieval concept of grace is *secularized* and turned into a normless exercise of *libertarian freedom,* as in Kant's *noumenal* world.

nature-grace scheme (4). In Dooyeweerd's understanding, the idea that Aquinas begins with the Greek view of nature, a combination of form and matter, and superimposes on that *form-matter scheme* a second layer of reality consisting of matters of salvation and God's grace. This, Dooyeweerd says, is the *nature* of scholastic thought. See *natural reason.*

necessary (7). Of or relating to what must be, as opposed to what merely happens to be.

necessary being (4). A being that by *nature* cannot fail to exist. Contrasted with *contingent being.*

necessary connection (1, 5). The relation between *cause* and *effect* on some traditional views of causality. Denied by Hume.

necessary truths of reason (6). Lessing's description of such fundamental metaphysical theological *truths* as the *existence* of God, which he claimed could not be established through historical investigation. Contrasted with *accidental truths of history.*

neoorthodoxy (10). Name given early to the theological movement of Barth, Brunner, and others because of their use of the language of Christian orthodoxy.

Neoplatonism (2, 3, 4). The philosophy of Plotinus and others, teaching that everything is an aspect of a oneness, embodying that oneness in varying degrees.

neo-Protestantism (10). Barth's name for the *liberal theology* of Schleiermacher and the Ritschlians.

Nestorian (5). Of or relating to the view (thought to be held by Nestorius) that the two *natures* of Christ constitute two distinct persons. This view was rejected by the church at Chalcedon in 451, but it became controversial again later in discussions between Lutherans and Calvinists. Contrasted with *Monophysite*.

new hermeneutic (10). Movement among Bultmann disciples to understand *revelation* as a *language event*, which interprets us rather than our interpreting it.

new quest (10). The effort of some disciples of Bultmann in the 1950s who sought to resume the quest of the historical Jesus, not to write a biography of him, but to understand how his historical *existence* is relevant to faith. Coordinated with *third quest*.

***Nichtige, Das* (10).** "Nothingness," which according to Barth constitutes evil. God overcame the nothingness in himself through grace, and he overcomes sin in the world in the same way.

noetic effects of sin (13). In Van Til, the suppression of *truth* (Rom. 1:18) because of sin.

nominalism (1, 4, 10). The view that only *particulars* exist, and that terms that seem to denote *universals* serve only to denote *particulars*. Contrasted with *realism*. In Barth, see *freedom of God*.

normal science (Kuhn) (12). The regular work of scientists, to apply an existing *paradigm* and solve *puzzles* arising from it.

normative perspective (1). A way of understanding the world by understanding God's norms for our knowing. Coordinated with *situational perspective* and *existential perspective*.

noumena (7). Kant's term for what really exists apart from our experience, also called *Ding an Sich* ("thing in itself"). Contrasted with *phenomena*.

***nous* (2).** Greek for "mind." Thought by Anaxagoras to be a principle of rationality in the world, similar to Heraclitus's *logos*. Also, the primary *emanation* of Plotinus's *One*.

objective idealism (7). See *idealism*.

objectively immortal (11). In process thought, of or relating to the state of each *actual occasion*, even after it perishes, of being available for *prehension* by other *actual occasions*.

objective spirit (7). In Hegel, see *spirit*.

object of knowledge (1). In *epistemology*, the content known by the subject. Contrasted with *subject of knowledge*.

objects (13). In Dooyeweerd, see *subjects*.

observation statements (12). In *logical positivism*, statements of empirical *fact*, recording observations that serve as the foundation of scientific theories.

Occam's razor (4). The principle of William of Occam that we should seek the simplest explanation for anything, positing no more entities than are absolutely *necessary*.

occasionalism (5, 6). The view that God is the only *cause* of events in the world.

old nature-religion (2). The religion of the Greeks that preceded the *religion of the Olympian gods*.

Olsen, Regina (8). Kierkegaard's fiancée at one time. He broke the engagement, precipitating much inconclusive discussion as to why.

One, the (2). In Plotinus's view, the highest being, the source of all plurality, who is perfectly one in such a way as to be incapable of analysis.

one and many (13). A problem in the *history* of philosophy that Van Til believed to be of fundamental importance. Van Til emphasized that the biblical doctrine of the Trinity explained it. That problem is that oneness cannot be understood without manyness, or vice versa.

Oneism (1). Peter Jones's term for *monism*, contrasted with *Twoism*.

ontological argument (4). Anselm's argument in the *Proslogium*: by definition, God has all perfections, and one of these is *existence*; therefore, God exists.

open future (11). Moltmann's view of eschatology, that since anything can happen in the future, we should have hope.

openness to the future (10). Bultmann's concept of *authentic existence*.

open theism (11). A position held among some theologians of evangelical background, who deny that God has exhaustive knowledge of the future.

operationalism (12, 13). The view that scientific statements are summaries of scientific operations, rather than statements about the *nature* of the world. Accepted by Gordon Clark in his Christian philosophy.

ordinary-language philosophy (12). The approach of the later Wittgenstein, who believes that ordinary language does not need to be reconstructed in order to do its job, as long as one employs it in its "proper use."

orthodoxastai (3). Term used by Clement of Alexandria to disparage those who prided themselves on perfect orthodoxy and who despised philosophy.

ostensive definition (12). The explanation of a term by pointing to its referent.

ousia (3). "Being" in Greek. Used to indicate the oneness of God in the Nicene formulation of the Trinity. Contrasted with *hypostasis*, which designated the threeness of God's Trinitarian *being*.

palingenesis (3). Regeneration as an individual and social reality, in Augustine and Kuyper.

panentheism (1, 8, 11). View that God is in the world and the world in God (as in process philosophy). Contrasted with *pantheism*, *deism*, and *theism*.

panpsychism (5). View that everything has the ability to think. Ascribed to Leibniz, Whitehead, and others.

pantheism (1, 5, 8). View that God is the whole universe and the universe is God (as in Spinoza's thought). Contrasted with *theism*, *deism*, and *panentheism*.

paradigm (12). One of the examples in Kuhn's assertion that "some accepted examples of actual scientific practice—examples which include law, theory, application, and instrumentation together—provide models from which spring particular coherent traditions of scientific research."

paradox (13). Either apparent or real contradiction. Gordon Clark believes that paradox in either form should be rejected as an aspect of human thought.

paralogisms (7). Fallacious arguments, according to Kant, that try to prove the *existence* of an eternal, immaterial soul, by confusing senses of "soul," "mind," and so forth. See *transcendental dialectic*.

***parole* (12).** In Saussure, the *surface structure* of language as we actually speak it. Contrasted with *langue*.

particulars (1, 4). Individual objects as opposed to qualities or properties. Contrasted with *universals*.

Pascal's "Memorial" (6). A document that Pascal sewed into his coat, recording his memory of the events of *Pascal's third conversion*.

Pascal's third conversion (6). A personal experience of God ("the God of Abraham, Isaac, and Jacob, not the god of the philosophers") that motivated Pascal to give up *secular* pursuits and give all his time to religious writing. See *Pascal's "Memorial."*

Pascal's three orders (6). In *Pensées*, body, mind, and *heart* as distinct ways by which we gain knowledge.

Pascal's Wager (6, 9). Famous argument of Pascal's *Pensées*. Pascal urges readers of his *Pensées* to wager (in effect) that Christianity is true, as a prudential decision. If you wager in favor of Christianity, and it turns out to be true, you win incomparable benefits. If you wager in favor of it, and it turns out not to be true, you have not lost anything. If you wager against it, and it is not true, you have not lost anything, but if you wager against it and it is true, you will suffer eternal punishment.

passive intellect (2, 4). In Aristotle, that part of the *intellect* that receives information from sensation. Contrasted with *active intellect*.

penal substitution (4). View of the atonement in which Jesus in death pays the penalty of human sin.

***Pensées* (6).** Pascal's greatest but unfinished work, an apologetic for Christianity.

***perichoresis* (1).** Synonymous with *circumcessio.*

person (1, 4). In ethics, the ethical agent. Contrasted with *law* and *situation.* Boethius uses the term in the context of the doctrine of the Trinity: a rational *substance.*

personal commitments (Polanyi) (12). The commitments, motivations, and *history* of the individual scientist as they affect his scientific conclusions.

personalism (10). In Barth, but especially in Brunner, the view that our relation to God is person-to-person (*I-thou*), not person-to-thing (*I-it*).

person-variable (13). Of or relating to the argument (of Mavrodes) that people differ as to the evidence they find persuasive.

perspectivism (9). Nietzsche's view that there is no distinction between *facts* and interpretations. We have no access to objective *truth*, only to one perspective or another.

persuasive (11). Of or relating to the *nature* of God's influence on *actual occasions*, according to process thought. Distinguished from *coercive.*

phenomena (7, 9). Kant's term for what appears to us in our experience. Contrasted with *noumena.* In Husserl, the appearance *is* the noumenon, the real world.

Philo Judaeus (3). Jewish philosopher-theologian, 20 B.C.–A.D. 50. Engaged in speculation about the *logos*, which influenced later Jewish, Christian, and pagan thinkers.

***Philosophia Reformata* (13).** "Reformed Philosophy," title of an academic journal that published the writings of Dooyeweerd and other members of his philosophical circle.

philosophy (Aquinas) (4). A means of understanding the natural world, without the need of supernatural *revelation.*

philosophy (etymology) (1). Love of *wisdom.*

philosophy (Frame) (1). A disciplined attempt to formulate, articulate, and defend a *worldview.*

physical pole (11). In process philosophy, one of the two poles of each *actual occasion* (the other being the *mental pole*). The physical pole is given by God and by past occasions, and cannot be changed.

physico-theological argument (7). In Kant, synonymous with *teleological argument.*

picture theory of language (12). In the early thought of Russell and Wittgenstein, the view that a perfect language should be a picture of the world.

pietism (5). Post-Reformation movement led by P. J. Spener and others, focusing on small-group Bible study, evangelism, and personal piety.

pineal gland (5). See *mind-body problem.*

Plato's three parts of the soul (2). The appetitive, the spirited, and the rational.

pluralism (1). The view that the universe consists of many entities. Contrasted with *monism* and *dualism*.

pneumatic sense (3). Origen's term for a reading of Scripture in a mystical, often allegorical manner. Contrasted with *somatic sense* and *psychical sense*.

point of contact (10). In Barth, something in man that makes it possible for God to reveal himself to him. Barth denied that there was any ongoing point of contact, preferring to say that God creates his own point of contact whenever he speaks to man.

Port Royal (6). Convent at which Pascal's sister was a nun. Pascal defended its *Jansenist* teaching.

posse peccare (3). Latin for "able to sin." One of Augustine's terms indicating the four moral states of man. Before the fall, man was able to sin. Because of the fall, he became *non posse non peccare*, unable not to sin. Redemption makes us able not to sin, *posse non peccare*, and in the consummation of redemption, we will be unable to sin, *non posse peccare*.

postliberalism (11). Position of some recent theologians such as George Lindbeck, who say that Scripture should be read not for its alleged connection to actual events in the past, but as the *canon* of the church, edifying and motivating us as it stands.

postmodern (12). Of or relating to a movement arising out of *poststructuralism*, including a general suspicion of *metanarrative*.

poststructuralism (12). Rejection of the idea of a *universal deep structure* of language and consequent suspicion of *metanarrative*.

potentiality (2). What something may possibly be. In Aristotle, the form of something defines not only what something is, but also what it may become. Contrasted with *actuality*.

pour soi (9). In Sartre, the status of beings that are free rather than designed or fated. Contrasted with *en soi*.

practical faith (7). In Kant's theology, seeking to follow Christ as a *moral archetype*.

pragmaticism (9). See *pragmatism (Peirce)*.

pragmatic maxim (9). In Peirce: "To ascertain the meaning of an intellectual conception one should consider what practical consequences might result from the *truth* of that conception—and the sum of these consequences constitute the entire meaning of the conception."

pragmatism (James) (9). The view that the *truth* is what works.

pragmatism (Peirce) (9). The view that the meaning of a statement is its practical consequences. Peirce restricted pragmatism to a theory of meaning and rejected James's pragmatic theory of *truth*. He changed the term to *pragmaticism*, which he described as a term "ugly enough to protect it from kidnappers."

praxis (11). Involvement in the sometimes revolutionary struggle for social justice, according to liberation theology. It does not require any theological justification; rather, theology itself must arise out of our involvement in this struggle.

pre-established harmony (5). God's ordination that all *monads* will work together in an orderly fashion, according to Leibniz.

prehension (11). In process thought, the taking account by *actual occasions* of one another, of *eternal objects*, and of God.

prescription (3). From Latin *praescriptio*, a legal document seeking to prohibit some party from addressing the court. Tertullian argued that *heretics* should be denied access to theological discussion in the church.

presence (1). God's nearness to his covenant vassals and to all creation. Coordinated with *control* and *authority* as an aspect of *lordship*.

presumption (11). Thinking that we can achieve justice in our own strength. Part of Moltmann's definition of *sin*.

presupposition (1, 3, 7, 13). What must be assumed as a basis for arguing something. An "ultimate presupposition" is what must be assumed as a basis for arguing anything at all.

presuppositionalism (4, 13). The view that one does not know God as he should unless he presupposes God as the basis of all meaning. In Clark, the *presupposition* is the Bible as God's revealed Word, understood as an *axiom* of a quasi-geometric system. In Van Til, the *presupposition* is God's whole *revelation*.

pretheoretical experience (13). Dooyeweerd's concept of experience that has not been structured into abstract categories for scientific investigation. Compare similar concepts in Husserl, Heidegger.

primacy of the intellect (13). Gordon Clark's view that the *intellect* should rule the *will* and *emotions*. Van Til rejects this notion.

primary qualities (5). In Locke, qualities that "really do exist in the bodies themselves." Primary qualities include solidity, extension, figure, motion, rest, and number. Contrasted with *secondary qualities*.

prime matter (2). In Aristotle, *matter* without any *form* at all.

Prime Mover (2). In Aristotle, the uncaused *cause* of all movement.

primordial nature of God (11). In process thought, the qualities that God must have in any possible world, not dependent on the *nature* of the present world. Those include *existence*, eternity, divine relativity. Contrasted with *consequent nature of God*.

principle of sufficient reason (4, 5). Principle that every true statement is true for a sufficient reason.

privation (3). Absence of something where it ought to be. Augustine saw evil as a privation of good.

problem of induction (6). The difficulty of showing that the future will be like the past and present.

problem of other minds (6). The difficulty of proving that other people have minds like mine.

proleptic (11). Of or relating to anticipating a later age, particularly the final judgment. Pannenberg sees the resurrection of Jesus as a proleptic anticipation of the last day.

proposition (12). A meaning complex that makes an assertion of *fact*.

propositional revelation (8). *Revelation* from God that tells us what to believe or do. Denied in various ways by liberal theologians.

protocol statement (12). *Observation statement* used in science as the basis of *theoretical statements* according to *logical positivism*.

***Provincial Letters* (6).** Pascal's defense of the *Jansenism* of *Port Royal*.

provisionality (11). In Pannenberg, the impossibility of having complete certainty about anything until the final judgment.

***psyche* (2).** Greek for "soul." The second *emanation* of Plotinus's *One*.

psychical sense (3). Origen's term for the moral and practical meaning of Scripture. Contrasted with *somatic sense* and *pneumatic sense*.

psychological Trinitarianism (3). View that emphasizes the analogy between the Trinity and a single human mind. Contrasted with *social Trinitarianism*.

public atheist (12). An atheist often quoted by the popular media. Bertrand Russell was one of these.

puzzles (12). Difficulties within *normal science* that can be worked out within an existing *paradigm*.

qualitative atomism (2). The views of Empedocles and Anaxagoras that the atoms that constitute the world have different qualities. See *atomism*. Contrasted with *quantitative atomism*.

quantitative atomism (2). The views of Democritus, Epicurus, and Lucretius that all atoms have the same qualities. Contrasted with *qualitative atomism*. See also *atomism*.

queen monad (5). In Leibniz, a particular *monad* that sets the course for an entire organism.

radical doubt (5). Descartes' resolve to doubt everything that could possibly be doubted, in order to determine whether any of our *ideas* constitute certain knowledge.

radical evil (7). The concept of sin in Kant's theology. It does not begin with Adam, but is a *necessary* element of human *nature*.

Radical Orthodoxy (13). A movement of John Milbank and others to develop a comprehensive critique of modern thought from a Christian standpoint. Relies heavily on a critique of *deconstruction*, and positively on the *Neoplatonic* notion of God as one who holds all things together.

radical theology (10). Synonymous with *Christian atheism*.

rapport (9). Direct involvement with other people (not just communication with them) to achieve *transcendence* in our relationships with them, according to Heidegger.

rational autonomy (2). The view that the human mind can know *truth* without reference to any supernatural being.

rationalism (1, 5). (1) The view that the human mind is the final judge of *truth* and falsehood. Contrasted with *irrationalism*. (2) Philosophical *epistemologies* that make *reason* decisive over against *sense experience* and inner subjectivity. Contrasted with *empiricism* and *subjectivism*.

realism (1). The view that *universals* are real objects in the world. Contrasted with *nominalism*.

reason (1, 5, 6). The human capacity for making inferences and detecting consistency. Often contrasted with *sense experience*. For Joseph Butler, a process that incorporates *sense experience*, thus the "reasonable use of reason."

receptacle (2). What receives Form, according to Plato. In Plato's *Timaeus*, the *Demiurge* copied the Forms onto the receptacle, which resisted his attempt to achieve perfection.

recollection (2). In Plato, the *nature* of knowledge. Plato believed that knowledge is a recollection of our prelife experience in the world of Forms.

recollection and expectation (Barth) (10). The results of *revelation*, according to Barth, as opposed to permanent, objective *truth*.

reference (Frege) (12). The function of language to designate a thing or *fact*. Cf. *sense*.

referential theory of meaning (12). The theory that the meaning of an expression is the reality or *fact* that it refers to. Held by Russell and Wittgenstein in their early work, rejected by Wittgenstein in his later work.

reformation (3). In Frame's parallel between fourth- and sixteenth-century historical developments, the movement toward orthodoxy as a reaction against *heresy*.

Reformed epistemology (Plantinga) (13). The view that some human *beliefs* are not derived from other *beliefs*, or from evidences or arguments. These *beliefs* arise when the mind is working properly and is placed in an environment likely to produce true *beliefs*. See also *basic beliefs* and *foundational beliefs*.

reformer (3). In Frame's discussion, one who detects the serious implications of a current *heresy* and presses the church to resist it. Contrasted with *synthesis*, *heretic*, and *consolidator*.

regulative use (7). The principle, in Kant, that *ideals of reason*, though they should not be used *constitutively*, may legitimately be used to regulate our decisions in a practical way. For example, we cannot prove that God actually exists, but assuming his *existence* may make us better persons.

relations of production (7). In Marx, the relations between groups involved in the production of goods: owners, workers, slaves, et al.

relativism (1, 2). The view that there is no *absolute* and *necessary truth*, but that all knowledge is relative to each subject.

religion (Barth, Bonhoeffer) (10). Man's self-righteous attempt to save himself.

religion (Clouser) (1). The practice of believing in something or other as divine. "Divine" means having the status of not depending on anything else.

religion (Frame) (1). The practice of faith.

religion (Hegel) (7). A set of symbols for what is literally expressed in Hegel's philosophy.

religion (Kant) (7). The practice of treating our ethical obligations as if they were divine commands.

religionless Christianity (10). In Bonhoeffer, serving God without the trappings of worship and religiosity, by serving the world.

religion of the Olympian gods (2). Successor to the *old nature-religion* of Greece, worship of personal but finite gods connected with various natural processes.

religious consciousness (8). Schleiermacher's feeling of *absolute* dependence. See *Gefühl*.

religious stage (8). The final stage, or stages, in Kierkegaard's "stages on life's way." Religion A is the traditionalist, ritualist faith of the Danish state church; Religion B is true faith in the paradox of the eternal God's entering time. Contrasted with *aesthetic stage* and *ethical stage*.

Renaissance (5). A period of restoration and renewal of European learning and culture, around 1350–1650.

***ressentiment* (9).** Nietzsche's term for a kind of envy that includes hatred of the strong and successful.

retrocipate (13). To reflect a lower *law sphere*. In Dooyeweerd, higher *modal aspects* reflect lower ones in various ways, called "retrocipation." Contrasted with *anticipate*.

revealed, ectypal knowledge of God (13). Kuyper's view of the knowledge of God available to human beings. It must be revealed by God himself, and it is *ectypal*, rather than *archetypal*. That is, it is not God's knowledge of himself, but something that images that knowledge and is analogous to it.

revelation. God's making himself known.

revivification (11). Raising of a dead body to life, as Jesus raised Lazarus. Pannenberg says that this is not the *nature* of resurrection.

richness (13). Philosophical systems' ability to deal with questions in many areas of life. Gordon Clark evaluates philosophical systems primarily by the test of logical consistency, but also by their richness.

righteousness (Luther) (5). Actions and character in keeping with God's moral standards.

rights (5). Benefits and freedoms due to people by virtue of their creation or social status. Sometimes these are deemed *inalienable* because of their source in God.

right-wing Hegelians (7). Thinkers who accommodated Hegel to traditional religion and philosophy. Contrasted with *left-wing Hegelians.*

right-wing Origenists (3). Followers of Origen who stressed his language about the ontological unity of the Father and the Son. This is the view that prevailed at the Nicene and Constantinopolitan Councils. Contrasted with *left-wing Origenists.*

risk (9). For Heidegger, a state that is *necessary* to transcend our *anxiety* as *being-toward-death.*

rule of faith (3). The early church's consensus on the meaning of the gospel. Eventually formulated into creeds and confessions.

rules (11). Function of *revelation,* according to Lindbeck. In Lindbeck's *postliberalism, revelation* should be considered not as informative *propositions,* nor as expressive feelings, but as rules for discourse in the church.

Russell tribunal (12). A mock trial of Western powers charging them with war crimes in Vietnam, presided over by Bertrand Russell.

sacred doctrine (4). Aquinas's term for a science distinct from philosophy that deals with matters of grace and salvation on the basis of *revelation.*

saga (10). A temporally sequenced narrative story, not necessarily inerrant. Barth believes that parts of Scripture are in this category. See *myth.*

satisfaction (4). In *Cur Deus Homo,* the principle argued by Anselm that the purpose of the atonement is to satisfy a breach of God's honor, that is, to make it right.

scholasticism (4, 5). The prevalent method of medieval theology, by gathering together the works of past theologians and evaluating their answers to common questions. *Protestant scholasticism* refers to a similar theological approach among Protestant theologians following the Reformation.

Schweitzer, Albert (8). See *consistently eschatological.*

scientific revolution (12). According to Kuhn, a period of *crisis* in which a *paradigm* is replaced by an incompatible new one.

scientism (9, 12). The view that the best (or only) way of determining *truth* is through the methods of natural science. Describes the views of Comte, Peirce, and the *logical positivists*. Opposed by phenomenologists and existentialists.

***Scopes* trial (8).** 1925 trial of John T. Scopes for teaching evolution in a Tennessee high school. Surrounding it was a publicity circus that turned the event into a serious setback for evangelical Christians.

scripturalism (13). Gordon Clark's view that the content of Scripture alone constitutes knowledge for human beings.

secondary qualities (5). In Locke, qualities that are in the mind of the thinker, not the physical body, though the body does have the power to create these qualities in the mind. Secondary qualities include colors, tastes, sounds, and odors. Contrasted with *primary qualities*.

secular (1). Not holy, common. Sometimes contrasted with *religious*.

secular theology (10). A school of theology affirming the *secular* (Harvey Cox et al.).

self-understanding (10). Idea of oneself and one's place in the world. In Bultmann's view, once Scripture is demythologized, it can be seen to communicate an existential self-understanding (similar to that of existential philosophy).

sense (Frege) (12). What must be added to *reference* to define the meaning of an expression.

sense experience (5). Ways in which human beings receive data about the world from outside themselves, as by seeing and hearing. Sometimes contrasted with *reason*.

sensuous consciousness (8). In Schleiermacher, the opposite of the feeling of *absolute* dependence; corresponding to the traditional concept of sin.

sentences (4). A collection of theological questions with the answers of prominent theologians of the past. See *Sic et Non*.

shadowside (10). According to Barth, an element of nonbeing that, though not evil in itself, made the entrance of sin and evil possible when God created the world. See *Nichtige*.

shapeless stream (2). The chaos underlying experience in ancient Greek religion according to Dooyeweerd. Predecessor of the principle of *matter* in Greek philosophy.

***Sic et Non* (4).** A work of Abelard gathering together answers of past theologians to current questions, emphasizing the disagreements among them.

signified (12). To Saussure, the concept in the mind that a linguistic sign refers to.

signifier (12). To Saussure, a concept in the mind that refers to something.

simple ideas (5). In Locke's *epistemology*, our *ideas* that come passively into our minds through the senses or through the reflective process. Contrasted with *complex ideas*.

simplicity of God (**3, 4**)**.** The doctrine that God has no parts, cannot be divided.

sin (**Moltmann**) (**11**)**.** Hopelessness, *presumption, desperation.*

situation (**1**)**.** The *facts* of the world, or some subset of them. In ethics, distinguished from *law* and *person.*

situational perspective (**1**)**.** A way of perceiving and knowing by knowing the *facts* of the world as under God's *control.* Correlated with *existential perspective* and *normative perspective.*

Skeptical Academy (**2**)**.** A phase in the later *history* of the Academy founded by Plato.

skepticism (**1**)**.** Doubt that knowledge is possible, either in general or in regard to a particular subject (e.g., God). Overlaps *irrationalism.*

slave morality (**9**)**.** A morality that favors humility and poverty over success and strength. Nietzsche thought that Christianity fostered such thinking.

social contract (**5**)**.** A historical or implicit agreement between people to respect certain rights, viewed as the source from which the authority of government derives.

social Trinitarianism (**3**)**.** View that emphasizes the analogy between the persons of the Trinity and a human society. Contrasted with *psychological Trinitarianism.*

societies (**11**)**.** In process thought, beings including more than one *actual occasion.* In process thought, such things and persons are understood to be societies of *actual occasions.*

somatic sense (**3**)**.** Origen's term for a literal reading of Scripture. Contrasted with *psychical sense* and *pneumatic sense.*

Sophists (**2**)**.** Traveling teachers in ancient Greece who claimed to prepare students for positions in public service and who taught a kind of *relativism.* Opposed by Socrates and Plato.

spectator model of knowledge (**9**)**.** In Dewey, the model "in which the mind stands outside of nature, observing and analyzing *facts* for its edification."

sphere sovereignty (**13**)**.** Principle of Abraham Kuyper that family, church, state are not hierarchically ordered, but are distinct spheres ordained by God. Each has its own sphere and should not encroach on the spheres of the others.

spirit (**7**)**.** In Hegel, a representation of a higher stage of *dialectic* than *subjective* or *objective* reality. The highest reality is *absolute spirit.*

state of nature (**5**)**.** In *social-contract* theory, the condition of mankind before they agree to a *social contract.* In Hobbes, the state of nature is the "war of all against all." In Locke, it is a more or less pleasant society governed by mutual respect for *rights.*

structuralism (12). Approach of Lévi-Strauss and others, building on the linguistics of Saussure, to see human language and activities as expressions of deep linguistic structures in the mind.

subjective idealism (5). See *idealism.*

subjective immediacy (11). In process thought, the inner feeling and thought of each *actual occasion.*

subjective spirit (7). In Hegel, see *spirit.*

subjective truth (Kierkegaard) (8). An objective uncertainty embraced with the most passionate inwardness.

subjective turn (in doctrine of revelation) (8). In *liberal theology,* the idea that *revelation* does not exist unless it makes a subjective impression on its hearers.

subjectivism (1). View that inner feelings or experience is most important in human knowing and choice. Contrasted with *empiricism, intellectualism,* and *voluntarism.*

subject of knowledge (1). The one who knows or seeks to know. Contrasted with *object of knowledge.*

subjects (13). In Dooyeweerd, the relation of things qualified by a particular *law sphere* to lower *law spheres.* Things qualified by a *law sphere* are subjects in the spheres below themselves and *objects* in the spheres above them.

subordinationism (3). The view that God's Son and Spirit are inferior in their *being* to God the Father.

substance (2, 4, 5). In Aristotle and Aquinas, a concrete object, consisting of both *form* and *matter.* An exception is God, who is a substance, but contains no *matter.* Contrasted with *accident.* Among *Enlightenment* thinkers (1650–1800), a substance is "what is in itself and conceived through itself" (Spinoza). Descartes, Locke, and others distinguished between *material substance* and *mental substance.*

summum bonum **(1).** Highest good. See *hedonism.*

supererogation (4). The principle of doing more than the law requires.

supertemporal heart (13). In Dooyeweerd, the internal core of a man's *being* as it is related to time. Dooyeweerd believes that if man is to know the eternal God, his own *heart* must be in some sense eternal.

supranaturalism (10). In Tillich, an inadequate method of theology that confuses the *depth of reason* with supernatural beings.

supreme monad (5). God, in Leibniz's thought.

surface structure (12). In *structuralism,* the obvious structure of language and human action, which points to *deep structure* beneath it.

sweetness (6). Emotional delight in our persuasion of the *truth* of God. Jonathan Edwards emphasized its importance.

swerve (2). The occasional path of atoms, according to Epicurus. He believed that atoms randomly swerve from their downward path, making it possible for them to bump against one another and form objects.

symbols (10). In distinction from signs, according to Tillich, language or ideas that participate in the reality to which they point.

synchronic (12). In Saussure, of or relating to analysis of language focusing on its present use. Contrasted with *diachronic*.

synthesis (Frame) (3). The attempt by someone (such as Origen or Aquinas) to integrate Christian theology with some form of non-Christian philosophy. This often leads to *heresy*, and the need for *reformation* and consolidation.

synthesis (Hegel) (7). See *dialectic*.

synthesis (Origen) (3). Understanding God by way of his *effects*. Same as Aquinas's *way of causality*. Contrasted with *analysis*.

synthetic (5). Of or relating to a sentence in which the meaning of the predicate is not part of the meaning of the subject. Contrasted with *analytic*.

synthetic *a priori* (7). In Kant, a sentence that we know to be true apart from experience, which is not *analytic*.

***tabula rasa* (5).** "Empty slate"; Locke's view of the *nature* of the human mind apart from *sense experience*.

tautology (12). A sentence that is necessarily true (*analytically*) because the predicate is included in the subject, such as "the bachelor was unmarried." Contrasted in *logical positivism* with *contradictions* and *empirical propositions*.

teleological argument (4). The fifth of Aquinas's *five ways*. It says that when unintelligent beings act for a purpose, they must be made to do this by an intelligent agent, which must be God. Contrasted with *ontological argument*, *cosmological argument*, and *e contingentia mundi*. See also *physico-theological argument*.

teleological suspension of the ethical (8). Kierkegaard's understanding of God's command to Abraham to sacrifice his son Isaac. For a purpose, God was suspending his own law.

teleologism (1). The view that ethics consists of formulating the *nature* of man's highest happiness or pleasure, and then seeking means to achieve it. Opposed to *deontologism* and *existentialism*.

teleology (1). That which pertains to the purpose or goal of something.

theism (1). View that some sort of God exists. Understood differently by Christianity, *pantheism*, *deism*, and other philosophies and religions.

theodicy (3). Justification of God, especially in the discussion of the problem of evil.

theology (1, 4, 11). Frame: The application of the Word of God by persons to all areas of life. In Aquinas, theology is the study of God, which combines the methods of *philosophy* and *sacred doctrine*. Gutierrez: the critical reflection on *praxis*, from within *praxis*.

theology of the word (10). Name given early to the theological movement of Barth, Brunner, and others.

theonomy (10). In Tillich, *autonomous reason* united to its own *depth*. Coordinated with *autonomy* and *heteronomy*.

theoretical statements (12). In *logical positivism*, formulations of scientific theory, necessarily dependent on the *truth* of *observation statements*.

therapeutic (12). Of or relating to the view of the later Wittgenstein that the work of philosophy is not to discover *facts* unavailable to the sciences, but to cure confusions and misunderstandings that have resulted, in many cases, from past philosophy.

thesis (7). In Hegel, see *dialectic*.

thinking reed (6). Pascal's description of the human being. He argues in the *Pensées* that man is a weak being, like a reed blowing in the wind, but nevertheless great, because he can understand and reason about his environment.

third man (2). A problem in Plato's philosophy: If there must be a Form for everything, must there be a Form of a Form, ad infinitum?

third quest (10). An interest by academic scholars such as N. T. Wright in the life of Jesus, following earlier quests among the Ritschlians and again among the disciples of Bultmann. Coordinated with *new quest*.

thisness (2). In Aristotle, what distinguishes two objects that have the same *form*: *matter*. Contrasted with *whatness*.

three forms of revelation (Barth) (10). Christ, Scripture, and preaching.

thrownness (9). In Heidegger's view, the quality of *Dasein*, finding itself in a reality that it did not choose.

tiny perceptions (5). In Leibniz, the way in which each *monad* gains knowledge of other *monads* at great distances.

***tolle lege* (3).** Latin for "take and read." In Augustine's conversion story, he heard children using this phrase, and he picked up a Bible to read a passage from Romans 13.

traditional method (13). In Van Til, the apologetic method of people such as Aquinas and Butler, of which he disapproves. He believes that these, and others in the tradition, begin by assuming non-Christian understandings of things in the world, and from those understandings try to prove the *existence* of God and the *truth* of Scripture.

traducianism (3). The view that the human soul derives from its parents rather than being a special creation of God. Contrasted with *creationism*. Tertullian was a traducianist.

transcendence (biblical) (1). God's *control* and *authority* over all the creation. Coordinated with divine *immanence* (biblical).

transcendence (Jaspers) (9). According to Jaspers, the opposite of finitude. When I become aware of my limits, I come to understand transcendence or God.

transcendence (nonbiblical) (1). The idea that God is so far removed from the world that he cannot be known. Denial of divine *presence.* Coordinated with divine *immanence* (nonbiblical).

transcendental aesthetic (7). The first mental process by which, according to Kant, the mind organizes its experience. In that step, we place all the data of the mind into a spatiotemporal sequence. Coordinated with *transcendental analytic, transcendental unity of the apperception,* and *transcendental dialectic.*

transcendental analytic (7). The second mental process by which, according to Kant, we organize our experience: the mind places experience under various *categories of the understanding,* such as unity, plurality, and causality. These list the *types of judgments* possible to the *intellect.* Coordinated with *transcendental aesthetic, transcendental unity of the apperception,* and *transcendental dialectic.*

transcendental argument (7, 13). In Kant and Van Til, an argument to show the ultimate *presuppositions* of meaningful thought.

transcendental dialectic (7). The attempt of the mind, according to Kant, to reason from the transcendental process to the *existence* of ideal realities beyond experience. This is fallacious when it attempts to identify real entities (*constitutive use*), but it could be a useful exercise in helping us to make practical decisions (*regulative use*). Coordinated with *transcendental aesthetic, transcendental analytic,* and *transcendental unity of the apperception.*

transcendental method (7). Kant's philosophical method, to show the conditions that make rational thought possible. Adopted also by Van Til.

transcendental unity of the apperception (7). The third unification of our experience, according to Kant: the integration of experience into a single consciousness capable of perceiving it. Coordinated with *transcendental aesthetic, transcendental analytic,* and *transcendental dialectic.*

transition (process thought) (11). One of two types of "process" among *actual occasions,* the other being *concrescence.* Transition is the passage from one *actual occasion,* which perishes, to another, which replaces it and *prehends* it.

transvaluation of all values (9). Nietzsche's goal for his philosophy: to overturn the values of Christianity and traditional ethics in favor of an ethic of strength and cheerful affirmation of the *will to power.*

tripersonality (1). God's quality of being personal, rather than impersonal, and his being three persons in one: Father, Son, and Holy Spirit.

Troeltsch, Ernst (8). Taught "historical relativism," the view (anticipated by Lessing) that the historical cultural distance between the biblical period and our time is so great that we cannot hope to make the Bible our rule of faith and life.

true individuals (11). In process thought, *actual occasions*. Cf. *fallacy of misplaced concreteness*.

trust (13). One of the elements of the traditional Reformed analysis of *faith*, the others being *knowledge*, *assent*, and *trust*. Gordon Clark believes that the concept can be reduced to *assent*. Also termed *fiducia*.

truth. (1) Metaphysical: what is *absolute* or complete. (2) Epistemological: a thought or verbal formulation that states what is. (3) Ethical: principle governing the way in which we ought to behave.

two ages (10). Structure of *history* according to *Heilsgeschichte* scholars. They distinguished in Scripture "this age" from the "age to come" and noted that in the NT the two ages overlap, since the age to come begins in Jesus.

Twoism (1). Peter Jones's formulation of the twofold (Creator and creature) *nature* of the universe. Contrasted with *Oneism* and *monism*.

two kinds of people (13). Kuyper's distinction between regenerate and unregenerate people working together in society. Cf. *two kinds of science*.

two kinds of science (13). Kuyper's distinction between the kinds of science practiced by the regenerate and the unregenerate. Kuyper concludes that because there are *two kinds of people*, regenerate and unregenerate, there are two kinds of science that reflect, respectively, the *worldviews* of the two groups.

types of judgments (7). See *transcendental analytic*.

***Übermensch* (9).** In Nietzsche, the "overman" or "superman" with qualities of excellence beyond the common man, worthy of admiration.

ubiquitous (5). Existing everywhere, as in the Lutheran doctrine of Christ's human *nature*.

ultimate concern (10). Tillich's definition of *faith*.

understanding (2). A relatively deep kind of knowledge. For Plato, it is higher than *conjecture* and *belief*, lower than *intuitive vision*.

universal (7). Pertaining to everyone and everything. For Kant, for example, ethical principles must apply the same way, in the same circumstances, to every person.

universalism (10). The belief that everyone will finally be saved.

universals (1, 4). Qualities or properties that describe many objects at once. Contrasted with *particulars*.

universal sacrament of salvation (11). Gutierrez's concept of the church as a community directed toward the future society. Contrasted with *Constantinian model*.

univocal (4). Of or relating to two pieces of language that are used in precisely the same sense. Contrasted with *equivocal* and *analogical*.

value judgment (8). In Ritschl, our forming of our theology not from historical *facts* as such, but from the values we find ourselves ascribing to them.

value theory (1). Division of philosophy that explores moral, aesthetic, and other kinds of value. Coordinated with *metaphysics* and *epistemology*.

Van Til-Clark controversy (13). Controversy that raged within the Orthodox Presbyterian Church during the 1940s. Clark believed that God and man sometimes share the same thought. Van Til denied that idea. This and other matters concerning these thinkers spurred the controversy.

verification principle (12). The *logical positivist* principle that no statement can be *cognitively meaningful* unless it can be verified or *falsified* by the methods of natural science.

***via negativa* (3, 4).** A way of gaining knowledge of something (particularly God) by discerning what it is *not*, rather than what it is. Same as Origen's *analysis*. Important to Dionysius, Aquinas.

voluntarism (1, 4). View that the *will* governs the *intellect* and the *emotions*. Contrasted with *intellectualism* and *subjectivism*.

vulnerability of Christianity (Pannenberg) (11). Susceptibility of Christianity to refutation by factual investigation.

warrant (1, 13). In *epistemology*, what confers on a *belief* the status of knowledge. Alvin Plantinga's preferred term to replace *justification*. Coordinated with *truth* and *belief*.

watchmaker illustration (6). Paley's version of the *teleological argument*: when you find a watch on the beach, you know that it has a designer. Same for the world.

way of belief (2). Parmenides' description of a philosophy other than the one he primarily recommends. Contrasted with *way of truth*.

way of causality (4). A way of coming to know God by means of his *effects* in the world. Aquinas distinguishes it from the *way of eminence* and the *way of remotion*. Similar to Origen's *synthesis*.

way of eminence (4). A way of coming to know God by ascribing to him the utmost perfection of all the good qualities of our experience. Aquinas distinguishes it from the *way of causality* and the *way of remotion*.

way of remotion (4). A way of knowing God by denying to him anything that seems to us unfit for him. Aquinas distinguishes it from the *way of causality* and the *way of eminence*. Same as the *via negativa* and Origen's *analysis*.

way of truth (2). Parmenides' description of his philosophy. Contrasted with *way of belief.*

Weiss, Johannes (8). See *consistently eschatological.*

whatness (2). In Aristotle, the *form* that makes anything what it is. Contrasted with *thisness.*

wholly other, wholly hidden (10). Phrases used by theologians (in Frame's view unwisely) to characterize the *transcendence* of God. These phrases normally connote that God is so far removed from us that we cannot know him or speak of him truly.

wholly revealed (10). Made known to man without reservation. According to Barth, God is both wholly hidden and wholly revealed. This paradox constitutes the fundamental *dialectic* of his theology. God is wholly revealed in Christ, according to Barth, for there is no secret *will* of God or hidden divine *nature* beyond the *revelation* of Christ.

will (4, 7). A person's capacity to choose a course of action. In Schopenhauer, a dark chaos lurking behind the world as *idea.*

will to believe (9). Man's voluntary choice of an *epistemological* conclusion. William James taught that when choice of a *belief* is forced on us and is otherwise undecidable, we may choose the *belief* that is likely to bring us the greatest benefit: a defense of *Pascal's Wager.*

will to power (9). In Nietzsche, the chief drive in human beings: not rational *truth*, but power over others and over the world.

wisdom (1, 2). An enhanced form of knowledge that penetrates to deeper understanding and practical usage.

wisdom literature (1, 2). A genre of literature in the ancient world in which someone collects wise sayings from many sources.

wish-projection (7). The *nature* of religion according to Feuerbach, Marx, and Freud. It is *belief* in something for which we have no evidence, because we wish it were true.

withering of the state (7). In Marx's eschatology, the inevitable consequence of the revolution and the *dictatorship of the proletariat.* Once people learn to work without the profit motive, the state will no longer be needed.

Wolfenbüttel Fragment (6). Part of a document from liberal Bible scholar Reimarus that Lessing claimed to have discovered in the library where he worked.

world come of age (10). In Bonhoeffer, the *secularization* of the world, so that modern culture no longer needs God as a stopgap.

world soul (2). In Plotinus, the Stoics, and others, a principle related to the world as the human soul is related to the body.

worldview (1). A conception of what the whole of reality is like.

Zealots (11). A Jewish faction that sought to overthrow the Roman oppressors by violent means. According to Gutierrez, Jesus agreed with them on some points, disagreed on others.

zero-sum (7). Of or relating to a relation in which, when one benefits, another must lose, as in Marx's view of the owners and the workers.

ANNOTATED BIBLIOGRAPHY OF PHILOSOPHY TEXTS

I HAVE LISTED here texts in philosophy (historical, topical, or both) that I consider to be useful for the student, with some comments about their distinctive content and approaches.

Allen, Diogenes. *Philosophy for Understanding Theology.* Atlanta: John Knox Press, 1985. Allen analyzes the thought of various philosophers to show how their work bears on the concerns of Christian theology.

Allen, Diogenes, and Eric O. Springsted. *Primary Readings in Philosophy for Understanding Theology.* Louisville, KY: Westminster John Knox Press, 1992. Readings in primary sources with brief introductions. A companion volume to the text in the previous entry.

Audi, Robert, ed. *The Cambridge Dictionary of Philosophy.* Cambridge: Cambridge University Press, 1995. Reference work on philosophers, ideas, and movements. Secular.

Bartholomew, Craig G., and Michael W. Goheen. *Christian Philosophy: A Systematic and Narrative Introduction.* Grand Rapids: Baker, 2013. An analysis of the whole history of philosophy, with an emphasis on Christian philosophy in the modern period. Bartholomew and Goheen are most indebted to the Christian philosophy of Herman Dooyeweerd, discussed briefly in chapter 13 of the present volume.

Brown, Colin. *Philosophy and the Christian Faith.* Downers Grove, IL: InterVarsity Press, 1968. Excellent textbook written from a Christian point of view. Brown says, "The aim of this book is to make a survey of the main thinkers and intellectual movements of western thought of the past thousand years, with a view to showing how they affect Christian belief." His limitation to the past thousand years keeps him, in my view, from giving sufficient attention to the thinkers from Thales to Plotinus, who certainly had a major effect on Christian belief. Deals with some modern theologians as well as philosophers.

———. *Christianity and Western Thought: A History of Philosophers, Ideas, and Movements from the Ancient World to the Age of Enlightenment.* Downers Grove, IL: InterVarsity Press, 2010.

Clark, Gordon H. *Thales to Dewey: A History of Philosophy.* Boston: Houghton Mifflin, 1957.

Clifford, W. K. *The Ethics of Belief and Other Essays.* New York: Prometheus Books, 1999. Clark was a Reformed Christian philosopher who defended biblical inerrancy. He sought to encourage more respect for logic and reason. See chapter 13 of the present volume. Clark's book is clearly written and focuses somewhat more on epistemology than on other areas of philosophy. It contains a Christian apologetic here, but that is fairly subtle.

Copleston, Frederick C. *A History of Philosophy.* 9 vols. Garden City, NY: Image Books, 1962–65. Nine-volume work by a scholarly Roman Catholic priest.

Edwards, Paul, ed. *The Encyclopedia of Philosophy.* New York: Macmillan/Free Press, 1967. Eight volumes of essays (later published as four) by experts on philosophical issues, movements, and thinkers. Highly authoritative, as of its publishing date. Most of the writers approach their subjects from secular points of view.

Hicks, Peter. *The Journey So Far: Philosophy through the Ages.* Grand Rapids: Zondervan, 2003. Discussion of the history of philosophy as a dialogue between Christian thought and philosophical schools.

Hoffecker, W. Andrew, ed. *Revolutions in Worldview: Understanding the Flow of Western Thought.* Phillipsburg, NJ: P&R Publishing, 2007. Generally excellent essays on the history of Christian thought as it responds to the developments of intellectual history.

Holmes, Arthur. *Philosophy: A Christian Perspective.* Downers Grove, IL: InterVarsity Press, 1975.

Kenny, Anthony. *A New History of Western Philosophy.* New York: Oxford University Press, 2010. A secular thinker, Kenny is well known as a philosopher in his own right.

Moreland, J. P., and William Lane Craig. *Philosophical Foundations for a Christian Worldview.* Downers Grove, IL: InterVarsity Press, 2003. Large, thorough discussion of philosophical problems from a Christian point of view.

Nash, Ronald H. *Life's Ultimate Questions: An Introduction to Philosophy.* Grand Rapids: Zondervan, 1999. Christian interpretation of several major philosophical issues and several major philosophical thinkers.

Naugle, David K. *Philosophy: A Student's Guide.* Wheaton, IL: Crossway, 2012. A brief, topical discussion of philosophical issues (prolegomena, metaphysics, philosophical anthropology, etc.) from a Christian point of view. Quite valuable.

Palmer, Donald. *Looking at Philosophy: The Unbearable Heaviness of Philosophy Made Lighter.* New York: McGraw-Hill, 2010. Accurate secular history of philosophy written in an engaging, witty style, illustrated with cartoons. I have often used it as a text in my seminary course on the history of philosophy.

Schaeffer, Francis A. *How Shall We Then Live?* Wheaton, IL: Crossway, 2005. Schaeffer was an evangelist rather than an academic scholar, but he popularized a broadly presuppositional apologetic that frequently appealed to the history of philosophy and culture. Many came to believe in Christianity through his work. He wrote many books, but this one summarizes his use of the history of philosophy.

Sire, James W. *Habits of the Mind.* Downers Grove, IL: InterVarsity Press, 2000.

———. *The Universe Next Door: A Basic World View Catalogue.* Downers Grove, IL: InterVarsity Press, 1975. Sire influenced many to think of the Christian faith as a worldview, in competition with other worldviews.

Stumpf, Samuel Enoch, and James Fieser. *Socrates to Sartre and Beyond: A History of Philosophy.* Boston: McGraw-Hill, 2003. Definitive, detailed, and often difficult secular treatment. Later, this book was combined with a group of primary source readings in *Philosophy: History and Readings* (New York: McGraw-Hill, 2011).

Tarnas, Richard. *The Passion of the Western Mind: Understanding the Ideas That Have Shaped Our World* (NY: Ballantine Books, 1993). This history of Western philosophy is similar to mine, but from a secular, pagan perspective that celebrates autonomous reason and emotion. Other secular thinkers have given it high praise.

Thilly, Frank, and Ledger Wood. *A History of Philosophy.* New York: Henry Holt, 1957. This was the textbook used at Princeton where I first studied the history of philosophy. It is a comprehensive secular text, very clearly written, judicious in its selections, generally well organized.

Van Til, Cornelius. *A Survey of Christian Epistemology.* Philadelphia: Den Dulk Foundation, 1969. Van Til's work has had much influence on the present volume. Van Til often refers in his many books to philosophers and philosophical issues. But this one, a revision of his early *Metaphysics of Apologetics*, is one of the few that deal with the history of philosophy in a systematic way. This book deals extensively with Plato, and then with Plato's repercussions through history.

———. *Who Do You Say That I Am?* Nutley, NJ: Presbyterian and Reformed, 1975. This is much shorter than the previous title, and gives the gist of Van Til's critique of non-Christian philosophical thought. The three sections deal with ancient, medieval, and modern replies to the titular question.

Wolterstorff, Nicholas. *Reason within the Bounds of Religion*. 2nd ed. Grand Rapids: Eerdmans, 1984. Note the reversal of Kant's title. This is a very important work on the nature of Christian thought. I discussed Wolterstorff in chapter 13 of the present volume.

GENERAL BIBLIOGRAPHY

PRINT RESOURCES

Abel, Donald C., ed. *Fifty Readings in Philosophy*. New York: McGraw-Hill, 2011.

Abel, Donald C., and Eric O. Springsted. *Primary Readings in Philosophy for Understanding Theology*. Louisville, KY: Westminster John Knox Press, 1992.

Abelard, Peter. *Abelard & Heloise: The Letters and Other Writings*. Edited by William Levitan. Indianapolis: Hackett Publishing, 2007.

Achinstein, Peter, and Stephen F. Barker, eds. *The Legacy of Logical Positivism*. Baltimore: Johns Hopkins Press, 1969.

Adam, Karl. "Die Theologie der Krises." *Das Hochland* 23 (June 1926): 276–77.

Alexander, Samuel. *Space, Time, and Deity*. New York: Macmillan, 1920.

Allen, Diogenes. *Philosophy for Understanding Theology*. Atlanta: John Knox Press, 1985.

Allen, Diogenes, and Eric O. Springsted. *Primary Readings in Philosophy for Understanding Theology*. Louisville, KY: Westminster John Knox Press, 1992.

Alston, William. *Perceiving God: The Epistemology of Religious Experience*. Ithaca, NY: Cornell University Press, 1991.

———. *Perceiving God: The Epistemology of Religious Experience*. Ithaca, NY: Cornell University Press, 1993.

Altizer, Thomas J. J. *The New Gospel of Christian Atheism*. Aurora, CO: Davies Group, 2002.

Anderson, James. *Paradox in Christian Theology*. Eugene, OR: Wipf and Stock, 2007.

———. *What's Your Worldview? An Interactive Approach to Life's Big Questions*. Wheaton, IL: Crossway, 2014.

Anderson, James N., and Greg Welty. "The Lord of Non-Contradiction: An Argument for God from Logic." *Philosophia Christi* 13, 2 (2011): 321–38. http://goo.gl/5Xn0w.

Anscombe, G. E. M. *The Collected Philosophical Papers of G. E. M. Anscombe*. Vol. 1, *From Parmenides to Wittgenstein*. Oxford: Blackwell, 1981.

———. *The Collected Philosophical Papers of G. E. M. Anscombe*. Vol. 2, *Metaphysics and the Philosophy of Mind*. Minneapolis: University of Minnesota Press, 1981.

———. *The Collected Philosophical Papers of G. E. M. Anscombe*. Vol. 2, *Metaphysics and the Philosophy of Mind*. Oxford: Blackwell, 1981.

———. *The Collected Philosophical Papers of G. E. M. Anscombe*. Vol. 3, *Ethics, Religion, and Politics*. Oxford: Blackwell, 1981.

Anselm of Canterbury. *St. Anselm: Basic Writings*. Edited by S. N. Deane. La Salle, IL: Open Court, 1962.

———. *St. Anselm's Basic Writings*. Edited by S. N. Deane. Chicago: Open Court, 1998.

Aquinas, Thomas. *Summa Theologiae: Complete Set Latin-English Edition*. Rochester, NY: Aquinas Institute, 2012.

———. *Summa Theologica*. In *Introduction to St. Thomas Aquinas*, edited by Anton C. Pegis. New York: Modern Library, 1948.

Aristotle. *The Basic Works of Aristotle*. Edited by Richard McKeon. New York: Random House, 1941.

Audi, Robert, ed. *The Cambridge Dictionary of Philosophy*. Cambridge: Cambridge University Press, 1995.

Austin, J. L. *How to Do Things with Words*. Cambridge, MA: Harvard University Press, 1975.

———. *How to Do Things with Words*. Oxford: Oxford University Press, 1976.

———. *Philosophical Papers*. Oxford: Clarendon, 1990.

———. *Sense and Sensibilia*. Oxford: Oxford University Press, 1962.

Ayer, A. J. *Language, Truth and Logic*. London: Gollancz, 1936.

———. *Language, Truth and Logic*. New York: Dover, 1946.

———. *Language, Truth and Logic*. New York: Dover, 1952.

———. *Logical Positivism*. Glencoe, IL: Free Press, 1959.

———. *Philosophy in the Twentieth Century*. New York: Random House, 1984.

Bahnsen, Greg L. "A Conditional Resolution of the Apparent Paradox of Self-Deception." Ph.D. diss., University of Southern California, 1978.

———. *Always Ready*. Atlanta: American Vision, 1996.

———. *Presuppositional Apologetics*. Atlanta: American Vision, 2008.

———. *Van Til's Apologetic*. Phillipsburg, NJ: P&R Publishing, 1998.

Barber, John. *The Road from Eden: Studies in Christianity and Culture*. Lakeland, FL: Whitefield Media Publications, 2008.

Barnes, Jonathan, ed. *The Complete Works of Aristotle*. Princeton, NJ: Princeton University Press, 1984.

Barr, James. *The Semantics of Biblical Language*. London: Oxford University Press, 1961.

Barth, Karl. *Anselm: Fides Quaerens Intellectum*. Richmond, VA: John Knox Press, 1960.

———. *Anselm: Fides Quaerens Intellectum*. Eugene, OR: Wipf and Stock, 1975.

———. *Church Dogmatics*. New York: Charles Scribner's Sons, 1936.

———. *Church Dogmatics*. Edinburgh: T&T Clark, 2004.

———. *Church Dogmatics: A Selection*. Edited by Helmut Gollwitzer. Louisville, KY: Westminster John Knox Press, 1994.

———. *The Doctrine of God*. Vol. 2 of *Church Dogmatics*. Edited by G. W. Bromiley and T. F. Torrance. Translated by T. H. L. Parker, W. B. Johnston, H. Knight, and J. L. M. Haire. New York: Scribner, 1957.

———. *The Doctrine of the Word of God*. Vol. 1 of *Church Dogmatics*. Edited by G. W. Bromiley and T. F. Torrance. Translated by G. T. Thomson. New York: Scribner, 1936.

———. *The Doctrine of the Word of God*. Vol. 1 of *Church Dogmatics*. Edited by G. W. Bromiley and T. F. Torrance. Translated by G. T. Thomson and Harold Knight. New York: Scribner, 1956.

———. *Dogmatics in Outline*. New York: Harper, 1959.

———. *The Epistle to the Romans*. London: Oxford University Press, 1933.

———. *The Epistle to the Romans*. New York: Oxford University Press, 1968.

———. *Evangelical Theology: An Introduction*. Grand Rapids: Eerdmans, 1992.

———. *Protestant Thought: From Rousseau to Ritschl*. New York: Simon and Schuster, 1969.

———. "Rudolf Bultmann: An Attempt to Understand Him." In *Kerygma and Myth: A Theological Debate*, edited by Hans Werner Bartsch, 2:83–132. Translated by Reginald H. Fuller. London: SPCK, 1962.

Barthes, Roland. "The Death of the Author." *Aspen* 5–6 (1967).

Bartholomew, Craig G., and Michael W. Goheen. *Christian Philosophy: A Systematic and Narrative Introduction*. Grand Rapids: Baker, 2013.

Berkhof, Louis. *Systematic Theology*. London: Banner of Truth, 1949.

Berkouwer, G. C. *Karl Barth*. Kampen: Kok, 1936.

———. *The Triumph of Grace in the Theology of Karl Barth*. Grand Rapids: Eerdmans, 1956.

Bloch, Ernst. *The Principle of Hope*. Translated by Neville Plaice, Stephen Plaice, and Paul Knight. 3 vols. Cambridge, MA: MIT Press, 1986.

Bochenski, Joseph M. *The Logic of Religion*. New York: New York University Press, 1965.

Boethius, Ancius. *The Consolation of Philosophy*. New York: Empire Books, 2012.

Boff, Leonardo. *Introducing Liberation Theology*. Maryknoll, NY: Orbis Books, 1987.

Bonhoeffer, Dietrich. *The Cost of Discipleship*. New York: Touchstone, 1995.

———. *Letters and Papers from Prison*. Edited by Eberhard Bethge. New York: Touchstone, 1997.

———. *Life Together*. New York: Harper, 2009.

Bonino, José Miguez. *Doing Theology in a Revolutionary Situation*. Minneapolis: Fortress, 1975.

Bouveresse, Jacques. *Wittgenstein Reads Freud: The Myth of the Unconscious*. Translated by Carol Cosman. Princeton, NJ: Princeton University Press, 1996.

Boyd, Gregory. *God of the Possible: A Biblical Introduction to the Open View of God*. Grand Rapids: Baker, 2000.

Bratt, James. *Abraham Kuyper: Modern Calvinist, Christian Democrat*. Grand Rapids: Eerdmans, 2013.

Bridgman, Percy. *The Logic of Modern Physics*. New York: Macmillan, 1927.

Brown, Colin. *Christianity and Western Thought: A History of Philosophers, Ideas, and Movements from the Ancient World to the Age of Enlightenment*. Downers Grove, IL: InterVarsity Press, 2010.

———. *Philosophy and the Christian Faith*. Downers Grove, IL: InterVarsity Press, 1968.

Brunner, Emil. *The Divine Imperative*. Louisville, KY: Westminster John Knox Press, 1979.

———. *Dogmatics*. Vol. 1, *The Christian Doctrine of God*. Translated by Olive Wyon. Philadelphia: Westminster Press, 1950.

———. *Dogmatics I: The Christian Doctrine of God*. Library of Theological Translations. Cambridge: James Clarke and Co., 2002.

———. *Dogmatics II: The Christian Doctrine of Creation and Redemption*. Library of Theological Translations. Cambridge: James Clarke and Co., 2002.

———. *Dogmatics III: The Christian Doctrine of the Church, Faith and the Consummation*. Library of Theological Translations. Cambridge: James Clarke and Co., 2002.

———. *Natural Theology: Comprising Nature and Grace by Professor Dr. Emil Brunner and the Reply No! by Dr. Karl Barth*. Eugene, OR: Wipf and Stock, 2002.

Buber, Martin. *I and Thou*. Translated by Ronald Gregor Smith. 2nd ed. New York: Scribner, 1958.

———. *I and Thou*. Translated by Walter Kaufmann. New York: Touchstone, 1971.

———. *I and Thou*. Translated by Walter Kaufmann. Eastford, CT: Martino Fine Books, 2010.

Budziszewski, J. *The Revenge of Conscience*. Dallas: Spence Publishing, 1999.

———. *What We Can't Not Know*. Dallas: Spence Publishing, 2003.

Bultmann, Rudolf. *Existence and Faith: Shorter Writings of Rudolf Bultmann*. Edited and translated by Schubert M. Ogden. New York: Meridian Books, 1960.

———. *New Testament and Mythology and Other Basic Writings*. Edited and translated by Schubert M. Ogden. Philadelphia: Fortress, 1984.

———. *Theology of the New Testament*. Translated by Kendrick Grobel. Waco, TX: Baylor University Press, 2007.

Bultmann, Rudolf, et al. *Kerygma and Myth: A Theological Debate*. Edited by Hans Werner Bartsch. Translated by Reginald H. Fuller. 2 vols. New York: Harper and Row, 1961.

———. *Kerygma and Myth: A Theological Debate*. Edited by Hans Werner Bartsch. Translated by Reginald H. Fuller. 2 vols. London: SPCK, 1962.

Butler, Joseph. *Analogy of Religion*. Philadelphia: J. B. Lippincott, 1865.

———. *The Works of Joseph Butler*. Chestnut Hill, MA: Adamant Media Corp., 2000.

Calvin, John. *Institutes of the Christian Religion*. Edited by John T. McNeill. Translated by Ford Lewis Battles. 2 vols. Philadelphia: Westminster Press, 1960.

Cantor, Georg. *Contributions to the Foundations of the Theory of Transfinite Numbers*. Translated by Philip E. B. Jourdain. Chicago: Open Court, 1915.

Childs, Brevard S. *Biblical Theology in Crisis*. Philadelphia: Westminster Press, 1970.

———. *Biblical Theology of the Old and New Testaments: Theological Reflection on the Christian Bible*. Philadelphia: Fortress, 1993.

———. *Biblical Theology of the Old and New Testaments: Theological Reflection on the Christian Bible*. Minneapolis: Fortress, 2012.

———. *Introduction to the Old Testament as Scripture*. Philadelphia: Fortress, 1979.

Chomsky, Noam. *Cartesian Linguistics*. New York: Harper and Row, 1966.

Christian, William A. *Meaning and Truth in Religion*. Princeton, NJ: Princeton University Press, 1964.

Clark, Gordon H. *A Christian Philosophy of Education*. Unicoi, TN: Trinity Foundation, 2000.

———. *A Christian View of Men and Things*. Grand Rapids: Eerdmans, 1952.

———. *A Christian View of Men and Things*. Unicoi, TN: Trinity Foundation, 1998.

———. *Dewey*. Philadelphia: Presbyterian and Reformed, 1960.

———. *The Johannine Logos*. Nutley, NJ: Presbyterian and Reformed, 1972.

———. *The Philosophy of Science and Belief in God*. Nutley, NJ: Craig Press, 1964.

———. *The Philosophy of Science and Belief in God*. Unicoi, TN: Trinity Foundation, 1996.

———. *Religion, Reason, and Revelation*. Philadelphia: Presbyterian and Reformed, 1961.

———. *Thales to Dewey: A History of Philosophy*. Boston: Houghton Mifflin, 1957.

———. *William James*. Philadelphia: Presbyterian and Reformed, 1963.

Clifford, W. K. *The Ethics of Belief and Other Essays*. New York: Prometheus Books, 1999.

Clouser, Roy A. *The Myth of Religious Neutrality: An Essay on the Hidden Role of Religious Belief in Theories*. Notre Dame, IN: University of Notre Dame Press, 1991.

Cobb, John B., Jr., and David Ray Griffin. *Process Theology: An Introductory Exposition*. Philadelphia: Westminster Press, 1976.

———. *Process Theology: An Introductory Exposition*. Louisville, KY: Westminster John Knox Press, 1996.

Cohen, S. Marc, Patricia Curd, and C. D. C. Reeve, eds. *Readings in Ancient Greek Philosophy: From Thales to Aristotle*. 4th ed. Indianapolis: Hackett Publishing, 2011.

Collett, Don. "Van Til and Transcendental Argument." *WTJ* 65, 2 (Fall 2003): 289–306.

Cone, James H. *A Black Theology of Liberation*. Maryknoll, NY: Orbis Books, 2011.

Cooper, David E., ed. *Epistemology: The Classic Readings*. Oxford: Blackwell, 1999.

Cooper, John M., and D. S. Hutchinson, eds. *Plato: Complete Works*. Indianapolis: Hackett Publishing, 1997.

Copleston, Frederick C. *A History of Philosophy*. 9 vols. Garden City, NY: Image Books, 1962–65.

Cowan, Steven B., ed. *Five Views on Apologetics*. Grand Rapids: Zondervan, 2000.

Cox, Harvey. *The Secular City*. New York: Collier Books, 1965.

———. *The Secular City*. Princeton, NJ: Princeton University Press, 2013.

Craig, William Lane. *The Kalām Cosmological Argument*. New York: Barnes and Noble Books, 1979.

———. *Reasonable Faith: Christian Truth and Apologetics*. Wheaton, IL: Crossway, 1994.

———. *Time and Eternity: Exploring God's Relationships to Time*. Wheaton, IL: Crossway, 2001.

Crampton, W. Gary. *The Scripturalism of Gordon H. Clark*. Unicoi, TN: Trinity Foundation, 1997.

Curd, Patricia, and Daniel W. Graham, eds. *The Oxford Handbook of Presocratic Philosophy*. Oxford: Oxford University Press, 2009.

Darwin, Frances, ed. *Autobiography of Charles Darwin*. N.p., n.d.

Descartes, René. *A Discourse on Method and Selected Writings*. New York: Dutton, 1951.

———. *The Philosophical Writings of Descartes*. 3 vols. Cambridge: Cambridge University Press, 1985.

Dewey, John. *A Common Faith*. New Haven, CT: Yale University Press, 1991.

———. *Experience and Nature*. New York: Dover, 1958.

———. *The Philosophy of John Dewey: Two Volumes in One*. Edited by John J. McDermott. Chicago: University of Chicago Press, 1981.

Dionysius the Areopagite. *Pseudo-Dionysius: The Complete Works*. Mahwah, NJ: Paulist Press, 1988.

Dooyeweerd, Herman. *In the Twilight of Western Thought*. Nutley, NJ: Presbyterian and Reformed, 1960.

———. *In the Twilight of Western Thought*. Grand Rapids: Paideia Press, 2012.

———. *A New Critique of Theoretical Thought*. 4 vols. Philadelphia: Presbyterian and Reformed, 1953.

Dreyer, J. L. E. *A History of Astronomy from Thales to Kepler*. 2nd ed. New York: Dover, 1953.

Duns Scotus, John. *Duns Scotus—Philosophical Writings: A Selection*. Translated by Allan Wolter. Indianapolis: Hackett Publishing, 1987.

Edgar, William. *The Face of Truth: Lifting the Veil*. Phillipsburg, NJ: P&R Publishing, 2001.

———. *Truth in All Its Glory: Commending the Reformed Faith*. Phillipsburg, NJ: P&R Publishing, 2004.

Edgar, William, and K. Scott Oliphint, eds. *Christian Apologetics Past and Present: A Primary Source Reader*. Vol. 1, *To 1500*. Wheaton, IL: Crossway, 2009.

———, eds. *Christian Apologetics Past and Present: A Primary Source Reader*. Vol. 2, *From 1500*. Wheaton, IL: Crossway, 2011.

Edwards, Jonathan. *Freedom of the Will*. Edited by Paul Ramsey. New Haven, CT: Yale University Press, 1973.

———. *The Works of Jonathan Edwards*. Edited by Edward Hickman. 2 vols. Amazon Digital Services, 2011.

Edwards, Paul, ed. *The Encyclopedia of Philosophy*. New York: Macmillan/ Free Press, 1967.

———, ed. *The Encyclopedia of Philosophy*. New York: Macmillan, 1967.

Erigena, John Scotus. *Treatise on Divine Predestination*. Notre Dame, IN: University of Notre Dame Press, 2003.

Evans, C. Stephen. *Existentialism: The Philosophy of Despair and the Quest for Hope*. Grand Rapids: Zondervan, 1984.

Evans, Ernest, trans. *Tertullian's Treatise on the Incarnation*. London: SPCK, 1956.

Ewing, A. C. *A Short Commentary on Kant's Critique of Pure Reason*. Chicago: University of Chicago Press, 1938, 1974.

Fairweather, Eugene R., ed. *A Scholastic Miscellany: Anselm to Ockham*. Louisville, KY: Westminster John Knox Press, 1956.

Fann, K. T. *Wittgenstein's Conception of Philosophy*. Berkeley, CA: University of California Press, 1969.

Ferm, Deane W. *Contemporary American Theologies*. San Francisco: Harper and Row, 1990.

Feuerbach, Ludwig. *The Essence of Christianity*. New York: Dover, 2008.

———. *The Essence of Christianity*. Seattle: CreateSpace, 2013.

Feyerabend, Paul. *Against Method: Outline of an Anarchistic Theory of Knowledge*. London: Verso, 1975.

Fieser, James, and Norman Lillegard. *A Historical Introduction to Philosophy: Texts and Interactive Guide*. New York: Oxford University Press, 2002.

Findlay, J. N., et al. "Can God's Existence Be Disproved?" In *New Essays in Philosophical Theology*, edited by Antony Flew and Alasdair C. MacIntyre, 47–75. London: SCM Press, 1955.

Fletcher, Joseph. *Situation Ethics: The New Morality*. Louisville, KY: Westminster John Knox Press, 1966.

Flew, Antony, et al. "Theology and Falsification." In *New Essays in Philosophical Theology*, edited by Antony Flew and Alasdair C. MacIntyre, 96–130. London: SCM Press, 1955.

———. *There Is a God: How the World's Most Notorious Atheist Changed His Mind*. New York: HarperOne, 2008.

Flew, Antony, and Alasdair C. MacIntyre, eds. *New Essays in Philosophical Theology*. London: SCM Press, 1955.

Frame, John M. *The Academic Captivity of Theology*. Lakeland, FL: Whitefield Media Publications, 2012.

———. *Apologetics: A Justification of Christian Belief*. Phillipsburg, NJ: P&R Publishing, 2015.

———. *Apologetics to the Glory of God*. Phillipsburg, NJ: P&R Publishing, 1994.

———. "Certainty." In *New Dictionary of Christian Apologetics*, edited by W. C. Campbell-Jack and Gavin J. McGrath, 141–45. Consulting ed. C. Stephen Evans. Downers Grove, IL: InterVarsity Press, 2006.

———. "Christianity and Contemporary Epistemology." *WTJ* 52, 1 (Spring 1990): 131–41.

———. *Cornelius Van Til: An Analysis of His Thought*. Phillipsburg, NJ: P&R Publishing, 1995.

———. "Determinism, Chance, and Freedom." In *New Dictionary of Christian Apologetics*, edited by W. C. Campbell-Jack and Gavin J. McGrath, 218–20. Consulting ed. C. Stephen Evans. Downers Grove, IL: InterVarsity Press, 2006.

———. *The Doctrine of God*. Phillipsburg, NJ: P&R Publishing, 2002.

———. *The Doctrine of the Christian Life*. Phillipsburg, NJ: P&R Publishing, 2008.

———. *The Doctrine of the Knowledge of God*. Phillipsburg, NJ: Presbyterian and Reformed, 1987.

———. *The Doctrine of the Word of God*. Phillipsburg, NJ: P&R Publishing, 2010.

———. *The Escondido Theology*. Lakeland, FL: Whitefield Media Publications, 2011.

———. "God and Biblical Language: Transcendence and Immanence." In *God's Inerrant Word*, edited by John W. Montgomery, 159–77. Grand Rapids: Bethany House Publishers, 1974.

———. "Greeks Bearing Gifts." In *Revolutions in Worldview: Understanding the Flow of Western Thought*, edited by W. Andrew Hoffecker, 1–36. Phillipsburg, NJ: P&R Publishing, 2007.

———. "Infinite Series." In *New Dictionary of Christian Apologetics*, edited by W. C. Campbell-Jack and Gavin J. McGrath, 353–54. Consulting ed. C. Stephen Evans. Downers Grove, IL: InterVarsity Press, 2006.

———. *No Other God: A Response to Open Theism*. Phillipsburg, NJ: P&R Publishing, 2001.

———. "Ontological Argument." In *New Dictionary of Christian Apologetics*, edited by W. C. Campbell-Jack and Gavin J. McGrath, 513–16. Consulting ed. C. Stephen Evans. Downers Grove, IL: InterVarsity Press, 2006.

———. "The Problem of Theological Paradox." In *Foundations of Christian Scholarship: Essays in the Van Til Perspective*, edited by Gary North, 295–330. Vallecito, CA: Ross House, 1976.

———. Review of *Belief Policies*, by Paul Helm. *WTJ* 57, 1 (Spring 1995): 248–51.

———. Review of *The Edges of Language*, by Paul M. Van Buren. *WTJ* 36, 1 (Fall 1973): 106–11.

———. Review of *The Grammar of Faith*, by Paul L. Holmer. *WTJ* 42, 1 (Fall 1979): 219–31.

———. Review of *Idols for Destruction*, by Herbert Schlossberg. *WTJ* 46, 2 (Fall 1984): 438–44.

———. Review of *The Legacy of Logical Positivism*, edited by Peter Achinstein and Stephen F. Barker. *WTJ* 34, 2 (May 1972): 199–201.

———. Review of *Longing to Know*, by Esther Lightcap Meek. *Presbyterion* 29, 2 (Fall 2003).

———. Review of *New Essays on Religious Language*, edited by Dallas M. High. *WTJ* 33, 1 (November 1970): 126–31.

———. Review of *On Theology*, by Schubert M. Ogden. *WTJ* 50, 1 (Spring 1988): 157–65.

———. "Scripture Speaks for Itself." In *God's Inerrant Word*, edited by John W. Montgomery, 178–200. Grand Rapids: Bethany House Publishers, 1974.

———. "Self-Refuting Statements." In *New Dictionary of Christian Apologetics*, edited by W. C. Campbell-Jack and Gavin J. McGrath, 660–62. Consulting ed. C. Stephen Evans. Downers Grove, IL: InterVarsity Press, 2006.

———. *Systematic Theology: An Introduction to Christian Belief.* Phillipsburg, NJ: P&R Publishing, 2013.

———. "Transcendental Arguments." In *New Dictionary of Christian Apologetics*, edited by W. C. Campbell-Jack and Gavin J. McGrath, 716–17. Consulting ed. C. Stephen Evans. Downers Grove, IL: InterVarsity Press, 2006.

———. "Unregenerate Knowledge of God." In *New Dictionary of Christian Apologetics*, edited by W. C. Campbell-Jack and Gavin J. McGrath, 732–35. Consulting ed. C. Stephen Evans. Downers Grove, IL: InterVarsity Press, 2006.

———. "The Uses of Scripture in Recent Theology." *WTJ* 39, 2 (Spring 1977): 328–53.

———. *Van Til: The Theologian*. Phillipsburg, NJ: Pilgrim Publishing, 1976.

Frame, John M., and Paul Kurtz. "Do We Need God to Be Moral?" *Free Inquiry* 16, 2 (1996).

Frei, Hans W. *The Eclipse of Biblical Narrative: A Study in Eighteenth and Nineteenth Century Hermeneutics*. New Haven, CT: Yale University Press, 1974.

———. *The Eclipse of Biblical Narrative: A Study in Eighteenth and Nineteenth Century Hermeneutics*. New Haven, CT: Yale University Press, 1980.

Funk, Robert W. *Language, Hermeneutic, and Word of God: The Problem of Language in the New Testament and Contemporary Theology*. New York: Harper and Row, 1966.

Gadamer, Hans-Georg. *Truth and Method*. New York: Crossroad Publishing, 1982.

Gamow, George. *One, Two, Three . . . Infinity: Facts and Speculations of Science*. London: Macmillan, 1946.

Gaussen, Louis. *The Inspiration of the Holy Scriptures*. Translated by D. D. Scott. Chicago: Moody Press, 1949.

Gay, Peter. *The Enlightenment: The Rise of Modern Paganism*. New York: W. W. Norton, 1995.

Geisler, Norman. "Process Theology." In *Tensions in Contemporary Theology*, edited by Stanley N. Gundry and Alan F. Johnson, 247–84. Grand Rapids: Baker, 1976.

Geivett, R. Douglas, and Brendan Sweetman, eds. *Contemporary Perspectives on Religious Epistemology*. New York: Oxford University Press, 1992.

Gettier, Edmund. "Is Justified True Belief Knowledge?" *Analysis* 23 (1966): 121–23.

Gier, Nicholas F. *Wittgenstein and Phenomenology*. Albany, NY: SUNY Press, 1981.

Gilson, Étienne. *The Spirit of Medieval Philosophy*. Notre Dame, IN: University of Notre Dame Press, 1991.

Gottlieb, Anthony. *The Dream of Reason: A History of Philosophy from the Greeks to the Renaissance*. New York: W. W. Norton, 2002.

Graham, Daniel W. *The Texts of Early Greek Philosophy: The Complete Fragments and Selected Testimonies of the Major Presocratics*. Cambridge: Cambridge University Press, 2010.

Grant, Frederick C. *An Introduction to New Testament Thought*. Nashville, TN: Abingdon Press, 1950.

Gundry, Stanley N., and Alan F. Johnson, eds. *Tensions in Contemporary Theology*. Grand Rapids: Baker, 1976.

Gutierrez, Gustavo. *A Theology of Liberation*. Maryknoll, NY: Orbis Books, 1973.

———. *A Theology of Liberation*. Maryknoll, NY: Orbis Books, 1988.

Guyer, Paul. *The Cambridge Companion to Kant's Critique of Pure Reason*. Cambridge: Cambridge University Press, 2010.

Gyula, Klima, ed., with Fritz Allhof and Arnand Jayprakash Vaidya. *Medieval Philosophy: Essential Readings with Commentary*. Hoboken, NJ: Wiley Blackwell, 2007.

Habermas, Jürgen. *Knowledge and Human Interests*. Boston: Beacon Press, 1972.

Hackett, Stuart C. *The Resurrection of Theism: Prolegomena to Christian Apology*. Chicago: Moody Press, 1957.

Hallett, Garth. *A Companion to Wittgenstein's Philosophical Investigations*. Ithaca, NY: Cornell University Press, 1977.

Hamilton, Kenneth. *The System and the Gospel: A Critique of Paul Tillich*. New York: Macmillan, 1963.

———. *The System and the Gospel: A Critique of Paul Tillich*. Charleston, SC: Nabu Press, 2011.

Hampshire, Stuart. *Spinoza*. Baltimore: Penguin, 1951.

Hanson, Norwood Russell. *Patterns of Discovery: An Inquiry into the Conceptual Foundations of Science*. Cambridge: Cambridge University Press, 1958.

Harnack, Adolf von. *What Is Christianity?* London: Williams and Norgate, 1901.

———. *What Is Christianity?* Eastford, CT: Martino Fine Books, 2011.

Hart, Hendrik, Johan van der Hoeven, and Nicholas Wolterstorff, eds. *Rationality in the Calvinian Tradition*. Lanham, MD: University Press of America, 1983.

Hartshorne, Charles. *The Divine Relativity*. New Haven, CT: Yale University Press, 1982.

———. "The Formal Validity and Real Significance of the Ontological Argument." *Philosophical Review* 53 (May 1944): 225–45.

Hasker, William. "Self-Referential Incoherence." In *The Cambridge Dictionary of Philosophy*, edited by Robert Audi, 721. Cambridge: Cambridge University Press, 1995.

Hegel, G. W. F. *Early Theological Writings*. Translated by T. M. Knox and Richard Kroner. Philadelphia: University of Pennsylvania Press, 1971.

———. *Hegel: Texts and Commentary*. Edited by Walter Kaufmann. Notre Dame, IN: University of Notre Dame Press, 1965, 1977.

———. *On Christianity: Early Theological Writings*. Introduction by Richard Kroner. New York: Harper, 1948.

———. *The Phenomenology of Spirit*. Translated by A. V. Miller. New York: Oxford University Press, 1976.

———. *Selections*. New York: Scribner's, 1929.

Heidegger, Martin. *Basic Writings*. Edited by David Farrell Krell. New York: Harper Perennial Modern Classics, 2008.

———. *Being and Time*. Translated by John MacQuarrie and Edward Robinson. New York: Harper Perennial Modern Classics, 2008.

———. *On the Way to Language*. New York: Harper, 1971.

Helm, Paul. *Belief Policies*. Cambridge: Cambridge University Press, 1994.

———. *Belief Policies*. Cambridge: Cambridge University Press, 2007.

———. *Eternal God: A Study of God without Time*. Oxford: Clarendon, 1998.

———. *Eternal God: A Study of God without Time*. New York: Oxford University Press, 2011.

———. *Faith and Understanding*. Grand Rapids: Eerdmans, 1997.

———. *Faith with Reason*. Oxford: Clarendon, 2000.

———. *The Providence of God*. Downers Grove, IL: InterVarsity Press, 1993.

———. *The Providence of God*. Downers Grove, IL: IVP Academic, 1994.

Henry, Carl F. H., ed. *Revelation and the Bible*. Grand Rapids: Baker, 1958.

Herrmann, Wilhelm. *The Communion of the Christian with God*. London: Williams and Norgate, 1906.

———. *The Communion of the Christian with God*. Charleston, SC: BiblioBazaar, 2009.

———. *Systematic Theology*. New York: Macmillan, 1927.

Hicks, Peter. *The Journey So Far: Philosophy through the Ages*. Grand Rapids: Zondervan, 2003.

High, Dallas M., ed. *New Essays on Religious Language*. New York: Oxford University Press, 1969.

Hobbes, Thomas. *Leviathan*. New York: Empire Books, 2013.

Hodge, Charles. *Systematic Theology*. 3 vols. Grand Rapids: Eerdmans, 1952.

Hoffecker, W. Andrew, ed. *Revolutions in Worldview: Understanding the Flow of Western Thought*. Phillipsburg, NJ: P&R Publishing, 2007.

Holmer, Paul L. *The Grammar of Faith*. San Francisco: Harper and Row, 1978.

Holmes, Arthur. *Philosophy: A Christian Perspective*. Downers Grove, IL: InterVarsity Press, 1975.

Holmes, Michael W., ed. *The Apostolic Fathers: Greek Texts and English Translations*. Grand Rapids: Baker, 2007.

Hume, David. *An Inquiry concerning Human Understanding*. New York: Liberal Arts Press, 1955.

———. *The Philosophy of David Hume*. New York: Random House, 1963.

———. *A Treatise of Human Nature*. New York: Dutton, 1911, 1956.

Husserl, Edmund. *The Essential Husserl: Basic Writings in Transcendental Phenomenology*. Indianapolis: Indiana University Press, 1999.

———. *Ideas: General Introduction to Pure Phenomenology*. New York: Routledge, 2012.

Hyman, Arthur, James J. Walsh, and Thomas Williams, eds. *Philosophy in the Middle Ages: The Christian, Islamic, and Jewish Traditions*. 3rd ed. Indianapolis: Hackett Publishing, 2010.

Israel, Jonathan I. *Radical Enlightenment: Philosophy and the Meaning of Modernity, 1650–1750*. New York: Oxford University Press, 2002.

James, William. "The Dilemma of Determinism." In *Essays in Pragmatism*, edited by Alburey Castell, 37–64. New York: Hafner Publishing, 1954.

———. *Essays in Pragmatism*. Edited by Alburey Castell. New York: Hafner Publishing, 1954.

———. *Pragmatism*. Seattle: CreateSpace, 2013.

———. *Pragmatism and the Meaning of Truth*. Cambridge, MA: Harvard University Press, 1979.

———. *Varieties of Religious Experience: A Study of Human Nature*. London: Longmans Green, 1902.

———. *The Writings of William James: A Comprehensive Edition*. Chicago: University of Chicago Press, 2011.

Jaspers, Karl, and Rudolf Bultmann. *Myth and Christianity: An Inquiry into the Possibility of Religion without Myth*. Translated by Norbert Gutermann. New York: Noonday Press, 1958.

Johnson, Elizabeth A. *She Who Is: The Mystery of God in Feminist Theological Discourse*. New York: Crossroad Publishing, 2002.

Jones, Peter R. *Capturing the Pagan Mind*. Nashville, TN: Broadman and Holman, 2003.

———. *The Gnostic Empire Strikes Back*. Phillipsburg, NJ: P&R Publishing, 1992.

———. *One or Two: Seeing a World of Difference*. Escondido, CA: Main Entry Editions, 2010.

———. *Spirit Wars*. Escondido, CA: Main Entry Editions, 1997.

Kähler, Martin. *The So-Called Historical Jesus and the Historic Biblical Christ*. Translated by Carl E. Braaten. Philadelphia: Fortress, 1964.

Kant, Immanuel. *Critique of Pure Reason*. Edited and translated by Norman Kemp Smith. New York: Modern Library, 1958.

———. *Critique of Pure Reason*. Edited and translated by Paul Guyer and Allen W. Wood. Cambridge: Cambridge University Press, 1999.

———. *Prolegomena to Any Future Metaphysics*. Translated by James W. Ellington. 2nd ed. Indianapolis: Hackett Publishing, 2002.

———. *Religion within the Boundaries of Mere Reason: And Other Writings*. Edited by Allen Wood and George di Giovani. Cambridge Texts in the History of Philosophy. Cambridge: Cambridge University Press, 1999.

Kaufmann, Walter, ed. *Basic Writings of Nietzsche*. New York: Modern Library, 2000.

———. *Critique of Religion and Philosophy*. Princeton, NJ: Princeton University Press, 1979.

———. *Existentialism from Dostoevsky to Sartre*. New York: New American Library, 1975.

———. *From Shakespeare to Existentialism*. Boston: Beacon Press, 1959.

———. *Hegel: A Reinterpretation*. Notre Dame, IN: University of Notre Dame Press, 1988.

———. *Hegel: Texts and Commentary.* Notre Dame, IN: University of Notre Dame Press, 1989.

———. *A New History of Western Philosophy.* Vol. 2, *Medieval Philosophy.* New York: Oxford University Press, 2007.

———. *Nietzsche.* New York: Meridian Books, 1950, 1956.

———, ed. *Nietzsche: Philosopher, Psychologist, Antichrist.* Princeton, NJ: Princeton University Press, 1975.

Kelsey, David H. *The Fabric of Paul Tillich's Theology.* Eugene, OR: Wipf and Stock, 2011.

Kenny, Anthony. *A New History of Western Philosophy.* New York: Oxford University Press, 2010.

Kierkegaard, Søren. *Attack upon Christendom.* Princeton, NJ: Princeton University Press, 1968.

———. *Concluding Unscientific Postscript.* Princeton, NJ: Princeton University Press, 1941, 1968.

———. *Concluding Unscientific Postscript.* Princeton, NJ: Princeton University Press, 1992.

———. *Either/Or.* New York, Penguin, 1992.

———. *The Essential Kierkegaard.* Princeton, NJ: Princeton University Press, 2000.

———. *Fear and Trembling.* New York: Penguin, 1986.

———. *On Authority and Revelation.* New York: Joanna Cotler Books, 1967.

———. *Philosophical Fragments.* Princeton, NJ: Princeton University Press, 1985.

———. *The Sickness unto Death.* Princeton, NJ: Princeton University Press, 1983.

———. *Stages on Life's Way.* Princeton, NJ: Princeton University Press, 1988.

Kirk, G. S., J. E. Raven, and M. Schofield, eds. *The Presocratic Philosophers: A Critical History with a Selection of Texts.* Cambridge: Cambridge University Press, 1983.

Kline, Meredith G. *Structure of Biblical Authority.* Grand Rapids: Eerdmans, 1972.

Kramnick, Isaac, ed. *The Portable Enlightenment Reader.* London: Penguin, 1995.

Kreeft, Peter. *Christianity for Modern Pagans: Pascal's* Pensées *Edited, Outlined, and Explained.* San Francisco: Ignatius Press, 1993.

Krell, David F., ed. *Martin Heidegger: Basic Writings.* New York: Harper and Row, 1977.

Kuhn, Thomas S. *The Structure of Scientific Revolutions.* Chicago: University of Chicago Press, 1962.

———. *The Structure of Scientific Revolutions*. 3rd ed. Chicago: University of Chicago Press, 1996.
———. *The Structure of Scientific Revolutions*. 50th anniversary ed. Chicago: University of Chicago Press, 2012.
Kuyper, Abraham. *Abraham Kuyper: A Centennial Reader*. Edited by James Bratt. Grand Rapids: Eerdmans, 1998.
———. *Encyclopedia of Sacred Theology*. London: Forgotten Books, 2012.
———. *Lectures on Calvinism*. Grand Rapids: Eerdmans, 1931.
———. *Lectures on Calvinism*. Edited by James D. Bratt. Grand Rapids: Eerdmans, 1943.
———. *Principles of Sacred Theology*. Translated by J. H. De Vries. Grand Rapids: Eerdmans, 1965.
———. *To Be Near unto God*. London: Forgotten Books, 2012.
———. *Wisdom and Wonder: Common Grace in Science and Art*. Grand Rapids: Christian's Library Press, 2011.
Lacugna, Catherine Mowry, ed. *Freeing Theology: The Essentials of Theology in Feminist Perspective*. New York: HarperOne, 1993.
Leibniz, G. W. *Philosophical Essays*. Indianapolis: Hackett Publishing, 1989.
———. *Selections*. New York: Scribner's, 1951.
Leithart, Peter J. "Medieval Theology and the Roots of Modernity." In *Revolutions in Worldview: Understanding the Flow of Western Thought*, edited by W. Andrew Hoffecker, 140–77. Phillipsburg, NJ: P&R Publishing, 2007.
———. "The Relevance of Eugen Rosenstock-Huessy." *First Things*, June 28, 2007.
Lévi-Strauss, Claude. *Structural Anthropology*. New York: Basic Books, 1974.
———. *Tristes Tropiques*. New York: Atheneum, 1964.
Lewis, C. S. *Mere Christianity*. London: Bles, 1952.
———. *Mere Christianity*. New York: Macmillan, 1958.
———. *Mere Christianity*. San Francisco: HarperCollins, 2001.
———. *Mere Christianity*. San Francisco: HarperCollins, 2009.
———. *Miracles: A Preliminary Study*. San Francisco: HarperOne, 2009.
———. *The Problem of Pain*. San Francisco: HarperOne, 2009.
———. "Surprised by Joy." In *The Inspirational Writings of C. S. Lewis*. New York: Harcourt Brace Jovanovich, 1987.
Lindbeck, George A. *The Nature of Doctrine: Religion and Theology in a Postliberal Age*. Philadelphia: Westminster Press, 1984.
———. *The Nature of Doctrine: Religion and Theology in a Postliberal Age*. Louisville, KY: Westminster John Knox Press, 2009.
Locke, John. *An Essay concerning Human Understanding*. 2 vols. New York: Dover, 1959.

Locke, John, George Berkeley, and David Hume. *The Empiricists*. New York: Anchor Books, 1960.

Luther, Martin. *The Martin Luther Collection: 15 Classic Works*. Kindle ed. Waxkeep Publications, 2012.

———. *Works of Martin Luther, with Introductions and Notes*. Vol. 1. Bel Air, CA: FQ Books, 2010.

Lyotard, Jean-François. *The Postmodern Condition: A Report on Knowledge*. Minneapolis: University of Minnesota Press, 1984.

Machen, J. Gresham. *Christianity and Liberalism*. Grand Rapids: Eerdmans, 1923.

———. *Christianity and Liberalism*. New York: Macmillan, 1923.

———. *What Is Faith?* New York: Macmillan, 1925.

MacIntyre, Alasdair C. *After Virtue: A Study in Moral Theory*. Notre Dame, IN: University of Notre Dame Press, 1981.

———. *After Virtue: A Study in Moral Theory*. 3rd ed. Notre Dame, IN: University of Notre Dame Press, 2007.

———. *Whose Justice? Which Rationality?* Notre Dame, IN: University of Notre Dame Press, 1988.

Mackenzie, Charles S. *Blaise Pascal: Apologist to Skeptics*. Lanham, MD: University Press of America, 2008.

———. *Pascal's Anguish and Joy*. New York: Philosophical Library, 1973.

Malcolm, Norman. *Ludwig Wittgenstein: A Memoir*. London: Oxford University Press, 1958, 1970.

Marsden, George M. *Jonathan Edwards: A Life*. New Haven, CT: Yale University Press, 2004.

———. *Karl Marx: Selected Writings*. Edited by David McLellan. 2nd ed. Oxford: Oxford University Press, 2000.

Marx, Karl, with Friedrich Engels. *The Communist Manifesto*. Seattle: CreateSpace, 2013.

———. *The German Ideology*. Includes: *Theses on Feuerbach* and the *Introduction to the Critique of Political Economy*. Amherst, NY: Prometheus Books, 1998.

Mavrodes, George I. *Belief in God: A Study in the Epistemology of Religion*. New York: Random House, 1970.

———. "Jerusalem and Athens Revisited." In *Faith and Rationality: Reason and Belief in God*, edited by Alvin Plantinga and Nicholas Wolterstorff, 192–218. Notre Dame, IN: University of Notre Dame Press, 1991.

McCormack, Bruce L. *Karl Barth's Critically Realistic Dialectical Theology*. New York: Oxford University Press, 1997.

McGowan, A. T. B. *The Divine Authenticity of Scripture: Retrieving an Evangelical Heritage*. Downers Grove, IL: IVP Academic, 2008.

McKeon, Richard, ed. *Basic Works of Aristotle*. Modern Library Classics. New York: Modern Library, 2001.

———, ed. *Selections from Medieval Philosophers II from Roger Bacon to William of Occam*. New York: Charles Scribner's Sons, 1930.

McPherson, Thomas. "Religion as the Inexpressible." In *New Essays in Philosophical Theology*, edited by Antony Flew and Alasdair C. MacIntyre, 131–43. London: SCM Press, 1955.

Meek, Esther Lightcap. *A Little Manual for Knowing*. Eugene, OR: Wipf and Stock, 2013.

———. *Longing to Know: The Philosophy of Knowledge for Ordinary People*. Grand Rapids: Brazos Press, 2003.

———. *Loving to Know: Introducing Covenant Epistemology*. Eugene, OR: Cascade Books, 2011.

Metaxas, Eric. *Bonhoeffer: Pastor, Martyr, Prophet, Spy*. Nashville, TN: Thomas Nelson, 2011.

Milbank, John. "Postmodern Critical Augustinianism: A Short Summa in Forty-two Responses to Unasked Questions." In *The Postmodern God: A Theological Reader*, edited by Graham Ward. Oxford: Blackwell, 2005.

Milbank, John, ed. *The Radical Orthodoxy Reader*. London: Routledge, 2009.

———. *Theology and Social Theory: Beyond Secular Reason*. Oxford: Blackwell, 2006.

———. *The Word Made Strange: Theology, Language, Culture*. London: Wiley-Blackwell, 1997.

Milbank, John, Catherine Pickstock, and Graham Ward, eds. *Radical Orthodoxy: A New Theology*. London: Routledge, 1999.

Moltmann, Jürgen. *The Crucified God: The Cross of Christ as the Foundation and Criticism of Christian Theology*. Translated by R. A. Wilson and John Bowden. Minneapolis: Fortress, 1993.

———. *Religion, Revolution and the Future*. Translated by Meeks M. Douglas. New York: Scribner's, 1969.

———. *Theology of Hope: On the Ground and the Implications of a Christian Eschatology*. Translated by James W. Leitch. New York: Harper and Row, 1967.

———. *Theology of Hope: On the Ground and the Implications of a Christian Eschatology*. Translated by James W. Leitch. Minneapolis: Fortress, 1993.

———. *The Trinity and the Kingdom: The Doctrine of God*. Translated by Margaret Kohl. San Francisco: HarperCollins, 1981.

———. *The Trinity and the Kingdom: The Doctrine of God*. Translated by Margaret Kohl. Minneapolis: Fortress, 1993.

Montgomery, John W., ed. *God's Inerrant Word*. Grand Rapids: Bethany House Publishers, 1974.

Mooney, Timothy, and Dermot Moran, eds. *The Phenomenology Reader*. New York: Routledge, 2002.

Moore, G. E. *Philosophical Papers*. London: Allen and Unwin, 1959.

———. *Principia Ethica*. New York: Dover, 2004.

———. *Selected Writings*. Edited by Thomas Baldwin. New York: Routledge, 1993.

Moreland, J. P., and William Lane Craig. *Philosophical Foundations for a Christian Worldview*. Downers Grove, IL: InterVarsity Press, 2003.

Morris, Thomas V. "Pascalian Wagering." In *Contemporary Perspectives on Religious Epistemology*, edited by R. Douglas Geivett and Brendan Sweetman, 257–69. New York: Oxford University Press, 1992.

Mouw, Richard. *Abraham Kuyper: A Short and Personal Introduction*. Grand Rapids: Eerdmans, 2011.

Murray, John. "The Attestation of Scripture." In *The Infallible Word*, edited by Ned Bernard Stonehouse and Paul Woolley, 1–54. 3rd rev. ed. Philadelphia: Presbyterian and Reformed, 1967.

———. *Principles of Conduct*. Grand Rapids: Eerdmans, 1957.

Nash, Ronald H. *Life's Ultimate Questions: An Introduction to Philosophy*. Grand Rapids: Zondervan, 1999.

Naugle, David K. *Philosophy: A Student's Guide*. Wheaton, IL: Crossway, 2012.

Nietzsche, Friedrich. *The Birth of Tragedy and the Genealogy of Morals*. Garden City, NY: Doubleday, 1956.

———. *The Gay Science: With a Prelude in Rhymes and an Appendix of Songs*. Translated, with commentary, by Walter Kaufmann. New York: Random House, 1974.

———. "On Truth and Lies in a Nonmoral Sense." Unpublished essay, 1873.

———. *The Portable Nietzsche*. Edited by Walter Kaufmann. New York: Viking, 1954.

North, Gary, ed. *Foundations of Christian Scholarship: Essays in the Van Til Perspective*. Vallecito, CA: Ross House, 1976.

Ogden, Schubert M. *Christ without Myth: A Study Based on the Theology of Rudolf Bultmann*. New York: Harper and Brothers, 1961.

———. *Faith and Freedom: Toward a Theology of Liberation*. Nashville, TN: Abingdon Press, 1979.

———. *On Theology*. San Francisco: Harper and Row, 1986.

———. *The Reality of God and Other Essays*. New York: Harper and Row, 1966.

Oliphint, K. Scott. *Covenantal Apologetics*. Wheaton, IL: Crossway, 2013.

Orr, James. *Ritschlianism: Expository and Critical Essays*. London: Hodder and Stoughton, 1903.

Pache, René. *The Inspiration and Authority of Scripture*. Translated by Helen I. Needham. Chicago: Moody Press, 1969.

Paley, William. *Natural Theology*. Chillicothe, OH: DeWard Publishing, 2010.

———. *The Principles of Moral and Political Philosophy*. Foreword by D. L. Le Mahieu. Indianapolis: Liberty Fund, 2002.

Palmer, Donald. *Looking at Philosophy: The Unbearable Heaviness of Philosophy Made Lighter*. Mountain View, CA: Mayfield Publishing, 1994.

———. *Looking at Philosophy: The Unbearable Heaviness of Philosophy Made Lighter*. New York: McGraw-Hill, 2010.

Pannenberg, Wolfhart. *The Apostles' Creed in the Light of Today's Questions*. Translated by Margaret Kohl. London: SCM Press, 1972.

———. *The Apostles' Creed in Light of Today's Questions*. Translated by Margaret Kohl. Eugene, OR: Wipf and Stock, 2000.

———. *Jesus, God and Man*. Translated by Lewis L. Wilkins and Duane A. Priebe. Philadelphia: Westminster Press, 1977.

———, ed. *Revelation as History*. Translated by David Granskou and Edward Quinn. New York: Sheed and Ward, 1969.

———. *Systematic Theology*. Translated by Geoffrey W. Bromiley. 3 vols. Grand Rapids: Eerdmans, 1991–98.

———. *Theology and the Kingdom of God*. Edited by Richard John Neuhaus. Philadelphia: Westminster Press, 1969.

Pascal, Blaise. *Pensées and Other Writings*. New York: Oxford University Press, 2008.

Pears, David. *Ludwig Wittgenstein*. New York: Viking Press, 1969, 1970.

Pegis, Anton C., ed. *Introduction to St. Thomas Aquinas*. New York: Modern Library, 1948.

Peirce, Charles S. *Collected Papers of Charles Sanders Peirce*. Edited by Charles Hartshorne and Paul Weiss. 6 vols. Cambridge, MA: Harvard University Press, 1931–35.

———. "How to Make Our Ideas Clear." *Popular Science Monthly* 12 (January 1878): 286–302.

———. *Philosophical Writings of Peirce*. New York: Dover, 1955.

———. *Philosophical Writings of Peirce*. Edited by Justus Buchler. New York: Dover, 2011.

Pinnock, Clark H. *Biblical Revelation: The Foundation of Christian Theology*. Chicago: Moody Press, 1971.

Pinnock, Clark H., Richard Rice, John Sanders, William Hasker, and David Basinger. *The Openness of God*. Downers Grove, IL: InterVarsity Press, 1994.

Piper, John. *Desiring God*. Sisters, OR: Multnomah, 1986, 2003.

Placher, William. *Readings in the History of Christian Theology*. 2 vols. Philadelphia: Westminster Press, 1988.

Plantinga, Alvin. "Advice to Christian Philosophers." *Faith and Philosophy* 1 (October 1984): 1–19.

———. *God, Freedom, and Evil*. Grand Rapids: Eerdmans, 1974.

———. *God, Freedom, and Evil*. New York: Harper and Row, 1974.

———. *God, Freedom, and Evil*. Grand Rapids: Eerdmans, 1977.

———. *God and Other Minds: A Study of the Rational Justification of Belief in God*. Ithaca, NY: Cornell University Press, 1967.

———. *God and Other Minds: A Study of the Rational Justification of Belief in God*. Ithaca, NY: Cornell University Press, 1990.

———. *The Nature of Necessity*. Clarendon Library of Logic and Philosophy. Oxford: Clarendon, 1974.

———. "Reason and Belief in God." In *Faith and Rationality: Reason and Belief in God*, edited by Alvin Plantinga and Nicholas Wolterstorff, 16–93. Notre Dame, IN: University of Notre Dame Press, 1983.

———. *Warrant and Proper Function*. New York: Oxford University Press, 1993.

———. *Warranted Christian Belief*. New York: Oxford University Press, 2000.

———. *Warrant: The Current Debate*. New York: Oxford University Press, 1993.

———. *Where the Conflict Really Lies: Science, Religion, and Naturalism*. New York: Oxford University Press, 2011.

Plantinga, Alvin, and Nicholas Wolterstorff, eds. *Faith and Rationality: Reason and Belief in God*. Notre Dame, IN: University of Notre Dame Press, 1983.

———, eds. *Faith and Rationality: Reason and Belief in God*. Notre Dame, IN: University of Notre Dame Press, 1991.

Plato. *Plato: The Collected Dialogues*. Edited by Edith Hamilton and Huntington Cairns. Princeton, NJ: Princeton University Press, 1961.

Plotinus. *The Enneads: Abridged Edition*. Edited by John Dillon. Translated by Stephen McKenna. New York: Penguin Classics, 1991.

Pojman, Louis P. *Classics of Philosophy*. New York: Oxford University Press, 1998.

Polanyi, Michael. *Personal Knowledge: Towards a Post-Critical Philosophy*. Chicago: University of Chicago Press, 1958.

———. *Personal Knowledge: Towards a Post-Critical Philosophy*. Chicago: University of Chicago Press, 1974.

———. *Science, Faith and Society*. Riddle Memorial Lectures. London: Oxford University Press, 1946.

Pollock, John L. *Contemporary Theories of Knowledge*. Totowa, NJ: Rowman and Littlefield, 1986.

Popper, Karl R. *The Open Society and Its Enemies*. Vol. 2, *Hegel and Marx*. Princeton, NJ: Princeton University Press, 1966.

Poythress, Vern S. *Chance and the Sovereignty of God*. Wheaton, IL: Crossway, 2014.

———. *God-Centered Biblical Interpretation*. Phillipsburg, NJ: P&R Publishing, 1999.

———. *Inerrancy and the Gospels: A God-Centered Approach to the Challenges of Harmonization*. Wheaton, IL: Crossway, 2012.

———. *Inerrancy and Worldview: Answering Modern Challenges to the Bible*. Wheaton, IL: Crossway, 2012.

———. *In the Beginning Was the Word: Language: A God-Centered Approach*. Wheaton, IL: Crossway, 2009.

———. *Logic: A God-Centered Approach to the Foundation of Western Thought*. Wheaton, IL: Crossway, 2013.

———. "Modern Spiritual Gifts as Analogous to Apostolic Gifts." *JETS* 39, 1 (1996): 71–101.

———. *Philosophy, Science, and the Sovereignty of God*. Nutley, NJ: Presbyterian and Reformed, 1976.

———. *Philosophy, Science, and the Sovereignty of God*. Phillipsburg, NJ: P&R Publishing, 2004.

———. *Redeeming Philosophy: A God-Centered Approach to the Big Questions*. Wheaton, IL: Crossway, 2014.

———. *Redeeming Science: A God-Centered Approach*. Wheaton, IL: Crossway, 2006.

———. *Redeeming Sociology: A God-Centered Approach*. Wheaton, IL: Crossway, 2011.

———. "Reforming Ontology and Logic in the Light of the Trinity: An Application of Van Til's Idea of Analogy." *WTJ* 57, 1 (Spring 1995): 187–219.

———. *The Returning King: A Guide to the Book of Revelation*. Phillipsburg, NJ: P&R Publishing, 2000.

———. *Science and Hermeneutics: Implications of Scientific Method for Biblical Interpretation*. Grand Rapids: Zondervan, 1988.

———. *The Shadow of Christ in the Law of Moses*. Phillipsburg, NJ: P&R Publishing, 1995.

———. *Symphonic Theology: The Validity of Multiple Perspectives in Theology*. Phillipsburg, NJ: P&R Publishing, 2001.

———. *Understanding Dispensationalists*. Phillipsburg, NJ: P&R Publishing, 1993.

———. *What Are Spiritual Gifts?* Phillipsburg, NJ: P&R Publishing, 2010.

Poythress, Vern S., and Wayne A. Grudem. *The Gender-Neutral Bible Controversy: Muting the Masculinity of God's Words.* Nashville, TN: Broadman and Holman, 2000.

———. *The TNIV and the Gender-Neutral Bible Controversy.* Nashville, TN: Broadman and Holman, 2004.

Quine, Willard Van Orman. *From a Logical Point of View: Nine Logico-Philosophical Essays.* Cambridge, MA: Harvard University Press, 1953.

———. *From a Logical Point of View: Nine Logico-Philosophical Essays.* 2nd rev. ed. Cambridge, MA: Harvard University Press, 1961.

———. *From a Logical Point of View: Nine Logico-Philosophical Essays.* 2nd rev. ed. Cambridge, MA: Harvard University Press, 1980.

———. "Two Dogmas of Empiricism." *Philosophical Review* 60 (1951): 20–43.

Ramsey, Ian T. *Religious Language: An Empirical Placing of Theological Phrases.* New York: Macmillan, 1957.

Reese, William L. *Dictionary of Philosophy and Religion.* Atlantic Highlands, NJ: Humanities Press, 1980, 1996.

Reid, Thomas. *Thomas Reid's Inquiry and Essays.* Long Beach, CA: Lexico Publishing, 2012.

Reno, R. R. "The Radical Orthodoxy Project." *First Things* 100 (February 2000): 37–44.

Rice, Richard. *God's Foreknowledge and Man's Free Will.* Grand Rapids: Baker/Bethany House, 1994.

Ridderbos, Herman N. *The Authority of the New Testament Scriptures.* Edited by J. M. Kik. Translated by H. de Jongste. Philadelphia: Presbyterian and Reformed, 1963.

———. *The Coming of the Kingdom.* Edited by Raymond O. Zorn. Translated by H. de Jongste. Philadelphia: Presbyterian and Reformed, 1962.

———. *Paul: An Outline of His Theology.* Translated by John Richard de Witt. Grand Rapids: Eerdmans, 1975.

Ritschl, Albrecht. *The Christian Doctrine of Justification and Reconciliation.* Edited and translated by H. R. Mackintosh and A. B. Macaulay. Edinburgh: T&T Clark, 1900.

———. *The Christian Doctrine of Justification and Reconciliation.* Edited and translated by H. R. Mackintosh and A. B. Macaulay. Whitefish, MT: Kessinger Publishing, 2006.

Robinson, John A. T. *Honest to God.* Philadelphia: Westminster Press, 1963.

———. *Redating the New Testament.* Eugene, OR: Wipf and Stock, 1976.

Rosenstock-Huessy, Eugen. *I Am an Impure Thinker.* Essex, VT: Argo Books, 2001.

———. *The Origin of Speech.* Essex, VT: Argo Books, 1981.

———. *Out of Revolution: The Autobiography of a Western Man*. Essex, VT: Argo Books, 1969.

———. *Speech and Reality*. Eugene, OR: Wipf and Stock, 2013.

Ross, James B., and Mary M. McLaughlin, eds. *The Portable Medieval Reader*. London: Penguin, 1977.

Russell, Bertrand. *The Basic Writings of Bertrand Russell*. Edited by Robert E. Egner and Lester E. Denonn. New York: Routledge, 2009.

———. "On Denoting." *Mind* 14 (1905): 479–93.

———. *The Problems of Philosophy*. Hollywood, FL: Simon and Brown, 2013.

———. *War Crimes in Vietnam*. London: Monthly Review Press, 1966.

———. *Why I Am Not a Christian and Other Essays on Related Subjects*. New York: Touchstone, 1967.

Russell, Bertrand, and Alfred North Whitehead. *Principia Mathematica*. 3 vols. Cambridge: Cambridge University Press, 1910–13.

———. *Principia Mathematica*. 2 vols. Seaside, OR: Rough Draft Printing, 2011.

Ryle, Gilbert. *The Concept of Mind*. Chicago: University of Chicago Press, 1949.

———. *The Concept of Mind*. New York: Barnes and Noble, 1949.

———. *The Concept of Mind*. Chicago: University of Chicago Press, 2000.

Sartre, Jean-Paul. *Being and Nothingness: An Essay on Phenomenological Ontology*. Translated by Hazel Estella Barnes. New York: Washington Square Press, 1984.

———. *Being and Nothingness: An Essay on Phenomenological Ontology*. Translated by Hazel Estella Barnes. New York: Washington Square Press, 1993.

———. *Critique of Dialectical Reason*. Vol. 1, *Theory of Practical Ensembles*. Edited by Jonathan Rée. Translated by Alan Sheridan. New ed. London: Verso, 2004.

———. *Critique of Dialectical Reason*. Vol. 2 (unfinished), *The Intelligibility of History*. Edited by Arlette Elkaïm-Sartre. Translated by Quintin Hoare. New ed. London: Verso, 2004.

———. *Existentialism Is a Humanism*. Translated by Carol Macomber. New Haven, CT: Yale University Press, 2007.

———. *No Exit (Huis Clos) and The Flies (Les Mouches)*. Translated by Stuart Gilbert. New York: Alfred A. Knopf, 1948.

———. *The Transcendence of the Ego: An Existentialist Theory of Consciousness*. Translated by Forest Williams and Robert Kirkpatrick. New York: Noonday Press, 1957.

Saussure, Ferdinand de. *Course in General Linguistics*. Edited by Charles Bally and Albert Sechehaye. Translated by Roy Harris. Chicago: Open Court, 1998.

Schaeffer, Francis A. *The God Who Is There*. Chicago: InterVarsity Press, 1968.

———. *How Shall We Then Live?* Wheaton, IL: Crossway, 2005.

Schaff, Philip, et al., eds. *Ante-Nicene Fathers*. 10 vols. Peabody, MA: Hendrickson Publishers, 1996.

———, eds. *Nicene and Post-Nicene Fathers*. 14 vols. Peabody, MA: Hendrickson Publishers, 1996.

Schleiermacher, Friedrich. *The Christian Faith*. Translated by H. R. Mackintosh and J. S. Stewart. Edinburgh: T&T Clark, 1928.

———. *The Christian Faith*. Edited by H. R. Mackintosh and J. S. Stewart. Berkeley, CA: Apocryphile Press, 2011.

———. *On Religion: Speeches to Its Cultured Despisers*. Translated by John Oman. New York: Harper and Brothers, 1958.

———. *On Religion: Speeches to Its Cultured Despisers*. Edited by Richard Crouter. Cambridge Texts in the History of Philosophy. Cambridge: Cambridge University Press, 1996.

Schlossberg, Herbert. *Idols for Destruction*. Nashville, TN: Thomas Nelson, 1983.

Schmitt, Richard. "Husserl, Edmund." In *The Encyclopedia of Philosophy*, edited by Paul Edwards. New York: Macmillan/Free Press, 1967.

Schopenhauer, Arthur. *The World as Will and Representation*. Translated by E. F. J. Payne. 2 vols. Mineola, NY: Dover, 1966.

Schroedinger, Andrew B. *Readings in Medieval Philosophy*. New York: Oxford University Press, 1996.

Schweitzer, Albert. *The Quest of the Historical Jesus: A Critical Study of Its Progress from Reimarus to Wrede*. Translated by W. Montgomery. London: A. and C. Black, 1910.

Searle, John R. *Speech Acts: An Essay in the Philosophy of Language*. Cambridge: Cambridge University Press, 1969.

Singer, C. Gregg. *From Rationalism to Irrationality*. Phillipsburg, NJ: Presbyterian and Reformed, 1979.

Sire, James W. *Habits of the Mind*. Downers Grove, IL: InterVarsity Press, 2000.

———. *The Universe Next Door: A Basic World View Catalogue*. Downers Grove, IL: InterVarsity Press, 1975.

Smith, James K. A. *Desiring the Kingdom: Worship, Worldview, and Cultural Formation*. Grand Rapids: Baker, 2009.

———. *Imagining the Kingdom: How Worship Works*. Grand Rapids: Baker, 2013.

———. *Introducing Radical Orthodoxy: Mapping a Post-Secular Theology*. Grand Rapids: Baker, 2004.

Spinoza, Baruch (Benedict de Spinoza). *Selections*. New York: Scribner's, 1930.

———. *Spinoza: Complete Works*. Edited by Michael L. Morgan. Translated by Samuel Shirley. Indianapolis: Hackett Publishing, 2002.

———. *Works of Spinoza*. 2 vols. New York: Dover, 1951.

Sproul, R. C. *If There's a God, Why Are There Atheists?* Wheaton, IL: Tyndale, 1988.

Sproul, R. C., John H. Gerstner, and Arthur Lindsley. *Classical Apologetics: A Rational Defense of the Christian Faith and a Critique of Presuppositional Apologetics*. Grand Rapids: Zondervan, 1984.

Steiner, George. *Martin Heidegger*. New York: Viking, 1979.

Stevenson, Charles L. *Ethics and Language*. New Haven, CT: Yale University Press, 1944.

Stonehouse, Ned Bernard. *J. Gresham Machen: A Biographical Memoir*. Edinburgh: Banner of Truth, 1987.

Stonehouse, Ned Bernard, and Paul Woolley, eds. *The Infallible Word*. 3rd rev. ed. Philadelphia: Presbyterian and Reformed, 1967.

Strawson, Peter F. *Individuals: An Essay in Descriptive Metaphysics*. London: Methuen, 1959.

———. *Individuals: An Essay in Descriptive Metaphysics*. London: Routledge, 1959.

———. *An Introduction to Logical Theory*. London: Methuen, 1952.

———. "On Referring." *Mind*, n.s., 59, 235 (July 1950): 320–44.

Strimple, Robert. "Roman Catholic Theology Today." In *Roman Catholicism*, edited by John Armstrong, 85–117. Chicago: Moody Press, 1994.

Stumpf, Samuel Enoch, and James Fieser. *Philosophy: History and Readings*. 8th ed. New York: McGraw-Hill, 2011.

———. *Socrates to Sartre and Beyond: A History of Philosophy*. Boston: McGraw-Hill, 2003.

Swinburne, Richard. *The Coherence of Theism*. Rev. ed. Clarendon Library of Logic and Philosophy. New York: Oxford University Press, 1993.

———. *The Existence of God*. 2nd ed. New York: Oxford University Press, 2004.

Talisse, Robert B., and Scott Akin, eds. *The Pragmatism Reader: From Peirce to the Present*. Princeton, NJ: Princeton University Press, 2011.

Tarnas, Richard. *The Passion of the Western Mind: Understanding the Ideas That Have Shaped Our World* (NY: Ballantine Books, 1993).

Thilly, Frank, and Ledger Wood. *A History of Philosophy*. New York: Henry Holt, 1957.

Thiselton, Anthony C. *The Two Horizons*. Grand Rapids: Eerdmans, 1980.

Tillich, Paul. *The Courage to Be*. New Haven, CT, and London: Yale University Press, 1952.

———. *The Courage to Be*. New Haven, CT: Yale University Press, 2000.

———. *Dynamics of Faith*. New York: Harper and Brothers, 1957.

———. *Dynamics of Faith*. New York: HarperOne, 2009.

———. *Systematic Theology*. 3 vols. Chicago: University of Chicago Press, 1951–63.

———. *Systematic Theology*. 3 vols. Chicago: University of Chicago Press, 1973.

Torrey, R. A., and Charles Feinberg, eds. *The Fundamentals*. Grand Rapids: Kregel, 1990.

Troost, Andree. *What Is Reformational Philosophy?* Grand Rapids: Paideia Press, 2012.

Turretin, Francis. *Institutes of Elenctic Theology*. Edited by James T. Dennison Jr. Translated by George Musgrave Giger. 3 vols. Phillipsburg, NJ: P&R Publishing, 1992–1997.

Urmson, J. O. *Philosophical Analysis: Its Development between the Two World Wars*. New York: Oxford University Press, 1956.

Van Buren, Paul M. *The Edges of Language*. New York: Macmillan, 1972.

Van Fraassen, Bas C. "Presupposition, Implication, and Self-Reference." *Journal of Philosophy* 65, 5 (1968): 136–52.

Vanhoozer, Kevin J. *The Drama of Doctrine: A Canonical-Linguistic Approach to Christian Doctrine*. Louisville, KY: Westminster John Knox Press, 2005.

———. *First Theology: God, Scripture, and Hermeneutics*. Downers Grove, IL: IVP Academic, 2002.

———. *Is There a Meaning in This Text?* Grand Rapids: Zondervan, 2009.

———. *Remythologizing Theology: Divine Action, Passion, and Authorship*. Cambridge Studies in Christian Doctrine. Cambridge: Cambridge University Press, 2010.

———. *Remythologizing Theology: Divine Action, Passion, and Authorship*. Cambridge Studies in Christian Doctrine. Cambridge: Cambridge University Press, 2012.

Van Riessen, H. *Nietzsche*. Philadelphia: Presbyterian and Reformed, 1960.

Van Til, Cornelius. *Christian Apologetics*. Phillipsburg, NJ: P&R Publishing, 2003.

———. *Christianity and Barthianism*. Philadelphia: Presbyterian and Reformed, 1962.

———. *Christianity and Barthianism*. Phillipsburg, NJ: P&R Publishing, 2004.

———. *A Christian Theory of Knowledge*. Nutley, NJ: Presbyterian and Reformed, 1969.

———. *The Defense of the Faith*. Philadelphia: Presbyterian and Reformed, 1963.

———. *The Defense of the Faith*. Edited by K. Scott Oliphint. 4th ed. Phillipsburg, NJ: P&R Publishing, 2008.

———. *The Doctrine of Scripture*. Ripon, CA: Den Dulk Foundation, 1967.

———. *Essays on Christian Education*. Nutley, NJ: Presbyterian and Reformed, 1971, 1974.

———. *An Introduction to Systematic Theology*. Nutley, NJ: Presbyterian and Reformed, 1974.

———. *An Introduction to Systematic Theology*. Phillipsburg, NJ: P&R Publishing, 2007.

———. *The New Modernism*. Philadelphia: Presbyterian and Reformed, 1946.

———. *The New Modernism*. Nutley, NJ: Presbyterian and Reformed, 1973.

———. *A Survey of Christian Epistemology*. Philadelphia: Den Dulk Foundation, 1969.

———. *The Triumph of Grace: The Heidelberg Catechism*. Philadelphia: Westminster Theological Seminary, 1958.

———. *Who Do You Say That I Am?* Nutley, NJ: Presbyterian and Reformed, 1975.

———. *Why I Believe in God*. Philadelphia: Orthodox Presbyterian Church, n.d.

———. *Why I Believe in God*. Chestnut Hill, PA: Westminster Theological Seminary, 1976.

Ward, Graham, ed. *The Postmodern God: A Theological Reader*. Oxford: Blackwell, 2005.

Ware, Bruce A. *God's Lesser Glory: The Diminished God of Open Theism*. Wheaton, IL: Crossway, 2000.

Warfield, Benjamin Breckinridge. *The Inspiration and Authority of the Bible*. Edited by S. G. Craig. Philadelphia: Presbyterian and Reformed, 1948.

Warner, Rex, ed. *The Greek Philosophers*. New York: Mentor, 1958, 1986.

Webb, Stephen H. *Re-Figuring Theology: The Rhetoric of Karl Barth*. New York: State University of New York Press, 1991.

Wells, D. F., and J. D. Woodbridge, eds. *The Evangelicals: What They Believe, Who They Are, Where They Are Changing*. Nashville, TN: Abingdon Press, 1975.

Welty, Greg. "Theistic Conceptual Realism: The Case for Interpreting Abstract Objects as Divine Ideas." D.Phil. dissertation (2006), University of Oxford. http://goo.gl/nrCP5o.

———. "Theistic Conceptual Realism." In Paul Gould, ed. *Beyond the Control of God? Six Views on the Problem of God and Abstract Objects*. London: Bloomsbury Academic, 2014. http://goo.gl/0Ahgdl.

Wenham, John William. *Christ and the Bible*. Downers Grove, IL: InterVarsity Press, 1973.

Wheatley, Jon. *Prolegomena to Philosophy*. Belmont, CA: Wadsworth, 1970.

White, Morton, ed. *The Age of Analysis*. New York: Meridian Books, 1955, 1983.

Whitehead, Alfred North. *Process and Reality: An Essay in Cosmology*. New York: Macmillan, 1929.

———. *Process and Reality: An Essay in Cosmology*. Edited by David Ray Griffin and Donald W. Sherbourne. Corrected ed. New York: Free Press, 1979.

———. *Religion in the Making: Lowell Lectures, 1926*. Cambridge: Cambridge University Press, 2011.

———. *Science and the Modern World*. New York: Free Press, 1925.

———. *Science and the Modern World: Lowell Lectures, 1925*. New York: Free Press, 1997.

Wild, John Daniel. *Existence and the World of Freedom*. Englewood Cliffs, NJ: Prentice-Hall, 1965.

Windelband, Wilhelm. *A History of Philosophy I*. New York: Harper, 1958.

Wittgenstein, Ludwig. "Lecture on Ethics." *Philosophical Review* 74, 1 (January 1965): 3–12.

———. *Lectures and Conversations on Aesthetics, Psychology, and Religious Belief*. Edited by Cyril Barrett. Compiled from notes by Yorick Smythies, Rush Rhees, and James Taylor. Oxford: Blackwell, 1966.

———. *Lectures and Conversations on Aesthetics, Psychology, and Religious Belief*. Edited by Cyril Barrett. Compiled from notes by Yorick Smythies, Rush Rhees, and James Taylor. Berkeley, CA: University of California Press, 2007.

———. *On Certainty*. Translated by Denis Paul and G. E. M. Anscombe. New York: Harper and Row, 1972.

———. *Philosophical Investigations*. Translated by G. E. M. Anscombe. New York: Macmillan, 1968.

———. *Philosophical Investigations*. Translated by G. E. M. Anscombe, P. M. S. Hacker, and Joachim Schulte. Rev. 4th ed. Oxford: Blackwell, 2009.

———. *Preliminary Studies for the "Philosophical Investigation": Generally Known as the Blue and Brown Books*. New York: Harper, 1964.

———. *Preliminary Studies for the "Philosophical Investigation": Generally Known as the Blue and Brown Books*. 2nd ed. Harper Torchbooks. New York: Harper and Row, 1965.

———. *Tractatus Logico-Philosophicus*. London: Routledge and Kegan Paul, 1963.

———. *Tractatus Logico-Philosophicus*. New York: Dover, 1998.

———. *Tractatus Logico-Philosophicus*. London: Empire Books, 2011.

Wolterstorff, Nicholas. *Art in Action: Toward a Christian Aesthetic*. Grand Rapids: Eerdmans, 1980.

———. *Divine Discourse: Philosophical Reflections on the Claim That God Speaks*. Cambridge: Cambridge University Press, 1995.

———. *Lament for a Son*. Grand Rapids: Eerdmans, 1987.

———. *On Universals: An Essay in Ontology*. Chicago: University of Chicago Press, 1970.

———. *Reason within the Bounds of Religion*. Grand Rapids: Eerdmans, 1976.

———. *Reason within the Bounds of Religion*. 2nd ed. Grand Rapids: Eerdmans, 1984.

———. *Reason within the Bounds of Religion*. 2nd ed. Grand Rapids: Eerdmans, 1988.

———. *Thomas Reid and the Story of Epistemology*. Cambridge: Cambridge University Press, 2001.

———. *Works and Worlds of Art*. Oxford: Clarendon, 1980.

Wood, W. Jay. *Epistemology: Becoming Intellectually Virtuous*. Downers Grove, IL: InterVarsity Press, 1998.

Wright, G. Ernest. *God Who Acts*. London: SCM Press, 1964.

Yolton, John W. *Perception & Reality: A History from Descartes to Kant*. Ithaca, NY: Cornell University Press, 1996.

Young, Edward J. *Thy Word Is Truth*. Grand Rapids: Eerdmans, 1957.

Young, William. *Hegel's Dialectical Method*. Nutley, NJ: Craig Press, 1972.

Zuidema, S. U. *Kierkegaard*. Philadelphia: Presbyterian and Reformed, 1960.

———. *Sartre*. Philadelphia: Presbyterian and Reformed, 1960.

ONLINE RESOURCES

Note: When possible, full bibliographical data has been provided for each entry.

Alston, William. *Perceiving God: The Epistemology of Religious Experience*. Ithaca, NY: Cornell University Press, 1993. Available at http://www.questia.com/library/103762715/perceiving-god-the-epistemology-of-religious-experience. Requires subscription for full text.

Anderson, James N. Analogical Thoughts. http://www.proginosko.com/.

Aquinas, Thomas. *On Being and Essence*. Available at http://faculty.fordham.edu/klima/Blackwell-proofs/MP_C30.pdf.

Austin, J. L. *How to Do Things with Words*. Cambridge, MA: Harvard University Press, 1975. Available at http://www.ling.upenn.edu/~rnoyer/courses/103/Austin.pdf.

Ayer, A. J. *Language, Truth and Logic*. New York: Dover, 1952. Available at http://archive.org/stream/AlfredAyer/LanguageTruthAndLogic_djvu.txt.

Barth, Karl. The Digital Karl Barth Library. http://solomon.dkbl.alexanderstreet.com/. Includes Barth's *Church Dogmatics* complete in both German and English, with other writings. Requires subscription.

Berkeley, George. *Three Dialogues between Hylas and Philonous*. Available at http://www.sacred-texts.com/phi/berkeley/three.txt.

———. *A Treatise concerning the Principles of Human Knowledge*. Available at http://www.gutenberg.org/catalog/world/readfile?fk_files=1983609&pageno=1.

Bonhoeffer, Dietrich. Dietrich Bonhoeffer Reading Room. http://www.tyndale.ca/seminary/mtsmodular/reading-rooms/theology/bonhoeffer. Most of these online versions are incomplete.

———. "Who Am I?" 1944. Available at http://neilwillard.com/2015/04/09/dietrich-bonhoeffer-who-am-i/.

Boyd, Gregory. "What Is Open Theism?" Video. http://www.youtube.com/watch?v=gApXDGjyksw.

Brunner, Emil. *Dogmatics I: The Christian Doctrine of God*. Translated by Olive Wyon. Philadelphia: Westminster Press, 1950. Available at http://archive.org/details/dogmatics01brun.

Bultmann, Rudolf. *History and Eschatology: The Presence of Eternity*. 1954–55 Gifford Lectures. Harper, 1962. Available at http://www.giffordlectures.org/books/history-and-eschatology.

———. "The Mythological Element in the Message of the New Testament and the Problem of its Re-interpretation" (also known as "New Testament and Mythology"). In *Kerygma and Myth: A Theological Debate*, edited by Hans Werner Bartsch. Translated by Reginald H. Fuller. London: SPCK, 1953. Available at http://www.sunysuffolk.edu/About/search.asp?cx=018295863947272962766%3An8erqd-hxfk&cof=FORID%3A9&ie=UTF-8&q=bultmann&x=0&y=0.

Bultmann, Rudolf, Ernst Lohmeyer, Julius Schniewind, Helmut Thielicke, and Austin Farrer. *Kerygma and Myth: A Theological Debate*. Edited by Hans Werner Bartsch. Translated by Reginald H. Fuller. London: SPCK, 1953. Available at http://www.sunysuffolk.edu/About/search.asp?cx=018295863947272962766%3An8erqd-hxfk&cof=FORID%3A9&ie=UTF-8&q=bultmann&x=0&y=0.

Burnet, John, trans. Fragments of Heraclitus. Available at http://en.wikisource.org/wiki/Fragments_of_Heraclitus.

Butler, Joseph. *Analogy of Religion*. Philadelphia: J. B. Lippincott, 1865. Available at http://www.ccel.org/ccel/butler/analogy.html.

Clark, Gordon H. A number of Clark's works and works about Clark are available at http://www.trinityfoundation.org/.

Clifford, W. K. "The Ethics of Belief." Originally published 1877. Now available as *The Ethics of Belief and Other Essays*. New York: Prometheus

Books, 1999. Available at http://infidels.org/library/historical/w_k_clifford/ethics_of_belief.html.

Cristaudo, Wayne. "Eugen Rosenstock-Huessy." *Stanford Encyclopedia of Philosophy* (June 14, 2012). http://plato.stanford.edu/entries/rosenstock-huessy/.

Descartes, René. *Discourse on the Method of Rightly Conducting One's Reason and of Seeking Truth in the Sciences*. Available at http://www.literature.org/authors/descartes-rene/reason-discourse/.

———. *Meditations on First Philosophy*. Available at http://faculty.ycp.edu/~dweiss/phl321_epistemology/descartes%20meditations.pdf.

Dewey, John. The Online Books Page. Numerous books by John Dewey. http://onlinebooks.library.upenn.edu/webbin/book/lookupname?key=Dewey%2C%20John%2C%201859-1952.

Dogmatic Definition of the Council of Chalcedon. Available at http://www.ewtn.com/faith/teachings/incac2.htm.

Dooyeweerd, Herman. A number of his works are published online. See the list at http://www.allofliferedeemed.co.uk/dooyeweerd.htm. See also http://reformatorische.blogspot.com/2009/11/herman-dooyeweerd.html. My critique of him can be found at http://www.frame-poythress.org/wp-content/uploads/2012/08/FrameJohnAmsterdamPhilosophy1972.pdf, developed further at http://www.frame-poythress.org/dooyeweerd-and-the-word-of-god/.

Dorrien, Gary. "The Origins of Postliberalism." *Christian Century* (July 4–11, 2001): 16–21. Available at http://thinkerkang.blogspot.com/2014/04/the-origins-of-postliberalism-by-gary.html.

Edwards, Jonathan. *Works of Jonathan Edwards*. 2 vols. Available at http://www.ccel.org/ccel/edwards/works1.html; http://www.ccel.org/ccel/edwards/works2.html.

Feuerbach, Ludwig. Ludwig Feuerbach Archive. His works and significant essays about him are available at http://www.marxists.org/reference/archive/feuerbach/.

Frame, John M. *The Academic Captivity of Theology*. Lakeland, FL: Whitefield Publishers, 2012. Available at http://whitefieldmedia.com/product/the-academic-captivity-of-theology/.

———. *The Amsterdam Philosophy: A Preliminary Critique*. Phillipsburg, NJ: Pilgrim Press, 1972. Available at http://www.frame-poythress.org/wp-content/uploads/2012/08/FrameJohnAmsterdamPhilosophy1972.pdf.

———. "Certainty." In *New Dictionary of Christian Apologetics*, edited by W. C. Campbell-Jack and Gavin J. McGrath, 141–45. Consulting ed. C. Stephen Evans. Downers Grove, IL: InterVarsity Press, 2006. Available at http://www.frame-poythress.org/certainty/.

———. "Infinite Series." In *New Dictionary of Christian Apologetics*, edited by W. C. Campbell-Jack and Gavin J. McGrath, 353–54. Consulting ed. C. Stephen Evans. Downers Grove, IL: InterVarsity Press, 2006. Available at http://www.frame-poythress.org/infinite-series/.

———. "Open Theism and Divine Foreknowledge." In *Bound Only Once*, edited by Douglas Wilson, 83–94. Moscow, ID: Canon Press, 2001. Available at http://www.frame-poythress.org/open-theism-and-divine-foreknowledge/.

———. Review of *The Nature of Doctrine*, by George A. Lindbeck. *Presbyterian Journal* 43 (February 27, 1985): 11–12. Available at http://www.frame-poythress.org/review-of-lindbecks-the-nature-of-doctrine/.

Frege, Gottlob. "On Sense and Reference." Translated by Max Black. Available at http://en.wikisource.org/wiki/On_Sense_and_Reference.

Gettier, Edmund. "Is Justified True Belief Knowledge?" *Analysis* 23 (1966): 121–23. Available at http://philosophyfaculty.ucsd.edu/faculty/rarneson/Courses/gettierphilreading.pdf.

Graham, Daniel W. "Heraclitus." *Internet Encyclopedia of Philosophy*. http://www.utm.edu/research/iep/h/heraclit.htm.

Harnack, Adolf von. *Works*. Includes *What Is Christianity?* and his six-volume *History of Dogma*. Available at http://www.ccel.org/ccel/harnack.

"Hartford Affirmation." Available at http://www.philosophy-religion.org/handouts/pdfs/Hartford-Affirmation.pdf.

Hegel, G. W. F. His main works are available at http://www.hegel.net/en/etexts.htm and http://www.hegel.org/links.html#texts.

Heidegger, Martin. His shorter articles and letters are available at http://archive.org/search.php?query=creator%3A%22Martin%20Heidegger%22.

Helm, Paul. Articles on many subjects are available at http://paulhelmsdeep.blogspot.com/.

Heraclitus. Fragments of Heraclitus are available at http://en.wikisource.org/wiki/Fragments_of_Heraclitus.

Herrmann, Wilhelm. *The Communion of the Christian with God*. Translated by J. Sandys Stanyon. Revised by R. W. Stewart. London: Williams & Norgate and New York: G. P. Putnam's Sons, 1906. Available at http://archive.org/details/communionofchris00herrrich.

Hobbes, Thomas. *The Leviathan*. Available at http://oregonstate.edu/instruct/phl302/texts/hobbes/leviathan-contents.html.

Hodanbosi, Carol. "Pascal's Principle and Hydraulics." National Aeronautics and Space Administration. http://www.grc.nasa.gov/WWW/k-12/WindTunnel/Activities/Pascals_principle.html.

Hume, David. *Dialogues concerning Natural Religion*. Available at http://latourgifford2013.wikispaces.com/Hume%27s+Dialogues+Concerning+Natural+Religion.

———. *An Enquiry concerning Human Understanding*. Available at http://ebooks.adelaide.edu.au/h/hume/david/h92e/index.html.

———. *An Enquiry concerning the Principles of Morals*. Available at http://www.gutenberg.org/files/4320/4320-h/4320-h.htm.

———. *A Treatise of Human Nature*. Available at http://www.gutenberg.org/files/4705/4705-h/4705-h.htm.

Husserl, Edmund. Online Texts. http://www.husserlpage.com/hus_online.html.

Internet Encyclopedia of Philosophy. http://www.iep.utm.edu.

James, William. The Online Books Page. Numerous books by William James. http://onlinebooks.library.upenn.edu/webbin/book/lookupname?key=James%2C%20William%2C%201842-1910.

———. *Pragmatism: A New Name for Some Old Ways of Thinking*. Available at http://www.gutenberg.org/ebooks/5116.

Kant, Immanuel. Kant on the Web. English translations of many of Kant's works are available at http://staffweb.hkbu.edu.hk/ppp/K2texts.html; http://ebooks.adelaide.edu.au/k/kant/immanuel/.

Kierkegaard, Søren. *Attack upon Christendom*. Translated, with an introduction, by Walter Lowrie. Princeton, NJ: Princeton University Press, 1946. Available at http://www.christianebooks.com/pdf_files/kierkegaard-satta00kier.pdf.

———. *Concluding Unscientific Postscript*. Edited and translated by Alastair Hannay. Cambridge: Cambridge University Press, 2009. Available at http://www.clas.ufl.edu/users/burt/KierkegaardConcludingUnscientificPostscript.pdf.

———. *Either/Or*. Edited and translated by Howard V. Hong and Edna H. Hong. Princeton, NJ: Princeton University Press, 1987. Available at http://sqapo.com/CompleteText-Kierkegaard-EitherOr.htm.

———. *Fear and Trembling*. Translated by Walter Lowrie. Princeton, NJ: Princeton University Press, 1941. Available at http://sqapo.com/CompleteText-Kierkegaard-FearandTrembling.htm.

———. *Philosophical Fragments*. Available at http://pol-ts.com/Research_files/Source%20Material/Kierkegaard/Philosophical%20Fragments.pdf.

———. Selections from the writings of Kierkegaard, including *Fear and Trembling*. Available at http://www.ccel.org/ccel/kierkegaard/selections.

———. *The Sickness unto Death*. Princeton, NJ: Princeton University Press, 1941. Available at http://www.naturalthinker.net/trl/texts/Kierkegaard,Soren/TheSicknessUntoDeath.pdf.

———. *Works of Love*. Translated by Howard and Edna Hong. New York: Harper and Row, 1964. Pages 58–98 only (out of 378 pages). Available at http://moe.machighway.com/~cliffor1/Site/EXSupplementalReadings_files/kierkegaard_works.pdf.

Kuhn, Thomas S. *The Structure of Scientific Revolutions*. 3rd ed. Chicago: University of Chicago Press, 1996. Available at http://moodle.eosmith.org/pluginfile.php/3436/mod_resource/content/1/The%20Structure%20OF%20Scientific%20Revolutions%203rd%20ed%20-%20Thomas%20Kuhn.pdf.

Kuyper, Abraham. Abraham Kuyper Translation Society. http://www.acton.org/research/kuyper-translation-project.

———. Six books by Kuyper, including his *Lectures on Calvinism* (the Stone Lectures), are available at http://www.ccel.org/ccel/kuyper. See also the Kuyper Digital Library at http://kuyper.ptsem.edu/. It contains most of his published works along with an archive of unpublished writings.

Leibniz, G. W. *Theodicy* and *Monadology*. Available at http://www.gutenberg.org/ebooks/author/7168.

Leithart, Peter J. "The Relevance of Eugen Rosenstock-Huessy." *First Things*, June 28, 2007. Available at http://www.firstthings.com/onthesquare/2007/06/the-relevance-of-eugen-rosenst.

Lessing, G. E. *The Dramatic Works of G. E. Lessing*. Edited by Ernest Bell. London: George Bell and Sons, 1878. Available at http://www.gutenberg.org/files/33435/33435-h/33435-h.htm.

———. "On the Proof of the Spirit and of Power." In *Lessing's Theological Writings*, edited by Henry Chadwick. Stanford, CA: Stanford University Press, 1956. Available at http://faculty.tcu.edu/grant/hhit/Lessing.pdf.

Lewis, C. S. The C. S. Lewis Reading Room. Articles by and about Lewis. http://www.tyndale.ca/seminary/mtsmodular/reading-rooms/theology/lewis.

———. *Mere Christianity*. London: Fontana, 1952. Available at http://lib.ru/LEWISCL/mere_engl.txt.

Locke, John. *An Essay concerning Human Understanding*. Available at http://oregonstate.edu/instruct/phl302/texts/locke/locke1/Essay_contents.html.

———. *The Works of John Locke in Nine Volumes*. 12th ed. Vol. 6, *The Reasonableness of Christianity*. London: Rivington, 1824. Available at http://oll.libertyfund.org/?option=com_staticxt&staticfile=show.php%3Ftitle=1438&Itemid=27.

———. *The Works of John Locke in Ten Volumes*. New ed. Vol. 5, *Two Treatises of Government*. London: Printed for Thomas Tegg, 1823. Available at http://www.efm.bris.ac.uk/het/locke/government.pdf.

Luther, Martin. Many of Luther's and Calvin's writings (including Calvin's *Institutes* and *Commentaries*) are available at http://www.ccel.org.

MacIntyre, Alasdair C. "Prologue" to *After Virtue: A Study in Moral Theology*. 3rd ed. Notre Dame, IN: University of Notre Dame Press, 2007. Available at http://www3.undpress.nd.edu/excerpts/P01162-ex.pdf.

Marx, Karl. Marx/Engels Library. Marx's writings are available at http://www.marxists.org/archive/marx/works/.

Meek, Esther Lightcap. *Loving to Know: Introducing Covenant Epistemology*. Eugene, OR: Wipf and Stock, 2011. Synopsis available at http://www.longingtoknow.com/loving-to-know-l2k.html.

———. Various resources are available on her website, http://www.longingtoknow.com/. Conversations with others on *Longing to Know* are available at http://www.missouriwestern.edu/orgs/polanyi/TAD%20WEB%20ARCHIVE/TAD31-3/TAD31-3-fnl-pg29-44-pdf. Her blog is available at http://www.longingtoknow.com/blog.

Milbank, John, et al. *Radical Orthodoxy: Theology, Philosophy, Politics*. Online journal, with many articles on Radical Orthodoxy. http://journal.radicalorthodoxy.org/index.php/ROTPP. See also Radical Orthodoxy Online. http://www.calvin.edu/~jks4/ro/.

Moltmann, Jürgen. *Theology of Hope: On the Ground and the Implications of a Christian Eschatology*. New York: Harper and Row, 1967. Concluding chapter available at http://www.pubtheo.com/page.asp?pid=1036.

Moore, G. E. "A Defence of Common Sense." In *Contemporary British Philosophy*, edited by J. H. Muirhead. 2nd ser. 1925. Reprinted in G. E. Moore, *Philosophical Papers*, 32–45. London: George Allen & Unwin, 1959. Available at http://www.ditext.com/moore/common-sense.html.

———. *Principia Ethica*. Amherst, NY: Prometheus Books, 1988. Available at http://fair-use.org/g-e-moore/principia-ethica/.

———. "Proof of an External World." In *Philosophical Papers*, 126–48. New York: Collier Books, 1962. Available at http://www.hist-analytic.com/MooreExternalWorld.pdf.

———. "The Refutation of Idealism." *Mind*, n.s., 12, 48 (October 1903): 433–45. Available at http://www.ditext.com/moore/refute.html.

Nietzsche, Friedrich. *The Complete Works of Friedrich Nietzsche*. Edited by Oscar Levy. Vol. 10, *The Joyful Wisdom*. New York: Macmillan, 1924. Available at http://www.archive.org/stream/completenietasch10nietuoft/completenietasch10nietuoft_djvu.txt.

———. *A Contemporary Nietzsche Reader*. Available at http://nietzsche.holtof.com/reader/index.html. Additional Nietzsche texts are available at http://nietzsche.holtof.com/.

———. The Online Books Page. Numerous books by Friedrich Wilhelm Nietzsche. http://onlinebooks.library.upenn.edu/webbin/book/search?amode=start&author=Nietzsche%2C%20Friedrich%20Wilhelm%2C%201844-1900.

Olson, Roger E. "Back to the Bible (Almost): Why Yale's Postliberal Theologians Deserve an Evangelical Hearing." *Christianity Today* 40, 6 (May 20, 1996). Available at http://www.christianitytoday.com/ct/1996/may20/6t6031.html. Requires subscription to read full article.

Paley, William. *Natural Theology*. Available at http://naturaltheology.us/table-of-contents/209.html.

Pannenberg, Wolfhart. "God of the Philosophers." Available at http://www.firstthings.com/article/2007/06/002-god-of-the-philosophers.

Parmenides. "On Nature." Edited by Allan F. Randall from translations by David Gallop, Richard D. McKirahan Jr., Jonathan Barnes, John Mansley Robinson, et al. Available at http://rhetcomp.gsu.edu/~gpullman/2150/parmenides.htm. Also see John Burnet's older translation at http://philoctetes.free.fr/parmenidesunicode.htm.

Pascal, Blaise. "Memorial." Available at http://www.users.csbsju.edu/~eknuth/pascal.html.

———. *Pensées*. Translated by W. F. Trotter. Available at http://www.ccel.org/ccel/pascal/pensees.html.

Peirce, Charles S. Peirce's Writings On Line. http://www.peirce.org/writings.html.

Plantinga, Alvin. "Advice to Christian Philosophers." *Faith and Philosophy* 1 (October 1984): 1–19. Available at http://www.calvin.edu/academic/philosophy/virtual_library/articles/plantinga_alvin/advice_to_christian_philosophers.pdf.

———. Many of Plantinga's papers are available under "Alvin Plantinga" at the Virtual Library of Christian Philosophy. http://www.calvin.edu/academic/philosophy/virtual_library/plantinga_alvin.htm.

———. "Two Dozen (or So) Theistic Arguments." Available at http://www.calvin.edu/academic/philosophy/virtual_library/articles/plantinga_alvin/two_dozen_or_so_theistic_arguments.pdf.

Poythress, Vern S. Most of Poythress's books and articles are available at http://www.frame-poythress.org.

Quine, Willard Van Orman. "Two Dogmas of Empiricism." *Philosophical Review* 60 (1951): 20–43. Reprinted in Willard Van Orman Quine, *From a Logical Point of View: Nine Logico-Philosophical Essays*. 2nd rev. ed. Cambridge, MA: Harvard University Press, 1961. Available at http://www.ditext.com/quine/quine.html.

Reid, Thomas. "Thomas Reid." Some Texts in Early Modern Philosophy. http://www.earlymoderntexts.com/authors/reid.html.

Reno, R. R. "The Radical Orthodoxy Project." *First Things* (February 2000). Available at http://www.firstthings.com/article/2000/02/the-radical-orthodoxy-project.

Ritschl, Albrecht. *The Christian Doctrine of Justification and Reconciliation*. Translated and edited by H. R. Mackintosh and A. B. Macaulay. 2nd ed. Edinburgh: T&T Clark, 1902. Available at http://archive.org/details/christiandoctri00edgoog.

Roberts, Lisa J. "Thomas Kuhn's *The Structure of Scientific Revolutions*." *ETC: A Review of General Semantics* 57, 1 (Spring 2000). Available at http://ebookbrowsee.net/thomas-kuhn-s-the-structure-of-scientific-revolutions-pdf-d94647007.

Rosenstock-Huessy, Eugen. Guide to the Papers of Eugen Rosenstock-Huessy, 1870–2001. http://ead.dartmouth.edu/html/ms522.html. See also Eugen Rosenstock-Huessy Society of North America. http://www.erhsociety.org/, with many resources available at http://www.erhsociety.org/documents/.

Russell, Bertrand. "A Free Man's Worship" (1903). Available at http://philosophicalsociety.com/Archives/A%20Free%20Man%27s%20Worship.htm.

———. "Has Religion Made Useful Contributions to Civilization?" Available at http://www.positiveatheism.org/hist/russell2.htm.

———. *Mysticism and Logic and Other Essays*. London: George Allen & Unwin, 1917. Available at http://en.wikisource.org/wiki/Mysticism_and_Logic_and_Other_Essays.

———. *Our Knowledge of an External World as a Field for Scientific Method in Philosophy*. London: George Allen & Unwin, 1914. Available at http://archive.org/details/ourknowledgeofth005200mbp.

———. *The Philosophy of Logical Atomism*. Oxford: Taylor & Francis e-Library, 2009. Available at http://www.ualberta.ca/~francisp/NewPhil448/RussellPhilLogicalAtomismPears.pdf.

———. *The Problems of Philosophy*. Oxford: Oxford University Press, 1959. Available at http://www.ditext.com/russell/russell.html.

Sartre, Jean-Paul. "Existentialism Is a Humanism." In *Existentialism from Dostoevsky to Sartre*, edited by Walter Kaufman. Translated by Philip Mairet. Meridian Publishing Company, 1989. Available at http://www.marxists.org/reference/archive/sartre/works/exist/sartre.htm.

———. Jean-Paul Sartre Archive. http://www.marxists.org/reference/archive/sartre/.

Schaff, Philip, et al., eds. *Ante-Nicene, Nicene, and Post-Nicene Fathers*. Christian Classics Ethereal Library. http://www.ccel.org/node/70.

Schaper, Eva. "Ernst Troeltsch." *Encyclopaedia Britannica*. Available at http://www.britannica.com/EBchecked/topic/606217/Ernst-Troeltsch.

Schleiermacher, Friedrich. Christian Classics Ethereal Library. http://www.ccel.org/ccel/schleiermach. Includes his *On Religion: Speeches to Its Cultured Despisers* and *Selected Sermons of Schleiermacher.* Translated by Mary F. Wilson. Some other English translations of Schleiermacher (but not *The Christian Faith*) are available at http://en.wikipedia.org/wiki/Friedrich_Schleiermacher#Works.

———. *The Christian Faith*. New York: Bloomsbury Academic, 1999. Available at http://books.google.com/books/about/The_Christian_Faith.html?id=8JiQhmLykAYC.

Schopenhauer, Arthur. Many of his works are available at http://ebooks.adelaide.edu.au/s/schopenhauer/arthur/.

Spinoza, Baruch (Benedict de Spinoza). *Ethics*. Available as free e-book at http://www.gutenberg.org/ebooks/3800.

———. *A Theologico-Political Treatise*. Translated by R. H. M. Elwes. New York: Dover, 1951. Available at http://www.spinozacsack.net78.net/Theologico-Political%20Treatise,%20Benedict%20de%20Spinoza.pdf.

Stanford Encyclopedia of Philosophy. http://plato.stanford.edu.

Swinburne, Richard. Selected full-text books and articles are available at http://www.questia.com/library/religion/philosophy-of-religion/richard-swinburne. Membership required for full texts.

Tillich, Paul. Articles by and about Paul Tillich are available at www.archive.org. Search "Paul Tillich."

Urmson, J. O. *Philosophical Analysis: Its Development between the Two World Wars*. Oxford: Clarendon, 1958. Available at http://www.questia.com/library/465525/philosophical-analysis-its-development-between-the. Membership required for full texts.

Vanhoozer, Kevin J., ed. *The Cambridge Companion to Postmodern Theology*. Cambridge: Cambridge University Press, 2003. Available at http://docs.google.com/viewer?url=http://assets.cambridge.org//052179/062X/sample/052179062Xws.pdf. Requires (free) Google account.

———. "The Inerrancy of Scripture." Available at http://www.theologynetwork.org/biblical-studies/getting-stuck-in/the-inerrancy-of-scripture.htm.

———. "Lost in Interpretation? Truth, Scripture, and Hermeneutics." *JETS* 48, 1 (March 2005): 89–114. Available at http://www.etsjets.org/files/JETS-PDFs/48/48-1/48-1-pp089-114_JETS.pdf.

———. Vanhoozer on the Net. Various articles, lectures, reviews. http://achorusofehoes.wordpress.com/2010/08/10/vanhoozer-on-the-net/.

Van Til, Cornelius. A number of works by and about Van Til are available at http://www.vantil.info/byauthor.html; http://presupp101.wordpress.com/2011/10/03/why-i-believe-in-god-by-cornelius-van-til/. Forty volumes of Van Til's works are available on CD-ROM at http://www.logos.com/product/3994/the-works-of-cornelius-van-til. His *Survey of Christian Epistemology* is available in a free PDF at http://veritasdomain.wordpress.com/2011/10/08/free-pdf-book-a-survey-of-christian-epistemology-by-cornelius-van-til/. His *Christianity and Idealism* is available at http://presupp101.wordpress.com/.

———. Van Til Info. "A comprehensive catalogue of online resources explicitly related to the theology, philosophy, and apologetics of Cornelius Van Til." http://www.vantil.info.

———. "Why I Believe in God." Available at http://www.the-highway.com/why_I_believe_cvt.html.

Welty, Greg. "An Examination of Theistic Conceptual Realism as an Alternative to Theistic Activism." M.Phil. thesis, Oriel College, Oxford University, 2000. Available at http://www.proginosko.com/welty/mphil.pdf.

Whitehead, Alfred North. "God and the World." In *Process and Reality: An Essay in Cosmology*. Edited by David Ray Griffin and Donald W. Sherburne. Corrected ed. New York: Free Press, 1978. Available at http://www.anthonyflood.com/whiteheadgodandtheworld.htm.

———. Various articles about Alfred North Whitehead are available at http://whiteheadresearch.org/.

Wikipedia, s.v. "Abraham Kuyper." http://en.wikipedia.org/wiki/Abraham_Kuyper.

Wikipedia, s.v. "Alasdair MacIntyre." See the section "Online videos of MacIntyre giving lectures." http://en.wikipedia.org/wiki/Alasdair_MacIntyre.

Wikipedia, s.v. "Auburn Affirmation." http://en.wikipedia.org/wiki/Auburn_Affirmation.

Wikipedia, s.v. "Ludwig Wittgenstein." http://en.wikipedia.org/wiki/Ludwig_Wittgenstein.

Wikipedia, s.v. "Open Theism." http://en.wikipedia.org/wiki/Open_theism.

Wikipedia, s.v. "Pietism." http://en.wikipedia.org/wiki/Pietism.

Wikipedia, s.v. "William Harry Jellema." http://en.wikipedia.org/wiki/William_Harry_Jellema#cite_note-2.

Wittgenstein, Ludwig. *The Blue Book*. Available at http://www.geocities.jp/mickindex/wittgenstein/witt_blue_en.html.

———. *On Certainty (Uber Gewissheit)*. Edited by G. E. M. Anscombe and G. H. von Wright. Translated by Denis Paul and G. E. M. Anscombe.

Oxford: Basil Blackwell, 1969–75. Available at http://web.archive.org/web/20051210213153/http://budni.by.ru/oncertainty.html.

———. *Tractatus Logico-Philosophicus (Logisch-philosophische Abhandlung).* Side-by-side-by-side ed. Version 0.41. February 11, 2014. Available at http://people.umass.edu/phil335-klement-2/tlp/tlp.pdf. Contains the original German, alongside both the Ogden/Ramsey and the Pears/McGuinness English translations. First published: London: Kegan Paul, 1922.

Wolterstorff, Nicholas. "The Grace That Shaped My Life." In *Philosophers Who Believe: The Spiritual Journeys of 11 Leading Thinkers*, edited by Kelly James Clark, 259–75. Downers Grove, IL: IVP Academic, 1997. Available at http://www.calvin.edu/125th/wolterst/w_bio.pdf.

Woodiwiss, Ashley. "What's So Radical about Orthodoxy?" *Christianity Today*, May 2005. Available at http://www.christianitytoday.com/ct/2005/mayweb-only/22.0c.html?start=1.

ILLUSTRATION CREDITS

The majority of the works listed below come from Wikimedia Commons. The eleven types of licenses involved are

Creative Commons CC0 1.0 Universal Public Domain Dedication (CC0 1.0). License terms available here: http://creativecommons.org/publicdomain/zero/1.0/.

Creative Commons Attribution 2.0 Generic license (CC-BY-2.0). License terms available here: http://creativecommons.org/licenses/by/2.0/.

Creative Commons Attribution 2.5 Generic license (CC-BY-2.5). License terms available here: http://creativecommons.org/licenses/by/2.5/deed.en.

Creative Commons Attribution-Share Alike 2.5 Generic license (CC-BY-SA-2.5). License terms available here: http://creativecommons.org/licenses/by-sa/2.5/.

Creative Commons Attribution 3.0 Unported license (CC-BY-3.0). License terms available here: http://creativecommons.org/licenses/by/3.0/deed.en.

Creative Commons Attribution-Share Alike 3.0 Unported license (CC-BY-SA-3.0). License terms available here: http://creativecommons.org/licenses/by-sa/3.0/deed.en.

Creative Commons Attribution-Share Alike 3.0 Germany license (CC-BY-SA-3.0-DE). License terms available here: http://creativecommons.org/licenses/by-sa/3.0/de/deed.en.

Creative Commons Attribution-Share Alike 3.0 Luxembourg license (CC-BY-SA-3.0-LU). License terms available here: http://creativecommons.org/licenses/by-sa/3.0/lu/deed.en.

Creative Commons Attribution 4.0 International (CC-BY-4.0). License terms available here: http://creativecommons.org/licenses/by/4.0/deed.en.

Free Art License (FAL). License terms available here: http://en.wikipedia.org/wiki/Free_Art_License.

GNU Free Documentation License, version 1.2 (GFDL). License terms available here: http://commons.wikimedia.org/wiki/Commons:GNU_Free_Documentation_License,_version_1.2.

Page 49, Homer. Anonymous / Wikimedia Commons / Public Domain.

Page 53, Thales. Anonymous / Wikimedia Commons / CC0 1.0.

Page 57, Parmenides. Anonymous / Wikimedia Commons / CC-BY-SA-3.0 / GFDL.

Page 61, Pythagoras. user:Galilea at German Wikipedia / Wikimedia Commons / CC-BY-SA-3.0 / GFDL.

Page 65, Plato. user:Jastrow / Wikimedia Commons / CC-BY-2.5.

Page 70, Aristotle. Eric Gaba (user:Sting) / Wikimedia Commons / CC-BY-SA-2.5.

Page 77, Zeno. user:shakko / Wikimedia Commons / CC-BY-SA-3.0.

Page 79, Plotinus. Anonymous / Wikimedia Commons / Public Domain.

Page 90, Justin Martyr. Anonymous / Wikimedia Commons / Public Domain.

Page 93, Irenaeus. user:Orf3us / Wikimedia Commons / Public Domain.

Page 97, Tertullian. user:Tomisti / Wikimedia Commons / Public Domain.

Page 101, Clement of Alexandria. Anonymous / Wikimedia Commons / Public Domain.

Page 103, Origen. Anonymous / Wikimedia Commons / Public Domain.

Page 104, Athanasius. Francesco Bartolozzi (1727–1815) / Wikimedia Commons / Public Domain.

Page 109, Augustine. Anonymous / Wikimedia Commons / Public Domain.

Page 124, Boethius. Anonymous / Wikimedia Commons / Public Domain.

Page 139, Anselm of Canterbury. Anonymous / Wikimedia Commons / Public Domain.

Page 142, Peter Abelard. © Marie-Lan Nguyen (user:Jastrow) / Wikimedia Commons / CC-BY-3.0.

Page 145, Thomas Aquinas. Anonymous / Wikimedia Commons / Public Domain.

Page 149, *Summa Theologiae*. Anonymous / Wikimedia Commons / Public Domain.

Page 154, John Duns Scotus. user:Faber / Wikimedia Commons / Public Domain.

Page 157, William of Occam. Moscarlop / Wikimedia Commons / CC-BY-SA-3.0 / GFDL.

Page 169, Martin Luther. Lucas Cranach / Wikimedia Commons / Public Domain.

Page 172, John Calvin. J. F. Cazenave / Wikimedia Commons / Public Domain.

Page 179, René Descartes. André Hatala / Wikimedia Commons / Public Domain.

Page 183, Baruch (Benedict) Spinoza. user:shop.mpiiir / Wikimedia Commons / Public Domain.

Page 186, Gottfried Wilhelm Leibniz. Anonymous / Wikimedia Commons / Public Domain.

Page 189, Thomas Hobbes. Anonymous / wpclipart / Public Domain.

Page 192, John Locke. Anonymous / Wikimedia Commons / Public Domain.

Page 197, George Berkeley. user:1wEMkObfE2BRpQ / Wikimedia Commons / Public Domain.

Page 201, David Hume. Anonymous / Wikimedia Commons / Public Domain.

Page 218, Edward, Lord Herbert of Cherbury. user:Dcoetzee / Wikimedia Commons / Public Domain.

Page 221, Gotthold E. Lessing. Gemälde von C. Jäger / Wikimedia Commons / Public Domain.

Page 225, Blaise Pascal. Anonymous / Wikimedia Commons / Public Domain.

Page 231, Joseph Butler. Anonymous / Wikimedia Commons / Public Domain.

Page 235, Jonathan Edwards. user:Flex / Wikimedia Commons / Public Domain.

Page 238, William Paley. Anonymous / Wikimedia Commons / Public Domain.

Page 241, Thomas Reid. Anonymous / Wikimedia Commons / Public Domain.

Page 252, Immanuel Kant. Anonymous / Wikimedia Commons / Public Domain.

Page 271, Georg W. F. Hegel. Anonymous / Wikimedia Commons / Public Domain.

Page 277, Arthur Schopenhauer. Anonymous / Wikimedia Commons / Public Domain.

Page 281, Ludwig Feuerbach. Anonymous / Wikimedia Commons / Public Domain.

Page 283, Karl Marx. John Jabez Edwin Mayall (1813–1901) / Wikimedia Commons / Public Domain.

Page 293, Friedrich D. E. Schleiermacher. Anonymous / Wikimedia Commons / Public Domain.

Page 301, Albrecht Ritschl. Anonymous / Wikimedia Commons / Public Domain.

Page 303, Wilhelm Herrmann. Anonymous / Teologia Liberal / Public Domain.

Page 307, Adolf von Harnack. user:Tagishsimon / Wikimedia Commons / Public Domain.

Page 309, *Auburn Affirmation*. © Anne Halsey. Used by permission.

Page 311, Albert Schweitzer. Bundesarchiv, Bild 183-D0116-0041-019 / Unknown / CC-BY-SA-3.0.

Page 314, Søren Kierkegaard. Neils Christian Kierkegaard / Wikimedia Commons / Public Domain.

Page 330, Friedrich W. Nietzsche. F. Hartmann / Wikimedia Commons / Public Domain.

Page 333, Charles Sanders Peirce. Anonymous / Wikimedia Commons / Public Domain.

Page 338, William James. Anonymous / Wikimedia Commons / Public Domain.

Page 341, John Dewey. Eva Watson-Schütze (1867–1935) / Wikimedia Commons / Public Domain.

Page 343, Edmund Husserl. Anonymous / Wikimedia Commons / Public Domain.

Page 347, Martin Heidegger. user:Hidalgo944 / Wikimedia Commons/ CC-BY-3.0.

Page 351, Jean-Paul Sartre. Anonymous / Wikimedia Commons / Public Domain.

Page 355, Karl Jaspers. Anonymous / Wikimedia Commons / Public Domain.

Page 356, Albert Camus. Photograph by United Press International / Wikimedia Commons / Public Domain.

Page 364, Karl Barth. © Karl Barth-Archiv. Used by permission.

Page 383, Emil Brunner. © Karl Barth-Archiv. Used by permission.

Page 387, Rudolf Bultmann. user:Ju / Wikimedia Commons / Public Domain.

Page 393, Paul Tillich. Richard Keeling / Wikimedia Commons / CC-BY-3.0 / GFDL.

Page 400, Dietrich Bonhoeffer. © Karl Barth-Archiv. Used by permission.

Page 407, Harvey Cox. Rob C. Croes / Anefo / Wikimedia Commons / CC-BY-SA-3.0.

Page 417, Ernst Bloch. Bundesarchiv, Bild 183-35545-0009 / CC-BY-SA-3.0-DE.

Page 418, Jürgen Moltmann. user:Orwell123 / Wikimedia Commons / CC-BY-3.0.

Page 425, Gustavo Gutierrez. user:Mohan / Wikimedia Commons / Public Domain.

Page 429, Wolfhart Pannenberg. Bundesarchiv, B 145 Bild-F065001-0017 / Reineke, Engelbert / CC-BY-SA-3.0-DE.

Page 439, Alfred North Whitehead. Wellcome Trust / Wikimedia Commons / CC-BY-4.0.

Page 442, John B. Cobb. The Center for Process Studies / Wikimedia Commons / CC-BY-SA-3.0.

Page 463, G. E. Moore. Filobotfil / Wikimedia Commons / CC-BY-SA-3.0.

Page 465, Bertrand Russell. Anonymous / Wikimedia Commons/ Public Domain.

Page 468, Ludwig Wittgenstein. user:rook76 / Fotolia / Extended License.

Page 471, *Tractatus Logico-Philosophicus*. Anonymous / Wikimedia Commons / Public Domain.

Page 483, Thomas Kuhn. Image Source: W. Andrew Hoffecker, ed., *Revolutions in Worldview: Understanding the Flow of Western Thought* (Phillipsburg NJ: P&R Publishing, 2007), 410. Used by permission.

Page 489, *Philosophical Investigations*. Public Domain.

Page 499, Willard V. Quine. user:Stampit at English Wikipedia / Wikimedia Commons / CC-BY-SA-2.5.

Page 501, Ferdinand de Saussure. Anonymous / Wikimedia Commons / Public Domain.

Page 503, Michel Foucault. user:Nemomain / Wikimedia Commons / CC-BY-SA-3.0.

Page 513, Abraham Kuyper. Anonymous / Wikimedia Commons / Public Domain.

Page 517, Herman Dooyeweerd. user:avc@vumc.nl / Wikimedia Commons / Public Domain.

Page 522, Gordon H. Clark. Public Domain.

Page 529, Cornelius Van Til. *The Works of Cornelius Van Til, 1895–1987*, CD-ROM (New York: Labels Army Co., 1997), ISBN 0875524613 / Wikimedia Commons / Public Domain.

Page 536, Greg Bahnsen. Anonymous / Wikimedia Commons / FAL.

Page 537, Francis Schaeffer. Used by permission of Crossway, a publishing ministry of Good News Publishers, Wheaton, IL 60187, www.crossway.org.

Page 538, Alvin Plantinga. user:Jonathunder / Wikimedia Commons / CC-BY-SA-3.0 / GFDL.

Page 543, Nicholas Wolterstorff. Nicholas Wolterstorff / Wikimedia Commons / CC-BY-SA-3.0 / GFDL.

Page 546, Kevin J. Vanhoozer. © Kevin Vanhoozer. Used by permission.

Page 547, C. S. Lewis. Used by permission of The Marion E. Wade Center, Wheaton College, Wheaton, IL.

Page 548, Alasdair MacIntyre. Sean O'Connor / Wikimedia Commons / CC- BY-2.0.

Page 549, Paul Helm. © Paul Helm. Used by permission.

Page 550, Eugen Rosenstock-Huessy. Photo courtesy of Mariot Huessy, Eugen Rosenstock-Huessy Fund / Wikimedia Commons / CC-BY-SA-3.0.

Page 551, John Milbank. user:Jwh at Wikipedia Luxembourg / Wikimedia Commons / CC-BY-SA-3.0-LU.

Page 554, Esther Lightcap Meek. © Gini Fanter. Used by permission.

Page 557, Vern S. Poythress. © Vern Poythress. Used by permission.

Page 579, *The Doctrine of the Knowledge of God* and *The Doctrine of God*. © P&R Publishing. Used by permission.

Page 580, *The Doctrine of the Word of God* and *John Frame's Selected Shorter Writings, Volume 1*. © P&R Publishing. Used by permission.

Page 580, *New Dictionary of Christian Apologetics*. © InterVarsity Press. Used by permission.

Page 590, William Lane Craig. ReasonableFaith.org / Wikimedia Commons / CC-BY-3.0.

Page 594, Anselm of Canterbury. Anonymous / Wikimedia Commons / Public Domain.

Page 620, Anthony Flew. Anonymous / Wikimedia Commons / Public Domain.

Page 644, Meredith G. Kline. Courtesy of Westminster Seminary California.

Page 660, Stephen Toulmin. Courtesy of the University of Southern California, on behalf of the USC Libraries Special Collections.

Page 669, Paul M. Van Buren. Used by permision of the Special Collections Research Center, Temple University Libraries, Philadelphia, PA.

Page 675, Paul L. Holmer. Courtesy of Yale University.

Page 687, Schubert M. Ogden. Courtesy of Bridwell Library Special Collections, Perkins School of Theology, Southern Methodist University.

Page 695, Paul Helm. © Paul Helm. Used by permission.

Page 701. Esther Lightcap Meek. © Gini Fanter. Used by permission.

Page 705, John L. Pollock. © Lilian Jacques. Used by permission.

Page 719, Gordon H. Clark. Public Domain.

Page 729, Herbert Schlossberg. © Herbert Schlossberg. Used by permission.

Page 733, Cornelius Van Til. *The Works of Cornelius Van Til, 1895–1987*, CD-ROM (New York: Labels Army Co., 1997), ISBN 0875524613 / Wikimedia Commons / Public Domain.

Page 871, Jesus Christ's crucifixion and resurrection. user:Krupo / Wikimedia Commons / Public Domain.

Page 871, Justin Martyr. Anonymous / Wikimedia Commons / Public Domain.

Page 871, Roman Emperor Constantine. Anonymous / Wikimedia Commons / Public Domain.

Page 871, Augustine. Anonymous / Wikimedia Commons / Public Domain.

Page 871, Thomas Aquinas. Anonymous / Wikimedia Commons / Public Domain.

Page 872, Martin Luther. Lucas Cranach / Wikimedia Commons / Public Domain.

Page 872, Edward, Lord Herbert of Cherbury. user:Dcoetzee / Wikimedia Commons / Public Domain.

Page 873, René Descartes. André Hatala / Wikimedia Commons / Public Domain.

Page 873, Immanuel Kant. Anonymous / Wikimedia Commons / Public Domain.

Page 873, Georg W. F. Hegel. Anonymous / Wikimedia Commons / Public Domain.

Page 873, Karl Marx. John Jabez Edwin Mayall (1813–1901) / Wikimedia Commons / Public Domain.

Page 873, Abraham Kuyper. Anonymous / Wikimedia Commons / Public Domain.

Page 874, Albrecht Ritschl. Anonymous / Wikimedia Commons / Public Domain.

Page 874, Karl Barth. © Karl Barth-Archiv. Used by permission.

Page 874, Ludwig Wittgenstein. user:rook76 / Fotolia / Extended License.

Page 875, Martin Heidegger. user:Hidalgo944 / Wikimedia Commons/ CC-BY-3.0.

Page 875, Cornelius Van Til. *The Works of Cornelius Van Til, 1895–1987*, CD-ROM (New York: Labels Army Co., 1997), ISBN 0875524613 / Wikimedia Commons / Public Domain.

Page 875, Alvin Plantinga. user:Jonathunder / Wikimedia Commons / CC-BY-SA-3.0 / GFDL.

Page 875, The Last Judgment. user:Jwh / Wikimedia Commons / CC-BY-SA-3.0-LU.

INDEX OF NAMES

INDEX OF SUBJECTS

INDEX OF SCRIPTURE

TURNING POINTS IN THE HISTORY OF PHILOSOPHY AND THEOLOGY

A.D. **33** Jesus is crucified and resurrected. The incarnation of God in Jesus Christ establishes the truth of the Christian worldview and fulfills the history in which redemption from sin and death forms the core of the Christian gospel.

165 Justin, of the first generation of Christian philosophers and apologists, dies as a martyr to his faith.

313 Roman Emperor Constantine issues the Edict of Milan, which ends empire-wide persecution of Christianity. In 325 he convened the first ecumenical council of the church at Nicaea, which affirmed the deity of Jesus Christ.

354–430 Augustine's writings culminate the theological and philosophical achievement of the patristic era and mark the beginning of the medieval, in which the church takes over from the Roman Empire the dominant role in philosophy and the preservation of ancient thought.

1274 Thomas Aquinas's *Summa Theologiae* combines Platonic, Aristotelian, and biblical elements to form the classical medieval synthesis of faith and reason. Aquinas relegates the Greek form-matter scheme to the realm of natural knowledge, and then adds a higher level in which faith and revelation supplement reason; see fig. T.1.

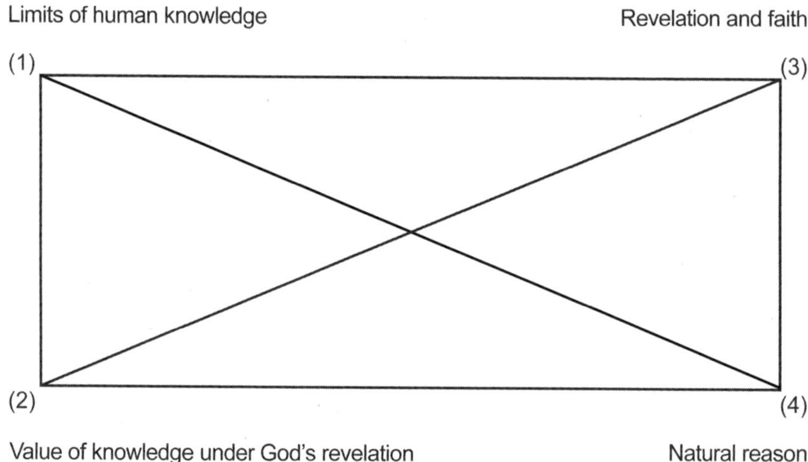

Fig. T.1. Rationalism and Irrationalism in Aquinas's Epistemology

1517 Martin Luther attaches Ninety-five Theses to the church door in Wittenberg, marking the beginning of the Protestant Reformation. Philosophically, the Reformation renounces the autonomy of reason (including Aquinas's "natural reason") and seeks to govern its thought by God's written Word; see fig. T.2.

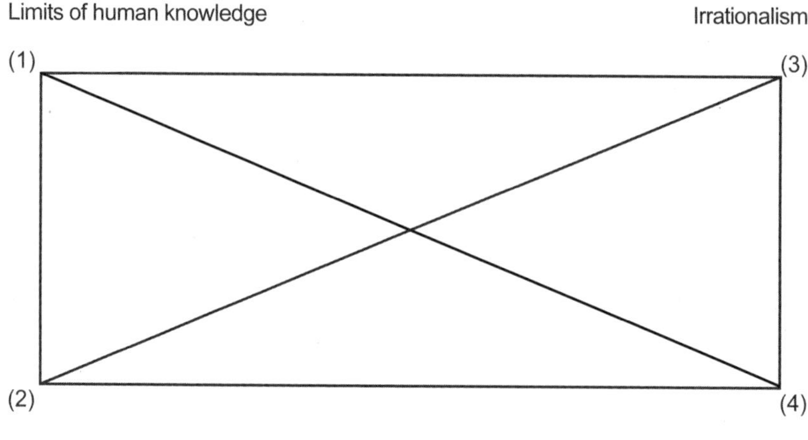

Fig. T.2. Luther's Epistemology Compared with Non-Christian Thought

1624 Edward, Lord Herbert of Cherbury enumerates fine points of natural religion in *De Veritate*, which marks the beginning of English deism and the liberal tradition in theology. The liberal tradition renounces biblical authority and seeks knowledge in ways that follow the autonomous pretensions of secular thought.

1637 René Descartes' *Discourse on Method* introduces a radically secular turn in philosophy, similar to the beginning of the discipline in 600 B.C. As Thales set aside all tradition and religion to think by reason alone, so Descartes sets aside everything he considers doubtful, including Scripture and Christian tradition.

1781 Immanuel Kant's *Critique of Pure Reason* creates a "Copernican revolution" in epistemology, in which the forms of experience are imposed on the world, not by God, but by the human mind. Thus Kant establishes human autonomy far more firmly as the fundamental authority for philosophy and theology. In *Religion within the Limits of Reason Alone*, Kant draws out the theological implications of this change, transforming the Christian gospel into an autonomous ethic. In Kant, the human mind essentially replaces God; see fig. T.3.

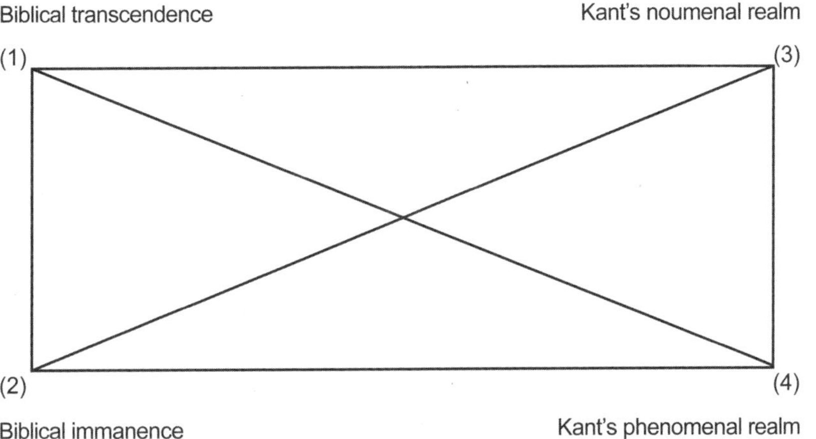

Fig. T.3. Transcendence and Immanence in Kant

1807 Georg W. F. Hegel publishes his *Phenomenology of the Spirit*, which renews the rationalist tradition after Kant's critique, but continues Kant's program of identifying God with the human mind.

1848 Karl Marx publishes his *Communist Manifesto*, which converts Hegel's neo-rationalism into a political ideology. Marx calls the proletarian working class to unite in a revolution to overthrow the capitalist bourgeoisie in order to establish a classless society.

1880 Abraham Kuyper, in his inaugural address as a professor at the Free University of Amsterdam, announces that there is not one square inch of territory over which Jesus Christ does not say, "Mine!" Kuyper's work begins a new era, in which Christians no longer seek to validate their work by secular models, but rather to assert forcefully the distinctive worldview of the biblical revelation.

1900 Albrecht Ritschl publishes *The Christian Doctrine of Justification and Reconciliation*, developing Kant's moralism into a theological movement with great influence in the churches.

1919 Karl Barth publishes *The Epistle to the Romans*, which fell "like a bombshell in the playground of the theologians" and proved the end of Ritschlianism. But in many ways, Barth's work was another synthesis with secular thought; see fig. T.4.

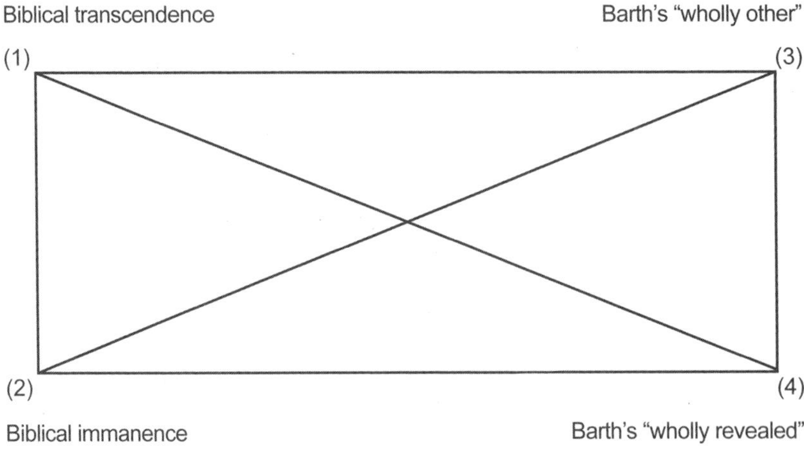

Fig. T.4. Transcendence and Immanence in Barth

1921 Ludwig Wittgenstein publishes his *Tractatus Logico-Philosophicus*, launching the method of solving all philosophical disputes by examination of language. But at the end of the book, he recognizes that his project is self-refuting; see fig. T.5.

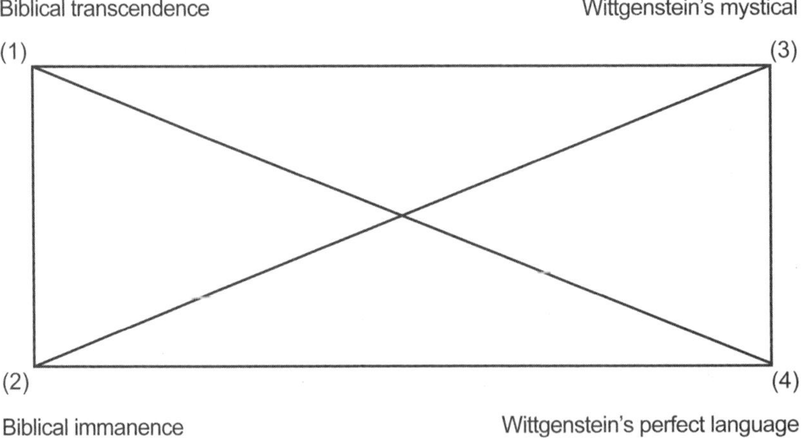

Fig. T.5. Transcendence and Immanence in Wittgenstein's *Tractatus*

1927 Heidegger publishes *Being and Time*, which (with the writings of Jean-Paul Sartre and others) seeks to reconstitute philosophy on a consistently atheistic basis.

1955 Cornelius Van Til publishes *The Defense of the Faith*, which seeks to establish philosophy and Christian apologetics on a distinctively biblical epistemology.

1967 Alvin Plantinga publishes *God and Other Minds*, beginning a new era of professional acceptance for Christian philosophers.

The Last Judgment Jesus Christ returns on the clouds with power and glory to judge the living and the dead, to vindicate his disciples, and to turn over his kingdom to his Father in the Holy Spirit. His appearance settles all arguments as to the truth of divine revelation and begins a new era of faithful human philosophic exploration. This philosophy will recognize all aspects of his lordship; see fig. T.6.

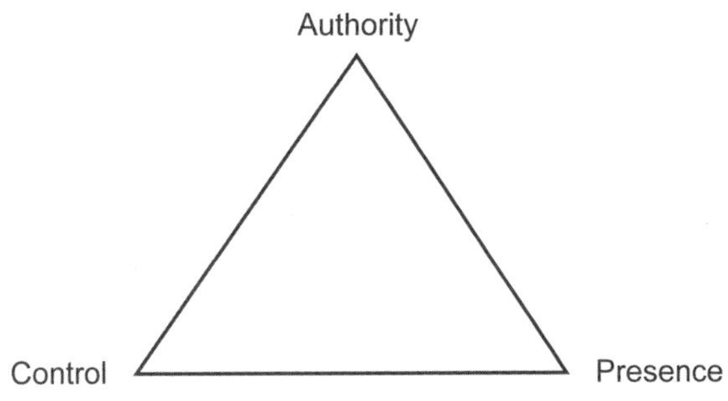

Fig. T.6. Jesus' Lordship

ALSO BY JOHN M. FRAME

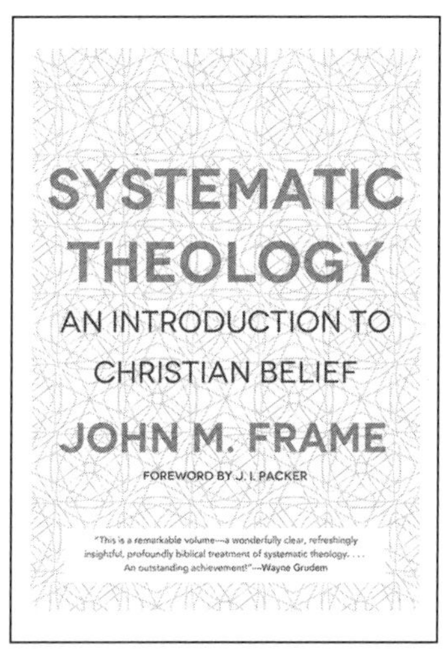

This magisterial opus—at once biblical, clear, cogent, readable, accessible, and practical—summarizes the mature thought of one of the most important and original Reformed theologians of the last hundred years. It will enable you to see clearly how the Bible explains God's great, sweeping plan for mankind.

"*Systematic Theology* brings together, slims down, sums up, and augments all the wisdom contained in Frame's four-volume Lordship series. It is a worthy climax to the life's work of one who has only ever sought to be a faithful servant of Christ, teaching in his church. . . . Thank you, John Frame, for this superb gift."

—**J. I. Packer,** Board of Governors' Professor of Theology, Regent College, Vancouver, British Columbia